The SAGE Handbook of
Responsible
Management
Learning and Education

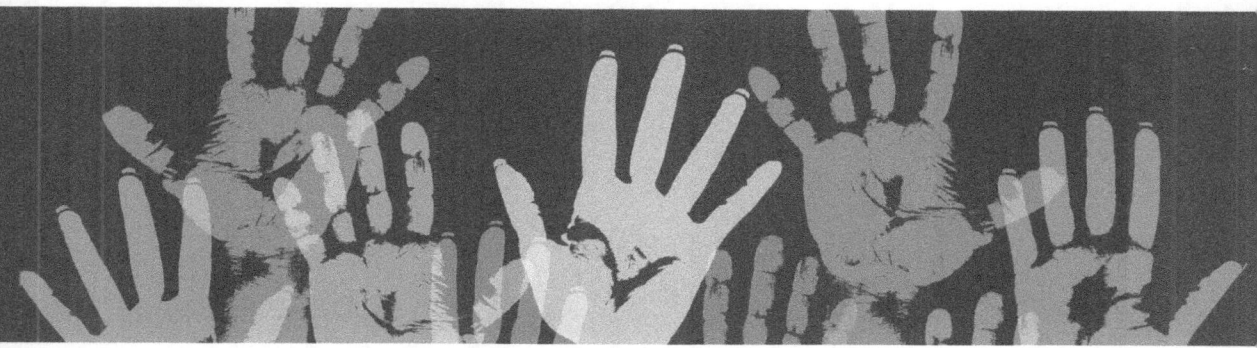

The SAGE Handbook of
Responsible Management Learning and Education

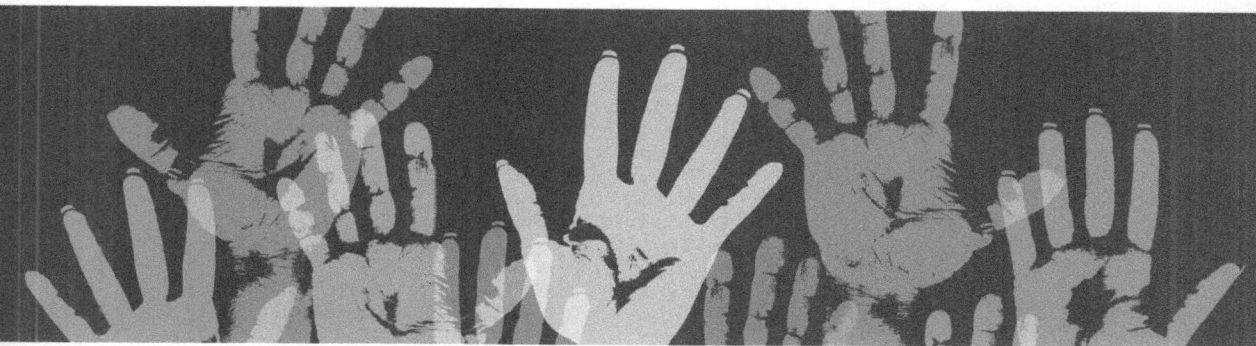

Edited by

Dirk C. Moosmayer
Oliver Laasch
Carole Parkes and
Kenneth G. Brown

reference

Los Angeles | London | New Delhi | Singapore | Washington DC | Melbourne

Los Angeles | London | New Delhi
Singapore | Washington DC | Melbourne

SAGE Publications Ltd
1 Oliver's Yard
55 City Road
London EC1Y 1SP

SAGE Publications Inc.
2455 Teller Road
Thousand Oaks, California 91320

SAGE Publications India Pvt Ltd
B 1/I 1 Mohan Cooperative Industrial Area
Mathura Road
New Delhi 110 044

SAGE Publications Asia-Pacific Pte Ltd
3 Church Street
#10-04 Samsung Hub
Singapore 049483

Editor: Matthew Waters
Editorial Assistant: Umeeka Raichura
Production Editor: Prachi Arora
Copyeditor: Elaine Leek
Indexer: Cathryn Pritchard
Marketing Manager: Lucia Sweet
Cover Design: Naomi Robinson
Typeset by Cenveo Publisher Services
Printed in the UK

Library of Congress Control Number: 2020936282

British Library Cataloguing in Publication data

A catalogue record for this book is available from the British Library

978-1-5264-6070-7

Contents

List of Figures and Tables

FIGURES

TABLES

Notes on the Editors
and Contributors

THE EDITORS

Dirk C. Moosmayer is a professor of Strategy at KEDGE Business School and member of the KEDGE CSR Research Group. Prior to this engagement he worked for eight years at the Nottingham University Business School China. In his research he integrates responsible management perspectives of firms, consumers, civil society players and higher education. Dirk serves as an associate editor of *Business Ethics: A European Review* and on the editorial boards of *Journal of Business Ethics*, *Business & Society* and *Academy of Management Learning & Education*, to which he had served as an associate editor (2015–17). Dirk won the University of Nottingham's Lord Dearing Award for teaching and teaching development. He also teaches on executive and MBA programmes globally in which a responsible lens is an inherent component of his business classes.

Oliver Laasch is a Senior Lecturer in Innovation and Entrepreneurship at the University of Manchester, UK and an Adjunct Associate Professor of Strategy at the University of Nottingham Ningbo China. Oliver is author of the United Nations PRME's first official textbook, *Principles of Responsible Management* (Sage, 2015, Spanish, Portuguese, Chinese, Indian editions), and of *Research Handbook of Responsible Management* (Edward Elgar, 2020). He has edited two inspirational guides of the PRME and 27 books as founding editor of the PRME/BEP book collection. Oliver founded the Center for Responsible Management Education (http://responsiblemanagement.net/) and co-convened the Responsible Management Education in Action workshop series at the Academy of Management meetings, which won the best PDW award in 2014. Oliver has edited special issues on responsible management in the *Journal of Business Ethics* and *Journal of Management Education*. He runs the Coursera MOOC Managing Responsibly and serves on the editorial board of *Academy of Management Learning and Education*.

Carole Parkes is Professor of Responsible Management at Winchester University Business School in the UK – a UN-backed PRME (Principles for Responsible Management Education) Champion School and has both a business and academic background. Carole is a member of the PRME Global Advisory Committee and former Chair of the PRME Chapter UK & Ireland. At the PRME 10th Anniversary Global Forum Carole was presented with a PRME Pioneer Award 'for her leadership and commitment to the development of PRME' and appointed a PRME Special Advisor. As an *International Journal of Management Education* (*IJME*) Associate Editor, Carole edited the PRME 10th Anniversary Special Issue of *IJME* and is an editor of Fighting Poverty as a Challenge for Management Education PRME Working Group publications. Carole is also an Inaugural Fellow of the Environmental Association of Universities and Colleges (EAUC) and serves on the editorial board of *Society and Business Review* (*SBR*).

Kenneth G. Brown is the Ralph L. Sheets Professor of Management and Associate Dean, Tippie College of Business, Iowa. Brown served as the editor of *Academy of Management Learning & Education* (2012–14) and on the editorial boards of *Academy of Management Review*, *Journal of Management*, *Journal of Applied Psychology*, *Journal of Management Education* and other journals. He edited *The Cambridge Handbook of Workplace Training and Employee Development* (Cambridge University Press, 2017) and co-authored *Human Resource Management: Linking Strategy to Practice* (4th ed., 2019, Wiley). Brown is also an award winning scholar and teacher, having received best paper awards from *Human Resource Management* (2003), *Academy of Management Learning & Education* (2010) and *Human Relations* (2016), and teaching awards from the University of Iowa, the Society of Industrial and Organizational Psychology and the HR Division of the Academy of Management.

THE CONTRIBUTORS

Ana Carolina Aguiar is currently a Researcher and Lecturer of Sustainability Education and Dialogic Organization Development at the Center for Sustainability Studies of Fundação Getulio Vargas-EAESP, Brazil. She is also a PhD student in the Organization Studies research line at the same university. Ana Carolina's current research interests are in sustainability education, social constructionism, dialogic organization development, embodied sensemaking and transdisciplinarity. She has published articles in the *Journal of Applied Behavioral Science*, the *International Journal of Management Education* and *Journal of Public Affairs*. She is responsible for sustainability courses offered by FGV-EAESP at the professional Master's level and supports other projects conducted by the Center for Sustainability Studies.

Raquel Antolin-Lopez is an Associate Professor of Management at the University of Almeria, Spain. She has also been visiting Scholar at Indiana University, University of Colorado at Boulder, Loyola Marymount Los Angeles University and City University of New York. Her main research interests include sustainable entrepreneurship, corporate sustainability, international business and sustainability, and sustainability education. Her research has been published in *Technovation*, *Academy of Management Learning & Education*, *Journal of Business Venturing*, among others. The quality of her research has been recognized with several awards (e.g., AOM best paper award, GRONEN best paper award, etc.). She acts as Associate Editor for *Business Ethics: A European Review*.

Markus Beckmann has been full professor for corporate sustainability management at Friedrich-Alexander University of Erlangen-Nuremberg, Germany, since 2012. Between 2009 and 2012 he was assistant professor for social entrepreneurship at the Centre for Sustainability Management at Leuphana University in Lueneburg. In 2009 Markus received his PhD from Martin-Luther-University Halle-Wittenberg. His research interests include corporate sustainability management, CSR, social entrepreneurship and business ethics. His work has appeared in journals such as *Business Ethics Quarterly*, *Business Strategy and the Environment*, *Business and Society*, *Journal of Business Ethics*, *Non-Profit and Voluntary Sector Quarterly* and *Technological Forecasting and Social Change*.

Lauren Beitelspacher received a PhD from the University of Alabama and is the Division Chair of the Marketing Division at Babson College, Massachusetts. Her research interests include:

buyer–supplier relationships, retail management and the retail supply chain. Her work has been published in numerous scholarly journals, including *Journal of Marketing*, *Journal of Applied Psychology*, *Journal of Retailing*, *Journal of the Academy of Marketing Science*, *Journal of Business Research* and *Industrial Marketing Management*. Lauren is also involved in pedagogical contributions for principles of marketing and retail management. Lauren is the author of the forthcoming *Connect Master Principles of Marketing* textbook, 1st edition, from McGraw Hill Publishing. In 2018 Lauren was named Faculty of the Year by the Undergraduate Class of 2018 at Babson College. Lauren won the Dean's Excellence in Undergraduate Teaching Award in 2017. Lauren was named one of the Top 40 under-40 Business Professors by Poets & Quants in 2016.

Ronald E. Berenbeim is an Adjunct Professor at the New York University Stern School of Business Administration where he has taught Professional Responsibility: Markets Ethics and Law since 1995. Professor Berenbeim is also a Senior Fellow at The Conference Board. From 2001 to 2003, he was a project director for a World Bank study of private sector anticorruption practices in East Asia. He is a member of the United Nations Global Compact Tenth Principle (anticorruption) Working Group, Transparency International's Steering Committee on Business Principles for Resisting Corrupt Practices, and the U.S. Advisory Board of FTSE4Good. In 2010, he received a Fulbright grant to teach business ethics and governance at the University of Cergy-Pontoise in Cergy, France. In 2011, he was selected by Trust Across America as one of 2010's Top 100 Thought Leaders in Trustworthy Business Behavior. In 2019, he taught Global Business Ethics to high school seniors at the Prudens Research Institute for the Arts and Sciences summer program at Donghua University, Shanghai.

Maribel Blasco is Associate Professor at the Department of Management, Society & Communication at Copenhagen Business School, Denmark. Her research focuses on learning, notably in management education, and with a particular focus on tacit dimensions of business school learning environments, including the hidden curriculum and spatial dimensions of curricula; and on how students acquire 'soft' skills such as creativity and innovativeness, responsibility awareness, and intercultural sensitivity. Her research has been widely published internationally, in journals such as *Academy of Management Learning and Education*, *Business & Society*, *Management Learning*, and *Journal of Management Education*. She received the award for Best Paper 2016 from the journal *Management Learning*, and the award for Outstanding Reviewer 2016 from the *Journal of Management Education*.

Karin Buhmann is Professor at Copenhagen Business School (CBS), Denmark, where she is charged with the field of Business & Human Rights (BHR). Her research and teaching focuses on how the ethical and legal human rights regimes can be transformed into responsible business conduct. Much of her work is poised in the interdisciplinary interaction between responsible management, business ethics and law. Her research interests include the evolution and implementation of normative guidance and other approaches related to business and human rights, both as an emergent but solidifying regime and as part of CSR. She has been looking at regulatory and communicative strategies for generating organizational buy-in without compromising the core objectives of the regulatory process. More recently she has begun looking at the interaction between the Sustainable Development Goals and human rights, and the role of BHR for enhancing climate justice and a socially responsible transition to low-carbon energy.

Anthony F. Buono is Professor of Management and Sociology at Bentley University, Massachusetts. He is also a former Chair of Bentley's Management Department and the founding director of the university's Alliance for Ethics and Social Responsibility, which he oversaw from its inception in 2003 through 2013. Tony's primary research, teaching and consulting interests include organizational change, inter-organizational strategies, management consulting, and ethics and corporate social responsibility. He has written or edited 20 books, including *The Human Side of Mergers and Acquisitions* (Jossey-Bass, 1989, 2003), *A Primer on Organizational Behavior* (Wiley, 7th ed., 2008) and, most recently, *Preparing for High-Impact Organizational Change* (Edward Elgar, 2019). He is also editor of the *Research in Management Consulting* series (Information Age Publishing), has received Bentley's highest honours for both teaching and research, and in 2017 was honored as a 'PRME Pioneer' with the UN Global Compact-sponsored Principles for Responsible Management Education (PRME) initiative.

Jon Burchell is a Senior Lecturer in CSR and Sustainable Development at the Sheffield University Management School. His research interests focus on the fields of cross-sectoral engagement and dialogue, CSR, Social Action and responsible management education. He has run a series of projects in collaboration with the Department for Digital, Culture, Media and Sport and is currently leading on the Enabling Social Action programme. He has published a range of academic articles on Green politics and CSR, and is the author of *The Evolution of Green Politics* (Routledge, 2002) and the *Corporate Social Responsibility Reader* (Routledge, 2008).

Fernanda Carreira is Coordinator and Researcher of Sustainability Education at the Center for Sustainability Studies of Fundação Getulio Vargas-EAESP, Brazil. Fernanda's current research focuses on responsible management education, education for sustainability and transformative learning in business schools. She has published articles in the *International Journal of Management Education* and the *Journal of Public Affairs*. She is responsible for sustainability courses offered by FGV-EAESP at both undergraduate and graduate levels and is involved in applied research projects conducted by the Center for Sustainability Studies.

Archie B. Carroll is professor emeritus of management in the Terry College of Business, University of Georgia, USA. Dr Carroll is senior co-author of *Business and Society: Ethics, Sustainability and Stakeholder Management* (10th ed., 2018), co-authored with Jill A. Brown and Ann K. Buchholtz, one of the leading books in the field. He is co-author of *Corporate Responsibility: The American Experience* (Cambridge University Press, 2012). This book won the prestigious Best Book Award at the 2014 Academy of Management Social Issues in Management (SIM) annual meeting. He was awarded the first Lifetime Achievement Award in Corporate Social Responsibility (CSR) by the Institute of Management, Humboldt University-Berlin in 2012. He is a Fellow of the Academy of Management (AOM), Southern Management Association (SMA) and International Association for Business & Society (IABS).

Molly Scott Cato is MEP for the South West of England and was previously a Professor of Economics at Roehampton University. She speaks for the Green Party of England and Wales on finance issues. Molly also has expertise in the issues of renewable energy, trade, food and farming, and cooperatives and mutuals. Molly studied Politics, Philosophy and Economics at Oxford University. Following a career in publishing she took a PhD in Economics from the University of Wales, Aberystwyth, focusing on employment in the South Wales Valleys. She has written several books, including *Green Economics* (2009), *Environment and Economy* (2011) and *The Bioregional Economy* (2012) as well as numerous academic papers.

Amelia Clarke is associate professor in the Faculty of Environment and the first director of the online Master of Environment and Business program at the University of Waterloo (Canada).

As director she oversaw the development and evolution of the program for the past 10 years. She also teaches two of the programme's online courses – Introduction to Sustainability for Business, and Strategies for Sustainable Enterprises.

Pamela Croney is Director of Recruitment, Outreach and Widening Participation at Newcastle Business School at Northumbria University where she is also Admissions Tutor. She is a Senior Fellow of the UK Higher Education Academy and has worked in a variety of roles within business education for many years as both a practitioner and as an examiner. Pam's research interests include Business Education pedagogy, student expectations, transition, psychological contracts and experiential learning. She recently designed and introduced a new year-long experiential learning module for all first-year students on programmes at Newcastle Business School. She holds a DBA in Psychological Contracts within Business Education, and MEd Practitioner Enquiry (Leadership) and BA (Hons) Business Studies.

Ann L. Cunliffe is Professor of Organization Studies at Fundação Getulio Vargas-EAESP, Brazil. She has visiting positions at Università Cattolica del S. Cuore, Italy; Aalborg University, Denmark; and the University of Bath, UK. Ann's current research interests lie at the intersection of organizational studies, philosophy and communications, to study leadership, qualitative research methods, embodied sensemaking, and reflexive approaches to research and practice. She has published articles in *Organizational Research Methods*, the *British Journal of Management*, *Human Relations*, *Management Learning* and the *Journal of Business Ethics*. She organizes the biennial Qualitative Research in Management and Organization Conference in New Mexico, USA.

Elaine E. Englehardt is Distinguished Professor of Ethics and Professor of Philosophy, Utah Valley University (UVU); President, Society for Ethics Across the Curriculum; directed seven multi-year national grants in the area of teaching ethics. She has authored or edited 10 textbooks (the most recent of which is *Ethics Across the Curriculum*), numerous articles and for several years co-edited (with Michael S. Pritchard) *Teaching Ethics*, the official journal of SEAC. She teaches courses in business ethics and media ethics, as well as an introductory course in ethics and values, which she developed, and which all UVU students are required to take. She has served in a variety of administrative positions at UVU.

Mathias Falkenstein is the Executive Policy Advisor at LUISS Business School, LUISS University, Rome (Italy); he is also the Managing Partner at XOLAS, a higher education consultancy firm. Dr Falkenstein's special focus is assisting global universities and business schools in designing and implementing institutional change, with particular attention to issues of sustainability and responsibility, quality management and internationalization. He is an expert in the transformation of management education and currently serves as the PRME Chair in Italy as well as a member of the EAIE General Council. Mathias worked in previous assignments as Director of Business School Services at the European Foundation for Management Development (EFMD), as Director of International Relations at IÉSEG School of Management in Paris, and Director of the International Summer University at the Free University in Berlin. Mathias is a research fellow and post-doctoral graduate at the International Centre for Higher Education Management (ICHEM) at the School of Management, University of Bath, UK.

Peter Jack Gallo is an Associate Professor of Strategy and Entrepreneurship at Creighton University's Heider College of Business, Nebraska. Professor Gallo holds a PhD and MBA from the Kenan–Flagler Business School of the University of North Carolina at Chapel Hill.

His primary research interest is the integration of social and ecological sustainability principles with strategy and entrepreneurship. His research has been published in *Business & Society*, *Journal of Cleaner Production*, *Journal of Business Ethics*, among others. He holds a BSE in Environmental Energy Engineering from Stanford University and he still maintains a significant interest in energy topics. This interest is manifest in both his teaching and research; particular areas of inquiry include renewable energy entrepreneurship, innovation in energy markets and electric utility deregulation.

Jennifer Gao is Lecturer at the Department of Management and Marketing, the University of Melbourne. She received her PhD in Management from the University of Auckland. Her research interests include human resource management, cultural effects on HRM, work and careers, development in East Asia, and university research commercialisation. She has also completed a global dairy industry research project for the International Union of Foodworkers. Her research publications have appeared in *The International Journal of Human Resource Management* and *R&D Management*.

Dirk Ulrich Gilbert is Professor of Business Ethics and Management at the University of Hamburg, Germany. His most recent research focuses on management education, international accountability standards and deliberative democracy. He published in internationally acclaimed journals such as *Business Ethics Quarterly*, *Business & Society*, *Academy of Management Learning and Education*, *Journal of Management Inquiry*, *Management International Review* and *Journal of Business Ethics*.

Vicente Góes is a psychologist, consultant and coordinator of training processes based on transdisciplinarity, and is a member of the Center for Transdisciplinary Education (CETRANS). He has been working at the Fundação Getulio Vargas Center for Sustainability Studies in São Paulo since 2015. He has been a guest professor at the Professional Master's Degree for Sustainability at the same institution, and also coordinates a journalism course at the Énois Association's School of Journalism. He has published articles, books and chapters on education, sustainability, transdisciplinarity, urban culture and Jungian psychology.

Christopher Gohl is a researcher and teacher at the Weltethos Institute at the University of Tübingen which specializes in responsible management learning with a cosmopolitan scope. He received his PhD degree in Political Theory from the University of Potsdam, and holds a Master's degree in American Studies and Jewish Studies. His research focuses on the epistemology, genesis and prevalence of values, on a pragmatist understanding of business ethics and global ethics, on issues of a learning democracy, and on civil society research. As a practising pragmatist, he has organized various stakeholder dialogues, such as the Regional Dialogue Forum Airport Frankfurt from 2005 to 2008, Germany's largest political mediation.

Jonathan Gosling is Emeritus Professor of Leadership at the University of Exeter and visiting scholar at universities around the world, including Indian Institute of Management in Ahmedabad and Renmin University of China. He is author of nine books and more than 100 articles. As a Director at Pelumbra Ltd he promotes thoughtfulness in confusing contexts, hosts writing retreats and educational programmes for experienced managers, and consults to international companies, agencies and multi-party projects. He is one of two lead faculty at the Forward Institute, and a co-founder of CoachingOurselves and the One Planet MBA.

Danna Greenberg is the Walter H. Carpenter Professor of Organizational Behavior at Babson College, Massachusetts. Danna's main area of research focuses on how individuals navigate the intersection between their work and non-work lives as they move through their careers. She has recently published a book on this topic entitled *Maternal Optimism: Forging Positive Paths Through Work and Motherhood*. Danna's second research stream centres on the scholarship of teaching and learning. Here she is focused on the changing landscape of higher education as it pertains to how we teach, what we teach and how we define our lives as academics. She has used this research expertise to lead curriculum innovation and has written a book related to this work entitled *The New Entrepreneurial Leader*. Danna has published more than 30 articles and book chapters in leading journals including *Academy of Management Journal*, *Human Resource Management* and *Academy of Management Learning and Education*. She serves as an Associate Editor for the *Academy of Management Learning and Education*.

Adam Grodecki is the Founder and CEO of the Forward Institute, a non-profit organization working to build a movement for responsible leadership. He set up the Institute with the support of the Boston Consulting Group (BCG), where he was a consultant for five years in their London office. He previously co-founded a student focused charity called Student Hubs. He is a member of the Advisory Board of the Evidence Initiative (an initiative of the Economist and Pew Charitable Trusts) and the NHS Frimley Leadership and Improvement Academy. Adam is also a Governor of Ark Academy.

Debbie Haski-Leventhal is a Professor of Management at Macquarie Business School, an expert of corporate social responsibility (CSR), responsible management education (RME) and volunteerism. Together with the United Nations Principles for Responsible Management Education (PRME), she conducts studies on business students around the world and their attitudes towards responsible management. She has published over 50 academic papers on CSR, RME, volunteering and social entrepreneurship in *Human Relations*, *Journal of Business Ethics*, *MIT Sloan Management Review*, *NVSQ* and other journals. Her work was covered many times by the media, including the *New York Times* and *Financial Review*. She is the author of *Strategic CSR* (Sage) with a foreword by David Cooperrider, and the upcoming books *The Purpose-Driven University* (Emerald) and *CSR and Employee Engagement* (Sage). She is a TED speaker and a public speaker on purpose, social responsibility and the future of higher education.

Christian Hauser is Professor of Business Economics and International Management at the University of Applied Sciences of the Grisons and Fellow at the Digital Society Initiative of the University of Zurich, Switzerland. He studied Latin American Studies at the Universities of Cologne, Germany, Lisbon, Portugal and Fortaleza, Brazil and earned his doctorate in Economics at the University of Cologne. He is a member of the topical platform Ethics of the Swiss Academy of Engineering Sciences (SATW), member of the United Nations Principles for Responsible Management Education (PRME) Working Group on Anti-Corruption and head of the first PRME Business Integrity Action Centre in Europe. His research interests include international entrepreneurship, SME and private sector development, corporate responsibility and business integrity.

Alex Hope is Head of Department for Leadership and Human Resource Management and Associate Professor of Business Ethics at Newcastle Business School, Northumbria University. He is responsible for the strategic leadership of the department and undertakes teaching, research and consultancy across topics such as responsible business, sustainable development, corporate social responsibility, energy policy and business ethics. Alongside his work at Newcastle

Business School Dr Hope is Vice-Chair of the UK and Ireland Chapter of the United Nations Principles of Responsible Management Education (UN PRME) initiative and Co-Chair of the UN PRME Climate Change and Environment working group. He holds a PhD in Sustainable Development, an MA in Academic Practice and BSc (Hons) in Environmental Management.

Dima Jamali has served as Professor in the Olayan School of Business, American University of Beirut from 2002 to 2018, where she made her way fast track through the ranks to Full Professor in 2010 and Endowed Chair in Responsible Leadership in 2014. She is the Editor of seven books dealing with different aspects of sustainability and sustainable development, and author of over 100 international and highly cited publications focusing on different aspects of sustainability and sustainable development in developing countries in general and in the Middle East specifically. Starting in 2015, she has founded and served as President and National Representative for UN Global Compact Network Lebanon (GCNL), a network of businesses committed to advancing Sustainability and the Sustainable Development Goals (SDGs) in Lebanon. In addition, she currently serves as Member of the Lebanese Parliament.

Maureen A. Kilgour is a Professor in the Faculty of Business and Economics at the University of Winnipeg. She is a co-founder and co-chair of the PRME Working Group on Gender Equality and was a member of the UN Women's Empowerment Principles Leadership Group from 2011 to 2018. She researches global governance, business and human rights and corruption, with a special focus on gender equality. She has co-edited three books, *Integrating Gender into Business and Management Education* (Emerald, 2015), *Overcoming Challenges to Gender Equality in the Workplace: Leadership and Innovation* (CTC Press, 2016) and *Gender Equality and Responsible Business: Expanding CSR Horizons* (Greenleaf, 2016). She has book chapters forthcoming on Canada's feminist foreign policy and the SDGs and on gender equality in higher education.

Tine Köhler is Associate Professor for International Management at the University of Melbourne, Australia. Her research interests include global teamwork, the management of cross-cultural differences in norms, communication and coordination, trust, and qualitative and quantitative research methods. Her methodological areas of expertise specifically revolve around quantitative methods including regression, meta-analysis and research design, as well as qualitative methods including grounded theory, case study analysis, ethnography and interviewing. She serves as an Associate Editor for *Organizational Research Methods* and was previously an Associate Editor for *Academy of Management Learning and Education*. She further serves on the editorial boards of *Journal of Management Studies, Journal of Management Education, Academy of Management Learning and Education, Small Group Research,* and the book series *Research Methods in Strategy and Management*. Her work has appeared in *Organizational Research Methods,* the *Journal of International Business Studies, Journal of Management, Academy of Management Learning and Education, Human Resource Management, International Journal of Human Resource Management,* and *Small Group Research*.

Florencia Librizzi is a PhD candidate at Universidad Nacional de Cordoba (UNC) and a sustainability/education professional and international attorney, licensed to practise law in Argentina and New York. She devoted over 6 years to building the Principles for Responsible Management Education (PRME) initiative at the United Nations Global Compact Office and her strategic leadership as Senior Manager contributed significantly to reaching 730+ participants in 90+ countries. She also served at the International Center for Transitional Justice (ICTJ), advising on issues of post-conflict societies and addressing human rights violations. Florencia has practised law since 2006, advising clients on a wide range of legal and sustainability issues, and has taught several courses and seminars at Universidad Empresarial Siglo 21, UNC, NYU School of Law and Columbia Institute for Study of Human Rights. She earned her first law degree magna cum laude at UNC and her Master of Law (LLM) at NYU School of Law.

Jennifer Lynes is associate professor in the Faculty of Environment at the University of Waterloo (Canada). For six years she was director of the Environment and Business undergraduate program – the only of its kind in North America. She has been designing and teaching online courses for almost 20 years, including being an instructor in the Master of Environment and Business program since its inception as well as the UC, San Diego's online specialized certificate in Sustainability & Behavior Change.

Geri Mason, is a Development Economist who focuses on microfinance performance and funding, micro–macro connections in responsible consumption and economic development, and poverty pedagogy in her research. Her research has been published in *World Development* and *Voluntas*. She is currently Associate Professor of Economics and Senior Economist at Seattle Pacific University. She teaches Macroeconomics (Micro & Macro) Development Economics, History of Economic Thought, and Global Encounters and Poverty.

Peter McKiernan, University of Surrey, England, is Professor of Management at the University of Strathclyde, Scotland, Distinguished Professor of Management at Vrje Universiteit Brussel, Belgium and Adjunct Visiting Professor at the University of Notre Dame, Australia. He has been President of both the British Academy of Management (BAM) and the European Academy of Management (EURAM) and is co-founder of the *European Management Review*. He has been awarded the BAM Life Time Achievement Award and the CEEMAN Institutional Champion of the Year Award. His research and practice examines how organizations make sense of their future landscapes and so make more informed strategy as a result. He is co-founder of the Responsible Research in Business and Management and helps support the global effort to transform business research into a force for the common good.

Marcel Meyer is Assistant Professor in the School of Economics and Business Administration at the University of Navarra (Spain). He holds a Bachelor's degree in International Business Studies from the University of Paderborn (Germany), a Master's degree in Business Management from the London Metropolitan University (England), and he obtained his PhD in Organizational Governance and Culture from the University of Navarra in 2017. Before he started his career in academia, Marcel worked as an International Affairs Manager. The focus of his research is on leadership, business ethics and organizational behaviour. His work has been published in *Business Ethics: A European Review*, the *Journal of Management* and in the *Journal of Business Ethics* among other journals.

Jill Millar is a Senior Lecturer in Business and Management at Oxford Brookes University, UK. She holds a PhD in socio-legal studies and is a qualified solicitor. Her research takes a critical approach to Higher Education as a social practice. Previous research projects have used the UN Principles for Responsible Management Education (PRME) and ideas of 'global citizenship' as prisms through which to explore pedagogic practices based on Habermasian ideas of communicative action. Adopting critical discourse analysis, her current research considers the implications of global standards, including PRME, in reinforcing and legitimating particular understandings of business responsibility and of the purpose of management education.

Petra Molthan-Hill leads the Green Academy at Nottingham Trent University since 2013. She won the Sustainability Professional Award in the Green Gown Awards 2016 and The Guardian University Award 2015 for Business Partnership (Greenhouse Gas Management Project) together with NetPositive Ltd. Molthan-Hill is Professor of Sustainable Management and Education for Sustainable Development at Nottingham Business School and Co-Chair of the United Nations Principles for Responsible Management Education (PRME) working group on climate change and environment. Recently, Molthan-Hill undertook research with *Coronation Street* – a popular TV soap opera in the UK – about their impactful carbon literacy training and has co-designed a Carbon Literacy Training for Business Schools based on this insight, which is currently rolled out as a PRME Champions Project.

Ivan Montiel is an Associate Professor of Management and the Area Coordinator for Business, Society and Sustainability at Zicklin School of Business at Baruch College, City University of New York. He is interested in understanding how businesses can tackle global grand challenges such as climate change with a special interest in emerging economies. He acts as Associate Editor for *Business & Society* and serves at the Editorial Review Boards of *Journal of Business Ethics, Organization & Environment* and *Journal of World Business*.

Jan Myers is Associate Professor of Business and Society at Newcastle Business School, Northumbria University. She has been a senior lecturer/assistant professor in business and management, organizational behaviour and HR, and leadership, individual and organizational development in both the UK and Canada. Before moving into academia, Jan was a senior manager, trainer and consultant working in and with third sector and public sector organizations, both in the UK and internationally.

Cristina Neesham is Director of Business Ethics and Corporate Social Responsibility (CSR) at Newcastle University Business School, Newcastle University, UK and Reader in Business Ethics and CSR. She is a Representative-at-Large for the Social Issues in Management division of the Academy of Management and serves as Associate Editor for *Business Ethics: A European Review.* Cristina's research interests focus on ethical issues raised by the introduction of new technologies (such as digitalization and artificial intelligence) in the workplace of the future. She also uses philosophical methods to inform the strategic management of systemic social problems. In particular, she investigates interdependencies between individual and group behaviours, social norms and institutional-regulatory regimes and their role in creating (as well as alleviating) social problems. She uses these findings to inform and design ethical capability building projects for industry, government and professional practice.

Mariam Patsatsia is an alum and former Communications Manager of oikos, an international student organization for sustainability in Economics and Management Education. She holds a Bachelor's degree in International Relations from Ivane Javakhishvili Tbilisi State University, Georgia, and is currently enrolled in the International Relations: Global Governance and Social Theories Master's programme at the University of Bremen and Jacobs University Bremen, Germany.

Michael S. Pritchard is Emeritus Professor of Philosophy, Founding Director of the Center for the Study of Ethics in Society, Western Michigan University, and Willard A. Brown Professor of Philosophy. His PhD in Philosophy is from the University of Wisconsin. He has directed several grants from the National Science Foundation to develop educational programmes in engineering and research ethics. He has authored or edited many books and articles, mostly in theoretical and practical ethics. For several years he co-edited *Teaching Ethics* with Elaine E. Englehardt. He is a founding board member of SEAC and the Association for Practical and Professional Ethics. His teaching areas include professional ethics, engineering ethics, and philosophy for children.

J. Christopher Proctor is the oikos Curriculum Research Manager. He studied Economics, Political Science and History at the University of Tulsa, Oklahoma, before enrolling in the Economic Policies in the Age of Globalization Master programme (EPOG) at Kingston University London and the University of Paris 13. He is a co-editor of the book *Rethinking Economics: An Introduction to Pluralist Economics* and the author of the oikos Guide to Pluralist Economics, and the oikos Mapping Pluralist Research report. He is currently working to promote more research activities within oikos.

Annie Snelson-Powell is a Lecturer of Business and Society at the University of Bath School of Management. She studies organizations in relation to their policies and practices for sustainability, responsibility, ethics and human rights. She focuses on how leaders respond to pressures to do more good and studies the causes and consequences of the gaps that emerge between organizational pledges, policies and strategies and the organizational activities that get implemented in practice. Annie's research involves institutional theory, organized hypocrisy and strategic paradoxes and she has published in leading academic journals including the *Academy of Management Learning and Education* journal and the *Journal of Business Research*.

Andreas Rasche is Professor of Business in Society at the Centre for Corporate Sustainability at Copenhagen Business School (CBS), Denmark. He also acts as the Associate Dean for the CBS MBA programme and is Visiting Professor at the Stockholm School of Economics. He has authored more than 40 academic articles in international top journals and published various cases on topics related to corporate sustainability. He authored and edited numerous well-known books, such as *Building the Responsible Enterprise* (Stanford University Press, 2012), *Corporate Social Responsibility: Strategy, Communication, Governance* (Cambridge University Press, 2017) and *Sustainable Investing* (Routledge, 2020). He is Associate Editor of *Business Ethics Quarterly*. More information is available at: www.arasche.com.

Rupert Read is an Associate Professor of Philosophy at the University of East Anglia, UK. He is author of eight books on a range of subjects and specializes in Wittgenstein, philosophy of film and ecological philosophy. Rupert formerly chaired Green House think-tank, and is a former Green Party of England and Wales councillor, spokesperson, European parliamentary candidate and national parliamentary candidate. Rupert is currently a national UK spokesperson for the Extinction Rebellion movement and is a frequent guest on a range of national UK television and radio programmes. He has articles in the *Guardian*, the *Independent* and in *The Ecologist*, and a number of other newspapers, magazines and websites.

Vikki Rodgers is a Professor of Ecology and current Chair of the Math and Science division at Babson College, Massachusetts. Vikki is a field ecologist and biogeochemist and her research specializes in climate change and plant invasion. She co-directs the Boston Area Climate Experiment (BACE) site in Waltham, MA and she is a board member for the Ecological Research as Education Network (EREN). Vikki's research is published in peer-reviewed, scientific journals, such as *BioScience, Journal of Ecology, Biogeochemistry* and *Reviews in*

Geophysics. Since being at Babson (2007) she has focused on teaching science and sustainability to undergraduate business students, allowing her to develop interdisciplinary and co-taught courses/activities addressing responsible management learning and education.

Philip Roscoe is Reader in Management at the University of St Andrews, Scotland. He is interested in the political and ethical dimensions of organizations. He has researched empirical sites from online dating to small company stock exchanges. He has been a Leverhulme Trust Research Fellow, and has published in leading sociology and management journals, notably *Organization Studies*, *Accounting Organizations and Society*, *Economy and Society* and *Organization*, with monographs published by Oxford University Press and Penguin. In 2011 he was one of 10 winners of the inaugural AHRC BBC Radio 3 'New Generation Thinkers' scheme and was shortlisted for the 2014 Deutscher Wirtschaftsbuchpreis. He holds a PhD in management from Lancaster University, an MPhil (taught) in medieval Arabic thought from the University of Oxford and a degree in theology from the University of Leeds.

Al Rosenbloom, PhD, is the John and Jeanne Rowe Distinguished Professor, Dominican University, River Forest, Illinois. He teaches marketing and international business. His research interests and publications have focused on the relationship between poverty and responsible management education as well as on global branding. He co-leads the Anti-Poverty Working Group, Principles of Responsible Management Education (PRME) and participates broadly in PRME. He was a Fulbright Scholar in Nepal and Bulgaria.

Quinn Runkle is the Director of Education for SOS-UK, the sustainability charity of the UK National Union of Students. She leads SOS' work on educational reform, focusing on transforming further and higher education into a force for good in creating a more just and sustainable world. Quinn joined NUS in 2014 and previously has a background in student and staff behaviour change, engagement and education for sustainable development programmes at the University of Bristol (UK) and the University of British Columbia (Canada). Quinn holds a Bachelor of Arts in Geography and Political Science with a specialism in Environment and Sustainability from the University of British Columbia. She is currently pursuing a Doctorate in Education at the UCL Institute of Education. In 2017, she was named among the 'Top 30 Under 30 Environmental Educators' by the North American Association for Environmental Education.

Georges Samara is the winner of the extraordinary doctorate award (2017–2018), the best family business paper award (Academy of Management, 2019) along with more than six international best research papers nominations and awards. A former visiting scholar at Florida International University, Dr Samara is currently in the professorial track at the American University of Beirut and affiliate researcher at the IPAG family business institute (IFBI). His main areas of research are family business management and ethical and socially responsible business behaviour, with a focus on non-Western contexts. His research has addressed both topics independently and simultaneously. His research has been published in reputable journals such as *Human Resource Management Review*, *Business Horizons*, *Journal of Family Business Strategy*, *Business Ethics: A European Review*, the *International Entrepreneurship and Management Journal*, *Management Decision*, and *Journal of Organizational Change Management*.

Maximilian J. L. Schormair is Assistant Professor in Business Ethics at Trinity Business School, Trinity College Dublin, Ireland. His research interests focus on multi-stakeholder governance, political CSR, stakeholder engagement, deliberative democracy, business & human rights, and the sharing economy. Maximilian's research has been published in *Business Ethics Quarterly, Business & Society*, the *Journal of Business Ethics* and in several edited volumes.

Stefan Schaltegger is full professor for corporate sustainability management, entrepreneurship and accounting at Leuphana University Lüneburg, Germany. Between 1996 and 1998 he was assistant professor of economics and public policy at the University of Basel, Switzerland. He received his PhD in business administration in 1992 and an honorary doctorate in 2017. His research interests include corporate sustainability management, sustainable entrepreneurship, managing stakeholder relationships, and sustainability accounting and performance management. He has more than 500 publications, including in leading journals such as *Journal of Business Ethics, Entrepreneurship Theory and Practice, R&D Management, Business Strategy and the Environment, Ecological Economics, Journal of Cleaner Production, Organization & Environment, Accounting, Auditing & Accountability Journal*, and *Accounting & Organizational Change*.

Alejo José G. Sison is a philosopher who teaches Business Ethics at the School of Economics and Business at the University of Navarre, Spain. He is Visiting Ordinary Professor at the Busch School of Business at the Catholic University of America and Adjunct at the McCourt School of Public Policy, Georgetown University. He was former President of the European Business Ethics Network (EBEN). He is section editor for Philosophy and Business Ethics in the *Journal of Business Ethics* and member of the editorial board of *Business Ethics Quarterly* and of the board of the *Society for Business Ethics*. His research deals with issues at the juncture of ethics, the economy and politics, examined from the perspective of the virtues and the common good. His latest books include *Happiness and Virtue Ethics in Business* (Cambridge University Press, 2015), *The Challenges of Capitalism for Virtue Ethics and the Common Good* (Edward Elgar, 2016), the *Handbook of Virtue Ethics in Business and Management* (Springer, 2016) and *Business Ethics. A Virtue Ethics and Common Good Approach* (Routledge, 2018).

Jeremy St John has a background in bioethics and political philosophy as well as psychology and neuroscience. He teaches business ethics and corporate social responsibility at Monash University and RMIT University, Australia. His research and teaching interests focus on the interaction between the political, economical, psychological and educational spheres of influence, and their effects upon our societies, institutions and selves, and the capacity for justice that flows between these.

Meredith Storey received her PhD in 2020 from the Kemmy Business School of the University of Limerick, Ireland, where her dissertation explored how the framing of sustainable development reporting by businesses and business schools has evolved over time. Other recent articles include 'Business Education for Sustainable Development' in *The Encyclopedia of Sustainability in Higher Education* (Springer, 2019) and 'Responsible Management Education: Mapping the Field in the Context of the SDGs' in *The International Journal of Management Education* (Elsevier, 2017). Meredith has served as a consultant with the UN Global Compact's Principles for Responsible Management Education (PRME) initiative. She currently works as an Education Manager for the UN Sustainable Development Solutions Network (SDSN) in New York City, where she helps create educational resources for the SDG Academy, SDSN's flagship education initiative. Her research interests include business education for sustainable development, ESD, RME, CME, and critical pedagogy.

Harriet Thiery is a Research Associate at the Sheffield University Management School. Her primary research interests are global poverty and development, neoliberal discourse and theories of neo-colonialism. She is in the process of completing her PhD in the School of Languages and Cultures. She has also worked on a number of research projects in the Management School in collaboration with the Department for Digital, Culture Media and Sport. She has taught across a range of subjects, including CSR, Management Themes and Perspectives and French colonial history.

Anne S. Tsui, PhD, University of California, Los Angeles, Honorary Doctorate, University of St Gallen, Switzerland, is Distinguished Adjunct Professor at the University of Notre Dame, Indiana, and Distinguished Visiting Professor at Peking University and Fudan University, China. She is the 67th President and Fellow of both the Academy of Management and the Academy of International Business, and 14th Editor of the *Academy of Management Journal*. Through founding the International Association for Chinese Management Research and *Management and Organization Review*, and working with leading business schools in China, she has contributed to the development of Chinese management research since 2000. She is a co-founder of Responsible Research in Business and Management, leading a global effort to transform business research into a force for the common good.

Sandra Waddock is Galligan Chair of Strategy, Carroll School Scholar of Corporate Responsibility, and Professor of Management at Boston College's Carroll School of Management. A winner of numerous awards, she has published 13 books and more than 150 papers on topics related to large system change, memes, intellectual shamanism, corporate responsibility, multi-sector collaboration, and management education, among others. Her latest books are *Healing the World* (Greenleaf, 2017) and *(Teaching) Managing Mindfully* (with Lawrence Lad and Judith Clair) (Global Jesuit Case Series, 2018). Other recent books include *Intellectual Shamans* (Cambridge, 2015), which was preceded by *Building the Responsible Enterprise* (with Andreas Rasche) in 2012. Current research interests include transformational change towards wellbeing, dignity and flourishing for all, corporate responsibility, intellectual shamanism, stewardship of the future, and management education.

Rachel Welton is a Principal Lecturer in International Business and Tourism at Nottingham Business School and a Senior Fellow HEA. Her expertise lies in the area of sustainable tourism. Her PhD was focused on the adaptation and mitigation of international tourism destinations to climate change, and this continues to be a research focus. She is currently involved in several pedagogic research projects in responsible management education, such as carbon literacy training and coaching and mentoring; the learning from these initiatives inform her teaching. Rachel is Course Leader for the undergraduate International Business suite of degrees and has embedded several student focused collaborative sustainability projects into the course, such as the Oath Project.

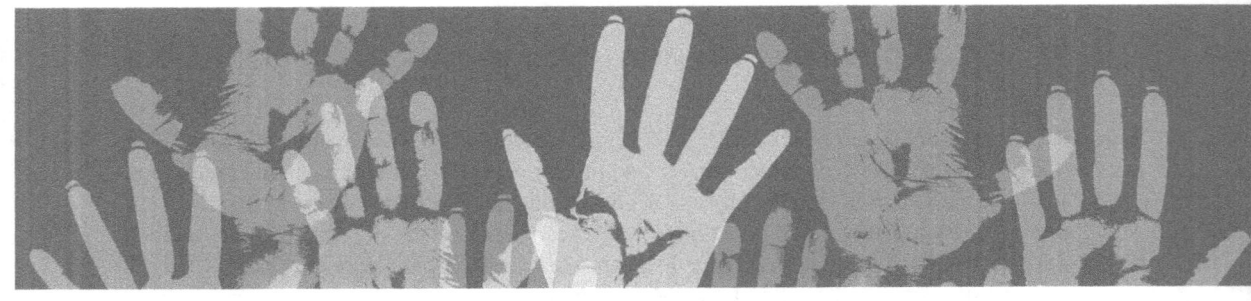

Introduction: Establishing and Questioning the Responsible Management Learning and Education Discipline

Dirk C. Moosmayer, Carole Parkes, Oliver Laasch and Kenneth G. Brown

This Handbook is published at the start of the 2020s and follows a decade of quite substantial development in the field of responsible management learning and education (RMLE). It brings together a broad range of voices and thoughts in the attempt to depict the field. In this introductory chapter, we first review the state of the world and highlight the need for RMLE. We then aim to define RMLE and discuss various definitions together with critical reflections of the field and its institutionalization. Finally, we offer our readers an overview of the 33 chapters in this Handbook.

The acceleration of development in RMLE followed the well-documented global financial crash in 2007/8 and the strident voices calling for change. This included accusations aimed at business schools and their culpability because of the fascination with particular forms of economics aimed solely at profit maximization (Starkey and Tempest, 2009) and a form of management built on a philosophy undermining responsibility (Painter-Morland, 2015), although there had been serious disquiet (even before the crash) that business and management education focused too narrowly on management practices designed to maximize returns, with greed being seen by many as the underlying catalyst for what was to come (Pfeffer and Fong, 2002). Similarly, Fassin (2005) analysed major business scandals in the preceding decades that appeared to lead to increasing distrust in business and a greater pressure for more transparency, accountability and change of underlying values. Finally, with the global COVID-19 pandemic, we expect even greater attention to questions about the ways that governments and large companies must balance public and economic health around the world.

Thus, although there have been major developments in RMLE, and we expect the field to continue to grow, to suggest that all is well would be a gross overstatement (Burchell et al., 2015; Louw, 2015). Advancements in the field could be in part due to a greater understanding of the nature of the subject with all its complexity and challenges, together with the different approaches and levels of engagement that is evident in the chapters of this Handbook. Indeed, its very existence can be seen as a major milestone. The commissioning of the Handbook recognizes RMLE as a distinctive subject area and sets out to address the following questions: What is the state of the art? Where is the discipline going? What are the key debates/issues that comprise the discipline?

Although many business and management educational institutions and academics have embraced RMLE, the extent to which this is fully integrated is debatable (Dyllick, 2015; Millar and Price, 2018). The criticism of business schools has continued to be made, including Martin Parker's provocative publication *Shut Down the Business School: What's Wrong with Management Education* (2018). PRME – the Principles for Responsible Management Education – is the largest UN-backed organization working with higher education on this agenda and has just over 800 signatory institutions (PRME, 2020). This does not reach anywhere near the over 13,000 business schools operating worldwide (Parker, 2018). There are, of course, many institutions working in other ways (and with other organizations) to integrate RMLE, and in particular, the Sustainable Development Goals (SDGs) (United Nations, 2019; Parkes et al., 2017; Storey et al., 2017) have become a catalyst to galvanize action across a range of issues previously underrepresented in the field, such as poverty and wider environmental concerns (Rosenbloom et al., 2017). The agenda set out in the SDGs brings many of the most pressing global challenges into sharp focus and it would be remiss of us as responsible management and leadership education academics and practitioners not to comment upon the state of the world as we publish the RMLE Handbook in this new decade (Laasch and Conaway, 2015).

As the Edelman Trust Barometer 2019 Report (that monitors trust in government, business, NGOs and media organizations across the world) noted, 'the last decade has seen a loss of faith in traditional authority figures and institutions' (Edelman, 2019). This lack of trust seriously inhibits progress towards resolving some of the world's greatest challenges, that include growing inequality and climate change. This is underlined by the rise of youth activism and social movements that have taken the debate to decision-makers.

In August 2018, at age 15, the Swedish schoolgirl Greta Thunberg began what has become a worldwide movement of youth activism, by striking outside the Swedish parliament to call for action on climate change. At the same time, Extinction Rebellion (XR, 2020) has developed as an international movement and held major protests across the globe. By the end of 2019, Thunberg had been nominated for a Nobel Peace Prize and was featured on the cover of *Time* magazine as the 'next generation leader' and credited with bringing the Climate Emergency to the fore of people's consciousness (TIME, 2019).

There are also reminders of the fragility of both the earth (including the unprecedented bushfires in Australia) (Attenborough, 2020) and the myriad reports of the loss of biodiversity worldwide. According to the Intergovernmental Science-Policy Platform on Biodiversity and Ecosystem Services (IPBES, 2019), nature is declining globally at rates unprecedented in human history – and the rate of species extinctions is accelerating, with grave impacts on people around the world.

The growing divide in wealth distribution worldwide has seen a profound increase in economic inequality, often driven by global forces but maintained by the perpetuation of economic systems that prioritize the 'haves' of the world (Ziblatt, 2020). The climate crisis exacerbates already stark global inequalities where its impacts are disproportionately felt by those least responsible and able to prevent, mitigate and rebuild after a climate-related disaster (Carter, 2020).

Similarly, the fragility of democracies and their communities is palpable. With the upsurge of populist parties and movements from Latin America and North America to Western and Eastern Europe, many populist outsiders have come to power speaking on behalf of 'the people' but often do so in ways that seem to challenge basic norms of liberal democracy. There has also been a rise in partisan polarization, with political opponents being regarded as existential enemies and in many countries migration being positioned as a threat to communities (Ziblatt, 2020).

One example of this was seen in the numerous broad-based immigration restrictions included in governmental COVID-19 responses, even when such restrictions were not widely regarded as useful for public health (WHO, 2020). https://www.who.int/news-room/articles-detail/updated-who-recommendations-for-international-traffic-in-relation-to-covid-19-outbreak/.

Given the context in which RMLE is now positioned, there is need for greater impetus to address not only the economic but the societal and environmental challenges faced by the world today (Parkes et al., 2018). When the SDGs were agreed in January 2016, the then Secretary General of the United Nations, Ban Ki-Moon, stated that 'solutions [for the SDGs] will involve everything from regulation to disruptive innovation – and everyone from world leaders and chief executives, to *educators*, activists and citizens' (Ban Ki-Moon, 2016).

There is also an implied urgency with the RMLE agenda because of the nature of the issues that have become an integral part of the agenda, such as the climate emergency and inequality (TIME, 2020). As we start this new decade, there are just 3653 days to 2030 when the SDGs are expected to be achieved. A stark reminder that to actually make a difference there needs to be an acceleration of the way and the rate at which all actors in society step up to these challenges which has been exacerbated by the Covid 19 pandemic. This is a humanitarian as well as an economic and financial crisis that highlights inequality of all types. Significantly, it disproportionately affects the billions of people living in poverty who are already severely threatened by the climate emergency; thus, time is of the essence. In addition, there is a governance crisis both internationally and locally with governments and organisations needing to respond to immediate and longer-term impacts. Responsible management and leadership have never been more important, and education is key to this.

(UN-) DEFINING RESPONSIBLE MANAGEMENT LEARNING AND EDUCATION

'"Responsible Management Education" sounds self-evident' (Forray and Leigh, 2012: 295), and RMLE is a vibrant topic that colleagues are interested in. This made it quite easy for us to get people interested in this handbook project, but even more difficult to develop a precise nuanced understanding of the domain. In this section we review different ways of defining the field of responsible management learning and education. We then critically reflect on these definitions by considering some of the aspects that are typically considered constitutive for the field. These include transdisciplinarity, institutionalization of the field, and impact on the real challenges.

Defining RMLE

'PRME's vision is to realize the Sustainable Development Goals through responsible management education' (www.unprme.org/about-prme/index.php). Thus

> RMLE is learning and education that targets the realization of the Sustainable Development Goals (UN SDGs). RMLE 'will develop the capabilities of students to be future generators of sustainable value for business and society at large and to work for an inclusive and sustainable global economy'. (PRME Principle 1 | Purpose)

A strength of this definition is that it defines RMLE from its outcome, the aim to contribute to the UN SDGs.

In targeting the UN SDGs, the PRME terminology focuses on the 'sustainability' (predominantly social and environmental) concept. Other definitions highlight the importance of integrating considerations of sustainability, responsibility and ethics as responsible management, which 'assumes responsibility for the triple bottom line (sustainability), stakeholder value (responsibility), and moral dilemmas (ethics)' (Laasch and Conaway, 2015: 25). With this in mind, *RMLE is the learning and education of a management approach that considers sustainability, responsibility and ethics in its decision making*. A connection of the integrated three fields with its wider educational implications is offered in Rasche and Gilbert's (2015) definition of responsible management learning and education as

> a descriptor for efforts aimed at embedding reflections about corporate responsibility (i.e., the social impact of businesses on society), environmental sustainability (i.e., the contribution of firms to a sustainable economy), and ethics (i.e., reflections about right and wrong in the context of business situations) into business schools' educational practices (Forray & Leigh, 2012; Godemann, Haertle, Herzig, & Moon, 2014). These practices are not limited to modifying the curriculum, but also include changes in research practices, pedagogies, organizational strategies, and extracurricular activities. (2015: 240)

Additional guidance for understanding the educational side of RMLE is offered by Nonet et al. (2016), who ask students about their understanding of responsible management and derive implications for RMLE. (Also see Haski-Leventhal et al. (2016) and Haski-Leventhal in this Handbook for a detailed students' view.) In addition to concepts such as the triple bottom line, Nonet's work is enlightening in its identifying *knowing*, *doing* and *being* as spheres of responsible managerial competence that need to be developed through RMLE.

The RMLE understanding in this Handbook is one of RM-LE, i.e. one of learning and education for and of responsible management. In their PRME special issue editorial, Forray and Leigh (2012: 295) ask 'how we educate responsibly'. This leads to an understanding of R-MLE, i.e. how to design and deliver management learning and education (MLE) responsibly, and thus offers an understanding of Responsible MLE that covers the consideration of educators' responsibility beyond the RM domain. This aspect is not explicitly addressed in this Handbook but is implicitly touched on in various chapters, e.g. in McKiernan and Tsui's chapter on doctoral education for RMLE.

Transdisciplinarity

In the initial call for this Handbook we suggested responsible management education is a transdisciplinary field related to learning for management sustainability, responsibility and ethics. Transdisciplinarity combines different academic research perspectives to jointly analyse an object or issue with diverse practitioner perspectives to jointly address complex real-world problems (Chapter 33 by Beckmann and Schaltegger). Transdisciplinary responsible management extends beyond the single discipline perspective in two ways.

First, it integrates the disciplines of sustainability, responsibility and ethics. Each of these three disciplines has different conceptual and pedagogical strengths and weaknesses. Integrating the three disciplines allows us to connect the answers to three fields of questions. Descriptive and behavioral *ethics* can tell us a lot on the *why* people behave good or bad. *Responsibility* can tell us a lot about stakeholders, their responsibilities and about relationships between stakeholders. *Sustainability* or sustainable development adds a systemic perspective as a strength and can thus serve as a more comprehensive framework. In addition, the traditions of corporate responsibility have a stronger emphasis on social impact and the people and society dimension while the sustainability discipline grew from an engagement with environmental impacts of business conduct. Transdisciplinarity between these three disciplines leads to better RMLE outcomes due to the complementarity of the disciplines. Transdisciplinary RMLE thus develops better competence in solving problems that have connections to more than one discipline. For example, addressing climate change (a traditional sustainability topic) would require understanding the nexus of climate change with poverty (a traditional responsibility topic) (Laasch et al., 2020).

Second, transdisciplinary RMLE extends beyond the academic domain and fosters strong exchange and integration of knowledge production and education with management practices in the business, governmental and non-governmental spheres. Hence, transdisciplinarity describes the expansion of our perspective beyond the boundaries of academia. The advent of the Sustainable Development Goals (SDGs) as an important pillar of RMLE underlines the need for more inter- and transdisciplinary approaches. More than ever before, this requires a collaborative approach with all actors in this space – not competing to be 'the best in the world but to be the best for the world' (The 50+20 Agenda, 2012; Muff et al., 2013). Diversity of actors and contributors is likely to provide more innovative solutions and collaborators for implementation. This view is also emphasized in a quote from Jon Khoo, Innovation Partner at Interface plc,[1] whom we interviewed in the scope of this handbook project:

> Our Founder Ray Anderson, was very good at ensuring he listened to the 'less obvious voices'. This could be the youngest person in the room who has the best ideas or scientists whose work on biomimicry significantly influenced our development of Entropy®, carpet tiles that reduced waste and use of chemicals.

Institutionalization

A further aspect of the RMLE project might be its institutionalization manifested in the establishment of RMLE as a discipline with a growing body of literature,[2] increasing number of related events, consideration of related expertise in hiring processes and its backing by the UN PRME. Work in the RMLE field self-identifies by using the *responsible management* label to reference its integrated use of the sustainability, responsibility and ethics concepts. The resulting shared body of RMLE literature thus interlinks more strongly than it would without an explicit RMLE label and without explicit reference to the emerging body of RMLE research, i.e. the existing work that explicitly integrates sustainability, responsibility and ethics views on one question (Setó-Pamies and Papaoikonomou, 2015).

In addition, the discipline is defined through an explicit strong link to the UN PRME and the Global Compact (UNGC) and thus an active community of practitioners under the RMLE umbrella (Rasche, 2020; Rasche and Waddock, 2014). The transdisciplinary RMLE definition is what defines, vitalizes and keeps alive the RMLE definition and the practices that belong to this definition. This handbook is thus an important step in defining the RMLE discipline. In becoming a clearly defined discipline, we can gain further impact. Elements in this institutionalization process may be the formation of RMLE-specific academic journals, academic interest groups or divisions, and perhaps the designation of academic positions as professor of RMLE.

PRME does offer a platform to gather, institutionalize and thus strengthen the consideration of transdisciplinarity, i.e. sustainability, responsibility and ethics across academia, businesses, and others. The institutional strength of the association with the United Nations, the UN Global Compact and the legitimacy of the PRME brand are elements that lead to bundling forces and increasing impact and the likelihood of real change by creating the necessary weight.

RMLE as Non-discipline

We identified transdisciplinarity, i.e. the fact that it spans beyond disciplinary boundaries, as a constitutive characteristic of the RMLE discipline. There seems to be an obvious contradiction:

the core idea of being transdisciplinary is exactly to not focus on disciplinary boundaries. So perhaps RMLE cannot or should not be a discipline.

By emphasizing the importance of self-identifying with the domain of responsible management and making explicit references to the RMLE domain, PRME initiative or a RMLE body of research, one establishes new disciplinary boundaries. These boundaries will guide the production of new knowledge as they guide academics in the choice of thoughts and evidence to build on. These boundaries guide the assessment of work, e.g. when reviewing the fit of a thought or an argument with the RMLE community. And the boundaries will guide the identity of RMLE practitioners and the shaping of practices (Laasch and Gherardi, 2019). This seems to be a step in the wrong direction for a 'discipline' that emphasizes transdisciplinarity and the overcoming of disciplinary boundaries.

By having more clearly defined boundaries, the community loses its inclusiveness and vibrant flexibility. We would not only define what is 'in', but also what is 'out'. In their editorial for a special issue on Responsible Management Learning, Laasch et al. (2020) distinguish disciplinary, interdisciplinary and transdisciplinary approaches. By a narrow definition of the RMLE discipline with transdisciplinary integration as a constitutive criterion, a consideration of Climate Change, a traditional sustainability topic (see, e.g., Chapple et al., 2019), would not be RMLE, unless it makes explicit its links with ethics and responsibility. Such an understanding would neglect that specialized knowledge (e.g. sustainability only) may be about as important as the integrated transdisciplinary perspective. In Chapter 11 of this Handbook Molthan-Hill, Hope and Welton build such a focused sustainability perspective and then add connections to responsibility and ethics in their final section.

Another aspect that should make us cautious of the institutionalization of RMLE and particularly of seeing its link with the UN-backed PRME initiative as a defining element is PRME's ideological underpinning. The PRME is an initiative convened by a group of accreditation bodies under the umbrella of the UN Global Compact and PRME Principle 2 makes explicit reference to the UNGC. The Global Compact is carried by the major corporations on this planet, by those who subscribe to fundamental business assumptions and values and many of them are stock listed and adhere to quarterly reporting. The Global Compact builds on the assumption that the global grand challenges (Van der Byl et al., 2020), which at least in parts were caused by businesses, can best be solved by businesses (see Chapter 25 by Jill Millar for a similar perspective). By institutionally connecting the RMLE field to the PRME, one might argue that we subscribe to UNGC values and prevent true systems change that might suggest radically different orchestrations of the roles of businesses, civil society and governments (Louw, 2015; Millar and Price, 2018; Painter-Morland, 2015).

RMLE has to better prepare students to develop creative visions of the future, to anticipate future challenges and to create innovative solutions to them (Laasch and Moosmayer, 2015; Nonet et al., 2016). It is important to learn lessons from the past but providing students with the skills and attributes to make a difference to current and future challenges is vital (TIME, 2020). In our interviews, Chris Harrop, Director of Sustainability and Marketing at Marshalls plc[3] summarized this:

One key area that business schools could improve on is getting students to think about the future and what kind of world and what kind of responses are needed from business. I see too many graduates who can tell you about business practices in the 1990s or 2000s but not able to plan and make decisions for the future.

The more the RMLE field institutionalizes, the more it risks to develop a narrow mindset of the themes, methods and internal incentive systems. The more we institutionalize as a discipline, the more we risk to replace the flexibility and dynamism of our field with inertia and stiff borders; and the more this happens, the more we lose the capacity to create something truly different that may be able to tackle the miseries of the future.

If we as the RMLE community want to be smarter than existing disciplines, if we want to be sustainable in a sense that we build ideas that carry through truly long term, then perhaps we should seek ways to stay out of common systemic mechanisms.

Challenge-centred Impact

We opened our introduction to this Handbook with a brief snapshot of the challenges, crises and miseries that our planet and our societies are currently going through. These crises could probably be described as the deficits that the UN SDGs address, including poverty, hunger, health, inequality, consumption, climate and other social and environmental challenges. Still, it seems important to connect these generic goals with the specific crises that we are experiencing today. RMLE aims at making a contribution to overcoming these crises, to creating solutions to the obvious challenges. RMLE's first and most important goal must be having impact in business practice and ultimately changing the environmental and social realities to the better.

Transdisciplinarity as defined above is a two-fold expansion beyond boundaries. First, beyond the boundaries of sustainability, responsibility and ethics; and second, beyond the boundaries of the academic sphere for stronger academic practice engagement. It is this second view that allows making the need for impact more explicit: In its attempt to address the grand challenges and contribute to the SDGs, RMLE needs to collaborate with practice and for practice and impact. The editors of this handbook, most of the contributors and probably many of our readers are academics. As academics, it typically appears relatively easy to us to conceptually integrate sustainability, responsibility and ethics. Integrating managerial practice in our work for creating real impact is much more difficult. It is thus even more important that we emphasize the influence on practices and the impact on our societal challenges in our understanding of RMLE.

> *RMLE should be the creation, dissemination and application of individual, organizational, and systemic level* **solutions to the pressing social and environmental challenges that our societies face today and in dynamic futures**. *To ensure impact in a dynamic future, RMLE regularly undefines itself.*

This definition acknowledges the inseparability of research (creation), teaching (dissemination) and business practices (application). It integrates the different levels of ethics (individual), responsibility (CSR, organizational) and sustainability (systemic). By setting the solution of social and environmental challenges as its goal, RMLE would acknowledge that economic goals need to serve society or the environment to be legitimate. By referencing a dynamic future, this definition suggests that RMLE needs to continuously question its own definition to ensure it still fits the dynamically changed future.

In this sense, this Handbook offers a range of perspectives that do all in some way aim to contribute to solving some of the big questions of our societies.

STRUCTURES OF RESPONSIBLE MANAGEMENT LEARNING AND EDUCATION – A GUIDE ON HOW TO READ THIS BOOK

In this section we develop a model that describes the field of responsible management learning and education (see Figure I.1). The model is congruent with the five sections of this handbook.

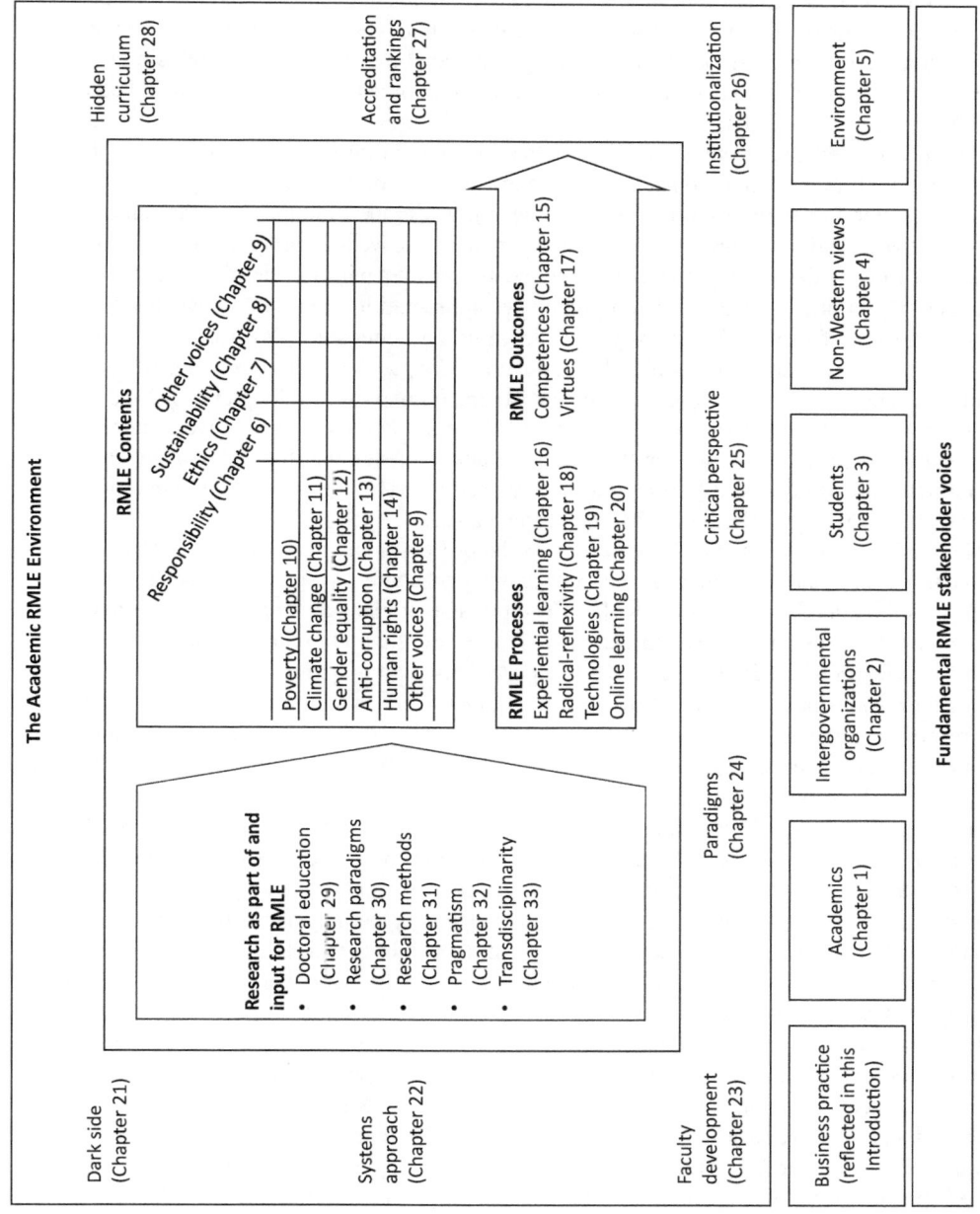

Figure I.1 The academic RMLE environment

In the first section we develop general perspectives on responsible management learning and education by exploring the views of different stakeholders in a wider sense: managers (taken into account in this introductory chapter), ourselves as academics (Chapter 1), PRME as topic-specific intergovernmental organization (Chapter 2), students (Chapter 3), culture (Chapter 4) and the environment (Chapter 5). The latter two are perspectives that extend the boundaries of traditional RLME by moving the still dominant Western view towards global and non-Western perspectives and by offering a perspective on green economics that suggests revising the traditional economic assumptions that are still very dominant in management studies and education (e.g. Moosmayer et al., 2019).

The second element of our model covers the educational purposes and contents of RMLE. This starts with reviews and considerations of (corporate) social responsibility (Chapter 6), of ethics (Chapter 7) and of sustainability (Chapter 8). While the fundamental assumption of our view on RMLE is that it integrates these three perspectives, we are still convinced that it is very important to consider each of these three concepts together with its traditions, its history and its genealogy in order to get a full comprehensive appreciation of possible contributions to the integrated field of responsible management learning and education. We further consider five challenges that are related to specific SDGs: poverty (Chapter 10), climate change (Chapter 11), gender (Chapter 12), anti-corruption (Chapter 13) and human rights (Chapter 14). Together, this section can be understood as a matrix built by the three fundamental perspectives on one dimension and the specific challenges on the other. We acknowledge that these perspectives may be incomplete and additional, different voices may need to be foregrounded (reflected in Chapter 10, which we include on both dimensions of the matrix).

The third section of this Handbook addresses the processes and outcomes of responsible management learning and education. In this section we first address responsible management competence as the intended outcome of RMLE. The purpose of management education is to develop certain competences among learners (Chapter 15). While the traditional competence debate has been very vibrant in the 1980s and 1990s it appears important to question and reconsider competences for responsible management. It seems that much work in the past built on the assumption that responsible management education just needs to produce, develop and nourish the same competences as traditional management and business education, but with application to responsibility management. However, building on the assumption that RMLE is a different type of management requires a different type of management and of management learning and education (MLE) than traditional MLE. We need to redefine the output more generally and thus identify a different set of processes to develop such competence. We include experiential learning (Chapter 16), as an approach to foster responsibility in and through management learning and education. Virtue ethics (Chapter 17) offers an integrated theoretical angle that specifies the virtuous manager as a desirable outcome of RMLE together with an educational process. We further cover a perspective on radical reflexivity (Chapter 18) that needs to be applied and developed. And we consider the aspects of technology in RMLE (Chapter 19) and the specific case of online education (Chapter 20).

In the fourth section, we offer perspectives on the prerequisites of RMLE implementation in the academic environment. We start from systemic views on RMLE (Chapters 21 and 22) and we reflect on what role we as academics may take (Chapter 24) and how we develop our own RMLE competences (Chapter 23). After a critical perspective (Chapter 25), we then offer institutional lenses on responsible management learning and education that consider the rhetoric and realities of RMLE institutionalization (Chapter 26), the role of accreditation and rankings in this context (Chapter 27), and finally the hidden curriculum underlying institutional realities (Chapter 28).

The fifth section of this Handbook sheds light on responsible management research as the fundamental supplier of the knowledge that is conveyed in responsible management learning and education, and of the knowledge that is applied in designing and delivering RMLE in programmes in business schools. We first consider how doctoral education needs to be and could be a crucial facilitator and driver of responsible management research and thus of responsible management knowledge and ultimately responsible management learning and education (Chapter 29). Then, different research paradigms (Chapter 30) and research methods (Chapter 31) in responsible management are reviewed with a discussion of how they influence, limit and facilitate the creation or discovery of responsible management knowledge that is conveyed in learning and education. A pragmatist perspective suggests a more integrated perspective on RMLE (Chapter 32). Finally, with the chapter on transdisciplinary RMLE (Chapter 33), we close the circle on the considerations presented earlier in this introductory chapter.

We introduce each chapter in more detail below.

Part One: Perspectives on Responsible Management Learning and Education

In Chapter 1, *Management Education Today and Tomorrow*, co-editor Kenneth (Ken) G. Brown presents 'Voices from the Contributing Authors' on their personal views and motivations in the field of RMLE. The fact that motivations of today's RMLE educators are not rooted in their own education and that they feel that our net impact is rather negative, emphasizes the need to change and do something significantly different in the way we teach management. The chapter also offers some big ideas that the authors find promising for this future avenue.

In Chapter 2, Florencia Librizzi and Carole Parkes depict *The United Nations-Backed Principles for Responsible Management Education (PRME): A Principles-Based Global Engagement Platform for Higher Education Institutions to Advance the Sustainable Development Goals (SDGs)*. The chapter offers a definition, a review of PRME's history, its principles, its organizational structure and engagement with stakeholders and a range of further aspects that are central to understanding the institutional impact of the PRME.

Debbie Haski-Leventhal, with Quinn Runkle representing Students Organising for Sustainability UK and with Mariam Patsatsia and J. Christopher Proctor for oikos International, review a wide range of studies that Debbie has done in an RMLE context. This chapter on *Responsible Management Education: The Voice and Perspective of Students* draws an optimistic outlook on students' RMLE-related perceptions, expectations and attitudes. This is further supported by voices from two global student organizations, Students Organising for Sustainability (SOS) and oikos. The chapter thus offers qualitative and quantitative support for the claim that the request for more responsibility is not just in our streets on Fridays but has arrived in our classrooms, thus strengthening the call for business schools to deliver RMLE to students' expectations.

With regards to the environmental impact of management decisions, RMLE calls for global inclusion and the consideration of effects in various localities. Dima Jamali and Georges Samara raise our awareness that within our own RMLE discipline we are yet quite unsensitive to being a global discipline and are very Western-dominated. Their chapter on *Non-Western Responsible Management Education: A Critical View and Directions for the Future* is a call for more consideration of non-Western perspectives in RMLE when it comes to understanding the institutional realities of business schools in which RMLE is taught and journals and funding bodies which influence the production of knowledge, when it comes to the contents and theories that are relevant to manage responsibly in specific non-Western local contexts, and when it comes to pedagogies that work in different cultures.

In Chapter 5 on *Green Economics: Rethinking Economics for Responsible Management Education*, Molly Scott Cato and Rupert Read engage with economic thinking as an important body of theories that determines our understanding and assumptions underlying management behaviours. They argue that a responsible approach to teaching economics needs to study the world as it really is rather than as it is described by economic theories. They demand a 'pluralist' approach to economic theory and practice.

Part Two: Educational Purposes and Contents

The purpose of Chapters 6, 7 and 8 is to review the three fundamental disciplines of RMLE, responsibility, ethics and sustainability. When we invited authors for these chapters, there was an apparent contradiction in the call for a review of a single discipline while at the same time building on an integrated understanding of responsible management {as sustainability, ethics, responsibility} as the fundamental assumption of this handbook project. In the initial chapter drafts, Archie B. Carroll had a strong emphasis on ethics in his responsibility chapter and Mike Pritchard and Elaine E. Englehardt worked on sustainability ethics when we thought we asked for an ethics chapter. This left us as editors with some challenges but even more so with a lot of hope: RMLE is understood as truly transdisciplinary and even to the authors who are pioneers in their fields, it would appear unnatural to disconnect the three streams. Chapter 9 connects well to this as it highlights the need to question the assumptions underlying current debates in the three disciplines in order to develop solutions that can stimulate the necessary systemic change that the grand challenges require.

In Chapter 6 on *Responsible Management Education: The Role of CSR Evolution and Traditions*, Archie B. Carroll offers an exciting, very personal account of the development of (corporate social) responsibility and how it found its way into management education. In this sense, the chapter is not only a review of the field but also an important case study of the institutionalization of the field from which we can all learn for our joint efforts in taking the field further. The chapter also offers strong links to ethics education in the management classroom and is thus well connected to the next chapter.

Michael S. Pritchard and Elaine E. Englehardt review ethics education in their chapter on *Ethics, Sustainability and Management Leadership*. They review how ethics has moved from a philosophical subject into the heart of leadership and management education. They put special emphasis on sustainability ethics, i.e. on clarifying why an emphasis on sustainability is ethically given. In doing so, they highlight the urgency of the RMLE project which we also outlined in our conceptual section.

The sustainability angle connects to Chapter 8 by Meredith Storey on *Critical Responsible Management Education for Sustainable Development*. Building on work from her doctoral dissertation, she applies critical theory to sustainability learning and education. This allows her to move sustainability away from an additional subject taught in the MBA towards a new educational paradigm that allows a comprehensive redefinition of management education as RMLE.

In Chapter 9 Jon Burchell and Harriet Thiery take the critical perspective further and find that it is *Time to Look Beyond the Business Case* and explain *Why Responsible Management Education Needs to Give More Time to Other Voices*. They cater to the institutionalization tension that we developed above and warn that institutionalization may limit the variety of voices that are considered. In particular, they identify a very instrumental approach to CSR as one dominant voice in RMLE. They critique this approach as it stays within the framework of existing economic assumptions which needs reconsideration to make MLE truly responsible.

Chapters 10 to 14 present five view on specific contents of responsible management, namely poverty, climate change, gender, corruption and human rights. We consider these five as threshold concepts, i.e. knowledge 'that alters the way we think about knowledge that is central to understanding a discipline' (Hibbert and Cunliffe, 2015: 180). In other words, without understanding the connections between business and management and each of these five themes, one cannot be a rounded responsible manager because it is too likely that one's actions are irresponsible in the way that they cause negative consequences.

In Chapter 10 on *Poverty and Responsible Management Education* Geri Mason and Al Rosenbloom make the consideration of poverty as a threshold concept explicit. They suggest that populations at the base of the pyramid, which are most exposed to poverty, need to be considered comprehensively in the business systems, e.g. as suppliers and customers and by taking into account their specific vulnerability, and that a responsible management system tackling the poverty issue needs to centre around human capital building, which is very compatible with the Handbook's learning and education angle. They further develop a teaching and learning programme that allows delivering the necessary concepts and experiences in the classroom or wider learning environment.

In Chapter 11, Petra Molthan-Hill, Alex Hope and Rachel Welton discuss *Tackling Climate Change through Management Education* and thus offer an example of an environmentally focused contents perspective. This chapter, which connects nicely with the concerns raised by the FFF – Fridays For Future – movement, connects common business practice with climate change and introduces the example of carbon literacy training as a way to tackle the issue. When engaging with the carbon literacy training, the perspective is one of the wider views on responsible management, as it develops knowledge on one specific aspect of RMLE. In the second part, the authors then put their climate change education concept in relation to ethics and responsibility, and thus take the perspective that we described above as that explicitly covers the first part of transdisciplinarity.

Maureen A. Kilgour engages with *Gender Equality: Taking Its Rightful Place at the Heart of Sustainability Education* in Chapter 12. While it is quite agreed that gender discrimination is unethical and by limiting the full use of human potential is unsustainable, the systemic view seems particularly interesting: The chapter shows how the dominant economic systems on private and public levels produce and maintain gender discrimination. An integrated view on addressing gender equality in RMLE is presented. The chapter seems also very valuable for readers who want to learn about addressing problems of discrimination by other human characteristics such as race and age.

In Chapter 13, Christian Hauser and Ronald E. Berenbeim review *Anti-corruption Education* and develop a path forward. They depict how the consideration corruption in academic curricula grew from compliance and financial risk management perspectives. More recent perspectives take a more comprehensive approach to explore institutional aspects and their interaction with individual behaviors. A learning and education programme is suggested.

Karin Buhmann discusses *Teaching Business and Human Rights: Past Approaches, Present State of the Art, and Opportunities for the Future* in Chapter 14. First, BHR – Business and Human Rights – is introduced as a distinct institutionalized area of concern and then profoundly developed together with its links to responsible management. In so doing, the chapter is exemplary in delivering the transdisciplinarity of RMLE issues as it provides a comprehensive consideration of the aspects that interact with the human rights issue in and beyond the business domain.

Part Three: Learning Outcomes and Processes

In Chapter 15 on *Competences for Responsible Management (and Leadership) Education and Practice* Jonathan Gosling and Adam Grodecki define the outcomes of RMLE: the competences that educators aim to instill and develop in the management learners. They develop their perspective on an individual, organizational and systemic level. Considering the negative consequences of some of today's business systems, they make a perspective explicit, that seems yet to be missing in many RMLE considerations: 'RMLE must foreground the possibility that the most "responsible" thing to do as a leader inside a large organisation may not be to balance stakeholder objectives (including shareholders) but actually to help cause the downfall of the organisation and its industry.'

In Chapter 16, Alex Hope, Pamela Croney and Jan Myers review concepts of *Experiential Learning for Responsible Management Education*, the probably most common *process* of RMLE. The authors review formal and informal approaches within and outside the academic institution. In this context, the external approaches to experiential learning are particularly valuable to the transdisciplinary understanding that extends RMLE beyond the academic discipline towards the realm of management practice.

Marcel Meyer and Alejo José G. Sison combine outcome and process in their chapter on *Virtues in Responsible Management Education: Building Character.* In Chapter 17, they introduce virtue ethics as a responsible educational process that builds a virtuous character as outcome. An interesting advancement seems to be the idea of taking virtues that are typically discussed as individual level concepts and applying them *in* and *through* organizational environments, i.e. to the organizational level.

In Chapter 18 Ann L. Cunliffe, Ana Carolina Aguiar, Vicente Góes and Fernanda Carreira review *Radical-Reflexivity and Transdisciplinarity as Paths to Developing Responsible Management Education.* They emphasize the idea that RMLE needs to develop the competence to reflect on the impact that applying taught theories in one's own living contexts will have. Their sound review of the reflexivity concept is followed by a very engaging example of how they use the reflexivity concept to design a master's programme in their business school. The chapter lends itself to be read together with Chapter 21, in which Philip Roscoe offers a critique of this individual focused idea on radical-reflexivity by exploring institutional level effects.

Peter Jack Gallo, Raquel Antolin-Lopez and Ivan Montiel explore the opportunities of *Technology in Responsible Management Education.* In Chapter 19 they offer the reader an overview of how games and simulation, social media and mobile apps can be used to facilitate RMLE. For each technology, the authors offer very applicable examples and discuss the advantages and disadvantages of each in obtaining specific RMLE goals.

In Chapter 20, Amelia Clarke and Jennifer Lynes review the advantages and disadvantages of *Online Education for Responsible Management Education.* Based on experiences with their online Master of Environment and Business programme, the authors explore in detail how the process and the content of an online programme needs to integrate sustainability thinking in order to build a convincing and successful online RMLE programme.

Part Four: Academic Environment

Philip Roscoe starts the section on the academic environment with his reflection on *The Dark Side of Responsible Management Education: An Ontological Misstep?* Chapter 21 explores the tension between individual level ethics and its organizational level effects (thus connecting to

Chapter 17 by Meyer and Sison). He suggests that many of the individual-level solutions that RMLE has to offer, e.g. in the domain of ethics, are ineffective as they are not able 'to transcend the calculative infrastructures of the organization'. The chapter implies a stronger consideration of how individual dispositions interact with organizational realities, and it further highlights the importance of the connection between academia and practices that we introduced above.

In Chapter 22, Danna Greenberg, Lauren Beitelspacher and Vikki Rodgers take *A Systems Approach to Transformational Responsible Management Learning and Education* and explore an institutional perspective of how RMLE can be implemented in a business school by changing its institutional logic. They identify four different processes that are centred around students (integration), around staff (collaboration), around the student–staff relationship (commitment and trust) and around a school's stakeholders (communication). The authors build on their own experiences from Babson college and integrate a vast range of examples from other institutions.

Chapter 23 engages with *Enhancing Responsible Management Education: Facilitating Faculty Development and Engagement*. This chapter addresses the question of how a faculty body that has been educated and trained in the pre-responsible management era should be able to deliver what is needed in RMLE. Drawing on his experiences at Bentley University, Anthony F. Buono points out that faculty comfort level with RMLE may be as important as expertise, and he discusses how to integrate the different initiatives and perspectives that one typically finds in a single academic organization. The reader is offered specific practical advice on how to design a development and engagement programme to ensure effectiveness at the individual and organizational level.

Whereas the previous chapter looked at faculty development at the organizational level, Sandra Waddock takes the perspective of the individual academic and calls for a new paradigm in Chapter 24. In *Reimagining Management Academics: The Emerging Responsible Management Education Paradigm* she develops an in-depth account of the assumptions and values on which traditional business theorizing builds and suggests a humanistic alternative that is centred around dignity and well-being. In a second step, she explores roles of business academics and develops an intellectual shamanic role model that is directed to delivering RMLE.

Jill Millar develops *Critical Perspectives on (and in) Responsible Management Education: The PRME Imaginary* in Chapter 25. The chapter connects well to the reflections on institutionalization of RMLE and the limits that result from PRME being an initiative of the corporate world's Global Compact. The author develops this idea in more detail and identifies and questions particular assumptions about sustainability, ethics and responsibility. She exposes their limiting effect on some of the conversations that might be necessary to achieve the fundamental change that might be necessary to address today's grand challenges. The chapter offers a path forward to open up the debates and bring them into the business curriculum through stronger consideration of critical theory.

In Chapter 26 Andreas Rasche, Dirk Ulrich Gilbert and Maximilian J. L. Schormair explore *The Institutionalization of Responsible Management Education*. The authors identify institutional pressures that have supported and hindered the institutionalization of responsible management within the management learning and education field. They highlight the importance of institutional entrepreneurs and thus offer mental support for all those readers who are passionate for RMLE but feel a bit alone in their academic environment. The authors further identify a decoupling of business school rhetoric from the educational realities, analyse this decoupling and discuss potential ways forward.

In Chapter 27, Mathias Falkenstein and Annie Snelson-Powell discuss *Responsibility in Business School Accreditations and Rankings* and thus closely connect to the institutional perspective developed in the chapter before. Specifically, the authors analyse how accreditation and rankings determine public perception of schools' quality, and thus connect school strategy and RMLE. They analyse how accreditation and rankings influence what RMLE is and is not and how it is disseminated, and thus offer a perspective on the interactions between RMLE at the levels of the individual organization and the business school industry.

Maribel Blasco concludes the section on the academic environment and engages with the implicit messages and learnings that the institutional academic environment sends to its students. In *The Hidden Curriculum: Can the Concept Support Responsible Management Learning?* she explores how values, assessment methods, cultural biases in textbooks etc. impact students' understanding of management and discusses to what extent this supports or hinders the RMLE agenda and the formal curriculum. In addressing potential negative effects of a hidden curriculum, business schools are advised to unhide the influences and explicitly discuss the implicit messages of various choices.

Part Five: Responsible Research

In their chapter on *Responsible Research in Business and Management: Transforming Doctoral Education,* Peter McKiernan and Anne S. Tsui introduce the RRBM – Responsible Research in Business and Management – community and their seven principles for designing and conducting responsible management research that fulfils the transdisciplinarity criterion with regard to its practice relevance. The authors then depict how these should be applied and conveyed in doctoral education to form responsible management researchers and thereby have a long-term socializing impact on the community that we are.

Jeremy St John and Cristina Neesham review *Paradigms in Responsible Management Learning and Education Research* in Chapter 30. As indicated above, research paradigms as manifestations of our ways of academic thinking determine to a large extent the range of possible solutions that we may create in research and thus in the knowledge we teach. The authors thus review positivism, post-positivism and critical realism, social constructionism, critical inquiry and critical theory, pragmatism and postmodernism, and discuss the implications for RM and RMLE for each paradigm. The authors identify a tension between a paradigm such as positivism that assumes and promotes measurable improvements and a paradigm like critical theory that promotes systems change as it assumes that incremental adjustments cannot solve the issue. Overall, the authors identify a trend towards multi-paradigm approaches, which reflect the idea of bridging disciplinary boundaries that underlies RMLE as a whole.

In Chapter 31 on *Methods in Responsible Management Learning and Education* Tine Köhler and Jennifer Gao discuss the methods we do and should use in research on RMLE. They find that survey, case studies and content analysis are the most common research methods. Qualitative studies outnumber quantitative studies by a factor of four and most often apply thematic analyses. This reflects the complexity and dynamic of the RMLE context and is thus a positive signal for the relevance of the discipline (we are doing the right thing). The authors further highlight games, simulations, service-learning and student consultancies as promising methodological approaches for future research.

Chapter 32 by Christopher Gohl on *A Pragmatist Approach to Responsible Management Learning and Education* nicely picks up the observation by Jeremy St John and Christina Neesham in Chapter 30 and explores pragmatism as a particularly promising research paradigm. The author introduces pragmatism as an approach that is as much a research method as a pedagogical approach as an approach to solving the problems associated with the UN SDGs. Based on a review that strongly engages with the works of John Dewey, he then develops a pragmatist RMLE programme that offers specific recommendations for us as management educators as well as responsible researchers and practitioners.

In Chapter 33, Markus Beckmann and Stefan Schaltegger reflect on *Responsible Management Learning and Education in Need of Inter- and Transdisciplinarity* and thus offer a nice round-up of this Handbook, which we built on the assumption of RMLE being a transdisciplinary project (or maybe discipline?). The authors engage with the concept of complexity that requires both specialization *and* integration and thus support the idea that singular specialized perspectives might be as important to RMLE as the integrated perspectives. The authors then develop a call for pedagogies and teaching and learning formats that integrate knowledge creation, application and dissemination, i.e. approaches to overcome the boundaries of management research, practice, and learning and education.

As educators in responsible management learning and education, we would like to sincerely thank the many colleagues, fellow academics and business professionals who have contributed to this volume and trust it will provide food for thought and inspiration for those engaged in RMLE scholarship in all its forms. The work goes on.

Notes

1 Interface plc is a global commercial flooring company with an integrated collection of carpet tiles and resilient flooring, with a strong sustainability mission that includes Climate Take Back™ 'running our business in a way that is restorative to the planet and creates a climate fit for life'.
2 See http://responsiblemanagement.net/literature-base/ for an up-to-date list of publications explicitly framed as RMLE.
3 Marshalls plc is an award-winning United Kingdom-based manufacturer of innovative hard products, supplying the construction, home improvement and landscape markets that prides itself in being a market leader in environmental and ethical business practice. See www.marshalls.co.uk/our-history.

REFERENCES

Attenborough, D. (2020) Australia's bushfires. *The Guardian*, 17 January. Available at: www.theguardian.com/tv-and-radio/2020/jan/17/david-attenborough-calls-australias-bushfires-the-moment-of-crisis-to-address-climate-change. Accessed 17 January 2020.

Ban Ki-Moon (2016) Address to High-Level Political Forum on Sustainable Development. Available at www.un.org/sg/en/content/sg/speeches/2016-07-19/secretary-generals-remarks-high-level-political-forum-sustainable. Accessed 17 January 2020.

Burchell, J., Kennedy, S. and Murray, A. (2015) Responsible management education in UK business schools: critically examining the role of the United Nations Principles for Responsible Management Education as a driver for change. *Management Learning*, 46(4), 479–497.

Carter, J. (2020) Half of UK universities divesting from fossil fuels isn't going far enough. Available at: www.timeshighereducation.com/blog/half-uk-universities-divesting-fossil-fuels-isnt-going-far-enough. Accessed 13 January 2020.

Chapple, W., Molthan-Hill, P. I., Welton, R. and Hewitt, M. (2019) Lights off, spot on: carbon literacy training crossing boundaries in the television industry. *Journal of Business Ethics*. doi:10.1007/s10551-019-04363-w.

Dyllick, T. (2015) Responsible management education for a sustainable world: the challenges for business schools. *Journal of Management Development*, 34(1), 16–33.

Edelman (2019) Edelman Trust Barometer. Available at www.edelman.com/research/2019-edelman-trust-barometer. Accessed 5 January 2020.

Fassin, Y. (2005) The reasons behind non-ethical behaviour in business and entrepreneurship. *Journal of Business Ethics*, 60, 265–279.

Forray, J. M. and Leigh, J. S. (2012) A primer on the principles of responsible management education intellectual roots and waves of change. *Journal of Management Education*, 36(6), 295–309.

Haski-Leventhal, D., Pournader, M. and McKinnon, A. (2016). The role of gender and age in business students' values, CSR attitudes, and responsible management education: learnings from the PRME international survey. *Journal of Business Ethics.* doi: 10.1007/s10551-015-2936-2.

Hibbert, P. & Cunliffe, A. (2015) Responsible management: Engaging moral reflexive practice through threshold concepts. *Journal of Business Ethics, 127,* 177–188. doi: 10.1007/s10551-013-1993-7.

Interface (2020) Available at: www.interface.com/EU/en-GB/about/modular-system/Microsfera-en_ GB. Accessed on 12 January 2020.

Intergovernmental Science-Policy Platform on Biodiversity and Ecosystem Services (IPBES) (2019) Available at: www.un.org/sustainabledevelopment/blog/2019/05/nature-decline-unprecedented-report/. Accessed 13 January 2020.

Laasch, O. and Conaway, R. (2015) *Responsible Business: The Textbook for Management Learning, Competence, Innovation.* Sheffield: Greenleaf Publishing.

Laasch, O. and Gherardi, S. (2019) Delineating and reconnecting responsible management, learning, and education: a research agenda through a social practices lens. Paper presented at the Academy of Management Annual Conference, Boston, MA.

Laasch, O. and Moosmayer, D. (2015) Competences for responsible management: a structured literature review. *CRME Working Papers,* 1(2).

Laasch, O., Moosmayer, D., Antonacopoulou, E. and Schaltegger, S. (2020) Constellations of transdisciplinary practices: a map and research agenda for the responsible management learning field. *Journal of Business Ethics.* doi: 10.1007/s10551-020-04440-5.

Louw, J. (2015) 'Paradigm change' or no real change at all? A critical reading of the UN Principles for Responsible Management Education. *Journal of Management Education,* 39(2), 184–208.

Millar, J. and Price, M. (2018) Imagining management education: a critique of the contribution of the United Nations PRME to critical reflexivity and rethinking management education. *Management Learning,* 49(3), 346–362.

Moosmayer, D. C., Waddock, S., Wang, L., Hühn, M. P., Dierksmeier, C. and Gohl, C. (2019) Leaving the road to Abilene: a pragmatic approach to addressing the normative paradox of responsible management education. *Journal of Business Ethics,* 157, 913–932.

Muff, K., Dyllick, T., Drewell, M., North, J., Shrivastava, P. and Haertle, J. (2013) *Management Education for the World: A Vision for Business Schools Serving People and the Planet.* Cheltenham: Edward Elgar.

Nonet, G., Kassel, K. and Meijs, L. (2016) Understanding responsible management: emerging themes and variations from European business school programs. *Journal of Business Ethics,* 139(4), 717–736.

Painter-Morland, M. (2015) Philosophical assumptions undermining responsible management education. *Journal of Management Development,* 34(1), 61–75.

Parker, M. (2018) *Shut Down the Business School: What's Wrong with Management Education.* London: Pluto Press.

Parkes, C., Buono, A. F. and Howaidy, G. (2017) The Principles for Responsible Management Education (PRME): The first decade – what has been achieved? The next decade – responsible management education's challenge for the Sustainable Development Goals (SDGs). *International Journal of Management Education,* 15(2), 61–65.

Parkes, C., Kolb, M., Schlange, L., Gudic, M. and Schmidpeter, R. (2018) Looking forward: leadership development and responsible management education for advancing the implementation of the Sustainable Development Goals (SDGs). *The International Journal of Management Education.* Available at https://docs.wixstatic.com/ugd/8be773_c2ee1e0f72334a9ab181b324ea043cac.pdf

Pfeffer, J. and Fong, C. (2002) The end of business schools? Less success than meets the eye. *Academy of Management Education and Learning,* 1(1), 78–95.

PRME (2020) Principles for Responsible Management Education. Available at: www.unprme.org. Accessed 10 January 2020.

Rasche, A. (2020) The United Nations Global Compact and the Sustainable Development Goals. In Laasch, O., Suddaby, R., Freeman, R. E. and Jamali, D. (Eds.), *The Research Handbook of Responsible Management.* Cheltenham: Edward Elgar.

Rasche, A. and Gilbert, D. U. (2015) Decoupling responsible management education: why business schools may not walk their talk. *Journal of Management Inquiry*, 24(3), 239–252.

Rasche, A. and Waddock, S. (2014) Global sustainability governance and the UN Global Compact: a rejoinder to critics. *Journal of Business Ethics*, 122(2), 209–216.

Rosenbloom, A., Gudić, M., Parkes, C. and Kronbach, B. (2017) A PRME response to the challenge of fighting poverty: How far have we come? Where do we need to go now? *International Journal of Management Education*, 15(2), 104–120.

Setó-Pamies, D. and Papaoikonomou, E. (2015) A multi-level perspective for the integration of ethics, corporate social responsibility and sustainability (ECSRS) in management education. *Journal of Business Ethics*, 136(3), 523–538.

Starkey, K. and Tempest, S. (2009) From crisis to purpose. *Journal of Management Development*, 28(8), 700–710.

Storey, M., Killian, S. and O'Regan, P. (2017) Responsible management education: mapping the field in the context of the SDGs. *International Journal of Management Education*, 15(2), 93–103.

The 50+20 Agenda (2012) Available at: https://grli.org/initiatives/the-5020-vision. Accessed 4 January 2020.

TIME (2019) TIME's Person of the Year. Available at: https://time.com/person-of-the-year-2019-greta-thunberg/. Accessed 12 January 2020.

TIME (2020) Hello from the Year 2050. We avoided the worst of climate change — but everything is different. Available at: https://time.com/5669022/climate-change-2050/. Accessed 17 January 2020.

United Nations (2019) UN Sustainable Development Goals. [Online] Available at: www.un.org/sustainabledevelopment/sustainable-development-goals/. Accessed 9 November 2019.

Van der Byl, C., Slawinski, N. and Hahn, T. (2020) Responsible management of sustainability tensions: a paradoxical approach to grand challenges. In Laasch, O., Suddaby, R., Freeman, R. E. and Jamali, D. (Eds.), *The Research Handbook of Responsible Management*. Cheltenham: Edward Elgar.

XR (Extinction Rebellion) (2020) International rebellion: worldwide. https://rebellion.earth/international-rebellion/worldwide/. Accessed 10 January 2020.

Ziblatt, D. (2020) Challenges to democracy. Available at: https://scholar.harvard.edu/dziblatt/challenges-democracy. Accessed 12 January 2020.

PART I

Perspectives on Responsible Management Learning and Education

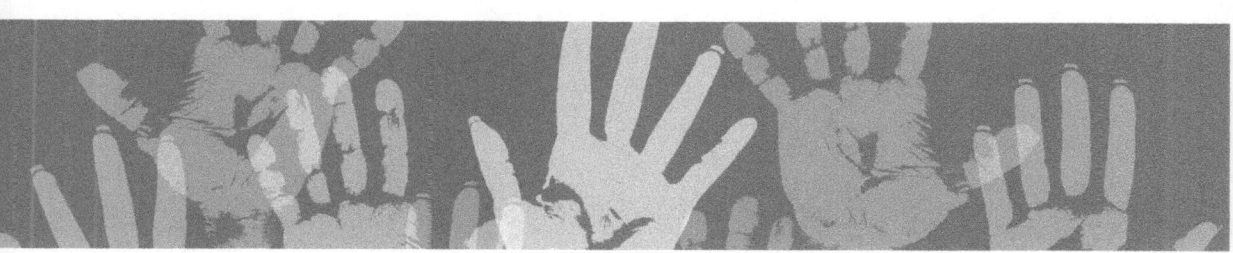

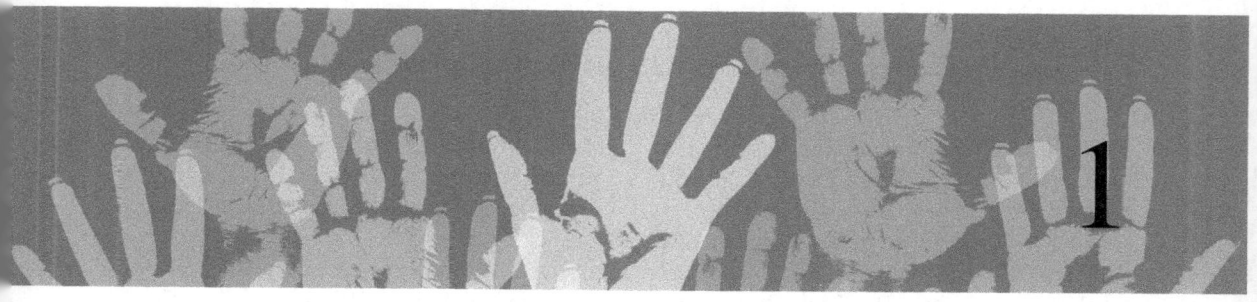

Management Education Today and Tomorrow: Voices from the Contributing Authors

Kenneth G. Brown

INTRODUCTION

Responsible management, as an umbrella concept, is a relatively young area of study. While business ethics, corporate social responsibility, and sustainability each have their own historical threads, responsible management's historical milestones are all relatively recent. The United Nations Global Compact for Principles of Responsible Management Education (PRME) was developed in 2007. The first textbook dedicated to responsible management, Laasch and Conaway's, was published in 2015. And while there are now multiple meetings and communities to host those who do this work, most are no more than 10 years old. For example, the PRME research conference was first held in 2009.

There is immense value in understanding history as a means for deep understanding that can foster future innovation (Cummings & Bridgman, 2016). In that vein, the editors of this volume asked authors to consider the historical context and development in their selected topic. But what about the chapter authors' personal histories? Rather than take an institutional perspective (e.g., Christensen, Peirce, Hartman, Hoffman & Carrier, 2007), the approach here is decidedly more personal. The short survey reported in this chapter is intended to capture the personal histories of scholars who contributed to this volume. Why did they decide to work in this area? Understanding their stories can help us better understand their work, and hopefully inspire others to join this growing community of responsible scholars.

We also sought contributing authors' assessment of the state of management education and plans for its future. Volume contributors were asked to consider whether management education is a force for good in society, particularly considering the sustained efforts to advance ethics, corporate social responsibility, sustainability, and now their umbrella concept of responsible management, in business curricula around the world.

This question was intended to see whether their overall assessment of management education's effectiveness was optimistic or pessimistic (or somewhere in between). Finally, adopting a 'burning question' approach employed by Robert P. Wright from Hong Kong Polytechnic (Wright & Brown, 2014), we asked for their single best piece of advice on how to make responsible management education more effective.

In asking these questions and reporting answers, we had two purposes. First, we wanted to give readers of this volume a better understanding of who the authors are. Their affiliations and bios are clearly displayed, but the deeper question is how they came to be RMLE scholars. Their answers reveal the authors' unique personal histories and the field's remarkable diversity. Second, we wanted to give the authors the opportunity to synthesize what they believe about both the current state and the future of management education, answering in effect 'where are we today,' and 'how can we make management education better tomorrow?' What follows is my synthesis of their voices.

QUESTIONS AND CODING

The editors brainstormed a list of questions related to scholars' histories, experiences and opinions about RMLE. By discussion we narrowed the list down to three that were broad enough to accomplish the goals we set for this chapter but concise enough to encourage responses: (1) What led you to thinking about and working in responsible management education? (2) Do you think the net impact of management education is becoming more positive or more negative to society? (3) What one big idea would you promote to ensure that the net impact of management education becomes more positive for society at large?

The questions were emailed to chapter authors, along with a reminder a month or so later. Eighteen complete responses were received, representing less than half of the volume contributors. I put all responses into a single document and began coding responses into categories once more than 10 were received. As more responses were received, I recoded and modified the coding. Final codes were set after three iterations, without any external reliability check. Reponses were generally short and clear, so coding was not challenging. I did not answer the survey myself, and I have little prior experience in this field of study except as a teacher of general management and a former editor of a generalist management education journal. As a result, I had no a priori sense for what a good or bad answer might be, nor for what themes might emerge.

QUESTION #1 RESPONSES AND THEMES

The first question asked why the author was active in this field of study. One author does not consider herself (much like me) to be in this field directly. Of the remaining 17 respondents, it was clear that some had decided quite early in their careers based on personal values and discipline. Early, in this case, is defined as early in their professional careers, such as with the choice of discipline for graduate school. In contrast, others arrived at the need to shift their focus because of life events after becoming a professional.

Most responses were coded as **early** (13, 76%). One example included an author who was involved in a prior job (before coming to academia) that revealed irresponsible practices that led to an interest in responsibility, and ultimately an academic identity as a student and now professor. Another author was involved in community development and came to graduate school in management with that framework as a guide. Yet another author reported that 'during my high school years and due to my exposure to the UN models, I became extremely interested in the most global issues of our time …' Others have simply done research in areas underneath the RMLE umbrella from the beginning of their careers, including pro-social behaviour, ethics, ecology, leadership and social philosophy. For these authors, responsible management is one label and community for their ongoing work.

A few indicated they came to this field **later** in life (4, 29%), either by accident or by personal insight. One author described discovering the field because he was assigned, by accident of being the youngest on faculty at the wrong time, to teach a Business and Society course. Over time, he fell in love with the field and began working in it despite the reservations of his colleagues. Another described the birth of children as being a factor, specifically wanting to be a solution to making sure their world would be better. And yet another described 'pitiful behavior of colleagues just publishing for publishing's sake'. This answer suggested that it was what he observed in the academic world, as much as the business world, that led him to work in responsible management.

QUESTION #2 RESPONSES AND THEMES

The second question was whether the author believed the net effects of management education today positive or negative. One respondent questioned the premise of quantifying impact in such a simple way, and three offered mixed appraisals. Many indicated that this was a hard question to answer given the enormous diversity of colleges and programmes around the globe. Never-the-less, the majority (56%) were negative in their assessment. Only a handful (28%) suggested the effects are net positive.

An example of a positive statement was, 'there is no question but that the net impact of responsible management has been strongly positive. It does not solve all societal challenge and problems, but the students exposed to this material are clearly better off in terms of their impact on organizations, society, and stakeholders.' Notably, this quote focuses on positive effect on students who participate in management education under the rubric of 'responsible management' rather than focusing on the totality of management education.

A sample of negative assessments include the following:

'Unfortunately, too much of management education today is business as usual…'

'False choices like this [profit or people] tend to be reinforced through disciplinary silos at business schools.'

'There is still much work to be done when it comes to (a) embedding competencies in students that actually allow them to move towards larger-scale implementation and (b) aligning the hidden curriculum in b-schools with the RME agenda.'

'Right now, I think the responsible management education field as a whole is just sobering up in front of the enormous systemic challenges created by climate change.'

'Unfortunately, I believe little is changing.'

QUESTION #3 RESPONSES AND THEMES

The third question asked authors for their idea of what would help management education have a more positive impact on society. One answer noted that the answers are too complex to simplify and summarize. Other answers fell into categories related to the management profession (4, 23%), the organization and administration of academia (4, 23%), and most common, the academic profession including the work of faculty as teachers and scholars (9, 53%).

Suggestions for the management profession include 'forming management as a profession could revolutionize management practice and thus education ... if management professionals were conceptualized as obliged to serve society rather than shareholders ...' and the narrative of the 'power of purpose ... especially a purpose that truly resonates with an organization's key stakeholders'.

Comments categorized as related to the organization and administration of academia included 'empowering faculty ... They are at the centre of everything we do' and 'Find different quality criteria based on which we measure the success of education.' This latter suggestion includes details about changing how we grade, what projects faculty and students complete, and changing how business schools run. Yet another respondent suggested that we 'adopt a holistic approach to responsible leadership ... embedding it in everything that you do ...'.

A sample of suggestions for the work of faculty include the following:

'Stop teaching about corporate social responsibility, business ethics and sustainable business ... it leads to a culture of blame of "the bad corporation" ... that puts the individual students and manager in a comfortable finger-pointing role without having to recognize our own responsibilities as individuals ....'

'I believe sustainability and responsible management education should be integrated in all studies across the board, and students should be exposed to more experiential and interdisciplinary learning.'

Finally, along the same lines, suggestions by others included '... all students take a business ethics course' and '... all business students need to take an ecology or environmental science course that focused on teaching system thinking, or better still, a co-taught systems course that combines ecology, society, and management education together'.

DISCUSSION

The responses across all three questions reveal a diversity of background and belief, even among the subset of scholars invited to contribute to this volume. The authors came to this work from different backgrounds, and assess the current state of the field in ways that range from optimistic to pessimistic. And when it came to pin-pointing a single way for management educators to do more for society, answers covered broad territory of the management profession, the conduct of business schools, and the work of individual faculty in the classroom and curriculum. This range of responses likely reflects the complexity of the concept of responsible management education, and the reality of a complicated and variegated present, and the need to pursue future progress along multiple fronts.

These results also suggest some interesting areas for further conversation and scholarly dialogue. Two such areas will be discussed here: (1) How to create opportunities for people to engage in the emerging discipline of responsible management, and (2) How to create desired changes in our school's faculty work and curricula.

Responses from the contributing authors revealed that most scholars came to the work of RMLE through early experiences outside of academia. And among those who came to the field later, the paths seem to reflect accidental departures. To help expand this community, a useful question to explore would be how to create opportunities for established scholars to transition into the discipline. Standalone conferences, such as the PRME Global Forum or regional conferences, are a great way for current scholars to convene and collaborate, but they may not be the best way to help faculty transition into this area. What are ways to encourage faculty to consider the responsible label? Perhaps more pointedly, would it be beneficial to advocate for those who study ethics, corporate social responsibility and sustainability to adopt this label, to gather forces and increase the visibility of the field? It seems likely that increasing the overall size of the field, in terms of scholars and papers using the term, would be likely to generate critical mass to attract even more scholars and scholarly work. Subfields in academic disciplines often pursue having separate journals (and scholarly volumes like this one), but this can serve both to increase work and isolate that work from the broader scholarly community. We should explore ways to balance the creation of specific outlets for RMLE work and the presence of that work in highly visible generalist settings (like Academy of Management conferences and existing journals).

A specific suggestion for recruiting new faculty into the discipline, or convincing them to use the RMLE terminology, is to build mid-career pathways. Specific writing about this transition, in the form of narratives like those in Frost and Taylor (1996), coupled with more concerted efforts to hold faculty development workshops at generalist conferences, could motivate established scholars to move into the community. As this recruitment effort unfolds, it would be useful to ask how broadly to construct RMLE, and whether in addition to the common three terms used in this book, we might recruit those doing work on purpose, spirituality, liberal arts and humanities in organizational research, and more (e.g., Mirvis, 1997; Statler & Guillet de Monthoux, 2015).

The second question to explore in future research is how to create movement toward integration of responsible management in business (and perhaps broader) curricula. More than a decade ago, AASB emphasized ethics to a greater extent, including commissioning a task force (AACSB International, 2004). The distinct emphasis on ethics has waned, in favor of what appears to be an emphasis on mission-driven and consistent curricula that promote responsible individual and organizational behaviour. Has the AACSB broadening helped bring new scholars and new schools to the table? Similarly,

UN PRME began with 60 schools, and now has over 650 signatory schools, suggesting a considerable expansion in the number of schools at least thinking and reporting on issues related to responsibility. But how far have we come, and how much further do we have to go? Additional scholarly work on ways to encourage both individual faculty and colleges to adopt new curriculum is warranted, and would help continue to broaden and deepen the RMLE community.

REFERENCES

AACSB International (2004). *Ethics education in business schools*. Tampa, FL: AACSB International.

Christensen, L. J., Peirce, E., Hartman, L. P., Hoffman, W. M., & Carrier, J. (2007). Ethics, CSR, and sustainability education in the Financial Times Top 50 Global Business Schools: baseline data and future research directions. *Journal of Business Ethics, 73*, 347–368.

Cummings, S., & Bridgman, T. (2016). The limits and possibilities of history: how a wider, deeper, and more engaged understanding of business history can foster innovative thinking. *Academy of Management Learning & Education, 15*(2), 250–267.

Frost, P. J., & Taylor, M. S. (Eds.). (1996). *Rhythms of academic life: personal accounts of careers in academia*. Thousand Oaks, CA: Sage.

Laasch, O. and Moosmayer, D. C. (2015) Responsible management competences: an integrative portfolio for sustainability, responsibility, and ethics. In: O. Laasch, and D. C. Moosmayer (Eds.)., *Critical Responsible Management Education* Working Paper, *Responsible management competencies*. Nottingham University Business School China. Available at http://responsiblemanagement.net/wp-content/uploads/2018/05/9LaaschMoosmayer2015RMCForOpen-PeerReview.pdf

Mirvis, P. H. (1997). 'Soul work' in organizations. *Organizational Science, 8*, 193–206.

Statler, M., & Guillet de Monthoux, P. (2015). Humanities and arts in management education: the emerging Carnegie Paradigm. *Journal of Management Education, 39*, 3–15.

Wright, R. P., & Brown, K. G. (Eds.). (2014). *Educating tomorrow's thought-leaders: distinguished scholars answer a burning question*. Chicago, IL: Strategic Management Society. (Available online at www.strategicmanagement.net/teaching/publications.)

2

The United Nations-Backed Principles for Responsible Management Education (PRME): A Principles-Based Global Engagement Platform for Higher Education Institutions to Advance the Sustainable Development Goals (SDGs)

Florencia Librizzi and Carole Parkes

THE PRINCIPLES FOR RESPONSIBLE MANAGEMENT EDUCATION (PRME)

The Principles for Responsible Management Education (PRME) has developed into the largest initiative backed by the United Nations as a platform to integrate principles of responsibility and sustainability in business and management-related higher education institutions globally (PRME, 2019a). The development of the Principles and the PRME initiative followed recommendations by academic stakeholders of the UN Global Compact (PRME, 2019b) who called for the creation of a 'principle-based global engagement platform' for higher education institutions with the aim of equipping students with the mind-set, skills and knowledge to become responsible leaders.

The stakeholder's recommendation constituted a global call for action 'to change the purpose of business education in order to adapt the teaching of business educators to a growing trend of corporate citizenship, corporate social responsibility and sustainability' (Alcaraz & Thiruvattal, 2010). The call promptly developed into a proposal that was introduced and discussed at the Global Forum 'Business as an Agent of World Benefit' at Case Western Reserve University in the fall of

2006 and subsequently in the official launch of the PRME initiative by UN Secretary-General Ban Ki-Moon at the opportunity of the 2007 UN Global Compact Leaders' Summit in Geneva. Head of the Global Compact Networks Manuel Escudero's concept paper entitled 'Global Corporate Citizenship and Academia: A Global Convergence' outlined a new vision for schools of business and management to meet the changing demands of the decades to come. It highlighted the failure of traditional approaches to be able to prepare graduates to respond to demands for a more responsible way of managing companies. In particular, Escudero identified business education as the key to creating responsible managers (Escudero, 2006).

The United Nations Global Compact (UNGC) – seen as a response to some of these perceived global problems facing the world – had been announced in 1999 by Kofi Annan and established a year later. Over the next few years it launched a number of initiatives designed to combat some of the worst social and environmental issues identified (Rasche, Waddock & McIntosh, 2013). PRME was seen as an opportunity 'not only to rethink what is being taught in business schools, but to question the pillars upon which management education was built' (Rasche & Escudero, 2010: 246).

The development and drafting of the Six Principles was driven by a global task force of 60 university presidents, deans and representatives of leading business schools and higher education institutions, as well as by following key organizations in the space who co-convened the process (in alphabetical order):

- AACSB International
- Aspen Institute Business and Society Program
- European Academy of Business in Society (EABIS – now ABIS)
- European Foundation for Management Development (EFMD)
- Globally Responsible Leadership Initiative (GRLI)
- Net Impact (student organization).

The concept of the Six Principles for Responsible Management Education as the framework for a global engagement platform was given support by its 'bottom-up' development by an expert task force, as well as by the 'top-down' political support of UN Global Compact and Ban Ki-Moon, the UN Secretary General at that time. In that sense, at the opportunity of the launch of PRME in 2007, Ban Ki-Moon declared his vision, stating that 'the Principles for Responsible Management Education have the capacity to take the case for universal values and business into classrooms on every continent' (PRME, 2008). The UN mandate to advance UN goals and priorities was further ratified in 2017, at the 10th Anniversary of the initiative, by United Nations Secretary-General António Guterres, who recognized that 'the PRME initiative was launched to nurture responsible leaders of the future. Never has this task been more important. Bold leadership and innovative thinking are needed to achieve the Sustainable Development Goals' (Guterres, 2017).

Following these endorsements, PRME forged partnerships with other UN entities to enable meaningful impact globally. With this purpose in mind, PRME became founding UN member of the Higher Education Sustainability Initiative (HESI), a partnership created in the run-up to the United Nations Conference on Sustainable Development (Rio+20) in 2012. HESI comprises United Nations Department of Economic and Social Affairs (UN DESA), UNESCO, United Nations Environment, PRME, United Nations University (UNU), UN-HABITAT, UNCTAD and UNITAR (HESI, 2019). By engaging in this multilateral UN partnership, PRME provides a larger higher education institution space to strengthen HESI's ability to create 'a unique interface between higher education, science, research and policy making' (HESI, 2019). Additionally, PRME has built a close relationship with other UN Global Compact's sister initiatives such as the Principles for Responsible Investment (PRI, 2019) and the Sustainable Cities Programme (2019).

The Six Principles: A Framework for Responsible Management Education Implementation

The Six Principles constitute a guiding framework for higher education institutions, including business and management schools, to advance in their journey to integrate responsible management and sustainability into teaching, researching, dialogue and partnerships, as well as into their own organizational practices (PRME, 2008, 2017b). By working through the PRME framework, higher education institutions commit and take steps to advance responsible management and sustainability education to ensure they form leaders with the mindset, skills and knowledge needed to deliver business profit while advancing sustainability goals. Higher education institutions that have joined the PRME initiative have indicated that using the Six Principles have helped them to integrate universal values into curriculum, research, organizational practices, dialogue and partnerships, and therefore are better suited to contribute to building a sustainable and inclusive global economy and prosperous societies (Alcaraz & Thiruvattal, 2010; Blasco, 2012; Sroufe, Sivasubramaniam, Ramons & Saiia, 2014).

The Six Principles, launched in 2007, remain mostly unchanged since they were introduced, however, an update to 'Principle 2 – Values' was publicly endorsed by the PRME community at the opportunity of the 2017 PRME Global Forum – 10 Years of PRME. This rather small but significant amendment includes 'organizational practices' to Principle 2 (italicized below) aiming to reflect signatories' commitment to incorporate and implement the values of the global social responsibility in their own 'organizational practices' by 'walking the talk' along with curricula, teaching, research and academic activities. The decoupling of engagement in responsible management education from organizational practices because of institutional pressures is recognized as a key

barrier to effective implementation as well as its legitimacy (Rasche & Gilbert, 2015) – see also Chapter 26 by Rasche et al. The intention of this change to 'emphasize the importance of our own organizations' practices as role models and to ensure that our own practices are consistent with what we teach and research' was made explicit and crystal clear by the 2017 Global Forum Outcomes Declaration (PRME, 2017b). Examples of such organizational practices include; fossil fuel divestment, campus-based waste management, carbon and energy reduction and HR policies and practices aligned with the Principles.

The text of the Principles is composed by a preamble declaration, followed by the Six Principles. The preamble states that 'As institutions of higher education involved in the development of current and future managers, we declare our willingness to progress in the implementation, within our institution, of the following Principles, starting with those that are more relevant to our capacities and mission. We will report on progress to all our stakeholders and exchange effective practices related to these principles with other academic institutions' (PRME, 2008). Following to the preamble, the Six Principles affirm:

Principle 1 – Purpose: We will develop the capabilities of students to be future generators of sustainable value for business and society at large and to work for an inclusive and sustainable global economy.

Principle 2 – Values: We will incorporate into our academic activities, curricula *and organizational practices*, the values of global social responsibility as portrayed in international initiatives such as the United Nations Global Compact.

Principle 3 – Method: We will create educational frameworks, materials, processes and environments that enable effective learning experiences for responsible leadership.

Principle 4 – Research: We will engage in conceptual and empirical research that advances our understanding about the role, dynamics and impact of corporations in the creation of sustainable social, environmental and economic value.

Principle 5 – Partnership: We will interact with managers of business corporations to extend our knowledge of their challenges in meeting social and environmental responsibilities and to explore jointly effective approaches to meeting these challenges.

Principle 6 – Dialogue: We will facilitate and support dialog and debate among educators, students, business, government, consumers, media, civil society organizations and other interested groups and stakeholders on critical issues related to global social responsibility and sustainability.

We understand that our own organizational practices should serve as example of the values and attitudes we convey to our students.

PRME Signatories and the Sharing Information on Progress (SIP) Report

Higher education institutions that wish to join the PRME initiative must be publicly recognized (i.e. legal/government recognition) and must have degree-awarding authority. PRME signatories commit to implement the Six Principles and report to stakeholders on the progress made against the Principles every 24 months together with (since January 2016) reporting on the Sustainable Development Goals (SDGs). The commitment to report on the implementation of the Principles stems from the Six Principles' preamble which states that signatories 'will report on progress to all … stakeholders and exchange effective practices related to these principles with other academic institutions'. The report, named 'Sharing Information on Progress' (SIP), was conceived as an integrity measure and for that reason, its main goal is 'to serve as a public vehicle for information on responsible management education' (PRME, 2017d). Additionally, the SIP report intended to encourage stakeholder dialogue, peer learning among signatories, and increase awareness and reflection on the vision, mission, strategy and activities of the reporting

institution. From a comprehensive approach, the Six Principles (informed by the 10 Principles of the UN Global Compact) and the Sustainable Development Goals (SDGs) (see Figure 2.1) now form the joint framing for PRME, in that the SDGs are the agenda (in line with Agenda 2030) for content of initiatives (the 'why' and 'what' – along with the 10 Principles of the UN Global Compact – for areas of action) and the Principles are the 'how' (for implementing strategies, plans and practices). Thus, all signatories are now expected to use the joint framework in their implementation as well as at the time of producing their SIP reports.

An underlying philosophy of PRME is the notion on continuous improvement. SIP reports, effectively produced, can provide important benefits to individual signatories as well as to the responsible management and sustainability education space. Signatories have appreciated the value of preparing, producing and sharing SIP reports since they help by creating awareness of the mission of PRME and their organization's commitment; giving a concise yet comprehensive picture of their institutions' activities; providing visibility and reputation; helping to define direction and strategy; and tracking and benchmarking progress (Weybrecht & SIP Working Group, 2015).

The SIP policy was developed in 2008 based on the consensus reached at the 1st PRME Global Forum for Responsible Management Education and was further updated in 2015 based on an extensive consultation with the PRME Working Group on SIPs and PRME Advisory Committee members. The reviewed policy was endorsed at the 2015 Global Forum for Responsible Management Education – 6th Annual Assembly in the Outcomes Declaration (PRME, 2015b). Since the 2017 Global Forum and PRME's 10th Anniversary the PRME community have been discussing the need for a further reform of the SIP policy to explicitly incorporate the SDGs as a cornerstone of these reports.

In order to maintain a 'communicating' status, a signatory must fulfill the following requirements which constitute the SIP policy:

Signatories are required to communicate their progress at least every 24 months by submitting a report that includes the following elements:

- A **letter signed by the highest executive of the organization** expressing continued commitment to PRME
- A **description of practical actions** (i.e. relevant policies, procedures, activities) that the institution has taken to implement one or more Principles during the past 24 months (since signing up to PRME or since last submission of SIP)
- An **assessment of outcomes** (i.e. the degree to which previously outlined goals were met, or other qualitative or quantitative evaluation of results)
- **Key, specific objectives** for the next 24-month period with regard to the implementation of the Principle(s). Concrete strategies and timelines are encouraged.

Signatories who do not comply with the SIP policy are listed as 'non-communicating' and therefore not eligible to take leadership roles within the community. In order to protect the integrity of the initiative, after a year of continuous 'non-communicating' status, the signatory is delisted from the initiative and reported publicly on the PRME website and other communication outlets. The policy of delisting followed UN Global Compact's decision to delist companies not complying with the requirement to submit 'Communicating on Progress Reports' (COPs) in 2010 that saw 859 companies publically delisted. This was followed by an upsurge in applications for membership as the integrity of the UN and UN Global Compact is seen to be linked to compliance (Sanquiche, 2010).

The PRME Community and Its Networks

In the years since its launch, PRME has become the largest organized relationship between the United Nations and management-related higher

education institutions, with over 730 signatories in 92 countries worldwide, including 45 of the Financial Times' Top 100 Business Schools. Since 2007, an estimated 23 million students have graduated from PRME signatory institutions (PRME Impact Report, 2017).

As a global learning community signatories are encouraged to get involved in a variety of platforms, activities and projects to scale up their commitment to implement the Six Principles and therefore transform business and management education. By joining PRME's networks, higher education institutions and partners can deepen their engagement with peers and be part of a larger movement for sustainability and responsible management education (Librizzi, 2019). In that sense, PRME provides a 'network of networks' that promotes a multiplier effect through dialogue and partnerships (Principles 5, 6 and SDG 17).

Regional chapters

PRME Chapters were first proposed and discussed at the occasion of the 2012 PRME Global Forum that took place at the United Nations Conference on Sustainable Development – or Rio+20 – in Rio de Janeiro. Since then, 14 Chapters emerged around the world and are working globally to help advance the Six Principles within particular geographic contexts, rooting PRME into different national, regional, cultural and linguistic landscapes (PRME, 2019b). These include established Chapters in: ASEAN+; Australia and New Zealand; Brazil; CEE (Central and Eastern European); DACH (Germany, Austria and Switzerland); India; Latin America and Caribbean; MENA (Middle East and North Africa); Nordic; North America; UK and Ireland; France BeNeLux (Belgium, Netherlands and Luxembourg); and emerging Chapters in East Asia and Iberia (Spain and Portugal).

With different levels of maturity, all Chapters enable local collaboration and partnership, engaging with relevant local stakeholders – including the Global Compact Networks – and thus contribute to a better aligned local–global strategy and implementation of the Six Principles and the SDGs. Chapters are empowered to develop their own governance arrangements within the PRME and Chapter policies as well as their locally adapted programs and activities, including:

- Providing a platform for dialogue, peer learning, and collective action
- Increasing the visibility of the Six Principles and its signatories in the region
- Adapting the Six Principles into a local context
- Developing and promoting activities in support to the Six Principles and the SDGs.

Chapters conduct a wide range of activities and projects; some key examples include:

- **Students' engagement**: Many Chapters' initiatives have made a priority to engage students directly from their own institutions or through student associations or initiatives that involve students such as WikiRate (2019), NetImpact (2019), Aim2Flourish (2019), and the Sustainability Literacy Test (Sulitest, 2019).
- **Regional meetings and other strategic events**: Most Chapters organize an annual regional meeting or Chapter meeting that includes high-level plenaries, interactive panels, roundtables and/or workshops focused on sustainability and responsible management education and the SDGs. These events are built around the mindset of how the Chapter can generate the collaboration and collective action to advance the SDGs and have also sessions to discuss the Chapter logistics, activities, governance, etc. Some Chapters have designed and are running the 'SDG Roadshows' series, which include multi-stakeholder roundtable events with Global Compact Local Networks to increase awareness and action around the SDGs at the local level (Chapters UK and Ireland and DACH).
- **Content creation, curriculum change and research**: Several Chapters have decided to focus much of their attention in producing resources to guide their members on how to advance the Principles and the SDGs, for instance the Chapter Brazil has issued the SDGs Good Practices Handbook to disseminate the SDGs in Educational institutions. The Chapter LAC has produced recently the Guide for Implementation

of the System of Indicators of University Social Responsibility (Yepes et al., 2018). Many Chapters conduct workshops to exchange experiences and learning on how to embed the SDGs into the curriculum and collaborate together and with businesses to produce applied research and SDG-relevant publications.

- **Peer learning and faculty development**: Chapters have also taken the initiative to organize workshops on faculty development as well as to exchange experiences and learning around integrated reporting, implementing the Principles, teaching the SDGs, etc. (Chapters MENA, ASEAN, North America, LAC, Brazil, UK and Ireland, DACH, etc.).
- **Chapter awards**: Some Chapters have developed Student Competitions (PRME UK and Ireland and North America) and Faculty Awards to recognize individuals who have demonstrated excellence in teaching, research and service (Chapter North America).
- **Advocacy, collaboration and partnerships on the SDGs**: Most Chapters have taken seriously their role of advocating for sustainability and responsible management education locally as well as pursuing collaboration and partnerships with relevant stakeholders to move the needle when it comes to SDG implementation in their context.

Additionally, Chapters are important drivers of the growth of the initiative in quantitative terms (e.g. recruiting and retaining signatories) as well as qualitatively (e.g. deepening the engagement and implementation of PRME in the local contexts). The ethos of PRME is one of inclusivity and collaboration and this chimes with the premise of the SDGs to 'leave no one behind'. In order to grow and fully realize the SDGs, growth in signatories and the development of Chapters in Asia (China, Indonesia and India) and Africa are seen as critical for the future.

PRME working groups

The PRME Working Groups were the first collective engagement platform created and crucially developed by members of the PRME community. These expert groups deepen collaboration within and across faculty and partners on specific issues relevant to sustainability and responsible management and related to the SDGs (PRME, 2013). Currently, there are eight active PRME Working Groups, including those on Innovation Challenge; Anti-Corruption in Curriculum Change; Business for Peace; Climate Change and Environment; Gender Equality; Humanistic Management; Poverty, a Challenge for Management Education; and on Sustainability Mindsets.

Many of the Working Groups predate the SDGs, for example the Poverty Working Group, developed a global survey on poverty as a challenge for management education in 2010 that was presented at the Rio+20 Earth Summit in 2012 (Gudić, Parkes & Rosenbloom, 2012). Thus, whilst some of them address SDG issues such as poverty, gender equality and peace, the grassroots nature of the Working Groups means that they can capture issues of broader and more specific interest to management education. Furthermore, PRME Working Groups foster collaboration among faculty, industry experts, business leaders and students with the aim to develop and publish relevant resources as well as cutting-edge research (PRME, 2013). Examples of these fruitful collaborations include publications such as *Socially Responsive Organizations and the Challenge of Poverty* and *Responsible Management Education and the Challenge of Poverty: A Teaching Perspective* (Gudić, Rosenbloom & Parkes, 2014, 2015), both books published by the PRME Working Group on Poverty in cooperation with Greenleaf Publishing. Another publication worth mentioning is *Beyond the Bottom Line: Integrating UN Global Compact into Management Education* (Gudić, Keong & Flynn, 2017), a joint effort of the PRME Working Group on Poverty with the Anti-Corruption and Gender Equality Working Groups. In addition to research and publications, these groups provide the community with SDG thematic events, workshops, training and webinars.

Going forward, consideration of more SDG-related Working Groups and other topic areas may be developed but this relies on PRME signatories and its community championing the issues. Further integration of the work among the different PRME Working Groups could also provide more interdisciplinary resources to address the interlinked challenges posed by the SDGs.

PRME champions

Champions of PRME exist in all signatory institutions and as a community-led initiative, individual and collective champions have contributed significantly to the development of PRME. Solitander, Fougère, Sobczak & Herlin (2011) found that Faculty Champions often need to work creatively to overcome some of the strategic, structural, cultural and political barriers to responsible management but can inspire transformation. The idea of a group of experienced and engaged PRME signatories committed to working collaboratively to develop and promote activities that address shared barriers to making broad scale implementation of sustainability principles a reality was envisioned and proposed during the 2012 Rio+20 PRME Global Forum (PRME, 2016).

The Champions group's mission is to 'contribute to thought and action leadership on responsible management education in the context of the United Nations sustainable development agenda' (PRME, 2016). Building on their mission, PRME Champions commit to working together to raise the bar on business and management education in curricula, research, educational frameworks, sustainability-based partnerships as well as thought leadership. Champions engages the different networks (e.g. Chapters, Working Groups, etc.) to support them through their implementation of the Principles and contribute to the broader UN goals, including the SDGs. In this regard, PRME Champions are seen as Champions *for* and not *of* PRME. An important distinction that prioritizes championing the initiative rather than individual champion institutions.

The PRME Champions two-year pilot started in 2013, aiming to address shared barriers to the implementation of responsible management education and making sustainability the rule rather than the exception. The second cycle of Champions took place during the years 2016–2017, focusing on undertaking advanced tasks and game-changing projects to address systemic challenges faced by the PRME community to integrating sustainability. These efforts include offering guiding resources such as the Transformational Model (PRME, 2015a), which focuses on the challenges and opportunities of embracing the journey of institutional transformation.

The third two-year cycle of the PRME Champions programme started in 2018. Guided by the framework provided by the PRME Transformational Model, and in support to the Champions' mission, this group is tasked to take transformative action on integrating the SDGs focusing in three main areas: curriculum, research and partnerships. In that sense, this project title, 'Mainstreaming the SDG in PRME Institutions', requires faculty and students to use their organizations as 'living labs' by integrating the SDGs into the curriculum, research and partnerships. The results of these experiences aim to help to co-design a blueprint 'to guide the next generation of business schools and management-related higher education institutions to achieve their SDG goals'.

PRME Signatory Events

The PRME initiative through its networks organize several events and meetings such as:

- **The Global Forum**, which is the PRME premier's global event convening over 350 thought leaders and experts of sustainability and responsible management education globally, including deans, university presidents, faculty, researchers, business school accreditation organizations, practitioners and students, in addition to high-level guests from the United Nations, the private sector and media. The Global Forum normally takes place every two years with the aim to celebrate and take stock of the achievements

and impact by the PRME community through individual signatories, networks and the overall initiative; increase the awareness about the SDGs and share good practices; as well as to establish the vision for the future of the responsible management education movement.

- **PRME Regional Meetings**, convened by Chapters around the world, play an important role in advocating for the Principles and to achieving progress on the SDGs in the local contexts. These meetings provide a regional platform for dialogue, collaboration and collective action among academia, civil society and business (PRME, 2019c). In any typical year, around 12–15 regional meetings take place around the world addressing local priorities under the PRME and SDG umbrella.

- The **Responsible Management Education Research (RMER) Conference** is another example of PRME grassroots activity, as it was conceived and created within the PRME Chapter DACH. This Chapter organized the first RMER Conference in the fall of 2014 with the vision to become 'a forum for ongoing research on the manifold initiatives undertaken to implement PRME in business teaching for the future we want' (PRME DACH, 2014). These series of events focused on research aim to facilitate exchange among PRME Chapters and Working Groups while catering 'to a wide audience ranging from academics to practitioners eager to advance their knowledge and skills integrating responsible management and sustainable development into their professional efforts' (PRME DACH, 2014). Since its first edition this event has been hosted in different regions driven by several Chapters in partnership with Working Groups and the Chapter DACH. These include HTW Chur (Switzerland), the American University in Cairo (Egypt), IMC University of Applied Sciences Krems (Austria), ISAE-FGV (Brazil), Cologne Business School (Germany) and, in 2019, Jönköping International Business School (Sweden).

PRME'S STRATEGIC DEVELOPMENTS

2016 PRME Strategic Review and the 10th Anniversary of PRME

In early 2016 (following the 2015 PRME Global Forum) and in advance of PRME's

10th Anniversary in 2017, it was clear for the PRME community and the Secretariat that there was a need for a strategic reflection. Its intention was to take stock on the progress of the initiative, including how to address its weaknesses and threats and leverage its strengths and opportunities as well as to understand how PRME could become the 'most effective link between the responsible management education community and the wider global sustainability landscape' (Haertle et al., 2017). Furthermore, while this relatively young initiative had become an important actor in the responsible management space, it seemed crucial at the time to establish a clear long-term vision that would take into account important UN priorities such as the Sustainable Development Goals.

Additionally, there was a need that the initiative should further reflect on the dynamic sustainability and responsible management education landscape, as well as the global and local challenges and opportunities, including a robust and active PRME community who had increasingly gained more ownership of the initiative. The last, meaning that the PRME community had grown in strategic involvement by directly funding an important portion of PRME's operations, influenced strategy through the voice of the PRME Advisory Committee, that captured the perspectives of the main networks and stakeholders of PRME; and run important projects, activities and events through the different networks. For that reason, the 2016 PRME Strategic Review was launched by the PRME Secretariat with the support of the PRME Steering and Advisory Committee, becoming the most comprehensive and inclusive strategic exercise that this initiative has undertaken, including a wide range of consultations with key PRME community members and stakeholder over a period of 4 months. The recommendations that emerged from this exercise focused on strategic areas and a number of operational aspects that needed to be addressed in order to scale up the impact of the initiative. Three 'Must-Win Battles' were

identified: Clarifying the brand (e.g. vision and mission); optimizing the global organization, including strengthening the demand side of responsible management education and aligning PRME's networks with new priorities; and creating balanced growth, including revising the governance and ensuring sustainable funding. Progress on these areas was considered essential to make PRME fit for purpose.

Key Recommendations and Outcomes

The 2016 strategic review became fundamental for the organization, since it meant a profound assessment of the initiative and laid the groundwork for the future of the initiative, aligning PRME's Vision and Mission to incorporate the SDGs and ensuring that all PRME's work streams explicitly aligned to advance the Global Goals. In that sense, several recommendations, goals and key performance indicators stemmed from the 2016 Strategic Review, including:

Clarifying the brand (e.g. vision and mission)

During the strategic review, participants shared their thoughts on some of the challenges they saw related to the PRME brand, as well as to how to best clarify what the initiative stands for.

In September 2015 all 193 Member States of the United Nations made a commitment to 'create a world we all want' in the next 15 years, adopting the Sustainable Development Goals (SDGs), also referred to as the 2030 Agenda for Sustainable Development ('2030 Agenda') (UN, 2019). Given the importance of this new agenda for sustainable development, a crucial outcome of the 2016 PRME Strategic Review was to align all PRME's work streams to focus on advancing the SDGs. In that sense, it was clear for all consulted stakeholders that the newly launched Sustainable Development Goals (SDGs) constituted 'a common framework to enable dialogue and action among the PRME initiative, the UN, the UN Global Compact, business and students, as well as other stakeholders and partners. The SDGs became a thematic umbrella to pointing to the most crucial challenges the world faces, enabling the PRME initiative to "bridge and catalyze" collaboration and action' (PRME, 2017c). The aim therefore, was not only to include the SDGs as part of the brand of PRME, but rather make the SDGs core to the PRME's mission. In that sense, key leaders involved in the strategic review recognized the following important roles of the PRME community: developing, through education, globally responsible citizens, managers and leaders with the commitment and capabilities to deliver on issues of sustainability; providing research that enables policy makers and organizations to serve on UN priorities, including the SDGs; as well as engaging in transforming business and societies by contributing actively on public debates. The SDGs would become the cornerstone

of PRME's programmatic and community work and this new focus was reflected in PRME's new vision, mission and strap line. The updated PRME's vision was 'Realizing the Sustainable Development Goals through responsible management education'; and the PRME's mission was 'Transforming business and management education, research and thought leadership to develop the responsible leaders for the world we want' with the strap line affirming that the initiative focused on 'developing responsible leaders of tomorrow.'

Optimizing the global organization

The second 'must win battle', optimizing the global organization included strengthening the demand-side of responsible management education as well as aligning PRME's networks to contribute with new priorities. Since 2012 when, as an outcome of the 3rd Global Forum on Responsible Management Education that took place in conjunction with the Rio+20 Summit, the PRME initiative officially launched PRME Chapters and the

Figure 2.1   The UN sustainable development goals (UN, 2019)

PRME Champions group, PRME had evolved into a global 'network of networks.' While the constituency became more robust and solid during the following years, it became clear during the strategic review process, that there was a need to strengthen a strategic link between the academic PRME signatories to other key constituencies: business and students.

The rationale to this recommendation was that both groups have 'considerable influence on the direction of management-related higher education institutions (HEIs)' (PRME, 2017c), apart from also being important drivers of sustainability and responsible management education.

Several targets were identified with the aim to align all work streams to the SDGs and ensure leverage of the demand side of responsible management education, as well as strengthen the links with relevant UN agencies and critical stakeholders such as business and students to enable systemic change. The targets included alignment of all PRME work streams (including Chapters, Working Groups and Champions) with the SDGs; leveraging business (including UN Global Compact) participants; to include student perspectives in all areas of activity and for Steering Committee members to promote PRME through the work of their organizations.

The PRME engagement model

An interesting outcome of the 2016 PRME Strategic Review is the 'PRME Engagement Model', stemming from the discussions with stakeholders particularly on the second 'must-win battle' and put together by the PRME Secretariat. This model aims to further explain the complex net system of collaborations and partnerships within the initiative (PRME, 2017a). In addition, as a United Nations and UN Global Compact-backed initiative, PRME has several partnerships with other UN entities and has aligned all its work streams to the SDGs. At the core, PRME engages higher education institutions

to become signatories by committing to the Six Principles, planning, implementing, reporting, communicating and recommitting to the Principles. Businesses, including participants of the UN Global Compact, and students and youth are key stakeholders to the initiative and are meant to be close partners in all work streams. PRME Networks are composed by the regional Chapters, the Champions leadership group, as well as the thematic Working Groups, advancing their work according to the priorities explained above. The PRME Secretariat, as the administrative body, and the Governance Bodies and partners are also important enablers of the PRME initiative (see also Figure 2.2).

Creating balanced growth

The third 'must-win battle' focused on creating 'balanced growth' for the PRME initiative. This aim included several important aspects such as quantitative and qualitative growth of the signatory base and engagement; as well as crucial operational elements such as sustainable funding and governance issues. All targets identified were coupled with several tactics to be implemented by the PRME Secretariat, the different PRME networks (Chapters, Champions, Working Groups), the governance bodies (i.e. Steering and Advisory Committees) and other partners. The PRME Secretariat also worked together with the community to spell out more detailed strategic work plans and regional targets to empower the constituency to make progress on these important aspects of the initiative. The targets included quantitative targets (to increase signatories and location countries) and qualitative targets to 'deepen' engagement with PRME at institutional, regional and global level. This would be supported by communication and engagement strategies and plans.

Part of the focus of this 'must-win battle' was given to creating sustainable funding for the PRME initiative. With that aim in mind, it was proposed that the funding model of the initiative would be reviewed and that a

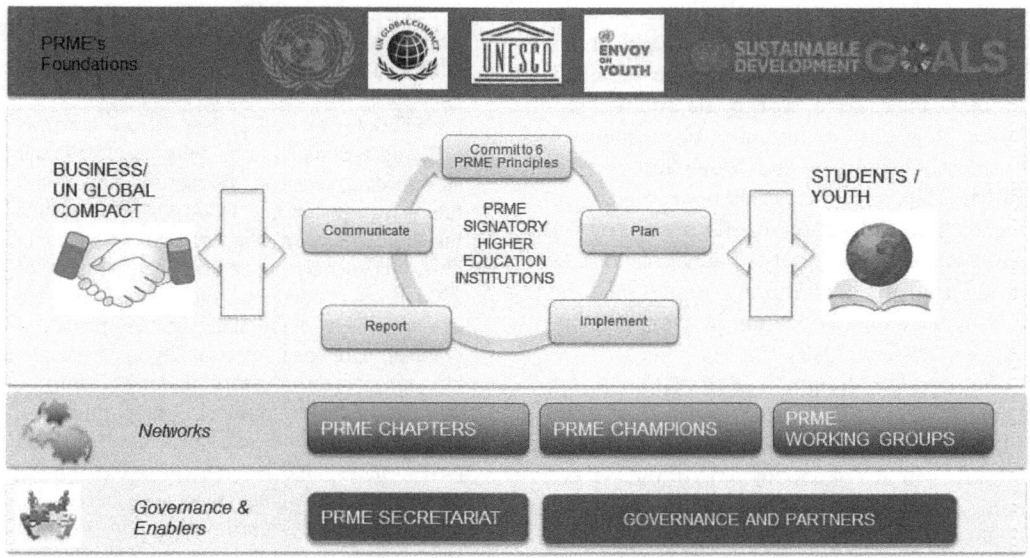

Figure 2.2   The PRME engagement model (PRME, 2017a)

pricing model would be developed in order to provide clear services to the PRME signatories. Finally, discussions around a more fit-for-purpose governance for the PRME initiative took place, such as some minor changes implemented in order to strengthen the voice of the PRME signatories through the PRME Advisory Committee, including linking this body more closely with the PRME Steering Committee.

TWELVE YEARS INTO PRME

Assessing the Impact of the Initiative: PRME's Development towards Contributing to the SDGs

Although the field of responsible management education is very dynamic and crowded, scholars agree that PRME has become a dominant actor, holding important symbolic capital and positioned to be a cornerstone supporting, connecting and promoting other actors in the space (Storey, Killian &

O'Regan, 2017). While the direct impact of PRME is hard to quantify, it is evident that this initiative has become an important catalyzer for debate and action around responsible management education and sustainability across the world. In that sense, many academics consider PRME as an opportunity to be 'a powerful driver of corporate sustainability considering the "long-term effect" of education' (UN Global Compact, 2015).

PRME embarked on an ambitious journey to engage critical global mass in a world whereby estimates there are over 16,000 business and management programs (AACSB, 2015). Yet, whilst the PRME signatory base has grown consistently over the years, PRME participants are still a minimal fraction of the overall amount of business and management programmes around the world, representing close to 5% of these institutions. Furthermore, if the amount of schools that are accredited or even top-ranked are considered, the number of schools reduces even further. It is also so important to PRME's DNA (conceived from the very beginning of its existence) to be inclusive and bottom-up because only by driving critical global mass can mainstreaming responsible business and management education to advance the SDGs be achieved. In that sense, as a worldwide multi-stakeholder learning community of academics, businesses, students, and leadership experts, PRME calls to business schools and management-related education institutions to commit and engage with a variety of networks to scale up their efforts toward transforming business and management education in support of the SDGs (Librizzi, 2019).

The explicit alignment of all PRME's work streams to the SDGs as a result of the 2016 PRME Strategic Review is indeed key, since, while Goal 4 (or 'SDG 4') of the SDGs, dedicated to ensuring 'inclusive and quality education for all and promote lifelong learning', is the specific goal that could swiftly be identified with PRME's work, in reality, the PRME community's work touches virtually on all SDGs, since education itself is one of the most critical vehicles (along with funding and partnerships) to ensure progress in achieving all 17 SDGs (Librizzi, 2019). This clear conviction, crystallized in the new PRME's vision and mission, was an important enabler for the vibrant PRME community to leverage the acquired social capital and PRME's very unique position to convene multi-stakeholder collaboration around the SDGs globally. In that sense:

- **PRME has become the largest organized relationship between the UN and management-related higher education institutions**: Counting over 730 signatories in more than 90 countries and reaching around 2.5 million students yearly (PRME, 2017b), PRME inspires and promotes responsible management education, research and thought leadership globally providing bridges for dialogue and partnerships with the business sector – in particular through the Global Compact Local Networks and UN Global Compact's business participants – in support of the SDGs.
- **PRME provides a framework for sustainability and responsible management education**: PRME's framework includes the Six

Principles that facilitate continuous progress on sustainability and responsible management education in support of the 10 Global Compact Principles. PRME participants commit to advance the Principles as well as report good practices and progress related to the Principles to all their stakeholders, aiming to develop the current and future leaders for 'the world we want'. While the Principles were launched at a key point in time, immediately before the financial crisis of 2008, they continue to show their relevance in the context of the SDGs, as they provide a roadmap to embed sustainability and responsible management education in values, curricula, research, methods, dialogue and partnerships. The breadth and interconnectedness of the SDGs have demonstrated how crucial is this shift of the educational paradigm to more connected and interdisciplinary approaches. More than ever the SDGs compel us to 'gather expertise from across disciplines and sectors to gain a more holistic view of the complex global issues and potential opportunities and solutions. Issues like poverty, climate change, human rights, equality, can only be tackled with a diverse and integrated knowledge approach' (Librizzi, 2019). Only by adopting an interdisciplinary focus as well as experiential learning methodologies, can a deeper understanding of the most pressing issues of our time properly address sustainable development.

- **PRME has become a 'network of networks' for collective action and partnership**: PRME has evolved into a 'network of networks' by developing 15 regional Chapters partnering around the world with the Global Compact Local Networks to advance the SDGs in the different local contexts. The Champions group, composed of 31 institutions, work globally to lead with innovation and raise the bar on responsible management education and sustainability. Additionally, eight Issue Working Groups produce SDG-relevant research and teaching resources. In 2016, PRME created a student engagement platform in partnership with organizations such as Wikirate, Aim2Flourish, Oikos and Sulitest. PRME has also realized the importance of understanding students' views and preferences on matters of sustainability and responsible management education, engaging with them and raising their voices. The fourth annual report on the international business student study led by the Principles of Responsible

Management Education (PRME) Secretariat and PRME Signatory Macquarie Graduate School of Management (MGSM) (Haski-Leventhal & Manefield, 2018) constitutes an ongoing initiative to gather students' perspectives into the sustainability and responsible management education conversations and actions. PRME also seeks partnerships with other relevant actors in the space such as ranking agencies, accreditation associations, publishers, NGOs, etc.

- **PRME has become the academic partner of the Global Compact Local Networks**: Across the world PRME Chapters and Global Compact Local Networks recognize their mutual value and appreciate working together as business and academic counterparts. The PRME-Global Compact Local Networks' collaboration creates a triple value proposition by 'bringing forth sustainable development challenges and the global–local practitioner agenda to enrich academic thinking, research and teaching of PRME institutions'; 'strengthening the capacities of Local Networks to build their SDG Action Plans on a sound and robust analytical basis supported by academic analysis and diagnosis'; 'providing a practitioner agenda for applied research, teaching and innovation on how sustainable business can have a significant impact in advancing the SDGs in the local-global context' (Cortes & Librizzi, 2016).
- **PRME is a content creator and disseminator**: The PRME initiative thematic work streams focus on research and teaching to advance the SDGs. In consequence, the eight PRME Working Groups enable content creation on issues such as addressing challenges posed by climate change, poverty and corruption; as well as advancing issues such as gender equality and human rights in business. At the regional and signatory level, Chapters and higher education institutions regularly produce good practices on how to incorporate the SDGs into their research and curricula. Chapters also support the dissemination of such content throughout their networks and members.

While the PRME initiative through its community has made progress on the objective to help advance the SDGs through responsible management education, much work still has to be done. In the sections below, we look at some potential next steps for the PRME initiative while also acknowledging some of the gaps of the responsible management education space in addressing the SDGs, as well as some recommendations that are relevant for both PRME and other organizations in the landscape.

PRME IN THE ERA OF THE SDGS

At the 2017 Global Forum for Responsible Management Education – 10 Years of PRME 'Bringing the SDGs to Every Classroom and Every Organization' – the PRME community celebrated a decade of achievements, while reflecting on the challenges and opportunities going forward (PRME, 2017b).

Based on the conversations of previous Global Fora, as well as the input received from different stakeholders, it seems clear that an important focus for PRME in the next years should be to continue strengthening the multi-stakeholder nature of the initiative to further support the implementation of the Six Principles and the SDGs worldwide. In this regard, the Outcomes Declaration of the 2017 Global Forum, section 3, entitled 'Our Results and Commitments' (PRME, 2017b) detailed the many great initiatives that have been undertaken for the last decade and the continuous need to take PRME to the next level through leadership at different levels (e.g. individual, institutional and collective level). Section 4 of the same document, entitled 'Partnerships and coalitions to accelerate change', spelled out the importance of collaborating and partnering with governments, businesses, non-governmental organizations, accreditation institutions, ranking agencies, student initiatives, media and other drivers in order to address fundamental issues of sustainability as well as to create tipping points for systemic change.

At this point in its existence, it becomes crucial to highlight and sharpen PRME's value proposition – serving as the largest higher education and responsible management education initiative of the United Nations – by:

- Further emphasizing PRME's principles-based approach to sustainability and responsible management education (e.g. thought leadership and policy developing functions) by promoting values and ethics globally, as well as by walking the talk as an organization.
- Strengthening multi-stakeholder 'bottom-up' collaboration and collective action among higher education institutions, business schools and management-related education institutions, the private sector, governments and the United Nations to pursue real transformation and meaningful impact on sustainable development (SDG 17).
- Bringing PRME to new heights through innovation and transformation by leveraging technology to allow more effective exchange within the constituency and beyond.

In this regard, it is key to tackle a few strategic areas to enable PRME to evolve into the primary convener and catalyzer to transform business and responsible management education worldwide.

Incubating Systemic Change through Partnerships and Collective Action

Further fortifying relationships among higher education institutions and business schools, the private sector, recent graduate, students and youth, publishers, ranking and accreditation associations, media and other levers becomes a priority. This is with the aim to create the conditions for systemic change to allow sustainability and management education to become the new normal. A recent example of how systemic change can be nurtured is a new report *Business School Rankings for the 21st Century*, authored by David Pitt-Watson and Ellen Quigley (2019) on business school rankings successfully launched in Davos in January 2019 at the PRME-Corporate Knights Luncheon. The report published under the aegis of the UN Global Compact and with the support of Aviva Investors, 'provides an overview of the current state of the business school rankings and suggests possible changes to help align business school education with the needs of the 21st century'. This report received input from the PRME Advisory Committee, business schools, progressive businesses, rankings publications, accreditation agencies and relevant civil society organizations convened by several organizations including PRME. PRME were pleased to contribute input and support this project, which has already resulted in positive discussions with some rankings agencies regarding the need to improve assessments and rankings to promote 'a race to the top' in business education. For instance, a few days after this report launch the *Financial Times* (FT) Work and Career Editor, Isabel Berwick, stated that just 'as business schools rethink what they do, so must the FT'. Therefore, FT is conducting a complete review of its methodologies (Berwick, 2019). This is the type of collaboration and advocacy that can result in creating effective tipping points for systemic change globally.

Raising the Bar: Driving Innovation and Thought Leadership

A crucial element of PRME's work is to advance thought leadership, research, policy development and content creation. It becomes key to fortify this objective by increasing the production of high-quality, innovative and interactive materials through the PRME Secretariat, Champions, Working Groups and other work streams that can be circulated and mainstreamed through PRME signatories, Chapters, Global Compact Local Networks and relevant partners. Additionally, it becomes necessary to foster interlinkages between academia and business on critical themes (e.g. anti-corruption, human rights, anti-poverty, gender issues, climate change, etc.) to produce applied research and tools to facilitate teaching and implementation of those topics. The PRME Inspirational Guides published by Greenleaf (now Routledge) both at the global and Chapter level provide institutional examples of such innovation.

The Responsible Management Education Research (RMER) Conferences (previously discussed) are also highly interactive events that bring together several PRME Chapters and Working Groups, as well as practitioners and experts, encouraging collaboration to breaking silos and advancing innovative solutions to elevate the ceiling of sustainability and responsible management education. Outcomes of these events include SDG- and PRME-relevant publications such as the PRME Journal Special Issues. The 10th Anniversary PRME Special Issue of the *International Journal of Management Education* was launched at the 2017 PRME Global Forum and 10th Anniversary featuring 26 articles looking back to the origins of PRME and its first decade as well as a look forward to the era of the SDGs. Another Special Issue of the same journal, 'In the era of the SDGs', is being published as follow-up to the 2018 RMER conference.

Scaling Up: Mainstreaming Sustainability and Responsible Management Education Everywhere

PRME as a platform of sustainability and responsible management education worldwide has the opportunity to leverage and scale up its convening power within and beyond the PRME community. This includes continuing to foster strategic partnerships with HESI, UN Envoy for Youth and other UN entities, business and youth to help mainstreaming sustainability and responsible management education globally.

Strengthening the engagement frameworks and building capacity will be crucial to nourish the multi-stakeholder of PRME and provide an increasingly robust dedicated platform for discussion and action on the SDGs. In order to increase interactivity and facilitate exchange within and beyond the PRME community, it is key to utilize the appropriate technology and media platforms and cater to the need of the constituency. The PRiMEtime platform developed by Giselle Weybrecht (PRiMEtime, 2019) brings together and shares good practices on how to mainstream sustainability and responsible leadership into management education globally. The blog serves as a platform to share and discuss inspirational activities that promote the development of responsible leaders.

Organizational Priorities

As discussed above, the 2016 PRME Strategic Review identified three 'must-win battles': (1) Clarifying the brand; (2) Optimizing the global organization; and (3) Creating balanced growth (including sustainable funding and governance revision). These strategic priorities are due to an assessment of progress and revision to ensure that the PRME Secretariat 'walks the talk' by living up to the higher standards of responsibility and sustainability that it promotes worldwide. The revision of priorities includes taking a hard look at the strategy and operations; the relationship between PRME and other UN entities – including the UN Global Compact; ensuring a sustainable funding, adhering to good governance practices and providing the PRME Secretariat with the adequate human resources. By conducting a proper revision of the progress attained since 2016, engaging key stakeholders in an inclusive and transparent manner, the organization aims to deliver meaningful impact and unleash its unlimited potential (Librizzi, 2019).

RESPONSIBLE MANAGEMENT EDUCATION AND THE SUSTAINABLE DEVELOPMENT GOALS (SDGS): ADDRESSING THE GAPS TO DELIVER THE 'WORLD WE WANT'

Why Responsible Management Education Is More Relevant Than Ever

In recent times we have witnessed the increase of inequalities – including related to gender – global warming, alarming decrease of biodiversity and an important portion of young people not employed, trained or educated (The 50+20 Agenda, 2012). In parallel, economic, political and demographic challenges continue to unfold, all of this, together with important technology advancements that accelerate change in a way never seen before. While technology and mass communication have brought together more transparency related to ethical scandals, it also often poses many risks to privacy and other human rights. On the flip side, studies show that closing the gender gap and developing responsible business that brings innovative solutions to the SDGs on areas of energy, cities, food and agriculture, health and wellbeing could bring trillions of dollars in market opportunities, as well as create millions of jobs around the world (World Economic Forum, 2017).

These challenges and opportunities have highlighted the importance of sustainability and responsible management and the key role of higher education institutions to integrate this content and teach the skills to form graduates with the mindset, abilities and knowledge to contribute to solve these complex issues. As educators of the next and current generation of leaders, business schools and management-related higher education institutions are in a unique position to shape the mindsets and influence the actions of those that will drive the largest and most powerful institutions around the world (Parkes, Buono & Howaidy, 2017).

Responsible Management Education (RME) seeks to best equip citizens and leaders to address the most pressing issues of our time and to enable them to implement meaningful change and avert future crises. The wider field of RME includes a range of organizations and initiatives which aim to progress RME. Even though the presence of the Agenda 2030 and the SDGs act to some extent as a unifying factor, these initiatives remain diverse in their approach (Storey et al., 2017). For instance, some actors focus on the ability of the SDGs to deliver sustainability or social changes, while others look at their potential for risk management of business or deliver goals within the corporate social responsibility (CSR) activities of business. Given the diverse institutional and cultural context of business education globally, there is a pluralistic approach to RME. Many of these groups have connection with PRME or are loosely aligned to its principles, approaching RME from different perspectives and methodologies.

Recognizing and Addressing the Gaps of Our Organizations for the Future

While there is much urgency in advancing the SDGs, there is common agreement that these goals are extremely ambitious and that progress is happening at a very slow rate. In addition, these demanding targets require not only doing the right thing but also doing things differently, meaning, there is a need of radical transformation beyond incremental progress, challenging the status quo and convening drivers for systemic change. Higher education institutions are enabled to act as facilitators and change agents, bringing rationality and scientific answers to the complex global issues at hand. Furthermore, they have the ability to convene multi-stakeholder dialogue and partnerships to discuss and propose adequate solutions. As educators and creators of content, higher education is called to form the current and future generation of responsible and sustainable leaders globally, able to drive the required changes forward. These changes can only happen if solutions come with input from different disciplines, as well as stakeholders, with a real inclusiveness that brings richness and reality to the process. These types of collaboration can only happen from a bottom-up perspective that genuinely integrates the different actors and enables effective collaboration and decision-making. As the 50+20 initiative articulated, we need to work together, not to be the best *in* the world but to be the best *for* the world (The 50+20 Agenda, 2012).

In 2019, the UN Global Compact commissioned a further Strategic Review to consider PRME's role in meeting these challenges. At the time of writing, the outcome of this review is not available. However, the 2030 Agenda is less than a decade away and its importance and urgency cannot be overstated, especially with the climate crisis and related issues.

It is also clear that all organizations in this space need to step up and be fit for purpose to make their contribution to these critical challenges of our time. Issues of transparency, accountability, lack of inclusion and responsibility can render organizations unable to deliver progress and fulfill its mission. We all need to build and contribute to effective, responsible and inclusive organizations to advance Responsible Management and Leadership Education within the context of the SDGs.

REFERENCES

AACSB (2015). Business School Data Guide. [Online] Available at: www.aacsb.edu/-/media/aacsb/publications/data-trends-booklet/2015.ashx?la=en. Accessed 19 February 2019.

Aim2Flourish (2019). [Online] Available at: https://aim2flourish.com/. Accessed 3 March 2019.

Alcaraz, J., & Thiruvattal, E. (2010). An interview with Manuel Escudero, The United Nations' Principles for Responsible Management Education: a global call for sustainability. *Academy of Management Learning & Education, 9*(3), 542–550.

Berwick, I. (2019). Financial Times 27 January 2019. [Online] Available at: www.ft.com/content/18bad724-14f5-11e9-a168-d45595ad076d. Accessed 30 January 2019.

Blasco, M. (2012). Aligning the hidden curriculum of management education with PRME: an inquiry-based framework. *Journal of Management Education, 36*(3), 364–388.

Cortes, J., & Librizzi, F. (2016). Making global goals local business: Global Compact local networks and PRME partnership to implement the SDG Action Plan. [Online] Available at: www.unprme.org/resource-docs/ConceptNoteSDGActionPlanswithPRMEandLocalNetworks.pdf. Accessed 25 February 2019.

Escudero, M. (2006). Global corporate citizenship and academia: a global convergence. A concept paper. New York: United Nations.

Gudić M., Keong T., & Flynn P. M. (2017). *Beyond the bottom line: integrating UN Global Compact into management education.* Greenleaf Publishing/Routledge, Taylor & Francis Group.

Gudić, M., Parkes, C., & Rosenbloom, A. (2012). Report on fighting poverty as a challenge for management education. UN PRME Global Forum & Corporate Sustainability Forum Rio+20 Earth Summit.

Gudić, M., Rosenbloom, A., & Parkes, C. (2015). *Responsible management education and the challenge of poverty: a teaching perspective.* (The Principles for Responsible Management Education Series.) Sheffield: Greenleaf Publishing.

Gudić, M., Rosenbloom, A., & Parkes, C. (2014). *Socially responsive organizations and the challenge of poverty.* Sheffield: Greenleaf Publishing.

Guterres, A. (2017). Secretary General Letter. [Online] Available at: www.unprme.org/resource-docs/SGLettersigned.pdf. Accessed 25 February 2019.

Haertle, J., Parkes, C., Murray, A., Hayes, R. (2017) PRME: Building a global movement on responsible management education. *The*

International Journal of Management Education, *15*(2), 66–72.

Haski-Leventhal, D., & Manefield, S. (2018). The state of CSR and RME in business schools: the Students' Voice Fourth Biennial Survey, 2018. [Online] Available at: www.unprme.org/resource-docs/PRMESurvey-2018FINAL.pdf. Accessed 3 March 2019.

HESI (Higher Education Sustainable Initiative) (2019). [Online] Available at: https://sustainabledevelopment.un.org/sdinaction/hesi. Accessed 22 February 2019.

Librizzi, F. (2019). Principles for Responsible Management Education (PRME) Initiative. In: Leal Filho, W. (Eds.), *Encyclopedia of sustainability in higher education*. Cham: Springer.

NetImpact (2019) [Online] Available at: www.netimpact.org. Accessed 27 February 2020.

Parkes, C., Buono, A., & Howaidy, G. (2017). PRME 10th Anniversary Special Issue. The Principles for Responsible Management Education (PRME): the first decade – what has been achieved? The next decade – Responsible Management Education's challenge for the Sustainable Development Goals (SDGs). *International Journal of Management Education*, *15*(2), 61–65.

Pitt-Watson, D., & Quigley, E. (2019). Business School Rankings for the 21st Century. [Online] Available at: www.unprme.org/resource-docs/60555MBAREPORT0119pr03.pdf. Accessed 27 February 2019.

PRI (2019). [Online] www.unpri.org/. Accessed 3 March 2019.

PRiMEtime (2019). [Online] http://primetime.unprme.org. Accessed 23 February 2019.

PRME (2008). The Six Principles. [Online] Available at: www.unprme.org/about-prme/the-six-principles.php. Accessed 19 February 2019.

PRME (2013). How to engage Working Groups. [Online] Available at: www.unprme.org/how-to-engage/display-working-group.php?wgid=3170. Accessed 27 February 2019.

PRME (2015a). Transformational Model. [Online] Available at: www.unprme.org/resource-docs/PRMETransformationalWeb.pdf. Accessed 27 February 2019.

PRME (2015b). 2015 PRME Global Forum Outcomes Declaration. [Online] Available at: www.unprme.org/resource-docs/2015PRME GlobalForumforResponsibleManagementEducationOutcomeStatementFINAL.pdf. Accessed 22 February 2019.

PRME (2016). PRME Champions. [Online]. Available from: www.unprme.org/working-groups/champions.php. Accessed 22 March 2016.

PRME (2017a). Engagement Model. [Online] Available at: www.unprme.org/resource-docs/PRMEEngagementModel.jpg. Accessed 3 March 2019.

PRME (2017b). 2017 Global Forum Outcomes Declaration. [Online] Available at: www.unprme.org/resource-docs/2017OutcomeDeclaration.pdf. Accessed 25 February 2019.

PRME (2017c). PRME Strategic Review. [Online] Available at: www.unprme.org/resource-docs/160517PRMEStrategicReviewFINAL.pdf. Accessed 22 February 2019.

PRME (2017d). SIP policy. [Online] Available at: www.unprme.org/reporting/sip-policy.php. Accessed 19 February 2019.

PRME (2019a). Overview. [Online] Available at: www.unprme.org/about-prme/index.php. Accessed 19 February 2019.

PRME (2019b). History. [Online] Available at: www.unprme.org/about-prme/history/index.php. Accessed 19 February 2019.

PRME (2019c). How to engage Chapters. [Online] Available at: www.unprme.org/how-to-engage/chapters.php. Accessed 19 February 2019.

PRME DACH (2014). 1st Responsible Management Education Research Conference. [Online] Available at: http://rmerconference2014.prmechapterdach.eu/?page_id=214. Accessed 27 February 2019.

PRME Impact Report (2017). Impact Report, pp. 21–23. [Online] Available at: www.unprme.org/resource-docs/PRMEImpactReport.pdf. Accessed 25 February 2019.

Rasche, A., & Escudero, M. (2010). Leading change – the role of the Principles for Responsible Management Education. *Journal of Business and Economic Ethics*, *10*(2), 244–250.

Rasche, A., & Gilbert, D. U. (2015). Decoupling responsible management education: why business schools may not walk their talk. *Journal of Management Enquiry*, *24*(3), 239–252.

Rasche, A., Waddock, S., & McIntosh, M. (2013). The United Nations Global Compact: retrospect and prospect. *Business and Society*, *52*(1), 6–30.

Sanquiche, R. (2010). Ethical markets. [Online] Available at: www.ethicalmarkets.com/un-global-compact-delists-companies/. Accessed 10 January 2019.

Solitander, N., Fougère, M., Sobczak, A., & Herlin, H. (2011). We are the champions: organizational learning and change for responsible management education. *Journal of Management Education*, *35*(3), 337–363.

Sroufe E., Sivasubramaniam, N., Ramons D., & Saiia, D. (2014). Aligning the PRME: how to study abroad nurtures responsible leadership. *Journal of Management Education*, *39*(2), 244–275.

Storey M., Killian, S., & O'Regan, P. (2017). Responsible management education: mapping the field in the context of the SDGs. *International Journal of Management Education*, *15*, 93–103.

Sulitest (2019). [Online] Available at: www.sulitest.org/en/index.html. Accessed 3 March 2019.

Sustainable Cities Programme (2019). [Online] Available at: https://citiesprogramme.org/partner/. Accessed 3 March 2019.

The 50+20 Agenda (2012). Available at: https://grli.org/initiatives/the-5020-vision. Accessed 4 February 2019.

United Nations (2019). UN Sustainable Development Goals. [Online] Available at: www.un.org/sustainabledevelopment/sustainable-development-goals/. Accessed 19 February 2019.

UN Global Compact (2015). Impact, transforming business, changing the world, p. 12´. [Online] Available at: www.unglobalcompact.org/library/1331. Accessed 25 February 2019.

Weybrecht, G., & SIP Working Group (2015). SIP Toolkit. [Online] Available at: www.unprme.org/resource-docs/2015PRMEGlobalForumforResponsibleManagementEducationOutcomeStatementFINAL.pdf. p. 7. Accessed 25 February 2019.

WikiRate (2019). [Online] Available at: https://wikirate.org/. Accessed 3 March 2019.

World Economic Forum (2017). The Inclusive Growth and Development Report 2017. Available at: www.weforum.org/reports/theinclusive-growth-and-development-report-2017. Accessed 3 March 2017.

Yepes, G. et al. (2018). University Social Responsibility Indicators System, sharing information on progress. PRME Guide for Implementation [Online] Available at: Guide for Implementation www.unprme.org/resource-docs/CARTILLAPRIMEINGLSONLINE.pdf. Accessed 3 March 2019.

3

Responsible Management Education: The Voice and Perspective of Students

Debbie Haski-Leventhal (with contributions by Quinn Runkle, Mariam Patsatsia and J. Christopher Proctor)

INTRODUCTION

In the last two decades an increasing number of businesses have demonstrated that they are attempting to be 'good' for the world – socially, environmentally and financially – while also creating value for their shareholders and other stakeholders. Mainly captured in the concept of corporate social responsibility (CSR), many businesses are presently aiming to demonstrate their accountability to all their stakeholders, not only shareholders (Haski-Leventhal, 2018).

In a similar vein, business schools are currently reflecting on their role in the development of business leaders who are ethical and responsible and how they could contribute to the shift towards responsible management. Some business schools are indeed shifting from being 'best *in* the world', with a focus on rankings and alumni salaries, to being 'best *for* the world', with a commitment to help in creating a more ethical and moral business environment (Haski-Leventhal, Pournader &

McKinnon, 2017). As part of this movement, the United Nations-supported Principles for Responsible Management Education (PRME) assists business schools in understanding what and how they can promote responsible management education (RME). With more than 700 PRME signatory schools all over the world, the discourse on RME is more vital than ever before. Just as companies came to realise that they cannot promote CSR without an integration of their most important stakeholders, such as consumers and employees, so do business schools now come to realise the importance of inclusion of the voice of their students in this discourse on RME.

Since business students collectively constitute the future leadership of corporations, it has been argued that they should be prioritised as a stakeholder group, and that their perspectives should be included in the discussion on RME (Albaum & Peterson, 2006). If business schools are to adopt a multi-stakeholder approach as part of their own social responsibility programmes (Boyle, 2004), including the students' voice is essential. Students have been an active player in voicing the importance they attribute to responsible management issues in their business education, and research shows the increasing percentage of students who expect their educators to deliver on RME (Haski-Leventhal et al., 2017). It is also essential to include the students' perspective in RME, not only as the main stakeholder of any business school and university, but also as the ones who will be implementing the knowledge gained as future business leaders.

However, the shift towards RME has not comprehensively incorporated the voice of the students, with most of the articles on the topic positioning students as passive learners (Holland & Albrecht, 2013; Rasche & Gilbert, 2013) or focusing on their (un)ethical behaviour (e.g. Segon & Booth, 2009). It is therefore important that the first handbook on RME will include the students' voice and perspective.

To address this issue, this chapter will include three parts. Firstly, it will cover the existing knowledge on RME and business students to also identify the gaps and the general exclusion of the students' perspective. The second part of the chapter will portray the results of four rounds of a study conducted with PRME on students' attitudes on CSR and RME. Finally, the third part will actually include the students' perspective by including two student bodies, enabling them to reflect on the first two parts and add their own story to the chapter. The chapter will end with reflection on all three parts of the chapter and the lessons they deliver on RME.

RESPONSIBLE MANAGEMENT EDUCATION

As the impact of unethical business conduct and notorious corporate scandals started to unfold in the 2000s, together with the global financial crisis, some of the responsibility was directed towards business management education (Crossan, Mazutis, Seijts & Gandz, 2013; Giacalone, 2007; Podolny, 2009). MBA programmes have been accused of producing 'number crunchers' and analysts, who are neither managers nor leaders (Mintzberg, 2004). Consequently, Matten and Moon (2004, p. 323) argued that business schools should stop being 'brain washing institutions educating their graduates only in relatively narrow shareholder value ideology' and instead become more socially responsible.

Scholars and practitioners criticised business education as partially responsible for unethical business conduct that leads to corporate scandals and unethical behaviour (Haski-Leventhal et al., 2017; Rasche & Gilbert, 2013). Business schools were held accountable for socialising business students into focusing only on profit with little consideration for ethics and social responsibility (Neal, 2017). Consequently, research showed that students saw the line between right and wrong as increasingly blurry and expect managers to behave unethically (Kidwell, 2001). Indeed, business students had a concerning 'disconnect' between ethics and professional performance, and students disagreed that it paid to be good (Luthar & Karri, 2005). Most concerning was the empirical evidence demonstrating that the more students progressed in their business education, the less ethical they became (Ferraro, Pfeffer & Sutton, 2005; Smyth & Davis, 2004). Business students were found to be more corruptible compared to students in other disciplines (Frank & Schulze, 2000), because certain elements of business education, such as economics courses, facilitated higher levels of greed (Wang, Malhotra & Murnighan, 2011).

Indeed, business schools were not doing enough to develop responsible management: only a minority of business schools were found to teach business ethics, particularly as a core unit (Cornelius, Wallace & Tassabehji, 2007; Evans, Treviño & Weaver, 2006; Matten & Moon, 2004). When business schools talk about responsibility but do not teach it as part of the core curriculum, the result is decoupling rhetoric from reality when referring to RME in MBA programmes (Rasche & Gilbert, 2013).

Boyle (2004) argued that business schools should develop their own social responsibility and the responsibility of the students by adopting existing CSR frameworks such as Carroll's Domain theory (Carroll, 1991). Boyle asserted that just like corporations, responsible business schools need to exhibit financial, legal and ethical responsibilities to model desired behaviour at the organisational level while instructing students in, and giving them experience in the practice of, good citizenship. Michaelson (2016) offered a novel approach to business ethics education by promoting a full integration of RME at all levels of business education to teach students not only how to manage but also how to live. Similarly, Shrivastava (2010) suggested that the role of business schools is to teach students by assisting students to develop passion for sustainability. Some scholars called to extend the purpose of business education to include issues such as poverty (Neal, 2017), the Sustainable Development Goals (Howard-Grenville et al., 2017), compassion and wisdom (Baden & Higgs, 2015).

As a result of the aforementioned criticism, empirical evidence and the general shift towards social responsibility, many business schools and universities began to reflect on their role in society and some underwent a shift towards RME (Rasche & Gilbert, 2013). In 2007, the United Nations Global Compact launched PRME, with the aim to inspire and champion responsible management education (RME), promote related research and encourage thought leadership globally in order to help in achieving the Sustainable Development Goals (Neal, 2017). There are currently over 700 PRME signatory schools that commit to the six principles (purpose, values, method, research, partnership and dialogue) and share mandatory reports (entitled 'Sharing Information on Progress' or SIP reports) on the PRME website (www.unprme.org).

PRME encourages the development and dissemination of socially responsible business practices and enlightened management education. Moreover, PRME offers means by which students may be introduced to the multifaceted issues involved in responsible management and develop the relevant necessary skills (Forray, Leigh & Kenworthy, 2015). According to Blasco (2012), one of the most laudable and engaging features of PRME is the profound respect for, and sensitivity to, the vast contextual diversity and complexity in which business schools, firms, and other organisations must operate. However, despite increasing efforts in the academic world to emphasise corporate social responsibility (CSR), sustainability, ethics and similar issues, the full scope of the above-mentioned view has not yet become embedded in the mainstream of business-related education (Alcaraz & Thiruvattal, 2010).

While PRME offers no universal definition of social responsibility or responsible management education (Blasco, 2012), Haski-Leventhal et al. (2017, p. 221) defined RME based on the six principles of PRME as 'the business education approach and method (including teaching, research and dialogue) purposed to develop the capabilities and perceived values of students to be responsible generators of sustainable value for business and society at large'.

In the last two decades, because of PRME and other aforementioned drivers, a shift occurs towards RME. There is a higher number of core and elective units on ethics and social responsibility in business schools listed in the Financial Times Top 50 Global Business Schools (Christensen, Peirce, Hartman, Hoffman & Carrier, 2007; Rasche & Gilbert, 2013), in AACSB-accredited business schools (Rutherford, Parks, Cavazos & White, 2012), and in PRME signatory schools (Rasche & Gilbert, 2013). However, we still lack knowledge about the impact of RME and what the students' perspectives are on all of the above.

RME AND STUDENTS

If RME is the 'business education approach and method [...] purposed to develop the capabilities and perceived values of students to be responsible generators of sustainable value for business and society at large' (Haski-Leventhal et al., 2017, p. 221) then it is vital to understand the students' perspective on RME and related issues. Furthermore, students are active in their education – rather than just passive learners – and a key stakeholder in the education universe. Erskine and Johnson (2012) stated that if businesses are embracing a triple bottom line, then business schools should prepare students for triple-bottom-line thinking, and, importantly, this is what students are expressing a desire for. In their research, these authors showed that 78% of business students agreed that sustainability is an important topic in business and 71% wanted to work for a company that embraced sustainability.

A review of the literature shows that continuing the PRME studies on understanding students' attitudes and perceptions contributes greatly to understanding the influence of RME programmes. If PRME is to meet its intended mission and goals then capturing the student experience that reflects all the challenges, ambiguities, complexity and often paradoxical demands faced by individuals in their work and personal lives (Millar & Koning, 2018; Painter-Morland, 2015) is a critical input into evolving business education programmes to support and equip future generations of responsible managers.

THE PRME STUDIES: BUSINESS STUDENTS' ATTITUDES AND BEHAVIOUR

Together with PRME and signatory schools around the world, I have been collecting data on the students' perspectives, particularly on CSR and RME, for nearly a decade, with four rounds of online surveys to date (2011, 2013, 2016 and 2018). The number of respondents varied by year: 1200 responses in 2018 compared to 2016 (1700 responses), 2013 (1285 responses) and 2011 (1250), bringing the total to nearly 5500 students. In all surveys, males were slightly overrepresented (55%) and most students were in their twenties (age range 18–65). Together, the four surveys collected data from across the globe, usually with the highest number of respondents coming from the US, the UK, Australia, China, Brazil, Germany, France and Iceland.

While the survey somewhat changed in each round, it always collected data on students' background, awareness of PRME, UN Global Compact and SDGs, sustainable behaviour, values, CSR attitudes, RME attitudes and ranking of business responsibilities. In the third and fourth round, we also asked students about their willingness to sacrifice a percentage of their future salary to work for responsible employers.

Awareness, Sustainable Behaviour and Values

Firstly, we asked the students to report on their awareness of PRME and the UN Global Compact, and since 2015 also on the SDGs. In 2018, 42.8% of students were able to confirm that their school is a PRME signatory, improving from 2016 (25.9%) and 2013 (36.4%). This result is lower than the 65% recorded in 2011, however, in that year respondents were reminded in the initial survey that they belonged to a PRME signatory school. Significantly, there was a large increase, up 81% from 2016 (37%), in awareness of the UN SDGs, with respondents reporting 67% had gained awareness within their specific study or through other sources.

In addition, we asked students about their community involvement and activism. As can be seen in Table 3.1, about 1 in 3 students

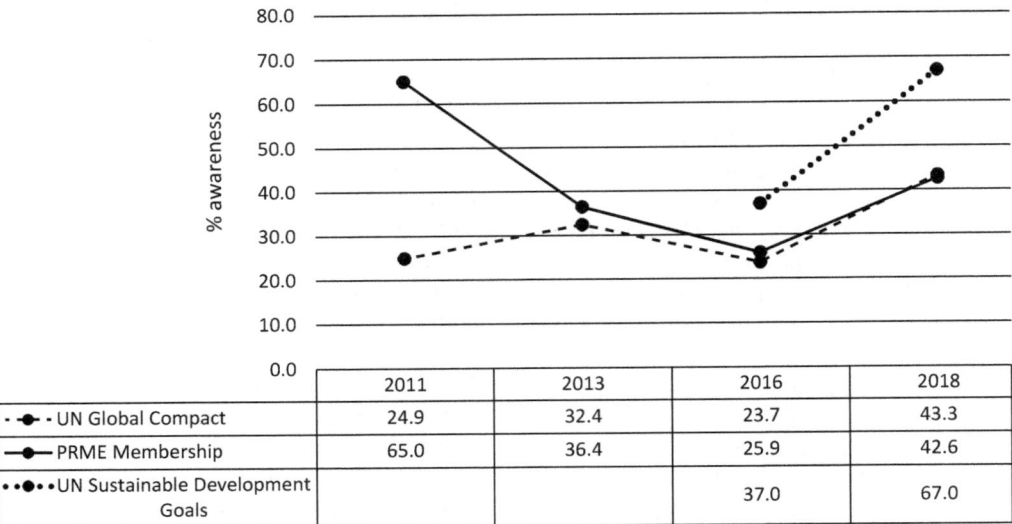

	2011	2013	2016	2018
· · ◆ · UN Global Compact	24.9	32.4	23.7	43.3
─●─ PRME Membership	65.0	36.4	25.9	42.6
· ·●· · UN Sustainable Development Goals			37.0	67.0

Figure 3.1   Level of students' awareness by year

Table 3.1   Students' community involvement and activism by year

Question	Measure	2011	2013	2016	2018
Volunteering	Average hours per month	N/A	9.1	4.0	3.8
	% volunteering	35.6	33.6	33.9	39.3
Philanthropic donations	Average $ per month	N/A	71.0	20.0	34.0
	% making donations	49.7	41.6	35.6	39.1
Social movement participation	Average hours per month	N/A	N/A	1.9	1.6
	% participating	N/A	24.0	21.0	21.0

N/A, data unavailable from previous surveys.

volunteered in the previous 12 months. Whilst the proportion of volunteering remains steady, the average hours of volunteering per month is declining across surveys. Percentage of respondents making financial philanthropic donations slightly increased from 35.6% in 2016 to 39.1% in 2018, with the average donation rising from $20 to $39 per month. Activism in social movements remained steady, with 21–25% of respondents participating. In 2018, older students ($\chi^2 = 455.506$, df = 215, p ≤ 0.001) and those in managerial positions ($\chi^2 = 82.238$, df = 41, p ≤ 0.001) reported higher levels of philanthropic donations.

In 2016 and 2018, students were then asked about their sustainable behaviour. 'Avoiding products or services that cause environmental damage' rated the highest amongst respondents, with a mean of 3.47 (34.8% = did it often, 17.5% = always), slightly higher than for 'Limiting energy use to reduce impact on the environment' (M = 3.46), reflecting similar results from 2016. 'Boycotting products and services' ranked third, with a mean of 3.38 up from fifth in 2016. 'Reducing air pollution' (M = 3.33) and 'Avoiding harm to animals' (M = 3.24) followed. 'Buying organic or fair-trade products' ranked the lowest (M = 3.03) for respondents, in line with results from 2016. In both surveys we found some degree of difference between gender and sustainable behaviour, with female students being more sustainable than males.

In 2018, for the first time, respondents were asked to rank the importance of the 10 dominant universal human values defined by Schwartz (1992). Schwartz's model (see Figure 3.2) arranges 10 values across four axes; openness to change, conservation, self-enhancement and self-transcendence (the latter including benevolence and universalism). 'Benevolence' was by far the most important (M = 4.47 between important and very important). This was followed by 'Self-direction' (M = 4.36) and 'Security' (M = 4.34). Respondents ranked 'Power' (M = 3.50), 'Hedonism' (M = 3.72) and 'Tradition' (M = 3.77) as lowest in importance, with 'Power' also attracting the highest rating from respondents for 'unimportant' (12.7%). In 2016, the survey measured values differently, making comparison difficult. Respondents ranked 'Living a happy, comfortable life' as the most important and 'Living according to your religious faith' ranked last.

Responsible Management and RME in the Eyes of the Students

Respondents were then asked to describe responsible management in their own words. Of the 427 respondents who provided additional comments in 2018, responses could be grouped into six categories to describe responsible management: care for the environment (163 times), followed by holistic management of stakeholders (154 times), sustainable management (104 times), behaving ethically (84 times), being socially responsible (63 times) and economic management (53 times). Respondents reflected on the need to balance the responsibilities to all stakeholders – direct and indirect – and the need for managers to be prepared to make decisions that go beyond just making a profit. Sustainability and concern for the welfare of future generations also featured strongly.

As for their own business management education, respondents identified RME-related topics taught within the current programme of study. The most common topics taught were CSR (M = 3.75) and business ethics (M = 3.68) – reflecting results from the 2016

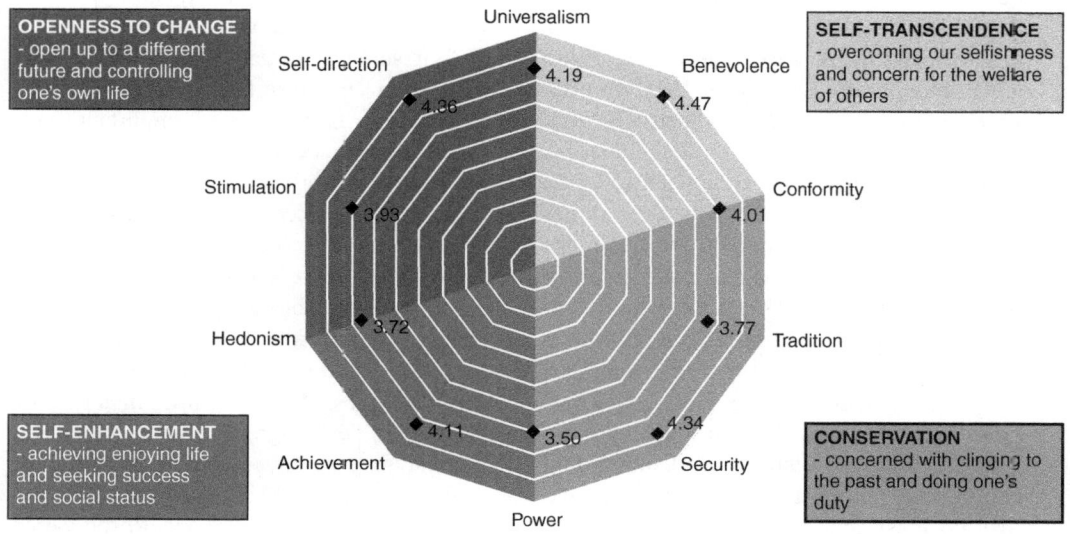

Figure 3.2   Mean level of value importance (based on Schwartz, 1992)

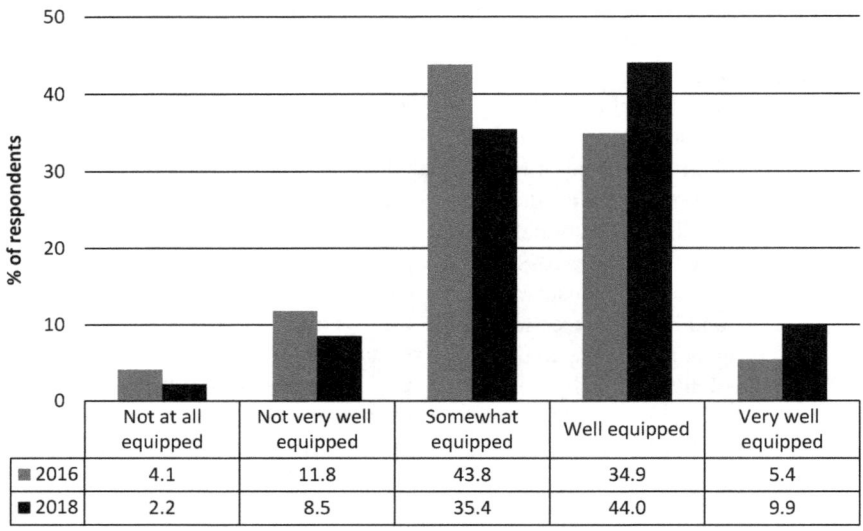

	Not at all equipped	Not very well equipped	Somewhat equipped	Well equipped	Very well equipped
■ 2016	4.1	11.8	43.8	34.9	5.4
■ 2018	2.2	8.5	35.4	44.0	9.9

Figure 3.3   Students' feeling of being well equipped to apply RME knowledge

survey – although the top two positions were reversed. Postgraduate students expressed the view that all subjects were more comprehensively studied than their undergraduate counterparts. Students reported an increase in how well equipped they felt to apply the RME topics in real life up from 2016 (40.3%) to 2018 (53.9%) (see Figure 3.3).

In 2018, 55.1% of students reported their school meeting their expectation regarding RME, compared to 43.3% in 2016. In both years about 80% of the students felt that their opinions were heard by their business schools. Over half of respondents (58.8%) felt that their business schools were doing enough (just enough or more than enough) to help develop responsible leadership, up from 54.9% in 2016. Asked about their suggestions on what their schools could do to improve RME, the first top three were: 'All business students should study business ethics' (85.9% agreed or strongly agreed); followed by 'All business students should study environmental sustainability'; and 'My business school should encourage students to have a critical analysis of all teaching they receive'.

CSR Attitudes and Commitment

This segment of the survey examined respondents' view of the importance of business responsibilities. Firstly, students were asked to rank business responsibility according to Carroll's pyramid (1991), namely financial, legal, ethical and philanthropic, and two additional (social and environmental). In all four surveys the emerging pyramid was exactly the same (see Figure 3.4), with ethical behaviour being the most important (with 93.5% of respondents rating this responsibility as important or very important in 2018).

Respondents were then asked to state their agreement with a series of seven questions designed to elicit respondents' CSR attitudes, regarding how a business demonstrates and balances their corporate social responsibilities, sustainability and other management responsibilities. In 2018, the majority of students (87.6%) agreed that business has a social responsibility beyond just making profits and that CSR and profitability were not mutually exclusive (86%). Respondents felt equally that companies could do more for society and the environment, and that good

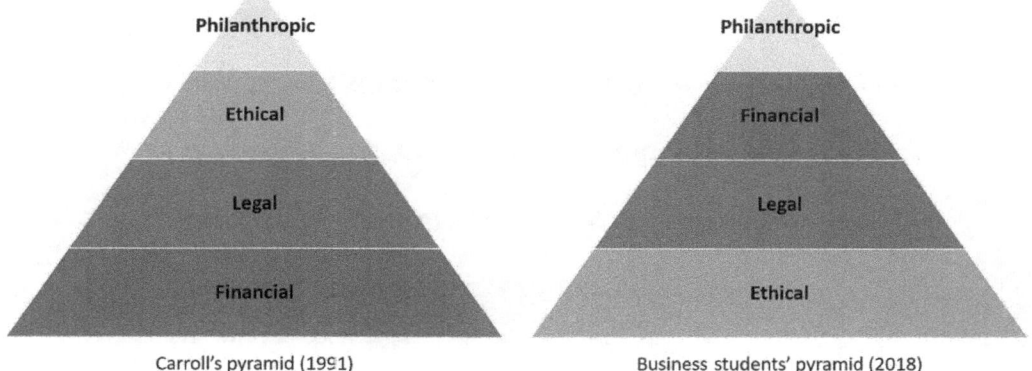

Figure 3.4   Carroll's and students' pyramids of business responsibilities

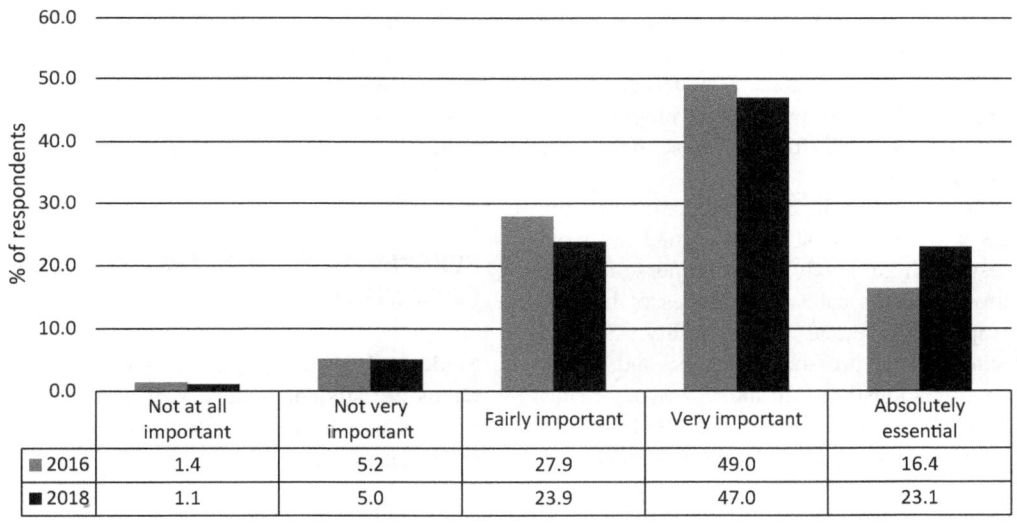

	Not at all important	Not very important	Fairly important	Very important	Absolutely essential
■ 2016	1.4	5.2	27.9	49.0	16.4
■ 2018	1.1	5.0	23.9	47.0	23.1

Figure 3.5   Students' CSR commitment by year

ethics is often good business (81%). Making a profit, even if it meant bending or breaking the rules, was not supported, with 71.3% of respondents disagreeing or strongly disagreeing with this statement.

In 2016 and 2018, students' CSR commitment was measured by how important it was for them to work for a responsible employer. Students were first asked how important it was to work for an employer that was operating responsibly, with 23.1% reporting it was 'absolutely essential', 47% reporting it was 'very important' and 23.9% reporting it was 'fairly important'. There was a large jump from 2016 to 2018 in respondents that rated this as 'absolutely essential' (see Figure 3.5).

Finally, respondents were asked how great a financial sacrifice they would make to work for a company that focused, in addition to making profits, on responsible management

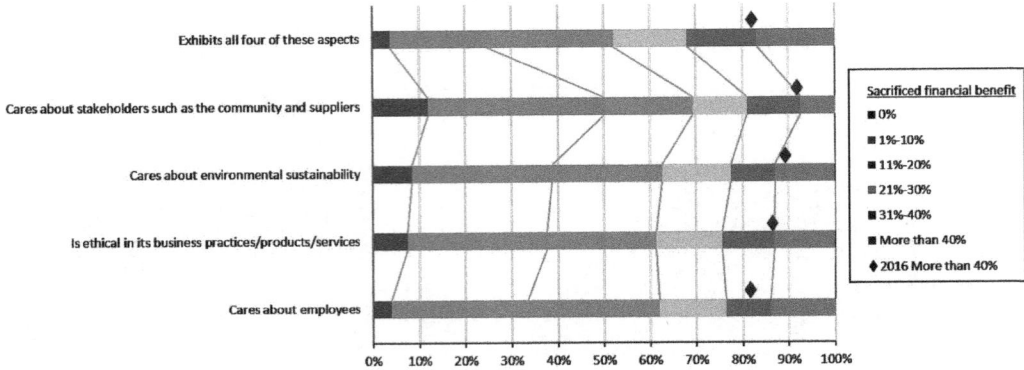

Figure 3.6   Students' expressed willingness to make a salary sacrifice

behaviours: caring for employees, being ethical, environmental sustainability and caring for stakeholders. In 2018 16.9% of respondents expressed that they would give up more than 40% of their financial benefits, up from 16.4% in 2016, to work for an employer that demonstrated all four of these behaviours (see Figure 3.6).

In summary, the four rounds of our studies with business students around the world display high levels of awareness and that most students care about issues of business responsibility and sustainability. Students demonstrate pro-social values and a personal responsibility in their everyday behaviour. Students who participated in this study over the years also consistently show

positive attitudes towards RME, expecting their schools to do more in this area and teach CSR to all students, as well as strong attitudes towards CSR, demanding ethical and responsible responsibility and behaviour of business. They also 'walk the talk', with most of them willing to sacrifice some part of their future salary to work for a responsible employer.

PERSPECTIVES FROM TWO STUDENT ORGANISATIONS

Students Organising for Sustainability and Oikos are student bodies with a mission to transform education. Their histories and reflections follow:

Students Organising for Sustainability: Engagement with Formal and Informal Curriculum[1]

Students Organising for Sustainability – UK (SOS-UK) is the new sustainability charity of the National Union of Students (NUS), which works to transform education to ensure all students learn and lead on sustainability, both during their studies and through their professional lives. Launched in summer 2019, SOS-UK is NUS' response to the growing demand from young people to see sustainability as part of their learning and the urgent need to take action on climate change (BBC, 2019; IPCC, 2018). NUS has tracked student opinion on climate change since 2012 and the spring of 2019 saw the highest-ever reported levels of concern, with 91% of students stating that they are fairly or very concerned about climate change (NUS, 2019c).

   SOS has three core aims: to move sustainability from being a niche subject to one that all students learn about; to create positive solutions-driven students who go on to make the world more just and sustainable; and to shift society from an obsession with short-term profit to long-term benefit. SOS does this through three programmes of activity:

engaging more students in leading on, and learning about, sustainability; embedding sustainability in the formal curriculum, from early years to adult learning; and making sustainability more inclusive, for everyone.

Universities educate future leaders and yet when one looks at most of today's political and business leaders, it is clear that their university experience failed to orient their understanding of the world around sustainability. UK universities have a global responsibility for the education of such world leaders, with 57 of all current prime ministers, presidents and monarchs having studied at a UK higher education institution (Hillman, 2018). As public institutions, one could argue that universities have a moral obligation to act for the public good and in society's best interest and that they must do so by educating future leaders who will be adept at solving the world's greatest challenges, rather than worsening them. Worldwide, just 6% of people attend university but make up 80% of those in the world's leadership positions (Hopkins, 2018). In order to ensure that the privileged minority who attend a university graduate with the ability to be positive agents of change, universities need to deeply and radically embed sustainability through their operations, teaching and learning, and research (Alabaster & Blair, 1996; Martin & Jucker, 2005).

For the past decade, NUS has tracked student interest in sustainability as it pertains to education. Consistently, 80% of students say that sustainability should be a priority for their institution and 60% say they would like to learn more about sustainability (NUS, 2018b). SOS embeds sustainability through all aspects of student learning (the formal, informal and subliminal curriculum) through top-down, middle-out and bottom-up interventions. The Responsible Futures programme works with institutions in partnership with their students' union to embed sustainability across the student experience (NUS, 2018a). To date, 30 institutions have taken part in this ground-breaking programme, which provides a supported framework approach to transforming further and higher education institutions' policies, leadership and practice (NUS, 2018a). The For Good suite of programmes (Dissertations, Projects, and Placements For Good) provide individual students with the opportunity to link their learning to a real-world challenge by matching students with community organisations that would benefit from their contributions (NUS, 2019b). Behaviour change and engagement programmes like the UNESCO-award-winning Green Impact programme and the Student Switch Off campaign work to empower students and staff to work together to make changes within their workplaces, academic departments and halls of residence (NUS, 2019a). As such, SOS' work empowers young people to change their education and, in doing so, change the world. SOS challenges the education sector to think beyond the current paradigm in which education seems to be seen simply as a means to future employment and a high(er) salary. NUS' longitudinal research has discovered that over two-thirds of students would choose a lower-paid job to work for an organisation with a stronger environmental and ethical record (NUS, 2018b). Jonathan Porritt, environmentalist and Chancellor of Keele University, sums this up well in saying that universities 'should be preparing students for the work of the world, not just the world of work' (Porritt, 2012). Today, the work of the world must be to solve the climate crisis and create a more just and sustainable future for all and the work of SOS-UK seeks to ensure our students will be at the forefront of this immensely important challenge.

oikos: Leadership for Sustainability and Responsible Management Education[2]

oikos is an international student network for sustainability in economics and management education. Against the background of ever-increasing problems in our economy and threats of climate change, oikos stands with a mission to transform economics and management education by empowering student change agents, raising awareness for sustainability opportunities and challenges, and building institutional support for curriculum reform.

A group of students bewildered by the lack of environmental awareness in economics and management came together to establish oikos in 1987, in St Gallen, Switzerland. They were convinced that only widespread understanding of ecological responsibility could guarantee long-term economic success (Barkawi, 2000). Now their concern is shared by students across the world.

Currently, 1,200 students in close to 50 local oikos chapters across 24 countries lead the process of transformation towards sustainability through hundreds of initiatives that reach over 50,000 people annually. What these young people of different social, economic and cultural backgrounds have in common is their shared conviction that the management practices that led to failures like the 2008 global financial crash, drastic inequality and climate crisis, cannot solve the very problems they created.

And yet today, these young people who have no choice but to remedy what has been damaged in the economy and environment, receive an education that is inapt to prepare them to overcome our sustainability challenges. Despite negligence on the part of higher education institutions, students have come to realise the value and importance of responsibility and sustainability in their education. They know that a new way of doing and thinking about business needs to be developed at universities worldwide. This new type of education should enable students to become change-makers for a more just and sustainable world, rather than mere managers within a broken system.

Creating this kind of education will take more than adding electives or improving teaching methods. While much of responsible management is framed in preventative terms – how do we teach students not to break laws or ethical norms – what is needed is a positive vision of what 'business as usual' for managers must look like for society to achieve an economic system that is both ecologically and socially sustainable. This will mean challenging some of the core principles of economics and management theory on which a standard business school curriculum is based and allowing new ideas and theories to form the educational building blocks. RME should enable students to embrace their values and encourage them to act accordingly, instead of overloading them with notions like hyper-rational economic man, unlimited growth, or 'efficiency' as they key measure of economic success.

To this end, oikos members are actively advocating for the integration of sustainability into the education system. To name but a few examples, oikos students in Copenhagen collaborated with faculty members to identify drawbacks of the existing curriculum, members in Maastricht designed a module on sustainability and the chapter in Lille has helped to launch a new Master's degree in Global and Sustainable Business (Robinson et al., 2019).

Furthermore, oikos students worldwide explore social, economic, as well as environmental problems and propose solutions to sustainability challenges in their local universities and communities. In doing so, students gain hands-on experience in responsible and ethical management. For instance, the oikos members place special attention on designing projects with as little as possible environmental impact, opting for zero-waste, carbon-neutral or other solutions.

The continuous success of oikos lies in the autonomy of chapters to decide on local priorities, as well as in its international programmes that prepare the next generation of sustainable leaders. These programmes provide guidance and support chapter members to develop responsible leadership skills. They equip students with the necessary insights, knowledge and tools for personal, professional and institutional development.

The oikos Leadership Program (LEAP), for example, inspires young leaders to reflect on their actions and become responsible in their decision-making. LEAP participants have consistently said that they actively seek meaningful employment opportunities and want to structure their career around achieving broader societal objectives. LEAP capitalises on this idea and allows chapter representatives to explore their values, attitudes and communication styles, draw insights and improve. In their local chapters these young people can practise their learnings, try out new leadership methods and galvanise fellow students to bring the necessary change in our education and beyond.

The oikos experience shows that introducing students to sustainability issues during their university education helps develop responsible leaders who think beyond profit maximisation and consider the environmental and social impact of their decisions. The youth hold the keys to solving the challenges of the 21st century and oikos is committed to creating a generation of sustainability change agents who can rise to meet the occasion.

DISCUSSION AND CONCLUSION

Based on the literature review, the findings from four rounds of international studies with business students, and the perspectives of two leading student organisations, this chapter aimed to bring the students' perspectives on business management and RME. While the older literature showed that many business schools educated their students with a narrow focus on profits only, resulting in business students' unethical attitudes and behaviour in their studies and later in life, the more recent literature is indicating a shift. In

the 1990s and in the 2000s much of the literature was criticising business education, based on research data showing the business students were more unethical than other students and that their degrees only made things worse, but also on the results of such management education, such as business scandals. More recently, however, the literature shows that the attitudes of business students are changing, and that they are now demanding their business schools educate them towards responsibility and sustainability.

The four international surveys conducted with PRME support this approach. They show that in the past decade, students demonstrate strong pro-social values, sustainable behaviour and positive attitudes towards RME and CSR. In fact, their commitment is so high, that 1 in 5 business students indicated, both in 2016 and in 2018, that they would be willing to sacrifice more than 40% of their future salary to work for an employer which demonstrates a holistic approach to CSR, caring about employees, stakeholders and the environment. These students completely shift away from the existing paradigm, showing that business responsibilities should be in this order: ethical, legal, financial and philanthropic, and not as previously thought.

Finally, the students who participated in this chapter, students who lead organisations that aim to change higher education institutions and the impact that they and their students can have on the world, further show that 'business as usual' is no longer an option – not for business nor for business schools. If the institutions fail to act in full responsibility, these students strive to change the world bottom-up. They take action and leadership in educating their peers towards a sustainable mindset, assuring that when they graduate, they will have the attitudes and capacities to lead business, not-for-profits and governmental institutions in a more responsible way.

Notes

1 This section of the chapter has been written by Quinn Runkle, SOS-UK (Students Organising for Sustainability – UK).
2 This section of the chapter has been written by Mariam Patsatsia and J. Christopher Proctor, oikos.

REFERENCES

Alabaster, T., & Blair, D. (1996). Greening the university. In J. Huckle and S. Sterling (Eds), *Education for sustainability* (pp. 86–104). London: Earthscan.

Albaum, G., & Peterson, R. A. (2006). Ethical attitudes of future business leaders: do they vary by gender and religiosity? *Business & Society*, *45*(3), 300–321.

Alcaraz, J. M., & Thiruvattal, E. (2010). An interview with Manuel Escudero, the United Nations' Principles for Responsible Management Education: a global call for sustainability. *Academy of Management Learning & Education*, *9*(3), 542–550.

Baden, D., & Higgs, M. (2015). Challenging the perceived wisdom of management theories and practice. *Academy of Management Learning & Education*, *14*(4), 539–555.

Barkawi, A. (2000) The need for student inputs: oikos – international student organization for sustainable economics and management in sustainability and university life. In W. Filho (Eds), *Sustainability and University life* (pp. 257–260, Appendix 2). Berlin: Peter Lang.

BBC (2019). Students walk out in global climate strike. Retrieved 29 July 2019 from: www.bbc.com/news/world-48392551.

Blasco, M. (2012). Aligning the hidden curriculum of management education with PRME: an inquiry-based framework. *Journal of Management Education*, *36*(3), 364–388.

Boyle, M. E. (2004). Walking our talk: business schools, legitimacy, and citizenship. *Business & Society*, *43*(1), 37–68.

Carroll, A. B. (1991). The pyramid of corporate social responsibility: toward the moral management of organizational stakeholders. *Business Horizons, 34*(4), 39–48.

Christensen, L., Peirce, E., Hartman, L., Hoffman, W. M., & Carrier, J. (2007). Ethics, CSR, and sustainability education in the Financial Times Top 50 Global Business Schools: baseline data and future research directions. *Journal of Business Ethics*, *73*(4), 347–368.

Cornelius, N., Wallace, J., & Tassabehji, R. (2007). An analysis of corporate social responsibility, corporate identity and ethics teaching in business schools. *Journal of Business Ethics*, *76*(1), 117–135.

Crossan, M., Mazutis, D., Seijts, G., & Gandz, J. (2013). Developing leadership character in business programs. *Academy of Management Learning & Education*, *12*(2), 285–305.

Erskine, L., & Johnson, S. D. (2012). Effective learning approaches for sustainability: a student perspective. *Journal of Education for Business*, *87*(4), 198–205.

Evans, J. M., Treviño, L. K., & Weaver, G. R. (2006). Who's in the ethics driver's seat? Factors influencing ethics in the MBA curriculum. *Academy of Management Learning & Education, 5*(3), 278–293.

Ferraro, F., Pfeffer, J., & Sutton, R. I. (2005). Economics language and assumptions: how theories can become self-fulfilling. *Academy of Management Review, 30*(1), 8–24.

Forray, J., Leigh, J., & Kenworthy, A. (2015). Special section cluster on responsible management education: nurturing an emerging PRME ethos. *Academy of Management Learning & Education, 14*(2), 293–296.

Frank, B., & Schulze, G. G. (2000). Does economics make citizens corrupt? *Journal of Economic Behavior & Organization, 43*(1), 101–113.

Giacalone, R. A. (2007). Taking a red pill to disempower unethical students: creating ethical sentinels in business schools. *Academy of Management Learning & Education, 6*(4), 534–542.

Haski-Leventhal, D. (2018). *Strategic corporate social responsibility: tools and theories for responsible management.* London: Sage.

Haski-Leventhal, D., Pournader, M., & McKinnon, A. (2017). The role of gender and age in business students' values, CSR attitudes, and responsible management education: learnings from the PRME International Survey. *Journal of Business Ethics, 146*(1), 219–239.

Hillman, N. (2018). UK slips behind the US, which takes the number one slot, for educating the world's leaders. Retrieved 29 July 2019 from: www.hepi.ac.uk/2018/08/14/uk-slips-behind-us-takes-number-one-slot-educating-worlds-leaders.

Holland, D., & Albrecht, C. (2013). The worldwide academic field of business ethics: scholars' perceptions of the most important issues. *Journal of Business Ethics, 117*(4), 777–788.

Hopkins, C. (2018). *Reorienting education and training systems to improve the lives of Indigenous youth: introducing the #IndigenousESD international research project.* Retrieved 29 July 2019 from: www.eiseverywhere.com/ehome/iau2018/815775.

Howard-Grenville, J., Davis, J., Dyllick, T., Joshi, A., Miller, C., Thau, S., & Tsui, A. S. (2017). Sustainable development for a better world: contributions of leadership, management and organizations. *Academy of Management Discoveries, 3*(1), 107–110.

IPCC (2018). Global warming of 1.5°C. Retrieved 29 July 2019 from: www.ipcc.ch/report/sr15/.

Kidwell, L. (2001). Student honor codes as a tool for teaching professional ethics. *Journal of Business Ethics, 29*(1–2), 45–49.

Luthar, H., & Karri, R. (2005). Exposure to ethics education and the perception of linkage between organizational ethical behavior and business outcomes. *Journal of Business Ethics, 61*(4), 353–368.

Martin, S., & Jucker, R. (2005). Educating earth-literate leaders. *Journal of Geography in Higher Education, 29*(1), 19–29.

Matten, D., & Moon, J. (2004). Corporate social responsibility education in Europe. *Journal of Business Ethics, 54*(4), 323–337.

Michaelson, C. (2016). A novel approach to business ethics education: exploring how to live and work in the 21st century. *Academy of Management Learning & Education, 15*(3), 588–606.

Millar, J., & Koning, J. (2018). From capacity to capability? Rethinking the PRME agenda for inclusive development in management education. *African Journal of Business Ethics, 12*(1), 22–37.

Mintzberg, H. (2004). *Managers, not MBAs: A hard look at the soft practice of managing and management development.* London: FT Prentice Hall.

Neal, M. (2017). Learning from poverty: why business schools should address poverty, and how they can go about it. *Academy of Management Learning & Education, 16*(1), 54–69.

NUS (2018a). Responsible Futures Programme. Retrieved 29 July 2019 from: https://sustainability.nus.org.uk/responsible-futures.

NUS (2018b). Sustainability Skills Survey 2017–18: Research into students' experiences of teaching and learning on sustainable development. Retrieved 29 July 2019 from: https://sustainability.nus.org.uk/our-research/our-research/skills-and-sustainable-development.

NUS (2019a). NUS' sustainability programmes. Retrieved 29 July 2019 from: https://sustainability.nus.org.uk/our-works.

NUS (2019b). For Good | National Union of Students. Retrieved 29 July 2019 from: https://forgood.nus.org.uk.

NUS (2019c). Student Opinion: Climate change. Retrieved 29 July 2019 from: https://sustainability.nus.org.uk/our-research/our-research-reports/energy-and-climate-change/climate-change-tracker.

Painter-Morland, M. (2015). Philosophical assumptions undermining responsible management education. *Journal of Management Development*, *34*(1), 61–75.

Podolny, J. M. (2009). The buck stops (and starts) at business school. *Harvard Business Review*, *87*(6), 62–67.

Porritt, J. (2012). Universities must lead the way on the sustainability agenda. *The Guardian*, 16 February. Retrieved 29 July 2019 from: www.theguardian.com/higher-education-network/blog/2012/feb/16/universities-lead-sustainability-agenda-porritt.

Rasche, A., & Gilbert, D. U. (2013). What drives ethics education in business schools? Influences on ethics in the MBA curriculum. *Academy of Management Proceedings*, *2013*(1).

Robinson R., Patsatsia M., Negacz K., & Proctor J. C. (2019). oikos, International Student Organization for Sustainability in Economics and Management Education. In W. L. Filho (Ed.), *Encyclopaedia of sustainability in higher education*. Cham: Springer.

Rutherford, M. A., Parks, L., Cavazos, D. E., & White, C. D. (2012). Business ethics as a required course: investigating the factors impacting the decision to require ethics in the undergraduate business core curriculum. *Academy of Management Learning & Education*, *11*(2), 174–186.

Schwartz, S. H. (1992). Universals in the content and structure of values: theoretical advances and empirical tests in 20 countries. *Advances in Experimental Social Psychology*, *25*, 1–65.

Segon, M., & Booth, C. (2009). Business ethics and CSR as part of MBA curricula: an analysis of student preference. *International Review of Business Research Papers*, *5*(3), 72–81.

Shrivastava, P. (2010). Pedagogy of passion for sustainability. *Academy of Management Learning & Education*, *9*(3), 443–455.

Smyth, M. L., & Davis, J. (2004). Perceptions of dishonesty among two-year college students: Academic versus business situations. *Journal of Business Ethics*, *51*(1), 63–73.

Wang, L., Malhotra, D., & Murnighan, J. K. (2011). Economics education and greed. *Academy of Management Learning & Education*, *10*(4), 643–660.

4

Non-Western Responsible Management Education: A Critical View and Directions for the Future

Dima Jamali and Georges Samara

INTRODUCTION

Corporate scandals, environmental scandals, food and energy crises, and complying with human rights international requirements are only a few of the complexities that businesses and their future managers will have to grapple with, continuously monitor, and manage (Alcaraz & Thiruvattal, 2010; Bendell, 2007). Management education, which contributes to the creation and formation of future managers, has been a point of blame when crises occur due to management malpractice (Beddewela, Warin, Hesselden & Coslet, 2017). To tackle the shortcomings of the current way management is being taught in higher education, different initiatives and frameworks began to gradually develop, as interdisciplinary approaches have been added to curricula that emphasize business ethics, corporate social responsibility and sustainability, all of which sit under the broad umbrella of Responsible Management Education (RME).

RME aims at instilling a sense of responsibility and practicality in the minds of fresh graduates who are about to enter the workforce, therefore contributing to a more responsible mindset and way of doing business and hence a more sustainable future. For example, Education for Sustainable Development (ESD), created by UNESCO, and the Principles for Responsible Management Education (PRME), introduced by the United Nations Global Compact, were instigators in changing thinking and learning mechanisms in relation to 'how to make decisions that consider the long-term future of the economy, ecology and equity of all communities' balancing triple bottom line considerations relating to people, planet and profits (Beddewela, Coslet & Warin, 2015; Cornuel & Hommel, 2015; Haertle, Parkes, Murray & Hayes, 2017).

In parallel, the research field of RME has significantly grown over the past decade, reflecting academics' amplified concern with current irresponsible patterns of business practices. Furthermore, there is increasing societal pressure on business schools to engage and promote responsible educational curricula and activities, consisting of, for example, staff- and/or student-led societies that encourage volunteering programmes that aim at promoting sustainability, ethics and social responsibility (Beddewela et al., 2015).

While historically the bulk of RME research has been situated in Western contexts, there is a more recent impetus into researching responsible management education in non-Western contexts. Indeed, the non-Western context may have significant cultural, regional and historical idiosyncrasies that make research and practice of RME peculiar and subject to a multitude of macro and micro forces affecting it. While the idea of whether we are doing enough to help future managers understand the challenges associated with responsible business management has been extensively debated in Western contexts, two important questions remain unanswered: How has research on RME developed in non-Western contexts? And where should research and educational programmes focused on RME go from here?

In this chapter we answer these questions through critically reviewing and discussing the results of research on responsible business education conducted in non-Western contexts and by offering suggestions that can move the research agenda on RME forward and that can help universities in turn to promote more RME within their programmes. We advocate for more indigenous research being conducted in non-Western contexts, focusing on local institutions and cultural peculiarities (Jamali & Caroll, 2017) as well as on the organizational setting prevalent in non-Western contexts, such as family businesses (Samara, Jamali & Parada, 2019). The future directions that we suggest can help glean finer-grained insights for practitioners and policy-makers about RME in non-Western settings and can potentially

help develop and refine current theoretical frameworks. We also suggest effective ways in which universities in non-Western contexts can promote RME among their faculty and students.

LITERATURE REVIEW

Below, we focus our review on three levels of analysis, namely the macro, meso and micro levels of analysis. This categorization allows us to better flesh out the multiple dimensions investigated in extant literature, therefore providing a holistic critical view on how RME research has developed in non-Western contexts, which also allows us to elaborate better on areas where we see opportunities for developing future research and practice.

Research at the macro level of analysis discusses how the broader institutional context affects the relationships investigated (Jamali, Samara, Zollo & Capapei, 2019). Dimensions at the macro level can relate to both formal and informal institutions (North, 1990). Formal institutions include the role of the state along with the written laws and codes of conduct common to a particular geographical setting. Informal institutions refer to the culture, traditions and customs embedded within a geographical context and that shape individuals' expectations and assumptions of what ethical and responsible management actually mean (Jamali et al., 2019).

Research at the meso level of analysis refers to studies that focus on the organizational setting, which can be the industry, organizational form, the social network, or the business environment under discussion. In RME research and practice, the meso context is important to investigate as each meso context (e.g. government-owned companies versus family-owned companies versus multinational companies or small/medium enterprises) can present idiosyncratic features that require specific ethical concepts to be discussed and particular educational programmes developed.

Research at the individual level of analysis focuses in turn on individual values, personality traits and how these affect actions and behaviours. Given that the informal macro contextual institutions, such as culture and religion, invariably shape personality traits and individual values below, we focus primarily on research discussing the macro and meso levels of analysis and how they affect RME.

Research at the Macro Level of Analysis

Research shows that, when it comes to RME, non-Western contexts may need a change in approach in designing curricula and in approaching students in the classroom. For example, when designing a business ethics course, in which teachings are essentially derived from theories and concepts developed in Western contexts, Chinese educators are facing a significant challenge, as what is being taught in the classroom does not resonate with the institutional context in which Chinese students are embedded (McCann, Chun Lam & Chiu, 2001). Issues like guanxi (connections in the social hierarchy), corruption, wide wage disparity, uncertain and differential rule of law across Chinese regions, and environmental concerns are all factors that need to be accounted for and effectively integrated and discussed when teaching ethics in China (Whitla, 2011). Additionally, the prevalence of these concepts differs between mainland China and Hong Kong. For instance, mainland China has stronger guanxi relationships compared to Hong Kong, which has a more rigid legal system in place.

Furthermore, when researching educational leadership and culture, dichotomies were found between Chinese and Anglo-American leadership and management traditions. The understanding of leadership in Anglo-American settings is marked by an individualistic-competitive orientation, emphasizing self-control, negotiated contracts, efficiency, professionalism, competition and personal interest/reward. However, in China, leadership is understood through a collectivist cooperative orientation, focusing on relationships, networks and the pursuit of group interests (Law, 2012). In the latter environment, individual interests are subordinate to group interests and the well-being of the in-group becomes the primary guideline that shapes the understanding of notions of ethics and social responsibility (Samara, Jamali & Parada, 2019). Accounting for these issues is of critical importance as they set the prerequisites for the understanding of leadership and the understanding of what is considered as responsible leadership practice across cultures.

In addition, in non-Western contexts, students seem to understand the Western model of RME as a matter of culture and personal lifestyle rather than normative ethical rules and prescriptions that need to be universally enforced. For example, in Saudi Arabia, the differentiation between gender roles has been historically and culturally accepted and expected, although this has been gradually changing in recent years (Murray & Zhang-Zhang, 2018). Indeed, not all citizens may understand or accept equal rights for men and women, which is often interpreted as a norm borrowed from the West and brought to the classroom, defying notions of cultural sensitivity and the acknowledgement of cultural differences. Socially constructed gender roles thus need to be carefully understood and dissected and this can be a good starting point for fruitful and informative RME discussions (Ourfali, 2015).

Moreover, it seems that adopting RME can present a different set of challenges in non-Western contexts compared to Western contexts. For example, when Huang & Wang (2013) compared US sustainability related curricula to those of the Chinese, they found that the United States typically paid more attention and gave more importance to RME compared to China. Moreover, there is some research in Western contexts suggesting that students are active players in raising the demand for RME as they consider such education as a relevant tool in today's world. This has been supported by research documenting the continuous increase in the percentage of students demanding that their educators provide some relevant material discussing responsible management (Haski-Leventhal et al., 2017). In contrast, there are threads of research suggesting that the demand from students for RME is declining (Cornuel & Hommel, 2015). Particularly, there are some students that favour acquiring career-relevant tools and skills, including primarily finance, accounting and audit skills, while not recognizing RME to be particularly relevant (Cornuel & Hommel, 2015). This may be interpreted in the context of a broader problem relating to how RME is understood and may also be attributed to mainstream academic journals not granting the required space for RME research. For example, in Western contexts, given the career focus of faculty and the current academic rewards structure, faculty members are not necessarily incentivized to conduct research on RME (Beddewela et al., 2017; Maloni et al., 2012). The lack of incentives to take courses related to RME may also reflect a general lack of knowledge of students in elementary schools and high schools about the instrumental and normative importance of RME. Clearly, given the Western-centric focus of these studies, there is an opportunity for future research to further explore the perceptions of both students and academics *vis-à-vis* RME in non-Western contexts.

In non-Western contexts, while the obstacles to RME highlighted above can persist, there might be different barriers to RME that stem from contextual embeddedness (Naeem & Neal, 2012). Interestingly, the barriers identified include the absence of qualified faculty able to teach RME courses. This lack of knowledge capital among faculty about ethical and socially responsible issues

increases the effort required to build an adequate RME syllabus and effectively deliver a course on responsible management, which in turn fosters uncertainty among students and university officials about the relevance of RME programmes and courses in the market. If the faculty member is not adequately qualified and is uncertain whether such RME is in fact needed, then students may also be swayed to taking other courses not related to RME, subduing in turn their sensitization to ethical and social responsibility issues that can be typically encountered in the workplace.

Furthermore, differences in opinion among faculty members concerning the need and urgency to integrate sustainability into their courses amplify the uncertainty problem and increase ambiguity about the relevance of RME among university administrators and among students (Naeem & Neal, 2012). Part of this problem can be attributed to RME not being perceived as needed in non-Western cultures because of the absence of a strong tradition of individual rights, such as the case in China and in Thailand, where priority is given to collective and state interests. For example, China, Japan and Thailand recently introduced comprehensive human rights legislation; however, these have created tensions between the values of the collective and the state (Brey, 2008).

Research at the Meso Level of Analysis

Interestingly, we found no research that discusses the impact or the practice of RME at the meso level of analysis. This kind of research would require the use of ethics and social responsibility education in discussing its practice in a particular organizational form, such as state-owned enterprises or family businesses. Finding no such research in non-Western contexts is surprising, especially given the prevalence of state-owned companies, semi-state-owned firms (e.g. public–private partnerships) and the predominance of family businesses (Fainshmidt, Judge, Aguilera & Smith, 2018) in such contexts. While this omission is unfortunate, it opens several opportunities for future research and several areas for future development of university curricula.

Research at the Micro Level of Analysis

Our review shows that, in Kuwait, the academic advancement of students is positively associated with their ethical attitudes (Al-Shaikh, Elian & Tahat, 2013). While this is an interesting finding, it can also set the ground for future research to examine whether the same results will hold in other Western and non-Western settings, again calling for more multi-level research with cross-national samples from Western and non-Western contexts.

The results presented above suggest the need for a critical analysis and some suggestions to advance research and practice relating to RME in non-Western contexts. Below, we attempt to provide avenues for future research and discuss practical measures to improve the current state of RME in non-Western contexts. We do so by discussing the prominent role of multiple stakeholders, such as academic journal editors, administrative units in management schools and universities, academics and students, in advancing research and teaching of RME in non-Western contexts that include topics such as sustainability, business ethics and CSR. We aim to provide faculty members, business school leaders and regulatory bodies with some suggestions to improve the research and practice of RME in a non-Western context. Future research can build on this initial pool of knowledge by leveraging the suggestions that we provide and by coupling RME curricula with local management actions, research, pedagogy and organizational strategies.

SUGGESTED WAYS TO ADVANCE RME RESEARCH AND PRACTICE IN NON-WESTERN CONTEXTS

Suggestions for Future Research

Macro RME research

While research on RME in non-Western contexts has grown in quantity and improved in quality in the last two decades, there are still some topics that deserve systematic attention in future research. In what follows, we use our critical analysis of extant literature and our experience in conducting research on business ethics and CSR in non-Western settings to propose an agenda for future research.

First, future research on RME in non-Western contexts should embrace the context dependence of their studies. In other words, research should not shy away from embracing that non-Western contexts are different from Western contexts, and that theories and results originating or in use in Western contexts cannot be transferred intact to non-Western settings. This is not to advocate that such theories and results should be automatically disqualified or ignored. Rather, we suggest that these theories and findings can be significantly tested, refined and contextualized and that this will contribute to a broader yet more nuanced understanding of RME in non-Western contexts.

One way to achieve this is to couple existing theories with institutional theory (DiMaggio & Powell, 1983) or institutional logics (Friedland & Alford, 1991), which allow to account for the peculiarities of the macro and meso context in which studies are conducted. For example, we note the absence of research on RME in many countries where such research is much needed. In this respect, we note scant research in countries embedded in socialist systems or in countries that rank low on human development indices. Research in those countries can provide a valuable contribution both to theory, through refining and expanding existing theoretical frameworks, and to practice through contributing to enhancing knowledge among universities and policy-makers about the importance of RME for the future and well-being of their citizens.

Relatedly, we also advocate for a more nuanced application of institutional theory and institutional analysis in research conducted in non-Western contexts. The Western versus non-Western dichotomies present simplistic assumptions about the institutional make-up of non-Western countries, assumptions that no longer hold given the advancements in describing the institutional make-up of non-Western countries in the international business literature (Fainshmidt et al., 2018; Witt, Kabbach de Castro, Amaeshi, Mahroum, Bohle & Saez, 2017). In this regard, future research can delve deeper into the institutional make-up of country clusters, using the national business systems categorization (Witt et al., 2017) or the varieties of institutional systems categorization (Fainshmidt et al., 2018). These two classifications show how non-Western countries are heterogeneous with respect to the various institutions operating within them, such as the state, the family, the importance of social capital, the functioning of the financial and control systems, the role of the state, the level and type of skill development, and trust and authority relationships, among others.

Another important area for future research is to encourage more collaboration and interdisciplinary research projects that investigate the impact of RME on other management practices such as human resources, accounting and finance. This kind of cross-disciplinary work will lead to important insights around the instrumental usefulness of RME programmes and can encourage faculty and students to engage more in RME. In non-Western contexts, the value proposition of RME is often challenged, as shown in our review. Interdisciplinary work can improve the perception of faculty, university administrators and students of the instrumental usefulness of RME.

Relatedly, we also advocate for more collaborations that are international in scope among scholars coming from Western and non-Western contexts. Such international collaboration between scholars can increase extant knowledge about the challenges and opportunities to RME across contexts. It can also lead to RME scholars learning from each other through integrating and analysing nuanced insights that are culturally sensitive, therefore reaching a better and more holistic understanding of the challenges and possible remedies for increasing the effectiveness and implementation of RME. This kind of research also helps set the boundary conditions over what kind of challenges are universal and what challenges are peculiar to a specific institutional setting or culture.

Finally, we recommend that academic journals grant more space to RME research in non-Western contexts. We, as editors of *Business Ethics: A European Review*, are trying to provide space and develop manuscripts that accord systematic attention to corporate social responsibility, business ethics and sustainability in non-Western contexts (Jamali, Barkemeyer, Leigh & Samara, 2020). We hope that more journals will do the same and will also grant the necessary space and adopt a developmental role when receiving manuscripts addressing RME in non-Western contexts.

Meso RME research

Future research at the meso level of analysis can investigate the risk of decoupling which universities can engage in by decoupling their claimed engagement in responsible management education from actual organizational practices (Rasche & Gilbert, 2015). As institutional pressures for RME coming from international organizations bodies increase, such as accreditation concerns, and as RME increases in popularity, universities can claim that they are supporting and are engaged in RME but, at the same time, do little to promote such practices (Rasche & Gilbert, 2015). Mimetic and coercive pressures might amplify these concerns. Accordingly, we advocate for research into actual university practices through qualitative research designs contextualized in non-Western contexts that can help get deep insights into whether decoupling happens or whether universities are walking the talk.

We also note scant research on different organizational forms typically encountered in non-Western contexts. For example, in China, Vietnam and other socialist economies, state ownership of companies is common (Brey, 2008). In most non-Western countries, family businesses constitute the most common organizational form (Samara & Berbegal-Mirabent, 2018; Samara, Jamali & Parada, 2019). Hence, we call for more focus on the meso level of analysis through context-sensitive research that takes into consideration meso-level contextual peculiarities in discussing responsible business management. For example, the family business literature has been gradually integrating and cross-fertilizing with the literature on corporate social responsibility and business ethics (Samara & Arenas, 2017; Samara, Jamali, Sierra & Parada, 2018; Samara & Paul, 2019; Vazquez, 2018). Issues of seeking family interest at the expense of society's welfare have been addressed along with problems of asymmetric treatment of family and non-family employees (Samara & Arenas, 2017; Samara et al., 2019). Also, the difficulties of integrating women non-family members into the workforce and the invisibility of women family members in the workplace have been highlighted as important ethical challenges that family businesses have to grapple with (Samara, Jamali & Parada, 2019). The invisibility of women family members in the family business workplace and the lack of opportunities for women non-family members have been largely attributed to biases that controlling owners and decision makers have towards women (Samara et al., 2019). It would therefore be interesting to investigate whether RME can help in addressing these biases and other irresponsible behaviour that can threaten the family business workplace, to

promote a meritocratic environment and equitable treatment of relevant stakeholders and to channel more attention towards issues like corporate social responsibility. Similarly, in countries where state ownership is common, such as China and Japan, it would be interesting to examine the impact of RME on the degree of corruption and on the overall level of ethicality of managers in performing their duties.

Micro level research

We thus far note scant research on RME in non-Western contexts at the micro level of analysis. Here we call for more multilevel research that accounts for micro, meso and macro effects simultaneously. Given its importance, multilevel CSR research has been on the rise in the past decade (Jamali & Karam, 2016; Jamali & Karam, 2018; Jamali et al., 2019). Such a perspective allows to investigate the context dependence of individual behaviour by exploring how the institutional context combines with the meso setting to influence the values and behaviours of individuals in relation to RME. For example, future research can investigate how the individual values or beliefs of university officials, academics and students shape their perception of RME. Of course, values and beliefs can be influenced by culture (Samara et al., 2018), but there is a need to better understand how culturally imbued values are synthesized at the individual level and are translated into action and behaviour.

Relatedly, given the plurality of religions present in the non-Western context, such as Buddhism, Islam, Hindu, among others, it will be interesting to explore how religion and religiosity affect the perception and the practice of RME. While religious denomination may be important, it is the level of religiosity that determines attitudes towards RME (Jamali & Sidani, 2013). This is particularly important in light of recent research showing that religiosity can indeed affect the attitudes of individuals towards CSR (Brammer et al., 2007).

We also advocate for more research into how RME has shaped the practices of future managers. Since RME continues to aim to make future managers more aware of and better able to understand the environmental and humanitarian challenges that the world grapples with and to raise awareness around the moral and instrumental incentives of companies to tackle such challenges, then there is a need to evaluate the effectiveness of such education in reaching its main goals. Longitudinal studies can be particularly relevant in this case (Choongo, 2017).

Suggestions for Practice

As shown in our literature review, university curricula developed in Western contexts cannot be used and taught without any adaptations in non-Western contexts, as they are decontextualized and therefore do not convey cultural sensitivity. However, we join George's (2014) call to bring context into management studies and into university curricula because bringing context can increase the interestingness, novelty and relevance of what is being taught in the classroom. Therefore, a starting point for any curriculum designed for RME is to incorporate cultural, historical and contextual variables that successfully convey the cultural setting in which RME is taught. In this way, rather than imposing Westernized knowledge on students, educational programmes need to embrace the preconceived expectations and understanding of students of what is fair and ethical, which should serve as a starting point for relevant RME. For example, in contexts where gender biases are prevalent, educational programmes can start by outlining the legal boundaries set by the state, and then show how we can alleviate gender discrimination within these legal boundaries. Furthermore, rather than directly promoting gender equality and automatically qualifying gender biases as unfair and unjust, a starting point would be in outlining the benefits of gender diversity, such as the benefits of having women actively serving on boards

(Samara, Jamali & Lapeira, 2019), and to then explain why gender biases would be considered as unfair and unethical.

Moreover, as our review indicates, students in non-Western contexts are not always convinced of the importance of responsible management education. Hence, curricula can start with some chapters discussing the instrumental and normative importance of socially responsible practices and ethical behaviour inside companies, especially in today's world where institutional investors are increasingly attracted to socially responsible companies and where unethical behaviour is harming the reputation and sometimes the performance of major companies. The latter can be done through inviting practitioners and consultants who can share their knowledge and experience regarding the instrumental importance of RME and the significant implications these might have on businesses and on people in the workplace.

We also advocate for more freedom in the classroom (Moosmayer, Waddock, Wang, Hühn, Dierksmeier & Gohl, 2019) to discuss sensitive contextual topics such as religion and politics in a respectful yet argumentative manner. Political turmoil is high in most non-Western contexts, which makes giving the students enough freedom to discuss these issues essential to promote an ethical environment where everyone feels empowered and free to discuss their ideas while having a moderator (usually the university professor) guiding the conversation and ensuring that conversations happen within the boundaries of respect and constructive argumentation. This will help remove cultural or political barriers between students and allow for richer and more fruitful discussions. This will also contribute to promoting social values and developing ethical habits and socially responsible mindsets within a safe educational environment (Moosmayer et al., 2019). Relatedly, laws differ across Western and non-Western contexts. Hence, RME in non-Western contexts needs to account for the legal boundaries within which the course is being taught. For example, respect for diversity in sexual preferences and respect for the sexual identity of the individual may have very different legal grounds in some non-Western contexts such as Russia and the Arab world than in Western contexts such as the United States.

Relatedly, we also encourage university officials to provide more academic freedom to professors to conduct research projects related to RME. One of the main obstacles to increasing the quality and relevance of RME in non-Western contexts is the lack of incentive systems that can promote the presence of a qualified faculty to teach courses related to RME. Here, we view that multiple stakeholders have a responsibility in developing faculty that are qualified and willing to teach RME. Foremost, university administrators and tenure committees should acknowledge the field of RME as equally important as other fields and not to discriminate against RME scholars. Moreover, we also see a prominent role for senior faculty members in hiring and promotion decisions. Senior faculty can also hold seminars discussing the potential obstacles in publishing related scholarship in top-ranked journals (Bendell, 2007).

In similar vein, there are some institutional settings where environmental challenges may be more urgent than humanitarian challenges or where humanitarian challenges may be more important than environmental challenges. Thus RME, while remaining inclusive and holistic, should place an emphasis on the institutional setting in which future managers will work. Students need to understand that distinctive contexts may have unique challenges and must understand that some challenges may be more pressing than others. For example, in the Arab world, some countries, such as Yemen, Comoros and Djibouti, have the lowest human development indices in the world, which indicates a pressing need to educate future managers on their role in reducing poverty, or providing healthcare to the less fortunate population and/or contributing to educational programmes for the illiterate and the less privileged (World Bank,

2014). Other countries, such as Saudi Arabia, Kuwait and Qatar, have the highest rate of CO_2 emissions in the world, which indicates a more pressing need for educational programmes that emphasize sustainability and socially responsible initiatives towards the environment and society.

It is also crucial to incorporate somewhat harmonized curricula in business and other disciplines towards Education for Sustainable Development and Business Ethics Education (Matten & Moon, 2008). This was evidenced by Matten and Moon (2004) who found over 40 different programme labels for RME across business schools in Europe with over 25% of these programmes using 'Sustainable Development' and 16% selecting 'Corporate Social Responsibility'. It seems therefore that in 'adopting' RME, business schools tend to integrate and confuse synonymous and associated concepts, such as CSR, Business Ethics and Sustainability amongst others (Beddewela et al., 2015).

Finally, in way of comprehensive assessment, it seems that the challenges facing RME are more or less universal, starting with challenging existing capitalistic paradigms, and making room in business schools for innovative human-centred teaching and learning programmes and activities, as well as building the capacity and alignment around these, both within the school and around it (through strategic partnerships). These seem to be common challenges to RME in Western and non-Western contexts. Perhaps the differences lie in the extent to which sustainable development is challenged in non-Western contexts, given that it is considered distant from current priorities relating to socio-economic development. Yet, this is a misperception and cannot be farther from the truth. RME is in fact crucially important for social and economic development, particularly in the way of equipping professionals with the necessary tools and values, and some appreciation of its importance in institution- and nation-building is starting to find traction in non-Western contexts as well.

Another potential difference lies in the issues that RME should focus on, which as indicated in this present chapter, needs to be invariably contextualized. Hence in non-Western contexts, and while staying within the broad guidelines of the triple bottom line (Carroll, 1991), more importance could be accorded to issues of alleviating corruption, reducing poverty and hunger, and empowering women, which seem to be common challenges across the developing world, and the role of business leaders in addressing them. Another potential difference is the possibly still attenuated appreciation in developing countries of the individual, organization, society and sustainability linkages, and that sustainable development is primarily a human-centred effort, focusing on the quality and mindset of professionals and business leaders. We need to build more awareness around this key point and reinforce the notion that RME and human-oriented patterns of education are in fact central to nation-building and balanced patterns of socio-economic development in non-Western contexts.

CONCLUDING REMARKS

Research on RME in non-Western contexts has been gradually developing. RME in universities has also improved and gained popularity in the past two decades. While much research work has come to the fore in recent years, increasing our understanding of the challenges that effective RME encounters, more work is needed in this critical space. We expect that our discussion in this chapter will encourage further enquiries into the challenges and opportunities for RME, particularly in non-Western contexts, which will result in more collaborative learning and innovations within the RME community.

While the importance of accounting for context and institutions applies perfectly to research and practice of RME in non-Western

contexts, the Western world can also benefit from such an approach. Indeed, not all Western contexts are similar, and dichotomies between many countries considered as Western have been documented in extant literature, such as the Anglo-Saxon/non-Anglo-Saxon dichotomy (García-Castro, Aguilera & Ariño, 2013; Samara et al., 2018) or the national business systems approach that differentiates between liberal market economies, coordinated market economies and European peripheral economies, to name a few (Witt et al., 2017). Hence, research and practice of RME in Western contexts can also benefit from accounting for the idiosyncratic features of the setting in which the research or the education is being conducted. Relatedly, we also advocate for future research on RME in Western contexts to adopt multilevel research, because it helps to capture the nested complexity of the Western context itself taking into account the organizational level and individual level of analysis, in addition to the peculiarities of the institutional context in which the study is conducted.

Going back to our original focus, RME in non-Western contexts, the time has come to move beyond a monolithic and simplistic understanding of RME in Western contexts to more organic conceptions that embrace contextual embeddedness and that develop and refine our theoretical understanding of RME across contexts. In parallel, educators must also acknowledge the cultural and institutional environment in which they are embedded and adapt their courses and curricula towards more context-sensitive applications. Jamali and Karam (2018) note significant differences between Western and non-Western countries with respect to their understanding and framing of business and society relationships and challenges. These idiosyncrasies need to be carefully accounted for in any research project or educational programme centred on RME.

With a view to moving the research and practice of RME forward, in this chapter we use current research shortcomings and our own experience in conducting corporate social responsibility and ethics research in non-Western contexts to provide some reflections that can move the research and practice of RME forward. Our main conclusion is that to effectively, and not ceremonially, improve the research and practice of RME, it takes a village or in other words, a complete ecosystem. Multiple stakeholders have a responsibility in facilitating such endeavour, including university officials, senior faculty, junior faculty, international bodies such as the UN global compact, networks and practitioners, and students. These stakeholders have a responsibility to combine forces and efforts to foster the development of educators and educational settings, with RME tools, incentives, and the flexibility to align with the peculiarities of the setting in question to make RME relevant and interesting to a pool of increasingly inquisitive and critical learners.

We hope that the insights that we have developed here and the avenues that we suggest will help in moving the research and practice of RME forward, particularly in developing country contexts where this sort of education is very valuable and much needed.

REFERENCES

Alcaraz, J. M., & Thiruvattal, E. (2010). An interview with Manuel Escudero: The United Nations' Principles for Responsible Management Education: a global call for sustainability. *Academy of Management Learning & Education*, *9*(3), 542–550.

Al-Shaikh, F., Elian, M., & Tahat, L. (2013). Business students' attitudes towards business ethics: evidence from Kuwait. *International Journal of Education Research*, *8*(1), 59–76.

Beddewela, E., Coslet, A., & Warin, C. (2015). Institutionalizing Responsible Management Education: a change process model. *Academy of Management Annual Meeting Proceedings*, *2015*(1), 3–10.

Beddewela, E., Warin, C., Hesselden, F., & Coslet, A. (2017). Embedding responsible management education – staff, student and institutional perspectives. *International Journal of Management Education*, *15*(2), 263–279.

Bendell, J. (2007). The responsibility of business schools. *Journal of Corporate Citizenship*, *29*, 4–14.

Brammer, S., Williams, G., & Zinkin, J. (2007). Religion and attitudes to corporate social responsibility in a large cross-country sample. *Journal of Business Ethics*, *71*, 229–243.

Brey, P. (2008). Global information ethics and the challenge of cultural relativism. Research Gate, 5. Available at: www.researchgate.net/publication/249713029_Global_Information_Ethics_and_the_Challenge_of_Cultural_Relativism.

Carroll, A. B. (1991). The pyramid of corporate social responsibility: toward the moral management of organizational stakeholders. *Business Horizons*, *34*(4), 39–48.

Choongo, P. (2017). A longitudinal study of the impact of corporate social responsibility on firm performance in SMEs in Zambia. *Sustainability*, *9*(8), 1300.

Cornuel, E., & Hommel, U. (2015). Moving beyond the rhetoric of responsible management education. *Journal of Management Development*, *34*(1), 2–15.

DiMaggio, P. J., & Powell, W. W. (1983). The iron cage revisited: institutional isomorphism and collective rationality in organizational fields. *American Sociological Review*, 147–160.

Fainshmidt, S., Judge, W. Q., Aguilera, R. V., & Smith, A. (2018). Varieties of institutional systems: a contextual taxonomy of understudied countries. *Journal of World Business*, *53*(3), 307–322.

Friedland, R., & Alford, R. R. (1991). Bringing society back in: symbols, practices, and institutional contradictions (2nd ed.). In W. W. Powell & P. J. DiMaggio (Eds.), *The new institutionalism in organizational analysis*. (pp. 232–263), Chicago: University of Chicago Press.

García-Castro, R., Aguilera, R. V., & Ariño, M. A. (2013). Bundles of firm corporate governance practices: a fuzzy set analysis. *Corporate Governance: An International Review*, *21*(4), 390–407.

George, G. (2014). Rethinking management scholarship. *Academy of Management Journal*, *57*, 1–6.

Haertle, J., Parkes, C., Murray, A., & Hayes, R. (2017). PRME: Building a global movement on responsible management education. *International Journal of Management Education*, *2*(15), 66–72.

Haski-Leventhal, D., Pournader, M., & McKinnon, A. (2017). The role of gender and age in business students' values, CSR attitudes, and responsible management education: learnings from the PRME International Survey. *Journal of Business Ethics*, *146*(1), 219–239.

Huang, S. K., & Wang, Y. L. (2013). A comparative study of sustainability management education in China and the USA. *Environmental Education Research*, *19*(1), 64–80.

Jamali, D., & Carroll, A. (2017). Capturing advances in CSR: developed versus developing country perspectives. *Business Ethics: A European Review*, *26*(4), 321–325.

Jamali, D., & Karam, C. (2016). CSR in developed versus developing countries: a comparative glimpse. In A. Örtenblad, (Ed.), *Research Handbook in Business and Management Series* (pp. 89–110), Cheltenham: Edward Elgar Publishing Limited.

Jamali, D., & Karam, C. (2018). Corporate social responsibility in developing countries as an emerging field of study. *International Journal of Management Reviews*, *20*(1), 32–61.

Jamali, D., & Sdiani, Y. (2013). Does religiosity determine affinities to CSR? *Journal of Management, Spirituality & Religion*, *10*(4), 309–323.

Jamali, D., Barkemeyer, R., Leigh, J., & Samara, G. (2020). A reinvigorated vision for BE: ER to sustain a trajectory of excellence. *Business Ethics: A European Review*, *29*(1), 1–2.

Jamali, D., Samara, G., Zollo, L., & Capapei, C. (2019). Is internal CSR really less impactful in individualist and masculine cultures? A multilevel approach. *Management Decision*, *58*(2), 362–375.

Law, A. (2012). Educational leadership and culture in China: dichotomies between Chinese and Anglo-American leadership traditions? *International Journal of Educational Development*, *2*, 273–282.

Maloni, M. J., Smith, S. D., & Napshin, S. (2012). A methodology for building faculty support for the United Nations Principles for Responsible Management Education. *Journal of Management Education*, *36*(3), 312–336.

Matten, D., & Moon, J. (2004). Corporate social responsibility. *Journal of Business Ethics*, *54*(4), 323–337.

Matten, D., & Moon, J. (2008). 'Implicit' and 'explicit' CSR: a conceptual framework for a comparative understanding of corporate social responsibility. *Academy of Management Review*, *33*(2), 404–424.

McCann, D. P., Chun Lam, J. K., & Chiu, R. K. (2001). Teaching business ethics in Hong Kong: challenges and response. *Journal of Teaching in International Business*, *12*(2), 23–33.

Moosmayer, D. C., Waddock, S., Wang, L., Hühn, M. P., Dierksmeier, C., & Gohl, C. (2019). Leaving the road to Abilene: a pragmatic approach to addressing the normative paradox of responsible management education. *Journal of Business Ethics*, *157*(4), 913–932.

Murray, J. Y., & Zhang-Zhang, Y. (2018). Insights on women's labor participation in Gulf Cooperation Council countries. *Business Horizons*, *61*(5), 711–720.

Naeem, M., & Neal, M. (2012). Sustainability in business education in the Asia Pacific region: a snapshot of the situation. *International Journal of Sustainability in Higher Education*, *13*(1), 60–71.

North, D. (1990). *Institutions, institutional change and economic performance*. Cambridge: Cambridge University Press.

Ourfali, E. (2015). Comparison between Western and Middle Eastern cultures: research on why American expatriates struggle in the Middle East. *Otago Management Graduate Review*, *13*, 36–37.

Rasche, A., & Gilbert, D. U. (2015). Decoupling responsible management education: why business schools may not walk their talk. *Journal of Management Inquiry*, *24*(3), 239–252.

Samara, G., & Arenas, D. (2017). Practicing fairness in the family business workplace. *Business Horizons*, *60*(5), 647–655.

Samara, G., & Berbegal-Mirabent, J. (2018). Independent directors and family firm performance: does one size fit all? *International Entrepreneurship and Management Journal*, *14*(1), 149–172.

Samara, G., & Paul, K. (2019). Justice versus fairness in the family business workplace: a socioemotional wealth approach. *Business Ethics: A European Review*, *28*(2), 175–184.

Samara, G., Jamali, D., & Lapeira, M. (2019). Why and how should SHE make her way into the family business boardroom? *Business Horizons*, *62*(1), 105–115.

Samara, G., Jamali, D., & Parada, M. J. (2019). Antecedents and outcomes of bifurcated compensation in family firms: a multilevel view. *Human Resource Management Review* doi: https://doi.org/10.1016/j.hrmr.2019.100728.

Samara, G., Jamali, D., Sierra, V., & Parada, M. J. (2018). Who are the best performers? The environmental social performance of family firms. *Journal of Family Business Strategy*, *9*(1), 33–43.

Vazquez, P. (2018). Family business ethics: at the crossroads of business ethics and family business. *Journal of Business Ethics*, *150*(3), 691–709.

Whitla, P. (2011). Integrating ethics into international business teaching: challenges and methodologies in the Greater China context. *Journal of Teaching in International Business*, *22*(3), 168–184.

Witt, M. A., Kabbach de Castro, L. R., Amaeshi, K., Mahroum, S., Bohle, D., & Saez, L. (2017). Mapping the business systems of 61 major economies: a taxonomy and implications for varieties of capitalism and business systems research. *Socio-Economic Review*, *16*(1), 5–38.

World Bank. (2014). *LAC Poverty and Labor Brief, February 2014: Social gains in the balance – a fiscal policy challenge for Latin America and the Caribbean*. Washington, DC: The World Bank.

5

Green Economics: Rethinking Economics for Responsible Management Education

Molly Scott Cato and Rupert Read

INTRODUCTION

As environmental crises crowd in from every side, the slogan for the 21st century should perhaps be 'We are all environmentalists now'.[1] Or perhaps, 'It's the ecosystem, stupid'. This might sound extreme to some readers, but as the global climate breaks down, we lose species at an unprecedented rate and hyper-mobility results in significant and civilisation-threatening increases in CO_2 emissions, as well as undermining community, this will become simply the reality for all the academic disciplines, beginning with natural and technological sciences and now moving through social sciences and philosophy, to art and literature. All the academic disciplines need to respond urgently and more or less revolutionarily to the most pressing issue-set of our time.

Yet, often sitting in the management school we find a discipline that seems largely oblivious to the urgent need to address environmental crisis. Economics defines problems from

human-triggered climate change to nuclear radiation as 'externalities' (see further discussion below) – seeming to imply that they are somebody else's problem – while continuing to produce its simplistic graphs and onanistic regression analyses that typically have little or no connection with reality.

Green economics begins, within the context of local and global ecosystems, with people and their concerns, rather than with theories or mathematical constructions of reality. Its central objective is to maximize human well-being while respecting the limits of the planet – in a real sense, not as a mere rhetorical flourish – and the other species we share it with. It also assumes that human well-being cannot be achieved without resources being shared fairly not just nationally but, eventually, globally. These objectives are obviously far from being achieved by the existing neoliberal economy – because they are not in actuality shared by that economy – which implies that any approach to management education by a green economist must be a fundamentally critical one, in relation to the status quo.

We recognise the achievement of the inspiring young people who have founded the Rethinking Economics movement and whose practice and experience we describe at the end of the following section. We believe that a responsible approach to teaching economics needs to follow their lead in beginning our study from the world (including the *Earth*) as it is and demanding a 'pluralist' approach to theory and practice, rather than assuming, rashly, that conventional economics has everything wrapped up.

RETHINKING ECONOMIC THEORY: NEOCLASSICAL VS GREEN

Economics is unusual amongst academic disciplines in having a dominant orthodoxy that is challenged by a small but growing minority of (various kinds of) 'heterodox economists'. In an opening and engaged academic discipline studying (and often offering advice with regard to) the human world, one might expect a plurality of views but in economics – at least, as taught in virtually all economics departments and most management schools; the situation is often different for development economics and agricultural economics – neoclassical economics rules supreme.

Most university teachers would find it strange to follow an economics course, where the established orthodoxy is in some key respects unchanging over the decades and which frequently has the quality of a theology class rather than one in what is, overwhelmingly, a 'social science'. Rather than remaining stuck in an outdated ideology, management students should be offered a range of economic prescriptions arising from a whole variety of ideological perspectives.[2] Most pressingly, economics needs to pay much greater heed to the dominant issue facing the social sciences and humanities: the environmental relationship crisis.

Environment is very much an afterthought in the standard economics curriculum, a situation that cannot be allowed to persist if we are to take a responsible approach to management education. Even 'environmental economics' mostly tacks on consideration of the environment to an unchanged neoclassical framework. By contrast, foundational for green economics is *ecological* economics, which, especially in the versions of it due to its founding figures Nicholas Georgescu-Rogen and his student Herman Daly, swaps the place of environment/ecology from being marginal to being non-negotiable, central.

In this section we are going to explore some of the central tenets of neoclassical economics and consider how each is incompatible with a responsible (green or ecological) approach to management education.

'We Understand the Economy by Reducing it to its Component Parts'

In the perspective of mainstream economics, economy and environment are separate spheres; they overlap when environmental resources are exploited to produce goods that can be sold, but they are not mutually dependent. From a green economic explanation perspective, this separation is itself at the heart of the problem. As the ecological crisis has inched (too) slowly towards the centre of political debate, the pioneers of policy responses have found their consensus over solutions challenged by newcomers with a more wholistic perspective.

Conventional economics will provide a graph with two straight lines representing 'supply' and 'demand' and then apply this to the complex relationships entailed by the production and exchange of goods. Green economics by contrast believes the word 'wholism' sums up the way in which we must learn to see the big picture when making economic decisions.

The economy needs to be understood as a subset of society, which needs to be understood as a subset of the planetary eco-system. And we need to recognise the principal lesson of ecology – that we live in a single interconnected system – and apply it to our economic activities.

'The Primary Objective of an Economy (and its Managers) is for it to Grow – Forever'

The metaphor of 'growth' is an imperialistic one. It tries to figure something which actually often means the proliferation of relatively pointless activity (e.g. most kinds of financial speculation) or of directly harmful activity (e.g. various forms of industrial activity) as if these were natural, biological processes, like the growth of an organism.

Furthermore, the idea that such growth should be endless then of course contradicts the biological ground-metaphor: for what organism grows endlessly bigger? There are no examples, thankfully for the viability of the biosphere. Any being that doubled its size without end – as endless economic growth would have us do, every generation or two – would quickly become too big to be even containable within its ecosystem, let alone provisioned by it.

The idea of endless economic growth is a fantasy, and a highly reckless one. Instead, economic growth should at best be considered as a temporary state of change from one 'scale' of economic activity to another. It is vital that the scale we settle on, in a post-growth 'steady state' economy, is very-long-term viable. That is not the case for the economy that we currently operate in most of the world, and certainly not in 'developed' countries (which, although they claim, hubristically, to be 'developed', are still endlessly seeking to 'develop' – i.e. grow – further).

Given this context, long-term sustainability certainly implies a post-growth perspective and probably implies some degrowth. It implies, furthermore, redistribution from the affluent to the non-affluent, from present to future generations, and from humans to non-humans.

'The Ideal Economic Agent is the Rational Economic Man'

Part of the simplification of the economy to enable mathematical modelling involves reducing economic agents to a generalised stereotype known as the rational economic man, or 'homo economicus'. It goes without saying that he is more representative of neo-classical economists than he is of the vast majority of global citizens. Unsurprisingly, the rational economic man has taken some sturdy criticism from feminist economics. Mary Mellor, for example, writes:

'Economic man is fit, mobile, able-bodied, unencumbered by domestic or other responsibilities. The goods he consumes appear to him as finished products or services and disappear from his view on disposal or dismissal. He has no responsibility for the life-cycle of those goods and or services any more than he questions the source of the air he breathes or his excreta. … Like Oscar Wilde's Dorian Gray, economic man appears to exist in a smoothly functioning world while the portrait in the attic represents his real social, biological and ecological condition.'[3]

The world as conceived by the rational economic man is the world we are confronted by, a world of ecological crisis, gross inequality and conflict. He is neither a representative nor a responsible characterisation of an economic actor. He is little more than a selfish semi-solipsist; thankfully, real economic actors often don't behave like him.

The advent of behavioural economics has brought the insights of psychological into economic analysis, although too often this is used to enable manipulation rather than empowerment; while the institutional school of economists has always considered people as fully rounded humans. Both these approaches should be included in responsible economics teaching.

'Markets Solve Problems'

The standard economics textbook will begin with a supply-and-demand diagram which is taken to be a schematic representation of a working market. Students will learn that scarcity drives rising prices and that the consumers who want the goods most will pay the price, thus allocating goods efficiently between those who wish to have them. This begs so many questions around how resources are allocated initially and what happens to those with fewer resources, as well as questions relating to the impact of acquiring resources on the environment. Orthodox economics will tend to relegate those questions to a final chapter or lecture and act as a cheerleader for 'markets' as universal problem-solving mechanisms.

Markets, as idealised by economic theory, are amoral and they are driven by profit. We have an object lesson on the consequences of this structure in the new and still evolving market for electronic information. The behaviour of Facebook has been irresponsible to a gross degree, allowing deceitful and anonymous political advertisements that appear to have affected the outcome of the 2016 US Presidential election and perhaps the Brexit referendum too.[4] Facebook have been equally lax about policing their site for the spreading of disinformation and racist or hate content.[5] While all the tech companies have resisted regulation, with some chagrin Mark Zuckerberg brought himself recently to acknowledge that European regulators were right to intervene in the market and that GDPR is, despite its flaws, a world-leading legislative framework to tame the Wild West of the internet.

A responsible approach to teaching economics would describe the extraordinary way in which markets can allocate goods between a vast number of consumers according to their preferences but it would also acknowledge that there are areas where markets will always under-supply (such as health care), where market sales are socially damaging (arms and drugs) and that in most areas legal regulation of markets is essential (environmental health law or the banning of bee-killing neonicotinoids in farming).

But, perhaps more important, the most crucial and urgent problems facing us have been caused by markets and will not be solved by them. Responsible educators should challenge the idea of 'market failure' which suggests that tweaking will solve these problems whereas the reality is that there are many problems facing the modern world – from climate change to biodiversity loss and marine pollution – where the market failure was *inevitable* and we need political solutions.

The very doctrine of 'market failure' is itself a piece of neoliberal and neoclassical ideology. It implies that the norm is for markets as idealised by economics to succeed; but, for the reasons we have already given, that just isn't so. The concept of 'externalities' is part and parcel of the concept of 'market failure'; but it is absurd to think of ecosystems, without which we are nothing, as 'external' to any economic setting. Thus the ecological economics revolution, which is part of green economics, would do away with or at least fundamentally recast both concepts.

The reality is that, from the point of view of selfish firms and actors as they are conceptualised by mainstream economics, 'market failure' is market-*success*, i.e the firm will succeed best which best succeeds in sloughing off all ethical responsibilities. Successfully dumping all of one's pollution onto the general public – getting away with this – is exactly what mainstream economic theory encourages firms to do. This in itself is a vast indictment of standard economic theory. (This is also why green economics considers seriously radical proposals such as corporate personhood being revocable in the event of firms behaving in the ways that, from a conventional economics point of view, are recommended and successful.)

'Free Trade Benefits All'

According to neoclassical economics, the factors of production (labour, capital and land – for which read resources)[6] are combined into a product which is then traded in a market. In this framing the resources of nature are considered as an infinite and free gift. From a green economics perspective the acquisition of those resources is of crucial importance, both in terms of its environmental impact and their origin. If trade statistics were to include data about the exchange of the biophysical factors embodied in a product, they would show an ecologically unequal exchange at the global level. The core regions of the industrialised world are net importers of the biosphere from other regions and, notwithstanding technological progress, they continue to import biosphere. The other regions are net exporters of their biosphere and, notwithstanding decades of trade, they need to continue to export their biosphere in order to maintain a positive trade balance.

The orthodox theory of trade falls under the rubric of 'the theory of comparative advantage', which posits that a country should direct their resources towards the production of those goods and services they produce most efficiently and import the others. This is to set the process of trade in a politically neutral sphere, whereas in the real world the relative geopolitical importance of states, as well as the strength of their currencies, is vital in deciding who benefits in negotiations over the terms of trade and in the process of trade itself. Politically determined unfair trade results in huge stresses to the countries that are net exporters of biosphere, leading to regional conflict and cross-border migration.

From a green economics perspective, 'free trade' then is not what it is invariably cracked up to be. Rather, the priority should be fair trade. And the direction of travel should be *less* trade:[7] to encourage resilience, and reduce the excessive and destabilising effects of the excessive trading patterns now characterising our overly globalised system. (We

offer greater detail, filling out these suggestions, in the section on 'Rethinking the pedagogy of economics'.)

Case study: rethinking economics pressure group

Rethinking Economics is a student-led pressure group to transform the economics discipline. It began in the early years of this century and was given a huge boost by the 2007/8 financial crisis, when students finally rumbled their professors who had no explanation for this worldwide disaster. They call themselves 'an international network of students, academics and professionals building a better economics in society and the classroom'. Their main call is for pluralism in economics education based on their critique:

> Economics in universities is narrow, uncritical and detached from the real world. It is dogmatically taught from one perspective as if it is the only legitimate way to study the economy. There is no room for the critical discussion and debate that is essential for any student to engage with real world economic problems. Seminars are focused on memorising and regurgitating academic theory whilst exams test how well students can solve abstract equations.

This is a truly global movement based around the International Student Initiative for Pluralism in Economics which has issued a statement of demands from economics students: that pedagogues can demonstrate a pluralist approach; that teaching is based on pluralist texts and teaching techniques; that economics joins the other social sciences and humanities and adopts an interdisciplinary approach.

RETHINKING THE ECONOMY

As we noted above, green economics begins with people in community, in the context of their ecosystem(s). Some green economists would take a stronger position and argue that the principle of Ubuntu[8] means that we cannot lead happy lives in the knowledge that other people – and perhaps other species – are being deprived of the ability to also lead lives of contentment and peace.

Economics is conventionally focused on one sort of value – which is monetary. One of the guiding principles of green economics is to extend the remit of economics to include a wider vision and deeper values. Three guiding principles to do this are: unity-in-diversity; interconnectedness; and immanence. The first describes the need to respect difference and to value the whole as requiring all of its different parts. The second is a belief in an inevitable relationship between all aspects of the planet, supported by ecology. The third refers to respecting the earth and thinking of it as a living thing – a 'thing' keeping us all alive, and thus thinking about the Earth's resources much more seriously than we do now. The values we need to build a sustainable economy are roughly as follows: recognition of self-determination; diversity and tolerance within an overall emphasis on a common vision and common destiny; compassion; upholding the principle of equality; recognition of the rights and interests of non-humans; respect for the integrity of natural systems; respect for the interests of future generations.

Green economics also extends the circle beyond our single species to consider the whole system of planet Earth, with its complex ecology and diverse species. Green economics is distinct then from the dominant economic paradigm as practised by politicians and taught in three main ways: (1) it is inherently concerned with social justice – for mainstream economics welfare is a minor part, for a green economist, equality and justice is at the heart; (2) green economics had emerged from environmental campaigners and green politicians due to their need for it; (3) green economics is not yet an academic discipline; this is due to the university itself having been captured by the globalised economic system – the motivations of which system are incompatible with green economics. Capitalism has

been touted as the only way of organising our economic life – like it or not, capitalism is said to be 'the only game in town'. But perhaps the town is about to enjoy some more enlightened form of urban planning.

Capitalism is running up severely now against (and over) the limits to growth.[9] Dangerous anthropogenic climate change, which is merely the most obvious and dire symptom of this, has moved from being a peripheral concern of scientists and environmentalists to being a central issue in policy-making. At least, that is supposedly so; witness the much-trumpeted Paris accord on climate. However, that accord barely mentions fossil fuels, tacitly relies on untested and reckless (highly unprecautious) 'geo-engineering' technologies,[10] and is in any case inadequate to rein in climate change to safe levels.[11] A green economics perspective would place safety first, and not allow 'the market' to let rip with our very futures. (We return below to discussing how Paris, despite its very real limits, allows a start to be made in the process of seeking to return to something like climate-safety.)

Green economics supports the use of the Precautionary Principle, that the lack of scientific certainty should not be used as a reason for postponing measures to prevent environmental degradation. (This applies widely, including very much still to some aspects of the climate crisis.[12]) It is better to not take the risk at all, than to perform an action that may cause catastrophic harm. This principle, along with the prevention principle, that prevention is better than harm, is essential for any true sustainability, and the chief responsibility for the avoidance of such harm lies within the corporations, scientists and politicians who make the salient decisions.

Mainstream economics favours forms of cost–benefit analysis that pretend that risk can be calculated numerically. Precaution eschews such pretence, and builds real safety into the system.

It bears repeating that the responsibility for ensuring such safety lies within 'market-forces', corporations, scientists and politicians who make economic decisions with more-than-merely-economic consequences. Green economics seeks to unify political economy with ecology in such a way that silent risks will not be imposed upon the general population in the name of 'efficiency'.

Case study: sustainable finance[13]

Within a capitalist economy acquiring finance is a crucial step in any economic enterprise. So shifting the finance system towards sustainability is like using a huge and powerful spanner on the whole system that is the global economy. This work is already under way in the EU institutions, which we will use as a case study here. The first priority is carbon stress tests for banks – a process of checking out what proportion of the assets they have that ensure they are solvent are linked to fossil fuels. Such fossil-fuel investments are considered 'stranded assets' meaning that, as we strengthen policies to tackle climate change in response to the Paris Agreement, they will lose value. The key to the sustainable finance agenda is making sure that this process happens in an orderly way. The European Systemic Risk Board has a group looking into how such a project might be undertaken. Since it protects the European financial system against systemic risks its decision about which assets have long-term value is vital.

Which brings us to definitions. European policy-makers are beginning to define what is a sustainable asset – and they are doing this in the economics committee rather than the environmental committee. European politicians are acknowledging what Greens have long understood – that if we destroy the planet we will not be able to generate any economic value. The European Commission has proposed a 'taxonomy', a way of categorising the sustainability of different kinds of assets. It begins with climate-positive investments, moves on through the circular economy, reducing pollution and

cleaning up waterways, and will eventually include socially beneficial and well-governed businesses.

Because the EU is a financial regulator, the European Supervisory Authorities can determine which assets are considered viable when determining whether banks are solvent or pension funds will be able to afford to pay out. So if we as regulators take the initiative to legislate that coal mines or intensive farms will not be viable assets after, say, 2030, we will ensure an orderly transition away from these assets and towards the assets of the future like windfarms and organic farms. This is the promise of the sustainable finance agenda: use finance as a lever on the whole economy. It is at its early stages but it helps us to create the incentives to ensure that future investment is compatible with the Paris Agreement and eventually with a whole raft of environmental, social and governance standards.

This agenda has actually not been led by politicians but by the finance companies themselves. They need to ensure that markets make an orderly transition away from stranded assets and this process will depend on clear market signals and unity of purpose amongst politicians framing the finance sector. That is why financial companies are not opposing the sustainable finance agenda and are often supportive, especially the insurance companies who are already seeing the threat that climate change poses to their business, and pension funds, whose managers need clear signals about how they will be able to generate value for their customers in the long term.

RETHINKING ECONOMIC ORGANISATION

Orthodox economics conventionally divides its consideration between macro – what happens in countries and the world at large – and micro – what happens at the level of the productive firm. We are going to largely follow this distinction in our consideration here, beginning with a consideration of how a green approach to economics would address the global trading system and alternative approaches to provisioning, and then moving on to consider the organisations that actually produce goods and services and how they should be owned and controlled.

It follows directly from the closing of the planetary frontier and the commitment to equality that the standard form of economic organisation in the modern economy – the shareholder-owned company – is not compatible with a green approach to the economy. Just and efficient allocation of resources cannot make space for the extraction of value by external shareholders.

The corporation hungry for profit and seeking to externalise as many costs as possible needs to be replaced as a goal: either by non-profits, social enterprises of various kinds, cooperatives (see below) and so forth, or by corporations that are legally obliged to pursue a wider range of objectives than profits. As mentioned above, a vital change in the law which would bring the possibility of a green economy closer would be for it to be made possible for corporations to have their charters revoked if they do not pursue objectives of ecosystem-maintenance (and indeed ecosystem-enrichment) social justice. Meanwhile, it is crucial to support alternative forms of economic organisation(s). Below we discuss cooperatives; another model well worth bearing in mind, because it is far bigger than most people realise, is the non-profit business. How many people know, for example, that Bosch is a non-profit, almost entirely owned by a charitable foundation, and donating most of its 'profits' to humanitarian causes?

The most renowned overarching principle of green economics is probably 'small is beautiful', so how does *this* impact on economic organisation? While Greens certainly would privilege the local and provide support for local economics and local communities this is always balanced by an acknowledgement that we cannot hide ourselves away from the global systems that will always impact on us. So rather than having a principle of always favouring the local we follow the principle of subsidiarity, meaning that power should be exercised at the lowest appropriate level. So Greens are stalwart defenders of the global institutions like UNCTAD and the UN tax body (especially as the US regime is trying to dismantle the global rules-based order that has prevailed since World War II); we favour European cooperation to achieve high standards preventing the use of conflict minerals or damaging pesticides; we believe that national (and local) governments should maintain control of vital public services such as transport, energy and water and that they should tax sufficiently to enable investment in services as well as crucial infrastructure; *but* we would enable the local economy to be the primary provisioning unit for most people.[14]

The EU has shown global leadership on policies to tackle climate change, especially since the global Paris Agreement reached on our continent in December 2015. This has led to policies to reduce CO_2 emissions directly via targets and investments as well as indirectly via a reshaped Emissions Trading Scheme. While, as we laid out earlier, none of this action is fast enough or strong enough for Greens, we use the Paris Agreement – almost daily – to justify stronger climate action and the sustainable finance agenda is one important outcome (as discussed in the Case Study, above). With President Trump pulling out of the Paris process it is more important than ever that the EU shows global leadership and Greens are proposing that we introduce a border adjustment mechanism – effectively a tax on goods from countries that do not meet Paris climate standards in production. This will allow us to use the purchasing power of 500 million wealthy global citizens to put upward pressure on other production markets.

The current global trading system privileges the demands of powerful countries and corporations who are able to benefit from the arbitrage between different markets to maximise their profits. Goods are made in countries where biosphere export is cheap and wages and environmental standards low, and exported to countries where consumers are wealthier, thus gaining a differential between the cost of production and the cost of sale, which generates a profit. This does not meet the fundamental Green criterion of maximising human well-being for the minimum use of energy and resources.[15]

We can extend the principle of subsidiarity into the realm of trade by proposing the principle of trade subsidiarity. Such a conceptualisation has two immediate contributions, one sustainable, one equitable. First, it suggests that we begin to seek resources locally only extending our provisioning circle as limited resources require, thus reducing energy-intensive transportation of like goods. Secondly, it enables us to reduce the impact of power imbalances between exporting and importing nations.

The distance that goods should flow depends on a number of factors: local seasonality, the complexity of the good, the size of the market and the availability of relevant skills. Products that are less labour-intensive and for which raw materials are plentiful need not travel the globe wasting energy and emissions. While this might in some cases mean an increase in prices, it would also onshore satisfying and productive employment, and would increase resilience against the shocks that are certainly coming, in the coming climate (and thus weather) chaos – on which, see more, below.

For complex products that require a high level of design and production skill and lengthy supply chains we need to raise questions about the efficiency of this production method and the control of 'intellectual property' that enables corporations to maximise profits while minimising wages and often ignoring the environmental impact of their production. Products that are labour-intensive or require specific raw materials

or climatic conditions cannot be acquired except by long-distance trade. In this case attention should focus on the quality of production, enforcing fair trade, decent working conditions and high environmental standards through EU external trade policies and initiatives like the UN binding treaty on business and human rights.[16]

Trade subsidiarity would change global biosphere trade patterns towards a fairer balance. Regions that so far have been net exporters would gain breathing-space for the regeneration of their ecosystems, if less biosphere were used for export. Regions such as the EU that so far have been net biosphere importers would need to accommodate new requirements for biosphere use and become much more innovative in finding appropriate solutions for minimising such needs to the utmost minimum.

Greens have written at length about the need to strengthen local provisioning systems as a unified means of mitigating and adapting to climate change.[17] Lengthy supply chains are wasteful of energy and can never be part of a sustainable future. Meanwhile, rising sea levels are likely to put our major ports out of action and other severe weather events are already beginning to disrupt the complex supermarket distribution systems. To make our systems resilient, they need to be much less globalised.

For many green economists, although the responsibilities rest within the authorities and governments, waiting for them to begin to support green economics is not an option: they believe that we need secure access to our basic resources and are working now to develop local systems of production and distribution. A system of interrelated but independent local economies can be described as an 'eco-localism'. This would include local currency systems, food cooperatives, microenterprise, farmers' markets, community-supported agriculture, car-sharing schemes and much more.

Beyond localisation, the concept now developing among green economists is that of a bioregional economy, an economy which is embedded within the environment. The crisis that we face is *essentially* an ecological crisis: if we fail to recognise our place within the complex system of interrelationships that life on earth represents, then the future of humankind as a species is under threat. Bioregionalism recognises, nurtures, sustains and celebrates our local connections with: land; plants and animals; rivers; lakes and oceans; air; families, friends and neighbours; community; native traditions; and traditional systems of production and trade.

As for the micro scale, g/Greens typically favour a form of organisation that allows power and the value of the productive process to be shared fairly. This arises partly from a moral commitment but also from a theoretical understanding that the acquisition of an inordinate amount of wealth creates an unnecessary environmental as well as social stress. The type of firm that best meets the requirements of green economics is the cooperative.

The story of cooperatives is the story of working people coming together to meet their own needs, in the UK initially as consumers but later through creating building societies to enable them to buy property. Elsewhere – as in France and Italy – the worker-managed firm has been the predominant form of cooperative. This model of common ownership and shared solutions is in sharp contrast to the market model where typically an individual who owns assets creates a private enterprise that makes goods or services available in exchange for the cash of those who need them. Cooperatives also seek to balance the needs of producers and consumers rather than pitting them against one another as is the case in the relationship assumed by neoclassical economics. Cooperatives furthermore neatly solve the problem of surplus value, the source of profit in a capitalist economy as the value difference between the cost of inputs and the market price is extracted by the owner in profit. In a cooperative there are no profits and surpluses are reinvested in

innovation, used to reduce prices, or shared with the cooperative members of the local community.

Cooperatives follow a series of principles and values which we do not have the space to lay out here, but what makes them special is that they serve the interests of either their own employees or their own customers rather than external shareholders. And the workers or members are also involved in deciding the direction and strategy for the cooperative. So if you become a member of a retail cooperative you could vote to stop them buying coffee that has not been fairly traded. If you were part of a worker cooperative you would be able to vote to set your own rates of pay. This is not as liberating or potentially irresponsible as it sounds, since it would also be your responsibility to make sure the business continued to be successful. So in a cooperative you have to take your responsibility as an owner very seriously. Hence cooperatives seem an ideal business form to share with students as part of a responsible approach to teaching about the economy in the management school, alongside the ordinary market model.

Case study: Mondragon Cooperative

Mondragon Cooperative demonstrates many of the key features of a green economy organisation. First, it is deeply embedded in its local community of the Spanish basque country and responds to the community's need for skilled employment. Mondragon is based around the 10 cooperative principles supplemented by four specific corporate values: cooperation, participation, social responsibility and innovation. It was founded in 1956 during a time when the Basque country suffered economic hardship under the Franco regime. It was focused around the production of white goods and vehicles, supported by a strong commitment to R&D reflected in the establishment of its own university, and the importance of control of finance leading to the establishment of the group's own bank the Caja Laboral. In addition, the group established the supermarket group Eroski. The 105 cooperatives that make up Mondragon constitute the largest industrial worker-owned business in the world and is in the top 10 of Spanish multinationals with more than €11bn turnover and 75,000 employees. In response to globalisation the cooperative expanded and now has production facilities in South America and Eastern Europe whose employees are not cooperative members, stretching the original principle. But Mondragon demonstrates that a participatory and egalitarian organisational structure does not prohibit success in a global and high-tech economic sector and is thus an inspiration to those committed to challenging the exploitative nature of global capitalism.

RETHINKING THE PEDAGOGY OF ECONOMICS

It is implicit in everything we have already written that green economics requires a paradigm shift in thinking about how our economy is structured and managed – and in how it is thought about, conceptualised. To achieve this, those who study sustainability education have suggested a distinct approach to pedagogy, and experiential learning has received particular attention.

Discussions with students have indicated that one of the reasons they choose to study economics is that it portrays the world to them as simple and controllable. In a world grown increasingly interconnected and complex this has an immediate appeal. But that appeal is meretricious because the world as portrayed by neoclassical economics is, as we have already discussed, based on false and often positively harmful assumptions. So the conventional approach to economics teaching is deceptive in a way that should be incompatible with minimum academic standards. It was the realisation that this was the case – that their professors had no

explanation for the financial crisis and no ability to explain how the global economy actually works – that inspired students in Paris to rebel against their academics and found the 'Post-Autistic Economics' movement, leading to the Rethinking Economics movement profiled above.

The reality is that any economy is a highly complex system involving a multitude of human (and non-human) actors in complex multi-dimensional relationships with multiple physical and non-physical variables. To produce a model to represent this complex system would be so time-consuming that it would be entirely counter-productive, although some economists are now developing a synthesis between scientific complexity theory and economic theory that may bear some fruit. If we connect this economic complexity with the complexity of the ecological system of planet earth we are left in the situation neatly encapsulated by Donella Meadows:

> Let's face it, the universe is messy. It is nonlinear, turbulent, and chaotic. It is dynamic. It spends its time in transient behaviour on its way to somewhere else, not in mathematically neat equilibrium. It self-organises and evolves. It creates diversity, not uniformity. That's what makes the world interesting, that's what makes it beautiful, and that's what makes it work.[18]

So how are we to help students learn about the economy in a way that empowers them and enables them to act responsibly? The first step is to acknowledge that all students are already economic actors. We need to begin by validating their own experiences with provisioning, creation, money and exchange from their earliest years to the present. We should consider adopting a broadly 'social constructionist' or at least bottom-up approach that considers all experience to have merit in building a shared understanding of how the economy functions. This will require an attitude of humility on the part of learner and educator alike.

Even so, this level of uncertainty presents significant problems for educators at all levels. It takes a brave lecturer to begin a course by admitting that s/he does not know the answers to all the most important questions. Accepting uncertainty, particularly when in contrast to the strident confidence of neoclassical economics, can lead to a lack of confidence amongst students, although it can also lead to positive outcomes, particularly in terms of building a relationship of trust between pedagogue and student.[19] Learning about a sustainable approach to the economy means learning to live in a different way. The process is itself relational: that is to say that we learn to develop better relationships between ourselves, between people and non-human animals, and between people and the natural environment.

The discussion that follows is situated in a broadly Freirean methodological framework. Paulo Freire's worldview can best be summed up in the phrase 'The world is emerging': 'Whenever people act creatively, they change the world and therewith themselves'. This view of learning as a shared experience between 'teacher' and 'taught' offers an empowering approach to sustainability educators, who are dealing with an area where change is inevitable and often unwelcome, which can leave students and citizens struggling with the size of the challenge. This is an approach that finds favour with theorists of sustainability pedagogy who strive for experiential learning and 'democratic learning contexts'.[20]

In an earlier paper,[21] one of the current authors proposed a way of considering sustainability education that draws on the tools of education more usually found in the development of craft skills than intellectual knowledge. Scott Cato posited the possibility that sustainability itself might be akin to a craft skill drawing on the work of Pamela Smith, and her study of the understanding of physical work during the European Renaissance. Smith explores the changing nature of skilled manual work at this time and in this place and how it came to define what she frames as an 'artisanal epistemology'.[22]

This epistemology arose as a result of the artisans' need to understand the natural materials that they used during their processes of creation: 'When artisans looked to nature, they were interested, not surprisingly, in its powers of generation and transformation, for they themselves worked with the materials of nature and struggled to manipulate and control them in order to produce objects' (p. 16). Through this process they came to regard nature as the source of secure knowledge: 'Nature increasingly came to be regarded as an authority to which to make appeal when other traditional sources of authority either failed or were not available' (p. 9) This knowledge arose through their direct experience of natural materials: 'certain knowledge can be extracted by engaging with nature, and …. this engagement takes place through a bodily encounter with matter' (p. 59).

This suggests a pedagogical approach in which students are encouraged to learn through reflecting on their real-time experiences in the existing economy. These might be brought into the pedagogical arena through discussions and debates, choosing different themes as the focus of each week's session. It goes without saying that the multicultural nature of most universities – where students have experiences from other parts of the world to share – would greatly deepen and enhance the learning experience. A technique might be to introduce popular culture considerations of economic situations and subject them to critical analysis using orthodox and heterodox economic theories. For example, one of the authors used the Nordic noir classic *Easy Money* by Jens Lapidus to consider the issue of competition for markets and different economic strategies.

Clearly, the teacher should take the lead in designing and managing the learning experience, but this should not be done in a hierarchical style. Again, the method of learning a craft can be instructive. Richard Sennett describes this process in his sociological analysis of *The Craftsman*.[23] His guiding principle is 'Show, Don't Tell' on the basis that 'Whoever has tried to assemble a do-it-yourself bookcase following written instructions knows the problem. As one's temper rises, one realises how great a gap can exist between instructive language and the body' (p. 179). Written or verbal instructions that do not connect with the learned experience of the student are much less likely to elicit enthusiasm or any kind of learning experience. Sennett dismisses such teaching (and perhaps most of the orthodox economics canon) as 'dead denotation' (p. 182): 'The challenge posed by dead denotation is precisely to take apart tacit knowledge, which requires bringing to the surface of consciousness that knowledge which has become so self-evident and habitual that it seems just natural' (p. 183). This is precisely how conventional economics teaching has managed to alienate many students, and perhaps the very ones whose creative thinking is most needed if we are to resolve the sustainability crisis.

The taking apart of tacit assumptions is exactly the task of philosophy.[24] It is therefore especially unfortunate that modern economics has typically repudiated its philosophical roots; in this respect, Adam Smith was a far deeper thinker than those who take his name (often, actually, in vain), today.[25] There should always be room for philosophical disputation and 'dialectic' in economics, and any true green economics encourages this.

Such taking apart (and reconstruction) cannot fail to be a question of some controversy; it isn't like a simple matter of data-collection nor even theory-articulation. This brings to manifestation the essential role of *debate* as a key aspect of (green economics) pedagogy. For to suppress the controversy hereabouts would be – is – an ideological imposition by a teacher on their students. Thus we recommend all those teaching economics to make prominent such a requirement of and engagement in debate. And this will, obviously, therefore inevitably be part of the methodology of green economics more generally. What human well-being is, potential 'trade-offs' between it and the well-being of other beings, and so forth, are inevitably

going to be matters for debate (which is not the same thing as saying that 'anything goes' in those debates; far from it. There are severe constraints: those of what makes for actual human happiness, what is ecosystemically long-term viable, as well as constraints of logic itself.)

In finding a method for learning-and-teaching Green economics we will also benefit from the insights of those teaching sustainability, particularly *their* emphasis on experiential learning. Wals and Van der Leij (2007: 18) define social learning as 'learning that takes place when divergent interests, norms, values and constructions of reality meet in an environment that is conducive to learning.'[26] Such experiential learning also builds on pre-existing understandings of the world rather than imposing the single, uniform understanding of the world that typifies neoclassical economics. The key question for the pedagogue is 'How can social learning build upon people's own knowledge, skills and, often alternative, ways of looking at the world?' (p. 19).

Given the destructive value system and behavioural patterns of the existing economics, what we are seeking when teaching green economics is nothing short of transformation and would therefore require the sort of 'transformative learning' proposed by Stephen Sterling.[27] Such an approach has also been supported by the United Nations: 'Higher education should emphasize experiential, inquiry-based, problem-solving, interdisciplinary systems approaches and critical thinking. Curricula need to be developed, including content, materials and tools such as case studies and identification of best practices' (pp. 22–3).[28]

What kinds of things does this mean in practice? Here are some possibilities, deliberately slightly radical ones, to seek to open the reader's mind in the very way that we should want the minds of our students to be opened:

- Abstractions such as 'natural capital' and 'ecosystem services' are in our view dangerous extensions of the neoclassical approach: they seek to turn nature itself into part of conventional economics.[29] In this way, they function as 'environmental economics' does: they keep the neoclassical paradigm alive by over-extending it; a dangerous move. This is exactly why a green ecological economics is needed. Thus we argue for resisting the 'natural capital' and 'ecosystem services' discourses, and instead engaging with the quiddities of place. That is, it is an antidote to those discourses to take seriously how each place has its own specific qualities, and you cannot simply 'offset' the destruction of one ecosystem by seeking to enrich another.[30]

- Thus green economics will thrive on the back of engagement and familiarity with real places. The teaching of green economics should ideally involve an exercise in de-abstraction of the kind that occurs if one takes a field trip not just into (say) an actual market-place, such as a farmer's market, but further, into nature itself. For example, connecting with the kinds of non-monocultural spaces produced by permacultural and other agroecological farming methods. Or going out foraging: a way of provisioning for one's needs that entirely bypasses 'the market'. (These kinds of 'field trips' would also have the immense benefit of undercutting the 'Nature Deficit Disorder', which is increasingly prevalent in our overly urbanised and suburbanised societies.)

- Extra-curricular interventions as a form of 'situated learning' (Lave and Wenger, 1991)[31] are favoured amongst sustainability pedagogues but are more challenging to those teaching economics. But one could imagine a site visit to a local food-bank or Job Centre as part of a critical approach to the provisioning system and labour market of the existing economy. The more creative approaches to pedagogy relating to Education for Sustainable Development (ESD) are identified in Table 5.1.

CONCLUSION

Post-growth economics is nothing less than the economics of the future. A green economics will either be adopted voluntarily, or it will be forced upon us by an 'enraged' nature – under human battering – ending growth for us, by its ending organised society.

It would be wise for humanity to get ahead of the game, and take the voluntary route, toward sanity.

In conclusion, it is apparent that, while green economics pedagogy is in its infancy[32] and in an experimental phase, it has much promise and already much to offer. As Cotton and Winter (2010: 41–2)[33] note about sustainability education in general:

> There are a number of general principles regarding sustainability pedagogies including participatory and inclusive education processes, transdisciplinary cooperation, experiential learning and the use of environment and community as learning resources; all of which involve student-centred and interactive enquiry-based approaches to learning and teaching.

We close then by mentioning the existence of certain institutions which place these kinds of values front and centre: institutions such as, for example, Schumacher College (in Devon), named after the great pioneer of green economics and green business-practice who famously authored 'Small is beautiful'. Those in management schools wishing to think more deeply about how to teach green economics as part of their curriculum could do a lot worse than try taking a course themselves at such an institution.

Table 5.1. Education for Sustainable Development teaching approaches

Personal	Reconnecting to reality	Holistic
Teachers as role models	Local communities	Interdisciplinarity
Teachers as learners/learners as teachers	Real-life experiences	Critical thinking
Lifelong learning	Connecting people with nature	Systems thinking
Transformative pedagogy	Enacting social change	Volunteering in local social economy or gift economy organisations

Clearly, there are going to be serious challenges in undertaking the kinds of institutional changes that we have proposed in this chapter. Overcoming those challenges is a topic for another time (and for practitioners in both 'institutional economics' and 'action-research' change-making). But if Extinction Rebellion can transform consciousness on the climate and ecological emergency within just a fortnight (as it did in April 2019) by non-violently breaking the law, then the least that academics and teachers can do is get serious about rapid paradigm-shift in their disciplines, classrooms and institutions.

ACKNOWLEDGEMENT

Thanks to Alexandra Steele for help researching this chapter.

Notes

1   In fact, taking up a stance such as this should not be considered radical at all: it should be considered merely sane. A more radical approach would suggest perhaps the need for a non-negotiably spiritual approach to our predicament, so extreme is that predicament; or would question the framing of the issue as one of 'environment'. (For the latter see e.g. www.futurelearn.com/courses/environmental-justice/0/steps/37226.) So what we are saying here in the main text is in fact the opposite of extreme.

2   We have taken just this approach in the textbook Reardon, J., Caporale Madi, A. M. and Cato, M. S. (2015) *Introducing a New Economics: Pluralist, Sustainable, and Progressive* (London: Zed). Cf. also https://rdcu.be/2Vw2.

3   Mellor, M. (2006) Ecofeminist political economy, *International Journal of Green Economics*, 1(1–2), 139–150; p. 143.

4   DCMS, Disinformation and 'fake news': Interim Report, 29 July 2018.

5   'Facebook protects far-right activists even after rule breaches', *Guardian*, 17 July 2018.

6   Karl Polanyi, in his great work *The Great Transformation*, called these 'fictitious commodities', because, unlike real commodities, their level of supply barely responds to demand. And moreover, because they are life itself. One of us (R. R.)

extends – generalises – Polanyi's argument, in his 2001 article 'There are no such things as commodities', published in the *Journal of Philosophical Economics*, IV(2), 93–104: www.jpe.ro/poze/articole/61.pdf.

7   See www.uea.ac.uk/arts-humanities/faculty-research-awards-and-fellowships/research-news/-/asset_publisher/DI5pwzXyqjAo/content/brexit-and-trade-moving-from-globalisation-to-self-reliance-rupert-read-ppl-?inheritRedirect=false for an important example of this in which we have both been involved: the direction of travel in which green principles would suggest trade policy be altered, if there is to be a 'green Brexit' in the UK.

8   www.huffingtonpost.com/reverend-william-e-flippin-jr/ubuntu-applying-african-p_b_1243904.html.

9   www.cusp.ac.uk/themes/p/limitsrevisited/.

10 See https://kevinanderson.info/blog/the-hidden-agenda-how-veiled-techno-utopias-shore-up-the-paris-agreement/.

11 See www.thelondoneconomic.com/opinion/climate-change-once-we-no-longer-deny-it-then-we-just-might-have-the-will-to-try-drastically-to-change-course/14/03/.

12 See e.g. https://agroecology-appg.org/ourwork/appg-briefings-on-the-precautionary-principle-climate-change-and-animal-welfare/.

13 Arguably, truly sustainable finance is necessarily finance that works precautionarily from both a financial and an ecological perspective, rather than creating black swans. We have no space to investigate this point further here; however, for some hints see Taleb, N. N. (2008) *The Black Swan*. Penguin Books: London, Taleb, N. N. (2012). *Anti-fragile*. Penguin Books: London, and also www.uea.ac.uk/research/explore-uea-research/are-some-risks-just-too-big-to-take, www.businessgreen.com/bg/opinion/2399759/evidence-or-precaution-a-new-way-of-looking-at-the-business-and-financial-worlds and https://bankunderground.co.uk/2017/01/27/how-should-regulators-deal-with-uncertainty-insights-from-the-precautionary-principle/.

14 See www.greenhousethinktank.org/uploads/4/8/3/2/48324387/post-growth-localisation_pamphlet.pdf for an overview of how our think-tank, Green House (in collaboration with Helena Norberg-Hodge, the world-leading localisationist), envisages this would work.

15 Scott Cato, M. (2012) *The Bioregional Economy* (London: Earthscan).

16 www.business-humanrights.org/en/binding-treaty.

17 Woodin, M. and Lucas, C. (2004) *Green Alternatives to Globalisation: A Manifesto* (London: Pluto

Press); Cato, M. S. (2009) *Green Economics* (London: Earthscan).

18 Meadows, D. (2002) 'Dancing with systems', *The Systems Thinker*, 13(2).

19 McWilliam, E. L. (2005) 'Unlearning pedagogy', *Journal of Learning Design*, 1(1), 1–11.

20 Springett, D. (2010) 'Education for sustainability in the business studies curriculum', in Jones, P., Selby, D. and Sterling, S. (Eds.), *Sustainability Education: Perspectives and Practice across Higher Education* (London: Earthscan).

21 Scott Cato, M. (2014) 'What the willow teaches: Sustainability learning as craft', *Learning and Teaching*, 7(2), 4–27.

22 Smith, P. (2004) *The Body of the Artisan* (Chicago: University of Chicago Press).

23 Sennett, R. (2008) *The Craftsman* (Harmondsworth: Penguin).

24 Although we note in passing that to say this is not to say that explicitising the implicit is always a good thing. On the contrary, sometimes leaving things implicit is precisely what is needful. If I seek to make my friendship with you entirely resolvable into the benefits that it brings the two of us, that will be the end of it as a *friendship*. (And this indicates a central aspect of what is wrong with the project of a narrowly economic valuation of humanity and/or of nature. Cf. n. 29 and text above.)

25 For a green take on what is of potential value in Adam Smith's philosophical orientation toward economics, the reader is recommended to begin with the opening pages of Woodin and Lucas, *Green Alternatives to Globalisation*. For a contemporary effort to recast economics as fundamentally a philosophical discipline, like it or not, see Read, R. (2007) 'Economics is philosophy, Economics is not science', *International Journal of Green Economics*, 1(3/4).

26 Wals, A. E. J. (Ed.) (2007) *Social Learning Towards a Sustainable World* (Wageningen: Academic Publishers).

27 Sterling, S. (2001) *Sustainable Education: Re-visioning Learning and Change* (Dartington: Green Books on behalf of The Schumacher Society).

28 UNESCO (2004) *United Nations Decade of Education for Sustainable Development (2005–2014): Draft International Implementation Scheme* (Paris: UNESCO).

29 See our co-authored paper 'The natural capital controversy', in the *Journal of Human Rights and the Environment*, 5(2) (2014), 153–167.

30 For more detail on why, see 'Offsetting Nature' by Mike Hannis: eprints.bbk.ac.uk/6031/1/Offsetting_nature_inner_final.pdf.

31 Lave, J, Wenger, E (1991) Situated Learning. Legitimate peripheral participation, Cambridge. Cambridge University Press.

32 Obviously, there is a need for the green economics materials and research that are already available to be more widely disseminated and understood – and for more research and more work on green economics pedagogy.

33 Winter J, Cotton D (2010) Embedding sustainability education into academic practice.

PART II

Educational Purposes and Contents

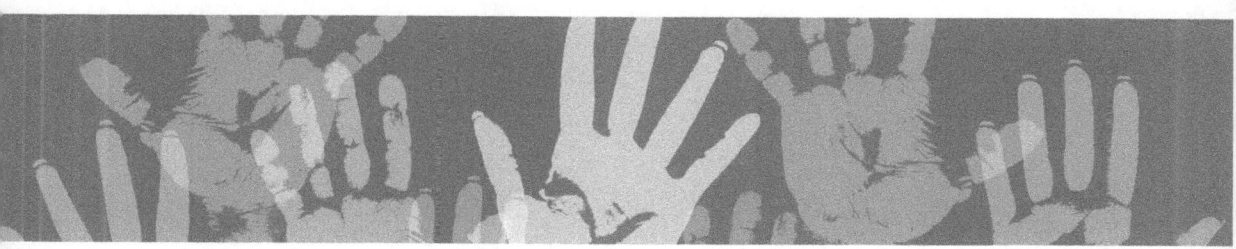

6

Responsible Management Education: The Role of CSR Evolution and Traditions

Responsible management (RM) is one of the most recent terminologies under which a concern for business's accountability, obligations and duties to society and stakeholders has been used, mostly by academics but also practitioners. Responsible management is the governance and supervision of the firm's social, public, and stakeholder issues to include corporate social responsibility (CSR), business ethics and sustainability as an integrated whole. It also embraces other socially-conscious concepts. It entails managing goals and processes related to the organization itself and organization members who have responsibility for these issues. It especially entails managing boundary-spanning activities and relationships between the organization and its stakeholder environments. Today, these topics are treated in a global business citizenship context.

Many different meanings of the term responsible management have been set forth. In addition to the characterizations above, another useful definition appeared in the *Financial Times* and it also provides an overall understanding: 'making business decisions that, next to the interests of the shareholders, also takes into account all the other stakeholders, such as workers, clients, suppliers, the environment, the community, and future generations' (quoted in Weybrecht, 2017). Of course, each of the various definitions of RM represents the content and sentiment of a number of different, popular concepts today, including not only corporate social responsibility, but also stakeholder management, corporate citizenship, business ethics, sustainability, creating shared value and managing with purpose.

RM is not a recent idea, as it has been around in one form or another since business enterprises began. To consider the seeds of the idea of responsible management, it should be noted that it has gone through a number of stages. It is easier because of written documentation to identify these stages as they evolved in the United States, where the popularity of the idea grew with the corporate form of organization, but parallel periods have occurred around the world, often simultaneously, as awareness became increasingly widespread. Indeed, recent research on the teaching of responsible management in other countries documents the degree to which this topic has proliferated and is now being taught around the world; for example, in Brazil, Australia, Britain and Spain, just to mention a few (Brunstein et al., 2018; Seto-Pamies et al., 2011; Stewart and Gapp, 2013).

Beginning with the period 1776–1880, some degree of management responsibility was present during the foundations of capitalism and the birth of the corporation. It grew in popularity during the turbulent rise of the corporate form (1880–1900). The notion of RM was present during the Progressive Era (1900–1918), and the corporation's case for responsibility to society strengthened during the 1929–1945 period and into the national and global crisis of the Great Depression. The idea of responsible management, or its more frequently used appellation, corporate social responsibility, came of age in the post-WWII period, especially becoming widespread during the 1950s and flourishing during the 1960s (Carroll et al., 2012).

The social consciousness that surfaced during the 1960s represented a period during which a revolution of rising expectations became prevalent and significantly compelled a closer scrutiny of business behaviors and decisions. This was in striking contrast to the 1940s and 1950s, when business enterprises sought improved legitimacy as a part of society, and their examples of responsible management were fewer and often unreported. The 1960s represented a crucible for change and social movements led to increased calls for responsibility on the part of companies and managements. In particular, the civil rights movement, the women's movement, the consumer movement and the environmental movement, along with a concern for worker safety and health, became the primary drivers of change in the relationship between business and society (Carroll et al., 2012).

To this list might be added related movements that began at about the same time, such as the youth movement, the anti-war, anti-militaristic movement, and a work ethic revolt (Frederick, 2006: 27–29). Clearly, the social contract between business and society began to change dramatically during the 1960s.

RESPONSIBLE MANAGEMENT'S CONCEPTUAL DEVELOPMENT

It can easily be argued that the modern era of CSR, and hence, responsible management, began in the 1950s with the work of Howard Bowen and the publication of his milestone book titled *Social Responsibilities of the Businessman* (Bowen, 1953). As the title of the book suggests, there were virtually no women prominent in business during this time. Bowen's motivation was significantly driven by his recognition that corporate power was rising during this period and how this was sometimes adversely impacting the lives of citizens in many different ways. Bowen gained prominence when he posed the question that even today still drives much of the literature and practice: 'What responsibilities to society may businessmen reasonably be expected to assume?' (p. xi).

Though Bowen did not dwell on defining social responsibility, academics, especially, began a process of delineating its meaning. Keith Davis was one of the earliest writers to describe what social responsibility meant when he argued that it referred to 'businessmen's decisions and actions taken for reasons at least partially beyond the firm's direct economic or technical interests.' (Davis, 1960: 70). William C. Frederick, another early and influential writer, contributed his view that business managers should oversee the economic system such that it 'fulfills the expectations of the public' and 'enhances total socio-economic welfare' (Frederick, 1960: 60). Joseph McGuire was another key contributor in the 1960s and in his book *Business and Society* (1963) he asserted that 'the idea of social responsibilities supposes that the corporation has not only economic and legal obligations but also certain responsibilities to society which extend beyond these obligations' (p. 144). Finally, Clarence C. Walton published a landmark book titled *Corporate Social Responsibilities* (1967) in which he provided a fundamental definition of CSR, as follows:

> In short, the new concept of social responsibility recognizes the intimacy of the relationships between the corporation and society and realizes that such relationships must be kept in mind by top managers as the corporation and the related groups pursue their respective goals. (1967: 18)

Definitions of CSR proliferated in the 1970s and the decade was ushered in with the book *The Social Responsibilities of Business: Company and Community, 1900–1960,* by Morrell Heald (1970). Heald did not dwell on definitions of SR or CSR as much as he described and commented on the concepts 'as businessmen themselves have defined and experienced it' (p. xi). Heald proceeded to chronicle business practices and policies that were community-oriented, and he concluded that business practitioners during this time were preoccupied with community relations and corporate philanthropy.

Following this, Harold Johnson presented a variety of definitions and discussed them in his book *Business in Contemporary Society: Framework and Issues* (1971). Johnson described what he termed the 'conventional wisdom' that socially responsible firms are ones in which 'managerial staff balances a multiplicity of interests' (p. 50). Johnson went on to say that these managers did not strive only for larger profits for stockholders, but that as responsible enterprises they also 'take into account employees, suppliers, dealers, local communities, and the nation' (p. 50). Johnson's views clearly presaged what we today recognize to be a stakeholder approach to enterprise management. Other important contributors to the definition and

understanding of CSR during the 1970s included the Committee for Economic Development (CED) (1971), Professor George Steiner (1971), Henry Manne and Henry Wallich (1972), Keith Davis (1973), Dow Votaw (1973), Richard Eells and Clarence Walton (1974), Lee Preston and James Post (1975) and Thomas Zenisek (1979). Further, Carroll (1977) sought to highlight the management and organizational dimensions of CSR with his book titled *Managing Corporate Social Responsibility.*

In 1979, this writer proposed a four-part definition of CSR that was embedded in a model of corporate social performance (CSP) (Carroll, 1979). The CSP model intended to bring together some of the CSR threads that had occurred in the literature up to this time. The three-dimensional CSP model contended that for managers to engage in CSP, they needed to have (a) a basic definition of CSR (the four-part definition), (b) a delineation of the issues and/or publics for which a social responsibility existed (today we call them stakeholders) and (c) a strategy or philosophy of responsiveness to the issues (1979: 499). Of interest here is the basic four-part definition of CSR. Carroll's observation was that to be comprehensive in describing business's responsibilities to society, it needed to embrace a broad range of activities and expectations that included but extended beyond business's economic and legal responsibilities to society. Therefore, the following definition was proposed: 'The social responsibility of business encompasses the economic, legal, ethical and discretionary expectations that society has of organizations at a given point in time' (1979: 500).

First and foremost, it was argued, business has a responsibility to society that is *economic* in nature. Before anything else, the business institution is the basic economic unit in society. As such it has a responsibility to produce goods and services that society wants and to sell them at a profit. All other business roles are predicated on this fundamental assumption (Carroll, 1979: 500). In addition, just as society expects business to produce goods and services it wants and needs, society expects business to obey the law. The law represents the basic 'rules of the game' by which businesses are expected to function. Thus, the *legal* responsibility became the second part of the definition.

The next two responsibilities address what today are more often thought of to be 'social' responsibilities – ones that extend beyond compliance with the law. The *ethical* responsibility addresses the kinds of actions, decisions, policies, practices and norms that society expects business to follow. These embrace a normative expression of what society expects of business beyond what the law addresses. These expectations always seem to be expanding as it becomes clearer what activities businesses engage in that may be deemed questionable. Finally, the fourth responsibility category was described as *discretionary* responsibilities. These represent voluntary roles and activities in which business engages but for which society does not provide a clear-cut expectation as to what is included. These activities and roles are guided by businesses' desire to engage in social roles not mandated or required by law, and not necessarily expected in an ethical sense. These discretionary responsibilities were later relabeled by Carroll to be 'philanthropic' responsibilities because at the time discretionary responsibilities were identified they tended to be illustrated by companies making philanthropic contributions such as donations, conducting in-house programs for drug abusers, training the hard-core unemployed, or providing day-care centers for working mothers (Carroll, 1979: 500). These acts of benevolence were activities that helped society but were not necessarily expected in an ethical sense. Since the time this category was defined, however, it has become ethically motivated by some companies and practically or instrumentally motivated by others as companies sought to be good corporate citizens. They are still at businesses' discretion, however.

As the 1980s arrived, we witnessed fewer new definitions of CSR, more empirical research on the topic, and alternative themes beginning to emerge. In 1980, Thomas Jones entered the CSR discussion. Jones contended that corporate social responsibilities ought to be voluntarily adopted and that the obligations are broad, extending beyond traditional duties to shareholders to other groups, such as customers, employees, suppliers and neighboring communities (Jones, 1980: 59–60). Once again, the stakeholder approach, later made well known by R. Edward Freeman (1984), is being presaged. Jones also concluded that since it is difficult to reach consensus as to what constitutes socially responsible outcomes, CSR should be seen as a *process*. Later in the 1980s, Edwin Epstein picked up on the process dimension and brought the collection of ideas that were emerging (CSR, social responsiveness and business ethics) into what he called the 'corporate social policy process' (Epstein, 1987: 106).

CSR thinking continued in the 1980s when the notion of stakeholders became popularized, by R. Edward Freeman in his landmark book on the subject (Freeman, 1984). Freeman's book was intended to be about strategic management, but the stakeholder theory and approach embedded in the book was quickly accepted by social issues scholars and became the centerpiece of its popularity and eventual impact in CSR, business ethics and sustainability.

During the 1990s, very few new or unique understandings of CSR emerged. More than anything else, the CSR concept had become a base point, point-of-departure or building block for concept extensions, elaborations and related themes or frameworks. Many of these embraced CSR-thinking and were quite compatible with it. Further development of the corporate social performance model was published by Donna Wood in 1991 and her work revisited and built upon Carroll's CSP model and refinements that had been made by Steve Wartick and Philip Cochran in 1985. Wood's contributions were significant as they placed CSR into a broader context than just a stand-alone definition.

In 1991, Carroll revisited his earlier four-part definition of CSR and emphasized how the discretionary component could be perceived as philanthropic in nature and that it embraced a 'corporate citizenship' perspective that was also becoming popular in the 1990s. Further, Carroll proposed that his four-part definition might be depicted as a pyramid of CSR in which the economic category was placed at the base since it was the foundation upon which the others rested. He then built upward through legal, ethical and philanthropic categories (Carroll, 1991: 40–42). Carroll made it clear that the pyramid was more of a graphical depiction of CSR than an attempt to add new meaning to the CSR definition. He also argued that businesses should not fulfill these responsibilities in a sequential fashion but that each is to be fulfilled simultaneously. He summarized, 'the CSR firm should strive *to make a profit, obey the law, be ethical*, and *be a good corporate citizen*' (Carroll, 1991: 43; italics added). This Pyramid of CSR became a centerpiece of much teaching in the RM field. Later, it became the subject of further research.

COMPETING AND COMPLEMENTARY FRAMEWORKS

From a historical perspective, the concept of corporate social responsibility (CSR) has been the dominant, core framework around which most discussions of responsible management have been centered. CSR represents a language and perspective familiar the world over and has become increasingly vital as both external and internal stakeholders have communicated that businesses need to do more than make money and obey the law. Today, the expectation of ethical and philanthropic policies and practices has become an integral part of the responsible management expectation, as organizations of all sizes are

striving to be legitimate and sustainable in a competitive, dynamic, global marketplace (Carroll, 2015).

Beginning in the 1980s and moving forward, a number of different alternative themes surfaced both in the literature of management responsibility and among business practitioners (Carroll, 1999). The basic concept of CSR began splintering into alternative themes or frameworks and this process seems to be ongoing. Among the most prevalent of these alternatives have included corporate social responsiveness, corporate social performance, corporate social policy, public policy, business ethics, stakeholder management, corporate citizenship, sustainability, creating shared value, and managing with purpose. In some instances, these represent different names for the same basic phenomenon; in other cases, particular dimensions of interest have been argued to be central or more important. Nuances differentiate these concepts from one another. The interest in CSR has not diminished, indeed it has escalated, but the core concept has been recast or reframed by some into what might be called 'competing and complementary' frameworks, concepts, theories, models or themes (Schwartz and Carroll, 2008; Carroll, 2015).

Each of the related concepts mentioned has its adherents and practitioners, but at their core they all focus on the same essential idea of management responsibility. Consequently, many writers and practitioners use these terms interchangeably; others acquiesce to their subtle differences or nuanced meanings. In terms of our present discussion and purposes of this chapter, our primary emphasis is on responsibility (as in responsible management or CSR). These other concepts are outside the scope of this chapter, but they intersect and overlap both in their meanings and issues related to their learning and education.

The final decade of the 20th century might be categorized as the period when corporate responsibility and responsible management were institutionalized and globalized and this era continued on into the 21st century as the idea that managements must be held accountable for their decisions, practices and actions became an accepted and required part of business enterprises of all sizes. What began as a preoccupation with large corporations in highly capitalistic societies, became a standard expectation for organizations of all sizes throughout the world, including in developing and less-developed regions.

BENEFITS OF TEACHING AND LEARNING RESPONSIBLE MANAGEMENT

Since a major concern in this chapter is on learning and education, it might rightly be asked who is interested in these topics and what are its benefits. A cursory review of literature and practice suggests that many different stakeholders think that the teaching and learning of RM, to embrace sustainability and business ethics, are important. Society wants these topics taught; the professions want these topics taught; the media wants these topics taught; the accrediting agencies want these topics taught; and, most important, students want these topics taught. Each of these groups has become a benefactor. As a consequence, there has been an explosion of courses in colleges and universities that focus on these topics and they appear under a host of similar titles – Business and Society; Business, Government and Society; Business *in* Society; Business and its Environment; Corporate Social Responsibility; Business Ethics; Management Ethics; Stakeholder Management; Sustainability; Responsible Management, and others.

APPROACHES TO RM EDUCATION

What are the different approaches that might be taken in responsible management (RM) education? To be sure, this topic and related topics have proliferated into colleges and departments in different schools across campus – business schools, law schools, journalism schools, education schools and many others. For sake of this discussion, we will focus on business schools, for that is where the bulk of relevant management education history resides. In addition, the business school's primary accrediting agency, the AACSB, has a long history with topics that fall under the RM umbrella and it is therefore desirable to focus on these experiences because most quality institutions around the world have or are pursuing AACSB accreditation (AACSB, 2018). Beginning in the early 1970s, the AACSB promoted its Standard IV(b), which maintained that a business school should provide its student learners with background teaching on the subjects of economics, legal environment and ethical considerations along with social and political influences as they affect such organizations. Unfortunately, the agency defined these responsibility-related terms quite broadly and were quite lax in their requirements.

The Social Issues in Management (SIM) Division of the Academy of Management, the primary academic professional association for management professors, in the mid-to-late 1970s, formed a task force with the intention of encouraging and lobbying the AACSB to strengthen its requirements for social responsibility education. Three suggested accrediting guidelines recommended by the SIM committee included (1) the curriculum should offer an opportunity to study a broad range of business and society relationships in an integrated fashion; (2) traditional functional courses (e.g. marketing, management, finance, and so on) should include social issues relevant to the subject matter; (3) the capstone business policy course (now called strategic management) should include a significant amount of material dealing with business's social, legal, and political environments, the social issues and problems that arise out of those environments, and the efforts of management to formulate and administer corporate social policies that would improve matters; (4) where possible, additional opportunities beyond the threshold, functional and policy courses should be given to students to delve into selected subject matter in the business and society area; (5) a variety of faculty members with contrasting disciplinary approaches is desirable for teaching the RM and business and society curriculum (Frederick, 2006: 217–220). The SIM committee, of which this author was a member, met with the AACSB standards committee several times. Since the standards committee was composed of business school deans, each member had a different perspective and the deans were constantly worried about how they would find 'shelf space' in the school curriculum to do all that was being asked. In short, the AACSB was never willing to accept all the SIM committee's recommendations.

By the 1990s, the AACSB had adopted a Content Standard C.1 which held that both undergraduate and MBA curricula should provide the student learners with an understanding of the perspectives that form the context for business to include ethical and global issues, influence of political, social, legal, regulatory, environmental and technological issues. AACSB also stressed the importance of the impact of demographic diversity on organizations. By the early 2000s, the AACSB passed its Assurance of Learning Standard in which it maintained that the curriculum ought to include learning experiences in such areas as ethical and legal responsibilities in organizations and society, understanding and reasoning abilities, analytical skills, and multicultural and diversity understandings. Other generic learning experiences were also supported, such as communication abilities and reflective thinking skills.

By 2013 and Revised in 2018, the AACSB had updated its standards though it made it clear that specific courses in the subject matters were not required. The AACSB held that for both undergraduate and graduate degree programs, learning experiences should be addressed in General Skill Areas such as *ethical understanding and reasoning (able to identify ethical issues and address the issue in a socially responsible way) and diverse and multicultural work environments* (italics added). In terms of AACSB's general Business and Management Knowledge Areas, the following topics should be addressed – *economic, political, regulatory, legal, technological, and social contexts of organizations in a globalized society; and social responsibility, including sustainability, and ethical behavior and approaches to management* (italics added) (AACSB, 2018). In short, virtually all the topics related to responsible management are now included in their standards, but the acid test arrives when the quality and extent of what business schools are actually doing are examined. This author, like many others, has strived to meet or exceed these requirements in teaching RM.

For business schools, the AACSB has laid out the standards for which accredited colleges and schools must adhere if they are to be accredited. But, since the AACSB does not require schools to have specific, dedicated courses in each of its standards areas, it is left to the various institutions to decide how this RM material is covered and, thus, instructors have considerable leeway in their teaching. In terms of prior practice and experience, there are three general ways that this material has been covered:

- A dedicated course on responsible management (RM) or related topics
- Infusing/integrating RM into many/all courses
- Employing both a dedicated course *and* infusing/integrating into other courses.

If one is seeking the maximal coverage, the third alternative seems to offer the best opportunity for full coverage but it is seldom achieved.

Dedicated course. Most experts in the field have long held that a specific, dedicated course on responsible management is needed to provide a foundation for their study elsewhere in the curriculum and to delve deeply into the concepts themselves so that they could be thoroughly understood before they were applied, perhaps in the various functional areas of business.

The earliest business school courses developed and offered to address responsible management topics were typically titled Business and Society or Business, Government and Society, or Business and Its Environment. The books that came to dominate the field in the mid-to-late 1960s and early 1970s were authored by George Steiner, Keith Davis and Robert Blomstrom, and by William T. Greenwood. As the business and society course matured, books and teaching evolved through an understanding of business's social responsibility (CSR) and businesses interrelationships with society and societal segments. Courses also evolved into focusing on one aspect of the business and society relationship such as advertising, marketing, minority affairs, philanthropy, business ethics, consumerism or other related focuses (Frederick, 2006: 227–229).

As the field of business and society continued to mature, the orientation of the courses became more managerial. Corporate social policy (Carroll and Hall, 1987) became a popular framework and an emphasis on managerially-related topics were treated more seriously. Moving into the 1980s and more recently, courses on business ethics, corporate citizenship and sustainability began appearing. At the heart of these dedicated courses, however, was always the concept of CSR or responsible management. Increasingly, these courses focused on educating managers for global business citizenship (Wood and Logsdon, 2008).

Infused/integrated. Many experts, and especially business school deans, thought that responsible management topics ought to be infused or integrated into core business courses and elective courses. From the deans' perspective, this could be more easily done. Simply have each course in the curriculum emphasize some coverage on the social, ethical, diversity, and global dimension of the topic at hand whether it be accounting, marketing, production or finance. What this meant was that each of these specialized professors was now expected to cover more topics and often topics for which they knew little. Textbooks began changing as each of the functional areas now had a chapter dedicated to CSR, business ethics and other values topics as it related to the main subject at hand. In an ideal world, infusing RM concepts into required and elective courses made perfect sense, but their implementation often left a lot to be desired because the topics were frequently neglected.

Dedicated and infused. The third alternative way to cover RM topics was to have both a dedicated course and require coverage be infused into other courses. For the most part, this is what is sought today in many business schools. Virtually all of them now have at least one dedicated course on RM topics, often as an elective, and the core courses are now covering social, legal, ethical, diversity and sustainability-related topics. This has been done because the AACSB requires it and the realization on the part of the instructors as to how integral and timely these issues have become for each of their fields. Today, CSR and RM topics are difficult to ignore in virtually any field or specialty of business or organization.

APPROACHES TO THE DEDICATED COURSE FOR RM EDUCATION

In virtually all business schools and other professional schools, a dedicated course focusing on responsible management education is found today. Over the past decades, this author has observed at least three identifiable approaches to the single course that has been offered. In the late 1960s and into the 1970s, what might be called an *issues/topics approach* was the central theme. This writer began his teaching career in RM using this modality. In this type of course, the focus was usually on a set of issues or topics that were in the news at the time and were interesting to be discussed, often on a chapter by chapter basis. In these early courses, they were structured around what were generally regarded as the social issues of the day. The early courses in the 1960s and 1970s focused on such issues as poverty, unemployment, urban renewal, civil rights, philanthropy, pollution and so on (Greenwood, 1964). These courses and books typically did not have any particular RM framework. They were simply discussion platforms for talking about the issues of the day. Very little attempt was made to relate them to what managers or organizations ought to be doing to address these social issues. The RM field was in its embryonic stage during this period.

Business-and-society approaches evolved next. This writer found that focusing on the business-and-society relationship was much more valuable than the 'issues/topics' approach. These approaches held that businesses needed to interact with many different 'publics' or 'constituencies' (consumers, environment, employees, communities, owners, government and so on) (Steiner, 1971). The stakeholder terminology was not used then. The predominant focus in most of these courses was on business's responsibilities to these various constituent groups. Some of these approaches claimed to pursue a managerial approach and they often were written from a managerial perspective though they did not get into specific management topics in detail. Quite often they were mostly focused on what good companies could contribute towards society.

Management/organization approaches were similar to the business-and-society approaches but they began to take more seriously the managerial and organizational dimension and implications of these topics. Stakeholders replaced publics and constituencies as the dominant nomenclature and most management approaches adopted the

ideas and language of stakeholder management. Corporate social responsibility continued to be a central paradigm and the concepts of business ethics and stakeholders were integral to the managerial approaches. More time was also spent on corporate governance and strategic management considerations, along with treatment of crisis management, issues management and public affairs management. Eventually, sustainability became another theme running throughout this set of approaches.

This latter approach, emphasizing a responsible management theme has become the most prevalent and one might argue, preferred, approach to teaching the subject today. Managers are practical people and they have begun to deal with corporate responsibility issues in ways similar to those they have used to manage traditional business functions such as marketing, finance, operations, risk management and so forth. Managers prefer a more rational, systematic and administratively sound approach to dealing with these topics today. By using a managerial approach, business people have been able to convert seemingly unmanageable issues into ones that can be dealt with in a more balanced fashion. The measure of success of this managerial approach has become the extent to which leaders have been able to improve upon the organization's social, ethical and sustainability performance rather than depending upon ad hoc measures or non-stop crisis management (Carroll et al., 2018: 22–23).

PEDAGOGICAL ISSUES IN RM EDUCATION

Pedagogy is the function or work of the instructor in an educational setting. It embraces all knowledge and methodologies that might be considered within the art and science of teaching and learning. It includes such topics as course objectives, framing the course or subject matter, selecting course materials to use, teaching methodologies, and the identification of methods, assignments, and testing. The role of pedagogy in teaching and learning cannot be overstated. Research and experience have demonstrated that no single approach or strategy in teaching responsible management has been demonstrated to be optimal. More often, a combination of goals, strategies or approaches have been successful. Relevant and critical variables are typically (1) the *instructor*, (2) the *subject* matter and (3) the *students*. The characteristics of each of these pertinent factors must be considered when selecting pedagogical approaches.

Instructors, for example, may come from different academic backgrounds, training and experience. A legal-environment-of-business professor is likely to teach best using an approach consistent with his or her background and experiences. The same would be true if the instructor's background, training or experience were in management, marketing, accounting or finance. An instructor with deep experience in the subject matter would best use an experiential approach than an approach used by an instructor with limited practical experience. The subject matter is another critical variable. Different colleges and universities have sought to cover RM topics in different departments and in different ways. In this writer's experience, RM was best taught in a management department since the notion of management is embedded in the concept's name and the management discipline has a history of supporting teaching and research in this area. Often for historical or other reasons, however, the topic may reside in a different department and then take on an alternative slant. In some limited circumstances, the course may be taught outside of the business school; for example, in a philosophy, religion or journalism department.

The students themselves are the third critical factor. Assuming for sake of argument that the students are located in a business school or a school of management, it then matters at what level (e.g. sophomore, senior, graduate) the course is taught. Whether the course is required or an elective makes a huge difference as well. If the course were taught in an executive education program, or management training program, where most of the students were older and more experienced, this would make a significant difference. In an ideal situation, courses of this type are offered at both undergraduate and graduate levels. In short, there are many variables to consider when thinking about RM education.

Using this writer's experience, let us assume that the RM course is taught in a business school to upper-level students (juniors or seniors). Let us also assume the course is taught in a management department wherein the emphasis is more likely to be on the managerial and organizational dimensions of the subject matter. Many of the characteristics of this situation would likely spill over or easily be adapted to different settings. Let us also assume the instructor has a business school background, most likely in one of the general or specialty fields of management and has some experience (actual or consulting) in the business world. This would be a typical situation in a college or university setting.

Using this set of circumstances, it is possible to think of the pedagogical issues that matter most to be the course goals or objectives, how the course is framed or introduced, the identification of course materials to be used, and the teaching methods, techniques and assignments that might follow. Another relevant issue might be testing and this will be briefly discussed.

COURSE GOALS OR OBJECTIVES

Depending on whether the course is primarily framed as responsible management, CSR, or some other complementary concept, the goals of the course might be stated in a variety of ways. Let us continue to use the more general course in RM which, of course, would likely include, but not emphasize, business ethics and sustainability and the other related concepts as well. It is all a matter of scope and interest.

Although there are some courses designed to be specific RM or CSR courses in name and scope, historically and currently, Business and Society courses represent the most frequent general context in which the topic is covered. We will use this as our example, knowing full well that it could be adapted to a similar or related course. Depending on the placement of the course in the curriculum and the individual instructor's philosophy or strategy, several essential goals such as the following might be appropriate. These are illustrative rather than comprehensive:

- The broad question of business's role and legitimacy as an institution in a global society is at stake and must be addressed from both business and societal perspectives.
- Students should be made aware of the expectations and demands that emanate from the stakeholder environment and are placed on business firms and their decision-makers.
- As prospective managers, students need to understand appropriate organizational and institutional responses and management approaches for dealing with social, ethical, environmental, technological, sustainability and global issues.
- An appreciation of business ethics and sustainability issues and the influence these have on society, management decision-making, behavior, policies and practices are essential.
- Students should be prepared to analyze the past, present and future progression of responsible management and be able to think through possible scenarios that might represent that future.

There are dozens of different ways in which these types of course goals might be presented. To be sure, the dimensions of CSR management, business ethics and sustainability should be interwoven into the course objectives, and when appropriate, other related concepts should be addressed and discussed in terms of their relevance and applicability.

FRAMING OR SETTING UP THE COURSE

The process of framing or setting up a course such as the one we are describing is a vital first stage in the pedagogical process. During this initial stage, appropriate coverage of *business*, *society* and *stakeholders*, and their dynamic interrelationships with one another, is vital. In doing this, business needs to be defined broadly to encompass the entire collection of private, commercially oriented organizations ranging in size from family proprietorships to corporate giants and all points in between. The global dimension is essential as virtually all medium and large enterprises today operate on the world economic stage, but the concepts of responsible management also apply to smaller, less visible organizational units as well (Spence, 2016). Likewise, the concept of a pluralistic society as a macroenvironment needs to be analyzed. This includes developing the thought of society being characterized by pluralism and multiple special interest groups and stakeholders.

One of the prominent issues in framing this global level of analysis is developing an understanding of the power and influence of the large, multinational enterprise. Most business criticism which sets the stage for responsible management is driven by business's perceived or actual abuse of power (Jacoby, 1973). Many different criticisms have been directed toward businesses over the decades and these continue – it is too big; it is too powerful; it pollutes the environment; it exploits workers and consumers; it does not tell the truth; its executives are too highly paid, and so on (Carroll et al., 2018: 10–18). These criticisms set the stage for the further discussion of responsible management, and the instructor should clarify the levels of interest that will be covered in the course. This concern with business criticism and power and balancing it with responsibility is a robust way to frame the study of RM.

Considering these factors, the stage is now set for a treatment of responsible management and its many related concepts and specifically an in-depth coverage of the role stakeholders and stakeholder management assume in RM and the relatedness of other topics such as business ethics and sustainability.

COURSE MATERIALS, METHODS AND ASSIGNMENTS

Course materials for education in responsible management run the gamut from the human to the technological and many points in between. The use of individual lectures and the presentation and analysis of case studies by the instructor has dominated the teaching methodologies of responsible management classes. Part of this, of course, involved students reading textbooks, articles and cases and preparing them for class analysis and discussion. With the passage of time, more diverse methodologies surfaced. Among these have been guest speakers, student presentations, case presentations, written papers, videos, movies and other computer-based technologies, including the use of the internet and social media. Digital platforms have become popular as well. There is no solid evidence regarding which of these or combinations of these works best. Sometimes it depends on the individual instructor and his or her interests and expertise.

In terms of teaching today and in the future, instructor-led teaching has been significantly augmented by technology-based approaches that range from movies or videos at one extreme to use of social media, such as Twitter, at the other. A brief mention of teaching methodologies is useful. The most frequently used have been instructor-directed lectures and discussions, and use of case studies, both instructor-directed and student group-directed.

Guest speakers. Guest speakers, often from the business, government or non-profit world, are a popular and useful teaching methodology in RM-type courses. Executives or managers in general or specific areas of responsibility can be quite educational in presenting and discussing the practical point of view. Directors or vice presidents of CSR, sustainability or business ethics often have many current and relevant examples to provide and students typically enjoy and learn from these presentations. Instructors may readily identify such individuals nearby and issue invitations to speak. An increasingly popular but often controversial guest speaker invitee is a manager or business person who committed some business fraud or crime, went to prison and once out began speaking to business school classes on responsible management (Porter, 2008). Many believe there is a lot to learn from such individuals if they have truly turned their lives around; however, some have raised questions about the appropriateness of inviting such speakers to campus. Regardless, many schools have used this technique.

Interestingly, there is a recent curiosity in the topic of corporate social *irresponsibility*, CSiR. CSiR might be broadly defined as management or organizational actions that cause harm to stakeholders, and it is often used loosely in conjunction with such topics as corruption, trust repair and crisis management (Carroll and Brown, 2018: 62–63). For example, researchers have studied stakeholder reactions to corrupt, irresponsible practices, the moral salience of misconduct and the repair of firm-stakeholder relationships following a breach of trust (Brown et al., 2016; Bundy and Pfarrer, 2015). Whether CSiR will emerge as its own distinct research and teaching construct is still to be seen, but it is the flip side of RM and there is much to be learned studying irresponsible organizations.

Student presentations. Student presentations of topics and case analyses have a deep history in the teaching of RM and it continues to this day. Often, instructors will provide guidelines for such presentations which often include such topics as method of presentation, dealing with nervousness and anxiety, the opening, making the presentation, engaging the audience, making an impression and using visual aids, among other topics (British Council BBC, 2018). Focusing on student presentations of case analyses in RM classes, students are often given a structure for their analysis to follow or are asked to use their own creativity in deciding the method of analysis and presentation. Student presentations of case analyses by groups have the benefit of getting the students more deeply involved in analysis and in the application of RM concepts and communications skills. Like all teaching techniques, student presentations have their benefits and drawbacks. Students often resist presentations in groups because such assignments come with complicated time constraints, equity issues and grading issues. In this writer's experience, student group presentations are best followed up by the instructor raising questions and making comments to ensure that all appropriate topics have been covered (Carroll, 2005).

Videos. Videos have long been an excellent source of teaching materials for RM courses. Brief videos, especially, are useful for illustrating and setting the stage for class discussions of concepts, principles, companies, industries or management issues. Today's students are highly attuned to videos, and their classroom use without much prior preparation makes them quite popular. Some research has suggested that students learn new, abstract and novel concepts when they are presented in visual formats. It has been shown that visual media make concepts more accessible than text media and facilitate later recall. Such media include short news clips, movies, documentaries, TV shows, facilitate interactive learning and thus are useful for teaching RM (Science Education and Resource Center, 2018).

Technology and social media. The use of computer-based technologies, the internet and social media has grown significantly in the past decade and they certainly characterize the future. The days of instructors going into class just with chalk and markers is history and the use of PowerPoint presentations has become routine, often to the point of boredom. Today, wireless classrooms are quickly becoming standard and students are seeking innovative teaching materials and methods. Most textbooks today are available in digital copies and digital platforms for courses are becoming commonplace. Social media is one of the most current, popular and dynamic developments in RM education. New technologies like Web 2.0 and social media (Facebook, Twitter, Instagram, LinkedIn, etc.) offer an opportunity for a more holistic, hands on and experiential learning experience. Social media, for example, the use of Twitter, is being experimented with more and more in RM-type classes.

There are a number of reasons why Twitter is appropriate and important to the field of responsible management, but one of the major reasons is that it is conducive to providing resources and communications on issues and topics that are changing daily, often hourly. And, Twitter is fast, fun and free (New Media, 2018). One of the major characteristics of the student age group currently studying responsible management is that they insist upon current, up-to-date, examples of and information about the matters that are making the news daily. In fact, the age group that would likely be studying RM is one of the largest groupings of Twitter users today (Statista, 2016).

At one time, students in business were content to study the classic, controversial social, environmental and ethical issues in the field (e.g., Enron, WorldCom, Tyco, BP oil spill, Flint, Michigan water crisis, etc.), but in recent years this author has discovered that students respond better to examples that have occurred within their recent, adult, memories. For university students, this typically means case studies or events that are less than about 3 years old, which to some extent defines their emerging adulthood period when they have begun to take an interest in these issues. In addition, today's students favor examples about companies with which they are quite familiar; for example, Google, Microsoft, Nike, Uber, Starbucks, Amazon, and Walmart, just to name a few. Indeed, with the use and popularity of social media, it can easily be argued that attention spans have greatly compressed to what is happening this month, week, or today.

In addition, the business world itself has been redefined by the digital revolution and social media accessibility; for example, Twitter, wherein information and opinions are disseminated on a real-time, instantaneous, basis (Euromonitor International, 2017). The digital times in which we live have changed the way business is conducted and it has changed how news, issues and CSR controversies have been reported, debated and resolved. And, it must be added, that this easy and quick availability of information and opinions is occurring on a local, national and global scale. Thus, it has been found that Twitter provides the ideal type of communication device for staying current in a field in which issues and examples are changing and occurring daily, even hourly. With the ubiquitous use of smart phones (everyone has one, all the time), including tablets and laptop computers, Twitter provides an almost perfect match for educational use in the field of responsible management (Seto-Pamies and Carroll, 2019).

Role playing. Role playing as a teaching strategy in management and business education has a long history with mixed results. Under the guidance of an experienced instructor, however, role playing offers definite benefits in teaching and learning responsible management. Role playing stresses the social nature of learning and offers the opportunity for cooperative behavior that may stimulate students' intellectual and social involvement. Role playing is an educational structure that allows the student participants an immediate opportunity to apply concepts and principles as they are placed in the role of an actor or decision-maker who must take some action

or make some decision regarding a situation, a policy or a decision (Carlton College, Science Education Resource Center, 2018). Among the most important advantages, students are able to immediately apply what they have learned in a relevant, real-world situation. They also may take on a decision-making role that allows or requires them to move beyond their own personal, normal behavioral restraints. In role playing situations, students are able to see the relevance of their own actions, decisions, and behaviors and they may receive immediate feedback from those with whom they are interacting. Instructors may easily and readily create scenarios that involve CSR or RM by using situations that appear in the daily news. Another major advantage is that students who have engaged in role playing report they remember their roles in these scenarios long after the semester ends (Carlton College, SERC, 2018). Feedback from students concerning role playing as a pedagogical device indicates that most students find the experience helpful in allowing them to practice key communicative behaviors and learning to manage their emotions involved in the exercise (Edwards and Gallagher, 2018: 10).

LOOKING FORWARD

It is easier to look back at the fields of CSR and RM, but looking forward is vital as well. Does the field of RM have a dismal or bright future? Where will CSR and RM venture in the future? These questions deserve some consideration. To begin with, the fields of study and practice may be thought of in terms of three conceivable scenarios – Gloomy, Hopeful and Probable (Carroll, 2015). In the Gloomy Scenario, CSR and RM and their related counterparts would begin to fade from the scene and eventually disappear from businesses' agenda. We can dismiss this prospect quickly barring some unforeseen global catastrophe or collapse.

Even in the dire days of the 2007–2008 global financial crisis, responsible management not only held its own but, if anything, became more important as scholars and practitioners came to realize that business irresponsibility helped to make all this a reality.

The Hopeful Scenario occupies the opposite end of the continuum. In this optimistic view, companies all over the globe would grow significantly their CSR commitments and think of RM as more transformational rather than transactional. In considering the current period of world affairs, it does not seem likely that companies will dramatically increase their CSR commitments across the board, although some companies will be more positive and expectant than others. A growing number of social-entrepreneurs, social-intrapreneurs and B Corporations, along with a rise in CSR exemplar firms, points to a bright future, but the sheer numbers of mainstream CSR adopters will far outnumber those establishing the cutting edge. These mainstream adopters pursue RM for a variety of practical motives – seeking competitive advantages, business case rationales, reducing costs, enhancing their reputations, emulating other firms in their industries or fulfilling their own self-identified versions of corporate citizenship. In brief, the companies pursuing instrumental motivations are likely to exceed those engaged in normative motivations such that the Hopeful Scenario is not likely to materialize speedily.

Though not particularly heartening to RM proponents, the Probable Scenario will likely dominate in the foreseen future. Most of the observable and predictable evidence points to the reality that CSR and RM have been stable and consistent in popularity and will continue to grow gradually in importance and implementation. This should be seen in a positive light because with each passing day it seems more and more evident that companies are jumping on board for either defensive or offensive justifications and RM growth continues in a constructive direction. To strengthen this Probable Scenario to reflect its positive trajectory, perhaps we should rename it the Probable *Plus* Scenario. There are a number of reasons why this Probable *Plus* Scenario is likely, but at least three driving forces are clearly identifiable – business acceptance, global growth, and academic passion and proliferation.

There was a time when *business acceptance* of RM was not almost universal, as it is today. We no longer hear of businesses and executives extolling the virtues of Milton Friedmann's preoccupation with profitability. For practical or inspirational reasons, most businesses today have embraced the idea of CSR and RM. They may prefer more fresh or faddish terminology such as sustainability, creating shared value, or managing with purpose, but at their core lies the underlying concept of CSR and RM. Businesses today, across the world, have adapted to society's expectations, maybe not as quickly nor as far as stakeholders would like, but businesses have demonstrably adapted and adopted some degree of RM as integral to their strategies for dealing with society and the public. These implementation postures have run the gamut of what Coro Strandberg, a consultant who has studied this topic, has termed CSR 'Lite,' to CSR Compliant, to CSR Strategic, to CSR Integrated, to Deep CSR (Strandberg, 2002). It is expected that the *compliant* → *strategic* → *integrated* range of postures will be most evident in the years ahead.

Reconcilability with profits is another part of business acceptance. Using 'the business case for CSR' thinking, companies have come to see that their investments in CSR are consistent with their financial pursuits. The 'business case for CSR' is the basic idea that CSR improves the 'bottom line'. Considerable evidence now supports the idea that it makes sound business sense to be engaged in CSR and RM (Carroll and Shabana, 2010). As a result of this business acceptance of CSR and RM, there has been a burgeoning profession of CSR positions appearing at mid-to-upper management levels in companies. They carry various titles such as CSR Officer, Vice President of CSR, Director of Philanthropy, Director of Sustainability, Compliance and Ethics Officers, and other variations. When this writer began teaching Business and Society in the early 1970s, a student one day said to me, 'Professor, I want to get a job in business and society.' I was shocked and laughed, telling him that there were no such jobs! Isn't it amazing how times have changed and CSR has become a mainstream management position over the past 50 years or so.

Global growth is the second driving force behind CSR's and RM's success and continuing expansion. Evidence of RM's growth and acceptance around the world has spanned from developed to developing economies. In Europe, for example, the growth of CSR and RM over the past decade or more has been remarkable. It has exceeded growth rates virtually everywhere else. Beyond Europe, CSR growth has proliferated in developing countries everywhere. CSR theory and research has exploded in Asia, Africa, India and South America, just to mention a few places. Almost every week this writer is contacted a couple of times by new and older scholars around the world seeking advice on CSR research or teaching. Many of them are just discovering the topic.

The third driving force behind CSR and RM's success has been *academic proliferation* of interest and research in the topics. Academic interest across many disciplines has greatly increased in the past decade. Books, articles, journals, encyclopedias, dictionaries, papers at meetings, blogs, postings on social media, and professional conferences have all increased in number, attendance and quality as attention is being drawn to CSR and RM. This has been occurring globally. These topics are gaining increased attention from within business schools and from other schools on campuses as well. Once these topics have been sanctioned with academic legitimacy, and they have, a whole new world of possible research is opened up. Recently, this writer visited with two academic scholars

from India who came to the United States to get caught up on all that is going on here in the realm of CSR and RM. This is the type of global exchange that is now taking place. In short, scholars are ramping up their interest and research on these topics and this portends a bright future for the topics from the halls of academe.

SUMMARY AND CONCLUSIONS

The field of responsible management teaching, research and learning has been growing steadily for over 50 years, driven significantly by the interest in and growth of the CSR movement. Since the new millennium, the field has increased exponentially in popularity and necessity in both developed and developing countries around the world. A field known as Responsible Management education has emerged and has led to improved management processes, policies, and decisions, improved organizational performance and more satisfied stakeholders both within and without enterprises of all sizes. The field has operated under a number of different nomenclatures as competing and complimentary frameworks have become the order of the day. At their core, however, they all build upon the ideas of CSR and the concept of responsible management.

Many benefits for students and society have occurred due to these trends, and instructors in colleges and universities have employed a variety of approaches, all striving to keep up with or exceed AACSB accrediting standards. Other groups have also participated in the development of standards and ideals; for example, the Principles of Responsible Management Education (PRME), an initiative of the UN Global Compact (PRME, 2019). The mission of PRME is to transform business and management education and to develop responsible leaders of tomorrow. Dedicated specialty courses have appeared alongside required and elective courses in offering the relevant concept coverage needed for effective responsible management. Many different approaches and pedagogical issues have arisen, and this chapter is but one in this volume aimed at improving the status of teaching and learning in this field.

The field of RM has experienced a robust past and it has an upbeat future. Three driving forces, in particular, have accelerated this trend. First, businesses all over the world have accepted the concepts of CSR and responsible management, and a burgeoning profession of organizational positions have been appearing in the mid-to-upper management levels of most companies – CR Officer, CSR Officer, Director of Sustainability, Director of Compliance, Ethics Officer, and so on. Business-related organizations advocating RM have emerged. For example, Business for Social Responsibility (BSR, 2020), a global business organization. A second driving force has been swift global growth and particularly developments in emerging economies. We have witnessed its mounting popularity and acceptance across the globe. In Europe, the growth of RM interest and programming over the past decade or more has clearly exceeded the interest anywhere in the world. Beyond Europe, RM thinking is rapidly catching on and growing in Asia, Australia, Africa, India and South America, and it continues in the United States and Canada, just to mention a few places. A third driving force behind RM's progress and stability has been academic acceptance, legitimacy and proliferation. Academic approval of teaching and research in RM has never been higher and the variety and quality of publications on the topic have been countless and they are increasing in number. The explosion of books, articles, conferences, websites, encyclopedias, social media postings, and blogs among academics have been staggering. RM is expected to endure and prosper on its rising trajectory and RM is quickly becoming one of the most vital topics in life-long learning for business education. Teaching, learning and research in responsible management is an industry that is on the rise.

REFERENCES

AACSB (2018) 2013 Eligibility Procedures and Accreditation Standards for Business Accreditation, Revised July 1, 2018. Tampa, FL. p. 35.

Bowen, H. R. (1953) *Social Responsibilities of the Businessman*. New York: Harper & Row.

British Council BBC (2018) Student presentations. [Online] Available at: www.teaching english.org.uk/article/student-presentations. Accessed 23 July 2018.

Brown, J. A., Buchholtz, A. and Dunn, P. (2016) Moral salience and the role of goodwill in firm–stakeholder trust repair. *Business Ethics Quarterly*, 26, 181–199.

Brunstein, J., Sambiase, M. F. and Brunnquell. C. (2018) An assessment of critical reflection in management education for sustainability: a proposal on content and form of shared value rationality. *Sustainability*, 10, June. doi:10.3390/su10062091.

Bundy, J. and Pfarrer, M. D. (2015) A burden of responsibility: the role of social approval at the onset of a crisis. *Academy of Management Review*, 40, 345–369.

Business for Social Responsibility (BSR) (2020) The business of a better world. [Online] Available at: www.bsr.org/en/about. Accessed 8 January 2020.

Carlton College, Science Education Resource Center (2018) Role playing. [Online] Available at: https://serc.carleton.edu/introgeo/ interactive/roleplay.html. Accessed 1 August 2018.

Carroll, A. B. (Ed.). (1977) *Managing Corporate Social Responsibility*. Boston, MA: Little Brown Company.

Carroll, A. B. (1979) A three-dimensional conceptual model of corporate social performance. *Academy of Management Review*, 4, 497–505.

Carroll, A. B. (1991) The pyramid of corporate social responsibility: toward the moral management of organizational stakeholders. *Business Horizons*, 34, 39–48.

Carroll, A. B. (1999) Corporate social responsibility: evolution of a definitional construct. *Business & Society*, 38(September), 268–295.

Carroll, A. B. (2005) An ethical education. *BizEd*, January–February, 136–140.

Carroll, A. B. (2015) Corporate social responsibility: the centerpiece of competing and complimentary frameworks. *Organizational Dynamics*, 44, 87–96.

Carroll, A. B. and Brown, J. A. (2018) Corporate social responsibility: a review of current concepts, research and issues. In Weber, J. and Wasieleski, D. (Eds.), *Corporate Social Responsibility*. Bingley: Emerald Publishing. pp. 39–69.

Carroll, A. B., Brown J. A. and Buchholtz, A. K. (2018) *Business & Society: Ethics, Sustainability and Stakeholder Management*, 10th ed. Boston, MA: Cengage Learning.

Carroll, A. B. and Hall, J. (1987). Strategic Management Processes for Corporate Social Policy. In King, W. R. and Cleland, D. I. (Eds.), *Strategic Planning and Management Handbook*. New York: Van Nostrand Reinhold Co. pp. 129–144.

Carroll, A. B. and Shabana, K. M. (2010) The business case for corporate social responsibility: a review of concepts, research and practice. *International Journal of Management Reviews*, 12, 85–105.

Carroll, A. B., Lipartito, K. J., Post, J. E., Werhane, P. H. and Goodpaster, K. E. (Executive editor) (2012) *Corporate Responsibility: The American Experience*. Cambridge: Cambridge University Press.

Committee for Economic Development (1971). *Social Responsibilities of Business Corporations*. New York: Committee for Economic Development.

Davis, K. (1960) Can business afford to ignore social responsibilities? *California Management Review*, 2, 70–76.

Davis, K. (1973) The case for and against business assumption of social responsibilities. *Academy of Management Journal*, 16, 312–322.

Edwards, M. S. and Gallagher, E. C. (2018). Oh, Behave! Insights and Strategies for Teaching Business Ethics to GenY Students. *Journal of Business Education and Scholarship of Teaching*, 2(1), 1–18.

Eells, R. and Walton, C. (1974) *Conceptual Foundations of Business*, 3rd ed. Burr Ridge, IL: Irwin.

Epstein, E. M. (1987) The corporate social policy process: beyond business ethics, corporate social responsibility, and corporate social responsiveness. *California Management Review*, 29, 99–114.

Euromonitor International (2017) The digital revolution mainstreaming in business operations. [Online] Available at: https://blog. euromonitor.com/2017/09/digital-revolution-mainstreaming-business-operations.html. Accessed 22 January 2018.

Frederick, W. C. (1960) The growing concern over business responsibility. *California Management Review*, 2, 54–61.

Frederick, W. C. (2006) *Corporation Be Good! The Story of Corporate Social Responsibility*. Indianapolis, IN: Dog Ear Publishing.

Freeman, R. E. (1984) *Strategic Management: A Stakeholder Approach*. Boston, MA: Pitman Publishers.

Greenwood, W. T. (1964) *Issues in Business and Society: Readings and Cases*. New York: Houghton Mifflin Publishers.

Heald, M. (1970) *The Social Responsibilities of Business: Company and Community, 1900–1960*. Cleveland, OH: Case Western Reserve University Press.

Jacoby, N. H. (1973) *Corporate Power and Social Responsibility*. New York: Macmillan.

Johnson, H. L. (1971) *Business in Contemporary Society: Framework and Issues*. Belmont, CA: Wadsworth.

Jones, T. M. (1980) Corporate social responsibility revisited, redefined. *California Management Review*, Spring, 59–67.

Manne, H. G. and Wallich, H. C. (1972) *The Modern Corporation and Social Responsibility*. Washington, DC: American Enterprise Institute for Public Policy Research.

McGuire, J. W. (1963) *Business and Society*. New York: McGraw–Hill.

New Media (2018) Characteristics of Twitter. [Online] Available at: https://impactoftwitter. weebly.com/characteristics-of-twitter.html. Accessed 2 August 2018.

Porter, J. (2008) Using ex-cons to scare MBAs straight. *Bloomberg BusinessWeek* 24 April. Available at: www.bloomberg .com/news/articles/2008-04-23/using-ex-cons-to-scare-mbas-straight. Accessed 22 July 2019.

Preston, L. E. and Post, J. E. (1975) *Private Management and Public Policy: The Principle of Public Responsibility*. Englewood Cliffs, NJ: Prentice Hall.

PRME (2019) Principles for Responsible Management Education: An initiative of the UN Global Compact. [Online] Available at: www.unprme.org/about-prme/index.php. Accessed 8 August 2019.

Schwartz, M. S. and Carroll, A. B. (2008). Integrating and unifying competing and complementary frameworks: the search for a common core in the Business and Society field. *Business and Society* 47(2), 148–186.

Science Education and Resource Center, Carlton College (2018) Why use media to enhance teaching and learning. Available at: https://serc.carleton.edu/econ/media/why.html. Accessed 23 July 2018.

Seto-Pamies, D. and Carroll, A. B. (2019) Education for business: using Twitter for teaching and learning in corporate social responsibility and sustainability courses. Unpublished manuscript in progress.

Seto-Pamies, D., Domingo-Vernis, M. and Rabassa-Figueras, N. (2011) Corporate social responsibility in management education: current status in Spanish universities. *Journal of Management and Organization*, 17, 604–620.

Spence, L. J. (2016) Small business social responsibility: expanding core CSR strategy. *Business & Society*, 55 (1), 23–55.

Statista (2016) Number of Twitter users in the US as of February 2016, by age group (in millions). [Online] Available at: www.statista.com/statistics/398152/us-twitter-user-age-groups/. Accessed 6 February 2020.

Steiner, G. (1971) *Business and Society*. New York: Random House.

Stewart, H. and Gapp, R. (2013) The complexity of teaching an emerging paradigm: understanding the university educator's view of CSR. *Journal of Business Ethics Education* 10, 1–22.

Strandberg, C. (December 2002) The Future of Corporate Social Responsibility, https://corostrandberg.com/publication/the-future-of-corporate-social-responsibility/. Accessed 6 February 2020.

Votaw, D. (1973) Genius becomes rare. In Votaw, D. and Sethi, S. P. (Eds.), *The Corporate Dilemma*. Englewood Cliffs, NJ Prentice-Hall.

Walton, C. (1967) *Corporate Social Responsibilities*. Belmont, CA: Wadsworth.

Wartick, S. L. and Cochran, P. L. (1985) The evolution of the corporate social performance model. *Academy of Management Review*, 10, 758–769.

Weybrecht, G. (2017) AACSB Blog: How we talk about responsible management education. [Online] Available at: www.aacsb.edu/blog/2017/june/how-we-talk-about-responsible-management-education. Accessed 5 July 2018.

Wood, D. J. (1991) Corporate social performance revisited. *Academy of Management Review*, 16, 691–718.

Wood, D. J. and Logsdon, J. M. (2008) Educating managers for global business citizenship In Swanson, D. L. and Fisher, D. G. (Eds.), *Advancing Business Ethics Education*. Charlotte, NC: Information Age Publishing pp. 265–284.

Zenisek, T. J. (1979) Corporate social responsibility: a conceptualization based on organizational literature. *Academy of Management Review*, 4, 359–368.

7

Ethics, Sustainability and Management Leadership

Michael S. Pritchard and Elaine E. Englehardt

INTRODUCTION: ETHICS TEACHING IN HIGHER EDUCATION

Beginning in the late 1960s in the United States, ethics in higher education expanded from being taught mainly in philosophy and religion programs to eventually finding a place in virtually every part of the academic curriculum.[1] This growing interest in teaching ethics in higher education seems to have been precipitated largely by public concern about a variety of ethically troubling matters arising in the non-academic world. In addition to intense controversy about the ongoing Vietnam War, there were reports of disastrous DC-10 airline crashes resulting from flawed equipment and poor safety maintenance, highly publicized stories about car safety (such as Ford Pinto gas tank explosions), reports of unsafe workplace conditions, polluted waterways and landfills, the abuse of human participants in medical research (including the infamous, government supported Tuskegee syphilis study), and so on. Philosopher Richard De George cites the US Civil Rights Act of 1964 as the first piece of legislation to result in significant changes in business practices regarding discrimination (De George, 2015: 7). Just a few years later, governmental regulatory bodies such as the Environmental Protection Agency (EPA) and the Occupational Health and Safety Administration (OSHA) were established. In response to widespread international bribery, in 1977 the US government passed the Foreign Corrupt Practices Act, the first legislation that tried to control the behavior of US corporations in foreign countries. In 1978 the National Commission for the Protection of Human Subjects of Biomedical and Behavioral Sciences issued its influential Belmont Report, which still serves as the foundation for ethical guidelines for conducting higher education research involving the use of human subjects. In short, ethics was in the news. There was much to discuss; and it was a good time for the academic world to become more involved in those discussions.

As De George and others have pointed out, many philosophers developed strong interests in trying to apply traditional philosophical theories of ethics (especially those grounded in utilitarian or respect for persons concerns) to the practical ethical issues that were engaging the attention of both the general public and those working in professional areas such as medicine, engineering and business. In 1975 philosopher Peter Singer's *Animal Liberation* targeted factory farming and the meat industry for practices he regarded to be cruel to animals, not the best route for healthful human diets, and ultimately posing serious threats to the environment. Among the first edited textbooks devoted to applying philosophical theories of ethics to a broad range of ethical issues in business were: Tom Beauchamp and Norman Bowie, *Ethical Theory and Business*; Thomas Donaldson and Patricia Werhane, *Ethical Issues in Business: A Philosophical Approach*; and Vincent Barry, *Moral Issues in Business*, all in 1979. In 1982 two more books with a strong philosophical flavor were published; Richard De George's *Business Ethics* and Manuel G. Velasquez's, *Business Ethics: Concepts and Cases*. Soon there were many more such philosophically grounded books on the market. According to De George, philosopher Norman Bowie is credited by many with identifying the 'birthdate' for this emerging academic field of business ethics. Bowie ties it to a business ethics conference held at the University of Kansas in 1974.

During this same period of time, many business schools were tackling the question of to what extent, if any, corporations have special social responsibilities to support the public good.[2] This idea was vigorously challenged by economist Milton Friedman and his followers. In a famous article published in 1970 in *The New York Times*, Friedman argued that the only social responsibility of business is to maximize profits for corporate shareholders (albeit, within the limits of law and ethical custom). This was by no means a consensus view among business leaders at the time, but it gained much support over the next several years.[3] In the mid-1980s Friedman's 'stockholder' view was vigorously challenged by Edward Freeman (1984), who articulated a 'stakeholder' view, insisting that corporations have direct obligations to employees, the communities within which corporations reside, and others who have a stake in how corporations affect the world in which they operate. According to Archie Carroll and Juha NaEsi (1997), a stakeholder view was firmly in place in Finnish business schools as early as 1965. It was developed by Eric Rhenman and Stylmne Bengt. They characterized stakeholders as 'individuals and groups who are depending on the firm in order to achieve their goals and on whom the firm is depending for its existence'. This mutual dependency is offered as an ethical basis for understanding the responsibilities of corporations to extend far beyond promoting the profits of stockholders.

Higher education's efforts to broaden ethics education in the 1970s and 1980s were aided by the establishment of ethics centers, both inside and outside of academic settings. Foremost among the first centers was New York's non-profit Hastings Center, which in 1969 established itself as the world's first bioethics institute. Soon, however, it expanded its range of interests to include ethics wherever it might be presented in higher education. In the late 1970s it sponsored a three-year interdisciplinary project that assembled a large group of distinguished ethics teachers from a broad range of academic disciplines to examine together the question of what should be the aims and goals of teaching ethics, given its growing place in higher education. In 1980, the Hastings Center published the results of its project. In addition to featuring a comprehensive volume on the teaching of ethics in higher education edited by Daniel Callahan and Sissela Bok, it published a set of modules on special areas that were emphasizing ethics education at that time.

The surprising result of the Hastings Center project was that, despite the large differences among the disciplinary areas represented, there emerged a consensus statement about what the basic aims and goals of teaching ethics in higher education should be. These aims and goals are presented and explained in the Callahan and Bok edited book, *Ethics Teaching in Higher Education* (1980: 61–74). They are also endorsed in each of the accompanying shorter monographs about teaching ethics in specific disciplinary areas, such as business, education, engineering, journalism, law, medicine, policy making, psychology and the social sciences.

The five aims and goals of teaching ethics in higher education are still regarded by many today (including us) to be as valuable today as when they were first articulated in 1980. The large and diverse Hastings Center team of ethics educators agreed that ethics education should strive to:

- Stimulate the moral imagination
- Provide assistance in recognizing ethical issues
- Provide assistance in analyzing key ethical concepts and principles
- Stimulate a sense of responsibility
- Suggest ways of dealing constructively with ethical disagreement and ambiguity in areas of practical, ethical concern.

A striking feature of this list is that each item presumes that the students engaged in the study of ethics in higher education, whether they realize it or not, are already somewhat familiar with the subject. Just as logic students come into their classes with some familiarity with the subject, ethics students come into their classes with some familiarity with ethics. An educational aim in both cases is to help students refine and improve abilities they have had for some time.

A second feature of this list is its emphasis on the importance of students attending to the details of specific contexts in which ethical concerns arise. On the one hand, ethical issues involving, say, civil engineering may require attending to details well understood only by those with engineering expertise of a certain sort. On the other hand, if the issues involve,

for example, how visually impaired pedestrians are expected to cross streets safely when a roundabout replaces the more traditional stop-and-go intersections governed by traffic lights or stop signs, more than engineering expertise is needed. What is needed is ethics education that helps students appreciate, not only the ethical significance of matters peculiar to their own areas of expertise, but the importance of being able to communicate well with those who have other relevant areas of expertise, experience, or competence.

It is clear that the Hastings Center aims and goals are offered with a steady eye on their practical implications. They focus on sensitivities and skills that can help students more reflectively deal with ethical problems they are likely to encounter. They emphasize the importance of being open to new ideas, many of which come from others, whether from within or outside one's own area of special expertise.

Many would argue that a solid grasp of the leading philosophical theories of ethics should have an important role to play in pursuing this end. It is interesting that the Hastings Center aims and goals do not suggest that the practical ends of ethics education require students to engage themselves fully with these theories, learning about their nuanced differences and similarities and how to apply them to the particular practical ethical issues of the day. Distinct from this is being able to recognize and employ many of the fundamental ideas that can be found in these theories. For example, utilitarian approaches to ethics emphasize the importance of the expected and actual consequences of decisions, Kantian approaches emphasize the importance of respect for persons, and virtue theories emphasize the importance of developing and putting into practice dispositions to act fairly, benevolently, and with integrity. But common morality supports all of these ethical values, as well.

Philosopher Michael Davis (2009) suggests that in having students in business or professional ethics classes examine the ethical appropriateness of options available to them as imagined practitioners, they should ask a series of questions that they can readily understand without having first to study the grand theories of philosophical ethics:

- Harm test – does this option do less harm than any alternative?
- Publicity test – would I want my choice of this option published in the newspaper?
- Defensibility test – could I defend my choice of this option before a Congressional committee, a committee of my peers, or my parents?
- Reversibility test – would I think the choice of this option good if I were one of those adversely affected by it?
- Virtue test – what would I become if I choose this option often?
- Professional test – what might my profession's ethics committee say about this option?
- Colleague test – what do my colleagues say when I describe the problem and suggest this option as my solution?
- Organization test – what does the organization's ethics officer or legal counsel say about this?

Davis does not offer this list as the only possible, or even the best, list that might be used. But he says that his students in practical ethics courses find it useful when they reflect on the practical ethical problems raised in those courses. They understand these questions and their appeal to what seems to them to be common sense. Those who are familiar with philosophical ethical theories might see connections between some of these questions and particular ethical theories, but Davis questions whether introducing those theories is wise in such courses. The basic problem he worries about is the amount of time that would have to be devoted to an adequate introduction (one that addresses philosophically nuanced aspects of the theories and points out commonly misunderstood basic features of the theories and their applications). Furthermore, says Davis, those teachers whose background in ethical theory is rather limited often fail to appreciate how problematic certain interpretations of the theories can be. So, Davis concludes:

Using moral theory in a course in business or professional ethics is like calculating logarithms from scratch when you have a reliable table available (and are not good at mathematics). You will take more time doing the calculation, have more errors (because of the complexity of the calculations), and (if, but only if, all goes well) end up with much the same result as if you had used the table. (2011: 56)

A notable feature of Davis's list is that the questions posed seem well suited for a defensive approach to ethical decision-making – posing a possible choice and then testing it against challenges. Going through such a defensive exercise certainly can require much careful reflection, perhaps resulting in better decision-making. However, in addition to taking up the task of asking such defensive questions, students should be encouraged to ask more positive questions about whether the options they favor can be expected to promote good consequences. Also, from a leadership perspective, they should ask how their favored option fares in contexts in which decisions are made with others, not simply as individuals.

Davis's questions take an individual, common sense approach to practical ethics and decision making. While this works well for situations calling for individual decision-making, it is important to consider relational complications that can arise for managers when operating in an organizational setting. A manager's responsibilities relate not only to discouraging harms of various sorts, but also to leading one's unit or even the entire organization in positive directions that are compatible with the organization's commitment to being socially responsible. When promoting sustainability is included among the organization's goals, managers need to realize that this requires the coordination of individuals in the organization to work together in figuring out ways to serve an end that is much larger than the organization's concern with profitability or even with enhancements of the local community within which the organization resides.

If we consider the role of leadership in business management, the importance of supporting a notion of shared responsibility, not just individual responsibility, becomes more evident. Philosopher Daniel Wueste sees leadership as relational in the sense that it is about 'relationships between and among persons that involve the potential for significant impact on human well-being' (2009: 7). Leadership's relational features, he says, make it evident that leadership has an ethical dimension. If we include ethical commitment to sustainability as a fundamental feature of managerial leadership, then it may also be necessary to include more than the impact on human well-being as a leadership concern. We will see this when discussing Randall Curren's approach to sustainability ethics below.

In any case, whether employing ethical theory or something like Davis's list of already familiar questions, rigorous, careful reflection is called for in the study of business ethics. The aims and goals of teaching ethics in business were subjected to close examination by the Hastings Center group. Topics typically taught included: general questions about relationships between laws, regulations and ethics in business; obligations to customers, stockholders and stakeholders, as well as employee rights and obligations; and more specific concerns about such matters as conflicts of interest, bribery, employee loyalty, hiring and firing practices, diversity in the workplace, and whistle-blowing. In addition, the establishment in the early 1970s of OSHA and the EPA, along with growing concerns about the long-term effects of business and industry on the environment brought new dimensions into the study of business ethics.

More recently, questions about the environmental sustainability of today's global business practices have entered center stage. This has given rise to an upsurge of programs in ethics and sustainability in business schools, particularly at the graduate and undergraduate levels in business management. How ethics and sustainability might be integrated effectively in such programs is a challenging question, and a central concern of what follows in this chapter.

SUSTAINABILITY ETHICS

At the outset it is important to say something about what the mix of 'ethics' and 'sustainability' involves. Attention needs to be given not simply to the sustainability of this or that way of doing things by a particular company for the near future. The fundamental questions are about whether present-day business practices collectively are sustainable in the long run. To explain how ethics relates to this broader, longer-term concern with sustainability, we will draw on the recent work of philosopher Randall Curren.[4] Curren advocates integrating sustainability ethics throughout the academic curriculum of higher education. He also advocates this for the K–12 curriculum. Our focus, however, is on undergraduate and graduate programs in management.

Sustainable behavior is characterized by Curren as living in ways that protect opportunities to live well far into the future, and not just for present generations, but for future ones as well. With this in mind, leaders in management should ask themselves what they might do in their business roles that will support a sustainable future. For example, even though the United States is not part of the 2016 Paris Agreement, this should not encourage ethical business leaders to lessen their goals and progress toward a more sustainable planet. Leaders in management should be concerned to join forces with business and industry to develop and implement practices for reducing the carbon footprint of facilities, product design, manufacturing and production processes, and consumptive practices such as travel. Curren (2019) offers several principles of sustainability ethics that can be applied to managerial leadership. He grounds these principles in basic features of common morality shared by nearly everyone.[5] This ensures that he is not relying on ethical perspectives understood and accepted only by, say, philosophers. His special focus is on ecologically sustainable practices and renewable natural capital.

Curren's first principle is to *'Take care to ensure that the totality of human practices is ecologically sustainable'* (p. 280). This is an ethical duty to not harm and to create well-being within renewable natural capital (RNC). It includes attending to areas of concern such as 'atmospheric carbon, phosphorus runoff, land cover conversion, atmospheric aerosol loading and nitrogen removal, and pollution' (p. 280). Managers have an ethical responsibility to favor choices that are harmonious with the long-term stability of these natural systems as well as others.

Curren's second principle also involves an ethical duty not to harm: *'Take care to ensure that the throughput requirements of human practices are compatible with the projected provisioning capacity of natural systems.'* To this he adds the corollary, *'Take care to ensure that the human attributes, practices, institutions, systems, and policies within your control, authority, or influence are conducive to ecological and throughput sustainability'* (p. 280).

Curren's third principle insists on fairness, another matter of ethical importance: *'Seek fair terms of cooperation conducive to sustainability. Actors whose actions affect each other have an obligation to cooperate in negotiating fair terms of cooperation in living in a manner that is collectively sustainable'* (p. 282).

The fourth principle ethically prescribes avoiding blocking maneuvers: *'Do not obstruct transparency and cooperation with regard to sustainability'* (p. 283).

Finally, the fifth principle ethically prohibits subjecting others to unreasonable risks: *'Do not subject individuals or collectivities to detrimental reliance. Do not cause anyone to be in a position of fundamental reliance on hazardous or vulnerable systems or resources – systems or resources that cannot be relied on without exposure to unreasonable risk to their fundamental interests'* (p. 284). Curren offers the Dust Bowl of the American prairies in the 1930s as an illustration violating

this principle. Homesteaders were offered inducements to farm land that was not suitable for that purpose, and this resulted in virtually destroying the grasslands that made up what was then the second largest ecosystem in North America.

To refer to something's sustainability is to attend to its ability to last or endure for some time into the future in its current or improved condition. An ice cube's ability to retain its solidity when exposed to temperatures well above freezing quickly diminishes – it will not be sustained. Ordinarily, the sustainability of a single ice cube does not raise ethical questions. However, the sustainability of ice formations in the Arctic Circle does, as their melting can have disastrous consequences for human and other life forms. Especially if human intervention can prevent these consequences from occurring, ethical questions about whether, when and what preventive measures should be undertaken loom large. Similar questions arise over the sustainability of our use of valued unrenewable natural resources.

Curren's contention is that sustainability ethics needs to become pervasive across academic curricula at every level. He begins his article thus:

> It is no exaggeration to say that the aggregate unsustainability of the ways we live now is diminishing the life prospects of the growing population we are collectively engendering, not to mention the prospects for countless other forms of life on this planet. This makes sustainability a matter of pervasive and fundamental importance, and it is one we would be well advised to teach systematically and at all levels of instruction. (p. 273)

Management programs help prepare students to assume roles in business and industry that can have a significant impact on how well environmental concerns are treated. Given their emphasis on leadership in management, undergraduate and graduate programs in management fall well within the scope of Curren's concern with teaching sustainable ethics. Our focus is on how these programs might effectively approach this task of teaching sustainability ethics.

RETROSPECTIVE AND PROSPECTIVE ETHICAL CONCERNS

It is clear that, to whatever extent the world of business and industry might have contributed to the environmental problems we face today, it must play a fundamental role in helping us to resolve, or at least mitigate, them. For corporations to try to avoid this role is to shun corporate responsibility. For them to accept present and future responsibility in addressing the sustainability challenges before us means that leaders in management need to play a key role. In regard to management in business and industry, ethical awareness, reflection and resolve are needed. A comprehensive study of the ethical issues this raises must include much more than looking back to try to determine who might be held responsible for causing the environmental challenges we face today. More importantly, it should include asking what roles various groups of people should play in attempting to remedy, or at least bring under better control, the sustainability problems we are now facing – however they might have come about. Our thesis is that managers in business have fundamental responsibilities in this future-oriented sense; and academic programs in business schools that focus on ethics and sustainability have an opportunity to lead the way.

In what follows, we outline some ways in which these programs might pursue this opportunity. In doing so, we emphasize the usefulness of discussing stories that illustrate the transformation of economically successful businesses from being unfriendly to the environment into companies that are adopting more environmentally sustainable practices, while at the same time attempting to retain their good standing economically. These stories can be

discussed in ways that embrace something like the Hastings Center ethical objectives in teaching and studying ethics.

INTERFACE CARPETS

The story of Interface Carpets is one of an already highly successful industrial firm that underwent a remarkable transformation in becoming a model of environmental leadership. From its inception in 1973 Interface had been on a consistent track of economic success. It specialized in the design, manufacture and sale of modular carpet tiles. Its modular approach to carpeting enables the easy installation and maintenance of carpets in ways that are adaptable to a variety of shapes and sizes of rooms, hallways and other areas suitable for carpeting.

The most celebrated figure in Interface's story is the late Ray Anderson, its founder and CEO until his death in 2011(Anderson, 2009). However, Interface's economic success and dedication to environmental sustainability did not stop with his passing, and his example continues to inspire others to undertake business ventures that are committed to environmentally friendly practices. Equally important, even during his career as the CEO of Interface, Anderson was not the only environmental leader in helping Interface make its transformation. In fact, as the Interface story will make clear, just launching a project like its 'Mission Zero' (discussed below) could not have been successful without relying on the leadership of many.

Through his strong, innovative leadership style, Ray Anderson helped take Interface during its first 20 years to the top of the carpet manufacturing industry. Part of his leadership style was to listen carefully to those around him at Interface, as well as to Interface's customers. In the mid-1990s, Jim Hartzfeld, an Interface manager with an MBA and background as a chemical engineer, reported to Anderson that a valued Interface customer wanted to know what impact Interface was having on the environment. Anderson had to admit that this was not a question he had ever seriously entertained.

Up to this point, Anderson had been satisfied that his company was in compliance with all the environmental regulations that applied to the carpet industry. Interface was a law-compliant operation, and a very profitable one at that. This, he had thought, was quite adequate. But, now wondering if this would seem adequate to Interface's questioning customer, Anderson for the first time began exploring literature that could help him give a more complete account of his industry's relationship to environmental sustainability. Among his readings was Paul Hawken's *The Ecology of Commerce* (1993). This book convinced him that he should take a critical look at how Interface was faring in regard to actual environmental challenges, rather than assume that satisfying current regulations was sufficient. He ordered detailed examinations of Interface's reliance on the use of unrenewable resources, its production and handling of excessive waste materials, and its release of emissions into the surrounding environment. Of course, he could not himself conduct all of these examinations. That would require the work of various Interface employees and consultants. No one person could have the necessary expertise in all of these areas. Nor did he have the time to conduct all of these examinations himself. However, he could read and discuss the results. What was required was a team of experts, each of whom would themselves serve as leaders in this intensive, comprehensive examination of the environmental impact of Interface as it was currently operating.

Anderson was not pleased with what this examination revealed. His own critical assessment involved looking imaginatively 'down the road' at the likely environmental impact his company would have on future generations unless radical changes were made. What he concluded was that simply continuing to satisfy current regulatory standards would fall far short of what was needed. Unless Interface and other industrial companies dramatically changed their ways now, he reflected, they could fairly be regarded as 'plunderers of the earth', at the expense of future generations. And he became concerned that, in just a short time, critics could justifiably argue that CEOs like himself should even be jailed. The impact of reading Hawken's book, Anderson said, was like being thrust in the heart by a spear.

How could Hawken's book have such an impact on Anderson? Interface was not specifically mentioned by Hawken. There was no analysis of the short- or long-term environmental impact of Interface's manufacturing processes beyond what might be required by law. Only a closer examination of Interface's operations could determine that. But current laws and regulations did not require that this be undertaken, at least not at the level of analysis that could show the need for Interface to change its ways. However, now aroused by Hawken's concerns, Anderson ordered that this task be undertaken at Interface. Others might attempt to avoid such a responsibility by simply looking the other way, but Anderson would not do this.

A SHARED ETHICAL CHALLENGE

As noted above, Anderson could initiate such an extensive examination of Interface's environmental impact, but he could not proceed alone. This task would require the cooperation and determination of many at Interface – managers, scientists, engineers and staff at several levels. Although Anderson was educated as an engineer, no single engineer has expertise in all the areas of science and engineering that Interface had to make use of in manufacturing and producing carpet tiles, including its production and disposal of waste materials. Hundreds of people were employed at Interface, including managerial leaders in the various areas that had an effect on the environment.

Eventually, based on the input of those enlisted to help analyze Interface's environmental impact, Anderson announced a plan for radical changes that would be needed at Interface. His team of analysts and advisors, both from within and outside of Interface, had provided him with critical information about Interface's current use of unrenewable resources, its production and handling of excessive waste materials, and its release of potentially harmful emissions into the surrounding environment. They also made suggestions about what might be done to dramatically reduce these negative factors without necessarily adversely affecting either Interface's product or its profitability. Called 'Mission Zero', Anderson's new program set 2020 as the target date for eliminating any negative impact that Interface might have on the environment. Anderson's death in 2011 meant that he would not be around to evaluate the degree of Interface's success in finally achieving this goal. But in 2009 he estimated that Interface was halfway there.

Interface has continued its commitment to 'Mission Zero' well after Anderson's passing. Anderson's efforts continue to inspire those at Interface and elsewhere. Each year an annual gathering of those inspired by Anderson, whether from Interface or other places that share Interface's commitment to environmental sustainability, celebrate his determination and declare their own commitment to furthering a more sustainable environment.

Although the story of Ray Anderson and Interface Carpets represents only a small segment of industry, it offers a rich and inspiring example for inclusion in ethics education in the areas of management, responsibility and sustainability in the business world.

Each of the Hastings Center objectives can be applied to the context of Interface Carpets. First, we can readily see how Anderson's moral imagination was stimulated. The key original stimulus came from outside the everyday operations of Interface – an unexpected question from a customer. Yet, Anderson's willingness to listen to others, his caring about satisfying customers, his inquisitiveness, and his courage to pursue matters to the point that new ideas might cause him to make radical changes all fed his moral imagination in this instance. The fact that he had never before asked these sorts of questions about his business does not indicate that he lacked the ability to engage them seriously. He did need some prodding, but this was provided by the inquisitive customer, a trusted Interface manager (Jim Hartzfeld), and author Paul Hawken.

What one needs to recognize about moral imagination is that it is engaged at a very early age and that it can continue to develop over a lifetime. Ray Anderson exhibited this continued development after he was well into his distinguished career as the CEO of a highly successful business. We might say that he was ready to have his moral imagination stimulated by some gentle prodding.

The second Hastings Center objective, recognizing ethical issues, is also never ending – at least for those like Ray Anderson who remain open to the likelihood that one's moral work is never done. The Hastings Center team of educators was particularly concerned to help us recognize moral issues sooner rather than later. Too often, recognition comes after several crucial oversights have been made and, as a result, greater complications make their entry. Realizing this can prompt being on the lookout for signs that trouble may lie ahead. Anderson might have regretted that he did not anticipate earlier any of the environmental concerns that Hawken's book raises. Even though Anderson eventually committed himself and his company to address these concerns, this happened only after years of contributing to serious environmental problems. With early reflection on the damage that might result from doing 'business as usual', Interface might have been able to avoid much of it earlier rather than later.

The third objective, analyzing key moral concepts and principles, could benefit from an early start, as well. Wastefulness and fairness, for example, are important concepts for young children, albeit in more limited contexts than adults. But they are not unrelated to ideas about what constitutes harm to the environment, what might count as sustainability, what leaving 'as much and as good' for future generations could mean, or what a fair distribution of benefits and harms for present and future generations requires. These are all notions that concerned Anderson as he began to 'look down the road' to try to come to an ethical assessment of the impact on the future Interface could have.

The fourth objective, stimulating one's sense of responsibility, can be seen to come into play throughout the Interface story. But this amounts to much more than simply urging oneself to do what is right. It also involves trying to determine what is right, taking on some responsibility, and doing something about it. At this point it should be clear that there were many more behind the Interface transformation than Ray Anderson. He was the Interface leader, but he was hardly the only doer – or the only one to have concrete ideas about what can and should be done. The task at hand in 'Mission Zero' could be successfully accomplished only by teams working together for a common end. Ray Anderson was fully aware of this, and he took on the responsibility of gathering together teams of experts who could help Interface figure out how best to undertake 'Mission Zero'.

This takes us to the fifth objective, reflecting on constructive ways of dealing with ambiguity, differences and even disagreement with others. This means that attitudes such as 'my way, or no way' need to be discouraged. What Anderson needed was a plan for 'our way' at Interface involving consensus on shared goals to be pursued together.

However, although it might contribute to group consensus, an Interface employee's willingness uncritically to agree with others for the sake of achieving their common goal could be problematic, too. This is a symptom of what sociologist Irving Janis (1982) calls 'groupthink'. Groupthink involves a set of shortcomings Janis says can be commonly found in cohesive groups that encourage their members to defer uncritically to others, especially when

it is believed (accurately or not) that this will help achieve the ends of the leader.[6]

However, as Janis argues, much depends on how those ends are understood. Without the aid of critical and diverse thinking, the results can be most unwelcome even by the leaders themselves. One of Janis's examples of groupthink leading to unwelcome consequences is the bombing of Pearl Harbor, causing much death and destruction and triggering the escalation of military conflict with Japan. U.S. military leaders failed to recognize indications that something like this might happen, something that none of them wanted. Absent from their deliberations was the sort of critical thinking that could have alerted them to the dangers at hand. Janis develops an account of a variety of ways in which cohesive groups can block critical thinking.

Janis suggests several ways in which group leaders can encourage the sort of critical thinking that can resist the pitfalls of groupthink. One line of resistance he suggests is for leaders sometimes to absent themselves from group meetings so their members will feel more free to exercise their own judgment in exploring alternatives. Another is for leaders to assign group members the responsibility to exercise their own critical thinking in assessing actions taken by the group. A third is to invite input from those outside the group who can be expected to bring up important matters for consideration that are likely to be overlooked by those on the inside. These strategies are not safeguards against groupthink, but they can be helpful.

Finally, leaders need to think deeply and carefully about the ends to be sought and acceptable means for pursuing of them. It took a long time for Ray Anderson, with the help of others, to take all these matters into account. And it took moral sensitivity, imagination, courage and the risk of business failure for him to move ahead despite the doubts of many of those around him.

So, Ray Anderson's story is one of both business and ethical success in management. But it is also the story of many others at Interface following his lead and exercising leadership of their own. To do this they had to be willing and able to explore new ways of doing things – and doing them together. Without the team's high degree of competence, determination and willingness to pursue 'Mission Zero', Ray Anderson would have failed. But strong, effective leadership requires strong, effective followers who themselves are also strong, effective leaders.

Fortunately, there were already a number of such follower/leaders employed at Interface who were prepared to respond positively to Anderson's 'Mission Zero' and to provide imaginative and critical leadership in advancing its ends. Anderson was also able to assemble a strong group of advisors outside of Interface.

WORKING TOGETHER

As could be expected, in order for 'Mission Zero' to be pursued effectively, Anderson's followers/leaders needed to commit themselves to the project and to be prepared to confront serious, different challenges – *together*. An important matter to be clarified is what 'working together' might mean. Here the writings of social and political philosopher Margaret Gilbert (1996) are particularly helpful. She begins with the seemingly simple example of taking a walk with someone.

Two people can, quite coincidentally, walk stride for stride next to each other for some distance and then, without exchanging a word, move off in different directions. In some sense, it might be said that they had walked together for a short while. However, in order for them to have been *taking a walk together*, more than this is needed. Going their separate ways at some point calls for no explanation or special acknowledgement. In fact, this is what both might expect if they were to give it any thought. However, even having the same destination (e.g., walking to the same department store) would not, by

itself, indicate that they were taking a walk together. Absent any special indicator that they had agreed to take a walk someplace together, there is no reason to suppose that they are.

Assuming that two people are taking a walk together, problems for them can arise that are different than those that can occur if they are simply walking side-by-side. Simply walking side-by-side next to Chris, for example, Alex might wonder, 'Which way should I go in order to get to the store, left at this corner or straight ahead? Straight ahead is the shorter, faster route, but I might get slowed down by my favorite ice cream shop on the way. It's hard for me to resist, but I really shouldn't allow myself to be distracted by it. So, I'll take the longer route.' Chris, however, may have no interest in the ice cream shop and, therefore, have no hesitation about walking straight ahead. That is, Alex has a problem that is Alex's alone, not Chris's. But if they are taking a walk to the store together, matters are different. For now *they* may have a problem about how to continue their walk *together*. If Alex simply turns to the left without saying anything to Chris, he will have failed to pay proper regard to the fact that they were taking a walk together. Even if it is important to Alex not to walk by the ice cream shop, it is also important to signal something to Chris and not simply walk silently in a different direction. This is an implication of their taking a walk together, rather than simply walking side-by-side for some distance.

Although Gilbert's primary interest is eventually to use her example of walking together to illuminate political relationships, it can also be used to help illuminate issues in management leadership in business. There is a sense in which leaders in management need to understand how they are 'taking a walk with' those to whom they are accountable as their leaders and with those whom they are leading, as well as with those outside their company with whom they are doing business. While these leaders need to understand how, important as it is to know how to work well with others, it is also important for them not to fall into, or to foster, the traps of Janis's 'groupthink' and Sunstein's 'group polarization'.

Although the notion of working together can apply within an organization that is working for its own ends, it can also apply to a much broader notion of working together. Anderson's vision was very broad – one that saw Interface as part of a large set of industries and businesses that collectively have a huge impact on the world that future generations will come into. 'Mission Zero' for Anderson was envisaged as a part of his much larger commitment to environmental sustainability. He saw his responsibility as a business leader to be to set an example to be followed by others. It is the *world*, not just Interface, nor just the carpet industry, that needs saving.

Of course, Anderson had to 'begin at home', but his aim ultimately was global. Hawken's *Ecology of Commerce* has this target as well. As he reflected on Hawken's book, Anderson broadened and deepened his vision – way beyond Interface. He began speaking to audiences everywhere he could, expressing disappointment and concern that so few seemed willing to join him for this needed walk together. His aim was not just for Interface to have 'clean hands', but for all to try, as best they can, to have the same end. Anderson saw this as a matter of leadership responsibility. Thus, he embraced a very inclusive *ethical* mission for leadership in a sustainable business world.

Fortunately, many already working at various levels at Interface were ready to follow Anderson's leadership when he announced 'Mission Zero' as his company's goal. Anderson formed a 'Dream Team' of sustainability advisors. These advisors were not CEOs, but they played essential roles as members of Anderson's team, each of whom was committed to environmental sustainability as a fundamental goal of Interface. He also enlisted the advice of people who previously had no connection with Interface, including Paul Hawken.

In 2012, shortly after Ray Anderson passed away, sustainable business writer and strategist Joel Makower published an article entitled 'Why aren't there more Ray Andersons?' in *Green Biz*. Makower characterizes Anderson as a 'truly enlightened business leader who understood the value of sustainability practices – to increase sales, cut costs, foster innovation, delight employees, engage customers, and build an enviable reputation for his company, even one whose products were based on materials as unnatural as nylon and vinyl.' Makower adds, 'He saw the potential to change the voice of business in the sustainability conversation.' But with Anderson's passing, Makower asked who will succeed him.

This is a good question. The answer, in part, is that there can be only so many CEOs, and few of them could be expected to combine the particular mix of qualities possessed by Ray Anderson to manage their companies. Fortunately, the qualities most essential for strong ethical leadership in sustainability in business can be present in non-CEOs, too. As we have emphasized, even Ray Anderson needed support teams; and he found them both at Interface and elsewhere. What is essential for such teams to be successful is that its members are knowledgeable, dedicated individuals who are committed to working together for the common end of environmental sustainability. Complementarity in their work is needed. Solitary efforts are not sustainable.

Good team members need to engage their moral imagination and have the determination and ability to work well with others. Perhaps most importantly, like Anderson, they need to be willing to continue learning what is needed, to re-examine their ideas and alter their course of action when needed. Although these were strong features of Ray Anderson, having them is not the special preserve of CEOs. However, their absence in a CEO can present a barrier for others in the company who are looking for opportunities to help it improve its environmental record. Anderson also effectively combined his engineering problem-solving ability with never being satisfied that he had learned enough. Thus, seeking answers to difficult questions seems to have whet his appetite for asking more questions. Makower noted in his article that Jim Hartzfeld said of Anderson: 'He was always throughout his entire life and career, learning and reading and talking to people. He was constantly learning in real time, translating into a better way to do something.' That it took special prodding to get him to seek answers about the environmental impact of Interface beyond satisfying regulations indicates that, like all of us, he sometimes needed others to get him started, but his openness to being so nudged seemed evident. As reported by Makower, Hartzfeld added, 'One of his daughters once told me that when she was growing up, they'd always go to the beach for vacation. Ray hated the beach, but everyone else loved it, so he went. Ray would take stacks of books. "We'd come home from vacation tanner," she told me. "Daddy always came back smarter."'

Anderson surrounded himself with environmental leaders both inside and outside Interface on whom he relied in pursuing the goals of 'Mission Zero.' In writing his article 'Why aren't there more Ray Andersons?' Makower interviewed many of these leaders. They noted an entrepreneur's vision in Anderson that centered around environmental sustainability, not just economic success. Still, Makower added: 'We've seen other founders whose companies pushed the envelope on sustainability — Patagonia's Yvon Chouinard, Stonyfield Farm's Gary Hirshberg, Seventh Generation's Jeffrey Hollender, Method's Adam Lowry and Eric Ryan – but none of these built billion-dollar industrial enterprises.' This raises another issue. A handful of CEOs who build billion-dollar enterprises would be helpful in fighting runaway unsustainable business practices. But this would not be sufficient to contain the problem. So, perhaps the question should be: 'Why aren't there many, many more in business, CEOs or managers at many levels, leading the fight against unsustainable practices?' They

are surely needed, as programs in management leadership need to emphasize.

Biologist Janine Benyus, co-founder of Biomimicry 3.8, an innovation consultancy, was a 'Dream Team' member. Makower noted her account of what she took to be Anderson's professorial manner: 'He was always reading. His talks were kind of pedantic – the professor telling you things. What Ray would do was call the authors of every one of these books he had read and get us all together.' Nevertheless, this seemed to work to his advantage, as his talks were well received. However, this is not an essential quality for business leaders in environmental sustainability, or for managerial leadership in general. Makower added yet another Jim Hartzfeld observation: 'He was a trained Georgia Tech engineer. He would wear you out analytically and logically, but he thought as hard and as deep and as powerfully with the intuitive side as he did the logic side.' Again, this seemed to work well for Anderson, but it is not a prerequisite for effective leadership in environmental sustainability.

Makower also discussed Anderson's persistence and determination to proceed even at the risk of serious failure. In the face of resistance by skeptical leaders in other businesses, Anderson seemed to become even more determined to push ahead. He refused to concede that there is an irresolvable conflict between the pursuit of profit and the pursuit of environmental sustainability. Benyus observed: 'This was a guy with an absolute iron fist. He did not suffer fools gladly. He had one of those leadership styles that was really low-key, but which was simmering. People wanted to please him. It wasn't that he was a pushover or trying to be everyone's best friend. He wasn't a softie.' Here what is most significant is Anderson's unwavering commitment, rather than his particular mode of making this evident to those whom he was leading.

A most important trait of Anderson noted by Makower was his willingness to rethink everything, a leadership trait much more common today than in the 1990s when Anderson laid out his 'Mission Zero'. 'Today,' said Makower, 'companies are embracing innovation in new ways, looking outside their walls for ideas and engaging in open innovation that entangles them in new kinds of partnerships with a wide range of external players.' If Makower is right about this shift in embracing innovation then this can be emphasized in teaching sustainability ethics in management, thus encouraging students to embrace this as well – at whatever level of management to which they might aspire.

Makower again cited Janine Benyus:

> Everyone talks about open-source innovation. Most companies bring in McKinsey. [Anderson] brought in Daniel Quinn. I think he brought in soul advice – the technical advice could have come from someone else. He brought in a conscience. He didn't bring in yes people – he brought in the crazies, the court jesters who would tell the truth. Everyone else in the room was squirming, because we brought up really hard things.

Questions about environmental sustainability have not gotten any easier since the 1990s. If anything, they have gotten harder – and more urgent. So, programs in ethics and sustainability in management need to take advantage of a seemingly more receptive atmosphere in today's business world to engage questions about how to tackle the challenges of environmental sustainability.

Makower concluded that Anderson's willingness to take seriously what the 'crazies' had to say helped him form much of his vision for the future. The example of the success of Interface in pursuing its 'Mission Zero' can offer an example of what might be possible for others. Ray Andersons may be rare, but even without more CEOs like him, the Interface story provides us with a model of the essential role that managerial leadership at other levels has to play.

Not only was Anderson the CEO of a very successful business, he was regarded by many he inspired as a 'rock-star' in the environmental sustainability arena. Not many can be expected to match his charisma on stage, CEOs or not. Makower did mention

Paul Polman, former CEO of Unilever, as some day possibly becoming a successor to Ray Anderson. Polman's Sustainable Living Plan for Unilever was launched in 2010. This plan emphasized the importance of trying to change consumer behavior in trying to change the company's sustainability footprint. It also rejected fixating on seeking short-term profits at the expense of a livable future environment.

Polman officially retired from Unilever in July of 2019 after years of advocating for environmental, social and cultural changes. In this same spirit, Unilever's new CEO, Alan Jope, announced plans that the corporation will cut its use of virgin plastic in half, by reducing its absolute use of plastic packaging by more than 100,000 tons and accelerating its use of recycled plastic. According to the Unilever website, this commitment makes Unilever the first major global consumer goods company to commit to an absolute plastics reduction. Jope asserts:

> Our starting point has to be design, reducing the amount of plastic we use, and then making sure that what we do use increasingly comes from recycled sources. We are also committed to ensuring all our plastic packaging is reusable, recyclable or compostable.

> This demands a fundamental rethink in our approach to our packaging and products. t requires us to introduce new and innovative packaging materials and scale up new business models, like re-use and re-fill formats, at an unprecedented speed and intensity. (Unilever, 2019)

Shortly after leaving Unilever in 2019, Polman created a firm called 'Imagine' with his own funds. In the spirit of Ray Anderson's global reach, its aim is to strengthen sustainable development while combating poverty and climate change. Polman's plan is to help companies pursue the sustainability goals of the United Nations with a collective sense of urgency:

> 'The imperative to eradicate poverty and inequality and stem runaway climate change has never been more acute,' Polman wrote in an email to former colleagues and business contacts detailing his new

project. What's more, 'we still miss the collective sense of urgency to move at scale and speed.' (Fourcade, 2019)

Polman may some day stand out with Ray Anderson as an environmental 'rock star.' Still, one need not seek out only environmental 'rock stars' as inspirational models. Helpful as charismatic qualities can be, this is so only insofar as they are joined with more central qualities of leadership in environmental sustainability. These include a basic understanding of what environmental sustainability involves, some ability to recognize what can support it and what threatens it, and a serious commitment to the values of environmental sustainability. It is clear that a charismatic personality can move in the opposite direction, at least in fiction. In the movie *Wall Street*, Gordon Gekko (played by Michael Douglas) certainly was charismatic when he proclaimed, 'Greed is good.' But what he was advocating paid no heed to environmental sustainability, nor sustainability of other sorts, for that matter. Shortly after his speech, he was jailed for his illegal undertakings. (Real-world Ivan Boesky suffered a similar fate. His University of California commencement address in praise of greed allegedly inspired the Gekko speech. Shortly after giving this address he was heavily fined and jailed for his business practices.)

THE NEED FOR 'LESSER LIGHTS' TOO

Admittedly, CEOs like Ray Anderson are inspirational leaders; and it would be good if more were like him. However, as we have insisted, such leaders cannot succeed alone. They depend on strong support at different managerial levels. Fortunately, Anderson had others in his employ, like Jim Hertzfeld, who were more than willing to assume leadership roles in transforming Interface. It is important to recognize that they, too, are exemplary managerial leaders who deserve accolades and emulation. Although less in the limelight

than CEOs, such managers can be found at many places other than Interface, and their stories can be quite compelling.

For example, 3M (Minnesota Mining and Manufacturing Company) adopted its 3M3P plan in 1975 and it is still in operation today. It was the brainchild of 3M environmental engineer and manager Joseph Ling. 3M was once regarded to be one of the largest polluters in the USA. Ling's response was to propose that 3M change its ways and adopt an aggressive pollution prevention program (3P).[7]

Ling's Memorial Tribute at the National Academy of Engineering celebrates his many accomplishments during his lengthy career as a leader in supporting environmental sustainability in industry:

> During his 32-year career in engineering, he had a profound influence worldwide on the direction of environmental policy, philosophy, and industrial environmental practices, as well as on government regulation and legislation. Joe retired in 1984 as vice president, Environmental Engineering and Pollution Control, 3M Company, but continued for another two decades as an advisor and a supporter of myriad academic, industrial, regulatory, and legislative organizations. He was known around the world for his foresight, innovative approaches, and effective implementation of advanced environmental technologies and policies.

Ling came to the United States from China in 1948. He received the University of Minnesota's first doctoral degree in sanitary engineering in 1952. In 1960, he became 3M's first professionally trained environmental engineer and head of the company's Water and Sanitary Engineering Department. In 1975, he established the 3P environmental policy (Pollution Prevention Pays), which specified that 3M would solve its own environmental problems, observe government regulations and assist the government with environmental regulatory matters.[8] In short, this meant that 3M would adopt practices that were designed to prevent pollution in its production processes rather than wait until waste was produced that would then require special treatment. The policy implemented the idea that pollutants are reclaimable natural resources, which properly handled could actually result in greater productive efficiency and cost savings for 3M.

Although Ling was responsible for proposing the 3P plan, he could hardly be credited with coming up with the 8500 pollution prevention activities and programs implemented by 3M in 23 countries around the world over the next 30 years. These activities and programs resulted from 3M encouraging its employees at all levels to propose innovative, cost saving ideas about how to eliminate or lower pollution in its operations. Management leadership at various levels had to play a key role in facilitating this. During this period 3M claims to have avoided producing 2.2 billion pounds of pollutants, thus saving nearly $1 billion.

A key to success in pollution prevention, Ling argued, is cooperation within and among industries. For Ling, worldwide environmental sustainability was the ultimate end. 3M's success in making advancements toward this end and saving money in the process sets an example that challenges the many skeptics who think that progress in environmental sustainability can come only at the expense of lowering profits.

CONCLUSION

Companies like Interface, Unilever and 3M provide large-scale success stories in maintaining their high levels of profitability while making significant strides in promoting environmental sustainability. Many such efforts can be found on a smaller scale as well, and they can all serve to inspire other businesses to make similar efforts. Management programs that are committed to helping their students prepare to play a vital role in transforming more and more businesses into environmentally sustainable enterprises are to be commended and encouraged. Studying businesses that are committed to environmental sustainability as an ethical responsibility should be a major feature of these programs.

Of course, the success some companies have had so far in their efforts to maintain or increase their high profit levels while undergoing major transformations in support of sustainability does not ensure that this can be done by all, or even most, companies. This leaves us with a fundamental question about business priorities: When they clash, which should take priority, sustainability or profits? Given the challenges that the idea of corporate social responsibility present to the stakeholder maximization view, it would seem that there should be a willingness to lower expectations somewhat in the pursuit of profits insofar as the vigorous pursuit of sustainability requires this. In any case, this is a topic well worthy of thoughtful discussion in management leadership programs that have sustainability as a central focus.

The emergence of the academic study of business ethics and corporate social responsibility in the 1970s, combined with more recent concerns about the sustainability of 'business as usual', make clear that ethics has become, and should remain, a central feature of the study of management leadership programs in higher education. Beyond this, books, journals, films and organizations that address ethical issues involving business continue to play a central role in helping all of us come to have a better understanding of the ethical challenges facing us today, and what responsibilities businesses have in addressing them.

Notes

1 See, for example, Englehardt and Pritchard (Eds.), *Ethics Across the Curriculum: Pedagogical Perspectives* (2019) and Callahan and Bok (Eds.), *Ethics Teaching in Higher Education* (1980).

2 For a detailed account of responsible management education from a stakeholder's perspective of corporate social responsibility, see Archie B. Carroll, 'Responsible management education: the role of CSR evolution and traditions', Chapter 6 in this volume.

3 Curious about the legal standing of Friedman's notion about the social responsibility of

corporations, legal scholar Lynn Stout researched this question for several years and found no legal basis for it. See Stout (2012).

4 Our account of Curren's views is based on his essay 'Sustainability ethics across the curriculum', pp. 273–287 in our edited volume *Ethics Across the Curriculum* (Englehardt and Pritchard, 2019).

5 We follow the now common practice of treating 'morality' as roughly synonymous with 'ethics'. The contexts within which these, and related terms, are used typically clarify what their referents are and enable readers to make necessary distinctions (e.g., between 'ethics' as the study of a subject, which can be called 'ethics' or 'morality', and 'ethics' as a prescriptive code of behavior, as in a professional code of ethics or a moral code of a profession).

6 Janis's concept of 'groupthink' has been widely valued, but there are some prominent critics. Cass Sunstein, for example, suggests that the idea of *group polarization* is simpler and it provides a more straightforward basis for predicting the sort of behavior that concerns Janis (Sunstein, 2009: 88). Sunstein recommends a system of 'checks and balances' for countering extremes associated with group polarization. In any case, Janis and Sunstein agree that, absent robust critical thinking, groups can interfere with rather than aid the sort of decision-making that is needed.

7 A detailed discussion of Ling's life and career can be found online under Joseph T. Ling, National Academy of Engineering (2008). Comments here on Ling are based on that memorial tribute. The success of the 3M3P program is prominently featured on 3M's website.

8 In 1976 Ling was elected to membership in the National Academy of Engineering 'For leadership in environmental engineering, specifically in pollution control of air and water.'

REFERENCES

Anderson, Ray, with Robin White (2009) *Confessions of a Radical Industrialist: Profits, People, Purpose – Doing Business by Respecting the Earth*. New York: St Martin's Press.

Beauchamp, Tom and Bowie, Norman (Eds.) (1979) *Ethical Theory and Business*. Englewood Cliffs, NJ: Prentice-Hall.

Barry, Vincent (1979) *Moral Issues in Business*. Belmont, CA: Wadsworth.

Callahan, Daniel and Bok, Sissela (Eds.) (1980) *Ethics Teaching in Higher Education*. New York: Plenum.

Carroll, Archie B. and NaEsi, Juha (1997) Understanding stakeholder thinking: themes from a Finnish conference. *A European Review*, 6(1), 46–51.

Curren, Randall (2019) Sustainability ethics across the curriculum. In Englehardt, Elaine E. and Pritchard, Michael S. (Eds.), *Ethics Across the Curriculum*. New York: Springer. pp. 273–287.

Davis, Michael (2009) The usefulness of moral theory in teaching practical ethics: a question of comparative cost. *Teaching Ethics*, 10(1), 73–4.

Davis, Michael (2011) The usefulness of moral theory in teaching practical ethics: a reply to Gert and Harris. *Teaching Ethics*, 12(1), 56.

De George, Richard (1982) *Business Ethics*. Englewood Cliffs, NJ: Prentice-Hall.

De George, Richard (2015) *A History of Business Ethics*. Markkula Center for Applied Ethics. 17 November, pp. 1–10.

Donaldson, Thomas and Werhane, Patricia (Eds.) (1979) *Ethical Issues in Business: A Philosophical Approach*. Englewood Cliffs, NJ: Prentice-Hall.

Englehardt, Elaine E. and Pritchard, Michael S. (Eds.) (2019) *Ethics Across the Curriculum: Pedagogical Perspectives*. New York: Springer.

Fourcade, Marthe (2019) Unilever former chief moves on with plan to fix the world. Bloomberg, 4 July 2019. [Online] www.bloomberg.com/news/articles/2019-07-04/unilever-s-former-chief-moves-on-with-plan-to-fix-the-world. Accessed 21 November 2019.

Freeman, Edward (1984) *Strategic Management: A Stakeholder Approach*. New York: HarperCollins College.

Friedman, Milton (1970) The social responsibility of business is to increase its profits. *The New York Times Magazine*, 13 September.

Gilbert, Margaret (1996) *Living Together: Rationality, Sociality, and Obligation*. Lanham, MD: Rowman and Littlefield.

Hawken, Paul (1993) *The Ecology of Commerce*. New York: HarperCollins.

Janis, Irving (1982) *Groupthink*, 2nd ed. New York: Houghton-Mifflin.

Ling, Joseph T., National Academy of Engineering (2008) Memorial Tributes: Volume 12. Washington, DC: The National Academies Press.

Makower, Joel (2012) Why aren't there more Ray Andersons? *Green Biz*, August.

Singer, Peter (1975) *Animal Liberation*. New York: HarperCollins.

Stout, Lynn (2012) *The Stakeholder Value Myth: How Putting Shareholders First Harms Investors, Corporations, and the Public*. San Francisco: Berrett-Koehler Publishers.

Sunstein, Cass (2009) *Going to Extremes: How Like Minds Unite and Divide*. Oxford: Oxford University Press.

Unilever (2019) Unilever announces ambitious new commitments for a waste-free world. [Online] 17 October. www.unilever.com/news/press-releases/2019/unilever-announces-ambitious-new-commitments-for-a-waste-free-world.html. Accessed 12 December 2019.

Velasquez, Manuel G. (1982) *Business Ethics: Concepts and Cases*. Englewood Cliffs, NJ Prentice-Hall.

Wueste, Daniel (2009) Ethics and leadership how long have they been together? *Teaching Ethics*, 10(1), 1–10.

8

Critical Responsible Management Education for Sustainable Development

Meredith Storey

INTRODUCTION

Education plays an unquestionable role in preparing students to deal with the sustainability challenges that presently face our planet, society and economy. Educating learners of every age level to understand these global issues and empowering them to act in the interest of our world is the fundamental backbone of education for sustainable development (ESD). If they are to become capable of forming a holistic response to the many sustainability challenges now facing our planet, today's students need to have the knowledge, tools and mindsets of sustainability ingrained in their learning process. Nowhere is this need for focused and embedded education for sustainable development more prevalent than in the curricula that will shape the education of future leaders. Business and management education will play a vital role in informing the future population of business employees and leaders. Students enrolled in business schools or those studying management will face the modern crises of sustainable

development in their future business-driven workplaces and should therefore be educated to address these crises. This bolsters the case (supply) for embedding sustainability in mainstream business and management teaching practices.

Besides the business-demand argument for sustainability-literate graduates, the role of education in shaping a sustainable future should be discussed in much greater depth. The application of critical pedagogy to the field of responsible management education (RME) provides a critical lens for understanding future applications of education for sustainable development. A critical framing of education, informed by critical pedagogy, moves the discussion of 'management education for sustainable development' from being a singular dimension of business schools to become a whole new educational paradigm.

This chapter contributes to the sustainable development conversation in business and management education. This is done by building on Paulo Freire's critical pedagogy, on the contemporary application of this praxis and on its relevance to RME. From this foundation, a larger discussion on critical management pedagogy is presented to establish the contemporary relevance of ESD criticality to RME and praxis. Just as education for sustainable development has been criticized for its lack of critical underpinning, RME practice and research must also address this gap in order to imbed the potential for meaningful change throughout the learning process. This critical underpinning must be supported by rich and dynamic pedagogical processes of action and reflection.

CRITICAL PEDAGOGY

Education is historically and socially bound, rooted in history and in the social constructs that form the context in which the discussion on education takes place. Education is a process of informing oneself, but it cannot be a neutral or objective process. The order and structure of education – the subjects that are addressed, those that are not addressed, and those that are assumed to be true – evoke a 'silent logic' that gives rise to assumed *truths* in the educational process.

It is *these assumed truths* that Paulo Freire sought to deconstruct through the process of critical pedagogy. Critical pedagogy is a social-movement-based philosophy of education that deconstructs major assumptions relating to education and society (Kincheloe and Steinberg, 1997). The critical-pedagogy process requires a rejection of the idea that knowledge is neutral, so that social injustices can be recognized and acknowledged throughout the pedagogical process. By questioning these social constructs, students engage in an emancipatory learning process that awakens their critical consciousness (Giroux, 2010).

Freire's work on critical pedagogy grew from his seminal work *Pedagogy of the Oppressed* (1968, 1970). This text documents Freire's lived experience during the Great Depression, and how this experience led him to reject class-based society (Freire, 1968, 1970). These experiences underpin Freire's radical understanding of the transformative power of education.

To establish his critical framework, Freire uses the term '*conscienctizacao*', which translates as 'critical consciousness' or 'conscientization' (Freire, 1968, 1970). In Freirean terms, critical consciousness is a means of understanding the role of oppression in sustained social inequality. Critical consciousness is a process of thought that encourages students to devise, implement, and evaluate solutions to the social inequalities they face (Freire, 1970). Through radical education, reflective learning and critical thinking, Freire's work aims to deconstruct the foundations of social inequality.

The term 'critical pedagogy' was first used in Henry Giroux's 'Theories of reproduction and resistance in the new sociology of education' (1983). This phraseology builds on Freire's '*conscienctizacao*' and aims to deconstruct the social realities first noted in *Pedagogy of the Oppressed*. Giroux frames an abstract discussion around progressive education for radical change, building on transformative social action (Giroux, 1983). Giroux's development of a critical pedagogy based on early Freirean ideals has become highly influential in the field of modern educational theory.

Foundations of Critical Pedagogy

The theory of critical pedagogy has been defined above, but the many interpretations and implications of this work must be further developed. To do so, the principles of critical pedagogy will be outlined below. Before that, the limitations governing the application of critical pedagogy in the present study will be outlined. A final section will note different interpretations of critical pedagogy, before furthering the contextual alignment with RME.

A basic understanding of critical pedagogy has been outlined above. In order to understand the theory and its many interpretations, the themes that are frequently drawn from critical pedagogy should be highlighted. Aliakbari and Faraji (2011) note nine major areas of focus across the critical-pedagogy literature: the educational process, politics, authentic materials, the roles of teacher and student, marginalization, levels of consciousness, praxis, dialogism and localization (pp. 78–83). Aliakbari and Faraji refer to these areas of focus as 'themes', but the implications of these areas of focus go far beyond thematic understanding to develop a deep context for the philosophy of critical pedagogy. Of these themes, areas that should be further examined for their intrinsic relevance to RME are developed below.

Processes of education

Kanpol (1998) emphasizes the urgent need to put the necessary educational structures and educators in place so that the vital objective of education for all can be achieved. Vandrick (1994) builds on this understanding when she states that the major goal of critical pedagogy is to emancipate and educate everyone, regardless of the inequalities that may face them. Education should depend only on one's willingness to learn, not on one's gender, class, race, or any other factor.

Freire's deconstruction of the educational process questions the structure of educational institutions and the top-down process of teaching and learning. The top-down approach begins by assuming that teachers are fountains of knowledge and that students are empty vessels that must be filled. This process unquestioningly places the authority of the teacher at the center of learning, leaving little or no room for the role of the students as questioning and active participants in their own education. Known as the banking model of education, this style of learning is one in which students are expected to receive, memorize and repeat knowledge. The result is a transaction-based process that mimics the act of depositing money and lacks room for original thought or critical thinking (Freire, 1968, 1970) (Table 8.1). This model has many shortcomings, particularly its tendency to substitute memorizing for real learning. An even greater problem is the banking model's tendency to act as an advocate for the fixation of reality. This tendency prevents it from addressing the context of the learning and leads it to replicate political oppression by refusing to share alternative perspectives (Joldersma, 2001).

In Freirean terms, the banking model's failure to contextualize the learning process is a serious problem. In other words, this model ignores the construction of education and its overall relationship with society. At a more basic level, the banking model fails to acknowledge that the passing on of easily transferable information is not at all the same thing as the sharing of deep knowledge (Joldersma, 2001). Packaging information to

Table 8.1   Mirrored relationship between the banking model of education and societal oppression as a whole (Freire, 1970)

(a) The teacher teaches, and the students are taught.
(b) The teacher knows everything, and the students know nothing.
(c) The teacher thinks, and the students are thought about.
(d) The teacher talks, and the students listen meekly.
(e) The teacher disciplines, and the students are disciplined.
(f) The teacher chooses and enforces her/his choice, and the students comply.
(g) The teacher acts, and the students have the illusion of acting through the action of the teacher.
(h) The teacher chooses the program content, and the students (who were not consulted) adapt to it.
(i) The teacher confuses the authority of knowledge with her/his own professional authority, which s/he sets in opposition to the freedom of the students.
(j) The teacher is the subject of the learning process, while the pupils are mere objects.

Table 8.2   Process of problematization in problem-based learning (Freire, 1970)

(a) Describing the content of discussion
(b) Defining the problem
(c) Personalizing the problem
(d) Discussing the problem
(e) Discussing the alternative understandings of and solutions to the problem

be shared and memorized dehumanizes the educational process and the related processes of psychological and sociological maturity required for critical learning. This dehumanization creates and breeds oppressive passivity in students (Freire, 1968, 1970a).

In response to the traditionalist banking model of education, Freire encourages a problems-based educational process that allows students to develop their own contextual understandings and critical consciousness. This process places the student at the heart of the learning process, frames the role of society and stakeholders in the greater discussion, and re-humanizes the educational experience. In Freire's words: 'In problem-posing education, people develop their power to perceive critically the way they exist in the world with which and in which they find themselves; they come to see the world not as a static reality, but as a reality in process, in transformation' (Freire, 1970: 71).

This transformative process of critical learning encourages students to inform their learning processes with past experiences and beliefs, allowing individual opinions to develop. In this process, the learner undergoes five steps of problematization, which are noted in Table 8.2.

According to Freire, both students and teachers must take active roles as subjects in the learning process. The teacher still has the top-down role of uncovering realities and creating knowledge of the world, but students command the learning process through critical reflection on their overall understandings of and relationships within the world.[1]

Understanding the process of education as an enlightenment through knowledge rather than as a technique of banking information

is a core component of critical pedagogy. This need for contextual understanding of the greater societal construct directly informs later work on education for sustainable development, environmental education and eco-pedagogy. To note, ecopedagogy refers to the application of Freire's critical pedagogy beyond the traditional social-specific context and expanding to the environmental contexts. Through the process of establishing an overall understanding of one's own beliefs, as well as one's place within society, learners are able to advance their own educations and make sense of large societal issues and possible solutions.

Curriculum for education

The critical-pedagogy discussion presented here has thus far examined the need for student-centered learning and critical reflection. However, there is no panacea for all of the potential problems and questions surrounding the critical-pedagogy methodology. There is no unique way of teaching that will meet the requirements of critical pedagogy in every case.

Giroux and McLaren (1992) contribute to the wide discussion about what a curriculum for critical pedagogy would look like. They note that critical pedagogy arises from a transformative curriculum, one that fosters students' development of strategies and skills for deep thinking. The kind of curriculum that would advance critical pedagogy should therefore help students to become critics of the economic, political and social realities that surround their learning processes. Bartolome (1994) notes that there is no set curriculum or program design that will inevitably engender critical pedagogy, because the material decisions to be made in each case need to reflect the interests of the specific students concerned. Building on these ideas in a more specific way, Ohara et al. (2001) align this discussion more closely with available resources. These authors state that meaningful critical pedagogy requires a foundation of 'authentic materials' that students can understand as truly representative within their culture. These authentic materials can serve as the basis for meaningful discussion, grounding their understanding in resources that have value across their culture. Developing a classroom construct with resources that hold the same symbolic value in the classroom that they do in the culturally understood reality allows students to experience deep learning and reflection in the pedagogical process.

Beyond critical pedagogy, the need for a varied curriculum based in reality is a key element of environmental education, education for sustainable development, and ecopedagogy. In order to understand the interrelation of human actions and their impact on the natural environment, one must in fact understand these human actions. Relating the curriculum to real-world examples, placing the student at the heart of the learning experience and citing ways to make meaningful societal change would advance critical pedagogy and provide interdisciplinary opportunities related to education for sustainable development.

Praxis of education

In *Pedagogy of the Oppressed*, Freire contextualizes and defines praxis:

> Revolution is achieved with neither verbalism nor activism, but rather with praxis, that is, with reflection and action directed at the structures to be transformed. The revolutionary effort to transform these structures radically cannot designate its leaders as its thinkers and the oppressed as mere doers. (1970: 125–126)

According to Freire, praxis can be understood as the process of developing critical awareness through action and reflection. Educational praxis aims to bridge theory and

transformational action. Freire further develops this context:

> Critical consciousness is brought about, not through intellectual effort alone, but through praxis, through authentic union of action and reflection. (1970: 48)

Praxis reflects the deep purpose of the educational process. Boyce (1996) characterizes praxis as a process that equips learners to be prepared for active participation in collective societal action. When praxis is understood in this way, its implications go far beyond the constructs of the individual classroom. Although there is no singular curriculum for critical pedagogy, a unified praxis of reflection, action and matured understanding is required for meaningful learning.

Praxis is the foundation of critical pedagogy. In order for deep learning to occur, the process of action and reflection must be actualized. This essential condition is not always present in discussions of environmental education and education for sustainable development. What separates critical pedagogy, and therefore ecopedagogy, from other means of learning for contextual change is the core mission of embedding the deep-learning process through praxis. Although not all constructs of the critical pedagogy have the same relevance to the ecopedagogy discussion, praxis is one area that must always be present to ensure purposeful learning.

Reflections on Critical Pedagogy

Critical pedagogy is an inspirational education philosophy that aims to spark revolutionary learning that will bring about change. In *Pedagogy of the Oppressed*, Freire developed the foundations of critical pedagogy, which he continued to refine throughout his later work and which is replicated across modern education and pedagogy texts. In order to understand the density and complexity of critical pedagogy, the areas of process, politics, curriculum, relationships, marginalization, consciousness, praxis and dialogism have been presented.

These primary elements of Freire's critical pedagogy open up possibilities for embedding critical pedagogy in business education for sustainable development and RME.

These ideas have been further developed in more recent scholarship and make contributions beyond the strictly social sphere. Moving beyond the examination of society in isolation, Freire's later work instead focuses on human effects on the natural environment. In his later work, the concept of ecopedagogy evolves from the philosophy of critical pedagogy. Whereas the theory of critical pedagogy is traditionally applied to social contexts, ecopedagogy expands its understanding to include the interrelationship between humans and the natural world (Freire, 2004). The personal growth that led Freire to redefine critical pedagogy through a more environmentally inclusive lens illustrates the innate undertones of sustainable development that are present in critical pedagogy. This process is similar to the present transition facing business and management schools. While the traditional curriculum emphasizes socially and economically derived outputs, the rise of RME demonstrates a matured understanding of all environmental, social and economic constructs in which management education is entangled. Critical pedagogy, and specifically ecopedagogy, bring an important level of rigor to discussions about sustainable development. They should therefore be given an important place within management and business curricula. Deeply embedding sustainable development in business and management classrooms will demand critical pedagogy to saturate teaching, learning and all experiences at business schools. Specifically, critical management pedagogy bridges the gap between traditional Freirean critical pedagogy and the RME paradigm rising in popularity across business schools and curricula.

CRITICAL MANAGEMENT EDUCATION

Critical management education (CME) is the business and management-focused pedagogy

derived in line with the traditional understanding of critical pedagogy (Freire, 1970). More specifically, CME (Grey, 2004) and critical management pedagogy (CMP) (Grey and French, 1996) pull from roots of Critical Theory. Reynolds (1999) develops the rich contextual underpinnings which inform critical management pedagogy, stating:

> Critical perspectives have been informed by different schools of thought, including Marxism, feminism, postmodernism, social constructionism, critical theory and liberationist (Freirean) theology. In adult education critical thought has been influenced by feminist scholarship [see for example Gore, 1993] and in particular, by Jurgen Habermas' [Habermas, 1972; Habermas and Lenhardt, 1973] writings in critical theory. Management educators have also drawn on Habermas' ideas, although not uncritically, the development of a critical pedagogy in management also having been influenced by post-structuralist critique. From this latter perspective, critical theorists are regarded as having taken insufficient account of the oppressive tendency inherent in making normative prescriptions from an all-embracing framework intended for universal application (Alvesson and Willmott, 1996) … Nevertheless, whether the terms used are 'critical reflection' (Kemmis, 1985), 'critical social science' (Nord and Jermier, 1992), or 'critical pedagogy' (Grey and French, 1996), there are some more or less shared principles which can provide a basis for understanding the more problematical consequences of introducing critical perspectives. (Reynolds, 1999: 172)

The rich theoretical underpinning of CME is further developed in Vince (1996). While critical of the experiential learning process which is so embedded in the action-and-reflection praxis of critical pedagogy, Vince articulates the innate relationship between learning and change, in that the process of learning *is* the process of changing, and that one's potential to change is directly influenced by ones capacity to learn. Vince develops a framework for understanding learning for change and experiential management education through understanding the four levels of human learning (Bateson, 1972), relationships between learning and power (see Freire, 1985), and organizational psychodynamics (Vince, 1996). This multi-lensed framework [and the processes of learning which derive from them] illustrates the sociological and interdisciplinary relationships within critical education and pedagogy. These frameworks can be applied within and beyond the context of management education.

CME bridges the gap between traditional critical theory and traditional management education, calling for learning which inspires changes within the classroom and across business schools. Moving from the traditional understanding of management education, Dehler et al. (2001) illustrates how the transition of business from traditional paradigms and orthodoxies, which have fallen by the wayside, to equal measures of innovative praxis that prepare students for the divergences from the traditional subject matter of business school curricula. Dehler et al. state: 'Understanding "management" in a new business context requires updated and richer conceptualizations, it follows that teaching and learning necessitates innovative pedagogies that both capture and convey these more complex notions' (2001: 507). While written at the turn of the millennium, these words still ring true, calling on richer conceptualizations, more thoughtful solutions, and more robust contextual understandings of the robust issues of society, economy and environment.

CME cannot be used as a panacea for all of the problems facing management education. However, the thoughtful, reflexive and critical elements of this body of educational practice do provide a framework for addressing the challenge of shifting mindsets within business schools. CME can be applied through core themes of management education to highlight opportunities for deep learning and creativity in the traditional process of education. Informing program design and pedagogy with CME allows for reinvention of these traditional subject matters to acknowledge progress in traditional management studies. Grey notes that management education has been historically informed by the interests of business [economy] rather

than the wider societal context (Grey, 2004). Grey states that the overt focus on economic well-being in management schools presents an opportunity to expand values-driven management education through CME. This understanding can be expanded to align with ecopedagogy and the modern definition of sustainable development. Therefore, CME can be used to embed societal and environmental values at the heart of management education praxis. Grey uses CME as a means to decouple management and values, so that management education may acknowledge the loaded issues that inform our global context[2]. In doing so, the process of learning and changing will expand beyond a singular individual's experiences [habitus] to be inclusive of a greater collection of issues, informed by experiences which confront social inequalities, and structural disparities in power. Individual experiences may inform the understanding of these sensitive issues, but collective change and action will inform the future of responsible management through CME (Grey, 2004).

The praxis of critical pedagogy requires the process of action and reflection to be present throughout the learning process. Brookfield (1987) developed reflexivity across professionals by noting the importance of developing a 'voice' to articulate lessons-learned. Ellsworth (1992) built the reflexivity conversation through the dialogue of educators, noting the need to articulate targets and inconsistencies across program design, curricula and reflections. This process is echoed through CME as well, arguing that students, educators and managers employing a critical perspective require critical reflexivity in order to question the management and processes of engagement (Reynolds, 1999). Going a step further, Grey and French (1996) stressed the need to recognize and articulate inconstancies, particularly those that present gaps in theory and practice and those that can be reconciled by teachers and learners. Because the ethical issues being brought to light through the CME process are innately open-ended and contested, a critical lens for questioning actions, perceptions and moral orientations must be considered (Fenwick, 2005: 45). The gap in addressing these contested areas may be mitigated though reflective practice on the part of the educator, learning activities that center on student experiences, and embedding critical theory in and out of the classroom to create elastic and action-based contexts for the learning process (Fenwick, 2005). Each of these steps plays an important role in shaping the educational process. In order to further contextualize critical pedagogy, CME and RME, the following section will outline work being done on the present economic, environmental and social-driven issues contested in business and management education.

APPLICATIONS TO RME

The pairing of action and reflection in ESD and RME praxis parallels the dynamic nature of sustainable development itself. Because sustainable development is an ever-evolving concept, no singular agenda or definition (beyond the broad framing of the Brundtland Report [United Nations, 1987]) will ever fully encompass all of the dimensions contributing to a sustainable future. Embedding an action-and-reflection-based praxis in business and management curricula gives RME the critical underpinning needed to truly teach individuals to account for their own experiences of and contributions to ecological, economic and social domains.

RME provides us with a thoughtful means of teaching sustainable-development-related content across business and management curricula. This is seen throughout RME research, particularly under the umbrella of UN Principles for Responsible Management Education (UN PRME) Working Groups (see Chapter 2). The UN PRME network has aided the production of sustainable-development-driven thematic research addressing climate change, human rights, gender equality, poverty reduction, anti-corruption and governance, and curriculum and mindsets. Practical examples of research addressing these themes can be seen across a number of different disciplines and regional contexts. Climate is addressed in a number of ways, including its relevance across economic and social contexts (Matei et al., 2012); sustainable development and climate action (Shrivastava, 2015); green human resources management (Sharma and Gupta, 2015); and the role of PRME in addressing climate (Hope, 2018). Human rights is addressed for its relevance to education for an inclusive and sustainable world (Palthe, 2013); and as a necessity for the new paradigm of RME (Albareda and Aguado, 2015). Gender equality is addressed in marketing studies centering on equality (Hein, 2015); research addressing obstacles to integrating gender equality in business schools, including pedagogical approaches to more inclusive teaching and learning (Flynn et al., 2015); and international survey research on the role of gender equality and its importance across varying cohorts of respondents, with findings noting the importance of gender equality as a transcending value across older generations (Haski-Leventhal et al., 2017). Poverty reduction is a central theme; texts focusing on this subject include a call to move beyond superficial social media to deep, academic commitment to responsible leadership development and poverty reduction (Marco, 2012; Tavanti, 2012); alignment of MBA and MPA courses to multidisciplinary education that addresses poverty reduction (Tavanti and Vedramini, 2014); and PRME Working Group research that discusses socially responsible organizations and poverty alleviation (Gudic et al., 2014, Gudic et al., 2017). Anti-corruption and governance are addressed in detail through best practices, methods and toolkits for action (Amann et. al., 2017); and through legal-related research (Becker et al., 2013; Verbos, 2016). Most relevantly to the core ethos of RME and sustainability in education, themes of curriculum, education and mindsets are developed throughout PRME-centric literature.

Unlike other thematic areas that have come into UN PRME research over time, this is a staple of the community that has been well developed since the founding of UN PRME. These texts broadly contribute to SDG 4: Quality Education, and demonstrate the alignment of business schools to RME and ESD. Within specific curricula, ESD in marketing education (Brennan et al., 2010; Wilhelm, 2008); sustainable tourism (Pomering et al., 2011); and MBA programs (Haski-Leventhal, 2013) are developed in the research. Curriculum development is more specifically noted in texts such as O'Connell and Sweeney (2015), which discuss curriculum development as an action plan for integrating PRME learning outcomes into business schools; and Hope (2015), which explicitly links curriculum development as the vehicle for the PRME community to contribute to the sustainable development agenda. Regarding the teaching and learning, Cezarino (2016) addressed curriculum development by understanding the opinions of teachers and educators on sustainable development, while Haski-Leventhal and Concato (2016) measured student attitudes on CSR and RME, emphasizing the importance of management and sustainable decision-making. Additionally, mindsets are explored through studies that examine competencies and understanding. One such example includes Laasch and Moosmayer (2015, 2016), which discusses competency development. This work aligns with sustainable mindsets, as it discusses a competencies-based approach to understanding sustainable, responsible and ethical business practice. An important essay by Rimanoczy (2016) explores holistic approaches to learning and addresses the questions of what to teach in RME and how to teach it. This research references content around knowledge, mindsets and capabilities and provides an example of how these contributions to the literature on UN PRME have become mainstreamed and

have inspired further educational development research.

The interplay between researchers and PRME has directly impacted research and knowledge creation around these areas of sustainable development. Texts specifically related to curriculum formation and mindset development have an innate relationship to the active and reflective processes of critical pedagogy, since the curriculum and mindsets are crafted and developed throughout praxis.

CONCLUSIONS

Since critical pedagogy was introduced by Freire, this foundational understanding has become an established presence in a number of different research areas. Among these areas are praxis philosophy (Giroux and McLaren, 1986; Kincheloe and McLaren, 2011; Lankshear et al., 1993; McLaren, 2003; McLaren, 2015), applied linguistics (Crookes, 2013; Crookes and Lehner, 1998; Crookes and Schmidt, 1989), cultural studies (Kincheloe and Steinberg, 1997), cognitive science/learning analytics (Blikstein, 2013; Blikstein and Krannich, 2013); adult education (Borg and Mayo, 2006; Darder et al., 2017; English and Mayo, 2012; Mayo, 1995), public policy (Amsler and Canaan, 2008; Amsler et al., 2010; Canaan, 2005, 2011, 2013), elementary education (DeMulder et al., 2009) and sustainability education (Kahn, 2008; Kahn and Kahn, 2010). These works demonstrate areas where critical pedagogy is especially evident, as the message of Paulo Freire has directly influenced the modern subject area in these texts. With particular reference to CME, management education is also deeply informed by criticality and reflexivity (Dehler et al., 2001; Ellsworth, 1992; Fenwick, 2005; Grey, 2004; Grey and French, 1996; Reynolds, 1999; Vince, 1996).

There is, however, a gap in the existing literature concerning the direct application of Freire's work to the disciplines of CME,

RME and business education for sustainable development. Texts such as Dehler et al. (2001), Closs and Antonello (2011) and Hibbert and Cunliffe (2015) have demonstrated the ability of reflexivity to enhance management-education learning. These three texts stand as best-practice examples leading CME or RME towards a more thoughtful and reflexive praxis. Going a step beyond this, the application of Freire's critical pedagogy provides a useful philosophy for a teaching and learning process that is engrained with personal action and reflection.

Additionally, as there is no one-size-fits-all recipe for integrating sustainable development into business or business education, these many resources and groups allow for engagement with the resource which best fits the needs of one's school, classroom, or research. This adaptability contributes to the narrative on critical pedagogy, as it allows educators to employ real-world scenarios and resources which shape the student experience. Through active and engaged processes of learning, teachers and learners are able to develop a deep understanding of the sustainable development goals (SDGs) in the classroom which aligns to the new doxa of sustainable development.

Critical pedagogy, and the praxis of action and reflection, has definitively underpinned this study. Freire's work has been explicitly discussed or developed in line with the relevant methods and findings throughout every section of this chapter. Social constructs and impacts on the natural environment should not only be questioned in research and reflection, but in active dialogue and classroom engagement. Underpinning the SDGs with critical pedagogy and ecopedagogy provide opportunities for educators to further develop their understanding of sustainable development and how these issues and themes can be developed in their own classroom, assignments, and overall praxis. Because ESD is an interdisciplinary area this is a process which should not be left to teachers and students in singular classrooms. Students should be questioned across all different courses and classes that they engage with. Beyond the student-and-teacher dynamic, teachers and researchers, support staff, department heads, deans, chancellors, and presidents should also engage with critical pedagogy to question their own actions; and reflect upon the outputs of the educational system in which they work. Neither critical pedagogy nor ESD are linear processes, and it is the responsibility of higher education institutions and educators to embody the inquisitive and reflective praxis needed to educate students and citizens for a sustainable future.

Sustainable development is '[d]evelopment that meets the needs of the present without compromising the ability of future generations to meet their own needs' (World Commission on Environment and Development, United Nations, 1987: 43). Business education *for* sustainable development builds on this understanding and reflects direction and urgency in educating future business leaders in-line with the sustainable development agenda. Critical pedagogy and ecopedagogy radically inform the educational process with action and reflection related to social and ecological development. Coupling ecopedagogy and business education for sustainable development, there is hope in learning for deep change which could shape the way future generations consider sustainable development. CME informs this gap in understanding and suggests an opportunity for management education and critical reflexivity in strengthening values-driven business education for sustainable development.

The current definition of sustainable development is presented above. While that understanding has remained the constant backbone of how sustainable development is articulated for more than 30 years, the ways in which sustainable development has been understood are constantly evolving. This evolution can be seen in high-level UN forums, the transition from eight poverty-centric global goals to 17 goals relating to economy, environment, governance and society. The dynamic shifts in how sustainability is popularly conceptualized illustrates a growth in holistic commitment to sustainable development. Changes can also be seen in the classroom; the shift from singular environmental economics classes to modules and programs that embed RME and sustainable development demonstrates increasing understanding within the academic community.

Both of these changes (how we understand sustainable development and how we educate for sustainable development) signal progress and deep commitment, moving sustainability beyond one-dimensional thinking about how to address issues concerning the degradation of ecology or humanity. The emphasis now is on the need to shape responsible and sustainable mindsets that consider the deeper interrelations at the heart of these issues. Educating future business leaders about sustainable development issues will be a continuous process, as will the larger project of addressing those issues. However, the SDGs have taken a large step forward by creating a platform through which a more holistic understanding of sustainable development can be achieved. As the new dominant doxa in the field of sustainable development, the SDGs provide a unifying set of concepts that can be used to inspire global action and critical reflection for change. RME leverages the sustainable development dialogue in the classroom. This ever-changing global sustainable development narrative must carry an equally dynamic praxis for critical, personal sense-making. The engrained process of action and reflection in the RME learning process will advance the way educated citizens conceptualize sustainable development in their own lives, as well as how we as a society broadly consider these issues globally. Sustainable development is a critical area that demands an equally critical praxis.

It is vital that businesses and business schools continue their actions, reflections and communications in support of the SDGs, and of sustainable development more generally. It is even more important that we consider the processes of sustainable development and

critical pedagogy in parallel so that education for sustainable development, and particularly RME, can inspire radical sustainable change for the future.

Notes

1   It is important too that Freire does acknowledge the necessity of including the global dimension when seeking to understand one's own educational context. When he wrote *Pedagogy of the Oppressed*, however, Freire still had a relatively traditional viewpoint that understood this context primarily in human terms. It was not until *Pedagogy of Indignation* (2004) that the definition of the world is expanded to include the natural world, and the footprint of humankind upon the natural world.

2   Grey (2004) acknowledges the 'political, ethical, and philosophical' challenges. To be explicit in understanding the relationship between these areas of concern and modern issues of sustainable development, one could also consider CME as a lens for examining issues of environment, economy and society; or each of the 17 Sustainable Development Goals.

BIBLIOGRAPHY

Albareda, L. and Aguado, R. (2015) *Integrating human dignity and human rights governance as a new management education paradigm*. Academy of Management Proceedings, 2015. Briarcliff Manor, NY: Academy of Management.

Aliakbari, M. and Faraji, E. (2011) Basic Principles of Critical Pedagogy. 2nd International Conference on Humanities, Historical and Social Sciences IPEDR. Citeseer, pp. 78–85.

Allen, S., Cunliffe, A. L. and Easterby-Smith, M. (2017) Understanding sustainability through the lens of ecocentric radical-reflexivity: implications for management education. *Journal of Business Ethics*, 1–15.

Alvesson, M. and Willmott, H. (Eds.). (1996) *Critical management studies*. New York: Sage.

Amann, W., Berenbeim, R., Tan, T. K., Kleinhempel, M., Lewis, A., Nieffer, R., Stachowicz-Stanusch, A. and Tripathi, S. (2017) *Anti-corruption: implementing curriculum change in management education*. Abingdon: Routledge.

Amann, W., Pirson, M., Dierksmeier, C., Von Kimakowitz, E. and Spitzeck, H. (2011) *Business schools under fire: humanistic management education as the way forward.* Basingstoke: Palgrave Macmillan.

Amsler, S. S. and Canaan, J. E. (2008) Whither critical pedagogy in the neo-liberal university today? Two UK practitioners' reflections on constraints and possibilities. *Enhancing Learning in the Social Sciences*, 1, 1–31.

Amsler, S., Canaan, J., Cowden, S., Motta, S. and Singh, G. (2010) Why critical pedagogy and popular education matter today. *Higher Education Academy, Centre for Sociology, Anthropology & Politics*.

Annan-Diab, F. and Molinari, C. (2017) Interdisciplinarity: practical approach to advancing education for sustainability and for the Sustainable Development Goals. *International Journal of Management Education*, 15, 73–83.

Azevedo, A., Apfelthaler, G. and Hurst, D. (2012) Competency development in business graduates: an industry-driven approach for examining the alignment of undergraduate business education with industry requirements. *International Journal of Management Education*, 10, 12–28.

Bartolome, L. (1994) Beyond the methods fetish: toward a humanizing pedagogy. *Harvard Educational Review*, 64, 173–195.

Bateson, G. (1972) *Steps to an ecology of mind.* San Francisco: Chandler Publishing.

Bebbington, J. and Unerman, J. (2018) Achieving the United Nations Sustainable Development Goals: an enabling role for accounting research. *Accounting, Auditing & Accountability Journal*, 31, 2–24.

Becker, K., Hauser, C. and Kronthaler, F. (2013) Fostering management education to deter corruption: what do students know about corruption and its legal consequences? *Crime, Law and Social Change*, 60, 326–347.

Blikstein, P. (2013) Digital fabrication and 'making' in education: the democratization of invention. *FabLabs: Of Machines, Makers and Inventors*, 4, 1–21.

Blikstein, P. and Krannich, D. (2013) The makers' movement and FabLabs in education: experiences, technologies, and research. Proceedings of the 12th International Conference on Interaction Design and Children, ACM (Association for Computing Machinery), pp. 613–616.

Borg, C. and Mayo, P. (2006) *Learning and social difference.* London: Paradigm.

Boyce, M. E. (1996) Teaching critically as an act of praxis and resistance. *Electronic Journal of Radical Organization Theory*, 2, 1–14.

Brennan, R., Eagle, L., Ellis, N. and Higgins, M. (2010) Of a complex sensitivity in marketing ethics education. *Journal of Marketing Management*, 26, 1165–1180.

Brookfield, S. D. (1987) *Developing critical thinkers.* Milton Keynes: Open University Press.

Canaan, J. (2005) Developing a pedagogy of critical hope. *Learning & Teaching in the Social Sciences*, 2.

Canaan, J. (2011) Critical pedagogy in, against and beyond the neoliberalised university. *ESRC seminar Global Citizenship as a Graduate Attribute, UCL*, 2011.

Canaan, J. E. (2013) Resisting the English neoliberalising university: what critical pedagogy can offer. *Journal for Critical Education Policy Studies (JCEPS)*, 11.

Cezarino, L. (2016) Teachers' opinion about sustainability on management education. *Business Management Dynamics*, 6, 01–08.

Christens, B. D., Winn, L. T. and Duke, A. M. (2016) Empowerment and critical consciousness: a conceptual cross-fertilization. *Adolescent Research Review*, 1, 15–27.

Cicmil, S. and Gaggiotti, H. (2018) Responsible forms of project management education: theoretical plurality and reflective pedagogies. *International Journal of Project Management*, 36, 208–218.

Closs, L. and Antonello, C. S. (2011) Transformative learning: integrating critical reflection into management education. *Journal of Transformative Education*, 9, 63–88.

Cockburn, T. and Jahdi, K. S. (2015) *Responsible governance: international perspectives for the new era.* New York: Business Expert Press.

Crookes, G. V. (2013) *Critical ELT in action: foundations, promises, praxis.* Abingdon: Routledge.

Crookes, G. and Lehner, A. (1998) Aspects of process in an ESL critical pedagogy teacher education course. *Tesol Quarterly*, 32, 319–328.

Crookes, G. and Schmidt, R. (1989) Motivation: reopening the research agenda. *University of Hawai'i Working Papers in English as a Second Language*, 8(1).

Cunliffe, A. L. (2009) Reflexivity, learning and reflexive practice. In: S. J. Armstrong & C. V. Fukami (Eds.), *The SAGE handbook of management learning, education and development.* London: Sage, pp. 405–418.

Darder, A., Mayo, P. and Paraskeva, J. (2017) *International critical pedagogy reader*. Abingdon: Routledge.

Dehler, G. E., Welsh, M. A. and Lewis, M. W. (2001). Critical pedagogy in the new paradigm. *Management Learning*, 32(4), 493–511.

DeMulder, E. K., Kayler, M. and Stribling, S. M. (2009) Cultivating transformative leadership in P-12 schools and classrooms through critical teacher professional development. *Journal of Curriculum and Instruction*, 3, 39.

Dewey, J. (1963) *Liberalism and social action*. New York: Capricorn Books.

English, L. M. and Mayo, P. (2012) *Learning with adults: a critical pedagogical introduction*. Netherlands: Brill Sense.

Ellsworth, E. (1992). 'Why doesn't this feel empowering? Working through the repressive myths of critical pedagogy'. In: C. Luke and J. M. Gore (Eds.), *Feminisms and critical pedagogy*. New York: Routledge, pp. 90–119.

Fenwick, T. (2005) Ethical dilemmas of critical management education: within classrooms and beyond. *Management Learning*, 36(1), 31–48.

Flynn, P. M., Haynes, K. and Kilgour, M. A. (Eds.) (2015) *Integrating gender equality into business and management education: lessons learned and challenges remaining*. Abingdon: Routledge.

Flynn, P. M., Haynes, K. and Kilgour, M. A. (2016) *Overcoming challenges to gender equality in the workplace: leadership and innovation*. London: Taylor & Francis Group.

Freire, P. (1968) *Pedagogia do oprimido [Pedagogy of the oppressed]*. Rio de Janeiro: Paz e Terra.

Freire, P. (1970). *Pedagogy of the oppressed*. New York: Herder and Herder.

Freire, P. (1973) *Education for critical consciousness*. London: Bloomsbury Publishing.

Freire, P. (1985) *The politics of education: culture, power, and liberation*. Wesport, CT: Greenwood Publishing Group.

Freire, P. (2004) *Pedagogy of indignation*. Boulder, CO: Paradigm (2016, Abingdon: Routledge).

Freire, P. and Ara, A. M. (1998) *Pedagogy of the heart*. New York: Bloomsbury Publishing USA.

Freire, P. and Macedo, D. (1987) *Literacy: reading the word and the world*. Abingdon: Routledge.

Giroux, H. (1983) Theories of reproduction and resistance in the new sociology of education: a critical analysis. *Harvard Educational Review*, 53, 257–293.

Giroux, H. A. (2010) Paulo Freire and the crisis of the political. *Power and Education*, 2, 335–340.

Giroux, H. and McLaren, P. (1986) Teacher education and the politics of engagement: the case for democratic schooling. *Harvard Educational Review*, 56, 213–239.

Giroux, H. A. and McLaren, P. (1992) Writing from the margins: geographies of identity, pedagogy, and power. *Journal of Education*, 174, 7–30.

Gore, J. M. (1993) *The struggle for pedagogies*. New York: Routledge.

Grey, C. (2004) Reinventing business schools: the contribution of critical management education. *Academy of Management Learning & Education*, 3(2), 178–186.

Grey, C. and French, R. (1996) Rethinking management education: an introduction. In: R.French and C. Grey (Eds.), *Rethinking management education*. London: Sage, pp. 1–16.

Gudic, M., Parks, C. and Rosenbloom, A. (2017) *Responsible management education and the challenge of poverty: a teaching perspective*. Abingdon: Routledge.

Gudic, M., Rosenbloom, A. and Parkes, C. (2014) *Socially responsive organizations and the challenge of poverty*. London: Taylor & Francis.

Gunarathne, A. (2018) Developing graduate competence in sustainability management. In: P. M. Flynn, T. K. Tan & M. Gudic (Eds.), *Redefining Success*. Abingdon: Routledge in association with GSE Research, pp. 86–96.

Habermas, J. (1972) Bewußtmachende oder rettende Kritik-die Aktualität Walter Benjamins. In: S UNseld (Ed.), *Zur Aktualität Walter Benjamins*. Frankfurt-am-Main: Suhrkamp, pp.173–223.

Habermas, J. and Lenhardt, C. (1973) A postscript to knowledge and human interests. *Philosophy of the Social Sciences*, 3(2), 157–189.

Haski-Leventhal, D. (2013) MBA students around the world and their attitudes towards responsible management. New York. PRME. Available at https://www.unprme.org/resource-docs/MGSMPRMEM-BAStudentStudy2013.pdf.

Haski-Leventhal, D. (2018) *Strategic Corporate Social Responsibility: tools and theories for responsible management*. London: Sage.

Haski-Leventhal, D. and Concato, J. (2016) The state of CSR and RME in business schools and the attitudes of their students. *Third bi-annual study*. New York. PRME. Available at https://www.unprme.org/resource-docs/MGSMPRMEReport2016.pdf.

Haski-Leventhal, D., Pournader, M. and Mckinnon, A. (2017) The role of gender and age in business students' values, CSR attitudes, and responsible management education: learnings from the PRME International Survey. *Journal of Business Ethics*, 146, 219–239.

Haynes, K. (2017) Gender equality in responsible management education and research. In: A. Murray, D. Baden, P. Cashian, A. Wersun & K. Haynes. (Eds.), *Inspirational Guide for the Implementation of PRME*. Abingdon: Routledge.

Heaney, T. (1995) Issues in Freirean pedagogy. *Thresholds in Education*. University of Chicago. Available at: https://people.well.com/user/willard/Heaney%20-%20Friere%20&%20Thresholds%20in%20Education.htm. Accessed 10 January 2020.

Hein, W. (2015) Defining the terrain for responsible management education: gender, gender equality and the case of marketing. In: P. Flynn, K. Haynes, M. Kilgour (Eds.), *Integrating Gender Equality into Business and Management Education*. Sheffield, England: Greenleaf Publishing, pp. 98–121.

Hibbert, P. and Cunliffe, A. (2015) Responsible management: Engaging moral reflexive practice through threshold concepts. *Journal of Business Ethics*, 127, 177–188.

Hope, A. (2015) Integrating principles of responsible management into undergraduate business curricula. The PRME Curriculum Tree. Available at https://www.researchgate.net/publication/280151096_Integrating_principles_of_Responsible_Management_into_Undergraduate_Business_Curricula_-_The_PRME_Curiculum_Tree. Accessed 10 June, 2020.

Hope, A. (2018) Combating climate change and its impacts through Responsible Management Education: business schools responses to SDG 13. Paper presented at 5th UN PRME Regional Chapter UK and Ireland Conference, London, United Kingdom.

Jarvis, P. (2012) *Paradoxes of learning: on becoming an individual in society*. Abingdon: Routledge.

Jickling, B. and Wals, A. E. (2008) Globalization and environmental education: looking beyond sustainable development. *Journal of Curriculum Studies*, 40, 1–21.

Joldersma, C. W. (2001) The tension between justice and freedom in Paulo Freire's epistemology. *Journal of Educational Thought (JET)/Revue de la Pensée Educative*, 129–148.

Kahn, R. (2008) Towards ecopedagogy: weaving a broad-based pedagogy of liberation for animals, nature, and the oppressed people of the earth. *The Critical Pedagogy Reader*, 2, 522–540.

Kahn, R. and Kahn, R. V. (2010) *Critical pedagogy, ecoliteracy, and planetary crisis: the ecopedagogy movement*. Bern: Peter Lang.

Kanpol, B. (1998). Critical pedagogy for beginning teachers: The movement from despair to hope. *Online Journal of Critical Pedagogy*, 2(1).

Karakas, F., Sarigollu, E. and Manisaligil, A. (2013) The use of benevolent leadership development to advance principles of responsible management education. *Journal of Management Development*, 32, 801–822.

Keesing-Styles, L. (2003) The relationship between critical pedagogy and assessment in teacher education. *Radical Pedagogy* 5(1). Available from http://radicalpedagogy.icaap.org/content/issue5_1/

Kemmis, S. (1985) Action research and the politics of reflection. In: D. Boud, R. Keogh and D. Walker (Eds.), *Reflection: turning experience into learning*. London: Kogan Page, pp. 130–163.

Kilgour, M. A. (2015) Gender inequality in management education: past, present and future. In: P. M. Flynn, K. Haynes, M. A. Kilgour, (Eds.), *Integrating Gender Equality into Business and Management Education*. Abingdon: Routledge, pp. 9–25.

Kincheloe, J. L. and McLaren, P. (2011) *Rethinking critical theory and qualitative research*. Key Works in Critical Pedagogy. Netherlands: Brill Sense.

Kincheloe, J. L. and Steinberg, S. R. (1997) *Changing multiculturalism*. Milton Keynes: Open University Press.

Kulkarni, S. R. and Kulkarni, S. S. (2014) Responsible management education: an emerging tool for sustainability. In: GLOBALETHICS.NET (Ed.), *Sustainability Ethics: Ecology, Economy & Ethics*. Shillong, India: International Conference SusCon III, pp. 201–216.

Laasch, O. and Conaway, R. (2017) *Responsible business: the textbook for management learning, competence and innovation.* Abingdon: Routledge.

Laasch, O. and Moosmayer, D. C. (2015) Responsible management competences: an integrative portfolio for sustainability, responsibility, and ethics. In: O. Laasch, and D. C. Moosmayer (Eds.)., *Critical Responsible Management Education* Working Paper, *Responsible management competencies.* Nottingham University Business School China. Available at http://responsible-management.net/wp-content/uploads/2018/05/9LaaschMoosmayer2015RMCForOpen PeerReview.pdf

Laasch, O. and Moosmayer, D. C. (2016) Responsible management competences: building a portfolio for professional competence. Academy of Management Proceedings, 2016. Briarcliff Manor, NY: Academy of Management.

Lankshear, C., McLaren, P. L. and McLaren, P. (1993) *Critical literacy: politics, praxis, and the postmodern.* New York: SUNY Press.

Marco, T. (2012) Eradicating world poverty requires more than Facebook likes: the academic commitment to educate socially responsible leaders. *International Journal of Cyber Ethics in Education (IJCEE)*, 2, 55–71.

Matei, M., Popescu, C. and Rădulescu, I. G. (2012) The consequences of climate change and social responsible behaviour. *WSEAS Transactions on Business and Economics*, 9, 29–38.

Mayo, P. (1995) Critical literacy and emancipatory politics: the work of Paulo Freire. *International Journal of Educational Development*, 15, 363–379.

McLaren, P. (2003) Critical pedagogy: a look at the major concepts. In: A. Darder, M. Baltodano, & R. D. Torres (Eds.), *The critical pedagogy reader*, New York; London: RoutledgeFalmer, pp. 69–96.

McLaren, P. (2015) *Life in schools: an introduction to critical pedagogy in the foundations of education.* Abingdon: Routledge.

McLaren, P. and Hammer, R. (1989) Critical pedagogy and the postmodern challenge: toward a critical postmodernist pedagogy of liberation. *Educational Foundations,* 3(3), 29–62. Available at https://digitalcommons.chapman.edu/education_articles/154/

McTiernan, S. and Flynn, P. M. (2011) 'Perfect Storm' on the horizon for women business school deans? *Academy of Management Learning & Education*, 10, 323–339.

Molthan-Hill, P. (2017) PRME, the UN Global Compact and the Sustainable Development Goals Tabani Ndlovu Introduction. In: *The Business Student's Guide to Sustainable Management.* Abingdon: Routledge. Available at https://books.google.com/books?id=p789DwAAQBAJ&pg=PT108&lpg=PT108&dq=molthan-hill+prme,+the+UN+Global+COmpact+and+the+sustainbledevelopment+goals&source=bl&ots=iafTXh2UWh&sig=ACfU3U0llSHcra0iHdYuNUM85p1dLUU3cA&hl=en&sa=X&ved=2ahUKEwjToterqYTqAhWjRzABHYxtApwQ6AEwAXoECAoQAQ#v=onepage&q=molthan-hill%20prme%2C%20the%20UN%20Global%20COmpact%20and%20the%20sustainbledevelopment%20goals&f=false

Moosmayer, D. C. (2017) Preaching to the unconverted – a cosmopolitan framework of PRME's influence on student satisfaction. Academy of Management Proceedings, 2017. Briarcliff Manor, NY: Academy of Management.

Nord, W. R. and Jermier, J. M. (1992) Critical social science for managers? Promising and perverse possibilities. In: M. Alvesson and H. Willmott (Eds.), *Critical management studies.* New York: Sage, pp. 202–222.

O'Connell, M. and Sweeney, L. (2015) An action plan for implementing the Principles for Responsible Management Education in college of business programme learning outcomes. DIT Teaching Fellowship Reports 2014–2015. Available at https://arrow.tudublin.ie/fellow/49/, https://arrow.tudublin.ie/cgi/viewcontent.cgi?article=1047&context=fellow, https://www.semanticscholar.org/paper/An-Action-Plan-for-Implementing-the-Principles-for-O'Connell-Sweeney/e85b06cf149f462a5eb79fb7fc476df07f0a5fd8

Ohara, Y., Saft, S. and Crookes, G. (2001) Toward a feminist critical pedagogy in a beginning Japanese-as-a-foreign-language class. *Japanese Language and Literature*, 35, 105–133.

Palthe, J. (2013) Integrating human rights in business education: embracing the social dimension of sustainability. *Journal of Education for Business*, 88, 117–124.

Pomering, A., Johnson, L. and Noble, G. (2011) Conceptualising a contemporary marketing mix for sustainable tourism marketing. *CAUTHE 2010: Tourism and Hospitality: Challenge the Limits*, 1129. Available at https://www.researchgate.net/publication/2329

59374_Conceptualising_a_contemporary_ marketing_mix_for_sustainable_tourism.

Reynolds, M. (1999) Grasping the nettle: possibilities and pitfalls of a critical management pedagogy. *British Journal of Management*, 10(2), 171–184.

Rimanoczy, I. (2016) *Stop teaching: principles and practices for responsible management education*. New York: Business Expert Press.

Rosenbloom, A., Gudić, M., Parkes, C. and Kronbach, B. (2017) A PRME response to the challenge of fighting poverty: how far have we come? Where do we need to go now? *International Journal of Management Education*, 15, 104–120.

Schlange, L. (2015) A case study of community learning and open innovation to reduce poverty at the base of the pyramid. In: M. Gudić, C. Parkes & Al. Rosenbloom, (Eds.), *Responsible management education and the challenge of poverty: a teaching perspective*. Sheffield, England: Greenleaf Publishing, pp. 191–206.

Shannon, P. (Ed.) (1992) *Becoming political: readings and writings in the politics of literacy education*. London: Heinemann.

Sharma, R. R. (2017) *A competency model for management education for sustainability*. New Delhi, India: Sage.

Sharma, R. and Gupta, N. (2015) Green HRM: an innovative approach to environmental sustainability. Twelfth AIMS International Conference on Management. Available at: http:// www.aims-international.org/aims12/12A-CD/ PDF/K723-final.pdf. Accessed March 1, 2020.

Shor, I. and Freire, P. (1987) *A pedagogy for liberation: dialogues on transforming education*. Westport, CT: Greenwood Publishing Group.

Shrivastava, P. (2015) Organizational sustainability under degrowth. *Management Research Review*, 38(6).

Stachowicz-Stanusch, A. (2011) The impact of business education on students' moral competency: an exploratory study from Poland. *Vision*, 15, 163–176.

Tavanti, M. (2012) Eradicating world poverty requires more than Facebook likes: the academic commitment to educate socially responsible leaders. *International Journal of Cyber Ethics in Education (IJCEE)*, 2, 55–71.

Tavanti, M. and Vedramini, E. A. (2014) Fighting poverty through practical, integrated and multidisciplinary education: The case of master programs in development practice. In: M. Gudic, C. Parkes and A. Rosenbloom (Eds.), *Socially responsive organizations and the challenge of poverty*. Sheffield, England: Greenleaf Publishing, pp. 197–208.

United Nations (1987) World Commission on Environment and Development: Our Common Future [Brundtland Report]. Available at: https://sustainabledevelopment.un .org/content/documents/5987our-common-future.pdf. Accessed 10 January 2020.

Vandrick, S. (1994) Feminist pedagogy and ESL. *College ESL*, 4, 69–92.

Verbos, A. K. (2016) Embedding the PRME in business law classes. *Journal of Higher Education Theory and Practice*, 16, 11.

Verbos, A. K. and Kennedy, D. (2015) Cleaning our houses: gender equity in business schools. In: P. M. Flynn, K. Haynes and M. A. Kilgour (Eds.), *Integrating gender equality into business and management education: lessons learned and challenges remaining*. Abingdon: Routledge, pp. 81–96.

Vince, R. (1996) Experiential management education as the practice of change. In: R. French and C. Grey (Eds.), *Rethinking Management Education*. London: Sage, pp. 111–131.

Visser, W. and Crane, A. (2010) Corporate sustainability and the individual: Understanding what drives sustainability professionals as change agents. SSRN Working Paper Series (1) Doi: . 10.2139/ssrn.1559087.

Viswanathan, M. (2012) Curricular innovations on sustainability and subsistence marketplaces: philosophical, substantive, and methodological orientations. *Journal of Management Education*, 36, 389–427.

Wilhelm, W. B. (2008) Marketing education for sustainability. *Journal for Advancement of Marketing Education*, 13, 8–20.

Young, G. L. (1974) Human ecology as an interdisciplinary concept: a critical inquiry. In: A. MacFadyen (Ed.), *Advances in ecological research*, vol 8. London: Academic Press, pp. 1–105.

9

Time to Look Beyond the Business Case: Why Responsible Management Education Needs to Give More Time to Other Voices

Jon Burchell and Harriet Thiery

INTRODUCTION

Without doubt the expansion and evolution of corporate social responsibility (CSR) in recent times can be seen to mark a significant process of change in the debates regarding the role and responsibility of business in society. Its growth within business practice has similarly been mirrored with a rapid expansion in scholarly research into CSR and subsequently with its adoption as an increasingly central aspect in undergraduate and postgraduate teaching provision. As the growing United Nations Principles for Responsible Management Education (PRME) membership demonstrates, notions of responsible management education (RME) are emerging as key facets of the contemporary business school world.

While there is much to regard as positive in these overarching developments, there is also important value in taking a step back and posing the question, what and how are we teaching students about responsible management, CSR and sustainability? For many of us, the predominant challenge of the past 10–20 years has been to actually get these topics recognised as important aspects of a management school curriculum, and to move them beyond the realm of 'nice to have' add-ons and optional topics. In this context we have maybe been preoccupied with making the case for responsible management education, and have largely just been pleased to see the growth of courses and modules labelled 'Business and Society' or 'Corporate Social Responsibility' popping up across business and management schools worldwide. However, we argue, with this continued engagement around the subject area, it is also crucially important that we take time to consider exactly what interpretations of CSR and responsible management are actually being prioritised within this growing curriculum.

This chapter offers a largely theoretical critique of the potential dangers and challenges of unquestioningly embracing the expansion of responsible management education without a more engaged debate about what this actually entails. With concepts such as RME and CSR so loosely defined and broad ranging, inevitably there are a plethora of approaches and frameworks through which we can encounter these issues and concepts. Indeed, a relatively brief examination of PRME-related case studies and teaching frameworks show that some truly innovative, challenging and in some cases, game-changing approaches to management education are being developed internationally (Setó-Pamies and Papaoikonomou, 2016). However, the challenge of getting greater engagement and awareness of RME within traditional established academic research and management programmes has led to an over-emphasis upon demonstrating its logical 'fit' with conventional business paradigms rather than embracing the contradictions and challenges that responsible business practice brings with it. Consequently, RME has been framed within the context of an ever-expanding CSR research field dominated by instrumental approaches centred around CSR as a strategic operational tool for business. The primary aim of much of this analysis is to seek to justify CSR's existence not on particularly moral grounds but upon the economic arguments of the business case and by evidencing correlations between responsible practice and profit.

In this chapter we seek to highlight the potential dangers of allowing the dominance of such instrumental approaches to CSR to provide the overarching framework for RME. While not denying the importance of business case logic as a primary channel for engaging business in processes of change, we argue that an over-reliance on these frameworks and arguments within both CSR research and RME course structures leads to a relatively narrow, normative interpretation. This interpretation connects 'responsibility' with 'profit' and places the firm – and its strategic interpretations of these concepts – centre-stage to the detriment of 'other' voices and interpretations. The long-term consequence of this might be to create a mainstream form of RME with a tendency

to focus upon how companies can manipulate ethical issues to gain competitive advantage rather than an educational environment, which encourages business and management students to consider the broader social context and challenges surrounding debates regarding the role of business in contemporary society.

In making the case for a broader conceptualisation of RME the chapter will firstly look at the evidence for the dominance of mainstream instrumental approaches to CSR within academic research. It will utilise this to draw out the core assumptions implicit within this instrumental approach and demonstrate how these assumptions have restricted the parameters of the research and debates that form the current foundations for the bulk of RME. Building from this critique, the chapter then looks at potential alternative framings of RME and the growing action and research that accompanies these interpretations. In doing so, we seek to champion an approach to RME that starts from a different point of departure and embraces a broad range of differing interpretations and expectations regarding the roles, responsibilities and impact of business in society. In particular, we argue, students should engage with a far broader range of actors and voices both within and outside of the business community, be introduced to competing conceptualisations of CSR and seek an expanded interpretation which goes beyond simply imposing Westernised notions of responsible practice onto an international stage.

BUILDING A MAINSTREAM CONCEPTUALISATION OF CSR

As previously mentioned, CSR research has blossomed in recent years providing an extensive analytical resource – both theoretical and empirically focused – upon which the framework for the bulk of RME has been developed. This material includes research on defining CSR (Carroll, 1991; McWilliams and Siegal, 2001), identifying correlations between responsible practice and business success (Cowe and Hopkins, 2008; Swanson, 1999; Waddock and Graves, 1997), CSR reporting and monitoring (Gray et al., 1997; Owen and O'Dwyer, 2008), the transition towards stakeholder management (Carroll and Buckholtz, 2002; Donaldson and Preston, 1995; Freeman, 1984) and the framing of corporations as citizens (Andriof and McIntosh, 2001; Matten and Crane, 2005; Zadek, 2001) amongst others. Central to all of these developments however is an overriding CSR paradigm that positions sustainability and responsibility as contemporary strands to the strategic objectives of the firm. CSR in this instrumental view is treated as an operational (Suchman, 1995) and manageable resource (Ashforth and Gibbs, 1990), which provides pragmatic legitimacy to corporate actions.

Overriding these perspectives on CSR is its predominant role in value creation for the contemporary company, through its ability to increase financial performance and efficiency, improve reputation, loyalty and brand awareness, and mitigate risk (see, for example, Orlitzky et al., 2003; Porter and Kramer, 2011; Waddock and Graves, 1997). Even where more critical perspectives on CSR emerge, they have a tendency to frame this critique within the parameters of CSR as a concept that is defined, shaped and controlled from within the business community. Hence Critical Management scholars paint a picture of CSR as a form of strategic manipulation creating an effective illusion of responsibility whilst continuing 'business as usual' (Hanlon, 2008; Parker, 2003). From both perspectives, however, we return to a central analytical discourse framed around prioritising what CSR represents for business and either why it will benefit from strategically engaging with the concept or how it seeks to manipulate it to its own ends. This relatively narrow framing of CSR from a predominantly instrumental

perspective has resulted in a series of dominant themes. In particular, three central tenets tend to dominate the presentation of CSR.

The dominant role of instrumental CSR and the business case

Building a business case for CSR has clearly been a key component of creating a level of legitimacy for the claims that companies could be simultaneously economically successful and socially and environmentally responsible. The embedding of concepts such as the 'triple bottom line' and 'creating shared value' into corporate practice since the 1970s represented a significant move forward in engaging businesses with the challenges of sustainability and responsibility. However, in many respects the business case arguments around both Ecological Modernisation and CSR have gained an overly dominant position within sustainability and responsibility narratives and the search for conclusive empirical evidence of the correlation between responsible practice and increased profit has emerged as a form of 'holy grail'. In a similar vein, the conceptualisation of 'win–win' scenarios as the basis upon which a successful CSR strategy can and should be positioned has become almost ingrained within company CSR reporting and strategic frameworks, however paradoxical these connections might appear (see Moosmayer et al., 2019).

While the search for 'win–win' CSR solutions to global problems has been central to RME case studies and analysis, there has really been little focus on the underlying suppositions on which these processes are based. In particular, little consideration is given to those perspectives that question whether the global challenges of creating a sustainable society can actually be achieved through 'win–win' solutions. The 'business case' frames CSR as a tool to rebuild reputation in the face of negative publicity, limiting the extent to which initiatives can address the root problems of far-reaching global issues, such as poverty or climate breakdown. Similarly Ecological Modernisation approaches focus upon the potential gains of channelling the competitive dynamics of advanced market economies, constantly producing new products, processes and forms of organisation, into an ecologically sustainable development path (Pataki, 2009: 83).

Firms are therefore likely to design their CSR strategies based on narrow calculations about profitability, restricted by the 'straitjacket of economic rationality' and the dominance of economic concerns over social values (Brooks, 2010: 604.). CSR becomes an exercise of reputation building, and the success of CSR initiatives is defined by its ability to achieve this, rather than by its social and environmental impacts. The Dow Jones Sustainability Index exemplifies this, defining a sustainable corporation as one that 'aims at increasing long-term shareholder value by integrating economic, environmental and social growth opportunities into its corporate and business strategies' (Dow Jones Sustainability Index, 2000, cited in Banerjee, 2008: 66).

By prioritising business case arguments, RME almost inevitably makes the predominant concern, does responsibility create economic value for the firm? The underlying doctrine of 'do good and you will do well' itself assumes that behaving more responsibly is in the self-interest of all firms at all times. Critics argue that this inevitably results in opportunism, where companies favour the most profitable CSR projects, rather than those that are most needed by society, effectively cherry-picking the social issues agenda (Nijhof and Jeurissen, 2010). This drives out intrinsic motivation for CSR and presents challenging questions which remain largely ignored: What are the repercussions if there is not a strong business case for all forms of responsible practice? Are we in danger of creating a discourse in which sustainability and social responsibility are only valid concerns as long as we can construct a business case for their consideration? Most importantly, the predominance of business case

arguments leaves us still having to justify why companies should behave responsibly rather than focusing upon whether there are ever circumstances in which companies can justify behaving irresponsibly.

The dominance of business-centric conceptualisations of CSR

The challenges identified within the discussion above are reflective of a broader weakness with the current normative conceptualisation of CSR; namely, that it is identified as a discourse and framework that is fundamentally defined and framed by business. While business practice inevitably sits at the heart of responsible management and corporate sustainability debates, this should not implicitly dictate that business perspectives are the only voices defining the parameters, definitions and constructs of responsible business practice. Broader consideration of the historical development of CSR and the debates around sustainability point to a far more expansive literature which incorporates a diverse and extensive set of voices and perspectives. However, much of this diversity appears to have been lost in both the predominant focus of research and subsequently the framing of CSR in contemporary business school curricula. The almost hegemonic position of this narrow, firm-centric conceptualisation reflects the way in which debates around responsibility and sustainability have been largely co-opted and institutionalised within conventional socio-political settings.

CSR and the business communities' broader engagement with sustainable development have often been portrayed as an attempt to champion a solution to this confidence crisis: a strategic response by the firm to increasing pressure from civil society to regulate against irresponsible corporate behaviour, and a desire to recognise a set of social responsibilities and obligations. While this business-centric approach is inherent in the instrumental approaches to CSR and sustainability, its position as a normative narrative extends beyond this sphere into competing conceptualisations.

The bulk of existing CSR research has arguably been devoted to understanding CSR from a business-led perspective. As a consequence, much CSR material focuses upon the different tools, strategies and management practices that companies can adopt in order to successfully engage with the CSR agenda. Areas that lend themselves to alternative voices such as stakeholder theory, again have been dominated by interpretations that place the company centre-stage and examine how companies 'manage' their stakeholders, defining which stakeholders are significant and the strategies firms can utilise to increase engagement. Analysis at individual micro-level, while still largely relatively limited in scope, has so far focused predominantly upon how company strategies impact upon employees, customers, etc. through changing perceptions, loyalty etc., rather than considering how these individuals might seek to influence and shape contested notions of CSR.

Even CMS (Critical Management Studies) perspectives that seek to challenge the very foundations of CSR, do so from a position that identifies businesses as the dominant voices in the CSR debate, seeing little agency in the positions of other actors to shape or determine the nature of responsible business practice.

A growing number of scholars see an increasing political role for the corporation (Crane et al., 2008; Frynas and Stephens, 2015; Scherer et al., 2016). This approach is framed around the concept of corporate citizenship, which extends the citizen metaphor to consider the firm and its relationship with society and politics. The corporate citizenship framework challenges the dominant business case paradigm, which sees a strict distinction between business and politics, understanding the role of the firm as a solely economic one. Scholars of the political CSR tradition argue that this classical liberal separation of private and public domains of society is outdated in the era of globalisation. In recasting the corporation as a political actor, this approach blurs the boundaries of political and economic societal spheres.

By contrast, scholars working within the tradition of CMS have taken both instrumental and political CSR to task for their failure to address the structural determinants of local and global societal and environmental issues (Banerjee, 2008; Fleming and Jones, 2012; Hanlon, 2008; Shamir, 2008). Political CSR is criticised for neglecting issues of social justice and basic structures when observing social processes affecting the distribution of benefits and burdens between people (Banerjee, 2010; Makinen and Kourula, 2012). These critics have questioned whether corporations can ever become reliable agents of positive societal change, since the damage inflicted by multinational corporations is systemic, rather than piecemeal. According to this literature, corporations continue to act in the interests of a small number of stakeholders (notably, senior managers and equity holders) and so are incapable of delivering outcomes that are beneficial to society as a whole.

CMS scholars argue that mainstream CSR and CSR research ignore these trends, whilst seeking to legitimise the practices of corporations. Rather than a sincere attempt to counteract the negative effects of companies on society, CSR represents instead no more than a PR strategy designed to convince audiences that it is possible to be both profitable and responsible. Understood through a CMS lens, CSR is therefore not only incapable of delivering on its promises, but also represents a way of helping corporations to evade public critique. Discourses around CSR, corporate citizenship and sustainability are used instrumentally to achieve the goals of powerful stakeholder groups, whilst creating the illusion of pursuing a more progressive agenda (Banerjee, 2008; Fleming and Jones, 2012; Hanlon, 2008; Shamir, 2008). Rather than representing a challenge to business, CSR represents a further embedding of neoliberal governmentalities and neoliberal visions of civil society, citizenship and responsible social action (Shamir, 2008). Importantly, CSR perpetuates the myth that social responsibility does not involve trade-offs but can be a matter of win–win solutions (Fleming and Jones, 2012).

However, even these more critical approaches to CSR continue to fall into the trap of according all agency to influence CSR discourse and practice to the firm, at the expense of other key societal actors in the business–society relationship.

The dominance of Westernised conceptualisations of responsible business

While the two sections above suggest the dangers of an overly business-focused conceptualisation of ideas such as sustainability and responsible management, the predominant voices are significantly narrower than even that position might suggest. Reflecting the evolution of CSR within a European and US context, the language and framing of responsible management has largely been set within a Westernised context. The global expansion of UN PRME clearly provides evidence that engagement with these agendas expands far beyond this initial locale. Similarly the economic growth of the BRIC countries (Brazil, Russia, India, China) signals a shift in corporate power and raises significant challenges for further engagement. However, these patterns are not reflected significantly within the academic literature, research and debates that frame RME. If anything, an initial examination of the emerging CSR literature within these contexts amounts to 'more of the same' as the debates continue to focus upon the well-worn paths of business case, and firm-centric analyses of CSR within these settings without really questioning their suitability or applicability to these cultural contexts and their bigger relational questions to human rights, political freedoms, etc. While these are arguably reflected in the PRME Six Principles (see Chapter 2), to what extent are these a predominant focus for RME?

The objectives of international development and CSR have become intertwined as policy-makers see businesses as integral to global sustainable development, not only through boosting economic growth but by building human capital and reducing poverty. However, once again the analysis and interpretation of CSR within a development context appears significantly restricted to a standardised logic. CSR initiatives in the developing world are too often conceptualised within the logic of the business case, defined by the financial imperatives of the firm and their success linked to stakeholder dialogue and management. In the developing country context, the engagement of stakeholders is complicated by factors such as language, culture, education and pluralistic values, all of which can influence the process of negotiation and decision-making (Blowfield and Frynas, 2005). As a result, the voices of the marginalised are often excluded from the engagement process and therefore there is inadequate representation of local perspectives and limited influence on corporate policies and practices.

An oft-cited example in RME textbooks of a 'successful' CSR initiative in the developing world is TOMS Shoes (Hill and Langan, 2014). In 2006, CEO Blake Mycoskie pioneered a 'one-for-one' model; for every pair of TOMS shoes purchased, the company donates a pair of shoes to children living in poverty. Framed as the classic CSR 'win–win' scenario, the TOMS one-for-one model allows the firm to pursue profits, whilst ostensibly helping people in need, and has become a blueprint for many firms engaging with CSR in the developing world. In the *Handbook of Research on Marketing and CSR*, Hill and Langan praised the initiative, stating that 'companies like TOMS Shoes focus on creating value for all stakeholders (from company employees to its customers) that will speak for itself' (2014: 296).

However, the TOMS model has drawn criticism from development theorists for neglecting one important group of stakeholders: local shoe producers. One-for-one models can undermine local enterprise; when shoes are donated for free, there is little incentive for people to buy local shoes. Donations are made irregularly, making it difficult for local shoe manufacturers and sellers to estimate their future sales. Furthermore, there is little evidence to support the purported impact of the free shoes on the health of the recipients. No independent evaluation has been commissioned by TOMS to substantiate the claim that free shoes improves health. Research in El Salvador found little evidence of a positive impact on the children, other than enjoying the shoes that they had been given, and spending marginally more time outside (Wydick et al., 2018). The praise that the TOMS model has received in mainstream CSR research, hailed as 'perhaps one of the best examples of CSR done right' by a popular RME textbook, is further evidence that the success of CSR initiatives is too often measured by the success of the firm (Hill and Langan, 2014: 296). Whilst evidence for the positive impact of the TOMS model on its beneficiary communities is far smaller than the $52 profit per pair of shoes (after donating the free pair).

BREAKING THE STRANGLEHOLD OF CONVENTIONAL APPROACHES TO CSR AND RME

While the discussion above is far from all-inclusive, and is merely indicative of the now rapidly expanding CSR/sustainability fields, there is an underlying trend within this discussion that has significant implications for how we approach RME, and the role of existing CSR research in encouraging a narrow conceptualisation of business engagement with sustainability and responsibility challenges. Importantly, we are not suggesting that alternative approaches, perspectives and interpretations are simply not available. Indeed there is a significant range of voices and perspectives, offering diverse and challenging interpretations of the roles and responsibilities of business and raising

important questions regarding whether contemporary business models have the potential to reframe their activities – or conversely if they should even have to. However, these alternative voices are getting limited attention within the research and management education fields. At present they are being marginalised within a more homogeneous perspective of CSR focused upon 'win–win' business case scenarios, Westernised conceptions of responsible practice and an overarching impression that CSR is business-instigated, defined and controlled with little room for the agency of other groups, individuals or perspectives to shape processes of change.

This stranglehold is the almost inevitable consequence of both CSR and RME being conceptualised as the response to the growing critique of the ethics of contemporary business practice and the underlying academic business and management programmes that championed these unethical approaches. Both CSR and RME, in trying to create a justification for responsible and sustainable practice and encourage engagement with these agendas, have focused on approaches that offer less direct challenge or conflict with traditional management approaches. Hence rather than focusing directly on the voices critiquing business and questioning whether management education actually encourages unethical practice, our attention has been directed towards business responses to these critiques, building a business case for justifying ethical practice and trying to conceptualise and measure the value of sustainability and responsibility. In so doing, we have created an approach that while developing a justification for its role within management education, does not actually focus on the broader understanding of the differing interpretations of the roles and responsibilities of business in society. CSR in this context has simply become shorthand for the strategic activities undertaken by business in responding to ethical and environmental challenges, rather than a broader field of debate.

Given the challenges outlined above, it appears that one must question whether within this context we can be confident that the current frameworks for RME can really be expected to deliver the sort of education likely to create the levels of change within mindsets and business practice that contemporary environmental and social challenges demand. In order to avoid the stranglehold of a relatively restricted interpretation of responsible management based around a limited conceptualisation of CSR, and embrace and engage with these broader challenges, requires a more expansive set of parameters for framing RME. While arguably there are many ways and approaches for achieving this, we would like to return to the three areas of dominance identified above and reflect upon how we might be able to break this stranglehold. In each of these areas, emerging bodies of research and practice are demonstrating an alternative perspective on responsible management. In particular, they reflect a broader range of voices and interpretations of what the role of business in society might be.

Embracing CSR as a Contested Concept: Making the Most of the Open and Contentious Nature of Responsible Business

While the focus of CSR must, by definition, be about 'corporate' responsibility, this does not dictate that research and debate must be framed and restricted within a business and management discourse (Burchell and Cook, 2006). We argue that individual actors and alternative organisations that can influence the definitions, parameters and impact of 'social responsibility' should be brought to the forefront of the discussion. Only by including these competing voices can management education achieve the levels of change within mindsets and business practice that the current environmental and social challenges demand.

As the first half of this chapter argued, the business community has successfully moulded the discourse of CSR in a direction that suits their interests. Firms have narrowed the definition of responsible business to the extent that CSR in practice, in literature and higher education, is too often narrowly framed within the three themes that we have explored in this chapter. The CMS response to this challenge has largely been to accept that within the current market-based political economy, CSR is fundamentally unable to shift corporate strategies away from serving the interests of a few shareholders, towards prioritising social justice and environmental sustainability (Banerjee, 2010). However, Burchell and Cook (2006) argue that the use of CSR as a hybridised discourse and the appropriation of the language of social responsibility, actually offers the opportunity for challenge. Indeed, Chouliaraki and Fairclough (1999) note that hybridity represents not just a struggle for domination, but also a process of resistance. In other words, the changing discourse of CSR is not simply a one-sided process of appropriation, but also a dialectical confrontation over the meaning of responsible business practice. The door is therefore open for other stakeholders to reinterpret CSR discourse from their own perspective; we must not underestimate the agency of other groups to scrutinise, shape and influence the language of CSR from outside of the firm (Burchell and Cook, 2006).

In accepting that CSR can only reflect a hollow form of ethical rhetoric that disguises a process of 'business as usual', Critical Management approaches neglect the reflexive potential that exists within a language that seeks to appropriate issues of sustainability within a context of business practice. This process has the power to shape the future of business practice, since discourses 'help to constitute and re-constitute the world, just as surely as do institutions or material forces' (Dryzek, 1997: 201). Although the relationship between business and society has largely been constructed around a discourse that is based upon corporate interests, not societal interests (Windsor, 2001, cited in Banerjee, 2008: 52), the parameters of this relationship are not preset.

Indeed, there are many credible voices, located outside of the firm, seeking to define the roles and responsibilities of ethical and sustainable businesses. We suggest that teaching CSR ought to begin with these alternative voices, emphasising the emerging critique of contemporary business activity which sees a different role and position for business within society. Whilst business interpretation of CSR must undoubtedly feature in the curriculum, we argue that RME should firstly introduce students to these critiques and challenges in order to present a more open and challenging definition of CSR. We suggest that courses return to the radical roots of CSR by exploring the anti-capitalist critiques of the 1990s, the growth of the ecological critiques challenging existing models of economic growth, and the questioning of the role of business in society. In doing so, this enables students to place the emergence of CSR within the wider socio-political context and to emphasise its inherent contestability as a concept. Consequently, students will develop a broader understanding of CSR which does not succumb to the lure of business-centric, Westernised mainstream approaches described here.

Furthermore, in teaching a more open definition of CSR, students are encouraged to think more ambitiously and more critically about its potential impacts. If we take as a starting point the social movements that drive the critique of contemporary business practice and CSR as a response to those criticisms, the objectives of CSR can be broadened, to consider more ambitious societal goals such as addressing the roots of poverty reduction or reversing climate breakdown. This will inevitably call into question the win–win premise upon which the business case is based, pushing students to consider the possibility that genuine progress and development in these areas may require a shift of resources and/or power from one group to another. Rather than focussing on a narrow selection of philanthropic CSR initiatives and projects, we argue that RME must

encourage students to consider how the core business operations of the firm impact upon society. In doing so, students might consider that not all socially responsible decisions will have a business benefit, and therefore not all ethical issues can be resolved through a win–win scenario. If we are seeking to restructure the business–society relationship in such a way that addresses the roots of poverty, caused directly by corporate lobbying, such as reducing labour rights or displacing people from land, for example, we may need to consider the possibility of 'win–lose' scenarios. Students should be encouraged to consider not only the alignment of social and economic responsibilities of the firm, but also the conflict between these two imperatives.

Through this approach, we would encourage students to consider where individual ethics reside – what is the philosophy or set of values that underpins CSR? The values dimension of CSR, often overlooked in RME, emphasises not only *what* firms do in the social arena but *why* they do it. In considering these aspects, RME could emphasise the relational, rather than economic impacts of contemporary business practice. This would represent a much-needed move away from the traditional myopic, short-termist, business focus on maximising shareholder value which fosters within students an individualistic ethic of personal advantage and materialistic gain (Kolodinsky et al., 2010).

Whilst we acknowledge a role for the business case within CSR education, we suggest that it be taught as a second-order driver, with more consideration given to the socio-structural factors that shift norms and values that drive change in the first order (Higgins, 2010). It is social movements that shift public perception around particular issues, forcing them onto the corporate agenda and providing the catalyst for business managers to seek a business case for CSR (Higgins, 2010). Only once managers accept that changes are required, does the business case become valuable for selling it to internal stakeholders. We argue that RME should de-centre the business organisation and place it in the broader context of sociopolitical challenge and debate.

Expanding Voice and Agency: Moving Away from Stakeholder Management Towards Stakeholder Engagement and Dialogue

Bringing forward a stronger emphasis upon competing voices and interpretations can also help to reinterpret the ways in which key aspects of the responsible business field are interpreted and contextualised. One good example of this is the way in which research has examined stakeholder literature. Focusing upon the competing interpretations and conceptions of responsible management can potentially reshape our conceptualisation of stakeholders and stakeholder management. Again, by changing the dominance of business within the dialogue of responsible management and opening the doors to competing voices, one is able to engage with the stakeholder debates from a slightly different angle. As mentioned previously, traditional stakeholder management literature takes as its starting point the central role of business, leading it to view the stakeholder debate in terms of which stakeholders companies identify as relevant and focusing upon how they can best 'manage' relationships with these stakeholders in order to improve business performance.

Within traditional stakeholder management approaches, CSR is organised and defined from within the organisation vis-à-vis its stakeholders, where external stakeholders are implicitly or explicitly subjugated to the corporate CSR policies communicated to them (Burchell and Cook, 2013). Effective stakeholder management is 'built upon managers and companies being able to improve their relationships with stakeholders and to balance their responses so that stakeholders are fairly and effectively dealt with' (Carroll,

2015: 92). As Coronado and Fallon articulate, 'this business-centric perspective is ingrained within stakeholder management, mapping the process like a wagon wheel with the company at its heart and the stakeholders around the periphery' (Coronado and Fallon, 2010).

In response to these challenges, a growing body of work is developing which seeks to redress the imbalance in stakeholder analysis by placing the primary focus on the perspectives and experiences of stakeholders, approaching CSR through a more nuanced, multi-actor lens, which does not always place the strategic objectives of the firm centre-stage (Burchell and Cook, 2013; Jonker and Nijhof, 2006). Analysis by den Hond and de Bakker (2007) and King (2008), for example, point towards the increasing influence of campaign organisations as 'secondary stakeholders' gaining their influence over the business community via their increased levels of public support and the successful championing of ethical and environmental claims onto both the political and business agendas. Similarly, Palacios (2010) highlights how the adoption of the language of corporate citizenship opens up channels for challenge, through which he sees NGOs and anti-globalisation movements developing new roles as 'civil regulators', constructing a governance framework challenging the power of multinationals.

Placing more emphasis upon the issues, debates and perspectives emerging within this literature, within responsible management education, will arguably challenge business and management students to consider more closely the roles and relationships between businesses and other social actors. Again such an approach offers much in the way of channelling the primary focus away from a business-centric, instrumental conceptualisation of responsible management based upon the prioritisation of the business organisation. Rather than placing business centre-stage, this more holistic framework places organisational engagement and strategic development in the more complex, contested terrain in which business approaches must engage with the perspectives, actions and abilities of the diverse range of stakeholders who are actually being impacted by business actions and decisions (Friedman and Miles, 2002; Frooman, 1999; Steurer, 2006). In particular, these approaches are moving away from a focus upon how businesses are able to 'manage' the demands of multiple stakeholders, and instead are focusing upon the ability of the different sets of stakeholders to exert influence over companies, and to reflect on and challenge the development and conceptualisation of CSR as a strategic frame (Burchell and Cook, 2008).

Approaching responsible management education from these alternative voices, we would argue, challenges students to engage with broader debates regarding the role of business in society. Developing a critical conceptualisation of stakeholder engagement and activity poses important questions regarding the innate contestability of the CSR concept and the failure of existing approaches to fully recognise the agency of individuals and organisations to reflect upon and utilise the concept in different ways. In doing so, it raises questions about exactly how stakeholder engagement can engage all actors so that business activity is seen to truly benefit society as a whole.

Stronger Understanding of CSR in a Developing Context

Since the global commitment to the Sustainable Development Goals (SDGs) in 2015, there have been renewed calls for multinational corporations to play a central role in the development agenda, not only from academia (Buhmann et al., 2018) but also from corporates themselves (KPMG, 2017). In a 2017 report, KPMG declared that 'though the SDGs are universally accepted by various governments, their success relies heavily on the action and collaboration with businesses and civil society', calling

on businesses to 'apply their creativity and innovation in solving the sustainable challenges' (KPMG, 2017). Given the increasing focus on businesses to make direct contributions to the development agenda, we argue that RME must emphasise a stronger understanding of CSR in a developing context.

This must involve engaging with theorists who critique the 'CSR as good development' perspective. An emerging literature has challenged the way that CSR is operationalised in the developing context, suggesting that it does not actually improve the conditions of its intended beneficiaries (Blowfield and Frynas, 2005; Jamali and Mirshak, 2007; Newell and Frynas, 2007). As Khan and Lund-Thomsen (2011) have observed, this represents a welcome addition to management-oriented CSR literature that has a tendency to uncritically embrace the notion of the firm as an appropriate agent of development. However, we argue that RME must go further and include the more radical voices, which offer a fundamental critique of the assumed benign nature of CSR in the developing world.

Rather than simply assessing the success or failure of CSR initiatives in Latin America, Africa and Asia, this academic niche combines perspectives of power and postcolonial thought to consider the dangers of traditional approaches to CSR in the developing world. By drawing on postcolonial theory, these theorists show how CSR dynamics in the developing world are affected by imperial history (Drebes, 2016; Jaya, 2001; Khan and Lund-Thomsen, 2011). We would encourage students to consider this broader sociopolitical historical context, with a view to fostering an understanding of the relationships and power inequalities between different stakeholders in CSR initiatives in the developing world, and the objectives pursued by those in the power network.

This more critical literature understands mainstream CSR initiatives as Eurocentric, developed and implemented without the inclusion of the subaltern stakeholder. This scholarship acknowledges that the ones 'taking responsibility' (driving CSR) are usually actors from developed nations, whilst those on the receiving end of 'responsible business practice' are stakeholders from the developing world (Drebes, 2016). RME should encourage students to consider what does CSR mean when it is articulated in the language of the West, and when many of the relevant stakeholders do not have the opportunity to take part in the debate, or when they do, their voices are too silent to be heard by drivers of the discussion (Drebes, 2016). Too often, academic discussion and practical implementation of CSR is based on the notion that there exist certain universal values and norms about the responsibilities of firms and about how to better improve the livelihood and well-being of all stakeholders. RME should encourage students to challenge this notion, and consider whether corporations, in their modern capitalist environment, can truly recognise values rooted in other cultures. In doing so, business schools could facilitate a context-based discussion that does not 'reproduce postcolonial power relations between the West and the rest' (Drebes, 2016: 105). Students ought to consider that by excluding the voice of the subaltern, and in their bold ambitions to save the planet and the natives from their corrupt and incompetent governments, mainstream CSR initiatives in the postcolonial world represent a form of stakeholder colonialism and a reimagining of the white man's burden (Drebes, 2016; Jamali and Mirshak, 2007).

Where RME does engage with positive case studies of successful CSR (their success measured by delivering on the needs of the stakeholders, and not on their ability to spin Eurocentric, problematic CSR initiatives like the TOMS case), it should look to alternative business and NGO models that seek to catalyse transformative social change by tackling deeper fundamental causes of power, rather than treating the symptoms. This will necessarily involve a move away from focusing on Western examples, but also applying appropriate scrutiny to those well-known case studies,

celebrated in the business community, that suffer from the criticisms outlined above. This ought to engage future business leaders in a much-needed more critical examination of relationships between corporations, NGOs, governments, community groups and funding agencies (Banerjee, 2006). RME must also engage with a deeper critique and be prepared to challenge students to question whether CSR is an appropriate vehicle for tackling key development issues like global poverty, human rights and climate breakdown.

CONCLUSION

The discussion above offers only a brief snapshot of some of the key areas in which RME could strive to move away from a business-centric, instrumentalist approach to CSR and sustainability issues. Other areas, such as the rise of Social Enterprise models, offer further areas for challenge and the potential to question whether the existing business frameworks are necessarily the best suited to responding to the social and environmental challenges facing contemporary society. In outlining the discussion above, we do not seek to prescribe a one-size-fits-all model for how to approach issues of responsible management; or to suggest that there are not exceptionally original and challenging approaches being adopted. Rather we seek to encourage those engaged within the field to consider whether there is more that we can do to push the boundaries of what and how some of these issues are being taught, and why we pushed to get these topics onto academic curricula in the first place.

As highlighted earlier, RME has in some ways become more constrained through its desire to become seen as part of the mainstream of business and management education. In seeking to get these issues adopted into curricula and accepted within research journals, we have 'softened' some of the sharper edges and framed the arguments, rationales and debates in language that is more palatable to mainstream management disciplines. In doing so, however, we are in danger of simplifying the debates about the role of business in society into a strategic framework for how business can marry increased profits with the perception of being socially responsible. The reason it was difficult for business schools to accept these issues as part of their curricula was precisely because they challenged some of the core preconceptions about the underlying principles of business. We need to ensure that the reason they have become more accepted now, is precisely because there is a recognition of the failures of those previous underlying principles and not because responsible management education no longer represents any challenge to the mainstream.

REFERENCES

Andriof, J. and McIntosh, M. (Eds.) (2001) *Perspectives on Corporate Citizenship*. Sheffield: Greenleaf Publishing.

Ashforth, B. E. and Gibbs, B. W. (1990) The double-edge of organizational legitimation. *Organization Science*, 1, 177–194.

Banerjee, B. (2006) Corporate citizenship, social responsibility and sustainability: corporate colonialism for the new millennium? In Jonker, J. and de Witte, M. (Eds.), *The Challenge of Organizing and Implementing Corporate Social Responsibility*. New York: Palgrave, 31–50.

Banerjee, B. (2008) Corporate social responsibility: the good, the bad and the ugly. *Critical Sociology*, 34(1), 51–79.

Banerjee, B. (2010) Governing the global corporation: a critical perspective. *Business Ethics Quarterly*, 20(2), 265–274.

Blowfield, M. and Frynas, J. G. (2005) Setting new agendas: critical perspectives on corporate social responsibility in the developing world. *International Affairs*, 81(3), 499–513.

Brooks, S. (2010) CSR and the strait-jacket of economic rationality. *International Journal of Sociology and Social Policy*, 30(11/12), 604–617.

Buhmann, K., Jonsson, J. and Fisker, M. (2018) 'Do no harm' and 'do more good' too: connecting the SDGs with business and human rights and political CSR theory. *Corporate Governance*, 19(3), 389–403.

Burchell, J. and Cook, J. (2006) Confronting the 'corporate citizen'. *International Journal of Sociology and Social Policy*, 26(3/4), 121–137.

Burchell, J. and Cook, J. (2008) Stakeholder dialogue and organisational learning: changing relationships between companies and NGOs, *Business Ethics: A European Review*, 17(1), 35–46.

Burchell, J. and Cook, J. (2013) CSR, co-optation and resistance: the emergence of new agonistic relations between business and civil society. *Journal of Business Ethics*, 115, 741–754.

Carroll, A. (1991) The pyramid of corporate social responsibility: towards the moral management of organizational stakeholders. *Business Horizons*, 34(4), 39–48.

Carroll, A. (2015) Corporate Social Responsibility: the centerpiece of competing and complementary frameworks. *Organizational Dynamics*, 44, 87–96.

Carroll, A. B. and Bickholtz, A. K. (2000) *Business and Society: Ethics and Stakeholder Management*. Cincinnati, OH: South Western Publishing.

Chouliaraki, L. and Fairclough, N. (1999) *Discourse in Late Modernity: Rethinking Critical Discourse Analysis*. Edinburgh: Edinburgh University Press.

Coronado, G. and Fallon, W. (2010) 'Giving with one hand', *International Journal of Sociology and Social Policy*, 30(11/12), 666–682.

Cowe, R. and Hopkins, M. (2008) Corporate Social Responsibility: is there a business case? In Burchell, J. (Ed.), *The Corporate Social Responsibility Reader*. London: Routledge.

Crane, A., Matten, D. and Moon, J. (2008) Ecological citizenship and the corporation: politicizing the new corporate environmentalism. *Organization and Environment*, 21(4), 371–389.

den Hond, F. and de Bakker, G. A. (2007) Ideologically motivated activism: how activist groups influence corporate social change activities. *Academy of Management Review*, 32(3), 901–924.

Donaldson, T. and Preston, L. (1995) The stakeholder theory of the corporation: concepts, evidence and implications. *Academy of Management Review*, 32(3), 901–924.

Drebes, M. (2016) Including the 'other': power and postcolonialism as underrepresented perspectives in the discourse on corporate social responsibility. *Critical Sociology*, 42(1), 105–121.

Dryzek, J. S. (1997) *The Politics of the Earth: Environmental Discourses*. Oxford: Oxford University Press.

Fleming, P. and Jones, M. T. (2012) *The End of Corporate Social Responsibility: Crisis and Critique*. London: Sage.

Freeman, R. (1984) *Strategic Management: A Stakeholder Approach*. Boston, MA: Pitman.

Friedman, A. and Miles, S. (2002) Socially responsible investment and corporate social and environmental reporting in the UK: an exploratory study. *Accounting Review*, 33(4), 523–548.

Frooman, J. (1999) Stakeholder influence strategies. *Academy of Management Review*, 24(2), 191–205.

Frynas, J. G. and Stephens, S. (2015) Political corporate social responsibility: reviewing theories and setting new agendas. *International Journal of Management Reviews*, 17(4), 482–509.

Gray, R., Dey, C., Owen, D., Evans, R. and Zadek, S. (1997) Struggling with the praxis of social accounting: stakeholders, accountability, auditing and reporting. *Accounting, Auditing & Accountability Journal*, 10(3), 325–364.

Hanlon, G. (2008) Rethinking Corporate Social Responsibility and the role of the firm – on the denial of politics. In Crane, A., Matten, D., McWilliams, A., Moon, J. and Siegel, D. S. (Eds.), *The Handbook of Corporate Social Responsibility*. Oxford: Oxford University Press, 157–172.

Higgins, C. (2010) Is a responsive business also a responsible business? *Journal of Business Systems, Governance and Ethics*, 5(3), 23–32.

Hill, R. P and Langan, R. (2014) *Handbook of Research on Marketing and Corporate Social Responsibility*. Cheltenham: Edward Elgar Publishing.

Jamali, D. and Mirshak, R. (2007) Corporate social responsibility (CSR): theory and practice in a developing country context. *Journal of Business Ethics*, 72(3), 243–262.

Jaya, P. S. (2001) Do we really 'know' and 'profess'? Decolonizing Management Knowledge. *Organization*, 8(2), 227–233.

Jonker, J. and Nijhof, A. (2006) Looking through the eyes of others: assessing mutual expectations and experiences in order to shape dialogue and collaboration between business and NGOs with respect to CSR. *Corporate Governance – An International Review*, 14(5), 456–466.

Khan, F. R. and Lund-Thomsen, P. (2011) CSR as imperialism: towards a phenomenological approach to CSR in the developing world. *Journal of Change Management*, 11(1), 73–90.

King, B. (2008) A social movement perspective of stakeholder collective action and influence. *Business and Society*, 47, 21–49.

Kolodinsky, R. W., Madden, T. M., Zisk, D. S. and Henkel, E. T. (2010) Attitudes about corporate social responsibility: business student predictors. *Journal of Business Ethics*, 91(2), 167–181.

KPMG (2017) Sustainable Development Goals (SDGs): leveraging CSR to achieve SDGs. First Sustainable Development Goals (SDGs) Summit 2017. Available at: https://assets. kpmg/content/dam/kpmg/in/pdf/2017/12/ SDG_New_Final_Web.pdf (Accessed 21 February 2020)

Makinen, J. and Kourula, A. (2012) Pluralism in political corporate social responsibility. *Business Ethics Quarterly*, 22(4), 649–678.

Matten, D. and Crane, A. (2005) Corporate citizenship: toward an extended theoretical conceptualization. *Academy of Management Review*, 30(1), 166–179.

McWilliams, A. and Siegel, D. (2001) Corporate social responsibility: a theory of the firm perspective. *Academy of Management Review*, 26(1), 117–127.

Moosmayer, D., Waddock, S., Wang, L., Huhn, M. P., Dierksmeier, C. and Gohl, C. (2019) Leaving the road to Abilene: a pragmatic approach to addressing the normative paradox of responsible management education. *Journal of Business Ethics*, 157(4), 913–932.

Newell, P. and Frynas, J. G. (2007) Beyond CSR? Business, poverty and social justice: an introduction. *Third World Quarterly*, 28(4), 669–681.

Nijhof, A. J. and Jeurisson, R. J. M (2010) The glass ceiling of corporate social responsibility. *International Journal of Sociology and Social Policy*, 30(11/12), 618–631.

Orlitzky, M., Schmidt, F. L. and Rynes, S. L. (2003) Corporate social and financial performance: a meta-analysis. *Organization Studies*, 24(3), 403–441.

Owen, D. and O'Dwyer, B. (2008) Corporate social responsibility: the reporting and assurance dimension. In Crane, A. et al. (Eds.), *The Oxford Handbook of Corporate Social Responsibility*. Oxford: Oxford University Press, 384–412.

Palacios, J. (2010) Corporate citizenship and social responsibility in a globalized world. *Citizenship Studies*, 8(4), 393–402.

Parker, M. (2003) Business, ethics and business ethics: critical theory and negative dialectics. In Alvesson, M. and Willmott, H. (Eds.), *Studying Management Critically*. London: Sage, 197–219.

Pataki, G. (2009) Ecological modernization as a paradigm of corporate sustainability. *Sustainable Development*, 17(2), 82–91.

Porter, M. and Kramer, M. R. (2011) The big idea: creating shared value. *Harvard Business Review*, 89, 2–17.

Scherer, A. G., Rasche, A., Palazzo, G. and Spicer, A. (2016) Managing for political corporate social responsibility: new challenges and directions for PCSR 2.0. *Journal of Management Studies*, 53(3), 273–298.

Setó-Pamies, D. and Papaoikonomou, E. (2016) A Multi-level Perspective for the Integration of ethics, Corporate Social Responsibility and Sustainability (ECSRS) in Management Education. *Journal of Business Ethics,* 136, 523–538.

Shamir, R. (2008) The age of responsibilisation: on market-embedded morality. *Economy and Society*, 37(1), 1–19.

Steurer, R. (2006) Mapping stakeholder theory anew: from the 'Stakeholder theory of the firm' to the three perspectives on business-society relations. *Business, Strategy and the Environment*, 15, 55–69.

Suchman, M. C. (1995) Managing legitimacy: strategic and institutional approaches. *Academy of Management Review*, 20(3), 729–757.

Swanson, D. (1999) Toward an integrative theory of business in society: a research strategy for corporate social performance. *Academy of Management Review*, 24(3), 506–521.

Waddock, S. and Graves, S. V. (1997) The corporate social performance–financial performance link. *Strategic Management Journal*, 18(4), 303–320.

Wydick, B., Katz., E., Calvo, F., Gutierrez, F. and Janet, B. (2018) Shoeing the children: the impact of the TOMS shoe donation program in rural El Salvador, *World Bank Economic Review*, 32(3), 727–751.

Zadek, S. (2001) *The Civil Corporation*. London: Earthscan.

10

Poverty and Responsible Management Education

Geri Mason and Al Rosenbloom

Poverty has been a persistent characteristic of human society throughout history (Beaudoin, 2006; Sachs, 2006). Yet, it was not until 1990, when the World Bank's *World Development Report* (WDR) chose poverty as its theme, that the issue of poverty was put firmly on the world's development agenda. Both the Millennium Development Goals and the Sustainable Development Goals had poverty eradication as Goal #1, thereby confirming the salience of poverty as the most important human development challenge the world faces. One decade later, the relationship between multinational corporations and the poor was transformed when C. K. Prahalad and colleagues defined the Base of the Pyramid (BoP) Proposition. Since that initial formulation, which reframed the poor as consumers (BoP 1.0), BoP insights have expanded to view the poor as both consumers *and* producers (BoP 2.0) as well as to include environmental sustainability, the triple bottom line and value-co-creation as integral to developing scalable BoP strategies (BoP 3.0).

Parallel to this evolution in thinking about the BoP was the emergence of the poor as a legitimate field of management inquiry and scholarship. Comprehensive literature reviews now exist for the BoP (Dembek, Sivasubramaniam & Chmielewski, 2019; Follman, 2012; Kolk, Rivera-Santos & Rufin, 2014) as well as for the disciplines of international business (Kolk, Rivera-Santos & Rufin, 2018), entrepreneurship (Sutter, Bruton & Chen, 2019), and marketing (Sridharan, Barrington & Saunders, 2017). Yet to be explored is the issue of poverty as a legitimate responsible management and learning topic. This chapter aims to fill that gap.

The chapter argues that while there are current touchpoints within management education where students and faculty discuss poverty, missing from most pedagogical approaches is the treatment of poverty as a threshold concept (Meyer & Land, 2003, 2005). When taught as a threshold concept, 'poverty' becomes a more complicated, more nuanced, more multidimensional concept that requires students to think through the interactions between business strategy, business ethics, sustainable development and responsibility. This places poverty squarely within the domain of responsible management learning. The chapter also summarizes the pedagogical literature on poverty in management education. Because faculty mediate what and how knowledge is developed, the chapter assesses the empirical research on faculty attitudes toward poverty. The chapter concludes with a look to the future as to how to integrate poverty further into responsible management education and learning.

POVERTY AND RESPONSIBLE MANAGEMENT

Previous to the development of the base of the pyramid concept, multinational firms engaged with the poor primarily through philanthropy (Kolk et al., 2018). The seminal work of Prahalad and Hart (2002), Prahalad and Hammond (2002) and Hart and Christensen (2002) challenged that perspective by radically repositioning the relationship between corporations and the poor. This initial formulation of the Base of the Pyramid (BoP) Proposition highlighted the untapped buying power hidden within poor communities when viewed as an aggregated market. Multinational firms could simultaneously 'address poverty while achieving profitable financial results', if multinational firms simply designed 'specific products and services for improving [the poor's] living standards' (Bisignano, Werhane & Ehret, 2017: 197). The initial BoP formulation had a strong marketing orientation: Find untapped needs and fill them.

However, as experience with low income markets increased, finding the 'fortune' *at* the base of the pyramid proved difficult and a more meaningful view of the poor emerged. The poor should be viewed as producers as well as consumers, which is fundamental

to the concept of inclusive markets (Mason, 2016). When viewed from this integrative view, the business case for targeting the poor is to facilitate human capital development and entrepreneurship (education, training, microfinance, productivity enhancing products, etc.). Inclusive market thinking squarely places the poor within the entire business eco-system for it identifies opportunities for inclusion from the beginning to ending of the value chain.

Nonetheless, managerial insights into the BoP have continued to evolve. London (2016) suggests that the poor should be engaged as 'partners', thereby allowing for new, entrepreneurial enterprises through co-venturing. Here the perspective shifted to finding 'fortune' *with* the base of the pyramid. The most recent formulation of the BoP proposition is 'now seeking a greater conceptual shift, away from singular solutions of poverty alleviation to understanding how wider innovation ecosystems and engagement through cross-sector partnership networks can be developed' (Mason, Chakrabarti & Singh, 2017: 267). In spite of the concerted attention given to understanding how business entities can profitably engage the poor, the BoP Proposition has proven elusive (Arora & Romijn, 2012). It has 'turned out to be a difficult endeavor calling for endurance, imagination, patient capital, and a willingness to build new skills and capabilities' (Hart, Sharma & Halme, 2016: 411.) Nevertheless, business engagement with the poor fits squarely within the domain of responsible management.

As defined by Laasch (2018), responsible management is 'a type of management that integrates sustainability, responsibility, and ethics into managerial practice(s)' (p. 2). The BoP Proposition expresses an organization's commitment to corporate social responsibility (Arnold & Valentin, 2013), while simultaneously raising ethical issues for individuals working with the poor and other marginalized communities (Laczniak & Santos, 2011; Wisor, 2017). For example, inadequate housing, coupled with low savings, means that the poor are disproportionately affected by environmental catastrophes and the lack of sustainable development (Hart et al., 2016; Khavul & Bruton, 2013).

It is sometimes overlooked, but the BoP Proposition has always been a statement about corporate responsibility: By targeting the poor with products and services designed specifically for them and by them, along with enhancing productive capacity for the poor, corporations could generate revenue for themselves *and* alleviate poverty. The BoP Proposition, thus, expresses an advanced view of the relationship between business and society: That business organizations 'are integrated within, rather than detached from, the rest of society' (Lindgreen, Maon, Vanhamme, Florencio, Vallaster & Strong, 2019: xxix). Business enterprises, therefore, have moral obligations for their behavior.

Stakeholder theory suggests that responsible firms engage in ongoing, reflective discussions with groups that will be affected by their actions. Responsibility derives from the firm's continuous assessment of impact, and the firm's willingness to change its strategies based on negative or harmful economic, social, or environmental stakeholder consequences. As organizations have sought to build inclusive supply chains and to think more fully about their relationships with the poor, 'the poor, the weak and the illiterate' have moved from being 'fringe stakeholders' to being simply 'stakeholders' (Hart & Sharma, 2004: 8). However, their lack of access to functioning institutions and decreased relative bargaining power places the responsibility to act consciously and strategically squarely on the firm. Therefore, the responsibility to develop a comprehensive understanding of poverty *before* engaging with these consumers and producers is essential.

Central to responsible management is the individual's ability to develop a reflexive response to the ethical issues that arise simply from doing one's job. In the BoP context, one such deeply embedded ethical issue is: How do firms and other business entities co-create and co-venture with the poor so as not to exploit them (Hahn, 2009)? For example, simply giving the poor a role in the value chain falls short of full responsibility. Karnani (2006) expresses the ever-present concern about exploitation resulting from the poor's vulnerability and marginalization.

Laasch (2018) notes that what distinguishes responsible management from other forms of responsible behavior is its application to the 'average,' practicing manager. The integrative justice model answers the practicing manager's question, 'What does it pragmatically mean [for me] to conduct business ethically when engaging impoverished market segments?' by providing a normative model for developing 'just' and 'fair' marketplace transactions (Santos & Laczniak, 2012: 2). This concern is a paramount reason for integrating a comprehensive understanding of poverty into responsible management education. Firms are called beyond the boundaries of their spreadsheets to engage with a highly vulnerable group: the poor. 'Business as usual' will not be enough to address the complex social and market facets of poverty sustainably, although it may be enough to extract profit from the base of the pyramid.

Multinationals that seek to do business with the BoP also suffer inherently from the liability of foreignness (London & Hart, 2004; Zaheer, 1995), that is, they are inevitably outsiders to the BoP and marginalized communities they seek to understand and serve. This implicit power imbalance creates another opportunity for exploitation. As Wettstein (2005) argues: Size obligates. Hahn (2009) grounds the moral obligation of corporations to act responsibly in relation to the BoP in the affirmative duties described in UN's Declaration of Human Rights, in Kant's categorical imperative and in Rawls' principles of justice. The BoP Protocol (Simanis, Hart & Duke, 2008) along with the Poverty Alleviation through Partnership Approach (Werhane et al., 2010), help translate these philosophical underpinnings of right action into a tangible, easy-to-understand framework that provides guidance to managers who work with the poor. All emphasize respect, empathetic listening and deep dialogue as foundational for responsibly working with the poor. In so doing, poverty and the poor fit directly within responsible management's domain.

Sustainable development further aligns responsible management with the poor. Frequently, the Brundtland Commission's definition of sustainable development as 'development that meets the needs of the present without compromising the ability of future generations to meet their own needs' (WCED, 1987: 16) is the starting point for sustainable development discussions. Often overlooked is the Brundtland Commission's reference to the poor: '[Sustainable development] contains within it ... the concept of "needs", in particular the essential needs of the world's poor, to which overriding priority should be given ...' (WCED, 1987: 43).

The centrality of poverty eradication as both a paramount sustainable development and a human development issue was codified in the Millennium Development Goals (2001) and their successor, the Sustainable Development Goals (2015). Both sets of goals had poverty eradication as Goal #1. Unlike the Millennium Development Goals which had eight goals and were meant as development goals primarily for the Global South (Vandemoortele, 2013), the Sustainable Development Goals (SDGs) have 17 goals, which are universal in terms of both their applicability to every country in the world and to all societal actors (e.g. cities, businesses, governments, schools, higher education institutions, civil society organizations, non-governmental agencies, and citizens) if all 17 goals are to be achieved by 2030.

The SDGs create a constructive framework for markets to address poverty alleviation. This is vital to every attempt to influence the lives of the poor. Responsible management, however, takes this one step further: it becomes the purview of companies engaged with the BoP to *take responsibility for* their own actions *and* the lives of the poor.

At the level of global institutions, the UN Global Compact and the UN Principles for Responsible Management Education (PRME) explicitly integrate management educators and businesses in their call to action, setting these two groups forward as the *primary* actors in the work for sustainable development. Higher education institutions shape thinking and philosophy regarding sustainable development and management, while businesses actively manage resources and drive sustainability results more than any other group. Responsible management education (RME) is therefore crucial in order to equip corporate leaders with the attitudes and knowledge to actuate the SDGs through all aspects of BoP encounters. Without this dimension, interactions with the poor are in a disengaged space where multinational corporations and other businesses may enter to seek profit with perhaps little regard for the lives of the poor, from whom they are earning their profits. This is why Jäger and Sathe (2015) insist that purpose must be part of the BoP recipe – and RME delivers just that.

Mason (2016) notes, 'Business is the farthest-reaching institution in human society and controls most of the Earth's resources, including natural resources, financial resources and human capital' (p. 79). Because of the amount of resources that businesses control (Vitali et al., 2011), change in how these resources are managed, utilized and targeted will not happen unless it happens through business management. This level of resource control mandates that business play a role in the SDGs. Responsible management will ensure that decision-makers in these roles are making choices that are responsible from a global perspective rather than limited to what is best for select stakeholders. Understanding the complexity of poverty (SDG #1: No Poverty) is the foundation for understanding the intricate links between the SDGs, and the key to achieving them through business.

POVERTY AND ITS NEXUS WITH RESPONSIBLE LEARNING

Discussion so far has focused on how poverty aligns with responsible management. The discussion now turns to responsible management *learning*, in other words, to the mechanics of implementation: how are business schools including poverty issues in their curricula and modules and what pedagogical techniques are being applied?

Godemann, Herzig and Moon (2011) and Ruskino (2010) provide two well-referenced frameworks for understanding how emergent topics, such as sustainability and poverty, can be integrated into responsible management curricula. Figure 10.1 simplifies these two frameworks by positing two dimensions to every curriculum: Knowledge and Experience. Knowledge is cognitive, theoretical and/or content oriented, and it is often developed in the classroom through lecture, homework, exams, quizzes and in-class, active learning. Experience is affective; it is the result of interaction and reflection, often – but not always – outside the classroom.

The experience dimension of Figure 10.1 acknowledges that business schools are complex learning environments, in which students can learn about poverty through the formal curriculum as well as through the hidden (Blasco, 2012), the informal (Caza & Brower, 2015), or the co-curriculum (Stirling & Kerr, 2015).

These latter three facets of curricula complement and often extend learning experiences from formal classroom instruction.

As Figure 10.1 indicates, courses, programs and/or curricula can exist anywhere within this two-dimensional space. For example, course A would be a course that spends little time discussing poverty and thus has little or no experiential activities related to the topic. In contrast, courses B and D combine both knowledge and experiential learning elements about poverty, although they do it at different levels of intensity. Course C represents a 100% lecture course with no experiential components. Figure 10.1 also is a framework to analyze and/or conceptualize any educational units larger than a course, such as a program, module, or curriculum, since each can be designed to include knowledge and experience dimensions (Fink, 2013).

Poverty: Knowledge Dimension

Poverty: A threshold concept

As Hibbert and Cunliffe (2015) summarize the work of Meyer and Land (2003, 2005), a threshold concept is 'a concept that alters the way we think about knowledge that is central to understanding a discipline' (p. 180). Poverty is a threshold concept in the BoP, economic development, sustainable development and/or subsistence marketplace contexts. Students must have an understanding

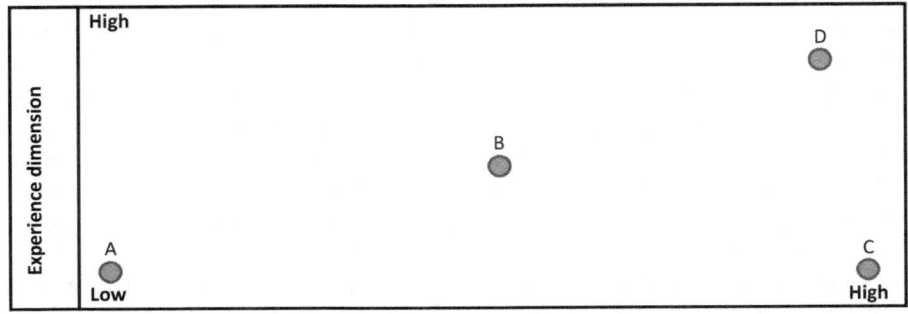

Figure 10.1   Knowledge–experience matrix with hypothetical plots

of poverty 'basics': what poverty is, its causes, its prevalence globally and locally, and how it is measured. Without this threshold knowledge, discussions about responsible management practice in the context of poor and marginalized communities become ungrounded and narrow.

This imperative to treat poverty as a threshold concept is underscored by Dembek et al.'s (2019) systematic review of the BoP literature that found that 'one-third of the 203 articles included in the review do not even define what poverty is' (Dembek & Sivasubramaniam, 2018: 244). And when researchers did define poverty, 'the majority of the of BoP research [used] an income-based definition' (Dembek et al., 2019: 17). A more nuanced, expansive view of poverty follows next.

Poverty is a multidimensional concept that defies easy definition, measurement and resolution (de Janvry & Sadoulet, 2016; Jefferson, 2018). Hulme (2010) states that, 'Poverty is not a set of self-evident "facts"; it has many potential dimensions and these can be presented in many different ways' (p. 51). Poverty may be construed as a narrow concept (conceptualized along one dimension, such as defining an absolute poverty line) or as a broad concept (including both material and nonmaterial deprivations, such as low income, poor health, financial exclusion, illiteracy, powerlessness, violence and marginalization). Additionally, different units of analysis (such as measuring poverty at the individual, family, household or country level) lead to different insights and understandings.

Historically, poverty has been understood in terms of income (Laderchi, 2000; Roundtree, 1901). As Ravallion (1992) states, 'The most important reason for measuring poverty is probably not the need for a single number for some place and date, but rather to make a poverty comparison. This is an assessment of which of two situations has more poverty' (p. 1).

Amartya Sen (1999) asks an important question: Why does low income matter as a measure of poverty? His answer is that it doesn't matter in its own right. For Sen, income is simply a means to an end. 'What really matters [is] the kind of life that a person is able to lead and the choices and opportunities open to her in leading that life' (Lister, 2004: 15). Persons living in poverty do not have the freedom 'to choose between different ways of living that they can have reason to value' (Sen, 1990: 114). Although Sen has his critics (Comiling & Sanchez, 2014; Dean, 2009; Pogge, 2010), his contribution to understanding poverty is significant (Desai, 2001). Sen's ideas link poverty with human development through the capabilities approach, and his early ideas served as foundational concepts for the UN's Human Development Index (Anand & Sen, 1997; UNDP, 1997).

Students need to understand Sen's perspective on poverty for a number of reasons. First, Sen's perspective expands the dimensions of poverty beyond the unidimensional criteria of income. Second, Sen's focus is on the individual and her lived experiences. This enables students to think of the poor as real people. '[W]e have to abandon the habit of reducing the poor to cartoon characters and take the time to really understand their lives, in all their complexity and richness' (Banerjee & Duflo, 2011: 9). Third, Sen's work helps make more visible to students the universal nature of such contemporary issues as gender inequality, which also exist within the poor (Bennett & Daly, 2014; Razavi, 2000). Fourth, because Sen redirects attention to ensuring that all individuals have the resources they need to lead lives of 'purpose, meaning, and fulfillment' (Jefferson, 2018: 36), poverty reduction is fundamentally repositioned as a responsible management topic in all countries, regardless of GDP per capita.

A complementary perspective

The subsistence marketplaces initiative seeks to understand how consumer consumption and exchange function in low income, thinly resourced communities. Consumers in subsistence marketplaces have low literacy, low education levels, low numeracy, and potentially misplace trust in those making the decisions about what to produce and market to them. Yet the subsistence marketplaces initiative is different from the BoP perspective. Whereas the BoP approach starts from the viewpoint of the enterprise and is therefore a top-down perspective, the subsistence marketplaces initiative is a bottom-up approach, which begins with the consumer living in subsistence (Venugopal & Viswanathan, 2017; Viswanathan, Shultz & Sridharan, 2014; Viswanathan & Venugopal, 2015). This bottom-up approach creates a rich picture of 'individual life circumstances at the micro level … providing understanding of what people in subsistence strive to sustain' (Gau & Viswanathan, 2018: 434). By engaging the realities identified in subsistence marketplaces, responsible learning now confronts this inescapable truth: 'Uncertainty and lack of margin of error [are] at the heart of low-income contexts' (p. 434).

Teaching for knowledge development

Students can gain threshold knowledge about poverty by reading Banerjee and Duflo's (2011) *Poor Economics. Poor Economics* is a non-technical introduction to poverty's multiple dimensions, and when coupled with the book's supplemental website (www. pooreconomics.com/) and occasional MOOC (www.edx.org/), provides students with a holistic picture of poverty. Similarly, subsistence marketplaces can also be brought to life through the MOOC that explains the focus of subsistence marketplaces through video profiles of various individuals living in subsistence (www.coursera.org/learn/subsistence-marketplaces).

From a faculty, course-development perspective, there is a small literature specifically focused on teaching about poverty in the context of responsible management. For example, Tripathi, Prakash and Amann (2016) provide an integrated flowchart that

strategically aligns what businesses are actually doing to engage the poor with educational course and program objectives. Their flowchart provides the intellectual linkages between knowledge created through research with the requirements for curricula in courses, modules and programs designed to reflect that knowledge (2016: 57).

Mason (2016) elucidates three key elements for the integration of poverty into any curriculum: a multifaceted understanding of the concept of poverty; the paradigm of incorporating the production capacity and role of the poor as a producer; and the ability to connect poverty research outcomes and business practices. Neal (2017) describes four thematic areas that can be used as pedagogical gateways for discussing poverty in a traditional management curriculum: multinational enterprises in developing countries; social enterprises; the poor as markets; and microfinance/microlending.

Gudić, Rosenbloom & Parkes (2014) place poverty discussions within the context of the 'socially responsive organization'. Their edited volume takes a broad view of management and its relation to poverty, by including underreported topics in management education, such as energy insufficiency, water scarcity, strategic design and crowdsourcing. That volume also discusses poverty prevalence in marginalized communities, such as Palestine or the Roma in Bosnia Herzegovina. The book includes a number of standalone cases that illustrate inclusive market development, responsible hiring, product innovation and responsible solutions to food insecurity.

At the course level, there are examples of what marketing and organizational behavior faculty have done to integrate poverty into their respective courses (Motta & Brashear, 2016; Rivera, 2016; Subramahniyan & Gomez, 2016). Further, Paton, Harris-Boundy and Melhus (2012) describe various class assignments that deepen student understanding of the BoP. Neal (2017) also provides a list of selected teaching resources relevant to poverty discussions, as does the online resource *Best Practices and Inspirational Solutions* (PRME Anti-Poverty Working Group, 2012). As might be expected, the published literature does not adequately capture the level of innovation that the global professoriate brings to the teaching of poverty in the responsible management classroom. Examples of these yet unpublished teaching innovations are in CEEMAN/PRME (2010).

Poverty: Experience Dimension

The importance of the experience dimension for responsible learning

Experiential learning has a long history in management education (Baden & Parkes, 2013; Kayes, 2002; Reynolds & Vince, 2007). Bilimoria (1998) describes experiential learning (what she calls 'real world learning') as 'premised on the notion that learning is best achieved when learners, steeped in complex contexts, personally work on and contribute to solving problems and issues that matter in the real world' (p. 266). Most often, Dewey's pragmatic philosophy of education, where learning is equated with doing, is cited as 'the founding voice' (Kezar & Rhoads, 2001: 150) and philosophical anchor for varied expressions of experiential learning (e.g., service learning, action research, analytic and field consulting projects, study away and study abroad programs, live cases and internships).

Moosmayer, Waddock, Wang, Hühn, Dierksmeier & Gohl (2018) also argue that Dewey's philosophy of pragmatism provides the philosophical rationale for responsible management learning. Responsible management learning is experiential because it is reflective and relational. It is 'the self' in conversation with others. Moosmayer et al. (2018) state: 'Pragmatist business education is responsible business education in a sense that it guides the learner through a reflection process that connects their role in processes of social inquiry with the question of *what person they want to be* in interaction with others and *what world they want to create*

through interdependent processes of social inquiry with others' (2018: 15–16; italics in the original).

Despite the well-known benefits of experiential learning, Meisel (2008) presents a reminder that 'Experiential learning that involves vulnerable populations deserves greater scrutiny from educators' (p. 196). In the context of student experiential learning with poor and marginalized groups, Simola (2016) writes that faculty should always 'exercise professional teaching responsibilities with care; demonstrate sensitivity to the potential personal discomfort of students; show sensitivity to social, emotional and physical risk; do no harm; afford dignity to participants; use noncoercive, voluntary participation; [and] obtain informed consent' (p. 18). Responsible management learning requires an ethic of care for participants, students, faculty, and organizational and community members (see GIBS in Appendix 10.A).

Experiential learning and poverty

Similar to the knowledge dimension discussions, the extant management literature on experiential learning that engages students deeply with poverty issues is limited. International service-learning (ISL) activities are the most reported experiential learning approach (see Gordon, 2008; Kellogg, 2014; Le, Raven & Chen, 2013; Schlange, 2016; Tyran, 2017; Wu & Martin, 2018 in Table 10.1). There is also a small, published literature on domestic experiential learning activities with impoverished, local communities (see Ortiz & Huber-Heim, 2017; Portales & de la Torre, 2015; Rosenbloom & Cortes, 2008; Vikhansky, Kiseleva & Churkina, 2016 in Table 10.1). Appendix 10.A in this chapter offers three more examples.

CEEMAN/PRME (2010) also indicates that business schools and programs located in transitional and developing economies may well be the leaders in integrating poverty within responsible management. This upends the more stereotypic view of who leads and who follows in innovative management education.

Table 10.1   Selected literature on experience-based projects related to poverty

Reference	Location	Purpose
Gordon (2008)	Various	MBA course focused on field work at the BoP
Rosenbloom and Cortes (2008)	Colombia	Field-based experiential assignments with low-income, local communities around Medellin
Le, Raven and Chen (2013)	Cambodia Vietnam	Students learn about global poverty issues in a context of [international business] education
Kellogg (2014)	Ghana	Service learning
Schlange (2016)	Ghana	Students participate in Global Brigades, an international service learning organization, where they conduct stakeholder analyses in community-based projects
Portales and de la Torre (2015)	Mexico	A social incubation project in which students deeply engage micro-businesses in local communities
Tyran (2017)	Kenya	Students work with a girl's academy situated in an area of high HIV prevalence, gender disparity, and limited educational opportunity
Vikhansky, Kiseleva and Churkina (2016)	Russia	Domestic student-led projects
Ortiz and Huber-Heim (2017)	Austria	Application of a five-level teaching concept, Public Participation Spectrum, to engage students with SDG #1: No Poverty
Wu and Martin (2018)	Honduras	Short-term service learning focused on writing an entrepreneurial business plan for an orphanage's small-scale uniform manufacturing enterprise in an extremely poor community
Appendix 10.1A	SPU, USA	Social Venture Plan Competition
Appendix 10.1A	GIBS, South Africa	Students engage in immersive, experiential-learning projects that foster emotional connectedness to issues articulated in the SDGs
Appendix 10.1A	INCAE, Costa Rica	Impact Course at Nosara bridges an MBA class with a course on social entrepreneurship that incorporates entrepreneurs from a poor region

Schools located in countries in which poverty is a challenge to global competitiveness and national cohesion may well be the global leaders, while the rest of business schools may learn from their practices.

Faculty Attitudes – a Mediating Factor for Integrating Poverty into Responsible Management Education

Faculty are the disciplinary gatekeepers for curricular content, timing and pedagogical techniques. 'What teachers think, what teachers believe, and what teachers do at the level of the classroom ultimately shapes the kind of learning that [students] get' (Hargreaves &

Fullan, 1992: ix). Research on integrating responsible management topics, such as sustainability and CSR, into contemporary management education frequently discusses faculty members' roles as facilitators and/or barriers to curricular change (Barber, Wilson, Venkatachalam, Cleaves & Garnham, 2014). Efforts to understand the relationship between poverty and responsible management must explore faculty attitudes and perspectives.

Global faculty attitudes

Empirical research on business/management faculty attitudes toward poverty alleviation is sparse. To date, there have been four surveys of the global business professoriate that specifically dealt with faculty perspectives on poverty. Rosenbloom, Gudić, Parkes and

Table 10.2   Faculty attitudes toward poverty and curricular change (CEEMAN/PRME, 2010)

	n	Mean*	S.D.
Poverty is a legitimate topic for management education.	226	5.68	1.14
There is general agreement among our professors that global poverty is a legitimate topic in management education.	186	4.24	1.69
The amount of time devoted to discussing global poverty in current curriculum is just about right.	217	3.00	1.63
I would like to see the number of courses that discuss global poverty increase in the next two years.	260	5.35	1.65
I would like to see the number of faculty willing to discuss global poverty increase in the next two years.	261	5.36	1.68

* Seven-point Likert scale where 1 = very strongly disagree and 7 = very strongly agree.

Kronbach (2017) provide an in-depth discussion of the first, second and third global surveys, while the fourth is yet to be analyzed for publication.

The first empirical research to suggest that poverty was an emerging responsible management topic was conducted in 2008 (CEEMAN, 2009). When asked whether 'Poverty is a legitimate topic for management education', 72% of respondents said 'yes'; 8% said 'no', and 20% were 'unsure'. In 2010, when the same question was asked of the global professoriate (CEEMAN/PRME, 2010), 90% of respondents either agreed, strongly agreed, or very strongly agreed that poverty was a legitimate topic for study in management education (see Table 10.2). Yet the same 2010 Survey (CEEMAN/PRME, 2010) also found that business faculty wanted more courses as well as more faculty beyond themselves to discuss poverty so that overall more time throughout the students' course study was spent on the topic (see Table 10.2).

Curricula and courses

The tension between 'what is' and 'what should be' is the central issue that defines curricular change (Barnett, Parry & Coate, 2001). Table 10.3 focuses on this issue by highlighting the top two curricular components recommended for greatest change in undergraduate-, master's/postgraduate- and executive-level business education.

Table 10.3 indicates consensus that the existing Business Ethics/Corporate Social Responsibility course is the place most ideally suited for poverty discussions for these three levels of management education. Interestingly, foundation courses were selected as the second most important place to include poverty discussions in the school or program's curriculum. This location is ideal for situating poverty as a threshold concept; instilling discussion and understanding of poverty early in the business curriculum ensures its integration into student learning at every stage thereafter. These findings suggest multiple opportunities to create a more coordinated responsible business curriculum by integrating poverty discussions from foundations through capstone courses.

In both the 2012 Global Survey (Gudić, Parkes & Rosenbloom, 2012) and the 2017 Global Survey faculty were asked to evaluate the perceived opportunities for undergraduate and master's/postgraduate students to study 14 specified responsible management topics. Table 10.4 compares the rank order of perceived opportunities to study these 14 responsible management topics for undergraduates, while Table 10.5 does the same for graduates.

In 2012, the top five topics in order of opportunity to study were ethics, corporate social responsibility, international development, corporate governance and sustainable development. The opportunity to study

Table 10.3 Faculty perceptions of current vs ideal placement for poverty discussion across undergraduate, master's/postgraduate and executive levels of management education (*n* = 377)

		Currently discussed in ...	Ideally discussed In ...
		Frequency	Frequency
Undergrad	Business ethics/CSR course	59	220
	All foundation courses	16	125
MBA/postgraduate	Business ethics/CSR course	61	213
	Selected foundation courses	46	159
EMBA	Business ethics/CSR course	29	176
	Selected foundation courses	29	102

Table 10.4 Perceived opportunities to study responsible management topics in undergraduate business programs

2012 Global Survey ranking (n = 477)			2017 Global Survey ranking (n = 297)		
Topic	Mean	S.D.	Topic	Mean*	S.D.
Ethics	3.77*	.993	Ethics	3.74	1.17
Corporate social responsibility	3.65	.992	Corporate social responsibility	3.67	1.16
International development	3.64	1.097	Corporate governance	3.64	1.08
Corporate governance	3.62	1.094	Sustainable development	3.48	1.08
Sustainable development	3.32	1.158	International development	3.39	1.22
Social entrepreneurship	3.07	1.148	Environmental sustainability	3.37	1.06
Environmental sustainability	3.02	1.095	Social entrepreneurship	3.34	1.18
Public policy/Governmental studies	3.01	1.227	Public policy/Governmental studies	3.07	1.12
Political stability	2.74	1.165	Human rights	2.87	1.04
Third sector/Civil society/ NGO relationships	2.71	1.137	Third sector/Civil society/ NGO relationships	2.84	1.02
Human rights	2.67	1.093	Climate change	2.78	1.13
Corruption	2.65	1.108	Poverty and inequality	2.77	1.07
Poverty and inequality	2.51	1.089	Corruption	2.75	1.15
Climate change	2.41	1.101	Political stability	2.72	1.08

* Scale: 1 = no opportunity to study, 2 = little opportunity to study, 3 = some opportunity to study, 4 = significant opportunity to study, 5 = extensive opportunity to study.

poverty and inequality, however, were ranked #13 – next to last in 2012. In 2017, the opportunity for undergraduates to study poverty and inequality issues increased minimally (now #12 out of 14), while ethics and CSR remained at the top.

At the graduate level, a similar pattern emerged. In the 2012 Global Survey, respondents ranked the top five responsible management topics as corporate governance, corporate social responsibility, international development, ethics and sustainable development (see Table 10.5). Because master's-level work often focuses on enterprise-level issues, it is not surprising that students had the most opportunity to study corporate governance. Similar to the rankings for undergraduates in 2012 (Table 10.4), the opportunity for master's-level students to study the issues of poverty

Table 10.5   Perceived opportunities to study responsible management topics in graduate/postgraduate business programs

2012 Global Survey rank order (n = 477)			2017 Global Survey rank order (n = 297)		
Topic	Mean	S.D.	Topic	Mean*	S.D.
Corporate governance	3.80*	1.034	Corporate social responsibility	3.82	1.02
Corporate social responsibility	3.77	.990	Corporate governance	3.80	1.05
International development	3.71	1.061	Ethics	3.76	1.06
Ethics	3.68	.998	Sustainable development	3.53	1.11
Sustainable development	3.42	1.115	International development	3.49	1.20
Social entrepreneurship	3.13	1.090	Social entrepreneurship	3.41	1.15
Environmental sustainability	3.07	1.110	Environmental sustainability	3.30	1.13
Public policy/Governmental studies	3.05	1.189	Public policy/Governmental studies	3.07	1.08
Third sector/Civil society/ NGO relationships	2.80	1.183	Third sector/Civil society/ NGO relationships	2.97	1.14
Political stability	2.74	1.140	Poverty and inequality	2.88	1.11
Corruption	2.73	1.132	Corruption	2.87	1.11
Human rights	2.66	1.128	Political stability	2.79	1.17
Poverty and inequality	2.60	1.082	Human rights	2.76	1.11
Climate change	2.46	1.140	Climate change	2.75	1.15

*Scale: 1 = no opportunity to study, 2 = little opportunity to study, 3 = some opportunity to study, 4 = significant opportunity to study, 5 = extensive opportunity to study.

and inequality was ranked #13 out of 14 topics (see Table 10.5). In the intervening five years, however, the rank order of responsible management topics for master's-level students changed significantly. In 2017, faculty members indicated that master's-level students had the most opportunities to study corporate social responsibility. Ethics (#3) and sustainable development (#4) increased in opportunities to study. Master's-level students also had more opportunities to study poverty and inequality, having moved to rank #10 from rank #13 in 2012 (see Table 10.5). Overall, responding faculty perceived not only an increased focus on responsible management but also increased opportunities for master's-level students to study poverty.

Student attitudes

A more recent study investigated student attitudes toward the legitimacy of poverty as a management education topic. Preliminary results found that only 39% of students considered poverty a legitimate or very important management topic (see Figure 10.2) (Mason, Marcheva, Rosenbloom & Gudić, 2018). The same study found only 12% of students thought themselves competent to address the SDGs and poverty alleviation (see Figure 10.3).

Mason et al. (2018) found faculty attitude to be a very important factor in whether or not students considered these topics important for 31% of the students surveyed, while 35% of the responding students reported that institutional voices, such as the university mission, the business school culture and scholarships for studying these topics, were very influential in their determination of whether or not poverty is a legitimate management topic. This reinforces the importance of faculty attitudes and the permeation of poverty within a program. Students are listening and being influenced by whether or not these topics are being taken seriously and imbedded into schools and curriculum, into mission statements and into the culture of the program.

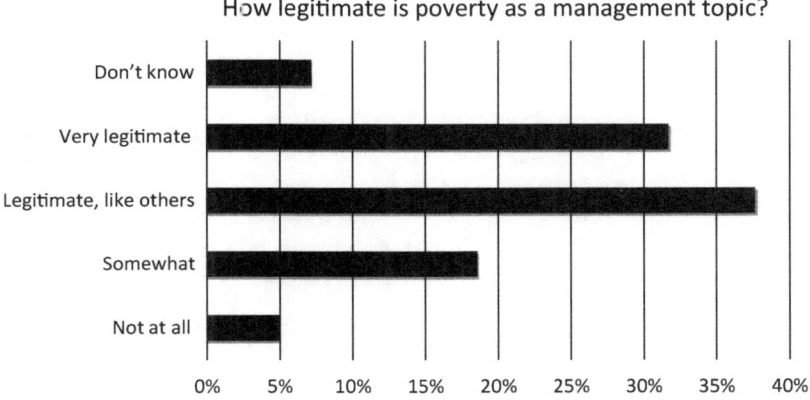

Figure 10.2   Student perceptions of poverty as a legitimate management topic (Mason et al., 2018)

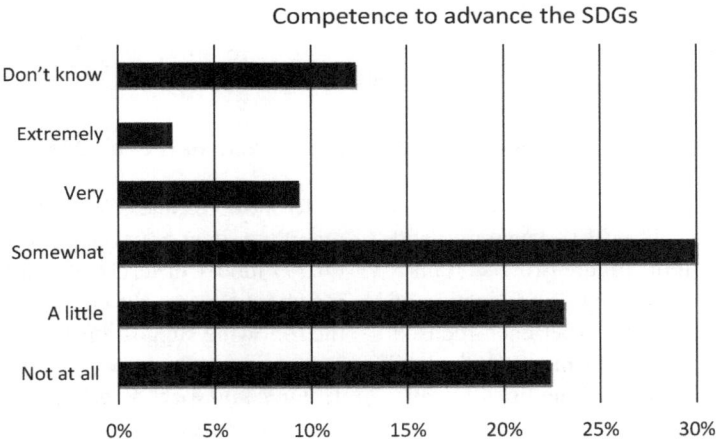

Figure 10.3   Perceived student competence in addressing the SDGs (Mason et al., 2018)

THE FUTURE FOR RESPONSIBLE MANAGEMENT EDUCATION AND POVERTY

Poverty is multifaceted and complex, and it needs to be better understood by those best positioned to impact it – the leaders and practicing managers of firms and corporations. As presented here, poverty is innately connected with each responsible management component and must be integrated more fully into management curricula and programs.

One model for developing a formative evaluation of where schools and programs of management currently stand in relation to poverty integration is provided by Hart, Fox, Korstad and Nill (2017). They studied the top 100 MBA programs in terms of each school's integration of sustainability into the curriculum. They developed a model differentiating amongst five levels of sustainability emphasis. Schools can be *silent, trivial, accepting, embracing* and *leading*. These same labels can be applied to curricular-level integration

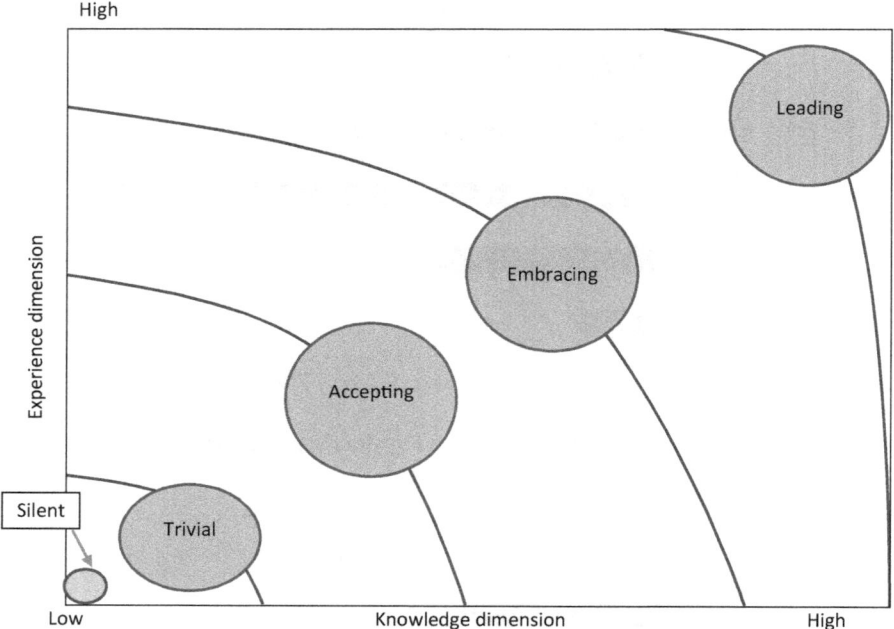

Figure 10.4   Formative evaluation framework (adapted from Hart et al., 2017)

and engagement with poverty. Figure 10.4 takes the Hart et al. (2017) categories and places them within Figure 10.1's framework of a curriculum being a combination of knowledge-building and experience-focused activities. Ideally, as a business curriculum includes poverty more intentionally and completely throughout the entire course of student study, the curriculum moves into higher levels of integration, with embracing and leading being the aspirational best.

As this chapter indicates, while there may be individual 'poverty champions' within a school or program (London, 2016), most business schools are probably in the silent or trivial phase of meaningfully including poverty within their curricula or programs. Nevertheless, Appendix 10.A indicates that some schools, while not yet in the literature, can be in the accepting or even embracing phase of integrating poverty in their curricula. These serve as exemplars of what can be done to fully engage students with poverty issues.

To move business schools and programs out of the silent or trivial phase of Hart et al.'s (2017) model in terms of responsible learning about poverty, the chapter concludes with the following suggestions:

1. *Find pathways within the curriculum to treat poverty as a threshold concept.*
Dembek et al. (2019) found an implicit bias towards thinking of poverty only in economic terms and only through an economic lens. Finding ways to infuse Sen's holistic view of poverty along with the subsistence marketplace's perspective throughout the curriculum are essential first steps for developing threshold knowledge about poverty. The importance of understanding the capability constraints for the poor is critical across business facets. It cannot be the role of a marketing department simply to convince the consumer that the product is necessary and desirable – it is not an even playing field. Marketing must carefully and responsibly explain the benefits and costs to using the product.

This means that responsible management learning must emphasize, for example, that the poor have important literacy and educational constraints. They may not be able to read and/or understand labels, warnings, or other documentation that would legally absolve a company from liability for harm. Company decision-makers must be equipped with an understanding not only of poverty, but also of their heightened responsibilities when they enter these markets. Good intentions are not enough. Responsible management learning requires that faculty stress these differences, that learners empathize with their low-income customers and that ethical considerations attendant to firm strategy be expressly considered. When poverty is treated as a threshold concept, more complex and nuanced discussions about business approaches to poverty alleviation can occur in responsible management classrooms.

2. *Confront the 'messiness' and 'uncomfortableness' that poverty discussions can surface.*

Deep, meaningful discussions of poverty have the possibility of making faculty and/or students feel uncomfortable. Poverty discussions can raise issues of privilege, unconscious bias, structural inequity, justice, and the institutionalization of any of the '-isms' (racism, sexism, etc.) – even within a business or management context. These can be difficult discussions to have. Yet as Hibbert and Cunliffe (2015) state, responsible management has an obligation to facilitate 'learning from what can be troublesome situations and experiences' (p. 177).

Moral reflective practice stands at the core of responsible management education (Hibbert & Cunliffe, 2015; Parkes & Blewitt, 2011). '[Moral reflective practice] requires engaging with the world around us and recognizing that feelings of discomfort and anxiety can offer opportunities to open up our actions and behaviors to reflexive examination' (Hibbert & Cunliffe, 2015: 180). Poverty

discussions fit squarely within this domain. Despite the messiness, uncomfortableness and tensions that may result from poverty discussions, it is essential to have them. To paraphrase Parkes and Blewitt's (2011) title, 'Ignorance of poverty was bliss. Now I am not ignorant, and that is more difficult.'

Gentile's Giving Voice to Values (Gentile, 2017) pedagogy might be one way forward. The Giving Voice to Values reframes values-based discussions around the question, 'How can one get the right thing done effectively?' so that faculty who teach core functional business/management courses can 'engage their students in applying the vocabulary, frameworks and analytics *of their own discipline* to a value-driven decision' (Gentile, 2017: 123; italics in the original). This reduces the perceived burden on faculty 'to lead philosophy discussions for which they feel unprepared' (2017: 123). Integrating poverty as part of the Giving Voice to Values pedagogy is one way of facilitating its discussion within the frame of responsible learning.

3. *Use the SDGs as a pedagogical gateway into poverty discussions.*

Because the SDGs are all interconnected, any SDG can be the entry point into class discussion about that particular SDG's relevance and relationship to poverty. The following extended quotation illustrates this point:

'Poverty is associated with other critical issues at the centre of the Sustainable Development Goals initiative and of the UN Global Compact. For example, poor households inefficiently use water and energy resources. They often settle on riverbanks and burn kerosene with detrimental impacts on water pollution (SDG6, SDG14, SDG15), on the air (SDG13) and on sustainable sources of energy (SDG7). Poverty forces families to prioritize basic needs, with negative effects on nutrition (SDG2), health (SDG3), and education (SDG4). The poor often live and work in informal economies, increasing the risks of inequality and exploitation at work (SDG8 and SDG9) and women remain especially vulnerable in these contexts (SDG5). Firms have the opportunity to tackle a variety of issues by empowering individuals and by creating robust partnerships across society. By tackling SDG1, firms can build stronger bases towards the achievement of all the other goals' (Bisignano et al., 2017: 199–200).

This suggests that most examples currently used in management classrooms can also serve as entry points for discussing poverty. A corollary is that poverty discussions must break out of being siloed in ethics, CSR or even sustainable development courses. When responsible management topics are confined to one class, the implicit message is that poverty is not applicable to other courses. This is clearly not the case.

4. *Change faculty and student perceptions that poverty alleviation is a problem only in developing economies.*

While the global development agenda focused on extreme poverty reduction (SDG #1), all countries have relative poverty (Atkinson, 2019). Poverty reduction is thus a local issue for all business schools and programs, and because it is a local issue, every business school and program has potential to increase both the knowledge and experience dimensions of student engagement with this issue (see Figure 10.1).

5. *View poverty as an opportunity to develop students' and faculty members' moral imagination.*

Mental models shape how individuals make sense of the world. Mental models can facilitate or hinder learning because when new facts, principles, ideas or concepts 'fit' within an individual's existing mental model, they are readily incorporated into it. When they don't 'fit', they are either rejected or held with a great deal of dissonance or unease. Poverty is an issue that engages an individual's mental model.

Werhane (2008) notes that an antidote to the limitations imposed by mental models is to develop the moral imagination, that is, 'the ability to discover, evaluate and act upon possibilities not merely determined by a particular circumstance, or limited by a set of

operating mental models, or merely framed by a set of rules' (p. 466). Cultivating students' moral imaginations 'entails the ability to escape from defective mental modes that dominate a particular situation, to envision new possibilities that are not so contextually dependent, and to evaluate and act on those possibilities' (Werhane et al., 2010: 75). SDG #1 (To end poverty in all its forms everywhere) is a catalyst for stimulating the moral imagination of students and faculty.

6. *Incentivize research that explicitly addresses one or more facets of a poverty as a multidimensional phenomenon.*

Unlike the growing literature on sustainability in education and sustainability for education, poverty has not received the same publication presence as the broader issues of sustainability. This is ironic because SDG #1 is No Poverty. Scholarly inquiry is uneven across the broad swath of business knowledge. The absence of comprehensive literature reviews in supply chain management, organizational behavior and logistics, just to name a few, suggests that there is yet to develop an adequate body of scholarly knowledge to make such reviews meaningful. There is much to be done to integrate poverty into management research, and incentives for faculty to enter this research space are an excellent way to begin this work. Work should also continue to highlight the student voices – student demand for learning from scholars who work on poverty issues will further lead faculty down this fruitful research stream (Mason et al., 2018).

CONCLUSION

Poverty is multifaceted and complex, and needs to be better understood by those best positioned to impact it – the leaders and practicing managers of firms and corporations. Firms control the greatest portion of the world's finite resources. Increasingly these firms' stakeholders expect that firms will provide solutions to the most pressing of all global issues: poverty. This cannot be done effectively, or indeed without harm, unless those making strategic and daily decisions have a firm grounding in responsible management practice. BoP, CSR and the SDGs are three of the most prominent invitations to firms to participate in the work of alleviating poverty. More will follow, and firms will be held increasingly responsible for impact on a range of global issues, of which poverty will always feature prominently because of its intricate connections to other global issues.

This begins with management faculty. Integrating poverty into all aspects of faculty work life is essential to the end goal of a multidimensional understanding of poverty permeating responsible management education. This includes faculty research, faculty development, curation of curricular resources for faculty use in classrooms, partnerships for working with and/or learning from peers who are doing this work at other institutions, support for difficult classroom discussions, and incentives for shifting both faculty and student perceptions regarding the importance of integrating poverty throughout the management curriculum.

Within the framework of responsible learning, poverty should no longer be confined within the boundaries of a single course on ethics or CSR. Students value the integration of poverty into their business education to the extent that they see this in the missions and curricula of their schools and universities, and the extent to which their faculty model making understanding the multifaceted nature of poverty paramount to understanding how to be a responsible business leader. It is therefore vital that poverty be acknowledged and embedded into curricula as a threshold concept by acknowledging that it is a problem in every country and business context, and by embracing the difficulty of confronting and discussing an uncomfortable topic. To this end, resources should be further devoted to supporting faculty undertaking this important task, developing pedagogy, and supporting/rewarding scholarship in this important area.

APPENDIX 10.A: PRME CHAMPION SCHOOLS – INNOVATIVE INTEGRATIONS OF POVERTY INTO CURRICULUM

INCAE: La Carpio

INCAE Business School and VIVA Idea's Impact Course[1] at Nosara[2] bridges an MBA class with a course on social entrepreneurship that incorporates entrepreneurs from a poor region in Costa Rica. The course aims to strengthen Nosara's social entrepreneurship ecosystem by including poor citizens into the booming high-end tourism sector in Costa Rica, while also generating significant impacts from business school students to society. The course is able to address local challenges by performing a Social Progress Index[3] (SPI) measurement in the region that enables the participants to identify the community's challenges for social progress. After the SPI results were obtained, a group of local leaders selected two core challenges of the region, that were social inclusion and recycling. The same leaders selected 20 Nosara entrepreneurs, who had been promoting business solutions for the selected problems. The selected entrepreneurs attended a six-module program held in Nosara and led by INCAE professors that fortified their knowledge on social entrepreneurship. In parallel, INCAE business school students learned about the same concepts in a class at INCAE. This built a bridge between the two groups generating a common language between the Nosara entrepreneurs and the INCAE students. After a theoretical preparation at INCAE, the INCAE students visited Nosara to work with the entrepreneurs of the Nosara course on their projects. The common work ended with a pitch in front of Nosara leaders. After the common work with the INCAE students, the Nosara entrepreneurs continued working on improving their business models. At the end of the course they held a presentation of their solutions in front of local and national leaders to receive the support they needed to continue implementing their ideas. After the course, another SPI was executed to measure the impact of the projects and to define a next cohort of Nosara students. As the course included a train-the-trainer model, two Nosara professors were able to continue the project on their own account, whereas the graduates of the first course became mentors of the next cohort of Nosara entrepreneurs. That way, the course intended to foster the dynamic of the social entrepreneur ecosystem in the low-income market of Nosara and to regularly measure its impact by executing an SPI.

Seattle Pacific University: Social Venture Plan Competition

The Social Venture Plan Competition[4] (SVPC) encourages teams of students from diverse disciplines to develop an entrepreneurial project that addresses dual bottom lines: social and financial. Participants tackle a felt social need while proposing a way to provide sustainable funding through a business activity. We ask teams to identify which SDG(s) their social enterprise is designed to address. SDGs addressed often include poverty, economic inequality and gender issues. All SVPC projects are required to demonstrate both their positive social/environmental impact *and* a feasible revenue-generating model. The fact that this is a required part of the one major (Global Development Studies) and a popular optional component of several Business and Economics major concentrations is also a sign of how a broader understanding of business has captured the imagination of this generation of idealistic students. While many are suspicious of business at the start, most come to see how business tools can become part of the solution to many of society's biggest problems. Students have the option to enroll in a two-course prep series (BUS 3680 + BUS 3682). BUS 3680 (3 credits) examines 'blended value' businesses designed to achieve both financial

return and social benefit, and includes initial preparation of a social enterprise business plan to study commercial ventures operated by nonprofit or for-profit organizations. BUS 3682 (2 credits) is a nontechnical, workshop-style course designed to help students develop an outstanding social venture plan and compete in the SVPC; each session of the course concentrates on a specific element of the SVPC planning template. During the Social Venture Plan competition, business people, entrepreneurs and other community partners evaluate and score the plans; student teams present their projects to faculty, staff, students and judges at a live trade-show display event (SVP Showcase) on the SPU campus. The teams with the highest cumulative scores from the two phases of the competition win cash prizes.

Gordon Institute of Business Science, University of Pretoria (GIBS): Multidimensional immersive experiences: creating emotional connectedness

GIBS is designing immersive experiences[5] for business students and program participants when addressing local challenges and developing business ideas that address the needs of society. The experiences are intended to expose participants to a particular problem and create an immersive experience where they can connect to the local context, meet the people, the local businesses and other organizations that are already tackling the problems. Challenges such as education – SDG #4, gender inequality in public services and institutions – SDG #5, 10 and 16, green energy – SDG #13 and 15, or inequalities – SDG #1 and 10 are a few examples.

Participants must consider what challenges are faced by the organization, what enablers will help address the challenges, and what the outcomes will be for the different stakeholders. To do this, a series of engagements are designed with local people, at local organizations, that expose the students to the situations that different stakeholders face in order to better understand the multidimensional nature of the challenge(s) they are attempting to address through business solutions. These immersions often include exposure to alternative contexts, including those where an innovative solution is being implemented. Experiences are designed to incorporate multiple stakeholders that live with, work with or experience the challenge on a day-to-day basis. This process allows participants to analyze a challenge and potential solution(s) from multiple perspectives.

Adequate preparation for the immersive experience is essential, including a foundational understanding of the SDG, such as poverty or inequality, the broader context, and some exploratory questions to interrogate the nature and impact of the challenges that are the lived experiences of the people in local communities.

This program creates a dual experience for participants. Students, participants and faculty are exposed to the challenges in context, allowing for a deeper and more complex comprehension of the issues that must be addressed at the same time as considering how viable business solutions might alleviate the problem and improve the lives of marginalized people in local communities. Furthermore, participants are directly connected with stakeholders, often creating an emotional connection to the people that will be most affected by the proposed outcomes. This allows for a richer engagement with the stakeholders, and a more empathetic consideration of the various stakeholder outcomes. Business solutions are then designed and implemented with follow-up in the engaged communities. This program is still in its design phase, with over 250 postgraduate business students having completed an applied business research project in 2019 using this approach, and another action research pilot conducted at four sites in March 2019.

Notes

1 This initiative is run by INCAE Business School and VIVA Idea. Contributed by José P. Valverde and Urs P. Jäger.
2 A village and Costa Rican district located in Guanacaste at the Nicoya Peninsula with a population of 5791 people.
3 The Social Progress Index is an aggregate index of social and environmental indicators that capture three dimensions of social progress (Basic Human Needs, Foundations of Well-being Opportunity).
4 This initiative is run by the SPU School of Business, Government, and Economics and the Center for Applied Learning. Contributed by Randy Franz and Mark Oppenlander.
5 Contributed by Jill Bogie, Gordon Institute of Business Science.

REFERENCES

Anand, S., & Sen, A. (1997). Concepts of human development and poverty: A multidimensional perspective. *United Nations Development Programme, Poverty and Human Development: Human development papers*, 1–20.

Arnold, D. G., & Valentin, A. (2013). Corporate social responsibility at the base of the pyramid. *Journal of Business Research*, 66(10), 1904–1914.

Arora, S., & Romijn, H. (2012). The empty rhetoric of poverty reduction at the base of the pyramid. *Organization*, 19(4), 481–505.

Atkinson, A. B. (2019). *Measuring poverty around the world*. Princeton, NJ: Princeton University Press.

Baden, D., & Parkes, C. (2013). Experiential learning: inspiring the business leaders of tomorrow. *Journal of Management Development*, 32(3), 295–308.

Banerjee, A. V., & Duflo, E. (2011). *Poor economics: a radical rethinking of the way to fight global poverty*. New York: Public Affairs.

Barber, N. A., Wilson, F., Venkatachalam, V., Cleaves, S. M., & Garnham, J. (2014). Integrating sustainability into business curricula: University of New Hampshire case study. *International Journal of Sustainability in Higher Education*, 15(4), 473–493.

Barnett, R., Parry, G., & Coate, K. (2001). Conceptualising curriculum change. *Teaching in Higher Education*, 6(4), 435–449.

Beaudoin, S. M. (2006). *Poverty in world history*. New York: Routledge.

Bennett, F., & Daly, M. (2014). *Poverty through a gender lens: evidence and policy review on gender and poverty*. Report for the Joseph Rowntree Foundation. University of Oxford, Oxford, May 2014.

Bilimoria, D. (1998). From classroom learning to real world learning: a diasporic shift in management education. *Journal of Management Education*, 22, 265–268.

Bisignano, A. P., Werhane, P. H., & Ehret, M. (2017). Designing sustainable business with the Base of the Pyramid. In Molthan-Hill, P. (Ed.), *Business Students Guide to Sustainability* (pp. 194–225). Sheffield: Greenleaf Publishing.

Blasco, M. (2012). Aligning the hidden curriculum of management education with PRME: an inquiry-based framework. *Journal of Management Education*, 36(3), 364–388.

Caza, A., & Brower, H. H. (2015). Mentioning the unmentioned: an interactive interview about the informal management curriculum. *Academy of Management Learning & Education*, 14(1), 96–110.

CEEMAN. (2009). Business school responses to the global crisis. Available at: www.ceeman.org/publications/ceeman-research-reports/survey-on-business-school-responses-to-global-crisis. Accessed 10 October 2016.

CEEMAN/PRME. (2010). Final Report: 2010 survey on global poverty as a challenge for management education. Available at: www.ceeman.org/docs/default-source/publications/poverty-survey-final-report-oct2010.pdf?sfvrsn=0. Accessed 14 January 2020.

Comiling, K. S., & Sanchez, R. J. M. O. (2014). A postcolonial critique of Amartya Sen's capability framework. *Perspectives in the Arts and Humanities Asia*, 4(1), 1–26.

de Janvry, A., & Sadoulet, E. (2016). *Development economics*. New York: Routledge.

Dean, H. (2009). Critiquing capabilities: the distractions of a beguiling concept. *Critical Social Policy*, 129(2), 261–278.

Dembek, K., & Sivasubramaniam, N. (2019). Examining Base of the Pyramid (BoP) venture success through the mutual value CARD approach.

In Grosse, R., & Meyer, K. E. (Eds.), *The Oxford handbook of management in emerging markets* (pp. 241–264). Oxford: Oxford University Press.

Dembek, K., Sivasubramaniam, N., & Chmielewski, D. A. (2019). A systematic review of the bottom/base of the pyramid literature: cumulative evidence and future directions. *Journal of Business Ethics*, 1–18. https://doi.org/10.1007/s10551-019-04105-y.

Desai, M. (2001). Amartya Sen's contribution to development economics. *Oxford Development Studies*, 29(3), 213–223.

Fink, L. D. (2013). *Creating significant learning experiences: an integrated approach to designing college courses*. San Francisco, CA: Jossey-Bass.

Follman, J. (2012). BoP at ten: evolution and a new lens. *South Asian Journal of Global Business Research*, 1(2), 293–310.

Gau, R., & Viswanathan, M. (2018). A bottom-up perspective on SDGs: the subsistence marketplaces approach. *Social Business*, 8(4), 429–444.

Gentile, M. C. (2017). Giving Voice to Values: a global partnership with UNGC PRME to transform management education. *International Journal of Management Education*, 15(2), 121–125.

Godemann, J., Herzig, C., & Moon, J. (2011). Approaches to changing the curriculum. In Presentation given on the ISIBS Workshop – Session II, University of Nottingham, October (Vol. 20, No. 21.10, p. 2011).

Gordon, M. D. (2008). Management education and the base of the pyramid. *Journal of Management Education*, 32(6), 767–781, 791.

Gudić, M., Parkes, C., & Rosenbloom, A. (2012). *Fighting poverty through management education: challenges, opportunities, solutions*. Report to the 3rd PRME General Forum, Rio de Janiero. Available at: www.unprme.org/resource-docs/FightingPovertythroughManagementEducationChallengesOpportunitiesandSolutions.pdf. Accessed 14 January 2020.

Gudić, M., Rosenbloom, A., & Parkes, C. (Eds.). (2014). *Socially responsive organisations and the challenge of poverty*. Sheffield: Greenleaf Publishing.

Hahn, R. (2009). The ethical rational of business for the poor – integrating the concepts bottom of the pyramid, sustainable development, and corporate citizenship. *Journal of Business Ethics*, *84*(3), 313–324.

Hargreaves, A., & Fullan, M. (1992). *Understanding teacher development*. New York: Teachers College Press.

Hart, S. L., & Christensen, C. M. (2002). The great leap: driving innovation from the base of the pyramid. *Sloan Management Review*, *44*(1), 51–56.

Hart, S. L., & Sharma, S. (2004). Engaging fringe stakeholders for competitive imagination. *Academy of Management Perspectives*, *18*(1), 7–18.

Hart, S.L., Sharma, S., & Halme, M. (2016). Poverty, business strategy, and sustainable development. *Organization & Environment*, *29*(4), 401–415.

Hart, T. A., Fox, C. J., Korstad, J , & Nill, E. E. (2017). Sustainable MBAs: A phase model development of sustainability in MBA education. In Arevalo, J. A., & Mitchell, S. F. (Eds.), *Handbook of sustainability in management education: in search of a multidisciplinary, innovative and integrated approach* (pp. 567–590). Cheltenham: Edward Elgar.

Hibbert, P., & Cunliffe, A. (2015). Responsible management: engaging moral reflexive practice through threshold concepts. *Journal of Business Ethics*, *127*(1), 177–188.

Hulme, D. (2010). *Global poverty: how global governance is failing the poor*. New York: Routledge.

Jäger, U., & Sathe, V. (2015). The importance of vision and purpose for BoP business development. In Cañeque, F. C. & Hart, S. L. (Eds.), *Base of the Pyramid 3.0.* (pp. 12–30). New York: Routledge.

Jefferson, P. N. (2018). *Poverty: a very short introduction*. Oxford: Oxford University Press.

Karnani, A. (2006). Misfortune at the bottom of the pyramid. *Greener Management International*, *51*, 99–110.

Kayes, D. C. (2002). Experiential learning and its critics: preserving the role of experience in management learning and education. *Academy of Management Learning & Education*, *1*(2), 137–149.

Kellogg, D. M. (2014). 'Partners in Learning' on the front lines of poverty. In Gudić, M., Rosenbloom, A., & Parkes, C. (Eds.), *Socially responsive organisations and the challenge of poverty* (pp. 220–229). Sheffield: Greenleaf Publishing.

Kezar, A., & Rhoads, R. A. (2001). The dynamic tensions of service learning in higher education: a philosophical perspective. *Journal of Higher Education*, *72*(2), 148–171.

Khavul, S., & Bruton, G. D. (2013). Harnessing innovation for change: sustainability and poverty in developing countries. *Journal of Management Studies*, *50*(2), 285–306.

Kolk, A., Rivera-Santos, M., & Rufín, C. (2014). Reviewing a decade of research on the 'base/bottom of the pyramid' (BOP) concept. *Business & Society*, *53*(3), 338–377.

Kolk, A., Rivera-Santos, M., & Rufín, C. (2018). Multinationals, international business, and poverty: a cross-disciplinary research overview and conceptual framework. *Journal of International Business Policy*, *1*(1–2), 92–115.

Laasch, O. (2018). Just old wine in new bottles? Conceptual shifts in the emerging field of responsible management. *Centre for Responsible Management Education Working Papers*, *4*(1).

Laczniak, G. R., & Santos, N. J. (2011). The integrative justice model for marketing to the poor: an extension of SD logic to distributive justice and macromarketing. *Journal of Macromarketing*, *31*(2), 135–147.

Laderchi, C. (2000). The monetary approach to poverty: a survey of concepts and methods. *QEH Working Paper 58, Queen Elisabeth House, Oxford*. [Online] Available at: https://pdfs.semanticscholar.org/2087/fba5d6104b9a6e2f1fb73f9c9a7aa5963f65.pdf

Le, Q. V., Raven, P. V., & Chen, S. (2013). International service learning and short-term business study abroad programs: a case study. *Journal of Education for Business*, *88*(5), 301–306.

Lindgreen, A., Maon, F., Vanhamme, J., Florencio, B.P., Vallaster, C., & Strong, C. (Eds.). (2019). Foreword. In *Engaging with stakeholders: a relational perspective on responsible business* (pp. xxix–xxxvii). Abingdon: Routledge.

Lister, R. (2004). *Poverty*. Cambridge, UK: Polity Press.

London, T. (2016). *The Base of the Pyramid promise: building businesses with impact and scale*. Stanford, CA: Stanford University Press.

London, T., & Hart, S. L. (2004). Reinventing strategies for emerging markets: beyond the transnational model. *Journal of International Business Studies*, *35*(5), 350–370.

Mason, G. (2016). Strategies for the integration of poverty alleviation into management curriculum. Poverty: how can business help? In Gudić, M., Rosenbloom, A., & Parkes, C. (Eds.), *Responsible management education and the challenge of poverty: a teaching perspective* (pp. 78–90). Sheffield: Greenleaf Publishing.

Mason, G., Marcheva, A., Rosenbloom, A., & Gudić, M. (2018). Students' voice on the SDGs in management education. 5th Responsible Management Research Conference, Cologne, Germany, November 2018.

Mason, K., Chakrabarti, R., & Singh, R. (2017). Markets and marketing at the bottom of the pyramid. *Marketing Theory*, *17*(3), 261–270.

Meisel, J. S. (2008). The ethics of observing: confronting the harm of experiential learning. *Teaching Sociology*, *36*(3), 196–210.

Meyer, J. H. F., & Land, R. (2003). Threshold concepts and troublesome knowledge: linkages to thinking and practicing within the disciplines. In Rust, C. (Ed.), *Improving student learning: theory and practice—ten years on* (pp. 412–424). Oxford: Centre for Staff and Learning Development.

Meyer, J. H. F., & Land, R. (2005). Threshold concepts and troublesome knowledge (2): epistemological considerations and a conceptual framework for teaching and learning. *Higher Education*, *49*(3), 373–388.

Moosmayer, D. C., Waddock, S., Wang, L., Hühn, M. P., Dierksmeier, C., & Gohl, C. (2018). Leaving the road to Abilene: a pragmatic approach to addressing the normative paradox of responsible management education. *Journal of Business Ethics*, 1–20.

Motta, P. C., & Brashear, T. (2016). A new vocabulary for teaching poverty in marketing. In Gudić, M., Parkes, C., & Rosenbloom, A. (Eds.), *Responsible management education and the challenge of poverty: a teaching perspective* (pp. 106–120). Sheffield: Greenleaf Publishing.

Neal, M. (2017). Learning from poverty: why business schools should address poverty, and how they can go about it. *Academy of Management Learning and Education*, *16*(1), 54–69.

Ortiz, D., & Huber-Heim, K. (2017). From information to empowerment: teaching sustainable business development by enabling an experiential and participatory problem-solving process in the classroom. *International Journal of Management Education*, *15*(2), 318–331.

Parkes, C., & Blewitt, J. (2011). 'Ignorance was bliss, now I'm not ignorant and that is far more difficult': transdisciplinary learning and reflexivity in responsible management education. *Journal of Global Responsibility*, *2*(2), 206–221.

Paton, B., Harris-Boundy, J., & Melhus, P. (2012). Integrating global poverty into mainstream business classrooms. *Journal of Teaching in International Business*, *23*(1), 4–23.

Pogge, T. (2010). A critique of the capability approach. In Brighouse, H., & Robeyns, I. (Eds.), *Measuring justice: primary goods and capabilities* (pp. 17–60). Cambridge: Cambridge University Press.

Portales, L., & de la Torre, C. G. (2015). The impact of university social services through social incubation and student engagement in poverty alleviation. In Gudić, M., Rosenbloom, A., & Parkes, C. (Eds.), *Responsible management education and the challenge of poverty: a teaching perspective* (pp. 179–190). Sheffield: Greenleaf Publishing.

Prahalad, C. K., & Hammond, A. L. (2002). Serving the world's poor, profitably. *Harvard Business Review*, *80*(9), 48–57.

Prahalad, C. K., & Hart, S. L. (2002). The fortune at the bottom of the pyramid. *Strategy+Business*, *20*, 1–13.

PRME Anti-Poverty Working Group (2012). *Collection of best practices and inspirational solutions for fighting poverty through management education*. [Online] Available at: www.ceeman.org/docs/default-source/publications/poverty_wg_collection_of_best_practices.pdf?sfvrsn=0. Accessed 14 January 2020.

Ravallion, M. (1992). *Poverty comparisons*. Washington, DC: World Bank.

Razavi, S. (2000). *Gendered poverty and well-being*. Oxford: Blackwell.

Reynolds, M., & Vince, R. (Eds.). (2007). *Handbook of experiential learning and management education*. Oxford: Oxford University Press.

Rivera, C. (2016). Educating young leaders for alleviating poverty through an organizational behavior course. In Gudć, M., Parkes, C., & Rosenbloom, A. (Eds.), *Responsible management education and the challenge of poverty: a teaching perspective* (pp. 121–133). Sheffield: Greenleaf Publishing.

Rosenbloom, A., & Cortes, J. (2008). Piercing the bubble: how management students can confront poverty in Colombia. *Journal of Management Education, 32*(6), 716–730.

Rosenbloom, A., Gudić, M., Parkes, C., & Kronbach, B. (2017). A PRME response to the challenge of fighting poverty: How far have we come? Where do we need to go now? *International Journal of Management Education, 15*(2), 104–120.

Roundtree, B. S. (1901). *Poverty: a study of town life*. London: Macmillan.

Rusinko, C. (2010). Integrating sustainability in management and business education: a matrix approach. *Academy of Management Education and Learning, 9*(3), 507–519.

Sachs, J. D. (2006). *The end of poverty: economic possibilities for our time*. New York: Penguin.

Santos, N. J., & Laczniak, G. R. (2012). Marketing to the base of the pyramid: a corporate responsibility approach with case inspired strategies. *Business and Politics, 14*(1), 1–42.

Schlange, L. (2016). A case study of community learning and open innovation to reduce poverty at the base of the pyramid. In Milenko, G., Carole, P., & Al, R. (Eds.), *Responsible management education and the challenge of poverty: a teaching perspective* (pp. 191–206). Sheffield: Greenleaf Publishing.

Sen, A. (1990). Justice: means versus freedoms. *Philosophy & Public Affairs*, 111–121.

Sen, A. (1999). *Development as freedom*. New York: Alfred A. Knopf.

Simanis, E., Hart, S., & Duke, D. (2008). The base of the pyramid protocol: beyond 'basic needs' business strategies. *Innovations: Technology, Governance, Globalization, 3*(1), 57–84.

Simola, S. (2016). Realising the promise of experiential learning in poverty-related management education. In Milenko, G., Carole, P., & Al, R. (Eds.), *Responsible management education and the challenge of poverty: a teaching perspective* (pp. 10–22). Sheffield: Greenleaf Publishing.

Sridharan, S., Barrington, D. J., & Saunders, S. G. (2017). Markets and marketing research on poverty and its alleviation: summarizing an evolving logic toward human capabilities, well-being goals and transformation. *Marketing Theory, 17*(3), 323–340.

Stirling, A. E., & Kerr, G. A. (2015). Creating meaningful co-curricular experiences in higher education. *Journal of Education & Social Policy, 2*(6), 1–7.

Subramahniyan, S., & Gomez, J. T. (2016). Poverty in a marketing class. In Gudić, M. Parkes, C., & Rosenbloom, A. (Eds.) *Responsible management education and the challenge of poverty: a teaching perspective* (pp. 91–105). Sheffield: Greenleaf Publishing.

Sutter, C., Bruton, G. D., & Chen, J. (2019). Entrepreneurship as a solution to extreme poverty: a review and future research directions. *Journal of Business Venturing, 34*(1), 197–214.

Tripathi, S. K., Prakash, A., & Amann, W. (2016). Management education with poverty alleviation focus. In Milenko, G., Carole, P., & Al, R. (Eds.), *Responsible management education and the challenge of poverty: a teaching perspective* (pp. 48–58). Sheffield: Greenleaf Publishing.

Tyran, K. L. (2017). Transforming students into global citizens: international service learning and PRME. *International Journal of Management Education, 15*(2), 162–171.

UNDP. (1997). *Human Development Report: Human development to eradicate poverty*. Oxford: Oxford University Press.

Vandemoortele, J. (2013). The limits of the MDGs' design: six caveats for human rights. In Langford, M., Sumner, A., & Yamin, A. E. (Eds.), *The MDGs and human rights: past, present and future* (pp. 49–66). Cambridge: Cambridge University Press.

Venugopal, S., & Viswanathan, M. (2017). The subsistence marketplaces approach to poverty: implications for marketing theory. *Marketing Theory, 17*(3), 341–356.

Vikhansky, O., Kiseleva, E., & Churkina, N. (2016). Challenges and opportunities for student engagement in university social projects in the current socioeconomic context of Russia. In Milenko, G., Carole, P., & Al, R. (Eds.), *Responsible management education and the challenge of poverty: a teaching perspective* (pp. 167–178). Sheffield: Greenleaf Publishing.

Viswanathan, M., & Venugopal, S. (2015). Subsistence marketplaces: looking back, looking forward. *Journal of Public Policy & Marketing*, *34*(2), 228–234.

Viswanathan, M., Shultz, C.J., & Sridharan, S. (2014). Introduction to the Special Issue on Subsistence Marketplaces: From micro-level insights to macro-level impact. *Journal of Macromarketing*, *34*(2), 119–121.

Vitali, S., Glattfelder, J., & Battison, S. (2011). The network of global corporate control. *PLoS ONE*, *6*(10): e25995. doi:10.1371/journal.pone.0025995.

WCED (World Commission on Environment and Economic Development). (1987). *Our common future*. Oxford: Oxford University Press.

Werhane, P. H. (2008). Mental models, moral imagination, and systems thinking in the age of globalization. *Journal of Business Ethics*, *78*, 463–474.

Werhane, P., Kelley, S., Hartman, L., & Moberg, D. (2010). *Profitable partnerships for poverty alleviation*. New York: Taylor & Francis.

Wettstein, F. (2005). From causality to capability: towards a new understanding of the multinational corporation's enlarged global responsibilities. *Journal of Corporate Citizenship*, *19*, 105–117.

Wisor, S. (2017). *The ethics of global poverty: an introduction*. New York: Routledge.

Wu, Y., & Martin, J. (2018). Incorporating a short-term study abroad service trip for educating international entrepreneurship in the BoP market. *Journal of Teaching in International Business*, *29*(3), 213–248.

Zaheer, S. (1995). Overcoming the liability of foreignness. *Academy of Management Journal*, *38*(2), 341–363.

11

Tackling Climate Change through Management Education

Petra Molthan-Hill, Alex Hope and Rachel Welton

INTRODUCTION

In 2015, the G20 leaders requested that the Financial Stability Board (FSB) launched a Task Force on Climate-Related Financial Disclosures (TCFD or Task Force). The Task Force chaired by Michael Bloomberg published its final recommendations in 2017 and requested that companies disclose their 'climate risks' – risks caused by climate change and linked to financial risks. In March 2018, the Climate Disclosure Standards Board (CDSB) in cooperation with the Carbon Disclosure Project (CDP) analysed 'the disclosures from 1681 companies across 14 countries and 11 sectors to the CDP Questionnaire in 2017, which were made around the time of the launch of the final TCFD recommendations in June 2017' (CDSB and CDP, 2018: 4). One recommendation by the TCFD was to report all scope 1[1] and scope 2 emissions; 9 out of 10 companies disclosed this information by 2017, with regards to scope 3 emissions 8 out of 10 disclosed at least one category. Despite this positive uptake, the report highlights several problems, for example:

> New supra-national and jurisdictional regulations are improving corporate climate disclosures and their integration into internal governance and risk management processes. However, they are also potentially widening the global gap between leaders and laggards. The research shows how companies in countries covered by higher (and most regularly updated) amounts of regulation, such as the EU Non-Financial Reporting Directive, have the most oversight of climate-related matters (9 out of 10 companies have board oversight). Geographies with higher perceived risk of litigation linked to disclosure, such as North America, lag behind (where only 7 in 10 do). (CDSB and CDP, 2018: 5)

Both the TCFD and CDP have placed pressure on businesses to take climate change more seriously, but as Patenaude (2011) pointed out, business schools are lagging behind in responding to the risks of climate change, which were established by the Intergovernmental Panel on Climate Change (IPCC).

IPCC CURRENT STATE OF CLIMATE CHANGE

In 1988, the Intergovernmental Panel on Climate Change (IPCC) was formed through a partnership with the United Nations Environment Programme (UNEP) and the World Meteorological Organization (WMO). The aim of the IPCC is to provide a clear scientific view on the current state of knowledge in climate change and its potential environmental and socio-economic impacts. The IPCC does not employ scientists to conduct research, it reviews the scientific research conducted by experts in a broad range of academic fields. The reviews are objective and rigorous and endeavour to provide information for decision makers in governments and business. The IPCC has released five assessment reports to date: 1990, 1996, 2001, 2007 and 2013/14, they include details of the methodology utilized, technical papers, and periodic special reports assessing specific impacts of climate change. To demonstrate the work of the IPCC, in the fifth assessment report experts from 80 countries reviewed research and synthesized the information (IPCC, 2014a). From time to time the IPCC also releases Special Reports with a specific theme, such as The Regional Impacts of Climate Change (1998), Carbon Dioxide Capture and Storage (2005), Renewable Energy Sources and Climate Change Mitigation (2011) and Global Warming of 1.5 °C (2018).[2]

The First IPCC Assessment Report (FAR), in 1990, developed the United Nations Framework Convention on Climate Change (UNFCCC) that established the political mechanism to address climate change. IPCC's Second Assessment Report (SAR), in 1996, covered the implications of potential emission limitations and the regional consequences associated, this information underpinned the Kyoto Protocol, a legally binding agreement. The Third Assessment Report (TAR), in 2001, stated that temperature increases in the 21st century were likely to be higher than previously thought and the evidence that human

influence on climate change was stronger than previously thought. In 2007, the Fourth Assessment Report (AR4) was released, which concluded that 'the warming of the climate system is unequivocal' and it is affecting global ecosystems. After a gap of six to seven years, the Fifth Assessment Report (AR5) was published, which affirmed that '[h]uman influence on the climate system is clear, and recent anthropogenic emissions of greenhouse gases are the highest in history (IPCC, 2014a: 2)'.

The findings within AR5 informed global political climate negotiations and resulted in the Paris Accord 2015. Whilst 197 countries signed and committed to limiting global warming below 2°C, it is a voluntary not legal agreement. Warming of the climate system is unequivocal, and since the 1950s, many of the observed changes are unprecedented over decades to millennia. Since the beginning of the industrial era, oceanic uptake of carbon dioxide (CO_2) has resulted in increased acidification of the ocean. The atmosphere and ocean have warmed, the amounts of snow and ice have diminished (both the Greenland and Antarctic ice sheets are losing mass), and sea level has risen (IPCC, 2014a: 3). See charts in Figure 11.1 for illustration.

The bottom chart in Figure 11.1 demonstrates that anthropogenic gas emissions have increased significantly since the industrial revolution, and this has been largely prompted by economic and population growth. These greenhouse gas emissions (carbon dioxide, methane and nitrous oxide) have largely resulted from pollution created as a result of industrial business processes. The concentrations and levels have been detected throughout the climate system (as seen in Figure 11.1). The AR5 states that the effects of these emissions are extremely likely to have been the dominant cause of observed warming since the middle of the 20th century (IPCC, 2014a: 4).

The popular media appear to report the consequences of global warming on a daily basis, with an alarming number of forest fires in all regions of the world, and heat waves and changes are recorded in areas not

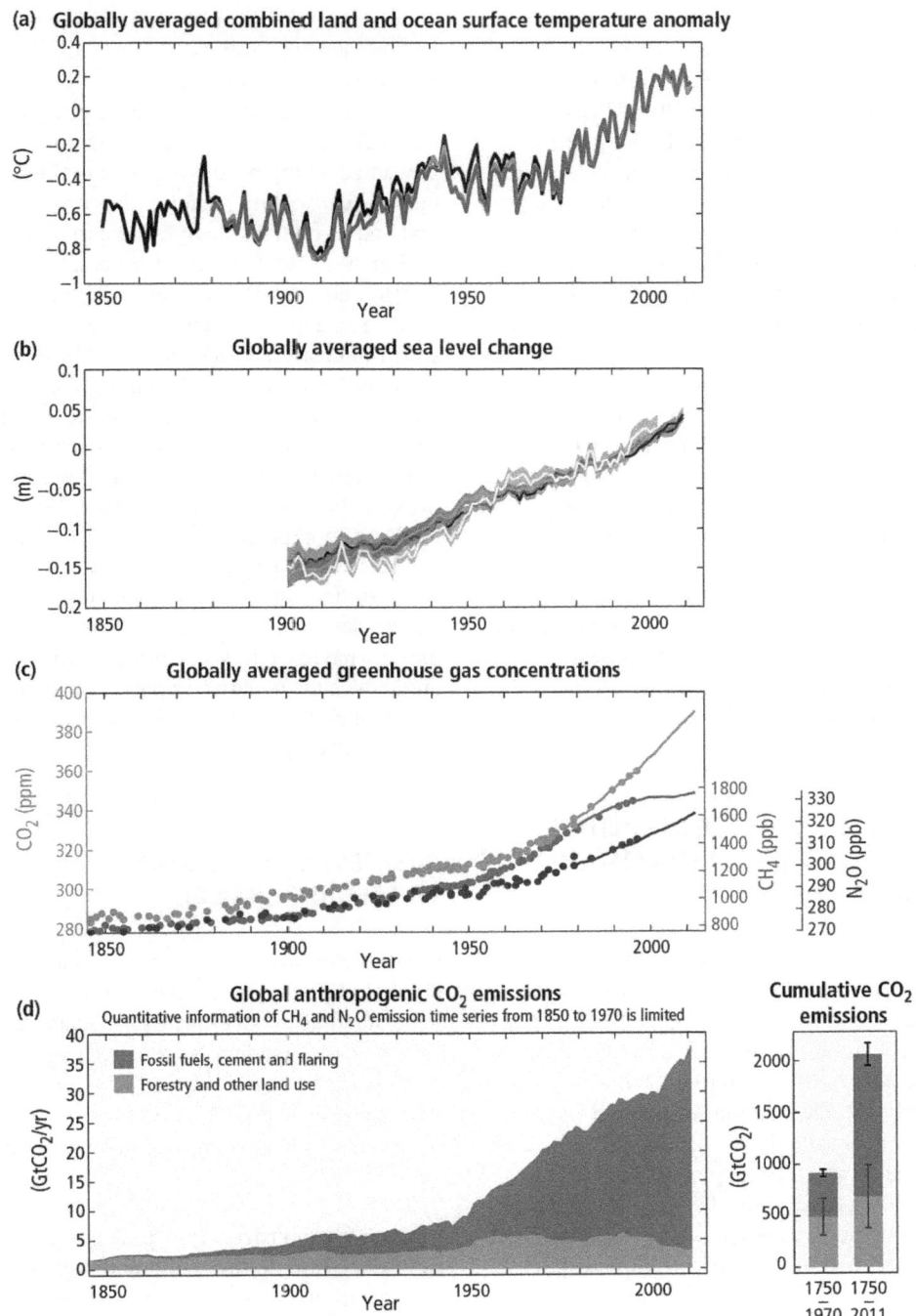

Figure 11.1   Indications and variability of the changing direct observations of climate change and anthropogenic global emissions (IPCC, 2014a: 3)

normally associated with warmer climates, such as Western Europe. Intensity in storms and the increased frequency of floods are also reported and the aftermath of these direct impacts is having considerable long-term consequences for governments, businesses and individuals. In 2018, the scientific evidence presented in AR5 was updated in a Special Report prepared to mark the IPCC's 30th anniversary. It is the first in a series of Special Reports to be produced during the IPCC's sixth assessment cycle (IPCC, 2018). The report highlights the stark differences in keeping global warming to 1.5°C rather than 2°C. Containing global warming to 1.5°C would require rapid, far-reaching and unparalleled changes within every facet of society, but could if successful provide a more sustainable and equitable society and help to achieve the Sustainable Development Goals (SDGs), especially those related to agriculture, water, energy, biodiversity, public health and cities – all of which influence business and are influenced by businesses.

environmental economics and climate change and he agrees with Stern that fossil fuel-based economies impose 'incalculable' costs on society and shifting to clean energy will pay off. Climate change is obviously an unwanted, complex and negative problem for businesses within society, the urgency to respond to climate change is clearly laid out within the IPCC's latest Special Report (2018) and the SDGs. Already the impact of climate change through flooding, increased storm intensity and less predictable weather patterns are negatively disrupting the supply chains, increasing the cost of basic supplies and insurance costs etc. Business schools are remiss towards their students if they do not provide them with an understanding, suitable skills and competencies covering the science, impacts and consequences of climate change. Once students graduate and are employed by businesses, they will be able to assist companies to navigate this changing environment and reduce the negative impacts whilst taking advantage of the sustainable business opportunities that emerge.

ECONOMIC DAMAGE RESULTING FROM UNCONTROLLED CLIMATE CHANGE

The UK government commissioned Nicholas Stern, an eminent economist, to conduct a review of the economic impacts of climate change, and it has been heralded as a seminal piece of research (Stern, 2007). He established that the economic damage resulting from uncontrolled climate change could cost between 5 and 20% of global GDP each year. He also stated that the cost of reducing carbon emissions would cost just 1% of GDP and that governments should respond quickly. The report also recognized that moving to a low carbon economy could provide many economic benefits, estimated to be in the region of $2.5 trillion a year, as well as opening up new low-carbon technology markets. Joseph Stiglitz (2018) has also researched

BUSINESS CONTRIBUTIONS TO CLIMATE CHANGE

Every sector has its own challenges and business students need to have some general understanding about climate change and some specific understanding of climate change mitigation tools to enable them to actively address the issues. Figure 11.2, provides an overview of various greenhouse gases (GHG) emissions by sector (IPCC, 2014b: 9).

There are different ways to analyse how much each industry or each sector is emitting. For example, the Food and Agriculture Organization of the United Nations highlights on their website that 'Total emissions from global livestock' represent '14.5 percent of all anthropogenic GHG emissions'. This figure, taken from a report by Gerber et al. (2013), would encompass companies

Greenhouse Gas Emissions by Economic Sectors

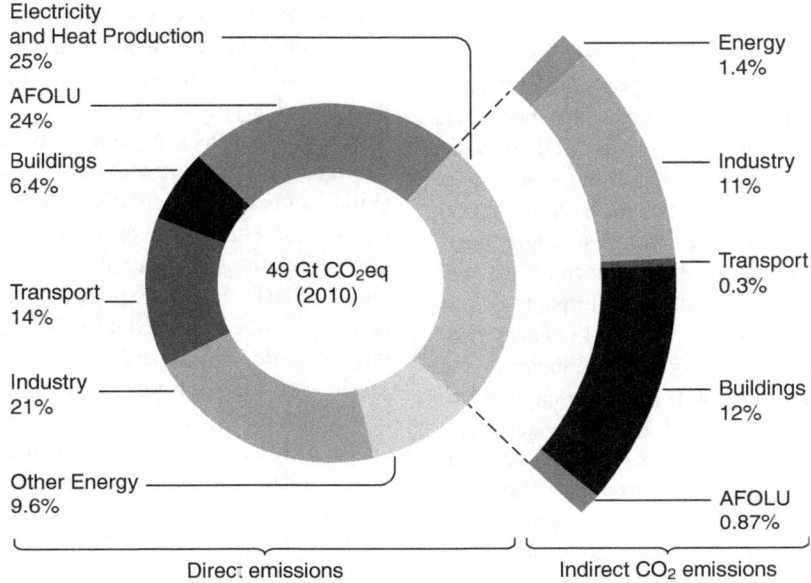

Figure 11.2   **Business contributions (sectors) to climate change (IPCC, 2014b: 9)**

and organizations in very different sectors, such as the food and drink sector but also the fashion industry. However, the overall message is clear, companies and organizations are responsible for high proportions of emissions or one could argue, through their products for all emissions we have. Addressing these emissions has, on the other hand, a strong financial benefit for a company. Even an SME can save thousands of pounds monthly through developing a carbon management plan to reduce carbon emission in their operations (Arora et al., 2018). However, owners of SMEs and employees generally often are not aware of their contribution to climate change nor of the opportunities to contribute to the reduction of climate change and save money at the same time.

There is contention regarding the amount of GHG emissions certain organizations contribute to climate change. Patenaude (2011: 259) calculated that during 2007–2009, using a range of publications (mostly from the Carbon Disclosure Project and UNFCC), 'Greenhouse gas (GHG) emissions from a selection of Global 500 companies approximate that of the United States and the EU 15 combined.' According to her calculations, Exxon Mobile in 2009 had higher GHG emissions than Belgium and Walmart's GHG emissions were nearly the same as Croatia and Volkswagen, the same as Iceland. Obviously, one could argue that every emission on a country level could be also allocated to an industry, e.g. the food we eat and associated carbon dioxide equivalents (CO_2e) to the food sector, the energy we use to heat our homes to energy providers, products we consume again to other industries. Clearly, when comparing organizations to countries, an understanding of the data and associated calculations would need detailed evaluation. However, the key underlying issue is that some businesses have extremely high GHG emissions and they need to reduce them.

BUSINESSES ARE PART OF THE SOLUTION TOO

Climate change permeates all sectors of industry and as a result provides extensive threats and opportunities for business. Clearly, some businesses will need to make significant adaptations to business processes and models, such as agriculture, construction and transportation. In contrast some businesses have seized the opportunities that have arisen as a result of the impacts of climate change, such as renewable energy producers. Business schools are educating the future leaders that will have the capacity to influence the policies, strategies, systems and practices that businesses will implement. This is why students need explicit knowledge about climate change to enable them to have effective discourse within organizations; in tandem with this they also require both hard and soft skills to influence the implementation of initiatives within businesses.

The Carbon Disclosure Project

While business schools have been very slow to respond to the challenge posed by climate change, the corporate sector has embraced the challenge, which is most evident by the growth and impact of the Carbon Disclosure Project (CDP), which was founded in 2002 as a NGO by 35 investors signing to ask companies to disclose their carbon emissions (CDP, 2018: 3); just 245 companies responded. The aim of the CDP has been from the beginning to provide investors and other stakeholders internationally with information about the voluntary carbon emission disclosure of companies and therefore increase transparency (de Faria et al., 2018). In 2010, questionnaires were sent to 4700 companies, including 500 S&P companies; 70% of S&P companies responded (CDP, 2010). By 2018, this had grown to 'over 650 global investors representing US $87 trillion in assets' (CDP, 2018: 3). In September 2018 this was further formalized by launching

the Investors Agenda (CDP, 2018) with the aim to accelerate the engagement of investors worldwide, which should lead to companies scaling up their actions as well. The philosophy behind this approach is that you can only manage what you measure.

Within business schools we have a responsibility to prepare students with appropriate skills to operate effectively within a changing world. This has been reinforced by the United Nations Sustainable Development Goals (SDG), which explicitly list Climate Action as one goal (SDG 13). One of its targets as developed and agreed at the 47th session of the UN Statistical Commission held in March 2016 requests: 'Improve education, awareness-raising and human and institutional capacity on climate change mitigation, adaptation, impact reduction and early warning' (United Nations Statistical Commission, 2017: Target 13.3). However, we do not appear to educate business students effectively about the science around climate change or the tools to respond to the impacts of climate change. There seems to be very limited research about climate change education (CCE) in business schools or any explicit evaluation of CCE/carbon literacy within responsible management education or ethics.

The Yale Study

A survey was undertaken by the Yale Centre for Business and the Environment in collaboration with the World Business Council for Sustainable Development and the Global Network for Advanced Management to understand among other objectives students' knowledge about climate change and their opinions on how this will impact business as well as their 'impressions of how well business schools prepare students to navigate issues at the intersection of business and the environment' (Yale et al., 2016: 6). The survey was distributed in 2015 to 27 business schools that are members of the Global Network for Advanced Management (25 countries on five continents) and two schools in the United States: Duke Fuqua School of Business and MIT Sloan School of Management. From the 17,600 students in the data set, 5135 responded. The median school response rate was 23%; 3711 contained all the key demographic information to be included in the analysis. One key insight from the analysis is the discrepancy between the demand of the students to learn about climate change, for example, and the learning opportunities given in business schools:

> While 94% of students consider t important for business leaders to be knowledgeable about environmental sustainability, many feel that they are not learning what they need to about this subject. More than three-quarters of all students say they feel only 'moderately' to 'not at all' knowledgeable across a range of related environmental concerns. Students generally feel less knowledgeable about the business solutions to environmental challenges than they do about the challenges themselves.

> To redress this gap, business students want the schools that they attend to integrate environmental sustainability into core curricula, programming, and career services. For instance, 61% of students want more faculty and staff with expertise in environmental sustainability and 55% think business schools should offer concentrations or joint-degree programs in this field; nearly two-thirds of students believe sustainability demands a more central position in the core curriculum. (Yale et al., 2016: 9)

WHY SHOULD WE TEACH CLIMATE LITERACY IN MANAGEMENT EDUCATION?

A climate-literate person is defined by the US Global Change Research Program (2009: 4) as someone who 'understands the essential principles of Earth's climate system, knows how to assess scientifically credible information about climate, communicates about climate and climate change in a meaningful way, and is able to make informed and responsible decisions with regards to actions that may affect climate.'

Education must play a key role in developing climate literacy at all levels of study and across all disciplines. This is one of the core challenges that faces educators: that introducing climate literacy topics is challenging because of its complexity and multidisciplinarity (Ekborg and Areskoug, 2006). A number of researchers have examined how climate literacy is dealt with in disciplines other than business. Many papers deal specifically with the issue of developing climate literacy in science-based disciplines. It is clear, however, that in order to develop a climate-literate society, climate issues need to be taught across disciplines other than the physical sciences. Dupigny-Giroux (2010) surveyed climate literacy literature and highlight six challenges to achieving a climate-literate population in both formal and informal learning settings. These challenges include: the language of climate science, the role of misconceptions, where to place climate change in curricula, the importance of learning styles, how educators can make a difference and the role of life experience. With regard to where to place climate change in curricula, the author makes the point that in order to create a climate-literate society, fundamental climate change concepts should be taught to all appropriate audiences. Traditionally climate principles tend to be taught in geography and earth science curricula, however not all students will benefit from such an education either at school or in further and higher education. Dupigny-Giroux (2010) concludes that achieving climate literacy will require a connected web of disciplinary, interdisciplinary, multidisciplinary and transdisciplinary approaches. This would require climate science and related topics to be taught in classes other than geography and earth science classes and embedded into social science curricula. Business and management is one such social science discipline where climate literacy can and should be addressed.

The challenge is that climate change is a 'super wicked problem', which according to

Bushell et al. (2017: 40) has the following key challenges:

Climate Change needs action now but the consequences cannot be seen easily nor understood and measured.

Climate is a public good and affects every person in the world, but the vested self-interests of certain actors hinder the debate.

Action (Decarbonisation) needs to happen on an unprecedented timescale.

Cognitive dissonance is common, with individuals believing that climate mitigation needs to happen e.g. reducing flights but not taking personal action to do so.

In line with cognitive dissonance many individuals feel that they do not need to act but someone else.

Integrating Climate Change mitigation is not seen as the social norm.

Given this background, it is understandable that climate change mitigation is rarely taught in management education. But especially with regards to climate change mitigation tools engineers can only provide part of the knowledge, such as the calculations of carbon emission (equivalents); this needs then to be translated into the business context as most of the reduction of carbon emissions will be achieved in business activities such as the energy-efficient transformation of processes in operations and the supply chain. Table 11.1 gives a very short summary of what each business discipline would contribute to climate change understanding and mitigation tools.

The research of climate change education could take any concept in RME and Education for Sustainable Development ESD) or Education for Sustainability (EfS) and explore whether this applies to climate change education or whether modifications need to be made. However, in Table 11.1 we have proposed some of the concepts that we consider as more relevant to climate change education given the nature of climate change and its standing in the corporate world and in business schools. We have focused on different disciplines. Each discipline could make its own contribution but also offers its own challenges. For this table we have defined climate change education as follows:

Climate change education is based on the assumption that climate change is anthropogenic and therefore any human activity that emits carbon emission or carbon emission equivalents contributes to changes in the Earth's climate. Given the scientifically predicted impact this will have on living conditions on Earth, climate change education aims to give every business student the tools and understanding to reduce their own impact on the climate and that of their future employer.

The ALBERT Carbon Literacy Training offered by BAFTA, BBC, ITV and Others

While the integration of carbon literacy training within business schools has been rudimentary, there is learning to take from businesses in the screen sector in the UK, which has embraced work-based carbon literacy training, embedding it within large corporations such as the BBC: BAFTA (British Academy of Film and Television Arts) in cooperation with the BBC, ITV and other television channels. In 2011, the BAFTA ALBERT Consortium was founded 'supporting the screen art industry's transition to an environmentally sustainable future' (ALBERT Consortium, 2018) and created a triple approach: Calculator, Certification and Carbon Literacy Training. Initially, ALBERT created the carbon calculator, so that production units could report on their carbon emissions (ALBERT Carbon Calculator, 2018). This was followed by an accreditation (ALBERT Certification, 2018), which appears as a logo at the end credits of popular TV productions such as *Downton Abbey* (Series 6). In parallel, they realized that the required carbon reduction can only be achieved if every employee in the different departments of the production process such as lighting, sounds and costumes understands how they contribute to carbon emissions. The Carbon Literacy Training (ALBERT Training, 2018) was initiated by the Carbon Literacy Project in Manchester, UK (Carbon Literacy Certificate, 2017). This is a wider project run by Cooler Projects CIC on behalf

Table 11.1 How to integrate carbon literacy/climate change in business curricula

Felds	Topic	Ethics/RME/ESD	Climate change education required
General	Climate change science and the anthropogenic nature of climate change	Utilitarianism, risk ethics, discourse ethics, social learning, system thinking	Business students need to understand the contributions business in all different sectors have on climate change and which impact climate change will have on business, e.g. through changes in the supply chain or flooding.
Corporate strategy	Long-term strategy versus short-term strategy	Ethical leadership, deontological ethics, system thinking	Climate change is already one of the risks a business is facing but also one of the opportunities, so tools such as SWOT or shared value can be applied.
Accounting	Carbon accounting, integrated reporting	Objects of ethical concern such as anthropocentric, etc. GRI, SDGs	Accountants need to translate the carbon (equivalents) into financial measures to inform the decision-making internally and report externally (integrated reporting).
Economics	Carbon tax, externalities	Utilitarianism	Economics has a crucial role to play to understand inventions to be taken on a policy level and their impact such as tax.
HR	Carbon literacy training, rewards scheme	Virtue ethics, locus of control, competencies, perceived self-efficacy	Behavioural changes need to underpin the technological changes at the workplace in order to achieve substantial reductions in carbon emissions.
Insurance	Risk assessment	Risk ethics, systems thinking	Pension fund managers need to understand the risks certain companies have in relation to climate change but also how to select companies who have an outstanding performance with regards to the reduction of carbon emissions.
Law	Regulations and policies	Deontological ethics	Internationally binding agreements such as the COP 21 [Paris Agreement] need to be translated into laws and policies.
Operations	Carbon measurement and reductions in operations	Virtue ethics	Efficient operations will reduce carbon emissions and costs simultaneously.
Marketing	Communication of climate change	Consumer ethics	Educate customers about behavioural changes, support reduction of carbon in buying decision such as rating systems.
Supply chain	Carbon measurement and reductions in supply chain	System thinking	Analyse the supply chain with regards to carbon emissions, such as logistics and risks, e.g. growing conditions for cocoa in relation to climate change.

ESD, Education for sustainable development; GRI, Global Reporting Initiative; RME, responsible management education; SDGs, Sustainable Development Goals.

of the Carbon Literacy Trust, which includes different sectors – for example, they also initiated a successful Carbon Literacy training scheme within Manchester Metropolitan University (Dunk et al., 2017). One of the principles of the Carbon Literacy Project is peer-to-peer teaching (Carbon Literacy Project, 2017), so in case of BAFTA, the Carbon Literacy trainers have a background in production, in the case of the university, students are trained by students.

Examples of Good Practice in Teaching Climate Change in Business Schools

The Frankfurt School of Finance and Management (2019) in Germany has run its 'Climate and Sustainable Energy Finance Summer Academy' to satisfy demands from the city's financial institutions every year since 2009. In 2016 an executive training was added to the portfolio and an e-course launched.

As outlined above, it is even more important that climate change education gets embedded into the core curriculum. At Nottingham Business School, UK (Chapple et al., 2020; Arora et al., 2018; Molthan-Hill et al., 2017) this has been done since 2011 as a student consultancy project linked to the core curriculum; at the time of writing this chapter it is in its seventh iteration. The project was first part of an option called 'The sustainable organization' and was a desk-based analysis of companies and how they could implement carbon management. However, the students had such fantastic ideas that the project was made a life consultancy project and moved into the core curriculum of BA Business. From 2011 to 2018, over 180 local SMEs took part but also some bigger organizations, for example four units of the NHS England (Clinical Commissioning Groups) or some units of the Nottingham City Council such as Newstead Abbey, the home of Lord Byron, an English poet. Each year, the students are allocated in groups of four to each participating

organization and over a course of 16 weeks apply the knowledge given to them in lectures to their 'own' organization. Tutors will have weekly seminars with students to check on progress and accuracy of the information later provided to the companies/organizations. The organizations have to provide their utility bills and other information to the students, the students will then have a site visit and meeting to ask questions of the organization. A few weeks later the students will send their remaining questions to the company and then present their final results and recommendations on a low-carbon event to their organization and the other attendees. The company will get the poster and the report a week before to give approval that this information can be presented in public.

At the beginning, the project followed the process outlined in Lingl et al. (2010), in 2013 NBS partnered up with Nottingham-based social enterprise NetPositive and the Investor in the Environment (iiE). From 2013 onwards, the final year undergraduate students helped local businesses and organizations to reduce greenhouse gas emissions and achieve at the same time Investor in the Environment (iiE) Accreditation. NBS was awarded the Guardian University Award 2015 in Business Partnership for this project together with its partner (Molthan-Hill et al., 2017).

Based on the principles of experiential learning, the scale-up methodology and crowdsourcing, over 600 students have developed very diverse solutions on how greenhouse gas emission can be reduced in business, ranging from a carbon-neutral Christmas decoration in a big shopping centre to advising a taxi company to be the first carbon-neutral transport provider in Nottinghamshire. Most companies reported that they have implemented the solutions of the students, one brewery for example invested in a whole new system suggested by the students, where they were turning the residues from the brewing process, which went to landfill before, into energy to run the machinery in the brewery. Using the data from 2014–2016, the total recommended greenhouse gas emissions savings from two years of the project are 507,435 kg CO_2e, averaging over 10 tonnes per organization and 2 tonnes per student (Molthan-Hill et al., 2020).

The Centre for Sustainable Global Enterprise at Cornell's Johnson Graduate School of Management has multiple courses that cover climate change and business, including issues of policy and compliance, and how climate change presents opportunities through product, service and business model innovation (Cornell, 2018). Additionally, students have the option of taking more traditional, case-based courses that look at climate change and business; lecture courses in which leaders from the private, public and non-profit sector discuss their approaches to climate change; and experiential learning-based practicum courses in which students work closely with companies to develop strategies to real climate change-related challenges and business opportunities (Cornell, 2018).

Climate Change Education might be taught in programmes and modules that focus on Education for Sustainable Development or more specifically in Environmental Sustainability Management Education. This is demonstrated for example in the paper by Montiel et al. (2018: 155) in AMLE, currently one of the leading journals in management education. The paper refers to climate change only twice in the main text and both times it is used only as an example such as: 'to address global environmental sustainability challenges such as **climate change**, income inequality, or deforestation'. Within the chosen 75 teaching case studies that are presented and analysed in this paper, only one refers to climate change, one to carbon-neutral (in the context of greenwashing) and one to GHG.

The main business school accrediting bodies do require institutions to commit to teaching on ethical, responsible and sustainability topics such as business ethics and corporate social responsibility (CSR), however teaching on climate change leadership is not explicitly required (Moules, 2015). Climate change education in business schools is well hidden if it happens at all. A survey analysing how climate change is taught in business schools worldwide has been conducted to produce a baseline, but also in order to understand whether climate change is only taught in very small units, for example in a case study. The results of this survey are currently being analysed.

RESEARCHING CLIMATE CHANGE EDUCATION AND CARBON LITERACY IN BUSINESS SCHOOLS

Wall et al. (2017) examined work-based learning as a catalyst for sustainability, including within their study work-based learning for climate change and climate literacy. They discovered just five full text academic peer-reviewed journal articles that dealt with climate literacy through a search on the EBSCO Business Source Elite databases when applying the search terms 'Climate Literacy', 'Climate Change Literacy', 'Climate Change Education', or 'Curriculum' and 'Climate Change'. Of these, none was published in mainstream business and management journals. We repeated this search, discovering an additional peer-reviewed article, taking the total to six (see Table 11.1). We build on this by broadening out the search using Google Scholar. Here the search term 'Climate Literacy' returns 243 results. Of these, none is published in peer-reviewed business and management journals, the majority being found in journals dealing specifically with geography, earth sciences and education in general. Using a Google Scholar search for the term 'Climate Change Education' in the title of the article yields 464 results. Again, none of these is published in business- and management-related journals.

This is not to suggest that business and management scholars are not interested in climate change as an issue, however. Using the search terms 'Climate Change' and

'Business' yields 223 publications of which 43 are published in peer-reviewed business- and management-oriented journals. Similarly, 'Climate Change' and 'Management' yields over 2500 results, although the vast majority of papers are focused on the management of climate change within specific disciplines rather than business and management responses to the issue. Finally, climate change as an issue is often bundled under the broader term 'sustainability'. Using the search term 'sustainability AND education AND business' returns 111 publications, the majority published within business and management affiliated journals. Many of these include climate change implicitly if not explicitly.

We suggest that this snapshot of the state of the literature on climate literacy and climate change education within the field of business and management and related disciplines indicates that academics in the field are interested in the issue of climate change from a practice perspective rather than an educational, curriculum or pedagogical viewpoint. In order to better understand the state of climate change education in business schools, we undertook an analysis of the six articles discovered through the EBSCO host search looking explicitly for linkages with and between business ethics, responsible management education (RME) and education for sustainable development (ESD). These are summarized in Table 11.2.

MAPPING RESEARCH OF CCE WITHIN ESTABLISHED RESEARCH FIELDS

Table 11.2 has also been compiled to establish the links having been made between climate change education (CCE) and more traditional fields such as ethics, RME and ESD.

Business Ethics

None of the papers explicitly discusses the issue of climate change or climate change education from a business ethics perspective, however ethics is mentioned as a discipline that may support climate change topics. Hess and Collins (2018) investigate climate change teaching in higher education across disciplines of liberal arts curricula, including business-related topics such as business ethics. They found that in the United States at least climate change issues are rarely included in the majority of such courses. Similarly, both Correia et al. (2010) and Takacs (2013) mention ethics as a subject within which one might seek to find climate change issues, however they also point out that this is rare. In order to address this issue, Correia et al. (2010) set out an epistemological framework though which climate change is taught across a broad range of first year undergraduate disciplines, including business-related courses such as Business Ethics. Overall the lack of discussion around the topic of business ethics is rather disappointing given that as Perkins et al. (2018) point out the United Nations Educational, Scientific and Cultural Organization (UNESCO) set out ethics as a thematic area within their Climate Change Initiative (UN, 2018).

Education for Sustainable Development

More prevalent across the literature examined is the concept of education for sustainable development (ESD), which is also referred to as education for sustainability (EfS). Perkins et al. (2018) use the term ESD to frame their study, which aims to provide an international perspective on the pedagogy of climate change. They report on the results of a questionnaire and interviews administered to a small sample of professors working in the area of climate change and sustainability across six geographic regions. Whilst limited in its scope, the study suggests that there is a very broad range of different conceptions as to what education for sustainability looks like and whether climate change issues are taught under this umbrella or not.

Table 11.2 Links between climate change education and more traditional fields such as ethics, responsible management education (RME) and education for sustainable development (ESD)

Author	Journal	Year	Title of paper	Focus of research	Ethics/ESD/RME
Hess and Collins	*Journal of Cleaner Production*	2018	Climate change and higher education: assesing factors that affect curriculum requirements	Investigation of climate change teaching in higher education across disciplines reporting that in the United States at least climate change issues are rarely included in the majority of liberal arts curricula, including business-related topics.	Passing comment on ethics as a discipline which may include climate issues. No mention of ESD or RME.
Perkins et al.	*Journal of Cleaner Production*	2018	International perspectives on the pedagogy of climate change	Investigation of the international perspective on the pedagogy of climate change.	Reference to ethics as a UNESCO climate change initiative theme. No mention of RME. Study is framed around the term ESD.
Rao et al.	*International Journal of Business Analytics and Intelligence*	2017	An application of structural equation modelling to determine the inclusion of climate change topics in MBA education	Investigation as to whether the inclusion of climate change education in MBA curriculum would inspire, encourage and equip managers to engage with climate change challenges.	No mention of the terms ethics, ESD or RME.
Takacs	*Journal of Education for Business*	2013	Teaching about climate change in the business curriculum: an introductory module and resource list	Presents a teaching module developed with the aim of integrating it into introductory business courses at the undergraduate level and a resource list for teaching climate change at all levels of study.	Discussion of how climate issues could be incorporated into Ethics courses. No detailed discussion of RME, although reference to UN PRME in the conclusion as a driver.
Paschall and Wustenhagen	*Journal of Management Education*	2012	More than a game: learning about climate change through role play	Report on a course taught to master's students in business with the goal of creating deep learning around the topic of climate change.	Presents the UNESCO definition of ESD, but not assessed in any detail. No mention of ethics or RME.
Correia et al.	*Journal of Cleaner Production*	2010	The importance of scientific literacy in fostering education for sustainability: theoretical considerations and preliminary findings from a Brazilian experience	Examination of the importance of scientific literacy in fostering education for sustainability using climate change as the main topic of study.	General commentary as to how ESD (termed 'education for sustainability' in the paper) interfaces with ethics. No mention of RME.

UN PRME, United Nations Principles for Responsible Management Education.

The findings of the study highlight the importance of cultural context, globalization and interdisciplinarity in curricula when teaching climate change. Correia et al. (2010) also seek to make explicit linkages between climate change and education for sustainable development, suggesting the creation of new interfaces between science, technology, society, environment and ethics. They assert that it is educators who are responsible for making changes to higher education curriculum in order to improve scientific literacy through dialogue and critical thinking.

This thinking is backed up by Takacs (2013), who begins her study by acknowledging that whilst general issues of sustainability and environmental management may have gained some foothold in business and management classrooms, topics that focus specifically on climate change are less widespread and certainly less documented. The author then presents a teaching module developed with the aim of integrating it into introductory business courses at the undergraduate level and a resource list for teaching climate change at all levels of study. The course in question is relatively short, comprising of two 75-minute classes, however it aimed simply to raise business and management students' awareness of the causes, consequences and responses to climate change. An evaluation of students' perceptions of climate change prior to undertaking the course and upon completion suggested that there was an increase in students' understanding of climate-related issues.

Responsible Management Education (Pedagogy)

Interestingly, none of the papers refers explicitly to the term 'responsible management education', despite presenting insights on teaching pedagogy and management education in general. This may simply be due to the relatively new use of the terminology rather than the implication that climate change has no part to play in the RME agenda.

Aside from the themes of ethics, ESD and RME, the additional theme of pedagogy comes up across a number of papers. For example, Perkins et al. (2018) suggest that the teaching of climate change and related issues necessitates a pedagogy that requires students to think critically, interdisciplinarily and globally about climate change. These findings can be useful for business school educators seeking to include climate-related issues in their teaching activities. Paschall and Wustenhagen (2012) agree that educating management students on the connections between business and climate change is essential to both their own careers and to societies' ability to solve climate change challenges and require different pedagogical approaches. They report on a course taught to master's students in business with the goal of creating deep learning around the topic of climate change. Specific learning outcomes were defined as: to understand climate change and the challenges it presents; to provide insight into the processes of international negotiation; to build negotiation skills for use in a variety of contexts; to understand the impact of climate change on business, and vice versa; and to invent creative and workable new solutions for climate negotiations. The course utilized a mixture of traditional lecture/seminar-based knowledge transfer sessions alongside role-playing and simulation pedagogies designed to bring the topic alive. Overall the authors report that despite initial scepticism or lack of interest from students, feedback was overwhelmingly positive, and the learning objectives met.

Additional Themes

Another topic which bears some consideration is that of extramural activities for education students on climate change issues. Rao et al. (2017) discovered that informal education in the business school has a powerful role to play in climate change education. This includes measures such as equipping the campus with conservation initiatives, climate change and renewable energy initiatives, as well as invited speakers. Clearly climate change education in the curriculum needs to be coupled with actions to improve campus sustainability.

Finally, the curriculum in general is a key consideration for researchers. Rao et al. (2017) set out to investigate if the inclusion of climate change education in MBA curriculum would inspire, encourage and equip managers to engage with climate change challenges. They employed a questionnaire administered to corporate managers to get responses as to their agreement on what categories of topics on climate change could be, have been and should have been included in their MBA curriculum both formally, and through informal actions. The results suggest that there was some demand amongst MBA students for the inclusion of climate-related topics in the taught curriculum. In particular, respondents indicated that they would like to learn more about specific climate change adaptation initiatives, which is perhaps unsurprising given that the majority of respondents were private sector managers seeking to better understand actions they could apply in their own organizations.

Hess and Collins (2018) identify three best practices for climate change education through reform of core curricula: the use of a core course required of all students, and increased volume of climate-related courses available as options across a programme of study, and a menu of courses that explicitly include climate science or climate change education (Hess and Collins, 2018). The study laments the fact that while climate change is arguably the most important global problem facing society, higher education institutions are failing to update the general curriculum to include education about climate change and climate-related topics.

Summary

In many articles, chapters, abstracts and books on ethics, RME and ESD, climate change is sometimes cited as an example when references are made to the challenges we face today. So, for example, research about competencies in ESD or/and RME might refer in the introduction to climate change as a challenge along with poverty, human rights, diversity etc. to name just a few. Recent research, for example, into the relationship between social learning and climate change education revealed that there is no article in any discipline explicitly linking these two concepts, however as demonstrated in our research, social learning was one of the key concepts underpinning the success of the carbon literacy training in the production unit of the TV soap opera *Coronation Street*, (Chapple et al., 2020). There might be the possibility that any insight gained in the research of ESD and/or RME is applicable to climate change education, however as Patenaude (2011) pointed out in her paper when debating why business schools are lagging behind in picking up the topic of climate change, climate change is highly abstract and very complex. The impact of individual actions cannot be measured, only the impact of whole nations, corporations, countries, humanity – a concept difficult to grasp. Citing Bleda and Shackley (2008: 518), she highlights: 'The belief that companies (and business scholars) hold in relation to the perceived reality or credibility of the "anthropogenic climate change" argument is a determinant factor of their willingness or reluctance to adapt.' She points out that in the corporate world fossil fuels are often linked with economic prosperity; in the insurance of industry, extreme weather events have been often framed as Acts of God. Therefore, climate change education offers its own challenges, which differ from other topics in RME or ESD/ESF.

Aside from the previously discussed papers that deal specifically with climate change education in the business school curriculum, a number of recent papers included in the EBSCO Business Source Elite database deal with climate change education more generally across higher educations. Some of these topics could form the base of some specific research in responsible management education.

VISION

What if every new recruit into corporations from the world's business schools was qualified as Carbon Literate? What if they knew the relevance of climate change to their chosen profession and could speak from the heart of its risks and opportunities to their future employers – *and* know how to act on that? (Phil Korbel, Carbon Literacy Project)

This chapter has shown that climate change education is in its infancy. We need to develop successful models of how to teach climate change in business schools and where and how to integrate it into the existing paradigms within ethics, responsible management education and ESD. Climate change education (CCE) therefore offers a rich field for researchers as so much is *not* known. A good way going forward would be to develop teaching methods/tools for climate change education and research their effectiveness simultaneously. As Fazey et al. (2018: 55) pointed out:

While science has so far excelled at understanding the climate problem and identifying techno-centric solutions, it has so far largely failed to seriously engage with the critical question of how to make transformational change happen. Addressing this and other related questions requires a diversity of approaches to knowledge production. ... As yet, however, there has been no integration of these insights specifically for researchers aiming to inform and facilitate the transformational changes necessary to address climate change and help achieve more sustainable societies. Further, while all forms of research have value, effective responses to climate change require a much more direct and concerted effort towards learning from and through action. (emphasis in original)

New tools for climate change education in all business disciplines could be developed or improved, their effectiveness in an organizational context tested, while at the same time the current best practice is embedded into the curriculum and taught while the impact is tested. This approach is quite different to the one used in research but would allow for a faster transformation of the business sector and management education. A paradigm shift might be also required; instead of looking backwards and analysing the gaps in existing research to define the next steps, researchers could start from the vision they want to achieve. For example, if we want to achieve that the climate change is stopped at $1.5°C$ increase, we might set this as our vision in 10 years. Then we would establish the knowledge we have already within the business discipline to achieve this vision and which could form part of our curriculum. In parallel, we can identity the gaps in our current knowledge, which might stand in the way of achieving our vision and this could form the base of our next research project. This approach could also be linked to a new form of knowledge management; instead of searching for the best knowledge in absolute terms, we could combine the sufficient knowledge we have for each of the challenges to achieve our vision and then concentrate on the one where we have no understanding at all. For example, if we have some sufficient understanding on how to transform an institution but very limited understanding why some departments engage with climate action and others do not, our research efforts could be dedicated to the latter.

It might be useful for the integration of climate change education into the curriculum of business schools to teach business students the underlying science of climate change so that they can understand why the business sector has such an impact on climate change. However, it is equally important that business students learn climate change mitigation tools that are relevant to their business discipline and would enable them in their profession to contribute to the reduction of carbon emissions and its equivalents. Therefore, climate change education needs to be integrated into every discipline such as carbon reporting into accounting, methods on how to improve energy efficiency into operations, employee engagement in carbon friendly behaviour into HR and so on (see Table 11.1). This opens up another rich field for research, whereby discipline-specific best practice in business schools and at the workplace are analysed and further improved; then transformed into teaching tools and linked to existing frameworks in management education such as experiential learning.

In summary, we suggest that where business and management academics are interested in the topic of climate change, the majority investigate issues from a practice perspective rather than an educational, curriculum or pedagogical viewpoint. This is a problem as the analysis of the papers above indicated that in order to deal with climate change-related challenges, business managers and leaders arguably need to become climate/carbon literate either through their higher education experiences or work-based learning programmes. There is a need then to further investigate the state of climate change education in business and management schools to gain a better understanding of how, where, when and why climate change issues are covered in curricula and syllabi and identify good practice as a means to assist management educators looking to develop climate literacy within their own courses.

Notes

1   Scope 1 are direct emissions from sources owned or controlled by the company; Scope 2 are indirect emissions from purchased energy. Scope 3 are indirect emissions from the operation of a company but are not directly controlled or owned by the company (Lingl et al., 2010:12).
2   All IPCC reports are available at www.ipcc.ch/reports/.

REFERENCES

ALBERT Carbon Calculator (2018) https://calc.wearealbert.org/uk/.

ALBERT Certification (2018) http://wearealbert.org/certification. Accessed on 10 June, 2020.

ALBERT Consortium (2018) http://wearealbert.org/about/the-consortium. Accessed 10 June, 2020.

ALBERT Training (2018) Sustainable film and TV production training – 'Albert' via BAFTA. http://wearealbert.org/help/get-trained. Accessed on 10 June, 2020.

Arora, A., Arora, A., Baddley, J., Molthan-Hill, P., and Leseane, R. (2018) Sustainable competitiveness: powering 'sustainability' through Investors in the Environment (iiE) initiative at Riverside Bakery. In McIntyre, J.R., Ivanaj, S. and Ivanaj, V. (Eds.), *CSR and Climate Change Implications for Multinational Enterprises*. New Horizons in International Business Series (pp. 162–195). Cheltenham: Edward Elgar Publishing.

Bleda, M. and Shackley, S. (2008) The dynamics of belief in climate change and its risks in business organisations. *Ecological Economics*, 66(2–3), 517–532.

Bushell, S., Buisson, G.S., Workmann, M. and Colley, T. (2017) Strategic narratives in climate change: towards a unifying narrative to address the action gap on climate change. *Energy Research and Social Science*, 28, 39–49.

Carbon Literacy Certificate (2017) www.carbonliteracy.com/individual/.

Carbon Literacy Project (2017) Carbon Literacy Course Kit. www.carbonliteracy.com/wp-content/uploads/2017/11/Carbon-Literacy-Course-Kit_v1.7.pdf.

CDP (2018) The Investor Agenda Factsheet. https://theinvestoragenda.org/wp-content/uploads/2018/09/The-Investor-Agenda-Fact-Sheet-final.pdf.

CDP (2010) Carbon Disclosure Project 2010 S&P 500 Report. https://ecometrica.com/article/cdp-releases-2010-reports-for-global-500-and-sp-500

CDSB and CDP (2018) Ready or not: are companies prepared for the TCFD recommendations? A geographical analysis of CDP 2017 responses. Joint CDSB and CDP report March 2018. https://6fefcbb86e61af1b2fc4-c70d8ead6ced-550b4d987d7c03fcdd1d.ssl.cf3.rackcdn.com/cms/reports/documents/000/003/116/original/TCFD-Preparedness-Report.pdf?1521558217.

Chapple, W., Molthan-Hill, P., Welton, R. and Hewitt, M. (2020) Lights off, spot on: carbon literacy training crossing boundaries in the television industry. *Journal of Business Ethics*, 162(4), 813–834.

Cornell University (2018) Johnson at Cornell: Center for Sustainable Global Enterprise, Curriculum. Retrieved 19 August 2018 from www.johnson.cornell.edu/Center-for-Sustainable-Global-Enterprise/Students/Curriculum.

Correia P.R.M., do Valle, B.X., Dazzani, M. and Infante-Malachias, M.E. (2010) The importance of scientific literacy in fostering education for sustainability: theoretical considerations and preliminary findings from a Brazilian experience. *Journal of Cleaner Production*, 18, 7, 678–685.

de Faria, J.A., Andrade, J.C.S. and da Silva Gomes, S.M. (2018) The determinants mostly disclosed by companies that are members of the Carbon Disclosure Project. *Mitigation and Adaptation Strategies for Global Change*, 23, 995–1018.

Dunk, R., Mörk, J., Davies, J., Davidson, J., Paling, C., Hindley, J., Leigh, S. and Tinker, H. (2017) Taking responsibility for carbon emissions – the evolution of a Carbon Literacy Living Lab. *Environmental Scientist*, 26(4), 88–95.

Dupigny-Giroux, L.-A. L. (2010) Exploring the challenges of climate science literacy: lessons from students, teachers and lifelong learners: challenges to addressing climate science literacy. *Geography Compass*, 4(9), 1203–1217.

Ekborg, M. and Areskoug, M. (2006) How student teachers' understanding of the greenhouse effect develops during a teacher education programme. *Nordic Studies in Science Education*, 5, 17–29.

Fazey, I., Schäpke, N., Caniglia, G., Patterson, J., Hultman, J., van Mierlo, B., ..., Wyborn, C. (2018) Ten essentials for action-oriented and second order energy transitions, transformations and climate change research, *Energy Research and Social Science*, 40, 54–70.

Frankfurt School of Finance and Management (2019) Key facts and findings at: www.frankfurt-school.de/en/home/international-advisory-services/development-finance-programmes/climate-sustainable-energy-finance-summer-academy-new.

Gerber, P.J., Steinfeld, H., Henderson, B., Mottet, A., Opio, C., Dijkman, J., Falcucci, A. and Tempio, G. (2013) Tackling climate change through livestock – a global assessment of emissions and mitigation opportunities. Rome: Food and Agriculture Organization of the United Nations (FAO). Key facts and findings at: www.fao.org/news/story/en/item/197623/icode/.

Hess, D.J. and Collins, B.M. (2018) Climate change and higher education: assessing factors that affect curriculum requirements. *Journal of Cleaner Production*, 170, 1451–1458.

IPCC (2014a) Climate Change 2014: Synthesis Report. Contribution of Working Groups I, II and III to the Fifth Assessment Report of the Intergovernmental Panel on Climate Change [Core Writing Team, R.K. Pachauri and L.A. Meyer (Eds.)]. Geneva: IPCC.

IPCC (2014b) Summary for Policymakers. In: Climate Change 2014: Mitigation of Climate Change. Contribution of Working Group III to the Fifth Assessment Report of the Intergovernmental Panel on Climate Change [Edenhofer, O., Pichs-Madruga, R., Sokona, Y., Farahani, E., Kadner, S., Seyboth, K., ... Minx, J. C. (Eds.)]. Cambridge and New York: Cambridge University Press.

IPCC (2018) Global Warming of 1.5 °C. An IPCC Special Report on the impacts of global warming of 1.5 °c above pre-industrial levels and related global greenhouse gas emission pathways, in the context of strengthening the global response to the threat of climate change, sustainable development, and efforts to eradicate poverty. Available at: www.ipcc.ch/report/sr15/. Accessed on 10 June, 2020.

Lingl, P., Carlson, D. and the David Suzuki Foundation (2010) *Doing business in a New Climate*. Abingdon: Earthscan.

Molthan-Hill, P., Winfield, F., Baddley, J. and Hill, S. (2017) Work based learning: students solving sustainability challenges through strategic business partnerships. In Flynn, P., Gudić, M. and Tan, T. (Eds.). *Redefining Success: Integrating the UN Global Compact into Management Education*, PRME Book Series. Sheffield: Greenleaf Publishing.

Molthan-Hill, P., Robinson, Z., Dharmasasmita, A., McManus, E. and Hope, A. (2020) Reducing carbon emissions in business through Responsible Management Education: influence at the micro-, meso- and macro-levels.

International Journal of Management Education, 18(1), 100328. https://doi.org/10.1016/j.ijme.2019.100328

Montiel, I., Antolin-Lopez, R. and Gallo, P.J. (2018) Emotions and sustainability: a literary genre-based framework for environmental sustainability management education. *Academy of Management Learning and Education,* 17(2), 155–183.

Moules, J. (2015) Teaching the impact of climate change to the leaders of tomorrow. *Financial Times*, 29 November. Available at: www.ft.com/content/96f662de-82db-11e5-a01c-8650859a4767. Accessed on 10 June, 2020.

Paschall, M. and Wuestenhagen, R. (2012) More than a game: learning about climate change through role play. *Journal of Management Education,* 36(4), 510–543.

Patenaude, G. (2011) Climate change diffusion: while the world tips, business schools lag. *Global Environmental Change*, 21(1), 259–271.

Perkins, K.M., Munguia, N., Moure-Eraso, R., Delakowitz, B., Giannetti, B.F., Liu, G., Nurunnabi, M., Will, M. and Velazquez, L. (2018) International perspectives on the pedagogy of climate change. *Journal of Cleaner Production*, 200, 1043–1052.

Rao, P.H., Pulupudi, R. and Sen, S. (2017) An application of structural equation modelling to determine the inclusion of climate change topics in MBA education. *International Journal of Business Analytics and Intelligence*, 5(1), 15–25.

Stern, N. H. (2007) *The Economics of Climate Change: The Stern Review*. Cambridge: Cambridge University Press.

Stiglitz, J. (2018) Nobel-winning economist to testify in children's climate lawsuit. Inside Climate News. Available at: https://insideclimatenews.org/news/11072018/joseph-stiglitz-kids-climate-change-lawsuit-global-warming-costs-economic-impact.

Takacs, H. (2013) Teaching about climate change in the Business curriculum: an introductory module and resource list. *Journal of Education for Business,* 88, 176–183. Accessed on 10 June, 2020.

United Nations (2018) Global Issues: Climate change. [Online] Available at: www.un.org/en/sections/issues-depth/climate-change/.

United Nations Statistical Commission (2017) Global Indicator Framework for the Sustainable Development Goals and targets of the 2030 Agenda for Sustainable Development. Available at: https://unstats.un.org/sdgs/indicators/Global%20Indicator%20Framework%20after%20refinement_Eng.pdf. Accessed on 10 June, 2020.

United States Global Change Research Program (2009) Climate Literacy: The Essential Principles of Climate. Washington, DC: USGCRP. Retrieved from www.globalchange.gov.

Wall, T., Hindley, A., Hunt, T., Peach, J., Preston, M., Hartley, C. and Fairbank, A. (2017) Work-based learning as a catalyst for sustainability: a review and prospects. *Higher Education, Skills and Work-Based Learning*, 7(2), 211–224.

Yale, CBE, GNAM, WBCSD (2016) Rising leaders on environmental sustainability and climate change: a global survey of business students. Available at: http://cbey.yale.edu/files/Rising%20Leaders%20on%20Environmental%20Sustainability%20and%20Climate%20Change%20Nov_2015.pdf. Accessed 15 November 2016.

12

Gender Equality: Taking Its Rightful Place at the Heart of Sustainability Education

Maureen A. Kilgour

INTRODUCTION

The goal of gender equality is central to any concept of sustainability, business ethics and corporate responsibility. Gender equality is also central to the attainment of the Sustainable Development Goals (SDGs), the current proxy for how sustainability is understood by the international community, governments, businesses and many management education (ME) institutions. It was designated as a stand-alone goal (SDG 5) and as a goal that cuts across all other goals – meaning that they must all be viewed from a gender-aware perspective to 'draw … attention to the gender dimensions of poverty, hunger, health, education, water and sanitation, employment, climate change, environmental degradation, urbanization, conflict and peace, and financing for development' (UN Women, 2018). The United Nations, the World Bank, major business organizations, governments and nongovernment organizations have all called for action on gender inequality. Public policy at the global level stresses the importance of gender equality.

The implications of this approach for a responsible management education (RME) that focuses on sustainability is significant – a gender-aware approach to education across all disciplines is required in order to prepare students to engage in the 'real world', to have the knowledge and competencies necessary to meet the challenges (as set out, for example, in the SDGs), to understand the preoccupations of the international business community, civil society and government institutions and to be agents of change toward a sustainable and ethical future for all.

Unfortunately, the lack of sufficient commitment to this goal by many actors means that it is unlikely to be achieved any time soon. Although the SDGs, launched in 2015, put gender equality front and centre, a recent audit on progress is not encouraging:

[T]he 2019 SDG Gender Index finds that, with just 11 years to go until 2030, nearly 40% of the world's girls and women – 1.4 billion – live in countries failing on gender equality. Another 1.4 billion live in countries that 'barely pass' (Equal Measures 2030, 2019a).

Management education institutions have a role to play in this persistent problem. Even though gender equality has been a longstanding goal in the international community and within management education institutions, many initiatives in the areas of sustainability, ethics and corporate responsibility appear to be gender-neutral at best and ignore gender at worst (Haynes, 2015). One of the first steps in addressing the lack of attention to gender equality in RME is to understand that there is a problem and that it can be fixed. A broad perspective on the problem would draw attention to pedagogy, organizational cultures and how ME is conceptualized and practised: since '[g]ender takes shape in, and is shaped by, teaching, learning, and leadership practices, and in relations between students, faculty, administrators, and communities' (Ropers-Huilman, 2003: 2).

Steps have been taken to make ME more responsible, as discussed throughout this *Handbook*. One of the major initiatives in management education which is focusing on sustainability is the UN Principles for Responsible Management Education (PRME), which aims 'to serve as a framework for gradual, systemic change in business schools and management-related institution' (PRME Secretariat, 2016). The domain of responsible management education (RME) is the perfect place for this systemic change to occur. Since ME is being asked to respond more directly to societal problems through initiatives on sustainability, ethics and corporate responsibility, there is a new imperative to ensure that gender inequality gets addressed.

This chapter explores issues around the integration of gender equality into RME, discusses how management education has addressed gender equality issues in the context of sustainability and suggests ways in which it can be improved. The chapter suggests that it is not possible to have sustainable, ethical

and responsible management education without having gender equality issues front and centre. The chapter begins with a brief overview of how gender equality has historically been addressed in management education (mostly, but not exclusively in the European/North American traditions). It reviews the evolution of gender issues as management education institutions began in significant numbers to discuss sustainability and responsible management education, including the ways in which organizations such as PRME began to make links between sustainability and gender equality. It concludes with suggestions on how those committed to RME can move toward a more gender-aware approach in their teaching on sustainability. Before looking at gender equality in management education in the context of sustainability, a brief overview of the concepts of sustainability, gender equality and RME will be provided in the next section.

KEY CONCEPTS

Why should gender equality be an essential component of RME? As Forray and Leigh ask, 'Who defines what is responsible among competing societal, organizational, and ecological values?' (2012: 295). While this is a topic outside the scope of this chapter, it is important to note that most current concepts of sustainability in the context of the United Nations and corporate responsibility initiatives such as the UN Global Compact do include gender equality in some form. It thus follows that if management education is striving to respond to these calls for action, such as action on the SDGs or PRME, by definition through this commitment to sustainability they are also committing to working toward gender equality. This chapter assumes the argument does not have to be made here as to why gender equality is important but it will discuss briefly below how gender equality is front and centre in current concepts of sustainability, including in the 2015 SDGs, which have had the effect of mobilizing universities, businesses and other organizations. Suffice it to say that it is not possible to have sustainable, ethical and responsible management education without foregrounding gender equality issues. This was articulated, for example, in the Outcome Declaration of the PRME 2017 Global Forum:

> Our vision and outlook for 2030 … is a world where extreme poverty is eradicated, all human beings are able to fulfil their potential in dignity and equality, the human rights of all are realized, gender equality is achieved … (PRME 2017 Global Forum, 2019).

Gender Equality

What does gender equality, mentioned in the SDGs and promoted by PRME, mean? Gender is an analytical category that is socially constructed – it also becomes 'the basis for relations of inequality between men and women' (Peterson and Runyan, 2010: 90). Although there are substantial differences across cultures, gender as a political system creates hierarchy and differential treatment in all societies throughout the world (UNRISD, 2005). In the context of what is now understood as sustainability, the 1970s concept of Women in Development (WID) was challenged for not drawing enough attention to how gender relations actually subordinated women (Pearson, 1998). The Gender Analysis in Development (GAD) approach was then adopted, which emphasized the importance of putting gender analysis at the heart of all development policies (Pearson, 1998). Gender plays a significant, if not central, role in structuring and reinforcing inequality (Peterson and Runyan, 2010). Given its historical uniqueness and pervasiveness, gender inequality should not 'be subsumed within a generic concept of inequality' (Walby, 2005: 372).

It is important to note that while the category of 'women' is not homogeneous, with multiple and concurrent levels of oppression that some women face, including racism, homophobia and indigeneity (Acker, 2006), women as a group suffer from gender-based inequality 'resulting in women's enduring and disproportionate economic, social and cultural disadvantage' (Otto, 2002: 5). In addition, gender is not a synonym for women. Attention must be paid to the ways in which men are affected by gender inequality, and the ways in which some benefit from the current system (Simpson, 2017). Recognition of the structural reasons for gender inequality is essential to understanding the concept of sustainability and to understand why women suffer such pervasive inequality. The world is gendered and this gendering has created different situations and life chances for women and for men. A gender-aware approach draws attention to such concepts as power, exclusion and marginalization (Ackerly, 2008: 28), as well as the concept of 'gender knowledge':

> … every form of knowledge is based upon a specific knowledge of gender. Accordingly, 'gender knowledge' pre-structures how problems are perceived and defined as well as the policy responses that result (Stone, 2010: 36).

Thus the use of a gender lens allows for a more thorough understanding of any phenomenon, including globalization and sustainability and an awareness of the concept of gender knowledge helps to draw attention to the ways in which gender equality and sustainability are understood in RME.

Sustainability's Many Meanings

There has been an evolution in ME in terms of the respective foci of corporate social responsibility (CSR), business ethics and sustainability (Christensen et al., 2007). Wu et al. noted in their 2010 study that their sample of US-based business schools tended to focus more on ethics and less on sustainability as understood in a broader sense (Wu et al., 2010). While business ethics and CSR in ME do explore issues outside of sustainability, there has been a turn toward sustainability as the goal of these other issues. This parallels what has gone on in discussions around CSR and business ethics in the business world. Given the emphasis on sustainability in many RME approaches, this chapter uses the concept of sustainability rather than CSR and business ethics.

For sustainability to have meaning in the context of RME and policy-making within the business community, it is necessary to acknowledge the complexity of the concept (Berger et al., 2017). One of the problems with the concepts of sustainability and sustainable development is the many meanings attributed to them. The Brundtland Report of 1987 popularized the term 'sustainable development', which embraced equality and environmental issues (Bennett, 2018). However, since Brundtland, there are so many different ways that sustainability has been used that some argue that this compromises the term's utility (Vallance et al., 2011). For example, the UN Global Compact (UNGC) website refers to 'corporate sustainability', 'market sustainability', 'sustainable business', 'sustainable development', 'sustainable markets' and the 'sustainability principles', among other terms (UN Global Compact, 2019). Corporate sustainability, used often by the UNGC among others, has multiple definitions (as discussed for example in Baumgartner and Ebner, 2010); one study showed companies had report titles such as 'Global Citizenship Report', 'Corporate Responsibility Report', 'Environmental Sustainability Report', 'Sustainability Report' and 'Environmental and Social Responsibility Report' to refer to their annual document summarizing their social and environmental initiatives'(Montiel, 2008). This lack of clarity opens up the possibility for various interpretations of what it means to be sustainable, with implications for RME.

Gender and Sustainability

Notwithstanding the Brundtland intention that sustainability be interpreted broadly,

there is evidence that for many actors the term refers to environmental issues rather than the broad range of issues which are captured by the SDGs (Schouten and Miklian, 2018; Tauszig and Toppinen, 2017). For example, prior to the Rana Plaza factory collapse, Canadian company Joe Fresh and its parent company promoted an almost exclusively environmentally focused notion of sustainability. The highly gendered aspects of the conditions leading up to the deaths of over 1000 people, mostly women and girls, were ignored in the company's CSR reports. This was not unusual, as '[g]ender issues are usually marginalized in most sustainability-oriented scenarios' (Littig, 2018: 573). Fukuda-Parr articulates why sustainability needs a broad interpretation:

> Unpaid labor and ... the vast amounts of time and effort spent raising the next generation ... are a fundamental aspect of sustainability, with important macroeconomic dimensions. If nonmarket caring labor did not take place, the economy would eventually grind to a halt; as an essential factor of production, the labor force would be compromised (Fukuda-Parr et al., 2013: 25).

The launch of the SDGs in 2015 have contributed somewhat to ensuring that gender equality is an essential element of sustainability, which should make it more difficult for actors to focus exclusively on environmental issues as part of their sustainability commitments, while neglecting others.

The SDGs

The SDGs, which are viewed as an expression of the international communities' interests on sustainability, make it clear that gender equality is an important and key aspect of the achievement of the goals as it is both a standalone goal (SDG 5) and a cross-cutting goal:

> ...With its emphasis on equity and on 'leaving no one behind', the SDG agenda also amplifies the importance of gender equality as an essential component for the achievement of every goal (Equal Measures 2030, 2019b).

Many global institutions such as the World Bank, the IMF, the World Economic Forum, the UNGC and PRME have turned their sustainability and SDG attention to gender equality and the empowerment of women and girls (Prügl and True, 2014). For example, the World Bank states that '[a]chieving gender equality … is central to the World Bank's goals of ending extreme poverty and boosting shared prosperity in a sustainable manner' (World Bank, 2019). The OECD also views gender equality from this instrumental perspective: 'Better use of the world's female population could increase economic growth, reduce poverty, enhance societal well-being, and help ensure sustainable development in all countries' (OECD, 2008).

These examples suggest that in order to understand the challenges of addressing gender equality through the paradigm of sustainability in RME, especially with such a focus on the SDGs as the current representation of sustainability, it is necessary to understand that the SDGs are firmly embedded in a more neoliberal paradigm (Fukuda-Parr, 2016; Weber, 2017). For example, SDG 17 ('Promote a universal, rules-based, open, non-discriminatory and equitable multilateral trading system under the World Trade Organization, including through the conclusion of negotiations under the Doha Development Agenda') embeds the global governance status quo in the SDGs. The significance of this for RME will be addressed later in the chapter. Having briefly explored the concepts of gender equality and sustainability, the next section will discuss how gender has been addressed in ME in the past.

Notwithstanding the recognition that gender equality is central to the achievement of the SDGs, there are concerns about the lack of specificity in the numerous indicators and measurement schemes (Equal Measures 2030, 2019b). The danger, bearing out in reality, is that it becomes difficult for initiatives in the support of the SDGs, including by RME actors, to focus on all 169 targets, and the result is that they pick and choose which

goals and targets to focus on. This has important implications for a wide range of issues, including gender equality, as respect for the goals and the rights that they imply becomes even more discretionary – a pick and choose approach can be adopted, with the potential for difficult goals like gender equality to be ignored in favour of goals which are more friendly to the market-based orientation of most ME institutions. The interpretation of sustainability and gender equality has led to a wide range of actions under the guise of addressing these issues.

Given its importance to society, the economy and business, gender equality should have been a focus of management education courses and programmes for decades, even before links were made with the sustainability issues that RME is now increasingly embracing. However, it has often remained on the margins in business schools or was viewed as an optional topic of study for management students and faculty, even despite initiatives to pay more attention to these issues throughout the business school environment: '[i]ssues of gender are often invisible in business schools … business school curricula continue to be designed almost exclusively around a male-dominated ethos' (Flynn et al., 2015: 26). The next section looks at how gender equality was addressed in ME in the past.

PAST APPROACHES TO GENDER IN MANAGEMENT EDUCATION

Limited Perspectives

Since the 1970s, attention has been paid to issues relating to gender in business schools but with a limited focus on four major areas: faculty and administration demographics and practices, the climate (the environment in which people study and work), students, including their attitudes and demographic profiles and programmes, such as the curriculum, sex-role stereotyping and the content of case studies (Kilgour, 2017). The demographic perspective centres around the paradigm of equal opportunity and can ignore the fundamental issues of gender inequality in management education, organizations and in society as a whole, especially in the context of sustainability. The issue of gender bias in the curriculum is perhaps most pertinent to the issue of RME. Concern about sex-role stereotyping go back decades (Foster, 1994). Even though 'the business school is under-researched in the literature of gender and higher education in relation to studies of other academic disciplines' (Reilly et al., 2016: 1027), there is academic literature discussing gender inequality in management education going back to the entry of women into business schools and one 1995 article entitled 'Sexism in the seminar strategies for gender sensitivity in management education' argued that gender is important to all students, not just female students (Thompson and Mcgivern, 1995). Outside of the ME literature, discussions about gender were limited. A content analysis of the gender issues in the *Academy of Management Journal (AMJ)* characterized the decades as: the 70s – 'acknowledging the plight of women'; the 80s – 'identifying and understanding the barriers'; the 90s – 'identifying (even more) barriers'; the 2000s – 'from sex differences to dissimilarity and diversity' (Joshi et al., 2015: 1461–1462). Gender was seen as something apart from other issues, and the research demonstrates the limited paradigms that were accepted for publication.

Gender in CSR Research

Many business disciplines have neglected gender issues. However, even those which have social change, human rights and corporate responsibility underpinning them have been slow to become gender aware. In the academic field of CSR within ME, gender and gender equality were not seen as significant, illustrating the challenge of getting RME

work on sustainability to take gender into consideration. Gender issues have not been prevalent in the field of CSR since its inception in the 1980s and 1990s (Coleman, 2002). A review of selected business ethics journals from 2006 revealed that there was rarely, if ever, gender content (Thompson, 2008). Grosser and Moon (2005) found that gender was not mainstreamed into CSR initiatives in the UK. In 2007, Pearson called for a 'gendering' of the discussions in the area of CSR and argued that it is essential the role that women play in reproducing the labour force be seen 'as a legitimate aspect of CSR concern' (2007: 745). The same year, an article on the UNGC was published which argued that gender equality was neglected by the initiative; when gender was mentioned, it was almost exclusively discussed in reference to the 'equal opportunity' paradigm and Principle Six (non-discrimination), despite its very strong mandate to address gender equality across the range of principles on human rights, labour rights, the environment and anti-corruption (Kilgour, 2007). Thompson concluded that '[g]ender equity does not appear to be a high priority in any CSR agenda, although it has been defined as a human and economic development priority by the United Nations' (Thompson, 2007: 88).

Despite these calls for CSR research and practice to be gender-aware, some significant publications on CSR illustrate how gender was neglected. The 2008 *Oxford Handbook of CSR*, a 570-page volume, contained no specific section referring to gender equality or women, despite the assertion that the 'volume contains findings from numerous experts … who have summarized the body of CSR literature and also outlined an agenda for additional research' (Crane et al., 2008). Gender was also missing from another ambitious 2008 compendium of research on corporate citizenship and CSR – the 640-page *Handbook of Research on Global Corporate Citizenship* (Scherer and Palazzo, 2008). Gender is to some extent still ignored in CSR research within management education, and published works on gender and CSR get fewer citations and lower profile than mainstream CSR publications (Spence, 2017). Even with the increase in attention to gender and women within CSR and business ethics research, much of this is 'mainly disengaged from feminist theory, feminist ethics apart' (Grosser and Moon, 2019: 321). Given what has happened in the past in ME, even in disciplines that deal with sustainability (CSR), it is not surprising that sustainability education still struggles to become gender-aware, despite it being so necessary.

CURRENT APPROACHES

It has been a challenge to get gender equality and sustainability issues integrated into ME; by definition they require a challenge to the status quo (as discussed in Perriton, 2007). One of the most persistent problems is that there is a tendency to view gender equality issues as limited to women working in the formal sector, most usually as white-collar or pink-collar workers in developed economies. This tendency is observed through the promotion of such themes as diversity, women on corporate boards and unconscious bias. In addition, attention to gender equality in ME is justified by the business case – the notion that gender equality is good for business and that is why it must be discussed. The UNGC, for example, despite having been critiqued for its earlier limited view of gender equality (Kilgour, 2007), indicated on their website in 2019 that SDG 5 (on gender equality) is linked to UN Global Compact Principles on human rights and non-discrimination (Principles 1, 2 and 6), implying that the other principles – labour rights, the environment and corruption – do not have anything to do with gender equality (Gender Equality | UN Global Compact, 2019). This continues to reinforce a very narrow, siloed approach to gender equality in sustainability practice; a limited understanding of what gender inequality is leads to a limited range of

remedies, both in management practice and in management education. This section will look briefly at these issues in order to draw attention to how they are used, and then proceed by discussing more systematic ways in which gender equality is viewed in RME.

Diversity

Diversity in management education has often been twinned with gender equality, resulting in a blurring of concepts and goals. The term diversity appears to have made its entrance into management studies in 1987 as a result of US workforce predictions for the year 2000 (Kapoor, 2011). Within the Academy of Management, 'gender' and diversity' have been merged into a community of 'Gender and Diversity in Organizations' (Ashcraft, 2009). It can often appear that a business school is addressing gender equality through the offering of diversity management courses or programmes, which usually are optional courses and are sometimes the only area where gender as an analytical category is discussed. Graduates of ME, who move to management positions in organizations, often have had little or no exposure to gender inequality. For example, in a comparative study of ME in India and the United States, the authors found that gender is often neglected in diversity issues, as 'gender is typically subsumed under the term diversity' (Moore et al., 2017: 273).

Some authors suggest that a focus on diversity tends to obscure the root causes of discrimination and disadvantage, such as inequality arising out of the current economic global structures (Michaels, 2008). One management educator wrote about her experience teaching gender issues in an MBA programme in the 1990s in a course option called 'gender and management'. This was converted to 'diversity and management'

...with some reservations...whilst 'diversity' is more inclusive in terms of potential differences and power dynamics considered, it can represent a muting of appreciations of power, political, economic and group level issues ... Diversity has also been adopted in some cases as a more business-friendly formulation, which might defuse valuable debate about fundamental assumptions and current practices (Marshall, 1999: 262).

Diversity management is important and should be included in RME (Symons and Ibarra, 2014). However, in the context of RME for sustainability, a singular focus on diversity management can draw attention away from gender inequalities and the disadvantage faced by women as a group in all societies.

Women on Boards

Another theme arising out of the diversity paradigm is that of women on corporate boards. When companies, industry associations, CSR initiatives and management education institutions are asked to report on gender equality in the context of sustainability or CSR, one often finds reference to this issue. While the lack of women's representation on corporate boards is worthy of attention and intervention, action in this area is not a substitute for significant attention to other forms of gender inequality. As Cook and Glass suggest in their mostly US-based research, 'most women who hold corporate leadership roles tend to be highly elite, white women' (Cook and Glass, 2018: 916). Gill et al. observe that '[in] the UK, the neoliberal feminist topic de jour – "women on boards" – has reached saturation point in the media, with the *London Evening Standard* championing the cause on its pages almost every day, whilst other feminist issues remain stubbornly ignored' (Gill et al., 2017: 226).

Unconscious Bias

Unconscious bias is a current preoccupation in management and academic settings and tends to get more attention than other concepts such as inequality and discrimination. In reference to the trend of offering unconscious bias training

(UBT) in the context of racism, one critic identifies the potential danger of focusing on unconscious bias to the detriment of discussions on discrimination and inequality:

> One danger is that UBT is adopted as a quick-fix ... it has the traits of a fad ... it is yet another distraction from the embedded, structural disadvantages within organisations; disadvantages that require far more radical solutions than introspective sessions that simply nudge managers and employees, often begrudgingly, into recognising that they are biased (Noon, 2018: 206).

While being aware of unconscious bias could be useful for understanding and taking action on gender inequality, it does not negate the need for external actions – either by organizations or individuals (Madsen and Andrade, 2018).

Women's and Girls' Empowerment

Another trend within CSR and RME which often appears as a proxy for gender equality, is the empowerment of women and girls. While this is an important goal in its own right, the concept of empowerment should be interrogated and should not act as a substitute for other issues in the area of gender inequality. Despite its recent appearance in the world of CSR, empowerment as a concept has been around for decades, and is prevalent in a wide range of areas. Cattaneo et al. observe that it is an overused concept that has 'lost its power' (their search on Google revealed 11 million hits and Google Scholar identified almost 900,000 articles and books), but argue that it still has potential as an 'orienting concept' (Cattaneo et al., 2014).

A prominent example of private sector engagement in women's empowerment is the UN Women's Empowerment Principles (WEPs). The assumption behind this initiative is that businesses can and should take steps to empower women in their 'workforces, marketplaces and communities' (EmpowerWomen, 2019). While the reach of the WEPs is broad, the focus is on economic empowerment and the promise that businesses stand to gain from promoting women's empowerment (referred to as 'the business case'). The theme of the initiative, 'Equality Means Business', draws attention to this promise. The framing of the WEPS in terms of the business case highlights one of the key debates in CSR generally and in gender and CSR specifically: gender equality is a 'business opportunity' (Bexell, 2012: 398). Women's empowerment is seen as instrumental to increasing value to the firm and its shareholders, and 'girls and women [are viewed] as untapped resources for economic growth and the resulting policy outcomes' which are closely tied to the advancement of a neoliberal economic policy agenda characterized by market fundamentalism, deregulation and corporate-led development (Calkin, 2016: 159). This is a problematic motivation for addressing gender inequality as there may not always be a business case for addressing women's inequality (Kilgour, 2007).

Business practices on sustainability and much of ME are anchored in a growth and neoliberal paradigm; this influences how gender is viewed in ME. As Gill, Kelan and Scharf summarize so well:

> [t]he contemporary analyst of gender, work and organizations is faced by a bewildering array of contradictions. Feminist 'manifestoes' and self-help books top the bestsellers list, enjoining (middle and upper class) women to 'lean in' (Sandberg 2013) or close 'the confidence gap' (Kay and Shipman 2014) yet official figures show the stubborn persistence of inequalities and how very far we are from 'getting to 50–50' (as another popular title would have it) … Hashtag feminism or 'clicktivism' marshal enormous energy and promise to change the world, yet empirical studies highlight the difficulty of even speaking about gender in many workplaces – the animosity, fatigue or simply blank incomprehension that makes inequality unspeakable or even unintelligible (Gill et al., 2017: 226).

Gender 'Blindness'

For those committed to sustainability in the context of RME, it is important to continually interrogate their own teaching in the area of gender equality and be on the lookout for 'gender blindness – appearing to be gender-neutral while actually ignoring the reality of gender, not mentioning gender inequality or failing to use a gender-aware lens on a particular issue (Grandy and Ingols, 2016). If gender is not being mentioned or considered in discussions on sustainability, it is possible that many of the structural and theoretical elements of a particular issue are being neglected.

Gender Missing from Teaching Materials

Many of the resources available to educators who are interested in RME and sustainability do not directly address the issue of gender inequality. Online compilations of resources and academic articles (for example, AOM, 2019; Center for Responsible Management Education, 2019) which in many ways are very useful and comprehensive in the area of sustainability and RME, do not often include material on gender inequality. Educators interested in ensuring that they teach sustainability in a comprehensive manner are often not directed to issues of gender equality via these materials, despite the best of intentions.

The case study method is an important pedagogical tool in RME. Grandy and Ingols ask 'Where are the women in teaching cases?' (Grandy and Ingols, 2016: 108). Their review reveals that the number of published cases with female protagonists is still very low (Grandy and Ingols, 2016). Despite the importance of having women featured in case studies in order to refute stereotypes, in a 2014 study only 9% of the HBS award-winning cases featured a woman as a protagonist (Symons and Ibarra, 2014). Even when women are mentioned, it is usually in reference to what is viewed as traditionally female roles or industries (Symons and Ibarra, 2014).

Notwithstanding that Harvard Business School (HBS) started admitting women to its MBA programme in 1962, it only had its first women tenured as faculty in 1980, and it is still trying to get gender equality right. Following very public criticism on their lack of progress on gender equality (as discussed in Kilgour, 2017), HBS launched The Gender Initiative to 'promote gender equity in business and society' and in 2019 hosted a symposium as part of The Gender Initiative. The theme of the event, 'The Courage of our Convictions' was 'inspired by the way resistance movements such as #MeToo and #BlackLivesMatter have prompted a widespread examination of power relationships in new, or newly urgent, ways … [our aim is to] more effectively engage the project of advancing structural equality in the workplace and beyond' (Harvard Business School, 2019).

While this does not explicitly focus on sustainability, drawing attention to the promotion of gender equality in society and discussing the concept of power are important steps in moving outside of the 'equal opportunity' paradigm of women's equality.

Gender Inequality Is Solved?

Perhaps one of the reasons why gender equality gets such little attention in ME is that there is a view that gender equality has been attained. This is described by some as a postfeminist view (Gill et al., 2017; Kelan, 2018; Rumens, 2018). Rumens, for example, discusses how some of the students in a business school environment believe that gender inequality was a problem of the past and does not concern them (Rumens, 2018). There may also be a gender element in terms of viewing certain sustainability issues as important. According to a recent report, examining 'how business students and people around the world prioritize the SDGs, and how they believe the goals might be achieved',

> [t]here was a significant divide along gender and regional lines when assessing the importance of gender equality [within the SDGS]. Over 31% of female respondents ranked gender equality as an SDG of immediate concern, compared to approximately 15% of male respondents (Cort and Frank, 2019: 10).

Another survey found that female students reported different attitudes toward CSR than male counterparts:

> Based on nearly 1300 responses to a survey, conducted with [PRME], we show that overall, female students placed a higher value on ethical responsibilities than male students. Female students were also more welcoming than male students regarding curriculum changes that were focused on CSR-related studies (or RME) (Haski-Leventhal et al., 2017: 219).

Lack of Attention to Rights

One of the barriers to ensuring that gender equality is a part of sustainability education in RME is the definition and understanding of sustainability in both the education and business contexts. This disconnect between sustainability and human rights, with consequences for gender equality (McPhail, 2013). Increasingly there are calls for ME to integrate human rights issues into sustainability discussions (McPhail, 2013): '[b]usiness leaders of the future need to be taught how to integrate human rights into business decision making and recognize that prudent strategic decision making incorporates economic, environmental, and social sustainability elements' (Palthe, 2013: 123). Winkler and Williams note that 'there was considerable disappointment that the SDGs had not reflected the advice provided by global leaders and grassroots activists to keep human rights central to the new development era' (Winkler and Williams, 2017: 1023). This has important implications for gender equality, among other goals (Bexell and Jönsson, 2017).

POLICY ATTEMPTS TO ADDRESS GENDER INEQUALITY

PRME

Among the initiatives that have emerged to support and promote RME, PRME, launched in 2007 as a complement to the UNGC, is perhaps the best known internationally (Haertle et al., 2017). In 2019 over 800 management education institutions have joined PRME, which indirectly commits them to address gender inequality, among other issues. On the face of it, the PRME Six Principles appear to be gender-neutral. However, each of the Six Principles cannot be respected without attention to gender equality, whether it is through the references to sustainability which inherently include gender equality, or through the reference to the UNGC (Kilgour, 2007).

PRME has been seen to be important in stimulating dialogue and action in ME (Cooper et al., 2014). However, there are criticisms that the PRME potential for transformation has been limited, with the observation that there is

disconnect between knowledge and practice … knowledge of principles [such as those of PRME] is inadequate unless we understand our own role in maintaining irresponsible practice and our ability to act differently in order to change the situation (Hibbert and Cunliffe, 2015: 179).

On gender issues specifically, there are concerns that PRME's ability to influence ME is limited; some authors call for:

inquiry into the PRME's capacity to radically impact trajectories of university governance, to attend to the employment conditions of their female scholars, and through support of the career aspirations of these scholars, provide leadership that enhances not only the vitality of women scholars in universities, but to manifest human organisations serving the vitality of all people and our life-sustaining planet (Asirvatham and Humphries-Kil, 2017: 126).

This lack of influence and impact may be due to the dominant way of thinking that fits into a more neoliberal approach to sustainability and to gender equality, which 'may serve not to disrupt universities as enabling institutions of neo-liberal market-driven or neo-nationalist globalisation, but to provide system preserving adaptations' (Asirvatham and Humphries-Kil, 2017: 126).

Communicating and Measuring Progress

It is difficult to measure progress on gender equality in relation to sustainability in management education. However, scholars have drawn conclusions based on what institutions self-report, which provides insight into their preoccupations. Even though it has been argued that 'gender equality related topics are a source of positive impact and legitimacy for top business schools' (Miotto et al., 2019: 1), ME institutions do not appear to prioritize reporting on gender equality (Haynes and Murray, 2015). The 2017 report to PRME from Copenhagen Business School, considered a leader in sustainability, contains few references to gender equality. Where gender is mentioned, it is most often in relation to hiring and bias. The list of goals in support of the SDGs does not include gender equality (Copenhagen Business School, 2020).

PRME Gender Equality Working Group

Notwithstanding concerns about the effectiveness of PRME, it has been the impetus for some important initiatives on gender equality. In 2010 the UNGC and UN Women launched the Women's Empowerment Principles (WEPs) to encourage signatories and the corporate community to pay more attention to gender equality. Less than a year later, in 2011, the PRME Gender Equality Working Group (GEWG) was bringing together scholars from around the globe to get ME attention focused on gender (PRME Working Groups, 2019). Given the critiques of RME being engaged in a restrictive paradigm on gender and on other issues, the GEWG has tried to go beyond the paradigms of equal opportunity and diversity management (both at the administrative and curricular levels) to a more thorough integration of gender equality into management education, with a strong focus on sustainability (such as

Flynn et al., 2015; Flynn et al., 2016). The GEWG has been successful in encouraging a broad interpretation of gender equality within sustainability and in forging partnerships with the other PRME Working Groups.

PRME Anti-Poverty Toolkit

Another PRME inspired RME initiative that pays attention to gender equality is the Anti-Poverty Toolkit, prepared by students at Radford University under the guidance of faculty members involved in the Anti-Poverty Working Group. Gender equality is one of the main areas of this RME toolkit, and it contains resources on the SDGs, hunger, climate change, and gender-based violence, among other issues (PRME Anti-Poverty Toolkit, 2019).

Accreditation

Accreditation bodies such as the AACSB and EQUIS have taken some steps to integrate concerns about sustainability in their work, providing an impetus for business schools to make commitments to address this (Doherty et al., 2015). Some of the more prominent accreditation bodies were even involved in the establishment of PRME and became involved in its governance when PRME was launched (Haertle et al., 2017). Given PRME's mandate in support of the UNGC and other UN principles, and given their power and influence on ME, one would expect that these accreditation bodies would lead PRME and the RME community toward addressing gender equality issues in the context of CSR and sustainability. There has been some movement linking diversity to sustainability in business school accreditation bodies. However, the direct link between gender equality and sustainability, and business schools for that matter, is not very strong. The AACSB has encouraged business schools to address diversity since the early 1990s, but there have been no mandatory elements required (Bell et al., 2009). The

AACSB revised standard mentions diversity approximately 40 times but gender only a few times in relation to a type of diversity (AACSB, 2019). The EQUIS accreditation criteria require that business schools demonstrate how they are integrating 'ethics, responsibility and sustainability' into their operations and practices (EQUIS, 2019). Gender is only mentioned four times in their Global Standards, and this in relation to statistics about students and faculty members.

There is no shortage of studies and recommendations about the problems of gender inequality in business schools in management education and what it will take to address these problems (Kilgour, 2017). In 2011, McTiernan and Flynn called for no less than a structural change. A systemic approach to dealing with systemic problems is required. The tools are available, the mandates are clear, and the knowledge and research exists. What is missing is awareness, the will and the execution of systemic change, which must include a challenge to the status quo.

THE WAY FORWARD

This section suggests some ways to increase the attention paid to gender equality in the context of sustainability-focused RME. That will be followed by some concluding comments.

Adopt the SDG Approach on Gender Equality

Although the SDGs have been critiqued on numerous grounds, they are a useful starting point for RME because they represent an international consensus on the concept of sustainability. RME should explicitly adopt the SDG approach to gender equality, which would be to make gender equality both a stand-alone goal and a cross-cutting goal, which would mean that every aspect of sustainability in RME would consider gender as an important variable.

Measure Progress

Measuring gaps and progress is important. Whether it is through the reporting progress for PRME or accreditation applications and reports, it is crucial that progress on gender equality in the context of RME and sustainability be measured and reported on (Haynes and Murray, 2015). RME could ensure that data that is used in teaching on sustainability is disaggregated by gender/sex and other social variables to ensure that a complete picture is obtained for decision-making. Some organizations have tried to develop gender-sensitive reporting. Even though gender equality is a stand-alone and a cross-cutting goal in the SDGs, measurement of progress on the SDGs and targets is often not broken down by gender/sex (Equal Measures 2030, 2019b). This lack of gender-specific data can translate into policy decisions that are not gender-sensitive in a context where gender may be (and often is) an important variable. Collecting gender disaggregated data, measuring and reporting are necessary prerequisites of systemic change (Walby, 2005).

Acknowledge Inequality Regimes and Organizational Change

The concept of inequality regimes is useful in understanding why, despite proclamations and signatures to incorporate gender equality into sustainability work, it is often neglected:

> All organizations have inequality regimes, defined as loosely interrelated practices, processes, actions, and meanings that result in and maintain class, gender, and racial inequalities within particular organizations (Acker, 2006: 443).

In addition, these regimes are perpetuated through numerous types of controls: direct, indirect and internalized (Acker, 2006). In the context of gender equality in ME, this means at a minimum that attention must be paid to the composition of the student body, the environment (the 'chilly climate', Dixon, 2013), the gender composition of the faculty

and leadership, as well as teaching materials, etc. that are used in the education process.

As discussed earlier in this chapter, ME in general has struggled to improve key areas of gender inequality, such as the underrepresentation of female faculty, pay inequities, the chilly climate and differential treatment of male and female students, among other issues. Even though the goal of RME is to ensure a focus on gender equality in the context of sustainability, the institutional and organizational environment is seen as an important starting point. In this vein, Cooper et al. argue that more effort at the institutional level is needed in RME:

> Alongside the six UN PRME principles is the expectation that the signatories should 'understand that our own organisational practices should serve as example of the values and attitudes we convey to our students'. We see this understanding as a critical aspect of the UN backed PRME and is essential if a Business School is to genuinely become more socially accountable and better engaged with the issues of ethics, social responsibility and sustainability (Cooper et al., 2014: 254).

Reflexivity Matters

Critical management education offers some avenues for going beyond the current business school paradigms to have a critical and more reflexive perspective (Simpson, 2006). A key problem has been identified in ME: the persistence of 'dominant masculine practices within what ought to be an inclusive and diverse academic community' (Hibbert and Cunliffe, 2015: 182). Reflexivity, both by the educator and the students, offers potential for confronting hesitancy to acknowledge and tackle gender inequality in RME, as it 'is a means of interrogating our taken-for-granted experience by questioning our relationship with our social world and the ways in which we account for our experience' (Hibbert and Cunliffe, 2015: 179–180). Hibbert and Cunliffe call for a more reflexive approach whereby students, in addition to studying ethical and sustainable practices, are encouraged to develop an 'engaged understanding of the responsibility of managers and leaders to actively challenge irresponsible practices' (Hibbert and Cunliffe, 2015: 176). The potential for impact in the area of gender equality is high.

The Personal Is Still Political

One 1969 call for reflexivity on gender issues, 'The Personal Is Political', considered the original feminist theory paper, has relevance today; it is a reminder of how little some things have changed and at the same time it can be a call that RME explicitly includes action on gender equality (Hanisch, 2006). The author looked back on its meaning in 2006:

> [Education activists] could sometimes admit that women were oppressed (but only by 'the system') and said that we should have equal pay for equal work, and some other 'rights.' But they belittled us no end for trying to bring our so-called 'personal problems' into the public arena [such as] [o]ur demands that men share the housework and child-care ... if women would just 'stand up for them-selves' and take more responsibility for their own lives, they wouldn't need to have an independent movement for women's liberation ... Heaven forbid that we should point out that men benefit from oppressing women (Hanisch, 2006).

This summary refers to many of the impor-tant issues arising out of the sustainability debates including those promoted by the United Nations and the SDGS. It also high-lights the limited approaches prevalent in RME when discussing gender equality in the context of sustainability – the limited focus on equal pay and women on corporate boards, the continued separation of the private and the public spheres, the promotion of a more individualistic view of women's economic empowerment, the lack of discussion of reproduction and the links to the labour force, and perhaps most importantly, a lack of discussion on how the current global gov-ernance regimes and economic systems that we teach about in business schools play an important role in creating and perpetuating gender inequality.

Power Matters

While management education has begun to discuss the concept of girls' and women's empowerment and girls' empowerment in the context of business activities, it has neglected to actually pay much attention to the concept of power itself, which is critical to understand the current system in which business operates and how to make this system (or a different one) more sustainable. Even when looking at diversity initiatives within organizations, the concept of power is often neglected (Zanoni et al., 2010).

Challenge the Dominant Paradigm

One of the problems with integrating gender into RME is that that ME tends to occur within a specific paradigm (Fleming and Banerjee, 2016). In an editorial 'Questions business schools don't ask', the authors iden-tify one of the problems of business school education: 'by propagating ideologically inspired amoral theories ... business schools have removed any sense of moral responsi-bility from their students' (Mabey et al., 2015: 535). Asking the right questions can improve how gender equality is addressed in management education. Grey argued that 'management needs always to be taught in ways that explicitly acknowledge the politi-cal, ethical, and philosophical nature of its practice' (Grey, 2004: 180). Calkin and others emphasize the importance of 'asking questions about how certain problems are framed, which issues are ignored, and how particular representations grant authority to an actor or policy direction' (Calkin, 2016: 160). An important way forward is to 'equip ... students with a plurality of theories, sup-plementing neoclassical economics with other economic perspectives (e.g., Post-Keynesian, Marxist, ecological, evolutionary and feminist economics) and views from other disciplines (e.g., sociology, psychology and political science)' (Moosmayer et al., 2019: 913).

Consider the Public and the Private

RME must consider globalization, the market and neoliberal paradigm, and the public and private debate. Globalization, underpinned by neoliberalism, is characterized by a focus on the market as the central means by which to address development problems and to achieve prosperity (Elson, 2002). Women have different relationships with the market than men. For example, 'a large proportion of the (female) population engages in unpaid production, only indirectly linked to the market' (Beneria, 1999: 69). In 2004, it was calculated that

> if unpaid activities were valued at prevailing wages, they would amount to $16 trillion or about 70 per cent of total world output ($23 trillion). Of this $16 trillion, $11 trillion, or almost 69 per cent, represent women's work (Beneria and Bisnath, 2004: 74–75).

Despite the importance of women's informal work, academic disciplines often neglect to account for it (Peterson, 2003).

The fact that women in developing economies often have a different relationship to the market than men underlines the importance of looking at the concepts of the public and private sphere. An important factor explaining women's inequality is the fact that women around the world shoulder most of the responsibility for care, especially for those who are very dependent. Making links between the private and public spheres in the context of sustainability automatically will help to incorporate a gender equality perspective.

Avoid the 'Flavour of the Month'

It is critical that RME avoids falling into the trap of viewing gender equality in the context of sustainability in limited terms, a phenomenon that Oloka-Onyango and Tamale referred to as the 'flavour of the month' in relation to women's human rights in the context of Africa: 'none of this will alter the fundamental basis on which gender domination and patriarchy is constructed, unless it attacks the broader framework in which such domination is embedded' (Oloka-Onyango and Tamale, 1995: 730).

Promote Interdisciplinarity

Management education has often been criticized for being ahistorical and for favouring an inter-disciplinary approach. One of the ways to increase attention and action on gender equality and other human rights and social justice issues in management education is to adopt a more interdisciplinary approach. This can promote useful areas of interaction on sharing knowledge and conceptual frameworks critical to understanding the global world order and what is required to move toward a more sustainable future for all.

Promote Human Rights and Social Justice

Despite numerous legitimate critiques of the SDGs and the lack of attention to rights (and the impact that may have on business and human rights voluntary activities), ongoing discussions about human rights and social justice suggest that a multi-pronged approach is still needed in order to fully promote sustainability and gender equality in RME. The SDGs, based on a relatively broad notion of sustainability, help draw attention to the needs facing the global community; despite their projected utility, however, there is concern that the enthusiasm for the SDGs is waning already (Winkler and Williams, 2017). Williams et al. argue that it is important to 'draw attention to the social justice aspect' of the concept of sustainability and to encourage students to question assumptions, as gender can be a difficult concept for them (Williams et al., 2017). A social justice approach would mandate action on gender equality (including having women on corporate boards but much more) because it is the right thing to do from an equality and rights perspective (McCann and Wheeler, 2011).

Education Is About Students

The concept of ecological illiteracy has been used to identify barriers to business action toward sustainability (Cooper et al., 2014). The same could be said about gender; there is a gender equality illiteracy amongst many graduates of management education, which means that they may be ill-prepared to understand the business world's stated commitments to gender equality. How will they understand and interrogate actions of the Global Economic Forum, which set 'Gender equality and the empowerment of women' as one of seven priority areas for 2019 (World Economic Forum, 2019). Or understand why the International Finance Corporation of the World Bank, whose mission is to promote the private sector in developing economies, has developed a guide for employers on childcare (IFC, 2019). They should understand why their firm has joined the UN WEPS, or why the Gates Foundation (or Nike, Oxfam, the fair trade movement, etc.) focuses on gender. Graduates should be able to understand why companies and organizations are engaging with the SDGs, why they launch initiatives on gender equality, what the political and economic considerations are for such behaviours, why some countries decide to adopt feminist foreign policies, what women's empowerment really can do for a sustainable economy and the planet and how these all fit into the current business paradigms as well as the broader goals of sustainability.

CONCLUDING COMMENTS: RME MATTERS

One of the challenges of looking at gender and sustainability in the context of RME

either for application in educational or management settings is that sustainability as a concept is vague and undefined. As discussed earlier, many companies have switched from using the term corporate responsibility to using the term sustainability to describe their voluntary activities which have some pertinence to social and environmental arenas. Even the concept of triple bottom line reporting, which is supposed to ensure that companies pay attention to their impacts on social, economic and environmental issues, seems to fall short. This vagueness makes it difficult to be specific about how to integrate gender equality issues into RME. One way around that is to ensure that everything has a gender-aware approach, that there is a recognition of the gendered impact of decision-making and corporate activities on women, and that gender is not invisible in the classroom.

One could argue that it is not responsible management education to graduate students who are ill-prepared for the debates and discussions and challenges of the 21st century. Educators need to ask themselves what they personally are doing to integrate gender equality into RME. Even the climate emergency has a gendered element that needs to be taken into consideration. Despite women being disproportionately affected by the consequences of climate change, the gendered aspects of the climate emergency tend to be ignored (Framework Convention on Climate Change, 2019; Quan, 2019). A 2019 UN report found that

> climate change impacts on women and men often differ and are more pronounced or severe in developing countries and for some local communities and indigenous peoples. Differentiation is widely considered to be based on pervasive historical and existing inequalities and multidimensional social factors …(Framework Convention on Climate Change, 2019).

RME has a significant role to play in addressing gender inequality in society. The mandate, tools and knowledge are there. Commitments have been made. With women and girls making up the vast majority of the billions of people living in poverty with precarious futures, which are disproportionately threatened by the climate emergency, time is of the essence.

REFERENCES

AACSB (Association to Advance Collegiate Schools of Business) (2019) AACSB Business Accreditation Standards. Available at: www.aacsb.edu/accreditation/standards/business. Accessed 2 December 2019.

Acker, J. (2006) Inequality regimes: gender, class, and race in organizations. *Gender & Society,* 20(4), 441–464.

Ackerly, B. (2008) Feminist methodological reflection. In Klotz, A. and Prakash, D. (Eds.), *Qualitative Methods in International Relations: A Pluralist Guide.* New York: Palgrave Macmillan. pp. 28–42.

AOM (2019) Principles for Responsible Management Education Virtual Collection. Available at: http://aom.org/Publications/AMLE/Principles-for-Responsible-Management-Education-Virtual-Collection.aspx. Accessed 8 November 2019.

Ashcraft, K. L. (2009) Gender and diversity: other ways to make a difference. In Alvesson, M., Bridgman, T. and Willmott, H. (Eds.), *The Oxford Handbook of Critical Management Studies.* Oxford: Oxford University Press. pp. 305–327.

Asirvatham, S. and Humphries-Kil, M. (2017) Feminist reflections on life in (im)balance, career praxis, and the PRME. *International Journal of Management Education,* 15(2, Part B), 126–137.

Baumgartner, R. J. and Ebner, D. (2010) Corporate sustainability strategies: sustainability profiles and maturity levels. *Sustainable Development,* 18(2), 76–89.

Bell, M. P., Connerley, M.L. and Cocchiara, F. K. (2009) The case for mandatory diversity education. *Academy of Management Learning & Education,* 8(4), 597–609.

Beneria, L. (1999) Globalization, gender and the Davos Man. *Feminist Economics,* 5(3), 61–83.

Beneria, L. and Bisnath, S. (Eds.) (2004) *Global Tensions: Challenges and Opportunities in the World Economy.* New York: Routledge.

Bennett, E.A. (2018) Voluntary sustainability standards: a squandered opportunity to improve workers' wages. *Sustainable Development,* 26(1), 65–82.

Berger, A., Blankenbach, J., Blumenschein, F. et al. (2017) Fostering the Sustainability of Global Value Chains (GVCs). G20 Insights Policy Brief. Available at: www. g20-insights.org/policy_briefs/fostering-sustainability-global-value-chains-gvcs. Accessed 13 January 2020.

Bexell, M. (2012) Global governance, gains and gender: UN–business partnerships for women's empowerment. *International Feminist Journal of Politics,* 14(3), 389–407.

Bexell, M. and Jönsson, K. (2017) Responsibility and the United Nations' Sustainable Development Goals. *Forum for Development Studies,* 44(1), 13–29.

Calkin, S. (2016) Globalizing 'girl power': corporate social responsibility and transnational business initiatives for gender equality. *Globalizations,* 13(2), 158–172.

Cattaneo, L.B., Calton, J.M., Brodsky, A.E. et al. (2014) Status quo versus status quake: putting the power back in empowerment. *Journal of Community Psychology,* 42(4), 433–446.

Center for Responsible Management Education (2019) Responsible Management (RM) Literature Base. Available at: http://responsiblemanagement.net/responsible-management-literature-list/. Accessed 8 November 2019.

Christensen, L.J., Peirce, E., Hartman, L.P. et al. (2007) Ethics, CSR, and sustainability education in the Financial Times Top 50 global business schools: baseline data and future research directions. *Journal of Business Ethics,* 73(4), 347–368.

Coleman, G. (2002) Gender, power and post-structuralism in corporate citizenship. *Journal of Corporate Citizenship,* 1(5), 9.

Cook, A. and Glass, C. (2018) Women on corporate boards: do they advance corporate social responsibility? *Human Relations,* 71(7), 897–924.

Cooper, S., Parkes, C. and Blewitt, J. (2014) Can accreditation help a leopard change its spots? Social accountability and stakeholder engagement in business schools. *Accounting, Auditing & Accountability Journal,* 27(2), 234–258.

Copenhagen Business School (2020) CBS PRME Reports. Available at: https://www.cbs.dk/en/knowledge-society/strategic-areas/principles-responsible-management-education/resources/cbs-prme-reports. Accessed 5 March 2020.

Cort, T. and Frank, T. (2019) Rising Leaders on the Sustainable Development Goals. The Yale Center for Business and the Environment. Available at: https://cbey.yale.edu/programs/rising-leaders-on-the-sustainable-development-goals. Accessed 15 November 2019.

Crane, A., McWilliams, A., Matten, D. et al. (Eds.) (2008) *The Oxford Handbook of Corporate Social Responsibility*. New York: Oxford University Press.

Dixon, K.M. (2013) How to warm the chilly climate, woman-to-woman. *Women in Higher Education*, 22(10), 8–9. doi: 10.1002/whe.10506.

Doherty, B., Meehan, J. and Richards, A. (2015) The business case and barriers for responsible management education in business schools. *Journal of Management Development*, 34(1), 34–60.

Elson, D. (2002) Gender justice, human rights, and neo-liberal economic policies. In Molyneux, M. and Razavi, S. (Eds.), *Gender Justice, Development and Rights*. Oxford: Oxford University Press. pp. 73–114.

EmpowerWomen (2019) UN Women's Empowerment Principles. Available at: www.empowerwomen.org/en/weps/about. Accessed 2 December 2019.

Equal Measures 2030 (2019a) Equal Measures. Available at: https://data.em2030.org/2019-global-report/. Accessed 28 October 2019.

Equal Measures 2030 (2019b) Harnessing the power of data for gender equality: Introducing the 2019 EM2030 SDG Gender Index. Available at: https://data.em2030.org/wp-content/uploads/2019/05/EM2030_2019_Global_Report_ENG.pdf.

EQUIS (2019) EQUIS Global Standards. Available at: https://efmdglobal.org/wp-content/uploads/EFMD_Global-EQUIS_Standards_and_Criteria.pdf.

Fleming, P. and Banerjee, S.B. (2016) When performativity fails: implications for Critical Management Studies. *Human Relations*, 69(2), 257–276.

Flynn, P.M., Cavanagh, K.V. and Bilimoria, D. (2015) Gender equality in business schools: the elephant in the room. In Flynn, P.M., Haynes, K. and Kilgour, M.A. (Eds.), *Integrating Gender Equality into Business and Management Education: Lessons Learned and Challenges Remaining*. Sheffield: Greenleaf Publishing. pp. 26–54.

Flynn, P.M., Haynes, K. and Kilgour, M.A. (Eds.) (2015) *Integrating Gender Equality into Business and Management Education: Lessons Learned and Challenges Remaining*. Sheffield: Greenleaf Publishing.

Flynn, P.M., Haynes, K. and Kilgour, M.A. (2016) *Overcoming Challenges to Gender Equality in the Workplace: Leadership and Innovation*. Sheffield: Greenleaf Publishing.

Forray, J.M. and Leigh, J.S.A. (2012) A primer on the principles of responsible management education: intellectual roots and waves of change. *Journal of Management Education*, 36(3), 295–309.

Foster, F. (1994) Managerial sex role stereotyping among academic staff within UK business schools. *Women in Management Review*, 9(3), 17–22.

Framework Convention on Climate Change (2019) Differentiated impacts of climate change on women and men; the integration of gender considerations in climate policies, plans and actions; and progress in enhancing gender balance in national climate delegations. FCCC/SBI/2019?INF.8. Available at: https://unfccc.int/sites/default/files/resource/sbi2019_inf8.pdf. Accessed 13 January 2020.

Fukuda-Parr, S. (2016) From the Millennium Development Goals to the Sustainable Development Goals: shifts in purpose, concept, and politics of global goal setting for development. *Gender & Development*, 24(1), 43–52. doi: 10.1080/13552074.2016.1145895.

Fukuda-Parr, S., Heintz, J. and Seguino, S. (2013) Critical perspectives on financial and economic crises: heterodox macroeconomics meets feminist economics. *Feminist Economics*, 19(3), 4–31.

Gender Equality | UN Global Compact (2019) Empower women in the workplace, marketplace and community. Available at: www.unglobalcompact.org/what-is-gc/our-work/social/gender-equality. Accessed 16 November 2019.

Gill, R. K., Kelan, E. and Scharff, C. M. (2017) A postfeminist sensibility at work. *Gender, Work & Organization*, 24(3), 226–244.

Grandy, G. and Ingols, C. (2016) Writing cases about women protagonists: calling for gender awareness in traditional case portraits. *Case Research Journal*, 36(4).

Grey, C. (2004) Reinventing business schools: the contribution of critical management education. *Academy of Management Learning & Education*, 3(2), 178–186.

Grosser, K. and Moon, J. (2019) CSR and feminist organization studies: towards an integrated theorization for the analysis of gender issues. *Journal of Business Ethics*, 155(2), 321–342.

Grosser, K.A. and Moon, J.A. (2005) The role of corporate social responsibility in gender mainstreaming. *International Feminist Journal of Politics*, 7(4), 532–554.

Haertle, J., Parkes, C., Murray, A. et al. (2017) PRME: building a global movement on responsible management education. *International Journal of Management Education*, 15(2), 66–72.

Hanisch, C. (2006) The Personal Is Political. The Women's Liberation Movement classic with a new explanatory introduction. Available at: www.carolhanisch.org/CHwritings/PIP.html. Accessed 17 November 2019.

Harvard Business School (2019) 2019 Symposium – Gender. Available at: www.hbs.edu/gender/symposium/Pages/2019-symposium.aspx. Accessed 30 October 2019.

Haski-Leventhal, D., Pournader, M. and McKinnon, A. (2017) The role of gender and age in business students' values, CSR attitudes, and responsible management education: learnings from the PRME International Survey. *Journal of Business Ethics*, 146(1), 219–239.

Haynes, K. (2015) Gender equality in responsible management education and research. In: Murray, A., Baden, D., Cashian, P., Wersun, A., and Haynes, K. (Eds.), *Inspirational Guide for the Implementation of PRME*. Abingdon: Routledge. pp. 21–27.

Haynes, K. and Murray, A. (2015) Sustainability as a lens to explore gender equality: a missed opportunity for responsible management. In Flynn, P.M., Haynes, K. and Kilgour, M.A. (Eds.), *Integrating Gender Equality into Management Education: Lessons Learned and Challenges Remaining*. Sheffield: Greenleaf Publishing.

Hibbert, P. and Cunliffe, A. (2015) Responsible management: engaging moral reflexive practice through threshold concepts. *Journal of Business Ethics*, 127(1), 177–188.

IFC (2019) Guide for employer-supported childcare. Available at: www.ifc.org/wps/wcm/connect/Topics_Ext_Content/IFC_External_Corporate_Site/Gender+at+IFC/Resources/Guide+for+Employer-Supported+Childcare. Accessed 18 November 2019.

Joshi, A., Neely, B., Emrich, C. et al. (2015) Gender research in AMJ: an overview of five decades of empirical research and calls to action. *Academy of Management Journal*, 58(5), 1459–1475.

Kapoor, C. (2011) Defining diversity: the evolution of diversity. *Worldwide Hospitality and Tourism Themes*, 3(4), 284–293.

Kelan, E. K. (2018) Men doing and undoing gender at work: a review and research agenda. *International Journal of Management Reviews*, 20(2), 544–558. (Epub ahead of print 30 May 2017 doi: 10.1111/ijmr.12146.)

Kilgour, M. A. (2007) The UN Global Compact and substantive equality for women: revealing a 'well hidden' mandate. *Third World Quarterly*, 28(4), 751–773.

Kilgour, M. A. (2017) Gender inequality in management education: past, present and future. In Flynn, P.M., Haynes, K. and Kilgour, M.A. (Eds.), *Integrating Gender Equality into Business and Management Education: Lessons Learned and Challenges Remaining*. Sheffield; Greenleaf Publishing. pp. 22–37.

Littig, B. (2018) Good work? Sustainable work and sustainable development: a critical gender perspective from the Global North. *Globalizations,* 15(4), 565–579.

Mabey, C., Egri, C.P. and Parry, K. (2015) From the Special Section Editors: Questions business schools don't ask. *Academy of Management Learning & Education*, 14(4), 535–538.

Madsen, S.R. and Andrade, M.S. (2018) Unconscious gender bias: implications for women's leadership development. *Journal of Leadership Studies*, 12(1), 62–67.

Marshall, J. (1999) Doing gender in management education. *Gender and Education*, 11(3), 251–263.

McCann, M. and Wheeler, S. (2011) Gender diversity in the FTSE 100: the business case claim explored. *Journal of Law & Society*, 38(4), 542–574.

McPhail, K. (2013) Corporate Responsibility to respect human rights and business schools' responsibility to teach it: incorporating human rights into the sustainability agenda. *Accounting Education*, 22(4), 391–412.

McTiernan, S. and Flynn, P. M. (2011) 'Perfect storm' on the horizon for women business school deans? *Academy of Management Learning & Education*, 10(2), 323–339.

Michaels, W. B. (2008) Against diversity. *New Left Review*, 52, 33–36.

Miotto, G., Polo López, M. and Rom Rodríguez, J. (2019) Gender equality and UN Sustainable Development Goals: priorities and correlations in the top business schools' communication and legitimation strategies. *Sustainability*, 11(2), 302.

Montiel, I. (2008) Corporate social responsibility and corporate sustainability: separate pasts, common futures. *Organization & Environment*, 21(3), 245–269.

Moore, L., Rajadhyaksha, U. and Blake-Beard, S. (2017) Still too soon to forget 'women'?: making the case for the importance of gender diversity in management education: a study of India and the United States. In Flynn, P.M., Haynes, K. and Kilgour, M.A. (Eds.), *Integrating Gender Equality into Business and Management Education: Lessons Learned and Challenges Remaining*. Sheffield: Greenleaf Publishing. pp. 272–297.

Moosmayer, D. C., Waddock, S., Wang, L. et al. (2019) Leaving the road to Abilene: a pragmatic approach to addressing the normative paradox of responsible management education. *Journal of Business Ethics*, 157(4), 913–932.

Noon, M. (2018) Pointless diversity training: unconscious bias, new racism and agency. *Work, Employment and Society*, 32(1), 198–209.

OECD (2008) Gender and sustainable development: maximising the economic, social and environmental role of women. Available at: www.oecd.org/social/40881538.pdf. Accessed 13 January 2020.

Oloka-Onyango, J. and Tamale, S. (1995) The personal is political, or why women's rights are indeed human rights: an African perspective on international feminism. *Human Rights Quarterly*, 17(4), 691–731.

Otto, D. (2002) Gender Comment: Why does the UN Committee on Economic, Social and Cultural Rights need a General Comment on women? *Canadian Journal of Women and the Law*, 14, 1.

Palthe, J. (2013) Integrating human rights in business education: embracing the social dimension of sustainability. *Journal of Education for Business*, 88(2), 117–124.

Pearson, R. (1998) 'Nimble Fingers' revisited reflections on women and Third World industrialisation in the late twentieth century. In Jackson, C. and Pearson, R. (Eds.). *Feminist Visions of Development: Gender Analysis and Policy*. New York: Routledge.

Pearson, R. (2007) Beyond women workers: gendering CSR. *Third World Quarterly*, 28(4), 731–749.

Perriton, L. (2007) Really useful knowledge? Critical Management Education in the UK and the US. *Scandinavian Journal of Management*, 23(1), 66–83.

Peterson, V. S. (2003) *A Critical Rewriting of Global Political Economy: Integrating Reproductive, Productive, and Virtual Economies*. New York: Routledge.

Peterson, V. S. and Runyan, A. S. (2010) *Global Gender Issues in the New Millennium*, 3rd ed. Boulder, CO: Westview Press.

PRME (2019) What is PRME? Available at: www.unprme.org/about-prme/index.php. Accessed 2 December 2019.

PRME 2017 Global Forum (2019) 2017 Global Forum for Responsible Management Education (18–19 July, New York). Available at: www.unprme.org/resources/display-resources-sub.php?scid=44. Accessed 18 November 2019.

PRME Secretariat, UN Global Compact (2016) *PRME Strategic Review 2016*. Available at: https://www.unprme.org/resource-docs/160 517PRMEStrategicReviewFINAL.pdf. Accessed 5 March 2020.

PRME Anti-Poverty Toolkit (2019) Home page. https://jenkinew.wixsite.com/anti-povertytk. Accessed 16 November 2019.

PRME Working Groups (2019) PRME Working Group on Gender Equality. Available at: www.unprme.org/how-to-engage/display-working-group.php?wgid=2715. Accessed 27 October 2019.

Prügl, E. and True, J. (2014) Equality means business? Governing gender through transnational public–private partnerships. *Review of International Political Economy*, 21(6), 1137–1169.

Quan, R. J. D. (2019) *Human Rights and the Gender Dynamics of Climate Change*. Cheltenham: Edward Elgar.

Reilly, A., Jones, D., Rey Vasquez, C. et al. (2016) Confronting gender inequality in a business school. *Higher Education Research & Development*, 35(5), 1025–1038.

Ropers-Huilman, B. (2003) *Gendered Futures in Higher Education: Critical Perspectives for Change*. Albany, NY: State University of New York Press.

Rumens, N. (2018) Teaching gender in a post-feminist management classroom. In Taylor, Y. and Lahad, K. (Eds.), *Feeling Academic in the Neoliberal University*. Basingstoke: Palgrave Macmillan. pp. 321–343.

Scherer, A. G. and Palazzo, G. (Eds.) (2008) *Handbook of Research on Global Corporate Citizenship*. Cheltenham: Edward Elgar.

Schouten, P. and Miklian, J. (2018) The business–peace nexus: 'business for peace' and the reconfiguration of the public/private divide in global governance. *Journal of International Relations and Development*, doi: 10.1057/s41268-018-0144-2.

Simpson, R. (2006) Masculinity and management education: feminizing the MBA. *Academy of Management Learning & Education*, 5(2), 182–193.

Simpson, R. (2017) Bringing critical masculinity studies into a gender-inspired paradigm. *Journal of Sociology*, 53(4), 771–773.

Spence, L. J. (2017) The obfuscation of gender and feminism in CSR research and the academic community: an essay. In Flynn, P.M., Haynes, K. and Kilgour, M.A. (Eds.), *Integrating Gender Equality into Business and Management Education: Lessons Learned and Challenges Remaining*. Sheffield: Greenleaf Publishing. pp. 16–30.

Stone, D. (2010) Knowledge and policy networks in global governance. In Scherrer, C. and Young, B. (Eds.), *Gender Knowledge and Knowledge Networks in International Political Economy*. Nomos Verlagsgesellschaft mbH & Co. KG. pp. 36–54.

Symons, L. and Ibarra, H. (2014) What the scarcity of women in business case studies really looks like. *Harvard Business Review* 28 April [Online] https://hbr.org/2014/04/what-the-scarcity-of-women-in-business-case-studies-really-looks-like. Accessed 13 January 2020.

Tauszig, J. and Toppinen, A. (2017) Towards corporate sustainability under Global Agenda 2030: insights from Brazilian forest companies. *BioProducts Business*, 65–76.

Thompson, J. and Mcgivern, J. (1995) Sexism in the seminar: strategies for gender sensitivity in management education. *Gender and Education* 7(3). Published online 1 July 2010. doi: 10.1080/09540259550039040.

Thompson, L J. (2007) Gender equity and corporate social responsibility in a post-feminist era. *Business Ethics: A European Review*, 17(1), 87–106.

Thompson, L. J. (2008) Gender equity and corporate social responsibility in a post-feminist era. *Business Ethics: A European Review*, 17(1), 87–106.

UN Global Compact (2019) Home page. www.unglobalcompact.org/. Accessed 2 December 2019.

UN Women (2018) *Turning Promises into Action: Gender Equality in the 2030 Agenda for Sustainable Development*. New York: UN Women.

UNRISD (United Nations Research Institute for Social Development) (2005) Gender equality: striving for justice in an unequal world. Available at: www.unrisd.org/research/gender/report. Accessed 13 January 2020.

Vallance, S., Perkins, H.C., and Dixon, J.E. (2011) What is social sustainability? A clarification of concepts. *Geoforum*, 42(3). Themed Issue: Subaltern Geopolitics: 342–348. doi: 10.1016/j.geoforum.2011.01.002.

Walby, S. (2005) Measuring women's progress in a global era. *International Social Science Journal*, 57(184), 371–387.

Weber, H. (2017) Politics of 'leaving no one behind': contesting the 2030 Sustainable Development Goals Agenda. *Globalizations*, 14(3), 399–414.

Williams, J., Meliou, E. and Arevalo, J.A. (2017) Gender and sustainable management education: exploring the missing link. In Arevalo, J. A. and Mitchell, S. F. (Eds.), *Handbook of*

Sustainability in Management Education. Cheltenham: Edward Elgar.

Winkler, I. T. and Williams, C. (2017) The Sustainable Development Goals and human rights: a critical early review. *International Journal of Human Rights*, 21(8). 1023–1028.

World Bank (2019) World Bank Sustainable development bond raises awareness for women and girls' empowerment. Available at: www.worldbank.org/en/news/press-release/2018/01/09/world-bank-sustainable-development-bond-raises-awareness-for-women-and-girls-empowerment. Accessed 9 November 2019.

World Economic Forum (2019) World Economic Forum and UN sign strategic partnership framework. Available at: www.weforum.org/press/2019/06/world-economic-forum-and-un-sign-strategic-partnership-framework/. Accessed 18 November 2019.

Wu, Y-C. J., Huang, S., Kuo, L. et al. (2010) Management Education for sustainability: a web-based content analysis. *Academy of Management Learning & Education*, 9(3), 520–531.

Zanoni, P., Janssens, M., Benschop, Y. et al. (2010) Guest Editorial: Unpacking diversity, grasping inequality: rethinking difference through critical perspectives. *Organization*, 17(1), 9–29.

13

Anti-corruption Education

Christian Hauser and Ronald E. Berenbeim

INTRODUCTION

Most scholars agree that corruption generates major societal costs. Corruption endangers political stability, undermines democratic values, provides fertile ground for organized crime and fosters a general loss of confidence in public institutions (Pacini et al., 2002; Frei and Muethel, 2017). Additionally, corruption contributes to market failure and hampers economic growth (Mauro, 1995; Pacini et al., 2002; Osuji, 2011; Frei and Muethel, 2017). Research indicates that corruption entails substantial risks and costs for businesses (Block et al., 1982; Wu, 2009; Hauser and Kronthaler, 2013; Ambler, 2014). Corruption undermines the social fabric by causing increased poverty, distorted access to public services and decreased public health (Frei and Muethel, 2017).

According to Transparency International's Corruption Perceptions Index (CPI) 2017, over two-thirds of the countries included in the CPI 2017 fall below the midpoint of the index ranging from 0 to 100, in which 0 indicates the highest and 100 the lowest level of perceived corruption. The global median is only 43. Moreover, there has been a global trend of declining anti-corruption activities rather than an improvement in individual countries (Transparency International, 2018). Equally significant is Transparency International's Bribe Payers Index (BPI). In its latest edition, the 2011 BPI ranks the propensity of companies from 28 top foreign direct investment (FDI) countries to bribe public officials abroad. The Netherlands and Switzerland finished first as the least likely. China and Russia tied for last, and the United States ranked 10th (Transparency International, 2011).

In light of the growing recognition of the importance of responsible management in business practices, there is a growing contribution to the academic literature in this regard. Having its origins in the academic debate on the United Nations Principles for Responsible Management Education (PRME), scholars have conducted research along three main avenues to tackle this issue: (1) responsible management, (2) responsible management learning and (3) responsible management education (Laasch and Moosmayer, 2015). In responsible management, issues related to sustainability, responsibility and ethics (SRE) are incorporated into management practices (Laasch and Moosmayer, 2015; Nonet et al., 2016). Responsible management learning takes place in a business environment, with professionals learning about SRE-related topics in the workplace either through explicit training programs or through implicit socialization (Verkerk et al., 2001; Antonacopoulou and Pesqueux, 2010; Verma et al., 2016; Hauser and Nieffer, 2018; Hauser, 2019b). Responsible management education, however, takes place in an academic context whereby future professionals are educated on SRE-related topics (Laasch and Moosmayer, 2015). Similar to responsible management learning, responsible management education can also be conducted explicitly or implicitly. In the former, students are educated on these topics through university education, such as lectures (Waples et al., 2009; Lavine and Roussin, 2012; Goodpaster et al., 2018). In the latter, universities' and business schools' 'hidden' curricula provide students with moral learning and socialization processes (Blasco, 2012; Borges et al., 2017).

Responsible management research and curricula are important components of the global fight against corruption (Hauser, 2019a). Awareness of situations that may raise corruption issues is vitally dependent on what practitioners are taught and, once employed, the examples that they set in collaboration with their colleagues (Hauser et al., 2020). Research is thus needed to enrich business curricula. Improving global resistance to corrupt practices also requires innovative pedagogical methods.

Against this background, the purpose of this chapter is to explore future research, curricula and teaching methods, which will be used in universities and business schools globally. In doing so, we will shed light on the past and present of anti-corruption education. The remainder of the chapter will therefore be structured as follows: first, we analyze the historic milestones that led to early anti-corruption education in universities and business schools; second, we examine the current situation in terms of the methods used and topics taught; and finally, we investigate future developments in this arena.

ANTI-CORRUPTION EDUCATION – PAST AND PRESENT

Past

Perceptions of what is desirable and acceptable managerial behavior evolve over time. Accordingly, standards and customs of business practices have also changed. For example, 50 years ago the mainstream business community probably agreed with the widely circulated view of Milton Friedman that profit is the primary, if not exclusive, objective of business enterprises. Friedman's 1970 *New York Times* article 'The social responsibility of business is to increase its profits' was frequently cited by supporters to emphasize the critical if not exclusive need to focus student attention on profit-making skills. An earlier article written by Levitt in 1958 compared running a business to fighting a war and the priority of combat skills over ethical sensitivities.

A few years later, public attention began to focus on the ethical performance and practices of business institutions. A 1973 follow-up investigation of the Watergate Scandal of illegal campaign contributions led by the United States Securities and Exchange Commission (SEC) found that a number of US corporations and executives had falsified company finances, improperly concealed and used company assets for campaign contributions and utilized hidden 'slush funds' (Koehler, 2012; Perlstein, 2018) in election campaigns. The investigation concluded that over 400 US companies made dubious or illegal payments, most commonly in the form of bribery and facilitation payments to government officials and other civil servants (House of Representatives, 1977). In this context, *bribery* is a payment to a public official or group of public officials to trigger an undue favorable decision in a business transaction. A *facilitation payment* is an informal payment to a public official or group of public officials for the acceleration of some aspect of the government's performance of a contract.

The SEC mid-1970s investigation determined that admissions of improper behavior occurred most frequently in the drug and healthcare, oil and gas production, services, food production, aerospace, airlines and air services, and chemical industries. Approximately one-quarter of the guilty companies were ranked in the Fortune 500, and most of the companies were publicly listed (House of Representatives, 1977). The investigation led to the passage of the Foreign Corrupt Practices Act (FCPA) 1977, which outlawed corporate bribery and provided criminal sanctions (Koehler, 2012). The FCPA requirements made it essential for businesspeople operating in an increasingly global environment to become conversant with the need for ethical conduct to resist corrupt practices. FCPA violations expose individuals and companies to severe financial penalties and, in extreme cases, can bar the company from doing business with the US government. At the same time, the law also gave companies incentives to mitigate legal penalties if the company could prove they had made a serious effort to communicate to employees by instituting compliance and training programs that corrupt behavior is not tolerated (Lange, 2011).

In response to these new demands, higher education institutions began to adapt their curricula to the ethical challenges of the new global environment by incorporating legal and ethical subject matter into their business curricula in the late 1970s (Sims and Sims, 1991). Even skeptics regarding ethics programs conceded that while ethics programs may not be effective, they were needed to meet societal and stakeholder expectations (McDonald and Donleavy, 1995). The increase in awareness of acts of, among others, corporate bribery and illegal political campaign contributions resulted in the establishment of academic centers dedicated to business ethics. One such center is the W. Michael Hoffman Center for Business Ethics established in 1976 by Bentley University (Bentley College, 1996, 2001; Bentley University, 2016). Within the next two decades, more universities and business schools in the United States began to integrate free-standing business ethics courses into their curricula (Sims and Sims, 1991). In a second example, in 1995, the New York University Stern School of Business engaged the entire business faculty in developing a program with a strong focus on cases and problems in traditional subject matter areas, such as marketing, finance, sales and human resources, regarding ethical practices (Berenbeim, 2018). Business scholars modeled the courses on professional ethics curricula (e.g. medicine, law) that promoted and established conduct as well as performance standards. Medical ethics, which already had well-established guidelines, was used as a model of an interdisciplinary applied area of study in developing business ethics curricula (Bentley College, 1996). In other business schools, these topics were often incorporated into traditional course material rather than taught as a stand-alone course.

Present

In the past two decades, several international conventions were established following the passage of the FCPA to promote global initiatives to combat corruption. These conventions included the 1997 OECD Convention on Combating Bribery of Foreign Public Officials in International Business Transactions, the establishment of the Council of Europe's anti-corruption monitoring body, GRECO, 1999, and the United Nations Convention Against

Corruption (UNCAC), which was signed in 2003. The conventions play a key role in the fight against corruption by creating an international framework for tackling corruption worldwide, including obligations for governments to criminalize corrupt behavior, extend and tighten existing criminal laws, foster domestic prevention measures, and cooperate internationally with other countries (Hauser and Hogenacker, 2014; OECD, 2018; UNDOC, 2018).

In 2011, PRME established an anti-corruption working group comprising approximately 30 scholars from around the world; the two authors are members. The working group aimed to develop source material and teaching methods for business schools to address the growing international problem of corporate corruption in business practices. This effort resulted in the creation of the PRME Anti-Corruption Toolkit (Amann et al., 2012). The earlier undertakings at US business schools were used as a foundation for development and enrichment. The working group utilized the participants' global experience to develop course materials that focused on a variety of teaching methods that can be used in different cultural environments and can address the broad range of concerns from one region to another.

Today, there is a growing recognition that business ethics in research and teaching is a stand-alone subject that recognizes evolving moral standards, decision-making methods, reasons for decisions and the extent to which, if at all, business objectives meet moral standards. Accordingly, a report by the PRME in 2015 found that 84% of the MBA programs at US business schools that are ranked in the top 50 by the *Financial Times* have ethics curricula, either as a standalone subject or integrated into other modules such as sustainability, human rights and corporate citizenship. It is less common for ethics to be taught at the bachelor's level, but there is an ongoing movement to integrate courses into undergraduate studies. Abend (2014) provides an in-depth discussion of the effort to include business ethics in business

studies and its antecedents. Research on ethics and anti-corruption education confirms that both theoretical and practical training in many European countries are still insufficient (Becker et al., 2013; Lisievici and Andronie, 2016; Kravchuk, 2017). This problem seems to be particularly acute in Eastern European countries, where there is a lack of knowledge regarding the developing global anti-corruption regime (Lisievici and Andronie, 2016). When anti-corruption disciplines have been integrated into curricula, they tend to be only for students of legal and administrative specializations rather than for business students (Kravchuk, 2017). Additionally, the topic is commonly included only at the master's level. Despite these documented shortfalls, there are some encouraging examples, which are described below.

Examples from Switzerland
The Zurich University of Applied Sciences in Switzerland uses both a real-life case study and an actual student business case. In cooperation with an internationally active company, students work on a case that includes assignments relating to strategic, financial and marketing management with a strong focus on corporate responsibility issues in the first semester. Building upon what they learn in the first semester, students then choose a business project in the second semester offered by companies in different industries that operate on an international scale. Playing the role of business consultants, the students are asked to devise a feasible and practice-oriented solution for the company (Prandini et al., 2012).

A second Swiss university and member of the PRME Champion leadership group, FHGR (University of Applied Sciences of the Grisons), is also taking a pedagogical approach to tackling anti-corruption issues. This program aims to address the sensitive issue of anti-corruption at an early stage in students' careers to prevent future malpractice. To do so, the university has built on the PRME Anti-Corruption Toolkit (Amann et al., 2012). Using the recommendations derived from the toolkit, lecturers help successfully educate current and future professionals on the topic of anti-corruption in a timely and responsive manner (Hauser, 2019a).

The Swiss chapter of Transparency International published a script for an anti-corruption curriculum to be taught in universities and business schools (Transparency International Schweiz, 2017). The framework provides an overview of the legal and risk areas relating to corruption in Switzerland in the context of both the public and private sectors. The curriculum is divided into two main parts. In the first stage, students learn about what constitutes corrupt behavior as well as the various impacts corrupt business practices can have on different stakeholders. The legal basis of corruption in Switzerland is taught in terms of the role of international anti-corruption conventions ratified by Switzerland and their respective implications for Swiss companies. Moreover, the script addresses methods that can be employed by companies to deter and react to corruption in addition to the benefits and potential drawbacks of each. Building upon prior learned knowledge, students are taught in the second phase about various risk areas related to corruption as well as how prevailing Swiss and international laws can be used to combat the identified risks. In particular, the curriculum covers risks related to the financing of political parties, public sector risks, potent funds, public procurement, risks within the sporting industry, development cooperation, and nepotism and favoritism.

Giving Voice to Values curricula

A further approach to developing anti-corruption curricula is the framework Giving Voice to Values (GVV). The GVV approach aims to address the knowledge–practice gap among professionals whereby professionals know what is right from an ethical perspective but are unable or unwilling to act accordingly in their day-to-day business lives (Hibbert and Cunliffe, 2015; Nonet et al., 2016). GVV thus takes a new stance upon how business ethics is taught to provide future professionals with the skills and knowledge to not only know what is morally correct but also know how to make it happen. Rather than merely teaching ethics, GVV aims to show students how they can voice their ethical concerns in a way that prompts change.

The use of case studies is central to this teaching method. In contrast to predecision case studies, where students are presented with a scenario and are instructed to choose the right decision from an ethical standpoint, GVV uses postdecision case studies. Here, an ethically grounded decision in response to the scenario has already been made, and the students must develop the most effective ethical strategy and action plan. All the participants then practice and rehearse the steps in the action plan, thus reinforcing the positive behavior. Many of the GVV cases include so-called A and B cases as well as teaching notes, which are available to faculty members for free. The so-called A cases are postdecision case examples originally provided to students. These cases indicate the context within which the protagonist made the decision to voice his/her values; the students must then decide the subsequent steps that must be taken. The so-called B cases provide greater detail and describe the actions the protagonists actually took in giving voice to his/her values and the resulting effect on the situation and the protagonist.

A few years ago, the PRME supported scholars writing 10 GVV anti-corruption cases about Indian companies and organizations, including, for example, 'When the boss is the barrier', 'Perils of collaboration' and 'The real cost of paying bribes'. Swamy and Detjen (2013) highlight that such GVV cases can help reduce the skepticism of students regarding anti-corruption education in India and show that GVV is a feasible approach to voicing values in the workplace. Furthermore, there are a number of other GVV-style corruption cases, including the case called 'Not an option even to consider'. In this case, students learn that when confronted with the issue of corruption, a systemic approach must be taken. The case illustrates that a series of steps must be applied in sequence to achieve the desired outcome. While critics of the framework note that corruption is an ingrained systematic phenomenon that seems almost impossible to fight, the reasoning behind the GVV approach is to get the students to understand that it takes a long-term stance to make systematic changes.

Modular framework from the Central European University (CEU)

The CEU is another institution with a focus on research in the field of anti-corruption education. To address the issue that there generally is no 'one size fits all' approach in regard to anti-corruption education, researchers at the CEU sought to develop a holistic modular framework for anti-corruption education in universities and business schools (Hardi, 2017). The characteristics of the modular design allowed for a multidisciplinary approach to be taken whereby anti-corruption is addressed across a series of core modules, with further discussions in elective subjects. Regardless of whether it takes place in core or elective courses, anti-corruption is largely discussed in the context of the macro- and micro-environments. The former represents the different economic, legal, political and sociocultural factors influencing anti-corruption. The latter concerns the managerial challenges for firms in relation to anti-corruption as well as the importance of factors such as risk assessments, corporate compliance, corporate culture and the leadership approach in tackling corruption. Other topics that are covered include the root cause of corrupt behavior, the coordination of public and private interests, and collective actions against corruption. The modular approach to the framework provides lecturers and institutions with the flexibility to address anti-corruption measures specific to the region.

To assess the impact and success of the modular anti-corruption education framework, different indicators were used. For example, participants in the course were asked to complete a pre- and postcourse survey, and the results were compared to indicate a change in students' attitudes. It was revealed that upon completion of the course, participants were generally more positive about anti-corruption in the sense that they viewed corruption as manageable. Moreover, faculty members were asked for feedback on the anti-corruption framework and its impact. The curriculum was well received and was able to meet expectations. It was said that the modules were often able to change students' perceptions in favor of ethical practices, and the curriculum looks promising in terms of having a lasting impact on students. In addition, the project steering committee and country-level project advisory councils were also asked for feedback. These responses illustrated that the program facilitated trust-building with the organization that partnered with the scheme, with the potential for future collaboration and cooperation on anti-corruption initiatives (KPMG, 2016).

Anti-corruption Education – Core Methods

The workplace is an arena for moral development that confronts business practitioners with temptations to be evil and opportunities to be virtuous. Optimally, teaching needs to enhance student understanding of the challenges with which this reality confronts them. Past and present curricula have emphasized the need for students to first master decision-making models for analyzing corruption challenges and related issues and to develop collaborative skills in formulating a (team) response. The individual issues and scenarios change over time. For these reasons, it is considered necessary that practitioners or academics with a thorough grounding in at least one traditional business subject undertake business ethics and anti-corruption research and education. Furthermore, business ethics and anti-corruption should be taught to students who have completed at least half of the conventional curriculum so that they are fully conversant with general management issues and the decisions and procedures that companies typically apply to resolve them.

Socratic method

Business ethics and anti-corruption pedagogy lends itself to a variety of approaches. The most commonly used method in business ethics and anti-corruption discussions is the Socratic method. Designed to stimulate critical thinking, business ethics and anti-corruption discussions seek to engage the entire classroom to achieve the best possible response to a context-specific situation. For future managers, executives and business leaders, effective peer collaboration must become a key learning objective in formulating a response to ethical challenges. These skills can be cultivated by dividing the class into teams and having them present and defend a course of action. Alternatively, assigning scenario roles to students that are 'performed' in a 'dramatization' of the case can also be effective. One of the advantages of this approach is that the teacher can 'cast against type' by using a student who has acquired a classroom reputation for a 'hard' or 'soft' approach to an issue to articulate a rationale that the class does not associate with their usual point of view. The utilization of a systematic 'casting' strategy in a designed experiment could yield learning outcomes that show (1) how individuals modify their responses over time, (2) the effect of group discussion on their changing attitudes and (3) the dynamics of group development into a 'team'.

Students need to be familiar with Jeremy Bentham and Immanuel Kant, who are the most influential modern thinkers on the two different forms of intuition that shape core beliefs: (1) utilitarianism and (2) empathy.

Utilitarianism: The business ethics literature has a more nuanced view of utilitarianism than the widespread definition of the 'greatest good for the greatest number'. The 'greatest number' is not 'me' or 'my company', which, in fact, is ethical egoism

(Bentham, 1996). True utilitarianism promotes a solution in which markets function efficiently and reward, to varying degrees, all the participants and, at the very least, harm none. It has become an easy stretch for a business practitioner to use the ethical egoism argument that if I benefit and my company succeeds, the rest of the world will inevitably profit. Enabling business practitioners to understand the difference between utilitarianism and ethical egoism, where conduct is defined by the role you play (e.g. advocate or defender of dubious behavior), is a key objective of business education (Applbaum, 2000).

Empathy: Kant's Categorical Imperative is the requirement that ethical choices be universal rules that the decision-maker would be willing to accept as a precedent for all similar situations. Furthermore, Kant argued in 1785 in his *Metaphysics of Morals* that the individual needs to reconcile concepts of duty to oneself with duty to others, which is a process that arguably requires empathy (Kant, 1948). Does this process leave open challenges in which evolving empathy standards can override a rationale that the categorical imperative might support? For example, capital punishment for a horrendous crime imposed after rigorous adherence to due process might meet categorical imperative standards but be overridden in some societies by evolving standards of empathy. See, for example, the Norwegian case of Anders Brevik.

The critical contribution of the Socratic method in a business ethics and anti-corruption curriculum is that it engages students in a dialogue between the utilitarian and the empathetic elements in their intuitive thinking. This dialogue illuminates the potential areas of convergence between utilitarianism and empathy and, in so doing, teaches students to be open and engaged with their colleagues in a lifelong process of sharing this common pursuit with others. Ultimately, it should be demonstrated that these two intuitions are potentially complementary and not necessarily diametrically opposed (Berenbeim, 2018).

Problem-solving method

A second commonly used method is the problem-solving method. A fundamental difference between ethics and anti-corruption dilemmas and other business cases is that the principals do not always agree that the problem *exists* and, if so, exactly *what it is*. The problem-solving method can teach students to think from different perspectives in relation to corruption. Teaching on this subject can be through experimentation with groups and case studies of recent problems (e.g. Siemens or Walmart) for insights into how decision-makers failed to identify potential issues. The Gibson Dunn website is perhaps the best authority for historical comparisons of US anti-corruption prosecutions and settlements (Gibson Dunn, 2019).

The key question in determining whether ethical analysis of a pending decision is needed is whether the agreed-upon facts constitute a finding of potential market failure. The US President John Adams is said to have remarked, 'facts are stubborn things'. However, there is seldom agreement as to what facts are or their relevance to the choices that need to be made. Invariably, the set of facts on which important decisions are based is in dispute or incomplete. Thus, students need to learn to supplement available information with reasonable assumptions based upon industry or local practices as well as personal experience.

After determining the facts and the alternative courses of action available to the decision-maker, he/she must determine if the outcome will give rise to one or more of the four forms of market failure. An efficient economy has (1) perfect competition, (2) no negative externalities, (3) no 'free riding' in the use of public goods and (4) perfect information (Edwards and Edwards, 1979). To the extent that any of these four conditions is deficient or absent, the market has failed to maximize the welfare of all participants and in so doing can give rise to rights violations. Arguably, corruption has the potential to give rise to any of these forms of market failure, and at least one of them is likely to be found in a corrupt act:

1 *Monopsony/monopoly buying power* – impairs market efficiency through excessive pricing of products (monopoly) or the lack of labor bargaining power (monopsony).
2 *Negative externalities* – add to the product's production and distribution costs and in so doing add to the ultimate price for the consumer. Other possible negative externalities include pollution, hazardous working conditions and unsafe products. These negative externalities are hidden costs that are imposed on the consumer and the community.
3 *Underpriced utilization of public goods* – (e.g. highways) can impose significant costs on adjacent communities.
4 *Information asymmetries* – corrupt acts may involve information asymmetries in which competitors and consumers may be unaware of the perpetrator's potential market pricing advantages and what they add to his/her purchasing price, stock value, or product risk (product liability).

When confronted with a market failure situation, the responsible manager or company has a choice between exploiting the market failure or exercising prudence and not engaging in the practice. Rightly or wrongly, decision-makers may believe that legal risks or competitor retaliation is unlikely. Alternatively, decision-makers may conclude that if retaliation does occur, the advantages still outweigh the cost. Hence, on a risk-adjusted basis, the company's interests are served at the cost of other stakeholder rights. Put simply, decision-makers may conclude that even in the worst case scenario, the outcome is an acceptable cost of doing business.

However, well-intentioned as the ethics and anti-corruption curricula and the research on which they are based may be, too much research and curriculum development effort has focused on deterrence. Thus, many students view these subjects as an opportunity to learn 'what can I do to avoid the risk of getting caught, or in the worst-case scenario, how can I minimize the resulting damages?' Hence, despite legal prohibitions, company compliance programs, and even some high-profile enforcement efforts, the aggregate level of global corruption has changed little in recent years, despite individual country or company improvements or declines during this period.

Developing proficiency in the application of problem-solving methods to specific dilemmas is the next step in business ethics research and education. It needs to be acknowledged at the outset that different analytical methods (e.g. consequentialism, deontology) often result in different preferred outcomes. The researcher and teacher's role in business ethics and anti-corruption education is to facilitate a discussion that helps students come to their own, often contradictory, conclusions (Mendelsohn, 2017). Business ethics researchers and teachers need to understand that their subject is a vital and unique part of the curriculum because student success depends on both conduct and performance; business ethics is the only subject that focuses on conduct-based decision-making. Put simply, other business courses teach students how to achieve success; business ethics shows them what they need to do to retain its benefits.

In fact, it is possible to make mistakes in the other business subject matter areas and nonetheless survive and prosper. For example, in 1985, Coca Cola's Chairman and CEO Roberto Goizueta made the 'New Coke' decision that is cited as a textbook example of bad marketing. Based on tasting samples, the Coke formula was changed. Coke fans hated the drink. Some even purchased cases of the beverage and shipped it back to the company. Goizueta admitted he was wrong. At the time of his death in 1997, he was still Coca Cola's CEO and one of the most admired CEOs in the United States (Benjamin, 2015). Had Goizueta made an ethical mistake of comparable significance his career would have ended.

Corruption in the context of agency and fiduciary duty

The minimal standard of business ethical obligation is defined by legal risk: (1) the entity vs. property view of corporate purpose, (2) fiduciary relationships and (3)

negligence and strict liability. The inclusion of these topics has been a response in large measure to the adoption of the United States Federal Sentencing Guidelines for Organizations and their 2004 revisions; similar incentives for ethics and compliance programs in other countries were increased after US enforcement in 2006 of the FCPA and the passage of the UK Bribery Act. In addition, there is a considerable body of research devoted to these subjects and professional organizations, publications and conferences where practitioners engage in discussions on issues of mutual concern, such as The Conference Board and the Society of Corporate Compliance and Ethics and its newsletter *Ethikos* (Conference Board, 2019; Society of Corporate Compliance and Ethics, 2019a, 2019b).

This topic begins with a discussion of to whom is the corporation responsible and for what. The issue of corporate purpose is at the heart of the directors' fiduciary duty to the company and the company's fiduciary obligation, if any, to individual stakeholder groups. Corporations engage in business pursuant to a license to operate in the state (in the United States) or country. As such, decision-makers must ask whether they are an 'entity' with an obligation to the state and its stakeholders (national and local governments, suppliers, employees, customers and owners/shareholders).

As noted by Allen (1992), the notion of corporate purpose depends on the extent to which the company is viewed in the legal sense as (1) *property* for which the performance test is the maximization of returns for the owners/investors (Friedman, 1970) or (2) an *entity* that exists pursuant to a license to operate from the state and has fiduciary obligations to other stakeholders besides the owners (e.g. employees, suppliers, customers). In the last 100 years, for example, US law and business practices have swung back and forth between these two extremes, but the variations have fallen within a narrow range (Allen, 1992).

In support of the entity view, the then President of General Electric, Owen Young, is reported to have stated in the 1920s that managers have a growing responsibility to be trustees of their institution rather than tailoring managerial decisions to the demands of shareholders. Nevertheless, Young also raised the question of who, if not the shareholders, are the beneficiaries of the trust and to whom do managers owe their responsibility (Dodd, 1932). Stating a current view that is widely but not unanimously held, Stout (2012) argues that even if the fiduciary obligation is exclusively to the owners, the narrow fiduciary 'shareholder value' interpretation reduces them 'to their lowest moral denominator'.

The second topic is fiduciary obligation and the question of to whom an agent/fiduciary is obligated and for what. According to DeMott (2006), an agent's duties to the principal typically fall into two categories: duties of loyalty and duties of performance.

Loyalty: Problems arise from the virtual impossibility of the complete alignment of objectives between the principal and agent. The example given by DeMott (2006) in this regard is instructive. The owner of a racehorse is the principal, and the jockey is the agent. Both want to win the race. While in the lead, the horse begins to stumble. At that point, the interests of the principal and agent diverge. The problem may be further complicated if the jockey has been paid an inducement by a bettor to focus exclusively on winning the race. The jockey whips the horse harder and stumbles over the finish line. Even if the horse wins the race, the owner's interest might have been better served by taking the horse out of the race and avoiding the danger of serious or permanent injury to the horse. As this example illustrates, in such a situation it is difficult to impose upon the agent the duty to act only as authorized by the principal (DeMott, 2006), particularly where the breach of loyalty flows logically from improper gifts, side deals and conflicts of interest (Clarkson et al., 2012; Mallor, 2016).

The jockey anecdote is an example of the kind of short- versus long-term choices that managers often face in business decisions regarding plant and product safety and many other issues that may have an impact on the company's long-term sustainability.

Examples of the jockey, owner and multiple fiduciary problem can be found in many current business issues: (1) factory conditions in less developed countries, (2) pharmaceutical prices and (3) advertisements for smoking products in countries where the government does not require the seller to identify health risks. In each of these examples, the company must decide whether profit maximization (fiduciary obligation to owners/shareholders) is its sole fiduciary obligation.

Performance: An agent's duties of performance include (a) reasonable diligence and skill, (b) notification with respect to all matters concerning the subject matter of the agency, and (c) accounting (DeMott, 2006).

Corruption in the context of the developing global anti-corruption regime

Business ethics and anti-corruption research and teaching also need to track the evolving global business ethics anti-corruption compliance regime and the ongoing discussions and controversies regarding the regime's organizations – public, private and civil society – for moral suasion and enforcement. The foundation document in this regard is the United Nations Universal Declaration of Human Rights. Subsequent national and global initiatives include the following:

National and international legislative and regulatory frameworks – such as the FCPA, OECD Anti-Bribery Convention, UNCAC and UK Bribery Act;

Voluntary codes – developed by Transparency International (TI), the International Chamber of Commerce (ICC), the World Economic Forum Partnering Against Corruption Initiative (PACI) and other organizations are significant tools for private organizations in terms of increasing (self-regulatory) responsibilities;

The new politics of organizational visibility, reputation and ethics – focuses on the developing links between the global anti-corruption regime and media globalization, social media, and citizen engagement in anti-corruption work.

Within the past two decades, incidents too numerous to mention involving corruption.

labor conditions and plant safety have attracted significant media attention and been the subject of unfavorable comment (*Wall Street Journal*, 2012). Some companies have responded to this development in positive ways through participation in the United Nations Global Compact and its various working groups. Another approach has been for companies to seek inclusion in ethical investor funds such as *FTSE for Good* by participating in annual transparency reporting requirements. Ultimately, companies need to find ways to coordinate their response to the three interlocking elements of the global best practices regime (national and international regulatory frameworks, voluntary codes and traditional and social media).

The teaching process entails equipping students with practical ways to decide between right and wrong (competing interests, individual versus company ethics) in the integration of ethical theory with specific case analysis, action planning, business decision-making and implementation.

The introduction of ethical subject matter into the business decision-making process requires a mastery of the skills needed for the development of five managerial processes:

1 *Ethical risk assessment* – entails the utilization of a confidential questionnaire in which employees share their perceptions of the frequency and nature of misconduct – particularly in situations where it contradicts the company's written policies and ethics codes.
2 *Ethics policies* – are based on stakeholder engagement and the formulation of a written document that states a leadership message, behavioral guidance and information on where to seek advice.
3 *Policy implementation* – utilizes training programs that discuss scenarios based on situations that the company has or is likely to confront.
4 *Ongoing program support* – is a program through which a senior-level executive serves as the ethics officer with direct reporting responsibility to the CEO and the board or its ethics committee. Other key features of successful ethics programs are a hotline (whistleblowing mechanism) that is usually outsourced and complemented by an internal mechanism (helpline) that offers employees an opportunity to seek advice before going to an outside source.
5 *Stakeholder engagement* – needs to be preceded by a rigorous analysis that identifies key stakeholders and the issues that concern them to maximize its effectiveness.

Corruption in the context of international supply chains

The globalization of markets and their increased role in the economies of the areas, countries, or regions in which companies are located has generated higher expectations regarding responsibility and accountability for the impact of firms' activities on the environment and society. In addition, advances in communications technology afford opinion-makers and stakeholders greater and faster access to information about corporate behavior. In the global business arena, governments, consumers and other stakeholders are demanding increasing transparency regarding supply chain performance – including, labor conditions, factory safety, environmental impact and corruption.

Differences in local customs can result in ethical dilemmas – particularly in regions and countries with weaker governments and poor law enforcement. Resistance to corrupt practices is fundamental in this environment. Corruption undermines a company's ethical environment and, in so doing, its capacity to responsibly manage supply chain issues for the proper tracking of risk. At the country level, corruption hinders development and deprives the citizenry of economic, social, environmental and political rights. This topic addresses five critical global ethical challenges and focuses on emerging standards of good 'sustainability' practices:

1 Understanding the risks, costs, dilemmas and rising expectations of company responsibilities with regard to companies' global and local business practices.
2 Developing an improved sense of the critical role that the company's ethical practices play in improving transparency regarding individual practices in the company's supply chains.

3 Improving awareness and understanding of the challenges of adhering to anti-corruption laws and the global anti-corruption regime's requirements in diverse environments with ingrained local customs and weak governance.
4 Discussing how business strategies and management practices can best adapt to improving global ethics standards.
5 Devising multifaceted implementation techniques, processes and metrics for anti-corruption programs that target all stakeholder groups (partners, intermediaries, suppliers, employees and local communities).

Corruption in the context of truth, disclosure, whistleblowing and loyalty

People whose ethical conduct subjects them or their companies to undue risk often engage in self-deception, and they are understandably reluctant to acknowledge, even to themselves, that they or their companies have engaged in harmful or illegal behavior (Trivers, 2011). Trivers (2011) argues that to deceive others, we must first deceive ourselves. The author describes how this process affects all aspects of life, including historical research, child-rearing, religion and science. In summary, the first step in becoming a whistleblower is to remove the wool that one has pulled over one's own eyes. Such an acknowledgment requires an admission and a fair apportionment of responsibility for the conduct and the harm that it has caused. This process is further complicated by the likelihood that the 'facts' of the case are subject to bias and distortion and are rarely complete. Factual determinations can also be complicated by a 'whistleblower's' involvement. A whistleblower's motives can often be challenged. The whistleblower may be a co-conspirator who wants to avoid blame or mitigate penalties against him or herself by accusing others. Alternatively, the whistleblower may be motivated by animus or revenge against the person(s) whom he/she has accused. There are also questions of timing. Employees who observe conduct that they believe to be improper rarely know all the facts, and they can be easily intimidated

by friends, colleagues, bosses, or senior managers who tell them that they do not know the whole story. At what point do such people have enough information to raise the issue within the company or in a public or legal forum? When these people do raise the issue, what is the next step?

Many companies have official reporting channels, through which potential informants can report concrete or suspected misconduct and/or 'helplines' through which they can seek confidential advice (Hauser et al., 2019). Does their organization's system command trust? When an employee is convinced that the situation is sufficiently urgent that he/she must blow the whistle, what is the next step? If there are internal procedures, do employees use them? Employee utilization depends significantly on ethnic and institutional cultural conditioning. The utilization or lack thereof of company hotlines has been the subject of considerable discussion. If the process begins with an internal complaint, at what point does the whistleblower decide that the matter is sufficiently urgent (or the process is unsatisfactory) to become an 'external' whistleblower who goes to the media or law enforcement?

Anti-corruption Education Research

Regarding actions under the PRME, Stachowicz-Stanusch and colleagues have edited two books on teaching anti-corruption in universities and business schools and how a foundation for business integrity can be developed. In the first book, Stachowicz-Stanusch (2013) discusses some anti-corruption solutions proposed by the PRME, which have been implemented globally by PRME signatories. Building upon these deliberations, Al-Arda and Islam (2013) consider how pedagogical practices such as the role of student participation and dialogue can contribute to tackling the endemic levels of corruption in Brazil. Furthermore, Jamali and Walburn (2013) set out a business case for implementing anti-corruption programs in MENA business schools, providing a set of recommendations for how such a program can be implemented as well as justifications. Moreover, Norris (2013) suggests that the role of learner autonomy, moral agency, traditional virtues and reflective practices should not be overlooked in education. Tavanti (2013) deliberates about the role of intercultural dimensions as a barrier to ethical business practices, examining the variation in prevailing corruption levels across cultures. As such, the author proposes a multilevel and multicultural model for anti-corruption education. In this vein, Goosby Smith and Schick Case (2013) further deliberate on the role of intercultural dimensions as well as the role of religion in relation to ethics. The authors argue that by appealing to the religious and spiritual beliefs in anti-corruption education, ethical behavior can be increased. The book also addresses alternative methods of anti-corruption teaching. For instance, Michael (2013) indicates how movies and the internet, along with thought-provoking questions, can help facilitate the ethical understanding of students and thus help facilitate an anti-corruption mindset. Against this background, Guidici et al. (2013) evaluate the effectiveness of contemporary anti-corruption methods used in universities and business schools. The authors conclude that since today's students are digital natives, it is vital that teachers adopt the same 'language' in their teaching methods, for instance, by using social networks, videos or comics to help teach anti-corruption programs.

The second book further explores the efforts made in anti-corruption education research. Here, topics such as the role of accounting in reducing corruption and its portrayal in US universities are described by Money (2019). The author reveals gaps in existing anti-corruption education in accounting curricula and presents a tool that can be used to close these gaps. Moreover, dela Rama (2019) discusses the mandatory nature of business ethics education for bachelor's students at an Australian university as well as the research undertaken in the field of anti-corruption. Furthermore, Sigri (2019) addresses criticisms of the implementation of anti-corruption education in business schools raised by professors by providing a case study that can be used within an educational framework to highlight the practical relevance of such an education.

Despite the visionary actions being taken by some universities, there is nevertheless still a further need for more business schools to implement business ethics and anti-corruption education. Business ethics and anti-corruption should become part of the curriculum as a separate foundational course as well as an integrative part of the different business disciplines. Powerful learning environments foster students' critical thinking and problem-solving abilities to identify dilemmas and blind spots in business realities. In summary, students, faculties and companies need to build a partnership to jointly explore effective approaches to business ethics and anti-corruption education (Prandini et al., 2012). This need is all the more significant since the research suggests that despite the calls for greater inclusion of business ethics and anti-corruption education in university curricula, many lecturers at such schools feel underqualified to teach such courses; these teachers often having little in the way of ethics training themselves (Wymer and Rundel-Thiele, 2017). Instead, Beggs and Dean (2007) find that lecturers base their teachings on legislative solutions rather than on ethical reasoning.

Although the aforementioned methods of anti-corruption education purportedly develop a sense of awareness of the risks of corruption and provide future professionals with the tools necessary to be able to stand up to corruption in the workplace, recent studies show that current approaches can have counterintuitive effects on students. While designing educational materials for an anti-corruption syllabus, Denisova-Schmidt et al. (2017) find that prior exposure to corruption and the familial level of education can influence the effectiveness of teaching approaches.

As such, the study found that standardized anti-corruption methods even increased the level of acceptance of corruption in students who had not previously engaged in such behavior and who come from families with a lower level of education. In a second study, Denisova-Schmidt et al. (2019) also finds that the presentation of anti-corruption information can influence the success of the training program. The study shows that educational videos, which are more factual and are presented in a documentary or news reporting style, do not generally stimulate negative attitudes in students towards corruption. Conversely, when students watch videos laden with emotion and show the impacts of corruption upon victims, more negative responses are generated, and corruption is perceived to be more of a crime. These studies show that while current methods can construct negative perceptions of corruption in some students, in others, current methods create an adverse effect and can even increase the acceptance of corrupt behavior. In this light, it can be said that current approaches to anti-corruption education are insufficient, and changes need to be made in the future to strengthen the outcomes.

ANTI-CORRUPTION EDUCATION – FUTURE

Business ethics in some form has been a subject of inquiry for centuries. For our purpose, the conversation began with the advent of anti-corruption standards in business practices and of anti-corruption curricula at universities and business schools. Unlike other professions, such as medicine or law, business lacks the disciplinary associations that can set and enforce these standards. By default, with varying degrees of success, this task has been undertaken by universities and business schools. Nevertheless, business education has a limited reach. The media expose company and individual behavior, and the courts ultimately establish and enforce the standards. Within the past 20 years, there has been a growing recognition by business associations that peer group councils of senior executives with ethics and compliance responsibilities can benefit from meetings and research that discuss program effectiveness issues within their companies. For example, The Conference Board, a global 'member-driven' organization that has a Global Business Conduct Council of Senior Executives who are responsible for Ethics and Compliance programs in major US and European companies. In the United States alone, The Conference Board has 103 other Councils, many of which, such as the Purchasing and Supply Leadership, Quality, Strategic Risk Management, Market Insight, Mergers and Acquisitions Councils, also focus on business ethics issues related to their individual functions.

The Limits of the Risk Management Compliance-Based Approach

Many academics recognize that the business ethics and anti-corruption project has reached a crucial juncture. Source material and teaching methods that focus on risk management through market failure analysis and legal and compliance-based instruction, training and systems for deterring wrongful conduct have achieved limited success in significantly improving business behavior that enhances long-term sustainability. While these traditional approaches have increased awareness of potential dilemmas, future research needs to devote more effort to developing teaching approaches and materials that enable and promote good behavior (see Hauser, 2020).

Corruption in the Context of Behavioral Issues

A growing number of business ethics scholars and teachers now recognize that an

understanding of behavioral issues is fundamental to the individual resolution of many
of the ethical challenges that individuals
encounter in the workplace, individual companies, business functions (e.g. marketing),
cultures and countries. The moral imagination and the behavior to which it gives rise is
shaped by culture, family and experience.

An increasing body of academic literature
on business ethics and anti-corruption efforts
highlights the need for students to understand
that in this lifelong process, practitioner intuitions of what is right and wrong will be challenged by the organization's own set of rules,
the intuition of their colleagues and the enterprise's strategies and objectives. Practitioners
need to find common ground with the rules
of society, the institutions they serve and the
people whose collaboration is vital to achieve
success. Practitioners need to understand how
and what to learn from experience to promote
their moral growth and development, which
will in turn improve their intuitive responses
to future situations and their ability to seek
common ground with the enterprises that
they serve without compromising their core
beliefs that develop over time from the lessons of experience. For the most up-to-date
thinking on these subjects, see the Ethical
Systems website (www.EthicalSystems.org).

Behavioral ethics examines the individual's
problem-solving skills when they perceive a
'moral dilemma' in confronting workplace
demands. This field also provides analytical tools to determine whether there may be
potential issues that they may not recognize
at the outset but that will arise at some point
before they complete their assigned task.
Ultimately, the discussion leads students to
examine their 'needs hierarchy' in terms of
career expectations to avoid career-ending
decisions and achieve both personal satisfaction and professional success (Ariely, 2013).

Kahneman (2011) offers a good description of the behavioral processes approach
to professional decisions that may have lifelong consequences. Two systems drive the
way we think. System 1 is fast, intuitive and

emotional; System 2 is slower, more deliberative and more logical. Kahneman exposes
the strengths as well as the faults and biases
of fast thinking and the pervasive effects of
intuitive thinking on thoughts and behavior.
The resulting 'cognitive biases' challenge
the ability to determine the actual risks of
workplace choices and their long-term effect
on personal satisfaction and happiness. The
managerial understanding of the Kahneman
'thinking fast – thinking slow' model also
enables companies to design organizational
management processes to improve human
resources management and devise performance incentive systems that encourage
integrity (thinking slow) and productivity
(thinking fast).

Haidt (2012) succinctly describes the case
for the inclusion of the 'fast' versus 'slow'
thinking academic literature and classroom
exercises and assignments: 'we're born to be
righteous, but we have to learn, what, exactly,
people like us should be righteous about.' The
logical application of this statement is that
the workplace is an arena for moral development that confronts us with temptations to be
evil and opportunities to be virtuous. Most
students now accept the need to include ethical analysis in the business decision maker's
toolkit.

Behavioral science research can enable
business organizations to balance the two
necessary and potentially conflicting requirements of the successful enterprise: (1) policies and processes that produce leaders who
are able to promote moral improvement and
excellence for all stakeholders and (2) well-
structured institutions that bear the primary,
if not exclusive, responsibility for the behavior of their employees, agents, and owners/
shareholders (Berenbeim, 2013).

With the introduction of behavioral science
into curricula, we have come full circle from a
path that begins with Aristotle's virtue ethics,
which prescribes the decision that contributes
most to the individual's moral improvement,
moves on to Bentham's 'greatest good for the
greatest number' and to Kant's Categorical

Imperative 'harmonizing each individual's freedom with that of everyone else' (Sandel, 2009) and returns back to Aristotle (Halbert/ Ingulli, 2009). Students need to recognize that Benthamite utilitarianism does not justify acting solely in their own or the company's interest. Nor does Kant's categorical imperative require that they act in accordance with a universal law for a particular transaction. These philosophical systems are not necessarily incompatible. Rather, in reconciling the outcomes prescribed by these two foundations of modern philosophy, students must strive to choose, as Aristotle would have done, the outcome that best promotes their own and their company's moral improvement (Haidt, 2012; Berenbeim, 2018).

Anti-corruption in the Context of other Study Programs

Business ethics and anti-corruption issues can also be taught as part of other study programs, such as a Liberal Arts curriculum. In 2019, the Prudens Research Institute for the Arts and Sciences offered a summer course on the subject in its Shanghai program for 'rising seniors' who want to study in English-speaking universities. The curriculum introduced basic concepts in ethics, law, economics and behavioral science to frame and resolve 'dilemmas' in business practice as well as career and life decisions. For a discussion of teaching and the importance of the Arts and Sciences curriculum, see Grayling (2015).

ACKNOWLEDGMENTS

We would like to dedicate this chapter to honor the memory of W. Michael Hoffman, a pioneer in the field of anti-corruption education, who passed away far too young. Furthermore, we would like to gratefully acknowledge writing assistance by Eleanor Jehan. The usual disclaimer applies.

REFERENCES

Abend, G. (2014) *The Moral Background: An Inquiry into the History of Business Ethics.* Princeton Studies in Cultural Sociology. Princeton, NJ: Princeton University Press.

Al-Arda, L. and Islam, G. (2013) Business ethics education in Brazil: pedagogical solutions for combatting corruption in Brazil. In A. Stachowicz-Stanusch and H. K. Hanser (Eds.), *Principles of Responsible Management Education (PRME) Collection. Teaching Anticorruption. Developing a Foundation for Business Integrity.* New York: Business Expert Press. pp. 41–56.

Allen, W. T. (1992) Our schizophrenic conception of the business corporation. *Cardozo Law Review*, 14(2), 261–281.

Amann, W., Berenbeim, R. E., Cecchihi, G., DePersis, D., Gentile, M. C., Haertl, J. et al. (2012) Anti-corruption Guidelines ('Toolkit') for MBA Curriculum Change July 2012: A Project by the Anti-Corruption Working Group of the Principles for Responsible Management Education (PRME) Initiative, United Nations Global Compact. Available at: www.unprme.org/resource-docs/ComprehensiveAntiCorruptionGuidelinesforCurriculumChange.pdf.

Ambler, L. (2014) Presentation of findings of the OECD Foreign Bribery Report. Available at: www.oecd.org/daf/anti-bribery/OECDFBR-Launch-Ambler.pdf.

Antonacopoulou, E. P. and Pesqueux, Y. (2010) The practice of socialization and the socialization of practice. *Society and Business Review*, 5(1), 10–21.

Applbaum, A. I. (2000) *Ethics for Adversaries: The Morality of Roles in Public and Professional Life.* Princeton, NJ: Princeton University Press.

Ariely, D. (2013) *The (Honest) Truth About Dishonesty: How We Lie to Everyone – Especially Ourselves.* New York: Harper Perennial.

Becker, K., Hauser, C. and Kronthaler, F. (2013) Fostering management education to deter corruption: what do students know about corruption and its legal consequences? *Crime, Law and Social Change*, 60(2), 227–240.

Beggs, J. M. and Dean, K. L. (2007) Legislated ethics or ethics education? Faculty views in the post-Enron era. *Journal of Business Ethics*, 71(1), 15–37.

Benjamin, J. (2015) Market research fail: How New Coke became the worst flub of all time. Business2Community, 22 June. Available at: www.business2community.com/consumer-marketing/market-research-fail-new-coke-became-worst-flub-time-01256904.

Bentham, J. (1996) *An Introduction to the Principles of Morals and Legislation.* Oxford: Clarendon Press.

Bentley College (1996) *Origins of a Movement: A 20-Year Retrospective of the Center for Business Ethics.* Waltham, MA: Bentley College.

Bentley College (2001) *Business Ethics: Reflections from the Center.* Waltham, MA: Bentley College.

Bentley University (2016) *Celebrating Its 40th Anniversary: Global Perspectives on Business Ethics.* Waltham, MA: Bentley University.

Berenbeim, R. (2013) Ethics classes don't need to make students more ethical to be worthwhile. EthicalSystems.org. Available at: https://ethicalsystems.org/content/ethics-classes-don't-need-make-students-more-ethical-be-worthwhile.

Berenbeim, R. E. (2018) The path to discovering the better angels of our nature. *Vital Speeches International*, 84(1).

Blasco, M. (2012) Aligning the hidden curriculum of management education with PRME: an inquiry-based framework. *Journal of Management Education*, 36(3), 364–388.

Block, W., Kinsella, N. S. and Hoppe, H.-H. (1982) The second paradox of blackmail. *Business Ethics Quarterly*, 10(3), 593–622.

Borges, J. C., Ferreira, T. C., Borges de Oliveira, M. S., Macini, N. and Caldana, A. C. F. (2017) Hidden curriculum in student organizations: learning, practice, socialization and responsible management in a business school. *International Journal of Management Education*, 1(2), 153–161.

Burchell, J., Kennedy, S. and Murray, A. (2015) Responsible management education in UK business schools: critically examining the role of the United Nations Principles for Responsible Management Education as a driver for change. *Management Learning*, 46(4), 479–497.

Clarkson, K. W. (2012) Duties of agents and principles. In K. W. Clarkson, R. L. Miller and

F. B. Cross (Eds.), Business Law. *Text and Cases: Legal, Ethical, Global, and Corporate Environment*, 12th ed. Mason, OH: South-Western Cengage Learning. pp. 931–933.

Clarkson, K. W., Miller, R. L. and Cross, F. B. (Eds.) (2012) *Business Law: Text and Cases: Legal, Ethical, Global, and Corporate Environment*, 12th ed. Mason, OH: South-Western Cengage Learning.

Conference Board (2019) The Conference Board. Available at: www.conference-board.org/us/.

dela Rama, M. (2019) After the compliance comes the practice: teaching business ethics and anti-corruption research in an AACSB accredited business school. In A. Stachowicz-Stanusch and W. Amann (Eds.), *Research in Management Education and Development. Anti-corruption in Management Research and Business School Classrooms.* Charlotte, NC: Information Age Publishing.

Denisova-Schmidt, E., Huber, M., Leontyeva, E. and Solovyeva, A. (2017) Combining experimental evidence with machine learning to assess anti-corruption educational campaigns among Russian university students. *Universität Freiburg Working Papers SES*, 487(8).

Denisova-Schmidt, E., Huber, M. and Prytula, Y. (2019) The effects of anti-corruption videos on attitudes towards corruption in a Ukrainian online survey. *Universität Freiburg Working Papers SES*, 499.

DeMott, D. A. (2006) Disloyal agents. *Alabama Law Review*, 58(5), 1049–1067.

Dodd, E. M., Jr (1932) For whom are corporate managers trustees? *Harvard Law Review*, 45(7), 1145–1163.

Edwards, L. N. and Edwards, F. R. (1979) *Differential State Regulation of Consumer Credit Markets: Normative and Positive Theories of Statutory Interest Rate Ceilings.* Columbia University Graduate School of Business.

Frei, C. and Muethel, M. (2017) Antecedents and consequences of MNE bribery: a multi-level review. *Journal of Management Inquiry*, 26(4), 418–432.

Friedman, M. (1970) The social responsibility of business is to increase its profits. *New York Times Magazine*, 13 September, pp. 122–124.

Gibson Dunn (2019) 2018 year-end FCPA update. Available at: www.gibsondunn.com/2018-year-end-fcpa-update.

Goodpaster, K. E., Dean Maines, T., Naughton, M. and Shapiro, B. (2018) Using UNPRME to teach, research, and enact business ethics: insights from the catholic identity matrix for business schools. *Journal of Business Ethics*, 14(4), 761–777.

Goosby Smith, J. and Schick Case, S. (2013) Applying a religious lens to ethical decision-making: my Ten Commandments of character for the workplace exercise. In A. Stachowicz-Stanusch and H. K. Hansen (Eds.), *Principles of Responsible Management Education (PRME) Collection. Teaching Anticorruption. Developing a Foundation for Business Integrity*. New York: Business Expert Press. pp. 181–210.

Guidici, E., Caboni, F. and Atzori, R. (2013) Testing the Effectiveness of innovative teaching tools to train anti-corruption students. In A. Stachowicz-Stanusch and H. K. Hansen (Eds.), *Principles of Responsible Management Education (PRME) Collection. Teaching Anticorruption. Developing a Foundation for Business Integrity*. New York: Business Expert Press. pp. 213–229.

Grayling, A.C. (2015) *The Challenge of Things: Thinking Through Troubled Times*. London: Bloomsbury.

Haidt, J. (2012) *The Righteous Mind: Why Good People Are Divided by Politics and Religion*. New York: Pantheon Books.

Halbert, T, and Ingulli, E. (2009) *Law and Ethics in the Business Environment. South-Western Legal Studies in Business*. Princeton, NJ: Recording for the Blind & Dyslexic.

Hardi, P. (2017) Anti-corruption education. In D. C. Poff and A. C. Michalos (Eds.), *Encyclopedia of Business and Professional Ethics*. Cham: Springer International Publishing. pp. 1–9.

Hauser, C. (2019a) Reflecting on the role of universities in the fight against corruption. *RAUSP Management Journal*. 54(1), 4–13.

Hauser, C. (2019b) Fighting against corruption: does anti-corruption training make any difference? *Journal of Business Ethics*, 159(1), 281–299.

Hauser, C. (2020) From preaching to behavioral change: fostering ethics and compliance learning in the workplace. *Journal of Business Ethics*, 162(4), 835–855. https://doi.org/10.1007/s10551-019-04364-9

Hauser, C. and Hogenacker, J. (2014) Do firms proactively take measures to prevent corruption in their international operations? *European Management Review*, 11(3–4), 223–237.

Hauser, C. and Kronthaler, F. (2013) Neue Märkte, neue Risiken: Empirische Evidenz zum Korruptionsrisiko für den international aktiven Mittelstand. *Zeitschrift für Betriebswirtschaft*, 83(SI 4), 37–60.

Hauser, C. and Nieffer R. (2018) Anticorruption in management training and the business game method. In A. Stachowicz-Stanusch and W. Amann (Eds.), *Fostering Sustainability by Management Education*. Charlotte, NC: Information Age Publishing. pp. 127–147.

Hauser, C., Hergovits, N. and Blumer, H. (2019) *Whistleblowing Report 2019*. Chur: HTW Chur Verlag.

Hauser, C., Simonyan, A. and Werner, A. (2020) Condoning corrupt behavior at work: What roles do Machiavellianism, on-the-job experience, and neutralization play? *Business and Society*. Advance online publication. https://doi.org/10.1177/0007650319898474

Hibbert, P. and Cunliffe, A. (2015) Responsible management: engaging moral reflexive practice through threshold concepts. *Journal of Business Ethics*, 127(1), 177–188.

House of Representatives (1977) Unlawful Corporate Payment Act of 1977 – Legislative History: House Report No. 95-640. Available at: https://www.justice.gov/sites/default/files/criminal-fraud/legacy/2010/04/11/houseprt-95-640.pdf

Jamali, D. and Walburn, A. (2013) Business schools as agents of change: addressing systematic corruption in the Arab world. In A. Stachowicz-Stanusch and H. K. Hansen (Eds.), *Principles of Responsible Management Education (PRME) Collection. Teaching Anticorruption. Developing a Foundation for Business Integrity*. New York: Business Expert Press. pp. 57–77.

Kahneman, D. (2011) *Thinking, Fast and Slow*. London: Penguin.

Kant, I. (1948) *The Moral Law: Kant's Groundwork of the Metaphysic of Morals*. London: Hutchinson.

Koehler, M. (2012) The story of the Foreign Corrupt Practices Act. *Ohio State Law Journal*, 73(5), 930–1013.

KPMG (2016) CEU Integrity Education final external evaluation: Siemens Integrity Initiative. KPMG.

Kravchuk, O. (2017) Anti-corruption education at technical university. *Advanced Education*, 4(8), 78–83.

Laasch, O. and Moosmayer, D. C. (2015) Competences for responsible management: a structured literature review (No. 2). CRME Working Papers. Available at: www.researchgate.net/publication/321327010_Competences_for_responsible_management_A_structured_literature_review.

Lange, C. J. (2011) The Foreign Corrupt Practices Act and its impact on the global movement of personnel. *Corporate Council Business Journal*, 3 April. Available at: https://ccbjournal.com/articles/foreign-corrupt-practices-act-and-its-impact-global-movement-personnel.

Lavine, M. H. and Roussin, C. J. (2012) From idea to action. *Journal of Management Education*, 36(3), 428–455.

Levitt, T. (1958) The dangers of social responsibility. *Harvard Business Review*, 36(5), 41–50.

Lisievici, P. and Andronie, M. (2016) Teachers assessing the effectiveness of values clarification techniques in moral education. *Procedia – Social and Behavioral Sciences*, 217, 400–406.

Mallor, J. P. (2016) *Business Law: The Ethical, Global, and e-Commerce Environment*, 16th ed. New York: McGraw-Hill Education.

Mauro, P. (1995) Corruption and growth. *Quarterly Journal of Economics*, 110(3), 681–712.

McDonald, G. M. and Donleavy, G. D. (1995) Objections to the teaching of business ethics. *Journal of Business Ethics*, 14(10), 839–853.

Mendelsohn, D. A. (2017) *An Odyssey: A Father, a Son and an Epic*. London: William Collins.

Michael, A. E. (2013) Understanding and reducing business corruption through movies and World Wide Web Videos. In A. Stachowicz-Stanusch and H. K. Hansen (Eds.), *Principles of Responsible Management Education (PRME) Collection. Teaching Anticorruption. Developing a Foundation for Business Integrity*. New York: Business Expert Press. pp. 157–179.

Money, E. T. (2019) Teaching anti-corruption in accounting in U.S. colleges and universities: the first step in the accounting

profession's fight against corruption. In A. Stachowicz-Stanusch and W. Amann (Eds.), *Research in Management Education and Development. Anti-Corruption in Management Research and Business School Classrooms*. Charlotte, NC: Information Age Publishing. pp. 13–29.

Nonet, G., Kassel, K. and Meijs, L. (2016) Understanding responsible management: emerging themes and variations from European business school programs. *Journal of Business Ethics*, 139(4), 717–736.

Norris, S. E. (2013) Learner autonomy, moral agency and ancient virtues: a curative constellation for the treatment of corruption in modern workplaces. In A. Stachowicz-Stanusch and H. K. Hansen (Eds.), *Principles of Responsible Management Education (PRME) Collection. Teaching Anticorruption. Developing a Foundation for Business Integrity*. New York: Business Expert Press. pp. 95–108.

OECD (2018) International Conventions. Available at: www.oecd.org/cleangovbiz/internationalconventions.htm. Accessed 10 July 2018.

Osuji, O. (2011) Fluidity of regulation–CSR nexus: the multinational corporate corruption example. *Journal of Business Ethics*, 103(1), 31–57.

Pacini, C., Swingen, J. A. and Rogers, H. (2002) The role of the OECD and EU Conventions in combating bribery of foreign public officials. *Journal of Business Ethics*, 37(4), 385–405.

Perlstein, R. (2018) Watergate scandal: United States History. Encyclopaedia Britannica [Online] www.britannica.com/event/Watergate-Scandal.

Prandini, M., Vervoort Isler, P. and Barthelmess, P. (2012) Responsible management education for 21st century leadership. *Central European Business Review*, 1(2), 16–22.

Sandel, M. (2009) *Justice. What's The Right Thing to Do?* New York: Farrar, Straus and Giroux.

Sigri, U. (2019) Can universities teach anti-corruption in business schools? In A. Stachowicz-Stanusch and W. Amann (Eds.), *Research in Management Education and Development. Anti-corruption in Management Research and Business School*

Classrooms. Charlotte, NC: Information Age Publishing. pp. 75–92.

Sims, R. R. and Sims, S. J. (1991) Increasing applied business ethics courses in business school curricula. *Journal of Business Ethics*, 10(3), 211–219.

Society of Corporate Compliance and Ethics (2019a) *Ethikos*. www.corporatecompliance. org/publications/newsletters/ethikos.

Society of Corporate Compliance and Ethics (2019b) We help you navigate compliance and ethics. [Home Page] www.corporate-compliance.org/.

Stachowicz-Stanusch, A. (2013) Alleviating the malady of low ethical awareness using PRME as a tonic lesson from Europe. In A. Stachowicz-Stanusch and H. K. Hansen (Eds.), *Principles of Responsible Management Education (PRME) Collection. Teaching Anticorruption. Developing a Foundation for Business Integrity*. New York: Business Expert Press. pp. 3–20.

Stout, L. A. (2012) *The Shareholder Value Myth: How Putting Shareholders First Harms Investors, Corporations, and the Public*. San Francisco, CA: Berrett–Koehler.

Swamy, R. and Detjen, J. (2013) Promoting ethical behaviour in India: an examination of the Giving Voice to Values (GVV) approach. In A. Stachowicz-Stanusch and H. K. Hansen (Eds.), *Principles of Responsible Management Education (PRME) Collection. Teaching Anticorruption. Developing a Foundation for Business Integrity*. New York: Business Expert Press. pp. 21–40.

Tavanti, M. (2013) The cultural dimensions of corruption: integrating national cultural differences in the teaching of anti-corruption in public service management sector. In A. Stachowicz-Stanusch and H. K. Hansen (Eds.), *Principles of Responsible Management Education (PRME) Collection. Teaching Anticorruption. Developing a Foundation for Business Integrity*. New York: Business Expert Press. pp. 129–155.

Transparency International (2011) *Bribe Payers Index*. Berlin: Transparency International. Available at: www.transparency.org/what-wedo/publication/bpi_2011.

Transparency International (2018) Corruption Perceptions Index 2017. Available at: www. transparency.org/news/feature/corruption_perceptions_index_2017. Accessed 10 July 2018.

Transparency International Schweiz (2017) *Korruption in der Schweiz: Einführung in die Rechtsgrundlagen und Risikobereiche*. Available at: https://transparency.ch/publikationen/ korruption-in-der-schweiz-rechtsgrundlagen-und-risikobereiche/. Accessed 14 January 2020.

Trivers, R. (2011) *The Folly of Fools: The Logic of Deceit and Self-Deception in Human Life*. New York: Basic Books.

UNDOC (2018) United Nations Convention against Corruption. Available at: www. unodc.org/unodc/en/corruption/uncac.html. Accessed 10 July 2018.

Verkerk, M. J., Leede, J. de, and Nijhof, A. H. J. (2001) From responsible management to responsible organizations: the democratic principle for managing organizational ethics *Business and Society Review*, 106(4) 353–378.

Verma, P., Mohapatra, S. and Löwstedt, J (2016) Ethics training in the Indian IT sector: formal, informal or both? *Journal of Business Ethics*, 133(1), 73–93.

Wall Street Journal (2012) Factory fire kills hundreds: locked doors, barred windows trap Pakistan workers; building owners sought. *The Wall Street Journal*, 12 September. Available at: www.wsj.com/articles/SB1 00008723963904438841045776466324 7 5170076.

Waples, E. P., Antes, A. L., Murphy, S. T., Connelly, S. and Mumford, M. D. (2009) A meta-analytic investigation of business ethics instruction. *Journal of Business Ethics*, 87(1), 133–151.

Wu, X. (2009) Determinants of bribery in Asian firms: evidence from the World Business Environment Survey. *Journal of Business Ethics*, 87(1), 75–88.

Wymer, W. and Rundle-Thiele, S. R. (2017) Inclusion of ethics, social responsibility, and sustainability in business school curricula: a benchmark study. *International Review on Public and Nonprofit Marketing*, 14(1), 19–34.

14

Teaching Business and Human Rights: Past Approaches, Present State of the Art, and Opportunities for the Future

Karin Buhmann

INTRODUCTION

Human rights are affected in a number of ways related to decisions or actions that are common in business management and operations. Business-related human rights impacts can be positive (e.g., improving occupational health and safety practices), or harmful (e.g., when suppliers' employees are pressured into excessive working hours). Yet, the inclusion of corporate responsibilities in the human rights in the responsible management curriculum is only starting to take off. Indeed, it is only during the past two decades that the connection between business and human rights has come to be recognised even with international organisations and human rights scholars. However, over the past decade, many companies and managers have adopted policies to take account of their human rights impacts, and expect their business relations to do the same. This chapter explains some essential features of what human rights mean in a responsible management context.

Human rights is an interdisciplinary topic, typically approached at universities from the perspective of philosophy and ethics, law or politics. This has influenced the incremental uptake of human rights into management education, including a reluctance in regard to recognising the relevance of a topic that is conventionally seen to relate to obligations of states, rather than responsibilities of companies. Even though many of the social issues inherent in concepts like corporate social responsibility (CSR) or the triple bottom line have a clear relation to international human rights standards, connecting human rights into management education has taken time. It has been advanced by a few business schools and scholars, with business ethics environments among those that pioneered human rights in management education. In this context human rights have been taught along with several other business ethics topics.

As a stand-alone topic of responsible management education, business and human rights (BHR) is more recent. Courses and textbooks on BHR took off around 2010, in tandem with the adoption by the United Nations of a set of guidance texts.

In a development that emerged in the 1990s and has solidified over the past two decades, human rights have come to feature as part of private or public–public (hybrid) standards of conduct for responsible management. One of the most well known among these is the United Nations (UN) Global Compact, which features human rights in the first two of its ten principles as well as in the four principles on labour rights.[1] However, in management education the Global Compact principles have generally been seen as CSR standards, and taught as such. Adopted by the UN Human Rights Council, the UN 'Respect, Protect and Remedy' framework ('UN Framework') (UN, 2008) and the UN Guiding Principles on Business and Human Rights ('UNGPs') (UN, 2011) broke ground by providing detailed normative guidance for companies and states for steps to be taken to prevent and manage business-related human rights abuse. This confirmed that respecting human rights is an inherent part of the normative foundations of responsible management and gave a decisive impetus for teaching BHR as a stand-alone topic. More recently, building on the United Nations 2030 Sustainable Development Agenda, the Sustainable Development Goals (SDGs) offer a catalogue of global development needs that businesses have been encouraged to look at as business opportunities.[2]

Considered current state of the art in regard to business responsibilities to respect human rights (Wettstein, 2012), both the UN Framework and the UNGPs display an explicit 'do no harm' focus. The SDGs have an explicit focus on how companies and governments can 'do good', however, their implementation provisions do encourage companies to ensure that they do not harm human rights in their efforts. Many issues covered by the SDGs are directly related to human rights, for example the right to food, education and gender equality. Hence, beyond the element of not doing harm, the

SDGs offer an opportunity for companies to contribute to human rights. Of course, knowledge of human rights advances the opportunities for doing so.

The chapter addresses BHR in responsible management education from the three perspectives guiding this book: past, present and future. The 'past' aspect is marked by the conceptual appreciation of human rights as relevant to responsible management. The 'current' aspect is dominated by the normative standards provided by the current state of the art, and what their implementation means for responsible business. The 'future' aspect is obviously more uncertain. This chapter approaches the future from the perspective of the SDGs.

The chapter is structured as follows: the next section explains what human rights are, sets out the interdisciplinary character of the topic, and explains some of the differences or challenges that the interdisciplinary features can cause in debates or application of human rights standards or theory in management education. Then follow three sections dealing with the past, the current and the future aspect of business and human rights in responsible management education, before the chapter draws its conclusions.

WHAT ARE HUMAN RIGHTS?

The Normative Foundations and Substantive Contents of Human Rights

Human rights are founded in several normative lines of thinking, in particular ethics and philosophy, political thinking on the relationship between individual and the state or other 'power holders', and law. Human rights are studied by several other disciplines as well, such as anthropology and sociology, and have more recently become recognised as relevant to responsible management.

The Universal Declaration of Human Rights (UDHR) (UN, 1948), adopted by the

UN in 1948, provides an authoritative list of human rights. That list has been elaborated by a series of detailed human rights conventions also developed by the UN or by regional human rights organisations. The right to freedom from discrimination based on race, sex, nationality, ethnicity, language, religion, or any other status is an inherent element in human rights. Human rights also include, for example, the right to freedom from slavery and torture, the right to food; to education (including free primary education); to form and join trade unions; to marry and have a family; to the highest attainable standard of health; to freedom of expression; to choose and change one's religion; and to move within one's country. Some rights are derived from others. For example, the UDHR does not mention a human right to water, but a right to water is derived from the right to food and the right to health. Studies show that companies have the capacity to affect all types of human rights (Ruggie, 2013). For teaching purposes it can be useful to provide overviews of human rights in order for students to grasp their broad coverage. This should be complemented by information that each right is complex, and human rights issues in a business context rarely come nicely wrapped as such (Ruggie, 2013). As a result, an analysis of perceived problems is often required to diagnose an issue as a human rights problem and develop appropriate solutions (see also Monash University, 2017, which is a great teaching resource for this). Table 14.1 provides a condensed overview of the human rights recognised by the United Nations (UN).

Labour rights are also human rights. Four are recognised as core labour standards: the eradication of slavery and forced labour; the elimination of child labour; the right of employees to form and join trade unions and engage in collective negotiations; and the rights of employees not to be discriminated at the workplace. The labour rights principles (3–6) of the UN Global Compact are derived from these rights. Other rights, such as to occupational health and safety, to rest and leisure and to fair wages and equal pay for work of equal value are covered by the UDHR as parts of the right to just and favourable conditions of work. Like the core labour rights, these are also covered by general conventions developed by the International Labour Organisation (ILO), a member of the UN family of organisations.

The modern notion of human rights is associated with the protection from interference from a powerful agent. This was originally understood to be the state. Today, non-state actors – and particularly business enterprises – are increasingly seen to have the capacity to infringe on human rights.

From the philosophical perspective, human rights are unconditional rights that derive from the inherent dignity of the human person. This means that we do not need to earn human rights: we have them simply because we are born human. They are in principle universal, indivisible and inalienable (Donnelly, 2013; Griffin, 2009; Spickard, 1999). Connecting back to the ethical aspect, freedom from want and from interference from powerful agents are at the core of the dignity of the person that underlies the human rights idea.

Human rights have evolved from moral, philosophical and political ideas developed and implemented in many traditions (e.g., Mahoney, 2008; Risse-Kappen et al., 1999). Scholars of anthropology, sociology and religious values have shown that the substantive contents inherent in the idea of human rights or in specific rights are found in cultures around the world (e.g., Goodale, 2008; Hastrup, 2001; Spickard, 1999; Twiss, 2004). With human dignity at its core, the basic idea inherent in what we refer to as 'human rights' today is a global concern (Shelton, 2014: 1–44), and the universal relevance and applicability of human rights are recognised to leave space for culturally diverse implementation (Donnelly, 2007). The UDHR was developed and deliberated by a multi-cultural group, which included representatives from China, India, the Philippines, Lebanon, Chile, South Africa, the Soviet Union, the

Table 14.1 Overview of human rights listed by the Universal Declaration of Human Rights

Article number	Summary of human right in article
1	All are born free and equal in dignity and rights.
2	Freedom from discrimination.
3	Right to life, liberty and personal security.
4	Freedom from slavery.
5	Freedom from torture and cruel, inhuman or degrading treatment.
6	Right to recognition before the law everywhere.
7	Right to equality before the law and equal protection without any discrimination.
8	Right to remedy.
9	Freedom from arbitrary arrest, detention or and exile.
10	Right to fair public hearing.
11	Right to be presumed innocent until proven guilty. No retroactive punishment.
12	Right to privacy.
13	Right to freedom of movement.
14	Right to seek asylum.
15	Right to a nationality.
16	Right to marry and to a family.
17	Right to own property.
18	Freedom of thought, conscience and religion.
19	Freedom of opinion, expression and information.
20	Right of peaceful assembly and association.
21	Right to public participation in government; right to free elections.
22	Right to social security.
23	Right to work; right to equal pay for equal work; right to remuneration that is just, and ensures a dignified existence for the employee and the employees' family; right to form and join trade unions.
24	Right to rest and leisure, reasonable working hours and holiday with pay.
25	Right to an adequate standard of living, including food, clothing, housing, medical care and social service.
26	Right to education, including elementary education.
27	Right to participate in cultural life.
28	Right to a social and international order supportive of human rights.
29	Community duties.
30	Freedom from interference in the above rights.

United States and other countries (Glendon, 2001). While the global applicability of the UDHR for a post-colonial world has been debated, studies show that the UDHR and other human rights instruments were applied in the 1960s–70s by several newly independent former colonies to advance their global political agendas, demonstrating the global relevance (Jensen, 2016).

Perhaps because they are 'rights', human rights are often associated with the field of law. However, the legal regime is only a recent development in the long history of human rights. The moral and political views above underpin the international legal regime on human rights. A moral justification is argued to be present behind and beyond any legal stipulation of human rights (Sen, 2004).

Human rights span freedoms (of speech, thought etc.) whose respect typically assumes non-interference by a powerful actor (hence also named 'negative rights') and claims to socio-economic human rights (e.g. education, health services, or 'rights at work', such as salary, rest, leisure and occupational health and safety) that assume active implementation on the part of a powerful actor for their implementation (therefore named 'positive rights'). In practice, most human rights rely on a combination of negative and positive aspects (non-action and action) (Shelton, 2014), therefore requiring those with the power to exert change to both refrain from interfering into the exercise and enjoyment of rights of individuals and supporting the development of practices and institutions necessary for their access to make use of their rights.

Typologies of Human Rights

We can distinguish between human rights in different ways. One distinction is between negative rights, where 'negative' simply means that the powerful actors (originally the state, but increasingly also companies) must refrain from a particular action because that action would infringe on the rights of a human being; and positive rights, which require the powerful actor to take specific steps to fulfil and respect human rights. For example, the (negative) human right to form a trade union requires the state or the company to abstain from interference with the efforts to form the union. The (positive) human right to access to free primary education requires the power holder to train teachers and build and fund schools.

Another distinction is between types of rights based on their substance: civil, cultural, economic, political and social. Civil and political rights are typically negative rights, whereas cultural, economic and social rights are typically positive. However, in practice the implementation of many human rights has both the negative and positive aspects. For example, the right of (members of a trade union) to association and assembly requires the power-holder to refrain from interference in the event, but it also requires it to protect the association or assembly against interference by others.

A third way to distinguish between human rights is based on whether the rights are to

be respected, protected, or fulfilled. Negative rights are typically rights to be respected, positive rights are to be fulfilled, and rights to be protected can include both types. This distinction has informed the evolution of standards on business and human rights which, however, operates with a right to access to remedy rather than a right to human rights fulfilment. This distinction is elaborated later in the chapter.

Why Human Rights Matter to Responsible Management

Understanding what human rights are about in terms of dignity, freedom from want and protection of integrity of the person, rather than looking for particular terminology may go a long way towards helping managers implement human rights in business practices.

Understanding, respecting and sometimes even contributing to fulfilling human rights matters to business for a range of reasons. Moral, strategic, economic and political reasons have been recognised in the literature and teaching as part of the general recognition of social issues in CSR and the triple bottom line. Corresponding to much of the 'past' of human rights in responsible management education, early incremental scholarship embodied views insisting that business enterprises do not cause harm (e.g. Clapham, 2006; Henkin, 1999; Jägers, 2002; Muchlinski, 2003) in line with Principles 1 and 2 of the UN Global Compact, and some suggestions that companies go beyond this to help advance the fulfilment of human rights, thereby doing good (e.g., Wettstein, 2005). Teaching and scholarship sought to seeking to develop ideas on business responsibilities for human rights with a foundation in the UDHR or other international human rights law as well as interdisciplinary human rights theory. As such law and theory is grounded in human rights as state obligations, that phase also aimed at advancing arguments for why human rights should matter to business enterprises at all, either on the basis of morals, strategy, economy, politics or law.

With the advent of authoritative guidance and its uptake in several private and public business governance instruments and regulatory schemes, human rights in responsible management have come to take on a more autonomous character (Buhmann and Wettstein, 2017; Ramasatry, 2015), which has reflected on the 'current' wave of human rights in responsible management education. This has been focused on the corporate responsibility to 'do no harm', in line with the focus of the authoritative guidance standards (the UN Framework and UNGPs). With their focus on 'doing good' and their reminder that business enterprises must not do harm and should observe the UNGPs, the SDGs hold promise of a renewed effort to combine the two aspects into a more comprehensive future wave of teaching, research and practice of integrating human rights into responsible management.

Moral reasons for corporate human rights responsibilities are often founded in philosophical ideas of human rights as perfect moral obligations (Fasterling and Demuijnck, 2013) that pertain to all actors in society, regardless of whether these are state bodies or private actors. Indeed, the UDHR's reference to 'all actors in society' has been assumed by several companies and argued by scholars to logically frame business commitments to human rights. Originally, there was no intention that companies were included as 'organs of society' (Henkin, 1999). The exclusion of companies was due to the limited political and economic role of companies at the time. Until well into the second half of the 20th century it was not commonly expected that the business sector would equal or even go beyond some states in economic power, and attain the political influence and impact that it now has.

Strategic reasons why human rights matter to responsible business are often linked to the 'business case' and therefore economic reasons why companies should respect human rights (Buhmann and Wettstein, 2017). Companies with pro-active human rights policies and initiatives may benefit from enhanced reputation, from a better and more motivated workforce, from decreasing staff fluctuation rates and so on.

Political reasons for managers to engage with human rights are closely related to governance structures at the global level. During the 20th century companies have been awarded an increase in economic rights (granted under international economic law, for example through the WTO and regional trade agreements). These economic rights have not, however, been matched by similar duties for companies to take account of and manage their adverse societal impacts, including those on human rights (Ruggie, 2013).

Many public goals of a political nature have a distinct human-rights-related character. This applies to political commitments at national as well as international level by governments to deliver solutions to socio-economic challenges like unemployment, inadequate living standards and housing conditions, access to health services and the protection of occupational health and safety (Buhmann, 2011). The same applies to policy goals like the elimination of poverty, child labour and discriminatory practices at the horizontal level between individuals and the protection of natural resources, whether marine or land-based, on which humans depend for their nourishment and incomes. Related public policy objectives inform several of the SDGs.

THE PAST: INCREMENTAL INTRODUCTION OF HUMAN RIGHTS INTO RESPONSIBLE MANAGEMENT EDUCATION

Human rights became part of the responsible management agenda because it became realised that human rights can be affected by a company in a number of ways. Whereas some managers and business ethics scholars found it natural to engage with human rights on a moral foundation, human rights implications for business became visible when it became clear that reputational damage led to economic losses or loss of the social licence to operate. An early example of this was Nike's exploitation of national governance gaps in Vietnam around working conditions and, in turn, of workers in the 1990s (see, e.g., Spar and La Mure, 2003). As that case shows, human rights problems for businesses were often seen to be a result of ineffective implementation of national law, but broader international governance gaps were also seen to be part of the reason for the problem. It was realised that institutional limits on the power of nation states and international organisations led to governance gaps that in turn caused opportunities for companies to exploit these gaps without legal or, often, political consequence (Buhmann, 2018a; Ruggie, 2004, 2013). A more recent example, the Rana Plaza collapse in 2013, which killed 1129 people and maimed many, drew attention to the adverse human rights impacts of economic decisions to produce under cheap conditions, which are unfortunately often sub-standard in terms of security, occupational health and safety, as well as salary, working hours and other working conditions.

Indeed, much of the debate on business and sustainability has been spurred by business-related human rights harm. From the health impact of multinational chemical companies, such as the Bhopal disaster in 1984 (Deva, 2012) to the employment practices of Nike in Asia in the 1990s and impacts on employees' working conditions (Spar and La Mure, 2003; Waddock and Rasche, 2012), and the human-rights-related impacts of environmental damage caused by oil extraction in the Niger (Frynas, 2001), the capacity of business to cause human misery that at the same time is costing society due to health expenses, conflicts, decreased tax payment and lost international trade has been well documented.

Overall, early steps to include human rights into responsible management education dealt with human rights as one among other aspects of CSR, socially responsible investment, supply chain management etc. rather than as a stand-alone topic. Hence, much

of the scholarship that touched on human rights occurred in a more general debate on corporate responsibilities (e.g., Paine, 1994; Bianchi, 1997; Elkington, 1998; Frynas, 2001; Margolis and Walsh, 2001; Ward, 2004; Bendell, 2004, 2005; Deakin, 2005; Prieto-Carron et al., 2006; Benedek, 2007; Black, 2008; Horrigan, 2010). However, in different contexts a small number of business ethics scholars, political scientists and international lawyers began to treat human rights as an issue that was not just another CSR issue (see also Buhmann and Wettstein, 2017). Some of these arguments made their way into management education, but still typically integrated into broader classes on responsible management. In particular, the message reflected in early research was that the moral foundations of human rights mean that any power-holder has responsibilities and that the ethical foundations that inform human rights can just as well apply to companies as to governments. Research by scholars of business ethics and law argued that companies have and should take negative as well as positive responsibility for human rights (Wettstein, 2010); that companies should be subject to accountability for their impacts on human rights (Jägers, 2002; De Schutter, 2006); and that national and international institutions must take account of business impacts on human rights and provide relevant responses (Clapham, 2006). Some of the key thoughts advanced were that as human rights are commonly viewed as a protection against the abuse of power, businesses should respect human rights when firms start to rival states in terms of economic or even political power. At least they should not benefit economically from gaps in governance or regulation that make the protection of human rights ineffective in some societies. For example, firms should not take advantage of sub-standard working conditions in certain states in order to produce or procure goods cheaply.

With the adoption of the UN Framework and the UNGPs, the normative foundations for the corporate responsibility to respect human rights shifted from the general recognition awarded by the human and labour rights principles of the Global Compact, to specific and comprehensive normative guidance in political and soft law form. This gave the impetus to the current stage of BHR in responsible management education.

CURRENT ISSUES AND STATE OF THE ART

When the UN launched the Global Compact in 2000 and five years later the process that led to the UN Framework and UNGPs, it took a course that diverted from the conventional state-centrist approach of both the UN and international human rights law. Drawing on a combination of moral obligations and expectations of responsible management and international standards of conduct originally developed for states, the Global Compact, UN Framework and UNGPs exemplify pragmatic efforts to overcome institutional and jurisdictional limitations on formal, enforceable regulation of companies in order to seek to contribute to reducing adverse impacts caused by business in a globalising world.

The UN Framework and the UNGPs both connect the public and the private interests in avoiding business-related human rights abuse. They do so through three interrelated 'Pillars', comprising the *state duty to protect* individuals and communities against human rights abuse caused by business, the *corporate responsibility to respect* human rights, and *access to remedy* through both state- and business-based institutions and mechanisms. The UN Framework and UNGPs do not develop new human rights, but explain the implications of existing human rights with regard to business impacts. The main focus is that businesses should 'do no harm', that states should contribute fully to avoid business-related human rights infringements, and that both businesses and states should offer access to remedy when infringements are nevertheless felt to have taken place. An allegation of

a human rights infringement is not the same as proof that human right abuse has occurred. Access to remedy offers an individual or community who have a sense that one or more of their human rights have been violated a grievance mechanism, which ideally may bring clarity, dialogue and learning to avoid similar occurrences in the future, and reparation in case a violation is found to have occurred.

The UN Framework and UNGPs define the International Bill of Rights (IBHR) and the core labour standards as the minimum baseline for the corporate responsibility to respect human rights. The International Bill of Rights comprises the UDHR and two detailed international conventions on human rights, one on economic, social and cultural rights and one on civil and political rights. These texts provide the basic reference point for businesses to understand what human rights are; how their activities and business relationships may affect them; and how to ensure that they prevent or mitigate the risk of adverse impacts. As these are minimum standards, companies may consider additional human rights standards relevant to a particular context. For example, when they operate in areas inhabited by indigenous people, they can consider ILO convention 169 or the UN Declaration on the Rights of Indigenous Peoples. Both of these underscore the right of indigenous people to be involved in decision-making relating to their lands.

According to the UN Framework and UNGPs, the responsibility of business enterprises to respect human rights applies to all enterprises regardless of their size, sector, operational context, ownership and structure.

The Academic Value and Theory Contributions of the UN Framework and UNGPs for Teaching BHR

For teaching purposes it can be useful to ask students to read the UN Framework as a theory of business responsibilities for human rights, and the UNGPs as an operational account of which the sections on the Corporate Responsibility to Respect Human Rights particularly address managers.

The UN Framework and UNGPs were developed through multi-stakeholder consultations as well as extensive studies by academically trained authors with experience in human rights, economy, business operations and ethics, and political science. The reports are not structured as academic articles, but elements of their processes of development and contents warrant their being considered key documents for teaching BHR. Unlike an international treaty or declaration (like the UDHR), which provide specific norms of conduct but not the academic reasoning, the Framework has academic value of its own in its analysis and elaboration of steps to reduce business-related human rights abuse. Combined with the UNGPs' operational steps and detailed explanations in commentaries, the Framework offers theoretical foundations for further guidance for companies to contribute societal value.

The UN Framework develops a contemporary theory of business responsibilities for human rights, taking account of moral arguments, economic realities, public policy needs and commitments, and international human rights law. The UNGPs spell out the general theory-based reasoning on business responsibilities for human rights into practical steps for companies as well as states. That is done based in a series of foundational principles that go back to the UN Framework. The foundational principles are followed by a series of operational principles. All are accompanied by detailed commentaries, also referring back to the UN Framework.

The reports set out the three pillars of: the *state duty to protect* human rights against abuse by companies, the *corporate responsibility to respect* human rights, and the joint responsibility to provide *access to remedy* for victims. When teaching responsible management, the main points are found in the second pillar, the *corporate responsibility to respect human rights*. Accordingly, businesses should

- avoid infringing on the human rights of others and should address adverse human rights impacts with which they are involved;
- respect internationally recognised human rights, understood, at a minimum, as those expressed in the International Bill of Human Rights and core labour rights;
- avoid causing or contributing to adverse human rights impacts through their own activities, and address such impacts when they occur; and
- seek to prevent or mitigate adverse human rights impacts that are directly linked to their operations, products or services by their business relationships, even if they have not contributed to those impacts.

To meet their responsibility to respect human rights, business enterprises should develop and apply

- a policy commitment to meet their responsibility to respect human rights;
- a human rights due-diligence process to identify, prevent, mitigate and account for how they address their impacts on human rights;
- processes to remedy any adverse human rights impacts they cause or to which they contribute.

Human Rights Due Diligence: A Core Risk-Management Process for Responsible Management

The UN Framework proposed a human rights due diligence process as a management process for companies to identify and manage their adverse human rights impacts. The steps set out by human rights due diligence support companies in navigating the complexity of social expectations and sometimes unclear normative specifications.

Under terms such as risk-based due diligence, following the UN Framework the approach has been adopted by other leading instruments for responsible management, including the Global Compact, the OECD Guidelines for Multinational Enterprises, the ISO 26000 Social Responsibility Guidance Standard and the International Finance Corporations (IFC) performance standards

(Buhmann, 2015, 2016). In other words, the risk-based due diligence approach has become widely adopted as a core process for responsible management, in several cases extended beyond human rights. For example, the OECD Guidelines since 2011 expect companies to exercise risk-based due diligence in regard to environmental and labour issues, anti-corruption and consumer protection, as well as human rights. Moreover, the EU's Non-Financial Reporting Directive asks companies to report on risk-based due diligence processes in regard to the diverse responsible management issues that are subject to a non-financial report.

Human rights due diligence and other so-called 'risk-based due diligence' is concerned with reducing and managing risks caused *by* a company *to* society. This differs from the financial or legal liability due diligence concept that is well known to many corporate lawyers and law students, as well as to many managers and management students. The latter concept is focused on reducing and managing risks *to* the company *by* factors in society, for example in the context of corporate mergers or acquisitions. This crucial difference offers a point of departure for understanding and teaching human rights due diligence. This chapter uses the terms risk-based due diligence to distinguish from liability-oriented due diligence.

By reducing its harmful social impact, a firm also reduces the risk to itself that may flow from reputational damage or economic sanctions by stakeholders. Thus, a well-performed human rights due diligence process may also serve as a risk management tool for the firm in reducing risks of reputational damage and potential economic loss.

Risk-based due diligence refers to a process through which companies identify, prevent, mitigate, account for and remedy their adverse impacts. The process entails a number of steps, each of which warrants specific attention in teaching and practice. Much of the process turns on assessing the company's impacts on human rights or responding to findings on adverse impacts. The process should be organised in such a way that it identifies the concerns of potential or actual victims ('affected stakeholders'). While other stakeholders should be included as well, the meaningful engagement of affected stakeholders is a significant element in adequately identifying and responding to human rights impacts. Moreover, transparency and information on responses to adverse impacts also forms part of risk-based due diligence.

The UNGPs specify that the process should involve external and internal *expertise* and *meaningful consultation* with (potential) victims ('affected stakeholders') and other stakeholders; that companies should *effectively integrate their impact assessment findings* across relevant internal functions and processes and take appropriate action; *track* the effectiveness of their responses through using qualitative and quantitative indicators and draw on feedback from internal and external sources, including victims; and *account for* how they address their human rights impacts by communicating this externally, through formal reports and/or in more informal manners.

Risk-based due diligence requires different types of responses based on the degree of involvement of the company (Ruggie, 2013). Companies may be involved in human rights abuse in different ways. A main distinction is between three situations: whether the company caused the adverse impact through its own activities; whether it contributed through its own activities; or whether the human rights impact is directly linked to its operations, products or services by its business relationship with another entity.

If the company *caused* the impact, simply put the company 'did it'. If the company *contributed*, someone else caused the impact but the company contributed, for example, by changing an order at the last minute without extending the time frame for delivery or the cost of the change. When a company is *directly linked*, it neither caused nor contributed to the adverse impact, but is in a relationship with an entity that is causing or contributing in another context. When involved in such a business relationship, the company has a responsibility to seek to prevent or mitigate the adverse impact, even if it has not contributed to the impact. A company that caused or contributed to an adverse impact is expected to act to cease that impact. A company that is directly linked is expected to use its influence ('leverage') with those who cause or contribute the impact so that they change their conduct. Leverage can take various forms, for example meetings or capacity building, and can be exercised in collaboration with other companies.

Differences between BHR and CSR

The CSR and BHR literatures have much in common, but also differ (Buhmann and Wettstein, 2017; Ramasatry, 2015). BHR attaches more emphasis to state obligations as well as private responsibilities, and its conception of business responsibilities explicitly recognises compliance with legal obligations as well as self-regulation going beyond legal requirements. The main difference may be described through the institutional perspective adopted: CSR theory tends to be anchored in the perspective of the business as a non-state actor; whereas BHR gives a more important role to states, whether on their own (as holders of duties to protect human rights against infringements by businesses) or in combination with business enterprises (recognised to have a separate responsibility to respect human rights and therefore avoid causing human rights harm, according to the UN Framework and UNGPs and literature learning on those texts).

THE FUTURE: THE SDGs AND HUMAN RIGHTS

As a result of strong business embrace of the SDGs, possibilities for combining doing good with not doing harm have risen alongside recognition that relevant guidance for doing so is lacking (Shift et al., 2017; Voegtlin and Scherer, 2017). A global rise in mandatory non-financial reporting, partly spurred by the UN Framework (Buhmann, 2018b), means that increasing numbers of companies engaging in CSR through contributing to the SDGs are expected or required to disclose information on their activities, policies related to responsible management, and impacts. Several studies suggest that such disclosure has reputational and financial implications, in particular in regard to firms causing adverse impacts, or even more seriously hide or mis-inform on such impacts (overview in Brooks and Oikonomou, 2018: sect. 3). This underscores the significance of an approach to doing good that integrates a process to avoid doing harm. The novelty of both BHR guidance for businesses and the SDGs underscores the need for responsible management education to take an integrated approach to both. The pertinence of theory-based explanations helping business and scholars integrate business and human rights (BHR) and the SDGs was reinforced in a 2018 speech by the CEO of the UN Global Compact (Kingo, 2018). The speech encouraged companies to adopt innovative approaches to identifying SDG contributions without, on the other hand, compromising good intentions by adverse impacts. It noted that 'leading companies and investors recognize there is no sharp line between the moral imperative and the business one', and on the other, that unlocking the interconnectedness of the SDGs means ensuring that action on one SDG does not undermine progress on another. It described the full SDG agenda as a human rights agenda: not just because numerous goals ('from Decent Work to Gender Equality and Clean Water and Sanitation') are directly related to human rights. But as importantly: because without adequate awareness of human rights impacts and processes in place to identify and manage adverse impacts, efforts to do good may lead to unintended harm. The Global Compact CEO observed that doing business through a human rights lens means considering the full spectrum of impacts, both positive and negative, when engaging in SDG contributions (Kingo, 2018). The SDGs therefore offer an interesting and pertinent perspective for integrating BHR into responsible management education.

Based on philosophical conceptions of human rights as entitlements, some authors have called for expanding the focus of BHR from 'do no harm' towards how business enterprises may contribute to the fulfilment of human rights (Kolstad, 2012; Wettstein, 2012). Critique of the UN's BHR regime for neglecting the potential of businesses to contribute to human rights fulfilment (and thereby doing good) points to the role and capacity of business enterprises to contribute to society through helping implement public policy objectives of a human rights character (such as access to health services or education) or to help address institutional defects that disrupt or delay the non-discriminatory delivery of public goods, many of which are of a human rights character. The SDGs aim to contribute to much of the same through the SDG 17 call on businesses to contribute to the implementation of SDG 1–16.

The SDGs in a Human Rights Context

Adopted by the UN General Assembly, the 17 SDGs are universal and relate to a range of societal needs that correspond to national and/or international public policy objectives, such as eliminating poverty and hunger (SDG 1–2), providing good health, education, clean water, gender equality (SDGs 3–6), industry and infrastructure (SDG 9) and ensuring life on land and below water (SDGs 14–15). As also indicated by the Global Compact CEO's statement above (Kingo, 2018), many of these goals are de facto about human rights implementation (see also Danish Institute for

Human Rights, 2019). Delivering the pertinent public goods – ranging from access to food and clean water to gender equality and sound institutions and governance – is the responsibility of governments, according to international human rights law that sets out the duties of governments. Most governments have undertaken such obligations, typically under the UN's multiple human rights treaties or in some cases regional human rights treaties. Like much other international human rights law, these international obligations are enforced mainly by 'naming-and-shaming'. However, similar commitments to provide for public goods are also often found as policy obligations at the national level. The SDG resolution reflects this in primarily relating to states' implementation of specific policy goals: SDGs 1–16 are addressed to states. SDG 17 also addresses business enterprises, calling on them to engage in partnerships that will help governments implement the goals set out in the previous 16 SDGs. This connection fuels the extensive efforts by initiatives like the UN Global Compact to encourage business to engage with the SDGs, and commitments by companies to the SDGs.

The risk that even responsible managers risk overlooking the combination between the prominent 'do good' focus of the SDGs and the moral imperative for companies to not cause harm can be explained by the fact that the SDGs are often displayed only in terms of brief catch-phrases or overall objectives of the 17 goals. Graphics presenting, e.g., SDG 1 as 'No poverty', SDG 2 as 'Zero hunger' and SDG 8 as 'Decent work and economic growth' (UN website 1) along with pictograms are useful as pointers but without elaboration risk overlooking the richness of each of the SDGs. The 17 SDGs are set out with detailed targets and means of implementation in a 35-page resolution (UN, 2015) adopted by the UN General Assembly. The resolution, which like the UN Framework can be likened to a rich academic report, explicitly notes that the role of business in regard to the SDGs should be implemented in a manner that protects 'labour rights and environmental and health standards in accordance with relevant international standards and agreements and other ongoing initiatives in this regard, such as the Guiding Principles on Business and Human Rights and the labour standards of the International Labour Organization, the Convention on the Rights of the Child and key multilateral environmental agreements, for parties to those agreements' (UN 2015, para. 67).

Both the SDGs and the UN's BHR guidance can be considered novelties in international business governance in that they explicitly reach out to businesses and through providing explicit guidance. As such, they are obvious candidates for teaching responsible management in the future.

Whereas the SDGs are basically about doing good by increasing the delivery of public goods and protecting the conditions for well-resourced societies (e.g. through sustainable energy and the preservation of marine resources), the implementation modalities set out in the SDG report contain a strong reminder that the ambitions should be honoured in a manner that does not cause harm. In particular, although so far somewhat overlooked both in the literature and in practice guidance, paragraph 67 refers explicitly to the UNGPs. The intention is that the implementation of all SDGs should be done in such a way as not, by itself, to cause harm. Consider SDG 7, which aims to ensure access to affordable, reliable, sustainable and modern energy for all, including renewable and clean energy. Such energy sources are increasingly drawn from agricultural products, which in turn leads to a surge in agri-industry. In Africa, Asia and Latin-America, agri-industry as well as wind-energy plants have been documented to result in human rights infringements on local communities, e.g. in regard to land rights and uncertainty on longer-term income for employees, and in many cases conflicts (Cotula and Berger, 2017; Gillespie, 2012; Mingorria et al., 2014).

Or, as explained by the Global Compact CEO, a company may invest in new climate infrastructure, such as wind farms, to advance Goal 13 on Climate Action. However, if local indigenous communities are disadvantaged or displaced as a result, the loss of livelihood or access to clean water cause decreased implementation of SDGs 8 and 6 (Kingo, 2018). Loss of livelihoods affects the human rights to food and an adequate standard of living, and inadequate access to clean water affects the human right to water.

Recent studies have shown that some SDGs are far from reaching their objectives. These include SDG 10, reduced inequality, and SDG 14, life below water (DNV-GL et al., 2018), both of which have clear human rights connotations in terms of non-discrimination and equal opportunities, not least in regard to land rights, as well as employment, working conditions and gender equality in the fisheries sector, including aquaculture. Addressing these as well as other gaps in SDG implementation can benefit from a stronger integration of BHR into SDG work. The precision of the normative standards of human rights, the theory basis provided by the UN Framework, and the operational guidance provided by the UNGPs can help companies identify SDG interventions in two ways. First, they can draw on the risk-based due diligence approach of the UN Framework and UNGPs to identify risks that their conduct may cause to specific SDGs. They can follow the steps set out by the UNGPs to develop human rights policies relevant to SDGs related to the company's operational focus and risk-profile, assess their impacts, integrate and follow up on action to prevent and manage harm. This can help them avoid harm and thereby honour the call of SDG 17, para. 62. Moreover, combining the 'do good' and 'do no harm' ambitions of the SDGs and the UNGPs, respectively, can be combined. In view of the resources that responsible companies invest in assessing and managing their human rights impacts can be turned into insights for SDG interventions. Companies can draw on the findings on causes for human rights risks that they generate from their impact assessment conducted as part of their due diligence, and turn this into foundations for developing SDG actions that are relevant to specific local needs and problems. For example, companies can identify problems related to institutional deficiencies with local public or private actors, which may raise the risk of the company causing human rights harm. This could relate to water provision deficiencies that cause health problems or perpetuate gender imbalances (Buhmann et al., 2018).

CONCLUSION

BHR is emerging as a specialised field of responsible management, characterised by features that define BHR in terms of normative guidance, expectations and responsibilities of businesses beyond voluntary action, and importantly, also responsibilities of home as well as host governments. The novelty of this means that BHR education as a specific topic of management education is a rather new field, increasingly taught both at business schools and some law schools. For this reason, the chapter's treatment of BHR as a specific topic of responsible management education in the past is quite limited, but the treatment of recent theory developments in BHR and implications for teaching BHR in context is more extensive.

Due to the interdisciplinary character of human rights, the BHR literature ranges across several disciplines. BHR shares much with business ethics theory, CSR and other disciplines of responsible management, but is increasingly solidifying into an independent strain with an emphasis on the roles and capacities of the public as well as private sector and recognition of both mandatory and voluntary action as pertaining to the field. Moreover, recent developments of BHR

theory are closely interwoven with the development of a UN-based normative regime, which also cuts across the public and the private. This, too, resembles the structure of the SDGs.

Over the past two decades, BHR has become a clearly defined field of responsible business in terms of business responsibilities to respect human rights. The UNGPs elaborate detailed steps for companies to identify and manage their impacts on human rights. The SDGs connect to the UNGPs and remind companies that in their efforts to do good by the SDGs they should not cause harm to human rights.

The emergence of the academic SDG debate had been preceded by other currents in theory and practice that relate to the social responsibilities of business. The BHR literature, which has mainly focused on how companies can avoid causing harm, is of relevance in this context, but the SDGs can also be seen in the context of the political CSR literature (PCSR), which takes its cue from the capacity of business to contribute to society by doing good. While also recognising societal contributions by business, the theory of creating shared value (Porter and Kramer, 2011), is less relevant to the current context because its point of departure is the strategic business perspective rather than public policy needs and implementation gaps.

Teaching human rights in responsible management education requires some in-depth knowledge of human rights in order to equip students and managers with the knowledge to be able to identify human rights issues in a management context where they often have to be unwrapped and identified in order to be handled responsibly. This chapter provides an entry point for that. Looking forward it is to be expected that human rights will not only remain a core element of responsible business, but that the need will increase for responsible management education (and research) to take account of positive as well as harmful human rights impacts that are potentially or actually caused by companies.

Notes

1 For the Ten Principles of the UN Global Compact see www.unglobalcompact.org/what-is-gc/mission/principles.
2 See 'SDGs explained for business' on the UN Global Compact website: www.unglobalcompact.org/sdgs/about.

REFERENCES

Bendell, Jem (2004) *Barricades and boardrooms: A Contemporary History of the Corporate Accountability Movement*. Technology, Business and Society Programme Paper Number 13. Geneva: United Nations Research Institute for Social Development (UNRISD).

Bendell, Jem (2005) Making business work for development: Rethinking corporate social responsibility, *Id21 insights* Number 54.

Benedek, Wolfgang (2007) The World Trade Organisation and human rights. In Benedek, Wolfgang, de Feyter, Koen and Marrella, Fabrizio (Eds.), *Economic Globalisation and Human Rights*. New York: Cambridge University Press. pp. 137–169.

Bianchi, Andrea (1997) Globalization of human rights: the role of non-state actors. In Teubner, Gunther (Ed.), *Global Law Without a State*. Brookfield: Dartmouth. pp. 179–212.

Black, Julia (2008) Constructing and contesting legitimacy and accountability in polycentric regulatory regimes. *Regulation and Governance*, 2, 137–164.

Brooks, Chris and Oikonomou, Ioannis (2018) The effects of environmental, social and governance disclosures and performance on firm value: a review of the literature in accounting and finance. *British Accounting Review* (forthcoming)

Buhmann, Karin (2011) Integrating human rights in emerging regulation of Corporate Social Responsibility: The EU case. *International Journal of Law in Context*, 7(2), 139–179.

Buhmann, Karin (2015) Business and Human Rights: Understanding the UN Guiding Principles from the perspective of Transnational Business Governance Interactions. *Transnational Legal Theory*, 6(1), 399–434, DOI 10.1080/20414005.2015.1073516

Buhmann, Karin (2016) Public regulators and CSR: the 'Social Licence to Operate' in recent United Nations instruments on Business and Human Rights and the juridification of CSR. *Journal of Business Ethics*, 136(4), 699–714.

Buhmann, Karin (2017a) *Changing Sustainability Norms through Communicative Processes: The Emergence of the Business and Human Rights Regime as Transnational Law*. Cheltenham: Edward Elgar.

Buhmann, Karin (2018a) *Power, Procedure, Participation and Legitimacy in Global Sustainability Regulation: a theory of Collaborative Regulation*. Abingdon: Routledge.

Buhmann, Karin (2018b) Neglecting the proactive aspect of human rights due diligence? A critical appraisal of the EU's Non-Financial Reporting Directive as a Pillar One avenue for promoting Pillar Two action. *Business and Human Rights Journal*, 3(1), 23–45.

Buhmann, Karin and Wettstein, Florian (2017) Business and human rights: not just another CSR issue? In Rasche, Andreas, Morsing, Mette and Moon, Jeremy (Eds.), *Corporate Social Responsibility. Strategy, Communication, Governance*. Cambridge: Cambridge University Press, pp. 379–404.

Clapham, Andrew (2006) *Human Rights Obligations of Non-State Actors*. New York: Oxford University Press.

Cotula, Lorenzo and Berger, Thierry (2017) Trends in global land use investment: implications for legal empowerment. International Institute for Environment and Development (IIED). Available at: http://pubs.iied.org/12606IIED/.

Danish Institute for Human Rights (2019) *Indicators and data for human rights and sustainable development: a practical approach to leaving no one behind*. Copenhagen: Danish Institute for Human Rights, Available at: https://www.humanrights.dk/sites/humanrights.dk/files/media/dokumenter/indicators_and_data.pdf

De Schutter, Olivier (2006) The challenge of imposing human rights norms on corporate actors. In De Schutter, Olivier (Ed.), *Transnational Corporations and Human Rights*. Oxford: Hart. pp. 1–40.

Deakin, Simon (2005) Social rights in a globalised economy. In Alston, Philip (Ed.), *Labour Rights as Human Rights*. New York: Oxford University Press. pp. 25–60.

Deva, Surya (2012) *Regulating Corporate Human Rights Violations: Humanizing Business*. London/New York: Routledge.

DNV-GL, UN Global Compact and Sustainia (2018) Global Opportunity Report 2018. Oslo: DNV-GL. Available at: f le:///C:/Users/kbu.msc/Downloads/GOR%202018%20FINAL_DIGITAL_SINGLE_PAGES.pdf.

Donnelly, Jack (2007) The relative universality of human rights. *Human Rights Quarterly*, 29(2), 281–306.

Donnelly, Jack (2013) *Universal Human Rights in Theory and Practice*. New York: Cornell University Press.

Elkington, John (1998) *Cannibals with Forks: The Triple Bottom Line of 21st Century Business*. Gabriola Island, BC: New Society Publishers.

Fasterling, Björn and Demuijnck, Geert (2013) Human rights in the void? Due diligence in the UN Guiding Principles on Business and Human Rights. *Journal of Business Ethics*, 116(4), 799.

Frynas, Jedrzej George (2001) Corporate and state responses to anti-oil protests in the Niger Delta. *African Affairs*, 100(398), 27–54.

Gillespie, P. (2012) Participation and power in Indonesian oil palm plantations. *Asia Pacific Viewpoint*, 53(3), 254–271.

Glendon, Mary-Anne (2001) *A World Made New: Eleanor Roosevelt and the Universal Declaration of Human Rights*. New York: Random House.

Goodale, Mark (2008) *Human Rights: An Anthropological Reader*. Hoboken, NJ: Wiley.

Griffin, James (2009) *On Human Rights*. Oxford: Oxford University Press.

Hastrup, Kirsten (2001) *Human Rights on Common Ground: The Quest for Universality*. The Hague: Kluwer.

Henkin, Louis (1999) The Universal Declaration at 50 and the challenge of global markets. *Brooklyn Journal of International Law*, 25, 17–25.

Horrigan, Bryan (2010) *Corporate Social Responsibility in the Twenty-First Century: Debates, Models and Practices Across Government, Law and Business*. Cheltenham: Edward Elgar.

Jägers, Nicola (2002) *Corporate Human Rights Obligations: In Search of Accountability*. Antwerp: Intersentia.

Jensen, Steven L. B. (2016) *The Making Of International Human Rights*. Cambridge: Cambridge University Press.

Kingo, Lise (2018) Executive update: How to put human rights at the heart of your business:

Four key steps. United Nations Global Compact. Available at: https://tinyurl.com/r9tu9x6.

Kolstad, I. (2012) Human rights and positive corporate duties: the importance of corporate–state interaction. *Business Ethics: A European Review*, 21(3), 276–285.

Mahoney, Jack (2008) *The Challenge of Human Rights: Origin, Development and Significance*. Hoboken, NJ: Wiley–Blackwell.

Margolis, Joshua Daniel and Walsh, James P. (2001) *People and Profits? The Search for a Link Between a Company's Social and Financial Performance*. Mahwah, NJ: Lawrence Erlbaum.

Mingorría, Sara, Gamboa, Gonzalo, Martín-López, Berta and Corbera, Esteve (2014) The oil palm boom: socio-economic implications for Q'eqchi'households in the Polochic valley, Guatemala. *Environment, Development and Sustainability*, 16(4), 841–871.

Monash University (2017) Human rights translated. Available at: www2.ohchr.org/english/issues/globalization/business/docs/Human_Rights_Translated_web.pdf.

Muchlinski, Peter (2003) The development of human rights responsibilities for multinational enterprises. In Sullivan, Rory (Ed.), *Business and Human Rights: Dilemmas and Solutions*. Sheffield: Greenleaf Publishing. pp. 33–51.

Paine, Lynn Sharpe (1994) Law, ethics and managerial judgment. *Journal of Legal Studies Education*, 12(2), 153–170.

Porter, Michael and Kramer, Mark (2011) Creating shared value. *Harvard Business Review*, 89(1/2), 62–77.

Prieto-Carron, Marina, Thomsen, Peter-Lund, Chan, Anita, Muro, Ana and Bhushan, Chandra (2006) Critical perspectives on CSR and development: what we know, what we don't know, and what we need to know. *International Affairs*, 82(5), 977–989.

Ramasatry, Anita (2015) Corporate Social Responsibility versus Business and Human Rights: bridging the gap between responsibility and accountability. *Journal of Human Rights*, 14, 137–159.

Risse-Kappen, Thomas, Ropp, Stephen C. and Sikkink, Kathryn (1999) *The Power of Human Rights: International Norms and Domestic Change*. Cambridge: Cambridge University Press.

Ruggie, John G. (2004) Reconstituting the global public domain – issues, actors and practices. *European Journal of International Relations*, 10 (4), 499–531.

Ruggie, John (2013) *Just Business*. Boston, MA: Norton.

Sen, Amartya (2004) Elements of a theory of human rights. *Philosophy and Public Affairs*, 32(4), 315–356.

Shelton, Dinah (2014) *Advanced Introduction to International Human Rights Law*. Cheltenham: Edward Elgar.

Shift, Danish Institute for Human Rights, Institute for Human Rights and Business, Business and Human Rights Resource Centre, Oxfam and ICAR (2017) An open letter to United Nations Secretary-General António Guterres and United Nations Private Sector Forum 2017 Participants, 13 September 2017.

Spar, Debora L. and La Mure, Lane T. (2003) The power of activism: assessing the impact of NGOs on global business. *California Management Review*, 45(3), 78–101.

Spickard, James V. (1999) Human Rights, religious conflict, and globalization. Ultimate values in a new world order. *MOST Journal on Cultural Pluralism*, 1(1), 2–19.

Twiss, Sumner B. (2004) History, human rights, and globalization. *Journal of Religious Ethics*, 32(1), 39–70.

UN (1948) The Universal Declaration of Human Rights (UDHR). Available at: www.un.org/en/universal-declaration-human-rights/.

UN (2008) Protect, Respect and Remedy: A Framework for Business and Human Rights. UN Doc. A/HRC/8/5.

UN (2011) Guiding Principles on Business and Human Rights: Implementing the United Nations 'Protect, Respect and Remedy' framework. UN Doc. A/HRC/17/31.

UN (2015) Transforming our World: the 2030 Agenda for Sustainable Development. UN Doc. A/Res/70/1.

Voegtlin, Christian and Scherer, Andreas G. (2017) Responsible innovation and the innovation of responsibility: governing sustainable development in a globalized world. *Journal of Business Ethics*, 143(2), 227–243.

Waddock, Sandra and Rasche, Andreas (2012) *Building the Responsible Enterprise: Where Vision and Values Add Value*. Stanford, CA: Stanford University Press.

Ward, Halina (2004) *Public Sector Roles in Strengthening Corporate Social Responsibility: Taking Stock*. Washington, DC: The World Bank Group.

Wettstein, Florian (2005) From causality to capability: towards a new understanding of the multinational corporation's enlarged global responsibilities. *Journal of Corporate Citizenship*, 19, 104–117.

Wettstein, Florian (2010) The duty to protect: corporate complicity, political responsibility, and human rights advocacy. *Journal of Business Ethics*, 96(1), 33–47.

Wettstein, Florian (2012) Human rights as a critique of instrumental CSR: corporate responsibility beyond the business case. *Notizie de POLITEIA* 116, 18–33.

PART III

Learning Outcomes and Processes

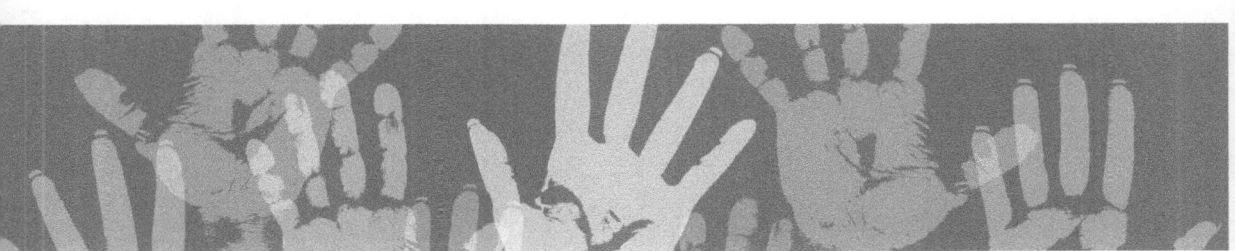

15

Competences for Responsible Management (and Leadership) Education and Practice

Jonathan Gosling and Adam Grodecki

INTRODUCTION

Our world needs responsible managers who, as Maak and Pless (2008) argue, lead with head, hand, and heart; have a responsible mindset, care for the needs of others, and act as global and responsible citizens. Yet, practically, what does it mean to be a responsible manager? What are the competences that enable leaders to act responsibly in world characterized by complex social, environmental and political challenges, and to do so at local and global scales? And just as importantly, how can educators, developers and organisations develop these qualities in their current and future leaders?

In this chapter we consider the contribution of 'competence' as a concept, how it's used in practice and the role of 'responsible management learning and education' (RMLE).

DEFINING TERMS

Responsibility

If we are to assess someone's competence in 'responsibility', we need an agreed notion of what that entails. The core questions are 'For what are we responsible? And to whom?'; competence to act responsibly only makes sense within the answers to those questions.

In this chapter we take responsible management and leadership to be fundamentally geared towards the concerns of others. Perhaps a foundational competence of responsible management and leadership is to clarify who the 'others' are and what is entailed in responding to their concerns. This clarification is itself a vital (and often contested) on-going task. For example, it might include human and non-human animals, the environment in general, some particular species, habitats or ecosystems, and future generations of all of these, all unable to represent their own interests.

Management and Leadership

It is rare to find organisations attempting to measure and develop separate 'management' and 'leadership' competences. Instead they typically have one framework, with differing expectations as people become more senior.

In recent times organisations have increasingly focused on leadership rather than management (with 'leadership programmes' for everyone from graduate trainees through to the board). Some of this represents a fashion-driven fetishisation of leadership, but some reflects a genuine attempt to encourage the capacity for initiative and accountability throughout an organisation.

We believe it is therefore more helpful to consider 'leader–managers' who embrace the role and its responsibilities in its most holistic form. So, like Mintzberg (2004), we will deal with competences in general and our comments apply equally to leadership and management competences. We will use the words 'management' and 'leadership' and 'manager' and 'leader' largely interchangeably and will draw on both the 'responsible leadership' and 'responsible management' literatures.

Where we think there is a difference worth making, we do so. For example over the past three decades there have been growing calls for leadership alongside a subtle denigration of management, famously articulated by (Bennis and Nanus, 1985: 21), 'Managers do things right, while leaders do the right things', and (Covey et al., 1994: 268), 'management works in the system; leadership works on the system'. Although this is clearly idealised – many leaders have no idea what the right thing is, and even if they did know, they wouldn't feel compelled to do it; conversely many people feel a responsibility to do the right thing, whether or not they are leaders. Yet 'ideal types' are foundational

to competence frameworks, which aim at explicitly articulated ideals, creating a developmental tension between what *is* and what *ought to be*. Where ideal and actual diverge, one might decide to modify idealisations in the light of experience (so to improve theory) or to urge more ideal behaviours (so to improve practice). This is what competence frameworks are supposed to do.

It is worth highlighting that in this chapter we are referring to, and interested in, competences of 'normal' mainstream managers. This is distinct from anything that may be required of specialised professionals, such as CSR managers, ethics officers or sustainability leaders (Grayson, 2017; Laasch, 2018). We are also referring to managers in all sectors because 'competences' are applied in widely private-sector companies, throughout the public sector (Hondeghem and Vandermeulen, 2000; Horton, 2000) and non-governmental organisations (Besler and Sezerel, 2011). Strangely, competency research has traditionally been weighted towards businesses, and *responsible* management/leadership research focuses mostly on the private sector, as if somehow leaders in politics, government, media, the military, NGOs, sports and other organisations somehow avoid dilemmas and other issues of responsibility.

Competences

An agent of responsible management and leadership might be an individual person, a team or board, a machine or system of machine + human processes, or perhaps an organisational tendency to take responsibility for a relatively wide set of stakeholders.

A competence can be considered to be an agent's ability to successfully perform a task or to tackle a problem in a specific context (Dale and Newman, 2005; Intagliata et al., 2000; Laasch and Moosmayer, 2016; Lans et al., 2014). But we will argue that this makes sense and is sustainable only in a culture of responsibility.

We consider various ways in which individual and collective competence are conceived and developed. We look mainly at competence as understood and used in large Western organisations. We believe our categories and typologies hold good in most industrialised countries but recognise that different cultural contexts influence the understanding of competence (Brewis, 1996; Cseh, 2003; Dai et al., 2019) and acknowledge that so-called indigenous cultures pay much more specific and consistent attention to development of socially responsible leadership (see Gosling and Case, 2013 for an example and further references).

DEVELOPMENT AND USE OF COMPETENCES

Modern use of 'competence' as a technical term dates to 1959, coined by American psychologist Robert White in an attempt to explain the seemingly natural desire of human children and animals to master their environment in playful exploration. It has been variously used since then, but perhaps the most influential definitional work for management literature appears in David McClelland's 1973 paper, 'Testing for competence rather than for intelligence.' McClelland's influential insight was that intelligence is not a guarantee of effective work. Rather, subtler and more variated qualities are at play; abilities which are 'causally related to [a manager's] effective or superior performance in a job or situation' (McClelland, 1973: 9). McClelland's work galvanised the academic community into attempts to describe comprehensive lists of managerial competences, perhaps the most publicised being Richard Boyatzis' list of 19 competences (Boyatzis, 1982, 2008).

By the 1990s, 'competence' was a near dominant theory in management strategy literature, especially in the United States, where it was seen as a way for organisations to gain competitive advantage (e.g. Campbell and Sommers Luchs, 1997; Mitrani et al., 1992; Nadler and Tushman, 1999). In addition to this positive incentive, organisations faced pressure from equal opportunities legislation, which stipulated that hiring should occur only on the basis of qualification and ability, e.g. the US Government's 'Uniform Guidelines on Employee Selection Procedures'. Competence-based assessment was an obvious means by which organisations could show they were complying with this legislation (Miller and Miller, 2001; Rankin, 2002).

Ideals of competence are commonly operationalised in competence frameworks, used by over 75% of large organisations in all sectors as a guiding standard for recruitment, development and promotion of their managers (Burns et al., 2012; Farnham and Horton, 2000; Sparrow, 2002).

Competence models have been enthusiastically taken up by organisations for two primary reasons:

- *Clarity*: They help organisations to translate the complex idea of leadership and management into a more concrete articulation of how it should be done, and in doing so send a message about the behaviours deemed necessary for corporate success. Setting clear expectations around the behaviour and standards of managers has become ever more important as transparency, media interest and pressure on organisations from stakeholders increases.
- *Consistency*: They provide a common framework and language for managers across an organisation, irrespective of function or location. They are frequently used to underpin training and development interventions, and form the base for many other HR systems and processes. Examples include performance management 360-degree feedback tools, promotion decisions, recruitment and selection criteria and remuneration decisions. Competency frameworks claim to offer a coherent approach to 'human resource' managing.

The impetus for competency frameworks emerged from practical questions in real-life organisations. It is therefore vital to keep this pragmatic perspective in mind when assessing them.

RESPONSIBLE MANAGEMENT COMPETENCE FRAMEWORKS: SOME EXAMPLES AND A SUMMARY OF COMMON FEATURES

Despite media interest in irresponsibility in many large organisations, increasing awareness of the social and environmental challenges facing the world, and despite the professed interest from most business schools in addressing the leadership and management problems exposed by the global financial crisis and ongoing organisational scandals, until recently there has been surprisingly little research on what counts as competent *responsible* management (Cullen, 2019). What there is seldom connects to practical application in competency frameworks (Groves and La Rocca, 2011; Maak and Pless, 2006; Stahl and De Luque, 2014; Voegtlin, 2011; Waldman and Balven, 2014).

Nonetheless two notable attempts have been made in recent years to consolidate the academic literature on responsible leadership and management competences. Both define competences as the integration of specific knowledge, skills and attitudes into a competence portfolio (Baartman et al., 2007; Cheetham and Chivers, 1996; Parry, 1998). The findings are summarised in Tables 15.1 and 15.2, and constitute normative statements of what *ought* to be the case.

The first of these (see Table 15.1) identifies three 'domains' of action, each of which implies rather different modes of competence development – there is more to competence than conceptual knowledge.

We reviewed responsible management/ leadership competency wish-lists created by initiatives explicitly established to promote responsibility (listed in Table 15.3). Although not reduced to specific competency frameworks, they express what they believe responsible management consists of, and what they expect responsible managers to be able to do.

The two literature reviews cited above focus almost exclusively on separate academic streams of work. Yet despite this different source material, there is a reassuring level of commonality across both, and when further compared with leadership frameworks proposed by the organisations listed in Table 15.3, some clear common clusters of competences emerge. We have summarised these below

Act ethically and virtuously: Leaders should be positive role models who act with integrity, have a strong values-based approach, make moral and principled decisions, ensure ethical and pro-social conduct in the workplace and are accountable to stakeholders beyond the corporation (Doh and Stumpf, 2005; Freeman and Auster, 2011; Muff, 2013; Pless et al., 2012; Treviño et al., 2000, 2003).

For some, responsible management requires leaders to go beyond avoiding harm and obeying rules (Brown and Treviño, 2006; Handelsman et al., 2002; Knight, 2018; Treviño et al., 2003;) or implementing duties (Rawls, 1971) or their own values. Instead leaders should cultivate the ability to do 'what is right, correct, or best' – to be 'virtuous' (Cameron and Winn, 2012). They should have the ability and skills to advance the best possible outcomes, to act towards the common good (Maak and Pless, 2006), rather than merely avoiding the negative (Cameron, 2011). Many organisations give this expression through statements of 'purpose', most of which are lofty and idealistic.

Work inclusively (because we value human dignity): Responsible leaders work generously with others. They care about those around them, appreciate and embrace diversity, are able to manage inclusively, are highly collaborative and involve others in decision-making and collective problem-solving. This builds on significant discussion about the responsibility for organisations to build inclusive cultures that value diversity, and that institutionalise policies of care for the mental, physical and emotional well-being of employees.

Engage stakeholders (to understand the concerns and impact on others): Responsible

Table 15.1 Overview of 45 sub-competencies for responsible leadership (Muff, 2016)

| Competency dimensions | *Domains of action* | | |
	Knowing (knowledge)	*Doing (skills)*	*Being (attitudes)*
Stakeholder relations	1. Methods to identify and integrate legitimate stakeholder groups 2. Seeing conflict as a foundation for creativity 3. Dealing with conflicting interests of stakeholders	4. Initiating and moderating a dialogue 5. Respecting different interests to find a consensus 6. Developing long-term relationships	7. Being empathic with a desire to help others 8. Being open and trustworthy 9. Appreciating the positive in diversity
Ethics and values	10. Knowing what is right and wrong 11. Knowing your own values 12. Understanding dilemmas	13. Critically questioning and adapting values 14. Acting according to ethics and own values 15. Acting as a role model	16. Being honest 17. Seeking fairness 18. Being responsible towards society and sustainability
Self-awareness	19. Understanding the importance of reflection in the learning process 20. Knowing oneself 21. Understanding one's own strengths and weaknesses	22. Learning from mistakes 23. Reflecting on one's behavior, mental models and emotions 24. Adapting the communication style	25. Reflecting about oneself 26. Reflecting about one's own behavior 27. Sharing one's developmental challenges
Systems thinking	28. Understanding how the systems work 29. Understanding inter-dependencies and inter-connections of systems 30. Understanding sustainability challenges and opportunities	31. Dealing with complexity and ambiguity 32. Estimating consequences of decisions on the system 33. Seeing the big picture and the connections rather than the parts	34. Working across disciplines & boundaries 35. Defending a long-term perspective 36. Providing a trans-generational perspective
Change and innovation	37. Understanding the significance of a motivating vision in change processes 38. Understanding the drivers and enablers of innovation and creativity 39. Understanding conditions, functioning and dynamics of change processes	40. Developing creative ideas 41. Acting to bring about change and translating ideas into action 42. Questioning the status-quo and identifying steps of change for a sustainable future	43. Being open, curious and courageous 44. Being flexible and adaptable for change 45. Being visionary in finding solutions for society's problems

leaders fundamentally are geared toward the concerns of others. Every organisation is embedded in a network of stakeholder relationships, so managing responsibly requires leaders to be able to understand the system around them. They need to have the ability to go beyond their direct reports and followers and build relations with a wide range of stakeholders inside and outside the organisation; listening to their concerns and considering the

impact on them in their decision-making. For some there is a need to go beyond 'considering' and 'listening' to stakeholders, to actively partnering with non-traditional stakeholders (Maak and Pless, 2006; Maak, 2007).

For many, it is this fundamental focus on stakeholders which most separates questions of responsible management/leadership from other leadership models (such as servant leadership, authentic leadership, transformational

Table 15.2   Overview of 'Competences for responsible management: a structured literature review' (Laasch and Moosmayer, 2016). There are three Areas, six Domains, 36 Themes of responsible management competence – Sustainability, Responsibility and Ethics (SRE)

Areas	Independent	Interdependent
Intellectual competence (extending 'knowledge')	**1. Knowledge (Know):** *Knowing about SRE, learning SRE knowledge* **Themes:** (a) Declarative knowledge, (b) Procedural knowledge, (c) Knowledge acquisition, (d) Knowledge handling	**2. Analysis (Think):** *Analysing and making multi-dimensional decisions in a SRE context* **Themes:** (a) Systems thinking, (b) Dealing with complexity, (c) Temporal thinking, (d) Strategic thinking, (e) Creative thinking, (f) Decision making, (g) Moral reasoning, (h) Critical thinking, (i) Analysing social relationships
Practical competence (extending 'skills')	**3. Action (Do):** *Initiating and sustaining action for SRE while managing with integrity* **Themes:** (a) Good behaviour and integrity, (b) Initiating action, (c) Sustaining action, (d) Dealing with issues, (e) Effecting change, (f) Managing sustainably, responsibly, ethics, (g) Mainstream management skills	**4. Interaction (Relate):** *Co-creating, leading and communicating in an actor-stakeholder network* **Themes:** (a) Group skills and collaboration, (b) Dealing with social complexity, (c) Dealing with dissent, (d) Communication, (e) Building and maintaining relationships, (f) Leadership
Personal competence (extending 'attitudes')	**5. Character (Be):** *Maintaining personal integrity, and strengthening SRE-conducive character and attitudes* **Themes:** (a) Sentiments and states of mind, (b) Motivations and aspirations, (c) Values, (d) Attitudes and consciousness, (e) Character traits	**6. Self-Adaptation (Become):** *Knowing oneself in context, governing states of mind, and shaping the self in interaction with personal context* **Themes:** (a) Self-image, (b) Introspection, (c) Self-control, (d) Self-direction, (e) Personal development

Table 15.3   List of normative responsible leadership/management frameworks from think-tanks and management developers

Blueprint for Better Business
Business for Social Responsibility (BSR)
Business in the Community (BIC)
Cambridge Institute for Sustainability Leadership
Forward Institute
Global Responsible Leadership Initiative (GRLI)
Strandberg Consulting
World Business Council for Sustainable Development (WBCSD)

leadership, ethical leadership, sustainability leadership or values-based leadership). For Pless, 'responsible leadership can be understood as the art of building and sustaining social and moral relationships between business leaders and different stakeholders (followers), based on a sense of justice, a sense of recognition, a sense of care, and a sense of accountability for a wide range of economic, ecological, social, political, and human responsibilities' (Pless, 2007: 438). Therefore we would expect to see these qualities represented in competency frameworks as well as the wishlists of the normative literature. We would also expect relevant skills and attitudes to be inculcated through RMLE.

Achieve change (to make the world a better place): Acting inclusively, ethically and with stakeholders is no good if no positive change occurs as a result. So implicit and explicit in most literature is the idea that responsible leadership requires the ability to successfully lead positive change.

Responsible leaders then must be '*response-able*,' possessing the capability and the capacity needed to respond to expressed need. To do this they should be sensitive, creative and innovative, question the status-quo, walk towards problems and translate ideas into action. They should be comfortable with ambiguity and able to manage complexity – to make decisions in the face of uncertainty, while continually testing and learning.

Readers will note the inward focus – they are primarily about how people get along – responsibly – within an organisation. There is little to say that leaders should be willing to initiate transformative responses to injustice, ecocide and inequality. The world of management competences has yet to catch on to calls for radical changes to (or of) capitalism.

WHAT GOES ON IN COMPETENCY MODELS OF ORGANISATIONS

To investigate this further we analysed the competency frameworks of 22 major organisations in the private, public and social sectors (see Table 15.4).

It is clear from this table that, perhaps unsurprisingly, there are some substantial gaps between what exists in organisations' competency frameworks, and our idealised list of responsible management competences. The clear focus for most organisations is on developing leaders that are skilled at working with their teams and others around them, and can get things done. There is little recognition of the need for managers to engage stakeholders or concern themselves with 'others' (especially others beyond customers, such as the environment, future generations, society at large). If there is a concern for virtue, it is usually implicit.

Much work then remains to be done to help organisations shift their understanding of important competences to those that are important for responsibility. If competency models express an aspirational ideal of what the organisation wants to be and do (and are supposed to be an instrument for realising this ideal) it is surprising that almost none of them explicitly aspire to responsibility. Their

public commitment to responsibility is not reflected in their models of good leadership or management.

However, a framework is like a map that describes only some aspects of the landscape. An organisation's competency framework will bear only limited relation to what goes on in practice. In the next section we enumerate some of these shortcomings and the potential contributions of RMLE.

LIMITATIONS OF COMPETENCY MODELS

As competency models have become widespread within organisations, they have faced increasing criticism and controversy from academics and HR practitioners alike (e.g. Bolden and Gosling, 2006; Briscoe and Hall, 1999; Carroll et al., 2008; Grzeda, 2005; Hollenbeck et al., 2006). Common criticisms refer to problems of universality, granularity and causality:

Universality: Competence models aspire to a 'holy grail' that, when found, would 'identify a small set of attributes that successful leaders possess, articulate them in ways that could be transferred across all leaders, and create leadership development experiences to ensure that future leaders possess these attributes' (Ulrich et al., 2000: 40). This universalism encourages conformity and inhibits diversity within organisations (Buckingham, 2001). We should ask if all competences are always useful, or if some that are responsible in one situation (such as loyalty) might be irresponsible in others (Bolden et al., 2003; Carroll et al., 2008; Grugulis, 2000; Hollenbeck et al., 2006; Loan-Clarke, 1996; Wood, 2005). Numerous studies show that effective leaders come in all sizes and shapes with unique combinations of strengths and weaknesses (Bennis and Nanus, 1985) and that individual leaders often succeed via different approaches (e.g. Hunt and Laing, 1997; McCall, 1998).

Table 15.4   Frequency of occurrence of competences in 22 frameworks

	Private sector	Public and social sectors	Total references
Working with others (e.g. developing others, communicating, collaborating internally)	35	26	61
Delivering results (e.g. analytical ability, cost focus, delivery focus, ability to simplify)	24	15	39
Achieving change (e.g. innovation, speaking up, curiosity, adaptability, dealing with ambiguity)	19	13	32
Working strategically (e.g. thinking for the long-term, having a vision)	9	9	18
External focus (e.g. working with stakeholders, a customer focus)	11	5	16
Demonstrating character (e.g. purpose, compassion, values)	4	12	16
Self-awareness (e.g. self-awareness, resilience)	9	6	15

RMLE can encourage appreciation of the contextual embeddedness of responsibility through empirical and reflective study of how it is accomplished *in situ* (Houtarri and Carroll, 2019; McKenna et al., 2004; Salaman, 2004; Turnbull and Ladkin, 2008).

Granularity refers to the level of specification. Competency frameworks by their nature fragment the management role rather than understanding it as an integrated whole (Grugulis, 1998; Hager and Beckett, 1995; Lester, 1994). Designed to be the basis of several other HR processes and systems, there is often a concentration on observable, measurable behaviour, usually at the cost of more interior, hard-to-assess or relational qualities. For example, 'reflectiveness' is a widely recognised component of responsible management, but is hard to measure or qualify, so is left out of many leadership competency frameworks (Bolden and Gosling, 2006 and see Table 15.4). Reducing the complexity of managerial and leadership work into lists of things 'to do' and 'to have' (Antonacopoulou and FitzGerald, 1996) excludes more subtle qualities and interactions (Bell et al., 2002) such as inter-personal relationships, the role of followers, and shared leadership. If they attempt to capture some of this subtlety they tend to become complicated – with multiple competences and even more behavioural indicators – which no manager can ever

remember and if they are known at all are typically regarded as a distraction from the real job of managing.

In any case, competency models may quickly become ossified and so can hinder attempts to become more 'agile' (Caldwell, 2003). If derived from past successes they may not represent skills that will be useful in the future, especially in a rapidly evolving context (Briscoe and Hall, 1999; Carroll et al., 2008).

While in-house leadership development is often concerned to reinforce institutional alignment and quell dissent, RMLE should counter this, offering external challenge to received opinions, and providing conceptual (and critical) understanding of such isomorphic processes. This 'critical studies' ability arguably constitutes a distinctive competence of RMLE.

Where competency frameworks are designed for performance assessment, they tend to gruesome granularity; but when lacking such specificity they become vaguely impressionistic. RMLE should therefore offer a more holistic, systemic perspective.

Causality: Leadership is inescapably morally hazardous. Despite many claims that successful leaders create 'win-win' outcomes the reality of management, and especially responsible management, more typically involves navigating dilemmas. Leaders and managers may be required to choose between evils, the outcomes of which are sure to be bad for significant numbers of people. Justifications can usually be made (for the nation, for the greater good, for investors, etc.), but a competent leader might with good intentions take a tough decision, things don't work out – and that leader is branded incompetent and irresponsible. History is written by the victorious, not the virtuous. Responsibility cannot be reduced to competences, and nor can good or bad outcomes be derived solely from motives or competences.

Given this, there is growing academic and practitioner consensus against reliance on competency models to define and evaluate management behaviours, or to define responsible management (Carroll et al., 2008).

BEYOND COMPETENCES?

If, in spite of the limitations described above, we want to describe what it is that responsible managers know and do, what other constructs are available, and how might they work alongside 'competences'?

Responsible Management 'Mindsets'

Kennedy et al. (2013) call for less focus on skills and more on mindset – on leaders' underlying assumptions and ways of understanding and approaching the world. This implies a shift in focus for those interested in developing responsible managers from changing *what* leaders know, to changing *how* they know. Gosling and Mintzberg (2003) propose five 'managerial mindsets', each distinct though all woven together in managerial practice (Table 15.5).

The concept of 'mindset' has been used to describe a combination of value-choices, attitudes and competences; for example, a global NGO dedicated to supporting girls and young women includes a 'gender equality mindset' in their leadership development programme.

Table 15.5   Mindsets for managers (Gosling and Mintzberg, 2003)

1. Managing self: the reflective mindset
2. Managing organisations: the analytic mindset
3. Managing contexts: the worldly mindset
4. Managing relationships: the collaborative mindset
5. Managing change: the action mindset

The construct of 'mindsets' does not replace 'competences' – one might be more or less competent at standing up for gender equality and the practices and techniques for promoting it. Developing a variety of mindsets suggests that responsible management involves thinking and relating in a range of ways.

But it still assumes that responsible management will result from an accretion of sufficiently broad-minded individuals; institutional and political aspects of responsible management are not really addressed.

A Responsible Management 'Concept'

Probert and Turnbull James (2011) argue that every organisation has strongly embedded assumptions about leadership and management – a 'leadership concept'. This is the set of assumptions, stories and ideas about leaders and leadership embedded consciously and unconsciously in the culture of an organisation or a whole sector such as financial services, a civil service, or amongst entrepreneurs. These deep-rooted assumptions profoundly shape the way that organisational members perceive, act and evaluate leadership and recruit new leaders. Responsible management education can help to make this explicit through collective reflection and analysis, opening the possibility of re-evaluation and critique, and a choice to shift assumptions about leadership and responsibility. Rasche, Gilbert and Schormair, in Chapter 26 of this Handbook note that in business schools quite separate to the formal curriculum there exists a 'hidden curriculum' that significantly affects students' moral learning.

This understanding emphasises the role of learning, reflection and critique. A competent educator, consultant or HR professional can deduce value not from applying a competence framework deductively (to identify and assess leaders), but rather in providing an opportunity to discuss and describe the kinds of leadership and management practice that one wants to develop. It's not the framework, but a challenging dialogue around it that matters.

Responsible Management 'Practices'

It might be argued that the character of the person is not as important as the actions that occur. As Rachel Dawes says to Bruce Wayne in *Batman Begins* (Roven et al., 2005), 'it's not who you are, but what you do that matters'. Rather than a bundle of individual character traits, managing and leading consists of everyday practices of organising, coordinating, cooperating, controlling, compromising and so forth. Importantly, this recognises that the work of managing and leading is effected through practices that are inherently relational.

Carroll et al. (2008) argues that this practice approach is directly opposite to the way of thinking that underpins competency (see Table 15.6) and is inherently more suited to developing and enhancing responsible management. If this is so, responsible management education should help to enhance these relational practices rather than individual competence (Raelin, 2011).

Reforming organisational practices might be easier and more effective than reforming people. This might involve finding more inclusive ways of running meetings, establishing psychologically safe conditions for people to compare and speak up for their values (Gentile, 2012), protections for whistleblowers, separating Chair and CEO roles, systematic attention to recruiting and valuing diverse backgrounds and ways of thinking.

The Forward Institute, an organisation established to build a movement for responsible leadership (and with which both authors are connected), articulates four practices that it believes underpin responsible leadership and management, and has designed a development programme that inculcates these practices within a 'fellowship' of peers, thereby making these practices salient to a social identity. Being 'one of us' means:

- observing and listening – observe and listen more deeply, and to wider groups of people
- working generously – collaborate, overcome divides, build alliances and offer help without expecting anything in return
- taking action – proactively experiment, make choices and act; actively strive to influence those around you for positive, considered outcomes
- reflecting more – take the process of reflection seriously; reflect often as an individual, encourage others to reflect and foster collective reflection. (Forward Institute, 2017)

DEVELOPING RESPONSIBLE MANAGEMENT COMPETENCES/ PRACTICES

We started this chapter stating that responsible management is fundamentally geared towards the concerns of others – and that a foundational

Table 15.6   The competency/practice distinction (Carroll et al., 2008)

Competency	Practices
Rooted in objectivism	Explicitly constructionist
Individual level of analysis	Inherently relational and collective
Quantifiable and measurable	Discourse, narrative and rhetoric
Unanchored in relationship and context	Situated and socially defined
Privileges reason	Privileges lived or day-to-day experience
Assumes intellect predominantly	Incorporates embodiment and emotion

competence of responsible management is to clarify who the 'others' are and what responding to their concerns entails. It follows that development of responsible management competences and practices must then also be rooted in helping managers develop the ability to do this difficult and contested task. Development activities should have a focus on others – on helping managers hear other perspectives and in doing so to gain perspective on their work, their organisation, and their impact in the world. This might involve engaging with different 'worlds', beyond their own. But it might also help managers be part of a moral community that considers and debates all of the inherently contentious questions around 'others' and 'responsibility'; issues of action and accountability as well as caring and listening, and of who gets to define what counts as responsible. RMLE interventions should give managers the ability to have these sorts of conversations.

A development approach that recognises management as a phenomenon that arises in relations amongst people requires a different approach to one rooted in a highly individualistic focus on developing a set of competences and mindsets. Here we highlight a few possible implications for *how* RMLE might be done:

- Leadership development must evolve from being seen as an 'event' or particular 'programme' to being an ongoing process without an actual end point (Conger, 2010). Managers should be constantly honing their craft via observation, reflection and critique. Organisations attempting to develop RMLE should ensure this commitment is embodied in the ongoing systems, processes and values of the organisation.
- RMLE should address actual dilemmas that people face: what's happening in the workplace and effects of the business, rather than being drawn into semi-fictional case studies. It should offer space and time for managers to reflect on, discuss and explore responsible use of power in all its permutations (Salaman and Butler, 1990; Raelin, 2008).
- If leadership is fundamentally relational then RMLE could develop responsibility as a team function. Coachingourselves.com is an example of RMLE in this mode (Senge and Kaeufer, 2001).

- RMLE ought to model the responsibility it is seeking to promote. For example while encouraging quiet reflection and mindfulness for stressed managers, questions might be asked about the use of luxury resorts safely cocooned apart from the very real issues of responsibility and social need that managers need to engage with if they are to successfully shift their mindset(s) and practice(s). 'Fly-in, fly-out' programmes that bring together participants from around the world might consider the justifiability of carbon emissions inherent in this. Residential formats may put unfair pressure on family life and exacerbate gender inequalities.
- Development focused on mindset rather than competence surfaces underlying assumptions about the nature of the world – and of human agency, leadership and management. Development is characterised less as gaining knowledge and more as questioning established patterns (Plowman et al., 2007; Weick and Sutcliffe, 2007), assumptions and thought processes (Kegan and Lahey, 2001; Petriglieri et al., 2011; Kennedy et al., 2013).

Framed like this, RMLE requires competences of its own: knowledge, skills and attitudes (to borrow from Muff et al., 2018, see Table 15.1; see also Grayson, 2017).

FAILURES OF COMPETENCE – CAN IRRESPONSIBILITY AND INCOMPETENCE BE AVOIDED?

How incompetent we seem to be about managing responsibly! Serious questions should be asked about why 'the severe erosion of leadership – the destructive, dramatic decline in *standards* … has coincided completely with the rise of, the burgeoning of … the leadership industry. The two axes intersect almost exactly. The decline of the one, leadership, intersects with the rise of the other, the leadership industry' (Kellerman, 2018: 5). This is perhaps because decision-making and behaviours of managers is highly dependent not just on the character of leaders, but also on their context and the company they keep (Grodecki, 2018; Grodecki and Turner, 2018a).

We have observed that responsible management and RMLE is contextual, relational and fundamentally about 'others'. It is therefore no surprise that *irresponsible* management often occurs due to system or cultural issues (Grodecki and Turner, 2018b). A wide range of contextual problems, lying outside any one individual manager, can make responsible management particularly difficult or create in-built incompetence and irresponsibility in a system:

- *Mindless bureaucracy*: Personified by the jobsworth official who won't take responsibility, bureaucracies dissipate accountability. A competent bureaucrat can avoid responsibility for any mishap. In principle this is not inevitable: a dynamic, responsible, responsive bureaucracy is conceivable, and sometimes experienced in practice. This is usually traceable to a deep-rooted ethic of service in which people collaborate across bureaucratic boundaries – they manage responsibly in spite of the formal system.
- *Cliques and elites*: Inclusion and exclusion work in many ways to undermine meritocracy. Conscious and unconscious bias is ubiquitous, evident in assumptions about who 'belongs' in leadership as well as, for example, recruitment processes that require qualifications or specified prior experiences might exclude competent people who never had the chance to access opportunities to prove their abilities.
- *Tribalism*: In many cultures primary loyalty is to the tribe, and people will seldom do anything contrary to in-group interests. Codes of ethics, transparency procedures and meritocratic criteria can give an appearance of impartial process, but the conflict of loyalties remains for the individual caught between system and culture.
- *Poor regulation*: The rules of the game establish boundaries and sanctions that articulate what is socially legitimate. Where regulation and enforcement are missing or corrupted, competent responsible leadership becomes much harder.
- *Time horizon and time pressure*: Many managers operate in systems highly orientated towards the short-term, creating challenges for gen-

eral long-term thinking and decisions. It makes particular difficulty for managers who try to competently engage with complex issues of responsibility such as climate change where the full impact will be felt beyond the time horizons of most organisations – the 'Tragedy of the Horizon' (Carney, 2015). Rasche et al. (Chapter 26 of this Handbook) refer to a conflict in business schools between 'external legitimacy demands' and 'internal efficiency requirements'.
- *Wilful blindness*: Many industries get so 'locked' in their point of view that they cannot see any other perspective. For example, Alice Stewart battled for 25 years to get medical institutions to accept the carcinogenic effects of X-rays – despite the existence of substantial evidence. No matter how competent or responsible the manager, it often requires an outsider's point of view – someone outside the system – to see what others are blind to (Heffernan, 2011).
- *Incomprehensible complexity*: The increasing scale, complexity and interconnectedness of large organisations means no one sees the whole – so the organisation is blind to the consequences of its decisions. This can be further compounded by layers of management who filter out non-conforming information from senior officers, and where specialist knowledge at the heart of a business model is beyond that of Directors or even executives.
- *Busyness*: Managers often face overwhelming pressure to be focused and deliver short-term goals, with organisations rarely creating time for managers or teams to reflect (Grodecki, 2018). Further, cognitive ability rapidly declines with tiredness – with a corresponding impact on ability to manage responsibly. Several large organisational failures have been impacted by overwork and tiredness, such as at the BP refinery in Texas City (Heffernan, 2011). Yet working hard is still often celebrated in many organisations, especially amongst senior managers.
- *Institutionalisation*: Organisations tend to be insular, with structures, rules and cultures that emphasise the organisation above all else. Managers are rewarded for complying with organisational 'norms', technical expertise is valued over broad perspective and so over time most managers naturally become 'institutionalised' in how they think and act (Brundrett, 2000; Grodecki, 2018; Grodecki and Turner, 2018b).

RESPONSIBLE MANAGEMENT COMPETENCE AS (CONTESTED) PRINCIPLES

Competence in responsible management requires more than the abilities or practices of individuals and teams. Instead, guiding principles of governance, ethical standards and structures of accountability may be the framework on which responsible management becomes possible (and without which it is always on the back foot).

Professional Standards

Barbara Kellerman (2018) argues for professional standards to which leaders are held, akin to professions such as law and medicine where status provides assurance of education and training (and continual professional development), and at least professed commitment to some standards of ethical and effective behaviour.

Kellerman describes standards that lift managers up to a level of conversation where they form part of a moral community in which these concerns are the norm. This idea is rooted in long-standing traditions such as the Hippocratic oath taken by physicians to swear that they will uphold specific ethical standards. The MBA Oath championed by Nitin Nohria, Dean of Harvard Business school from 2009, aspired to establish such standards, and is allegedly voluntarily signed by up to 50% of graduates from that business school. Whilst there remains significant debate about the efficacy of such oaths, they at least encourage debate and act as a powerful signal about expected behaviours. The Salz Review (2013), an independent assessment of Barclays' business practices, supported the creation of professional standards in banking – and of an overarching, principles-based code of conduct for both individuals and firms. Salz hoped this would encourage bankers to recognise 'that they are part of a community, constituted by the

vocation or profession, with responsibilities for the industry and not just the bank for which the individual is working' (2013: 2).

In a similar vein the UK government introduced 'The 7 Principles of Public Life (Nolan, 1995) after British MPs were accused of accepting money from lobbyists for asking specific questions in parliament. The Principles have been applied across much of the UK public sector and in the authors' experience are widely known, understood and respected by public servants. So they succeed as a set of clear standards about how leaders in public life (from police officers and civil servants to school governors) are expected to operate, and to which those leaders have to explicitly agree. Nonetheless, evidence of ongoing irresponsible management in the UK public sector reminds us that developing professional standards cannot in itself prevent incompetence or irresponsibility.

Organisational Practices

As we discussed earlier, organisational context plays a major role in influencing management behaviour. Too often organisations exhort managers to act responsibly when organisational process, structures and systems encourage irresponsible behaviour. It is important then to think not just about what responsible 'competences' organisations want to see in managers but how they can create contexts that are conducive to these behaviours.

Perhaps the most obvious way that organisations shape management behaviours is through their remuneration and performance management systems. These send powerful signals about what an organisation values – explicitly communicating desired behaviours and implicitly sending powerful signals of what really matters. The way that 'talent' is managed in an organisation – e.g. through promotions, appointments and other recognition – matters as much as direct financial measures. For 'humans are highly attuned to what elicits respect, praise, and status, and in many ways these intangible rewards are more motivating than money' (Moore, 2018: 61). These and other important organisational practices (e.g. strategic planning processes, budget allocation and governance structures) are underutilised levers in the effort to increase responsible management behaviour. Shifting 'due process' and the organisational systems is a powerful and probably necessary way to institutionalise responsible management practices and competence.

RMLE may contribute to responsible leadership, rather than heroic leaders, by engaging in the more mundane work of building good structures, accountable processes and management practices.

Various international and trans-institutional initiatives have been established to create frameworks, audits and rankings to help organisations create more responsible management contexts. These include, for example, the United Nations Global Compact (UNGC), the Global Reporting Initiative (GRI) and the Principles for Responsible Investment (PRI) (see Rasche et al., Chapter 26 in this Handbook). These mostly focus on sustainability reporting and codes of conduct, rather than reforming the core levers of organisational behaviour. Perhaps significant in this regard is B Lab, a non-profit organisation which certifies that companies are doing business in a way that meets rigorous standards of social and environmental performance, accountability and transparency – and explicitly aim to create value for society, not just shareholders. B Lab has to date focused mostly on small and medium privately held companies, but since 2015 Danone has been working with them to define a model suitable for publicly listed multinationals and has since been joined by a number of large organisations such as Natura, Patagonia, Bancolombia and Guardian Media Group.

Cultural Systems

Rules-based governance systems that provide a level playing field, common boundaries of acceptable behaviour and socially legitimised goals enable appeals to responsibility and critiques of shortcomings. Where such principles are lacking or where they are not embedded in institutions, responsibility is reduced to personal morals. Therefore the competence to manage responsibly may be seen as an effect of formal treaties. An example is the Sustainable Development Goals agreed in the Paris Accord of 2015. However, in the context of contemporary globalisation, definitions of responsibility are contested and contingent; un-noticed effects could emerge at any moment, and legitimate authority is constantly under critique.

There are obvious areas of dispute – for example globalisation itself: is it responsible to further the reach of global capital (and global institutions) which largely serve vested interests of an elite at the expense of many others? Established orders of authority under serious critique include the post-colonial dominance of 'Western values' in relation to governance and business practice, patriarchal authority, market mechanisms as a means of efficient resource allocation, and so on.

Underlying all commitments to responsible action is the assumption that relevant others will reciprocate and 'behave well'. Trust in cultural norms and institutions is fundamental but fragile. Responsible management competence may therefore exist at a cultural systemic level. For individual leaders and managers this requires the ability, willingness and status to engage in building, critique and reform of institutions.

TRAJECTORIES AND CONCLUSIONS

Artificial Intelligence (AI)

As artificial intelligence (AI) becomes more commonly used in high-profile and public-facing services such as transport, defence and medical treatment, questions about its responsible use will become ever more important. Already significant challenges include lack of accountability, hidden biases and the 'black box' nature of decisions which even the people who built the technology struggle to fully understand.

The competence to act responsibly (according to current standards) could be built into algorithms, and the ability to deal with enormous data sets could enable many more collateral effects to be factored into decision-making. On the other hand, we are reluctant to define responsibility as the automatic application of a set of rules. Can there be such a thing as artificial, or autonomous, or automatic responsibility? If it requires iterative negotiation and intuition of moral standards and norms, does this discount the possibly of a machine that can do this with less bias, more inclusivity, and much larger samples than any human could handle? If so, what would be the 'responsible management competences' defining the starting point of such a machine? Alternatively, instead of trying to programme 'responsibility' into machines, perhaps there will be a growing need to help AI to 'learn' responsibility; responsible AI can be achieved if we 'raise' the technology right. Maybe we should aim to educate and nurture the moral development of AI as we do with children, who we don't expect to act ethically without guidance. So perhaps the field of developing responsible management will become even more critical as the responsible agent becomes an inseparable hybrid of human and machine competences.

Climate Change

Probably the most significant challenge to responsible management arises from the diverse effects of climate change (and related risks to planetary boundaries and biodiversity loss). The Sustainable Development Goals have become headings under which corporate, civil and governmental policy and behaviour is judged; it is fast becoming impossible to consider any activity contrary to the SDGs as 'responsible'.

Yet there is mounting evidence that the effects of historic industrial activity and colonial exploitation have already initiated a cascade of effects that will extend catastrophic social and economic disorder throughout the world. Is it responsible, therefore, to abide by commonly agreed SDG targets, even when these perpetuate the destruction of planetary systems?

Responsible management and leadership education may therefore now need to include three new areas of competence:

1   How to radically transform industrial systems towards regenerative economics, including but not limited to innovation, disruption, protest and rebellion.
2   How to prepare for chaotic effects of climate change (at personal, community, national and global scales).
3   How to live well with failure to halt or mitigate these effects, even to the point of social collapse. So-called 'deep adaptation'. (Bendell, 2018)

RMLE must foreground the possibility that the most 'responsible' thing to do as a leader inside a large organisation may not be to balance stakeholder objectives (including shareholders) but actually to help cause the downfall of the organisation or reform of its industry.

Responsible Management Competences in 'Non-Traditional' Organisations

Issues of inequality, climate change and AI require strong and responsible action on the part of governments, the wider public sector and many 'plural sector' actors. RMLE should at least emphasise areas such as multi-stakeholder working, cross-sector collaboration and citizen and employee participation. Arguably it should also encompass competences for radical, even rebellious change.

Wellbeing and 'Human' Workplaces

RMLE will also need to take account of increasing concerns in many parts of the world to well-being and bringing more 'humanity' into the workplace. Many organisations extract too significant a personal toll on their people, and in subtle ways the workplace dehumanises – with often significant mental health implications. These challenge traditional concepts of 'management' and 'competences', both of which reside, or at least originate in, a mechanistic and not very 'human' way of thinking about organisations.

Examples of responsible modes of organising often attempt to move away from traditional notions of management completely. Social care co-op Buurtzorg explicitly rejects the hierarchical construct of traditional management, replacing it with self-managed teams.

Mass grassroots movements such as Extinction Rebellion are emerging that explicitly reject the 'patriarchal, heroic forms of leadership', which, they argue, are 'what have got us into this life-threatening situation' (Taylor, 2019: 63). For Extinction Rebellion, traditional models of leadership and management are fundamentally rooted in old ideas of oppression, empire, conquest and the marginalisation of women – so they are trying to run themselves in fundamentally different ways, to 'make sure that we work in a way that helps us all to learn, grow and care for each other' (Taylor, 2019: 67).

CONCLUSIONS

We have suggested that 'competence' is a flawed but useful construct; and shown that applied to responsible leadership, management, learning and education it opens challenging and fruitful questions about individual and collective agency, ethical relativism and uncertainty in the face of contested futures. As an educational topic, it deserves complex treatment.

REFERENCES

Antonacopoulou, E. P. and FitzGerald, L. (1996) Reframing competency in management development. *Human Resource Management Journal*, 6(1), 27–48.

Baartman, L. K. J., Bastiaens, T. J., Kirschner, P. A. and Van der Vleuten, C. P. M. (2007) Teachers' opinions on quality criteria for Competency Assessment Programmes. *Teaching and Teacher Education*, 23, 857–867.

Bell, E., Taylor, S. and Thorpe, R. (2002) A step in the right direction? Investors in people and the learning organization. *British Journal of Management*, 13, 161–171.

Bendell, J. (2018) Deep adaptation: a map for navigating climate tragedy. IFLAS Occasional Paper 2. www.iflas.info.

Bennis, W. (2007) The challenges of leadership in the modern world: introduction to the special issue. *American Psychologist*, 62(1), 2–5.

Bennis, W. and Nanus, B. (1985) *Leaders: The Strategies for Taking Charge*. New York: Harper and Row.

Besler, S. and Sezerel, H. (2011) Core competences in non-governmental organizations: a case study. *Procedia Social and Behavioral Sciences*, 24, 1257–1273.

Blueprint for Better Business – *A framework to guide decision making*. Available at http://www.blueprintforbusiness.org/principles-and-framework/ Accessed on 26 February 2020.

Bolden, R. and Gosling, J. (2006) Leadership competencies: time to change the tune? *Leadership*, 2(2), 147–163.

Bolden, R., Gosling, J., Marturano, A. and Dennison, P. (2003) *A Review of Leadership Theory and Competency Frameworks*. University of Exeter, Centre for Leadership Studies.

Boyatzis, R. (1982) *Competent Manager: A Model for Effective Performance*. New York: John Wiley & Sons.

Boyatzis, R. (2008) Competencies in the 21st century. *Journal of Management Development*, 2 (1), 5–12.

Brewis, J. (1996) The making of the 'competent' manager – competency development, personal effectiveness and Foucault. *Management Learning*, 27(1), 65–86.

Briscoe, J. P. and Hall, D. T. (1999) The interplay of boundaryless and protean careers: combinations and implications. *Journal of Vocational Behavior*, 69(1), 4–18.

Brown, M. E. and Treviño, L. S. (2006) Ethical leadership: a review and future directions. *Leadership Quarterly*, 17, 595–616.

Brundrett, M. (2000) The question of competence: the origins, strengths and inadequacies of a leadership training paradigm. *School Leadership and Management*, 20(3), 353–369.

Business for Social Responsibility (BSR) (2012) Sustainability and Leadership Competencies for Business Leaders. Available at https://www.bsr.org/reports/BSR_Sustainability_Leadership_Competencies.pdf Accessed on 26 February 2020.

Business in the Community (2010) Leadership Skills for a Sustainable Economy. Available at http://efsandquality.glos.ac.uk/toolkit/BITC_Leadership_Skills%20Report_July10.pdf Accessed on 26 February 2020.

Buckingham, M. (2001) What a waste. *People Management*, October 11, 36–39.

Burns, E. W., Smith, L. and Ulrich, D. (2012) Competency models with impact: research findings from the top companies for leaders. *HR People & Strategy*, 35(3), 16–23.

Caldwell, R. (2003) Models of change agency: a fourthfold classification. *British Journal of Management*, 14(2), 101–187.

Cambridge Institute for Sustainability Leadership. Cambridge Impact Leadership Model. Available at https://www.cisl.cam.ac.uk/about/leadership-hub/cambridge-impact-leadership-model Accessed on 26 February 2020.

Cameron, K. S. (2011) Responsible leadership as virtuous leadership. *Journal of Business Ethics*, 98(1), 25–35.

Cameron, K. S. and Winn, B. (2012) Virtuousness in organizations. In Cameron, K. S. and Spreitzer, G. M. (Eds.), *Oxford Handbook of Positive Organizational Scholarship*. New York: Oxford University Press. pp. 231–243.

Campbell, A. and Sommers Luchs, K. (1997) *Core Competency-Based Strategy*. London: International Thomson Business Press.

Carney, M. (2015) 'Breaking the tragedy of the horizon – climate change and financial stability'. Speech at Lloyd's of London, London, 29 September 2015. Accessed at https://www.bis.org/review/r151009a.pdf.

Carroll, B., Levy, L. and Richmond, D. (2008) Leadership as practice: challenging the competency paradigm. *Leadership*, 4(4), 363–379.

Cheetham, G. and Chivers, G. (1996) Towards a holistic model of professional competence. *Journal of European Industrial Training*, 20(5), 20–30.

Conger, R. D. (2010) Leadership development interventions: ensuring a return on the investment. In: Nohria, N. and Khurana, R. (Eds.), *Handbook of Leadership Theory and Practice: and HBS Centennial Colloquium on Advancing Leadership*. Boston, MA: Harvard Business Press. pp. 709–738.

Covey, S., Merrill, A. R. and Merrill R. R. (1994) *First Things First: To live, to love, to learn, to leave a legacy*. New York: Simon & Schuster.

Cseh, M. (2003) Facilitating learning in multicultural teams. *Advances in Developing Human Resources*, 5(1), 26–40.

Cullen, J. (2019) Varieties of responsible management learning: a review, typology and research agenda. *Journal of Business Ethics*. 10.1007/s10551-019-04362-x.

Dai, W., Gosling, J. and Pye, A. (2019) The inclusiveness and emptiness of Gong Qi: a non-Anglophone perspective on ethics from a Sino-Japanese corporation. *Journal of Business Ethics*, Oct. doi.org/10.1007/s10551-019-04308-3.

Dale, A. and Newman, L. (2005) Sustainable development, education and literacy. *International Journal of Sustainability in Higher Education*, 6(4), 351–362.

Doh, J. P. and Stumpf, S. A. (2005) Towards a framework of responsible leadership and governance. In Doh, J. and Stumpf, S. (Eds.), *Handbook on Responsible Leadership and Governance in Global Business*. Cheltenham: Edward Elgar. pp. 3–18.

Farnham, D. and Horton, S. (Eds.) (2000) *Human Resources Flexibilities in the Public Services: International Perspectives*. Oxford: Palgrave.

Forward Institute (2017) Our Principles and Practices. Available at: www.forward.institute/our-principles-practices.

Freeman, R. E. and Auster, E. R. (2011) Values, authenticity, and responsible leadership. *Journal of Business Ethics*, 98(1), 15–23.

Gentile, M. (2012) *Giving Voice to Values: How to speak your mind when you know what's right*. New York: Yale University Press.

Global Responsible Leadership Initiative, *50 + 20 Vision*. Available at https://grli.org/initiatives/the-5020-vision/ Accessed on 26 February 2020.

Gosling, J. and Case, P. (2013) Social dreaming and ecocentric ethics: sources of non-rational insight in the face of climate change catastrophe. *Organization*, 20(5), 705–721.

Gosling, J. and Mintzberg, H. (2003) The five minds of a manager. *Harvard Business Review*, 81(11), 54–63.

Grayson, D. (2017) New leadership competencies for corporate sustainability. Retrieved from www.cranfield.ac.uk/som/thought-leadership-list/new-leadership-competencies-for-corporate-sustainability.

Grodecki, A. (2018) The permafrost problem: from bad apples to excellent sheep. Creating an environment where we can truly think. Financial Conduct Authority Discussion Paper 18/2: Transforming Culture in Financial Services. Available at: https://www.fca.org.uk/publication/discussion/dp18-02.pdf.

Grodecki, A. and Turner, R. (2018a) Leading responsibly through change: a call for creative conflict. *Leadership Insight*, no. 8 (1). Centre for Army Leadership.

Grodecki, A. and Turner, R. (2018b) Leading responsibly through change: 'Fix the system, not the people'. *Leadership Insight*, no. 8 (2). Centre for Army Leadership.

Groves, K. S. and La Rocca M. A. (2011) An empirical study of leader ethical values, transformational and transactional leadership, and follower attitudes toward corporate social responsibility. *Journal of Business Ethics*, 103(4), 511–528.

Grugulis, I. (1998) 'Real' managers don't do NVQs: a review of the new management 'standards'. *Employee Relations*, 20(4), 383–403.

Grugulis, I. (2000) The management NVQ: a critique of the myth of relevance. *Journal of Vocational Education and Training*, 52, 79–99.

Grzeda, Maurice (2005) In competence we trust? Addressing conceptual ambiguity. *Journal of Management Development*, 24(6), 530–545.

Hager, P. and Beckett, D. (1995) Philosophical underpinnings of the integrated conception of competence. *Educational Philosophy and Theory*, 27(1), 1–24.

Handelsman, M. M., Knapp, S. and Gottlieb, M. C. (2002) Positive ethics. In Snyder, C. R. and Lopez S. J. (Eds.), *Handbook of Positive Psychology*. New York: Oxford University Press. pp. 731–744.

Heffernan, M. (2011) *Wilful Blindness: Why We Ignore the Obvious at Our Peril*. New York: Walker & Company.

Hollenbeck, G. P., McCall, M. W. and Silzer, R. F. (2006) Leadership competency models. *The Leadership Quarterly*, 17(4), 398–413.

Hondeghem, A. and Vandermeulen, F. (2000) Competency management in the Flemish and Dutch civil service. *International Journal of Public Sector Management*, 13(4), 342–353.

Horton, S. (2000) Competency management in the British civil service. *International Journal of Public Sector Management*, 13(4), 354–368.

Houtarri, V. and Carroll, B. (2019) An archaeological dig into leadership competencies in the 21st century. In Carroll, B., Wilson, S. and Firth, J. (Eds.), *After Leadership*. New York and Abingdon: Routledge. pp. 19–34.

Hunt, J. W. and Laing, B. (1997) Leadership: the role of the exemplar. *Business Strategy Review*, 8(1), 31–42.

Intagliata, J., Ulrich, D. and Smallwood, N. (2000) Leveraging leadership competencies to produce leadership brand: creating distinctiveness by focussing on strategy and results. *Human Resources Planning*, 23(3), 12–23.

Kegan, R. and Lahey, L. (2001). The real reason people won't change. *Harvard Business Review*, November, 84–93.

Kellerman, B. (2018) Standards. BK – Barbara Kellerman blog, 29 October 2018. Available at: http://barbarakellerman.com/standards/.

Kennedy, F., Carroll, B. and Francoeur, J. (2013) Mindset not skill set, evaluating in new paradigms of leadership development. *Advances in Developing Human Resources*, 15(1), 10–26.

Knight, B. (2018) Behavioural competencies of sustainability leaders: an empirical investigation. *Journal of Organizational Change Management*, 31(3), 557–580.

Laasch, O. (2018) Just old wine in new bottles? Conceptual shifts in the emerging field of responsible management. *CRME Working Papers*, 4(1).

Laasch, O. and Moosmayer, D. (2016) Responsible management competences: building a portfolio for professional competence. Paper presented at the Academy of Management Annual Conference, Anaheim.

Lans, T., Blok, V. and Wesselink, R. (2014) Learning apart and together: towards an integrated competence framework for sustainable entrepreneurship in higher education. *Journal of Cleaner Production*, 62, 37–47.

Lester, S. (1994) Management standards: a critical approach. *Competency*, 2(1), 28–31.

Loan-Clarke, J. (1996) The Management Charter Initiative – a critique of management standards/NVQs. *Journal of Management Development*, 15(6), 4–17.

Maak, T. (2007) Responsible leadership, stakeholder engagement, and the emergence of social capital. *Journal of Business Ethics*, 74(4), 329–343.

Maak, T. and Pless, N. M. (2006) Responsible leadership in a stakeholder society – a relational perspective. *Journal of Business Ethics*, 66(1), 99–115.

Maak, T. and Pless, N. M. (2008) Responsible leadership in a globalized world: a cosmopolitan perspective. In Scherer, A. G. and Palazzo, G. (Eds.), *Handbook of Research on Global Corporate Citizenship*. Cheltenham: Edward Elgar Publishing. pp. 430–453.

McCall, M. W. (1998) *High Flyers: Developing the Next Generation of Leaders*. Boston, MA: Harvard Business School.

McClelland, D. (1973) Testing for competence rather than for intelligence. *American Psychologist*, 28(1), 1–14.

McKenna, M., Gartland, M. and Pugno, P. (2004) Development of physician leadership competencies: perceptions of physician leaders, physician educators and medical students. *Journal of Health Administration Education*, 21, 343–354.

Miller, T. W. and Miller, J. M. (2001) Educational leadership in the new millennium: a vision for 2020. *International Journal of Leadership in Education*, 4(2), 181–189.

Mintzberg, H. (2004) Enough leadership. *Harvard Business Review*, 82(11), 22.

Mitrani, A., Dalziel, M. and Fitt, D. (1992) *Competency Based Human Resource Management*. London: Kogan Page.

Moore, C. (2018) How do organisations motivate people to act? *Financial Conduct Authority Discussion Paper 18/2: Transforming Culture in Financial Services*. Available at https://www.fca.org.uk/publication/discussion/dp18-02.pdf Accessed 26 February 2020.

Muff, K. (2013): Developing globally responsible leaders in Business schools: a vision and transformational practice for the journey ahead. *Journal of Management Development*, 32 (5), 487–507.

Muff, K. (2016) The collaboratory: a common transformative space for individual, organizational and societal transformation. *Journal of Corporate Citizenship*, 18(2), 91–108.

Muff, K., Liechti, A. and Dyllick, T. (2018) *The Competency Assessment for Responsible Leadership (CARL): consolidating the responsible leadership discourse into an operationalized definition and an online tool for practice and education*. Available at https://carl2030org/wp-content/uploads/2017/11/Muff-Liechti-Dyllick-CARL-consolidating-the-RL-discourse-into-an-online-tool-210817-002.pdf Accessed 26 February 2020.

Nadler, D. A. and Tushman, M. L. (1999) The organization of the future: strategic imperatives and core competencies for the 21st century. *Organizational Dynamics*, 28(1), 45–60.

Nolan, M. (1995) The 7 principles of public life. Available at www.gov.uk/government/publications/the-7-principles-of-public-life/the-7-principles-of-public-life–2 Accessed on 28 February 2020.

Parry, K. W. (1998) Grounded theory and social process: a new direction for leadership research. *The Leadership Quarterly*, 9(1), 85–105.

Petriglieri, G., Wood, J. and Petriglieri, J. (2011) Up close and personal: building foundations for leaders' development through the personalization of management learning. *Academy of Management Learning & Education*, 10(3), 430–450.

Pless, N. M. (2007) Understanding responsible leadership: role identity and motivational drivers. *Journal of Business Ethics*, 74(4), 437–456.

Pless, N. M., Maak, T. and Waldman, D. (2012) Different approaches toward doing the right thing: mapping the responsibility orientations of leaders. *Academy of Management Perspectives*, 26(4), 51–65.

Plowman, D., Solansky, S., Beck, T., Baker, L., Kulkarni, M., and Travis, D. (2007) The role of leadership in emergent, self-organization. *The Leadership Quarterly*, 18, 341–356.

Probert, J. and Turnbull James, K. (2011) Leadership development: crisis, opportunities and the leadership concept. *Leadership*, 7, 137–150.

Raelin, J. (2008) *Work-Based Learning: Bridging Knowledge and Action in the Workplace*. San Francisco: Jossey-Bass.

Raelin, J. (2011) From leadership-as-practice to leaderful practice. *Leadership*, 7(2), 195–211.

Rankin, N. (2002) Raising performance through people: The Ninth Competency Survey. *Competency and Emotional Intelligence*, Jan, 2–21.

Rawls, J. (1971) *A Theory of Justice*. Cambridge, MA: Harvard University Press.

Roven, C., Thomas, E., Franco, L. and Nolan, C. (2005) *Batman Begins* [Motion Picture]. United States: Warner Bros.

Salaman, G. (2004) Competences of managers, competences of leaders. In Storey, J. (Ed.), *Leadership in Organizations: Current Issues and Key Trends*. London: Routledge.

Salaman, G. and Butler, J. (1990) Why managers won't learn. *Management Education and Development*, 21(3), 183–191.

Salz, A. (2013) *Salz Review: An Independent Review of Barclays' Business Practices*. Available at http://online.wsj.com/public/resources/documents/SalzReview04032013.pdf. Accessed 26 February 2020.

Senge, P. and Kaeufer, K. (2001) Communities of leaders or no leadership at all. In Chowdhury, S. (Ed.), *Management 21C*. New York: Prentice Hall. pp. 186–204.

Sparrow, P. (2002) 'To use competencies or not to use competencies? That is the question'. In Pearn, M. (Ed.), *Individual Differences and Development in Organizations*. Chichester: Wiley. pp. 107–129.

Stahl, G. K. and De Luque, M. (2014) Antecedents of responsible leader behavior: a research synthesis, conceptual framework, and agenda for future research. *Academy of Management Perspectives*, 28(3), 235–254.

Taylor, C. (2019) Circles of power: Extinction Rebellion's approach to organising. In Amory, E. (Ed.), *Unfollow: Redefining Leadership in a Changing World*. London: The Brewery. pp. 61–70.

Treviño, L. K., Hartman, L. P. and Brown, M. (2000) Moral person and moral manager: how executives develop a reputation for ethical leadership. *California Management Review*, 42, 128–142.

Treviño, L. K., Brown, M. E. and Hartman, L. P. (2003) A qualitative investigation of perceived ethical leadership: perceptions from inside and outside the executive suite. *Human Relations*, 55, 5–37.

Turnbull, J. K. and Ladkin, D. (2008) Meeting the challenge of leading in the 21st century: beyond the deficit model of leadership development. In Turnbull James, K. and Collins, J. (Eds.), *Leadership Learning: Knowledge into Action*. Basingstoke: Palgrave. pp. 13–34.

Ulrich, D., Zenger, J. and Smallwood, N. (2000) Building your leadership brand. *Leader to Leader*, Winter, 40–46.

Voegtlin, C. (2011) Development of a scale measuring discursive responsible leadership. *Journal of Business Ethics, Special Issue on Responsible Leadership*, 98(1), 57–73.

Waldman, D. and Balven, R. M. (2014) Responsible leadership: theoretical issues and research directions. *Academy of Management Perspectives*, 28(3), 224–234.

Weick, K. and Sutcliffe, K. (2007) *Managing the Unexpected: Resilient Performance in an Age of Uncertainty*. San Francisco, CA: Jossey-Bass.

Wood, M. (2005) The fallacy of misplaced leadership. *Journal of Management Studies*, 42(6), 1101–1121.

World Business Council for Sustainable Development (2011) *Enabling Leadership for Sustainability*. WBCSD working paper. Conches-Geneva, Switzerland.

16

Experiential Learning for Responsible Management Education

Alex Hope, Pamela Croney and Jan Myers

INTRODUCTION

In recent years there has been much debate within business and management schools and higher education institutions in general as to whether business schools are providing students with the learning they require in order to build essential business knowledge and competencies to practise effectively once in employment (Levy & Petrulis, 2012; Scherpereel & Bowers, 2014; Tynjälä, 2008). In addition to this, many business leaders are questioning whether business schools are able to produce new graduates with the requisite skills and knowledge required to behave ethically and deal with responsibility and sustainability challenges (Carroll & Buchholtz, 2014; Colby, Ehrlich, Sullivan & Dolle, 2011; Datar, Garvin & Cullen, 2010). The charge has been made that business education is 'too much about rigour and not enough about relevance' (Smith, 2005: 357) and 'does not prepare students for the realities of business life' (Scherpereel & Bowers,

2014: 13). Similarly, within business schools there are many concerns and issues related to student learning; that students are too passive in their learning, have poor motivation and poor self-directed learning skills (Croney, 2016; Rolfe, 2002; Taylor & Bedford, 2004). As Baden and Parkes (2013) suggest, it is not enough to simply raise awareness of issues in business, particularly in the areas of sustainability, ethics and responsibility, rather educators should be developing future business leaders and managers who are able to influence workplace behavior.

These criticisms of management learning are levelled not just at traditional business school educators, but also at those who espouse responsible management education. Whilst experiential learning as a pedagogical approach to learning and teaching has been around since the late 20th century, the challenge is how to embed experiential learning techniques in the formal and informal curricula both internally in business schools and externally within community partners. As business education continues to grow in popularity, there is a need to understand how to build experiential learning into educational experiences from undergraduate to postgraduate courses, within executive education through to doctoral and graduate research studentships. Before examining the opportunities that experiential learning offers responsible management educators, it is useful to examine how management education has evolved over time and some of the key criticisms both traditional and responsible management education have received.

EVOLUTION OF MANAGEMENT EDUCATION

Management education has been around in some form since the mid-1300s (Richardson, 1940), however, as Spender (2005) points out, some forms of administration and administrative education must have taken place in ancient eras as our ancestors passed on techniques for counting sticks, granary management or within the wine supply-chain in the cities of Rome. The parentage of the US business schools can be traced back to German institutions such as the University of Halle or the University of Frankfurt-am-Oder, who appointed their first professors of Administration in 1727 (Forrester, 1990). In the United States the Wharton School of Business was established in 1881, Harvard Business School 1908 and Stanford Graduate School of Business in 1925. The British business schools came a little later, with the Oxford Centre for Management Studies, the precursor to today's Said Business School, was established in 1965, the City Business School of City University London (now Cass Business School) in 1966 and Cambridge University's Judge Institute for Management Studies (now Cambridge Judge Business School) not appearing until 1990. Whilst management education goes back a

long way and co-evolved with management itself, so does the criticism of the management learning.

A key criticism of management education is that it suffers from a gap between theory and practice. Redlich (1957) relates the cautionary tale of a 19th-century German steel-town which, its business failing, employed the local business school principal to take charge. The business failed despite his efforts and he died in jail after pondering the gap between theory and practice. The challenge of developing business education which delivers knowledge that relates to practice continues to be one of the wicked problems facing the discipline. Key voices leading the critique of management education include Henry Mintzberg, who through his book *Managers Not MBAs* (Mintzberg, 2005), argues that there is plenty of business education, but hardly any management education. The charge is that business schools teach *about* business as opposed to how to manage one. Mintzberg asserts that we are teaching the wrong people, the wrong thing, the wrong way. This challenge is taken on by Jeffery Pfeffer, who suggests that business and management schools create the gap between theory and practice through poor teaching and that we should emulate the teaching of the 'hard' sciences such as physics and engineering. He pointed out in 2002 that business schools tended to rely on a combination of lectures and case study approaches to learning rather than learning by doing through experiential learning techniques such as those used in professions such as medicine (Pfeffer & Fong, 2002).

Another criticism of traditional management education has been that it is simply unable to provide the necessary behavioural competencies required for leaders and managers to deal with their complex environments. Specifically, many have pointed out that there is a need for education to renew its orientation toward self-awareness and interpersonal skills and not just learning concepts and techniques (Waddock & Lozano, 2013).

Some of these critiques are about the way the knowledge is delivered; others are attacks on the body of knowledge itself (Spender, 2005). Acquiring competencies is not comparable with learning as knowledge acquisition, rather competencies can be described as learnable but not teachable (Weinert, 2001). When considering these criticisms, Parker (2018) provocatively suggests that we should simply shut down the business schools. In his view they continue to act as loudspeakers for neoliberal capitalism with all its injustices and planetary consequences (Parker, 2018). His key thesis is that business and management schools have produced a generation of unreflective managers, primarily interested in their own personal rewards. Instead he advocates 'School for Organising' which would critique the dominant corporate model, enabling individuals to discover alternative responses to the pressing issues of inequality and sustainability. Perhaps such schools would facilitate a shift towards education for sustainable development and responsible management education.

Responsible Management Education

As the debate as to the purpose and effectiveness of management education has evolved, a parallel discussion has emerged on the need to embed the concepts of ethics, sustainability and responsibility into business and management education. It is not the intention of this chapter to provide a detailed discussion of the evolution of responsible management education, rather make the case that many critiques of the concept mirror those levelled at business and management education in general.

One of the key criticisms of traditional responsible management education, in particular the teaching of business ethics, is that it is abstract in nature, intellectual in approach and deeply theoretical (McDonald & Donleavy, 1995). The charge is that it is not translated into action and behavioural change

in the real world of business and management. This view is confirmed by many business educators themselves with research by Dean and Beggs (2006) finding that tutors had very little confidence that their teaching practice impacted on students' behaviour. Similarly, through a meta-analysis of the effectiveness of ethics education, Waples et al. (2009) found that business ethics programmes had little impact on increasing ethical outcomes, perceptions, behaviour or awareness. As Lozano et al. (2013) set out, pedagogy for teaching sustainability in classrooms needs to be a participative process, one that includes opportunities for students to experience dynamic, problem-solving methods. In such there is a shift from a content-centred to a more student-centred curriculum alongside an understanding that the student learning experience is key. It is about the full and active engagement of learners including affective, cognitive and active dimensions. Many core principles of integrating sustainability into higher education require substantial shifts in thinking and practice. Sterling (2011, 2013) argues that sustainability education implies a transformation in educational thinking and practice through which education becomes more transformative learning. This indicates a paradigm that is holistic, systemic and participative. Learning for sustainability moves beyond education in and about sustainability and responsible management topics to a focus on equipping students with the conceptual frameworks required to develop skills to effect change towards the sustainable world of the future.

Sunley and Leigh (2016) discuss how there is a need to move beyond discussing the business case for responsible management education towards how to educate managers and leaders through experiential, engaged and ethics-focused approaches to learning. They go on to say that it is important that management educators understand that there is a range of pedagogical approaches and strategies that may provide effective learning experiences for responsible management-related topics above and beyond traditional lecture and case study formats (Sunley & Leigh, 2016). In short, they argue that it is not enough to simply teach responsible management content, rather that the way in which we inspire and enrich the education of the future business leaders must be broadened and enhanced (Sunley & Leigh, 2016).

With this in mind, addressing sustainability in the business and management curriculum requires more than simply the addition of content (Iyer-Raniga & Andamon, 2016; Sterling & Thomas, 2006). In the past emphasis has been placed primarily on building awareness of sustainability issues, learning about sustainability not how to address sustainability-related issues. Education about sustainability focuses on developing knowledge and understanding about key concepts and sustainability issues rather than learning that engages and equips students for change towards sustainability and responsible management (Tilbury, 2004). In particular, responsible management education shares some traits with the concept of education for sustainable development (ESD) in that it requires an in-depth learning approach that focuses on communication, innovation and critical thinking (McPherson et al., 2016) and an understanding of the importance of generating mindset shifts among students (Backman, Pitt, Marsden, Mehmood & Mathijs, 2019). Such shifts happen when learning is transformative in the way in which experiential learning has been shown to be (Taylor, 1998). UNESCO set out the importance of teaching life skills as means to tackle sustainability challenges. Educating for responsible management and sustainable development requires the re-examination of educational policy to shift the focus toward the development of knowledge, skills, perspectives and values related to sustainability (UNESCO, 2004). Here it is suggested that higher education requires a review of recommended and mandated approaches to teaching, learning and assessment to enable lifelong learning skills to be fostered. Such

skills include creative and critical thinking, oral and written communication, collaboration and cooperation, conflict management, decision-making, problem-solving and planning, using appropriate ICTs, and practical citizenship (UNESCO, 2004).

There is a broad consensus that sustainability education requires active, participative and experiential learning methods that engage the learner and make a real difference to the learner's understanding, thinking and ability to act. Sterling (2012) sets out a range of assumptions that underlie thinking and practice in education for sustainable development that also relate to responsible management education. These include:

- individuals, organisations and society need to shift values, thinking, policies and practices towards those that can help ensure a more sustainable future;
- sustainability and RME issues may be characterised by complexity and uncertainty and as a result cannot be understood adequately through single discipline approaches;
- sustainability and RME issues often present ethical challenges and dilemmas;
- sustainability and RME issues are often marked by rapid change which can be seen in the news coverage of topics such as energy, health, social justice, migration, environmental stresses, climate change, globalisation, etc.

Sustainability and RME requires learning that engages and develops the 'whole person': affective, cognitive and practical dimensions and abilities, and in relation to 'real-world' issues and concerns. The complex challenges associated with sustainability issues are difficult to grasp through abstract and theoretical knowledge alone (Perlstein, Mortimer & Robertson, 2017; Ramey, 2013). Perhaps more importantly, it has been suggested that the breadth and complexity of sustainability challenges can in fact lead to student apathy in that they feel overwhelmed and incapable of acting (Álvarez-Suárez, Vega-Marcote & Mira, 2013; Savage, Tapics, Evarts, Wilson & Tirone, 2015). Experiential learning has been shown to help overcome these challenges as dealing with complex problems through a combination of theory and practice develops a sense of urgency among learners (Hensley, 2017). Within the limits of business and management course requirements, learning methods and approaches should be much more open-ended, participatory, diverse and interactive than is often the case in business school education.

EXPERIENTIAL LEARNING

The term 'experiential learning' rose to prominence in the late 20th century and was initially used to describe the relationship between *experience* and *learning* that underwrote experiential education in the 1970s. The most widely used definition of experiential learning is Kolb's (1984) model articulated as 'The process whereby knowledge is created through the transformation of experience'. Kolb went on to assert that 'Knowledge results from the combination of grasping and transforming experience' (Kolb, 1984: 41). The roots of experiential learning can, however, be traced back much further to philosophers and educational reformists such as John Dewy in the early 20th century through to the psychologist Kurt Lewin in the 1940s, Benne and Tuckman in the 1960s, through to Joplin and Gass in the mid 1980s alongside Kolb (for a comprehensive history of experiential learning see Seaman, Brown & Quay, 2017). Today many educators see experiential learning as a broad umbrella term to describe approaches to learning that are driven by a process of enquiry, are 'student-centred' and can take therefore many forms (see Figure 16.1). What underpins all these pedagogical approaches however are their constructivist principles, i.e. that learners are actively involved in constructing their own knowledge and understanding, and the fact that none of them is a rigid instructional programme (Smith, 2005).

An experiential learning approach to university teaching has long been established as an effective pedagogy for student learning (Boud, Cohen & Walker, 1993; Moon, 2013).

It is suggested that experiential-based curriculums can provide a deep and student-centred learning type of environment which

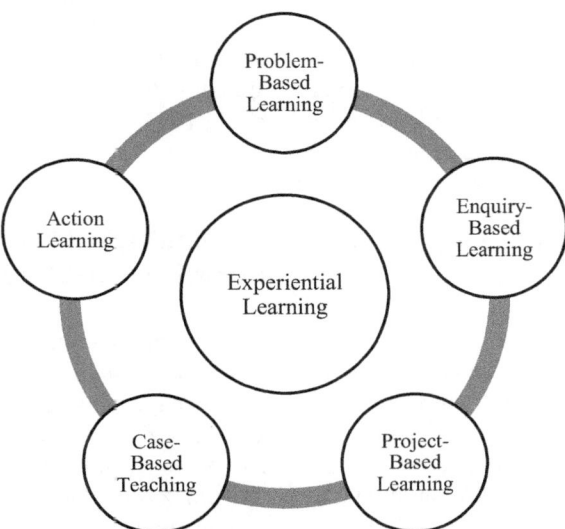

Figure 16.1 Different forms of experiential learning

is important for good learning (Chan, 2016) and that learning becomes more interesting and engaging for students (Zimitat, Hamilton, Dejersey, Reilly & Ward, 1994) as by its very nature it requires more student participation and the development of leadership skills. Furthermore it can deliver lifelong, key skills such as critical thinking, teamwork, creativity, problem-solving, leadership and communication (Bradley-Levine et al., 2010; Chan, 2016; Delaney & Kelleher, 2008; Savery, 2006) benefiting students by making them more employable and providing them with 'higher order thinking skills and learning abilities as demanded by today's economy' (Chan, 2016: 26).

Research reviewed by Tynjälä (2008) has 'shown that learning in authentic working life environments is very important in helping students to develop their competencies, skills and vocational identity' (p. 148). Within business education, it is seen as a particularly effective aspect of the curriculum helping students to manage challenges (AACSB, 2002) and become less passive and instrumental in their learning (Kahn & O'Rourke, 2005).

Experiential learning, however, is not without its critics. It has been suggested that there is no body of research supporting its use and indeed that there is evidence to the contrary to suggest that strong instructional guidance is more effective, especially with first-year and intermediate learners (Kirschner, Sweller & Clark, 2006; O'Hanlon, Winefield, Hejka & Chur-Hansen, 1995); a point which is refuted by others (Chan, 2016: 26; Hmelo-Silver, Duncan & Chinn, 2007) with some advocating it can improve the period of transition from secondary education (Barrett & Cashman, 2010; Croney, 2016). Within business it is intimated to be ineffective in delivering an 'agreed' management curriculum with specific learning objectives and can be a challenge to the educational institution in which it is situated (Reynolds & Vince, 2007).

From a purely pragmatic perspective the introduction of EL is resource-intensive.

The instructional responsibilities of academics change from that of a 'front of house oracle' to primarily having to manage students in small teams, keep them focused on important content and concepts and maintain student motivation (Ertmer & Simons, 2005). This requires significant institutional support at its inception and further ongoing support and professional development to develop academics as reflective EL practitioners (Joham & Clarke, 2012; Lee, Blackwell, Drake & Moran, 2014). Academics need to have good facilitation skills (Barrett, 2010; Chan, 2016: 26; Kahn & O'Rourke, 2005) which requires further training and guidance to cope with student enquiry, providing feedback and adopting new types of classroom management (Ertmer & Glazewski, 2015).

Employability is also of concern to both universities and students and a key challenge for curriculum developers within business schools is to develop programmes that will produce both students *of* business as well as students *for* business. Despite these challenges, many universities and business schools faced with these challenges have looked to introduce modules that adopt an experiential learning approach which by its very nature requires more student participation (Fenwick, 2005) and has been cited as being more interesting and engaging for students (Ocak & Uluyol, 2010; Zimitat et al., 1994).

EXPERIENTIAL LEARNING IN BUSINESS EDUCATION

Experiential learning, in its many guises, has been a dominant concept in business and management education for the past 20 years (Illeris, 2007) aiming to build capability as well as competence in students (Remidez & Fodness, 2015). Some subjects in universities such as medical schools, immerse students in real-world or simulated real-world scenarios to prepare them for decision-making when they enter their profession. In contrast to this, the majority of business education still relies on teaching concepts, theories and beliefs (Hodge, Proudford & Holt, 2014). Whilst students are taught real life skills, such as report writing, how to prepare presentations or pitch projects, until relatively recently has the idea of providing the opportunity for students to work on real-world problems with real clients taken hold. Today many business schools do seek to utilise experiential learning into their learning and teaching. The most common forms tend to include simple team-building exercises, business games and simulations, guest speakers and opportunities to take part in internships (Baden & Parkes, 2013). Whilst such activities can assist in connecting business students to business practice, students need opportunities to be more fully engaged as individuals and have the opportunity for self-reflection to truly gain the full benefits of experience-based learning (AACSB, 2002).

It is becoming increasingly understood that traditional methods of teaching business and management do not always prepare students adequately for the workplace. Fourcade and Go (2012) set out three key challenges faced by business managers which cannot be addressed through traditional teaching methods: (1) ongoing crisis and short-term focus of results which equates to a loss of meaning among managers; (2) how to deal with the proliferation of often contradictory and confusing standards; and (3) increasing demands and shrinking resources. When considering these challenges, it could be argued that all three can be seen as sustainability challenges. Firstly, business leaders are increasingly facing sustainability- and ethics-related crisis challenges, such as having to deal with the impacts of climate change or ethical scandals. These challenges are exacerbated when coupled with the often short-term focus of business strategies and financial models. Second, it could be argued that the proliferation

of environmental and social sustainability standards and reporting mechanisms are second only to those that cover health and safety. Third, nowhere are the challenges of increased demand and shrinking resources more evident than when considering research depletion and the need to diversify from non-renewable resources. So if experiential learning methods are important to teaching and preparing business and management students for the world of work in general, more so are they important when preparing them to address sustainability and ethical challenges.

Experiential Learning for Responsible Management Education

All the arguments above lead us to the same point. How do we develop business and management education to be able to addresses the grand challenges that face both the business world and society as a whole? We have learnt that business education must be experiential in nature in order to address the gap between knowledge and experience. But it should also act across discipline boundaries in the same way in which global sustainability challenges do. Experiential approaches tend to combine theory with practice. In the context of responsible management education, it has been suggested that the type of pedagogical method required to positively influence behaviour in a more sustainable manner would be one that is able to generate positive beliefs and attitudes towards sustainability and related issues (Baden & Parkes, 2013). For example, if students believe that it is possible for businesses to be both successful and ethical, that such ethical/sustainable businesses exist and are something to be aspired to. Finally, sustainability is inherently a transdisciplinary subject which adds a multidisciplinary dimension to experiential learning. This leads us to consider how experiential learning is being used in an increasing number of educational institutions and beyond. Experiential leaning to enhance students' understanding of responsible management and sustainability issues can take place in a variety of contexts; formal and informal; inside the higher education institution and externally.

Formal Institutional Approaches

An example of formal, curriculum-embedded experiential learning can be found in Newcastle Business School, Northumbria University. The institution, based in the North-East of England, is one of the largest in the country, with approximately 38,000 enrolled students, over 5000 of whom study in the business school. In 2018, the university released its new five-year strategic plan which includes 'business outcomes' that break the overall strategy down into operational objectives. Business Outcome 52 sets out the intention to achieve an 'Enhanced reputation for Sustainability' using the Sustainable Development Goals (SDGs) as a framework to map the current and potential contributions to be made through teaching and research activities. In response to the strategy, the business school has designed its programmes alongside the principles of 'Engaged Learning; Experiential Learning; Enquiry Based Learning; and Education for Entrepreneurship'. These principles are operationalised through an experiential spine embedded within taught programmes which introduces students to collaborative, problem-based learning designed to equip them to tackle complex sustainability challenges.

All undergraduate students begin by studying a core module titled 'Building Business Practice', which seeks to facilitate student learning through student research projects delivered over the course of a year through a two-hour workshop each week plus a one-hour facilitated group working session. Whilst the module itself is not inherently focused on ethics, responsibility or sustainability, the projects through which students apply their knowledge and skills are. Care is

taken to refer to the global challenges articulated through the SDGs to help students better understand the responsibility of business in dealing with such issues and the role they play as individuals. The result is that students are exposed to responsibility issues through their general educational experience which helps to normalise these topics, rather than isolate them which may lead the students to perceive responsibility as an additional consideration. In the second-year students study a 'Building Professional Practice' module focused exclusively on the social economy and social enterprise organisations as well as alternative business and service delivery mechanisms. This design is driven by a desire to expose students to different business models and organisational forms that exist or are emerging, as well as issues of ethical practice, sustainable organisations and responsible management. Student 'consultancy teams' work remotely with real organisations on a range of development, growth and sustainability issues ranging in complexity that challenge students to provide recommendations for client organisations. Students are asked to reflect on their learning and experiences, both in relation to employability skills and competence and in providing a critical reflection on enquiry-based learning in this context, emphasising that the practical accomplishment of learning requires some degree of critical reflective thinking (Scott-Cato & Myers, 2010).

In the final year, the focus shifts to undergraduate project work. There are three project pathways at the time of writing, with a fourth in development. The underlying rationale through all the business degrees is that every student can gain a 'real-world' experience and develop and enhance key transferable employability skills. Again, projects are not all explicitly linked to ethical, responsible or sustainable business, however increasingly these are exactly the type of projects that students seek to take on, and the skills employers are seeking. Many of the businesses who use the clinic are not-for-profit organisations who are looking to grow by taking their business in a new direction, explore new challenges or simply require fresh eyes to help them succeed (Hope, 2018). The embedded nature of experiential learning for responsible management education means that every student is exposed to sustainability issues and therefore leaves the university with an understanding as to the real-world challenges facing business organisations.

External, Informal Approaches

Experiential learning does not only have to take place within formal educational settings. Learning by doing can be most effective within the workplace and as such higher education institutions can act by facilitating partnership with organisations, signposting to students or offering their time and experience to assist extramural activity and nurture and develop links between different community stakeholders (Hope, 2016). An example of such a project is the Umuzi Academy, which offers a free one-year programme of learning that produces high-calibre, entry-level designers, copywriters, digital and multimedia professionals. The academy was established in response to what was described as a crisis in South African education. High fees in the tertiary education sector put university level education out of reach for many South Africans resulting in protests in 2015/2016. Of those who did manage to enter higher education, 50% would drop out within the first year. In order to address this Umuzi works with leading employers to equip talented young people with the digital skills the job sector in South Africa requires, thus enabling them to access high-value careers (Umuzi, 2019). Many of the students at Umuzi are university dropouts who, whilst bright and engaged learners, could not afford to continue paying university fees. Students are sponsored by companies who offer work experience and contribute to their training and development and more than 80% of the recruits get full-time jobs after completing the programme (Mail & Guardian, 2018).

Umuzi has experimented with various modes of education finding that by far the most effective has been on-the-job, experiential, engaged. Umuzi runs out of a large open-plan studio in Johannesburg where they don't employ traditional educators, instead hiring experienced, senior creatives, from leading agencies, to manage and mentor students to undertake real work. Briefs come from clients, community-based organisations and partnerships with advertising agencies. The business organisations find benefits in collaborating with young Umuzi students as they simply do not have access to young, black people who represent much of their target demographic in their own creative departments (Pooley, 2016). Umuzi has emerged as a response to the state of higher education in South Africa and lack of formalised opportunities to engage with experiential learning.

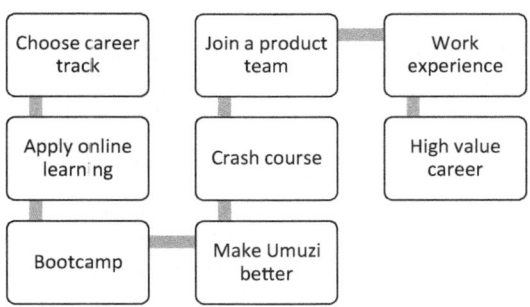

Figure 16.2　The Umuzi learning journey

It has clearly demonstrated the power of 'on the job' experiential learning in assisting students to enter high-value careers. By offering these opportunities to students from some of the more disadvantaged communities in South Africa, the organisation is helping not only individual learners, but also enhancing the economic sustainability of the entire country.

INFORMAL APPROACHES

The importance of exposing business and management students to real-life experiences, problems and sustainability issues is highlighted by one such project in the La Carpio district of San Jose, Costa Rica, one of Costa Rica's poorest slums. The project demonstrates how a research study may be used to offer informal approaches to experiential learning through the relationships built between a higher education institution and local community actors. La Carpio is a poor neighbourhood of approximately 40,000 residents, about half of whom are impoverished, Nicaraguan immigrants (Morgan & Vardell, 2010). Over half of the population lives below the poverty line (compared with 22% of the national population), and few residents have formal employment or title to their land (Morgan & Vardell, 2010). The project is led by the social venture System of Art Education for Social Inclusion (SIFAIS) and the Latin American Center for Competitiveness and Sustainable Development (CLACDS) and has created strong ties with INCAE Business School, one of the top business schools in Latin America. The project explores La Carpio's access to water, personal security, health, housing, education, information and communication, environmental quality, personal freedoms and higher education with an end goal to assess collective well-being and sustainability in a largely immigrant community that has been historically marginalized by the state and stereotyped by much of

society (Lang & Zúñiga, 2018). At the same time, SIFAS exists to provide support and mentorship to local entrepreneurs who out of necessity have had to find innovative ways in which to build businesses whilst faced with extremely limited resources (Resio, 2017).

Students studying in INCAE's Global MBS programme are engaged in assisting to analyse issues that residents of La Carpio experience whilst living and working in the district as well as attempting to take entrepreneurial action to start small businesses. This provides them with the opportunity to experience the environment at first hand and immerse themselves in an unfamiliar environment helping to expand their knowledge and understanding of sustainability issues. The role of such 'immersion experiences' as an experiential learning method is well understood in fields such as healthcare, multicultural studies, social work and general education. Such experiences can result in improved cultural awareness, help build empathy among teachers and enhance their understating of the range of issues facing different stakeholder groups. For the students of INCAE, engagement with the community of La Carpio assists them as future leaders and managers to consider the importance of community investment and that the business world should be sensitive to social needs (INCAE, 2018).

CONCLUSION

The teaching of ethics, responsibility, sustainability and other responsible management topics often necessitates educators to employ experiential and problem-based learning approaches. In doing so there is perhaps a greater opportunity to generate positive beliefs and attitudes among students towards sustainability and related issues. Whilst not all experiential learning activity can be explicitly linked to responsible management topics, it is the skills and competencies inherent in problem-based learning which equip students with the ability to deal with complex sustainability challenges. When students work collaboratively to co-develop solutions to sustainability problems, they are replicating the practices necessary within organisations in real life. This chapter has set out the different approaches that can be employed when considering how to enable students to engage in experiential learning for responsible management education. The three examples demonstrate that experiential learning can occur in different ways, in different contexts and within different countries. The results, however, are similar in that exposing students to a 'real life' learning experience, whether it be in the classroom or extramural, can assist students in developing the necessary skills, knowledge and empathy to respond to global responsibility challenges. The examples also indicate how experiential learning can be applied at any level of study across a range of management education programmes such as undergraduate, postgraduate, executive development and doctoral studies. Experiential learning techniques can also facilitate partnerships between educational institutions, businesses and other stakeholder to further the role of business in society, sustainable development, responsible management and the advancement of the SDGs.

If the intention is to learn and teach about sustainability, then we need to consider how learning approaches and pedagogies might be designed to enable students (and academics) to both learn about and question current management ideology, theory and practice. Students should be engaged in a supportive environment where they may work alongside academic tutors to co-produce knowledge linked to 'live' issues that organisations are facing. Such issues may include economics students exploring the value of green space in urban environments, or finance students investigating avenues for social as well as economic investment, or even students examining awareness of the SDGs and how

they may be implemented in the workplace. Business and management schools can achieve this by working in partnership with local social economy organisations, which provides opportunities for shared learning and curriculum development as students' videos and evaluations are provided to partner organisations who in turn feedback their actions and reactions.

REFERENCES

AACSB. (2002). *Management education at risk: report of the Management Education Task Force to the AACSB International Board of Directors.* Tampa, FL: AACSB International

Álvarez-Suárez, P., Vega-Marcote, P., & Mira, R. G (2013). Sustainable consumption: a teaching intervention in higher education. *International Journal of Sustainability in Higher Education, 15*(1), 3–15.

Backman, M., Pitt, H., Marsden, T., Mehmood, A., & Mathijs, E. (2019). Experiential approaches to sustainability education: towards learning landscapes. *International Journal of Sustainability in Higher Education, 20*(1), 139–156.

Baden, D., & Parkes, C. (2013). Experiential learning: inspiring the business leaders of tomorrow. *International Journal of Management & Enterprise Development, 32*(3), 295–308.

Barrett, T. (2010). The problem-based learning process as finding and being in flow. *Innovations in Education and Teaching International, 47*(2), 165–174.

Barrett, T., & Cashman, D. (2010). *A practitioners' guide to enquiry and problem-based learning.* Dublin: UCD Teaching and Learning. Available at: www.ucd.ie/t4cms/ucdtli0041.pdf.

Boud, D., Cohen, R., & Walker, D. (1993). *Using experience for learning.* Maidenhead: McGraw-Hill Education.

Bradley-Levine, J., Berghoff, B., Seybold, J, Sever, R., Blackwell, S., & Smiley, A. (2010). What teachers and administrators 'need to know' about project-based learning implementation. Annual Meeting of the American

Educational Research Association. Denver, CO. Available at: www.dr-hatfield.com/science_rules/articles/WHAT%20TEACHERS%20AND%20ADMINISTRATORS%20NEED%20TO%20KNOW%20ABOUT.pdf.

Carroll, A. B., & Buchholtz, A. K. (2014). *Business and Society: Ethics, Sustainability, and Stakeholder Management.* Cengage Learning.

Chan, C. K. Y. (2016). Facilitators' perspectives of the factors that affect the effectiveness of problem-based learning process. *Innovations in Education and Teaching International*, 53(1), 25–34.

Colby, A., Ehrlich, T., Sullivan, W. M., & Dolle, J. R. (2011). *Rethinking Undergraduate Business Education: Liberal Learning for the Profession.* John Wiley & Sons.

Croney, P. (2016). Undergraduate student expectations of role requirements and pedagogic relationships in a business school: a psychological contract approach. Doctoral thesis, Northumbria University. Available at: http://nrl.northumbria.ac.uk/27929/.

Datar, S. M., Garvin, D. A., & Cullen, P. G. (2010). *Rethinking the MBA: Business Education at a Crossroads.* Harvard Business Press.

Dean, K. L., & Beggs, J. M. (2006). University professors and teaching ethics: conceptualizations and expectations. *Journal of Management Education*, 30(1), 15–44.

Delaney, K., & Kelleher, J. B. (2008). *Real-world process design for mechanical engineering students: a case study of PBL in DIT.* Available at: https://arrow.dit.ie/engschmeccon/16/.

Ertmer, P. A., & Glazewski, K. D. (2015). Essentials for PBL implementation: fostering collaboration, transforming roles, and scaffolding learning. In Walker, H., Leary, H., Hmelo-Silver. C.E. and Ertmer, P. A. (Eds.), *Essential readings in problem-based learning* (pp. 89–106). West Lafayette, IN: Purdue University Press.

Ertmer, P. A., & Simons, K. D. (2005). Scaffolding teachers' efforts to implement problem-based learning. *International Journal of Learning*, 12(4), 319–328.

Fenwick, T. (2005). Ethical dilemmas of critical management education: within classrooms and beyond. *Management Learning*, 36(1), 31–48.

Forrester, D. A. R. (1990). Rational administration, finance and control accounting: the experience of cameralism. *Critical Perspectives on Accounting*, 1(4), 285–317.

Fourcade, F., & Go, N. (2012). Towards a new paradigm in experiential learning: lessons learned from kindergarten. *International Journal of Management & Enterprise Development*, 31(3), 198–208.

Hensley, N. (2017). The future of sustainability in higher education. *International Journal of Sustainability in Higher Education*. Available at: www.susted.com/wordpress/wp-content/uploads/2017/03/Hensley-JSE-March-2017-Future-Casting-Issue-PDF.pdf.

Hmelo-Silver, C. E., Duncan, R. G., & Chinn, C. A. (2007). Scaffolding and achievement in problem-based and inquiry learning: a response to Kirschner, Sweller, and Clark. *Educational Psychologist*, 42(2), 99–107.

Hodge, L., Proudford, K. L., & Holt, H., Jr. (2014). From periphery to core: the increasing relevance of experiential learning in undergraduate business education. *Research in Higher Education Journal.* Available at: https://eric.ed.gov/?id=EJ1055308.

Hope, A. (2016). Creating sustainable cities through knowledge exchange: a case study of knowledge transfer partnerships. *International Journal of Sustainability in Higher Education*, 17(6), 796–811.

Hope, A. J. (2018). The PRME Curriculum Tree: a framework for responsible management education in undergraduate business degree programmes. In Flynn, P. M., Tan, T. K., & Gudic, M. (Eds.), *Redefining success: integrating sustainability into management education.* Abingdon: Greenleaf/PRME.

Illeris, K. (2007). *How we learn: learning and non-learning in school and beyond.* Available at: https://content.taylorfrancis.com/books/download?dac=C2009-0-22893-9&isbn=9781134071371&format=google PreviewPdf.

INCAE. (2018). INCAE analyzes the exceptional case of SIFAIS Foundation in La Carpio. Available at: www.incae.edu/en/blog/2018/01/09/incae-analyzes-exceptional-case-sifais-foundation-la-carpio.html

Iyer-Raniga, U., & Andamon, M. M. (2016). Transformative learning: innovating sustainability education in built environment.

International Journal of Sustainability in Higher Education. doi:10.1108/IJSHE-09-2014-0121.

Joham, C., & Clarke, M. (2012). Teaching critical management skills: the role of problem-based learning. *Teaching in Higher Education*, *17*(1), 75–88.

Kahn, P., & O'Rourke, K. (2005). Understanding enquiry-based learning. In Barrett, T., Mac Labhrainn, I., & Fallon, H. (Eds.), *Handbook of Enquiry & Problem Based Learning* (pp. 1–12). Galway: CELT.

Kirschner, P. A., Sweller, J., & Clark, R. E. (2006). Why minimal guidance during instruction does not work: an analysis of the failure of constructivist, discovery, problem-based, experiential, and inquiry-based teaching. *Educational Psychologist*, *41*(2). 75–86.

Kolb, D. (1984). *Experiential learning as the science of learning and development.* Englewood Cliffs, NJ: Prentice Hall.

Lang, E., & Zúñiga, A. (2018). By the community, for the community: measuring progress in La Carpio. The Tico Times. Costa Rica. Available at: https://ticotimes.net/2018/04/12/by-the-community-for-the-community-new-measures-of-progress-in-la-carpio.

Lee, J. S., Blackwell, S., Drake, J., & Moran, K. A. (2014). Taking a leap of faith: redefining teaching and learning in higher education through project-based learning. *Interdisciplinary Journal of Problem-Based Learning*, *8*(2), 2.

Levy, P., & Petrulis, R. (2012). How do first-year university students experience inquiry and research, and what are the implications for the practice of inquiry-based learning? *Studies in Higher Education*, *37*(1), 85–101. doi:10.1080/03075079.2010.499166

Lozano, R., Lukman, R., Lozano, F. J., Huisingh, D., & Lambrechts, W. (2013). Declarations for sustainability in higher education: becoming better leaders, through addressing the university system. *Journal of Cleaner Production*, *48*, 10–19.

Mail & Guardian. (2018). Gilbert Pooley. From Mail & Guardian 200 Young South Africans website. Available at: https://200youngsouthafricans.co.za/gilbert-pooley/.

McDonald, G. M., & Donleavy, G. D. (1995). Objections to the teaching of business ethics. *Journal of Business Ethics: JBE*, *14*(10), 839–853.

McPherson, S., Anid, N. M., Ashton, W. S., Hurtado-Martín, M., Khalili, N., & Panero, M. (2016). Pathways to cleaner production in the Americas II: Application of a competency model to experiential learning for sustainability education. *Journal of Cleaner Production*, *135*, 907–918.

Mintzberg, H. (2005). *Managers not MBAs: a hard look at the soft practice of managing and management development.* San Francisco: Berrett-Koehler.

Moon, J. A. (2013). *A handbook of reflective and experiential learning: theory and practice.* Abingdon: Routledge.

Morgan, M. Y., & Vardell, R. (2010). Empowering women through photo-voice: women of La Carpio, Costa Rica. *Journal of Ethnographic & Qualitative Research*, *5*, 31–44.

Ocak, M. A., & Uluyol, Ç. (2010). Investigation of students' intrinsic motivation in project based learning. *Journal of Human Sciences*, *7*(1), 1152–1169.

O'Hanlon, A., Winefield, H., Hejka, E., & Chur-Hansen, A. (1995). Initial responses of first-year medical students to problem-based learning in a behavioural science course: role of language background and course content. *Medical Education*, *29*(3), 198–204.

Parker, M. (2018). *Shut down the business school: what's wrong with management education.* London: Pluto Press.

Perlstein, A., Mortimer, M., & Robertson, D. (2017). Making sustainable development real through role-play: 'The Mekong Game' example. *Journal of Sustainability Education*, 12. Available at: www.susted.com/wordpress/wp-content/uploads/2017/02/Perlstein-et-al-JSE-Feb-2017-General-Issue-PDF1.pdf.

Pfeffer, J., & Fong, C. T. (2002). The end of business schools? Less success than meets the eye. *Academy of Management Learning & Education*, *1*(1), 78–95.

Pooley, G. (2016). Here are alternative solutions to the higher education crisis. HuffPost, 2 December. Available at: www.huffingtonpost.co.uk/gilbert-pooley/alternative-solutions-to-the-higher-education-crisis_a_21618415/.

Ramey, L. (2013). Engaging learners in community service learning to enhance teacher preparation curriculum. *Journal of Sustainability Education*, 5. Available at: www.jsedimensions.org/wordpress/wp-content/

uploads/2013/06/LindaRameyOpinionPiece PDFReady.pdf.

Redlich, F. (1957). Academic education for business: its development and the contribution of Ignaz Jastrow (1856–1937) in commemoration of the Hundredth Anniversary of Jastrow's birth. *Business History Review*, *31*(1), 35–91.

Remidez, H., & Fodness, D. (2015). An experiential approach to building capability in business and IS students. *Journal of the Academy of Business Education*, Spring, 175–191. Available at: www.researchgate.net/profile/ Herbert_Remidez/publication/276278556_ An_Experiential_Approach_to_Building_ Capability_in_Business_and_IS_Students/ links/555526a008aeaaff3bf459b3.pdf.

Resio, P. (2017) Learning entrepreneurship through a Central American lens. *Global Network for Advanced Management website*, 30 August. Available at: https:// globalnetwork.io/news/2017/08/learning-entrepreneurship-through-central-american-lens.

Reynolds, M., & Vince, R. (2007). *Handbook of experiential learning and management education*. Oxford: Oxford University Press.

Richardson, H. G. (1940). Business training in medieval Oxford. *American History Review*, *46*, 259–278.

Rolfe, H. (2002). Students' demands and expectations in an age of reduced financial support: the perspectives of lecturers in four English universities. *Journal of Higher Education Policy and Management*, 24(2), 171–182.

Savage, E., Tapics, T., Evarts, J., Wilson, J., & Tirone, S. (2015). Experiential learning for sustainability leadership in higher education. *International Journal of Sustainability in Higher Education*, *16*(5), 692–705.

Savery, J. R. (2006). Overview of problem-based learning: definition and distinctions, The interdisciplinary. *Journal of Problem-Based Learning*. Available at: http://citeseerx. ist.psu.edu/viewdoc/summary?doi= 10.1.1.557.6406.

Scherpereel, C. M., & Bowers, M. Y. (2014). Using critical problem based learning factors in an integrated undergraduate business curriculum: a business course success. *Developments in Business Simulation and Experiential Learning*, 33.

Scott-Cato, M., & Myers, J. (2010). Education as re-embedding: Stroud Communiversity, walking the land and the enduring spell of the sensuous. *Sustainability: Science Practice and Policy*, *3*(1), 51–68.

Seaman, J., Brown, M., & Quay, J. (2017). The evolution of experiential learning theory: tracing lines of research in the JEE. *Journal of Experiential Education*, *40*(4), NP1–NP21.

Smith, G. F. (2005). Problem-based learning: can it improve managerial thinking? *Journal of Management Education*, *29*(2), 357–378.

Spender, J.-C. (2005). Speaking about management education. *Management Decision*, *43*(10), 1282–1292.

Sterling, S. (2012). *The Future Fit Framework*. Available at: www.heacademy.ac.uk/system/ files/future_fit_270412_1435.pdf.

Sterling, S. (2011). Transformative learning and sustainability: sketching the conceptual ground. *Learning and Teaching in Higher Education*, *5*(11), 17–33.

Sterling, S. (2013). An analysis of the development of sustainability education internationally: evolution, interpretation and transformative potential. In Blewitt, J., & Cullingford, C. (Eds.), *The sustainability curriculum: the challenge for higher education* (pp. 56–75). Abingdon: Routledge.

Sterling, S., & Thomas, I. (2006). Education for sustainability: the role of capabilities in guiding university curricula. *International Journal of Innovation & Sustainable Development*, *1*(4), 349–370.

Sunley, R., & Leigh, J. (Eds.) (2016). *Educating for responsible management: putting theory into practice*. Sheffield: Greenleaf.

Taylor, E. W. (1998). The theory and practice of transformative learning: a critical review. Available at: https://eric.ed.gov/?id=ED423422.

Taylor, J. A., & Bedford, T. (2004). Staff perceptions of factors related to non-completion in higher education. *Studies in Higher Education*, 29(3), 375–394.

Tilbury, D. (2004). Environmental Education for sustainability: a force for change in higher education. In Corcoran, P. B., & Wals, A. E. J. (Eds.), *Higher education and the challenge of sustainability: problematics, promise, and practice* (pp. 97–112). Dordrecht: Springer Netherlands.

Tynjälä, P. (2008). Perspectives into learning at the workplace. *Educational Research Review*, *3*(2), 130–154.

Umuzi. (2019). Umuzi. Retrieved 27 October 2019 from Umuzi website at https://www.umuzi.org/.

UNESCO. (2004). United Nations Decade of Education for Sustainable Development: Draft International Implementation Scheme (IIS). Paris: United Nations Educational, Scientific and Cultural Organization.

Waddock, S., & Lozano, J. M. (2013). Developing more holistic management education: lessons learned from two programs. *Academy of Management Learning & Education*, *12*(2), 265–284.

Waples, E. P., Antes, A. L., Murphy, S. T., Connelly, S., & Mumford, M. D. (2009). A meta-analytic investigation of business ethics instruction. *Journal of Business Ethics: JBE*, *87*(1), 133–151.

Weinert, F. E. (2001). Concept of competence: a conceptual clarification. In Rychen, D. S., & Salganik, L. H. (Eds.) *Defining and selecting key competencies* (pp. 45–65). Boston, MA: Hogrefe & Huber.

Zimitat, C., Hamilton, S., Dejersey, J., Reilly, P., & Ward, L. (1994). *Problem-based learning in metabolic biochemistry*. Brisbane: Florey Institute, University of Queensland.

17

Virtues in Responsible Management Education: Building Character

Marcel Meyer and Alejo José G. Sison

INTRODUCTION

In today's business world the focus lies on accomplishments. The means with which they were achieved are at best secondary, and in a society where money 'rules', even less attention is paid to the moral value of outcomes. The emphasis is on 'what works'. Thus, it does not come as a surprise that virtues are commonly perceived as the product of naïveté and considered irrelevant in corporate environments. Business scholars have largely ignored the role of virtues in organizational life (Cameron & Caza, 2002; Cameron, Bright & Caza, 2004). However, in Anglo-American philosophy, virtue ethics has recently made a comeback vis-à-vis consequentialism and deontology (Snow, 2015). This resurgence has led to a growing number of organizational and management scholars paying more attention to the virtues (Ferrero & Sison, 2014). Perspectives from philosophy, theology and psychology regarding the cultivation of virtue have begun to influence not only business ethics, but also leadership and management studies, among other areas of the administrative sciences. Positive Organizational Scholarship (POS), for example, a novel, but rapidly growing field of research, studies extraordinary individual and organizational performance, concerning itself with conditions that promote and enable *virtuous behaviours* and positive emotions (Meyer, 2015). This should not come as a surprise when organizational misbehaviour and cases of environmental destruction are getting more attention (Meyer, Sison & Ferrero, 2018) and many employees and leaders describe their environment as gloomy (Youssef-Morgan & Luthans, 2013).

'Over the last 10 years we have seen a plethora of ethical scandals, along with financial crises and leadership controversies' (Hibbert & Cunliffe, 2013: 178). What is more, scandals such as the 'Dieselgate' (Huehn, Meyer & Racelis, 2018) or the Theranos scandal (Ramsey, 2018) have shown that corporate social responsibility (CSR) marketing campaigns and corporate compliance programmes do not make a company more ethical. It needs more than rules and policies for a company to avoid wrongdoing (Reeves, Dierksmeier & Chittaro, 2018). Gleaming CSR projects might help create the image of an ethically run company, but do not assure corporate ethical behaviour in the long term. Neither do corporate compliance or CSR campaigns help develop the moral identity (as a set of character traits) of employees or a morally sound organizational culture. Thus, organizational and management scholars have now started to emphasize the role of character for businesses and leadership (Crossan, Byrne, Seijts, Reno, Monzani & Gandz, 2017) and point to the virtues to create more ethical, responsible and sustainable organizations.

This chapter starts by laying out the nature of the virtues and clarifying their importance in business. This first segment, apart from showcasing the evolution of Virtue Ethics in business and management, explains how the virtues refer to the 'nature' and 'final end' of human beings, applying to a full range of dispositions to action. A careful reading of Aristotle shows that the virtues, as 'character excellences', also refer to inclinations and tendencies, actions and habits, and, indeed, even lives taken as a whole (Sison, 2003).

The second part of this chapter focuses on the development of the virtues *in* organizations. It highlights two essential aspects of virtue. Initially, we show the crucial role of growing routines in business ethics education. We explain how habits are acquired, nurtured and finally perfected. We describe how the conscious and reflective repetition of virtuous actions can positively transform the character of an agent. Hereby we refer to the craft analogy in the virtues (Russel, 2015). The similarity between learning a craft or skill and becoming virtuous leads us to the subsequent part. There we describe the crucial role of 'practical wisdom' (*phronesis*) for the development of the virtues. *Phronesis* is essential for the virtues to evolve and has been

identified as an important feature for leadership and management education (Huehn 2016; Melé, 2010). Aristotle describes *phronesis* in the Nicomachean Ethics as the virtue of choosing the suitable means to the right end. Since observable conduct alone, without knowledge of underlying feelings and motivations, is not enough for practical wisdom or the development of virtue in general, we underscore the importance of the alignment of emotions and action in virtue ethics education. This leads us to a discussion of the different Aristotelian character types.

The third and final section illuminates the function of organizational conditions and the major role of leadership for the development of the virtues *through* businesses (Cameron, 2003; Meyer et al., 2018). We draw not only from accounts of Aristotelian virtue, but also from positive organizational virtuousness (Meyer, 2016; Cameron & Winn, 2012). Notwithstanding that virtue ethics means to provide guidance beyond context, we explain, through the lens of Positive Organizational Scholarship, how formal organizational features (e.g. structures, rules, policies) in combination with the right leadership can foster the development of environments conducive to the virtues, thus helping organizations to do *good* and well in a sustainable manner (Meyer, 2015). Finally, conclusions and some practical advice complete this chapter. Through a focus on moral character building, we aim to stimulate a lively discussion integrating ethics, sustainability, and responsibility.

ARISTOTELIAN VIRTUE ETHICS IN BUSINESS

The word 'virtue' has its origin in the Greek concept of 'arête', which signifies 'what is best' or 'excellent' in human beings. Thus, virtue describes 'human excellence' and refers to 'what is best in human beings'.

This part starts by laying out the 'nature' and the 'final end' of human beings as understood by Aristotle. Building on these antecedents, we, then, expound on virtues as 'character excellences' and explain how they can also refer to inclinations and tendencies, actions and habits, and, indeed, even lives taken as a whole. Finally, we briefly showcase the evolution of virtue ethics in business and management.

The 'Nature' and 'Final End' of Human Beings

To know what is best *in* and *for* human beings, Aristotle stresses the importance of discovering first and foremost (a) what human beings are and (b) what the aim of human life is. Regarding the former, Aristotle refers to the 'nature' (*physis*) of human beings, describing their characteristic activity or function (*ergon*) in the Nicomachean Ethics (henceforth NE) and the Politics (henceforth Pltcs). He comprehends humans to be 'political animals' (NE: 1097b; Pltcs: 1253a), 'living creatures that use words' (Pltcs: 1253a; Metaphysics 1037b), and beings capable of rational thought (*logos*). Apart from considering the individual aspect of human beings, Aristotle also highlights their social dimension, as beings that can intelligently communicate and live in dynamic, but stable structures. Concerning the latter, Aristotle proposes the 'final end' of human beings as happiness or flourishing (*eudaimonia*) (NE: 1097b–1098a).

Flourishing depends, first, on the individual itself, because it requires the perfection of a person's nature as a social and rational creature through the practice of the virtues, the quest for excellence, which leads to personal thriving. 'Virtues are necessary for and partially constitutive of flourishing' (Sison, Ferrero & Guitián, 2018). However, flourishing, as described by Aristotle, depends further on two important aspects. It rests on (a) an individual's community and (b) to a certain extent, also on material means.

Firstly, as the individual and social characteristics of humans are interconnected, Aristotle thinks that people cannot flourish without being part of some sort of society. No person can thrive without other people achieving a certain level of well-being too. Flourishing is a common good. The individual and its community are linked in the pursuit of excellence and, especially, flourishing, which for Aristotle represents a fully developed human existence (Pltcs: 1252b). Secondly, even though one needs virtues to thrive, one also needs material means, because flourishing not only includes *doing well*, but also *living well* (NE: 1098a). Thus, Aristotle distinguishes between virtues, which he considers to be 'goods of the soul' and material resources, which are 'external goods' (NE: 1098b; Pltcs: 1323a). Even though Aristotle considers both necessary to flourish, he clearly states that external, bodily goods are of less importance. They are significant only in so far as they are indispensable for the performance of excellent actions, for becoming virtuous (Pltcs: 1324a). Material goods are mere means to achieve the supreme goal of flourishing, the final end that we desire only for itself and nothing else (Meyer, 2015).

The 'Nature' of the Virtues

Virtues usually refer to 'excellences' found in a person's character. However, they can also denote other capacities or dispositions typical for human beings, such as habits (NE 1103a). A virtuous character results from the development and realization of virtuous habits. Habits derive from the frequent repetition of virtuous actions, caused by virtuous inclinations or tendencies consistent with human nature and its final end. Therefore, a careful interpretation of Aristotle discloses that virtues not only imply character traits, but also signify, analogously, inclinations and tendencies, actions, habits and, indeed, even lives taken as a whole. As Flynn highlights: 'In Aristotle's view, a fulfilled life is a life lived *kat' aretên* – in accordance with virtue' (2008: 363). Let us now explain these different, but interwoven parts of virtue.

Aristotelian ethics is based on the idea of 'proper human functioning' (*ergon*), which indicates 'some sort of life of action of the [part of the soul] that has reason' (NE: 1098a). Hence, actions are the building blocks of virtue. Not only are they easily observable but also fundamental, because an agent's emotions, thoughts or inclinations obtain moral relevance only through deeds. In contrast, happenings or events external to an individual's sphere of responsibility cannot be understood as an indication of the ethical quality of a person. To account for the moral significance of actions, one must make a distinction between acts that are performed willingly and freely, on the one hand, and actions performed against one's will, on the other hand. Like fortuitous occurrences (e.g. winning a lottery), involuntary actions take place by force of nature; people are passive subjects (NE: 1110a). The human actions that are related to the character are those performed intentionally after deliberation; acts that express feelings, desires or will. For this reason, to evaluate whether an action is good or evil, it is essential to comprehend (a) an action's aim, (b) an agent's motivation and (c) the conditions surrounding the deed. Even though the object of an act is the most significant aspect in the evaluation of deeds, for a correct assessment we also need to consider an actor's intentions. It is not enough to give the *impression* of being good; an agent's intentions need to be aligned with his or her final end as a human being to make a deed virtuous. Similarly, the circumstances under which an action is performed must also be considered. Consider, for example, a courageous, hard-working manager trying to avoid layoffs in times of crisis. However, due to unfortunate and biased negative media coverage all the manager's efforts are in vain, and she is forced to close the business. While adverse conditions can devalue an 'a priori' good action or even turn it evil, advantageous situations do not change the moral quality of an action from evil to good. In sum, a virtuous act entails the integrity and confluence of its object, intention and circumstances.

Habits are a second level of Aristotelian virtue ethics. A habit can broadly be described as a firm disposition of being, doing, or acting. Habits result from the frequent repetition of voluntary actions (NE: 1103a). Voluntary actions and their transformation into habits presuppose freedom on three different levels: (1) physical freedom, (2) psychological freedom and (3) moral freedom. Physical freedom means that an agent is, for example, not held prisoner in a penitentiary, but has the capacity for motion/movement. Psychological freedom means that an agent's decision is based on free choice, taking for granted that this agent's independent will is the determining factor in the decision-making process, and that he or she takes full responsibility for his or her decisions. Physical freedom and psychological freedom relate to our natural condition and are thus freedoms from contrary physical forces and psychological factors. Moral freedom is different. It means the free choice to seek something larger and nobler than our natural condition. One attains such freedom when he or she grows virtues as good habits.

Virtuous habits aid an agent to perform more good actions better. Habits, in general, do not only improve an agent's set of skills through continuous practice or training, but also increase the level of pleasure and satisfaction derived from repeated performance. The same is true for 'moral' skills. Imagine, for example, the executive of a small company, who improves her feedback techniques by being more compassionate. Habits or routines, enhanced and strengthened dispositions, constitute something like a 'second nature'. Sooner than later, our executive would *be seen* not only as more caring, but also *become* more concerned and benevolent. Ideally, she would even be considered a role-model and her conduct would start to positively influence her co-workers' conduct as well. Such an effect would not be considered rare, because leaders, as role models, can have a strong impact on their employees through their performance (Cameron & Caza, 2002).

Both virtues and vices arise from the repetition of actions (NE: 1103b), but only good deeds produce virtues. For example, in face of adversity, only those who have the habit of responding with courage will be valiant and self-assured. Those who do not are paralysed by fear. Only a person prepared to react courageously would opt to reveal managerial malpractice to the relevant authorities or the public as a result.

Character is the third and most common level in which we find the virtues. Virtue theories solely based on behaviour generally count as weak conceptions of virtue. Aristotle considers character states the proper locus for virtue (NE: 1106a). Character means a more precise and complete depiction of a human being than habits or actions alone because it displays greater permanence and is more difficult to alter. Even though character, in some way, is constituted by habits, as with successful work teams, the sum is greater than the mere aggregation of parts.

Character incorporates various habits. These habits, unsurprisingly, can be found in various stages of development. While a person might be courageous and compassionate, this same person might be, at the same time, more caring than brave. What is more, one habit might influence another habit positively or negatively. A prudent person, for example, is more likely to be brave, just or temperate. Thus, character describes the entirety of a person's habits plus their degree of development, providing a person with an inimitable touch.

Lifestyle embodies how a person feels, behaves and lives. A lifestyle is an all-inclusive choice. It represents, first and foremost, a person's aim in life and corresponds to a person's ideals and moral point of view. Most people would agree that human beings ultimately seek *eudaimonia* or a flourishing life. Therefore, all our actions are directed towards this final goal, which is desirable in itself. Everything else becomes significant because of it. Flourishing exemplifies the absolute form of virtue or moral excellence and can be understood as human nature in its perfect state. Still, even

though most human beings agree that they seek flourishing (*eudaimonia*), there are different interpretations of what exactly this means and involves. Ideally, an individual's goals and moral points of view are in line with the principles and values of the corporation he or she works for.

Aristotle differentiated between four main lifestyles: (a) one focused on wealth or money (NE: 1096a), (b) one aimed at pleasure (NE: 1095b), (c) one that pursues honour (NE: 1095b) and (d) one directed toward knowledge or study (NE: 1098b). His deliberations show that not the search for money, nor pleasure, nor honour lead to true flourishing; the life of study and the search for knowledge is what represents the highest form of virtue (NE: 1177a). Even though Aristotle acknowledged that a certain level of wealth can be useful for attaining a flourishing life, money is only of instrumental value. Similarly, Aristotle acknowledged the appeal of pleasure, but argues that such a life would be somewhat 'slavish', and that human beings should aspire instead for higher things. The third option, a life of action, a political life that pursues honour, is certainly more elevated than a life dedicated to gratification. Still, even such a lifestyle appears somewhat 'superficial' (NE: 1095b). Finally, Aristotle explained why a life of study is the best option to attain flourishing. A life dedicated to knowledge and study is self-contained and includes its own end (NE: 1098b). It is also pleasant in itself, embodying an important part of the soul's proper activity (NE: 1099a). Lastly, a life of study is in accordance with reason and sound judgment (NE: 1099a). Hence, a person devoted to study and knowledge pursues the noblest objects (NE: 1100b). A life of study is in accordance with a life of virtue.

In a certain way we can observe this reasoning among many corporations and their human resources practices. Many successful organizations acknowledge that simply paying a monthly salary, even though an essential part of any serious workplace is not enough to truly motivate employees. Thus companies such as Google, Starbucks, Reebok, or Spotify offer their employees additional compensations (i.e. *pleasures*) such as free food, free education, sports classes and free concerts (Schrodt, 2017). As the 2018 Global Talent Trends survey reveals, nowadays, that employees highly value a focus on well-being at their company, including perks such regular health screenings and frequent 'lunch and learn' sessions (Kohll, 2018). On top of such sweeteners many organizations tend to give credit to their employees for work well done (i.e. recognize and *honour* their accomplishments) through award programmes such as peer-to-peer recognition, customer service awards, volunteer awards, and so forth. Finally, many companies not only opt for stressing a *'higher purpose'* in their vision and mission statements, but also ingrain it into their corporate culture (e.g. Patagonia, Zingerman's, Warby Parker). Motivation can come from different sources at once (Hilliard, 2013), and these business examples show how companies can combine extrinsic and intrinsic motivations.

The Evolution of Virtue Ethics in Business and Management

Together with utilitarianism and deontology, virtue ethics is largely recognized as one of the three major schools of ethics. In business and management literature, however, the other two schools have long been dominant, virtue ethics being only of marginal importance. This near absence of virtue ethics in business and management was probably not because scholars and practitioners were ignorant about virtue ethics, but because virtue ethics was simply not thought fit for business. So, despite their long history, business scholars mostly avoided considering virtues in organizational life (Cameron et al., 2004; Cameron and Caza, 2002). Still today, the virtues are sometimes perceived as naive and inappropriate in corporate environments. Lately, however, virtue ethics has returned to the forefront (Petri, 2017),

especially in Anglo-American philosophy as an alternative to consequentialism and deontology (Snow, 2015). This resurgence has led to a growing number of organizational and management scholars paying more attention to the virtues (Ferrero & Sison, 2014). Perspectives from philosophy, theology and psychology regarding the cultivation of virtue have started to influence not only research in business ethics, but also leadership and management studies among other areas.

In the 1980s, the rebirth of virtue ethics was a rather slow process. The first mention of virtue ethics back then was in relation to marketing (Robin & Reidenbach, 1987). However, in the 1990s the topic gained more influence, and by 1999, the rate of articles published on virtue ethics rose steadily. The virtues also reappeared in teaching. Then, from the turn of the millennium until 2009, articles concerning virtue ethics nearly doubled compared to the previous decade (Ferrero & Sison, 2014).

BUSINESS ETHICS EDUCATION: DEVELOPING VIRTUES *IN* ORGANIZATIONS

Growing virtuous habits and developing practical wisdom together leads to character excellence. In other words, being good at living one's life means to have the right goals (i.e. virtues) and to know how to realize those goals (i.e. practical wisdom).

This section focuses on the development of virtues. First, we highlight the role of growing routines in business ethics education. We explain how virtuous habits are acquired, nurtured and finally perfected. Second, we illustrate the crucial role of practical wisdom (*phronesis*) in virtue ethics. Aristotle describes 'practical wisdom' as the virtue of choosing the suitable means to the right end. Phronesis is essential for virtues to develop. However, since observable conduct alone, without knowledge of underlying feelings and motivations, is not enough for practical wisdom or the development of virtue in general, this part also deals with the importance of the alignment of emotions and action for becoming virtuous. This leads us finally to the different character types which Aristotle distinguishes.

Growing Habits: The Power of Having Routines

Following Hursthouse and Pettigrove (2016) virtues are 'multi-track dispositions' attributable to a 'certain sort of person with a certain complex mindset'. Hence, (1) no one is born virtuous and (2) to become virtuous is an achievement. In other words, virtues are not given to us; they do not simply appear, but virtues are something we must develop (Russel, 2015). To be virtuous or not is not an 'act of nature' or a biological occurrence beyond one's dominion. It is, rather, the result of decisions made in accordance with reason. No one can be forced to become virtuous. What is more, virtues can be gained, but they can also be lost. The development of virtues is not a unidirectional, accumulative process. There is no guarantee that one will become a virtuous person – it is an individual choice, which implies dedication and needs time. Aristotle was aware that complete virtuousness might not be reachable in a single lifetime and that highly virtuous persons are rare, but he also affirmed that all human beings have the capacity to develop virtues and become virtuous. One crucial step to becoming virtuous is to develop virtuous routines. So, how do we grow such habits, and how do we distinguish between right and wrong habituation?

As a famous radio commercial in Spain says: You expect the doctor performing your surgery to have done the procedure many times before. You also expect the pilot taking you from Madrid to New York to have thousands of flight hours. So, why would you listen to a radio station playing hits from singers or groups that have only recently gained popularity through a casting show? In short, the message from this radio station (ROCK FM) is that people who have ample experience do a better job. Having experience means that one has probably gone through a long process of learning. An assignment we have completed many times becomes easier every time we perform it, because the development of a habit or routine regularly includes an integrated feedback loop. Thus, habits result from the repetition of voluntary actions (NE 1103a). Such routines, then, create capacities and lead us to develop our full potential. Hence, we know exactly how to perform a certain task and how possible mistakes can be avoided. We find better ways to react when something unpredictable comes up and we know how to successfully finish the task. At its core, developing a habit means the conscious repetition of a certain type of action until it forms part of our 'nature' (Sison & Ferrero, 2015). Consider, for example, an employee that has recently started to use new software. At first the employee struggles with all the new tools it includes and has problems using them. She feels overwhelmed by all the information and the possibilities the new software offers. Still, despite her uneasiness, she decides to give the computer program a chance and learns how to use it. Every time she uses it, she makes mental notes on how the different tools function. Whenever she uses the new system, she discovers that she becomes better at using it. After a few weeks she feels confident using the software. Half a year later she cannot imagine herself using any other software.

Even though learning how to use a new software is not the same as developing a virtue, it exemplifies how the conscious repetition of actions functions. Eventually, developing a virtue is not that different from learning a skill (Russel, 2015). Both are acquired through practice. 'Becoming virtuous is a special case of the general phenomenon of getting better – better at succeeding in the sorts of things where succeeding is not the default' (Russel, 2015: 18).

Thinking of a virtue as some sort of skill is useful when it comes to developing them. Still, it does not help us to decide between good and bad habits, and it does not fully explain how one acquires *proper* habituation. So, what can we learn from Aristotle about the right kind of habituation? There are three important aspects which Aristotle highlighted when it comes to properly developing a habit: (1) actions should express proper reasoning (NE: 1103b), (2) right habituation shuns excess and defect (NE: 1104a), and (3) proper habituation comes from an individual's experiencing pleasure or pain in the appropriate kind of action (NE: 1104b).

Let us explain these three aspects of habituation. First, Aristotle linked actions (and therefore also habits) to correct reasoning. Hence, individual actions whose repetition creates a habit should be done thoughtfully, minding what is opportune in each case, as good surgeons, architects, or airplane pilots do in practice. Next, as Aristotle pointed out, right habituation does not involve excess or defect. Every habit should be oriented towards a 'golden mean', defined with regard to the individual agent. For example, someone who is courageous is neither too fearful nor too confident. Third, to develop the right kind of habits signifies that an individual experiences pleasure or pain in the appropriate kind of action. Action and emotions such as pleasure and pain are very much interconnected. Just consider that we all begin to develop a better or worse personality through pleasures and pains experienced during childhood. These two emotions can, however, also serve as important indicators for developing the right habits (the ones which are in line with our nature) during adulthood and for avoiding the bad ones (the ones which are contrary to our nature). On the one hand, excessive eating and drinking produces stomach pain, abusing drugs can cause serious health issues, hearing excessively loud music can cause hearing problems, working too much over a longer period can lead to burn-out, etc. On the other hand, playing tennis or the piano for one or

two hours can produce pleasure, eating some ice cream on Sundays can make us happy for a while, or learning a new language can help staying mentally fit during old age. Listening to our inner voice and being conscious about our habits is crucial when developing virtues and avoiding vicious habits.

Similarly, Hibbert and Cunliffe (2013) suggest that *moral reflexive practice* (i.e. a certain manner of being that comprises questioning who we are and the way we interact in responsible and ethical ways; see Cunliffe, 2009) offers a possibility to foster responsible and ethical practices. At the workplace, that could mean slowing down from time to time and reflecting on our behaviour and that of others. This habit is mostly long lost in business nowadays. Instead, the environment is commonly described by the acronym VUCA (volatile, uncertain, complex and ambiguous), showcasing the growing inability of employees to grasp the world and deal with what is happening to and around them (Kraaijenbrink, 2018). Thus, as the architects of our lives one must (continuously) study one's habits, practices and routines. To ask questions about ourselves (and others) is key to eradicating irresponsible actions and habits, and to becoming more responsible (Hibbert and Cunliffe, 2013). In practice that could mean avoiding any habits that jeopardize oneself; getting rid of any routines that do not lead us towards our personal flourishing. To start such an endeavour is certainly not easy. Bad habits are hard to break. However, for starters, it might be enough to eliminate practices we do not want to have, because these habits keep us away from what is important. Through such a simple process of elimination we will automatically find ourselves doing more of the things we are really interested in.

Practical Wisdom: The Mother of All Virtues

Virtuous actions result from the pairing of conscious decisions and right reasoning. Virtuous habits, then, come from the repeated performance of such actions, which are consequently perfected through a feedback loop. Since virtuous actions occur in concrete situations, to become virtuous, it is indispensable to develop also proper appreciations of situations and knowledge of how to proceed. We cannot become virtuous simply by studying the virtues theoretically. Aristotle pointed out that for the appropriate development of the virtues, one needs to obtain practical wisdom (*phronesis*): 'the right way to do the right thing in a particular circumstance, with a particular person, at a particular time' (Schwartz & Sharpe, 2010: 3–4). Practical wisdom signifies the alignment among right thinking and perception, right desire and right action. It creates harmony among reason, sensibility or emotions, and behaviour. Rules do not apply to practical wisdom, which can only be learned through practice, experience and constant training. Practical wisdom is an ideal that is hard to achieve and has even been considered a 'sixth sense' (Malan & Kriger, 1998: 246; see also McKenna et al., 2009). Thus, it does not come as a surprise that Aristotle indicated that practical wisdom usually comes with age and experience.

Together with Aristotle (NE: 1145a), medieval scholars considered practical wisdom as the mother of all other virtues because, essentially, all virtues involve practical, normative knowledge. What is more, without practical wisdom, no other virtue is possible because knowledge must be essentially unified; to evaluate something is to compare its relative value to others. Nowadays, according to Bachman et al. (2017) 'virtue ethicists consider practical wisdom as a sine qua non condition of becoming a virtuous leader' (p. 153). They suggest that managers who develop practical wisdom become more effective, as they become more morally tuned, integrate better ethical considerations with instrumental ones, start to give better advice, become experts at solving complex problems, and develop a fine sense of how to inspire colleagues and followers.

Developmental Stages of Virtuousness

Developing virtuous habits is not easy; especially because it is extremely complex to obtain practical wisdom. Thus, it does not come as a surprise that each individual human being will have reached a different level of virtuousness towards the end of his or her life. Aristotle (NE: 1145a–1152a) differentiated between four general levels of virtuousness (see also Curzer, 2012; Homiak, 2016; Kraut, 2018).

Let us start with the vicious (*kakia*) character. Not being conscious of his or her selfish inclinations, a person with a vicious character does not distinguish between what is morally right or wrong (NE: 1150b–1151a). Such an individual lacks any moral sense of the good and, thus, does not have any sense for justice either (Kraut, 2018). He or she is careless of the feelings of others and is strongly dominated by his or her tendencies to excessively accumulate material goods and pursue bodily pleasures (NE: 1151a). The vicious person fails to take the right decisions because he or she does not comprehend what is right. What is more, as such a person does not sense any tension between his or her (self-centred) tendencies and possible moral implications; he or she might easily mistake what is right for what is wrong. For example, a vicious MBA-student would cheat in an exam without feeling any guilt. Instead, such a student would rather be concerned with assuring him or her a good mark (no matter what), and the professor not finding out about the betrayal to avoid any troubles that might result in negative consequences.

Then there is the incontinent (*akrasia*) character. In contrast to the vicious person, the incontinent is aware of his or her wrongdoing. He or she distinguishes well what is right from wrong. Individuals with this character know what they should ideally do but see themselves unable to control their inclinations. They lack self-discipline and act against their better knowledge (NE: 1152a).

A person with an incontinent character might wish to do the right thing but finds him or herself failing to do so. This type of character is internally conflicted and, in contrast to the vicious person, suffers from inner remorse (Homiak, 2016). Coming back to our example from above, an MBA-student with an incontinent character would cheat in an exam to assure a good mark. However, this student would feel guilty about it. He or she knows that cheating in an exam is morally blameworthy. He or she might even think afterwards about how to correct the misbehaviour, because the betrayal would put him or her at unease with him or herself.

Thirdly, Aristotle refers to the continent (*enkrateia*) character. On the one hand, this type of individual resembles the incontinent person because he or she knows to distinguish between what is morally right and wrong. However, in contrast, the continent character not only chooses to do good, but also acts upon his or her decisions (Curzer, 2012). He or she has the ability to stand his or her ground (NE: 1152a). This person has learned to control him- or herself. In this way, continence can be understood as a form of self-mastery. On the other hand, from an external perspective, the continent character resembles the virtuous person very much, because he or she has learned to act properly (Kraut, 2018). Nevertheless, he or she struggles to do so. Acting appropriately does not come easy to him or her because such a person's actions do not resemble his or her feelings (NE: 1151a). Hence, the continent person is also internally conflicted (Homiak, 2016). This state of character requires a strong will and the ability to suffer for the right reasons. In the case of our MBA student, we would observe a person that would like to cheat but decides not to. Instead, such a student would opt to study hard to obtain a good grade. He or she might, however, find it hard to make this decision, as cheating still appears attractive.

Finally, Aristotle considers the virtuous character as the highest ideal. A person with this character type knows and chooses the right thing. Additionally, the virtuous person enjoys performing the right action. There is no intra-psychological conflict. Emotions and reason are in harmony. He or she does not have any inclination toward acting selfishly or amorally; he or she deeply desires to do good. The virtuous person could, thus, be considered the natural progression from the continent character. Such an individual not only chooses the right thing, but also desires it. His or her emotions, feelings and wishes are in line with his or her decisions.

Most people would certainly fall into the second (incontinent) or third (continent) group. However, a clear distinction is a rather complicated process. That is because the virtuousness of a person can only be evaluated by a truly virtuous individual. Also, it would be difficult to expect a person to have developed all the virtues to the same degree. Thus, one must consider the possibility that a person might have achieved the ability to suppress a certain type of desire, but not have control over others. On the one hand, one could easily imagine a husband that is committed to his wife and, even though he desires other women, has mastered control over these desires. He is 100 per cent loyal to his better half. From this example, such a person would be considered to fall into the continent character group. On the other hand, the same man might accept from time to time bribes at work. Even though he does not feel comfortable to do so, he lacks the self-control to say no to such 'sweeteners', because they permit him and his family to maintain a certain lifestyle which would otherwise be impossible. Evaluating from this example only, such a person would have to be considered incontinent. What is more, looking at a single action or the behaviour of a person in only one domain does not allow for a generalization on the virtuous development of a human being. It is easy to imagine a person saying no to a bribe on one occasion and accepting a bribe on another. Hence, the importance of character as a whole in evaluating the virtuousness of a person.

BUSINESS ETHICS EDUCATION: DEVELOPING VIRTUES *THROUGH* ORGANIZATIONS

A leader is someone who helps improve the lives of other people or improve the system they live under. (Sam Houston)

This section illuminates the role of organizational conditions and the importance of leadership for the development of the virtues *in* and *through* business. Here we not only draw from accounts of neo-Aristotelian virtue, but also from Positive Organizational Scholarship (e.g. positive organizational virtuousness). We explain how organizational features such as structures, rules or policies in combination with the right leadership can foster the development of environments conducive to the virtues.

Organizational Conditions

Organizations are composed of people. However, they are not merely loosely connected clusters of various individuals. Generally, organizations have rules, structures, processes, routines and so forth. All these characteristics influence the members of an organization and help create its culture.

The behaviour of the organization's stakeholders is influenced by its features. For this reason, Positive Organizational Scholarship (POS), a research field inspired by Positive Psychology (PP), considers organizational features to be important for the ethical development of organizational members. Even though POS's idea of virtue is not entirely in line with the idea of many Aristotelian virtue ethicists (Meyer, 2016), their notion of (organizational) virtuousness can help to better understand the relationship between an organization's members and its features.

Positive Organizational Scholarship is a rapidly developing field of research founded shortly after the turn of the century. It centres around that which impacts organizations and individuals positively with a focus on virtuous

behaviours and positive emotions. Among other things, it studies human strength, resilience and flourishing. 'At the heart of POS is what leads to prosperous results and the best of the human condition' (Meyer, 2015: S175). The word 'positive' has created some confusion as there is still no final answer to what it exactly signifies (Caza & Carroll, 2012). However, since the early stages of the research field, 'positive' has been taken to mean: excellence, thriving, flourishing, abundance, resilience and virtuousness. Gittel, Cameron, Lim and Rivas (2006) and Hess and Cameron (2006) have also considered it a synonym for extraordinary performance.

(Organizational) virtuousness is a core concept of POS (Cameron & Winn, 2012), mainly inspired by Aristotle's notion of virtue. Positive (organizational) virtuousness is also motivated by research in positive psychology, biology, sociology, socio-biology, social psychology and genetic psychology among others. Positive (organizational) virtuousness is, at its core, the result of a mixture of research findings from multiple scientific disciplines plus POS's understanding of Aristotle's concept of virtue (Meyer, 2016).

At the most elementary level, positive (organizational) virtuousness is about human nature, human behaviour and its interaction with that of co-workers in organizations and with the rest of society. A deeper look, however, reveals that also organizational features such as a company's structure play an important part in positive (organizational) virtuousness. For example, a specially designed organizational structure, such as in the case of the firm AES, exemplifies 'one key aspect of virtuousness in organizations' (Cameron, 2003: 49). Consequently, the definition of organizational virtuousness encompasses organizational features as *enablers* of virtuous deeds (i.e., Cameron, 2003; Cameron et al., 2004). In this sense, POS suggests that such formal features (e.g. structures) can be understood as an extension of the virtuousness of the organization's members. They provide a favourable setting for the development of virtues in organizations. The organization fosters the practice of virtues *through* its context. Imagine, for example, a company designed to increase their members' level of courage to help employees to speak up if they discover any wrongdoing. To start, the company decides to (1) reward courageous behaviour with extra days off (e.g. speaking up against misconduct), (2) introduce an annual award for courageous behaviour at work and (3) promote the introduction of a 'courage working group' where employees are not only encouraged to participate, but also get paid extra for doing so. The company wants to institutionalize courage; it wants to make it part of its 'nature'. Similar to this example, the German *manager magazin* suggests an 'anti-bullying company agreement' as a possible start for VW to cope with its current 'Dieselgate' scandal (Claassen, 2017). As the journal explains, such an agreement would sanction non-information as a discriminatory act, normatively guaranteeing the best possible information for the entire workforce. Every employee who courageously tells and shares the truth must and could be effectively protected. Such an agreement describes one possible step to protect the truth, openness and information culture by promoting courage.

These examples show how a company, by introducing new rules, structures, norms and so forth can influence the behaviour of its members. From an Aristotelian perspective, however, it is not the environment which changes the behaviour of a virtuous agent, but it is rather the virtuous person that alters his or her surroundings. Thus, Aristotle would probably not entirely agree with the importance given to non-human elements in positive (organizational) virtuousness. Still, he would probably admit that situations can be powerful and sometimes even overpowering influences upon behaviour (see Alzola, 2012; Tenbrunsel and Smith-Crowe, 2008; Treviño, den Nieuwenboer & Kish-Gephardt, 2014). Even a virtuous person would deteriorate in an extremely vicious environment.

Because the surrounding environment can facilitate (or hinder) the development of virtuous actions and habits, organizations should pay attention to how their structures, rules, etc. impact upon its members.

Organizational Leadership

At its core, leadership deals with the problem of how to shape the behaviour of individuals or groups (Huehn, 2014). Above we explained how organizational conditions can impact the behaviour of organizational members. A leader can, through the introduction of new rules, structures, or strategies, change the conduct of employees. Now we want to concentrate on how leaders can influence upon an organization's stakeholders more directly, through their communication skills and, also, through their own actions, behaviour and even through their character. Thus we will refer first to positive leadership, and second, to neo-Aristotelian leadership.

Positive Leadership means the application of research findings from POS to organizational governance. Thus, not surprisingly, the above-mentioned concept of positive (organizational) virtuousness counts among the leadership theory's key aspects.

To describe a virtuous leader, Cameron (2011) conflates virtuousness with responsibility. He sticks to Pless's idea of responsible leadership as 'the art of building and sustaining social and moral relationships between business leaders and different stakeholders (followers), based on a sense of justice, a sense of recognition, a sense of care, and a sense of accountability for a wide range of economic, ecological, social, political, and human responsibilities' (Pless, 2007: 451). A positive and virtuous leader is accountable, empowered and faithfully pursues outcomes (Meyer, 2016). To this, Cameron (2011) adds the ability 'to act in an appropriate fashion', finding the right or best way to handle situations, not in general or in the abstract, but in specific circumstances (p. 26).

Regarding outcomes, positive organizations aim at *doing good* and *doing well*. Doing good refers to individuals or organizations that undertake actions 'to create a beneficial and sustainable situation for a company, the stakeholders and the community, the environment, and for society as a whole' (Meyer, 2015: 188). Doing well stands for 'marked improvements in terms of a multilevel performance including economic, human, and environmental aspects, indicating the magnitude of change in an upward trajectory, and highlighting future viability and sustainability' (p. 188).

Within the notion of positive (organizational) virtuousness, we find two attributes that explain how a leader can affect the behaviour of employees and mould a positive organization: the amplifying and buffering effects. The amplifying effect describes an ascending and self-reinforcing spiral produced by the repetition of virtuous conduct in groups (Cameron & Winn, 2012). The buffering effect clarifies how virtuousness operates as a protection mechanism against dysfunction (Seligman & Csikszentmihalyi, 2000). The buffering effect makes organizations more robust, strengthens group cohesion, and helps organizational members better deal with challenges (Cameron & Caza, 2002). Let us explain how these two attributes can help a leader to influence the behaviour of individuals and groups.

The amplifying quality of virtuousness is based on studies by Fredrickson (1998, 2001, and 2003) and Fredrickson and Joiner (2002). When individuals observe or experience positive deeds, they sense the urge to also act virtuously. Positive emotions trigger positive activities. These positive acts, then, produce more positive feelings. Thus, a virtuous cycle is set in motion (Meyer, 2016). In Aristotelian virtue ethics, this is traditionally known as 'feedback loops' (Sison, 2003). This mechanism is closely linked to social capital and prosocial behaviour (Cameron, 2003). Regarding the former, virtues like caregiving, empathy and trust help to improve a workplace's flow of information, enrich the

interactions between employees and, in general, lead to more dynamism and more efficient resource-sharing (Dutton and Heaphy, 2003; Cameron et al., 2004). They create social capital in organizations. Similarly, regarding prosocial behaviour, witnessing excellent or moral behaviour inspires people to echo such conduct on their own (Cameron, 2003; Cameron and Winn, 2012). Employees observing their co-workers behaving in a prosocial way, tend to imitate them. Hence, by, for example, acting in a prosocial way, or by living virtues such as the ones mentioned above, the leader, as a *role model*, can help to set into motion a process of virtuous transformation.

The buffering effect of virtuousness goes back to research by Seligman and Csikszentmihalyi (2000). It works in the same way as the amplifying effect, but it describes another outcome. The buffering effect explains how virtuousness enables resiliency (Cameron et al., 2004). It makes individuals and organizations more robust because it strengthens group cohesion and aids organizational members to better cope with challenges (Cameron & Caza, 2002). Among other advantages, the buffering effect helps organizations protect themselves against the negative effects usually linked to downsizing. For example, imagine a company that has just downsized. Rationalization generally affects employees' lives negatively. The morale deteriorates, abuse intensifies and employees typically even see their private lives adversely affected. However, if the leader is able to institutionalize forgiveness, in the sense that the company adopts a positive attitude towards challenges, the organization can recuperate more easily and even flourish again (Shannon, 2013). This does not mean that any harm must not be acknowledged or that any damage is denied. It solely means to go ahead with optimism and not to be stuck in the past. In contrast, most companies, which do not have a culture of forgiveness, usually have a hard time to recover (Shannon, 2013).

Positive Leadership, via the concept of (organizational) virtuousness, offers (potential) leaders ways to develop virtues in institutions through implementing the right organizational conditions (e.g. structure, routines, norms) and through being a positive leader (e.g. being a role model that actively promotes virtuous behaviours).

In Aristotelian virtue ethics, when it comes to leadership, the focus is on 'rhetoric' (Sison, 2003, Meyer et al., 2018), that is, an individual's ability to persuade or convince other people through peaceful means, respecting their freedom and rationality. In the Rhetoric, Aristotle enlisted three instruments to bring this about: the argument or speech (*logos*), the audience or listeners' emotional condition (*pathos*), and the leader or speaker's character (*ethos*). Although all three are necessary, Aristotle believes that the speaker's character (*ethos*) is the critical factor for successful leadership; it determines one's credibility. This way Aristotle established the link between leadership and virtue insofar as virtue denotes, among other things, excellence in character. Granted such a leader's commitment to moral excellence, economic outcomes are clearly directed to a lower level of importance. A virtuous leader would rather renounce economic success than put virtue in jeopardy. Hence, such a leader would certainly not consider any shady organizational practices (e.g. harming the environment, child labour and so forth) to boost financial results.

CONCLUSIONS

The purpose of this chapter is to explain how character-building through the development of the virtues contributes to good business and responsible management practices. To do so, we first had to make clear how virtue refers primarily to excellence in character, perfects human nature and brings each person closer to his or her flourishing (*eudaimonia*) or 'final end'.

Inasmuch as virtues are not innate properties in human beings, they need to be acquired and nurtured through conscious and deliberate actions. These actions, on the one hand, reinforce certain inclinations and tendencies, and on the other, create habits, which, in turn, determine one's character and condition one's lifestyle choices. Practical wisdom, the intellectual and moral habit of doing the right thing the right way for the right reason, is crucial for acquiring all the other virtues. Without practical wisdom, no other moral virtue is possible. In response to objections of circularity we have traced how practical wisdom can be advanced through different character stages.

We have also demonstrated how Positive Organizational Studies (POS) draws inspiration from neo-Aristotelian virtue ethics. The synergy between the two is helpful in clarifying how institutional contexts such as management structures, rules and policies in business organizations can either help or hinder the virtues and virtuousness. In particular, positive leadership styles ensure that managers promote and protect virtue among individuals under their charge, mainly through different amplifying and buffering effects. In a sense, responsible management education is none other than encouraging the practice of virtues and virtuousness through one's organizational leadership.

FUTURE PRACTICE

In this chapter we put the emphasis on the development of virtue *in* and *through* organizational environments. Hence, we offer two mutually supportive ways for leaders to encourage virtuousness at work. On the one hand, leaders can create *organizational settings* conducive to the virtues. On the other hand, leaders, as role models, can foster virtuous habits in organizations *through their own behaviour and character*. Both ways are crucial in the development of virtues in organizations. Both ways should, ideally, be further reinforced through virtue education in the form of in-company trainings. Thus, to finish this chapter, we present three ideas on how to teach the virtues in the classroom.

One way to teach the virtues in the classroom is to combine *case studies* with *reflection logs*. While the case study presents students with the opportunity to discuss, for example, vicious behaviour or exceptionally ethical conduct, it further offers the opportunity to learn from others and reflect upon these individuals' behaviour. These insights can then be used to contemplate over one's own behaviour using reflection logs. For example, one of the authors, in his role as Business Ethics professor at the University of Navarra, started to incorporate (real-life) case studies of notorious business scandals combined with positive business examples. Students discussed these in class and, then, were encouraged to further reflect upon their thoughts, feelings and ideas later on. This combination of negative and positive examples helped students to elaborate fruitful discussions about the underlying motivations of human behaviour and the importance of having a '*higher purpose*' in business organizations. Some commendable (real-life) case studies to introduce students to business ethics have been developed by the Virtue Ethics in Business Research Group, which consists currently of over 60 professors, researchers and practitioners from all over the world (see: www.unav.edu/web/virtue-ethics-in-business/home). Initiatives like these, which understand the purpose of a firm to not only be the efficient production of goods and services, but also as a place to provide a community in which employees can learn and grow as real human beings, are important for the promotion of sustainable and responsible management practices.

A further way to foster virtuous behaviour through classroom sessions is through *positive 360° feedback* (see and compare to: 'The reflected best-self feedback', Cameron, 2008). By obtaining information from multiple sources about one's talents, capabilities and attributes, the student gets crucial feedback about his or her behaviour. Such feedback can help students to guide them through a process of discovering, analysing and reinforcing the positive characteristics that are observed by their peers, superiors, employees or even family members. Through positive 360° feedback students are encouraged to further build upon their already positive behaviours, which might lead them to discover their full potential to become virtuous. Multiple source or multiple rater feedback is a tool, which should be incorporated more often into business ethics classes as it might help students to engage into self-reflexive questioning. Hibbert and Cunliffe (2013) believe this to be crucial in realizing what is culturally acceptable is not necessarily morally responsible.

A third method to teach virtues in the classroom is through *storytelling,* a technique used, for example, at Sloan School (MIT) or the University of Virginia's Darden School (Forman, 2013). We do not refer to telling the classical stories of fictional heroes and their adventures such as *The Odyssey*. Rather we refer to real-life stories about actual leaders and their virtuous behaviour or characters. (As an alternative to the lecturer telling the stories, students can also be encouraged to present their own narratives based on their own experiences.) Such narratives can help students uncover what it means to act virtuously in face of adversity and find new role-models they can relate to. Telling stories about exceptional positive behaviour such as virtuous deeds in company environments abates the fact that business ethics almost always only hits the headlines in the wake of scandals, but hardly ever when businesspersons do good deeds. These are often met with a disbelief for, given the profit motive, such stories are just 'too good to be true'. Why so? Making employees or students aware that the firm, through proper ethical development, could actually be a potent force toward attaining the common good, is one of the most crucial tasks a leader or business ethics lecturer has. As best-selling author and psychologist Wayne Walter Dyer (2008) said: 'If you change the way you look at things, the things you look at change.'

REFERENCES

Alzola, M. (2012). The possibi ity of virtue. *Business Ethics Quarterly*, *22*(2), 377–404.

Aristotle (1985). *Nicomachean ethics* (trans. T. Irwin). Indianapolis, IN: Hackett Publishing.

Aristotle (1990). *The politics* (Everson, S., Ed.), Cambridge: Cambridge University Press.

Bachman, C., Habisch, A., & Dierksmeier, C. (2018). Practical wisdom: management's no longer forgotten virtue. *Journal of Business Ethics*, *153*, 147–165.

Cameron, K. S. (2003). Organizational virtuousness and performance. In Cameron, K. S., Dutton, J. E. and Quinn, R. E. (Eds.), *Positive Organizational Scholarship – foundations of a new discipline* (pp. 48–65). San Francisco: Berrett-Koehler.

Cameron, K. S. (2008). *Positive leadership: strategies for extraordinary performance*. San Francisco: Berrett-Koehler.

Cameron, K. S. (2011). Responsible leadership as virtuous leadership. *Journal of Business Ethics*, *98*(S1), 25–35.

Cameron, K. S., Bright, D. S.. & Caza, A. (2004). Exploring the relationships between organizational virtuousness and performance. *American Behavioral Scientist*, *47*(6), 766–790.

Cameron, K. S., & Caza, A. (2002). Organizational and leadership virtues and the role of forgiveness. *Journal of Leadership and Organizational Studies*, *9*(33), 34–48.

Cameron, K. S., & Winn, B. (2012). Virtuousness in organizations. In Cameron, K. S., & Spreitzer, G. M. (Eds.), *The Oxford handbook of POS* (pp. 231–243). New York: Oxford University Press.

Caza, A., & Carroll, B. (2012). Critical theory and POS. In Cameron, K. S., & Spreitzer, G. M. (Eds.), *The Oxford handbook of POS* (pp. 965–978). New York: Oxford University Press.

Claassen, U. (2017). Die wahren Ursachen der VW-Krise. *manager magazin*. 24 July. Available at: www.manager-magazin.de/ unternehmen/autoindustrie/volkswagen-die-wahren-ursachen-der-krise-a-1159434.html.

Crossan, M. M., Byrne, A., Seijts, G. H., Reno, M., Monzani, L., & Gandz, J. (2017). Toward a framework of leader character in organizations. *Journal of Management Studies*, *54*(7), 986–1018.

Cunliffe, A. (2009). The philosopher leader: on relationalism, ethics and reflexivity – critical perspective to teaching leadership. *Management Learning*, *40*(1), 87–101.

Curzer, H. J. (2012). *Aristotle and the virtues*. New York: Oxford University Press.

Dutton, J. E., & Heaphy, E. D. (2003). The power of high quality connections. In Cameron, K. S., Dutton, J. E., & Quinn, R. E. (Eds.), *POS. Foundations of a new discipline* (pp. 263–278). San Francisco: Berrett-Koehler.

Dyer, W. W. (2008). Wayne Dyer – when you change the way you look at things. YouTube Available at: www.youtube.com/watch?relo ad=9&v=urQPraeeY0w.

Ferrero, I. & Sison, A. J. G. (2014). A quantitative analysis of authors, schools and themes in virtue ethics articles in business ethics and management journals (1980–2011). *Business Ethics: A European Review*, *23*(4), 375–400.

Flynn, G. (2008). The virtuous manager: a vision for leadership in business. *Journal of Business Ethics*, *78*(3), 359–372.

Forman, J. (2013). *Storytelling in business: the authentic and fluent organization*. Stanford, CA: Stanford University Press.

Fredrickson, B. L. (1998). What good are positive emotions? *Review of General Psychology*, *2*(3), 300–319.

Fredrickson, B. L. (2001). The role of positive emotions in positive psychology: the broaden-build theory of positive emotions. *American Psychologist*, *56*(3), 218–226.

Fredrickson, B. L. (2003). Positive emotions and upward spirals in organizations. In Cameron, K. S., Dutton, J. E., & Quinn, R. E. (Eds.), *POS: Foundations of a new discipline* (pp. 163–175). San Francisco: Berrett-Koehler.

Fredrickson, B. L., & Joiner, T. (2002). Positive emotions trigger upward spirals toward emotional well-being. *Psychology Science*, *13*(2), 172–175.

Gittell, J. H., Cameron, K. S., Lim, S., & Rivas, V. (2006). Relationships, layoffs, and organizational resilience: airline industry responses to

September 11. *Journal of Applied Behavioral Science*, *42*(3), 300–328.

Hess, E. D., & Cameron, K. S. (2006). *Leading with values: positivity, virtue, and high performance*. New York: Cambridge University Press.

Hibbert, P., & Cunliffe, A. (2013). Responsible management: engaging moral reflexive practice through threshold concepts. *Journal of Business Ethics*, *127*, 177–188.

Hilliard, I. (2013). Responsible management, incentive systems, and productivity. *Journal of Business Ethics*, *118*, 365–377.

Homiak, M. (2016). Moral character. In Zalta, E. N. (Ed.), *The Stanford encyclopedia of philosophy*. Stanford, CA: Stanford University. Retrieved from: https://plato.stanford.edu.

Huehn, M. P. (2014). You reap what you sow: how MBA programs undermine ethics. *Journal of Business Ethics*, *121*(4), 527–541.

Huehn, M. P. (2016). Ethics as a catalyst for change in business education? *Journal of Management Development*, *35*(2), 170–189.

Huehn, M., Meyer, M., & Racelis, A. (2018). Virtues and the common good in leadership. In Sison, A. J. G., Ferrero, I., & Guitán, G. (Eds.), *Business ethics: a virtue ethics and common good approach* (pp. 24–50). New York: Routledge.

Hursthouse, R., & Pettigrove, G. (2016) Virtue ethics. In Zalta, E. N. (Ed.), *The Stanford encyclopedia of philosophy*. Stanford, CA: Stanford University. Retrieved from http://plato.stanford.edu.

Kohll, A. (2018). What employees really want at work. *Forbes,* 10 July. Available at: www.forbes.com/sites/alankohll/2018/07/10/what-employees-really-want-at-work/#6aaac5425ad3.

Kraaijenbrink, J. (2018). What does VUCA really mean? *Forbes,* 19 December. Available at: www.forbes.com/sites/jeroenkraaijenbrink/2018/12/19/what-does-vuca-really-mean/#70a1e03717d6.

Kraut, R. (2018). Aristotle's ethics. In Zalta, E. N. (Ed.), *The Stanford encyclopaedia of philosophy*. Stanford, CA: Stanford University. Retrieved from: https://plato.stanford.edu.

Malan, L. C., & Kriger, M. P. (1998). Making sense of managerial wisdom. *Journal of Management Inquiry*, *7*(3), 242–251.

McKenna, B., Rooney, D., & Boal, K. (2009). Wisdom principles as a meta-theoretical basis for evaluating leadership. *The Leadership Quarterly*, *20*(2), 177–190.

Melé, D. (2010). Practical wisdom in managerial decision making. *Journal of Management Development*, *29*(7/8), 637–645.

Meyer, M. (2015). Positive business: doing good and doing well. *Business Ethics: A European Review*, *24*(S2), 175–197.

Meyer, M. (2016). The evolution and challenges of the concept of organizational virtuousness in POS. *Journal of Business Ethics*, *153*(1), 245–264.

Meyer, M., Sison, A. J. G., & Ferrero, I. (2018). How positive and neo-Aristotelian leadership can contribute to ethical leadership. *Canadian Journal of Administrative Science*, *36*(3), 390–403.

Petri, A. A. (2017). Leadership and moral excellence: cultivating virtue through moral imagination. In Sison, A. J. G., Beabout, G. R., & Ferrero, I. (Eds.), *Handbook of virtue ethics in business and management* (pp. 973–983). Dordrecht, Netherlands: Springer Science + Business Media.

Pless, N. M. (2007). Understanding responsible leadership: role identity and motivational drivers. *Journal of Business Ethics*, *74*(4), 437–456.

Ramsey, L. (2018). The rise and fall of Theranos, the blood-testing startup that went from Silicon Valley darling to facing fraud charges. *Business Insider*, 25 May. Available at: www.businessinsider.es/the-history-of-silicon-valley-unicorn-theranos-and-ceo-elizabeth-holmes-2018-5?r=US&IR=T.

Reeves, M., Dierksmeier, C., & Chittaro, C. (2018). The humanization of the corporation. BCG Henderson Institute. 8 February. Available at: https://www.bcg.com/publications/2018/humanization-corporation.aspx.

Robin. D., & Reidenbach, E. R. (1987). Social responsibility, ethics, and marketing strategy: closing the gap between concept and application. *Journal of Marketing*, *51*(1), 44–58.

Russel, D. C. (2015). Aristotle on cultivating virtue. In Snow, N. E. (Ed.), *Cultivating virtue* (pp. 17–49). Oxford: Oxford University Press.

Schrodt, P. (2017). 12 companies with the most luxurious employee perks. *Money,* 9 October.

Available at: http://money.com/money/4972232/12-companies-with-the-most-luxurious-employee-perks/.

Schwartz, B., & Sharpe, K. E. (2010). *Practical wisdom: the right way to do the right thing.* London: Riverhead.

Seligman, M. E. P., & Csikszentmihalyi, M. (2000). Positive psychology. *American Psychologist, 55*(1), 5–12.

Shannon, P. (2013). Virtuous business practices: an interview with Dr. Kim Cameron. *Positive Psychology News.* Available at: https://positivepsychologynews.com/news/shannon-polly/2013071826735.

Sison, A. J. G. (2003). *The moral capital of leaders – why virtue matters.* Northampton, MA: Edward Elgar.

Sison, A. J. G., & Ferrero, I. (2015). How different is neo-Aristotelian virtue from positive organizational virtuousness? *Business Ethics: A European Review, 24*(S2), 78–98.

Sison, A. J. G., Beabout, G. R., & Ferrero, I. (2017). *Handbook of virtue ethics in business and management.* Dordrecht: Springer.

Sison, A. J. G, Ferrero, I., & Guitián, G. (2018). Virtues and the common good. In Sison, A. J. G., Ferrero, I., & Guitán, G. (Eds.), *Business ethics: A virtue ethics and common good approach* (pp. 1–23). New York: Routledge.

Snow, N. E. (2015). *Cultivating virtue: perspectives from philosophy, theology, and psychology.* New York: Oxford University Press.

Tenbrunsel, A. E., & Smith-Crowe, K. (2008). Ethical decision making: where we have been and where we are going. *Academy of Management Annals, 2*(1), 545–607.

Treviño, L. K., den Nieuwenboer, N. A., & Kish-Gephardt, J. J. (2014). (Un)ethical behavior in organizations. *Annual Review of Psychology, 65*, 635–660.

Youssef-Morgan, C. M., & Luthans, F. (2013). Positive leadership: meaning and application across cultures. *Organizational Dynamics, 42*(3), 198–208.

18

Radical-Reflexivity and Transdisciplinarity as Paths to Developing Responsible Management Education

Ann L. Cunliffe, Ana Carolina Aguiar, Vicente Góes and Fernanda Carreira

INTRODUCTION

In January 2019, Brumadinho, Brazil, a tailings dam owned by Vale Mining collapsed, resulting in toxic sludge containing mining by-products engulfing the cafeteria where employees were eating lunch, and the surrounding area. Two hundred and forty-eight people died and there are still people missing. Five company and subsidiary company officials were arrested, the courts froze £2.2bn company assets, bonuses to company managers and dividends to shareholders were halted. Criminal charges have been brought against Vale company officials and workers at the German company who audited the dam's stability. Investigations are continuing and Vale has agreed to pay $107,000,000 in 'moral damages' to affected families. Employees say that a leak the previous year compromised the dam. And this is not the first incident. In November 2015, a Vale company dam in Mariana burst, killing 19, resulting in Brazil's worst environmental disaster to that date.

As exemplified above, the need for responsible management, particularly in relation to communities and the natural environment, has never been more urgent, as, by extension, is the need for responsible management education and learning (RMLE) around sustainability. As Kurucz, Colbert and Marcus (2014: 437) note, 'our dominant approaches to wealth creation degrade both the ecological systems and the social relationships upon which their very survival depends'. Our chapter addresses this issue by drawing upon and furthering the call set forth by Allen, Cunliffe and Easterby-Smith (2019) for an ecocentric approach to sustainability grounded in radical-reflexivity, by proposing transdisciplinarity as an additional underpinning strand of responsible management education. In contrast to a neoclassic perspective, which assumes that humans are separate from the physical world and that natural resources are there to be exploited and 'managed', ecocentrism has its antecedents in Bateson's (1972) work and embeds humans *in* the natural environment.

Accordingly, education based on an ecocentric perspective means 'educating students in ways that bring attention to interactions between values, actions and our social and material world' (Allen et al., 2019: 782). Radical-reflexivity means working at the borders of society and work (Kessel & Maurer, 2012), which when extended to incorporate transdisciplinarity also means working across academic disciplines, accepted perceptions, truths, spaces/places, self/other, communities and groups.

In this chapter, we introduce and review the concepts of reflexivity and transdisciplinarity, focusing on: the differences between reflection, reflexivity and radical-reflexivity; the origins and development of transdisciplinarity; and their relevance to responsible management education and learning. We then illustrate how radical-reflexivity and transdisciplinarity can enhance RMLE by discussing our experience working with an 18-month postgraduate master's program for practitioners at the Center for Sustainability Studies at FGV-EAESP, Brazil. By doing so, we offer resources for others interested in embedding these two concepts in RMLE. The program, 'Integrated Education for Sustainability' (IES), has been running since 2016 and is oriented around the Principles of Responsible Management Education (PRME). Its purpose is to facilitate the development of participants who are responsible, ethical, reflexive and sensitive in their relationships with others and with the world around them, i.e., responsible ecocentric professionals (Allen et al., 2019). It does so by facilitating personal identification with our physical world (Whiteman, Walker & Perego, 2013) through a pedagogy that draws on radical-reflexivity and transdisciplinarity. The uniqueness of the program is reflected in the diversity of students, who come from various sectors (private, public, nonprofit) and backgrounds (engineering, economics, business administration, journalism, social sciences, psychology, etc.), some of whom travel from outside São Paulo State to attend.

Two key theoretical trajectories run through the program – radical-reflexivity and transdisciplinarity – used as a means of embedding ecocentricism. While there have been calls to connect both in sustainability research (e.g., Popa, Guillermina & Dedeurwaerdere, 2015), little has been written in relation to responsible management education. We will first give a theoretical overview of each trajectory and examine the implications for responsible management education and learning, before going on to discuss how they are enacted in the program.

REFLEXIVITY

Reflexivity is the antithesis of the 'scientific' preoccupation with objectivism, neutrality and technocentrism that underpins many business school curricula, because it requires us to problematize conventional knowledge and discourse, to challenge and unsettle conventional taken-for-granted ways of understanding and acting by highlighting contradictions, tensions and the values, practices and processes that underpin them. Reflexivity means 'questioning what we, and others, might be taking for granted – what is being said and not said – and examining the impact this has or might have' (Cunliffe, 2016a: 741). In other words, it is the capacity for examining, in critical terms, the assumptions behind texts (e.g., organizational policies, procedures), decisions and actions and the impact of these upon others. Radical-reflexivity focuses on ourselves in relation to others and our world. This form of reflexivity is not done from a detached perspective, rather it recognizes that we are embedded within our social and material world and therefore need to interrogate our place, activities and responsibilities from within our experience (Allen et al., 2019; Pollner, 1991; Shani and Docherty, 2009; Shrivastava, 2010). Simply put, it means asking 'What am I/are we taking for granted?' 'What are my/our assumptions and how do they influence the way I speak/act/relate with others and the world around me?' Radical-reflexivity can provide a basis for acting and relating differently with each other and the environment.

Traditionally, management education is based on facilitating reflection, and the terms reflection and reflexivity are often used interchangeably. However, it is important to distinguish between them because the difference is an ontological one (Cunliffe, 2009). Reflection draws on an objectivist ontology in which social realities exist independently from us – we are born into a reality in which we have to learn to become an effective member of society. To reflect means to be able to stand back from that reality, to identify how 'it' works and how we may become an effective manager, professional, educator etc., by comparing ourselves with ideal social categorizations. It therefore embodies neoclassicalism, analyzing situations using already established concepts, categories, models and theories – from an outside 'objective' perspective. Reflexivity draws on a subjectivist ontology and often a social constructionist epistemology to suggest that we are not separate from an objectified reality, rather we both shape and are shaped by our social and organization realities in our conversations, actions and interactions with others. In other words, we create, sustain and transform our realities and ourselves in a social and physical landscape of possibilities (Shotter, 2008).

Reflexivity thus complexifies our thinking and experience by exposing contradictions, doubts, dilemmas and possibilities – within ourselves (*self-reflexivity*), and in relation to the world around us (*critical-reflexivity*) (see Cunliffe, 2014; Hibbert & Cunliffe, 2015). *Self-reflexivity* means accepting responsibility for shaping our world: questioning our ways of being and acting. It involves thinking about how our assumptions, actions, responses and the words we use in our living conversation with others influence meaning and help create, sustain

and/or transform 'realities', ourselves and others. As such, self-reflexivity embraces an embodied and dialogical understanding in which we think and act *from within our experience* of relating with other people. *Critical-reflexivity* takes a more intellectualized approach by questioning the assumptions underlying theoretical, ideological, rational and normalized texts and practices to understand their impact – how they may privilege particular groups or positions and marginalize others. For example, how the wording of a performance evaluation system might be culturally or gender-biased. Such practices can also exclude people from participating in issues that concern them.

Based on these concepts, Allen et al. (2019) go a step further by proposing an 'ecocentric radically-reflexive approach' in the context of sustainability practice and education. Radical-reflexivity as an ecocentric attitude to sustainability invites us to understand ourselves as *embedded in*, rather than *detached from*, nature, in a larger whole. The authors argue that a reflexive understanding of sustainability sees the environment as shaped and enacted by people, organizations and materialities and a radical-reflexive understanding of 'the environment and human experience as reciprocally, ongoingly and multiply constructed as they come together in lived experience' (p. 790). In terms of RMLE, this requires a paradigm shift: from the neoclassical view of sustainability as managing the environment based on the triple bottom line, providing individual courses on sustainability and ethics, or developing management competencies and techniques, to integrating sustainability, ethics and responsibility (Laasch & Moosmayer, 2015), self and the environment, body and mind, mind and nature, subject and object, possibility and actuality. Reflexivity in general, and a radically-reflexive approach specifically, provides a fundamental perspective for dealing with major contemporary challenges around sustainability and can therefore form the bedrock for ecocentric RMLE.

TRANSDISCIPLINARITY

A process in which members of different fields work together over extended periods to develop novel conceptual and methodologic frameworks with the potential to produce transcendent theoretical approaches. (Klein, 2008: S117)

The notion of transdisciplinarity is closely connected to responsible management because its roots lie in a concern for developing a socially responsible science that creates knowledge and facilitates social change around global issues and society's grand challenges, including environment problems (e.g., climate change); issues of health and social justice; bioeconomy; and global food security (see Bernstein, 2015 for an overview). It is also aptly suited to researching and enacting sustainability issues (Jahn, Bergmann & Keil, 2012) because it embraces the complexity around the involvement and conflicting goals, interests and values of many stakeholders (economic, political, social, academic, community, etc.). Indeed, Polk (2014) argues that transdisciplinarity is particularly relevant to addressing sustainability issues for three main reasons: (1) multiple stakeholder participation is key to solving problems at a societal level; (2) the complex nature of sustainability requires a broad knowledge/expertise base and therefore calls upon a wide range of perspectives. Transdisciplinary research and education involve creating initiatives that integrate knowledge from non-academic sources as well as different academic disciplines including science, social science and cultural studies; and (3) the collaboration of multiple academic/non academic actors ensures the 'scientific rigor, practical legitimacy and usability of the results' (p. 441).

The origin of the term transdisciplinarity is attributed to Swiss psychologist Piaget (1972), but has been more recently developed by Romanian theoretical physicist Nicolescu (1996, 2012), who urges us to move beyond interdisciplinarity (which mainly involves the transfer of methods across disciplines) to transdisciplinarity, which 'is at once between

the disciplines, across the different disciplines, and beyond all disciplines' (Nicolescu & Montuori, 2008: 2; italics in original). We further define and situate transdisciplinarity within Gibbons, Limoges, Nowotny, Schwartzman, Scott and Trow's (1994) modes of knowledge production, while recognizing a degree of fluidity in relation to our 'disciplinary' categorization:

Mode 1: Academic-driven research, theoretically oriented and mainly discipline based with little or no collaboration across disciplines and application being a secondary (if any) concern, i.e., uni-disciplinarity.

Mode 2: Applied research focusing on real-world problems, and which can involve interdisciplinary research in that different disciplines may collaborate over the term of a project, but use their own methods and theoretical orientations to develop knowledge within a discipline. This is often linked to the triple helix model of government, industry and academia (Etzkowitz & Leydesdorff, 1995).

Mode 3: Trans-disciplinary. Long-term partnerships between disciplines to invent 'new science' by integrating knowledge and collaboratively developing new methodologies, theories and solutions to social problems. This is achieved by working at 'the intersection of their respective fields' (Gray, 2008). This is linked to the quadruple helix model of civil society and the media, university, government and industry (Carayannis & Campbell, 2009). However, from a sustainability perspective, transdisciplinarity takes us to the quintuple helix, which adds the natural environment into the mix (Carayannis & Campbell, 2010).

These distinctions are important to responsible management and sustainability education because they implicitly and/or explicitly impact the focus of pedagogy, with mainstream business school research and curricula often based on a Mode 1 approach. There have been calls for business schools to take a more interdisciplinary approach to education and research, particularly in addressing issues of social value and sustainability (Currie,

Davies & Ferlie, 2016). Even applied Mode 2 forms of research and education tend to focus on creating impact through the application of theory to practice rather than impact within practice (Cunliffe & Scaratti, 2017).

In exploring the connection between knowledge and nature, Nicolescu (2010) sees reality as complex, multidimensional and contradictory, which provides an impetus for creativity. The multilayered nature of reality connects subjectivity and objectivity through a 'hidden third' that lies between and beyond them. Although subjects (humans) and objects (the physical and material world) are conceptualized as separate, they are related through a 'third', which is a form of understanding that fuses both knowledge and being as a way of becoming sensitized to the different layers of reality. We can interpret this idea as an ecocentric radically-reflexive one in the sense that sustainable development requires us to know both ourselves as subjects and how we are embedded in and relate to the material world. We come to understand this 'beyond disciplines' through science, philosophy, art, spirituality, imagination and so on, which involves cognitive knowledge (abstract representations), embodied knowledge (feelings, intuition, imagination) and enacted knowledge (experience and know-how) (Dieleman, 2017).

For Dieleman (2017), Nicolescu's construction of reality requires us to be reflexive about our subjective experiences and how we produce knowledge because reality 'changes according to how we feel, think, and act' and we create our understanding of reality 'out of many possible realities we potentially can create' (p. 172). This understanding emerges from integrating scientific knowledge, senses, emotions and our bodily interactions with others and the environment. It is never complete because 'it emerges in the spontaneous, taken for granted, subjective, un/conscious ways in which we respond to others' (Cunliffe, 2002: 37) and is therefore open to our continuous articulation in response to particular circumstances. A simple summary of transdisciplinarity is that it is problem-oriented, transformational in addressing real societal and environmental issues, involves collaborative (across traditional knowledge boundaries) action-oriented research, and a mutual embedded learning process. By re-approaching the living connection between subject and reality, transdisciplinarity proposes a paradigm shift in the way we produce knowledge and how we relate to and engage with the world and, we argue, embraces radical-reflexivity.

Questioning assumptions (reflexivity) and realizing embedded knowledge from within and through interactions (radical-reflexivity) also means interrogating and narrowing the gap between perceiving and acting/reacting upon reality by heightening our sensitivity of reality *as it unfolds*. So it is with the transdisciplinary concept of emergence of the subject, meaning our subjectivity arises from the conscious embodied relationship between self, other and environment. This means that we understand our self, social and natural worlds from within the present emerging context. It requires us to facilitate RMLE as learning from within situations to produce knowledge and transform those situations. What emerges from such a radically-reflexive and transdisciplinary attitude is both a more integrated pragmatic solution in which students understand complexity and the need for change. We now turn to the implications for RMLE.

RADICAL-REFLEXIVITY AND TRANSDISCIPLINARITY IN LEARNING

Much of the literature around sustainability leadership focuses on identifying generalized competencies and skills, which are divorced from the context in which sustainability issues are embedded (Heizmann & Liu, 2018). It also tends to take an individualized 'heroic' leader approach situated in a 'reflective' perspective on managing the environment. To sociologist Edgar Morin (2011), the major challenge for education in the 21st century is to overcome the primacy of such fragmented and individualized forms of knowledge by creating new ways of understanding reality that create and consolidate 'the ethics of a planetary education' (pp. 15–18). His work connects with reflexivity and transdisciplinarity by arguing the need for inquiry based on identifying underlying assumptions, contradictions and recognizing the embodiedness and embeddedness of the inquirer/learner in a complex whole. Nicolescu assesses the educational implications of transdisciplinarity[1] around four pillars of learning: *learning to know* means being able to make connections and bridge the gap between disciplines; *learning to do* is an 'apprenticeship in creativity' that goes beyond learning a profession or occupation; *learning to live together with* means understanding and respecting our own and others' culture; and *learning to be* is an ongoing search for selfhood and (we suggest) what it means to be an ethical person in relation with others. This approach to learning highlights our responsibility as educators and learners to work collaboratively and reflexively across boundaries (discipline, functional, community, etc.) in order to address society's problems. It also involves temporality, in terms of addressing how current problems and issues relate to practices and traditions embedded in the past that need to be reconfigured for future benefit. In terms of RMLE, this means re-visioning learning across disciplinary boundaries.

Compared to reflexivity, there are fewer efforts to embed transdisciplinarity into the business school curriculum (see Marques, 2016 and Paschall & Wüstenhagen, 2012 for exceptions). This is perhaps because management and business education is generally discipline-based and 'interdisciplinary' is often viewed as accounting, strategy, marketing and organizational behavior faculty working together. One exception is Bissola, Imperatori and Biffi's (2017) experimental postgraduate entrepreneurship education project based on a transdisciplinary rhizomatic pedagogical model where the program content draws on science, business studies and arts, and participants complete courses in an emergent way. An example outside business schools is that at the University of Tokyo, which has a transdisciplinary Graduate Program in Sustainability Science in its Graduate School of Frontier Sciences, which involves a collaborative effort across five universities and between the university departments of Natural Environmental Studies, Environment Systems, Human and Engineered Environmental Studies, Socio-Cultural Environmental Studies, and International Studies (Onuki & Mino, 2009). The purpose of these programs is to create a more wholistic approach to RMLE by integrating disciplines, research and practice, and learning strategies (e.g. through analysis, experience, senses, intuition). Gröschl and Gabaldon (2018) discuss how Morin's notion of transdisciplinarity can be incorporated into business school curricula as a means of developing responsible leaders, offering examples of seminars and business simulations – but no complete programs. We found only a few instances in the literature of business school programs connecting both transdisciplinarity and reflexivity in one MBA module (Parkes & Blewitt, 2011).

To summarize, we argue that both radical-reflexivity and transdisciplinarity are central to an ecocentric approach to RMLE in recognizing that reality emerges intrinsically in the interaction between people, their circumstances and their selves: in the hidden third between, across and beyond the moment-to-moment relationships between ourselves and our world. Thus, as 'subjects' we play an active role in the constitution of our world and our knowledge about it. How we experience and understand these relationships therefore, becomes a crucial part of learning and we move from being reflective practitioners operating *on* a *real* world to reflexive authors embedded *in* and shaping our worlds (Cunliffe, 2014). In terms of the Integrated Education for Sustainability (IES) program, these principles are enacted through reflexive dialogue, mindfulness, experiential and arts-based methods of inquiry that harness feelings and emotions, bodily sensations and movement, imagination and intuition. Through the hidden third of affective engagement a new 'subject' and 'object' may emerge.

We now turn to the topic of responsible management education as an important conceptual and practical background in positioning FGV's Integrated Education for Sustainability program.

The 2007 Principles for Responsible Management Education (PRME) aimed to drive curriculum changes in business and management schools around three core themes of social responsibility, ethics and sustainability. Rasche and Escudero (2010) argued that PRME's aspirational principles offer a way of educating students to commit to responsible management practice. Based on voluntary commitment and self-regulation, recent evaluations indicate that although PRME is being increasingly supported, it has not had the desired impact and little work has been done to assess the impact on students (Carteron, Haynes & Murray, 2014; Perry & Winn, 2013). And while integrated and interdisciplinary approaches to research and education in sustainability, responsibility and ethics have been called for, little progress has been made (Burchell, Kennedy & Murray, 2015; Laasch & Moosmayer, 2015). We now illustrate how one university in Brazil has integrated PRME principles into a postgraduate master's program for sustainability practitioners based on an ecocentric pedagogy that incorporates radically-reflexive and transdisciplinary principles.

Integrated Education for Sustainability (IES) is a pedagogy used in a master's program[2] offered to senior sustainability professionals from different sectors and backgrounds. Developed by the Center for Sustainability Studies at FGV-EAESP, Brazil in 2009, it is one of the school's responses to the United Nations' Principles of Responsible Management Education. IES meets PRME's principles in the ways illustrated in Table 18.1.

The program is 'integrated', i.e., adopts an ecocentric, transdisciplinary philosophy at many levels in order to help students to become more sensitive in their relationships with themselves, others and the whole. To do so, IES works with four components:

- The *Reference Project* – a challenge chosen by the students relating to a real and complex sustainability issue, i.e., ecocentric radical-reflexivity and Nicolescu's learning pillars of learning to know and do.
- The *Self Project* – inviting students to experience activities and practices that seek to expand their perception of themselves, others and reality, i.e. to engage in both self-reflexivity and radical-reflexivity, i.e., self-reflexivity and Nicolescu's learning to be.
- *Thematic courses:* 2–4-month courses exploring key sustainability issues in transdisciplinary and reflexive ways, such as Climate Change, Culture of Consumption, Local Development, Sustainable Cities, Ecosystem Services and others, i.e., critical-reflexivity and Nicolescu's learning to know.
- *Sustainability in the field*: an immersive course based on ecocentric and radically-reflexive principles in which students spend four days in an Atlantic Forest region (in southern Brazil), experiencing different aspects of sustainability by interacting with and questioning members of public, private and non-governmental organizations, and local community members in the field, i.e., radical-reflexivity and Nicolescu's learning to know, to live together and to be.

These components are explained in more detail in the following section.

RADICAL-REFLEXIVITY AND TRANSDISCIPLINARITY IN IES

The IES program combines three sources of learning (*formal*, *experiential* and *sensitive/sensible*), which embed transdisciplinarity and ecocentrism, with three dimensions of reflexive learning (individual or *self-reflexivity*, group or *dialogic reflexivity*, and whole or *radical-reflexivity*). Together, they embrace two core principles of ecocentrism: (1) wholeness and (2) embodiedness and embeddedness in the natural world. Figure 18.1 visualizes how reflexivity, transdisciplinarity and ecocentrism are integrated in the program.

Table 18.1 IES meets PRME

Principles for Responsible Management Education (PRME)	Integrated Education for Sustainability (IES)
 Methodology: Create educational frameworks, materials, processes and environments that enable effective learning experiences for responsible leadership  Purpose: Develop capabilities of students to be future generators of sustainable value for business and society at large and to work for an inclusive and sustainable global economy	IES's purpose is to create conditions to extend learners' perception and to help a more 'responsible leadership' to emerge. To accomplish this purpose, it offers a new methodology based on ecocentric, reflexive and transdisciplinary principles, with activities that integrate formal, experiential and sensible sources of learning and expression
 Values: Incorporate into academic activities and curricula, and organizational practices the values of global social responsibility as portrayed in international initiatives such as the United Nations Global Compact	IES incorporates PRME's values into academic activities both in terms of content (curricula development based on relevant topics for the sustainable development agenda) and process (a methodology based on ecocentric, reflexive and transdisciplinary principles)
Partnerships: Interact with managers of business corporations to extend the knowledge of their challenges in meeting social and environmental responsibilities and to explore jointly effective approaches to meeting these challenges	IES fosters partnerships with public and private institutions, and with participants from civil society through the development of multi-stakeholder projects (Reference Projects) around sustainability issues
 Dialogue: Facilitate and support dialogue and debate among educators, students, business, government, consumers, media, civil society organizations and other interested groups and stakeholders on critical issues related to global social responsibility and sustainability	Dialogue is key to our operation through a process that encourages active listening and reflexive communication among educators, learners, organizations, community members and all other actors or stakeholders involved in the process
 Research: Engage in conceptual and empirical research that advances the understanding about the role, dynamics, and impact of corporations in the creation of sustainable social, environmental and economic value	The Center for Sustainability Studies at FGV EAESP develops applied research in key areas such as climate, ecosystem services, local development, value chains and empirical studies around the IES pedagogy

Source: Adapted from Aguiar, Carreira and Góes (2015)

Ecocentrism is embedded in IES through the principles of learning *to know, do, live with, and be,* which are reflected in formal, experiential and sensible forms of learning combined with a focus on reflexive learning as individuals, groups and wholes. In this way, students begin to understand that they are embedded in the world around them and therefore have an ethical responsibility for their relationship with the social and physical world as individuals, professionals and managers. Transdisciplinarity and reflexivity are emphasized in thematic courses, which address formal theories that gain meaning through experiential work-based projects in which students adopt a critically-reflexive stance to question both theory and

sustainability-related practices in their organization. In doing so, they work also from a radically-reflexive perspective by seeing themselves as embedded in that practice and therefore responsible for consequences. Thus, each program component includes different combinations of one or more dimensions and sources of learning. We now describe each part of the matrix in more detail.

Dimensions of learning (embedding reflexivity)

• Individual self-reflexivity puts students in relation to themselves and the whole by encouraging them to engage in a self-reflexive questioning

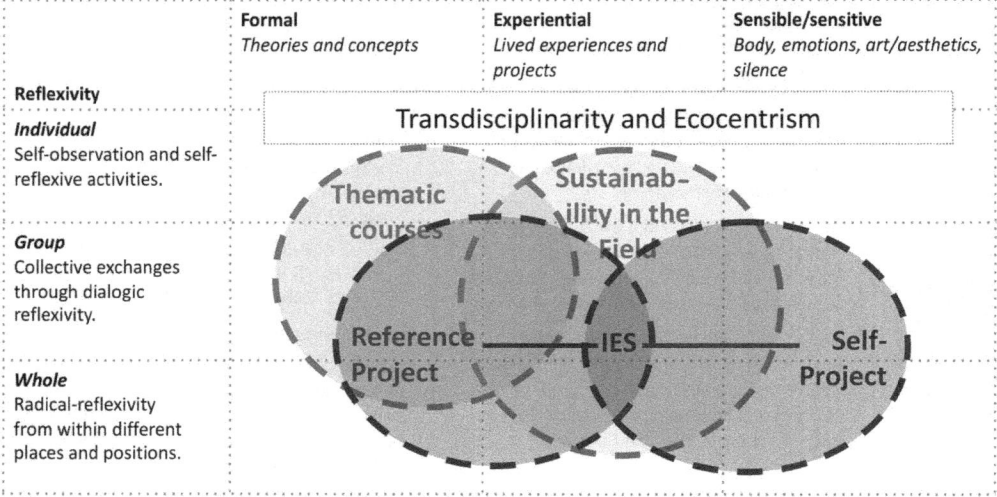

Figure 18.1   Reflexivity and transdisciplinarity in the Integrated Education for Sustainability program

of how they experience themselves in relation to the world around them. This questioning is facilitated through artistic activities aimed at expressing and examining personal meanings in relation to the course; bodily expressions and movements by which a student can perceive and interpret his/her assumptions, ways of thinking, acting and relating; and 'presencing' (being silent for 1–2 hours to meditate on what may emerge between what students are 'letting go' and 'letting come' (Scharmer, 2009).

- Group dialogic reflexivity refers to students' relationships with others (within the group and outside) and involves group discussion and questioning around how worldviews, cultural meanings and identity are constructed through relationships and language. Dialogic reflexivity involves conversations that surface, question and explore 'multiple meanings and imagining new possibilities for moving on' (Cunliffe & Scaratti, 2017: 29). These include debriefings after formal team assignments and social activities and aim to facilitate ecocentrism by helping students perceive and interpret their relational environment.
- Whole radical-reflexivity refers to highlighting students' relationships to natural, cultural and social environments. Assignments around organizational problems form the basis for examining

how one shapes and is shaped by institutional dynamics, social-economic and macro-political contexts and the field trip places students in contact with the natural environment and their local communities and government administrators in more experiential terms.

Sources of learning (embedding ecocentrism and transdisciplinarity)

- Formal learning refers to theories and concepts. It helps to organize, integrate and articulate lived experience into coherent concepts and representations through lectures, papers, case studies, and reflexive dialogue circles.
- Experiential learning refers to practical and concrete experiences and memories, helping students construct meaning through practice. It is experienced through games, role-plays, projects and fieldtrips.
- Sensitive/sensible learning incorporates emotions and imagination, perceptions and impressions. Triggering personal meanings and an ontological and ecocentric consciousness in terms of how one is situated in the world, it is experienced through body, artistic and contemplation activities.

Table 18.2   Thematic (transdisciplinary) courses: engaging students in *critical-reflexivity*

Course name	Examples of critically-reflexive questions
Sustainable Development: Agenda and Governance	What is development? How has this concept evolved? What are the constraints of such conceptions? How does freedom and development relate? What is sustainable development?
Climate Change: Regulation and Business Management	What are the fundamental challenges and dilemmas of the transition from a carbon-intensive and climate-vulnerable economy to a low-carbon and resilient economy? What are the roles of regulation, governance and companies at global and national levels currently and in post-2020?
United Nations Role Play	How does the multilateral system for sustainable development operate at the UN level? How do the intense and complex ways of negotiating occur at UN conferences and consider the 2030 agenda? How are key stakeholders involved and what factors influence them to take certain positions?
Local Development: Companies and Territories	What is territory? What is local development in a territory? How can the effects of significant installation's and operations of infrastructure, logistics and mining projects in Brazil be understood from a local perspective, considering concepts of local development, territory governance and social license to operate? What are the challenges and opportunities to public policies, corporate practices and civil society initiatives to planning and management of such installations?

Thematic courses: engaging students in critical-reflexivity

The thematic courses enable students to think in a critically-reflexive way about important sustainability issues by questioning taken-for-granted assumptions in key course content areas. Courses also embody principles of transdisciplinarity by being organized around themes that cross disciplines and sectors. Table 18.2, highlights 4 of the 11 thematic courses with examples of the critically-reflexive questions promoted.

As the questions above reveal, a common objective among all thematic courses is not only to present content about sustainability, but through a critically-reflexive questioning of taken-for-granted assumptions and practices to promote new perspectives that cross disciplinary boundaries. Challenging students in this way helps present new lenses for understanding the dilemmas, tensions and paradoxes in managing the organization–environment relationship in more responsible and ethical ways. Essentially, the reflexive questions draw attention to the sustainability paradox of how to focus on wealth creation and nurture a sustainability ethos (Kurucz et al., 2014) in organizational policies, strategies and practices.

The IES program enables students to understand and practice sustainability in a more integrated way as former students noted:

'The Masters journey turned my perspectives about the world, providing new lenses for interpreting it and allowing new ways to interact with and to modify my environment. In each course, new concepts were shared, complementing each other in connections that simply made sense together. It is difficult then, to segregate how each concept and experience has influenced me in isolation. I noticed different vectors of influence that complemented and mixed together, as if several flows of thought and energy converged harmonically, guiding new actions ('Nano steps') that emerged spontaneously … both in my professional and personal lives.' (M.G. – former student)

'Perhaps one of the greatest lessons to me has been to develop an integrated view of the concept of sustainability. Although we tend to segment the elements to facilitate their understanding, we cannot dissociate the components of the whole. Sustainability involves the individual, the collective and the environment, and the connections and interactions that happen at all times between them; … it is the integrated understanding of this complexity and of this network of relationships that will allow us to seek solutions that bring meaning to the concept and allow a more harmonious experience in the whole.' (D.P. – former student)

The Reference Project: Thinking and acting reflexively on issues of sustainability

The objective of the Reference Project is to expand students' perception of their relationships with the social and natural environment by seeking practical solutions to real sustainability challenges. They do so by connecting concepts and tools with management practices; integrating knowledge with a reflexive stance; and acting as change agents towards sustainable development. By 'drawing attention to the interrelated nature of individual and collective worldviews, social and material space and power relations' (Allen et al., 2019: 788) each project provides a field experience in which radical-reflexive engagement is cultivated.

Each semester, students are encouraged to choose a challenge related to a real and complex sustainability issue. Using the Open Space Technology method (Owen, 2008) students propose a sustainability-related topic of personal or professional strategic importance as the class agenda. Students self-organize into groups of 3–7 members, around each challenge, thus encouraging dialogic reflexivity. The results should be practical in co-creating applicable solutions, which are accessible to anyone interested. Teams are encouraged to develop their projects following three main stages, which are inspired by the Theory U method (Scharmer, 2009): (i) *Observe, observe, observe:* a 2-month investigation stage that includes an open event to key stakeholders to explore key questions around the challenge, plus data collection by the group (e.g. interviews, observation, literature review); (ii) *Retreat and reflect:* an introspective stage in which students are invited to somehow 'silence' the inner noise of information collected. The group spends 2–4 days outside the city going through experiences of meditation, nature contemplation, self-assessments and body activities to encourage reflexivity around the project's challenge and how each group member feels and relates personally to that challenge; and

(iii) *Act in an instant:* a prototyping stage that lasts around 2 months and includes group activities for solutions design.

To be effective in solving sustainability issues necessarily involves not only integrating different stakeholder perspectives but also formulating new perspectives of relationships and reality itself. The Reference Project facilitates radical-reflexivity as students begin to notice how their own patterns and habitual mindsets are involved in constituting reality. In a transdisciplinary view, to be immersed in a complex context means to face contradiction, and reflexive and responsible engagement with contradiction involves learning from a cognitive and embodied sense of emergence within complex and multilayered realities. By questioning the habitual neoclassical separation of mind from social, material and environmental realities and recognizing that we are embedded in the natural world (ecocentrism), students can become agents of radical change in themselves and their working contexts. For example, one student working on climate change developed a simulator to connect carbon emission costs to financial statements:

'The group was able to open and research to understand in greater depth the issues related to climate change and carbon pricing that were being discussed with Professor G. In this project we made 'a trip around the world' to understand how the topic was being developed in different countries and at the same time a 'parallel trip' with companies, banks and investors to understand the topic relevance. By combining all this information, we understood that bringing a carbon pricing simulator (EBITDA) into the companies' results would be appropriate. We validated this understanding with several stakeholders, who ratified our proposal and suggested improvements. As a result, we came up with something unexpected, a tool that managed to extrapolate the physical boundaries of scholarly work and reverberate into several extra-class forums ... The simulator brings transparency, isonomy and eases the competitive opportunities (or risks) that companies will absorb when Brazil formally adopts one of the forms of carbon pricing ... It has been presented to 30 different banks associated with the [Brazilian Federation of Banks]'. (R.O. – former student)

The Self Project: Turning the reflexive act upon ourselves

The objective of the *Self Project* is to enable students to acquire a new repertoire (spoken and unspoken languages) for perceiving, relating and acting in complex and multilayered environments and relationships. It does so by integrating subjective dimensions (emotions, intuition, spirituality) as a source of knowledge. Students expand their perception of themselves, others and reality by engaging in radically-reflexive dialogue around activities and practices. Such activities occur throughout the program, from small practices during thematic courses, reference project stages, and field trips, to entire classes dedicated to such practices. These practices include:

- *Journaling*: From Day 1, each student receives a notebook, which they customize aesthetically, to express, elaborate and reflexively question all sorts of inputs.
- *Body*: Different activities that use movement and sensation (interacting with others or not) as means of perceiving and interpreting reality, be it internal, relational or of a larger context. By these activities, students learn to process sensitive information about themselves, others, and the environment. One example uses Capoeira (a traditional Brazilian dance/martial art/game) to create a non-verbal experience for creating an embodied reflexive understanding of being in the world and metaphorical bridges with concepts.[3]
- *Tradition*: From a transdisciplinary perspective, the oral reading of traditional stories (e.g., Christian, Jewish, Arab, Hindu, Chinese, Japanese or Congolese) exposes students to a broader repertoire of metaphors and symbols, which are a great source for seeing and understanding multiple realities and understanding Others differently.
- *Mindfulness*: Short meditations of 5–10 minutes are a common practice in class for emphasizing some aspect of sensation, thought or imagination. Students often suggest the practice of mindfulness between themselves. The practice contributes greatly to sensitizing students to the incessant flux of perceptions from within the moment and encourages self-reflexivity.

- *Art* (poetry, music, aesthetics): in a transdisciplinary view art facilitates a reflexive understanding of different realities and forms of knowledge through a synthesis of the aesthetic and cognitive. Students produce drawings, body movements, sculptures, poetry, music, videos, games and performances either to address 'objective external' issues or 'subjective internal' ones.

While the transdisciplinary thematic courses and the Reference Project promote outside-in perspectives, encouraging students to ask critically-reflexive questions about real life challenges and stakeholders, the Self Project promotes a self-reflexive inside-out perspective, putting students in contact with themselves in relation to others (to multiple meanings, perceptions, feelings, assumptions etc.): a more embodied form of knowledge. In this sense, the Self Project and Reference Project combined connect subjectivity and objectivity through Nicolescu's notion of the 'hidden third' by fusing knowing and being. Students begin to appreciate new ways of thinking about themselves and how they relate with/in the world and to the quality of relationships they cultivate. Self-reflexivity encourages students to think about their own assumptions, bodily practices, relationships and radical-reflexivity encourages them to see themselves in relation to others and social realities as characterized by inherent tensions, dilemmas and challenges. The Self Project is the very essence of reflexive transdisciplinary, and ecocentric RMLE since it stresses the importance of *being* and perceiving oneself as an integrated whole, transcending rational cognition and self-centered perspectives (egocentric approach). The quotes below exemplify the impact of the Self Project on students:

'Reconnection. This is the word that describes my feeling at this end of the journey. It was a profound and transformative cycle, which generated anxieties, reflexivity and moments of happiness and fulfillment. ... I was encouraged to seek a new way of thinking, a different perspective at my own attitudes, practices, and everyday decisions. I learned to deal with the paradoxes and accept contradictions. I understood that disorder is part of our thoughts, so I realized there is a false idealization about stability and certainty … This is my greatest discovery.' (S.S. – former student)

'Something that I have been practicing is the sensitive listening that I call complete listening. A phrase marked me at the beginning of this discipline: 'we are our relationships'. During the course I realized that in order to be better we needed to be open to interaction with others, not only in personal life as in professional life. Today I am a more open person, more reflective in both opinions and ideas, so I had to be less critical and demanding at work, I am learning to separate the moments and to understand the other points of view, not seeking the quickest and objective solutions.' (A.M. – former student)

Sustainability in the field: Embedding radically-reflexive ecocentrism in RMLE

The aim of the field trip is to experience different 'realities' relating to sustainability and to understand how neoclassic and ecocentric paradigms work in practice. Students develop a map of actors, relationships, challenges and opportunities in the region, analyzing the territory as a space of articulation and disputes. This helps them realize how local realities are influenced and can be co-created. Students and educators spend 4 days in the region of Guaraqueçaba, Brazil, to experience different aspects of sustainability, including the relationship between public, private and non-governmental organizations, institutions and local actors. During the trip we visit one of the largest ports in Brazil, which exemplifies the sustainability paradox by bringing expansive economic development while at the same time having a significant environmental and social impact on local communities and the surrounding Atlantic forest – Brazil's richest biome in terms of biodiversity. Students also visit a live session of a local meeting of councilors; three protected forest areas; and experience contrasting models of conservation (public, private and non-governmental).

Sustainability in the field enables students to *be* reflexive (Cunliffe, 2016a) as they

question stakeholders in their context and begin to understand how people, communities and the environment shape each other in mutually defining ways as they interact in lived experiences. The trip facilitates radical-reflexivity through a deeper contact between themselves and nature, promoting moments of contemplation and silence (mindfulness). As one student commented:

'Another important point was to provide moments of individual connection with the environment. The exercises of the practice of silence, as a vector of reflection and interaction, were extremely beneficial in this sense. … Moments of introspection experienced in the midst of nature on the trip to Guaraqueçaba were important for me to reconnect with myself at a time when I experienced situations of extreme agitation at work. The readings of Manoel de Barros's poems, in turn, generated reflexivity, reflected in my aesthetic synthesis, coming from past ages … to build a smoother path in the future. Today the silence and the moments of individual connection and with the environment have been my allies to walk a more serene and sustainable way.' (D.P. – former student)

'My vision was amplified. Self-knowledge, learning to perceive myself, allowed me to develop mindfulness, sensitive listening and self-positioning, overcoming polarities. … How good to realize that I can interfere in the World.' (A. – former student)

RADICAL-REFLEXIVITY AND RMLE: THE FUTURE

We began the chapter with a current (at the time of writing) horrific case, which highlights why we need reflexive responsible management research and education initiatives that fundamentally reconceptualize our relationship with the natural and social world from a neoclassical to an ecocentric perspective. Instead of the traditional focus on managing the environment taught through discipline-based courses, and perhaps requiring students to *reflect on* the environment as if it were separate from us, we argue that incorporating radical-reflexivity and transdisciplinarity as core principles of an ecocentric

RMLE can result in a deeper and more embedded understanding of the relationship between ourselves, organizations and the environment.

One of the present authors (A. L. C.) began working with reflexivity over 20 years ago, as a concept and as a practice – believing that managers, educators, researchers and students needed to begin to think about the world and their responsibilities differently. At that time, reflexivity was rarely addressed within organization and management studies. It has become more evident over the years, especially in critical management studies and critical management education, where critical reflexivity is often used as a method of critiquing ideologies, intellectual suppositions, forms of knowledge and the lack of reflexivity of others (leaders, managers, etc.) without necessarily being reflexive oneself: in other words, reflexivity from an external, detached stance. Radical-reflexivity is more than a concept and a practice, more than a technique or a tool to criticize others – it is *a way of being in the world* where we accept responsibility for our actions, relationships with others, and for the world around us (Cunliffe, 2016a). It is fundamental to what it means *to be an ethical person* caring for our community and environment. This was embodied in young climate activist Greta Thunberg's impassioned speech to the United Nations,[4] when she rebuked world leaders for continuing to talk about 'fairytales of eternal economic growth' while 'entire ecosystems are collapsing'. She highlighted the desperate and urgent need to address world problems by questioning neoclassical assumptions and strategies.

We argue that radical-reflexivity and transdisciplinarity are critical to this effort because they highlight the need to confront normalized ways of thinking and acting in order to take responsibility for tackling sustainability issues in new ways. In educational terms, designing programs around radical-reflexivity requires us to understand that a different form of knowledge is required: in addition to knowing about (e.g. information, techniques), we also need to facilitate knowing from the inside – knowing-from-within (Shotter, 2008) – a reflexive understanding from which we begin to see ourselves in the world in different and more embedded ways. This form of radically-reflexive knowing embraces Nicolescu's knowing how to live together and how to be and can be powerful, exemplified in a manager's comments.

> 'Knowing is an ongoing process ... almost the intersection of experience, environment and knowledge becomes knowing ... it happens in time, it affects your future knowing but it's not like knowledge in the sense that you can take it off the shelf. Knowing changes you ...' (quoted in Cunliffe, 2016b)

As educators we need to recognize our responsibility for harnessing our students' 'moral and critical engagement' with sustainable management practices (Heath, O'Malley & Tynan, 2019: 442). The IES program aims to facilitate the development of responsible practitioners who understand and engage with sustainability from a more embedded, embodied and reflexive perspective that highlights their relationship with and responsibility for the world around them.

To have an impact on our world both now and in the future – and prevent disasters such as Brumadinho from occurring again – we need to embrace more self-reflexive and radically-reflexive forms of learning that emphasize a manager's responsibility for the community and environment. We have encountered few examples in the literature of sustainability programs that encourage reflexivity or are designed around transdisciplinary principles. Business schools need to begin taking responsibility for moving beyond the myopic neoclassical mentality to incorporate radical-reflexivity and transdisciplinarity in course design. By doing so, we can begin to address societal and environmental issues in problem-oriented and collaborative ways that move beyond our disciplinary mindset and even beyond the triple bottom line to the quintuple helix.

We end with an excerpt from a poem 'Culture and the Universe' by Simon Ortiz, a Native American poet from the Acoma Pueblo in New Mexico. In Native American life, people, land and nature belong together, often with the earth as creator, an affinity – a relationship – we might learn from.

Lean into me

The universe

sings in quiet meditation.

We are wordless:

I am in you.

Without knowing why

culture needs our knowledge,

we are one self in the canyon.

Simon J. Ortiz (2002)

Notes

1   http://ciret-transdisciplinarity.org/bulletin/b12c8. php. (accessed 25 October 2018).
2   https://eaesp.fgv.br/en/courses/professional-masters-management-competitiveness-sustainability.
3   see www.youtube.com/watch?v=MqTn7d-Q6EE to see the studio visited.
4   www.bbc.com/news/av/world-49795221/thunberg-if-you-choose-to-fail-us-we-will-never-forgive-you. Accessed 24 September 2019.

REFERENCES

Aguiar, A. C., Carreira, F., & Góes, V. (2015). Integrated Education for Sustainability – Guide to fundamentals and practices – Version 1.0. Available at: http://gvces.com. br/integrated-education-for-sustainability-guide-of-fundamentals-and-practices-version-1-0?locale=en.

Allen, S., Cunliffe, A. L., & Easterby-Smith, M. (2019). Understanding sustainability through the lens of radical reflexivity. *Journal of Business Ethics*, *154*, 781–795.

Bateson, G. (1972). *Steps to an ecology of mind*. Aylesbury: Intertext.

Bernstein, J. H. (2015). Transdisciplinarity: a review of its origins, development, and current issues. *Journal of Research Practice*, *11*(1), 1–20.

Bissola, R., Imperatori, B., & Biffi, A. (2017). A rhizomatic learning process to create collective knowledge in entrepreneurship education: open innovation and collaboration beyond boundaries. *Management Learning*, *48*(2), 206–226.

Burchell, J., Kennedy, S., & Murray, A. (2015). Responsible management education in UK business schools: critically examining the role of the United Nations Principles for Responsible Management Education as a driver for change. *Management Learning*, *46*(4), 479–497.

Carayannis, E. G., & Campbell, D. F. J. (2009). 'Mode 3' and 'Quadruple Helix': toward a 21st century fractal innovation ecosystem. *International Journal of Technology Management*, *46*(3/4), 201–234.

Carayannis, E. G., & Campbell, D. F. J. (2010). Triple helix, quadruple helix and quintuple helix and how do knowledge, innovation and the environment relate to each other? A proposed framework for a trans-disciplinary analysis of sustainable development and social ecology. *International Journal of Social Ecology and Sustainable Development*, *1*, 41–69.

Carteron, J-C., Haynes, K., & Murray, A. (2014). Education for sustainable development, the UNGC PRME initiative, and the sustainability literacy test: measuring and assessing success. *SAM Advanced Management Journal*, *79*(4), 51–58.

Cunliffe, A. L. (2002). Reflexive dialogical practice in management learning. *Management Learning*, *33*, 35–61.

Cunliffe, A. L. (2009). Reflexivity, learning and reflexive practice. In Armstrong, S., & Fukami, C. (Eds.), *Handbook of management learning, education and development* (pp. 405–418). London: Sage.

Cunliffe, A. L. (2014). *A very short, fairly interesting and reasonably cheap book about management* (2nd ed.). London: Sage.

Cunliffe, A. L. (2016a). 'Becoming a critically reflexive practitioner' redux: what does it mean to BE reflexive? *Journal of Management Education*, *40*, 740–746.

Cunliffe, A. L. (2016b) Twenty-one words that made a difference: shifting paradigms. In Corcoran, T., & Cromby, J. (Eds.), *Joint action: Essays in honour of John Shotter* (pp. 173–190). London: Taylor & Francis, Psychology Press.

Cunliffe, A. L., & Scaratti, G. (2017). Embedding impact: developing situated knowledge through dialogical sensemaking. *British Journal of Management, 28*, 29–44.

Currie, G., Davies, J., & Ferlie, E. (2016). A call for university-based business schools to 'lower their walls': collaborating with other academic departments in pursuit of social value. *Academy of Management Learning & Education, 15*(4), 742–755.

Dieleman, H. (2017). Transdisciplinary hermeneutics: a symbiosis of science, art, philosophy, reflective practice, and subjective experience. *Issues in Interdisciplinary Studies, 35*, 170–199.

Etzkowitz, H., & Leydesdorff, L. (1995). The triple helix – university–industry–government relations: a laboratory for knowledge-based economic development. *EASST Review, 14*(1), 14–19. Available at SSRN: https://ssrn.com/abstract=2480085

Gibbons, M., Limoges, C., Nowotny, H., Schwartzman, S., Scott, P., & Trow, M. (1994). *The new production of knowledge: the dynamics of science and research in contemporary societies.* London: Sage.

Gray, B. (2008) Enhancing transdisciplinary research through collaborative leadership. *American Journal of Preventative Medicine, 35*(2S), S124–S132.

Gröschl, S., & Gabaldon, P. (2018). Business schools and the development of responsible leaders: a proposition of Edgar Morin's transdisciplinarity. *Journal of Business Ethics, 153*, 185–195.

Heath, T., O'Malley, L., & Tynan, C. (2019). Imagining a different voice: a critical and caring approach to management education. *Management Learning, 50*(4), 427–448.

Heizmann, H., & Liu, H. (2018). Becoming green, becoming leaders: identity narratives in sustainability leadership development. *Management Learning, 49*(1), 40–58.

Hibbert, P., & Cunliffe, A. L. (2015). Responsible management: engaging moral reflexive practice through threshold concepts. *Journal of Business Ethics, 127*(1), 177–188.

Jahn, T., Bergmann, M., & Keil, F. (2012). Transdisciplinarity: between mainstreaming and marginalization. *Ecological Economics, 79*, 1–10.

Kessel, F., & Maurer, S. (2012). Radical reflexivity as a key dimension of a critical scientific understanding of social work. *Social Work and Society, 10* (2). Available at: www.socwork.net/sws/article/view/335/672.

Klein, J. T. (2008). Evaluation of interdisciplinary and transdisciplinary research: a literature review. *American Journal of Preventative Medicine, 35*(2S), S116–S123.

Kurucz, E. C., Colbert, B. A., & Marcus, J. (2014). Sustainability as a provocation to rethink management education: building a progressive educative practice. *Management Learning, 45*(4), 437–457.

Laasch, O., & Moosmayer, D. (2015). Competences for responsible management education: a structured literature review. *CRME Working Papers, 1*(2).

Marques, J. (2016). Shaping morally responsible leaders: infusing civic engagement into business ethics courses. *Journal of Business Ethics, 135*, 279–291.

Morin, E. (2011). Os sete saberes necessários à educação do futuro (Seven complex lessons in education for the future). Brasília: Cortez Editora, UNESCO (United Nations Educational, Scientific and Cultural Organization).

Nicolescu, B. (1996). *La transdisciplinarité.* Paris: Rocher.

Nicolescu, B. (2010). Methodology of transdisciplinarity – levels of reality, logic of the included middle and complexity. *Transdisciplinary Journal of Engineering & Science, 1*(1), 19–38.

Nicolescu, B. (2012). Transdisciplinarity: the hidden third, between the subject and the object. *Human & Social Studies, 1*(1), 13–28.

Nicolescu, B., & Montuori, A. (Eds.). (2008). *Transdisciplinarity: theory and practice.* New Jersey: Hampton Press.

Onuki, M., & Mino, T. (2009) Sustainability education and a new master's degree, the Master of Sustainability Science: the Graduate Program in Sustainability Science (GPSS) at the University of Tokyo. *Sustainability Science, 4*, 55–59.

Ortiz, S. J. (2002). 'Culture and the universe'. In *Out there somewhere.* Tucson: University of Arizona Press.

Owen, H. (2008). *Open space technology: a user's guide*. San Francisco, CA: Berrett-Koehler.

Parkes, C., & Blewitt, J. (2011). 'Ignorance was bliss, now I'm not ignorant and that is far more difficult'. Transdisciplinary learning and reflexivity in responsible management education. *Journal of Global Responsibility*, *2*(2), 206–221.

Paschall, M., & Wüstenhagen, R. (2012). More than a game: learning about climate change through role-play. *Journal of Management Education*, *36*(4), 510–543.

Perry, M., & Win, S. (2013). An evaluation of PRME's contribution to responsibility in higher education. *Journal of Corporate Citizenship*, *49*, 48–70.

Piaget, J. (1972). The epistemology of interdisciplinary relationships. In Apostel, L., Berger, G., Briggs, A., Michaud, G. (Eds.), *Interdisciplinarity: Problems of teaching and research in universities* (pp. 127–139). Paris: OECD.

Polk, M. (2014). Achieving the promise of transdisciplinarity: a critical exploration of the relationship between transdisciplinary research and societal problem solving. *Sustainability Science*, *9*(4), 439–451.

Pollner, M. (1991). Left of ethnomethodology: the rise and decline of radical-reflexivity. *American Sociological Review*, *56*(3), 370–380.

Popa, F., Guillermin, M., & Dedeurwaerdere, T. (2015). A pragmatist approach to transdisciplinarity in sustainability research: from complex systems theory to reflexive science. *Futures*, *65*, 45–56.

Rasche, A., & Escudero, M. (2010). Leading change: the role of the principles of responsible management education. *Journal of Business and Economic Ethics*, *10*(2), 244–250.

Scharmer, O. (2009). *Theory U: leading from the future as it emerges. The social technology of presencing*. San Francisco, CA: Berrett-Koehler.

Shani, A. R., & Docherty, P. (2009). *Learning by design: building sustainable organizations*. Oxford: Wiley Blackwell.

Shotter, J. (2008) [1993]. *Conversational realities revisited: life language, body and world*. Chagrin Falls, OH: Taos Institute Publications.

Shrivastava, P. (2010). Pedagogy of passion for sustainability. *Academy of Management Learning & Education*, *9*(3), 443–455.

Whiteman, G., Walker, B., & Perego, P. (2013). Planetary boundaries: ecological foundations for corporate sustainability. *Journal of Management Studies*, *50*(2), 307–336.

19

Technology in Responsible Management Education

Peter Jack Gallo, Raquel Antolin-Lopez and Ivan Montiel

INTRODUCTION

Technology can be crucial to enhance the learning process required for effective responsible management education (RME). Despite the interdisciplinary nature of RME and the various tensions between sustainability, responsibility and ethics; the three dimensions of RME do share one commonality. This commonality is the role of interrelating the perspectives of multiple actors in the solution of sustainability, responsibility and ethics challenges. It is exactly this type of relational competence (Laasch & Moosmayer, 2016) for which technology provides very specific means of learning, application and assessment. Whether it is the use of pre-programmed actors in games and simulations, or the social network building of Web 2.0, a variety of new technologies facilitate the introduction of multiple actor perspectives and dynamic environmental contexts that are crucial in honing essential RME skills.

The importance of context has always been a unique attribute of management education as a whole. The role of introducing context when teaching new management theories and skills explains why the case study, borrowed from Harvard Law School (Hoskin, 1998), became such an integral part of management pedagogy. However, the written case study can only go so far in helping students grasp the multiple perspectives and various contexts of management, and thus technology has increasingly played a role in the management classroom.

History of Technology in RME

Probably the earliest example of technology applied to management pedagogy is the use of audio-visual equipment. That is, using videos to supplement students' grasp of contextual elements of a given case study or management issue (Lacho & Herring, 1996). Videos can include interviews with managers, employees and customers that help students get a richer grasp of the issues, emotions and perspectives of various parties in a management situation. Videos have become such an accepted technology that some cases now include video supplemental material. In RME, context is equally as important but perhaps more complex to grasp. Each element of RME introduces multiple additional and sometimes conflicting dimensions that require considerable effort to make sense of. Sustainability, for example, introduces a focus on the triple bottom line that requires an understanding and analysis of the social, environmental and financial dimensions inherent in a particular management decision. With sustainability alone, the challenge of designing a 30-page written case study that can elucidate all of these dimensions is quite challenging. This is not even considering the contextual variety needed to understand the stakeholder value optimization of responsibility and the moral excellence challenge of ethics (Laasch & Conway, 2015). Therefore, the use of video technology has been a very important element in successful RME pedagogy.

Since RME requires an understanding of dynamic and multiple perspectives on both the physical and social environment; a number of video sources are available that convey these complexities to students. Excerpts from the evening news that portray any number of social or environmental challenges that face managers or result from management decisions can be utilized. Additionally, documentaries (Comer & Holbrook, 2012) and Hollywood movies can be utilized to convey social and environmental realities relevant to a particular RME challenge or theory. For example, in expressing the devastation of corporate environmental disasters certain movies provide excellent portrayals, such as *Silkwood* (1983) or *Bhopal: A Prayer for Rain* (2013). While dramatizations may not be historically accurate, they provide a level of detail and emotional impact that cannot be captured solely in written case studies or class discussion.

While videos still represent a useful technology applicable to the RME classroom, a number of technological advances have introduced new opportunities for management pedagogy. These include the rapid development and acceptance of the World Wide Web, starting in the mid-1990s to the explosion of portable computing power made available from the smartphone revolution of 2007. The Internet proved useful in a number of ways critical to RME pedagogy, not the least of which included the greater availability of firm specific information (annual and sustainability reports) available at corporate websites. Professors could supplement discussion of particular RME practices with exercises that challenged students to identify and criticize the practices of specific firms through searches of corporate websites. The Internet also provided a new means of distribution for management simulation software, rather than requiring individual software purchases or that course simulation assignments be run exclusively on a university server. Finally, the early web provided blogging sites that could be utilized to encourage student dialogue and discussion through blog post entries (Quible, 2005). Since discussions of RME can include topics of ethics and personal morals, students may be less likely to share in classroom discussion. Therefore, online blog diaries or discussions allow students the digital distance to open up more than they might in face-to-face discussion.

Assessing Current State of Technology in RME

All of these historical technologies continue to be a part of the RME classroom, however the dynamics of Web 2.0 and mobile computing power have contributed multiple new pedagogical opportunities. In today's RME courses, instructors have the option of multiple new technologies that can be accessed via students' own devices and are available outside of classroom management software and traditional text and case publishers. These new technologies provide great learning opportunities, however they can also present considerable new challenges in course design and course management. Despite these challenges, a comprehensive introduction to the emerging technologies used in today's RME classrooms will provide any instructor the ability to combine the exact mix of pedagogies to achieve their teaching goals.

The use of multiple and innovative pedagogies is linked to positive learning outcomes in the educational psychology literature (Khoo & Bonk, 2014). Therefore, teaching effective responsible management, as with many topics, requires using a wide range of approaches (Figueiró & Raufflet, 2015; Starik, Rands, Marcus & Clark, 2010). Technology has introduced a number of novel learning tools to the management classroom, and today's students are more and more comfortable shifting between the various learning environments provided by different technologies. Understanding the depth of technology options available, and how they may work in conjunction to create a holistic learning environment is essential for RME. To that end, this chapter will evaluate the effectiveness of three such interactive technological tools currently used in RME courses: games/simulations, social media and mobile apps.

ONLINE GAMES/SIMULATIONS

Gamification consists of the introduction of game elements, characteristics and dynamics into non-game contexts, for example in an educational context (Buckley & Doyle, 2016). Learning through games falls into the category of experiential learning of Kolb's (1984) model, since learning takes places not only by reading and studying material, but also by reflection on doing – *playing*. Students learn by playing, which helps to engage and motivate students since they perceive the learning process as fun, obtain rapid and continuous feedback on how to improve at the game, and have to solve a challenge that has to be solved through their progress at the game (Buckley & Doyle, 2016). Gamification promotes active participation, personal experience and problem-based learning (Hansmann, 2010).

Specifically, technological advances have contributed to the spread of online and digital games and gaming-based software that involve modern media as a means to improve instruction and the learning experience in higher education (Fletcher & Tobias, 2011), becoming a trend in business education (Seaborn & Fels, 2015; Veltsos, 2017). Examples of digital games used in management-related classes are World of Warcraft, railroad tycoon and civilization. Gaming-based software and digital games not only provide the advantages derived from using gamification but also fit well with the new types of students, digital native, that prefer and widely use new technologies in all aspects of their daily life (Rodriguez, Ajjan & Honeycutt, 2014; Wankel, 2009). However, their potential for learning remains underexploited (Pivec, 2007).

Digital Simulations in Responsible Management Education

Recent studies have also proposed digital games as an effective and engaging approach in responsible management education; for example, in the domain of corporate sustainability learning (e.g. Dieleman & Huisingh, 2006; Gatti, Ulrich & Seele, 2018; Heuer, 2010; Mercer, Kythreotis, Robinson, Stolte, George & Haywood, 2017) or business ethics learning (e.g., Dubbelt, Oostrom, Hiemstra & Modderman, 2015; Jagger, Siala & Sloan, 2016). Within digital games, the use of simulation games as a teaching methodology is increasingly becoming a trend in responsible leadership, business ethics and sustainability related courses. The main reason is their ability to imitate the operation of real-world complex processes or systems (Doyle & Brown, 2000; Salas, Wildman & Piccolo, 2009).

Simulation games provide a realistic business environment that resembles real life where students have to make decisions or solve challenges organized as a sequence of steps involving different thinking processes, knowledge and skills (decision-making, critical thinking, problem-solving, etc.) and can experiment with the consequences of their choices and actions (Salas et al., 2009). This is important because ethics and sustainability are complex domains that require more dynamic and holistic pedagogical approaches to understand their multi-dimensional and inter-temporal characteristics (Starik et al., 2010), as well as, their cognitive and emotional effects (Montiel, Antolin-Lopez & Gallo, 2018; Shrivastava, 2010).

Recent studies have recognized that despite effort and research, to date, the Principles of Responsible Management Education have not significantly impacted practice (Hibbert & Cunliffe, 2015; Hilliard, 2013). According to Hilliard (2013) the existing disconnect between responsible management theories and their application in real-life organizations is due to the complexity and holistic nature of the field. Simulation games might be an effective teaching tool to educate managers and students to behave responsibly and significantly impact practice since they might help build bridges between knowledge and practice in responsible management. Simulation games engage students to develop a critical reflexive practice about business, sustainability and ethics issues (Gatti et al., 2018), a key competency recently identified as essential to achieving transformational learning that leads to the development of more responsible behaviors (Brunstein, Sambiase & Brunnquell, 2018; Hibbert & Cunliffe, 2015).

Games/simulations learning advantages for RME

The main pedagogical potential of simulation games as a teaching tool in responsible management education is their ability to place students in learning environments that present ethics and sustainability-related challenges that they can only solve through the development of mindsets capable of dealing with complexity. In other words, simulation games promote the development of systems thinking that is required for effective responsible management, compared to other teaching methods focused solely on the acquisition of factual knowledge. Creating responsible management solutions requires the ability to deal with the complex dynamics that characterize the world in which we live and focus on the world as a whole, considering both immediate problems and long-term consequences that decision-making processes could generate, and the interconnectedness of multiple factors exerting influence on it. Students must learn that a business is part of a much larger system involving other competitors, a wide variety of stakeholders and natural ecosystems.

Scholars have acknowledged a number of specific learning advantages of simulation games for responsible management learning. First, multi-player simulation games can create shared learning experiences that allow bringing students together to reach solutions (Dieleman & Huisingh, 2016). Students make decisions whose outcomes on their organization, society and the natural environment are constantly updated, not only on the basis of the results of their own decisions but with the results of the other participating groups or students. If the dilemma is raised in an international context, simulation games have the potential of contextualizing transboundary and cross-cultural conflicts as well. In addition, some simulation games even allow for performing different roles with varying points of view that interact with complex responsible management issues that do not have a single correct outcome (Maier, Baron & McLaughlan, 2007). This is an important pedagogical advantage because most of the ethics and sustainable challenges require agreement and collaboration from multiple organizations and stakeholders with conflicting interests. For example, the United Nations included 'partnerships for the goals' as the 17th goal in its list of Sustainable Development Goals to emphasize the role of collaboration and cooperation to address global sustainability-related grand challenges.

Furthermore, simulation games help to promote an interdisciplinary learning since they present scenarios where students can learn that developing responsible management solutions require handling multiple and diverse factors (Dieleman & Huisingh, 2016; Gatti et al., 2018; Heuer, 2010). For example, simulation games can be helpful in responsible management learning on corporate sustainability since they provide students with the opportunities to struggle with how to integrate dynamic natural systems and complex social dilemmas with profit-oriented management. The skills required for an effective integration of multiple, often opposing, factors in the design of a responsible organizational strategy can only be learned through experience. Simulation games allow the students to see, feel and experiment several aspects of the systemic behavior.

Third, simulation cases also seem to be well suited to help students to learn about the inter-temporal nature of responsible management. Irresponsible business practices have negative consequences in the short-term, but also mid- and long-term effects that are difficult to observe and learn though traditional teaching methodologies. Even changes in one dimension of responsible management might have consequences in other dimensions that are only felt in the long term. For example, the importance of time and the interaction between its dimensions over time have recently been proposed as one of the major issues to take into account for a comprehensive understanding of corporate sustainability and its practice (Bansal & DesJardine, 2014; Sweeney & Sterman, 2000). Through different rounds of decision-making that represent different time horizons, simulation games allow students to learn about the consequences of their decisions in the short, mid and long-term.

Another advantage of using simulation games for responsible management learning resides in that games allow students to learn by doing, as previously stated, but also learning by failing, an important aspect of learning (Dieleman & Huisingh, 2006). Trial and error is a core characteristic of game playing since the main goal of games is to develop a positive relationship with failure by creating rapid feedback cycles and promoting reflection (Buckley & Doyle, 2016). Just-in-time feedback about success or failure helps students develop a systemic understanding of the consequences of their actions when dealing with ethics and sustainability issues without negative consequences to the real world. However, learning by failing is frequently absent in traditional pedagogical approaches (e.g. in corporate sustainability classes) since failure usually leads to lower grades (Mercer et al., 2017).

Games also promote self-knowledge in different personal spheres. When addressing complex decision-making, interacting with students from different backgrounds, and observing the consequences of their actions, students develop knowledge on themselves, for example about their own values, beliefs, and attitudes. Simulation games create realities where students can put themselves in others' shoes, developing an emotional understanding of their and others' behaviors (Jagger et al., 2016). This creates an emotional link and allows for experiencing emotions connected with ethics and sustainability. For example, horror when experiencing a natural catastrophe derived from their decision making or hope when developing a technology that allows for the integration of sustainability, responsibility, and ethics. This is important because responsible management is strongly connected with values and personal attachment. For instance, recent scholars in the corporate sustainability domain of responsible management education have highlighted the need for developing and using teaching methodologies that help students not only to engage in cognitive, but also emotional learning (Montiel et al., 2018; Shrivastava, 2010).

Taken all together, simulation games might be seen as an effective tool to learn about the complexities of responsible management related dilemmas since they can foster integrative values and cognitions that can lead students towards a transformational learning necessary for behavioral change towards responsible behaviors (Mercer et al., 2017). Traditional pedagogical methods, for instance the case method, might be less effective to address systemic nature and complexity that responsible management requires.

Games/simulations examples for RME

We provide a list of simulation games that might be used in the classroom to teach responsible management. Table 19.1 describes the domains of responsible management and specific themes. Additionally, the table explains the simulation games in terms of the context, objective and game process description, and provides the link where they can be found.

Fishbanks, *World Climate*, *Shortfall* and *Cesim SimPower* might be excellent simulation games to learn about environmental sustainability as students assume the role of a business leader making decisions involving trade-off between environmental and economic aspects in different organizational contexts. For instance, *Fishbanks* is a simulation game used in corporate sustainability courses to explain a core foundation of environmental sustainability: The Tragedy of the Commons (Hardin, 1968). Students play the role of fishermen that make decisions on buying, selling, building ships, where to fish, participate in policy options, etc. All these decisions have an impact on the natural environment and the availability of natural resources. If decisions are made from a profit-maximizing perspective, students will face the problem of the depletion of fishery resources which challenge their survival. Students learn that the lack of a sustainable management of natural resources hampers carrying out their business goals.

As can be seen in the table, *Social Progress Index* takes a step further by involving the three elements of sustainability in decision-making. It is a digital simulation game that

helps to understand the trade-offs between the triple bottom line at a country level: social well-being, GDP growth and environmental progress. Students perform the role of country leaders as decision-makers that have the main aim of turning their countries into prosperous but sustainable economies. By playing this simulation game, students learn about the interplay and trade-offs between the economic, social and environmental dimensions of sustainability.

The rest of the simulation games add complexity to students' decision-making by covering the three pillars of sustainability but also business ethics or corporate social responsibility. For example, *Sustentics* is an appealing simulation software that combines the learning advantages of the case method with the potential of simulations to enhance the use of case studies in the classroom. It consists of a simulation software system that supports decision-making derived from cases studies. Students first read the cases that present ethical and sustainability dilemmas, and then, *Sustentics* is used as a digital platform that allows different rounds of decision-making, which allows students to see the impact and consequences of their decisions and lead them to different subsequent scenarios. Therefore, decision-making is expanded compared to the traditional use of the case method, making the case method more dynamic and interactive.

Napuro is another interesting example of a simulation game that can be applied in responsible management education. It presents students with a futuristic scenario where they run companies that produce sustainable cleaning robots. Their main goal is developing a sustainable strategy that allows for success in their competitive environment. It involves many aspects connected with business ethics and corporate sustainability such as designing a sustainability strategy, both internal and external actions connected with sustainability and ethics, stakeholders' management, governance, etc. It is a complete simulation with a lot of potential to bring the student closer to business realities.

Table 19.1   Examples of games/simulation to teach sustainability, responsibility and ethics

Simulation game	RME field	Specific themes	Context	Objective	Description	Further information
Fishbanks	Environmental sustainability	Tragedy of Commons Managing resources sustainably	Participants play the role of fishermen that make decisions on buying, selling, building ships, where to fish, participate in policy options, etc.	Maximizing the net worth as they compete against other players and deal with variations in fish stocks and their catch	Different years (rounds) of choices on boats purchases, place of fishing, etc.	https://mitsloan.mit.edu/LearningEdge/simulations/Pages/Sustainability.aspx
World Climate	Environmental sustainability	Climate change Stakeholders' involvement and cooperation Environmental impact Emotions and sustainability	World Climate is a team role-play simulation of the international climate change negotiations	This exercise provides participants the chance to explore the risks of climate change and the challenges of negotiating international agreements to reduce greenhouse gas (GHG) emissions. They have to come to an agreement on the quotas by country	Participants play negotiators representing countries and regional blocks that work to create an agreement that limits climate change by reducing GHG emissions. Proposals are tested using a climate policy simulation model that provides participants science-based feedback on the implications of their proposals for atmospheric carbon dioxide concentrations, global mean surface temperature, sea level rise, and other impacts	https://mitsloan.mit.edu/LearningEdge/simulations/worldclimate/Pages/default.aspx
Shortfall	Environmental sustainability	Green supply chain Sustainable manufacturing	Students run an automobile manufacturer company in a competitive environment. They have to plan and make decisions that involve economic and environmental trade-offs along the supply chain	Developing a supply chain that is sustainable and economically profitable	The game is played in a series of rounds, each of which represent a fiscal quarter. In the final round, teams 'sell off' their companies, and the team with the most money and that performs well environmentally wins Students play in teams	http://www.coe.neu.edu/Groups/shortfall/

(Continued)

Table 19.1 Examples of games/simulation to teach sustainability, responsibility and ethics (Continued)

Simulation game	RME field	Specific themes	Context	Objective	Description	Further information
Cesim Sim-Power	Environmental sustainability	Renewable energy investment Environmental sustainable policies Risk-management	Student teams manage a power utility that has its own production with coal-fired, gas-fired, and wind power plants. The company uses forward contracts for hedging against market price fluctuations and it operates in markets where greenhouse gas regulations and carbon emissions trading take place	The success of the teams is measured by their ability to generate sustainable shareholder returns. The returns are dependent on how teams are able to incorporate the impact of regulatory policies, customer preferences, sustainable development and risk-management policies in their investment decisions	There are different rounds of decision-making. During the rounds, participants experience how variations in the electricity spot price, pricing policies to customers, customers' demand for renewable energies, and regulations impact the company's profits	https://www.cesim.com/simulations/compare-business-simulations
Social Progress Index (SPI)	Sustainability	Social progress: basic human needs, health status Economic growth: GDP Environmental progress: future generations' resources, long-term environmental impacts	In a fictional country, players make economic, social and environmental decisions The conditions are endogenously determined, with no price shocks or variance in the relationships	Becoming an economic prosperous society that is also sustainable The simulation shows the interdependency of multiple variables and economic sectors at country level	The instructors determine the length of the game in terms of years (different generations) and the number of rounds (choices). Students are divided into teams where they can play different roles	http://procesimlabs.com/
Cleanstart	Sustainability Ethics	Sustainable venture creation (Sustainable entrepreneurship) Business ethics decisions: employee salaries, firing, etc.	Participants play the role of the founder of a new startup company in the clean tech sector	Developing the technology into a successful company	In each year quarter, teams must set prices, hire engineers and sales people, set compensation, (salary, stock, options and profit sharing), select sources of funding, etc.	https://mitsloan.mit.edu/LearningEdge/simulations/Pages/Sustainability.aspx

Napuro	Sustainability CSR	Sustainability strategy design Sustainability communication Sustainability practices Relationships with stakeholders (e.g. clients, NGOs) Product sustainability Governance	It simulates a set of four to six companies of the future that produces sustainable cleaning robots competing in one common market. The companies can distinguish themselves through defining internal and external measures for corporate sustainability	Developing a sustainable strategy that allows them being successful in the competitive environment. Companies have to be profitable, while sustainable, and manage well the relationships with the stakeholders	Students have to make different decisions regarding both internal and external factors for strategy making and execution. The simulation takes places in different years. Students play in teams The game lasts 4-8 hours	http://www.simxp.com/SimulationExperience/en/catalogue-with-our-selection-of-our-ready-to-play-simulations-and-games/11-napuro/
Sustentics	Sustainability CSR Ethics	Universal principles (life, peace, justice, liberty and love) Ethics (personal, social, global) Sustainability Development Goals (e.g. water security, health, etc.)	It is a simulation system that makes the use of case studies more dynamic and interactive. Decision-making is extended and the choices are followed by different implications and scenarios	Students read cases that present ethical and sustainability dilemmas and then use Sustentics to make choices that generate impacts and observable consequences Example of cases: Paradoxical Blessings, Indupalma, Coca Cola	In each case there are three decision moments. Each alternative represents a different path with its own implications and unique scenario Student feedback is based on eight badges	http://sustentics.aguascordobesas.com.ar/course/index.php?categoryid=2

SOCIAL MEDIA

In the past 10–15 years, social media platforms of different natures have emerged to become the most used communication and information sharing tools globally. People, especially the younger generations, e.g. millennials, spend substantial time on social media platforms. In fact, millennials, who were born between 1980 and 1999, are often called 'digital natives' because they grew up with digital technology in their homes and they are likely to turn to technology when gathering any type of information (Hesel & Williams, 2009). This new reality needs to be recognized and embraced as significant novel opportunities to educate managers and future managers can emerge from an effective use of social media platforms in responsible management education.

In addition, the use of social media platforms such as Facebook and Twitter to enhance student interaction in management courses is becoming a trend (Lantz-Andersson, Vigmo & Bowen, 2013). It is therefore very important for educators to understand how different social media platforms like Facebook, Twitter, or Instagram work as they may offer opportunities for a more holistic experiential learning experience that may enhance responsible management behaviors.

Social media learning advantages for RME

Using social media provides several pedagogical advantages in responsible management education. First, the convenience of such platforms for learners who are already users. Most learners are already predisposed to use social media platforms for educational purposes as they already spend substantial amounts of time checking their different social media accounts like Facebook, Instagram or Twitter. Thus, there will be only an extra-step to reach relevant information

which may only require learners to become a fan of a particular Facebook page, or follow a particular Instagram or Twitter account. In fact, it is likely that most leaners will appreciate the bundling of educational content into their daily routines of checking their different social media accounts. The learning experience becomes embedded into their lives rather than having to deal with the usual divide between personal and educational/professional informational platforms.

Second, social media platforms have the ability to enhance collaboration between learners as these platforms are based on interaction between users to function. For example, in business communication courses the use of social media has facilitated group decision making but also generated individual responsibility for their ideas (Buechler, 2010). In addition, previous studies have noted positive reasons to educate students on the appropriate use of social media as they should learn how to use the different platforms responsibly (Hagler, 2013).

Social media examples for RME

Several studies have already showcased the opportunities that social media platforms provide for responsible management education. Here we provide a couple of examples from three of the most used social media platforms: Facebook, Instagram, and Twitter.

Facebook was released in 2004 as a social media and networking service that quickly grew to become the number one global social media platform. In January 2018, Facebook claimed to have more than 2.2 billion monthly active users. Of those users, many of them consider Facebook as their 'home site' and visit the site multiple times throughout the day. Facebook has been adopted by companies for marketing and communication purposes because it provides a rich user environment to disseminate information about their products and services, to build brand awareness and to establish relationships with consumers (Hyllegard, Ogle, Yan & Reitz, 2011). Furthermore, Facebook offers extensive learning opportunities for responsible management. The platform is easy to use, most people are already part of the network and it includes tools to create closed groups to share materials, comment and engage in conversations about any relevant topic on responsible management. Additionally, students can be asked to analyze the social network strategies of different organizations and their legitimacy. In the context of sustainable development agendas, learners can be assigned to analyze how companies develop legitimacy using social media when addressing stakeholders' multiple demands (Castelló, Etter & Årup Nielsen, 2016).

Instagram was launched in 2010 as a photo and video-sharing social media platform and was quickly acquired by Facebook in 2012. This social media app has recently gained popularity to become the most popular platform among younger generations, the post-millennials. It has even helped create a new marketing figure, the 'influencer' – individuals and organizations with a large number of followers who can be used to disseminate ads and information very efficiently. In fact, according to a recent study, 78% of the social influencers for brand collaboration use Instagram as their preferred social media platform (Zine, 2017). The opportunity that Instagram offers for responsible management education relies on identifying the right influencers for learners to follow, those that can enhance education on responsible management topics. These influencer accounts can be either individuals or organizations that post pictures and videos with relevant content. Some examples include B Corporation (@bcorporation), UN Sustainable Development Goals (@sdgaction) or individual influencers in areas like environmental sustainability and zero waste.[1] Identifying the right accounts and influencers to follow can be an effective way to ensure that users receive relevant information to become more responsible managers.

First released in 2006, Twitter is a microblogging service that has become extremely popular as a form of disseminating concise information in a very fast fashion. Users interact by posting and re-posting short messages, 'tweets', that were originally limited to 140 characters but later this limit was doubled. Twitter has since become a very powerful communication tool, with the most relevant example being the US President, Donald Trump, who is an avid Twitter user to quickly disseminate any type of information or thought that crosses his mind. Ten years ago, shortly after Twitter had been released, Reuben (2008) predicted the immense potential of Twitter as a learning tool and Dunlap and Lowenthal (2009) pointed out how Twitter would become a powerful tool to enhance social presence. In fact, no global company or CEO can exist these days without a Twitter account and this provides enormous opportunities to create exercises around responsible management education. For example, students can analyze how different companies and business leaders disseminate information about their corporate social responsibility and sustainability practices. Alternatively, students can also examine how different business crises have been managed on Twitter, the types of responses that companies have released and how their followers have reacted to such responses. Another interesting exercise could involve testing the effectiveness of such tools and how responsive companies and executives are to questions raised by their followers. Students could test communication effectiveness and responsible management by tweeting questions to specific companies or CEOs and analyzing their responses (or non-responses) to their requests as well as different communication strategies between competing companies.

MOBILE APPS

In addition to the social media explosion, the use of smart phones has also brought additional technology tools for information dissemination: the mobile app. Recent statistics show that

60% of the time spent by Americans on the Internet is done through their smartphones (Techcrunch, 2014), which explains why smartphone app design is one of the fastest-growing tech industries. For instance, since 2008, over 100 billion apps have been downloaded (*The Economist*, 2016). Academics have also started to investigate the potential of mobile apps to be used in management education. For example, a recent call for papers on 'There is an App for that! The use of new technologies and apps for ethics, CSR and sustainability education' was recently released at the *Journal of Business Ethics* (Montiel, Delgado-Ceballos, Ortiz-de-Mandojana & Antolin-Lopez, 2020).

Mobile apps learning advantages for RME

This technology boom founded on the development of smartphones and mobile apps has also created new opportunities in responsible management education (Montiel, Delgado-Ceballos & Ortiz-de-Mandojana, 2017). Some have a pedagogy component (e.g. math fluency apps for children, language-learning apps or brain-training apps for seniors), and instructors may benefit from them. Some of these mobile apps may offer the opportunity to educate managers in responsible management. Mobile apps are very convenient to use since everyone now has a mobile device and they are already using those devices at all times. The identification and use of apps that can help educate managers on responsible behaviors seems natural.

Mobile apps examples for RME

Mobile apps may offer the opportunity to educate managers in responsible management. In fact, within the entire universe of mobile apps that are currently available in our smartphones, one can find multiple apps that are useful to educate on different aspects of responsible management. These apps are also useful to educate managers about the

importance of all the different stakeholders since they cover issues related to different stakeholders such as government, employees, consumers, communities, civil society organizations (NGOs), and the natural environment. Next, we provide a few examples that try to tackle different aspects of ethical business, corporate social responsibility and environmental sustainability.

Philanthropy apps are apps aimed at facilitating philanthropic activities of different types of organizations such as non-profits or private companies. Some examples include *Donate a Photo* and *Google One Today*. *Donate a Photo* is an initiative developed by Johnson & Johnson that takes phones and turns them into a way to do good. For every photo shared through the Donate a Photo app, Johnson & Johnson donates $1 to the charity of choice such as Save the Children or Girl Up. Similarly, *Google One Today* facilitates users to support nonprofit causes they believe in.

Employee fair wages apps provide a mechanism for consumers to learn about fair wages by providing information on wages. For example, *ROC United* (Restaurant Opportunities Centers United) is a mobile app that provides information on whether a particular restaurant is paying fair wages or not to its employees. Another interesting app named *Sweatshop* allows users to play the role of a sweatshop owner who has to hire staff, make them work and make decisions on sales and salaries.

Consumer protection apps are apps aiming at providing transparent and accurate information to consumers. For example, the *GoodGuide* app provides health attributes information on personal care, cosmetics, and household cleaning when users scan the product barcodes. *Piensa en Clima* app was developed by a Spanish non-profit, Fundacion Economia y Desarrollo to help consumers in their purchasing decisions. The apps provide information on the climate change actions (or lack of) undertaken by corporations.

Business political involvement apps are apps that provide information on the political involvement of businesses. For example, *BuyPartisan* in the United States allows users to scan a product's barcode and find out the political contributions of each company's CEO, Board of Directors, political action committees and employees. Similarly, *Dollarocracy* is an app developed by OpenSecrets.org that provides information about money in politics in the United States. Both apps are aimed at providing more transparency to the American political process.

Community activism apps provide opportunities to engage users in community activism in different ways. For example, the *Buycott* app is an app with barcode scan capabilities that suggests whether consumers should buy or avoid a particular product based on how well it aligns with the consumer's values and principles. The app also allows consumers to join boycott campaigns to express their support or opposition to various issues. *Joulebug* is an app game that helps users to be more sustainable and compete with their friends and contacts towards being more environmentally sustainable in their daily lives at work and at home. Users gain points by changing their behaviors towards being more environmentally sustainable.

Finally, there are hundreds of apps available that aim at helping users become more environmentally sustainable. For example, *Seafood Watch* is an app developed by the Monterey Bay Aquarium in California that provides information on how to consume seafood and fish in a sustainable way. It reveals whether a particular seafood item can be consumed in a sustainable way in a particular season. Another example is *Air4U*, an app developed at the University of California, Los Angeles, that provides real-time air quality information based on location.

FUTURE TRENDS

The technologies we have discussed in the RME environment are focused on providing

the additional context that we mentioned as being lacking in written case studies and traditional class discussion. We see two themes emerging from these technologies: first there are the technologies that achieve a connection between the management challenge being studied and the student's personal life. The location apps that allow learners to connect sustainability concepts with their daily consumption, philanthropic and waste disposal decisions are just one example of making a particular RME issue concrete and relevant for the student's daily life. The second theme emerging from this group of current technologies is the connection with the perspectives, needs and desires of others; separate from the personal experience of the student. Social media interaction is a perfect example of how the technology can help expose the student to issues and beliefs outside of their own lived experience and allow them to approach management decisions with the multiple perspectives of various stakeholders. It is through this enhanced exposure to personal connection and outsider perspectives that these technologies allow for better engagement with the sustainability, responsibility, and ethics pillars of RME.

While we cannot fully speculate about what great technologies are around the corner that may benefit management education, there are certain technologies that are almost reaching the level of maturity needed for effective utilization in the management classroom. As we look at these maturing technologies, we can identify direct connections with the two contextual themes of personal connection and outsider perspective we found in the current technologies. The two technologies we see as having a significant potential to impact RME pedagogy in the future are virtual reality (VR) and artificial intelligence (AI). We see these technological advances less as standalone pedagogical technologies and more as advancements that may influence some of the tools we have already identified.

Virtual reality is the use of technology to simulate a 3D immersive experience for the user of the technology. This is separate from virtual worlds, which are simulated artificial environments that exist in a digital space and have been used by businesses to create simulated meeting or teamwork environments. These virtual worlds do not necessarily include the level of sophisticated visual immersion of virtual reality. The focus on immersion and rich visual detail makes VR a perfect extension of the traditional use of videos in the management classroom. Rather than observe a video of a manufacturing process, customer service interaction, or human resource management situation, VR would allow students the opportunity to experience these management scenarios as if they were real to life. Using VR technology, a professor can expose students to a rich experience that might not be possible to recreate through field-trips or other pedagogical tools. For example, a VR experience could place a student in the heart of the Bhopal disaster, rather than watch a Hollywood film. VR technology has a significant impact for RME pedagogy specifically because it can place the student in an interactive environment that might not be easily experienced in the real world (Eschenbrenner, Fui-Hoon Nah & Keng Siau, 2008).

VR technology builds on those technologies that seek to build a personal connection for the student with the material being studied. Obviously, the material will be more immersive than videos or images on Facebook and Instagram, however it is unclear whether the greater depth of immersion heightens the learning and personal connection of the management material. Studies have shown that VR can improve students' enjoyment and interest with the learning material but has no improved impact on reliability and understandability (Lee, Sergueeva, Catangui & Kandaurova, 2017). A counterpart to VR technology is augmented reality (AR), which provides the user with additional objects and environments overlaid with their true reality. This technology has implications for the ability to introduce class concepts to the student's everyday life. Rather than ask students to utilize a mobile app when

shopping, these future technologies might allow the instructor to create an overlay that highlights environmental or social issues as the student passively goes by their daily life. For example, such AR may highlight a diesel bus with text or colors to suggest their negative environmental impact in comparison to a natural-gas bus. Again, this focuses on bringing the classroom material alive for the student throughout their daily life which allows them to reinforce cognitive learning and build a personal emotional connection with RME concepts of sustainability, responsibility and ethics.

The second maturing technology that has significant implications for RME pedagogy is artificial intelligence (AI). There are a multitude of different opinions and definitions of AI, but in the simplest terms it concerns the simulation of human intelligent behavior. AI can refer to physical robots, but the technology is equally impressive even if it only exists as a software program that one interacts with through voice or type inputs. As computing power grows, and programming prowess improves these simulations can appear more and more realistic. The Touring test refers to a diagnostic process whereby an AI is tested to see whether it can appear indistinguishable from an actual human subject to an outside observer. These ever more realistic AI technologies have significant implications for the game/simulations we have covered extensively in the earlier sections of this chapter. Most of those simulations rely on simplistic agent behavior models or at most some stochastic processes in their interaction with students. However, more sophisticated AI would significantly impact the quality of interaction in these simulations and would go much further in exposing students to the dynamic perspectives of various stakeholders. RME simulations based on advanced AI could truly duplicate the complex and unpredictable behaviors of various stakeholders faced with an ethical challenge, sustainability misstep, or effort to create shared stakeholder value.

AI technology is also playing an ever-increasing role in mobile app technology.

From music apps that help you identify new music that fits your past tastes, to virtual assistants that automate some of your daily tasks. Therefore, advances in AI may modify the existing mobile apps we have identified in this chapter, or more interestingly, allow for the development of new apps that provide further opportunities to explore RME issues. Imagine an app that is designed to play an ethical devil's advocate. Students may be tasked to make an ethically challenging management decision. After applying all course tools in a comprehensive analysis, students may then be challenged to justify their decision to this devil advocate app. Finally, they could then provide a written reflection on the outcome of the AI assisted discussion.

Both virtual reality and artificial intelligence have been around for many years, therefore we are not predicting the emergence of new technologies. However, if these technologies follow their existing development curves, they will inevitably play a greater role in the management classroom. RME pedagogy relies on the particular exposure to personal connection and outsider perspectives. We identify a relation between VR and the creation of deeper personal experiences and AI and the exposure to almost infinite possibilities of outsider perspectives. Therefore, these two technologies will play an important role in the evolution of technologies used in the RME classroom.

CONCLUSION

We provide a survey of three technology domains for their effective use in RME. Games/simulations, social media and mobile apps were introduced as the domains with the greatest relevance to current RME pedagogy. We define each technology for the reader and provide a general analysis of how it provides useful learning outcomes in the three dimensions of RME, sustainability, responsibility and ethics. For each technological domain we introduce specific examples of how to apply

them in the management classroom. Finally, we argue that these technologies address the need for introducing two main contextual elements to RME courses: a personal connection to the material and a greater exposure to outsider perspectives on the material.

Note

1   www.skinnyfit.com/blog/eco-friendly-influencers/.

ACKNOWLEDGMENTS

We acknowledge the financial support from the Spanish Ministry of Economy, Industry and Competitiveness, Agencia Nacional de Investigación-AEI, and the European Regional Development Fund-ERDF/FEDER-UE (R&D Project ECO2015-66504).

REFERENCES

Bansal, P., & DesJardine, M. R. (2014). Business sustainability: it is about time. *Strategic Organization, 12*(1), 70–78.

Brunstein, J., Sambiase, M., & Brunnquell, C. (2018). An assessment of critical reflection in management education for sustainability: a proposal on content and form of shared value rationality. *Sustainability, 10*(6), 2091.

Buckley, P., & Doyle, E. (2016). Gamification and student motivation. *Interactive Learning Environments, 24*(6), 1162–1175.

Buechler, S. (2010). Using Web 2.0 to collaborate. *Business Communication Quarterly, 73*(4), 439–443.

Castelló, I., Etter, M., & Årup Nielsen, F. (2016). Strategies of legitimacy through social media: the networked strategy. *Journal of Management Studies, 53*(3), 402–432.

Comer, D. R., & Holbrook, R. L. (2012). Getting behind the scenes of Fleetwood Mac's Rumours: using a documentary on the making of a music album to learn about task groups. *Journal of Management Education, 36*(4), 544–567.

Dieleman, H., & Huisingh, D. (2006). Games by which to learn and teach about sustainable development: exploring the relevance of games and experiential learning for sustainability. *Journal of Cleaner Production, 14*(9–11), 837–847.

Doyle, D., & Brown, F. W. (2000). Using a business simulation to teach applied skills – the benefits and the challenges of using student teams from multiple countries. *Journal of European Industrial Training, 24*(6), 330–336.

Dubbelt, L., Oostrom, J. K., Hiemstra, A. M., & Modderman, J. P. (2015). Validation of a digital work simulation to assess Machiavellianism and compliant behavior. *Journal of Business Ethics, 130*(3), 619–637.

Dunlap, J. C. and Lowenthal, P. R. (2009). Tweeting the night away: using Twitter to enhance social presence. *Journal of Information Systems Education, 20*, 129–135.

Eschenbrenner, B., Fui-Hoon Nah, F., & Siau, K. (2008). 3-D virtual worlds in education: applications, benefits, issues, and opportunities. *Journal of Database Management, 19*(4), 91–110.

Figueiró, P. S., & Raufflet, E. (2015). Sustainability in higher education: a systematic review with focus on management education. *Journal of Cleaner Production, 106*, 22–33.

Fletcher, J. D., & Tobias, S. (Eds.). (2011). *Computer games and instruction.* Charlotte, NC: IAP.

Gatti, L., Ulrich, M., & Seele, P. (2018). Education for sustainable development through business simulation games: an exploratory study of sustainability gamification and its effects on students' learning outcomes. *Journal of Cleaner Production.* doi: 10.1016/j. jclepro.2018.09.130.

Hagler, B. (2013). Value of social media in today's classroom. *Journal of Research in Business Education, 55*(1), 14–23.

Hansmann, R. (2010). 'Sustainability learning': An introduction to the concept and its motivational aspects. *Sustainability, 2*(9), 2873–2897.

Hardin, G. (1968). The tragedy of the commons. Science, *13*(162), 1243–1248.

Hesel, R. A., & Williams, R. C. (2009). Social networking sites and college-bound students. *StudentPoll, 7*(2), 1–8.

Heuer, M. (2010). Foundations and capstone; core values and hot topics; ethics-lx; skytech; and the green business laboratory: simulations for sustainability education. *Academy of Management Learning & Education, 9*(3), 556–561.

Hibbert, P., & Cunliffe, A. (2015). Responsible management: engaging moral reflexive practice through threshold concepts. *Journal of Business Ethics, 127*(1), 177–188.

Hilliard, I. (2013). Responsible management, incentive systems, and productivity. *Journal of Business Ethics, 118*(2), 365–377.

Hoskin, K. (1998). The mysterious case of the case study: a re-thinking. *Accounting Education, 7*, S57–S70.

Hyllegard, K., Ogle, J., Yan, R., & Reitz, A. (2011). An exploratory study of college students' fanning behavior on Facebook. *College Student Journal, 45*(3).

Jagger, S., Siala, H., & Sloan, D. (2016). It's all in the game: a 3D learning model for business ethics. *Journal of Business Ethics, 137*(2), 383–403.

Khoo, E. G., & Bonk, C. J. (2014). *Adding some TEC-VARIETY: 100+ activities for motivating and retaining learners online.* Open World Books/Amazon CreateSpace.

Kolb, D. A. (1984). *Experiential learning.* Englewood Cliffs, NJ: Prentice Hall.

Laasch, O., & Conway, R. (2015). *Principles of responsible management: glocal sustainability, responsibility, ethics.* Boston, MA: Cengage.

Laasch, O., & Moosmayer, D. (2016). Responsible management competences: building a portfolio of professional competence. *Academy of Management Annual Meeting Proceedings, 2016*(1).

Lacho, K. J., & Herring III, R. A. (1996). Use of videotape in the management classroom. *Mid-American Journal of Business, 11*(2), 35–42.

Lantz-Andersson, A., Vigmo, S., & Bowen, R. (2013). Crossing boundaries in Facebook: students' framing of language learning activities as extended spaces. *International Journal of Computer-Supported Collaborative Learning, 8*(3), 293–312.

Lee, S. H. (Mark), Sergueeva, K., Catangui, M., & Kandaurova, M. (2017). Assessing Google Cardboard virtual reality as a content delivery system in business classrooms. *Journal of Education for Business, 92*(4), 153–160.

Maier, H., Baron, J., & McLaughlan, R. G. (2007). Using online roleplay simulations for teaching sustainability principles to engineering students. *International Journal of Engineering Education*, 6(23), 1162–1171.

Mercer, T. G., Kythreotis, A. P., Robinson, Z. P., Stolte, T., George, S. M., & Haywood, S. K. (2017). The use of educational game design and play in higher education to influence sustainable behaviour. *International Journal of Sustainability in Higher Education*, 18(3), 359–384.

Montiel, I., Antolin-Lopez, R., & Gallo, P. J. (2018). Emotions and sustainability: a literary genre-based framework for environmental sustainability management education. *Academy of Management Learning & Education*, (172), 155–183.

Montiel, I., Delgado-Ceballos, J., & Ortiz-de-Mandojana, N. (2017). Mobile Apps for sustainability management education: the example of GoodGuide. *Academy of Management Learning & Education*, 16(3), 488–491.

Montiel, I., Delgado-Ceballos, J., Ortiz-de-Mandojana, N., & Antolin-Lopez, R. (2020). New ways of teaching: using technology and mobile apps to educate on societal grand challenges. *Journal of Business Ethics*, 161(2), 243–251.

Pivec, M. (2007). Play and learn: potentials of game-based learning. *British Journal of Educational Technology*, 38(3), 387–393.

Quible, Z. K. (2005). Blogs: a natural in business communication courses. *Business Communication Quarterly*, 68(1), 73–76.

Reuben, R. (2008). The use of social media in higher education for marketing and communications: a guide for professionals in higher education. www.fullerton.edu/technologyservices/_resources/pdfs/social-media-in-higher-education.pdf. Accessed 11 January 2019.

Rodriguez, M., Ajjan, H., & Honeycutt, E. (2014). Using technology to engage and improve millennial students' presentation performance. *Atlantic Marketing Journal*, 3(2), 3.

Salas, E., Wildman, J., & Piccolo, R. (2009). Using simulation-based training to enhance management education. *Academy of Management Learning & Education*, 8(4), 559–573.

Seaborn, K., & Fels, D. I. (2015). Gamification in theory and action: a survey. *International Journal of Human-Computer Studies*, 74, 14–31.

Shrivastava, P. (2010). Pedagogy of passion for sustainability. *Academy of Management Learning & Education*, 9(3), 443–455.

Starik, M., Rands, G., Marcus, A. A., & Clark, T. S. (2010). From the guest editors: in search of sustainability in management education *Academy of Management Learning & Education*, 9(3), 377–383.

Sweeney, L. B., & Sterman, J. D. (2000). Bathtub dynamics: initial results of a systems thinking inventory. *System Dynamics Review*, 16(4), 249–286.

Techcrunch. (2014). Majority of digital media consumption now takes place in mobile apps. https://techcrunch.com/2014/08/21/majority-of-digital-media-consumptionnow-takes-place-in-mobile-apps/. Accessed 5 September 2016.

The Economist. (2016). Bots, the next frontier. Business, 9 April. Available at: www.economist.com/news/business-and-finance/21696477-market-apps-maturing-now-one-text-based-services-or-chatbots-looks-poised?fsrc=rss. Accessed 10 May 2018.

Veltsos, J. R. (2017). Gamification in the business communication course. *Business and Professional Communication Quarterly*, 80(2), 194–216.

Wankel, C. (2009). Management education using social media. *Organization Management Journal*, 6(4), 251–262.

Zine. (2017). Influencer marketing: science, strategy and success. https://blog.zine.co/2018-influencer-marketing-report-post. Accessed 11 January 2019.

20

Online Education for Responsible Management

Amelia Clarke and Jennifer Lynes

INTRODUCTION

For us in the School of Environment, Enterprise and Development (SEED) at the University of Waterloo (Canada), responsible management is closely tied with sustainable development. We consider business operationalization of environmental sustainability, social responsibility and ethics in an integrated way through sustainable business and sustainable development lenses. This chapter focuses specifically on our Master of Environment and Business (MEB) online degree and considers what lessons can be learned for teaching and learning responsible management through online courses. In this chapter we argue the value of fully integrating sustainability thinking within business education. We also argue how technology now makes online learning quite comparable to in-person courses, with some specific advantages and disadvantages for responsible management education (RME).

The chapter starts with a brief introduction to Education for Sustainable Development as well as a short history of online learning. Next, detail is provided about the online Master of Environment and Business program, explaining how we have chosen to integrate environmental sustainability, social responsibility and ethics throughout the program design. The chapter then explores the opportunities and challenges of online learning for RME. This focuses on the process of online learning, and also on the responsible management content that is easier/harder to teach through this platform. The chapter ends with thoughts about the future of online learning as a means of teaching and learning responsible management.

Education for Sustainable Development

The United Nations held a Decade of Education for Sustainable Development (ESD) from 2005 to 2014 (UNESCO, 2019). In 2019, in follow-up to that, and in an effort to support the implementation of the United Nations' Sustainable Development Goals (SDGs), the United Nations Educational, Scientific and Cultural Organization (UNESCO) developed a framework entitled *Education for Sustainable Development: towards achieving the SDGs (ESD for 2030)* (UNESCO, 2019). This ESD for 2030 will be an integral element of implementing SDG 4 (the SDG on quality education), but also relevant for implementing all 17 SDGs (United Nations, 2015).

UNESCO, in developing the ESD for 2030, determined three key notions that are critical for education that aims to make significant progress on sustainable development: (1) transformative action; (2) structural changes; and (3) technological future. While these are not specific to management education, they do provide insight into the latest thinking about what is required to fully integrate a strong sustainability approach into business education. We revisit these three key notions of Education for Sustainable Development through the chapter when considering if responsible management is fully integrated into a program.

As an institution, the University of Waterloo is committed to teaching, researching and operationalizing sustainable development. It has been recognized as a global leader in social and economic impact, including being ranked 13th in the world by the Times Higher Education (THE) University Impact Rankings (THE, 2019). These newly established rankings focus specifically on assessing educational institutions against the United Nations' SDGs. As noted by the University of Waterloo's president and vice-chancellor, Feridun Hamdullahpur: 'The University of Waterloo has long valued the principles underpinning the United Nations SDGs, particularly as they relate to gender equality, innovation and sustainability' (University Relations, 2019: 1).

The Master of Environment and Business degree is built on the premise that any effort to bring responsible management thinking into business education needs to consider the ecological, social and economic challenges of our times. The SDGs provide a key framework for approaching the three pillars of sustainability (United Nations, 2015). Given that the latest report by the Intergovernmental Panel on Climate Change (IPCC) gives humanity until 2030 to make significant progress on climate action (i.e., 45% reduction in greenhouse gas emissions) or the planet will surpass 1.5 °C warming (IPCC, 2018), the urgency of responsible management education is clear. Business has many roles to play in providing products and services needed for the transition to a low carbon economy and should be doing so in an ecologically sustainable, socially responsible and ethical way. In the MEB program we fully integrate sustainability content into every course. It is not an elective, or one module within a course; rather, it is core to the curriculum in every course throughout the online degree program.

Online Education

Correspondence education dates back to 1889 in Canada (Caputo, Christofides & De Pasquale, 2018). With the advent of the Internet, this shifted to online learning (and online learning management systems) in the late 1990s. Massive Open Online Courses (MOOCs) were first coined in 2008, and evolved into open courses by 2011. Many universities now offer online credit courses for in-person degree programs, and fully-online degrees. Online learning is now considered to be as effective, if not more so, than in-person instruction; though this also depends on the type of material being delivered, the quality of the course design and the extent of institutional support (Siemens, Gašević & Dawson, 2015). The Ontario government's Ministry of Advanced Education and Skills Development definition of an online course or program is one that can be completed primarily (80% or more) online (Caputo et al., 2018).

In terms of online education in business schools, there is a relative lack of coverage about this in mainstream teaching and learning journals (Arbaugh, 2010). That said, online and blended learning offerings are increasing in business schools, and there is a body of literature in management education journals on this topic. Given the epistemological and behavioral differences between traditional business disciplines, online course designs differ to accommodate more or less emphasis on learner–learner discussion to co-create knowledge versus learner mastery of concepts and techniques (Arbaugh, 2010). The same is true for introductory versus more advanced courses, where the emphasis switches from foundational knowledge to analysis and application.

The University of Waterloo has been offering correspondence courses since 1968, and online courses since 1997 (Caputo et al., 2018). In 2008, the University of Waterloo Task Force on Online Learning determined that online courses should be considered a normal part of teaching load, and equivalent to their on-campus counterparts. As of 2018, the University has 23 online degree programs, and 511 online courses. At a university of approximately 39,000 students, 11% of undergraduate students and 24% of graduate students are enrolled in an online course (Caputo et al., 2018). One of the fully online degrees is the Master of Environment and Business degree.

and motivated individuals with the information, tools and expertise to integrate environment with business in very practical ways' (University of Waterloo, 2019: 1). The last time the MEB was rated by Corporate Knights, it ranked second in Canada for MBA (and MBA equivalent) degrees with sustainability content (SEED, 2016).

Most MEB students take the degree over three years on a part-time basis, while working full-time (and often while also starting or caring for young families). A subset of students takes it full-time, on a one- or two-year track. There are about 75 students in the program at any given time, with slightly more females than males. The average age of an incoming student is approximately 35 years old, and about 40% are already sustainability professionals. Another 40% are in careers they like (accounting, marketing, finance, engineering, etc.) but they want to make a difference with their careers and build in more sustainability management. Only about 20% of the students are looking to make a career shift or to launch a new career. Most of the students are located somewhere in Canada (as it is an online degree, they are generally not located in Waterloo), with a sub-set located in another country (China, Afghanistan, Bangladesh, Brazil, Germany, UK, USA, etc.). Completion rate is around 90% and our outgoing surveys indicate that 92–100% of the students are either 'highly' or 'very highly' satisfied, depending on the cohort.

MASTER OF ENVIRONMENT AND BUSINESS (MEB) PROGRAM

Launched in 2010 with its first cohort, the MEB program has a mission: 'to equip working professionals with the knowledge, tools and expertise to integrate environment with business' (Clarke, 2018: 5). The program is aimed at 'meeting the growing need for business sustainability professionals as a distinct group of knowledgeable, skilled, confident

Program Design

The MEB is a professional course-based master's degree with a two-week in-person residency, followed by online courses (Clarke, 2014). It ends with a three day in-person residency. There are eight courses plus a two-course research project for a total of ten courses. In addition to the coursework, students are required to attend two professional conferences as milestones in the degree. The program is strongest in environmental sustainability (as it

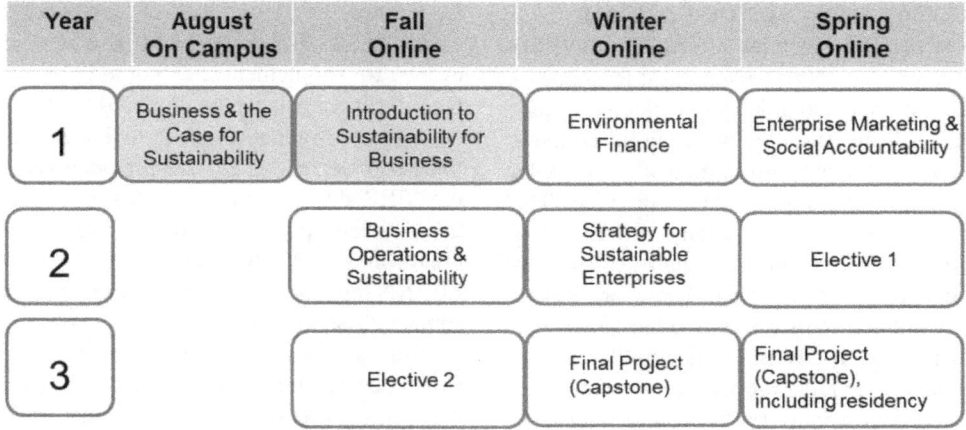

Year	August On Campus	Fall Online	Winter Online	Spring Online
1	Business & the Case for Sustainability	Introduction to Sustainability for Business	Environmental Finance	Enterprise Marketing & Social Accountability
2		Business Operations & Sustainability	Strategy for Sustainable Enterprises	Elective 1
3		Elective 2	Final Project (Capstone)	Final Project (Capstone), including residency

Figure 20.1   MEB program design – 3-year part-time version (Clarke, 2018: 11)

relates to business), but takes a sustainable business approach (i.e., integrating environment, social and economic elements of sustainability). Figure 20.1 shows the course sequence for a part-time student.

Foundation and core courses

The program begins with two foundation courses – shaded grey in Figure 20.1 – which ensure all students have an introductory knowledge of business basics, sustainability basics, and integrated sustainability and business concepts. These two courses are designed to be taught at two levels; a base knowledge that all students must learn (and which is assessed through exams) and leading-edge knowledge to further the understanding of those with an existing background in the topics. The true integration of 'sustainability' and 'business' concepts is a key differentiator of the MEB program. Courses in MEB are purposely designed to approach traditional business material through a sustainability lens.

The next four core courses teach graduate-level business content about: operations, marketing, strategy and accounting and finance. At the same time these courses teach the integrated responsible management content as it relates to the core business area.

For example, the Strategy for Sustainable Enterprises course uses a MBA textbook and lectures to teach business strategy, while at the same time uses readings and assignments to adapt business strategy concepts into a sustainable business strategy. One of the core readings and concepts that frames part of the course is Hart and Milstein's (2003) Creating Sustainable Value 2x2. Their today/tomorrow and internal/external framework provides direction on the content to be included in a sustainability strategy; the strategy should have content relating to each box. There are many other business sustainability readings in the course, some of which are updated each year to capture the latest thinking in the field. The main assignment in the strategy course is to develop a growth strategy for a company that is inherently based on sustainable development. As another example, in our Enterprise Marketing and Social Accountability course, students learn the same basic principles of marketing as one would in an MBA-style marketing course but each assignment is tied into how these concepts can be applied in a more holistic way. What are the implications of an organization's choice of distribution system, for instance, when also taking one's carbon footprint into consideration?

Electives and capstone project

There are five electives offered by the MEB program. Students have to take at least one of these options, and at least two electives total. The MEB electives are all 'how-to' courses, and offer students with frameworks and skills that are highly applicable to practice. The second elective can be any pre-approved graduate-level course that relates to sustainability, business, or both. These are online and in-person electives from other University of Waterloo programs, or students in Canada can take a graduate-level course at another Canadian university (with a lot of approvals and paperwork).

The final two courses are a capstone project. This can be done as a team or an individual and includes a full research project (including literature review, methods, ethics approval, data collection, data analysis, a report and a final presentation). The projects are done for a client and overseen by a professor as part of the course. The topic and client is of the student's choosing (though we help with matches if need be). The project itself pulls together knowledge and skills learned throughout the degree, and ensures the students are able to use research to develop sustainability-related recommendations for the client. The capstone course wraps up with a final weekend residency that allows the students to present their projects in person and gather one more time as a cohort before completing the program.

Milestone requirement

The MEB degree requires two milestone conferences and also participation in two residency periods. The purpose of our milestone conferences (in order of importance) is: (1) networking and connecting in-person with other MEB students in the same cohort and in other cohorts; (2) networking with sustainable business leaders; (3) learning the leading-edge conversation; (4) experiencing an MEB-endorsed professional conference and determining how to make the most of this type of event; and (5) seeing how the larger movement continues to stay informed. Students must choose one

conference from our list of pre-approved events, and at that event the MEB offers side-events to supplement the conference. The second conference can be proposed by the student; something that relates to their career and the MEB degree. These are pre-approved by the MEB director. After a milestone conference, students post a reflection on a discussion board in the MEB Community Group in LEARN (our online platform) and comment on someone else's reflection.

MEB is designed as a course-based professional degree, modeled on an MBA. The program has a list of learning outcomes related to content and skills, which are informally assessed with incoming and outgoing surveys. Formally they are evaluated through course assessments and students are expected to maintain an overall average of 75% to obtain the degree. In the program, as it is a professional degree, more emphasis is placed on teamwork, applied knowledge and professional skills-building than a research master's degree would have. That said, students are also taught to critically analyze material, build an argument with evidence, understand the role of research, and present their thoughts in well-written and cited documents (targeted at different academic and non-academic audiences).

Unique MEB Program Considerations and Tools

As the MEB is an online degree, we nurture the learning community in a different way than an in-person degree would. The first residency period creates a cohort dynamic that is continued online. In addition, at the first residency period, the students meet their future professors and a number of senior sustainability professionals. Care is taken during the residency period to demonstrate sustainability considerations in the organization of the event itself, where feasible. For example, all the food is provided on reusable dishes, the teas and coffees offered during breaks are fair trade certified, the food is locally sourced and organic (where possible), accommodation options are provided within walking distance of the venue, and public-transit options are promoted in the travel information. There is even an electric vehicle charging station, should a student need this. A tour of our LEED Platinum certified building and an opportunity to meet with the university's sustainability coordinator is part of the two-week schedule.

Throughout the degree, there is considerable engagement with key sustainability practitioners and between students. In each course generally there are at least two senior sustainability professionals that join the class as guest experts. Also, the students themselves have considerable expertise to share, given their work experience. The MEB milestone events enable students to interact with each other and with leading edge professionals in our field. In addition, the MEB Community Group is an online forum in LEARN where students can post announcements or items to all other MEB students. This is also where milestone reflections are posted to enable discussion and sharing between students on their experiences at various events in our field.

All MEB courses have core design elements in common. Each course is 12 weeks long, with approximately 7–10 hours of asynchronous work each week, inclusive of all activities (reading, watching videos, writing, etc.). Courses are designed with a steady volume of work, numerous small deliverables, and no crunch periods in order to accommodate and pace the working professionals. Each has an interactive schedule with hyperlinks to content, a syllabus section, 12 content modules (one per week), individual and group assignment descriptions, discussion boards, weekly announcements, drop boxes for student submissions and a gradebook. The content modules each contain the learning objectives and description for the week, links to the assignments for the week and a mix of pre-recorded webinar style presentations, videos, readings, cases and so on. Instructors individualize not just their content, but also their other activities (see Table 20.1). For example, in the marketing course the students record elevator-style

Table 20.1 Examples of online activities used in the Master of Environment and Business program

Sample activity	Examples of how it has been used
Guest experts	• Q & A on a discussion board • Feedback on elevator pitch drafts
Online wikis	• To build a glossary of definitions of key terms related to sustainable development • To build on and provide real-life examples to support existing sustainability frameworks (e.g. 'the 20 rules of green marketing')
Stakeholder negotiation	• Stakeholder engagement/negotiation simulation through discussion boards
Pre-recorded webinar-style videos	• As an alternative to in-person lectures
Scaffolded group assignments	• To build a business or marketing strategy for a 'real-life' organization piece by piece • Group work – proposal and then final presentation (with peer-feedback through a discussion board)
Individual assignments	• Critical analysis of a case • Prepare a memo for your workplace on course learnings • Course reflection
Quizzes	• For self-assessment by students of the concepts they are learning
Surveys	• Feedback for the professor on course content
Class discussions	• Weekly discussion on a key question that enables reflection on the week's content or case
Exam	• End of term assessment; conducted through examination centres and proctors
Projects	• Capstone project to integrate course learning and produce relevant recommendations for a real client

pitches, and a guest expert is brought in to provide feedback on these pitches. In the strategy course, there is a stakeholder negotiation activity, where each student represents a different stakeholder. Multiple negotiations can run simultaneously on different discussions boards; after the exercise is over the boards can be shared so other groups can see each other's outcomes to view the difference that negotiation and facilitation style makes to the results. As another example, in the introduction to sustainable business course, there is a wiki where students build a glossary of definitions, using proper APA formatting. Also, guest experts engage with students through discussion boards or assignments. The courses all have a doctoral-level teaching assistant to support the volume of interaction and grading needed.

OPPORTUNITIES AND CHALLENGES FOR ONLINE RME

There are a number of opportunities and challenges that are related to online learning for RME. This section opens with a discussion on the advantages of online learning generally, followed by a discussion on the advantages and challenges of online learning for RME in particular. Reflections are then offered on the MEB program's content in relation to RME. The section concludes by offering key elements of a successful online program.

Advantages of Online Courses

All online programs have a certain set of advantages over in-person courses, if designed well. A September 2018 study conducted at the University of Waterloo about our own online education courses discussed some of the advantages from the student perspective (Caputo et al., 2018). From an MEB student perspective, some of the advantages of learning online are:

- Accessible education for adult learners and those with other commitments
- Flexibility (enrolment options, where and when students do work; meetings by appointment)
- Interpersonal connections (e.g., learning virtual teamwork skills)
- Different learning styles are catered to.

From an MEB instructor perspective, some of the implications of online teaching are:

- Flexibility (where and when you teach)
- Course design (opens up options; but eliminates others)
- Instructor knowledge (can look up and/or ponder responses)
- Global reach (for guests and for students).

Many of these have been discussed in the management education literature, often overly-focused on student engagement, sometimes at a loss of focus on student learning (Morgan-Thomas & Dudau, 2019).

RME and Online Learning

There are some features of the online nature of the degree that enable deep learning for sustainability. For example, the fact that students are living in different cities and countries enables a breadth of participants that is harder to achieve with an in-person course. The experiences these students bring to the discussion enable us to delve deeply into sustainability considerations from different cultural/regional perspectives. Related to this diversity is the range of workplaces and sectors that the students work in. These range from extraction (e.g. oil and gas), to manufacturing, retail and service (e.g. banking, insurance and finance) companies. There are also students who work for governments, Indigenous communities, non-profit organizations, consulting firms, and co-operatives. This multi-sector perspective brings a richness to course discussions, to the point where about half the learning in the program is from other students. While we attract international students and mature students to our in-person graduate programs in our school, it is very different having a class of students who can relate the class material to their ongoing work situation. This is only possible because the degree is online.

Other advantages of the online design for RME are that we can use live case studies and guests from anywhere in the world. The guests engage with the students through a week-long discussion board. While we could bring a virtual speaker into the classroom through video conferencing, the online asynchronous course does not create time zone challenges or depend on the reliability of the connection. It is very easy for someone from the other side of the world to fully engage with the students at times that are convenient for them. It is also easier to confirm guests as we are not asking for a specific time slot and do not require travel time. For example, in the Introduction to Sustainability for Business course, we have a guest from a company based in the USA answering very specific questions from students about their leading-edge sustainable business practices. As many of the 'best' sustainable business experts and companies are located in other countries, it is wonderful to be able to access them for our classes.

The online discussions, while perhaps frustrating for that student in your in-person class who likes to talk at length, are actually ideal for ensuring all students are heard. Asynchronous discussions are known to be effective for deep learning (DeLotell, Millam & Reinhardt, 2010). This is particularly important for teaching responsible management as we are not just building skills or departing knowledge; we are changing mindsets and supporting students to become changemakers. We are aiming for deep learning by every member of the class. As each student is required to post weekly, and to reply to a post weekly, it is easy to tell who has really understood the material in an integrated and transferable way. It is then possible to target specific students with additional

support to further their understanding, if need be. For more sensitive topics, the discussion boards enable a considered response or intervention.

There are also some disadvantages of online teaching. In the more technical electives in the MEB, the instructors have struggled to help students apply the software in their assignments. For example, we had a course on carbon accounting that the instructor found difficult to convert effectively for online delivery. The online students struggled to understand and complete the assignments. We currently have a course on life cycle assessment that has the same challenge. The instructor has resorted to creating a less technical stream of assignments for those students without an engineering degree (or equivalent technical expertise). She teaches the same course in-person, and says it is the online platform that creates the challenges.

Group work can have its challenges in-person or online. Some of the challenges are related to personalities and the students' skills related to teamwork. Online adds another element, where all the meetings are virtual. Time zone differences, and the reliance on virtual communication tools, can make group assignments more complicated. The positive side of this is that the students learn virtual teamwork, which is actually how many projects are managed in companies, so they are learning useful skills.

For instructors, one of the challenges is that we are unable to update the content to reflect the specific needs and interests of a given cohort. All the material is prepared in advance, as the courses are asynchronous. As there is considerable preparation in creating the webinar style presentations, and building the site, it must all be done months before the course goes live. We can use announcements and discussion boards to introduce very current content, but the core content is not flexible after the course starts. As the cases and stories we bring into responsible management education are often very current, this is a barrier. One solution is to invite students to bring current content into the discussions, or to post links during announcements.

These days, the online tools have developed to a point where the online courses are of equal quality to an in-person course. Retention of course content is higher, as the students can stop and start the lecture, re-listen to parts, and engage when they are most interested. Most content and activities are adaptable to the online platform; in fact, most in-person courses at the University of Waterloo now have an online site to complement them. For our in-person courses, professors post lecture slides online instead of using handouts in class, students submit assignments through online drop boxes and receive their feedback the same way, and students see their grades on the course site. What is different about the fully online course is the amount of content available, the virtual activities and discussions, and the fact there is no in-person interaction.

RME and MEB Online Content

The MEB program was built for deep learning about sustainable business (for more on this see Clarke, 2014). When considering the content, from an Education for Sustainability (ESD) for 2030 perspective (UNESCO, 2019), the responsible management content is fully integrated into the MEB program. To enable transformative action by the learner, from the very start of the degree we emphasize the importance of being a changemaker, and how we are training students to leverage business to help society move towards sustainability. While we provide the knowledge and skills they need, we also work to build their confidence and support network. They are asked to consider their own behavior and their spheres of influence to create change. For example, in the second course in the degree, the first activity is an ecological footprint exercise. Students complete the online activity (offered by the Global Footprint Network and many others) and then share

their footprint through an online discussion board. They are asked to comment on their footprint in relation to the global ecological and social trends we learn about that week. This makes the trends personal, and helps students to realize that their behavior and individual choices matter.

Another example of encouraging students to be changemakers is the individual assignment in the Introduction to Sustainability for Business course. Students prepare a backgrounder memo for their employer (current or past or future) on a list of five topics we cover in the course. For most students, this is their current employer. This assignment allows them to demonstrate their understanding of the course material, but perhaps more importantly they relate the material to their individual sector and company, allowing them to see its immediate relevance. On occasion students even adapt the completed assignment to actually use at work.

As the degree is designed to move from introduction, to core content, to the how-to courses, to the capstone project, there is a progression in the expectation of the students' ability to recommend transformative action. As sustainability thinking is fully integrated into the design of the degree, it enables this level of deep learning.

In terms of the second ESD for 2030 – consideration about teaching structural changes – this is also inherent in the MEB design. While the MEB program is much more focused on solutions than the problems, we do cover social, ecological and economic challenges faced by people, and the planet. This is from a Sustainable Development Goals perspective that is external to the firm. We then relate these larger systemic challenges to the roles and functions of business, and what it means to pursue sustainable business practices.

Probably the area we are weakest is the third ESD for 2030 – consideration about the technological future. While the MEB program and its online education for responsible management is a living example of the potential benefit (and challenges) of technological solutions for management education, the MEB program also has the potential to provide students with an opportunity to consider responsible management in relation to technology companies and their products. While we consider technology companies (in relation to sustainable business considerations) and technological solutions (e.g. blockchain and renewable energy trading), and we teach critical analysis, the larger discussion about the underlying ethical, social and environmental considerations of technology are not as deeply considered as they perhaps should be. The University of Waterloo, with its focus on innovation and entrepreneurship, has started conversations about 'technology for good', ethical considerations of technology and sustainable entrepreneurship tools for tech start-ups. For example, our social innovation incubator GreenHouse (one of many incubators/accelerators on campus), recently held their Social Impact Showcase. Almost all the finalists this term had developed new software to help people or organizations in a way that also solved a social challenge. There are opportunities for us to further integrate discussions and case studies related to topics such as 'ethics and technology', 'technology for good' and 'sustainable technology' into the MEB program, particularly given how core technology is to the future of work and the economy.

Necessary Components for Successful Online Programs

In our experience, a successful online program will have the following elements:

- *Institutional support*: this includes technical and design support for online platforms; acknowledgement of additional time needed to develop material for online courses; and financial support to re-design and update online material every few years. At the University of Waterloo, there is a centralized unit called Centre for Extended Learning. Their staff build and update all online courses, and provide technical support to students and professors throughout the term. The first time an online course is developed, it counts as a course in a professor's teaching load.
- *A flexible online learning platform* that has the capacity to integrate a variety of teaching and learning tools, from the ability for students to record and share audio/video, to voiceover slides and interactive material. The platform also needs to be easily managed by the professor and intuitive for students. It needs to be accessible from a number of different devices, running a range of operating systems and software. At the University of Waterloo we are currently using D2L's LEARN platform.
- *A community-building component* such as an initial in-person residency/introductory course for each cohort or an activity at the beginning of each course that allows students to get to know each other. In our program, most students in a cohort go through the program together so that by the end of the first course they know each other quite well and are comfortable sharing thoughts and ideas on discussion forums, etc.
- *Fully integrated responsible management content* as part of the core degree components, including taking both a sustainable business and sustainable development perspective and supporting students to become changemakers. Related to this is updating the content to reflect the latest thinking and practices in our field.

CURRENT TRENDS AND FUTURE DIRECTIONS IN ONLINE LEARNING FOR RME

The MEB degree was designed to train sustainability professionals, and therefore has RME at its core. This raises questions as to how much integration is needed to train all business students to consider social, environmental and ethical considerations in their respective degrees. If our world requires we transition to a sustainable pathway, and urgently so, does it require all students to have a base understanding and work with integrity? Yes. Can this be achieved with just one core course on 'business and society' or equivalent? Probably not. We think that capstone projects should have sustainability considerations built into their requirements, and enough training needs to happen before that stage at which students are able to do this effectively.

Today's young people desire to work in meaningful careers. This is true for Millennials, and it is expected to be even more so for the generation behind them (Gen Z). Teaching them to use 'business for good', how to help solve the world's challenges as outlined in the UN Sustainable Development Goals, and how to do it in an environmentally, socially and ethically responsible manner will set them up to have meaningful careers. Youth are wired for innovation (Dougherty & Clarke, 2018), and thus we need them to help create the solutions to our world's economic, social and environmental problems.

Online courses offer considerable potential for extending the reach of RME. It is possible to have an introductory course with a high number of students, for example. At the University of Waterloo we have just created a Sustainability Diploma that will be open to all undergraduate students, regardless of degree program. An online core course is being developed that will not have a cap on the number of students. While a large online course is designed differently than the MEB courses described earlier in the chapter, it can still be a very effective way of offering an introductory course.

Online courses are not geographically restricted, except by Internet bandwidth. We have had an MEB student take the degree from a rural community in Guyana where the whole community shared an Internet connection. The course material was put on a disk so he did not have to watch the videos online. He used his online time for discussions and teamwork. It was tricky, but feasible.

MOOCs and other online courses have already introduced many people to the potential of lifelong learning through online courses. Compared to 10 years ago, when we first started the MEB program and perhaps one or two students had taken an online class, now it is more likely that the majority of students entering the program took online courses in their undergraduate degree or through their professional associations.

The online courses also open up more opportunities for joint degrees from multiple universities or shared courses. For RME, this might enable more elective offerings for students at smaller universities or those without much selection in this space. The online nature enables shared content to be developed by people or organizations external to your university too. Publishers are starting to move into this space, by not only offering textbooks, slides, and test banks, but also offering the course website to go with it. As with many technology innovations, online education has potential to really evolve over the coming years. More tools are being built into learning management systems every year.

In the future, we expect online education to offer more adaptive technology allowing courses to be more responsive to individual students' needs and learning styles (e.g., software and online platforms that can adapt teaching materials and strategies to individual learning styles/needs/progress). This will also accommodate students with learning disabilities to ensure they can access the material and are assessed appropriately. Also, crowd marking and tools for adding 'template' comments are advancing considerably, and we anticipate these will make marking more efficient while not reducing effectiveness.

For the past few decades, online educators have discussed the idea of bringing together achievements and reflections from individual courses in the form of an e-portfolio. E-portfolios are especially worthwhile for online learning that results in a certificate/diploma/degree as they allow students to bring together learning and concepts from different courses while also showcasing achievements such as outputs from assessment items. While the desire to have this capability has been there since the early 2000s (e.g. Downes, 2008), the platform was not. This is no longer the case, with several online e-portfolio platforms now available.

In the future these will likely be tied to storage in the cloud so alumni can still access them.

Some extended learning centres are trying to move towards more 'generic' course content that does not require updating from year to year, but we disagree with this approach. Because online learning can be more isolating for both students and instructors than in-person classes, the personal and individualized touch needs to be integrated into the course content and design wherever possible. For online learning in responsible management to work it *needs* to be current. Related to this desire to reduce the workload of the course designers and move the updates towards professors, is a desire to create more generic designs. Our experience is that they are not as ideal for accommodating the needs of different business disciplines and for courses with varied learning outcomes. For those of you who are new to online teaching, push for a design that fits your learners and learning outcomes, instead of one that is easily developed (assuming you have technical support).

While we are not supportive of making all courses delivered with the same content formats and assessment tools, there is considerable benefit to standardizing the look of core components so the students in an online program only have to learn the platform once. While the number of tools available for online learning continues to grow, in our experience one needs to approach these new opportunities with some caution. New technologies need to be considered for their suitability not only for one's own online course, but also for how it fits in with the larger program of courses. If students need to adapt to new platforms and tools for each course they take, they spend too much time learning the tool, rather than the content. Question the pedagogical benefit of the tool, not just look/slickness of the tool.

In conclusion, we have made two main arguments throughout this chapter. First, given the need for sustainable development, and in particular the urgency for addressing climate change, fully integrating responsible management into business education is critical for our planet's and humanity's future. Second, online teaching and learning presents both opportunities and challenges for furthering responsible management education, but is certainly an important part of the story now.

REFERENCES

Arbaugh, J. B. (2010). *Online and blended business education for the 21st century: current research and future directions*. Oxford: Chandos Publishing.

Caputo, A., Christofides, E., & De Pasquale, D. (2018). Assessing the impact of online learning: a model and case study (Report for eCampusOntario). Waterloo, Canada: Centre for Extended Learning, University of Waterloo.

Clarke, A. (2014). Building an online master's program for deep learning in sustainability. In Azeiteiro, U. M., Leal Filho, W., & Caeiro, S. (Eds.), *E-learning and sustainability* (pp. 237–246). Frankfurt, Germany: Peter Lang Scientific Publishers.

Clarke, A. (2018). Master of Environment and Business – orientation presentation slides. Waterloo, Canada: University of Waterloo.

DeLotell, P. J., Millam, L. A., & Reinhardt, M. (2010). The use of deep learning strategies in online business courses to impact student retention. *American Journal of Business Education*, 3(12), 49–55.

Dougherty, I., & Clarke, A. (2018). Wired for innovation: valuing the unique innovation abilities of emerging adults. *Emerging Adulthood*, 6(5), 358–365.

Downes, S. (2008). *The future of online learning: ten years on*. Ottawa, Canada: National Research Council Canada. Available at: www.downes.ca/files/books/future2003. pdf.

Hart, S. L., & Milstein, M. B. (2003). Creating sustainable value. *Academy of Management Perspectives*, 17(2), 56–67.

IPCC. (2018). Summary for policymakers of IPCC Special Report on Global Warming of 1.5 °C. Available at: www.ipcc.ch/2018/10/C8/

summary-for-policymakers-of-ipcc-special-report-on-global-warming-of-1-5c-approved-by-governments/.

Morgan-Thomas, A., & Dudau, A. (2019). Of possums, hogs and horses: capturing duality of student engagement in eLearning. *Academy of Management Learning and Education*, Online First. doi: https://doi.org/10.5465/amle.2018.0029.

SEED. (2016). Report for augmented academic program review degrees. In B.E.S. Honours Co-Op – Environment and Business; B.E.S. Honours (Regular) – Environment and Business; Master of Environment and Business; M.E.S. – Sustainability Management; M.A.E.S. – Local Economic Development, Volume I – Self-Study Report. Waterloo, Canada: School of Environment, Enterprise and Development (SEED), University of Waterloo.

Siemens, G., Gašević, D., & Dawson, S. (2015). *Preparing for the digital university: a review of the history and current state of distance, blended, and online learning*. Arlington, TX: Link Research Lab.

THE. (2019). Times Higher Education – World University Rankings – University Impact Rankings 2019. Available at: www.timeshighereducation.com/rankings/impact/2019/overall#!/page/0/length/25/sort_by/rank/sort_order/asc/cols/undefined.

UNESCO. (2019). *SDG 4 – Education 2030: Part II – Education for Sustainable Development Beyond 2019*. (206 EX/6.II). Paris: United Nations Educational, Scientific and Cultural Organization (UNESCO).

United Nations. (2015). Sustainable Development Goals. Available at: https://sustainabledevelopment.un.org/?menu=1300.

University Relations. (2019). Waterloo ranks 13 in global University Impact Rankings 2019. https://uwaterloo.ca/stories/waterloo-ranks-13-global-university-impact-rankings-2019.

University of Waterloo. (2019). Master of Environment and Business (MEB). https://uwaterloo.ca/school-environment-enterprise-development/graduate-programs/master-environment-and-business.

PART IV

Academic Environment

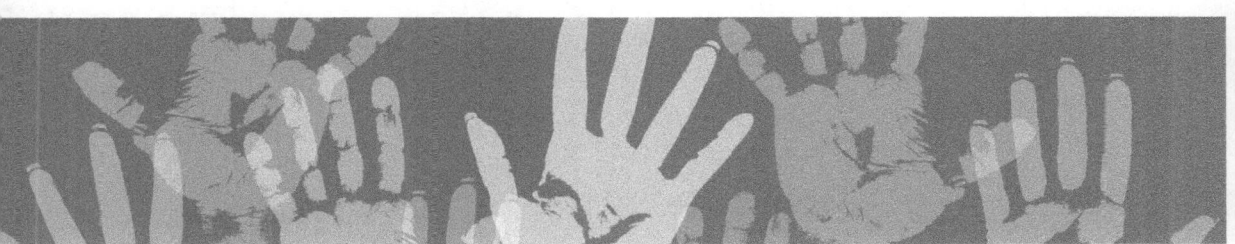

21

The Dark Side of Responsible Management Education: An Ontological Misstep?

Philip Roscoe

The SAGE Handbook is a collective celebration of all that we have achieved in the domain of responsible management education, a recognition that the endeavour of responsibility has been successfully embedded in the curricula and discourses of business schools. We have done well, surely? It's a big, happy party, and we can all pat ourselves soundly on the back! It will be no surprise, then, that the present chapter has been difficult to write. I am grateful to the editors for their invitation to contribute to this volume, and always willing to provoke the reader in the name of scholarly debate – why do I think I was invited anyway? – but it has been harder than usual to marshal the arguments that follow. Responsible management education (RME) seems such a vitally important undertaking. It has its own United Nations principles. I work at a school of management committed to responsible enterprise, where I am surrounded by critically minded, liberal colleagues. I teach a course on ethics and management. I have tried, when it has

been necessary, to manage responsibly. I am wholly implicated in this project, and yet … I have persevered with this chapter because of a nagging sense that something is missing, that responsible management education has made a misstep, an ontological wrong turn that threatens to undermine the entire programme.

There is a famous remark that the journey from 'hippy to yuppie is not nearly as convoluted as some people like to believe'. It comes from a British music journalist named Charles Shaar Murray, who saw that the intellectual underpinnings of the summer of love translated seamlessly into the acquisitive ideals that powered the 1980s (Green, 1988). I propose a similar aphorism: that the road from idealistic MBA to corporate zealot is wide, straight and paved with the very best intentions. I worry that responsible management education, with its focus on individual responsibility and its simultaneous, almost wilful, ignorance of the sociological construction of that same responsibility prepares the ground for a corporate good citizen who – taking all the best decisions for all the right reasons – simply reproduces existing arrangements. The present chapter is an attempt to think through and articulate this troubling concern.

THE ONTOLOGICAL MISSTEP

How, then, should we educate the next generations of managers to be responsible? Not, as responsible management educators have already realised, by stuffing them with values, well-meaning turkeys fattened for the Thanksgiving of graduation and employment. Nor by encouraging reflection on their pre-existing prejudices – their formative years in the Scout troop or football team, what they learnt at mother's knee – as if such tortured introspection were the only source of personal authenticity and moral rectitude. Ken Blanchard's interminable 'leadership point of view' offers a precise example of what we should *not* do. The present thrust of RME is on the individual nature of ethical choice and the need for reflexive questioning of one's ethical taken-for-granteds. One should, writes Cunliffe (2004, 2016) be both self-reflexive in terms of one's relation with others and critically reflective in terms of the norms and culture of the organisation. For Cunliffe, the basic ethical question is 'who am I?' and all else follows. For me, this is the misstep, an ontological inadequacy in the way we understand how responsible management might work in organisations. I will argue that responsible management education's rootedness in the field of pedagogic theory (Laasch, 2018) causes it to overlook some crucial aspects of sociological construction of management ethics. We have, as Laasch argues, little grasp of the practices and processes of managing responsibly. We are inadequately sociological.

It would be churlish to criticise responsible management education for being inadequately sociological without acknowledging that sociology itself largely ignored the topic of ethics through the second half of the 20th century (Bykov, 2018). Psychology stepped into the gap, offering accounts of morality based environmental, evolutionary concerns, an approach that risks downgrading moral action to 'just' individual responses to given stimuli. Yet moral responses clearly differ across groups, and an emerging 'new sociology of morality' (Hitlin & Vaisey, 2013) is attempting to theorise these same in terms of the social structures surrounding moral choice. Philosophers have for centuries debated appropriate conduct, but have framed this as a matter of individual choice; a sociology of morality, on the other hand, seeks to explore the social construction of ethics, beginning from the simple observation that moral norms vary between cultures and across time. Work in organisation studies has framed ethics in terms of 'culture', while research in the science-and-technology studies tradition has offered an account of decision-making as distributed across heterogeneous, 'cyborg' assemblies, and drawn attention to the social and organisational work involved in constituting things as valuable.[1] To approach the moral agent in this way is to see her, not as an individual making choices, but as something constructed through the interplay of the social, material, epistemic and technical. Such morality is qualitatively – ontologically – distinct from the reflexive self-examination of RME's virtuous executive.

My chapter will draw on these resources to give an account of morality as embedded in organisational practices and sociotechnical assemblies (Callon, 2008). It will suggest that we do future managers a disservice by positing organisational ethics as a matter of individual responsibility, to be changed by charismatic leadership or individual consumption practices, what Banerjee (2003) calls 'designer environmentalism'. Where responsible management discussion supposes an empty space at the centre of 'social responsibility' that the ethical persona of the manager will come to occupy, our survey will show that space to be very much full. It is overflowing with theoretical models, organisational culture and practices, and socio-technical constructions. Such a recognition will make us think differently about responsible management. Rather than worrying how managers use theory (Ghoshal, 2005), we should consider how theory uses managers (Ferraro, Pfeffer & Sutton, 2005). We might recognise the moralities baked into some kinds of organisation, and move away from seeing management and business as synonymous (Parker, 2002). We might start to understand management in terms of the occupational virtues specific to a given practice (MacIntyre, 1981) rather than aiming at a generalised, transferrable profession (Rubin & Dierdorff, 2013). Finally, we might speculate on what this means for us as management scholars, for it is here – not on our students – that I discern the most unexpected and untoward consequences of responsible management education.

WHERE RME IS NOW

Responsible management education is underpinned, as readers of this volume must certainly know, by the United Nations Principles of Responsible Management Education (PRME). These six principles are: purpose – that students should be 'future generators of sustainable value for business and society'; values – incorporating the values of global social responsibility; method – creating educational frameworks that enable effective learning for responsible leadership; research – into the 'role, dynamics, and impact of corporations in the creation of sustainable social, environmental and economic value'; partnership – 'interact with managers of business corporations to extend our knowledge of their challenges'; and finally, dialogue – with everybody and anybody, 'educators, students,

business, government, consumers, media, civil society organisations and other interested groups and stakeholders' (United Nations, n.d.). These are laudable statements, aiming to repair the contract between business and society (Setó-Pamies & Papaoikonomou, 2016). At the same time, they follow the current vogue for self-governance and soft regulation (Burchell, Kennedy & Murray, 2015). The principles encourage schools to sign up and self-report, and there is widespread disagreement about the extent to which such actions are being taken, or if they are being taken in a largely symbolic manner (Rasche & Gilbert, 2015). Compliance with the principles may be driven by work on league tables or through the processes of accreditation with an umbrella group. One such, EQUIS, demands that a school should have a

> clear understanding of its role as a 'globally responsible citizen' and its contribution to ethics and sustainability. This understanding should be reflected in the School's mission, strategy and activities. There should be evidence that the School's contribution is reflected in its regular activities, covering education, research, interactions with businesses and managers, community outreach and its own operations. (Rasche & Gilbert, 2015: 242)

Another, the AACSB, appears to suggest that a much more symbolic commitment to the principles is all that is necessary (Solitander, Fougere, Sobczak & Herlin, 2012). Unsurprisingly, this flexibility is reflected in the content of courses actually delivered by business schools, as the meta-review provided by Setó-Pamies and Papaoikonomou (2016) shows. To the extent that social responsibility and ethics are taught in business schools, they are provided as stand-alone units or topics within more general courses, and rarely systematically integrated into the pedagogic structures of the institution. There are geographical variations in provision. Corporate social responsibility (CSR) teaching occupies a mainstream position in European undergraduate curricula, but does not in Australia and the United States (Matten &

Moon, 2004; Nicholson & De Moss, 2009). It is interesting to note that there appears to be less provision of ethics teaching in high-ranked business schools than lower-ranked ones (Cornelius et al., 2007).

Prescriptions for change abound in the literature, largely seeking to inculcate young learners with an understanding of global problems and a passion for change: 'Individuals with an understanding of sustainability and a positive attitude towards it can be creative, generating sustainable innovative solutions that correspond to the local needs of their communities' (Setó-Pamies & Papaoikonomou, 2016: 523). Teaching ethics, say Giacalone and Thompson (2006: 262), 'must result in a more constructively critical view of businesses' place in the world and willingness to teach students to confront accepted practices as ethically questionable'. To do so will require change at the institutional, curricular and instrumental levels – much in the spirit of the United Nations principles (Setó-Pamies & Papaoikonomou, 2016). Institutional reform will require champions (Fougere, Solitander & Young, 2014; Matten & Moon, 2004) while curriculum innovation might invoke reflexive learning (Gray, 2007; Hibbert & Cunliffe, 2015) or 'live cases' that 'allow for training transfer from classroom to real life ... one of the most challenging components of teaching ethics' (McWilliams & Nahavandi, 2006: 425). Such cases, they argue, will allow 'exposure to philosophical and theoretical concepts of ethics, practical application of the concepts ... critical thinking ... relevance – a connection between personal values and problems ... accountability', and so forth. Solitander et al. (2012: 340) argue that the principles encourage business schools to set their own house in order first and that such 'a transformation will require that those involved – teachers, researchers, students, and administrators – engage in a reflexive learning process that will at times question the adequacy of the educational institution itself.' Responsible education champions drive the process of deep, double-loop learning that

questions the organisation's underlying values and habitual practices. Many follow Cunliffe's (2004, 2016) work on reflective learning and practice here; Cunliffe stresses the relational, socially constituted nature of our social and organisational worlds and encourages managers to be both self-reflexive (critically examining one's own taken-for-granted norms and values) and critically reflective, turning the same lens upon organisational practices. So Solitander et al. (2012: 344) see it as 'central that champions are faculty members who dare to enact their own criticality, as we cannot expect the future managers we educate to be reflexive of the very system they (and we) are part of if they are being challenged to do so by the "comfortable" and unreflexive academic.' Such aspirations are bland enough to find a place in the high temples of mainstream management theory; when esteemed scholar C. K. Prahalad, originator of the bottom (base) of the pyramid, shared his capstone aphorisms on responsible management with the *Harvard Business Review*, they comprised calls to authenticity, honesty, bravery and inclusivity (Prahalad, 2010).

Laasch (2018) argues that discussions of responsible management education are hindered by the field's origins in the pedagogic literature and a lack of exposure to the practicalities of management. Responsible management education, he writes, must emancipate itself. In fact, these discussions of management education resemble many accounts of organisational ethics in the critical management literature where the discharge of ethics is understood in terms of an individual, embodied encounter that stands up against corrupt institutional structures. Bauman's (1989) reading of Weber – accusing bureaucracy of replacing this regard for persons with a purely technical responsibility – has set the tone for much subsequent work on organisational ethics. Scholars have tended to see ethics as individual and subjective behaviour set against the rule-bound frameworks of organisation (Jackall, 2010; Rhodes & Wray-Bliss, 2013). Rationality corrupts the ethical impulse

(Jones, 2003). For these writers, technical and ethical responsibility are fundamentally incompatible phenomena. So, for example, McMurray, Pullen and Rhodes (2011) offer an account of ethics as a means of moral agency and freedom in organisations. Munro (2014) argues that ethics should be understood as a spiritual discipline through which novel subjectivities can arise, a means of resisting the discursive disciplining demanded by employers (Halsall & Brown, 2013). For Weiskopf and Willmott (2013) 'ethics' is most properly understood as a mode of individual agency displayed in the face of organisational power structures, norms and moral orders. Even bureaucrats, those most Weberian of organisational citizens, manage to combine the dispassionate aspects of their office with an understanding that, 'bureaucracies are essentially immoral and allow for injustice and atrocities because of emotional detachment, distance and rationalization' (Eggebø, 2013: 314). In Eggebø's study, ethics flow from the emotional responses of the officials, which offer a means of negotiating the grey areas and blurred lines of formal organisation. In the same way, Pullen and Rhodes (2015: 160) suggest that, 'affectual relations, care, compassion or any other forms of feeling that are experienced pre-reflexively through the body' form the basis for ethical agency.

We can pursue the parallels further. The critical management perspective on ethics is distinguished by its determination to move away from rational–philosophical accounts, which it critiques as thinly disguised regimes of domination, embedded in relations of gender as well as race (Contu, 2018; Knights, 2015; Swan, 2017). Compare Cunliffe on managerial reflexivity:

> The managers in my study rarely spoke in ideological or critical ways about their actions. Rather they spoke in practical terms about relational issues: what they did, who said/did what to whom, how they felt, and the dilemmas they faced. They use the everyday language of participants within the situation; 'grappling with stuff' and 'railroad trains' hitting them. (Cunliffe, 2002: 40)

The ethical subject is one who manages to articulate a moral position within the confines of organisational action; ethical responsibility becomes a feat of rebellion (McMurray et al., 2011). For Cunliffe, learning happens around moments when participants are 'struck', encountering a spontaneous response – emotional, physiological, cognitive – a feeling there is something important we cannot quite grasp in the moment. Most of all, ethics that emphasise their claim on the individual as a whole must be universal and consistent. 'The possibility of categories and practices of personhood', writes du Gay (2008: 132), 'expressing distinctive ethical comportments, irreducible to common principles, appears quite foreign to those for whom a common or universal form of moral judgement is held to reside in the figure and capacities of the self-reflective person'.

THE INTRANSIGENCE OF ORGANISATIONAL CULTURE

These critical voices speak in the same register as those who bemoan the existential crisis of the business school. Rubin and Dierdorff (2013: 128), reviewing a decade of scholarship on the MBA curriculum, suggest that researchers have largely argued 'that curriculum is deficient or contaminated in some significant way'. Perhaps the most significant of these critiques comes from Ghoshal (2005), whose highly cited paper chastises the MBA curriculum for its emphasis on, and ideological commitment to, the rights of shareholders, thus distancing students from moral responsibilities. Hühn (2014) argues that a simultaneous focus on transformational leaders – a great man theory of business history – and on a pseudo-scientific account of decision-making as based on economising trade-offs has left potential managers deeply confused. The international business curriculum, a staple of business school pedagogy, concentrates on international enterprises and their managers, thus marginalizing those others caught up in the tendrils of globalisation; it offers, say Śliwa and Cairns (2009: 229), a 'historically fragmented, decontextualized and instrumental approach to presentation of the subject'. Rubin & Dierdhorff (2013) recognise that the search for professionalisation – including appropriate normative codes – underpins the creation of the business school and yet has been undermined by the success of those same institutions, while Solitander et al. (2012) suggest that a commitment to rankings may lead to the pursuit of short-term goals at odds to a genuinely ethical organisation. Some critical scholars dispute the very basis of social responsibility, arguing that it simply represents a novel form of colonialism (Banerjee, 2003, 2008) or that capital has consumed and metabolised the responsibility critique and now deploys it in pursuit of further accumulation (Chiapello, 2013). The argument has been made most recently by Parker (2018), who argues that business schools are so contaminated by their commitment to managerial capitalism that they should be closed. Collectively, one might take these arguments to suggest that the business school is a morally bankrupt institution, in need of a dose of its own medicine to restore a responsible pedagogy. But empirical work shows this not to be the case.

Let me illustrate this point with a vignette, a case well known in the management literature. It concerns the implementation of an honour code at a large business school in a public research university in the United States and shows the complex, emergent nature of any new moral practices. Gehman, Treviño and Garud (2013) dispense with the suggestion that the code, enthusiastically supported by a new Dean, is part of a top-down implementation of organisational values. The honour code is viable only because it becomes entangled in a nexus of pre-existing values work several years old. The authors are able to identify critical incidents where values practices from other institutions collide with this one. These include the presence of an accountant on the advisory board, shocked that students would not report a misdemeanour (for that is what auditors are professionally instructed to do); student reaction to a scandal elsewhere; student reaction to the less-than-transparent dealing with an internal scandal; and a small group gathering cross-institutional data on honour codes to present to senior management who were understood to be susceptible to the carrot and stick of comparison. These entanglements gathered force as the network of practices connected to a value-laden discourse invoking accountability, honesty, integrity, responsibility and transparency. The code therefore emerged organically from diffuse actions within the school, until it was enacted in a signing ceremony which became a hallowed institutional moment. After all, as one Dean remarked, 'who could be against honesty? It's like apple pie' (p. 98).

It turned out, however, that many people were against honesty. The form of honesty written into the code challenged the many value practices already embedded in the institution. The code lead to contrary effects. A faculty member was hounded out following disputes over trust in exams; a clash arose between the 'disciplinary implications of peer surveillance' and 'other long-standing MBA practices of teamwork, helping each other through the ups and downs of the programme, and the ethos of community' (p. 99); and new power struggles came into play following the perception that administrators had taken too tight a hold over a student-led initiative. Later cohorts of students, less connected to the original values work, began to rebel against the code. At the same time, the code became entangled with other sets of practices and its influence spread. The case concludes with the observation that, by the end of the research period, the code had reshaped admissions into the programme and job search after it, and was informing an ongoing cultural mission among stakeholders beyond the institution itself.

The saga of the honour code makes us aware of some uncomfortable truths. Students cheat, and students in business schools cheat more (McCabe, Butterfield & Treviño, 2006). Economic students cheat too, and are given to freeriding and other kinds of antisocial behaviour (Frank, Gilovich & Regan, 1993, 1996). What constitutes good behaviour in the mind of one person may represent awkward compromises to another; even the most general and incontrovertible virtues, such as honesty, can collide with existing organisational mores. Differing strategic perspectives cause actors to respond in different ways and to pursue heterogeneous courses of action. Most of all, the episode shows that responsible management education, however lofty its ideals, is not easily transformed into responsible management practice. A code of conduct – a solution beloved of those advocating the professionalisation of management – cannot easily be imposed on a practice that is already value-rich, given to its own kinds of occupational virtues (MacIntyre, 1981). Gehman et al. (2013) are still keen to emphasise the role of human agency in values work, which they conceptualise as based on a process of 'knotting' local values into emergent action networks. They show that values become organisational attributes when they are enrolled into networks of practice; the values that 'succeed' are those that speak to underlying, or pre-existing values work. Moreover, values are performative, or world-making; 'values practices actively intervene in situations', they write, 'contributing to the enactment of normative realities' (p. 104). The study shows how an intervention might produce consequences the very reverse of those expected, 'misfires' or 'counterperformatives' as the literature has termed such outcomes (Callon, 2010; MacKenzie, 2006).

WHO – OR WHAT – AM I?

Gehman et al. (2013) locate their concept in opposition to two concepts prevailing in the literature. On the one hand, values are understood in cognitive terms and can be analysed accordingly (and objectively). On the other, scholars have argued that organisational values are dependent upon organisational narratives, rituals and symbols, as well as language and meaning-making within the organisation, factors that can be broadly understood as cultural perspectives and are often linked to the role of leaders in instilling values across an organisation. These perspectives correspond broadly to the positions taken in the literature on ethics and organisation that I have sketched out above; we find on the one hand the organisation as the source of all malfeasance, and on the other the individual as the ethical subject capable of free choice. Responsible management educators seem convinced that an emphasis on the latter can overcome the problems of the former. Champions of RME can tackle organisational silos, structural barriers and defensive routines (Solitander et al., 2012). The honour code episode suggests that this is the case: values work is hard work and organisational culture is intransigent. But this does not, as yet, constitute an ontological misstep for responsible management education. Such a misstep requires a misunderstanding of the nature of the world, and it comes in a failure to understand the nature of choice available to individuals.

Despite the heterogeneity of scholarship concerning responsible management, it is united by a common understanding of how managers take decisions, as individual, freely choosing moral agents. In this it inherits the fundamental position of a Western intellectual paradigm that can be traced back to Kant. The understanding of individual agency also clearly demonstrates the field's roots in the world of pedagogic theory. What is good in the classroom must also be good in the office. Complaints about an excessive reliance on, for example, cost–benefit analysis imply that authentic moral judgement demands a move into the self, a break with organizational routine justified by the 'recognition and openness to the face of the Other, which entails

… a total question, a distress and denuding, a supplication, a demanding prayer' (Jones, 2003: 227). Cunliffe (2016) locates the problems of the business school in the ontological underpinnings of management education, manifested as an objectivist view that sees the world as testable and predictable, and management knowledge as a morally-neutral set of instruments to be deployed in the pursuit of efficiency and to be valued on account of utility and effectiveness. She advocates instead a constructivist, relational perspective that understands ethics as springing from the foundational moral question, 'Who am I?'

'Who' is the wrong pronoun. The existential self-examination that the question prompts should eventually arrive at 'what'. The manager must be considered as an organisational cyborg, a hybrid entity (Latour, 1993) that spans metrological and calculative devices, organisational structures, co-workers, and even the material architectures of the workplace. This assertion comes from work in the science and technology studies tradition, where scholars have advanced on account of organisational decision-making that sees choices made across socio-material 'agencements', and constructed by the performative role of management theory. Agency is distributed across these networks, as the French neologism 'agencement' implies, and such entities are never free of the entanglements of culture and morals (Latour, 1993). Let me unpack this rather dense idea further, and then illustrate with another vignette – perhaps even better known – from the literature.

Managers must take decisions in complex and dynamic environments. Their cognitive work is therefore difficult, and managers are quick to employ tools to simplify these tasks and thereby enact some kind of organisational reason. As Hutchins' (1995) important study of the cognitive arrangement of a warship shows us, managers 'distribute' cognition. Managers analyse using tools, systems of measurement and organisational procedures. Cabantous, Gond and Johnson-Cramer (2010) show this process at work, highlighting the 'complex and fragile socio-technical infrastructure' underlying the production of organisational rationality. A body of literature has applied this perspective to finance and illustrates how decisions become shared across socio-material networks, forming hybrids that become market 'actors' including a hedge fund (Hardie & MacKenzie, 2007), a trading desk (Beunza & Stark, 2004), even a solitary non-professional investor plugged into his analytic software and trading interface on a desktop PC (Roscoe & Howorth, 2009). The importance of mundane, material devices cannot be understated. MacKenzie's (2006) study of options pricing, for example, shows how the traders' rationality is configured by mundane material artefacts – printed lists of numbers worn on the sleeve.

Decision-making agencements therefore comprise human agents, technical devices, metrological arrangements, and are held together by organisational routines (Feldman & Pentland, 2003). All of this is underpinned by theory, inscribed into technical devices (D'Adderio & Pollock, 2014; Gond, Cabantous, Harding, & Learmonth, 2016). Such a claim takes us back to where we began, with the popular lament that business schools corrupt young minds through the provision of analytic tools predicated on theories of economic maximisation (Ghoshal, 2005; Hühn, 2014). But it also allows us to understand the impossibility of stepping outside of some kind of socio-technical frame of reference. As understandings of economised rationality become more widely accepted as the paradigms for decision-making, so these assemblages proliferate. Human agents are guided by cognitive 'prostheses' (Callon, 2008) to appropriately rational decisions, whether as tourists (Jeacle & Carter, 2011) or lonely hearts (Roscoe & Chillas, 2014). Even the central values underpinning 'responsibility' are subject to prolonged social construction. Research has sensitised us to the emergence of value as an ongoing practice dependent upon systems of measurement, incentive structures, material technologies and understandings of the world (Dussauge, Helgesson, & Lee, 2015; Kornberger, Justesen, Madsen, & Mouritsen, 2015; Stark, 2011). These processes extend to the epistemic realm and our account of 'what matters' that is so central to any moral decision. Dussauge et al. (2015) draw attention to the relations between value and epistemology, arguing that what we deem to be worth knowing is itself the outcome of values work. Scientific practices, for example, produce values, rather than being underpinned by values.

The study of valuation points to a broader understanding of social life and scientific fact – two crucial aspects of moral behaviour – as performed through and held in place by networks of relations (Latour, 2007). Returning to the MBA clutching her suite of rational, cost–benefit-based analysis tools we can start to form another argument, ontologically distinct from the position of responsible management education. It is not that the methods corrode her innate moral goodness. Instead, the cost–benefit analysis is part of a much greater sociotechnical infrastructure that *constitutes* her as manager. This infrastructure itself depends upon particular forms of language and calculative strategies, and gives rise to particular forms of action in the world. As Foucault reminds us, we must recognise that power makes possible as well as restricts. The manager is inseparable from her socio-technical network; the moral cyborg can never transcend itself.

THE MORAL CYBORG IN ACTION

I will draw this out through a second vignette, also well known among management scholars, Gioia's (1992) reflective account of his role in the Ford Pinto scandal. The story of the Pinto fires is familiar enough to skip much of the detail. Ford put into production a car with a safety defect, a petrol tank located by the boot that could be ruptured by collision. Crash tests had identified this defect but were new, unfamiliar to engineers, and not legally binding. Margins were thin enough to make management resistant to small production fixes. Media reports later claimed that Ford had used a cost–benefit analysis to determine whether to fit this modification. Doing so was in line with Federal guidelines and followed the classic Coasian insight that those presenting the cheapest solution to a problem should bear the cost; it is not clear that the calculation played a part in Ford's decision to launch the car (Lee & Ermann, 1999; Schwartz, 1990), but it provoked a furore nonetheless, and Gioia brings these considerations into his introduction.

The chapter's narrative begins with Gioia, later an eminent organisation theorist, as a young idealist at a business school. He found himself,

> In MBA classes railing against the conduct of businesses of the era, whose actions struck me as ranging from inconsiderate to indifferent to simply unethical ... I wanted something to change ... I cultivated my social awareness; I held my principles high; I espoused my intention to help a troubled world; and I wore my hair long. (p. 379)

To the surprise of his classmates, the young man took a job at Ford, hoping to change the system from the inside. Gioia tells us how he quickly became caught up in the norms of the corporation, competing with other new arrivals for progress in the firm's fast track. In 1973 he became field recall coordinator, a job that brought him into contact with the notorious Pinto fires. Reports began trickling in of Pintos being consumed by fire after low-speed accidents:

> Was there a problem? Not as far as I was concerned. My cue for labelling a case as a problem either required high frequencies of occurrence or directly traceable causes. I had little time for speculative contemplation on potential problems that did not fit a pattern that suggested known courses of action leading to possible recall. I do, however, remember being disquieted by a field report

accompanied by graphic, detailed photos of the remains of a burned-out Pinto in which several people had died ... I did not flag it as any special case. (p. 382)

Gioia stresses the complexity and pace of the job, 'the busiest, most information-filled job' he ever held. He recognised that he was responsible for life and death matters and took his job very seriously, waking up at night to worry about particular cases. He describes the process of suppressing some of these emotions to make the job manageable, concentrating on the most pressing risks with the resources at hand. Pintos were not one of these risks, yet the reports continued and he saw a wreckage first hand.

The revulsion on seeing this incinerated hulk was immediate and profound. Soon afterwards, and despite the fact that the file was very sparse, I recommended the Pinto case for preliminary departmental review concerning possible recall. (p. 382)

So far, the case fits our account of embodied morals. The busy mid-level manager, overwhelmed by the cognitive and emotional demands of the job, seeking technical 'cues' to avoid a direct confrontation with the harm, is struck by an unavoidable, embodied response to the 'incinerated hulk'. Yet the story takes an unexpected turn:

After the usual round of discussion about criteria and justification for recall, everyone voted against recommending recall – including me. It did not fit the pattern of recordable standards; the evidence was not overwhelming that the car was defective in some way ... (p. 382)

The recall team did not know, at this point, about the damning crash test data. Following a comparative analysis of other small cars the team once again voted against the recall. Reason, it seems, triumphed over affect.

Gioia finishes his account with a personal reflection. Plagued over the years by doubts over his own culpability he built the story into a case for MBA students, revealing his role in the saga at the end. He writes: 'After getting to know me for most of the semester, and then finding out that I did not vote to recommend

recall, students are often incredulous, even angry at me for apparently not having lived what I have been teaching' (p. 384). He concludes that while his actions were legal, and probably also ethical in the perspective of the time, they were still a moral failure, and that he should have done everything possible to get the cars off the road.

Although Gioia's *mea culpa* is the only way this narrative could have ended, the case provides us with a careful exploration of the sociological construction of the good – what matters – and furthers my cautionary tale about responsible moral education. The young MBA Gioia is everything we would want our students to be, politically committed, angry at corporate indifference to the state of the world in the Vietnam era, eager for change, possessing high moral standards. Despite his rapid adaption to the corporate tournament – the hippy to yuppie, perhaps – he is a committed manager, reflecting in the small hours on decisions that he knows could be life or death to a driver. He is principled and reflexive, he believes he is doing the right thing, and yet he is caught up in the waves of this terrible scandal. Gioia is very clear that the reports of Pinto fires did not match the models of recallable faults that the department used. We might argue that these models inhibited his ability to exercise moral judgement, or sympathy. But this does not seem to be the case, for he found the wrecks disquieting enough to prompt action.

Instead, following the literature sketched out above, we might say that the models underpinned a calculative assemblage that performed a certain moral position. That position was genuinely concerned with effectiveness and need, but these value-laden moral criteria *could only be understood* within the calculative apparatus of the office, one manifested in files, test results, computations and procedures. Tools, models (Pollock & D'Adderio, 2012) and accounting inscriptions (Qu & Cooper, 2011) are all devices that perform certain kinds of organisational reality and organisational processes depend on accepting these as valid. Models have path dependencies and organisational trajectories. As MacKenzie (2011) has shown so well in his study of the credit crisis, different models inhabit different organisational provinces and rarely communicate, and this was certainly the case in the Pinto affair. Tools do not simply constrain, but also make possible. The job, busy and information-filled, is only manageable through this apparatus; it is these models that help the young coordinator distinguish between the magnitude of different potential recalls and to determine what matters – what is worth knowing and talking about (Dussauge et al., 2015). Like the values work described by Gehman et al. (2013), models are bigger than any individual.

The story offers a cautionary tale about responsible management education. If the idealistic, young Gioia could find himself in such a position, why should any new graduate be any different? No matter how reflexive, no matter how conscientious, it seems impossible to transcend the calculative infrastructures of the organisation. The ethical framing of the decision – what is in and what is out, what matters and what does not – is entirely contingent upon the sets of sociotechnical relations that surround the manager. The moral being is complex, distributed and cyborg. To complicate matters further, it is clear that many bureaucratic roles do have their own internal values, such as fairness and an even-handed disregard for rank and status (du Gay, 2000). There is already values work going on within the department and Gioia alludes to this throughout. It is a small step from good student to good manager, in all the polysemic senses of the word: the path from MBA ideology to organisational zealotry is straight, wide and paved with the very best intentions.

RETOOLING MANAGEMENT, REORGANISING MANAGERS

At the risk of oversimplification, let me characterise the debate around responsible management education in a few lines. Business schools have been guilty of advocating a particular kind of worldview, an objectivist account underpinned by economic theory, where the role of managers is to employ certain tools for instrumental purposes. This approach, scholars claim, is morally corrosive. The solution is to encourage managers to be more reflexive about their practice, allowing more scope for judgement, humanity and other such virtues. Those advocating a reflexive approach to management see managers as caught up in social interactions that determine the form of the institution, understanding organisations as ongoing conversations that can be reshaped by a few deft tugs on the discursive threads. I have made use of two vignettes, well known in the literature, to illustrate the pitfalls of such an approach. First of all, I have highlighted the intransigence of organisational culture and the efforts involved in 'values work'. Gehman et al. (2013) chronicle a business school's honour code to show how complex and unpredictable, even contrary, this process may be. Where organisational norms emerge organically from an institution, they may be contrary in their results; a code of conduct designed to combat cheating leads to new circuits of power within the organisation, and the hounding of one faculty member to a position elsewhere. It is hard, on this basis, to understand how the most reflexively aware manager can hope to make material change to an institution. But this view seems pessimistic and susceptible to exhortations that we must simply try harder, so I supplement it with an ontological objection centring on the nature of moral personhood in the manager.

The arguments I have offered are based on understanding organisations, not as discursively constructed from tapestries of ephemeral discourse, but as substantial, obdurate realities embedded in networks of sociotechnical relations. As Law and Urry (2004) argue, while 'the "real" is indeed "real" it is also made, and … it is made within relations'.

Gioia's (1992) case study of the votes not to recall the Pinto shows these processes at work. It is not a case of monstrous behaviour facilitated by bureaucratic dispassion and moral distance (Bauman, 1989) or rational trade-offs and organisational groupthink (Kühl, 2016). Nor is it a case of would-be good citizens hemmed in by misleading pedagogy, so much as an organisational world constituted by particular technical modes of valuation distributed across calculative and metrological devices. This is no scholastic distinction. Advocating reflexivity suggests that there is something beyond the model, a socially constructed organisational world which the intellectual pilgrim might discover and re-work through sheer force of reflexive will. A Latourian (1999, 2004) approach, on the other hand, suggests that tools, devices and practices should occupy our attention as the source of managerial responsibility. Rather than worry what managers do with tools (Ghoshal, 2005), we should draw attention to what tools do with managers (Ferraro et al., 2005).

If tools and devices are the source of organisational morality, they must also represent a potential mechanism for change. Law and Urry (2004) argue that many of the relations underlying our modernity are constituted by social science. It is certainly the case for management theory. The business school curriculum transmits modes of knowledge that construct a particular world. We should start, therefore, by recognising the constitutive ontological power of management models. We might speculate that the Ford recall department would have come to different conclusions had it counted in different ways. The challenge becomes a technical one, understanding how to recast engineering measures in pursuit of certain aims. But better ways of counting leave the basic problem unchanged. Under the more modern 'value of statistical life' methods (Viscusi & Aldy, 2003), themselves highly problematic, a different conclusion might have been reached,

the underlying mechanism untouched. We need, but do not have, other ways of articulating moral demands that can be made meaningful in an organisational setting, a problem recognised by MacIntyre (1992) himself. Finding a solution here requires not more disengaged economising (Roscoe, 2014) but an interdisciplinary engagement between engineers, philosophers and management scholars. Or consider the problem of the honour code, nicely demonstrating the inability of a generic solution to prevent an ongoing and endemic problem within a certain kind of institution. Tackling the widely recognised problem of cheating is likely to involve curriculum reform, changes in the manner and structure of assessment, and a much broader change in the understanding of the purpose of executive education. In other words, this is a problem that calls for solutions collaboratively crafted by students and faculty. These are technical issues, not in the sense of making it harder to cheat, but in the sense of constructing assessments that reward honesty, engagement and contribution, however that might be defined in a particular context. It might also involve sociological work, attempting to move beyond fixation on final grades, not only on the part of students (where it is understandable, in view of the obstacles that they face) but also on the part of employers. Today's students will be tomorrow's recruiters, and in the long term, the curriculum must be one of the most promising vehicles for affecting such change. Such possibilities speak to the specific academic expertise of faculty, rather than increasingly generic management solutions set out by those who treat university education as a form of industrialised production.

We have to distinguish between the manner of our pedagogy and its intention. I wholeheartedly concur with theories of learning seeking to move to active participation in the classroom and reflexive, double-loop learning (Argyris, 1991). As responsible management educators, part of our mission must be to produce critically self-aware, open-minded learners able to question their dearly-held assumptions. In terms of the intention (and therefore content) of our pedagogy, we should pursue a different agenda. We must explain to them how management models structure the world in a particular way, and how certain kinds of organisational framing facilitate certain aims and preclude others. I worry, for example, that by emphasising the ability of managers to effect transformational change within and through organisations we implicitly accept those organisations as appropriate means for change. As Parker (2018) has pointed out at length, business schools teach managerial capitalism. He argues that we should be teaching students other ways of organising, those that permit different kinds of moral calculus and different kinds of social relation within the world. *Forbes'* magazine's colourful answer to Parker, dismissing him as 'a little-known professor from a business school that fails to make either the Financial Times or The Economist rankings', states that 'the need for a moral compass and ethical behaviour is drummed into business students *ad nauseam*'. Ignoring the painfully literal truth of *ad nauseam*, this answer captures my misgivings perfectly. All we need is a little bit of self-reflection and the world will be just fine.

Perhaps the most responsible kind of management education would be one that simply showed how difficult an endeavour responsible management can be, and this brings me to my final caution about responsible management education. I wonder if its most corrosive consequences – unexpectedly – bear on faculty and the business school itself, rather than students. In view of the arguments marshalled above, it cannot be the job of managers to be responsible, not only for the effective and humane discharge of their daily work, but also in a transcendental, but very real, sense for the survival of the planet and the emancipation of humanity. Just as supermarkets and industrial food producers have moved the ethical onus for their bad

practices onto consumers, so responsible management education, with its focus on the individual, not the organisation, has shifted the burden to our students. We recognise that consumers are powerless (Banerjee, 2008) and yet we pin our hopes on young people, keen and ambitious, but indebted and precarious, soon to become entry-level employees in tournament-style graduate training schemes. We should extend our critical logic and take account of our own responsibilities.

The business school is the pre-eminent source of management knowledge and tools, the stuff from which worlds are made. We are implicated in shareholder theory, globalisation, and up to our neck in agency-based approaches to management. When radical approaches to organisation are most needed, we who have the luxury of scholarly distance and intellectual freedom prefer to pass the baton. Colleagues, we must roll up our sleeves. The party is over, and we management academics have got a lot of clearing up to do.

Note

1 'Cyborg' strictly refers to physical combinations of person and machine (Warwick, 2003). My use here is less specific, suggesting that human decision-making is distributed (Hutchins, 1995) across assemblages of human, material and technical. Here, I follow a well-established usage in the literature of science and technology studies and critical theory (e.g. Haraway, 1985; Callon, 2008).

REFERENCES

Argyris, C. (1991). Teaching smart people how to learn. *Harvard Business Review*, 63(3), 99–109.

Banerjee, S. B. (2003). Who sustains whose development? Sustainable development and the reinvention of nature. *Organization Studies*, 24(1), 143–180.

Banerjee, S. B. (2008). Corporate social responsibility: the good, the bad and the ugly. *Critical Sociology*, 34(1), 51–79.

Bauman, Z. (1989). *Modernity and the holocaust*. Cambridge: Polity Press.

Beunza, D., & Stark, D. (2004). Tools of the trade: the socio-technology of arbitrage in a wall street trading room. *Industrial and Corporate Change*, *13*(2), 369–400.

Burchell, J., Kennedy, S., & Murray, A. (2015). Responsible management education in UK business schools: critically examining the role of the United Nations Principles for Responsible Management Education as a driver for change. *Management Learning*, *46*(4), 479–497.

Bykov, A. (2018). Rediscovering the moral: the 'old' and 'new' sociology of morality in the context of the behavioural sciences. *Sociology*, *53*(1), 192–207.

Cabantous, L., Gond, J.-P., & Johnson-Cramer, M. (2010). Decision theory as practice: crafting rationality in organizations. *Organization Studies*, *31*(11), 1531–1566.

Callon, M. (2008). Economic markets and the rise of interactive agencements. In Pinch, T. & Swedberg, R. (Eds.), *Living in a material world* (pp. 29–56). Cambridge, MA: The MIT Press.

Callon, M. (2010). Performativity, misfires and politics. *Journal of Cultural Economy*, *3*(2), 163–169.

Chiapello, E. (2013). Capitalism and its criticisms. In Du Gay, P. & Morgan, G. (Eds.), *New spirits of capitalism?* (pp. 60–81). Oxford: Oxford University Press.

Contu, A. (2018). '… the point is to change it' – yes, but in what direction and how? Intellectual activism as a way of 'walking the talk' of critical work in business schools. *Organization*, *25*(2), 282–293.

Cornelius, N., Wallace, J., & Tassabehji, R. (2007). An analysis of corporate social responsibility, corporate identity and ethics teaching in business schools. *Journal of Business Ethics*, *76*(1), 117–135.

Cunliffe, A. L. (2002). Reflexive dialogical practice in management learning. *Management Learning*, *33*(1), 35–61.

Cunliffe, A. L. (2004). On becoming a critically reflexive practitioner. *Journal of Management Education*, *28*(4), 407–426.

Cunliffe, A. L. (2016). 'On becoming a critically reflexive practitioner' redux: what does it mean to be reflexive? *Journal of Management Education*, *40*(6), 740–746.

D'Adderio, L., & Pollock, N. (2014). Performing modularity: competing rules, performative struggles and the effect of organizational theories on the organization. *Organization Studies*, *35*(12), 1813–1843.

du Gay, P. (2000). *In praise of bureaucracy*. London: Sage.

du Gay, P. (2008). Max Weber and the moral economy of office. *Journal of Cultural Economy*, *1*(2), 129–144.

Dussauge, I., Helgesson, C.-F., & Lee, F. (2015). *Value practices in the life sciences*. Oxford: Oxford University Press.

Eggebø, H. (2013). 'With a heavy heart': ethics, emotions and rationality in Norwegian immigration administration. *Sociology*, *47*(2), 301–317.

Feldman, M., & Pentland, B. (2003). Reconceptualizing organizational routines as a source of flexibility and change. *Administrative Science Quarterly*, *48*, 94–118.

Ferraro, F., Pfeffer, J., & Sutton, R. I. (2005). Economic language and assumptions: how theories can become self-fulfilling. *Academy of Management Review*, *30*(1), 8–24.

Fougere, M., Solitander, N., & Young, S. (2014). Exploring and exposing values in management education: problematizing final vocabularies in order to enhance moral imagination. *Journal of Business Ethics*, *120*, 175–187.

Frank, R. H., Gilovich, T., & Regan, D. T. (1993). Does studying economics inhibit cooperation? *Journal of Economic Perspectives*, *7*(2), 159–171.

Frank, R. H., Gilovich, T. D., & Regan, D. T. (1996). Do economists make bad citizens? *Journal of Economic Perspectives*, *10*(1), 187–192.

Gehman, J., Treviño, L. K., & Garud, R. (2013). Values work: a process study of the emergence and performance of organizational values practices. *Academy of Management Journal*, *56*(1), 84–112.

Ghoshal, S. (2005). Bad management theories are destroying good management practices. *Academy of Management Learning & Education*, *4*(1), 75–91.

Giacalone, R. A., & Thompson, K. R. (2006). From the guest editors: Special issue on ethics and responsibility. *Academy of Management Learning & Education*, *5*(3), 261–265.

Gioia, D. A. (1992). Pinto fires and personal ethics: a script analysis of missed opportunities. *Journal of Business Ethics*, *11*, 379–389.

Gond, J.-P., Cabantous, L., Harding, N., & Learmonth, M. (2016). What do we mean by performativity in organisational and management theory? The uses and abuses of performativity. *International Journal of Management Reviews*, *18*(4), 440–463.

Gray, D. E. (2007). Facilitating management learning: developing critical reflection through reflective tools. *Management Learning*, *38*(5), 495–517.

Green, J. (1988). *Days in the life: voices from the English underground, 1961–1971*. London: Pimlico.

Haraway, D. (1985). A manifesto for cyborgs: science, technology, and socialist feminism in the 1980s. *Socialist Review*, *80*, 65–108.

Halsall, R., & Brown, M. (2013) Askēsis and organizational culture. *Organization*, *20*(2), 233–255.

Hardie, I., & MacKenzie, D. (2007). Assembling an economic actor: the agencement of a hedge fund. *The Sociological Review*, *55*(1), 57–80.

Hibbert, P., & Cunliffe, A. (2015). Responsible management: engaging moral reflexive practice through threshold concepts. *Journal of Business Ethics*, *127*(1), 177–188.

Hitlin, S., & Vaisey, S. (2013). The new sociology of morality. *Annual Review of Sociology*, *39*(1), 51–68.

Hühn, M. (2014). You reap what you sow: how MBA programs undermine ethics. *Journal of Business Ethics*, *121*(4), 527–541.

Hutchins, E. (1995). *Cognition in the wild*. Cambridge, MA: MIT Press.

Jackall, R. (2010). Morality in organizations. In Hitlin, S., & Vaisey, S. (Eds.), *Handbook of the sociology of morality* (pp. 203–209). New York: Springer.

Jeacle, I., & Carter, C. (2011). In TripAdvisor we trust: rankings, calculative regimes and abstract systems. *Accounting, Organizations and Society*, *36*(4–5), 293–309.

Jones, C. (2003). As if business ethics were possible, 'within such limits'. *Organization*, *10*(2), 223–248.

Knights, D. (2015). Binaries need to shatter for bodies to matter: do disembodied masculinities undermine organizational ethics? *Organization*, *22*(2), 200–216.

Kornberger, M., Justesen, L., Madsen, A. K., & Mouritsen, J. (2015). Introduction: Making things valuable. In Kornberger, M., Justesen, L., Madsen, A. K., & Mouritsen J. (Eds.), *Making things valuable* (pp.1–17). Oxford: Oxford University Press.

Kühl, S. (2016). *Ordinary organizations*. Cambridge: Polity Press.

Laasch, O. (2018). Just old wine in new bottles? Conceptual shifts in the emerging field of responsible management. CMRE Working Papers. Centre for Responsible Management Education.

Latour, B. (1993). *We have never been modern*. Cambridge, MA: Harvard University Press.

Latour, B. (1999). *Pandora's hope*. Cambridge, MA: Harvard University Press.

Latour, B. (2004). *Politics of nature*. Cambridge, MA: Harvard University Press.

Latour, B. (2007). *Reassembling the social: an introduction to actor-network-theory* (new edition). Oxford: Oxford University Press.

Law, J., & Urry, J. (2004). Enacting the social. *Economy and Society*, *33*(3), 390–410.

Lee, M., & Ermann, D. (1999). Pinto 'madness' as a flawed landmark narrative: an organizational and network analysis. *Social Problems*, *46*(1), 30–47.

MacIntyre, A. (1981). *After virtue: a study in moral theory*. London: Duckworth.

MacIntyre, A. (1992). Utilitarianism and cost benefit analysis: an essay on the relevance of moral philosophy to bureaucratic theory. In Gillroy, J. M., & Wade, M. (Eds.), *The moral dimensions of public policy choice* (pp. 179–194). University of Pittsburgh Press: Pittsburgh.

MacKenzie, D. (2006). *An engine, not a camera: how financial models shape markets*. Cambridge, MA: MIT Press.

MacKenzie, D. (2011). The credit crisis as a problem in the sociology of knowledge. *American Journal of Sociology*, *116*(6), 1778–1841.

Matten, D., & Moon, J. (2004). Corporate social responsibility education in Europe. *Journal of Business Ethics*, *54*, 323–337.

McCabe, D. L., Butterfield, K. D., & Treviño, L. K. (2006). Academic dishonesty in graduate business programs: prevalence, causes, and proposed action. *Academy of Management Learning & Education*, *5*(3), 294–305.

McMurray, R., Pullen, A., & Rhodes, C. (2011). Ethical subjectivity and politics in organizations: a case of health care tendering. *Organization, 18*(4), 541–561.

McWilliams, V., & Nahavandi, A. (2006). Using live cases to teach ethics. *Journal of Business Ethics, 67*(4), 421–433.

Munro, I. (2014). Organizational ethics and Foucault's 'art of living': lessons from social movement organizations. *Organization Studies, 35*(8), 1127–1148.

Nicholson, C. Y., & DeMoss, M. (2009). Teaching ethics and social responsibility: an evaluation of undergraduate business education at the discipline level. *Journal of Education for Business, 84*(4), 213–218.

Parker, M. (2002). Utopia and the organizational imagination: Outopia. *The Sociological Review, 50*(S1), 1–8.

Parker, M. (2018). *Shut down the business school*. London: Pluto Press.

Pollock, N., & D'Adderio, L. (2012). Give me a two-by-two matrix and I will create the market: rankings, graphic visualisations and sociomateriality. *Accounting, Organizations and Society, 37*(8), 565–586.

Prahalad, C. K. (2010). The responsible manager. *Harvard Business Review, Jan–Feb*.

Pullen, A., & Rhodes, C. (2015). Ethics, embodiment and organizations. *Organization, 22*(2), 159–165.

Qu, S. Q., & Cooper, D. J. (2011). The role of inscriptions in producing a balanced scorecard. *Accounting, Organizations and Society, 36*(6), 344–362.

Rasche, A., & Gilbert, D. U. (2015). Decoupling responsible management education: why business schools may not walk their talk. *Journal of Management Inquiry, 24*(3), 239–252.

Rhodes, C., & Wray-Bliss, E. (2013). The ethical difference of organization. *Organization, 20*(1), 39–50.

Roscoe, P. (2014). *I spend therefore I am*. London: Penguin Viking.

Roscoe, P., & Chillas, S. (2014). The state of affairs: critical performativity and the online dating industry. *Organization, 21*(6), 797–820.

Roscoe, P., & Howorth, C. (2009). Identification through technical analysis: a study of charting and UK non-professional investors. *Accounting, Organizations and Society, 34*(2), 206–221.

Rubin, R. S., & Dierdorff, E. C. (2013). Building a better MBA: from a decade of critique toward a decennium of creation. *Academy of Management Learning & Education, 12*(1), 125–141.

Schwartz, G. T. (1990). The myth of the Ford Pinto case. *Rutgers Law Review, 43*, 1013–1068.

Setó-Pamies, D., & Papaoikonomou, E. (2016). A multi-level perspective for the integration of ethics, corporate social responsibility and sustainability (ecsrs) in management education. *Journal of Business Ethics, 136*(3), 523–538.

Śliwa, M., & Cairns, G. (2009). Towards a critical pedagogy of international business: the application of phronēsis. *Management Learning, 40*(3), 227–240.

Solitander, N., Fougere, M., Sobczak, A., & Herlin, H. (2012). We are the champions: organizational learning and change for responsible management education. *Journal of Management Education, 36*(3), 337–363.

Stark, D. (2011). *The sense of dissonance: accounts of worth in economic life*. Princeton, NJ: Princeton University Press.

Swan, E. (2017). What are white people to do? Listening, challenging ignorance, generous encounters and the 'not yet' as diversity research praxis. *Gender, Work & Organization, 24*(5), 547–563.

United Nations. (n.d.). Our 2030 vision. Available at: www.unprme.org/about-prme/the-six-principles.php.

Viscusi, W. K., & Aldy, J. E. (2003). The value of a statistical life: a critical review of market estimates throughout the world. *Journal of Risk and Uncertainty, 27*(1), 5–76.

Warwick, K. (2003). Cyborg morals, cyborg values, cyborg ethics. *Ethics and Information Technology, 5*(3), 131–137.

Weiskopf, R., & Willmott, H. (2013). Truth-telling, and the unsettling of organizational morality ethics as critical practice: the 'Pentagon Papers', deciding responsibly. *Organization Studies, 34*(4), 469–493.

22

A Systems Approach to Transformational Responsible Management Learning and Education

Danna Greenberg, Lauren Beitelspacher and Vikki Rodgers

Close to a decade ago, the UN established the PRME, Principles of Responsible Management Education, to encourage businesses schools to develop curricula and research that contributes to a more sustainable and inclusive global economy. Since its inception, over 700 higher education institutions have committed to the PRME. In so doing they have joined the UN in their commitment to educating responsible leaders who have the skills and mindset to pursue both economic and sustainability goals. PRME has become an influential stakeholder in bringing responsible management learning and education (RMLE) into the mainstream of management education (see Chapter 2 by Librizzi and Parkes in this Handbook).

Despite the growing interest in RMLE, many scholars continue to question the effectiveness of the UN PRME initiative. PRME is based on a 'voluntary, soft governance' model in which business schools are not forced to comply with a specific model but allowed to craft their own distinct approach to RMLE (Burchell, Kennedy & Murray, 2015). This self-directed approach is sensible as it is difficult to design a one-size-fits-all strategy given the varied cultural and regulatory contexts in which business schools are situated. This approach also fits the culture of broader models of higher education reform, monitoring and evaluation (Lowrie & Willmott, 2009). Academic accreditation, which is usually done by academic leaders at peer institutions, is rarely compulsory though it can be necessary for securing federal funding and research grant access. Still, some scholars have criticized this loose approach as they argue it enables business schools to engage in incremental reform rather than commit to comprehensive, transformational pedagogical changes (Burchell et al., 2015). An incremental approach can be problematic as it rarely results in the development of a new generation of leaders who are committed to responsible management (Rasche & Gilbert, 2015; Painter-Morland, Sabet, Molthan-Hill, Goworek & de Leeuw, 2016). Unfortunately, few business schools have engaged in a more transformational approach to RMLE which integrates multiple facets of sustainability (Finlay & Massey, 2012).

A second challenge business schools face when engaging with RMLE is the tendency to focus primarily on student learning. Even when defining transformational RMLE, some management education scholars focus entirely on student learning. For instance, Visser (2016: ix) states RMLE requires integrating 'social, ethical, and environmental considerations into all management subjects'. There has also been a tendency among management educators to center RMLE discussions on the barriers and enablers that support transformational *pedagogical* change (e.g. Solitander, Fougere, Sobczak & Herlin, 2012). While curricular change is an essential component of transformational RMLE, it cannot be the only component. A transformational model of RMLE should challenge faculty and staff to go beyond curriculum change to also reimagine how we teach, where student learning occurs, and how the college operates.

In this chapter, we introduce a systems approach to transformational RMLE that considers multiple stakeholders as it emphasizes student learning, faculty and staff engagement, and the business school's operations. We begin by identifying lessons and insights that can be drawn from universities that have taken an incremental approach to responsible management education as well as other higher education institutions that have engaged a transformational approach to sustainability education specifically. By connecting these insights to current models of transformational change, we identify four processes that form the basis of a systems approach to transformational RMLE. These processes include: (1) integrated student learning, (2) collaboration among internal stakeholders, (3) commitment and trust and (4) communication that builds shared understanding. We draw upon our experiences at Babson College to provide specific examples

of each process. In providing these examples, we are not suggesting that Babson College is operating out of a transformational model to RMLE. Rather we hope other business schools can draw upon our experiences to develop their own systems approach to transformational RMLE.

LEARNING FROM OTHER INSTITUTIONS

As we noted in our introduction, to date few business schools have effectively implemented transformational approaches to RMLE. As such, we begin by exploring further the more common incremental approach and then compare it to higher education institutions which have engaged a transformational approach to sustainability education specifically. We conclude with a discussion of the insights that can be drawn from this comparison as we develop a systems approach to RMLE.

Rusinko (2010) outlines a matrix of three options for integrating RMLE into business education. Option one is to integrate RMLE into an existing course. This is easy to implement and requires little additional resources. Option two is to create a new discipline-specific course which allows for a more standardized approach. Neither of these approaches is transformational as RMLE remains isolated with the faculty and students who engage with the particular course or discipline. Furthermore, a compulsory, stand-alone module rarely supports student learning of the integrative systems thinking that is central to responsible leadership (Visser, 2016).

There are many legitimate reasons for adopting an incremental approach to RMLE. Business school leadership may be concerned that a transformative approach to RMLE will be met with resistance. An incremental approach may be more fitting with a particular business school culture and may be a better way to gain early support if there is resistance. Alternatively, a business school may have limited financial capital or faculty bandwidth to support a transformational approach. While they may not be transformational, these incremental approaches to RMLE have yielded many valuable pedagogical initiatives, including case studies (Steiner & Posch, 2006; Stubbs & Cocklin, 2007); projects, modules and activities (Roome, 2005; MacVaugh & Norton, 2011; Rodgers, 2015; Beitelspacher & Rodgers, 2018); and standalone courses (Kurland et al., 2010; Lester & Rodgers, 2012).

Rusinko (2010) introduces option three as a more significant pedagogical change. Here RMLE is integrated into core business courses. If done well, faculty from different disciplines work together to provide learning opportunities which expose all students to systems thinking towards responsible leadership. In comparing the teaching of ethics, social responsibility, and sustainability across the top 50 global MBA programs, Christensen and colleagues (2007) found that integration of these topics into core courses had the most lasting impact on student learning.

The fourth and most comprehensive option noted by Rusinko (2010) is the creation of new structures, such as programs or majors/minors that are transdisciplinary and are further supported by co-curricular offerings. This approach has been adopted by Arizona State University (ASU) and the University of Vermont (UVM), two business schools that have received awards for their commitment to sustainability. In ASU's Executive Masters of Sustainability Leadership program students learn to embed sustainability throughout their organizations by focusing on global context, strategy, communication and leadership (Wiek, Xiong, Brundiers & van der Leeuw, 2014; Business Fights Poverty, 2018). UVM created the Sustainable Entrepreneurship MBA Program (SEMBA), which 'represents a bold new venture where a major university has sought to fundamentally reinvent business education and the MBA degree to address the challenges we face in the 21st century – environment, ethics, entrepreneurship, poverty, and inequality' (Sharma & Hart, 2014: 14). The program aims to develop the next generation of leaders who will transform, disrupt, innovate and build sustainable business and enterprises in a world that demands it (University of Vermont, 2018). This program has recently been ranked by the Princeton Review as the '#1 Best Green MBA'. In both of these new programs, faculty have collaborated to develop exciting new curricula in which embedding sustainability is integrated across the entire curriculum (Sharma & Hart, 2014).

While both programs represent transformational pedagogical models of RMLE, they do not represent a comprehensive transformational approach for the entire business school. These programs, for all their progress and recognition, do not fundamentally shift learning, pedagogy and operations across the business school as a whole. Instead, changes focus on a subset of students and faculty in a particular program. Furthermore, these programs are not directed to research, co-curricular learning, or campus operations. A transformational approach would engage all these stakeholders, not just those associated with a particular program.

Transformational Models of Sustainability Education Beyond Business Schools

Without many exemplars of system-wide transformational approaches to RMLE in business schools, we focus our attention on other higher education institutions that have adopted transformational approaches to environmental sustainability education. To identify transformational models of sustainability education, we rely on ranking systems of university commitment to sustainability. Evaluating schools on environmental sustainability is difficult, due to the many dimensions of sustainability. Sustainability ranking systems tend to focus on institutional policies and practices, such as carbon footprint reduction, rather than curriculum. Keeping the above caveat in mind, as well as the limitations that come with all ranking systems, we look at three prominent ranking systems to identify trends of success in sustainability transformation, The Princeton Review Guide to Green Colleges, the AASHE STARS, and the Sierra Club Cool Schools.

The Princeton Review uses school-reported data and student opinion to rank the top 50 'Green Colleges' (Princeton Review, 2018). The Association for the Advancement of Sustainability in Higher Education (AASHE) created the Sustainability Tracking, Assessment & Rating System™ (STARS) in 2005 as a transparent, self-reporting framework for colleges and universities to measure their sustainability performance (Best Colleges, 2018). The Sierra Club has used its Cool School Rankings to assess colleges on environmental performance for the past 12 years (Sierra Club, 2018).

Although these three systems score slightly different aspects of sustainability, Colorado State University (CSU), Dickinson College and American University are the only schools ranked top 15 on all three lists (see Table 22.1). Interestingly, none of these universities was initially founded with a mission for sustainability. Therefore, their transformation stories are relevant to business school stakeholders who are interested in shifting an established business school towards a transformational approach to RMLE. Below, we briefly review key learnings from each of these universities.

CSU is a public research university located in Fort Collins, Colorado. Although CSU had been a leader in alternative energy research since the 1960s, the transformation toward environmental sustainability only emerged over the past two decades. As a land-grant university, CSU has relied on stewardship and conservation to embrace environmental sustainability in academics, research, operations and outreach (Rentsch, 2016). The university

Table 22.1 Top-ranked US colleges and universities based on three 2018 sustainability ranking systems

Ranking	Princeton Review	AASHE STARS	Sierra Cool Schools
#1	College of the Atlantic	**Colorado State University**	(Tied) Green Mountain College University of California, Irvine
#2	State University of New York College of Environmental Science and Forestry	Stanford University	University of New Hampshire
#3	University of Vermont	Sterling College	University of Connecticut
#4	**Dickinson College**	University of Connecticut	**Colorado State University**
#5	St Mary's College of Maryland	University of Washington	Arizona State University
#6	**Colorado State University**	Appalachian State University	**Dickinson College**
#7	Pitzer College	Green Mountain College	University of Massachusetts, Amherst
#8	Cornell University	Chatham University	Seattle University
#9	Randolph College	Colby College	California State University, Chico
#10	Stanford University	**American University**	Middlebury College
#11	University of California, Davis	**Dickinson College**	Sterling College
#12	Seattle University	University of California, Santa Barbara	**American University**
#13	Santa Clara University	Oregon State University	Santa Clara University
#14	**American University**	State University of New York College of Environmental Science and Forestry	Chatham University
#15	Goucher College	Middlebury College	Oregon State University

offers 962 credit courses with sustainability content and an additional 532 non-credit continuing education courses. In addition, sustainability-related research is conducted in more than 90% of the academic departments at CSU (Colorado State University, 2015). CSU is committed to a broad spectrum of operations initiatives, including alternative transportation options available to faculty, staff and students, an Energy Reserve Fund, which pays for energy efficient upgrades in buildings, and a number of innovative social, energy and outreach programs (Colorado State University, 2015). In 2015, CSU earned the first platinum rating ever awarded by STARS (Sustainability Tracking, Assessment and Rating System).

Dickinson College, a private, residential liberal arts college in Carlisle, Pennsylvania, represents a radically different educational context in which we see a transformational approach to environmental sustainability. Dickinson was founded on principles of active engagement. It is home to 'one of the only community studies centers in the US, where students can perform field research and take oral histories in local communities from different academic perspectives' (Dickinson College, 2019). In 2008, building off of its commitment to active engagement, the college founded its Center for Sustainability Education while also launching a comprehensive, institution-wide sustainability initiative. Students study Dickinson's LEED Gold buildings, solar arrays and energy efficiency, recycling and composting programs, and they collaborate with Campus Operations staff to analyze and recommend actions for reducing greenhouse gas emissions (Dickinson College, 2019). The college envisioned environmental sustainability would become a defining characteristic of a Dickinson education (Dickinson College, 2019). Neil Leary, Director of the Center for Sustainability Education, states that 'sustainability is part of the academic and co-curricular experience of every Dickinson student. It is also a guiding

principle for campus strategic planning and operations' (The Sentinel, 2018).

American University (AU), the third university that appears on all three rankings, is a private research university in Washington, DC, originally chartered by the US Congress in 1893. It is the first urban-based research university to reach carbon neutrality. This transformation toward environmental sustainability began in 2009 when they integrated sustainability into the university's overall strategic plan. The university created an Office of Sustainability and proposed a carbon action plan, which they completed two years earlier than planned (American University, 2019). AU presidents have demonstrated leadership in sustainability and 500+ faculty members have been certified through the Green Teaching Program which focuses on recognizing teachers who use green practices in the classroom. There are four interdisciplinary programs focused on sustainability (Environmental Science, Global Environmental Politics, Environmental Film-Making, and MS in Sustainability Management) and over 300 courses that include sustainability (American University, 2019). Across the entire curriculum, sustainability is central to pedagogy and student learning.

In comparing these three universities, we see a number of similarities that provide insight for developing a systems approach to transformational RMLE. First, in each institution, there was a university-wide strategic initiative focused on sustainability which included high-level administrative leadership, commitment and support. The process toward transformation in these schools may have initially been slow, but once an institutional commitment was made, collaborative efforts from motivated faculty fueled the creation of new sustainability initiatives and programs. Integration across different disciplines and pedagogical approaches resulted in new courses which were the basis for transformational learning opportunities. Finally, in each institution sustainability programs or centers were established that created integrated curricular and co-curricular learning opportunities. In summary, commitment, collaboration, and integrated learning were the foundation of these transformational approaches.

A SYSTEMS APPROACH TO TRANSFORMATIONAL RMLE

Shifting an established business school to a transformational approach to RMLE is not a simple, straightforward change. Organizational transformation encompasses a 'radical shift' in an organization's value system, culture and practices (Canterino, Cirela & Shani, 2018). One institutional logic is replaced with another (Rao, Monin & Durand, 2003) with institutional logic being a 'set of material practices and symbolic constructions that constitute a society's organizing principles', (Kurtmollaiev et al., 2018: 60). Shifting an established business school to be fully aligned with RMLE requires a fundamental shift in institutional logic.

For these reasons, we suggest a systems approach provides a holistic strategy for

supporting transformational RMLE. Relying on the insights from the prior section, we suggest a systems approach includes reimagining student learning, faculty pedagogy and scholarship, and how the institution operates internally and externally. We propose four processes that form the basis for this transformation. The first process, *integration*, centers on student learning. The second process, *collaboration*, concentrates on how faculty, staff and administrators work across the institution to support RMLE. The third process, *commitment and trust*, is the basis from which collaboration and integration emerge. The fourth process, *communication*, highlights how key stakeholders communicate their support for RMLE and collaborate to make change happen (see Figure 22.1). In proposing this systems-approach to transformational RMLE, we are suggesting transformational RMLE is not a static end-goal to be achieved. Rather it represents dynamic iteration and improvement as an institutional logic emerges and evolves which fundamentally embraces responsible pedagogy, scholarship and institutional operations.

Below, we discuss each of these four processes in more detail using examples from

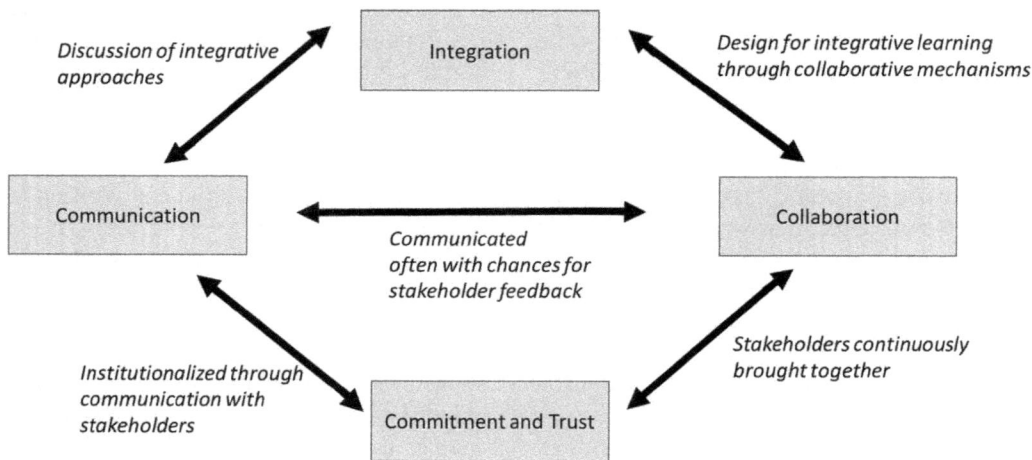

Figure 22.1   A systems approach to transformational responsible management learning and education

our own experiences at Babson College. As we noted in the introduction, we are not suggesting Babson is operating out of a transformational model of RMLE. More changes will need to be undertaken before these four processes are fully integrated into a systems model of transformational RMLE. Nonetheless, our experiences to date can provide examples other institutions can draw from as they pursue a systems approach to transformational RMLE.

Integration

For students, transformational RMLE involves developing an integrated systems thinking mindset to solve societal and business problems. With systems thinking students move beyond causal relationships to explore complex underlying structures and problems. Students learn how a system works as they explore the relationships between the structure of the system and the associated behaviors and feedbacks. A systems approach is especially effective for addressing social challenges and fostering meaningful and thoughtful insights into responsible leadership (Patel & Mehta, 2017).

For students to develop this systems thinking perspective, they have to engage in integrative learning opportunities across multiple dimensions. For example, at Babson, we offer students a sustainable course that is led by marketing faculty but also involves arts and humanities, science and organizational behavior faculty. This integrated approach teaches students to see multiple perspectives in product development and the consequences of decisions throughout the value chain. This dynamic perspective helps students reconsider the costs when delivering low price products or engaging in marketing campaigns which invoke stereotypes of customers. A pedagogy that is based in integration supports a more holistic approach to management in which students explore all dimensions of what it means to be human and

to understand how the individual fits *vis-à-vis* their community and the world (Palmer, Zajonc & Scribner, 2010). Below, we discuss further the different dimensions across which integration can occur.

Integrating across disciplinary standpoints

To teach students to see an organization as an integrated system, business schools have been moving beyond stand-alone required disciplinary courses to developing more integrated learning opportunities. Courses and curricula are being redesigned to integrate across core business disciplines. Yet, to develop a holistic understanding of responsible leadership, students also need to learn how the organization is linked to the wider social, economic and ecological systems of the world. To help students develop this type of systemic thinking, a transformational approach to RMLE needs to include opportunities to integrate across liberal arts, science and business. For example, when business students understand scientific principles and the environment, they can use this knowledge to critically think about the environmental impact of marketing, operational and financial decisions. Similarly, if students understand the social, political and historical issues of a particular context they can use this knowledge to make more responsible business decisions. Students learn to integrate critical thinking about ethical and social systems into their understanding of how to take responsible action.

We are not the first to draw attention to the benefits of a pedagogy that integrates across liberal arts, science and business. In 2011, the Carnegie Foundation suggested that to develop leaders who will engage responsibly in business and the world, students need to understand their place in the world as they develop the necessary skills and knowledge to take responsible action (Colby, Ehrlich, Sullivan & Dolle, 2011). Management students benefit from a holistic curriculum from which they can cultivate a pluralistic way of thinking and acting which is necessary in today's complex, rapidly changing world (Colby et al., 2011).

At Babson, we have tried to rely on the UN Sustainable Development Goals to provide an overarching umbrella from which to support this integrative learning. One such course is entitled Art and Ecology in the Anthropocene. This advanced elective for business students is co-developed and co-taught by an artist and an ecologist. The course specifically addresses SDGs #6 (clean water), #10 (reduced inequality), #13 (climate action), #14 (life below water) and #15 (life on land). The faculty do this by challenging students to focus on integrating visual art practices with scientific methodologies as a means of observing, understanding, interpreting and creatively responding to human-driven disturbances. Students engage art and science to investigate ecological integrity and social injustice by building from an understanding of the hydrosphere (water), lithosphere (soil), atmosphere (air) and biosphere (living organisms, including the role of humans within nature) to a large-scale, systems-approach of landscape understanding.

Another example of integrative learning can be found in the course Case Studies in Ecosystem Management. In this applied ecology course students perform primary research to analyze the socio-ecological impact of the life cycle of a product they select. Students use complex systems-thinking to synthesize their perspectives of impact for society, the environment and economics. They are also empowered to create positive change by working in the lab to change the design, packaging, or materials of their product to make them more sustainable (Rodgers, 2015). Within this project, students integrate their understanding of ecological integrity and responsible consumption and production, with creativity, innovation and design thinking.

Integrating critical thinking with critical action

To develop a holistic, systems-thinking approach that forms the basis of responsible leadership, students must also become comfortable operating in uncertain, even unknown situations. Given the interconnected, ever-changing relationship between society, an organization and the environment, it may not always be clear which data are best to use, how to gather that data, or even if data are available to make a decision and pursue an opportunity. In these situations, leaders must rely upon action, not just analysis, to cope with uncertainty and ambiguity as they make responsible business decisions and adjust accordingly (Greenberg, McKone-Sweet & Wilson, 2011).

Across all of Babson's undergraduate and graduate programs, a foundational principle of our curriculum is teaching students how to analyze and act their way into an opportunity. All students take a version of a course in which organizational behavior, design thinking and entrepreneurship principles are integrated as students learn to make decisions and pursue an opportunity in unknowable situations. Students learn how to analyze data to inform decisions as well as how to use action to make decisions when data are unavailable. We refer to this approach as *analyzing* and *acting* one's way into an opportunity. For instance, in our graduate program students combine analysis and action as they work through a year-long group project in which they identify an opportunity or problem to pursue and develop a prototype and business plan for a venture in this opportunity space. Many students will use this project as an entry point for starting their own ventures. A key learning objective in this course is to teach students how to consider the perspective of diverse stakeholders as they pursue an opportunity. Students are taught to analyze an opportunity from an economic, social, and environmental standpoint and how to assess competing priorities. This analysis process rarely yields a clear decision so students are also taught how to use action to explore multiple perspectives and priorities. Through these entrepreneurial projects, students develop a more nuanced understanding of responsible leadership. Teaching students to integrate thinking and acting supports the development of responsible leaders who have the capabilities, curiosity, and flexibility that is needed to cope with the uncertainty of 21st-century problems (Sunley & Coleman, 2016).

Collaboration

Integrated learning opportunities emerge when faculty, staff, administrators and other internal stakeholders move beyond their individual areas of responsibility and commit to working more collaboratively. Collaboration affects what occurs in the classroom, in the broader curriculum, in scholarship and in school operations. Here, we discuss the different forms of collaboration that are needed to support transformational RMLE.

Collaboration among faculty

In most universities, there are boundaries between management, general liberal arts and science faculty which creates boundaries in how we construct our pedagogy. While these boundaries support deep learning in a discipline, these boundaries also limit holistic, systems thinking which is the basis of responsible leadership. Transformational RMLE requires faculty to collaborate across these divides.

For instance, at Babson, a creative collaboration has emerged as entrepreneurship faculty partner with philosophy and ethics faculty. Entrepreneurship centers on the pursuit of new venture creation. Students and even faculty may initially assume that the pursuit of high growth opportunities conflicts with an emphasis on ethics and societal responsibility. To manage this tension, students are taught to evaluate a venture opportunity on the financial growth potential of the venture and on its ethical basis, particularly as it pertains to society and the environment. Philosophy faculty are invited to co-teach modules in the entrepreneurship course. By attending to the theoretical basis of each

discipline, faculty expand their understanding of RMLE and students learn the interconnected systems thinking which is necessary for responsible leadership.

Collaboration also means arts and sciences faculty value and actively engage management faculty as they consider the applied aspects of their discipline. For instance, in a Biomimicry (imitation of the models, systems, and elements of nature for the purpose of solving complex human problems) course, students are taught to integrate science with operations. In this course, students connect nature's principles to sustainable design, integrate ecology with supply chain management, and engage life cycle assessments to analyze the entire socio-ecological system. These learning modules are taught collaboratively by science and operations faculty. By collaborating across disciplinary lines, faculty integrate business, liberal arts and science to develop a pedagogy that develops responsible leaders who are attending to the environmental and social impact of organizational initiatives and innovation.

These pedagogical collaborations have also fueled scholarly collaborations. As faculty have uncovered the creativity and innovation that arises from these pedagogical collaborations, they have become passionate about sharing these insights with the wider academic community. Numerous cross-disciplinary teams are engaged in research and writing about RMLE and specifically about pedagogical innovations pertaining to RMLE (e.g. Beitelspacher & Rodgers, 2018; Greenberg et al., 2017; Lester & Rodgers, 2012). Beyond contributing to the college's reputation with regards to RMLE, this scholarship has led to new insights as we continue to pursue transformational RMLE.

Collaboration among faculty and staff

Collaboration also refers to how faculty and staff partner with regards to curriculum development and scholarship. Faculty have a tendency to focus primarily on student learning as it pertains to the classroom or activities that are associated with a course (i.e. service learnings, consulting projects). A more expansive notion of student learning embraces campus experiences and work and volunteer experiences as opportunities for learning. On residential campuses, co-curricular experiences are particularly important to student learning (Colby et al., 2011). Although higher education may have embraced the premise that learning occurs in and out of the classroom, there are rarely opportunities for students to connect what they learn across these two contexts.

To pursue transformational RMLE, faculty and staff need to collaborate across these spheres of learning. To do so requires faculty to look beyond their own classroom as they explore co-curricular opportunities that can connect to a course curriculum. On the other side, administrators and staff who are designing and overseeing co-curricular opportunities also need to connect with faculty to engage frameworks and concepts that are taught inside the classroom. In this way, students learn to seamlessly integrate the frameworks and theories from a management class to the organizational challenges and opportunities they are exploring outside of class. In so doing, students develop a fuller understanding of the complexity of engaging as a responsible leader.

At Babson College, in the Center for Faith and Community Service, a collaborative learning experience has been created by connecting community service to classroom learning. To enhance the learning experience of students who are interested in careers in community activism and community service, the center has created a fellowship program. Students apply to the program, which involves curricular and co-curricular experiences and culminates in a capstone senior project in which they lead a social change project. Leading up to this capstone project students participate in immersion service experiences and take a required course in community activism and engagement. The course is co-taught by a political science professor and the Faith and Service Director, an administrator. Other business school faculty are brought in as guest lectures. The course is linked to students' community work in such a way that students eventually will apply this learning as they pursue their independent social change projects, projects that could not be executed within the context of a traditional course. The collaboration between these two spheres enriches students' learning of responsible leadership in this context.

Collaboration among faculty, staff and operations

Finally, faculty and administrators can pursue collaborative opportunities between learning and scholarship and how the business school itself engages in responsible management practices. This is a school-wide approach in which curriculum and research are integrated with campus operations to create transformational RMLE (Mcmillin & Dyball, 2009). By explicitly aligning the core school functions with RMLE, the college is modeling for students a real-life case of how to practice responsible leadership. Business schools that are not integrating across campus operations, curriculum research and outreach are not modeling the responsible leadership they are attempting to teach, which can result in a lack of trust and confidence in leadership's commitment to RMLE (McMillian & Dyball, 2009). When RMLE is supported by collaborative endeavors among these stakeholders, it becomes more deeply institutionalized across the business school. Once institutionalized, it is less likely that faculty and staff turnover will threaten practices, and more difficult for resisters to block continued progress.

At Babson College, faculty and staff have collaborated with campus operations to improve the university's commitment to responsible leadership and to provide students with unique learning experiences. For instance, in a foundational science course students design a renewable energy system to replace the energy demands of a campus dorm which currently runs on the traditional electrical grid. Students obtain energy use data from the facilities department and evaluate different renewable energies. They present their findings to the campus facilities department as proposals that include financial analysis and tradeoffs of implementation (Winrich, Rodgers, MacLean, Blodgett & Schaefer, 2015). In an operations course, students work with the sustainability office to explore new strategies to improve upon the college's food waste, grounds maintenance, and water usage and waste. Students use design thinking and operations management principles to develop innovative solutions that could improve the college's ESG goals. The sustainability office partners with students by providing access to information and data and offering feedback on student's final presentations. Beyond supporting student learning, both of these courses have resulted in new initiatives that are being further integrated into the university's operations. Over the years some of the campus changes include early adoption of tray-less dining and hydration stations, surplus food donations, and 'slash-the-trash' programs during student move out. In this way, students learn that responsible leadership informs and is informed by campus operations.

Trust and Commitment

Trust and commitment refer to the culture that is necessary to support the integrative learning and collaboration that was discussed in the prior sections. To define trust and collaboration in this context, we draw on work from Morgan and Hunt (1994), who contend that trust and commitment are the basis for any collaborative relationships. Trust is the belief in an exchange partner's 'reliability and integrity, credibility and benevolence, and word that an obligation will be fulfilled' (Lambe, Spekman & Hunt, 2000: 217). When trust exists between individuals and in

the wider organizational system, individuals can be confident that other organizational members can be relied upon to move the organization forward (Morgan & Hunt, 1994). Trust then supports relational commitment, which means when individuals have confidence that in spite of occasional conflicts and challenges a relationship is worth continuous effort and will endure (Morgan & Hunt, 1994). Relationship commitment is essential to the long-term collaboration that is needed to support transformational RMLE.

A systems approach to transformational RMLE requires internal and external business school stakeholders to work through complex, competing ideas. Individuals will have diverse perspectives on what a transformational approach to RMLE is and how best to pursue it. We see these differing perspectives as essential to developing a shared commitment to a transformational approach. By bridging these differences, a business school can build its own systems approach to RMLE, which will be transformational for all stakeholders.

At Babson, the trust and commitment that exists among faculty have been essential to supporting transformational RMLE. Within the college, there is a history of faculty from different disciplines working collaboratively on research, curriculum redesign and strategic committees. This history has helped create a foundation of trust and commitment that we have built upon as we pursue our own transformational approach to RMLE. For instance, when an interdisciplinary committee of faculty from business, liberal arts and sciences was assembled to create a more transformational approach to RMLE, it helped that the committee members already had a basis of trust and commitment from which to work. This trust and commitment made it easier to debate the radically different views committee members held about the vision of transformational RMLE for the college, how to take action to move towards this vision, and even details about how the current pedagogy and student context would need to shift. Trust and commitment enabled the committee to reconcile their differences.

This foundation of trust and commitment has also been essential to how the committee engaged with the broader faculty. As individuals challenge the recommendations of the committee and introduce alternative perspectives, their ideas are not taken as a criticism of the committee. The faculty trust the committee and are committed to their colleagues and the direction that is being set. This trust enables these debates to be intellectual and not relational.

While there is trust among the faculty, a challenge we have faced at Babson is building the same trust and commitment among the diverse organizational stakeholders. Because our approach to RMLE grew organically, different internal stakeholders are engaged with their own unique activities related to responsible leadership (Greenberg et al., 2017). For instance, the college has two different centers whose activities support responsible leadership in different ways. These centers are not always aligned and supportive of one another. The administrators who oversee these centers are not always willing to collaborate with faculty to develop a shared commitment to a transformational model of RMLE as they have been successful at pursuing their own agendas. When stakeholders are not willing to put aside their individual interests to focus on the collective, higher goals it is difficult to form the trust and commitment needed to support a transformational approach to RMLE.

Similarly, trust and commitment between faculty and administrators have also challenged Babson's ability to pursue a transformational approach to RMLE. The administration verbally supports RMLE and has shown its commitment to RMLE through the college's formal vision. Yet, administrators have not always made the financial investment needed to elevate the college's pursuit of a transformational approach to RMLE. This has led to breakdowns in the trust and commitment between the faculty and the administration. As Babson commits to its next iteration of RMLE and to pursuing a more transformational approach, trust and commitment will need to be repaired along these fault lines.

Communication

The final process of a systems approach to transformational RMLE is communication. Communication refers to both the communication between individual members of the community as well as how the institution communicates and messages its strategy and branding. High-quality communication enables trust and collaboration to form while also creating strong integrative learning experiences and collaborative partnerships. Communication quality refers to the 'accuracy, timeliness, adequacy, and credibility of information exchanged' (Mohr & Spekman, 1994: 138). Accuracy is the extent to which communication is factual. Timeliness and adequacy refer to the frequency of communication and the robustness of the information being communicated. Communication quality falters if it is too frequent or not frequent enough or if it is over- or under-detailed. Finally, the source and content of the information also need to be credible. Determining appropriate communication quality requires finesse and careful planning.

Communication is critical to embarking on transformational RMLE as it is the basis for integration, collaboration, and communication and trust. For collaboration and integration to exist, there needs to be strong, open lines of communication among administration, faculty, students, staff and external stakeholders. All parties involved have to feel their voices are heard and they are receiving the information they need to support the transformation. Communication improves the sharing of information which drives individual and collaborative initiatives that support transformational RMLE.

As Babson moves toward a transformational approach to RMLE, we are focused on increasing communication quality in all directions in order to support trust, commitment and collaboration. An important starting point of quality communication has been developing shared language regarding responsible leadership. In the past, Babson had a cumbersome acronym, SEERS (social, environmental, economic, responsibility and sustainability), to reference our own brand of responsible leadership. The cumbersome acronym was accompanied by a long definition. Faculty, staff and students struggled to define and use the concept, which kept it from being widely integrated into students' learning. Students were exposed to different language and models of responsible management depending on the class they took or the co-curricular experience in which they were engaged. This prevented students from forming an integrated, systems thinking perspective. The term was even less understood and adopted when engaging with external stakeholders. Faculty rarely connected their scholarship to the SEERS construct. Our lack of quality communication became a stumbling block to a transformational approach to RMLE.

As we now envision our next iteration of RMLE, which we aspire to be more transformational, we have revised the language we use to communicate responsible leadership. We are using the construct, Integrated Sustainability, to frame how we discuss systems thinking and business decisions related to complex social and environmental challenges. For faculty, we are holding regular informal workshops to discuss integrated sustainability-related topics around scholarship and teaching. This language is already being engaged to drive curriculum development and curriculum strategy. Faculty have presented this construct to college marketing and to the trustees so that they will begin engaging with it as they communicate the college's commitment to transformational RMLE. In so doing, the new language has the potential to better a systems approach to transformational RMLE.

CONCLUSION

In this chapter, we develop a systems approach to transformational RMLE as we identify the processes needed to integrate RMLE into an established business school. Transformational RMLE is an evolving, dynamic process that emerges when commitment to RMLE comes from and is apparent to all stakeholders and when RMLE is fully integrated into the business school's entire systems, including curriculum, co-curricular activities, research and university operations. With this definition, transformational RMLE is a continuing process. As the world of higher education changes rapidly and the landscape of business shifts with respect to ethics, the environment and social responsibility, transformational RMLE must also be able to adapt and evolve.

The four processes we have described form the basis for this evolving dynamic viewpoint of transformational RMLE. Commitment and trust lay the foundation for understanding the importance of RMLE across the organization. This commitment becomes institutionalized through communication and collaboration among all stakeholders. To be effective communication needs to be high quality with opportunities for feedback, which further builds trust and innovative new ideas. In order to sustain transformational RMLE, the goal must be ongoing improvement and redesign of the systems that constitute the college.

REFERENCES

American University. (2019). Sustainability. www.american.edu/about/sustainability.

Beckhard, R. (2006). What is organization development? In Gallos, J. V. (Ed.), *Organization development* (pp. 3–12). San Francisco, CA: Jossey-Bass.

Beitelspacher, L., & Rodgers, V.L. (2018). Integrating corporate social responsibility awareness into a retail management course.

Journal of Marketing Education, *40*(1), 66–75.

Best Colleges. (2018). Greenest universities. www.bestcolleges.com/features/greenest-universities.

Burchell, J., Kennedy, S., & Murray, A. (2015). Responsible management education in UK business schools: critically examining the role of the United Nations Principles for Responsible Management Education as a driver for change. *Management Learning*, *46*(4), 479–497.

Business Fights Poverty. (2018). The role of business in education and training for sustainable development. https://businessfightspoverty.org/articles/the-role-of-business-in-eduction-for-sustainable-development.

Canterino, F., Cirela, S., & Shani, A. B. (2018). Leading organizational transformation: an action research study. *Journal of Managerial Psychology*, *33*(1), 15–28.

Christensen, L. J., Peirce, E., Hartman, L. P., Hoffman, W. M., & Carrier, J. (2007). Ethics, CSR, and sustainability education in the Financial Times Top 50 Global Business Schools: baseline data and future research directions. *Journal of Business Ethics*, *73*, 347–368.

Colby, A., Ehrlich, T., Sullivan, W. M., & Dolle, J. R. (2011). *Rethinking undergraduate business education: liberal learning for the profession*. San Francisco, CA: Jossey-Bass.

Colorado State University. (2015). CSU named nation's most sustainable university. https://source.colostate.edu/colorado-state-university-named-nations-most-sustainable-university.

Dickinson College. (2019). History of the college. www.dickinson.edu/info/20048/history_of_the_college/1404/the_dickinson_story.

Finlay, J., & Massey, J. (2012). Eco-campus: applying the ecocity model to develop green university and college campuses. *International Journal of Sustainability in Higher Education*, *13*(2), 150–165.

Greenberg, D. N., Deets, S., Erzurumlu, S., Hunt, J., Manwaring, M., Rodgers, V., & Swanson, E. (2017). Signing to living PRME: learning from a journey towards responsible management education. *International Journal of Management Education*, *15*(2), 205–218.

Greenberg, D., McKone-Sweet, K., & Wilson, H. J. (2011). *The new entrepreneurial leader: developing leaders who shape social and economic opportunity*. San Francisco, CA: Berrett-Koehler.

Kurland, N. B., Michaud, K. E. H., Best, M., Wohldmann, E., Cox, H., Pontikis, K., & Vasishth, A. (2010). Overcoming silos: the role of an interdisciplinary course in shaping a sustainability network. *Academy of Management Learning & Education*, *9*(3), 457–476.

Kurtmollaiev, S., Fjuk, A., Pedersen, P. E., Clatworthy, S., & Kvale, K. (2018). Organizational transformation through service design: the institutional logics perspective. *Journal of Service Research*, *21*(1), 59–74.

Lambe, C., Spekman, R. E., & Hunt, S. D. (2000). Interimistic relational exchange: conceptualization and propositional development. *Journal of the Academy of Marketing Science*, *28*(2), 212–226.

Lester, T., & Rodgers, V. L. (2012). Teaching a cross disciplinary environmental science, policy and culture course on Costa Rica's ecotourism to business students. *Journal of Environmental Studies and Sciences*, *2*(3), 234–238.

Lowrie, A., & Willmott, H. (2009). Accreditation sickness in the consumption of business education: the vacuum in AACSB standard setting. *Management Learning*, *40*(4), 411–420.

MacVaugh, J., & Norton, M. (2011). Introducing sustainability into business education contexts using active learning. *Higher Education Policy*, *24*(4), 439–457.

Mcmillin, J., & Dyball, R. (2009). Developing a whole-of-university approach to educating for sustainability: linking curriculum, research and sustainable campus operations. *Journal of Education for Sustainable Development*, *3*(1), 55–64.

Mohr, J. & Spekman, R. (1994). Characteristics of partnership success: partnership attributes, communication behavior, and conflict resolution techniques. *Strategic Management Journal*, *15*(2), 135–152.

Morgan, R. M., & Hunt, S. D. (1994). The commitment–trust theory of relationship marketing. *Journal of Marketing*, *58*(3), 20–38.

Painter-Morland, M., Sabet, E., Molthan-Hill, P., Goworek, H., & de Leeuw, S. (2016). Beyond the curriculum: integrating sustainability into business schools. *Journal of Business Ethics*, *139*(4), 737–754.

Palmer, P. J., Zajonc, A., & Scribner, M. (2010). *The heart of higher education: a call to renewal*. San Francisco, CA: John Wiley & Sons.

Patel, S., & Mehta, K. (2017). Systems, design, and entrepreneurial thinking: comparative frameworks. *Systemic Practice and Action Research*, *30*(5), 515–533.

Princeton Review. (2018). Top 50 green colleges. www.princetonreview.comcollege-rankings?rankings=top-50-green-colleges.

Rao, H., Monin, P., & Durand, R. (2003). Institutional change in Toque Ville: nouvelle cuisine as identity movement in French gastronomy. *American Journal of Sociology*, *108*(4), 795–843.

Rasche, A., & Gilbert, D. U. (2015). Decoupling responsible management education: why business schools may not walk their talk. *Journal of Management Inquiry*, *24*(3), 239–252.

Rentsch, J. (2016). A brief history of sustainability initiatives at Colorado State. https://collegian.com/2016/04/a-history-of-sustainability-initiatives-at-colorado-state.

Rodgers, V. L. (2015). A SEERS approach to analyzing impact: using an ecology research project to evaluate product life cycle sustainability. In Crittenden, V. L., Esper, K., Karst, N., & Slegers, R. (Eds.), *Evolving entrepreneurial education: innovation in the Babson classroom* (pp. 399–410). Bingley: Emerald Publishing.

Roome, N. (2005). Teaching sustainability in a global MBA: insights from the OneMBA. *Business Strategy and the Environment*, *14*(3), 160–171.

Rusinko, C. A. (2010). Integrating sustainability in management and business education: a matrix approach. *Academy of Management Learning & Education*, *9*(3), 507–519.

Sharma, S., & Hart, S. L. (2014). Beyond 'saddle bag' sustainability for business education. *Organization & Environment*, *27*(1), 10–15.

Sierra Club. (2018). The top 20 coolest schools 2018. www.sierraclub.org/sierra/cool-schools-2018/top-20-coolest-schools-2018.

Solitander, N., Fougere, M., Sobczak, A., & Herlin, H. (2012). We are the champions: organizational learning and change for responsible management education. *Journal of Management Education*, *36*(3), 337–363.

Steiner, G., & Posch, A. (2006). Higher education for sustainability by means of transdisciplinary case studies: an innovative approach for solving complex, real-world problems. *Journal of Cleaner Production*, *14*, 877–890.

Stubbs, W., & Cocklin, C. (2007). Teaching sustainability to business students: shifting mindsets. *International Journal of Sustainability in Higher Education*, *9*(3), 206–221.

Sunley, R., & Coleman, M. (2016). Establishing a foundational responsible learning mind-set for business in the 21st century. In Sunley, R., & Leigh, J. (Eds.), *Educating for responsible management: putting theory into practice* (pp. 28–51). Sheffield: Greenleaf Publishing.

The Sentinel. (2018). Dickinson College ranked first in sustainability. https://cumberlink.com/news/local/communities/carlisle/dickinson-college-ranked-first-in-sustainability/article_d2c8b28a-8bde-5ea3-a743-2fb16af824b9.html.

University of Vermont. (2018). The Sustainable Innovation MBA. www.uvm.edu/sites/default/files/media/SI-MBA_eBook.PDF.

Visser, W. (2016). Foreword. In Sunley, R., & Leigh, J. (Eds.), *Educating for responsible management: putting theory into practice* (pp. vii–x). Sheffield: Greenleaf Publishing.

Wiek, A., Xiong, A., Brundiers, K., & van der Leeuw, S. (2014). Integrating problem-and project-based learning into sustainability programs: a case study on the School of Sustainability at Arizona State University. *International Journal of Sustainability in Higher Education*, *15*(4), 431–449.

Winrich, C., Rodgers, V. L., MacLean, M. G., Blodgett, D., & Schaefer, J. (2015). Science education as entrepreneurial thought and action methodology. In Crittenden, V., Karst, N., Slegers, R., & Esper, K. (Eds.), *Evolving entrepreneurial education: innovation in the Babson classroom*. New York, NY: Emerald Publishing.

23

Enhancing Responsible Management Education: Facilitating Faculty Development and Engagement

Anthony F. Buono

INTRODUCTION

Business schools are being increasingly challenged to instill a more conscious approach to business practice, ensuring that sustainability, social responsibility and ethics are reflected across the curriculum, ingrained in faculty research and embedded in their operational practices. As part of a responsible approach to management education, greater attention is being placed on a 'beyond the bottom line' orientation, a stakeholder-oriented mindset reframing the role of business as an integral part of the larger society as an agent of social change (e.g. Buono, 2018; Buono & Nichols, 2005). In essence, rather than defining success solely in terms of profit and economic prowess (e.g. Collins, 2001), profitability is being increasingly linked to those success factors that resonate with key stakeholders and the firm's broader social connectedness (see, for example, Mackey & Sisodia, 2013; Purnell & Freeman, 2012).

As a driving force underlying the need to refocus organizational strategy and policy decisions and practices, the UN Global Compact's (UNGC) Principles for Responsible Business and the subsequent Sustainable Development Goals (SDGs) raise a number of challenges for educating the next generation of business leaders and professionals – especially in terms of faculty development, curriculum innovation and institutional practice (e.g. Fort, 2016; Hockerts, Borgbo, Srkoc, Goldberg & Chaudry, 2015; Shrivastava, 2010). Drawing on a case example of a long-time signatory of the UNGC's Principles for Responsible Management Education (PRME), the chapter explores the implications for how we think about ways to enrich responsible management education (RME): (1) enhancing individual learning as a foundation for organizational learning and (2) envisioning new ways of approaching RME in practice. The focus of the chapter is on two key aspects of this challenge: (1) developing faculty expertise and comfort level in areas that traditionally have not been part of their discipline and (2) creating integrative structures that bring together the myriad individual, departmental and institution-wide perspectives, initiatives and endeavors that typically exist in varied forms on college and university campuses.

It is clear, of course, that an approach that works well in one context might not necessarily be as effective or even applicable in a different context – a reality that underscores the fallacy of simplistic notions of transferring 'best practice' from one setting to another (Newell, 2005). As a study of conceptions of responsible management education across different European business schools indicates, the interpretation and implementation of RME practices range from thinking through needed changes to our current economic paradigms and developing a more robust sense of corporate citizenship, to an emphasis on sustainability and a focus on the triple bottom line, to attempts to make students more mindful within a virtue ethics and values-based notion of appropriate managerial decisions and organizational practices (Nonet, Kassel & Meijs, 2016). Thus, largely out of respect for such varied perspectives and contextual differences in institutional norms and practices across its global signatories, the UN PRME initiative has stopped short of offering specific guidelines for how such development might be accomplished (Rasche, Gilbert & Schedel, 2013; Waddock, Rasche, Werhane & Unruh, 2010). Yet, even within such realistic constraints there are broad lessons that can be gleaned from different endeavors that draw on a multi-level approach to responsible management education (Setó-Pamies & Papaoikonomou, 2016) that can be adapted to fit the context, culture and practices of different business schools.

RME AS A HOLISTIC CHALLENGE

The UN PRME emphasizes the need for a holistic approach to responsible management education (e.g. Forray & Leigh, 2012; Kell & Haertle, 2011), drawing on collective actions and collaborative activities that cut across traditional boundaries (Haertle, Parkes, Murray & Hayes, 2017). In essence, if a responsible management mindset is to be instilled in the next generation of business professionals our efforts must go beyond siloed, piecemeal approaches – no matter how well intentioned and thought out they may be. While dedicated courses across the curriculum are clearly an important part of responsible management education, the need to look beyond individual courses as well as the classroom itself should be just as obvious. As Blasco (2012) has argued, the myriad signals that students are given about appropriate conduct – communicated in many subtle ways across our campuses – go well beyond formal curricular content. These inherent dimensions of the education process – codes of conduct and honor codes, socialization routines and extracurricular activities, testing and assessment procedures, faculty comments and behaviors in and out of the classroom, the use of different pedagogical approaches – significantly influence student values, attitudes and behaviors (Blasco, 2012; Gair & Mullins, 2001; Setó-Pamies & Papaoikonomou, 2016; Trevino & McCabe, 1994). Reflecting Argyris and Schön's (1978) distinction between espoused values (what people say they do) and 'theory-in-use' (i.e., enacted values that reflect what they actually do), the notion of the 'hidden curriculum' differentiates the 'curriculum as designed and curriculum in action' (Barnett & Coate, 2005: 3; Blasco, 2012; Buono, 2018).

There are, of course, myriad ways in which curricula and school-specific practices can be recast, enhanced and extended, ensuring a greater diversity of thought throughout the educational process. Such innovations can range from developing a more nuanced understanding of the history and development of management thought (Cummings & Bridgman, 2016) and incorporating novels in reading assignments as a way of creating empathy and notions of the 'good life' (Michaelson, 2016), to integrating poverty-related issues and challenges (Neal, 2017) and innovative approaches to sustainability (Aragon-Correa et al., 2017) across the curriculum, to drawing on multidisciplinary pedagogical approaches and experiential learning (Cajiao & Burke, 2016; Setó-Pamies & Papaoikonomou, 2016; Tyran, 2017), among others. The underlying key appears to be the extent to which such initiatives cut across the institution, leading to true systemic integration (see Painter-Morland et al., 2016) – in ways that fit the unique nature of individual business schools, supporting adoption, adaptation and application rather than a decoupling of practice from RME rhetoric (see, for example, Rasche & Gilbert, 2015). As research has indicated, while many business schools have added a broad array of courses on ethics, corporate responsibility, and sustainability in their curricula, the majority of these courses are electives that are disconnected from core business disciplines (e.g. accounting, finance, operations) and institutional practices (Rasche, Gilbert & Schedel, 2013; Solitander, Fougère, Sobczak & Herlin, 2012; Sterling, 2004).

The UNGC PRME principles reflect this challenge, capturing the essence of responsible management education in terms of the: underlying *purpose* (Principle 1) and (2) *values* (Principle 2) of our business schools (to develop the capabilities of our students to be future generators of sustainable value in the context of global social responsibility); *methods and educational frameworks* (Principle 3) we use to create effective learning experiences; *research* (Principle 4) that provides insight into the role of business in creating sustainable social, economic, and environmental value; and *partnerships* (Principle 5) that we develop and *dialogue* (Principle 6) we engage in around these issues, also ensuring that our own institutional practices reflect the values and mindsets we convey to our students.

The chapter will examine two approaches to this holistic challenge, focusing on a developmental approach to enhancing RME-expertise among faculty members and creating an integrative structure that can facilitate collaborative activities across traditional institutional boundaries.

Enhancing Faculty Development: Creating RME 'Gadflies'

Many, if not most, business schools have informal RME-oriented initiatives on their campuses, from ongoing conversations among interested faculty and occasional workshops on related topics, to guest lectures and school-wide programs that address issues of ethics, responsibility and sustainability. Research suggests, however, that most of these efforts are not directly focused on faculty development and even for those that are roughly only one-third of faculty at a given school participate in these activities. Moreover, the majority of these participants teach dedicated courses in the RME realm, such as business ethics, environmental management and corporate social responsibility (Hockerts et al., 2015). For the most part, faculty development in these areas is left to the discretion and commitment of individual professors – which presents a significant challenge, especially since most faculty are less and less comfortable when they extend themselves beyond their discipline-based expertise.

Responsible management education, however, requires reinforcement and guided reflection on its underlying principles (Prandi, Martell & Lozano, 2018) across the curriculum. The challenge is to formalize a process of developing faculty capabilities in this area in ways that do not impinge on academic freedom and meet the needs of different institutions while providing opportunities for a broad range of faculty to engage in the learning processes that identify RME and make it possible. This need is increasingly recognized across the globe, with ample material to enhance the RME process. As an example, the Central and Eastern European Management Association's (CEEMAN) International Management Teacher Academy (IMTA) focuses on enhancing case teaching and experiential learning activities in the context of RM practice. Copenhagen Business School has an assistant professor program that helps develop pedagogical skills that enhance student learning and instructor competence in the classroom. The Shumacher Institute in the United Kingdom, an independent think-tank focused on environmental, social and economic issues and the sustainability of complex systems, provides resources that support systems learning aimed to 'free [people] from the existing limitations of business as usual'[1]. The Global Reporting Initiative (www.globalreporting.org) provides significant resources on sustainability reporting. Case Western University's Fowler Center for Business as a World Benefit emphasizes ways to create value for society and the environment in ways that create even more value for stakeholders.[2] In essence, there are myriad opportunities for faculty to draw on materials and build partnerships – core principles of the UNGC PRME – that frame key aspects of the RME process.

Another such approach, which has been in place for over 25 years at Bentley University, a US business school, is the 'Gadfly Project'. The intent of the initiative is to encourage faculty to address ethical issues and questions of RME in their discipline-based courses across the curriculum. The program name dates back to Socrates, who described himself as a 'gadfly', a stinging insect whose purpose was to harass and 'sting' the citizens of Athens out of their ignorance and intellectual complacency. By 'seeding' each academic department with such gadflies, the goal was to develop a core group of faculty across the institution who would 'light the path' for their colleagues (see Solitander et al., 2012)– developing and sharing their own discipline-based materials, prodding and influencing

others to incorporate informed discussions of ethical issues and responsible management in their courses.

The general format of the workshop, which takes place over a week-long time-frame, engages a cross-departmental group of faculty to explore ways of integrating ethical issues into their disciplinary courses. The workshop is designed to accomplish this goal through: (1) facilitated discussions among faculty from several different disciplines intended to provide them with a basic grounding in ethical theory and corporate responsibility; and (2) presentations by the faculty participants on integrating ethics into their courses, with the opportunity for feedback from the workshop facilitators and other participants. Initially supported solely by the institution, the program has received corporate support over the past decade that funds visiting scholars from other colleges and universities around the world to come together to explore these issues. Reflecting on the impact of the program, a senior executive from the sponsoring company noted, 'We are committed to supporting this program because good behavior needs to be modeled and encouraged; we know all too well what happens when values are ignored' (Buono, 2018: 139).

The basic objective of the Gadfly workshop is to assist faculty to feel more comfortable with ethics and RME concepts, analysis, and application – placed in the context of their own discipline – so that they are better able to work with students in raising their ethical awareness and ability to make rational, responsible choices. In the workshop and accompanying readings and materials, an attempt is made to balance exposure to ethical theory and frameworks with hands-on practice in analyzing cases and other teaching materials (such as films, simulations, role plays, and service-learning) from an ethical as well as discipline-based perspective. The mix of faculty from different departments, disciplines and institutions – sharing their ideas, experiences and concerns about these important issues – further contributes to a rewarding, developmental experience.

By focusing on pedagogical tactics and approaches to incorporating ethical and RME issues, the teaching workshop has stimulated a greater comfort level across the faculty. Over time, our experience suggests that faculty become increasingly skilled at engaging students in in-depth discussions of ethical and RME-related issues, going beyond planned activities (cases, exercises, videos) to drawing on student work-related experiences and issues that emerge 'in the moment'. As illustrated in Figure 23.1, a basic objective is to broaden the ways in which faculty think about drawing discussions of ethics and responsible behavior into their discipline-based courses. Although stand-alone courses are important and can provide in-depth coverage of RME-related issues, there are clear limits as to what any individual course can accomplish in this realm. The key is to ensure that the underlying message and mindset are infused across the curriculum, drawing on an interdisciplinary approach to better understand the complex challenges we are facing (see Annan-Diab & Molinari, 2017). While there are differences of opinion as to the most

appropriate pedagogical approaches and curricular activities, especially across different disciplines (e.g. Roome, 2005), as Figure 23.1 suggests an important goal is to ensure broad coverage across curricula in ways that play to the strengths of individual courses and instructors. As examples, philosophy courses can include a focus on ethical theory, management courses can draw on case studies and simulations about responsible management challenges, accounting courses can explore the ethical responsibilities of auditors, finance courses can examine the ethics of backdating stock options and the role of micro-financing in facilitating social change, and so forth. The key is to draw these issues into different courses as appropriate to their focus and content.

As faculty become more comfortable with these issues, we have found that they are increasingly comfortable engaging in 'teachable moments', drawing on emergent discussions of RME-related issues 'in the moment' focused on student experience, as suggested by Mintzberg's (2004) notion of 'experienced reflection' and Gentile's (2012) 'giving voice to values.' Infusing RME across the curriculum can also include experiential

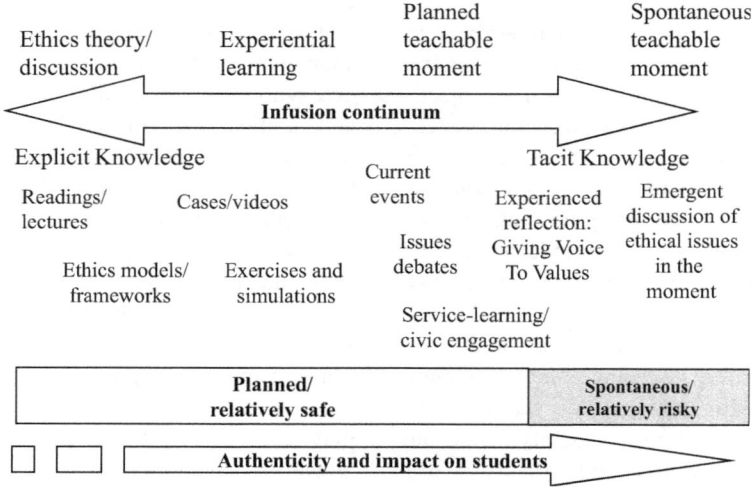

Figure 23.1   Business ethics pedagogical infusion: the 'gadfly' approach across the curriculum (Buono, 2018)

learning and immersion techniques such as service-learning and community engagement, which can readily be integrated into a wide range of business and also arts and sciences courses (see, for example, Christensen et al., 2007; Salimbene, Buono, LaFarge & Nurick, 2005). These latter techniques tend to have a greater impact on student learning in terms of their perceived authenticity, although they do bear increased risk as the experience itself is less controllable than traditional classroom pedagogies. Students begin to realize the impact they have on others, prompting them to reflect on how they are relating and responding to them. This process can be facilitated through focused self-reflection, examining relationships for which they want to be responsible. By experimenting and taking responsibility for their actions and their outcomes, research suggests that students begin to develop a foundation for their own approach to responsible management decisions and actions (see Eriksen & Cooper, 2018).

An underlying challenge is to prompt students to truly reflect on their experience as it relates to the nature and substance of responsible management in practice. Students need to understand their responsibility for developing the skills needed to create their own knowledge, developing their own points of view rather than simply repeating what they hear in the classroom. If we are to create a responsible management mindset in the next generation of business professionals, it is critical to enhance the learning process – helping students reflect on and learn from their immediate experience, connecting theory to practice, and creating life-long learners who are knowledgeable about how to gain insights from future experiences (Wagenheim, 2019).

One way to facilitate this process is through focused debriefing, using a series of open-ended questions presented in a sequential manner paralleling the way the human mind absorbs and processes new information – going from observation (e.g. 'What did you see?') and reflection ('What did you feel?'), to interpretation ('What insights did you gain?') and decision-making ('What will you do?'). The main goal of this focused discussion method is to help individuals and groups come to a deeper understanding of the subject they are studying and direct their thinking toward making a decision (Buono, 2019; Wagenheim, 2019).

While the specific format and nature of the Gadfly Workshop may not be appropriate for all business schools and institutions of higher learning, drawing on these general approaches which have been referred to as 'second-best solutions' that fit the reality and resources of different institutions (Cotton, Bailey, Warren & Bissell, 2009) may be the most appropriate course of action. An underlying goal is to encourage faculty to reflect on what they are teaching (RME content) and just as importantly how they are teaching it (RME pedagogy). It is becoming clear that given the growing importance of RME and the complex nature of its multidisciplinary content, some type of formalized structure and process to support faculty development in this area is clearly needed (see Setó-Pamies & Papaoikonomou, 2016).

Building an Institution-wide RME Network

Given the multidisciplinary reality of responsible management, efforts to enhance faculty expertise in the RME arena reflect only one component – albeit an important one – of a much larger challenge. As a number of observers argue, we must move beyond mere modifications to our pedagogy and curricula to include greater attention to research, campus operations, and the ways in which our institutions engage with their stakeholders (cf. Beddewela, Warin, Hesselden & Coslet, 2017; Haski-Leventhall, Pournader, McKinnon, 2017; Rasche & Gilbert, 2015) – in essence, reflecting the full range of the PRME principles discussed earlier.

Most schools of business, of course, have a number of successful, co-curricular initiatives in the RME realm, focusing on ethics, responsibility and sustainability. These efforts are often started by dedicated faculty and administrators, described as *internal* RME champions (Solitander et al., 2012), who engage their teaching, research and institutional service to push for change (much like the ethical 'gadflies' discussed earlier), attempting to balance individual preferences for responsible management education with institutional priorities. Yet, while these efforts typically have a positive effect on parts of the institution, a limiting factor is that they are often isolated and disconnected from each other. This reality has been described as a 'saddle bag' approach, where the RME focus is compartmentalized into isolated, albeit visible, courses and/or programs in parts of an institution (Sharma & Hart, 2014).

The challenge is to build on these existing initiatives within the broader institutional context – cultural, political, economic – of different colleges and universities in ways that support RME (Wersun, 2017), encouraging greater collaboration and integration on an institution-wide basis. In essence, the task is to create linkages across these programs and initiatives in ways that seek out synergies while preserving the independent nature of the various efforts. Emphasis can be placed on amplifying and extending these initiatives, supporting and encouraging greater awareness of, respect for and commitment to RME in faculty research, campus culture, stakeholder engagement and institutional practices. The overall effectiveness of such networks, of course, is dependent on the commitment of a broad range of internal and external stakeholders, including faculty, staff, students and alumni, as well as business executives, corporate and community partners, and relevant associations in an effort to enhance and disseminate responsible management education across the institution.

The initial challenge in our business schools – as with any cross-institutional initiative – is

to seek out and build on the dedication, commitment and creativity of individuals – the RME champions – throughout the organization. While there are a number of ways to approach this challenge, a starting point is bringing together those faculty who are already committed to these ideas, in essence 'preaching to the choir' through 'management by *talking* around' (Buono, 2012). Given the different types of barriers and enablers that exist across university campuses (see Wersun, 2017), emphasis should be placed on leveraging such institutional strengths, drawing on social capital, and creating 'small wins' (see Weick, 1984) as a way of building communities of practice. Others have conceptualized this process as setting the scene for RME, integrating and embedding RME principles and practices across the institution, and empowering an RME community through the creation of an enabling environment (Weybrecht, 2017).

Management by 'talking around'

A starting point for creating an institutional network of like-minded, RME-oriented faculty can be thought of as *management by talking around*, beginning with one-on-one conversations with key players across campus, and gradually building to one-on-two, one-on-three, two-on-two (and so forth) interactions. The key is to identify and engage key players across the institution whose support would facilitate the type of changes necessary for an integrated RME platform.

These discussions can focus on understanding and honoring past programs and activities at the institution, conceptualizing potential linkages across campus, and thinking about ways to engage key internal and external stakeholders. The underlying idea is to build on these smaller interactions to transition to wider community conversations with the goal of what organization development guru Marvin Weisbord referred to as 'getting the whole system in the room' (Weisbord & Janoff, 2010).

This process also helps to identify key aspects of the institution that can be critical for long-term success. As an example, drawing on our case study, there were two key centers that had a long and influential presence on campus – a business ethics center and a service-learning program. Focusing on their accomplishments and how they might further contribute in the future, the approach was to honor their past contributions and leverage their visibility and impact on the institution, exploring how these endeavors might further contribute to and benefit from collaboration with other programs, centers, and campus initiatives. A series of 'Bringing the Centers to the Center' programs were held as a way of increasing their visibility and exploring potential collaborative opportunities, where the directors of different programs and initiatives had the opportunity to share their past, present and future activities and plans with faculty, staff and students across campus.

The 'talking around' strategy can also be useful in creating an initial benchmark for what has already been accomplished in the RME arena, from gathering information on the number of faculty involved in ethics-, social responsibility- and sustainability-related research and course development, to creating a web-based repository of information that can be shared across the institution (Buono, 2018).

Preaching to the choir

A noted barrier to the institutionalization of RME focuses on the faculty, where discipline-focused faculty members fail to see RME's relevance for their own courses and research (Warin & Beddewela, 2016). While these individuals can create an impediment for the type of institution-wide change that is called for, a basic tactic is to limit initial interaction with them. As part of the 'talking around' strategy, emphasis can be initially placed on *preaching to the choir*, starting, as noted above, with faculty across the institution who are already committed to the goals of RME as a way of building communities of

practice. The idea is to build on the energy and enthusiasm of these individuals, providing support and visibility for their efforts, and linking them with like-minded colleagues in different departments. By uniting them in a value-sharing environment, the intent is to facilitate their ability to deepen their insights and influence through mutual interaction across disciplinary boundaries (Borges, Cezarino, Ferreira, Muniz Sala & Unglaub, 2017; Wenger, McDermott & Snyder, 2002).

Based on our experience, the resulting 'small wins' from these interactions and conversations can gradually lead to a tipping point, where the beliefs and energies of this critical faculty group begin to influence a gradual conversion to an RME-oriented mindset across campus. Over time, a small group of motivated individuals can generate pockets of commitment that can readily influence large-scale institutional change (see Kim & Mauborgne, 2003).

Providing context, creating content

The next phase focused on ways to (1) enhance individual learning as a foundation for organizational learning and (2) envision new ways of thinking about responsible management. As discussed earlier, an underlying challenge is to support faculty in drawing in responsible management-related concepts into their discipline-based courses. As a way of conceptualizing the process of mainstreaming this focus, business schools have gradually moved from dedicated courses, to building aspects or modules of RME across the curriculum, to more explicit partnering between academic departments, to true integration, where RME is part of a broad, normative framework across the institution (see Kolb, Frohlich & Schmidpeter, 2017).

As discussed earlier, as a way of facilitating this process the Business Ethics 'Gadfly' Workshop was created, with the intent of 'seeding' every academic department on campus with 'ethical gadflies' who would develop and share materials for their courses and encourage their departmental colleagues to do the same. These internal RME champions evolve their own teaching – in terms of both content and pedagogy – and through structured exchanges with other faculty encourage similar explorations and development. While the integration of RME practices will vary from institution to institution (see Alcarez & Thiruvattal, 2010), these types of collaborative interactions can help to establish communities of practice that focus on different dimensions of the RME challenge, providing further intellectual and emotional support among the faculty involved (Borges et al., 2017).

A related set of parallel process can focus on ground-breaking research, recognizing and supporting research that translates and illustrates responsible management education in practice. As an example, the GAP frame, a normative framework that translates the SDGs into relevant actions across different countries (Dyllick & Muff, 2016; Muff, Kapalka & Dyllick, 2017) can be used as both a strategic tool for businesses and an educational platform for business schools. The UN's SDG Fund, an international multi-donor and multi-agency development program created to support sustainable development activities through integrated, multidimensional joint programs, has an online database of sustainable development case studies that illustrate how the SDGs have been advanced, especially through public–private partnerships.[3]

As another example of supporting this contextual effort with content, the ideal of Conscious Capitalism reflects a new way of thinking about the role of business, emphasizing commitment to a higher purpose (beyond profits *per se*) and a multi-stakeholder engagement orientation, supported by conscious leadership and the development of a facilitative culture (Mackey & Sisodia, 2013). Research found that these 'firms of endearment' (Sisodia, Wolfe & Sheth, 2007) paid their rank-and-file employees much

better than their peers, had suppliers who were profitable, invested heavily in their communities, paid taxes at a higher rate than their corporate counterparts, provided remarkable customer service, invested in making their operations more environmentally sustainable, and did not externalize costs onto society. As other observers have also noted (Schwartz, 2013; Simpson, Fischer & Rohde, 2013), while such spending would suggest that there would simply be less left for investors, the opposite was true. These companies had dramatically outperformed the market over a 15-year period. Beyond financial wealth, these companies also created many other kinds of societal wealth: more fulfilled employees, happy and loyal customers, innovative and profitable suppliers, thriving and environmentally healthy communities, and more (Buono & Sisodia, 2011).

There are myriad examples that can be drawn on from around the world – from companies committed to a long-term orientation with deep roots in their communities (Sternad, Kennelly & Bradley, 2017) and corporations committed to economic *and* social outcomes (Honeyman, Gilbert & Houlahan, 2014), to firms that embody 'integrated bottom-line performance' and a socio-economic-environmental focus (Ehrenfeld & Hoffman, 2013; Sroufe, 2018). The key is to underscore that the essence of these approaches – which highly resonate with the UNGC principles on human rights, labor, environmental protection and anti-corruption – lies in stark contrast to traditional approaches to business. The content provides strong evidence of the utility of a more conscious orientation toward business.

Making it real

Finally, as a way of solidifying this effort, it is important to 'make it real', linking RME-related practices and goals with other structures, systems and processes on campus (Buono & Sisodia, 2011). As examples, this step can include integration with academic honesty systems, institutional ethics policies and related ethics committees, Institutional Review Boards (focusing on ethical issues in research with human subjects), students as colleagues initiatives (engaging them in community projects, domestic and international service-learning, and research initiatives), and related institutional programs, initiatives and experiences. The goal is to ensure that RME's ideals are reflected not only in the classroom, but also in faculty research, campus life and engagement with external stakeholders.

A Unified Approach to Responsible Management Infusion

Drawing on our case study, a key result of the collective effort and process described above is the Alliance for Ethics and Social Responsibility (see Figure 23.2). The Alliance's mission was to *amplify and extend the work of the autonomous centers and initiatives on campus, supporting and encouraging greater awareness of, respect for, and commitment to ethics, service, social responsibility, and sustainability in faculty research, curricula, and campus culture.* Reflecting the goal of institutionalizing a focus on RME, the internal network sought to: (1) support and encourage collaborative, transdisciplinary applied *research* that has the potential to significantly affect current practice; (2) influence *curriculum* development and pedagogical innovations intended to make students more ethically sensitive and socially aware; (3) ensure a broader application of these principles and ideals in *campus life*; (4) attempt to foster life-long *civic engagement* and a commitment to *responsible management* among the students; and (5) work closely with external organizations,

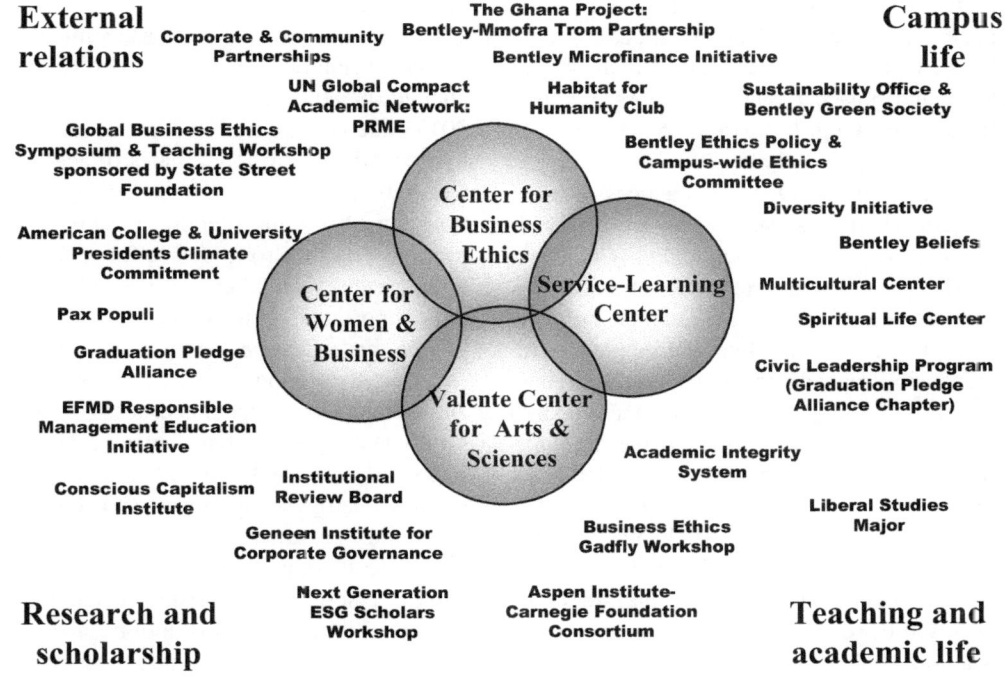

External relations

Corporate & Community Partnerships

Global Business Ethics Symposium & Teaching Workshop sponsored by State Street Foundation

UN Global Compact Academic Network: PRME

American College & University Presidents Climate Commitment

Pax Populi

Graduation Pledge Alliance

EFMD Responsible Management Education Initiative

Conscious Capitalism Institute

Institutional Review Board

Geneen Institute for Corporate Governance

The Ghana Project: Bentley-Mmofra Trom Partnership

Bentley Microfinance Initiative

Habitat for Humanity Club

Center for Business Ethics

Center for Women & Business

Service-Learning Center

Valente Center for Arts & Sciences

Academic Integrity System

Business Ethics Gadfly Workshop

Campus life

Sustainability Office & Bentley Green Society

Bentley Ethics Policy & Campus-wide Ethics Committee

Diversity Initiative

Bentley Beliefs

Multicultural Center

Spiritual Life Center

Civic Leadership Program (Graduation Pledge Alliance Chapter)

Liberal Studies Major

Research and scholarship

Next Generation ESG Scholars Workshop

Aspen Institute-Carnegie Foundation Consortium

Teaching and academic life

Figure 23.2   The Alliance for Ethics and Social Responsibility

partnering with academic and professional associations, corporations and civil society organizations in pursuit of these goals.

As illustrated in Figure 23.2, the Alliance was built on four key centers in the institution that continued to operate as autonomous entities, but collaborated under the aegis of the initiative. Combined with a series of programs and activities across the institution, this initiative has facilitated a multi-pronged approach that attempts to shape and influence a sense of ethics, service, responsibility and sustainability in: (1) the classroom; (2) campus life; (3) the university's research agenda; and (4) outreach to the academic, corporate, and not-for-profit worlds. While this particular configuration of centers, programs and initiatives may be unique to this particular institution, the general framework for thinking about how to instill RME across courses, programs and a wide array of endeavors is applicable to any business school.

One foundational aspect of RME lies in the integrity of the educational process itself. In essence, students who 'cut corners' in their education – engaging in questionable and unacceptable behaviors ranging from 'borrowing the work of others' to outright plagiarism and cheating – are likely to engage in similar types of practices in their careers, when the stakes and consequences of their actions are that much higher (Callahan, 2004). Thus, an important part of any RME program must deal with academic honesty and integrity. Much like our approach to responsible management education itself, it is critical to develop student understanding and the concomitant desire to embrace the shift from an acceptance of cheating to demanding integrity, by understanding objectives and removing barriers to the change, making it personal and providing incentives for the changed behaviors. Similar to the pressures they will be under during their careers, if we want our students to make better ethical decisions under stress and pressure, we need to equip them with the skills necessary to make those better decisions (Gallant, 2008).

CONCLUDING THOUGHTS

If business schools are serious about instilling a commitment to responsible management education in all that they do, it is critical to take a broader view of the institution in its totality. A unique feature of the approach described in this chapter is its collaborative and integrative focus, drawing together an emphasis on ethics, social responsibility, civic engagement and sustainability – the essence of responsible management education – across the entire campus. Drawing on the experience presented in this chapter, this type of network increases the visibility of these activities and programs, both on campus and with external stakeholders. As business schools continue to move forward in this realm – in essence, continuing a journey toward responsible management in all facets of the educational experience – proponents must continue to explore, improvise, learn and redesign their approaches.

Business schools, as with academic institutions in general, are particularly difficult to change (Greenberg et al., 2017; Weybrecht, 2017) due to a myriad of factors, including long-standing traditions, issues of academic freedom, pressures for high-level publications in discipline-specific peer-reviewed journals, and a strong desire for autonomy among faculty members among others. It is thus important to conceptualize such change as iterative in nature, beginning with small steps, creating opportunities for faculty, staff and students to engage in a process of exploration, testing, self-reflection and redesign.

As suggested by Figure 23.3, although the journey analogy is appropriate for the challenge that lies ahead, the path is not linear. This type of transition also runs counter to what is emerging as a basic acceleration of academic life, where institutions and their faculty are expected to do more at an increasingly faster pace (Berg & Seeber, 2016). The reality is that the underlying development inherent in this process is far from being

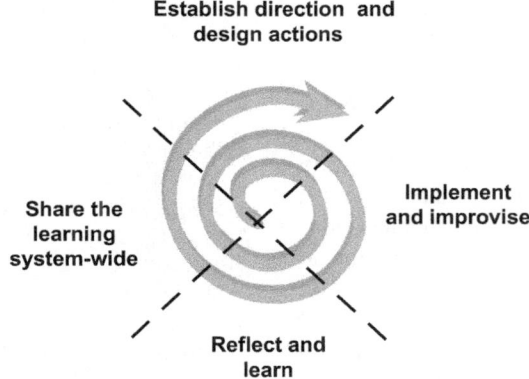

Figure 23.3   An iterative approach to RME program creation (adapted from Kerber & Buono, 2018)

straightforward, where one set of learnings morphs predictably into another on a continual basis. We clearly need to move beyond such 'single-loop' conceptions of the learning and development process (Argyris & Schön, 1978). It is thus important to rethink the challenge of developing our capabilities to deliver a truly responsible management learning experience.

The approach presented in this chapter is iterative in nature, one that takes time to develop and continuously improve due to the inherent complexity and uncertainty involved in the process. The underlying change process is experimental in nature, focused on a loosely defined direction where the process involves action, improvising, learning from and sharing that experience, and then acting again based on what was learned, thereby becoming clearer about both the RME change goal and the process for changing over time (see Kerber & Buono, 2018). The challenge is to prompt 'double-loop' learning (Argyris & Schön, 1978) that revisits, tests, questions, rethinks and ultimately modifies these initiatives in light of experience.

As an example of this iterative cycle, as noted earlier many business schools have introduced the Sustainable Development Goals into their curricula as well as research and institutional practices. Beginning with an initial discipline-based view of the SDGs, over time iterations encourage more of a cross-disciplinary perspective, looking at challenges from a variety of perspectives. As faculty continue to iterate, learning from their experiences and sharing that learning with colleagues across the institution, an ultimate transdisciplinary realization of both the problem and how it might be dealt with will emerge. As a growing body of work suggests, the result can be a new vision for business and management, one that embraces a broad array of stakeholders with the goal to create a more inclusive and sustainable world informed by responsible research and practice (e.g. Amabile, 2019; Davison, 2018). The AIM2Flourish initiative hosted by the Fowler Center at Case Western University is a good example of this vision, encouraging and emboldening future business leaders to achieve the SDGs, creating a 'flourishing world for all' with business as 'an agent of world benefit' (Aim2Flourish, 2019).

Of course, given the differences across business schools and the global nature of the RME challenge – from different societies and cultures, to school size and distinct missions – it is clear that we cannot superimpose a set of practices from one school to another if we expect to be successful. As other attempts to move from initial intent to institutional integration of responsible management education (Greenberg et al., 2017; Wersun, 2017) suggest, such alignment can take years to develop and it can unfold in intended and unintended ways. The approach to enhancing responsible management education presented in this chapter is thus meant as a reference point, a general framework that has the potential to be changed, modified and adapted to fit the unique configuration of specific business schools. The underlying process also clearly takes time for thoughtful reflection and development. Perhaps we can ultimately do more by doing less at a particular point, creating the time and space for the creation of cross-institutional partnerships that encourage deep immersion into and reflection on the subtleties and nuances associated with the RME challenge.

Notes

1   See www.schumacherinstitute.org.uk.
2   See weatherhead.case.edu/centers/fowler/about/.
3   See www.sdgfund.org/case-studies.

REFERENCES

Aim2Flourish. (2019). Aim2Flourish: celebrating business innovations for global good. https://aim2flourish.com. Accessed 15 July 2019.

Alcarez, J., & Thiruvattal, E. (2010). An interview with Manuel Escudero, the United Nations principles for responsible management education: a global call for sustainability. *Academy of Management Learning & Education*, 9(3), 542–550.

Amabile, T. M. (2019). Educating leaders who make a difference in the world. *Perspectives on Psychological Science*, 14(1), 7–11.

Annan-Diab, F., & Molinari, C. (2017). Interdisciplinarity: practical approach to advancing education for sustainability and for the Sustainable Development Goals. *International*

Journal of Management Education, 15(2, Part B), 73–83.

Aragon-Correa, J. A., Marcus, A. A., Rivera, J. E., & Kenworthy, A. L. (2017). Sustainability management teaching resources and the challenge of balancing planet, people, and profits. *Academy of Management Learning & Education*, 16(3), 469–483.

Argyris, C., & Schön, D. (1978). *Organizational learning: a theory of action perspective*. Menlo Park, CA: Addison-Wesley.

Barnett, R., & Coate, K. (2005). *Engaging the curriculum in higher education*. Maidenhead: Open University Press.

Beddewela, E., Warin, C., Hesselden, F., & Coslet, A. (2017). Embedding responsible management education – staff, student and institutional perspectives. *International Journal of Management Education*, 15(2, Part B), 263–279.

Berg, M., & Seeber, B. K. (2016). *The slow professor: challenging the culture of speed in the academy*. Toronto, CA: University of Toronto Press.

Blasco, M. (2012). Aligning the hidden curriculum of management education with PRME: an inquiry-based framework. *Journal of Management Education*, 36(3), 364–388.

Borges, J. C., Cezarino, L. O., Ferreira, T. C., Muniz Sala, O. T., & Unglaub, D. L. (2017). Student organization and communities of practice: actions for the 2030 agenda for sustainable development. *International Journal of Management Education*, 15(2, Part B), 172–182.

Buono, A. F. (2012). How to get started: management by talking around. In Escudero, M. et al., (Eds.), *Inspirational guide for the implementation of PRME: placing sustainability at the heart of management education* (pp. 33–36). Leeds: GSE Research Ltd.

Buono, A. F. (2018). Beyond the classroom: instilling responsible management principles, practices, and possibilities in our business schools. In Flynn, P. M., Gudić, M., & Tan, T. K. (Eds.), *Redefining success: integrating sustainability into management education* (pp. 131–144). Sheffield: Greenleaf Publishing.

Buono, A. F. (2019). Facilitating focused debriefing: connecting experience with theory and reflection – the three-part journal. In Schwarz, G., Buono, A. F., & Adams, S.

(Eds.), *Preparing for high impact organizational change: experiential learning and practice* (pp. 225–228). Cheltenham: Edward Elgar.

Buono, A. F., & Nichols, L. T. (2005). Stockholder and stakeholder interpretations of business's social role. In McDonald, M. (Ed.), *Ethics readings handbook* (pp. B2:13–B2:17). Vancouver, BC: Certified General Accountants' Association.

Buono, A. F. & Sisodia, R. (2011). A conscious purpose. *EFMD Global Focus, 5*(2), 56–59.

Callahan, D. (2004). *The cheating culture: why more Americans are doing wrong to get ahead. New York: Mariner Books.*

Cajiao, J., & Burke, M. J. (2016). How instructional methods influence skill development in management education. *Academy of Management Learning & Education, 15*(3), 508–524.

Christensen, L. J., Pierce, E., Hartman, L. P., Hoffman, W. H., & Carrier, J. (2007). Ethics, CSR, and sustainability education in the *Financial Times* top 50 global business schools: baseline data and future research directions. *Journal of Business Ethics, 7*(4), 347–368.

Collins, J. (2001). *Good to great: why some companies make the leap and others don't.* New York: HarperBusiness.

Cotton, D., Bailey, I., Warren, M., & Bissell, S. (2009). Revolutions and second best solutions: education for sustainable development in higher education. *Studies in Higher Education, 34*(7), 719–733.

Cummings, S., & Bridgman, T. (2016). The limits and possibilities of history: how a wider, deeper, and more engaged understanding of business history can foster innovative thinking. *Academy of Management Learning & Education, 15*(2), 250–267.

Davison, R. M. (2018). Editorial: researchers and the stakeholder's perspective. *Information Systems Journal, 28*, 1–5.

Dyllick, T., & Muff, K. (2016) Clarifying the meaning of sustainable business: introducing a typology from business-as-usual to true sustainability. *Organization & Environment, 29*(2), 156–174.

Ehrenfeld, J. R., & Hoffman, A. J. (2013). *Flourishing: a frank conversation about sustainability.* Palo Alto, CA: Stanford Business Books.

Eriksen, M., & Cooper, K. (2018). On developing responsible leaders. *Journal of Management Development, 37*(6), 470–479.

Forray, J. M. & Leigh, J. S. A. (2012). Primer on the principles of responsible management education: intellectual roots and waves of change. *Journal of Management Education, 36*(3), 295–309.

Fort, T. (2016). Adding ethics to the classroom. *BizEd, 15*(1), 48–49.

Gair, M., & Mullins, G. (2001). Hiding in plain sight. In Margolis, E. (Ed.), *The hidden curriculum in higher education* (pp. 21–41). New York: Routledge.

Gallant, T. B. (2008). *Academic integrity in the twenty-first century.* San Francisco, CA: Jossey-Bass.

Gentile, M. (2012). *Giving voice to values. How to speak your mind when you know what's right.* New Haven, CT: Yale University Press.

Greenberg, D. N., Deets, S., Erzurumlu, S., Hunt, J., Manwaring, M., Rodgers, V., & Swanson, E. (2017). Singing to living PRME: learning from a journey towards responsible management education. *International Journal of Management Education, 15*(2, Part B), 205–218.

Haertle, J., Parkes, C., Murray, A., & Hayes, R. (2017). PRME: building a global movement on responsible management education. *International Journal of Management Education, 15*(2, Part B), 66–72.

Haski-Leventhall, D., Pournader, M., & McKinnon, A. (2017). The role of gender and age in business students' values, CSR attitudes, and responsible management education: learnings from the PRME international survey. *Journal of Business Ethics, 146*(1), 219–239.

Hockerts, K., Borgbo, P., Srkoc, T., Goldberg, E. S., & Chaudry, R. (2015). *Faculty development for responsible management education.* New York: PRME Champions Report.

Honeyman, R., Gilbert, J. C., & Houlahan, B. (2014). *The B Corp handbook: how to use business as a force for good.* Oakland, CA: Berrett-Koehler.

Kell, G., & Haertle, J. (2011). UN global compact and principles for responsible management education: The next decades. *Global Focus, 5*(2), 14–16.

Kerber, K. W., & Buono, A. F. (2018). The rhythm of change leadership. *Organization Development Journal*, *35*(3), 55–72.

Kim, W. C. & Mauborgne, R. (2003). Tipping point leadership. *Harvard Business Review*, (March-April), 37–47.

Kolb, M., Frohlich, L., & Schmidpeter, R. (2017). Implementing sustainability as the new normal: responsible management education – from a private business school's perspective. *International Journal of Management Education*, *15*(2, Part B), 280–292.

Mackey, J., & Sisodia, R. (2013). *Conscious capitalism: liberating the heroic spirit of business*. Boston, MA: Harvard Business Review Press.

Michaelson, C. (2016). A novel approach to business ethics education: exploring how to live and work in the 21st century. *Academy of Management Learning & Education*, *15*(3), 588–606.

Mintzberg, H. (2004). *Managers, not MBAs: a hard look at the soft practice of managing and management development*. Oakland, CA: Berrett-Koehler Publishers.

Muff, K., Kapalka, A., & Dyllick, T. (2017). The gap frame: translating the SDGs into relevant national grand challenges for strategic business opportunities. *International Journal of Management Education*, *15*(2, Part B), 363–383.

Neal, M. (2017). Learning from poverty: why business schools should address poverty, and how they can go about it. *Academy of Management Learning & Education*, *16*(1), 54–69.

Newell, S. (2005). The fallacy of simplistic notions of 'best practice'. In Buono, A. F., & Poulfelt, F. (Eds.), *Challenges and issues in knowledge management* (pp. 51–68). Charlotte, NC: Information Age Publishing.

Nonet, G., Kassel, K., & Meijs, L. (2016). Understanding responsible management: emerging themes and variations from European business school programs. *Journal of Business Ethics*, *139*(4), 717–736.

Painter-Morland, M., Sabet, E., Molthan-Hill, P., Goworek, H., & de Leeuw, S. (2016). Beyond the curriculum: integrating sustainability into business schools. *Journal of Business Ethics*, *139*, 737–754.

Prandi, M., Martell, J., & Lozano, J. M. (2018). *Learning in a social context*. New York:

UNGC PRME. www.unprme.org/resource-docs/LearninginaSocialContextReport.pdf. Accessed October 2018.

Purnell, L. S., & Freeman, R. E. (2012). Stakeholder theory, fact/value dichotomy, and the normative core: how Wall Street stops the ethics conversation. *Journal of Business Ethics*, *109*, 109–116.

Rasche, A., & Gilbert, D. U. (2015). Decoupling responsible management education: why business schools may not walk their talk. *Journal of Management Inquiry*, *24*(3), 239–252.

Rasche, A., Gilbert, D. U., & Schedel, I. (2013). Cross-disciplinary ethics education in MBA programs: rhetoric or reality? *Academy of Management Learning & Education*, *12*(1), 71–85.

Roome, N. (2005). Teaching sustainability in a global MBA: insights from the OneMBA. *Business Strategy and the Environment*, *14*(3), 160–171.

Salimbene, F. P., Buono, A. F., LaFarge, V. V., & Nurick, A. J. (2005). Service-learning and management education: the Bentley experience. *Academy of Management Learning & Education*, *4*(3), 336–344.

Schwartz, T. (2013). Companies that practice 'conscious capitalism' perform 10x better. *Harvard Business Review*, April 4. Available at: https://hbr.org/2013/04/companies-that-practice-conscious-capitalism-perform.

Setó-Pamies, D., & Papaoikonomou, E. (2016). A multi-level perspective for the integration of ethics, corporate social responsibility and sustainability (ECSRS) in management education. *Journal of Business Ethics*, *136*, 523–538.

Sharma, S., & Hart, S. (2014). Beyond 'saddle bag' sustainability for business education. *Organization and Environment*, *27*(1), 10–15.

Shrivastava, P. (2010). Pedagogy of passion for sustainability. *Academy of Management Learning & Education*, *9*, 443–455.

Simpson, S., Fischer, B. D., & Rohde, M. (2013). The conscious capitalism philosophy pays off: a qualitative and financial analysis of conscious capitalism firms. *Journal of Leadership, Accountability and Ethics*, *10*(4), 19–29.

Sisodia, R., Wolfe, D. B., & Sheth, J. N. (2007). *Firms of endearment: how world-class companies profit from passion and purpose.*

Upper Saddle River, NJ: Wharton School Publishing.

Solitander, N., Fougère, M., Sobczak, A., & Herlin, H. (2012). We are the champions: organizational learning and change for responsible management education. *Journal of Management Education*, 36(3), 337–363.

Sroufe, R. (2018). *Integrated management: how sustainability creates value for any business*. Bingley: Emerald Publishing.

Sterling, S. (2004). Higher education, sustainability and the role of systemic learning. In Corcoran, P. B., & Wals, A. E. J. (Eds.), *Higher education and the challenge for sustainability: problematics, promise and practice* (pp. 47–70). Dordrecht, Netherlands: Kluwer Academic.

Sternad, D., Kennelly, J., & Bradley, F. (2017). *Digging deeper: how purpose-driven enterprises create real value*. Sheffield: Greenleaf Publishing.

Trevino, L. K., & McCabe, D. (1994). Meta-learning about business ethics: building honorable business school communities. *Journal of Business Ethics*, 13, 405–416.

Tyran, K. L. (2017). Transforming students into global citizens: international service learning and PRME. *International Journal of Management Education*, 15(2, Part B). 162–171.

Waddock, S., Rasche, A., Werhane, P. H., & Unruh, G. (2010). The principles for responsible management education. In Swanson, D. L., & Fisher, D. G. (Eds.), *Towards assessing business ethics education* (pp. 13–28). Charlotte, NC: Information Age.

Wagenheim, G. (2019). Debriefing change exercises: end-point engagement. In Schwarz, G., Buono, A. F., & Adams, S. (Eds.), *Preparing for high impact organizational change: experiential learning and practice* (pp. 206–224). Cheltenham: Edward Elgar.

Warin, C., & Beddewela, E. (2016). Drivers barriers and enablers of institutionalizing responsible management education. In Sunley, R., & Leigh, J. (Eds.), *Educating for responsible management* (pp. 301–323) Sheffield: Greenleaf Publishing.

Weick, K. (1984). Small wins: redefining the scale of social problems. *American Psychologist*, 39(1), 40–49.

Weisbord, M., & Janoff, S. (2010). *Future search: getting the whole system in the room for vision, commitment, and action*. San Francisco, CA: Berrett-Koehler Publishers.

Wenger, E., McDermott, R. A., & Snyder, W. (2002). *Cultivating communities of practice: a guide to managing knowledge*. Cambridge, MA: Harvard Business Press.

Wersun, A. (2017). Context and the institutionalization of PRME: the case of the University for the Common Good. *International Journal of Management Education*, 15(2, Part B), 249–262.

Weybrecht, G. (2017). From challenge to opportunity – management education's crucial role in sustainability and the Sustainable Development Goals: an overview and framework. *International Journal of Management Education*, 15(2, Part B), 84–92.

24

Reimagining Management Academics: The Emerging Responsible Management Education Paradigm

Sandra Waddock

THE NEED FOR A NEW PARADIGM

In 1962, Thomas Kuhn published the first edition of *The Structure of Scientific Revolutions* (Kuhn, 1970), in which he argued that most scientists spend their careers doing what he called normal science. Normal science means that scientists do their thinking, research and teaching in the context of an existing paradigm. Most of today's management and education is set in the context of today's dominant neoliberal economics paradigm, with its assumptions (memes) of rationality, self-interest, free markets and continual growth (Monbiot, 2016; Waddock, 2016). Scientific revolutions or new paradigms develop, according to Kuhn, when anomalies arise that cannot be explained by the currently dominant paradigm and its explanatory power begins to fray.

This chapter argues that today's dominant economic ideology, neoliberalism, which shapes most of management thinking, curriculum and research in business schools, is badly fraying. The tenets of responsible management learning and education (RMLE) emphasize human and natural flourishing, well-being and dignity for all, sustainability and a solid foundation in responsible and ethical practice. These RMLE tenets represent a significant paradigm shift in the responsibilities and functions of management educators if they are to successfully negotiate the shift towards an RMLE paradigm, and educate tomorrow's leaders, thinkers and citizens.

Today's Dominant Narrative: Neoliberalism

What is currently being taught in management education largely rests on a bedrock of neoliberal thought. Neoliberalism, which also manifests as neoclassical economics, argues that markets and trade are and need to be 'free', that responsibility is individual (either person or company) and not shared, that private property and private goods are essential to successful economies. In this frame, competition is fierce and unrelenting, and unfettered globalization and endless growth, without regard for ecological, equity, or societal consequences, are good things (Monbiot, 2016; Waddock, 2016). As articulated by Friedman (1970), perhaps its most prominent proponent, the only responsibility of firms under neoliberalism is to increase their profits and, as many economists would still argue, 'maximize shareholder wealth', where wealth is solely associated with financial wealth.

Responsible Management (Education): Shifting Paradigms

Responsible management learning and education, recognizing the cracks in the neoliberal paradigm or ideology, offers a substantially different, more humanistic (Pirson, 2017) paradigm for businesses, the economy and, consequently, management educators, if fully implemented (Dyllick, 2015). Paradigm shifts are hard and the transition toward RMLE is no different (e.g. Louw, 2015). As Kuhn notes (1970: 151), quoting physicist Max Planck, paradigms change or science advances most rapidly when 'opponents eventually die' or, to paraphrase, one funeral at a time. Paradigm shift is difficult in the context of what Kuhn called 'normal science', which is what most academics and scientists do most of the time, because theories, ideas, expertise, and entrenched research and teaching interests are embedded in the existing paradigm.

As the emergent RMLE paradigm attempts to replace neoliberalism, the transition raises similar difficulties. Making a paradigm shift away from core assumptions in neoliberalism about self-interested materialism, power aggrandizement and (financial) wealth maximization is very difficult (Frederick, 1995; Painter-Morland, 2015). Many businesses and other leaders are currently benefitting from the current system. Educators themselves are entrenched in the existing set of ideas, having built their careers around them. As novelist Upton Sinclair famously stated, 'It is difficult to get a man [sic] to understand something, when his salary depends on his not understanding it.'[1] That maxim applies as well to scientists and management educators as it does to business people.

This particular paradigm shift is difficult because it seeks explicit incorporation of a normative, whole-systems perspective into the 'rational reductionist' or positivist mindset of many management scholars today. It also shifts fundamentally away from an understanding that science is 'objective' towards recognition that values and perspectives are embedded in all human activities. Further, it moves beyond the idea that the only value(s) that is(are) valuable are financially or economically measurable towards consideration of a broader set of relational and ecological values that are important to humankind (Painter-Morland, 2015; Pirson, 2017). Instead of emphasizing individualistic, rationalist and materialistic values, RMLE demands that management education emphasize a more complex and sometimes seemingly conflicting set of goals. For example, RMLE emphasizes cooperation *and* competition, individual results *and* relationality, holistic, systemic thinking *and* understanding of the disciplines and functions (atomization or fragmentation), rationality *and* ambiguity and paradox, focus *and* breadth (Painter-Morland, 2015; Schoemaker, 2008). It also emphasizes interpersonal practices, informational practices and decision-making (Laasch, 2017), incorporating important issues of sustainability, responsibility and ethics through practices that emphasize knowing, doing, interacting and being (Laasch et al., 2015; also Rimanoczy, 2017) rather than just cognitive (knowing) learning, as well as modes of knowing that involve 'doing' or action and presence or 'being' (Rimanoczy, 2017).

Today's management education emphasizes relatively narrow functional and discipline-based, analytical knowledge rather than the 'soft skills' of leading (Mintzberg, 2004) embedded in RMLE. RMLE argues that narrow functionalism needs to be supplemented by systemic understanding, ethics, responsibility and ecologically sustainable understanding/ knowing, inter- and transdisciplinary learning, and critical thinking that enlarge the role of business and other enterprises in society, and integrated perspectives (e.g. Dyllick, 2015) that foster self-, other- and systemic-awareness. RMLE also advocates emphasis on the 'soft skills' of leading and managing (Dyllick, 2015; Mintzberg, 2004), to be added to analytical, functional and discipline-based knowing. Laasch and Moosmayer (2015) uncovered six integrative competency domains: knowledge (knowing), analysis (thinking), action (doing), interaction (relating), character (being) and self-adaptation (becoming), all of which are important elements of the emerging RMLE paradigm. Further, RMLE offers fundamentally different and more humanistic assumptions about the nature of humans, e.g. away from self-interest towards (more realistic) caring, collaborating and relational values sometimes (but not always) supported by rational reasoning (Pirson, 2017).

Many of these changes fly in the face of traditional management education's norms and values (e.g. Rasche & Gilbert, 2015). Making things even more problematic is the fact that entrenched interests, knowledge bases and specialized expertise limit the perspective and understanding of management education itself of many faculty members, and make diffusion of RMLE throughout curricula, research programs and institutions difficult (cf. Setó-Pamies & Papaoikonomou, 2016). All of this makes curriculum change, never mind changing research focus, akin to 'moving a graveyard' because 'you never know how many friends the dead have until you try to move them', as an old saw variously attributed to Calvin Coolidge or Woodrow Wilson goes.

THE CHALLENGE FOR RMLE ACADEMICS

In implementing the emergent RMLE paradigm, management academics implicitly (or explicitly) assume the mantle of the intellectual shaman, i.e., incorporating the shamanic functions of healing, connecting and sensemaking into their sets of responsibilities (Waddock, 2014). RMLE is oriented towards creating a more equitable, flourishing world with dignity and well-being for all (The 50+20 Agenda, ca. 2012; Muff, Dyllick, Drewell, North, Shrivastava & Haertle, 2013; Pirson, 2017; Solitander, Fougere, Sobczak & Herlin, 2012). Academics focusing on RMLE face a set of challenges and emerging tasks that expand significantly beyond the traditional responsibilities of teaching, research and service (Mitchell, 2007). In part this situation exists because the practice-based competencies of doing, relating, being and becoming (Laasch & Moosmayer, 2015) needed for responsible management are far broader than are the cognitive and analytic skills emphasized in traditional management education.

Below I will argue that under the emerging RMLE paradigm, academic responsibilities expand accordingly, so that teaching morphs into facilitating learning, doing research morphs into explicitly becoming an intellectual shaman (though teaching and service are also implicated in that process) and service morphs into being a change agent. Of course, these expanded responsibilities also cover traditional responsibilities of teaching, research and service, and notably, it is not always easy to tease out what are teaching vs research vs service responsibilities, since they can overlap.

The next three sections elaborate these expanded sets of responsibilities of RMLE academics, with the clear limitation that it is probable that no one individual can undertake all of these tasks. RMLE academics will likely select from among these (and possibly other) responsibilities as best suits their own interests and talents. The key in thinking of management academics in the RMLE context is that, as intellectual shamans, they perform their work with either implicitly or explicitly the healing, connecting and sense-making responsibilities of the intellectual shaman in mind. The expansion of management academic responsibilities closely follows the demand for management education to fundamentally transform in order to sustain its legitimacy in the context of ongoing business ethics scandals and lack of responsibility for growing crises of sustainability, climate change and inequality (Dyllick, 2015), factors that are associated with civilizational collapse (Diamond, 2005). The US-based accrediting agency AACSB has recognized the importance of many of these issues with its 'Collective Vision' statement (AACSB, 2016), which calls for business education and educators to be co-creators of knowledge, catalysts for innovation, hubs of lifelong learning, leaders on leadership and enablers of global prosperity, an agenda that incorporates may aspects of RMLE. Globally, the European Foundation for Management Development (EFMD)'s EQUIS accreditation guidelines[2] recognize many similar issues.

From Teaching to Facilitating Learning

Teaching is perhaps the most fundamental aspect of responsible management education. Yet in many management disciplines, both pedagogical approaches and content need to significantly shift to meet the demands of preparing leaders and citizens for the fraught future they will undoubtedly face (e.g. Muff et al., 2013). Bloom's Taxonomy of Educational Objectives[3] (Anderson, Krathwohl & Bloom, 2001; Krathwohl, 2002) can be helpful in understanding why teaching with the RMLE paradigm in mind demands that instructors move from being 'teachers' in front of the class to facilitators of learning.

Bloom argued that there were six levels of cognitive learning objectives, the first of which is knowledge acquisition or recall. The second level is comprehension, in which learners can translate, interpret and extrapolate from basic knowledge but may not yet be able to understand the full implications of what knowledge they have acquired or be able to transfer that knowledge to new contexts. The third level is application, where learners can take abstract concepts, general principles and methods, and begin to apply them to specific new situations. The fourth level, analysis, implies that learners can break down knowledge into its component elements, and understand the principles on which that knowledge is organized. The fifth level, synthesize, means that learners can create new ideas and concepts linking multiple sources or arenas of knowledge into integrated and meaningful patterns, resolving contradictions in the process. The sixth and highest level is that of evaluation, which implies the ability to assess or judge the appropriateness of relevant ideas, approaches and methods for a given context using criteria that fit the situation.

Understanding Bloom's taxonomy is important because the foundational element of responsible management education is that learners go well beyond knowledge acquisition (understanding relevant language and concepts) and comprehension (Muff et al., 2013) towards practicing new competencies that engage their character development, their presence in the world, their interpersonal abilities and how they act (Laasch & Moosmayer, 2015; Rimanoczy, 2017). Further, RMLE learners need to be able to work towards changing organizations, communities and even the world for the better. Being a change agent (as leader) explicitly implies the ability to apply, analyze, synthesize and evaluate learning and use it appropriately, all the while understanding the broader context of society and ecology that affects and interacts with managerial decisions (The 50+20 Agenda, ca. 2012; Dyllick,

2015; Muff et al., 2013; Painter-Morland, 2015). Below I briefly explore how Bloom's levels of educational objectives shift in the context of RMLE.

Facilitating learning

RMLE places significant new demands on the traditional paradigm of 'teaching' in which the instructor serves as the 'sage on the stage' (King, 1993), mostly lecturing to learners, an approach that emphasizes lower-level learning objectives of knowledge acquisition and comprehension. In contrast, RMLE shifts learning towards understanding, application, analysis and evaluation in Bloom's terminology, once the first two objectives are accomplished, and towards new interpersonal and personal practices as well (Laasch, 2017; Laasch & Moosmayer, 2015). Achieving these different types of objectives consequently moves the instructor away from traditional lecture-based models towards becoming a facilitator of learning, since these objectives cannot be achieved through passive learning and probably require significant personal practice for learners to become accomplished. King (1993) called this transition shifting from the 'sage on the stage' to the 'guide on the side'.

Lecturing means that the instructor serves as the expert who conveys knowledge to passive students who are 'absorbing' the lecture, typically in a one-way process that goes from instructor to student. That learning paradigm simply assumes that the instructor knows what students need to learn and that they will absorb that learning by listening, reading relevant texts and taking exams. About this approach the French novelist Albert Camus said, 'Some people talk in their sleep. Lecturers talk while other people sleep.'[4] Another relevant quote, attributed to scientist and author Edwin Emery Slosson by Harry Lloyd Miller in 1927, claimed, 'Lecturing is that mysterious process by means of which the contents of the note-book of the professor are transferred through the instrument of the fountain pen to the notebook of the student without passing through the mind of either.'[5]

Lectures can be appropriate for conveying information and are useful at early stages of cognitive learning, that is, when memorization and basic recognition of terms, ideas, and procedure are desired, i.e., knowledge acquisition and comprehension. RMLE demands something more than simple memorization or acquisition of facts and 'knowledge'. Indeed Rimanoczy (2016) argues that faculty should 'stop teaching' in favor of more engaged learning styles, particularly to help learners gain what she terms the sustainability mindset. Essential to RMLE, then, are facilitated learning strategies variously called engaged learning (Kenworthy-U'Ren, Zlotkowski & Van de Ven, 2005), experiential learning (Kolb, 2014; Kolb & Kolb, 2005), and active learning (Auster & Wylie, 2006; King, 1993; Kolb & Kolb, 2005; Loeb, 2015). Such facilitated learning strategies are very much a part of what are now being called 'flipped' classrooms, which improve student learning possibly mainly because they foster active learning approaches (O'Flaherty & Phillips, 2015).

Shifting content

For many academics, the content to be 'delivered' to learners also shifts significantly with RMLE, away from traditional understandings of the firm, competition and how businesses operate in societies and the natural environment. RMLE has taken an individually, ecologically and societally aware, i.e., systems, perspective on how businesses need to operate, asking learners to become responsible leaders in the process.

Responsible leadership emphasizes accountability, moral decision-making (ethics), responsibility and trust, plus focusing on relationships ('connecting' in the language of the intellectual shaman) (Maak & Pless, 2006; Pless & Maak, 2011), as well as sustainability and responsibility (Laasch, 2017). Responsible leadership, like responsible learning, inherently recognizes the importance of ethical and responsibility considerations integrally embedded in all managerial decisions. Responsible leaders take a systemic perspective that follows the logic of impacts, consequences and implications that managerial and leader decisions have on other people, on societies and on the natural environment (Maak & Pless, 2006, 2009). This capacity for thinking through the consequences of actions is how Ackoff defined wisdom (Ackoff, 1999).

RMLE further recognizes that leadership takes place today in the context of what Maak & Pless (2009) called a global stakeholder society, an inherently relational, network-based way of conceiving the world (cf. Freeman, 1984). Indeed, emphasizing the healing function of responsible leadership, Maak & Pless (2009) argue for leaders and their enterprises becoming 'agents of world benefit' (Adler, Scherer & Palazzo, 2008; Cooperrider, 2017). Still others similarly argue for more humanistic approaches to management education (e.g. Amann, Pirson, Dierksmeier, Von Kimakowitz & Spitzeck, 2011).

Shaper of change agents, artist, designer

In the context of RMLE, instructors take on additional roles, including (but perhaps not limited to): shaper of social change agents to improve the world, artist, designer and translator. Arguing for an ethics of care, connection and relationships, and the common good, Giacalone & Promislo (2013) promote ethical decision-making and values that can potentially override what they term the materialistic values and 'win at any cost' mentality of many management education programs. Such approaches to RMLE can help learners avoid 'taking the red pill' of ethical disempowerment (Giacalone, 2007), and enable constructive ethical decision-making. They can also help learners shift away from the 'worldview' that underscores today's management education, which Giacalone & Thompson

(2006: 266–267) state 'undermines and countermands the most basic tenets of ethics and social responsibility', towards the more humane, ethical and ecologically respectful stance – or ways of being and doing in the world (Laasch & Moosmayer, 2015; Rimanoczy, 2017) articulated by RMLE.

Similarly, moves to establish or 'reclaim' professionalism' (Khurana, 2010; Trank & Rynes, 2003) in management education can potentially ensure that learners can engage in the so-called 'soft' skills of actually leading and managing (Mintzberg, 2004) required by the RMLE paradigm. Business schools' attempts to better meet the needs of businesses (Jain & Stopford, 2011), among other critiques, can also be viewed as part of reshaping not only management education but also the ways in which graduates fulfill the enlarging set of managerial and leader responsibilities they will face. RMLE can help intellectual shamans fulfill emerging responsibilities as change agents who ultimately are responsible for the system as a whole and foster new ways of being, knowing and doing in the world.

Facilitating the development, even the transformation, of learners is fundamental to building responsible management education, since at the core of responsible leadership is self- and other-awareness (interpersonal and being realms), the ability to perspective-take (interpersonal realm), and socio-ecological consciousness (responsibility, ethics, sustainability orientation) fostering the emergence of wisdom (Waddock, 2010). Core to processes of transformation involved in RMLE is the work of the instructor as artist and designer, since art can be defined as the skill of transformation (Orr, 2009). Art and design are fundamental processes, part of what Orr (2009) calls aesthetic practice in building courses and whole curricula that foster the types of changes in worldview RMLE seeks.

Instructors have to learn to design new types of active-learning-based courses, design specific activities for learners, and develop whole curricula 'beautifully', keeping in mind their broader responsibilities for the planet as well as their local enterprise (see Adler, 2011). That imperative becomes more important because the future leaders who are being educated also need to be able to lead 'beautifully' (Ladkin, 2008), i.e., artistically in a sense. Doing so engenders much-needed spontaneity and innovation that can help them cope with the exigencies of a planet in trouble (Adler, 2006, 2011; Adler & Delbecq, 2017), where enterprise of all sorts is undergoing rapid change and experiencing increased pressures from many different stakeholders. As Orr (2009: 66) states, 'Art is a vehicle of commonality; it illuminates the unspoken rules, values, truths, and priorities of a culture.' That response is important because, as Orr (p. 66) also notes, 'By the responses that we ourselves create, we learn what we find promising, frightening, and exciting in the future,' something that RMLE hopes to inspire in learners.

As designer and artist, the RMLE instructor is responsible for thinking through innovative ways that engage learners and broaden their perspectives so that they understand the individual, organizational and systemic consequences of their decisions. Using design thinking is one way to do so (Liedtka & Ogilvie, 2011). There are many other possible approaches, including Scharmer's Theory U (2009, 2013), Cooperrider's Appreciative Inquiry (Cooperrider & Whitney, 2005), and Senge's *Fifth Discipline* (2006). Such systemic approaches present routes to active learning and systems understanding so necessary to achieving wisdom (Waddock, 2010) and developing leaders capable of acting effectively in the 21st century (Adler & Delbecq, 2017).

Translator and sensemaker

The last emerging functions for instructors as facilitators of learning are serving as translator and sensemaker. The translation role is itself a sensemaking practice (Weick, 1995; Weick, Sutcliffe & Obstfeld, 2005), in which

the instructor (and scholar) takes what has been learned through research and perhaps consulting practice and 'translates' it for use in the classroom, in other arenas of practice, and in organizational and community life more generally. As translators, RMLE educators need to take what they understand about leading and managing, organizing and structuring healthy systems and be able to explain those ideas to others in ways that are readily understandable. Many times, of course, those 'others' will be students. There are, however, other ways, particularly in this era of social media, in which the translator role can be fulfilled, some of which will be discussed briefly below in discussing the responsible management educator as public intellectual. Gioia and Chittipeddi (1991) called this responsibility for leaders 'sensemaking and sensegiving in strategic change', while Frost and Egri (1994) illustrate it as the spiritual leadership role in change management, and the seminal shamanic function of sensemaking (also Waddock, 2014). Increasingly, as the need for responsible, visionary, systems-oriented leadership embedded in the heart of RMLE becomes ever-clearer, this sensemaking becomes important for achieving the values-based, systemic orientation of what Giacalone (2004) called 'transcendent management education', and what today is being cast as RMLE.

From researcher to intellectual shaman

A major policy document by the Community for Responsible Research in Business and Management (RRBM, 2016) strongly posits that management research, theorizing and idea development need to adapt to demands for greater sustainability, responsibility and ethics. The RRBM position paper argues for seven core principles that define responsible research. Such research should: (1) be of service to society, (2) create stakeholder involvement, (3) have an impact (positive) on stakeholders, (4) value both basic and applied contributions, (5) value plurality and multidisciplinary collaboration, (6) employ sound methodology and (7) have broad dissemination (RRBM, 2016). Set in the context of the UN's Global Goals, also called the Sustainable Development Goals (Sustainable Development Goals Knowledge Platform, n.d.), RRBM is calling for 'science for better business and a better world', explicitly putting values and research that matters front and center, highlighting the role of academics as value influencers (Moosmayer, 2012). Doing so also fits well with the RMLE agenda (Dyllick, 2015) and pushes researchers and scholars towards (perhaps finally) what Academy of Management Past President Don Hambrick first called for in 1994 – doing research that 'actually matters', and moving away from an overemphasis on theory (Hambrick, 1994, 2007).

Indeed, management education has been subject to serious critiques over the years. Critics charge, for example, that business schools have 'lost their way' (Bennis & O'Toole, 2005), that they are responsible for teaching bad theories that destroy good managerial practices (Ghoshal, 2005), and even that they were partly responsible for the global financial crisis of 2007–2008 (e.g. Podolny, 2009). In the face of these sometimes devastating critiques (e.g. Datar, Garvin & Cullen, 2010; Ghoshal, 2005; Khurana, 2010; Mintzberg, 2004; Pfeffer & Fong, 2002 to name only a few) and the sustainability, responsibility and ethical challenges posed by RMLE (Dyllick, 2015), management education needs to work to retain – or perhaps regain – legitimacy (Boyle, 2004; Thomas & Cornuel, 2012; Wilson & Thomas, 2012). Ratings and rankings drive much of today's business school research and curricula with results that are not always salutary (Adler & Harzing, 2009; Devinney, Dowling & Perm-Ajchariyawong, 2008; Mingers & Willmott, 2013; Morgeson & Nahrgang, 2008).

Additionally, the way management academics conduct research and the topics studied are also subject to serious critiques about relevance to practice in what is sometimes called the rigor–relevance debate or creating 'actionability' from research (e.g. Bartunek & Egri, 2012; Bennis, 2010; Gulati, 2007; Lorsch, 2009; Pearce & Huang, 2012; Rousseau, 2012; Worrell, 2009). This debate argues in general that too much management research is oriented towards 'gap finding' in the literature, resulting in trivial or irrelevant questions of little interest to practicing managers and leaders. In a sense, RLME calls for moving away from academics playing the 'game' of getting ever-more citations, publishing in 'high impact', 'A' level, or first-tier journals (which mainly means that scholars are citing each other) (e.g. Aguinis, Suárez-González, Lannelongue & Joo, 2012; Mingers & Willmott, 2013). The movement is towards doing more meaningful research and scholarship addressing the so-called 'grand challenges' of our era, many of which are outlined by the SDGs (Sustainable Development Goals Knowledge Platform, n.d.)

To reclaim research legitimacy, management scholars need to go 'beyond the dehydrated language of management' in the colorful phrase of Adler (2010). They need to move beyond the 'sense and nonsense' of academic rankings, impact factors, and citation counts (Adler & Harzing, 2009; also David, David & David, 2011). In doing so, they need to build responsible research programs that can be communicated to a variety of interested parties in comprehensible ways. In a sense, RRBM is calling for many more academics to take necessary intellectual and scholarly risks to become intellectual shamans, acknowledging their intent to do work that heals, connects and makes sense of the world (Waddock, 2014).

The RMLE paradigm thus pushes scholars towards a different research paradigm that complements the shifting instructional paradigm. From armchair or 'ivory tower' academics, the charge from RMLE is that researchers become 'engaged' in various communities through what is called engaged scholarship in a variety of ways (Boyer, 1996; Van de Ven, 2007). Engaged scholarship means integrating research, scholarship and teaching with building a better world, that is, dealing with serious ethical, societal and, today, ecological problems through research and scholarship (Boyer, 1996). Engaged scholarship by definition tends to have a multi- or transdisciplinary orientation, involves relevant stakeholders, and uses multiple methodological approaches as they are relevant to the situation. Engaged scholarship connects rigorous research with innovative community involvement explicitly directed at 'healing' what is wrong and improving overall community function, at whatever level of engagement is relevant to a given project. It means focusing questions that affect, in real ways, the 'real world,' not simply addressing 'gaps' in the research literature or abstract theorizing, though rigorous scholarship certainly requires that some of both be done.

RMLE research in the context of the RRBM's guidelines calls for collaboration and means that research is difficult for one researcher to devise and implement. Although traditional research approaches will likely continue, emphasis on responsible research, like responsible teaching, calls for a shift in orientation to encompass a wide variety of approaches, collaborators and research designs. Such research, for example, might take the form of action research on big system questions (Burns, 2014) in which the researcher is engaged in the processes. It can involve stakeholders in both qualitative and quantitative approaches, where stakeholders are co-creating the research design and processes rather than simply being viewed as 'subjects' (Bradbury & Reason, 2003; Bradbury-Huang, 2015). Engaged scholars can also work with 'big data' and other sources of quantitative data to tackle important questions, while ensuring emphasis on the ethical and values-based implications of the scholarship.

In other words, engagement means just that – not (solely) sitting in one's office and testing abstract theories (though obviously,

writing and reading the literature demand office time). Sometimes, somehow, engaged scholarship means getting out into the world or working with people where actual things are happening and learning from those experiences. Devising new types of truly impactful research also draws on the skills of the designer, who must put together creative research designs that address difficult questions in a collaborative context under the engaged scholarship rubric. Those kinds of skills, and the ability to 'connect' (as shamans do) with others who are different from the scholar become important. Stakeholders to a research project will bring different perspectives, questions, skills, functions and disciplines to bear on research questions and designs can be helpful in pushing scholarship towards important questions and issues.

While approaches that integrate stakeholders into research designs can be complicated and time-consuming, they can also shed important light on questions and issues that might not otherwise be addressed. Such work can also foster innovation or pioneering, because it engenders new ways of thinking about how organizations and the world operate effectively, and in harmony with nature. Scholars and researchers who directly engage with practice, whether with individuals, organizations, or broader communities (or even nations) are taking on the 'shift shaping' role of the shaman because they can become deeply involved in change practices (Waddock, 2019). Shaping needed shifts is also part of the transformative power that ideas have, for as Kurt Lewin wrote, 'nothing is as practical as a good theory' (1945: 129), and the management field as it transitions to the new RMLE paradigm needs many new and practical theories.

Management education, of course, deals with managerial, leadership and organizational practice – or at least it does so theoretically. In the push for rigor, many management academics seem to have forgotten the underlying reality that ideas have

REIMAGINING MANAGEMENT ACADEMICS

impacts – and that management is an applied discipline. RMLE seeks in part to redress this gap by better linking managerial theory to practice, and acknowledging the implications of managerial/leader decisions on the broader world, not to mention the natural environment. The intellectual shaman serves as thought leader and intellectual pioneer, risk-taker and collaborator, and connector among the many different stakeholders in any real-world research context (Waddock, 2014). Part of the 'call' to RMLE, then, is that more academics take on these types of intellectual challenges. In doing that, however, the third traditional role of the management academic, service, tends to shift towards becoming both an internal institutional and external change agent.

From Service to Change Agentry

Service or 'being a good citizen' is the third role that traditional management academics assume (Mitchell, 2007). Traditional service activities within one's academic institution mean sitting on committees, using existing criteria to tenure and promote others, developing courses and curriculum that fall within the realm of business as usual. Service does involve being a good organizational citizen, though service is typically considered the least important of the three main academic activities (Mitchell, 2007). That is the case despite that such service is vital to the internal functioning of institutions – and that such service can play important roles in field building, and public service. Professional service, means taking on vital leadership and committee roles in professional organizations, editorial roles on journals, reviewing and otherwise serving and developing the field. Professional service, both internally and externally, can also mean mentoring junior colleagues (and, of course, students), much within the construct of normal science, i.e., accepting things as they are while trying to do them better.

RMLE will still require that all of these tasks be done, and it takes service to another place and potentially increases its salience. Under the RMLE paradigm, service arguably means becoming a change agent. Among other tasks, RMLE change agentry means working to incorporate issues of ethics, responsibility and sustainability into management educational strategies, curricula, course design and internal decisions around promotion, tenure and other rewards. Bringing such ideas into the broader professional arena, e.g. through professional associations, setting of academic and professional standards, and shaping new ideas for the field also represent important service activities – and put the academic into the role of change agent.

Change agentry involves seeking out and helping implement new standards of practice and assessment criteria within the institution and the profession. Through such activities, 'impact' and 'quality' of research, scholarship and teaching incorporate standards, values and practice associated with responsible management education – and practice. Sometimes RMLE scholars may well need to serve not just as teachers and scholars, but also as public intellectuals, especially in this dynamic era of cultural and societal change, and facing the sustainability issues of the world (Dyllick, 2015; Hoffman, 2017).

While public intellectuals are sometimes thought of as 'free spirits' (Dallyn, Marinetto & Cederström, 2015), today there is increasing call for scholars to make their work both practical and relevant to specific audiences and to the general public. That means occasionally (or more often) stepping into the public limelight, sometimes weighing in on policy and practice issues relevant to one's research. Further, public intellectuals operating in the public sphere, on social media and in policy debates can help in shaping and disseminating novel or important, scientifically-based ideas. The public intellectual can draw from his/her and others' excellent and rigorous research, then engage with that work in a public setting, e.g. via social media, public appearances and talks, in social and other types of media so that ideas move into the public sphere rather than simply remaining in largely unread academic journals (Hoffman et al., 2017).

This increasing expectation that community service for at least some management educators means serving as public intellectual puts pressure on another emerging role, that of translator. If ideas are to be transmitted to the general public, knowledgeable leaders and managers, and more specialized audiences, those ideas need to be 'translated' away from academic jargon to language that can be understood by an educated public.

In most institutions it is still unusual for management educators to incorporate criteria around scholars serving as public intellectuals and translators, or otherwise engaging social and traditional media into their evaluation criteria. The American Sociological Association (ASA), however, issued an important policy statement in 2016 called 'What counts? Evaluating public communication in tenure and promotion'. It calls for researchers to 'move their work beyond journals and libraries into the public realm, where they can contribute to public conversations as well as disciplinary ones' (McCall et al., 2016: 2). Can management education be far behind in making a similar call for public engagement by management scholars as part of their service commitment, particularly under the emerging RMLE/RRBM paradigm, which seeks engagement and involvement in major issues and problems?

Because management is an applied discipline, found in organizations of every type, management academics have frequently also been consultants to organizations and their leaders. Consulting activities can manifest as process consulting, strategy consulting, more technical consulting and executive education, among other ways. As RMLE's new paradigm takes hold, management educators can probably expect that requests for such services will increase as RMLE's ideas begin to take hold in practice. Because awareness of what is going on in the world beyond academia is likely to become increasingly important, the RMLE paradigm is likely to value such activity more than it does today.

Some management educators in the RMLE paradigm shift will fulfill their service responsibilities by establishing centers, new programs in which they serve as administrators, or similar initiatives within the context of their institutions. One example of an initiative that creatively brings together researchers and business practitioners in the interests of building a sustainable future is the Network for Business Sustainability at the Ivey Business School in Canada. Under an RMLE paradigm, it seems that many more such activities and initiatives can be expected.

CONCLUSIONS AND IMPLICATIONS

Shifting to a new paradigm of responsible management education and learning is likely to put even more pressure on scholars than they are already experiencing, with potential corresponding shifts in academic priorities. A move to RMLE means engaging in much the same RMLE learning practices of knowing, doing, interacting and being (Laasch & Conaway, 2015; also Rimanoczy, 2017) that they expect of their students. Similarly, if students are to learn about ethics, responsibility and sustainability (Laasch & Moosmayer, 2015), then so must the instructors teaching them. This shift also puts significant strain on the evaluation systems that universities and colleges employ to evaluate their faculty members, demanding a reshuffling of academic priorities, probably geared to the specific strategy and position of a given institution.

At the same time, RMLE poses a new and more demanding set of criteria that faculty members are likely to be expected to attain – with the same 24 hours a day, family and personal demands, and constraints that have always existed. Thinking through the implications of the shift towards RMLE and how to balance competing demands will be increasingly important in the future to the extent that RMLE takes hold. In that context, the reflective practices associated with 'being' and the capacities for interpersonal relationships embedded in RMLE (Laasch & Moosmayer, 2015) become vitally important skill sets for academics.

Where today research is highly valued, particularly research published in 'high impact' journals with large citation counts and a great deal of prestige and status, perhaps in the world of RMLE, other types of impact will be valued. For example, RMLE may favor impacts that change management practice for the better, impacts that incorporate ethical, societal and ecological responsibilities, or impacts that help with the grand challenges of the world, or that foster greater reflective practice. As Mitchell (2007: 240) pointed out in discussing the traditional academic roles of research, teaching and service, 'Thinking, reading, and writing demand hours of uninterrupted work. ... [T]eaching and service work, are filled with deadlines NOW, [and] will overwhelm discretionary time allocated for research.'

As expectations shift so that 'teaching' becomes facilitating learning, 'research' becomes taking on the healing, connecting and sensemaking challenges of the intellectual shaman, and service expands to encompass public intellectualism and translation of ideas, demands on faculty skills, expertise and time will only accelerate. What that means in practical terms is that individual academics will have to make choices about where to apply their talents most effectively in the face of a wider array of demands. Demands to publish 'only' in tier one or 'A' level journals may also need to shift to match reality, with publications in both context-specific journals and practice-oriented publications equally valued. RMLE expectations from management academics are for useful, practical and relevant management and leadership

ideas for organizations that work effectively in a troubled context, that balance their own needs for profitability and effectiveness with very real ecological and societal constraints, and that help develop future and current leaders and managers capable of dealing well in these contexts. If that is the case, then expectations and, particularly, reward systems for academic work and life need to shift accordingly to value these expanded responsibilities and corresponding achievements.

It is clear that the emerging RMLE paradigm poses a significant shift for many academics across all of the responsibilities that management academics assume. Given the grand challenges facing the world, however, it seems only proper that management educators do their bit to bring about healing, to connect where connections need to made, and to make sense of it all for themselves and for others.

Notes

1 Goodreads, Upton Sinclair, www.goodreads.com/quotes/21810-it-is-difficult-to-get-a-man-to-understand-something.
2 EFMD(2020),https://efmdglobal.org/accreditations/business-schools/equis/equis-guides-documents/.
3 For an excellent and simple overview, see The Center for Teaching and Learning, UNC Charlotte, Bloom's Taxonomy of Educational Objectives, https://teaching.uncc.edu/services-programs/teaching-guides/course-design/blooms-educational-objectives.
4 Goodreads, www.goodreads.com/author/show/957894.Albert_Camus.
5 Quote Investigator, https://quoteinvestigator.com/2012/08/17/lecture-minds/.

REFERENCES

AACSB (2016). A collective vision for business education. AACSB International. Available at: www.aacsb.edu/~/media/Management-Education/docs/collective-vision-for-business-education.ashx.

Ackoff, R. L. (1999). On Learning and the Systems that Facilitate It. *Reflections*, 1(1):

14–24. [Reprinted from The Center for Quality of Management, Cambridge, MA, 1996].

Adler, N. J. (2006). The arts and leadership: now that we can do anything, what will we do? *Academy of Management Learning & Education, 5*(4), 486–499.

Adler, N. J. (2010). Going beyond the dehydrated language of management: leadership insight. *Journal of Business Strategy, 31*(4), 90–99.

Adler, N. J. (2011). Leading beautifully: the creative economy and beyond. *Journal of Management Inquiry, 20*(3), 208–221.

Adler, N. J., & Delbecq, A. L. (2017). Twenty-first century leadership: a return to beauty. *Journal of Management Inquiry, 27*(2), 1–19. doi: 10.1177/1056492617710758.

Adler, N. J., & Harzing, A. W. (2009). When knowledge wins: transcending the sense and nonsense of academic rankings. *Academy of Management Learning & Education, 8*(1), 72–95.

Adler, N. J., Scherer, A., & Palazzo, G. (2008). Global business as an agent of world benefit: new international business perspectives leading positive change. In Scherer, A., & Palazzo, G. (Eds.), *Handbook of research on global corporate citizenship* (pp. 374–401). Cheltenham: Edward Elgar.

Aguinis, H., Suárez-González, I., Lannelongue, G., & Joo, H. (2012). Scholarly impact revisited. *Academy of Management Review, 16,* 586–612.

Amann, W., Pirson, M., Dierksmeier, C., Von Kimakowitz, E., & Spitzeck, H. (2011). *Business schools under fire: humanistic management education as the way forward.* Basingstoke: Palgrave Macmillan.

Anderson, L. W., Krathwohl, D. R., & Bloom, B. S. (2001). *A taxonomy for learning, teaching, and assessing: a revision of Bloom's taxonomy of educational objectives.* Boston, MA: Allyn & Bacon.

Auster, E. R., & Wylie, K. K. (2006). Creating active learning in the classroom: a systematic approach. *Journal of Management Education, 30*(2), 333–53.

Bartunek, J. M., & Egri, C. P. (2012). Introduction: can academic research be managerially actionable? What are the requirements for determining this? *Academy of Management Learning & Education, 11*(2), 244–246.

Bennis, W. (2010). Comment on 'Regaining lost relevance'. *Journal of Management Inquiry, 19*(1), 22–24.

Bennis, W. G., & O'Toole, J. (2005). How business schools lost their way. *Harvard Business Review, 83*(5), 96–104.

Boyer, E. L. (1996). The scholarship of engagement. *Bulletin of the American Academy of Arts and Sciences, 49*(7), 18–33.

Boyle, M.-E. (2004). Walking our talk: business schools, legitimacy, and citizenship. *Business & Society, 43,* 37–68.

Bradbury, H., & Reason, P. (2003). Action research: an opportunity for revitalizing research purpose and practices. *Qualitative Social Work, 2*(2), 155–175.

Bradbury-Huang, H. (Ed.) (2015). *The Sage handbook of action research* (3rd ed.). Los Angeles, CA: Sage.

Burns, D. (2014). Systemic action research: changing system dynamics to support sustainable change. *Action Research, 12*(1), 3–18.

Cooperrider, D. (2017). Agents of world benefit: businesses and communities: business as an agent of world benefit: why do good things happen to good companies? *AI Practitioner, 19*(2).

Cooperrider, D., & Whitney, D. D. (2005). *Appreciative inquiry: apositive revolution in change.* San Francisco, CA: Berrett-Koehler Publishers.

Dallyn, S., Marinetto, M., & Cederström, C. (2015). The academic as public intellectual: examining public engagement in the professionalized academy. *Sociology, 49*(6), 1031–1046.

Datar, S. M., Garvin, D. A., & Cullen, P. G. (2010). *Rethinking the MBA: business education at a crossroads.* Cambridge, MA: Harvard Business Press.

David, F. R., David, M. E., & David, F. R. (2011). What are business schools doing for business today? *Business Horizons, 54*(1), 51–62.

Devinney, T., Dowling, G. R., & Perm-Ajchariyawong, N. (2008). The *Financial Times* business schools ranking: what quality is this signal of quality? *European Management Review, 5*(4), 195–208.

Dyllick, T. (2015). Responsible management education for a sustainable world: the challenges for business schools. *Journal of Management Development, 34*(1), 16–33.

Diamond, J. (2005). *Collapse: how societies choose to fail or succeed*. New York: Penguin.

Frederick, W. C. (1995). *Values, nature, and culture in the American corporation*. Oxford: Oxford University Press.

Freeman, R. E. (1984). *Strategic management: a stakeholder approach*. Boston, MA: Pitman.

Friedman, M. (1970). 'The social responsibility of a business is to increase its profits'. *The New York Times Magazine*, September 13, pp. 122–124.

Frost, P. J., & Egri, C. P. (1994). The shamanic perspective on organizational change and development. *Journal of Organizational Change Management*, 7(1), 7–23.

Ghoshal, S. (2005). Bad management theories are destroying good management practices. *Academy of Management Learning & Education*, 4(1), 75–91.

Giacalone, R. A. (2004). A transcendent business education for the 21st century. *Academy of Management Learning & Education*, 3(4), 415–420.

Giacalone, R. A., & Thompson, K. R. (2006). Business ethics and social responsibility education: Shifting the worldview. *Academy of Management Learning & Education*, 5(3), 266–277.

Giacalone, R. A. (2007). Taking a red pill to disempower unethical students: Creating ethical sentinels in business schools. *Academy of Management Learning & Education*, 6(4), 534–542.

Giacalone, R. A., & Promislo, M. D. (2013). Broken when entering: the stigmatization of goodness and business ethics education. *Academy of Management Learning & Education*, 12(1), 86–101.

Gioia, D. A., & Chittipeddi, K. (1991). Sensemaking and sensegiving in strategic change initiation. *Strategic Management Journal*, 12(6), 433–448.

Gulati, R. (2007). Tent poles, tribalism, and boundary spanning: the rigor–relevance debate in management research. *Academy of Management Journal*, 50, 775–782.

Hambrick, D. C. (1994). What if the academy actually mattered? *Academy of Management Review*, 19(1), 11–16.

Hambrick, D. (2007). The field of management's devotion to theory: too much of a good thing. *Academy of Management Journal*, 50, 1346–1352.

Hoffman, A. J. (2017). *Finding purpose*. New York: Taylor & Francis.

Hoffman, A. J., Ashworth, K., Dwelle, C., Goldberg, P., Henderson, A., Merlin, L., ... & Wilson, S. J. (2017). *Academic engagement in public and political discourse: Proceedings from the Michigan Meeting, May 2015*. Ann Arbor, MI: University of Michigan.

Jain, S. C., & Stopford, J. (2011). Revamping MBA programs for global competitiveness. *Business Horizons*, 54(4), 345–353.

Kenworthy-U'Ren, A., Zlotkowski, E., & Van de Ven, A. H. (2005). Toward a scholarship of engagement: a dialogue between Andy Van de Ven and Edward Zlotkowski. *Academy of Management Learning & Education*, pp. 355–362.

Khurana, R. (2010). *From higher aims to hired hands: the social transformation of American business schools and the unfulfilled promise of management as a profession*. Princeton, NJ: Princeton University Press.

King, A. (1993). From sage on the stage to guide on the side. *College Teaching*, 41(1), 30–35.

Kolb, A. Y., & Kolb, D. A. (2005). Learning styles and learning spaces: enhancing experiential learning in higher education. *Academy of Management Learning and Education*, 4(2), 193–212.

Kolb, D. A. (2014). *Experiential learning: experience as the source of learning and development*. Upper Saddle River, NJ: FT Press.

Krathwohl, D. R. (2002). A revision of Bloom's taxonomy: an overview. *Theory into Practice*, 41(4), 212–218.

Kuhn, T. S. (1970). *The structure of scientific revolutions*. Chicago: University of Chicago Press.

Laasch, O. (2017). Delineating the blurry boundaries of responsible management, responsible management education, and responsible management learning? A social practices perspective. CRME Working Papers, 3(1).

Laasch, O. & Conaway, R. (2015). *Principles of responsible management: global sustainability, responsibility, ethics*. Mason: Cengage.

Laasch, O., & Moosmayer, D. C. (2015). Responsible management competences: an integrative portfolio for sustainability, responsibility, and ethics. CRME Working Papers 1(2).

Laasch, O., with Tanaka, A. C., Thiruvattal, E., Rimanoczy, I., Haertle, J., Ogunyemi, K., Tripathi, S. K., Hügli, T., & Kocollari, U. (2015). Management: basics and processes. In Laasch O. and Conaway, R. N. (Eds.), *Principles of responsible management: glocal sustainability, responsibility, ethics* (pp. 23–51). Mason: Cengage.

Ladkin, D. (2008). Leading beautifully: how mastery, congruence and purpose create the aesthetic of embodied leadership practice. *The Leadership Quarterly, 19*(1), 31–41.

Lewin, K. (1945). The Research Center for Group Dynamics at Massachusetts Institute of Technology. *Sociometry, 8*(2), 126–136.

Liedtka, J., & Ogilvie, T. (2011). *Designing for growth: a design thinking toolkit for managers.* New York: Columbia University Press.

Loeb, S. E. (2015). Active learning: an advantageous yet challenging approach to accounting ethics instruction. *Journal of Business Ethics, 127*(1), 221–230.

Lorsch, J. W. (2009). Regaining relevance lost. *Journal of Management Inquiry, 18,* 108–117.

Louw, J. (2015). 'Paradigm change' or no real change at all? A critical reading of the UN Principles for Responsible Management Education. *Journal of Management Education, 39*(2), 184–208.

Maak, T., & Pless, N. M. (2006). Responsible leadership in a stakeholder society – a relational perspective. *Journal of Business Ethics, 66*(1), 99–115.

Maak, T., & Pless, N. M. (2009). Business leaders as citizens of the world. Advancing humanism on a global scale. *Journal of Business Ethics, 88,* 537–550.

McCall, L., Hetland, G., Kalleberg, A., Nelson, A., Ovink, S. Schalet, A. …. Wray, M. (2016). What counts? Evaluating public communication in tenure and promotion. Final Report of the American Sociological Association on the Evaluation of Social Media and Public Communication in Sociology, August 2016. Available at: www.asanet.org/sites/default/files/tf_report_what_counts_evaluating_public_communication_in_tenure_and_promotion_final_august_2016.pdf.

Mingers, J., & Willmott, H. (2013). Taylorizing business school research: on the 'one best way' performative effects of journal ranking lists. *Human Relations, 66*(8), 1051–1073.

Mintzberg, H. (2004). *Managers, not MBAs: a hard look at the soft practice of managing and management development.* San Francisco, CA: Berrett-Koehler.

Mitchell, T. R. (2007). The academic life: realistic changes needed for business school students and faculty. *Academy of Management Learning & Education, 6*(2), 236–251.

Monbiot, G. (2016). Neoliberalism – the ideology at the root of all of our problems. *The Guardian,* 15 April. www.theguardian.com/books/2016/apr/15/neoliberalism-ideology-problem-george-monbiot.

Moosmayer, D. C. (2012). A model of management academics' intentions to influence values. *Academy of Management Learning & Education, 11*(2), 155–173.

Morgeson, F. P., & Nahrgang, J. D. (2008). Same as it ever was: recognizing stability in the BusinessWeek rankings. *Academy of Management Learning & Education, 7*(1), 26–41.

Muff, K., Dyllick, T., Drewell, M., North, J., Shrivastava, P., & Haertle, J. (2013). *Management education for the world: a vision for business schools serving people and the planet.* Cheltenham: Edward Elgar.

O'Flaherty, J., & Phillips, C. (2015). The use of flipped classrooms in higher education: a scoping review. *The Internet and Higher Education, 25,* 85–95.

Orr, D. (2009). Aesthetic practice: the power of artistic expression to transform organizations. *Revue Sciences de Gestion,* 63–82.

Painter-Morland, M. (2015). Philosophical assumptions undermining responsible management education. *Journal of Management Development, 34*(1), 61–75.

Pearce, J. L., & Huang, L. (2012). Toward an understanding of what actionable research is. *Academy of Management Learning & Education, 11*(2), 300–301.

Pfeffer, J., & Fong, C. T. (2002). The end of business schools? Less success than meets the eye. *Academy of Management Learning and Education, 1,* 78–95.

Pirson, M. (2017). *Humanistic management: protecting dignity and promoting well-being.* Cambridge: Cambridge University Press.

Pless, N. M., & Maak, T. (2011). Responsible leadership: pathways to the future. *Journal of Business Ethics, 98,* 3–13.

Podolny, J. M. (2009). The buck stops (and starts) at business school. *Harvard Business Review*, *87*(6), 62–67.

Rasche, A., & Gilbert, D. U. (2015). Decoupling responsible management education: why business schools may not walk their talk. *Journal of Management Inquiry*, *24*(3), 239–252.

Rimanoczy, I. (2016). *Stop teaching: principles and practices for responsible management education*. New York: Business Expert Press.

Rimanoczy, I. (2017). *Big bang being: developing the sustainability mindset*. Abingdon: Routledge.

Rousseau, D. M. (2012). Designing a better business school: channeling Herbert Simon, addressing the critics, and developing actionable knowledge for professionalizing managers. *Journal of Management Studies*, *49*(3), 600–618.

RRBM (Community for Responsible Research in Business and Management) (2016). A vision of responsible research in business and management: striving for credible and useful knowledge. Responsible Research in Business and Management Network, Position Paper, www.rrbm.network/position-paper/.

Scharmer, C. O. (2009). *Theory U: learning from the future as it emerges*. San Francisco, CA: Berrett-Koehler.

Scharmer, O. (2013). *Leading from the emerging future: from ego-system to eco-system economies*. San Francisco: Berrett-Koehler.

Schoemaker, P. J. H. (2008). The future challenges of business: rethinking management education. *California Management Review*, *50*(1), 119–139.

Senge, P. M. (2006). *The fifth discipline: the art and practice of the learning organization*. New York: Broadway Business.

Setó-Pamies, D., & Papaoikonomou, E. (2016). A multi-level perspective for the integration of ethics, corporate social responsibility and sustainability (ECSRS) in management education. *Journal of Business Ethics*, *136*(3), 523–538.

Solitander, N., Fougere, M., Sobczak, A., & Herlin, H. (2012). We are the champions: organizational learning and change for responsible management education. *Journal of Management Education*, *36*(3), 337–363.

Sustainable Development Goals Knowledge Platform (n.d.) Sustainable Development Goals. https://sustainabledevelopment.un.org/sdgs.

The 50+20 Agenda (ca. 2012). The 50_20 agenda. Management education for the world. Available at: www.unprme.org/resource-docs/5020ManagementEducationfortheWorld.pdf.

Thomas, H., & Cornuel, E. (2012). Business schools in transition? Issues of impact, legitimacy, capabilities and re-invention. *Journal of Management Development*, *31*(4). 329–335.

Trank, C. Q., & Rynes, S. L. (2003). Who moved our cheese? Reclaiming professionalism in business education. *Academy of Management Learning & Education*, *2*(2), 189–205.

Van de Ven, A. H. (2007). *Engaged scholarship: a guide for organizational and social research*. New York: Oxford University Press.

Waddock, S. (2010). Finding wisdom within – the role of seeing and reflective practice in developing moral imagination, aesthetic sensibility, and systems understanding. *Journal of Business Ethics Education*, *7*, 177–196.

Waddock, S. (2014). *Intellectual shamans: management academics making a difference*. Cambridge: Cambridge University Press.

Waddock, S. (2016). Foundational memes for a new narrative about the role of business in society. *Humanistic Management Journal*, *1*, 91–105.

Waddock, S. (2019). Shaping the shift: shamanic leadership, memes, and transformation. *Journal of Business Ethics*, 155, 931–939.

Weick, K. E. (1995). *Sensemaking in organizations*, Vol. 3. Thousand Oaks, CA: Sage.

Weick, K. E., Sutcliffe, K. M., & Obstfeld, D. (2005). Organizing and the process of sensemaking. *Organization Science*, *16*(4), 409–421.

Wilson, D. C., & Thomas, H. (2012). The legitimacy of the business of business schools: what's the future? *Journal of Management Development*, *31*(4), 368–376.

Worrell, D. L. (2009). Assessing business scholarship: the difficulties in moving beyond the rigor–relevance paradigm trap. *Academy of Management Learning & Education*, *8*(1), 127–130.

25

Critical Perspectives on (and in) Responsible Management Education: The PRME Imaginary

Jill Millar

INTRODUCTION

Responsible management learning and education (RMLE) has a ground-breaking ambition, to transform management practice through rethinking management education, reconnecting academics and practitioners. It represents a challenge to mainstream business orthodoxies in business schools and businesses, demanding a broadening of focus from concerns with profitability, efficiency and effectiveness, to include the recognition that sustainability, responsibility and ethics are integral to how business is taught, researched and practised. In this chapter I will argue that while such a transformation of management education is much needed, some current initiatives to bring about change have, paradoxically, the potential to perpetuate existing orthodoxies, closing down the conversations in business schools that might enable necessary change. In making this argument my purpose is to provide a counter-narrative to a responsible management education (rME with a small 'r') as framed by PRME. Using critical theory and critical discourse analysis, I present PRME as an 'imaginary' of rME (Fairclough, 2010; Jessop, 2009), through which underlying assumptions of the current version of capitalism are 'sedimented' in business school practices. The seeds for this approach were sown in the outcomes of a small-scale research project examining responses to PRME within my own business school, the details of which can be found elsewhere (Millar and Price, 2018). I develop the thinking stimulated by this project, exploring ways in which conversations about the nature and purpose of management education can be reopened in order to re-imagine and re-politicise management education. In so doing I suggest that it is necessary to move beyond PRME, to develop more disruptive and inclusive imaginaries of responsible management education (RME with a capital 'R'), as part of the RMLE project discussed in this Handbook.

SETTING THE CONTEXT

There is a growing crisis of legitimacy in the capitalist economy. A developing policy discourse highlights the problems of increasing economic inequalities generated through current economic practices, with the World Economic Forum (WEF) Inclusive Growth and Development Report a significant example (2017). In its introduction the report asks: 'Can rising in-country inequality be satisfactorily redressed within the prevailing liberal international economic order? Can those who argue that modern capitalist economies face inherent limitations in this regard – that their internal "income distribution system" is broken and likely beyond repair – be proven wrong?' (2017: vii). As might be expected, the answer to these questions appears to be 'yes'. The problem is not with the capitalist system itself, but with the way in which the benefits of growth are diffused across different countries, 'Inequality is largely an endogenous rather than exogenous challenge for policymakers' (WEF, 2017: xii). What is needed, it is argued, is a 'new social contract' which better distributes the benefits of economic growth in order to achieve greater equity (WEF, 2019: 2–3). Indeed, a crucial response to the problems attending the 'New Economy' (WEF, 2019) has been to promulgate a specific normative agenda for economic enterprise. Notions of global social responsibility (GSR) and sustainable growth have been embedded in current international and national initiatives, including the UN Global Compact (United Nations, 2019), and the UN Sustainable Development Goals, or SDGs (United Nations, 2015).

Capitalism's crisis of legitimacy has been mirrored in debates about what is happening in business schools. Fundamental questions about the content, values and purpose of management education have been raised. Central to these concerns is the suggestion that business schools continue to fail in their responsibilities to students in delivering a narrowly focussed curriculum that is over-reliant on ideas of abstract rationality, scientific rigour and value neutrality (Waddock et al., 2010). As a consequence it is argued that business-school-educated managers were ill equipped to deal with the recent financial crisis (Colby et al., 2011; Ghoshal, 2005; Painter-Morland, 2015), and remain unprepared to address crucial issues facing business in the 21st century, including sustainability and social justice (Kurucz et al., 2014).

To address these concerns, a rethinking of the purpose and values of management education has been proposed, that has generated responses including the Carnegie Report (Colby et al., 2011), the Globally Responsible Leadership Initiative (GRLI), the Global Business School Network (GBSN) and the UN Principles for Responsible Management Education (PRME). Central to these initiatives is the idea that management education should be re-moralised, extending a normative agenda from business practice into business schools.

This chapter focuses on PRME, as a dominant and potentially unifying actor in the field of rME (Storey et al., 2017). Developed in 2007 by a task force of representatives from the elite of business schools (PRME, 2019), by 2019 it had been adopted by over 750 business schools worldwide (PRME, 2019). As a change initiative, PRME is an example of soft governance and voluntary regulation, a light touch route to necessary changes in management education (Burchell et al., 2015). Participants are encouraged to embark on a process of continuous improvement, self-reporting their progress to interested stakeholders (PRME, 2019). There are no substantive sanctions beyond de-listing a non-communicating signatory (which by the end of 2018 constituted around one-seventh of the total signatories; PRME, 2019). However, the significance of PRME to the business school community has been enhanced by the participation of accreditation bodies (including the Association for the Advancement of Collegiate Schools of Business (AACSB) and the European

Foundation for Management Development (EFMD)) on the PRME steering committee (Burchell at al., 2015). In addition, Storey et al. (2017) suggest that the integration of criteria relating to responsibility and sustainability for accreditation purposes by, amongst others, the EFMD's quality improvement system (EQUIS) has led to PRME adoption being seen as valuable for accreditation purposes, signalling engagement with rME.

The UN PRME secretariat presents PRME as a 'global learning community' with signatories encouraged to participate in global, regional, and thematic networks, and engage with a range of platforms and projects (PRME, 2019). As Storey et al. comment, 'UN PRME's main contribution may be as a connector … uniting signatories for a common purpose, and providing a platform on which to share resources to develop the RME [*sic*] discussion' (2017: 96). In the next section I look at what the common purpose might be, and where PRME takes the discussion of management education, describing the concepts that underpin the PRME agenda.

PRME – PURPOSE, SUSTAINABILITY AND RESPONSIBILITY

The PRME initiative rests on six principles (see full text on the PRME website [PRME, 2019]). The content of the principles can be briefly summarised as follows. Principles 1 and 2 set out the purpose and values of PRME. Principles 3 to 6 set out a framework for implementing both purpose and values, through educational and organisational practices (Principle 3 and epilogue to the principles); research priorities (Principle 4); partnerships with businesses (Principle 5); and stakeholder dialogues (Principle 6). In order to focus my discussion of PRME, I will concentrate on the first two principles:

Principle 1. Purpose: We will develop the capabilities of students to be future generators of sustainable

value for business and society at large and to work for an inclusive and sustainable global economy.

Principle 2. Values: We will incorporate into our academic activities, curricula, and organisational practices the values of global social responsibility as portrayed in international initiatives such as the United Nations Global Compact. (PRME, 2019)

These two principles are particularly important when considering PRME, because they articulate both what PRME is for, and what the discourse represents as responsibility and sustainability in a PRME-driven rME. Thus, Principle 1 identifies the purpose of management education as developing the 'capabilities of students to be future generators of sustainable value'. Interestingly, the term 'future generators' is rarely considered in the PRME literature, instead there is a tendency to link Principle 1 to potential business roles of graduates including responsible managers and responsible leaders (Prandini et al., 2012), or more generally to graduates 'who have the competencies and attitudes link to operate sustainably as people and business people' (Stubbs, 2013). Although the nature of future generators is left opaque, considerable attention in the literature is paid to the knowledge, attitudes competencies and behaviour that management education should instil in order to develop student capabilities (Ollala and Merino, 2019; Prandini et al., 2012; PRME Inspirational Guide, 2015; Sharma, 2017).

The second part of Principle 1 highlights the connection between management education, sustainable value and an inclusive sustainable economy. Since 2016 PRME has been explicitly linked to the SDGs (PRME Strategic Review, 2016, PRME, 2019), with the expectation that Principle 1 will be understood in terms of 'the common language' of sustainable development (Weybrecht, 2017: 85). Indeed, the SDGs have become 'the unspoken rules of the game' for management education (Storey et al., 2017: 95). As a consequence, rME becomes aligned with a multifaceted (17 goals; 169 targets) collaborative and integrated programme aimed at addressing economic, social and environmental development.

Principle 2 states that the values of 'global social responsibility' (GSR) will be incorporated into the range of activities undertaken in an adopting business school, becoming the underpinning values of PRME. Like 'future generators', GSR is undefined, but some meaning is imported by the direct link made in Principle 2 to the UN Global Compact. It is on this basis that PRME proponents argue that the principles articulate, in a relatively straightforward way, a universal internationally accepted set of values (Haertle and Miura, 2014). GSR can also be seen as the development of the more familiar concept of corporate social responsibility (CSR), and reflects the same tensions and uncertainties in pinning down meaning and implications (Windsor, 2006).

I will return to these concepts and to their meanings (as more or less defined) later. First though, I want to discuss what I mean by describing PRME as an imaginary (based on my argument in Millar and Price, 2018).

PRME AS IMAGINARY

> Discourses include not only representations of how things are, they can also be representations of how things could be, or 'imaginaries'. (Fairclough, 2010: 444)

Conceptualising PRME as an imaginary draws on critical discourse theory, including the work of Fairclough and Jessop. A key element of this strand of critical discourse thinking is the argument that social actors are not sovereign agents, but operate within social practices. Here the concept of social practice has a specific meaning, that of 'relatively stabilised forms of social activity' (Fairclough, 2003: 205). More expansively, as Gherardi proposes, practices are persistent patterns of activities, (re)-combinations of human and non-human elements that conform to socially negotiated norms, through

which institutions are (re)-constituted, and collective and individual experiences given form (Gherardi, 2006). From this perspective, course preparation, assessment setting, funding applications, validation panels, departmental meetings, university open days and dissemination events are all practices within the field of management education. These practices are not simply social practices, but *discursive* social practices – practices involving the use of language in interaction. As such, management education operates as sites of *mutual constitution*, involving 'particular ways' of using space and language, acting and interacting, that operate to shape 'more or less' what is actually said and done by social agents (Fairclough, 2003: 25). While emphasis may vary among the thinkers who engage with discourse theories, there is a shared understanding that it is within social practices that meaning and identities are generated. Meaning is thus *situated* in social practice, with social practices understood as sites that set limits of intelligibility (Contu, 2014). In Fairclough's terms, the discourse elements in social practice 'constitute distinctive resources for meaning making' (Fairclough, 2010: 74), acting as 'filtering mechanisms' (p. 74), selecting some meanings and excluding others with selected meanings in turn constituting social action. As a consequence, the way that individuals – academics, students and administrators in business schools – engage with the practices within their institutions is circumscribed by the meanings and identities available to them through discourses such as PRME.

In conceptualizing the way that discourse elements act as filtering mechanisms, Fairclough (2010) and Jessop (2014) have developed the notion of 'imaginaries', as described at the start of this section. Imaginaries are assemblages of discourse elements, that operate, in Jessop's words, to 'frame individual subjects' lived experience of an inordinately complex world and/or guide collective calculation about that world'

(2014). As a result imaginaries help to deal with complexity, enabling social actors to make sense of the world, and give it meaning by focussing selectively on some aspects rather than others (Jessop, 2014). However, this process of complexity reduction is not neutral. In framing experience it makes available some interpretations of the world, while excluding others. Understood in this way imaginaries not only address complexity but do so in a way that limits available meaning making resources.

Further, imaginaries as representations of how things should be, are predicated on specific value assumptions. For PRME this includes the assumption that it is desirable that management students should become generators of sustainable value, governed by ideas of GSR. Where such visions articulate with other discourses and resonate with influential social actors they may be shared, collective visions, that become organizationally and institutionally dominant, through interactions with material practices and relations (Jessop, 2014). Potentially the PRME process reflects just such a trajectory, of a particular imaginary of management education in a re-moralised capitalist system (Jessop, 2009), an imaginary that appears to resonate with a range of institutions and is accompanied by strategies for integrating change. It is becoming a vision of rME that construes (interprets) practices in business schools.

PRME AS AN IMAGINARY: WHAT DOES THAT MEAN?

I have already mentioned that key PRME concepts seem to be endowed with a certain flexibility of meaning. However this apparent openness to debate is more limited than it first appears, contradicting claims made by proponents of the initiative (Burchell et al., 2015; Rasche and Escudero, 2010; Verbos and Humphries, 2015). As I now suggest, the PRME discourse represents a promulgation of *particular* understandings of the purpose of education, of sustainability and social responsibility, that bolstered by assumptions of universality and consensus, operate to constrain debate.

Turning first to purpose, while it is not clear what 'future generators of sustainable value' are, there is sense of predetermination (Louw, 2015) that students will go on to perform the role of manager, entrepreneur or leader, and in a specified way. This expectation links to a broader literature on the role of universities as socially and economically accountable institutions (Larran and Andrades Pena, 2017), in which it is understood that business schools in particular will 'meet the increasing societal demands for a responsible economy' (Godemann et al., 2014: 17). While it might be acknowledged that education has a social purpose, or a value to the individual (Storey, 2017), there is a bias in favour of economic activities reflected in the roles envisaged for students as future generators, and in the focus on work-related skills, attitudes and behaviours. In fact, it can be argued that PRME contributes to an entrenchment of the discourse of employability in business schools driven by the expectation that universities promote economic development through the production of 'oven-ready' graduates and postgraduates, ready to take on traditional business identities (Boden and Nedeva, 2010: 46). This economic logic is only reinforced by the linkage of PRME to the SDGs.

Although the SDGs are explicitly aimed at addressing the three dimensions of sustainability: economic, social and environmental (United Nations, 2015: Preamble), there is a growing literature that suggests an overemphasis on economic priorities (Gupta and Vegelin, 2016). Thus economic discourse shapes understandings of what sustainable development is, with economic growth as the driver of development, the achievement of development measured through a 'conservative economic framework' (Pouw and Gupta, 2017: 105), and social well-being defined in terms of economic security and access to income (Pouw and Gupta, 2017; WEF, 2019). It seems that the global north has achieved this form of development, and the global south is in the process of being developed. Further, the SDGs reproduce a particular form of economic organisation. Although the term 'capitalism' is absent from the text, rules and institutions of capitalism are restated (United Nations, 2015: Declaration, 21; Implementation 39–48; and Call for Action) and embedded through the goals and targets (for example Goals 8, 10, 12). The role of the state in promoting development is diminished, with an expectation that the private sector will take increased responsibility (see Goals 10.5 and 8.3 for instance), and it is this expectation that is reflected in the PRME literature. Indeed this expectation legitimates the linkage between PRME and the SDGs, creating the opportunity for business schools to be 'a [sic] true driver and enabler of change' (Weybrecht, 2017: 85). Thus the PRME agenda serves to reproduce the dominant economic narrative of the role of education and the nature of development, in which specific social identities are available (the manager, the business leader) and particular ways of achieving justice and prosperity can be articulated (based on growth).

Similarly, to represent business responsibility as involving CSR and GSR, is to reflect understandings of the relation between business and society, rooted in 19th and 20th century Anglo-American jurisprudence. The nature of that relation is debated and the location of moral agency troubling (Donaldson, 2017). However the fundamentals remain unchallenged, involving a more or less narrow set of legal responsibilities, attributed to corporations as legal persons, together with a nebulous and uncertain collection of moral responsibilities applied to the organisation, board of directors and employees. At the same time, the attachment of an increasing range of voluntary obligations to corporations reflects a privatisation of social responsibilities, a process in which corporations

are reconceived as corporate citizens, albeit citizens who do not necessarily meet those obligations (Banerjee, 2010).

While ideas of responsibility and sustainability may reflect a particular set of understandings and values, this is obscured in the PRME agenda by assumptions of universality, expressly articulated in Ban Ki-Moon's claim that PRME 'have the capacity to take the case for universal values and business into classrooms on every continent' (PRME, 2019). There is though a distinction between international endorsement and universal acceptance. If GSR is understood to reflect universal values, this understanding effectively excludes alternative accounts of the nature of corporations as social structures, as well as different versions of the nature of business responsibility, beyond conceptualisations based on versions of self interest (Carroll, 1991; Freeman, 1994; Friedman, 1970; Porter and Kramer, 2011). I could go further and suggest that presenting GSR in terms of universal values effectively excludes alternative versions of responsibility itself (Spivak, 2004).

In addition to claims of acceptance and universality, the PRME imaginary sets boundaries to debate through the notion of consensus (Millar and Price, 2018). In the principles themselves an assumed consensus is achieved through the reiteration of the pronoun 'we' throughout the text – with 'we' as a subject position slipping between an institutional 'we', to a 'we' as the deans of business schools (Louw, 2015). Indeed, as argued elsewhere (Millar and Price, 2018), the 'we' could also be taken to refer to the concrete PRME 'learning community' constituted by PRME signatories, as well as to an abstract global academic community. As a result, not only are alternative understandings of educative purpose and business responsibility excluded by PRME, but no such understandings are required since 'we' are all already in agreement, whoever 'we' are.

Arguably PRME represents less a process of glocalisation as claimed by Haertle and

Miura (2014), a process in which the local and the global adapt and combine (Laasch and Conaway, 2015) to shape the outcomes of interactions with heterogeneity the end state (Roudometof, 2016: 399). Rather it more nearly resembles Ritzer's (2003) notion of 'grobalisation', of a growing, even aggressive push for consensus and homogeneity, in which local management education is assessed in terms of presumed universal standards, promulgating an imaginary in which alternative meanings have no place.

CLOSING DOWN A CONVERSATION?

The articulation of PRME in 2007 can be seen to represent a point at which a conversation about the nature and purpose of management education ended, and a conversation about how this particular imaginary should be implemented began. Since 2007 we have seen the increasing introduction of ideas of responsibility, employability and sustainability into management education. Cullen (2017) indicates an upsurge in recent publications on sustainability (understood as environmental social and economic sustainability). Equally, as Storey et al. (2017) comment, the rME field is crowded and dynamic, involving a range of different groups and initiatives, among which PRME is dominant, but not determinant. Thus I am not asserting here that PRME is the sole catalyst for the increased focus on responsibility and sustainability. Indeed, as Burchell et al. (2015) argue, it may have had limited impact in terms of absolute numbers of CSR and sustainability-related courses in business schools. Rather, as several authors, including Burchell et al., suggest, PRME acts as a way of endorsing activities already occurring within business schools as well as encouraging new engagement with rME. This is particularly so when combined with the necessity to gain and maintain accreditation from the AACSB and other similar bodies (Burchell et al., 2015).

Whatever the reason for PRME adoption, my analysis of it as an imaginary suggests that it contributes to an ongoing 'sedimentation' of meaning. Jessop uses this evocative term to indicate that as meanings are embedded there is a 'forgetting' of the 'contested origins of discourses, structures and processes' (Jessop, 2014) that naturalises particular assumptions (in respect of the purpose of education, of the nature of business responsibility, of social justice and well-being), thereby legitimating the existing economic paradigm.

The small-scale research project in which I was involved, investigating colleagues' responses to PRME following its introduction to my own business school, serves to demonstrate Jessop's ideas of sedimentation and forgetting. The effect of the imagined consensus on PRME was reflected in the discomfort evident in the way that Sam, the only participant who challenged its vision of management education, articulated his/her position. At the same time we found that none of the participants, not even Sam, appeared to question either the universal claims of the PRME imaginary, or that social responsibility *per se* should underpin management education (Millar and Price, 2018).

In this reading of PRME, then, I am arguing that it does *not* simply create opportunities to question assumptions, or to interpret norms and adjust regulations, but rather constrains debate and closes down conversations. If this reading is persuasive, we are still missing an opportunity in management education (Rasche and Escudero, 2010). Rather than simply doing the same but better there is the chance to use a sense of crisis to generate scope for fundamental change (Jessop, 2014), for allowing variation, the toppling of dominant ideas and a shift from rME to RME.

REOPENING – THE FUTURE

Jessop's focus is on the role of language in constructing and reproducing economic and political institutions. Specifically, the aim is to explore the role of discourse in stabilising and reproducing such institutions, and in so doing to enable what he refers to as the re-politicisation (Jessop, 2009) or disinterring of contested origins and assumptions underlying the imaginaries that sustain social structures. In this regard he would argue that imaginaries are only ever partially constituted and it is this partial constitution that permits change and the evolution of meaning (Jessop, 2014).

Jessop (2009) identifies a sequence of factors that influence the constitution and reconstitution of imaginaries. The sequence starts with responses to changing circumstances and perceived crises, which generate an ongoing variation of discourses and social structures. Some emerging discourses become selected as resources for interpreting events and legitimating actions, and as they are increasingly privileged they become embedded in material practices, and ultimately institutionalised into orders of discourse. In the concluding sections of this chapter, I use Jessop's sequence as a structure for identifying strategies for re-politicising and re-imagining management education, starting with the availability of alternative discourses through which to talk of responsibility, well-being and sustainability, before discussing the selection and embedding of these discourses within new imaginaries. In so doing I draw on the insights of scholars already writing in terms of RMLE, particularly Contu and Gherardi, as well as others including Cunliffe and Banerjee.

New Imaginaries of RME: Alternative Discourses

The implication of business schools in a broader crisis of capitalism has led to a proliferation of studies on management education. Although lack of moral responsibility has emerged as an influential interpretation of the cause of previous failings, what is

meant by 'responsibility' itself, as distinct from responsible management, is not always conceptualised in the literature (but see Hibbert and Cunliffe, 2015; Painter-Morland, 2015). Taking the question of 'responsibility' as my starting point, I now develop a brief illustrative discussion, framed by the work of Gayatri Spivak, so as to suggest discursive resources that can contribute to the replacement of the PRME imaginary with new imaginaries of RME.

Responsibility and the other

Spivak's 2004 essay 'Righting wrongs' offers a way in to the question of responsibility through postcolonial discourse. In this essay Spivak argues that in seeing responsibilities as duties held by individuals in relation to others, there is an understanding, as Spivak puts it, that we are responsible *for* others (Spivak, 2004). This conceptualisation reflects an understanding that 'we' are distinct from, defined by, the 'other', a distinction that has shaped colonial and postcolonial processes of subjectification. It is a distinction in which the 'we' of colonial and postcolonial powers are juxtaposed with the 'other' of colonised cultures and societies. This understanding informs ideas of developed and developing; cosmopolitan and traditional; metropolitan and subaltern populations (where subaltern is understood as peoples outside the hierarchies of power). In this framing, the 'fitter self' (Spivak, 2004: 535), developed countries, development agencies and now corporations and business people, are presented with a sense of mission, not far detached from the white man's burden. A mission in which we are responsible *for* subaltern populations, responsible for leading them in an upward trajectory of development to become more like us, a journey that they cannot take without our intervention. Crucially, this idea of development embodies an assumption that we know the other and *know what the other needs*, delegitimating local knowledges.

In rethinking the nature of responsibility Spivak (influenced by Levinas and his notion of the Other) proposes a necessary change in the way it is understood, arguing that rather than considering us responsible for others, we should consider ourselves as having a responsibility *to* others. This is a small prepositional change, but one with significant implications. Shifting from 'for' to 'to' involves a sense of accountability to the other, and an openness to the other, beyond what Spivak (2004) refers to as crude cultural relativism or ideas of cultural sensitivity. It implies an acceptance that we do not know the other, that we need to listen, respond and learn from them. At bottom it requires an 'othering' of ourselves, a recognition that we are 'not the end product for which history has happened' (Spivak, 2004: 532), and that different ways of being and doing are available and should be pursued. It is a risky strategy, involving a shift in power from 'us' to 'them' with the effect that it is, as Spivak (2004) suggests, a more robust imperative of responsibility than capitalist social productivity may be comfortable with.

Listening to the other: ideas of development and CSR

What would this change in understandings of responsibility mean to rethinking management education? To begin with, responsibility *to* calls into question the sense of knowing integral to the PRME/SDGs nexus. A knowing that suggests a comprehensive recipe for development to which the objects of that knowing have not yet contributed (Gupta and Vegelin, 2016). PRME, in aligning rME with SDGs, has inserted this knowing into business school curricula and research. In response the work of inclusive development theorists is useful in providing alternative multidisciplinary languages of development-Pouw and Gupta, 2017). This literature highlights the need for the inclusion of local knowledges in the development process (Gupta and Vegelin, 2016), and provides a dynamic definition of development that

focuses on social well-being and ecological protection, while arguing for alternatives to growth (Demaria and Kothari, 2017). Complementary to inclusive development discourses, Sen's work on social justice and capability theory provides a language through which to re-balance ideas of well-being. His theoretical perspective reverses the focus on economic growth as the end goal of development, seeing it rather as a contributing factor to a development, understood as enabling people to 'live the lives that they would like' (Sen, 1999: 41). Crucially, what the lifestyles (or 'functionings' to use Sen's terminology) that constitute lives of value might be are not pre-defined by Sen (contra Nussbaum). Instead he presents functionings and the freedoms (or the capabilities) that support them, as 'inescapably pluralist' (1999: 76), arguing that social participation and public discussion are required to explore the valuation of functionings and capabilities in different contexts and regions, implicitly recognising Spivak's call to connect with different knowledges.

Again, inserting responsibility *to* rather than *for* into constructions of CSR would have important consequences, this time reversing the organisational priorities structured into current ways of thinking about business responsibilities that shape our curricula. Formulating CSR in terms of creating shared value by addressing those social problems that enhance a firm's competiveness (Porter and Kramer, 2011); or identifying a business case for CSR (Carroll and Shabana, 2010); or even of managing stakeholders for reasons of efficiency as well as ethics (Freeman, 1994); is to allow corporate interests to set the agenda. As Banerjee comments, there is 'too much "corporate"' in ideas of corporate social responsibility (2010: 266). In the context of CSR, the 'other' to whom we should be responsible goes beyond marginalised groups and includes society as a whole. Having such a sense of responsibility would require an openness to allowing a multiplicity of knowledges frame the corporate agenda, with the risky possibility that corporate strategy rather than harnessing social needs would be harnessed by them. There is so far limited research on how to achieve such an openness and accountability (Voltan et al., 2017), or on how to address the challenge of a cacophony of different knowledges (Richter and Dow, 2017), suggesting that this is an area for further investigation.

The human and non-human other: discourses of relationality

Relationality is a current theme in approaches to rethinking management education (for example, Moosmayer et al., 2018; Painter-Morland, 2015; Verbos and Humphries, 2015). This theme is particularly highlighted in Cunliffe's discussion of a 'relationally responsive social constructionism' (2008: 124), one that reflects the inter-subjective nature of reality and interdependence of self and other, and its implications for management education and research. Spivak's conceptualisation of responsibility makes a helpful contribution here, adding a further dimension to the relation of self and other in her claim that 'we are angled to the other before will'. By this she means we, as individuals, are embedded physically (through our bodies) and culturally (through language) in structures and material realities that exist beyond/before us (2004: 545). She points to a sense of visceral connectedness that enhances the idea of responsibility to the other, in that we are part of the other, and the other is part of us, and our responsibility exists irrespective of our decision to act upon it. This profound sense of relationality reverberates with a range of alternative discourses exploring relational ontologies and ethics. Such discourses include feminist analyses (Phillips, 2019), which envisage us as immersed in a web of human and non-human relations, and advocate an ethic of care. Similarly, work on More Than Human geographies (Thomas, 2015) presents a relational ethics that emerges from our (human) experiences with human and non-human 'kin'

(2015: 978). Drawing on indigenous understandings of connectedness, it provides the language for Western as well as non-Western practitioners and policy-makers to talk of a deep relationality. Finally, for this is not an exhaustive survey, Barad's body of work encapsulates insights from quantum physics, queer theory, feminism and philosophy. Her theory of agential realism challenges 'foundational dualisms' (Juelskjaer and Schwennesen, 2012: 18). Instead, she proposes an 'ethico-epistem-ontology' (Juelskjaer and Schwennesen, 2012: 12), which sees responsibility as an 'incarnate relation' that is prior to choice (Barad, 2010 cited in de Freitas, 2018: 745); and points to an inseparability between human and non-human agents that undermines stewardship accounts of sustainability.

Each of these discourses then provides a language to enrich imaginaries of RME, imaginaries that question the instrumentalism of corporate sustainability management (Schuler et al., 2017), the individualism that influences Western ethical traditions (Crane and Matten, 2016) and the assumptions of voluntarism that appear to inform understandings of CSR (Carroll and Shabana, 2010).

New Imaginaries: Privileging Alternative Discourses

How do some discourses become selected, and others discarded, in the construction of imaginaries? None of the discourses mentioned above are 'new', why are they not already central to an rMe imaginary? These questions bring us to ideas of agency. In this chapter I argue that imaginaries such as PRME constrain agency, however that is not the whole story. Relevant here is Fairclough's (2003) recognition that while imaginaries structure action, social actors are not totally socially determined. Rather, as Jessop (2009) argues, semiotic (meaning-making) and extra-semiotic forces (material and agential) interact to shape social action. In other words discourse and material structures constrain social actors, but individuals do have a degree of agency with respect to the discourses to be deployed and privileged and those to be rejected. Meanings, interpretations and identities are thus not simply produced but are *negotiated*, suggesting that there is scope for the construction of alternative imaginaries of management education within business schools. However, the process by which this occurs needs to be examined, as Fairclough indicates:

> One of the mysteries of the dialectics of discourse is the process in which what begins as self conscious rhetorical deployment [of emergent discourses] becomes ownership – how people become unconsciously positioned within a discourse. (2003: 208)

Contu's recent research (2014) is relevant to Fairclough's mystery. Taking a practice-based approach, she explores the way that interpretations and identities are negotiated and produced within 'local economies of meaning' (Wenger, 1998: 199). She refers to 'political moments' (2014: 311), moments of conflict, tension, continuity and discontinuity that are inherent in community interactions and in which meanings are rejected or become owned and acquire authority, reflecting local relations of power. In so doing, Contu makes two important connected points. First, that local economies of meaning are not 'indigenous' to settings and context, as Wenger would have it (1998: 80, 125); there is a continuity and co-constitution of meaning across macro/micro social structures (captured in the idea of site ontology [Contu, 2014: 292]). Secondly, political moments operate to sediment *particular* and *hegemonic* meanings and relations of power within communities of practice, fixing and privileging some discourses at the expense of others. As a result, Contu is able to identify potential for resistance and change, with political moments as sites of struggle in which difference is articulated and

boundaries drawn. Tensions between members of communities of practice, conflicts over the purpose and content of joint activities, and disagreements over the interpretation of artefacts and shared repertoires, along with the negotiation and renegotiation of identities, create opportunities for conversation and debate, enabling social actors to draw on alternative discourses, challenge assumptions, potentially re-politicising management education.

For management education what is at stake are pedagogies and practices that capitalise on political moments, that create the space to construct alternative imaginaries. Here critical pedagogies constitute a rich resource, influenced by Freirian ideas of emancipation, praxis and social justice (Dirkx and Mezirow, 2006; Hibbert and Cunliffe, 2015; Kurucz et al., 2014; Lange, 2018; Martin and Brown, 2013). Within the critical pedagogy 'big tent' (Martin and Brown, 2013: 384) there is a shared understanding that learning is a social practice and that knowledge is constructed through interaction. Critical pedagogues point to the value of critical reflexivity (Dirkx and Mezirow, 2006; Hibbert and Cunliffe, 2015); senses of perturbation (Lange, 2018); dialogic encounters (Kurucz et al., 2014); forms of argumentation (Englund, 2006); and respectful responses to patterns of thinking (Juelskjaer and Schwennesen, 2012), *including economic logics*, as ways of provoking the questioning of assumptions within this process of (re)construction. Or as Kurucz et al. put it, moving from 'improving within the rules of the game [to] … questioning the rules of the game [to] … questioning the game itself' (2014: 451). Ultimately the expectation is that, by engaging in critical pedagogy, the understandings and values of students will be transformed, developing competencies including: listening, observation, inquiry, empathy, imagination (Kurucz et al., 2014) and moral judgement (Englund, 2006; Hibbert and Cunliffe, 2015). Similarly, facilitating critical pedagogies offers the possibility of alternative identities with students becoming agents of change rather than 'servants of power' (Kurucz et al., 2014: 439), responsible people, rather than generators of sustainable value.

Martin and Brown (2013) comment that discussions of critical pedagogies can sound idealistic, especially in a higher education context in which teaching is understood in terms of logics of demand, customer satisfaction and learning outputs. Questioning habitual assumptions is painful (Hibbert and Cunliffe, 2015). The space for story-telling, for real world encounters, and for initiating openness in seminar discussions with moments of meditative stillness (Lange, 2018), feels limited. Standing outside the claimed consensus of current imaginaries of management education is uncomfortable (Millar and Price, 2018). Being involved in critical pedagogy though can allow us (participants in management education) to recognise that we do have agency and can enact different choices (Shahjahan, 2014: 230). As a consequence, it is important to explore further how to translate 'idealistic' critical pedagogies into practice.

Retaining Imaginaries

As emergent imaginaries become embedded into material practices and ways of being, the capacity for them to become retained and reinforced is enhanced. Here the PRME initiative models an effective strategy for achieving retention through its local and international networks, its linkage to both education and economic policy structures and its perceived role as connector across a range of rME initiatives. Indeed, this chapter could end here, with the recommendation that proponents of a new imaginary of RME could do worse than to use PRME as an instructive example of how to secure the retention of such an imaginary.

There is though more to be said about the process of privileging and retaining imaginaries. As Jessop argues, for new imaginaries

to 'stick' or be retained, they must have a stronger resonance than existing imaginaries with a wide range of social actors (Jessop, 2009). In critical discourse analysis literature, resonance is discussed in terms of the discursive capacity of imaginaries to make a new sense of multiple real material economic and social relations. Yet as we know, Fairclough acknowledges there is something of a mystery in the process by which people come to own discourses and available identities, 'how people become unconsciously positioned within a discourse' (2003: 208). It seems something else is happening here, suggested by the use of the words resonance and unconscious. To explore Fairclough's mystery a little further, I will end by going outside the questions of discourse discussed in the rest of this chapter, to mention briefly what has been labelled 'the turn to affect' (Gherardi, 2017a).

'Feelings are important' (Humphries-Kil, 2017: 386). A growing literature highlights the need to supplement the cognitively based rational analyses of social practice that discourse analytic approaches exemplify (Ahmed, 2010; Anderson, 2016; Contu, 2014; Gherardi, 2017a, 2017b). The focus in this literature is on affect, conceptualised variously as emotions, senses (Ahmed) or intensive capacities (Gherardi) for the way that groups, organisations and social formations operate. Affect is implicated in social practice (Gherardi, 2017b).

Integral to the affective turn is an understanding that affect exceeds the individual subject and that it is contagious (Ahmed, 2010), illustrated by the experience that many have had of feeling the atmosphere of a room when we enter it, being affected by it and affecting it in our turn (Ahmed, 2010; Gherardi, 2017a, 2017b). Affective atmospheres, ephemeral or more long standing (Anderson, 2016: 745–747), are seen to permeate and inform the ownership of discourses. Ahmed provides one version of the way that this is achieved, arguing that affect is 'sticky', linking objects, values and ideas together to influence behaviour and practice. Applying Ahmed's analysis to management education, (as object) we can see that it may be linked by an atmosphere of hope (affect) to the social goods (ideas) claimed by the PRME imaginary, and the potential of business schools to be a force for (values of) inclusion and justice (Humphries-Kil, 2017). Even where day-to-day experiences demonstrate that our activities may not deliver the desired objects, affect, affective bargains, can keep us attached to such imaginaries (Gheradi, 2017b).

Incorporating these insights into a process of re-politicising management education demands that we recognise the affective dimensions of the PRME imaginary. As I suggested above, space feels limited for alternative pedagogies. It is uncomfortable to challenge an imagined consensus. Taking up Ahmed's phrase, we need to explore ways to empower colleagues (staff, students, administrators) to be 'affect aliens' (2010: 30) to take positions outside the affective atmospheres that permeate PRME, in order to create the emotional space for alternative imaginaries of RME to develop and have the potential of being retained and embedded in their turn.

CONCLUSION

Imaginaries are coagulations of discourse elements, genres, discourses and identities, which act as sources for meaning-making, that frame our experience of a complex world, legitimating some meanings and excluding others. Presenting PRME as an imaginary uses critical theory to provoke important insights. As an imaginary, PRME becomes shorthand for a rethought management education, a ready-made, complexity-busting solution for a crisis that appears to overshadow business schools. As a dominant vision of rME, PRME short-circuits debate, obscuring and sedimenting assumptions about business responsibility and the purpose

of management education. Recognition that imaginaries work in this way allows us to look for ways to re-politicise management education, disinterring and discussing hidden assumptions, so as to facilitate the constitution and re-constitution of new imaginaries of management education.

In this chapter I have pointed to trends in a range of literatures that can provide the resources for different imaginaries, imaginaries that would be inclusive of the other, embracing critical perspectives on responsibility, growth and the purpose of management education. Developing such imaginaries would require us, as participants in management education, to engage in forms of debate in order to explore issues of care, relationality and responsibility, to question enduring dichotomies between 'us' and 'them', human and non-human, to ask why we hold some ideas dear, and to recognise that we live in a world in which there are multiple ways of being and doing. Perhaps as a result we can contribute to a transformation of rME into a radical RME.

REFERENCES

Ahmed, S. (2010) Happy objects. In M. Gregg and G. Seigworth (Eds.), *The Affect Theory Reader.* London and Durham, NC: Duke University Press. pp. 29–51.

Anderson, N. (2016) Neoliberal affects. *Progress in Human Geography*, 40(6), 734–753.

Banerjee, S. (2010) Governing the global corporation: a critical perspective. *Business Ethics Quarterly*, 20(2), 265–274.

Boden, R. and Nedeva, M. (2010) Employing discourse: universities and graduate 'employability'. *Journal of Education Policy*, 25(1), 37–54.

Burchell, J., Kennedy, S. and Murray, A. (2015) Responsible management education in UK business schools: critically examining the role of the United Nations Principles for Responsible Management Education as a driver for change. *Management Learning*, 46(4), 479–497.

Carroll, A. (1991) The pyramid of corporate social responsibility: toward the moral management of organizational stakeholders. *Business Horizons*, 34(4), 39–48.

Carroll, A. and Shabana, K. (2010) The business case for corporate social responsibility: a review of concepts, research and practice. *International Journal of Management Reviews*, 85–105.

Colby, A., Ehrlich, T., Sullivan, W., Dolle, J. and Shulman, L. (2011) *Rethinking Undergraduate Business Education: Liberal Learning for the Profession*. San Francisco, CA: Jossey-Bass.

Contu, A. (2014) On boundaries and difference: communities of practice and power relations in creative work. *Management Learning*, 45(3), 289–316.

Crane, A. and Matten, D. (2016) *Business Ethics*, 4th ed. Oxford: Oxford University Press.

Cullen, J. (2017) Educating business students about sustainability: a bibliometric review of current trends and research needs. *Journal of Business Ethics*, 145, 139–149.

Cunliffe, A. (2008) Orientations to social constructionism: relationally responsive social constructionism and its implications for knowledge and learning. *Management Learning*, 39(2), 123–139.

de Freitas, E. (2018) Karen Barad's quantum ontology and posthuman ethics: rethinking the concept of relationality. *Qualitative Inquiry*, 23(9), 741–748.

Demaria, F. and Kothari, A. (2017) The post-development dictionary agenda: paths to the pluriverse. *Third World Quarterly*, 38(12), 2588–2599.

Dirkx, J. and Mezirow, J. (2006) Musings and reflections on the meaning, context, and process of transformative learning: a dialogue between John M. Dirkx and Jack Mezirow. *Journal of Transformative Education*, 4(2), 123–139.

Donaldson, T. (2017) Donaldsonian themes: a commentary. *Business Ethics Quarterly*, 27(1), 125–142.

Englund, T. (2006) Deliberative communication: a pragmatist proposal. *Journal of Curriculum Studies*, 38(5), 503–520.

Fairclough, N. (2003) *Analysing Discourse: Textual Analysis for Social Research*. London: Routledge.

Fairclough, N. (2010) *Critical Discourse Analysis: The Critical Study of Language*, 2nd ed. Essex: Longman.

Freeman, E. (1994) The politics of stakeholder theory: some future directions. *Business Ethics Quarterly*, 4(4), 409–421.

Friedman, M. (1970) 'The social responsibility of business is to increase its profits'. *New York Times*, 13 September 1970. Available at: www.umich.edu/~thecore/doc/Friedman.pdf. Accessed 12 July 2019.

Gherardi, S. (2006) *Organizational Knowledge: The Texture of Workplace Learning*. Oxford: Blackwell.

Gherardi, S. (2017a) One turn … and now another one: do the turn to practice and the turn to affect have something in common? *Management Learning*, 48(3), 345–358.

Gherardi, S. (2017b) Which is the place of affect within practice-based studies? *M@n@gement*, 20(2), 208–220.

Ghoshal, S. (2005) Bad management theories are destroying good management practices. *Academy of Management and Learning Education*, 4(1), 75–91.

Godemann, J., Haertle, J., Herzig, C. and Moon, J. (2014) United Nations supported Principles for Responsible Management Education: purpose, progress and prospects. *Journal of Cleaner Production*, 62(2014), 16–23.

Gupta, J. and Vegelin, C. (2016) Sustainable development goals and inclusive development. *Int Environ Agreements*, 16, 433–448.

Haertle, J. and Miura, S.(2014) Seven years of development: United Nations-supported principles for responsible management education. *SAM Advanced Management Journal*, Autumn, 8–17.

Hibbert, P. and Cunliffe, A. (2015) Responsible management: engaging moral reflexive practice through threshold concepts. *Journal of Business Ethics*, 127, 177–188.

Humphries-Kil, M. (2017) Telling (emotional) stories about management education. *International Journal of Management Education*, 15, 384–392.

Jessop, B. (2009) Cultural political economy and critical policy studies. *Critical Policy Studies*, 3(3–4), 336–356.

Jessop, B. (2014) Imagined recoveries, recovered imaginaries: a cultural political economy of crisis construals and crisis management in the North Atlantic Financial Crisis. Available at: https://bobjessop.wordpress.com/2014/04/06/recovered-imaginaries-imagined-recoveries-a-cultural-political-economy-of-crisis-construals-and-crisis-management-in-the-north-atlantic-financial-crisis/. Accessed 24 May 2019.

Juelskjaer, M. and Schwennesen, S. (2012) Intra-active entanglements – an interview with Karen Barad. *Kvinder, Kon &Forskning*, 1–2, 10–23.

Kurucz, E., Colbert, B. and Marcus, J. (2014) Sustainability as a provocation to rethink management education: building a progressive educative practice. *Management Learning*, 45(4), 437–457.

Laasch, O. and Conaway, R. (2015) *Principles of Responsible Management: Glocal Sustainability, Responsibility, and Ethics*. Mason: Cengage.

Lange, E. (2018) Transforming transformative education through ontologies of relationality. *Journal of Transformative Education*, 16(4), 280–301.

Larran, J. M. and Andrades Pena, F. (2017) Analysing the literature on university social responsibility: a review of selected higher education journals. *Higher Education Quarterly*, 71(4), 302–319.

Louw, J. (2015) 'Paradigm change' or no real change at all? A critical reading of the U.N. principles for responsible management education. *Journal of Management Education*, 39(2), 184–208.

Martin, G. and Brown, T. (2013) Out of the box: making space for everyday critical pedagogies. *The Canadian Geographer*, 57(3), 381–388.

Millar, J. and Price, M. (2018) Imagining management education: a critique of the contribution of the United Nations PRME to critical reflexivity and rethinking management education. *Management Learning*, ePub ahead of print 26 March 2018, doi.org/10.1177/1350507618759828.

Moosmayer, D., Waddock, S., Wang, L., Hühn, M., Dierksmeier, C. and Gohl, C. (2018) Leaving the road from Abilene. *Journal of Business Ethics*, 157, 913–932.

Ollala, C. and Merino, A. (2019) Competences for sustainability in undergraduate business studies: a content analysis of value-based course syllabi in Spanish universities. *International Journal of Management Education*, 17, 239–253.

Painter-Morland, M. (2015) Philosophical assumptions undermining responsible management education. *Journal of Management Development*, 34(1), 61–75.

Phillips, M. (2019) 'Daring to care': challenging corporate environmentalism, *Journal of Business Ethics*, 156, 1151–1164.

Porter, M. and Kramer, M. (2011) Creating shared value. *Harvard Business Review*, 89(1/2), 62–77.

Pouw, N. and Gupta, J. (2017) Inclusive development: a multi-disciplinary approach. *Current Opinion in Environmental Sustainability*, 24, 104–108.

Prandini, M., Vervoort, I. and Barthelemess, P. (2012) Responsible management education for 21st century leadership. *Central European Business Review*, 1(2).

PRME (2015) *Inspirational Guide for the Implementation of PRME: UK and Ireland edition*. Sheffield: Greenleaf Publishing.

PRME (2016) *Strategic Review 2016*. Available at: https://www.unprme.org/resources/display-resources.php?cid=9. Accessed 14 June 2019.

PRME (2019) Home page. Available at: www.unprme.org/index.php. Accessed 14 June 2019.

Rasche, A. and Escudero, M. (2010) Leading change: the role of the principles for responsible management education. *Zeitschrift fuer Wirtschafts- und Unternehmensethik*, 10(2), 244–250.

Richter, H. and Dow, K. (2017) Stakeholder theory: a deliberative perspective. *Business Ethics: A European Review*, 26, 428–442.

Ritzer, G. (2003) Rethinking globalization: glocalization/grobalization and something/nothing. *Sociological Theory*, 2(3), 193–209.

Roudometof, V. (2016) Theorizing glocalization: three interpretations. *European Journal of Social Theory*, 19(3), 391–408.

Schuler, D., Rasche, A., Etzion, D. and Newton, L. (2017) Corporate sustainability management and environmental ethics. *Business Ethics Quarterly*, 27(2), 213–237.

Sen, A. (1999) *Development as Freedom*. Oxford: Oxford University Press.

Shahjahan, R. (2014) From 'no' to 'yes': postcolonial perspectives on resistance to neoliberal higher education. *Discourse: Studies in the Cultural Politics of Education*, 35(2), 219–232.

Sharma, R. (2017) A competency model for management education for sustainability. *Vision*, 21(2), x–xv.

Spivak, G. (2004) Righting wrongs. *The South Atlantic Quarterly*, 103(2/3), 523–581.

Storey, M., Killian, S. and O'Regan, P. (2017) Responsible management education: mapping the field in the context of the SDGs. *International Journal of Management Education*, 15, 93–103.

Stubbs, W. (2013) Addressing the business-sustainability nexus in postgraduate education. *International Journal of Sustainability in Higher Education*, 14(1), 25–41.

Thomas, A. (2015) Indigenous more-than-humanisms: relational ethics with the Hurunui River in Aotearoa New Zealand. *Social & Cultural Geography*, 16(8), 974–990.

United Nations (2015) General Assembly Resolution 70/1. Transforming Our World 2030 Agenda for Sustainable Development. A/Res/70/1 (25 September 2015). Available at: https://sustainabledevelopment.un.org/post2015/transformingourworld. Accessed 2 June 2019.

United Nations (2019) Global Compact. Available at: www.unglobalcompact.org/. Accessed 2 June 2019.

Verbos, A. and Humphries, M. (2015) Indigenous wisdom and the PRME: inclusion or illusion? *Journal of Management Development*, 34(1), 90–100.

Voltan, A., Hervieux, C. and Mills, A. (2017) Examining the win–win proposition of shared value across contexts: implications for future application. *Business Ethics: A European Review*, 26, 347–368.

Waddock, S., Werhane, G. and Rasche, A. (2010) The principles for responsible management education – where do we go from here? In D. Fisher and D. Swanson (Eds.), *Assessing Business Ethics Education*. Charlotte: Information Age Publishing. pp. 13–28.

Wenger, E. (1998) *Communities of Practice: Learning Meaning and Identity*. Cambridge: Cambridge University Press.

Weybrecht, G. (2017) From challenge to opportunity: management education's crucial role in sustainability and the Sustainable Development Goals. An overview and framework *International Journal of Management Education*, 17, 84–92.

Windsor, D. (2006) Corporate social responsibility: three key approaches. *Journal of Management Studies*, 43(1), 93–114.

World Economic Forum (2017) The inclusive growth and development report. Available at: www.weforum.org/reports/the-inclusive-growth-and-development-report-2017. Accessed 1 June 2019.

World Economic Forum (2019) *Dialogue Series on New Economic and Social Frontiers Shaping the New Economy in the Fourth Industrial Revolution: White Paper*. www3.weforum.org/docs/WEF_Dialogue_Series_on_New_Economic_and_Social_Frontiers.pdf. Accessed 1 June 2019.

26

The Institutionalization of Responsible Management Education

Andreas Rasche, Dirk Ulrich Gilbert and
Maximilian J. L. Schormair

INTRODUCTION

Responsible management education (RME) has proliferated throughout the past decade. Currently, more than 700 schools have signed up to the Principles for Responsible Management Education (PRME) and thereby promised to align their research and teaching practices with basic values relevant to corporate responsibility, sustainability and ethics. Also, accreditation agencies like the Association of MBAs (AMBA) as well as professional networks like Net Impact and the Globally Responsible Leadership Initiative (GRLI) have supported the diffusion and adoption of relevant practices by business schools. Few schools would question the significance and diffusion of RME by now. It is therefore appropriate to view RME as an institutionalized social practice – that is, a practice by which 'social processes, obligations, or actualities come to take on a rule-like status in social thought and action' (Meyer & Rowan, 1977: 341). Institutionalized practices

are widely followed and exhibit permanence (Tolbert & Zucker, 1983: 25) and therefore have moved beyond being perceived as an unstable 'fashion' (Abrahamson, 1996). RME can be perceived as an institution to which organizations (like business schools) respond because they seek legitimacy.

Based on institutional theory in general and organizational institutionalism in particular (Meyer & Rowan, 1977; Zucker, 1988), this chapter discusses the institutionalization of RME in business schools and theoretically frames consequences of its widely diffused nature. We believe this analysis is important and timely for at least two reasons. First, it helps us to better understand why schools respond to this emerging agenda and the manifold changes in the institutional context. The institutionalization of RME and its influence on organizational practices is not a natural process. Rather, it is the result of (a) the existence of different types of institutional pressures that make the implementation of an emerging practice like RME seem inevitable for an organization to appear legitimate and (b) the work of different types of institutional entrepreneurs who leverage resources to either transform existing institutions or to create new ones (Battilana, Leca & Boxenbaum, 2009). Second, an analysis of the institutionalized nature of RME also highlights whether or not schools actually 'walk their talk' and engage in substantive or only symbolic adoption of the practice (Høgdal, Rasche, Schoeneborn & Scotti, 2019; Rasche & Gilbert, 2015). Such an analysis is important, as the institutionalization of a practice by itself says little about its actual impact on adopting organizations. We argue that there is always a risk that schools will decouple formal structures (e.g. committees and new policies regarding RME) from their everyday organizational practices.

Our analysis proceeds as follows. The following section takes a brief look back and discusses what has shaped the institutionalization of RME over time. We review different types of institutional pressures that have shaped the diffusion of the practice, and we also discuss the relevance of selected institutional entrepreneurs that have influenced the acceptance of RME as a legitimized social practice. The next section then focuses more on the current status of the institutionalization by demonstrating that many schools only symbolically adopt RME and hence decouple their public commitments from actual implementation practices. We review different types of decoupling in the business school context and discuss what determines whether a school decouples or not. The final section takes a look into the future and outlines an agenda for forthcoming scholarly work in this area. This section also discusses in what ways educational and organizational practices can be improved to avoid decoupling and to therefore move more strongly towards substantive implementation of RME.

INSTITUTIONALIZATION OF RME

The institutionalization of practices like RME is the result of different pressures that exist in organizations' environment and also the explicit work of selected actors who 'push' their practices towards institutionalization.

Existence of Isomorphic Pressures

Following DiMaggio & Powell (1983), we argue that (1) coercive, (2) mimetic and (3) normative pressures affect the diffusion of RME policies and practices in business schools over time (see also Rasche & Gilbert, 2015). First, coercive pressures induce the adoption of a policy or practice because organizations tend to avoid expected negative consequences whenever non-compliance with relevant rules or regulations occurs. In the context of business schools, these pressures result mostly from accreditation agencies – like the Association for MBAs (AMBA), the European Foundation for Management Development (EFMD) and the Association to Advance Collegiate Schools of Business (AACSB) – which have acknowledged the need for RME and, in some cases, have added relevant criteria to their guidelines. AACSB, for instance, requires business schools to commit themselves 'to address, engage and respond to current and emerging corporate social responsibility issues … through its policies, procedures, curricula, research, and/or outreach activities' (2018: 7). Business schools increasingly depend on accreditations to uphold their legitimacy as well as to differentiate themselves from competitors (Doherty, Richards & Meehan, 2015; Durand & McGuire, 2005). Schools' RME-related activities are also influenced by coercive pressures that originate from ranking providers. For instance, the *Financial Times*' well-known MBA ranking just recently included a criterion focusing on ethics and sustainability (FT, 2018).

Second, business schools are exposed to mimetic pressures, that is, forces that cause organizations to adapt their behavior towards the actions of peers. This means that under conditions of uncertainty schools adapt their programs and commitments to what other schools have done. They imitate peers that are perceived to be influential or successful in the organizational field of RME. Since leading business schools have adopted RME around the world (e.g. by joining the PRME), other schools have to respond in order to be perceived as legitimate by social actors. This emerging market trend, in combination with the rather unspecific conceptualization of RME, induces business schools to adapt their behavior towards the RME measures that other schools have already implemented. Prestigious schools such as INSEAD and the London Business School were among the first signatories of PRME and received positive media coverage for changes in curricula or programs. This inspired other schools to follow suit, as demonstrated by the increasing number of PRME signatories (PRME reported an average global signatory growth of 12% in 2017). Such mimetic pressures are further strengthened by the existence of elite groups like the PRME Champions, which were explicitly set up to encourage RME newcomers to learn (and copy) best practices from 'Champions'. Currently, 29 business schools from all over the world are part of this group and committed themselves to 'serve the broader PRME community through active engagement' with RME stakeholders (PRME, 2018b).

Finally, business schools also face normative pressures in that their organizational environment increasingly perceives RME to reflect a proper course of action. Even before the 2007–2008 financial crisis, business schools were criticized for 'propagating ideologically inspired amoral theories' (Ghoshal, 2005: 76) that neglect the ethical dimension of business and management. Prominent business schools, such as Harvard, were accused of being (at least partially) responsible for the 'moral failure of the MBA elite' by fostering a culture of narrow self-interest

that contributed to the crisis of capitalism (McDonald, 2017). Parker (2018) takes this critical diagnosis as a starting point for his call to 'shut down the business school' by suggesting radical reform of the conventional business school model.

These criticisms have been echoed broadly by the media, which increased the normative pressure on business schools to change course. In addition, several surveys suggest that students demand more courses on ethics and sustainability in their curricula. An online survey by PRME (2016) with nearly 1,800 participants finds that 79% of students agree or strongly agree that 'all business students should study business ethics' and 68% call on business schools to integrate ethics and sustainability into the core curriculum. Another survey suggests that 64% of Millennials would not work for a company that lacks strong CSR values while 88% perceive a job with a positive societal impact as more fulfilling (Cone Communications, 2016). Hence, business schools are also increasingly confronted with students who expect curricula to include courses and activities that provide qualifications and skills in RME-related topics.

Institutional Entrepreneurs Supporting Responsible Management Education

The existence of different isomorphic pressures highlights the importance of the environment in which business schools are embedded. However, merely focusing on these pressures would unnecessarily downplay the role of certain actors and hence result in an over-socialized view of institutionalization. We therefore also account for the role of different individual and organizational actors, who have influenced the institutionalization of RME. We label these actors institutional entrepreneurs and define them as 'actors who leverage resources to create new or transform existing institutions' (Battilana et al., 2009: 69). Such entrepreneurs usually do not just have sufficient financial and non-financial resources at hand to support institution building, they also see the creation or transformation of an institution as an opportunity to further their own interests (David, Sine & Haveman, 2013; DiMaggio, 1988). Institutional entrepreneurs usually launch proto-institutions (i.e. not yet institutionalized practices) and work for these proto-institutions to be widely acknowledged and legitimized. Ideally, proto-institutions become recognized as legitimate and appropriate social objects that are widely viewed as possessing a taken-for-granted status (Berger & Luckmann, 1966). Our discussion will primarily focus on PRME as an example for such an institutional entrepreneur, but it will also consider organizations that have acted as important allies.

Although RME was discussed long before the launch of PRME (see e.g. Teece & Winter, 1984), relevant debates were often ad hoc and lacked organizational support. For instance, Windsor (2002) criticized AACSB's curricular flexibility approach and called for the mandatory inclusion of RME-related courses. However, these early attempts did not result in a wide diffusion of relevant practices, as there was no organization that could support these claims and keep them on the agenda of decision-makers. The debate became more organized with the introduction of PRME, which were launched in the midst of the financial crisis in 2007 (Rasche & Escudero, 2010; Waddock, Rasche, Werhane & Unruh, 2011). Rather than impeding success, the financial crisis helped PRME and the RME debate to gain traction. Crisis situations often act as enabling field-level conditions for institutional entrepreneurs to be successful (Fligstein, 2001). Although the financial crisis did not motivate the creation of PRME, it helped to disrupt the existing field-level consensus that business schools were sufficiently covering responsibility, sustainability and ethics. The financial crisis created a situation in which business schools were suddenly criticized for educating rogue bankers who put profit above everything. *The New York Times* even asked: 'Is it time to retrain b-schools?' (Holland, 2009). The launch of PRME therefore helped to legitimize changes to educational practices.

Another factor that enabled the role of PRME as an institutional entrepreneur was its social position. PRME's affiliation with the United Nations Global Compact (UNGC) and its recognition as an initiative that is officially backed by the UN provided access to an important resource: social legitimacy. As the UN enjoys high levels of trust and legitimacy (Barnett & Finnemore, 2008, Torgler, 2008), PRME profited from positive legitimacy spillover effects and therefore increased its capacity to diffuse RME. These high degrees of legitimacy supported the institutionalization of RME in two different ways. First, it helped to legitimize PRME's vision for divergent change, which is reflected in its six core principles. The principles enjoyed a high degree of communicative legitimacy because they were drafted by an international task force that was tied to the UNGC (Rasche & Escudero, 2010). Second, PRME's perceived legitimacy was helpful in mobilizing important allies. The following organizations co-convened the drafting of the principles, then officially endorsed them, and later on served on the PRME Steering Committee: AACSB International, EFMD, the Aspen Institute Business in Society Program, the Academy of Business in Society (ABIS), the GRLI and Net Impact. Mobilizing these organizations as allies also implied gaining access to resources, most importantly the formal authority that is attached to accreditation agencies. The support of these allies also enabled PRME to frame the emerging RME discourse in a way that it resonated with the values and interests of major business schools. This further supported the institutionalization of RME, as it prevented the field from being dominated by different, competing groups of actors.

THE SYMBOLIC ADOPTION OF RME: DECOUPLING

Institutional theory argues that organizations may respond differently to institutionalized practices (Oliver, 1991). While some organizations will implement the relevant practice, others may resist environmental pressures leading to a situation in which conformity to institutional pressures may only be ceremonial (Meyer & Rowan, 1977). In such cases, the need to respond to institutional pressures contradicts schools' internal needs for efficiency. Schools then decouple their implementation activities (e.g. curriculum change) from formal structures (e.g. policies) to secure and preserve their organizational efficiency (Boxenbaum & Jonsson, 2008). Such decoupling between business schools' public commitment to RME (reflected in their formal structures) and their actual organizational practices (reflected in their day-to-day activities) has formed an important part of the scholarly debate (see e.g. Burchell, Kennedy & Murray, 2015; Rasche & Gilbert, 2015; Rasche, Gilbert & Schedel, 2013).

What Causes Decoupling of RME?

Four main factors drive decoupling of RME in business schools (see also Rasche & Gilbert, 2015): (1) some business schools have only limited resources available, (2) there can be resistance against RME by some powerful actors, (3) schools often have to respond to multiple institutional pressures at the same time, and (4) organizational actors can perceive RME demands as ambiguous and vague. These factors describe conditions that make it more *likely* for business schools to decouple without, however, determining that decoupling will always be induced by these factors. Ultimately, decoupling rests upon highly contextual conditions that can vary significantly between individual business schools (Snelson-Powell, Grosvold & Millington, 2016).

First, decoupling can be the result of a conflict between external legitimacy demands and internal efficiency requirements (Meyer & Rowan, 1977; Westphal & Zajac, 1998). Business schools need to mobilize significant material and immaterial resources to integrate RME into their organization. Depending on the scale and scope of a school's RME efforts, courses, curricula and programs need to be modified, internal governance structures altered and, at least in some cases, additional staff needs to be hired. The overall costs of integrating RME across all programs and courses can be expected to be high, since a full integration requires the implementation of RME not only within selected courses but also across the entire program portfolio. At the same time, the competition among business schools for students and financial funding has increased significantly over the past years. Governments have reduced public funding for higher education on a per student basis in several countries, while business schools face strong competition on the global market (Fethke & Policano, 2013). Tuition fees cannot be increased indefinitely, as student debt has already reached unsustainable levels in countries with a high international market share in higher education, such as the USA or the UK. Therefore, many business schools are likely to encounter a tension between the external demand for RME and their internal resource constraints. This tension, in turn, can induce business schools to adopt RME only on a symbolic rather than a substantial level. Recent research points to the diversity of material and immaterial resources that are associated with either tight coupling or decoupling (see Snelson-Powell et al., 2016). In other words, a lack of financial resources does not necessarily lead to decoupling, while other material resources such as an experienced faculty or a business school's reputation appear to foster a substantial implementation of RME.

Second, the decoupling of RME can be caused by power dynamics within business schools. Prior research has shown that decoupling can be the result of powerful actors opposing relevant reforms within an organization (Westphal & Zajac, 2001). Business schools allocate most of the decision-making authority to faculty and provide tenured professors with considerable academic freedom (Mortimer & Sathre, 2010). Studies stress that tenured faculty show only limited interest in changing teaching materials and that they invest less time and effort in teaching (compared to research; Premeaux, 2012). This tendency to prioritize research over teaching is passed on to junior faculty as doctoral programs typically put only limited emphasis on teaching skills (Brightman & Nargundkar, 2013). Therefore, reforming courses and programs largely depends on individual faculty members' willingness to embrace change (Antonacopoulou, 2010; Doherty et al., 2015).

Faculty members might resist change because they do not believe in the RME agenda, for instance, because they perceive such education as a largely futile exercise within the constraints of a free market system. Some faculty may also view RME as threatening their professional identity as 'neutral' and 'value-free' scientists who avoid being associated with a political agenda. Since implementing RME into the curriculum ultimately affects syllabi and course content, faculty has significant leeway to oppose these changes also in more subtle and covert ways. For instance, teachers can ignore RME-related topics in the classroom or teach them with a high degree of cynicism, while formally modifying their syllabus (Høgdal et al., 2019; McLaughlin & Talbert, 2001). This form of decoupling at the classroom level is difficult to prevent, as tenured professors are used to high levels of freedom and low levels of control. Although the majority of deans publicly support RME, deans' influence on tenured professors and the curriculum is limited.

Third, as suggested by institutional theorists (Ruef & Scott, 1998), decoupling of RME can be related to business schools

being simultaneously exposed to multiple demands from their organizational environment. This can lead to a situation where schools implement selected institutional requirements in a substantial way, while only symbolically adopting other field-level requirements. Many business schools, for instance, face conflicting demands concerning the policy implications of major rankings, such as from *The Economist, The Financial Times* or *Forbes*. Since rankings are widely perceived as a valid signal of quality (Wedlin, 2007), they exert considerable influence on strategic decisions of business schools regarding staff, programs and research priorities (Morgeson & Nahrgang, 2008). Although rankings from different outlets and their underlying criteria do not necessarily contradict RME, they only rarely encourage its adoption. *The Financial Times* and *Forbes*, for instance, assign high weights in their ranking methodology to salary prospects incentivizing business schools to invest in placement and career services rather than RME. Although *The Financial Times* included CSR/sustainability as a criterion in their 2018 ranking for the first time (FT, 2018), the criterion only carries a weight of 3% compared to the 40% weighting for the whole salary category (20% for the average salary 3 years after graduation as well as 20% for the average salary increase).

It is therefore reasonable to expect that business schools prioritize investments in areas that affect their ranking position the most, while they could decouple the structural effects of RME. However, as sustainability and CSR-oriented rankings are becoming more popular (e.g. the ranking by Corporate Knights), business schools increasingly are confronted with field-level pressures towards adopting RME (Doherty et al., 2015). These rankings, at least for now, largely address a niche market segment in higher education that focuses on sustainability and CSR and remain less prestigious and less well known. Business schools may therefore feel compelled to focus their attention mainly on the core criteria of conventional rankings, while, at the same time, adopting more symbolic RME measures to also appeal to sustainability-oriented audiences.

Finally, RME decoupling can also be induced by the ambiguity of institutional demands that business schools are facing. Ambiguity can cause decoupling because it creates considerable room for interpretation concerning the specifics of the institutional requirements to which an organization is exposed to (George, Chattopadhyay, Sitkin & Barden, 2006). Such ambiguity may motivate some schools to implement RME policies in ways that have a small or no effect. Ambiguity is likely to be an important driver of decoupling as the institutional demands related to RME are usually rather vague. The PRME (2018a), for instance, requires business schools to adopt 'the values of global social responsibility' and to 'create educational frameworks, materials, processes and environments that enable effective learning experiences for responsible leadership'.

Although PRME argues that such vagueness is intentional, it seems reasonable to expect that some business schools will exploit such vagueness in their favor by avoiding substantial changes to the status quo. This vagueness can also be identified in the requirements of accreditation agencies. AACSB (2018: 7), for instance, states that 'sustainable development, environmental sustainability, globalization, and other emerging corporate and social responsibility issues are important and require proactive engagement between business schools and business students', without providing further specifics on what 'proactive engagement' actually means and how schools should translate these ideas into concrete action.

Types of RME Decoupling

RME decoupling can occur in three different ways: (1) schools do not redesign their curriculum substantially, (2) changes of the curriculum are not transferred into actual classroom practices and (3) schools avoid the integration of RME into their hidden curriculum. First, there is the case where schools decouple their public claims around RME from the content of their formal curriculum. This type of decoupling has been observed by analyses of schools' curricula. Rasche et al. (2013), for instance, analysed RME in the context of MBA programs and found that, while schools doubled the number of RME-related courses between 2005 and 2009, about 75% of these courses were electives that were not tied to disciplines like finance and accounting. Based on these insights, they claim that there is a risk that schools decouple their public commitments from actual implementation, for instance, because it is questionable whether the bulk of MBA students are exposed to relevant content, if the vast majority of courses are electives and thus 'preach to the converted' (Rasche et al., 2013: 78). Burchell et al.'s (2015) analysis of RME content in UK business schools points in a similar direction. While they also observed a general increase in RME content over time, they did not find evidence that PRME signatory schools performed better than non-signatories. This calls into question how far initiatives like PRME really act as a catalyst for curriculum change. Snelson-Powell et al. (2016) extend these insights by finding that smaller, prestigious schools tend to be associated with tighter couplings, while larger, less prestigious schools tend to be associated with decoupling.

A second type of decoupling occurs between schools' formal curricula and actual classroom practices. As teachers possess high degrees of autonomy (McLaughlin & Talbert, 2001) and do not necessarily have to fully follow the formal curriculum (see e.g. Meyer & Rowan, 1983), they can decouple their actual teaching practices from statements around RME in the formal curriculum. Although this type of decoupling has not been empirically observed so far, it is likely to exist.

One key reason for such decoupling could be the existence of different ideological positions regarding core themes within the RME agenda. Most RME content is critical of the neo-classical model of welfare economics and the assumptions that are attached to this model (e.g. that profit maximization should be the only business objective). It is likely that economics and finance instructors cannot really identify with such criticism and therefore rather avoid relevant discussions in the classroom. Nicholson and DeMoss (2009), for instance, find that coordinators from accounting and finance departments attached much less importance to topics related to ethics than coordinators from management and marketing departments. Given the freedom attached to the tenure system (see above), it is likely that tenured faculty feel less pressure to change actual classroom practices even if they symbolically support a school's emphasis on RME (e.g. by changing parts of the syllabus).

Finally, it is also possible that schools decouple RME content that is fixed in the formal curriculum from the organization's hidden curriculum. We use the term 'hidden curriculum' to emphasize the role of implicit learnings that occur alongside the more formal learnings in educational institutions (Blasco, 2012). The hidden curriculum encompasses the socialization processes about norms and values that schools pass on to their students. To our knowledge, only the study by Høgdal et al. (2019) has discussed the role of decoupling in the context of the hidden curriculum so far. Their analysis of a PRME signatory showed that some of the messages that were attached to the school's hidden curriculum contradicted the institution's official goal to integrate RME throughout its programs. For instance, faculty often sent messages to students that made them perceive RME content as 'soft' and 'non-theoretical' (e.g. by emphasizing that such kind of topics are subjective and only based on one's personal opinion). This last type of decoupling seems particularly important, as

prior studies have emphasized that the hidden curriculum can significantly affect students' moral learning (Hafferty & Gaufberg, 2017).

Although the discussion of RME decoupling still lacks broad empirical support, the existing scholarly work in this area shows the relevance of the topic. Decoupling seems at least likely, as many of the conditions that enable the symbolic adoption of RME are fulfilled. The rather high environmental pressures to show *some degree* of involvement in RME paired with the rather vague nature of relevant requirements create a situation in which decoupling becomes a strategic option for those schools who lack the resources and/or interest to show substantive implementation.

AGENDA FOR FUTURE RESEARCH AND EDUCATIONAL PRACTICES

The institutionalization of RME provides an interesting area for future scholarly activity. In this section, we highlight three research areas that deserve more scrutiny in upcoming scholarly work before we conclude with some final implications for educational and organizational practices.

Decoupling of RME and the Hidden Curriculum

Our discussion of decoupling showed that we still lack empirical insights on whether a school's hidden curriculum contradicts its public claims around RME. Studies in this direction would need to carefully unpack the hidden curriculum concept in the context of RME (see e.g. Blasco, 2012) to then investigate whether schools send implicit messages to students about RME (e.g. through their teaching and assessment practices). Such research would be important and timely, as it includes students' experience of RME in future scholarly discussions. As most studies of decoupling focus exclusively on the curriculum or faculty (Doherty et al., 2015; Rasche et al., 2013), including a student perspective would be important and timely. Relevant research has to unpack the tacit and contextual dimension of implicit messages that are sent by schools through the hidden curriculum. We therefore suggest a much stronger consideration of ethnographic fieldwork (Goffman, 1989), for instance, through observations of curricular and non-curricular activities. Such in-depth ethnographic accounts can help us to better understand the life-worlds in which students, faculty and administrative staff are embedded. One important advantage of an ethnography is that it allows to reach beyond what actors consciously make sense of and, therefore, share during interviews (Bourdieu, 1990).

Institutional Maintenance of RME

Current scholarly work primarily focuses on the practices associated with creating RME as an institution. While institutional creation is an important facet, the institutional work of maintaining RME as an institution has received relatively little empirical or theoretical attention. Even powerful and non-contested institutions like RME require maintenance so that they remain relevant to social actors (Lawrence, Suddaby & Leca, 2009). Topics for future research include, but are not limited to: (a) studying how actors like PRME aim to preserve the normative underpinnings of RME and thus stabilize the institution, (b) investigating whether a broad-based observation of decoupling could endanger the existence of RME, for instance, because it undercuts its legitimacy and perceived relevance and (c) researching whether some actors try to establish higher coercive barriers that would prevent deinstitutionalization (e.g. when accreditation agencies further tighten their criteria). Reflecting on institutional maintenance is important, as RME is a fairly recent institution and hence

requires ongoing support by different actors, especially if the relevant organizational field moves in new and unexpected directions. Research in this direction needs to consider that maintaining RME as an institution means to actively work for its relevance and legitimacy and is therefore more than a simple absence of change.

Institutional Entrepreneurs in Support of RME

Finally, research has to better understand the role of institutional entrepreneurs in the context of RME. While it is clear that these entrepreneurs have succeeded in creating RME as an institution, there are at least two issues that have remained unaddressed so far. First, while numerous studies have highlighted the role of PRME as an important organization that has shaped the institutionalization of RME (see e.g. Godemann, Haertle, Herzig & Moon, 2014; Rasche & Escudero, 2010; Solitander, Fougère, Sobczak & Herlin, 2012), there is almost no discussion of the role of other actors. In particular, we need to know more about the role of individual school-based champions that drive the RME agenda (see e.g. Solitander et al., 2012 for case examples). These individual champions can help to legitimize divergent or contested aspects of RME (see e.g. Maguire, Hardy & Lawrence, 2004). They can also engage in motivational framing (Misangyi, Weaver & Elms, 2008) – that is, they can offer their schools compelling reasons (beyond compliance) to adopt RME as an institution. Such institutional entrepreneurs work against decoupling in various ways, for instance, by organizing resources and navigating through political difficulties (Solitander et al., 2012) or also by 'translating' the rather vague requirements of RME initiatives into contextualized solutions at the school level. Second, we need a stronger focus on how those individual actors, who operate outside of business schools and in the broader organizational field, act as institutional entrepreneurs. Certain individuals have shaped the institutionalization of RME in significant ways, for instance, Jonas Heartle (former Head of PRME) or Eric Cornuel (Director General and CEO of EFMD). Future research can study how these actors used their social capital (e.g. their informal network positions) to build alliances that impacted the institutionalization of RME.

Implications for Educational and Organizational Practices

Our discussion also has implications for the design of future educational and organizational practices. In particular, we want to highlight the importance of recoupling. Often, RME decoupling occurs unintentionally, for instance, because a school signed up to an initiative like PRME without having properly checked whether it has the financial and non-financial resources for substantive implementation (see e.g. Hillon, 2017). In such cases, it is possible to recouple, because schools have the intention to improve their practices (and do not exploit RME as a public relations smokescreen). Recoupling can be tied to 'aspirational talk' (Christensen, Morsing & Thyssen, 2013): i.e. schools that publicly talk about changes may create this very reality, because key organizational stakeholders hold them accountable and initiate relevant change processes. Such a perspective assumes that communication is action and has the potential to initiate incremental change processes that slowly alter a school's identity. For such recoupling to occur there needs to be support from a school's senior management. Although senior managers are rarely directly in charge of RME (Solitander et al., 2012), it is important that those internal champions, who are tasked with implementing relevant practices (e.g. driving curriculum change), have good access to decision-makers at the top of a school's hierarchy.

This ensures that necessary resources can be mobilized and that emerging discussions are not quickly silenced by internal politics, ideological differences and power games.

Schools that want to recouple also need to better understand and assess their hidden curriculum. Blasco's (2012) inquiry-based framework provides an important yardstick for such analysis. Considering the role of the hidden curriculum is essential, because it points to issues that often escape the attention of decision-makers and can therefore lead to unintentional decoupling. For instance, existing collaborations between a school and its corporate partners can strengthen or weaken the perception of RME. Høgdal et al.'s (2019) analysis is a case in point. They discuss how students perceived the sponsorship of the business school by a tobacco company as a misalignment between the school's public position on RME and its actual behavior. Although the implicit dimension of educational experiences cannot be directly managed (like a curriculum), it is essential that (a) relevant actors are aware that the hidden curriculum manifests itself in three main message sites (i.e. school governance, interpersonal interactions and the formal curriculum; Blasco, 2012) and (b) it is possible to influence these sites in various, often indirect, ways. One important aspect, which has been highlighted by research on corporate culture (Sathe, 1983), is to more carefully listen to what actors have to say (and also to realize what they do not talk about) and to acknowledge the importance of informal carriers of values. Storytelling in and outside of the classroom can be a powerful source to nudge people, as numerous studies on narratives and change have shown (see e.g. Brown, Gabriel & Gherardi, 2009). After all, the stories, jokes, rituals, anecdotes, and stereotypes that faculty and senior management share with students may be more important for a recoupling of RME than significant financial investments in the curriculum.

REFERENCES

AACSB. (2018). Eligibility Procedures and Accreditation Standards for Business Accreditation. Available at: www.aacsb.edu/-/media/aacsb/docs/accreditation/business/standards-and-tables/2018-business-standards.ashx?la=en.

Abrahamson, E. (1996). Management fashion. *Academy of Management Review, 21*(1), 254–285.

Antonacopoulou, E. P. (2010). Making the business school more 'critical': reflexive critique based on phronesis as a foundation for impact. *British Journal of Management, 21*(s1), s6–s25.

Barnett, M., & Finnemore, M. (2008). Political approaches. In Weiss, T. G., & Daws, S. (Eds.), *The Oxford handbook on the United Nations* (pp. 41–57). Oxford: Oxford University Press.

Battilana, J., Leca, B., & Boxenbaum, E. (2009). How actors change institutions: towards a theory of institutional entrepreneurship. *Academy of Management Annals, 3*(1), 65–107.

Berger, P. L., & Luckmann, T. (1966). *The social construction of reality: a treatise in the sociology of knowledge.* Garden City, NY: Doubleday.

Blasco, M. (2012). Aligning the hidden curriculum of management education with PRME: an inquiry-based framework. *Journal of Management Education, 36*(3), 364–388.

Bourdieu, P. (1990). *The logic of practice.* Cambridge: Polity Press.

Boxenbaum, E., & Jonsson, S. (2008). Isomorphism, diffusion and decoupling. In Greenwood, R., Oliver, C., Lawrence, T. B., & Meyer, R. E. (Eds.), *The SAGE handbook of organizational institutionalism* (pp. 78–98). Los Angeles, CA: SAGE Publications.

Brightman, H. J., & Nargundkar, S. (2013). Implementing comprehensive teacher training in business doctoral programs. *Decision Sciences Journal of Innovative Education, 11*(4), 297–304.

Brown, A. D., Gabriel, Y., & Gherardi, S. (2009). Storytelling and change: an unfolding story. *Organization, 16*(3), 323–333.

Burchell, J., Kennedy, S., & Murray, A. (2015). Responsible management education in UK business schools: critically examining the role of the United Nations Principles for Responsible Management Education as a driver for change. *Management Learning, 46*(4), 479–497.

Christensen, L. T., Morsing, M., & Thyssen, O. (2013). CSR as aspirational talk. *Organization, 20*(39), 372–393.

Cone Communications (2016). *The 2016 Cone Communications Millennial Employee Engagement Study.* Available at: https://www.conecomm.com/research-blog/2016-millennial-employee-engagement-study.

David, R. J., Sine, W. D., & Haveman, H. A. (2013). Seizing opportunity in emerging fields: how institutional entrepreneurs legitimated the professional form of management consulting. *Organization Science, 24*(2), 356–377.

DiMaggio, P. J. (1988). Interest and agency in institutional theory. In Zucker, L. G. (Ed.), *Institutional patterns and organizations: culture and environment* (pp. 3–22). Cambridge, MA: Ballinger.

DiMaggio, P. J., & Powell, W. W. (1983). The Iron Cage revisited: institutional isomorphism and collective rationality in organizational fields. *American Sociological Review, 48*(2), 147–160.

Doherty, B., Richards, A., & Meehan, J. (2015). The business case and barriers for responsible management education in business schools. *Journal of Management Development, 34*(1), 34–60.

Durand, R., & McGuire, J. (2005). Legitimating agencies in the face of selection: the case of AACSB. *Organization Studies, 26*(2), 165–196.

Fethke, G. C., & Policano, A. J. (2013). Public no more universities: subsidy to self-reliance. *Journal of Management Development, 32*(5), 525–536.

Fligstein, N. (2001). Social skill and the theory of fields. *Sociological Theory, 19*(2), 105–125.

FT. (2018). Executive MBA Ranking 2018. Available at: http://rankings.ft.com/businessschoolrankings/executive-mba-ranking-2018.

George, E., Chattopadhyay, P., Sitkin, S. B., & Barden, J. (2006). Cognitive underpinnings of institutional persistence and change: a framing perspective. *Academy of Management Review, 31*(2), 347–365.

Ghoshal, S. (2005). Bad management theories are destroying good management practices. *Academy of Management Learning & Education, 4*(1), 75–91.

Godemann, J., Haertle, J., Herzig, C., & Moon, J. (2014). United Nations supported Principles for Responsible Management Education: purpose, progress and prospects. *Journal of Cleaner Production, 62*, 16–23.

Goffman, E. (1989). On fieldwork. *Journal of Contemporary Ethnography, 18*(2), 123–132.

Hafferty, F. W., & Gaufberg, E. H. (2017). The hidden curriculum. In Dent, J. A., Harden, R. M., & Hunt, D. (Eds.), *A practical guide for medical teachers* (pp. 35–41). Edinburgh: Elsevier.

Hillon, Y. C. (2017). Heroic narratives of intentional non-compliance with PRME. *Society and Business Review, 12*(3), 256–273.

Høgdal, C., Rasche, A., Schoeneborn, D., & Scotti, L. (2019). Exploring student perceptions of the hidden curriculum in responsible management education. *Journal of Business Ethics*, ePub 7 June. doi.org/10.1007/s10551-019-04221-9.

Holland, K. (2009). Is it time to retrain b-schools? *The New York Times*, 14 March. Available at: www.nytimes.com/2009/03/15/business/15school.html.

Lawrence, T. B., Suddaby, R., & Leca, B. (2009). Introduction: theorizing and studying institutional work. In Lawrence, T. B., Suddaby, R., & Leca, B. (Eds.), *Institutional work: actors and agency in institutional studies of organizations* (pp. 1–27). Cambridge: Cambridge University Press.

Maguire, S., Hardy, C., & Lawrence, T. B. (2004). Institutional entrepreneurship in emerging fields: HIV/AIDS treatment advocacy in Canada. *Academy of Management Journal, 47*(5), 657–679.

McDonald, D. (2017). *The golden passport – Harvard Business School, the limits of capitalism, and the moral failure of the MBA elite*. New York: Harper Business.

McLaughlin, M. W., & Talbert, J. E. (2001). *Professional communities and the work of high school teaching*. Chicago: University of Chicago Press.

Meyer, J. W., & Rowan, B. (1977). Institutionalized organizations: formal structure as myth and ceremony. *American Journal of Sociology, 83*(2), 340–363.

Meyer, J. W., & Rowan, B. (1983). The structure of educational organizations. In Meyer, J. W. & Scott, W. R. (Eds.), *Organizational environments: ritual and rationality* (pp. 71–97) Beverly Hills, CA: Sage.

Misangyi, V. F., Weaver, G. R., & Elms, H. (2008). Ending corruption: the interplay among institutional logics, resources, and institutional entrepreneurs. *Academy of Management Review, 33*(3), 750–770.

Morgeson, F. P., & Nahrgang, J. D. (2008). Same as it ever was: recognizing stability in the businessweek rankings. *Academy of Management Learning & Education, 7*(1), 26–41

Mortimer, K. P., & Sathre, C. O.'B. (2010). *The art and politics of academic governance: relations among boards, presidents, and faculty*. Lanham, MD: Rowman & Littlefield.

Nicholson, C. Y., & DeMoss, M. (2009). Teaching ethics and social responsibility: an evaluation of undergraduate business education at the discipline level. *Journal of Education for Business, 84*(4), 213–218.

Oliver, C. (1991). Strategic responses to institutional processes. *Academy of Management Review, 16*(1), 145–179.

Parker, M. (2018). *Shut down the business school: what's wrong with management education*. London: Pluto Press.

Premeaux, S. R. (2012). Tenure perspectives: tenured versus nontenured tenure-track faculty. *Journal of Education for Business, 87*(2), 121–127.

PRME. (2016). The state of CSR and RME in business schools and the attitudes of their students. Available at: www.unprme.org/resource-docs/25MGSMPRMEReport2016.pdf.

PRME. (2018a). Principles of Responsible Management Education. Available at: www.unprme.org/resource-docs/10SixPrinciples.pdf.

PRME. (2018b). PRME Champions. Available at: www.unprme.org/working-groups/champions.php.

Rasche, A., & Escudero, M. (2010). Leading change – the role of the principles of responsible management education. *Journal of Business and Economic Ethics, 10*(2), 244–250.

Rasche, A., & Gilbert, D. U. (2015). Decoupling responsible management education: why business schools may not walk their talk. *Journal of Management Inquiry*, *24*(3), 239–252.

Rasche, A., Gilbert, D. U., & Schedel, I. (2013). Cross-disciplinary ethics education in MBA programs: rhetoric or reality? *Academy of Management Learning & Education*, *12*(1), 71–85.

Ruef, M., & Scott, W. R. (1998). A multidimensional model of organizational legitimacy: hospital survival in changing institutional environments. *Administrative Science Quarterly*, *43*(4), 877–904.

Sathe, V. (1983). Implications of corporate culture: a manager's guide to action. *Organizational Dynamics*, *12*(2), 5–23.

Snelson-Powell, A., Grosvold, J., & Millington, A. (2016). Business school legitimacy and the challenge of sustainability: a fuzzy set analysis of institutional decoupling. *Academy of Management Learning & Education*, *15*(4), 703–723.

Solitander, N., Fougère, M., Sobczak, A., & Herlin, H. (2012). We are the champions: organizational learning and change for responsible management education. *Journal of Management Education*, *36*(3), 337–363.

Teece, D. J., & Winter, S. G. (1984). The limits of neoclassical theory in management education. *American Economic Review*, *74*(2), 116–121.

Tolbert, P. S., & Zucker, L. G. (1983). Institutional sources of change in the formal structure of organizations: the diffusion of civil service reform, 1880–1935. *Administrative Science Quarterly*, *28*(1), 22–39.

Torgler, B. (2008). Trust in international organizations: an empirical investigation focusing on the United Nations. *Review of International Organizations*, *3*(1), 65–93.

Waddock, S., Rasche, A., Werhane, P., & Unruh, G. (2011). The principles for responsible management education: implications for implementation and assessment. In Swanson, D. L., & Fisher, D. G. (Eds.), *Toward assessing business ethics education* (pp. 13–28). Charlotte, NC: Information Age Publishing.

Wedlin, L. (2007). The role of rankings in codifying a business school template: classifications, diffusion and mediated isomorphism in organizational fields. *European Management Review*, *4*(1), 24–39.

Westphal, J. D., & Zajac, E. J. (1998). The symbolic management of stockholders: corporate governance reforms and shareholder reactions. *Administrative Science Quarterly*, *43*(1), 127–153.

Westphal, J. D., & Zajac, E. J. (2001). Decoupling policy from practice: the case of stock repurchase programs. *Administrative Science Quarterly*, *46*(2), 202–228.

Windsor, D. (2002). An open letter on business school responsibility. Available at: http://info.cba.ksu.edu/swanson/Call/Call.pdf.

Zucker, L. G. (Ed.) (1988). *Institutional patterns and organizations: culture and environment.* Cambridge, MA: Ballinger.

27

Responsibility in Business School Accreditations and Rankings

Mathias Falkenstein and Annie Snelson-Powell

INTRODUCTION

This chapter explores the role of accreditations and rankings in shaping business schools' progress in relation to the responsible management learning and education (RMLE) agenda. We take an institutional perspective (Meyer & Rowan, 1977; DiMaggio & Powell, 1983) and consider how these two 'mechanisms' or 'institutions' influence business school strategies at the organizational level, and at the sector level, and examine the extent to which their stipulations influence business school behaviour and inform the institutional template for legitimate business school behaviour (Wedlin, 2007).

This perspective allows us to better understand the limited progress of RMLE content in the curriculum in the past (e.g. Moratis, 2016; Navarro, 2008; Rasche & Gilbert, 2015). The case has been made that business schools have not yet overcome the 'tipping' point (Hommel & Thomas, 2014) required to fundamentally change such that

they re-focus on their role in and to society, to remain relevant and responsible (Ferlie, McGivern & De Moraes, 2010; Wilson & Thomas, 2012). We are thus interested in examining the ways in which accreditation and rankings bodies have played a role in inhibiting progress of RMLE.

In doing so, we also seek to examine the ways in which these mechanisms are also promising tools for the future, with potential to overcome barriers and galvanize otherwise shallow commitments and speed up the progress of RMLE integration. Accreditation bodies and ranking frameworks are considered to be important institutions in their ability to directly influence business school strategies (Wilson & McKiernan, 2011). But it has only been in recent developments that accreditation bodies and ranking criteria have begun to set out RMLE expectations. We thus also seek to form a view of future prospects in this evolving area.

To underpin the discussion of how business schools are shaped by the two institutions of accreditation bodies and ranking frameworks we will explore how these mechanisms have been examined in scholarly research. The literature finds that the combination of business school accreditations and rankings together, has promoted isomorphism, a convergence of schools to behave similarly, and decoupling, a phenomenon where policies are adopted for legitimacy purposes but where corresponding practices are absent (Alajoutsijärvi, Juusola & Siltaoja, 2015; Pfeffer & Fong, 2004; Wedlin, 2011) through the sector. Business school accreditations and rankings substantially determine the nature of the institutional pressures that impact business schools' strategic decisions (Adler & Harzing, 2009; Wilson & McKiernan, 2011), including how, and indeed if, business schools might approach the RMLE agenda (Solitander, Fougere, Sobczak & Herlin, 2012). We are therefore interested in the question of how RMLE in business schools is stimulated through adherence to accreditation and ranking criteria.

However, it is not likely to be a simple case of including RMLE criteria amongst the accreditation and ranking stipulations, and expecting progress to follow naturally. It is not a new theme within the literature to identify rhetoric vs. reality gaps (Cornuel & Hommel, 2015) where business schools' appearances endorse commitment towards RMLE, but actual practices are less evident (Rasche & Gilbert, 2015). The literature notices that while many business schools exhibit behaviours that say they are committed to RMLE, only few schools really do promote and enable RMLE in practice (e.g. Moon & Orlitzy, 2011; Snelson-Powell, Grosvold & Millington, 2016; Wu, Hang, Kuo & Wu, 2010). This chapter takes an institutional perspective, drawing on concepts such as institutional pressures, institutional fields and means–ends decoupling, to consider both how business school accreditations and rankings are in a position to advance the range of RMLE activities pursued by business schools, as well as recognizing they

can also operate to inhibit progress (Adler & Harzing, 2009; Solitander et al., 2012).

This chapter begins by providing a brief overview of the role of business school accreditations and rankings in general and then in relation to RMLE. This overview situates the discussion broadly, before providing a more in-depth study of, firstly, business school accreditations and then, secondly, business school ranking frameworks. A discussion then follows to offer a synthesis of these two mechanisms in relation to the prospects for RMLE, before concluding with a summary of the implications raised by the chapter.

THE ROLES OF BUSINESS SCHOOL ACCREDITATIONS AND RANKINGS

There are two mechanisms in particular that play a decisive role in determining how business schools are judged and inform how they behave (Wilson & McKiernan, 2011). Together these mechanisms establish the cross-border reputation of business schools through what can be thought of as a two-stage filtering system, with international accreditations providing access while acting as 'certifiers' and international rankings defining the relative competitive position. These mechanisms operate together to inform opinion, while at the same time it is also argued that together they drive homogenization (Gioia & Corley, 2002) and define the institutional norms and accepted culture in the global business school sector (Hommel & Thomas, 2014). While we acknowledge they function in combination, they are in fact differently motivated and structured mechanisms, having come about in different ways. We therefore treat them separately in the discussion that follows.

Business School Accreditations Overview

Business school accreditation agencies are seen as drivers for development that influence the transformation process in business and management education (Bryant, 2013). Decisions on governance, programme portfolio and design, faculty composition, internationalization and overall strategy are often linked to standards provided by accreditations. Business schools also use accreditation seals extensively for positioning in the global market (Cornuel, Thomas, Lejeune & Vas, 2009).

International business school accreditations began to understand that continued demand for management education and market growth is not in itself an adequate indicator of the value and success of management education (Thomas, Lee, Wilson & Thomas, 2014). Many different approaches have been encouraged to reconnect management education with business and society. However, beside the many commitments from accreditations, Dyllick (2015) argues that most business and management schools continue to teach biased content in business functions, often ignoring the fact that these functions have negative effects on the sustainability performance of companies (Bondy & Starkey, 2014). Although accreditations are not the only factor that determines what business schools believe, do and become, it certainly is an important shaper of the direction in which they find their way forward in the face of 21st century management education imperatives (Harvey, 2004; Hedmo, Sahlin & Wedlin, 2001, Lindstrom & Word, 2007; Prøitz, Stensaker & Harvey, 2004).

While there are different national and international business school accreditation bodies, this paper focuses on international accreditations such as EQUIS and AACSB, given its relevance and impact in management education. They have especially become relevant since the integration of a strong RMLE narrative in the prestigious European Foundation for Management Development's Quality Improvement System (EQUIS) accreditation as well as for business schools' eligibility to the Association to Advance Collegiate Schools of Business (AASCB) accreditation.

Within this context, international accreditations are playing a dual role in the development of RMLE. While they arguably had their share in business schools' narrow-minded approach to research and education in the past, they also play an important role by driving processes and acting as a change agent in business schools' development (Canals, 2010).

Business School Rankings Overview

Not without controversy (Adler & Harzing, 2009), national and international rankings continue to gain in relevance and influence (Naidoo & Pringle, 2014). As an assessment and marketing tool, international rankings such as the Financial Times European Business School Ranking receive substantial attention from internal and external stakeholders (Hedmo et al., 2001). According to the Graduate Management Admissions Council (Arbaugh, 2016), prospective students often use rankings to inform their decision as to which school they will apply to, while employers use rankings to identify schools from which they want to hire students (Petriglieri, 2015). According to Wedlin (2007), rankings influence faculty in their career paths and choice of future employers. In addition, ministries of higher education and national accreditations consult rankings when they assess quality, award research grants and distribute financial support, and when they define academic and institutional excellence (Thomas et al., 2014). Rankings also support schools in their differentiation from direct competitors, and they are used extensively for branding and marketing purposes (Naidoo, Gosling, Bolden, O'Brien & Hawkins, 2014). Rankings are also influential in determining business school strategy (Martins, 2005) and what comes to be regarded as legitimate organizational behaviour in business schools (Rasche, Hommel & Cornuel, 2014) since the activities of those business schools that perform highly informs the template more broadly of how a business school should behave (Wedlin, 2011).

Traditional business school rankings inhibit RMLE progress in the sector in two important ways. Firstly, RMLE-related objectives remain outside the criteria adopted by rankings of business schools and rankings of the quality of research performed by the school's academics. Secondly, they tie business schools to short-term strategic goals as rankings become more important in the competition for students. RMLE, by contrast, requires a long-term perspective (Brundtland Report; United Nations, 1987), while business schools are influenced by the shorter-term goals to improve rankings (Gioia & Corley, 2002; Wilson & McKiernan, 2011; Wilson & Thomas, 2012). Solitander et al. (2012) identify short-termism as a key strategic barrier to business schools implementing sustainability and RMLE.

BUSINESS SCHOOL ACCREDITATIONS

Background of Business School Accreditation

Business school accreditation has its roots in the US higher education system (Khurana, Nohria & Penrice, 2005). Since the early 20th century, accreditation has been the main monitoring regulator of North American business and management schools, with pre-defined quality standards in various academic areas, administered by independent, non-governmental organizations (Locke, 1989; Porter & McKibbin, 1988). The most important and oldest American accreditation body is the Association for the Advancement of Collegiate Schools of Business (AACSB); founded in 1916, AACSB has been accrediting business schools for over 100 years. Another important American accreditation organization is the Accreditation Council for Business Schools and Programs (ACBSP).

Other national and international accreditation agencies such as the European Foundation of Management Development (EFMD) and the Association of MBAs (AMBA) subsequently developed in Europe. While in the beginning both accredited mainly European business schools, they are now global organizations.

The rise of business school accreditations and assessments during the 1980s and 1990s can be seen as part of a larger societal trend. In a world that is increasingly characterized by variations and differences, accreditations are one way to bridge those differences and facilitate the flow of information (Thomas & Cornuel, 2012). Quality audits are considered as a reaction to the evolving risk society (Hood, 2004), with its increasing demand for transparency and accountability (Khurana, 2010; Locke, 1989), which appear in parallel with increasing access to higher education through globalization and mobility (Power, 1999). Moreover, the emergence of new regulations has been further analysed as an aspect of rationalization in management education that is increasingly challenged by growing competition and deregulation (Moran, 2002). Other studies suggest that the growing importance of business school accreditations could rather be described as a fashion, in a search for additional certifications, standardization and quality assurance systems, all in order to achieve differentiation in competitive, globalized markets (Engwall & Morgan, 2002; Hood, James, Scott, Jones & Travers, 1999; Meyer, 1994). In response, management scholars suggest that the growing importance of accreditations could be rather described as a fashion and search for additional certifications, standardization and quality assurance systems in order to achieve differentiation in competitive, globalized markets (Engwall & Morgan, 2002; Hood et al., 1999; Meyer, 1994). The increasing pressure in management education, resulting from globalization and internationalization as well as the intensification of transnational competition, led to an 'explosion' of regulations and accreditations (Djelic & Sahlin-Andersson, 2006).

International business and management school accreditations now describe a new method of assessment. With a transnational identity, these accreditations are mostly voluntary and include large elements of self-assessment and self-regulation (Bryant, 2013). Voluntary accreditation standards are soft rules and processes with complex procedures of self-presentation, self-reporting and self-monitoring (Power, 2000). The accreditation criteria are framed by science, expertise and experience, but are described in general terms (Morsing & Schultz, 2006; Starkey & Madan, 2001). Thus, they are open to interpretation, translation, editing and negotiation by both those that are being regulated and the regulators (Friga, Bettis & Sullivan, 2003). The accreditation incentives include quality improvements as well as building reputation, trust, and legitimacy (Bryant, 2013). Moreover, international accreditations are often not directly linked to systems of sanctions or resource allocation, and neither the regulators nor the regulatees are hierarchically coupled (Rayment & Smith, 2010; Thomas, Hommel, Muff, King & Roos, 2013a). In consequence, these accreditations are very different from those of the national accreditation systems, which provided the main regulation and recognition in management education (de Onzono, 2011) before international accreditations were established (Thomas et al., 2013b). While in some cases accreditation is driven by those that are being assessed, such as management education institutions (Hood, 2004), in other cases, those that are performing the accreditation (professional organizations, governments, etc.) are the driving force (AACSB, 2011b, Thomas et al., 2013a). It is therefore necessary to differentiate between mandatory accreditations that are often conducted on a national platform versus voluntary accreditations, which in most cases are provided by transnational organizations (Hedmo et al., 2001).

While some schools experienced positive external effects in terms of visibility and image from obtaining the accreditation label, others see internal effects as more important, to reinforce strategies and to benchmark development issues towards other accredited schools (Lindstrom & Word, 2007). A different approach can be found in Prøitz et al.'s (2004) paper 'Accreditation, standards and diversity', which is based on an analysis of several EQUIS peer review reports. Scholarly research finds an initial limitation in business schools' responses, which results from an accreditation process where recommendations are rather abstract and general, often lacking clarity on how to implement them. Further on, research observes an impact of accreditation systems that links directly to quality improvement in management education, but also detects limitations due to accountability and transparency issues in accreditation provided by peer-review teams (Prøitz et al., 2004, Frølich, Huisman, Slipersæter, Stensaker & Bótas, 2012). Along the same lines (Harvey, 2004) argues that accreditations are incompatible with the improvement of organizational effectiveness, as it overloads higher education institutions with the production of public relations documents.

A number of insightful studies have evaluated the impact of this accreditation and how schools respond to the auditing process. Roller, Andrews & Bovee (2003) discussed the benefits of three leading US accreditations by analysing their impact with regard to programme goals, competitiveness and student learning. The results show significant qualitative and quantitative differences across the categories in response to the individual accreditation demands (Roller et al., 2003). In addition, Zoffer (1987) sees the AACSB accreditation process as generally for the benefit of institutions through self-assessment, accountability, the establishment of a legal standard and competition, while providing access to status, ranking or other types of public exposure. In a thought-provoking essay, Julian and Ofori-Dankwa (2006) suggest that the AACSB accreditation process may hinder business schools' ability to adapt to changing environments. Bailey and Dangerfield (2000) point out that institutions may experience the accreditation process and its specific benefits differently, depending on their status, management strength and structure. In addition, the impact of the different accreditation systems may be influenced by factors such as timing, relation to other accreditations and institutional development activities undertaken by the business school (Pupius & Brusoni, 2000).

Lejeune and Vas (2014) analyse in their paper 'Institutional pressure as a trigger for organizational identity change' the case of accreditation failure within seven European business schools. In this study, the authors suggest that accreditation standards represent an important institutional influence in an increasingly competitive European business school environment. They see in EQUIS a label that provides legitimacy and identity to the schools, and the case study suggests that accreditation standards influence the schools' organizational identities through changes in resources and activities (Lejeune & Vas, 2014). However, the study also finds conflicting institutional logics, leading to different identity understandings within the schools. The authors see a risk that the differentiation effect progressively decreases with a constant increase in the number of accredited schools. In a previous study, Lejeune and Vas (2014) analyse the impact of accreditation by studying organizational culture and effectiveness in business schools. This empirical research suggests that EQUIS accreditation may not lead to improvements in student satisfaction with academic programmes. The study argues that the schools' management emphasized more the impact of accreditation on the attractiveness and brand of their school as an indicator of improved performance, rather than students' satisfaction with their curricula (Beehler & Luethge, 2013; Friga et al., 2003). Further, the

dimensions of effectiveness that seem most improved through accreditation are linked to schools' resources, and to qualified faculty and academic partners in particular (Cornuel et al., 2009). Lejeune and Vas further suggest that the EQUIS audit process plays a major role in cultural changes as well as in the effectiveness of the schools. However, as EQUIS expects schools to become more international, it seems unsurprising that the schools are developing a corporate culture through accreditation, which also engenders increased competition in a larger field (Cornuel et al., 2009; Lejeune, 2011; Vas & Lejeune, 2004).

Accreditations and RMLE

The economic crisis resulted in pressure from both internal and external stakeholders on business schools and national as well as international accreditation bodies. The EFMD revised its EQUIS accreditation standards in 2013 and established far-reaching changes by integrating ethics, responsibility and sustainability (ERS) transversally into all of its accreditation criteria (see Figure 27.1) (EFMD, 2016a, EFMD, 2016b). The change implies that responsible and ethical behaviour should be an integral part of a business school's mission, vision, values and strategies, and that it should be reflected in all of the school's regular activities (Rasche & Gilbert, 2015; Thomas et al., 2014).

Equally, AACSB also introduced new criteria for responsible management education in their 2013 revised Business School Accreditation Standards (AACSB, 2015). By linking responsibility and sustainability to the initial eligibility phase, AACSB expects substantial developments to be in place prior to a school entering the accreditation process. One of the guiding principles is that 'The school must encourage and support ethical behaviour by students, faculty, and professional staff' (AACSB, 2011a, 2015). A strong commitment to corporate and social

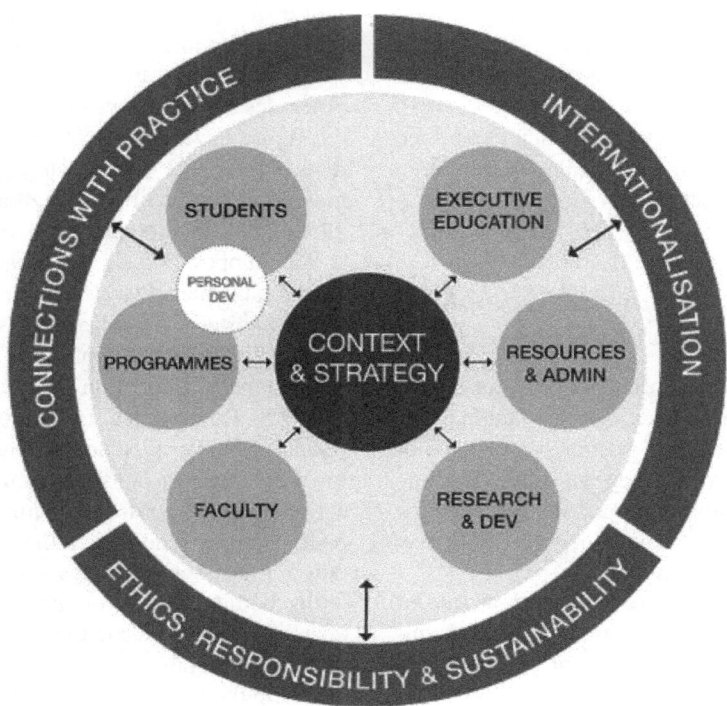

Figure 27.1   EQUIS criteria framework (EFMD, 2016a)

responsibility is demanded and 'The school must demonstrate a commitment to address, engage, and respond to current and emerging corporate social responsibility issues (e.g. diversity, sustainable development, environmental sustainability, globalization of economic activity across cultures) through its policies, procedures, curricula, research, and/or outreach activities' (AACSB, 2015).

Business schools are considered to be in an identifiable 'institutional field' subject to similar pressures and expectations (Wedlin, 2007). While not all business schools participate in the global accreditation schemes nor the various rankings systems, their prevalence amongst the recognized leaders in the sector establish them as relevant and influential institutions across the wider institutional field. In fact international business school accreditation agencies are considered to be one of the most important

sources of pressures in the business school field (Rasche & Gilbert, 2015). Although the accreditation standards give room for interpretation, business schools cannot ignore their call for RMLE, as accreditations such as EQUIS and AACSB act as an important source of legitimacy (McKiernan & Wilson, 2014). The substantial change in accreditation standards, while well intended, may induce business schools to appear to conform and adopt RMLE, but in practice there is no guarantee that corresponding change will be implemented.

Business schools struggle with the development of a coherent and substantial response to the RMLE accreditation standards. As business school activities are highly visible and their success is measured by accreditations, decoupling of this kind, where responsibility-related policies serve as window-dressing, can be risky for a business school. Discrepancies between claims and actual engagement, practices and integration can challenge legitimacy, if discovered by stakeholders (Rasche & Gilbert, 2015). Nonetheless, these inconsistencies continue to be observed in empirical research (e.g. Snelson-Powell et al., 2016).

What Next for Business School Accreditations and RMLE?

With a history of more than 100 years, business schools have been instrumental in shaping the economic and business paradigms of the past century and they will not escape the tumultuous processes occurring among various stakeholders involved in co-creating new directions for the future.

With so much of the system in a state of flux, attention and resources must be committed towards new ways of thinking and practice, being and doing, and a commitment to a period of trial and error in order to find directions for the future that are both prudent and practical. The distinction between those that 'walk the talk' versus those that only engage in superficial changes is descriptive of the challenges and tensions inherent in adaptive change within institutions – namely, maintaining integrity whilst working simultaneously on both reputation and identity amidst the conflicting expectations of various stakeholders.

Accreditations such as EQUIS and AACSB International can play a key role in this development and are prominent examples. They have shown that accreditation systems are able to change, guide and drive business schools effectively in their challenge to become more ethical, responsible and sustainable. The new RMLE standards and criteria are also in line with accreditations' mission to raise the standard of management education worldwide and to foster a sense of global responsibility in management education. With a substantial revision of all accreditation standards, accreditations have

sent a strong signal, highlighting the importance of responsible management education. With this important change, accreditation processes not only contribute substantially to the future development of business schools, they also ensure their own legitimacy and mandate as influential change agents in the global management education arena.

With support from the European Foundation for Management Development, the AACSB and important organizations such as the United Nations' Principles for Responsible Management Education (PRME) and the Globally Responsible Leadership Initiative (GRLI), business schools have advanced towards a more responsible management education model. In order to continue along this path, business schools together with accreditation processes, rankings and other regulating bodies need to cooperate and further develop a responsible management education agenda. A stronger sense of accountability will help the business school sector to evaluate those activities and measure the real relevance and impact they provide for society at large. This will require business schools to further reinvent themselves and find a common purpose for their existence, which includes a radical rethinking of management education paradigms.

BUSINESS SCHOOL RANKINGS

Background of Business School Rankings

Having established both the background and modern role of accreditations in relation to business school strategy and its engagements with RMLE, this section similarly seeks to explore the role of business school rankings in explaining business school behaviour. Like accreditation mechanisms, business school rankings stipulate particular criteria, which come to shape the norms within the institutional context governing how society expects its business schools to behave (Rasche et al., 2014). Unlike accreditation bodies, however, business school rankings systems do not currently specify requirements that directly relate to RMLE. Nonetheless, how business schools respond to business school rankings remains a pertinent question, since they shape the development of business schools and influence their behaviour (Wedlin, 2007; Wilson & McKiernan, 2011).

This section therefore sets out something of the nature of business school rankings, and establishes how they function as institutional actors (Lawrence & Suddaby, 2006) to determine what comprises legitimate behaviour in the business school sector (Rasche et al., 2014). This broader discussion is then followed by the introduction of RMLE rankings for business schools, namely the Corporate Knights Better World MBA ranking.

There are different kinds of business school rankings. Those that relate to the quality of the research at the level of the institution, for example the UK's Research Excellence Framework (REF), or those at a programme level such as the international Financial Times' Global MBA ranking. Regardless of whether the accolade is determined by a government body or media actor, the rankings share a common approach (Wilkins & Huisman, 2012), with indicators that are weighted and aggregated to yield a relative score. These kinds of methods and means are not always aligned with the best interests of society, despite the fundamental role rankings play in the development of business schools and thus should arguably be a concern of society (Wilson & McKiernan, 2011). Enders (2014) argues that these kinds of indicators invite active engagement to influence image and rankings performance, drawing the measures into the internal dynamics of the business school. Criticisms of rankings abound (Gioia & Corley, 2002) and their role as a measure of quality is questioned (Pfeffer & Fong, 2004). Two particular criticisms are explored here in as much as they impact

RMLE – firstly, related to the narrowness of their measures when RMLE requires broad perspectives and, secondly, related to the short-term nature of their assessments, when RMLE requires a longer-term approach.

Scholars approaching this first criticism have argued that rankings measures propagate narrow perspectives (Rasche et al., 2014) since they measure performance on the basis of faculty publications in a limited set of pre-determined, and often North American, journals (Adler & Harzing, 2009). RMLE, on the other hand, requires the development of broader multidisciplinary intellectual capability, not usually synonymous with what rankings measure as a strong academic profile (Hommel & Thomas, 2014). The limited set of measures that rankings use to assess business schools is also at odds with the great variety of activities schools need to engage in, to involve a large number of heterogeneous stakeholders in an RMLE vision. Inevitably these efforts of engagement fall outside the domain of the rankings bodies and are overlooked. RMLE requires an approach to management education that broadly encompasses the role of the responsible business in its interactions with society and the environment, and considers a multitude of stakeholders.

Secondly, playing the rankings game is sometimes thought of as a tyranny (Khurana, 2007) in that it ties business schools to short-term perspectives, compelling them to resist any change that could displace their reputational standing. Scholars find that business schools adjust strategy to offset rankings changes (Martins, 2005), implying a short-term approach where longer-term plans are at risk. And yet for business schools intending to implement RMLE, they need instead a longer-term approach that is tied to stable strategic goals that have meaning beyond the annual publications of the rankings list. If business schools fear that change may possibly impact reputational standing the next year, it is not hard to see that the change may be resisted (Solitander et al., 2012).

While rankings are culturally supported by business schools (Rasche et al., 2014), providing a much-needed platform for differentiation and international comparison, as the sector marches to commercialization (Gumport, 2000), rankings are also a force or institutional pressure that restricts change that deviates from a set template of established legitimate behaviours (Wedlin, 2007). Until these criteria are updated to embrace RMLE or at least enable broader and longer-term approaches, then progress of this crucial agenda is at risk.

Business School Rankings of RMLE

While the traditional business school rankings schemes do not feature RMLE elements, there are other rankings that focus on green credentials of universities, for example the People and Planet Green League. Further, there is one ranking that focuses on business schools and the RMLE imperative, which is currently known as the Corporate Knights Better World MBA ranking.

The Corporate Knights report (2017) suggests that business schools have a particular responsibility in relation to society, the environment and the economy, and that the sector fails to sufficiently recognize the responsibilities and opportunities offered by the United Nations Sustainable Development Goals (SDGs). The Corporate Knights ranking thus aims to encourage a change amongst business schools to better address this potential to do a better, more responsible job of this in the MBA programme.

In terms of whom it involves, the Corporate Knights Better World MBA ranking is an annual assessment of full-time MBA programmes at business schools worldwide. The top 40 are selected from a population of business schools that includes all the top Financial Times Global MBA programmes as well as other business schools who choose to voluntarily opt in to the Corporate Knights

processes of evaluation. The methodology for evaluation involves three key criteria – the presence of sustainability-related courses as core, or compulsory in the MBA curriculum; the business school's links or affiliation with centres and institutes in a related subject area; and the faculty of the school's research as judged by the quantity of publications and citations in the field.

That prestigious business schools feature highly in the Corporate Knights rankings, is notable for the RMLE agenda. The actions of the most prestigious serve to define and redefine what an ideal business school should do (Wedlin, 2007), and hence eventually influence behaviour in the sector overall. This link between prestige and RMLE is therefore encouraging as it serves to suggest a spread of RMLE in the MBA as, over time, other business schools observe the behaviours of the prestigious institutions and follow suit.

Despite the clear view of progress these kinds of rankings provide, a question remains about whether they drive substantive change for RMLE. Looking more carefully at the MBA curriculum itself, one-fifth of those schools evaluated in the top 40 in 2017 were found to be graded at the lowest level as having none, or only one, core dedicated course on the subject. Even at these exemplar 'greenest' schools, which should provide the definitive model of the best education for future managers, there is clearly still more that can be achieved.

Aside from the Corporate Knights there are several other organizations that exist to further the agenda of RMLE in society and which have a focus on business schools as a provider of education for future managers. They believe that the provision of this management education underpins society's success in the management of the complex and uncertain challenges of the future, which requires responsible leadership. This argument is important and common to a set of initiatives and networks such as the United Nation's Principles for Responsible Management Education (PRME), the

Academy of Business in Society (ABS), the Globally Responsible Leadership Initiative (GRLI) and the recently founded Responsible Research in Business and Management (RRBM) initiative.

While there are positives to these kinds of focused initiatives, they are also prone to the same weaknesses as other kinds of frameworks, which we can ascertain from our study in this chapter of the business school accreditation and ranking systems. Specifically, there remains scope amongst the criteria for participating business schools to become adept at featuring in the rankings or membership by displaying compliance with these criteria, without necessarily requiring fundamental change. There is thus a relatively low bar to achieve membership or compliance with an institute that produces a legitimacy earning RMLE signal at the business school level. What will help us bridge the rhetoric reality gap?

What Next for Business School Rankings and RMLE?

While there is debate surrounding rankings, and what they mean (Gioia & Corley, 2002), given they lack precision, they are nonetheless 'reified' (Wilson & McKiernan, 2011: 462). We have established that since business school rankings shape the development of business schools (Rasche et al., 2014) rankings thus influence business schools' approach to RMLE.

We therefore suggest that business school rankings seek to include RMLE criteria in the mainstream business school rankings in the future, and this chapter outlines some risks and opportunities. Specifically, that supporting the strongest of the accreditations' RMLE criteria and the criteria of the RMLE-specific rankings bodies, such as the Corporate Knights for example, has the potential to stimulate a greater emphasis on adherence in practice. These institutional actors together can reinforce the norms in the

sector. If rankings bodies follow suit with the accreditation bodies to help shape the social landscape (Espeland & Sauder, 2007) there is scope for the institutional pressure to accumulate in this sphere, thereby underpinning a propagation of RMLE through the sector.

Given that business schools themselves are in a position to influence the institutional norms, we also call on all business schools, but especially those in positions of influence. These include those business schools that are relatively more visible through their success, size or prestige (Pfeffer & Salancik, 1978). The behaviour of these business schools is respected and imitated and can therefore be important if we are to speed the diffusion of RMLE through the sector.

A recent report (Pitt-Watson & Quigley, 2018) suggests that some further simple changes to rankings criteria can help the RMLE agenda. They argue that the emphasis on salary metrics favours developing graduates for the highly paid financial sector over other kinds of organizations, such as public sector or charity roles, where pay is relatively low. De-emphasizing graduate salary would thus serve to broaden what business schools conceive of as successful graduates who need to be educated to serve a much wider set of social constituents. The report also suggests reconsidering the requirement for 100% of faculty to have a PhD (Pitt-Watson & Quigley, 2018) and instead introducing other notions that relate to faculty's experiences in practice and their teaching abilities.

We also see new ranking and rating initiatives such as the Positive Impact Rating (PIR) entering the business school markets. After many years of criticism of existing rankings, the desire and need to enable business schools to play a more positive role in society has grown steadily. As leading rankings such as the FT are recognizing a need to entirely review their methodology, the Positive Impact Rating was initiated with the intention to support fundamental change in the business school landscape with regards to the schools' societal responsibility.

Today, business schools are called upon to contribute to the UN SDGs introduced in 2015.

These kinds of initiatives are required on multiple fronts, simultaneously, if they are to be successful in driving change. Scholars have observed that business schools have increasingly signed up for discrete RMLE initiatives, such as PRME, but have failed or been hampered in delivering on the promises of these RMLE principles (e.g. Doherty, Meehan & Richards, 2015). There is a danger of *'responsibility erosion'* (Moratis, 2016: 237) when social and environmental principles are implemented through such commitments, but are prone to becoming detached from actual practices. The discussion that follows explores this phenomenon where we aim to highlight the risk that there is only a weak connection to progressing RMLE, despite growing external commitment to RMLE criteria in business school RMLE initiatives and via accreditation membership.

DISCUSSION: TAKING RMLE BEYOND 'COMPLIANCE' TO IMPACT

The literature that surveys the progress of RMLE into business schools and into the management curriculum, gives us a positive starting point. Sustainability, ethics and corporate social responsibility (CSR) are at least on the agenda for some business schools (Christensen et al., 2007; Matten & Moon, 2004; Moon & Orlitzky, 2011; Snelson-Powell et al., 2016). There are a range of activities that many business schools adopt that are materially advancing the imperative.

That said, this does not represent the case for all business schools, where at the same time as these pockets of progress, other business schools have been slow to move in terms of responding to RMLE in practice, despite the inclusion of RMLE criteria in accreditation bodies, and the growing support among increasing business school members of PRME (Doherty et al., 2015). There is evidence that efforts to date have been partial where many MBA programmes, even at the most engaged business schools that are recognizable for the attention they appear to pay to these matters, still may not include responsibility-related content in the MBA curricula (Corporate Knights, 2017).

It is therefore argued that efforts to date have emphasized rhetoric over the reality (Cornuel & Hommel, 2015). This disconnect is one that involves the dominance of a tick-box or compliance-oriented approach that prioritizes achieving an auditable display of the accreditation criteria, above a substantive and genuine responsive that delivers on the goals of RMLE. Accreditation bodies in particular are prone to this kind of decoupling, noticed by Alajoutsijärvi, Kettunen and Sohlo (2018: 203), where 'accreditation agencies frame their core missions around improving the quality of management education, [while] paradoxically, they reinforce a positional competition that overemphasizes the ends (accreditation labels) over the means (quality improvement)'.

This kind of disconnect, in this instance relating to RMLE commitments which are implemented for accreditation purposes, can be described as a situation of means–ends decoupling (Bromley & Powell, 2012). Here, business schools ensure they are compliant with accreditation criteria, and may often allocate high levels of resources to this effort (Wijen, 2014, but the goal of improving RMLE remains disconnected from the eventual activities, which could be less impactful than planned. This is because the *way* business schools handle the implementation can be narrowly or minimally constructed, particularly in a scenario of high ambiguity or high opacity (Wijen, 2014). What it means to deliver RMLE remains a contested space, with differing opinions on what these concepts might mean in practice (Moon, 2007) and in particular in RMLE where 'there is no formula for how these [responsibility-related concepts] are integrated into the curriculum'

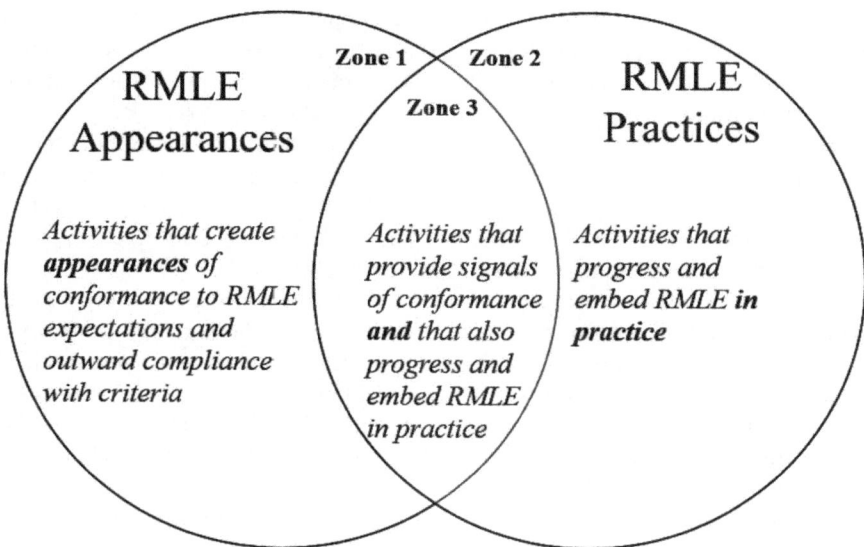

Figure 27.2   RMLE activities can support RMLE appearances and practices

(Stubbs & Schapper, 2011: 259). This definitional uncertainty in RMLE provides scope for a minimalistic interpretation of what it means to demonstrate engagement.

Figure 27.2 reflects how business schools can adopt a range of activities that can vary in terms of the degree to which they are helpful to the school to signal RMLE behaviour and the degree to which they promote a deeper embedding of responsibility.

Zone 1 of Figure 27.2 represents activities that seemingly convey compliance with expectations about proper RMLE behaviour, but in reality may allow the business school to continue to operate as before. This could relate to mission statements that involve the word responsibility or signing up to become a member of an organization that promotes responsible business (such as the Institute for Business Ethics) or responsible business education (such as the UN's PRME), without engaging with the commitments such membership entails. Alvesson and Gabriel (2016) discuss the urge business schools experience to look good; activities to enhance the business school's image are appealing (Alvesson & Gabriel, 2016) but can eventually damage

legitimacy as time passes and the absence of practice becomes conspicuous (Bowen, 2015).

Zone 2 of Figure 27.2 are those activities that really do deliver impact in terms of driving responsibility into management education in a variety of ways, through curriculum transformations to include ethics, sustainability and responsibility, new programmes with a responsibility focus (Rusinko, 2010), promoting research into corporate responsibility, by embodying responsibility organizationally and by considering the hidden curriculum (Blasco, 2012). These activities individually may be insufficient to progress RMLE, however, together and across a variety of domains within the business schools they can generate impactful change.

Zone 3 represents the intended outcome of compliance with the responsibility standards and expectations (Wijen, 2014), as set out in rankings and accreditation mechanisms. This is where organizational plans, processes and practices that flow from compliance with the criteria really do result in the impacts to embed responsibility and deepen the school's engagement with RMLE. We argue that this is frequently not the case in reality, where the idea that impact in achieving RMLE automatically follows from compliance with RMLE criteria is flawed.

To achieve activities in the overlapping zone requires progress on two fronts; one in relation to how accreditation and rankings bodies develop their responsibility criteria and effectively measure schools' actual performance and the other is more movement amongst business schools to break out of the rankings 'tyranny' (Khurana, 2007), which obscures the business schools' social mission in favour of short-term objectives. The progress required by the accreditation and rankings bodies relates to the way performance is stipulated and measured, perhaps involving more stringency in terms of evidence of change and impact, rewarding sustained efforts over time, rather than looking at performance in the previous 12 months alone. This would support the progress required by business schools that take actions to move up the rankings list which are not aligned with their public policy commitments (Enders, 2014). Business schools will face great difficulty in escaping the 'academic arms race' (Enders, 2014: 155) without these developments by accreditation and rankings bodies.

Limitations of a Western Perspective of RMLE

To complete our analysis we also note limitations of the developing RMLE perspective in relation to the emphasis of a Western viewpoint of these accreditations and rankings, calling into question the 'global' boundaries of the field they relate to and their broader relevance. Darley and Luethge (2019) summarize how Western accreditation standards do not address pertinent business problems in African contexts, given the differing needs of their stakeholders. This is not surprising given that management education will naturally mean different things in different geographic contexts and that historically, non-North American authors in management research have been generally under-represented (Baruch, 2001; Burgess & Shaw, 2010). In terms of what RMLE might mean in alternative contexts, we know there is a 'highly diverse understanding, contextualisation and packaging of CSR teaching' (Matten & Moon, 2004: 334).

We have seen that the Corporate Knights ranking list of the Better World MBAs identifies only one of the 40 business schools featured that is not from a typically Westernized country. That the countries in North America, Europe and Australasia might alone determine what an MBA for a better world is, is blinkered and unrealistic. We should therefore seek to consider how business schools in Africa, Asia and elsewhere in the world are viewing RMLE and explore the question of how non-Western schools might benefit from participating in this kind of assessment or other RMLE initiative. While the Corporate Knights efforts progress the initiative, there is still more work to do to establish a global understanding of what comprises an MBA programme that really delivers on the goal of a better world.

CONCLUSION

Business schools are under increasing pressure to respond to societal needs (Pfeffer & Fong, 2004). This means they have to exhibit a true commitment to ethics, responsibility and sustainability at an organizational level or face the loss of mandate and legitimacy that they derive from internal and external stakeholders as well as society at large. In this context, business schools are required to 'walk their talk' (Boyle, 2004; Rasche & Gilbert, 2015). However, when schools address sustainability imperatives, they face internal and external resistance as well as limitations in strategy and resource autonomy. Complex governance structures combined with diverse coercive, formal and normative pressures lead often to only superficial changes (Doherty et al., 2015) to maintain an impressive external image (Alvesson & Gabriel, 2016).

Business schools are perceived as slow adopters of responsible management education; despite some visible activities, there is evidence that RME remains largely as an 'unfulfilled promise' (Cornuel & Hommel, 2015). While many schools have been active in developing RMLE courses and research centres, the core of their academic activities (research and teaching) appears largely immune to societal and environmental issues (Hommel, Painter-Morland & Wang, 2012). The question is raised inside and outside of business schools whether management educators were at all ready to equip their students for leadership in a world faced by crucial economic, social and environmental challenges. Therefore, business and management schools have been criticized for failing to educate responsible managers that are able to respond adequately to demands from internal and external stakeholders as well as society at large (Alvesson, 2013; Aspling, 2013; Dyllick, 2015; Ghoshal, 2005, Muff, Dyllick, Drewell, North, Shrivastava & Härtle, 2013). It is widely argued that business schools continue to deliver a narrow view on responsible management education, while many of their primary stakeholders, such as students, governments and companies, demand a greater sense of purpose (de Onzono, 2011).

This chapter has taken an institutional perspective and focused on two important institutions that shape the behaviour of business schools and the management education they deliver. These are the accreditation bodies and the rankings institutions. In important ways the accreditation bodies, with RMLE stipulations for members, are driving the implementation of these concerns into the business schools sector. However, at the same time, studies note that these very same mechanisms present the risk of compliance over an impact orientation (Wijen, 2014), where

business schools may be more concerned by creating the appearance that they satisfy the accreditations criteria (Alajoutsijärvi et al., 2018) rather than actually satisfying the first-order requirement of developing an environment that stimulates real RMLE. Further the relevance of the notions of RMLE developed in, by and for the predominantly Western business schools that define the global management education context, might require adaption to address and include other geographical contexts where responsible business practice may be differently constructed, but remain as crucial.

While business schools are subject to institutional pressures (Lawrence & Suddaby, 2006; Wilson & McKiernan, 2011) relating to a need to convey institutional conformance and win social approval, this chapter proposes that there is on-going potential for business schools together with the accreditations and rankings to be more centrally involved in RMLE. What appear to be positive RMLE strategies but actually serve purposes relating to satisfaction of accreditation and ranking criteria could be redirected to engage with RMLE more substantively.

Therefore, both accreditation and rankings bodies have a duty to recognize the very real potential for their initiatives in relation to RMLE to be harnessed for window-dressing purposes. They must work to ensure more commitment to actual RMLE performance improvement and adjust their processes accordingly. We recommend a continued push by these bodies to reinforce each other with more specificity relating to the kind of practices expected and to drive through ever-higher expectations of their members with more rigorous criteria that contain less scope for manipulation.

REFERENCES

AACSB. (2011a). *Globalization of management education: changing international structures, adaptive strategies, and the impact on institutions*. Bingley: Emerald Group.

AACSB. (2011b). *Globalization Task Force Recommendations to AACSB International 2011*. Tampa, FL: AACSB International.

AACSB. (2015). Business Accreditation Standards. [Online] Available at: www.aacsb.edu/en/accreditation/standards/2013-business.aspx.

Adler, N., & Harzing, A. (2009). When knowledge wins: transcending the sense and nonsense of academic rankings. *Academy of Management Learning and Education*, 8(1), 72–75.

Alajoutsijärvi, K., Juusola, K., & Siltaoja, M. (2015). The legitimacy paradox of business schools: losing by gaining? *Academy of Management Learning and Education*, 14(2), 277–291.

Alajoutsijärvi, K., Kettunen, K., & Sohlo, S. (2018). Shaking the status quo: business accreditation and positional competition. *Academy of Management Learning and Education*, 17(2), 203–225.

Alvesson, M. (2013). *The triumph of emptiness: consumption, higher education, and work organization*. Oxford: Oxford University Press.

Alvesson, M., & Gabriel, Y. (2016). Grandiosity in contemporary management and education. *Management Learning*, 47(4), 464–473.

Arbaugh, J. (2016). Where are the dedicated scholars of management learning and education? *Management Learning*, 47, 230–240.

Aspling, A. (2013). Business, management education, and leadership for the common good. In Hardy, D. & Everett, G. (Eds.), *Shaping the future of business education: relevance, rigor, and life preparation* (pp. 40–58). Basingstoke: Palgrave Macmillan.

Bailey, J. J., & Dangerfield, B. (2000). Viewpoint: applying the distinction between market-oriented and customer-led strategic perspectives to business school strategy. *Journal of Education for Business*, 75, 183–187.

Baruch, Y. (2001). Global or North American? A geographical based comparative analysis of publications in top management journals. *International Journal of Cross Cultural Management*, 1(1),109–126.

Beehler, J. M., & Luethge, D. J. (2013). Achieving success through quality: the role of accreditation and continuous improvement in management education. In Altmann, A., & Ebersberger, B. (Eds.), *Universities in change* (pp. 277–291). Cham: Springer.

Blasco, M. (2012). Aligning the hidden curriculum of management education with PRME: an inquiry-based framework. *Journal of Management Education*, 36(3), 364–388.

Bondy, K., & Starkey, K. (2014). The dilemmas of internationalization: corporate social responsibility in the multinational corporation. *British Journal of Management*, 25, 4–22.

Bowen, F. (2015). *After greenwashing: symbolic corporate environmentalism and society*. Cambridge: Cambridge University Press.

Boyle, M. E. (2004). Walking our talk: business schools, legitimacy, and citizenship. *Business & Society*, 43(1), 37–68.

Bromley, P., & Powell, W. W. (2012). From smoke and mirrors to walking the talk: decoupling in the contemporary world. *Academy of Management Annals*, 6, 483–530.

Burgess, T., & Shaw, N. (2010). Editorial board membership of management and business journals: a social network analysis study of the Financial Times 40. *British Journal of Management*, 21(3), 627–648.

Bryant, M. (2013). International accreditations as drivers of business school quality improvement. *Journal of Teaching in International Business*, 24, 155–167.

Canals, J. (2010). *The future of leadership development: corporate needs and the role of business schools*. Basingstoke: Palgrave Macmillan.

Christensen, L. J., Peirce, E., Hartman, L. P., Hoffman, W. M., & Carrier, J. (2007). Ethics, CSR, and sustainability education in the Financial Times top 50 global business schools: Baseline data and future research directions. *Journal of Business Ethics*, 73(4), 347–368.

Cornuel, E., & Hommel, U. (2015). Moving beyond the rhetoric of responsible management education. *Journal of Management Development*, 34(1), 2–15.

Cornuel, E., Thomas, H., Lejeune, C. & Vas, A. (2009). Organizational culture and effectiveness in business schools: a test of the accreditation impact. *Journal of Management Development, 28,* 728–741.

Corporate Knights Report (2017). The 15th annual Corporate Knights Better World MBA ranking. Corporate Knights website: www.corporateknights.com/reports/2017-better-world-mba-ranking/.

Darley, W. K., & Luethge, D. J. (2019). Management and business education in Africa: a post-colonial perspective of international accreditation. *Academy of Management Learning & Education,* 18(1), 99–111.

de Onzono, S. I. (2011). *The learning curve: how business schools are re-inventing education.* Basingstoke: Palgrave Macmillan.

DiMaggio, P. J., & Powell, W. W. (1983). The iron cage revisited: institutional isomorphism and collective rationality in organizational fields. *American Sociological Review,* 147–160.

Djelic, M.-L. & Sahlin-Andersson, K. (2006). *Transnational governance: institutional dynamics of regulation.* Cambridge: Cambridge University Press.

Doherty, B., Meehan, J., & Richards, A. (2015). The business case and barriers for responsible management education in business. *Journal of Management Development,* 34(1), 34–60.

Dyllick, T. (2015). Responsible management education for a sustainable world: the challenges for business schools. *Journal of Management Development, 34,* 16–33.

EFMD. (2016a). *EQUIS Standards and Criteria 2016.* Brussels: European Foundation of Management Education.

EFMD. (2016b). *EFMD Annual Report 2016.* Brussels: European Foundation of Management Education.

Enders, J. (2014). The academic arms race. In Pettigrew, A. M., Cornuel, E., & Hommel, U. (Eds.), *The institutional development of business schools* (pp. 155–175). Oxford: Oxford University Press.

Engwall, L., & Morgan, G. (2002). 5 regulatory regimes. *Regulation and Organisations: International Perspectives,* 82.

Espeland, W., & Sauder, M. (2007). Rankings and reactivity: how public measures recreate social worlds. *American Journal of Sociology,* 113(1),1–40.

Ferlie, E., McGivern, G., & De Moraes, A. (2010). Developing a public interest school of management. *British Journal of Management,* S60–S70.

Friga, P. N., Bettis, R. A., & Sullivan, R. S. (2003). Changes in graduate management education and new business school strategies for the 21st century. *Academy of Management Learning & Education, 2,* 233–249.

Frølich, N., Huisman, J., Slipersæter, S., Stensaker, B., & Bótas, P. C. P. (2012). A reinterpretation of institutional transformations in European higher education: strategising pluralistic organisations in multiplex environments. *Higher Education, 65,* 79–93.

Ghoshal, S. (2005). Bad management theories are destroying good management practices. *Academy of Management Learning & Education, 4,* 75–91.

Gioia, D., & Corley, K. (2002). Being good versus looking good: business school rankings and the Circean transformation from substance to image. *Academy of Management Learning and Education,* 1(1), 107–130.

Gumport, P. (2000). Academic restructuring: organizational change and institutional. *Higher Education, 39,* 67–91.

Harvey, L. (2004). The power of accreditation: views of academics 1. *Journal of Higher Education Policy and Management, 26,* 207–223.

Hedmo, T., Sahlin, K., & Wedlin, L. (2001). *The emergence of a European regulatory field of management education: standardizing through accreditation, ranking and guidelines.* SCORE (Stockholms centrum för forskning om offentlig sektor).

Hommel, U., Painter-Morland, M., & Wang, J. (2012). Gradualism prevails and perception outbids substance. *Global Focus, 6,* 30–33.

Hommel, U., & Thomas, H. (2014). Research on business schools: themes, conjectures, and future directions. In Pettigrew, A. M., Cornuel, E., & Hommel, U. (Eds.), *The institutional development of business schools* (pp. 6–35). Oxford: Oxford University Press.

Hood, C. (2004). The middle aging of new public management: into the age of paradox? *Journal of Public Administration Research and Theory, 14,* 267–282.

Hood, C., James, O., Scott, C., Jones, G. W., & Travers, T. (1999). *Regulation inside government: waste watchers, quality police, and sleaze-busters.* Oxford: Oxford University Press.

Julian, S. D., & Ofori-Dankwa, J. C. (2006). Is accreditation good for the strategic decision making of traditional business schools? *Academy of Management Learning & Education, 5*, 225–233.

Khurana, R. (2007), *From higher aims to hired hands: the social transformation of American business schools*. Princeton, NJ: Princeton University Press.

Khurana, R. (2010). *From higher aims to hired hands: the social transformation of American business schools and the unfulfilled promise of management as a profession.* Princeton, NJ: Princeton University Press.

Khurana, R., Nohria, N., & Penrice, D. (2005). Is business management a profession? *Harvard Business School Working Knowledge, 21.*

Lawrence, T., & Suddaby, R. (2006). Institutions and institutional work. In Clegg, S., Hardy, C., Lawrence, T., & Nord, W. (Eds.), *The SAGE handbook of organization studies* (2nd ed.) (pp. 215–254). London: Sage.

Lejeune, C. (2011). Is continuous improvement through accreditation sustainable? A capability-based view. *Management Decision, 49*, 1535–1548.

Lejeune, C. & Vas, A. (2014). Institutional pressure as a trigger for organizational identity change. In Pettigrew, A. M., Cornuel, E., & Hommel, U. (Eds.), *The institutional development of business schools* (pp. 95–25). Oxford: Oxford University Press.

Lindstrom, P., & Word, W. R. (2007). Accreditation of European management schools: the EQUIS system. *Palmetto Review,* 10.

Locke, R. R. (1989). *Management and higher education since 1940: the influence of America and Japan on West Germany, Great Britain, and France.* Cambridge: Cambridge University Press.

Martins, L. (2005). A model of the effects of reputational rankings on organizational change. *Organization Science, 16*(6), 701–720.

Matten, D., & Moon, J. (2004). Corporate Social Responsibility Education in Europe. *Journal of Business Ethics, 54*, 323–337.

McKiernan, P., & Wilson, D. (2014). Strategic choice. In Pettigrew, A. M., Cornuel, E., & Hommel, U. (Eds.), *The institutional development of business schools* (pp. 248–270). Oxford: Oxford University Press.

Meyer, J. W. (1994). Rationalized environments. In Scott, W. R., & Meyer, J. W. (Eds.), *Institutional environments and organizations* (pp. 28–54). London: Sage.

Meyer, J. W., & Rowan, B. (1977). Institutionalized organizations: formal structure as myth and ceremony. *American Journal of Sociology, 83*(2), 340–363.

Moon, J. (2007). The contribution of CSR to sustainable development. *Journal of Sustainable Development, 15*, 296–306.

Moon, J., & Orlitzky, M. (2011). Corporate social responsibility and sustainability education: a trans-atlantic comparison. *Journal of Management and Organization, 17*(5), 583–603.

Moratis, L. (2016). Decoupling management education: some empirical findings, comments and speculation. *Journal of Management Inquiry, 25*(3), 235–239.

Moran, M. (2002). Understanding the regulatory state. *British Journal of Political Science, 32*(2), 391–413.

Morsing, M., & Schultz, M. (2006). Corporate social responsibility communication: stakeholder information, response and involvement strategies. *Business Ethics: A European Review, 15*, 323–338.

Muff, K., Dyllick, T., Drewell, M., North, J., Shrivastava, P., & Härtle, J. (2013). *Management education for the world: a vision for business schools serving people and the planet.* Cheltenham: Edward Elgar.

Naidoo, R., Gosling, J., Bolden, R., O'Brien, A., & Hawkins, B. (2014). Leadership and branding in business schools: a Bourdieusian analysis. *Higher Education Research and Development, 33*, 144–156.

Naidoo, R., & Pringle, J. (2014). Branding business schools. In Pettigrew, A. M., Cornuel, E., & Hommel, U. (Eds.), *The institutional development of business schools* (pp. 176–196). Oxford: Oxford University Press.

Navarro, P. (2008). The MBA core curricula of top-ranked US business schools: a study in failure. *Academy of Management Learning & Education, 7*(1), 108–123.

Petriglieri, G. (2015). Disrupt or be disrupted: a blueprint for change in management education. *Academy of Management Learning & Education, 14*, 133–139.

Pfeffer, J., & Fong, C. (2004). The business school 'business': some lessons from the US experience. *Journal of Management Studies*, 1501–1520.

Pfeffer, J., & Salancik, G. (1978). *The external control of organizations: a resource dependence perspective*. New York: HarperCollins.

Pitt-Watson, D., & Quigley, E. (2018). Business School Rankings for the 21st Century Report. Available at https://www.cser.ac.uk/media/uploads/files/Jan_2019_Business_School_Rankings.pdf

Porter, L. W., & McKibbin, L. E. (1988). *Management education and development: drift or thrust into the 21st century?* New York: McGraw-Hill.

Power, M. (1999). *The audit society: rituals of verification*. Oxford: Oxford University Press.

Power, M. (2000). The audit society – second thoughts. *International Journal of Auditing*, 4, 111–119.

Prøitz, T. S., Stensaker, B., & Harvey, L. (2004). Accreditation, standards and diversity: an analysis of EQUIS accreditation reports. *Assessment & Evaluation in Higher Education*, 29, 735–750.

Pupius, M., & Brusoni, M. (2000). Comparing and contrasting the EFQM excellence model and the EQUIS accreditation process for management in higher education. International Conference 'Quality in Higher Education in the New Millennium'. University of Derby, UK, 2000, pp. 24–25.

Rasche, A,. & Gilbert, D. U. (2015). Decoupling responsible management education why business schools may not walk their talk. *Journal of Management Inquiry*, 24, 239–252.

Rasche, A., Hommel, U., & Cornuel, E. (2014). Discipline as institutional maintenance: the case of business school rankings. In Pettigrew, A., Cornuel, E., & Hommel, U. (Eds.), *The institutional development of business schools* (pp. 196–220). Oxford: Oxford University Press.

Rayment, J. J., & Smith, J. A. (2010). The current and future role of business schools. Research report, Anglia Ruskin University, Cambridge. Available at: www.g-casa.com/conferences/budapest/papers/Rayment.pdf.

Roller, R. H., Andrews, B. K. & Bovee, S. L. (2003). Specialized accreditation of business schools: a comparison of alternative costs, benefits, and motivations. *Journal of Education for Business*, 78, 197–204.

Rusinko, C. A. (2010). Integrating sustainability in management and business education: a matrix approach. *Academy of Management Learning & Education*, 9(3), 507–519.

Snelson-Powell, A., Grosvold, J., & Millington, A. (2016). Business school legitimacy and the challenge of sustainability: a fuzzy set analysis of institutional decoupling. *Academy of Management Learning & Education*, 15(4), 703–723.

Solitander, N., Fougere, M., Sobczak, A., & Herlin, H. (2012). We are the champions: organizational learning and change for responsible management education. *Journal of Management Education*, 36(3), 337–363.

Starkey, K., & Madan, P. (2001). Bridging the relevance gap: aligning stakeholders in the future of management research. *British Journal of Management*, I, S3–S26.

Stubbs, W., & Schapper, J. (2011). Two approaches to curriculum development for educating for sustainability and CSR. *International Journal of Sustainability in Higher Education*, 12(3), 259–268.

Thomas, H., & Cornuel, E. (2012). Business schools in transition? Issues of impact, legitimacy, capabilities and re-invention. *Journal of Management Development*, 31, 329–335.

Thomas, H., Hommel, U., Muff, K., King, R., & Roos, J. (2013a). Promising direction in management education. *Journal for Management Development*, 37, 377–385.

Thomas, H., Lorange, P., & Sheth, J. (2013b). *The business school in the twenty-first century: emergent challenges and new business models*. Cambridge: Cambridge University Press.

Thomas, H., Lee, M., Wilson, A. & Thomas, L. (2014). *Securing the future of management education: competitive destruction or constructive innovation?* Sheffield: Emerald.

United Nations. (1987). World Commission on Environment and Development: Our common future (Brundtland Report). Available at: https://sustainabledevelopment.un.org/content/documents/5987our-common-future.pdf.

Vas, A., & Lejeune, C. (2004). Revisiting resistance to change at the university: an interpretative approach. IAG Working paper.

Wedlin, L. (2007). The role of rankings in codifying a business school template: classifications, diffusion and mediated isomorphism in organizational fields. *European Management Review*, 4, 24–39.

Wedlin, L. (2011). Going global: Rankings as rhetorical devices to construct an international field of management education. *Management Learning, 42*(2), 199–218.

Wijen, F. (2014). Means versus ends in opaque institutional fields: trading off compliance and achievement in sustainability standard adoption. *Academy of Management Review, 39*(3), 302–323.

Wilkins, S., & Huisman, J. (2012). UK business school rankings over the last 30 years (1980–2010): trends and explanations. *Higher Education, 63*, 367–382.

Wilson, D., & McKiernan, P. (2011). Global mimicry: putting strategic choice back on the business school agenda. *British Journal of Management, 22*, 457–469.

Wilson, D., & Thomas, H. (2012). The legitimacy of the business of business schools: what's the future? *Journal of Management Development, 31*(4), 368–376.

Wu, Y., Huang, S., Kuo, L., & Wu, W. (2010). Management education for sustainability: a web-based content analysis. *Academy of Management Learning & Education, 9*(30), 520–531.

Zoffer, H. (1987). Accreditation bends before the winds of change. *Educational Record, 68*, 43–46.

28

The Hidden Curriculum: Can the Concept Support Responsible Management Learning?

Maribel Blasco

INTRODUCTION

'Perhaps the greatest of all pedagogical fallacies,' wrote the famous American educationalist John Dewey (1938: 48) more than 80 years ago, is 'the notion that a person learns only the particular thing he is studying at the time'. To capture this elusive parallel learning, Dewey coined the notion of *collateral learning*, defined as 'the way of formation of enduring attitudes, of likes and dislikes' that occurred through the formation of habits in schools (1938: 48). He was convinced that this collateral learning left a deeper impression than regular lessons, and was more important for students' future attitudes, even though it sometimes seemed to bear little relation to intended learning outcomes. The key message of Dewey's 'collateral learning' idea – that schools 'teach more than they claim to teach'[1] (Vallance, 1974: 5) – was taken up by Dewey scholar Phillip Jackson, in his (1968) book *Life in Classrooms*, in which the first reference to the 'hidden curriculum' (HC) reportedly appears;[2] and quickly adopted by numerous scholars who used it to draw attention to the *implicit* dimensions of learning environments that are embedded in routines, taken-for-granted structures (physical, spatial, temporal), implicit biases, incentives, rules and discipline, expectations and interaction, among other things (Dreeben, 1967; Giroux & Purpel, 1983). These scholars brought into the mainstream the idea that learning involves 'a socialization process, quietly transferring social norms and values to the student' (Gofton & Regehr, 2006: 22), and is not merely a straightforward and value-neutral process of transferring objective knowledge, and functional skills, to learners.

Why does this matter for responsible management learning (RML)? First, the HC concept offers a lens for exploring unquestioned, undisclosed or unintended learning processes and outcomes (Cotton, Winter & Bailey, 2013: 195) at business schools and potentially also in management learning more broadly, as I shall argue. This is clearly of pertinence to RML scholars, since such implicit dimensions of learning environments are believed to have a powerful socializing effect by tacitly conveying norms that influence learners' values and behaviour (Välimaa & Nokkala, 2014). Sometimes, as Dewey (1938) noted, these norms and values may even be at odds with an institution's stated objectives; and Ottewill, McKenzie & Leah, (2005), writing about the HC in business education, similarly write: 'there is a danger that the aims of the formal curriculum could be undermined'. We must suppose that business schools and other organizations with an explicit responsibility agenda would be loath to unwittingly sabotage their own explicit RML agendas because they are oblivious to the existence of a counterproductive HC. Second, because the HC concept has a long history of empirical operationalization at all levels of education, it can enable targeted investigation of the kind of 'meta-messages' (Blasco, 2012) that are communicated about responsibility in business schools and other organizations, by pointing to specific dimensions and concrete tools that can reveal aspects of the learning environment that might otherwise be overlooked. Third, the HC concept can help to broaden our bandwidth as RML educators so that we become equally alert to how students *apprehend* and *respond to* implicit aspects of the learning environment as we are to course content and delivery. This, in turn, enables a simple but powerful shift in perspective away from our usual concern with how to change *students*, and instead turns a reflexive lens on what *we*, as teachers and managers, may need to change in our own practices and in the academic environment in order to better support RML. Focusing on student reception, in turn, also puts *resistance* – a concept that has fallen out of favour since it became unfashionable to speak of power relations and social control in regard to schooling (Vallance, 1974) – back on the radar, as well as the forms that resistance can take, not only among students but also among teachers and other school actors,

some of which may be counterproductive to RML. Fourth, the HC concept can help to debunk the axiom that business education is value-neutral (Amann, Pirson, Dierksmeier, Von Kimakowitz & Spitzeck, 2011; Grey, 2004), since from a HC perspective, education is never value-neutral, since values are communicated in *all* learning situations, through inclusions and omissions, incentives, rewards, interactions (however seemingly trivial) and implicit messages about 'the right way to be', whether or not this is conscious or acknowledged (Gair & Mullins, 2001; Kohlberg, 1975). We need think no further than standard theories and models taught at business schools, which are rife with assumptions about how the world works but are often taught as value-neutral 'truths' (Ghoshal, 2005). Finally, the HC concept compels us to critically heed the connections between what is learned in business schools and other organizations, and the wider society in which that learning is embedded. It impels us to confront the fundamental question of whether business schools should educate students to conform to existing societal structures, or to instigate social change. And, perhaps most importantly today, it reminds us to be wary of attempting to align education with 'societal needs' that may be defined by powerful interest groups that are not necessarily representative or in step with broader responsibility imperatives. I unfold these points further below. Irrespective of whether one buys into the existence of a 'real' HC, the concept is, in my view, an invaluable heuristic device for exploring taken-for-granted dimensions of learning environments that might otherwise go unnoticed, though it must be used with caution, as I outline in the section on critique of the HC.

My overall goal is to raise awareness about the strengths and weaknesses of the HC concept among scholars and teachers interested in RML. The chapter is structured as follows. First, I present key definitions of the HC concept, and I offer a brief account of its history, development and theoretical underpinnings. This paves the way for the following section, in which I outline how the concept can prove insightful for current RML scholarship, and I present examples of how it has been deployed in the field. I then address some critiques of the HC concept and explain their relevance for RML research. Finally, I tackle the question of what a *Responsible* Hidden Curriculum (RHC) might look like, and whether and how business schools and other organizations might implement such a RHC. I conclude by outlining some avenues for future research through which I believe the HC concept may support the RML agenda.

THE HIDDEN CURRICULUM: DEFINITIONS AND THEORETICAL UNDERPINNINGS

Definitions of the HC

The HC has been defined in different ways and the idea behind it has been expressed using a range of related terms, such as: the 'implicit', 'unstudied', 'covert', 'latent', 'unwritten', 'invisible' and 'silent' curriculum, or simply the 'by-products of schooling' (see overview in Portelli, 1993: 344). This terminological medley notwithstanding, most concur that the HC involves aspects of schooling that are typically 'unwritten' (Kentli, 2009: 83) and which somehow take place under the radar of the formal, explicit or declared curriculum; that it has to do with implicit and interactional aspects of learning environments; and that it plays a meaningful role in the learning of values and ideologies (Gair & Mullins, 2001). Jackson, who is credited with coining the term 'hidden curriculum' in his 1968 book *Life in Classrooms*, describes it thus, ascribing to the HC a critical role in students' academic performance:

> the crowds, the praise, and the power that combine to give a distinctive flavor to classroom life collectively form a hidden curriculum which each student (and teacher) must master if he is to make his way satisfactorily through the school. The demand

created by these features of classroom life may be contrasted with the academic demands – the 'official' curriculum, so to speak – to which educators traditionally have paid the most attention ... the reward system of the school is linked to success in both curriculums. Indeed, many of the rewards and punishments that sound as if they are being dispensed on the basis of academic success and failure are really more closely related to the mastery of the hidden curriculum'[3] (Jackson, 1968: 33–4).

Others definitions of the HC include the following, some of which refer explicitly to the often unacknowledged ideological dimension of schooling:

- 'What is implicit and embedded in educational experiences in contrast with the formal statements about curricula and the surface features of educational interaction' (Sambell & McDowell, 1998: 391–392).
- '"Curriculum as designed" versus "curriculum in action"' (Barnett & Coate, 2005, 3).
- 'All the ideological instances of the schooling process that "silently" structure and reproduce hegemonic assumptions and practices' (Giroux & Purpel, 1983: 71).
- 'The tacit teaching to students of norms, values, and dispositions that goes on simply by their living in and coping with the institutional expectations and routines of schools day in day out for a number of years' (Apple, 1990: 14).

Scholars have pointed out that that there is not necessarily one, monolithic HC; rather, various different types of HC may operate in a given learning environment at any one time. Portelli (1993, summarized in Orón Semper & Blasco, 2018) unfolds four possible types of HC:

1 The HC as the unofficial or implicit expectations, values, norms and messages conveyed by school actors.
2 The HC as unintended learning outcomes.
3 The HC as implicit messages emanating from the structure of schooling.
4 The HC as created by the students who infer and anticipate what they need to do to be rewarded.

Thus, different actors may experience different HCs, or experience the same HC differently (Anijar in Gair & Mullins, 2001: 24). For instance, a particular HC may be concealed from teachers, managers and administrators, but obvious to students (Martin, 1976; Portelli, 1993); students may try to 'game' the system (Baker, Walonoski, Heffernan, Roll, Corbett & Koedinger, 2008; Gordon, 1982) or engage in superficial or work-avoidant learning strategies (Dweck, 1986; Meece, Blumenfeld & Hoyle, 1988), without the knowledge of their teachers; and teachers or managers may perpetuate a HC that is embedded in school structures or rituals without being aware that they are doing so.

Scholars have also debated the extent to which the HC is hidden or not. Gair and Mullins (2001) consider the term 'hidden curriculum' misleading, suggesting that the HC merely hides 'in plain sight' – we are blind to it exactly because it is right under our noses the whole time. Others have scrutinized the question of intentionality in thinking about the 'hidden' dimension of the HC. Portelli (1993), for instance, remarks that 'hidden' implies a relationship – something is being hidden *by* somebody *from* somebody else. Martin (1976) similarly observes that 'hidden' may mean intentional concealment – but also perhaps simply that something has not yet been discovered. Margolis, Soldatenko, Acker and Gair remark that curricula 'can be hidden by a general social agreement not to see': in the case of universities, for instance, they argue that this pact is that students are not taught to produce for use or exchange, but rather to produce ideologies that underpin the needs of contemporary capitalism – how to manage, communicate, advertise and so on. In this sense, the authors argue, the curriculum 'may be seen as a "hide", like a duck blind' (Margolis et al., 2001: 2).

Some hidden curricula may even be quite overt, although not strictly speaking part of the formal curriculum, for instance implicit socialization into particular social class dispositions, manners, or entrepreneurial and leadership qualities that are regarded as perfectly

legitimate and are merely 'hidden by a wink' (Margolis et al., 2001: 3). The HC may therefore also manifest on or through the bodies of students, teachers and others, by implicitly encouraging conformity to a particular habitus, behaviours and self-presentation deemed acceptable in a given environment, e.g. attire and grooming, gait, physical expressiveness or restraint, or food consumption, all of which may be further shaped, in turn, by gender and other norms specific to the environment in question (Margolis et al., 2001).

Within the overall framework of these definitions, the HC concept covers a wide range of aspects of learning environments, including but not limited to: the structuring of time and space, including architecture and the layout and feel of classrooms and other aspects of the physical environment; traditions, routines and socialization rituals, extracurricular activities such as associations and clubs, rules of conduct, assessment, interaction, endorsers and the composition of boards of governors, incentives and sanctions, teachers' delivery of the curriculum, curricular content (including skills, knowledge, theories and models taught and omitted), students' characteristics and reception of learning, and unintended outcomes of learning (Gair & Mullins, 2001; Margolis et al., 2001; Martin, 1976; Sambell & McDowell, 1998).

Theoretical Underpinnings of the HC Concept

Early HC scholars such as Jackson (1968) and Dreeben (1967), mobilized the HC concept within a broadly functionalist approach to education that regarded implicit socialization as a necessary aspect of schooling that prepared students for post-school life, even while (in Jackson's case) recognizing that the outcomes of this socialization process were often directly at odds with key explicit or purported functions of schooling – notably the development of intellectual, critical and creative faculties (Jackson, 1968). Thus, if society were competitive and bureaucratic, students should learn to adapt to and comply with these values in school (Kohlberg, 1975). This functionalist perspective is also known as the 'consensus' approach, which views the function of education as broadly supportive of societal harmony and a well-functioning workforce. Schools achieve this by providing students with secondary socialization that they are not usually able to receive during their primary socialization within the family, notably specific professional/occupational skills, as well as particular social norms and behaviour such as discipline, social solidarity and a feeling of belonging to a wider community. Seen from this perspective, the goal of business education would be to ensure that graduates are equipped with the values, behaviours, skills and knowledge to slot seamlessly into the business community.

As a backlash against this functionalist view of the HC, scholars working with so-called 'correspondence' or 'conflict' theories of education began to examine schooling through a more critical lens, as an instrument of social control and dissent rather than emancipation. This work, much of which was based on in-depth ethnographic fieldwork in primary and secondary schools, concurred with functionalism that the role of schools was to assure consensus or 'correspondence' between the school's structures and the structures of production (Margolis et al., 2001: 7), but viewed this as dysfunctional rather than necessary or socially beneficial. Thus, the social reproduction engineered by the school was viewed as politically motivated and controlled by the interests of powerful groups, and not as benignly representing society as a whole and ensuring its seamless functioning, as in the functionalist view. Key scholars working within this perspective used the HC concept to reveal how schools legitimize and serve the unequal social structures, control and power relations inherent in capitalism (Apple, 1980; Bowles & Gintis, 1976; McLaren, 1989). They showed how, despite the high hopes invested in education as a remedy for many of the social challenges of the day, certain aspects of what went on in schools actually produced behaviours and attitudes that were inimical to equality, ethics and democracy (Giroux & Penna, 1979).

What is more, these scholars asserted that schools achieved this by legitimizing and naturalizing certain values, behaviours and ways of being – typically white, middle-class, competitive, individualist and conformist – and delegitimizing others, thereby tacitly grooming students for their preordained positions either as labourers or white-collar workers (Gair & Mullins, 2001). There was little agreement about how this grooming process occurred. Some argued that through their routine practices, sanctions and incentives, schools trained students in discipline, punctuality, conformity, self-denial and in the acceptance of power relations and the lack of intrinsic rewards associated with dutiful compliance (Bowles & Gintis, 1976; Lynch, 1989). Some proposed that the linguistic codes of schools were biased towards middle-class students, putting working-class or ethnic minority students at a cultural disadvantage and making them more likely to be perceived by teachers as academically weaker, and more likely to perform poorly (Bernstein, 1971). Others noted that through schools' seemingly objective grading procedures students are implicitly socialized to buy into the societal ideology of individual meritocracy since they experience it in schools as natural and personal rather than structural (Giroux & Penna, 1979). Overall, the correspondence perspective opened up for the view that schools are not necessarily an emancipatory, democratizing, progressive force, or even a neutral one, but may actually tacitly endorse the diametrical opposite by reinforcing selected cultural and ideological messages that serve the dominant classes and market interests (Anyon, 1979; Apple, 1980; Giroux & Penna, 1979).

As can be seen from the above, overall, theorizing about the HC concept has mainly been carried out from a sociological point of view, targeting the relationship between the school as an institution and society. From a more psychological perspective, Kohlberg (1975) has argued that moral learning, in particular, is influenced to a greater extent by the HC than by the formal curriculum, since learning takes place through social relationships, in particular the teacher–student relationship. Teachers, Kohlberg argued, send powerful moral signals about 'good and bad' through their admonitions and reactions, and the rewards and sanctions they distribute, as well as the fact that they represent an ultimate authority over students. For these reasons, Kohlberg claimed that moral education based on cognitive knowledge transmission and taught through offering, e.g., theories and cases in the formal curriculum, was unlikely to be effective compared to the implicit modelling of values that took place in the academic environment. He proposed that countering these tendencies required establishing a 'just community' in the learning environment that reflected the (democratic, participatory and egalitarian) values that schools wished to inculcate. In other words, he emphasized the importance, for moral learning, of *modelling* desired behaviours in academic environments.

The above definitions of the HC and theoretical approaches underpinning the concept raise pertinent issues for RML. The *first* issue has to do with the tension between consensus and conflict in terms of the business school's role in society, i.e., should business schools socialize their students to fit uncritically into the capitalist system, or should they train them to act as change agents who hold that system to account, even as they equip them with the functional skills for business? Today, the conflict perspective may seem outmoded in its uncompromising critique of capitalism, as business schools increasingly face calls to legitimize themselves in terms of their usefulness in the 'real world' (Thomas & Cornuel 2012), making it seem not only unremarkable but perfectly obvious and proper that business students should be trained and socialized

into the requisite competences and habitus for business under modern capitalism. Yet in critical management education scholarship, the conflict approach remains very much alive, and is still raising the alarm about a 'school–business alliance' that supports the production of efficient, compliant workers or 'adapted individuals' (Gorz in Giroux & McLaren, 1989: xv) who fail to question the system. Ehrensal darkly declares that: 'By the time a student successfully leaves a business school program, he or she is a ready foot soldier for the capitalist enterprise' (Ehrensal, 2001: 109). Mills (1997: 331) argues that business curricula are 'profoundly wedded to the status quo, embedding the business professor in what Clegg (1981) has termed *reproduction rules*, that is, a system dedicated to the reproduction, maintenance and rationalization of existing ideologies and power structures'. Grey (2004: 179) remarks that 'the supposedly scientific approach of management studies actually conceals its commitment to a normally unstated set of values, for example and in particular, those of the competitive market economy and private corporations'. Antonacopoulou (2010) raises concerns about the absence of critical thinking teaching at business schools. And McIntosh (2017: 6–7) offers this damning assessment of business school complicity in underpinning the capitalist elite: 'most business and management schools have tended to teach the prevailing neoliberal orthodoxy and uphold the current dominant model of capitalism and incorporation. They are not agents of change or enlightened thinking in the main, but institutions for the maintenance of the elite.' We see, then, that the original conflict–consensus debate over the HC concept remains highly pertinent to business schools in contemporary capitalist societies.

The *second* issue is that the HC draws attention to the *micromechanisms* of educational processes at business schools that tend to be overlooked as seemingly trivial or neutral (Margolis et al., 2001: 13), are only visible to some of the involved actors, or are simply unaligned with the school's explicit goals and values. A simple example of this could be a school that brands itself grandly as promoting social responsibility and inclusion, but whose teachers do not feel obligated to reply to students' emails in a respectful and timely manner. However minor this discrepancy may seem, it undermines consistency between the school's declared values and the practices of its teachers, making the former at best seem meaningless and at worst cynical. By drawing attention to such inconsistencies, HC concept invites business schools to walk the talk, and in particular to 'sweat the small stuff', recognizing that this also sends important signals to students about the type of behaviour that is implicitly acceptable to, if not explicitly endorsed by, their school. Crucially, this puts the onus on the school, notably its teachers, managers and other significant actors to model responsible behaviours through their *own* actions and relationships, rather than merely on how to change the *students* so that they become more responsible (cf. also Brown in Caza & Brower, 2015: 103).

USE AND OPERATIONALIZATION OF THE HC CONCEPT IN MANAGEMENT EDUCATION

The HC concept has so far not been widely used in studying management education, with a few exceptions, which I discuss below. However, it should be noted that much critical management education-oriented scholarship reflects the HC mode of thought without actually using the term. Indeed, if we take on board the definitions of the HC outlined above, any scholarship that addresses learning beyond the formal overt curriculum, or looks at its biases and unintended effects, or lacunae between schools' stated values and their practices, may be said to be working within the spirit of HC research. In the following section, I offer an overview of how

the HC concept has been used explicitly within management education, including examples of other RML-pertinent research that reflects the HC idea, albeit not explicitly.

Several authors have drawn on the HC to understand moral learning processes at business schools. Echoing Kohlberg (cf. above), Trevino and McCabe (1994: 406) use the HC concept to support their argument that business schools must *model* the kind of behaviours and attitudes they want from their students. They propose that 'much, if not most ethics and values learning takes place outside the classroom, within the "hidden curriculum" of the business education program, where messages about ethics and values are implicitly sent and received' (1994: 406). Accordingly, they suggest building 'honourable business school communities' in which students can enact and debate real ethical issues. They further posit that since values are learned in interaction, student–faculty dialogue should explicitly challenge students' assumptions, thereby fostering cognitive disequilibrium and preparing the way for values learning. Caza and Brower (2015) point out that business schools' formal goals are not always reflected in their practices. They note that although the formal curriculum looks remarkably similar across most business schools, the quality of the education provided varies considerably, a paradox that they explore using the concept of the 'informal curriculum' which they defined as activities that 'are not linked to formally stated goals, or [they] have no formal assessment' Caza and Brower see the HC as part of the informal curriculum, but consider the latter a broader construct that covers activities which the HC does not.[4] The informal curriculum, they propose, 'may have a powerful influence on learning outcomes'. Failing to take it into account, they warn, 'may result in students learning the "wrong" things' (2015: 96). Along similar lines, Ottewill et al. (2005: 90) argue that 'there needs to be an affinity between what is usually understood by ...

the formal or taught curriculum, and the hidden curriculum' – if this is lacking there is a risk that the goals of the formal curriculum may be undermined. And, although their article is not specifically about the HC, Rasche and Gilbert (2015) propose that if business schools fail to integrate responsible management education into their organizational culture, this can give rise to a HC that plays a role in decoupling the formal structures of business schools, for instance policies and committees, from the school's everyday practices. They point to the risk of cynicism developing when action fails to live up to talk in an organization in this way.

In an earlier article (Blasco, 2012: 366) I argued that business schools should pay attention to the HC, as focusing exclusively on explicit dimensions of the formal curriculum, for instance by adding courses on social responsibility, is not enough to improve students' sense of social responsibility given that 'signals about appropriate conduct are communicated in many subtle ways beyond formal curricular content', notably through socialization that takes place through social interaction in communities of practice. Accordingly, I attempted to operationalize the HC concept specifically for business schools, conceptualizing the latter as 'multi-level learning environments comprising various message sites[5] where students undergo moral learning and socialization processes'. These message sites are: the *formal curriculum* (e.g. course organization, delivery, assessment, etc.), *interpersonal interactions* (e.g. teacher–student dialogue, jokes, anecdotes, competitions, etc.), and *school governance* (e.g., hiring of endorsers, school sustainability/diversity practices, explicit enforcement of good conduct). These sites transmit *meta-messages*, defined as 'the messages about appropriate conduct that students apprehend, and which may differ significantly from intended formal curricular messages' (Blasco, 2012: 374).

In the following, I draw on existing critical management education literature in offering some examples of how meta-messages may be transmitted through the different HC message sites at business schools.

Biases in Theories and Textbooks

Ehrensal (2001) uses the HC concept to argue that business schools exercise 'symbolic violence' over students through various types of pedagogic authority, and by training and socializing them in the skills, habitus, values and ideologies required by employers so that they internalize the legitimacy of the business world. This authority is established and maintained by exposing students to repeated, seemingly banal pedagogic actions that constitute standard fare in formal curricula in business schools worldwide, such as the same textbooks and theories that portray simplified, normative, certain and universalizing takes on the world – but which are presented as neutral truths. Ehrensal (2001: 104) argues that all undergraduate business students, are 'exposed to the same core of courses' and textbooks that portray a particular world view of 'simplified certainty', with knowledge presented as 'normative, certain, and based on universal precepts'. Antonacopoulou (2010: 10) similarly warns that 'The economic logic propounds corporate profitability as the core of effective management and a signal of efficient managers. This uncritical orientation to teaching and learning about management provides little space for experimenting with ideas that operate outside the dominant economic logic, and hence social and political aspects within management are frequently neglected.' The theories learned at business school are a case in point, as robustly shown in Ghoshal's (2005: 84) landmark article, in which he argued that 'Friedman's version of liberalism has indeed been colonizing all the management-related disciplines over the last half century', and showed how standard theories taught at business schools, such as Porter's five forces, transaction cost theory and neo-classical economics propound and legitimize 'pessimistic assumptions' (2005: 77) about individuals and institutions, as well as particular ways of being such as extreme individualism and competitiveness, distrust and an instrumental and opportunistic approach to others. Most would concur that none of these dispositions are defensible outcomes in business schools claiming to promote social responsibility among their students.

Others have pointed out how through such theories, texts and other teaching practices, business schools promote traits such as aggression, competitiveness and objectivity, which constitute 'gendered aspects of managerial archetypes', noting that the study of gender at business schools – despite the acute need to redress the glaring gender imbalance in the business world (Coder & Spiller, 2013) – is sparse to say the least (Mills, 1997). In like manner, Smith (2000: 159) observes that management education and training are characterized by a 'masculine culture' that reflects that of the labour market, with lectures mainly delivered by male professors and textbooks that are largely written by men and which omit women's contributions and points of view (see also Kelan & Jones, 2010). When gender is included as an issue, the messages are often based on outdated perspectives, and are often inconsistent and confusing (Coder & Spiller, 2013). Finally, Rumens (2016: 38) draws attention to the 'heteronormative bias' that characterizes business schools, a problem reflected in their lack of engagement with theories from other disciplines such as the humanities, arts and that could draw students' attention to issues of 'social justice, equality and diversity'.

Similar arguments have been made about the limited regional representation in business school textbooks and curricula, with management texts and other teaching material heavily biased towards the US context, making it of little relevance for the local concerns that students need to learn about in other contexts (cf. Nkomo, 2015). Godwyn (2015: 1) remarks that 'course material [is] often predicated on a Western, White male

protagonist in a time when international business interactions are growing exponentially and business students are increasingly non-Western and increasingly female'. Research from the UK similarly shows that textbook content and other teaching resources fail to represent cultural diversity, instead featuring Western perspectives that for many students leads to 'a disconnect within the learning process' (Jabbar & Hardaker, 2013: 282).

As with the above selective biases, all textbook content (as well as the formal curriculum more broadly) is also a result of *omission* – a notion captured by Eisner's (1985) concept of the 'null curriculum', meaning what is not taught or left out of the curriculum. Omissions arguably also form part of the HC at business schools. As Grey (2004: 179) points out, 'Facts are always impregnated with values ... The very selection of what we study is bound up with judgments about what is worth studying.' Anyon (1979: 50) writes: 'by identifying and analyzing textbook omissions, distortions and rationalizations, one reveals the workings of society ... textbook misrepresentations ... identify deep characteristics of the economic and political order: through them one highlights those arrangements that must be justified in order to secure support and future participation in social institutions'. All curricula are obviously necessarily the end result of selection and de-selection, but the key point of the null curriculum concept is that such selection processes do not merely constitute neutral, strictly 'academic' choices, but involve prioritization about the kind of skills and knowledge needed to produce a certain type of graduate. Such prioritization inevitably precludes alternative intellectual experiences, perspectives and skills that could otherwise be offered to students (Eisner, 1985). At the very least, teachers and curriculum designers should be alert to these exclusion processes and to their significance in terms of the broader values endorsed and communicated by the business school, as well as to their possible effects on students.

These are but a few examples of the kind of biases in business school curricula that a HC analysis can reveal. These biases send meta-messages about what is considered normal and appropriate which are so deeply embedded in business school curricula that they are seldom questioned. Below, I address another aspect of the formal curriculum which communicates meta-messages that are routinely taken for granted – namely the teaching methods through which content is *delivered* at business schools. These didactic forms are pertinent to the HC, since, as Burbules and Callister (1999: 2) note, '[t]eaching is not just a delivery system — in pedagogy, form shapes content'. I address this point primarily using the example of the case study.

Meta-Messages Enshrined in 'Gold Standard' Teaching Methods

Case studies are so widespread and influential a teaching method in business schools that it is fair to say they form an integral part of their teaching lifeblood, although clearly there are differences in the type and format of cases used and the way they are taught (Rippin, Booth, Bowie & Jordan, 2002). The idea behind case studies is to present students with holistic, real-world scenarios that reflect real-life complexity, can trigger debate in the classroom and can enable students to engage in vicarious problem-solving and decision-making (Aharoni, 2011; McCarthy & McCarthy, 2006).

Applying a HC lens to case teaching, however, means examining how it can represent business in a skewed or uncritical manner. Starkey and Tempest (2009) draw attention to a heavy bias towards presenting the point of view of senior managers in many case studies, rather than that of employees or customers, for instance. As they write (2009: 582), 'This sets a poor example for students, who might well be persuaded that interviewing the CEO is a sufficient method of researching an organization.' Rather than encouraging a

critical perspective, the authors argue, 'Many cases simply recycle traditional assumptions about how business – and indeed society – should be run, in an unquestioning way. The emphasis is more advocacy than inquiry, one-dimensional narratives rather than grappling with complexities. The CEO is king, the workforce is silent, success is all about inspirational, omniscient leadership' (Starkey & Tempest, 2009: 582). I have found this to be true in my own teaching practice, where I must often remind students eager to interview top management that there is more to companies than just their leaders.

Not only the content, but also the *form* of the case study, has been subject to critique. Ehrensal (2001) argues that the case study implicitly teaches students to translate the abstract into the concrete by applying 'universal' theories to specific examples; and socializes students into the 'right' way of thinking by favouring certain theories for solving certain cases and by showing students what problems, and problem-solvers, look like in practice. Aharoni (2011) notes, however, that case studies teach the reverse manoeuvre too – to extrapolate from specific situations to generalizable principles, and that this (among other strengths) is a valid and worthy learning outcome of case studies. Finally, after a nuanced and thoughtful presentation of the pros and cons of case studies, Rippin et al. (2002: 440) conclude that due to the massification of HE, these advantages may be difficult to leverage, with the result that the case teaching method 'can reinforce, rather than challenge homogeneity and increasing managerialism; can package and contain, rather than celebrate and explore, ambiguity and uncertainty'.

In addition to case studies, other exercises often used in business teaching, such as role-playing, games and student presentations, also encourage a similar kind of 'behavioural modelling' (Ehrensal, 2001). Ehrensal (2001: 108) describes how these techniques implicitly socialize students by encouraging mastery of 'appropriate management behaviors in the simulated organizational situations in which they are placed', through critique by their teacher or peers; as well as by more subtly modelling business-appropriate forms of attire, hairstyles and (if relevant) facial hair grooming (Ehrensal, 2001: 107).

The Hidden Curriculum of Space and Time

Among the most 'hidden' or taken-for-granted aspects of educational institutions – and therefore important elements of the HC – are the spatial and temporal dimensions of learning environments, including the formal curriculum. These dimensions are fundamental to the experience of learning, yet little work has been carried out on this in management education to date, despite increasing attention to these issues in the social sciences and humanities more broadly (Edwards & Usher, 2003: 1) and notably in fields such as education, management and organization studies, and geography, which recognize the importance of both dimensions for learning, performance, power and social relations, among other things (Alhadeff-Jones, 2016; Clegg & Kornberger, 2006; Edenius & Yakhlef, 2007; Kornberger & Clegg, 2004; Lefebvre, 2004; Lefebvre & Nicholson-Smith, 1991; Rosa, 2013; Vostal, 2015).

Regarding space, some scholars have explored how physical spaces such as classroom architecture and furniture layout can further or inhibit particular teaching styles, as well as shaping students' attitudes to learning and collaboration (Brooks, 2012; Carmean and Haefner, 2002; Oblinger, 2006; Park & Choi, 2014). Hargreaves (1978) found that the organization of space and time in classrooms – such as seating arrangements, being at liberty to move around (teachers) or not (students) – symbolically expressed and reproduced power relations between teachers and students. Others have addressed space in a more abstract fashion as a *potential* for learning that can be expanded or shrunk

depending on the way the formal curriculum is administered. For instance, Marton, Tsui, Chik, Ko and Lo (2004) show how teacher and classroom discourse – for instance the type of questions asked – can shape the nature of the learning space, with the result that learning is either minimized or maximized. Beyes & Michels (2011) draw on Lefebvre's theorizing about, and Foucault's concept of, heterotopia, to explore ways in which heterotopic educational spaces of innovation and experimentation might be fostered within business schools. They conceive of such spaces as sites where the real and the imaginary intersect, producing arenas with learning potential, positing that experimenting with such spaces offers a means to 'unsettle taken-for-granted practices' and stimulate the imagination (2011: 522). In Blasco (2016), I argued that spaces for thinking, autonomy and reflection are being crowded out at business schools by cramped, rushed curricula, with potentially deleterious effects on students' engagement, imagination and deep learning. Using the Japanese concept of *ma* to reclaim the value of empty space, I devised a framework for conceptualizing curricular space at business schools in terms of curricular structures that enable *cognitive*, *autonomy* and *reflective* space. I argue that to enable these spaces, curricula should take into account both the vertical 'stacking' of classes and assignments, as well as the horizontal flow of tasks, as experienced by students.

Regarding time, temporal structures such as deadlines, schedules, routines and timelines are crucial to the experience of learning, shaping subjects' experience of pace, workload and satisfaction, impacting performance, and may also give rise to strategies such as multi-tasking and prioritization, for instance (Benabou 1999). Alhadeff-Jones (2016) points out how time compression (arising, e.g., from squeezing courses into ever-shorter time slots), alters the rhythm, pace and overall experience of learning encounters, accelerating that experience, with implications for the development of trust and collaboration, self-reflection and introspection, and autonomy and emancipation. He notes how contemporary tensions between the drive for efficiency and the pursuit of excellence are deeply intertwined with temporal structures and the idea of time as a finite and exploitable resource, producing a sense of rush, urgency and disempowerment, and what he calls 'temporal alienation' among learners. These effects may be said to be a product of the temporal and spatial features that form part of the HC as it manifests through the formal curriculum at business schools.

THE HIDDEN CURRICULUM: VALUABLE INSIGHTS FOR RML – BUT PROCEED WITH CAUTION

It is hopefully evident by now that the HC concept constitutes a potentially valuable 'vehicle of criticism' (Cornbleth, 1984: 29) in the RML arsenal, since it enables scrutiny of fine-grained aspects of learning environments that matter for RML but which tend to be overlooked. However, the HC concept is not without its snags and I therefore recommend its careful deployment in RML analyses and practice. In this section, I discuss some important critiques that have been levelled against the concept, and I suggest how these may be addressed by RML scholars and others interested in using it anyway.

The first snag has to do with the way the HC has sometimes been used rather uncritically to critique the consensus model of the school–society relationship – or for present purposes, the school–business 'alliance', which, as outlined above, holds that it is the school's proper role to produce graduates aligned with the needs of the labour market and (implicitly) that there is nothing wrong with that. Correspondence- and conflict theory-inspired critiques do not buy this innocent role of the school, instead holding that through the HC, a kind of 'hidden agenda'

is asserted in which the school becomes – consciously or not – complicit in furthering powerful interest groups, notably capitalist elites, that perpetuate social inequality and injustice.

This consensus–conflict conceptual duo, although necessary and productive in enabling a critical eye to the link between schools (or other organizations where learning takes place) and society, if crudely applied risks oversimplifying matters and portraying that link with an iron-clad, gloomy determinism. In that regard, Dewey – himself a staunch proponent of progressive, critical, democratic education – aptly reminds us that society functions not only through transformation but also in large part through *transmission* – of values, functional skills and dispositions that enable people to channel their capabilities, enhance their personal autonomy, exercise a profession and cooperate (often enjoyably) with one another (Cornbleth, 1984; Hlebowitsh 1994: 343). In other words, schools afford opportunities both 'for domination and resistance or transformation', and they can both limit and enhance students' personal autonomy (Cornbleth, 1984: 31). In like manner, Gordon (1982: 189) points out that although correspondence theorists may have a valid point in drawing attention to the darker sides of schooling, this does not make schools all-out pernicious institutions; rather, they are likely to reflect, as well as resist, the differences and tensions in the societies they are presumed to 'correspond to'. Just as capitalism is far from a monolithic or unchanging phenomenon (Amable, 2003; Hall, 2015; Walker, Brewster & Wood, 2014), so are schools also heterogeneous and often internally contradictory institutions: they vary enormously in their ethos and learning climate, teachers teach differently, courses communicate different types of message and students are a heterogeneous crowd both within and across cohorts, among other things (Cornbleth, 1984). We need only look to the highly variegated landscape of business schools to see such tensions and contradictions played out daily: both within and among schools, there is great variation in, for instance, the emphasis given to responsibility issues and the way these are taught (Maloni, Smith & Napshin, 2012). The doleful shadow of correspondence theory also seems to preclude the possibility that *positive* HCs may also exist, which combat undesirable societal ideologies and tendencies and promote RML-friendly ones instead. Blasco and Tackney's (2013) analysis of the (formerly) positive HC at a Danish business school, for instance, shows how HC elements, including a unique combination of particular didactic techniques and incentives, can promote collaboration, participation, collective accountability and independent thinking.

Second, scholars have raised serious questions about the *implicit* nature of the HC. Some have questioned whether it is even viable to research something that is concealed: 'Technically speaking, if it is hidden, it is not really known and thus not really intelligible' (Hlebowitsh, 1994: 349). Vallance (1980) remarked of the HC concept that it is 'as powerful as it is elusive', observing that 'it is both a strength and weakness of the hidden-curriculum concept that it is nearly impossible to pin down'. Because of this, a major challenge for researching the HC at business schools remains how to operationalize the concept convincingly. However, as discussed earlier, this depends greatly on whether one understands 'hidden' to mean literally invisible and incognizable; or simply ignored or taken-for-granted but otherwise plain for all to see. And indeed, based on the latter definition, a great deal of studies have designed and deployed plausible methodologies to study the HC, typically using in-depth ethnographic methods akin to those used to study culture (Vallance, 1980; Willis, 1977). Similarly, if one conceptualizes the HC according to Portelli's (cf. 1993, above) four possible definitions, then eminently researchable aspects such as unintended learning outcomes, expectations and incentives, also become salient.

Others have questioned the theoretical assumptions that underpin the HC concept. Assor and Gordon (1987: 331), for instance, criticize the HC concept for being a 'one-factor' theory that can hardly be sufficient to explain the powerful learning effects that have been attributed to it. That 'one factor' is implicit learning theory which, due to the paucity of psychological research on the HC, scholars have tended to accept quite uncritically (Assor & Gordon, 1987). Implicit learning theory is premised on the idea that the implicit dimensions of learning, such as the form through which learning occurs, are more effective, in terms of values learning, than the explicit dimensions, such as content – quite an extravagant claim, and one for which there is, as yet, little evidence. In that connection, Hlebowitsh urges scholars not to underestimate the manifest, or be taken in by rhetoric which presumes that 'the latent is the real and the manifest is the unreal' (Jackson, 1977 in Hlebowitsh, 1994: 343–4). Gordon (1982: 189) similarly questions why the hidden curriculum should be regarded as more effective than the formal curriculum; and in particular why the social environment should be attributed with such extraordinary powers for the teaching of values and norms compared to the formal curriculum and cognitive learning environment. Gordon (1982: 195) further critiques what he calls 'the problem of non-events', namely the notion that students learn something from the '*non-occurrence* of certain events' in teaching (p. 195) – such as the failure to present students with certain views on a topic (cf. the arguments about selective bias in textbooks, outlined above). He wonders which of a potentially infinitesimal number of non-events can be singled out as being significant in a given learning context ('the teacher is not standing on his/her head', for example).

Specifically, Assor and Gordon (1987) argue that the main assumption underpinning the HC concept – namely that prolonged exposure to certain repeated rituals, actions and interactions in schools results in students absorbing these messages to a greater extent than those communicated via the formal curriculum – begs empirical verification. This assumption, they hold, reflects behaviouralist approaches to education which assume that recurrent, dominant elements in the learning environment are almost automatically internalized by students (Assor & Gordon, 1987), a perspective that has long been criticized for ignoring students' agency, negotiation, creative resistance or other spontaneous and unruly reactions to learning environments (Cornbleth, 1984).

It has, moreover, long been known that students' existing mental schemas influence how they receive external stimuli: when their schemas match those stimuli, learning is facilitated, and the opposite occurs when there is no match (Assor & Gordon, 1987). Moreover, in processing stimuli, people typically reorganize and recategorize them, and in that process they may completely redefine their meanings (Assor & Gordon, 1987). Related to this, Assor and Gordon (1987) draw attention to the principle of *hedonic relevance* in learning, i.e. that the greater the reward value (emotional or in terms of identification) of the information received, the more attention a student will give to it. So, for instance, students 'may learn more effectively the liberal views of the one teacher who rewards him [*sic*] greatly (or with whom he identifies) than the conservative views of the rest of the teachers, who do not pay attention to him (or with whom he does not identify)' (Assor & Gordon, 1987: 333–4). The effects of repeated exposure to one dominant message are, in this case, completely annulled by the reward value effect for the student in question (Assor & Gordon, 1987). A high reward for a single explicit or formal curriculum intervention could therefore, in principle, cancel out the effect of repeated HC messages with little reward value. Seen through this lens, it becomes implausible that students will seamlessly absorb certain HC messages even if they are repeatedly exposed to them. For instance, if a student

with a strong sense of social responsibility is exposed to 'irresponsible' messages in the business school learning environment, s/he may simply reject these all the more roundly, thereby disarming and even undermining the supposed 'power' of the HC in question.

In short, in much HC research, the mere *existence* of implicit messages has 'tended to be equated with effects' (Cornbleth, 1984: 30) – an elision that RML scholars should be wary of. Like all academic endeavours, then, HC analyses should be open and sensitive to inconsistencies and tensions and avoid conspiracy theory-type assessments for which there is, as yet, scarce evidence (Cornbleth, 1984). Indeed, rather than buying wholesale into the notion of a 'hidden curriculum', Cornbleth (1984: 30) suggests that it may be more advisable to think in terms of an 'implicit curriculum' and to 'directly examine … the seemingly contradictory messages that are communicated by the school milieu and how they are mediated by students.'

TOWARDS A RESPONSIBLE HIDDEN CURRICULUM?

How can we use the HC concept to rethink RML, while bearing in mind the above-mentioned strengths and weaknesses? I should preface this section by saying that, in my view, it would be remiss to recommend a one-size-fits-all recipe for a RHC, since each school or organization is likely to have its own, idiosyncratic hidden curricula, shaped by its unique constellation of actors, its particular regional, societal and cultural context, its institutional culture, teaching traditions, working conditions and other factors. Vallance (1980) reminds us, too, that even making a HC explicit does not necessarily render it controllable. Attempting to define a responsible HC would also necessarily require a *definition* of what constitutes RML – something that is likely to cause controversy at business schools, where faculty do not always agree on whether values should be taught at all, and if so, which ones. PRME acknowledges this diversity, having resisted imposing a specific model for RML (Solitander, Fougere, Sobczak & Herlin, 2012). Defining what is meant by RML, and then attempting to root out HC elements that do not support that definition, also risks replacing one set of values with another, equally dogmatic set, which would surely generate a possibly counterproductive HC all of its own.

Instead, based on the foregoing discussion, I show how business schools might diagnose elements that are known to be 'vehicles of the hidden curriculum' (Vallance, 1980: 140), and which they should be alert to, so that they can further explore whether and how these elements may manifest in their particular context. I then suggest ways to make the HC explicit at business schools, which can then devise their own strategies to address any problems they see connected to it.

Diagnose

A first step in addressing the HC at business schools is obviously to diagnose elements of the existing HC that may be dysfunctional in terms of a particular school or other organization's RML goals. Martin (1976: 141) proposes attempting to identify which elements produce a particular HC in a given learning environment, by examining the 'practices, procedures, rules, relationships, structures, and physical characteristics' of that environment. Apple (1990: 210–211) suggests searching for the HC in the following areas of school life: (1) basic everyday institutional routines; (2) how particular types of curricular knowledge reflect these ideologies; and (3) how these ideologies may be reflected in the way teachers organize and give meaning to their own activities. Portelli's (1993) four-pronged framework (outlined earlier) proposes different types of HC that might be investigated in such a diagnosis.

Vallance (1980: 144–145) recommends four ways of studying the HC: (i) looking into the 'kinds of learnings provided by the school environment outside its formal curriculum'; (ii) inquiry into how such learnings are transmitted to students, when, and by whom; (iii) an evaluation of the educational significance of such learnings; (iv) an evaluation of what, if anything, to do about them. And finally, as mentioned earlier, I have suggested a framework, designed specifically for business schools, to facilitate a HC diagnosis (Blasco, 2012), consisting of various aspects to look out for in (i) the formal curriculum, (ii) interpersonal interactions and (iii) school governance.

I should like to add some further areas which, in my experience, constitute important elements for HC analysis:

> *Walking the talk:* If business school staff are autocratic, inconsiderate, tight with their time, unengaged, cynical, chauvinistic or shoddy, or otherwise display unprofessional or unethical behaviour, we cannot expect our students to miraculously morph into model responsible business citizens. We must remain acutely aware that students take their cues from us about what constitutes acceptable professional behaviour, and monitor our behaviour accordingly. This includes 'sweating the small stuff', as I mentioned earlier, since one of the most valuable insights of HC research is that small things matter. Rituals, off-hand remarks, jokes, punctuality, keeping one's word and tone, among others, communicate volumes about the 'right way to be' and influence students' socialization in academic environments.
>
> *Pay attention to the informal discourse on responsibility at your business school*: Faculty often resort to 'hard–soft' dichotomies to describe their own and other teachers' subjects, where subjects such as CSR, cultural and diversity studies, sustainability etc. may be depicted as 'soft', as talking shops or overly-easy; and, conversely, subjects such as economics and finance may be branded as 'hard', narrow-minded, cynical and antisocial. This may be because faculty often have 'narrow disciplinary orientations' (Waddock, 2005: 147) and lack insight into the nuances of what is being taught, and how, in each other's

classes, resorting to stereotypes about different disciplinary areas; in my experience, students are very sensitive to this language and tend to reproduce it. This can undermine the legitimacy of RML initiatives at business schools, and we must be mindful of it.

Reflect on how political–institutional pressures trickle down to the academic environment: Current pressures on business schools to compete for rankings and publications trickle down to myriad aspects of the academic environment (Mingers & Wilmott, 2013; Morrish, 2017). We must be vigilant about how such pressures manifest in our relations with students as well as colleagues, and in the way we administer our time and structure the learning process (Contu, 2011). For instance it may be tempting to minimize contact time with students, to cram more and more students into classes, or to compress courses into ever-shorter time spans in an effort to free up resources and research time. Such measures may respond to the needs of managers and faculty in the current 'accelerated academy' (Carrigan & Vostal, 2017) but they shrink the time–space available for learning, and send unfortunate messages to students that learning is about rushing rather than dwelling (cf. Blasco, 2016).

Make Explicit

Diagnosing the HC is just the first step, however. It does not solve the vexed question posed by Martin (1976) over 40 years ago, namely: 'What should we do with a hidden curriculum when we find one?'. Vallance (1980: 140–141) proposes that we can use the HC in different ways to study, and improve, academic environments: as a tool for educational dialogue; as a tool to describe a problem; as a 'vehicle for the social criticism of schooling'; or simply as a 'point of view' that allows acknowledgement that there may be aspects of the academic environment that behave unpredictably and escape our control. Echoing some of Vallance's points, Greene (in Portelli, 1993: 343) argues that once a HC is discovered, educators have an obligation to make it explicit, a point echoed by Cornbleth (1984:

34), who asserts that 'A hidden curriculum is not merely to be made visible but is to be interrogated as to its nature and function.'

Arguably, a HC can never be made perfectly explicit, since it is to a large extent created in interaction, and is therefore unpredictable – and not least, as Orón Semper and Blasco (2018: 490) point out, because 'it is the teacher who teaches, not the official documents'. However, several authors have proposed ways to attempt this. Following Apple, Gair and Mullins (2001: 37) propose the following strategy for exposing and addressing the HC at universities:

> At universities the hidden curriculum must be brought to an overt level, it must be thought about, it must be talked through and the kinds of norms and values you want to organize the workplace. ... All of that should be brought to a level where people can participate in it, struggle over it, talk about it but it's got to be done in a way where people feel they can speak honestly and where the norms that are supposed to be usually hidden are democratic, participatory, and organized around critical intellectual and pedagogic work.

Giroux and Penna (1979) likewise recommend discussing, together with the students, how particular aspects of knowledge come to be represented as objective and factual, what kind of ideological interests the curriculum represents, and how the school itself endorses such knowledge as 'truth'. Orón Semper and Blasco (2018: 491) propose making the HC explicit by abandoning the notion of 'a technical, value-free education' and strengthening the interpersonal relationship among and between teachers and students through, inter alia, improved access to one another, self-disclosure in large classes that otherwise tend to remain highly impersonal, arenas and activities where different school actors can meet and discuss school issues on an equal footing, student–faculty commissions to look into implicit biases in textbooks and other teaching materials, and peer mentoring both for students and teachers.

A major challenge is how to clear spaces for such discussions at business schools.

At my own school, we have done this mainly in collaboration with the PRME office, which has organized focus group interviews with students, as well as faculty development courses about the hidden curriculum both for local and visiting staff.

CONCLUSION AND SUGGESTIONS FOR FUTURE RESEARCH ON THE HC AT BUSINESS SCHOOLS

Whether or not one buys into the existence of a 'real' HC at business schools, the concept remains, in my view, a valuable tool for attaining 'a state of mind [that is] by definition open to unknowns and attuned to the subtle qualities of schooling' (Vallance, 1980: 138). The concept can also help us to interrogate 'the implicit and taken-for-granted rationality of most "modern" curricula and the totality and coherence of the belief systems which inform them' (Skelton, 1997: 177). The HC concept obliges its users to acknowledge that learning is not just a matter of planning the right lessons and content, but is far more complex, power-laden and less controllable than we like to admit. In that sense, if we acknowledge the basic premise of the HC, i.e. that much is learned at schools that is not intentionally taught; and much is taught that is not necessarily learned (Dewey, 1938; Gordon, 1982; Kohlberg, 1975), the HC concept 'opens the door to a perhaps more realistic view' of education (Vallance, 1980: 139). It also encourages a renewed focus at business schools on the 'Big Questions' that dominated early HC research, such as what is *actually* learned in schools? What knowledge should be taught, and should it be taught explicitly or implicitly? What is – and should be – the relationship between the values taught in schools and those of the societies in which schools are embedded? (Vallance, 1980: 139). Some of these questions are already being carefully addressed within the critical management

education community, notably in connection with PRME initiatives (cf. Forray & Leigh, 2012; Forray, Leigh & Kenworthy, 2015; Laasch & Conaway, 2017). Indeed, a HC perspective is perfectly consistent with a critical management education approach (see Perriton & Reynolds, 2004), and further research on the topic could usefully link the two fields.

In addition, the review and critiques of the HC concept that I have presented in this article raise a number of theoretical, methodological and empirical issues and questions which I outline below as a first step towards sketching out an agenda for future research on the HC in RML. I believe that these issues must be rigorously interrogated if the HC concept is to gain traction in RML analyses.

In terms of *theoretical issues*, first, research should level a critical eye at the implicit learning theory that underpins the HC concept, as outlined above, in order to avoid conflating the existence of a HC with an automatic impact on student learning assumed. Second, following the insights of hedonic relevance theory, we need to know much more about students' initial value orientations and expectations when they arrive at business schools, in order to assess how receptive they are to various aspects of the formal curriculum and to a possible HC. Of interest here, clearly, is to investigate how reward value is experienced by students when it comes to learning about responsibility, CSR and related subjects, compared to other subjects at business schools. We need theories that can explain the dynamics underpinning the 'meta-messages' that students pick up, why they sometimes differ from student to student, and which environmental factors play in? What does it mean for RML if a learning environment pays lip service formally to social responsibility through courses and other initiatives, but promotes individualism and profit maximization through its HC – will students 'buy' the HC rather than the messages they receive in their RML-friendly courses in the explicit curriculum, and if so why? (Cf. Gair & Mullins, 2001: 35–36.) Third, we need theorizing that addresses whether and how the HC influences efforts to introduce RML at business schools. Revisiting the conflict–correspondence debate, notably finding ways to theorize societal influence on the business school HC, as well as seeking to shed light on the tensions and contradictions that surround discussions about responsibility in business schools, would be a good place to start (see Maloni et al., 2012 for a good example of such a study in connection with the implementation of PRME).

In terms of *methodological issues*, as outlined above, frameworks do exist for researching the HC not only for schools generally, but for business schools, but we need much more experience with applying these frameworks at business schools in different contexts. In connection with that, existing research into the HC has tended to be qualitative, and often ethnographic, notably participant observation and interviews (Cotton et al., 2013; Vallance, 1980). Quantitative and/or comparative inquiry might add insights concerning the pervasiveness and generalizability of HC elements at business schools – a point also made for schools more generally by Vallance (1980: 146), who endorses the mass application of quantitative instruments such as the Flanders Interaction Schedule,[6] to detect 'subtle learning patterns and educational inequalities'. A complementary emphasis on positivistic types of enquiry in HC research, seeking generalizable phenomena and causal mechanisms, may also help to address the question of *how* HC dynamics operate – so far much HC research has been dedicated to *describing* how the HC manifests rather than to *explaining* it (Vallance, 1980; (Phillips, 1980 and Burbule, 1980 in Portelli 1993: 344; see also my points on theorizing the HC, above).

In terms of *empirical questions*, first, detailed ethnographic studies of interaction at business schools are rarely compared to other educational settings (although see, e.g., Anteby, 2013; Arbaugh, 2000, 2001; Northcott, 2001). To properly understand the HC, we need to know much more about the kind of socialization that occurs through interaction at business schools – not only between teachers and students, but also among managers and faculty, and among students – and we need rigorous studies that can document the effects, if any, of such socialization on students and other school actors. Second, we also lack a rich picture of the variation in RML teaching at business schools, for instance studies might investigate what different *strains* of capitalism are taught at business schools, through which theories and means, and whether they are taught as dogma or with a critical intent. In which situations are students trained to think critically and to act as change agents as opposed to conformists? Third, we need studies of strategies and initiatives to redress HC elements that are diagnosed as being counterproductive to RML: such studies would serve as templates and inspiration for other schools wishing to tackle these issues. And finally, we need studies that investigate possible links between the HC at business schools and that which students encounter at their workplaces post-graduation, in terms of responsibility learning: for instance, does the immediate work environment 'override' prior HC learning at business schools?

In that connection, although developed in relation to schools, the HC concept could, I believe, potentially also yield fruitful analyses of how managers and employees in other organizations learn responsibility – or irresponsibility – while on the job, since just like schools, workplaces are sites of socialization, informal and incidental learning (Hafferty & Hafler, 2011; Watkins & Marsick, 1992). Also, French and Bazalgette (1996: 117) point out that, although the word 'teach' is seldom explicitly used, from a HC perspective teaching is a 'systemic organizational function' – one carried out not only by mentors, consultants and managers but by *all* organizational actors, who implicitly model behaviours to their co-employees; as well as by 'decisions, rituals and structures [that] communicate powerful messages'. A HC perspective applied to the workplace would, therefore, regard all organizational actors simultaneously both as learners susceptible to workplace socialization *and* as teachers socializing their colleagues through interaction and other mechanisms, thus potentially obliging all organizational actors to ask themselves 'What responsibility message am I sending if I do X, and will my action align with the organization's explicit values?' The critical spirit of a HC analysis also lends itself to deliberate investigation of mismatches between an organization's explicit responsibility messages, and the implicit messages received through the HC. In the sense that it also manifests through concrete artefacts and interactions (Kuenzi & Schminke, 2009; Schein, 2004), the HC concept bears similarities to the concepts of organizational culture and climate (French & Bazalgette, 1996), although the HC concept focuses more on the tacit messages conveyed by concrete micro-practices and interactions, and how they are perceived, than on underlying assumptions as an organizational culture analysis would (Kuenzi & Schminke, 2009). Future work might theorize interfaces and distinctions between the HC concept, and organizational learning, socialization, culture and climate literatures; and apply the HC framework in non-school organizations to examine how the HC supports or combats the unequal social structures and power relations inherent in capitalism (Apple, 1980; Bowles & Gintis, 1976).

Such analyses could feed into targeted interventions that have an eye to counterproductive elements while preserving and strengthening what already works to support an RML agenda in business schools and other organizations. This represents a major task, but also a colossal opportunity for RML scholarship.

Notes

1 An idea also earlier expressed by Durkheim (2012) in *Moral Education*, and which also influenced Jackson, as he explicitly states in *Life in Classrooms* (Jackson, 1968).

2 Some scholars have, however, traced the idea behind the HC concept back to Plato (Barrow, 1976 in Portelli, 1993), while Vallance (1974) argues that the normative, socializing (and some would say also disciplining) function of the HC was, in fact, the overt purpose of schooling in the 19th century, only becoming 'hidden' once it was so widely accepted that it was no longer necessary to state this explicitly.

3 Ramsden (2003: 8) similarly writes that a lot of what students learn is not directly related to the subject matter at hand, but 'about learning how to please lecturers and gain high marks'.

4 The authors refer specifically to activities such as 'a multicultural celebration of food and dance' which is not part of the formal curriculum but which students are encouraged to attend, as an example of something not encompassed by the HC concept but covered by the 'informal curriculum' construct. I differ from the authors on this point – in my view the celebration in question would be perfectly consistent with definitions of the HC, since school's endorsement of this event sends tacit signals to students about what constitutes appropriate behaviour and attitudes.

5 The concept of 'multi-level learning environments' is drawn from Hafferty (1998); 'message sites' is drawn from Hafferty & Franks (1994).

6 An observational instrument that 'captures the verbal behaviour of teachers and students that is directly related to the social–emotional climate of the classroom' (Amatari, 2015: 43).

REFERENCES

Aharoni, Y. (2011). Fifty years of case research in international business: the power of outliers and black swans. In Piekkari, R., & Welch, C. (Eds.), *Rethinking the case study in international business and management research* (pp. 41–54). Cheltenham: Edward Elgar.

Alhadeff-Jones, M. (2016). *Time and the rhythms of emancipatory education: rethinking the temporal complexity of self and society*. New York: Routledge.

Amable, B. (2003). *The diversity of modern capitalism*. Oxford: Oxford University Press.

Amann, W., Pirson, M., Dierksmeier, C., Von Kimakowitz, E., & Spitzeck, H. (2011). *Business schools under fire: humanistic management education as the way forward.* Basingstoke: Palgrave Macmillan.

Amatari, V. O. (2015). The instructional process: a review of Flanders' Interaction Analysis in a classroom setting. *International Journal of Secondary Education, 3*(5), 43–49.

Anteby, M. (2013). *Manufacturing morals: the values of silence in business school education.* Chicago, IL: University of Chicago Press.

Antonacopoulou, E. P. (2010). Making the business school more 'critical': reflexive critique based on phronesis as a foundation for impact. *British Journal of Management, 21*(s1).

Anyon, J. (1979). Education, social 'structure' and the power of individuals. *Theory & Research in Social Education, 7*(1), 49–59.

Apple, M. W. (1980). The other side of the hidden curriculum: correspondence theories and the labor process. *Interchange, 11*(3), 5–22.

Apple, M. (1990) *Ideology and curriculum.* New York: Routledge.

Arbaugh, J. B. (2000). Virtual classroom versus physical classroom: an exploratory study of class discussion patterns and student learning in an asynchronous Internet-based MBA course. *Journal of Management Education, 24*(2), 213–233.

Arbaugh, J. B. (2001). How instructor immediacy behaviors affect student satisfaction and learning in web-based courses. *Business Communication Quarterly, 64*(4), 42–54.

Assor, A., & Gordon, D. (1987). The implicit learning theory of hidden-curriculum research. *Journal of Curriculum Studies, 19*(4), 329–339.

Baker, R., Walonoski, J., Heffernan, N., Roll, I., Corbett, A., & Koedinger, K. (2008). Why students engage in 'gaming the system' behavior in interactive learning environments. *Journal of Interactive Learning Research, 19*(2), 185.

Barnett, R. and Coate, K. (2005). *Engaging the curriculum in higher education.* Berkshire, GBR: McGraw-Hill Education.

Benabou, C. (1999). Polychronicity and temporal dimensions of work in learning organizations. *Journal of Managerial Psychology, 14*(3/4), 257–270.

Bernstein, B. (1971). *Class, codes and control: theoretical studies towards a sociology of language.* London: Routledge & Kegan Paul.

Beyes, T., & Michels, C. (2011). The production of educational space: heterotopia and the business university. *Management Learning, 42*(5), 521–536.

Blasco, M. (2012). Aligning the hidden curriculum of management education with PRML: an inquiry-based framework. *Journal of Management Education, 36*(3), 364–388.

Blasco, M. (2016). Conceptualising curricular space in busyness education: An aesthetic approximation. *Management Learning, 47*(2), 117–136.

Blasco, M., & Tackney, C. (2013). 'If it ain't broke, don't fix it': internationalisation and the erosion of the positive hidden curriculum in Danish higher education. *International Journal of Management in Education, 27*(4), 341–359.

Bowles, S., & Gintis, H. (1976). *Schooling in capitalist America: educational reform and the contradictions of economic life.* New York: Basic Books.

Brooks, D. C. (2012). Space and consequences: the impact of different formal learning spaces on instructor and student behavior. *Journal of Learning Spaces, 1*(2), n2.

Burbules, N. C. (1980). The hidden curriculum and the latent functions of schooling: twooverlapping perspectives, 2: Who hides the hidden curriculum? In C. J. B. Macmillan (Ed.), *Philosophy of Education* (pp. 281–29). Normal, IL: Philosophy of Education Society.

Burbules, N. C., & Callister, T. A. (1999). Universities in transition: the challenges of new technologies. Paper presented to the Cambridge Philosophy of Education Conference, 18 September.

Carmean, C., & Haefner, J. (2002). Mind over matter: transforming course management systems into effective learning environments. *Educause Review, 37*(6), 26–34.

Carrigan, M., & Vostal, F. (2017) An introduction to the second Accelerated Academy. Available at: http://accelerated.academy/. Accessed 16 August 2018.

Caza, A., & Brower, H. H. (2015). Mentioning the unmentioned: an interactive interview about the informal management curriculum.

Academy of Management Learning & Education, *14*(1), 96–110.

Clegg, S. (1981). Organization and control. *Administrative Science Quarterly*, *26*(4), 545–562.

Clegg, S., & Kornberger, M. (Eds.). (2006). *Space, organizations and management theory*. Oslo: Liber.

Coder, L., & Spiller, M. S. (2013). Leadership education and gender roles: 'Think, manager, think'?. *Academy of Educational Leadership Journal*, *17*(3), 21–51.

Contu, A. (2011). Critical management education. In Alvesson, M., Bridgman, T., & Willmott, H. (Eds.), *The Oxford handbook of critical management studies* (pp. 536–550). Oxford: Oxford University Press.

Cornbleth, C. (1984). Beyond hidden curriculum? *Journal of Curriculum Studies*, *16*(1), 29–36.

Cotton, D., Winter, J., & Bailey, I. (2013). Researching the hidden curriculum: intentional and unintended messages. *Journal of Geography in Higher Education*, *37*(2), 192–203.

Dewey, J. (1938). *Experience and Education*. New York: Kappa Delta Pi.

Dreeben, R. (1967). The contribution of schooling to the learning of norms. *Harvard Educational Review*, *37*(2), 211–237.

Durkheim, E. (2012) *Moral education*. Courier Corporation.

Dweck, C. S. (1986). Motivational processes affecting learning. *American Psychologist*, *41*(10), 1040–1048.

Edenius, M., & Yakhlef, A. (2007) Space, vision and organizational learning the interplay of incorporating and inscribing practices. *Management Learning*, *38*(2), 193–210.

Edwards, R., & Usher, R. (2003). Putting space back on the map of learning. In Edwards, R., & Usher, R. (Eds.), *Space, curriculum, and learning* (pp. 1–12). Charlotte, NC: Information Age Publishing.

Ehrensal, K. N. (2001). Training capitalism's foot soldiers: the hidden curriculum of undergraduate business education. In Margolis, E. (Ed.), *The hidden curriculum in higher education* (pp. 97–113). New York: Routledge.

Eisner, E. (1985) *The educational imagination: on the design and evaluation of school programs*, 2nd ed. New York: Macmillan.

Forray, J. M., & Leigh, J. S. (2012). A primer on the principles of responsible management education: intellectual roots and waves of change. *Journal of Management Education*, *36*(3), 295–309.

Forray, J., Leigh, J., & Kenworthy, A. L. (2015). Special section cluster on responsible management education: Nurturing an emerging PRML ethos. *Academy of Management Learning & Education*, *14*(2), 293–296.

French, R., & Bazalgette, J. (1996). From learning organization to teaching–learning organization? *Management Learning*, *27*(1), 113–128.

Gair, M., & Mullins, G. (2001). Hiding in plain sight. In Margolis, E. (Ed.), *The hidden curriculum in higher education* (pp. 21–41). New York: Routledge.

Ghoshal, S. (2005). Bad management theories are destroying good management practices. *Academy of Management Learning and Education*, *4*(1), 75–91.

Giroux, H. A., & Purpel, D. E. (1983). *The hidden curriculum and moral education: Deception or discovery?*. Mccutchan Pub Corp.

Giroux, H. A., & McLaren, P. (1989). Introduction: Schooling, cultural politics, and the struggle for democracy. In Giroux, H. A., & McLaren, P. (Eds.), *Critical pedagogy, the state, and cultural struggle* (pp. xi–xxxiv). Albany, NY: SUNY Press.

Giroux, H. A., & Penna, A. N. (1979). Social education in the classroom: the dynamics of the hidden curriculum. *Theory & Research in Social Education*, *7*(1), 21–42.

Godwyn, M. (2015). *Ethics and diversity in business management education: A sociological study with international scope*. Springer.

Gofton, W., & Regehr, G. (2006). What we don't know we are teaching: unveiling the hidden curriculum. *Clinical Orthopaedics and Related Research*, *449*, 20–27.

Gordon, D. (1982) The concept of the hidden curriculum. *Journal of Philosophy of Education*, *16*(2), 187–198.

Grey, C. (2004). Reinventing business schools: the contribution of critical management education. *Academy of Management Learning & Education*, *3*(2), 178–186.

Hafferty, F. W. (1998). Beyond curriculum reform: confronting medicine's hidden curriculum. *Academic Medicine, 73,* 403–407.

Hafferty, F. W., & Franks, R. (1994). The hidden curriculum, ethics teaching, and the structure of medical education. *Academic Medicine, 69,* 861–871.

Hafferty, F. W., & Hafler, J. P. (2011). The hidden curriculum, structural disconnects, and the socialization of new professionals. In Hafler, J. P. (Ed.), *Extraordinary learning in the workplace* (pp. 17–35). Dordrecht: Springer Netherlands.

Hall, P. A. (2015). Varieties of capitalism. In *Emerging Trends in the Social and Behavioral Sciences.* Wiley Online. https://doi.org/10.1002/9781118900772.etrds0377.

Hargreaves, D. (1978). Power and the paracurriculum. In Richards, C. (Ed.), *Power and the Curriculum: Issues in Curriculum Studies* (pp. 97–108). Driffield: Nafferton.

Hlebowitsh, P. S. (1994). The forgotten hidden curriculum. *Journal of Curriculum and Supervision, 9*(4), 339–349.

Jabbar, A., & Hardaker, G. (2013). The role of culturally responsive teaching for supporting ethnic diversity in British University Business Schools. *Teaching in Higher Education, 18*(3), 272–284.

Jackson, P. (1968). *Life in Classrooms.* New York: Holt, Rinehart 8c Winston, Inc.

Kelan, E. K., & Jones, R. D. (2010). Gender and the MBA. *Academy of Management Learning & Education, 9*(1), 26–43.

Kentli, F. D. (2009) Comparison of hidden curriculum theories. *European Journal of Educational Studies, 1*(2), 83–88.

Kohlberg, L. (1975). Moral education for a society in moral transition. *Educational Leadership, 33*(1), 46–54.

Kornberger, M., & Clegg, S. R. (2004). Bringing space back in: organizing the generative building. *Organization Studies, 25*(7), 1095–1114.

Kuenzi, M., & Schminke, M. (2009). Assembling fragments into a lens: A review, critique, and proposed research agenda for the organizational work climate literature. *Journal of Management, 35*(3), 634–717.

Laasch, O., & Conaway, R. (2017). *Responsible business: the textbook for management learning, competence and innovation.* New York: Routledge.

Lefebvre, H. (2004). *Rhythmanalysis: space, time and everyday life.* London: Continuum.

Lefebvre, H., & Nicholson-Smith, D. (1991). *The production of space.* Oxford: Blackwell.

Lynch, K. (1989). *The hidden curriculum: reproduction in education, a reappraisal.* Hove: Psychology Press.

Maloni, M. J., Smith, S. D., & Napshin, S. (2012). A methodology for building faculty support for the United Nations Principles for Responsible Management Education. *Journal of Management Education, 36*(3), 312–336.

Margolis, E., Soldatenko, M., Acker, S., & Gair, M. (2001). Peekaboo. In Margolis, E. (Ed.), *The hidden curriculum in higher education* (pp. 1–20). New York: Routledge.

Martin, J. R. (1976). What should we do with a hidden curriculum when we find one? *Curriculum Inquiry, 6*(2), 135–151.

Marton, F., Tsui, A. B., with Chik, P. P., Ko, P. Y., & Lo, M. L. (2004). *Classroom discourse and the space of learning.* Mahwah, NJ: Lawrence Erlbaum.

McCarthy, P. R., & McCarthy, H. M. (2006). When case studies are not enough: integrating experiential learning into business curricula. *Journal of Education for Business, 81*(4), 201–204.

McLaren, P. (1989). *Life in schools: an introduction to critical pedagogy in the foundations of education.* White Plains, New York: Longman.

McIntosh, M. (Ed.). (2017). *Business, capitalism and corporate citizenship: a collection of seminal essays.* Abingdon: Routledge.

Meece, J. L., Blumenfeld, P. C., & Hoyle, R. H. (1988). Students' goal orientations and cognitive engagement in classroom activities. *Journal of Educational Psychology, 80*(4), 514–523.

Mills, A. J. (1997). Gender, bureaucracy, and the business curriculum. *Journal of Management Education, 21*(3), 325–342.

Mingers, J., & Willmott, H. (2013). Taylorizing business school research: on the 'one best way' performative effects of journal ranking lists. *Human Relations, 66*(8), 1051–1073.

Morrish, L. (2017). Academic identities in the managed university: neoliberalism and resistance at Newcastle University, UK. *Australian Universities' Review, 59*(2), 23–36.

Nkomo, S. M. (2015). Challenges for management and business education in a 'developmental' state: the case of South Africa. *Academy of Management Learning & Education*, *14*(2), 242–258.

Northcott, J. (2001). Towards an ethnography of the MBA classroom: a consideration of the role of interactive lecturing styles within the context of one MBA programme. *English for Specific Purposes*, *20*(1), 15–37.

Oblinger, D. G. (2006). *Learning spaces*. Washington, DC: Educause.

Orón Semper, J. V., & Blasco, M. (2018). Revealing the hidden curriculum in higher education. *Studies in Philosophy and Education*, *37*(5), 481–498.

Ottewill, R., McKenzie, G., & Leah, J. (2005). Integration and the hidden curriculum in business education. *Education + Training*, *47*(2), 89–97.

Park, E. L., & Choi, B. K. (2014). Transformation of classroom spaces: traditional versus active learning classroom in colleges. *Higher Education*, *68*(5), 749–771.

Perriton, L., & Reynolds, M. (2004). Critical management education: from pedagogy of possibility to pedagogy of refusal? *Management Learning*, *35*(1), 61–77.

Phillips, D. C. (1980). The hidden curriculum and the latent functions of schooling: two overlapping perspectives. 1: why the hidden curriculum is hidden. In C. B. J. Macmillan (Ed.), *Philosophy of Education* (pp. 274–280). Normal, IL: Philosophy of Education Society.

Portelli, J. P. 1993. Exposing the hidden curriculum. *Journal of Curriculum Studies*, *25*(4), 343–358.

Ramsden, P. (2003). *Learning to teach in higher education*, 2nd ed. Abingdon: Routledge.

Rasche, A., & Gilbert, D. U. (2015). Decoupling responsible management education: why business schools may not walk their talk. *Journal of Management Inquiry*, *24*(3), 239–252.

Rippin, A., Booth, C., Bowie, S., & Jordan, J. (2002). A complex case: using the case study method to explore uncertainty and ambiguity in undergraduate business education. *Teaching in Higher Education*, *7*(4), 429–441.

Rosa, H. (2013). *Social acceleration: a new theory of modernity*. New York: Columbia University Press.

Rumens, N. (2016). Towards queering the business school: a research agenda for advancing lesbian, gay, bisexual and trans perspectives and issues. *Gender, Work & Organization*, *23*(1), 36–51.

Sambell, K., & McDowell, L. (1998). The construction of the hidden curriculum: messages and meanings in the assessment of student learning. *Assessment & Evaluation in Higher Education*, *23*(4), 391–402.

Schein, E. H. (2004). *Organizational culture and leadership*, 3rd edition. San Francisco: John Wiley & Sons.

Skelton, A. (1997). Studying hidden curricula: developing a perspective in the light of postmodern insights. *Curriculum Studies*, *5*(2), 177–193.

Smith, C. R. (2000). Notes from the field. Gender issues in the management curriculum: a survey of student experiences. *Gender, Work & Organization*, *7*(3), 158–167.

Solitander, N., Fougere, M., Sobczak, A., & Herlin, H. (2012). We are the champions: organizational learning and change for responsible management education. *Journal of Management Education*, *36*(3), 337–363.

Starkey, K., & Tempest, S. (2009). The winter of our discontent: the design challenge for business schools. *Academy of Management Learning & Education*, *8*(4), 576–586.

Thomas, H., & Cornuel, E. (2012). Business schools in transition? Issues of impact, legitimacy, capabilities and re-invention. *Journal of Management Development*, *31*(4), 329–335.

Trevino, L. K., & McCabe, D. (1994). Meta-learning about business ethics: Building honorable business school communities. *Journal of Business Ethics*, *13*, 405–416.

Välimaa, J., & Nokkala, T. (2014). The dimensions of social dynamics in comparative studies on higher education. *Higher Education*, *67*(4), 423–437.

Vallance, E. (1974). Hiding the hidden curriculum: an interpretation of the language of justification in nineteenth-century educational reform. *Curriculum Theory Network*, *4*(1), 5–22.

Vallance, E. (1980). The hidden curriculum and qualitative inquiry as states of mind. *Journal of Education*, *162*(1), 138–151.

Vostal, F. (2015). Academic life in the fast lane: the experience of time and speed in British academia. *Time & Society*, *24*(1), 71–95.

Waddock, S. (2005). Hollow men and women at the helm … hollow accounting ethics?. *Issues in Accounting Education*, *20*(2), 145–150.

Walker, J. T., Brewster, C., & Wood, G. (2014). Diversity between and within varieties of capitalism: transnational survey evidence. *Industrial and Corporate Change*, *23*(2), 493–533.

Watkins, K. E., & Marsick, V. J. (1992). Towards a theory of informal and incidental learning in organizations. *International Journal of Lifelong Education*, *11*(4), 287–300.

Willis, P. (1977). *Learning to labour*. London: Saxon House.

PART V

Responsible Research

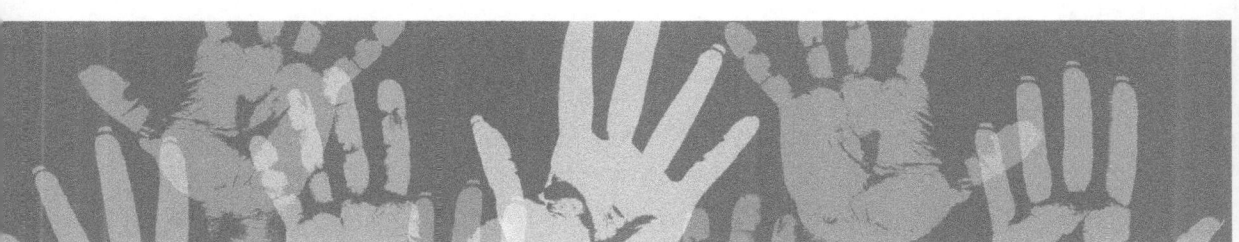

Responsible Research in Business and Management: Transforming Doctoral Education

Peter McKiernan and Anne S. Tsui

INTRODUCTION

Rigour and relevance have been topics of rich debate in the recent business and management literature. Over the past three decades, scholars have been accused of low internal scientific standards of published research (Bedeian, Taylor & Miller, 2010; Honig, Lampel, Siegel & Drnevich, 2014; Tsui, 2016) along with limited external impact (Aguinis, Suárez-González, Lannelongue & Joo, 2012; Ghoshal, 2005; Harley & Cornelissen, 2019; Tsui, 2015). Harley and Cornelissen (2019) argue that the situation is so desperate that senior academics must intervene and help to create and support a new, corrective forward pathway. As a rejoinder to Harley, McKiernan and Tsui (2019) even encourage emiriti to engage with doctoral education actively and inject sound science and a better understanding of societal needs into its programmes and thus, lever their considerable influence and academic legitimacy to force a generational transformation. This chapter explores the historical context of business schools (especially in the United States), highlighting both their 'golden age' and their 'dark age', in order to situate the problematique; analyses the causes of research despair in the latter; introduces the new responsibility turn in business and management research; focuses on the seven Principles of responsible research in business and management research; and, calls for a transformation in doctoral education to help propel the generational change required to re-route the research enterprise. This treatise opens up the opportunity for a valuable contribution to sound science and useful knowledge by our younger generations of scholars.

A BRIEF HISTORY OF BUSINESS SCHOOLS IN THE UNITED STATES

In a book titled *From Higher Aims to Hired Hands: The Social Transformation of American Business Schools and the Unfulfilled*

Promise of Management as a Profession, Khurana (2007) provides a historical account of the rise, development and 'fall' (unfulfilled promise) of American business education and management as a profession. The important milestone in this history was the publication of both the Gordon and Howell report (1959) – funded by the US Ford Foundation – and the Pierson report (1959) – funded by the Carnegie Council, whose recommendations helped transform US business schools from 'trade schools' to applied social science departments (Pfeffer & Fong, 2002). The reports called for 'improving the academic quality of business schools by raising the intellectual calibre of the faculty' (Khurana, 2007: 273). US business schools responded to this call by hiring new faculty with doctoral degrees in economics, psychology, sociology and even mathematics and statistics, since quantitative analysis has become the centre of business research. By 1969, business schools at Stanford, Chicago, Northwestern, Wharton, Columbia and MIT have gained reputation as the premier research-oriented business schools. From then on and even today, any respectable business school would have a research mission with a commitment to develop a research-guided business education curriculum. Many scholarly journals in business and management were founded around this time (e.g. *Management Science* in 1954, *Administrative Science Quarterly* and the *Journal of Accounting Research* in 1956, the *Academy of Management Journal* in 1958) and they 'modelled themselves on scholarly journals in the social sciences, featuring blind reviews and theoretical and empirical articles that would fall under the Kuhnian category of "normal science"' (Khurana, 2007: 274).

Enter the 'Golden Age' of Business and Management Research

The next thirty-plus years following these instrumental reports may be considered the 'Golden Age' of business and management

research in terms of building the legitimacy and reputation of quantitative social science research. Many important contributions to practice through the theoretical and empirical discoveries by the research faculty in business schools were made during this time. Below are a few illustrative examples of such contributions.

In finance, several ideas have revolutionized the finance industry. The Black–Scholes asset-pricing model (1973) and Malkiel and Fama's efficient market hypothesis (1970) transformed investment management. Meckling and Jensen's agency theory (1976) led to the widescale adoption of stock options in executive compensation by the listed corporations in the United States and beyond. In the marketing area there is consensus that a most influential stream of research that has made a major contribution to practice began with the article on service quality by Zeithaml, Parasuraman and Berry (1985). The original paper stimulated large numbers of academic and practitioner papers, books, presentations and applications across industries. The PZB model in the Zeithaml et al. (1985) paper is the organizing framework for the leading textbook *Services Marketing* (Zeithaml, Bitner & Gremler, 2018), which is in its 7th edition in 2018. There are also significant contributions in production and operations management (POM), which grew out of both economics and engineering. Important discoveries in POM were usually based on studying systems that have been shown to be effective, e.g. the Toyota Production System (Ohno, 1988) or phenomena that are surprising, e.g. the 'bullwhip effect' observed by Lee, Padmanabhan and Whang (1997). This effect, which was observed in the P&G Company, suggests that a minor variability in downstream customer demand can create a huge variability in the order quantity by upstream partners along the supply chain. In the management discipline, there are a number of theories that have influenced practice. The matrix organizational structure (Galbraith, 1971) came from the research on contingency theory (Burns & Stalker, 1961; Donaldson, 2001; Lawrence & Lorsch, 1967). A popular management tool, Management by Objectives, had its foundation on a strong tradition of goal-setting research (Locke & Latham, 2002). Research on performance appraisal and feedback has greatly improved the performance management process in organizations (Latham, 1981). Influenced by developments in industrial economics, Porter (1980) made widespread and influential contributions on industry structure (5-force analysis) and competitive strategy (the generic strategies of low cost, differentiation and focus). As business school academics interacted with practitioners, a host of useful competitive matrices (e.g. the Boston Consulting Group; GE Matrix, Shell Portfolio Matrix) were developed that gained traction in strategy, international business, consultancy and finance.

An interesting revelation from this brief review of the contribution of research on practice is that most of the greatest high-impact ideas were developed in the 30 years after the two reports in 1959, so we might call this the 'Golden Age'. Furthermore, the book *Great Minds in Management* (Smith & Hitt, 2005) features 24 scholars whose ground-breaking works sustained the test of time. Most of these works were developed in the 1960s to 1980s. However, since the early 1990s, instead of great theories, there has been a steady flow of papers criticizing how management theory development has stalled (e.g. Buckley, 2002).

Enter the 'Dark Age' of Business and Management Research

The dominant research approach in business schools was influenced heavily by quantitative, statistical analyses as scholars 'enthusiastically seized on and applied a scientific paradigm that applies criteria of precision, control, and testable models' (Bailey & Ford, 1996: 8). This positivist approach became

path-dependent in the profession, influencing career prospects through faculty incentive systems. More, the eagerness of business school research to gain legitimacy as a 'new' social science led to rigour in method and theory being emphasized ahead of the relevance of the topic being studied. Over time, an unintended consequence of this rise of science in business schools was that the original goal of building an integrated body of knowledge of management theory and practice in different disciplines working side by side, recommended by Gordon and Howell, did not materialize. Instead, 'individual faculty members were more concerned with building a reputation in their respective disciplines than with making contributions to multidisciplinary team projects' (Khurana, 2007: 283).

Clearly, solving real, complex problems in the practical world was not the aspiration of rigorous, theory-oriented social scientists in the late 1980s. The gulf between the research interests and disciplinary orientation of business school faculty and the practical and multidisciplinary interests of students and business practitioners grew over time. Arguably, 1993 marked the second milestone of this history in the United States. Donald Hambrick, the President of the Academy of Management, gave his Presidential address at the 1993 national meeting, entitled 'What if the Academy actually mattered?' In this speech, he challenged the academy to pay more attention to the world outside of its ivory tower in its research (Hambrick, 1994). In the following years, many presidential addresses of the Academy of Management were along the same theme, calling for increasing relevance of research and for research that examined the conditions of the stakeholders beyond shareholder wealth (Tsui, 2013).

In the late 1990s and early 2000s, business schools entered a 'dark age', becoming the faces of scandal. Institutionalized fraud at Enron and the toxic bank trading that foreshadowed the 2008 global financial crisis and led to the bankruptcy of Lehman Brothers; the collapse of AIG, Fanny Mae and Fanny Mac shocked the business world. Interconnected banking systems translated these issues into a global crisis and the international response was massive financial intervention, with consequent widespread austerity for more than a decade thereafter. Accused of preparing hyper-competitive, unethical and greedy managers, business school teaching, especially the MBA, came under heavy accusation (Machold & Huse, 2010).

Sadly, business school research, with its theoretical and methodological obsession, had little to say that might have guided policymakers and practitioners through these crises. In reviewing business and management articles in top US-based journals from the crisis years of 2007/08 to 2015, Starkey reported that 'The silence of management research on the subject suggests that our research seems to have almost entirely ignored probably the biggest economic and business event of our lives'(Starkey, 2015: 657). Detached from reality, the embrace of theory with the associated laboratory pretence in business and management research had become *de rigeur.* This dominant paradigm in research process, together with creeping managerialism in business schools, helped promulgate powerful isomorphic pressures (Wilson & McKiernan, 2011) of rankings, ratings, journal lists, KPIs and a 'publish or perish' culture that was marked by acceptable research – defined as only that published in a narrow set of elite journals. For instance, global output of publications in CABS 4 and 4-starred journals grew from just under 6000 in 1996 to nearly 10,000 in 2016 and a good proportion of these (17%) were by faculty in the top 73 AACSB-accredited schools (Mijnhardt, 2017[1]). The costs of producing such elite articles was estimated at $400,000 each in faculty time and research support (Terwiesch & Ulrich, 2014) and calculated at an investment of over $3.9bn per annum from the 780 AACSB-accredited schools (Glick, Tsui & Davis, 2018).

Generous incentives for academics to publish in these journals, which were meant to increase the productivity of good scientific output, led to perverse outcomes like an avalanche of papers with only incremental contributions (though dressed in the cloak of novelty and non-intuitive discoveries with complex theoretical models and rigorous analysis); a dilution of the peer review process as junior staff adopted this role; a corrosion of acceptable scientific method and increases in false discovery rates (Smaldino & McElreath, 2016). Schwab and Starbuck (2017) accused business and management research of both 'Big Lies' and 'Little Lies' in their published output. The former was an intentional (and maybe elaborate) deviation from ethical norms (Bakker & Wicherts, 2011; Honig & Bedi, 2012) but, thankfully, these were less pronounced in the system. More common were the little lies of research that skirted at the edges of what was ethically acceptable (Honig et al., 2014).

Among the 64 research studies that they examined, Banks and colleagues (Banks et al., 2016) found that 91% of them showed evidence of covert, undesirable practices. Such practices might include, but are not limited to, the selective reporting of hypothesis tests; problems with replication rates (Bergh, Sharp & Li, 2017); non-reporting of non-significant findings (Biemann, 2013); tough reviews for papers that challenged the accepted theoretical view (Siler & Strang, 2017); a proliferation of erroneous results in strategy research (Goldfarb & King, 2016); and, extensive HARKing (Bedeian et al., 2010) and p-hacking (Bedeian, Sturman & Streiner, 2009). Analogously, the desperate search for high citations and H-indices to achieve tenure and promotion led to extended reference lists, increases in self-citation and a tendency among reviewers to ask writers to cite their work (Edwards & Roy, 2017). Consequently, the number of articles suffering retraction increased and spawned its own 'policing' system.[2]

Institutional mimicry, spurred on as lower-ranked schools copied the actions of higher-ranked ones on the research ladder, spread worldwide from the developed regions (e.g. the United States, Europe – the UK, in particular) to the developing regions (e.g. Asia) as standard practices and norms were consumed voraciously. System homogeneity was the natural consequence, but such homogenization suppressed the creativity that came from divergence and pluralism in research topics and methods, especially in a global context (Tsui, 2007).

Unsurprisingly, much of the positivist, scientific narrative in business and management research was alien to business managers. Though academic journals flourished from 1996 to 2016, despite the heavy investment in producing articles, their technical content and lack of impact meant that their content had little practical utility. Research in cognate domains like engineering and medical science had retained an active engagement with practitioners in their fields and so held greater appeal for them. The interchange between academia and practice held mutual benefit for both and, importantly, for the public good. In contrast, the major beneficiaries of business and management research were the academics who both produced and consumed it. Because of entrenched norms and perverse incentive structures, this became one of the few academic domains that spoke to itself. The system only *hoped* for relevance, while rewarding productivity. Inside academia, the benefits were well known to those scholars who could master elite publishing, yet outside the benefits to a broader society were less obvious. As much academic research and, indeed, academic salaries were funded from public monies, the issue of social justice reared its head and public research agencies (e.g. the UK's Research Evaluation Framework) began to clamour for greater impact. Glick and McKiernan lamented that the state of business and management research had become '… a self-centred, self-serving, self-feeding process, a form of academic narcissism that parallels the salons of Marie Antoinette' (Glick & McKiernan, 2017: 14).

Clearly, there was a need for serious change. Senior scholars (e.g. Harley, 2019) called upon their peers to end the pretence of science mimicry, heroic publishing and their support of an unsupportable system. Many called for a better science in making business and management research meaningful and useful to policy and practice (Grote, 2017; Tourish, 2019). The current *responsibility turn* in business and management research (www.rrbm.network) called for a much more reliable and a much more diverse scientific approach and an urgent return to the applied roots of relevance. The re-discovery of the need to include 'practice' and societal impact in the research purpose and process returns the business school research function back to some of its original ground. The circle was complete. The intervention of responsibility initiatives began to alter our understanding of the purpose of research in business schools.

THE RESPONSIBILITY TURN IN THE SCIENCES

The *responsibility turn* in business and management has been some time in coming. The underlying rigour–relevance debate had developed into a small, internally focused industry that became endlessly protracted. It heralded many suggestions yet, few workable solutions (Bartunek & Rynes, 2014). It transitioned from an early focus on a gatekeeper's orthodoxy and the collaboration with practitioners (Starkey & Madan, 2001; Tranfield & Starkey, 1998) to posturing on paradigmatic shifts in research and, more recently, to purposive research on that elusive societal contribution (Carton & Mouriccu, 2017), all inherently recognizing its lack of relevance in the past.

Business and management research is situated within a larger community of both natural and social sciences. Similar problems had beset a broader scientific domain which had recognized the serious consequences of wrongful conclusions from scientific studies. A requirement of scientific work is not to overreach, based on conclusions from weak evidence; or, to provide random findings from improper research procedure or deliberate research misconduct. Ioannidis' (2005) paper 'Why most published research findings are false' is a wake-up call for the scientific community. This 'irreproducibility crisis' got the attention of the field and, luckily, self-correction occurred (Alberts et al., 2015).

Traditionally, the necessary evaluation of scientific research within academia and by interested stakeholders (e.g., funding agencies) was a human affair, where panels of peers prevailed over the written words of their colleagues. But, as the availability of data in the profession accelerated globally, this human touch declined, being replaced by the convenience and accessibility of measures that were often calculated for quite different reasons. Hence, there were flaws in both the science and in the use of the metrics to judge the quality of that science. Indeed, this growing metrification may have helped disguise the malpractice in scientific rigour as decisions on academic careers became more influenced by machine, than by man. As Hicks and colleagues describe:

> Before 2000, there was the Science Citation Index on CD-ROM from the Institute for Scientific Information (ISI), used by experts for specialist analyses. In 2002, Thomson Reuters launched an integrated web platform, making the Web of Science database widely accessible. Competing citation indices were created: Elsevier's Scopus (released in 2004) and Google Scholar (beta version released in 2004). Web-based tools to easily compare institutional research productivity and impact were introduced, such as InCites (using the Web of Science) and SciVal (using Scopus), as well as software to analyse individual citation profiles using Google Scholar (Publish or Perish, released in 2007). (Hicks, Wouters, Waltman, De Rijcke & Rafols, 2015: 429)

Soon, international researchers across the scientific spectrum became increasingly frustrated with the use of such instant codification for the assessment of methodological rigour and the progression of academic careers. They

proceeded to design self-correcting criteria for an educational system where the damaging processes were deeply embedded. For instance, a gathering of American cell biologists in San Francisco in 2012, annoyed at the misuse of the ubiquitous Journal Impact Factor (JIF), were determined to offer alternatives. The JIF was designed as a tool to assist the purchasing policies of librarians, and not one to assess the scientific quality of articles in a particular journal – as many institutions had begun using it for. The biologists identified a litany of weaknesses of the JIF in its latter role and made a series of recommendations to stakeholders warning them against its broad misuse and urging them to use a variety of measures to assess both scientific content and impact. These policies became known as the *San Francisco Declaration on Research Assessment* [3] (DORA) (Munafò et al., 2017). They spoke to the primacy of scientific rigour over journal metrics; the combination of both quantitative and qualitative measure when assessing output; an emphasis on impact; a reinforcement of the JIF with other measures to assess journal quality; transparency and openness in the calculation of metrics; and the making of allowances for the type of article under scrutiny (a review versus original research).

The DORA was followed quickly by the establishment of the *Center for Open Science* (COR) in 2013 by cognitive psychologists Nosek and Spies, at the University of Virginia. COR's original mission was to 'increase the openness, integrity and reproducibility' of scientific research. Specifically, its strategic plan was concerned with the engagement of stakeholders in the research life cycle and the training, evidence, connectivity, infrastructure and incentives required to enact the major cultural change required to overturn the existing business model of research production – metrics and misuse included. COS became a champion of open sourced outputs and its Open Science Framework, with primary focus on the natural sciences, has over 10,000 subscribers.

In Europe, the search for more responsible science in the social sciences continued at a conference of the European Network of Indicator Developers in the Dutch city of Leiden, in 2014. Alarmed by the serious problems of data-driven assessment of academic output by many institutions, Hicks and colleagues developed the *Leiden Manifesto for Research Metrics*[4] to re-emphasize the importance of judgement in performance appraisal. They distilled best practice into 10 Principles which, inter alia, covered the use of both quantitative and qualitative measures to support expert judgement; the measurement of performance with regard to its institutional and personal context; an emphasis on local research; the real time scrutiny of all assessment indicators; and, the accounting for variations across different fields with respect to publication practices and associated citations, H-indices etc.

Each of these three initiatives is concerned with openness, integrity and output assessment by human judgement rather than metrics alone in their attempts to re-engineer scientific practice and its evaluation. We might call this intervention to arrest the paucity of rigour in the conduct of science a 'responsibility turn'. However, in the domain of business and management, the issue was not simply the restoration of scientific rigour but also the absence of practical relevance. Hence, this 'turn' developed and continued apace with the creation of the Community for Responsible Research in Business and Management (cRRBM) at the suggestion of the European Foundation for Management Development (EFMD) – better known amongst global business schools for housing the accreditation agency EQUIS – in 2015.[5] Its objective was to change research practices for a better science and towards having a greater impact, especially on society as a whole. The assumption is that relevance (knowledge from research that is applicable for practice) needs credible research findings. Neither credible findings without relevance nor relevant ideas without credible research evidence are useful for society. RRBM declares that research should strive

to produce knowledge that is *both* credible and useful. The 28 founders of RRBM wrote a position paper (Co-founders of RRBM, 2017) which offered a vision of responsible research, to be achieved by 2030. The paper suggests possible actions that stakeholders of the research ecosystem can take to transform current practices to practices that encourage, support and reward responsible research.

In addition, the position paper offers seven Principles to guide research to ensure both credible and useful knowledge. The ultimate purpose is to use the skills of business and management researchers to build a better world through creating knowledge that will enable better business practices that contribute to solving the world's grand challenges e.g. poverty, water supply, migration, climate change, justice, inequality.

Of the seven principles, Principle 1 is core, and reminds us crucially that science is in service of society. Of the other six principles, three are dedicated to improving the scientific rigour of studies and three are dedicated to ensuring that the research outcomes are relevant to society. Table 29.1 presents the seven Principles. Column one defines each principle that is intended to guide business and management research to build a sound body of knowledge that serves society. Column two offers further clarification on each one and its implications for implementation.

TRANSFORMATIVE DOCTORAL EDUCATION

Translating these principles into business schools' research activity requires long-term, or generational, planning. Of course, a number of immediate actions might bring quick results, e.g. persuading deans to adjust research incentives or convincing accreditation agencies to demand the adoption of such principles as a condition for retaining or receiving approval. But, sustained change with an enduring impact is unlikely to happen

Table 29.1   The RRBM principles of responsible research

Principle	Clarification and implications for implementation
1. *Service to society*: Business research aims to develop knowledge that benefits business and the broader society, locally and globally, for the ultimate purpose of creating a better world.	The aim of research is to systematize knowledge of best practices, past and current, and to shape the future by creating knowledge based on emerging scenarios. Innovative research can inform future practice. Business and management research serves a critical social function by observing the blind spots and potential downsides of the business world. Business education focuses not only on knowledge of the past, but also upon knowledge, skills and values that are relevant to both managing in the current context and dealing with emerging trends that signal the shape of future domains.
2. *Valuing both basic and applied contributions*: Business school deans, journal editors, funders, accrediting agencies, and other stakeholders respect and recognize contributions in both theoretical and applied research.	Theories are important to guide our collective understandings and to explain empirical patterns that defy common sense. Applied research aims to analyse management practices such as incentive systems and governance (economics, finance, management); consumer and firm behaviour (marketing, strategy); customer service; and supply chain processes (marketing, operations, information systems). Integrating theory- and practice-led problems in business research will both contribute to basic knowledge development and enhance its applied utility for stakeholders who support this research.
3. *Valuing plurality and multidisciplinary collaboration*: Business school deans, senior leadership, journal editors, funders and accreditation agencies value diversity in research themes, methods, forms of scholarship, types of inquiry and interdisciplinary collaboration to reflect the plurality and complexity of business and societal problems.	Business and management research supports pluralism in its theories, grounded in different assumptions about human nature, multiple perspectives and, alternative models of business and its role in society. Rich, in-depth ethnographic studies of corporate practices yielding reflective and imaginative thinking that contribute to new theorizing are as valuable as quantitative or experimental studies. In the global context, business and management research values both 'global and local' knowledge development. Stakeholders value both multi- and inter-disciplinary research, both within business disciplines and across other social science disciplines, as well as engineering, medicine, education, or humanities. Multi- and inter-disciplinary research has the potential to provide new understandings of business due to synergies amongst disparate disciplines.
4. *Sound methodology*: Business research implements sound scientific methods and processes in both quantitative and qualitative or both theoretical and empirical domains.	Robustness of empirical work in business and management research takes into account emerging practices in good science. For example, empirical research practices that value replication, falsification of theory and reproducibility are encouraged. Journals and professional societies adopt open science practices such as data, materials, and code repositories, and transparency of sample construction and measures. Similar expectations though different criteria of rigour may apply to in-depth, ethnographic field studies with qualitative data in contrast to quantitative, lab or field experiments. The expectation of data transparency might reduce the volume of investigations but could improve the quality and comprehensiveness of studies by discouraging data slicing and other questionable practices. Mathematical models are calibrated using real data and assumptions are validated ultimately using empirical evidence.

(Continued)

Table 29.1   The RRBM principles of responsible research (Continued)

Principle	Clarification and implications for implementation
5. *Stakeholder involvement*: Business and management research values the involvement of different stakeholders who can play a critical role at various stages of the scientific process, without compromising the independence or autonomy of inquiry.	The research ecosystem consists of many participants including the researchers as the producers of knowledge, journal editors, tenure and promotion committee members, school leadership, directors of PhD programs, accreditation agencies, funding organizations, ranking publishers, and business leaders, public and third sector managers, policy makers and students as beneficiaries of knowledge. Also, broader society has a stake in business and management research. Research can benefit from the 'co-creation' of knowledge with all types of organizations (businesses, NGOs, trade unions, governments, industry associations, social enterprises, customers, charities and consumers). However, academic integrity and independence require that research is not captured, or reported findings not influenced, by vested interests.
6. *Impact on stakeholders*: Business and management schools, funders and accrediting agencies acknowledge and reward research that has an impact on diverse stakeholders, especially research that contributes to better business and a better world.	Business and management schools recognize that the publication itself is not the outcome or the end goal, but a step in the journey to scholarly and/or societal impact. Assessing influence may require multiple papers, dissemination of findings to non-academic circles, and tracking whether companies, communities or policy makers benefit from this program of research. Also, impact includes the teaching of the findings from evidence-based responsible science in undergraduate, masters, doctoral and executive education programs. Promotion and tenure requirements reflect this requirement to institutionalize research's positive influence on society.
7. *Broad dissemination*: Business and management schools value diverse forms of knowledge dissemination that collectively advance basic knowledge and practice.	The digitization of the global economy has suggested new forms of dissemination of research findings, including online, open source and open access publishing. Business schools have opportunities to improve the visibility of ongoing research through creative translation, publishing and dissemination methods, as well as drawing insights in simple and powerful ways to influence the target audience and non-academic stakeholder communities. Open source and access publishing embrace rigorous peer review for building and disseminating credible knowledge.

Source: RRBM (2017) position paper, www.rrbm.network.

through such simple, tactical switching by deans or established researchers. Nor is such sustained change likely to emerge from junior scholars, stressed and trapped by the top journal publication expectation for their tenure and promotion. But deans and senior faculty could provide an internal force for generational change and secure the next generation of sensible scholars by addressing the content and process of doctoral training. Dr Aliotta, Professor of Nuclear Astrophysics at the University of Edinburgh, documented that most Nobel winners developed their ideas in their dissertation research.[6] In management, Smith and Hitt (2005) feature the groundbreaking work of 24 scholars whose ideas stood the test of time. Most of these works were based on the scholars' dissertations.

Also, Kuhn (1996) observed that young entrants, who were not so committed to the old paradigms, are more likely to introduce paradigmatic changes. Conversion is difficult for those entrenched in the existing paradigms. Sometimes change will have to wait until the opponents grow old and die. Hope lies in 'young and rising naturalists, who will be able to view both sides of the question with impartiality' (Kuhn, 1996: 151). The history of scientific progress encourages us to place our trust in the new generation of scholars.

The RRBM focuses on the research ecosystem and encourages journals and school leadership to open up to opportunities for responsible research. These changes will unlock the iron cage of top journal publications – a practice that focuses primarily on the quantitative number and much less on the content or the ideas of the research. However, we cannot assume that young entrants will know how to pursue responsible research without proper training. Revisions in the doctoral curriculum will be important to prepare young scholars with the necessary understanding of science and associated responsibilities in addition to technical skills of sound research.

Toward a Deeper Understanding of Social Science and Scientific Responsibility

Business and management academia can do better in preparing its new entrants to make meaningful contributions to society. Given the dramatic changes in the economic landscape, where the sustainability of both the social and natural worlds is at risk, this task is especially urgent. These two worlds are interdependent, since human actions have influenced our nature in profound ways. Nature offers the human world resources that it can enjoy but rapid human exploitation of them has reached the point of dangerous depletion. Social science research in business schools can offer remedies to these challenges by turning businesses into a force for good – for instance, through the adoption of practices informed by responsible scientific research. Many doctoral programmes do not emphasize the deep understanding of social science and the responsibility of a social scientist to society that can make this happen.

Two responsibilities underlie the responsible research framework. The first responsibility is to science. Science is to understand and to explain nature. Puzzles (ranging from the microscopic living cell to the infinite universe) and anomalies (unexpected or unexplained physical and social phenomena) are the appetite of curious scientists. Science can provide sound solutions through the excellent execution of both theory and method. Theories are conjectures about why the anomaly exists and explanations of possible outcomes. Methods are means to collect, analyse and explain observations or data. A major responsibility of the scientist is to ensure that the explanations are valid and that the method yields reliable conclusions. To make the most valid conclusions from scientific inquiries, nascent social scientists should know the limits to inductive and deductive reasoning. Inductive reasoning is to make general statements from some specific empirical observations. Since we cannot possibly exhaust all observations, we have to infer from limited observations what might be true in general. Since we cannot assume that the next observation will be identical to previous observations (e.g, the possibility that black swans exist, even though all the swans we have seen are white[7]) we cannot confidently conclude that our general statement based on the empirical observation is valid. This is referred to as 'Hume's problem', after David Hume (the 18th-century Scottish philosopher), who pointed out the problem with the assumption of a 'uniformity of nature'. Repeated observations with the same conclusion would increase our confidence that the probability of the next swan being white is high. The importance of replication is clear. This example illustrates the importance of a deeper understanding of the philosophy of science to guide high-quality empirical research by doctoral students.

Though scientific process appears to be similar between the natural and social sciences to seek explanation and understanding, to be a responsible social scientist includes a deep understanding of the basic differences between natural and social phenomena. Can people or social systems be treated like physical or biological objects? Human societies have both collectives and norms while natural objects (physical or biological) may have grouping but they do not have norms. For understanding, physical objects can be broken down into the most basic molecules. Is this reductionist approach sufficient for a full understanding of social systems? Can social institutions be explained solely by individual actions? Topics like normativity, naturalism and reductionism offer fascinating discussions of some fundamental similarities or differences between social and natural phenomena, with implications for epistemology and ontology (Risjord, 2014). Further, the dynamic, complex and reactive nature of the human person implies that extra consideration is necessary for studying social phenomena. Furthermore, the responsible researcher understands and appreciates that reality is contextual. Imposing the reality of the researcher onto the subject (when we define a concept unilaterally or develop a measurement without the subject's input) may be a recipe for failure in understanding the subject's world. These philosophy of science issues may influence the credibility of the research findings in the business and management domain. Ensuring the reliability of evidence is the first major responsibility of the researcher.

The second responsibility of research is to society. The scientific process begins with defining the problem to be solved. Who decides what problem is worthy of the scientists' time and attention? Usually, members of the scientific community work on a set of problems that they find to be important and interesting. The scientist who first noticed and reported on a puzzle becomes the trail blazer.

Then, others follow. The funding agencies can influence the attention of the scientific community by awarding funding to work on the problems they identify to deserve research attention. Douglas (2009) devoted an entire book to discuss the role of values in scientific work and the role of both values and scientists in policies. She distinguishes epistemic values (those that determine the quality of evidence) from social values (those that influence the choice of topics and use of research results). But values also influence the choice of theories, methods or preferences of how to disseminate the research results (Tsui, 2016).

The scientific process does not end with reporting the findings. A responsible scientist also engages in assessing the risks or consequences of wrongful conclusions from induction (type I and type II error). The risk assessment should evaluate the cost to society associated with type I (false positive) or with type II (false negative) errors. It should also include a consideration of any unintended consequences with the application of an idea – similar to the estimation of 'side effects' in medicines or biomedical research. For example, global warming is an unintended consequence of carbon emission. Boredom is an unintended consequence of work simplification in the form of assembly lines for production efficiency. Social values determine whose interests are to be protected or advanced. In business and management research, most attention has been focused on improving firm performance, often at the cost of the interests of consumers, employees, suppliers or the society at large (Walsh, Weber & Margolis, 2003; Tsui & Jia, 2013). Risk assessment is absent in our current research practices. Further, it has been observed that 'social scientists are agents of social change, whether they want it or not' (Risjord, 2014: 52). This suggests the need for a much deeper understanding of scientific responsibility than most doctoral programmes in business and management currently offer. Inclusion of this, and other related topics in responsible doctoral education, is essential in preparing the future generation of responsible business and management researchers.

The searchlight to good science has three lenses: the first is a focus on epistemic values to ensure the technical quality of a study; the second is a focus on social values to ensure the research to ensure the research "study is free of personal and disciplinary biases; the third is a focus on the purpose of research. Who is being served? What kind of problems should a scholar study? How to ensure that science is a blessing and not a curse for our world? Scientific independence is sacred, but this privilege must be accompanied by a responsibility of producing knowledge that is relevant and useful to the society that has entrusted the scientific community with tremendous resource investment.

The learning of these topics in an analytical and critical fashion is a necessary" foundation for the preparation of foundation for the preparation of the next generation of scholars. A deep understanding of these topics will prepare students to live up to the expectations of society and become responsible public servants of knowledge. The well-being of society is improved markedly through the accumulation of credible and useful knowledge that informs business practices and develops responsible leaders for a world in need.

How Today's Social World Offers Opportunities for Responsible Research

We have raised many questions about the natural sciences and the social sciences, the responsibility of scientists and how they might go about their work to foster a better world. Finding answers means understanding two related cultural issues within the business and management arena. The first lies in the fundamental difference between the natural sciences and the social science of the study of management. Dynamic change is the key. In a relatively stable laboratorial world, the former can search for universal laws, ceteris paribus.

While the latter is subject to dynamic change in its outer and inner contexts, forcing the intellectual menu of managerial work to produce fresh models to guide practice. Besides a supply of established concepts (study-deductive), this constant supply of new ones requires considerable field work (study-inductive). Research in business and management requires a broad set of methods and epistemic stances. But much existing research has favoured narrow deductive approaches, incremental additions to knowledge, fine technical analysis, single disciplinary lenses and the prosperity of the individual researcher rather than the community.

Simply, this research approach does not capture the dynamic change in the world of managers, who need to know how to act and what decisions to make in different circumstances. So, we call upon doctoral researchers to supply *more inductive-based field studies* to play an informative role in rectifying the imbalance. The 2019 Nobel prize in Economics went to three development economists who, over 20 years of field studies, sought new ways to alleviate poverty. Closer to home, Mintzberg's early work is an example of how studying the gap between normative views and field-based ones can be queried to provide a better understanding of the managerial world. Many early management textbooks (e.g. Cole, 1982) *prescribed* that management *should* be about the interaction and execution of the functions of Planning, Organizing, Leading and Controlling. Mintzberg's (1973) seminal field work *described* the messiness of what management *is* about, showing how managerial work can switch suddenly between 10 different, but related roles. Clearly, what Mintzberg saw (the *is*) was not what *should* be. We might call this gap between what *should* be and what *is*, gap one.

The second issue lies in the normative axioms embedded in these cultures – views of how the world *should* be. These are rarely challenged, e.g, the ubiquitous acceptance of growth, technological sophistication, consumerism and constant innovation as always good. They represent the status quo for many Western economies, India and China and, an aspirational objective for others in less developed worlds. In marketing, there is an often-used expression that consumers 'always know what they want but they don't always know what they need'. This plays to a global problem of constant personal product acquisition driven by advertising campaigns and reinforced by peer pressure and perceived fashion. In turn, those supplying corporations play to stock markets that demand growth in measurable performance indicators and quarter-by-quarter results. Consumers want product variety and technological sophistication and corporations want growth and profit. Wants are not necessarily responsible needs. Perhaps what *is*, is not what *should* be. In addressing responsible themes for research, doctoral colleagues might interrogate the gap between the *should* and the *is* in their chosen domain. This means questioning the *is* from a number of standpoints, e.g. moral, ethical, responsible, sustainable, citizenship, humility etc., to try to shape up what the broader societal need might be. A helping hand can be provided by the concept of 'counter-factual' reasoning, incarnate of the Greek philosophers and often used by historians to check the validity of what happened in the past (see, for instance, Byrne, 2015). To enact this process means imaging what would have happened if the event under study (e.g. the strike on the Twin Towers of 9/11) had not happened. In other words, *what if* 9/11 had not happened, what would American foreign policy have looked like? If it would have looked much different from what it looks today, then the event is likely to have happened – as it can explain the policy today better than any alternative reasoning. Of course, there is no doubt that 9/11 happened – as millions witnessed it for the permanent record – but, imagine asking the question what would have happened to Western civilization had the Assyrians captured Jerusalem nearly 3000 years ago? Documentary evidence is lightweight so, historians use the counterfactual to try to establish whether this event happened or not. We see the *what if* question used regularly in the sustainability literature with *what if* questions over single use plastics and CO_2 emissions. *What if* society didn't do this or did do that? Hence it is a powerful way of getting answers for a responsible doctoral theme.

Clearly, the gap between what *should* be and what *is* can be a fruitful pathway in the search for answers. But what *should* be is often locked up in the dominant paradigms of yesterday and may have become path-dependent – especially as presented in textbooks. Hence, it is worth taking this thinking a step further and examining a second gap between what *is* and what *could* be, i.e. extending thinking into a better world for society than what is imagined at the moment (the *should*). Scenario thinking (see, for instance, MacKay & McKiernan, 2018) can be a wonderful friend in this theatre, exploring a range of alternative futures and interpreting their meaning for where society is today. The study of both gaps can be major instructional components of both responsible doctoral research and responsible management education (ME) – (see, for instance, Meirovich, 2015).

Responsible Management Education Needs Responsible Research

Though responsible management research and management education have not yet benefited from a productive interaction, the potential for synthesis, synergy and a reinforcement of strategic direction in the profession is exciting. For centuries, environmental pollution has been identified as a crippling feature of the societal common good (see, for instance, Ibsen's play 'Enemy of the People', 1882). Eventually, management education scholars have taken the first steps in encouraging business schools to bring Earth Systems Science (ESS) into their pedagogy. ESS deals with the impact and interaction of physical, chemical, biological and human systems on the planet:

> ESS-inspired research is showing that the planetary level, as a subject of both study and action, is a

legitimate and important scale for scientific research, one that increasingly needs to be of concern for the corporate world and for business and management education. (Edwards, Alcaraz & Cornell, 2018: 2)

In particular, these authors call for major reformulation of curricular design and pedagogical practice within management education to stress the direct linkage between the economic and social spheres with the biosphere. This involves a deep recognition of planetary boundaries – especially where assessable risks drift into the domain of uncertainty and impending danger. This learning requires a multidisciplinary effort from chemists, geographers, ecologists, biologists working alongside management scholars in theme-based rather than silo-based management education and research programmes. It demands a high level of engagement with a new collection of stakeholders within management education, e.g. the cultural arts (including science and climate fiction writers), community groups (Ibsen understood this well in is 'enemy' play), global NGOs and biodiversity groups, as central to the framework is nature as a 'primordial stakeholder' (Driscoll & Stark, 2004).

Amid the principles of responsible research (see above), such stakeholder engagement is paramount. But, the rhetoric of 'research-driven teaching', though having some success in management education, has not yet touched the surface of the deep contribution that it can make. Examinations of these grand challenges through the lenses of multidisciplinary teams is an expensive and time-consuming process. But if they are not addressed, schools may lose their legitimacy in society. So, the business school community might ask direct questions like – what is the impact of businesses on planetary boundaries? And, what is the impact of shareholder value theory on global ecosystems? The search for answers means moving up from incremental studies at the micro level to grander macro- and meso-level activity. If this progression is not made, it is likely that their teaching and learning will lag behind progressive organizations, who will have to ask such questions to survive as consumers become more eco-knowledgeable. As witnessed, ecological change causes societal crisis and this, in turn, can destroy whole markets for corporations.

Doctoral research can play a major part in addressing these fundamental planetary survival issues. A new generation of researchers, unencumbered and energized, can lead fresh scholarly activity towards a more sustainable and responsible society.

CONCLUSION

Business school research has a relatively short history, of slightly over 100 years. Alas, though it traversed from a descriptive to an applied scientific base from the 1950s to 1990s, it then lost its way. Many scholars have cried out for a self-correction to the associated poor science and lack of impact that followed. We assert that senior scholars, through their interaction with doctoral education, have both a moral duty and a ripe opportunity to change the status quo and, to pave the way for a second 'golden age'.

Doing nothing about the *problematique* questions the veracity of our educational mission, slows our response to major global challenges and risks political concern over the use of public funds in higher education. Many of the current research practices are highly unsatisfactory, with much talent and money wasted on research that contributes to neither science nor society. Social scientists in business schools enjoy a significant resource base and skillset that can prosper in searching for solutions to pressing global issues and in providing greater sustenance for the quality of life. Through the advent of modern science, business and technology have contributed much and can contribute much more to human progress. In this chapter, we hope to have made a strong case for a new generation of doctoral students to carry the flag of transformative change. We have provided some suggestions on how to prepare them better to become the future agents of influence in creating a more positive society, through their dedication to responsible research.

Notes

1   Figures calculated by Wilfrid F. Mijnhardt (2017), Policy Director RSM at the Rotterdam School of Management, Erasmus University (RSM): https://orcid.org/0000-0001-9066-0798

2   See, for instance, http://retractionwatch.com.

3   https://sfdora.org/.

4   www.leidenmanifesto.org/.

5   See www.rrbm.network. The cRRBM Principles for business and management focused around *research* and its work was followed quickly (in 2018) by the Central and Eastern European Management Development Association's (CEEMAN) Manifesto that focused upon changing the pathway of management development by combining excellence and relevance in the *teaching* domain.

6   https://marialuisaaliotta.wordpress.com/2014/10/01/the-burden-of-knowledge/.

7   For example, black swans inhabit large tracts in South East and South West Australia, with Europeans seeing them for the first time in the late 17th century.

REFERENCES

Aguinis, H., Suárez-González, I., Lannelongue, G., & Joo, H. (2012). Scholarly impact revisited. *Academy of Management Perspectives*, *26*(2), 105–132.

Alberts, B., Cicerone, R. J., Fienberg, S. E., Kamb, A., McNutt, M., Nerem, R. M., & Zuber, M. T. (2015). Self-correction in science at work. *Science*, *348*(6242), 1420–1422.

Bailey, J., & Ford, C. (1996). Management as science versus management as practice in postgraduate business education. *Business Strategy Review*, *7*(4), 7–12.

Bakker, M., & Wicherts, J. M. (2011). The (mis)reporting of statistical results in psychology journals. *Behavior Research Methods*, *43*(3), 666–678.

Banks, G. E., O'Boyle, J., Pollack, C., White, J., Batchelor, C., Whelpley, K., Abston, A., Bennett, A. A., & Adkins, C. (2016). Questions about questionable research practices in the field of management: a guest commentary. *Journal of Management*, *42*(1), 5–20.

Bartunek, J. M., & Rynes, S. L. (2014). Academics and practitioners are alike and unlike: the paradoxes of academic–practitioner relationships. *Journal of Management*, *40*(5), 1181–1201.

Bedeian, A. G., Sturman, M. C., & Streiner, D. L. (2009). Decimal dust, significant digits, and the search for stars. *Organizational Research Methods*, *12*(4), 687–694.

Bedeian, A. G., Taylor, S. G., & Miller, A. N. (2010). Management science on the credibility bubble: cardinal sins and various misdemeanors. *Academy of Management Learning & Education*, *9*(4), 715–725.

Bergh, D. D., Sharp, B. M., & Li, M. (2017). Tests for identifying 'red flags' in empirical findings: demonstration and recommendations for authors, reviewers, and editors. *Academy of Management Learning & Education*, *16*(1), 110–124.

Biemann, T. (2013). What if we were Texas sharpshooters? Predictor reporting bias in regression analysis. *Organizational Research Methods*, *16*(3), 335–363.

Black, F. and Scholes, M. (1973). The pricing of options and corporate liabilities. *Journal of Political Economy*, *81*(3), 637–654.

Burns, T., & Stalker, G. M. (1961). *The management of innovation*. London: Tavistock. pp. 120–122.

Buckley, P. J. (2002). Is the international business research agenda running out of steam? *Journal of International Business Studies*, *33*(2), 365–373.

Byrne, R. M. J. (2015) *The rational imagination: how people create alternatives to reality*. Boston, MA: MIT Press.

Carton, G., & Mouricou, P. (2017). Is management research relevant? A systematic analysis of the rigor-relevance debate in top-tier journals (1994–2013). *Management*, *20*(2), 166–203.

Co-founders of RRBM (2017, revised 2020). A vision for responsible research in business and management: striving for useful and credible knowledge. Position Paper, accessible from www.rrbm.network.

Cole, G. A. (1982) *Management: theory and practice*. Eastleigh: DP Publications

Donaldson, L. (2001). *The contingency theory of organizations*. London: Sage.

Douglas, H. (2009). *Science, policy, and the value-free ideal*. Pittsburgh: University of Pittsburgh Press.

Driscoll, C., & Stark, M. (2004). The primordial stakeholder: advancing the conceptual consideration of stakeholder's status for the natural environment. *Journal of Business Ethics*, *49*, 55–73.

Edwards, M. A., & Roy, S. (2017). Academic research in the 21st century: maintaining scientific integrity in a climate of perverse incentives and hypercompetition. *Environmental Engineering Science*, *34*(1), 51–61.

Edwards, M. G., Alcaraz, J. M., & Cornell, S. E. (2018). Management education and earth system science: transformation as if planetary boundaries mattered. *Business & Society*, DOI: 10.1177/0007650318816513.

Galbraith, J. R. (1971). Matrix organization designs: how to combine functional and project forms. *Business Horizons*, *14*(1), 29–40.

Ghoshal, S. (2005). Bad management theories are destroying good management practices. *Academy of Management Learning & Education*, *4*(1), 75–91.

Glick, W., & McKiernan, P. (2017). Why care about impact? *EFMD Global Focus*, *11*(1), 12–15.

Glick, W. H., Tsui, A., & Davis, G. F. (2018). The moral dilemma of business research. *BizEd*, *17*(3), 32–38.

Goldfarb, B., & King, A. A. (2016). Scientific apophenia in strategic management research: significance tests & mistaken inference. *Strategic Management Journal*, *37*(1), 167–176.

Gordon, R. A., & Howell, J. E. (1959). Higher education for business. *New York: Columbia University Press*.

Grote, G. (2017). There is hope for better science. *European Journal of Work and Organizational Psychology*, *26*(1), 1–3.

Hambrick, D. (1994). What if the academy actually mattered? *Academy of Management Review*, *19*(1), 11–16.

Harley, B. (2019). Confronting the crisis of confidence in management studies: why senior scholars need to stop setting a bad example. *Academy of Management Learning & Education*, *18*(2), 286–297.

Harley, B., & Cornelissen, J. (2019). Reframing rigor as reasoning: challenging technocratic conceptions of rigor in management research. In Zilber, T. B., Amis, J. M., Mair, J. (Eds.), *The production of managerial knowledge and organizational theory: new approaches to writing, producing and consuming theory* (pp. 59–76). Sheffield, UK: Emerald.

Hicks, D., Wouters, P., Waltman, L., De Rijcke, S., & Rafols, I. (2015). Bibliometrics: the Leiden Manifesto for research metrics. *Nature News*, *520*(7548), 429.

Honig, B., & Bedi, A. (2012). The fox in the hen house: a critical examination of plagiarism among members of the academy of management. *Academy of Management Learning and Education*, *11*(1), 101–123.

Honig, B., Lampel, J., Siegel, D., & Drnevich, P. (2014). Ethics in the production and dissemination of management research: institutional failure or individual fallibility? *Journal of Management Studies*, *51*(1), 118–142.

Ioannidis, J. P. (2005). Why most published research findings are false. *PLoS Medicine*, *2*(8), e124.

Khurana, R. (2007). *From higher aims to hired hands: the social transformation of American business schools and the unfulfilled promise of management as a profession.* Princeton, NJ: Princeton University Press.

Kuhn, T. (1996). *The structure of scientific revolutions.* 3rd edition. Chicago, IL: University of Chicago.

Latham, G. (1981). *Increasing productivity through performance appraisal.* Boston, MA: Addison-Wesley.

Lawrence, P. R., & Lorsch, J. W. (1967). Differentiation and integration in complex organizations. *Administrative Science Quarterly*, 1–47.

Lee, H. L., Padmanabhan, V., & Whang, S. (1997). Information distortion in a supply chain: the bullwhip effect. *Management Science*, *43*(4), 546–558.

Locke, E. A., & Latham, G. P. (2002). Building a practically useful theory of goal setting and task motivation: a 35-year odyssey. *American Psychologist*, *57*(9), 705.

Machold, S., & Huse, M. (2010). Provocation: business schools and economic crisis – The emperor's new clothes: learning from crisis? *International Journal of Management Concepts and Philosophy*, *4*(1), 13–20.

MacKay, R. B., & McKiernan, P. (2018) *Scenario thinking: the historical evolution of strategic foresight.* Cambridge: Cambridge University Press.

Malkiel, B. G., & Fama, E. F. (1970). Efficient capital markets: a review of theory and empirical work. *Journal of Finance*, *25*(2), 383–417.

McKiernan, P., & Tsui, A. S. (2019). Responsible management research: a senior scholar legacy in doctoral education. *Academy of*

Management Learning & Education, 18(2), 310–313.

Meckling, W. H. & Jensen, M. C. (1976). Theory of the firm: managerial behavior, agency costs and ownership structure. *Journal of Financial Economics, 3*(4), 305–360.

Meirovich, G. (2015). Normative and descriptive aspects of management education: differentiation and integration. *Journal of Educational Issues, 1*(1), 97–113.

Mintzberg, H. (1973). *The nature of managerial work.* New York: Harper and Row.

Munafò, M. R., Nosek, B. A., Bishop, D. V., Button, K. S., Chambers, C. D., Du Sert, N. P., & Ioannidis, J. P. (2017). A manifesto for reproducible science. *Nature Human Behaviour, 1*(1), 0021.

Ohno, T. (1988). *Toyota production system: beyond large-scale production.* Portland: Productivity.

Pfeffer, J., & Fong, C. T. (2002). The end of business schools? Less success than meets the eye. *Academy of Management Learning & Education, 1*(1), 78–95.

Pierson, F. C. (1959). The education of American businessmen. *Journal of Business Education, 35*(3), 114–117.

Porter, M. (1980). *Competitive strategy: techniques for analysing industries and competitors.* New York: Free Press.

Risjord, M. (2014). *Philosophy of social science: a contemporary introduction.* New York: Routledge.

Schwab, A., & Starbuck, W. H. (2017). A call for openness in research reporting: how to turn covert practices into helpful tools. *Academy of Management Learning & Education, 16*(1), 125–141.

Siler, K., & Strang, D. (2017). Peer review and scholarly originality: let 1,000 flowers bloom, but don't step on any. *Science, Technology, & Human Values, 42*(1), 29–61.

Smaldino, P. E., & McElreath, R. (2016). The natural selection of bad science. *Royal Society Open Science,* DOI 10.1098/rsos.160384.

Smith, K. G., & Hitt, M. A. (Eds.). (2005). *Great minds in management: the process of theory development.* Oxford: Oxford University Press.

Starkey, K. (2015). The strange absence of management during the current financial crisis. *Academy of Management Review, 40,* 652–663, DOI: 10.5465/amr.2015.0109.

Starkey, K., & Madan, P. (2001). Bridging the relevance gap: aligning stakeholders in the future of management research. *British Journal of Management, 12,* S3–S26.

Starkey, K. (2015). The strange absence of management during the current financial crisis. *Academy of Management Review, 40*(4), 652–663.

Terwiesch, C., & Ulrich, K. T. (2014). Will video kill the classroom star? The threat and opportunity of massively open on-line courses for full-time MBA programs. Mack Institute for Innovation Management at the Wharton School, University of Pennsylvania.

Tourish, D. (2019). *Management studies in crisis: fraud, deception and meaningless research.* London, UK: Cambridge University Press.

Tranfield, D. and Starkey, K. (1998). The nature, social organisation and promotion of management research: towards policy. *British Journal of Management, 9*(4), 341–353.

Tsui, A. S. (2007). From homogenization to pluralism: international management research in the academy and beyond. *Academy of Management Journal, 50*(6), 1353–1364.

Tsui, A. S. (2013). 2012 Presidential address—On compassion in scholarship: why should we care?. *Academy of Management Review, 38*(2), 167–180.

Tsui, A. S. (2015). Reconnecting with the business world: socially responsible scholarship. *EFMD Global Focus, 9*(1), 36–39.

Tsui, A. S. (2016). Reflections on the so-called value-free ideal. *Cross Cultural & Strategic Management, 23*(1), 4–28.

Tsui, A. S., & Jia, L. (2013). Calling for humanistic scholarship in China. *Management and Organization Review, 9*(1), 1–15.

Walsh, J. P., Weber, K., & Margolis, J. D. (2003). Social issues and management: our lost cause found. *Journal of Management, 29*(6), 859–881.

Wilson, D., & McKiernan, P. (2011). Global mimicry: putting strategic choice back on the business school agenda. *British Journal of Management, 22*(3), 457–469.

Zeithaml, V., Bitner, M. J., & Gremler, D. (2018). *Services marketing: integrating customer focus across the firm.* 7th edition. New York: McGraw-Hill Education.

Zeithaml, V. A., Parasuraman, A., & Berry, L. L. (1985). Problems and strategies in services marketing. *Journal of Marketing, 49*(2), 33–46.

30

Paradigms in Responsible Management Learning and Education Research

Jeremy St John and Cristina Neesham

INTRODUCTION

In this chapter, we take the view that responsible management learning and education (RMLE) is not reducible to teaching the sustainability, responsibility and ethics (SRE) curriculum (Laasch & Moosmayer, 2015) in management programmes. It involves teaching management, in all its forms, in ways that embed principles of business ethics, corporate social responsibility and sustainability in how the content is presented, problematized, debriefed and assessed. It means adopting and applying particular assumptions about the SRE of management practices in the teaching and learning of management, both as a practice and as an academic discipline.

We can discern research in RMLE as an area of inquiry with a distinct history comprising two stages:

1   A fragmented stage, characterized by iterative but irregular feedback relations between SRE research,

on the one hand, and critical management education (CME) research, on the other hand, leading, in time, to closer dialogue and mutual acknowledgment of common purpose; and

2   A catalyzing stage, marked by the United Nations' introduction of the Principles of Responsible Management Education (PRME) in 2007, and spurring a consistent stream of RMLE research that promotes responsible management beyond units dedicated to the SRE nexus, and using a shared language and discourse that is now well established. Within this stage, which includes the state-of-the-art RMLE research literature, we further distinguish two research methodology streams that build on, and feed off, each other: one that supports the philosophical assumptions of the PRME manifesto, and one that challenges these assumptions to improve RMLE practices and to generate new, more radical-emancipatory social movements. Both contribute to developing the RMLE research field to maturity.

This chapter follows the past–present–future logic and structure promoted throughout the Handbook, and summarizes the evolution of

RMLE literature through the prism of research paradigms. This prompts us to also reflect on the scope and limits of using paradigms as analytical-organizing instruments in a historical account of the field. In doing so, we explain the role of paradigmatic thinking in research design; document the main paradigms that have influenced RMLE research to date; and suggest future directions in RMLE research methodology, including an alternative solution to the use of (single and multiple) paradigms and paradigmatic thinking.

RESEARCH PARADIGMS: ROLE, SCOPE AND LIMITS

The concept of paradigm has its origins in the philosophy and sociology of the natural sciences. Kuhn (1962) defines a paradigm shift as a moment of disruption in scientific thinking, where the accumulation of evidence in response to particular research questions leads to the formulation of new questions, due to a change in worldview that generates new assumptions about reality and knowledge. This concept has been given a new life in the social sciences. Significantly, it has gradually been accepted that multiple worldviews can co-exist and co-evolve in an agonistic relationship, as social science researchers have grown to understand that irreducible conflict can be used constructively to advance knowledge (Lyotard, 1984). While social theorists tend to share Kuhn's assumption that paradigms are mutually exclusive (see Burrell & Morgan, 1979/2017), they also note that different paradigms are contemporaries that interact in a climate of ongoing competition (Guba & Lincoln, 1994), without destroying and replacing each other in a linear historical sequence, as in Kuhn's scenario. Simply defined, paradigms are 'basic belief systems' whose key components are 'ontological, epistemological and methodological assumptions' (Guba & Lincoln, 1994: 107). They are basic

because they refer to first-order philosophical tenets about the nature of reality (*ontology*), human knowledge (*epistemology*) and the research process (*methodology*); they are beliefs because their truthfulness has not been (and perhaps cannot be) demonstrated beyond doubt; and they are systems because relationships of logical coherence tend to group particular assumptions together, in particular ways.

However, as we shall see in the case of RMLE research, there is some flexibility in how this coherence may be achieved, which does not always lead to mutually exclusive paradigmatic groupings. We argue that it is in the nature of the social sciences to generate new combinations of philosophical assumptions, across paradigms – and, therefore, to proliferate new paradigms. We also argue that one of the key responsibilities of all management education research is to make its paradigmatic assumptions explicit and to reflect on these in order to improve them.

Typically, a paradigm is defined by a set of philosophical premises working together to form a coherent view about the world in which research is conducted and knowledge is produced. But paradigms are also cultural products generated by research practice traditions with specific histories and path dependencies. Furthermore, paradigm theorizations themselves are such cultural products. Consequently, paradigm theorists do not always agree on the same set of philosophical premises to be used in classifying paradigms, and the results of their classifications are also divergent. Burrell and Morgan (1979), for instance, find it difficult to separate between ontological and epistemological assumptions in the research process. Their matrix-based taxonomy of social science research paradigms (identifying functionalism, interpretivism, radical humanism and radical structuralism) combines two dimensions explaining the nature of science and, respectively, the nature of society through philosophical premises about reality, knowledge and human nature;

while drawing methodological conclusions from the combination of these three types of premises.

Other theorists note that different research orientations emphasize different types of philosophical premises. This has prompted authors like Guba and Lincoln, for example, to modify their earlier work on classifying paradigms into positivism, post-positivism, critical theory and constructivism (Guba & Lincoln, 1994) and acknowledge the primacy of axiological premises, i.e. about the values of the researcher and their interpretation of the purpose of research, in defining paradigms (Guba & Lincoln, 2005). Indeed, while ontological and epistemological differences traditionally drawn between positivism and social constructionism can account for their different methodologies, the emancipatory focus of critical inquiry, as highlighted by Habermas (1971/2015), can only be accounted for by appeal to a certain interpretation of research axiology. Furthermore, Neesham (2018) discusses the importance of praxeological premises, referring to the nature and intelligibility of purposeful human action, in the study of organizations. Together with axiology, praxeology makes a decisive contribution to explaining and justifying pragmatism, for instance, as a particularly relevant paradigm in the organization studies field. This variability in philosophical premises across paradigms suggests that RMLE research may also have its specific interests and emphases, which may not be included in the already theorized paradigms. The most prominent of these specific interests and emphases are discussed, with examples, in each paradigm-descriptive subsection below, and summarized in the conclusion of this chapter.

We ground the selection of paradigms discussed here in the available RMLE research literature. Also, in agreement with Laasch and Moosmayer (2015), we emphasize the need for researchers to adopt a paradigm based on the inherent features of the specific area under investigation and not on the conventional authority of dominant research traditions.

ORIGINS AND DEVELOPMENT OF RMLE RESEARCH: A PARADIGMATIC ACCOUNT

The disciplines of business ethics, corporate social responsibility and sustainability have been identified as the intellectual roots of the United Nations' Principles for Responsible Management Education (PRME) (Forray & Leigh, 2012). We examine these roots here, from a paradigmatic perspective, taking into consideration the period prior to (and roughly contemporaneous with) the establishment of these Principles by UN Secretary General Ban Ki-Moon in 2007. To this corpus we add the critical management education (CME) research developed during the same period, given the overlaps and affinities of purpose that exist between the critical management and responsible management fields, and given their ongoing, productive interaction (despite, or perhaps precisely due to, methodological debates and disputes). Proceeding from this, within the discussion of each paradigm, we examine the RMLE literature since the establishment of the PRME.

Our incursion into paradigmatic approaches to RMLE research reveals a preference for positivism, with openings into post-positivism and critical realism, social constructionism, critical inquiry and pragmatism intensifying only more recently. Although well represented in the SRE 'roots' literature, the postmodern stream has found little resonance in the post-2007 RMLE research to date, despite relevant and profoundly transformative conceptual contributions that can be stimulated by its challenges. We have organized our presentation of all these paradigms in a combination of historical sequencing and logical progression from status quo to increasing possibilities for transformative research. In addition, each of the following subsections is dedicated to one of these paradigms, first describing its philosophical foundations and then documenting the evolution of RMLE research from its SRE roots and CME influences to post-PRME developments, with a view to identifying important aspects or issues that remain unaddressed. We summarize those issues in the last section of the chapter, where we also suggest future approaches to paradigms and paradigmatic thinking that are more likely to develop the field to its full potential.

Positivism

Grounded in the traditional philosophies of the natural sciences and extending these philosophies into the realm of social science with the works of Comte (1844/2019) and Durkheim (1895/2013), positivism is characterized by ontological realism and epistemological objectivism. The former assumes a single reality existing independently of our perception; and the latter that human beings can access this reality directly, and know it as it is, most commonly through observation. Hence, positivist epistemology often informs (and is informed by) empiricism, i.e. the assumption that all knowledge is derived from experiencing reality through our senses.

Research in empirical business ethics has been found to be predominantly, if often implicitly, positivist, although calls have been made to address the imbalance (Brand, 2009; Crane, 1999; Laasch & Moosmayer, 2015). In corporate social responsibility, positivism dominates the instrumental stream (Laasch & Moosmayer, 2015; Scherer & Palazzo, 2007), i.e. research that subordinates its objectives to the priorities and values of business as usual, particularly where emphasis is placed on empirical research into measuring the effect of CSR on financial performance (Berman, Wicks, Kotha & Jones, 1999). In the field of corporate social performance (CSP), positivism is favoured by a focus on measurable outcomes (Wartick & Cochran, 1985),

diagnosis (Carroll, 1979), practical outcomes (Wood, 1991) and integration of the field with other positivist disciplines such as economic theory and behavioural science (Jones, 1995).

The positivist bias in the SRE literature has been charged with reducing paradigm variety (Brand, 2009) and marginalizing more reflective approaches (Ählström et al., 2009; Welford, 1998). Critics have pointed out the inability of positivism to account for moral values in business ethics (Crane, 1999) or to offer a foundation for normative corporate social responsibility, hence driving the discipline towards instrumentalization (Scherer & Palazzo, 2007). As such, positivist approaches have been criticized for maintaining an artificial separation between the empirical and the normative (Rosenthal & Buchholz, 2000; Wicks & Freeman, 1998) and for its blindness to the political and cultural embeddedness of the issues under examination (Laasch & Moosmayer, 2015; Meppem & Gill, 1998). This limitation is particularly obvious, and harmful, in cross-cultural research (Brand, 2009), and has more recently been found to lead to reductionism and lack of sensitivity to context (Buckley, 2013).

Furthermore, the focus of positivist methodology on quantitative measurement has had reductionist effects in business ethics research, especially in assessing normative concepts that are difficult to quantify, and has demonstrated lack of interpretive depth and specificity, as well as a propensity for avoiding the sensitive and the controversial (Crane, 1999). In the sustainability literature, it has been found to claim to be value-free despite demonstrable subjectivity in process, and to lack transparency and reflexivity regarding its own epistemological positions (Meppem & Gill, 1998). This has led to a co-optation of the sustainability discourse by market-liberal ideology, at the expense of more radical perspectives (Jensen, 2007). In CME, the positivist professional education model has been criticized for separating theory from praxis (Raelin, 2007), for privileging technicism (as the authority of technical expertise) at the expense of lived experience, and for misplaced assumptions of rational, disinterested neutrality (Hay & Hodgkinson, 2008). Furthermore, Perriton and Reynolds (2004) find positivist reflexes so entrenched in management education research that, in examining CME practice itself, they appraise it as too rationalist and masculine, thus replicating inside the academy precisely those power structures that it seeks to change outside it.

Regarding the RMLE literature as developed after the UN's PRME landmark moment, a positivist paradigm dominates here too but it is mostly implicit – and often, out of necessity, combined with interpretive tools. The widespread interest in measuring the achievements of the PRME, as a policy instrument, with respect to making management education more responsible has produced, for example, studies that routinely collect and analyse self-reported experiences of PRME implementation and results in business schools (Hervieux, McKee & Driscoll, 2017; Perry & Win, 2013; Stachowicz-Stanusch, 2011). This stage is undoubtedly necessary in RMLE research, as it allows us to ascertain in a timely manner what is happening, what can be improved and (further) how the existing conceptual frameworks may be reinterpreted and transformed to induce radical change. It also means that research methodology has to increase its efforts to catch up with the empirical research needs of this fast-growing field.

As with instrumentalizing CSR and CSP, limiting RMLE research to the positivist approach leads to constraining the valuable to the measurable and to excluding intrinsic values from discussion. This trend, manifested in both the SRE roots and the later RMLE literature, has been recognized as part of a wider reflex to apply the assumptions of physical science to management education (Clegg & Ross-Smith, 2003; Louw, 2014). In response to it, we observe an increasing self-reflective concern over those effects of dominant positivist methodology and

discourse that undermine the pursuit of normative imperatives and, in particular, of those values that, while difficult to measure, are central to the very objectives of the PRME (Lozano, 2012; Painter-Morland, 2015). The inadequacy of positivism in accounting for contextual differences in the interpretation of key values in RMLE practice calls for a thorough, well-documented consideration of alternative paradigms. Several potential candidates for supporting RMLE more successfully are discussed below.

Post-Positivism and Critical Realism

Following the epistemological critiques of positivism in the natural sciences by Heisenberg (1930/2015) and Popper (1959/2005) and, in the philosophy of logic, by Gettier (1963), post-positivism in the social sciences maintains the ontological assumptions of positivism but accepts that human knowledge is fallible and can never be complete. While retaining the assumption of a single, objective reality independent of perception, post-positivism recognizes that our methods of accessing this reality are necessarily bounded. Post-positivists pursue probable rather than certain truth but maintain some of the core methodologies associated with positivist research to draw as closely as possible to the nature of reality, while cognizant of their limitations. Critical realism, the social-science-based counterpart of natural-science-based post-positivism, shares with the latter the acceptance of a realist ontology while holding human observations of reality's phenomena to be conditioned by the specific scope and limits of human knowledge formation. Moreover, critical realism is actively interested in avoiding the traditional positivist pitfalls of confusing perception with reality and, consequently, in pursuing more complex forms of 'knowing' deeper levels of reality that are underlying our perceptions. Emblematic of critical realism in the social sciences is the work of Roy Bhaskar (1975, 1979, 1987), whose theoretical perspective is both transcendental realist, in that it defines science as seeking knowledge of things as they are (rather than of things as they appear to the researcher), and critically naturalist, in that it assumes (1) that this transcendental realism also applies in the study of social phenomena; and (2) that critical epistemology and methodology are essential to accessing the deeper nature of these phenomena. According to Bhaskar's ontology, reality is stratified into the 'empirical' (what we can observe), the 'actual' (what actually occurs) and the underlying 'real', which is not directly observed but may influence both the empirical and the actual.

An overview of SRE research prior to the PRME 2007 reveals critical realism as emerging rather slowly and less frequently, in the interstices of a field consumed by radical tensions between positivism and critical inquiry (more about the latter will be discussed further below). Notwithstanding, Bhaskar's critical realism was used in sustainability research by Carolan (2005) to frame a conceptual typology of nature comprising the three fluid categories of 'nature', nature, and Nature, corresponding to Bhaskar's three levels of reality. It has also been utilized in business and society scholarship, for example by Wry (2009), who critiques simplistic economic and behaviourist explanations of individual and organizational behaviour in order to effect social change.

Despite timid beginnings, however, critical realism is becoming increasingly interesting to RMLE researchers and is likely to become a prominent paradigm. By way of example, some of the post-PRME literature can be seen as explicitly post-positivist. Sunley and Leigh (2016) note the limits of positivism and embrace a wider range of epistemological avenues. Haski-Leventhal, Pournader and McKinnon (2017) research the effects of gender and age attitudes to, and interpretations of, the PRME and highlight subjective reactions to a phenomenon that, in essence,

is assumed to exist as some independent form of reality. It is also in this context that Nonet, Kassel and Meijs (2016) examine the differences in interpreting the PRME across European schools, and seek to establish a framework for organizations to define their own interpretation of responsible management. Similarly, Wersun (2017) emphasizes the contextual dependence of the articulation and practice of the PRME across institutions. In highlighting the context-dependent interpretation, implementation and pedagogical communication of the PRME while acknowledging their ongoing value and indeed necessity, these works echo the critical realist's rejection of objective phenomenological access to reality without rejecting the ontologically objective reality – although the reality to which they speak, in the case of RMLE, is more normative than empirical.

Critical realism introduces new ways of accounting for contextual differences in projects still driven by measurable goals, which can usefully extend the boundaries of teaching practice. The examples mentioned here suggest significant potential for critical realism in RMLE research, and we feel that a greater prevalence of critical realist approaches in the field could help to alleviate the limitations of positivism discussed earlier. That said, we note that current assessments of the PRME via critical realist perspectives tend to stop short of critically examining the fundamental assumptions underpinning the PRME themselves. Extension in this direction is an avenue for further research, where it may intersect with the critical inquiry and critical theory approaches discussed further below.

Social Constructionism

Challenging both positivism and critical realism, social constructionism rejects the ontological realist premise altogether, arguing instead that we (human beings, or researchers) participate in creating the reality we perceive. In rejecting the idea of a single, objective (social) reality, this paradigm contends that we constantly co-construct multiple, subjective realities through our social interactions. As meaning is similarly co-constructed in this fashion, and knowledge (and the research that pursues it) is dependent upon and suffused with meaning and interpretation, knowledge itself is subject to this process of construction. Hence, to understand the nature of knowledge we need to de-construct the social processes that give rise to it – in other words, to examine how this meaning has been socially constructed and so question the objectivity and dominance of systems of meaning, as well as the architecture of knowledge based upon them. Theorized in Berger and Luckman's *The Social Construction of Reality* (1966), social constructionism has been enriched, in the social sciences, through Weick's (1995) theory of sensemaking and Latour's (2005) actor-network theory. Methodologically, social constructionist researchers are therefore interested in studying those/these/the social processes that lead to the formation of meaning, communication and discourse. They are, however, only observers of (other) subjectivities, and seek to capture these as they 'encounter' them, without upholding social change programmes of their own.

SRE literature has been significantly enriched by field work undertaken from constructionist perspectives. In the area of sustainability, Murdoch (2001) adopts an interdisciplinary approach utilizing co-constructivism (in particular, actor-network theory) and social analysis to explore a link between the social and the natural in order to establish an ecological sociology. Within CSR research, Nijhof and Jeurissen's (2006) special issue of *Business Ethics: A European Review* coordinates the application of sensemaking (and sensegiving) to a variety of managerial topics, including stakeholder relations and CSR communication (Morsing & Schultz, 2006), collective stakeholder sensemaking in response to supply chain issues such as child labour (Pater & van Lierop,

2006), the collective creation of a proactive process for managing the impacts of extractive industry activities on various stakeholders (Schouten & Remme, 2006) and the development of a contextualized and organization-specific concept of CSR (Cramer, Van Der Hiejden & Jonker, 2006). Further, Basu and Palazzo (2008) draw upon Weick's work to explore sensemaking at the managerial and organizational level through a cognitive, linguistic and conative (attitudinal) lens.

Post PRME, researchers' interest in social constructionism has increased, reflecting more recent advances in the study of communities of practice in the wider SRE literature. Accordingly, Young and Nagpal (2013) undertake an ethnographic study of management graduates' responsible leadership capabilities at an Australian university, and conclude that change is more profound when grassroots movements take hold, with students' values and perspectives shaping the PRME adoption process. These findings suggest a stronger impetus towards learner-centred education, especially when considered in the aftermath of Prandini, Vervoort Isler and Barthelmess (2012), who contrast objectivist and constructivist assumptions underpinning pedagogical methods that are passive and educator-directed and, respectively, creative and student-directed. This momentum is continued in the organizational learning space (see Benn, Edwards & Angus-Leppan, 2013).

In a similar trend, Eiríksdóttir and Engelmark (2016) offer a more thorough application of Weick's sensemaking approach in examining how business schools adopt, interpret and understand the PRME, their requirements and the role they can be brought to play in the business school as a particular type of institution with a specific social mission, influencing the attitudes and behaviour of those who will in turn influence, and perhaps determine, the economic trajectory of society and its consequences for social well-being. Borges, Ferreira, Borges de Oliveira, Macini and Caldana (2017) offer an optimistic account of how students can co-create, outside the classroom, a 'hidden curriculum' and discourse about ethical responsibility that may provide fertile grounds for enhancing the PRME in institutionalized practices.

Recent studies such as these demonstrate that the social constructionist paradigm has room to flourish in the RMLE literature. But, as indicated by Godemann, Bebbington, Herzig and Moon (2014), substantially more needs to be done in this direction. Although cognizant of the risks posed by excessive emphasis on subjectivism and relativism (as we shall discuss in relation to postmodernism later on), we see this as an opportunity for extending the social constructionist contribution to RMLE, as also recommended by Laasch and Moosmayer (2015). This priority is reinforced by the social nature of management practice and management education, and the need for critical examination of the origin, implementation and pedagogical communication of the PRME. The next paradigm presented here has made significant contributions to meeting this need.

Critical Inquiry and Critical Theory

Focused on examining and challenging the social structures of power, critical inquiry was defined as a social research paradigm in the taxonomy formulated by Guba and Lincoln (1994). This paradigm claims its roots in the critical theory approach of the Frankfurt School of philosophy, reflected in the works of Adorno (1966), Horkheimer (1974) and, later, Habermas (1971/2015, 1984, 1985). Different critical theorists have covered a nuanced ontological-epistemological spectrum, from post-positivism to assuming that social reality is created by all those who participate in it. In contrast with social constructivism, however, this process of creation does not emphasize the subjectivity of the individual but the complex inter-subjectivity of individuals interacting in groups,

communities and societies across generations. It is on this basis that the formation of social structures of power is explained, and their conventional nature makes them open to challenge. Metaphysical ambiguity does not disquiet critical scholars as much as it would positivists or social constructionists – because, in contrast with the preceding paradigms, critical inquiry is primarily an axiological paradigm, rejecting the positivistic notion that research is or can be purely descriptive and value-neutral, and considering that such assumptions simply reinforce the status quo. Critical research embraces the culturally determined, value-laden, political nature of the pursuit of knowledge, interrogating systems of oppression and seeking methods of emancipation and empowerment of the disadvantaged and the vulnerable.

Critical inquiry perspectives have produced new theoretical foundations for business ethics and CSR. Unlike more traditional frameworks, such as Kantian ethics (Bowie, 1999), virtue ethics (Solomon, 1993), social contract theory (Donaldson & Dunfee, 1999) and Rawlsian ethics of justice (Freeman, 2002), discourse ethics has been advanced as a more effective alternative that accounts for the political relations and power differentials influencing organizational interactions. Mingers (2009), for instance, proposes an ethics based on a dialectic between discourse ethics and Bhaskar's critical realism. Discourse ethics has informed normative stakeholder management theory (Reed, 1999) and the communicative theory of the firm (Smith, 2004). From the same tradition, Habermas's theory of communicative action is engaged to ground the corporate legitimacy of the firm (Palazzo & Scherer, 2006). Furthermore, Jones and Fleming (2003) draw on Habermas's ideas as well as Burrell and Morgan's (1979) radical structuralism in a critical stakeholder theory-based analysis of globalization, emphasizing the socio-economic and political embeddedness of stakeholder groups and questioning the legitimacy of stakeholder relations as accepted in traditional stakeholder management. Applying Habermas's later work, Scherer and Palazzo (2007) draw on the framework of deliberative democracy. Positioning the firm as a political actor in a democratic society, they argue that a focus on civic self-determination and collective civil society actors in deliberative democracy offers a more pragmatic grounding for corporate social responsibility, reconciling the normative and the empirical in a political theory of CSR. Furthermore, Banerjee (2003) discusses stakeholder colonialism and the contest between national and indigenous interests, in a critique of colonial, anticolonial and postcolonial narratives.

In this context, CME research has made significant contributions, as it naturally builds on the critical inquiry paradigm and the traditions of critical management studies (Grey, 2002, 2004). By way of example, Dehler (2007) applies the ideas of Habermas and the Frankfurt School in the development of critical pedagogy. Morrow (Morrow & Torres, 2002) seeks a fusion between Freire's critical pedagogy (Freire & Freire, 1994) and Habermas's critical theory in order to link social theory and education. Raelin (2007) combines critical theory and social constructionism to produce an epistemology of practice that challenges the tradition of the professional education model, emphasizing tacit knowledge, social information processing as knowledge creation, and critical reflection as praxis.

Since the establishment of the PRME, critical inquiry-based approaches have been, progressively, better represented than alternatives such as critical realism or social constructionism. Millar and Price (2018) utilize critical reflexivity (Archer, 2012) and critical discourse analysis (Fairclough, 2010) to examine whether the PRME enable critical discourse. Their conclusions suggest that the Principles themselves represent and generate a dominant discourse, unable to admit the possibility of questioning the functionalist assumptions of management education. Also drawing on critical discourse analysis

and critical realism, Louw (2014) questions the capability of the PRME movement to challenge the dominance of neoliberal discourse, suggesting that the Principles are the product of a consensual approach to traditional management education that maintains academic institutions' subservience to the corporate sector. In this context, Blasco (2012) pushes for a critical pedagogical approach to teaching the PRME, to enable transformational learning – namely, learning that changes a student's entire frame of reference (their thoughts, feelings, associations, values and responses) and not merely their body of knowledge. Asirvatham and Humphries-Kil (2017) draw on radical feminism and critical organizational studies to examine the PRME aspirations and achievements, and to challenge the mechanism of global capitalism considered to underpin ongoing gender disparity. They encourage scrutiny of the unexamined assumptions and values at work in management education, to enable the PRME as a platform of genuine change.

Critical inquiry and critical theory have maintained an appreciable presence in the RMLE discourse, engaging with the processes of PRME application and communication within the RMLE curriculum. Overall, these approaches have been beneficial and seminal for the field, having produced a wide spectrum of positions towards PRME, from conditional support (Burchell, Murray & Kennedy, 2014) and methodological suggestions for effective PRME communication in management teaching (Blasco, 2012) to outright rejection of the PRME as unreflectively implemented (Millar & Price, 2018) ideological products (Louw, 2014). While critical inquiry and critical theory offer the promise of comprehensive and radical examination, by rejecting the framing of existing contexts they also tend to delay or inhibit action within those contexts. Therefore, moving forward, it is worth seeking a balance between lofty ideals and more achievable targets. A pragmatic turn may assist in this endeavour.

Pragmatism

Pragmatism emphasizes praxeological premises, focusing on purposeful action and rejecting methods of inquiry that fail to demonstrate utility in relation to this focus. Pragmatism recognizes that questioning the relevance of all ontological, epistemological and axiological assumptions renders practical action difficult, if not impossible, for without knowledge of reality we have little indication of how to act, and absent any system of values we are denied a motivation as to why to act. Where critical inquiry or postmodern interrogation may recommend suspending action for purposes of inquiry (justifiably so if these actions are explicitly or implicitly oppressive), pragmatism recommends suspending inquiry to enable purposeful action, where such inquiry may prove an obstacle to initiating change. Championed in philosophy by James (1907), Dewey (1916, 1929), Peirce (1934) and Rorty (1992), pragmatism embraces a contextualist ontology, emphasizing the relevance of situational and circumstantial detail in defining desirable action. It rejects the objectivism and universalism of positivism, while falling short of the relativism underpinning some strains of social constructivist and postmodern thought. Here, knowledge is what a community of inquiry finds useful and relevant in solving its problems (Peirce, 1934). Of the paradigms discussed, pragmatism is perhaps the most flexible in its utilitarian formulation of philosophical premises. It embraces, without doctrinal restraint or inertia, those methods of inquiry that may prove useful in any given situation, without extrapolating them to unrelated contexts. Its emphasis on predictable beneficial outcomes shares some of the methodological assumptions embraced by positivism and post-positivism, while grounding the benefit of research in practical outcomes and rejecting universal measures of that practicality acknowledges some social construction of value. As such, we might see pragmatism as ontologically and epistemologically ambivalent, axiologically relativist, and praxeologically positivist (in that it prefers taking purposeful action to not doing so).

Within business ethics, pragmatism has been embraced as an alternative, transcending the positivist/non-positivist conflict and strengthening the link between theory and practice (Wicks & Freeman, 1998), bridging the divide between the normative and the empirical in research (Rosenthal & Buchholz, 2000; Wicks & Freeman, 1998), and collapsing the fact-value distinction (Rosenthal & Buchholz, 2000). It has been offered as a foundation for virtue in business ethics (Jacobs, 2004), and applied to specific learning–teaching approaches inside and outside the academy (Ruhe & Nahser, 2001). Pragmatism has been promoted as an alternative to integrated social contract theory (ISCT) as more reflective of the contextually embedded and historical–evolutionary process of norm generation (Frederick, 2000), and as a refinement to ISCT (Scherer & Palazzo, 2007), contributing reflexivity and institutional thickness to what these authors otherwise see as the thin, decontextualized application of the hypernorm. In the field of sustainability, Scholz, Lang, Wiek, Walter and Stauffacher (2006) focus on the necessarily probabilistic nature of knowledge due to our limited access to reality, and on its relationship to purposeful, functional behaviour. While not specifically pragmatist, their assumptions of a limited representation of reality and their satisficing approach with regard to the purpose of research resonate with pragmatism's acknowledgment of epistemological limitations and the dependence of a finding's value upon its usefulness.

Pragmatism has also gained increasing ground in the RMLE literature post-PRME. Painter-Morland (2015) appeals to it when outlining a human-centred (rather than organization-centred) framework as a counterforce to the reductive, rationalist neoliberal perception of human nature, well-being and organizational behaviour. Extending on Buchholz and Rosenthal's (2008) critique of the scientific model of education, Painter-Morland examines the effects of the fact-value distinction in projecting management as an objective profession, excluding morality from its discourse and processes, and thus hamstringing responsible management. Similarly critical of the portrayal of management as an objective, value-free science, Fougère, Solitander and Young (2014) draw on Rorty's work on final vocabularies and moral imagination, on Flyvbjerg's (2006) conception of phronesis (practical wisdom) and on critical pedagogy (Cunliffe, 2002; Grey, 2002) to look at a critical application of the PRME to the classroom and the business community, and, drawing from Clegg, Kornberger and Rhodes' (2007) ethics as practice, seek to offer a polyphonic discourse exploring the values and power relations inherent in management education. Phronesis is also emphasized by Laasch (2018), with the aim to embed the PRME in a community of practice. Moosmayer, Waddock, Wang, Hühn, Dierksmeier and Gohl (2018) draw on Dewey's articulation of reflective, potential freedom to recommend multidisciplinary economic education and broaden teaching perspectives beyond the neoclassical norm, to liberate management discourse from quantitative limitations, and to enable social freedom through pragmatic RMLE. Furthermore, Kelley and Nahser (2017) draw on pragmatic inquiry to envision meaningful implementation of the PRME objectives.

Pragmatism promotes the practical pursuit of comprehensive well-being within the RMLE literature, though alone may lack the positioning and instruments to critically evaluate the nature of this well-being. However, authors like Fenwick (2005) and, later, Fougère et al. (2014) illustrate approaches that complement pragmatism with more critical frameworks, thus helping to address this limitation.

Postmodernism

Although less represented in RMLE, postmodernism is worth discussing here for two reasons. Firstly, in stark contrast with pragmatism, it pushes the limits of scepticism and questions the appropriateness of utility as a criterion for defining knowledge. Secondly, unlike the previous paradigms, it questions the very possibility and meaning of general philosophical assumptions, be they ontological, epistemological or axiological. Hence, postmodernism offers a stance wherefrom we may be able to consider progressing RMLE research by moving beyond the existing paradigms, and perhaps even beyond paradigmatic thinking.

As a reaction of resistance to the material, social and historical positivism characteristic of the modernist period, postmodernism questions the grand, unifying historical narratives, value systems, socio-political structures and knowledge systems that inform contemporary society (Aylesworth, 2015). Perhaps the most thematically diverse of the paradigms discussed here, the postmodern literature can be characterized by a rejection of the universal in favour of the relative, and of the objective in favour of the subjective. It emphasizes personal, lived, intuitive experience – but without claiming that a unified, context-independent perspective can be achieved. Postmodernism re-conceptualizes both knowledge and the socio-political condition of individuals as contingent (Lyotard, 1984; Heller & Feher, 1989). Clearly opposed to positivism and post-positivism, postmodernism finds some common cause with social constructionism and critical inquiry in seeking to examine and deconstruct systems of meaning and power – but without investing in constructive political programmes.

In relation to business ethics, Willmott (1998) draws on the works of Derrida (e.g. 1967, 1992), Foucault (e.g. 1979, 1984) and Bauman (e.g. 1993) to offer a poststructuralist, post-humanist analysis of the tensions between descriptive ethical codes used in organizations, the values imposed via organizational culture, and the individual's (employee's) normative ethical values in the hierarchical organization. Similarly, Clegg et al. (2007) seek to liberate organizational ethics from mere rule-following and the narrow, constrained assumptions of selfhood and agency so conferred. Jones (2003) draws on Levinas (e.g. 1985) and Derrida (e.g. 2002) to question the possibility of ethics in the business domain while it remains tied to calculative reasoning and regimented rule adherence, and calls for a postmodern deconstruction of business ethics to resolve these aporias. Later on, Jones (2007) returns to Derrida in order to examine tensions within neoliberal conceptions of society versus the economy, business and CSR – and to interrogate the notion and nature of responsibility. In the sustainability field, Newton (2002) draws on Bauman (1997) and Elias (e.g. 1994) to explore the limits of power, intention, agency and ordering in examining ecocentrism, deep ecology and the greening movement, offering an interdependency network analysis in organizational and global contexts. Dey and Steyaert (2007) draw on Derrida, Foucault, and Lyotard to recommend a process of deconstruction and re-imagination of management education, which they see as too commodified and Taylorized – i.e. uniform, repetitive and mass produced. Perriton and Reynolds (2004) refer to Bauman's work and feminist theory to question the capacity of critical management education to achieve its emancipatory goals. Furthermore, drawing on Ellsworth's (1989) earlier critique of critical pedagogy (for replicating within the classroom the very power structures that it criticizes outside it), they discuss the recalcitrance of authoritarian power structures within the critical classroom. They recommend, therefore, a pedagogy of refusal over one of emancipation, in an attempt to extend Ellsworth's challenge to the whole CME domain, and to critique the masculine domination of the critical management field.

By comparison to the SRE 'roots' literature, the postmodern paradigm is notably under-represented in the discussion of RMLE post-PRME – with some exceptions, such as Clegg and Ross-Smith's (2003) use of Foucault's contextual examination of power relations to critique what they see as a modernist-Kantian emphasis on universalism. While postmodernism's tendency to question all knowledge and assumptions may lead to nihilism, thus paralysing any impulses to implement PRME goals within RMLE, its challenges to grand narratives may still prove useful in providing ongoing reflection and critique of RMLE as a maturing field.

CONCLUSION: MAPPING THE FIELD

We summarize the key features of the above paradigms in Table 30.1 – which indicates the key philosophical premises founding each paradigm, together with its representative theorists and preferred research methodologies and/or methods.

Furthermore, building on Laasch and Moosmayer's (2015) evaluation of research paradigms in the broader SRE literature, we highlight three notable features of RMLE research in relation to paradigm use. Firstly, the insights of their conceptual analysis are confirmed by the history of RMLE research itself. For those who initially embraced the PRME as an effective guide for a valuable research programme, and who also invested confidence in its effectiveness as an instrument for assessing the outcomes of RMLE research, relying on positivism seemed sufficient. This accords with the observed predominance of a (largely implicit) positivist skew in the RMLE literature thus far. However, as research in this direction proliferated and matured, it became clear that many initially positivistic assumptions had to be questioned. Progressively, critical realism, social constructionism, critical inquiry and pragmatism have made their way into

Table 30.1 RMLE research paradigms – key philosophical premises, representative theorists, and preferred methodologies

Paradigm	Ontology	Epistemology	Axiology	Representative theorists	Preferred methodologies/methods
Positivism	*Realist*: a single reality exists that the researcher investigates	*Objectivist, empiricist*: phenomena are perceived as they are; our senses are accurate recorders	*Value neutral*: findings are assumed to be independent of the researcher's values	Comte (1844) Durkheim (1895)	*Empiricism:* Quantitative measurements Statistical methods Direct observation
Post-positivism, critical realism	*Realist*: a single reality exists that the researcher investigates	*Bounded objectivist*: phenomena are accessed through perception, which is limited (post-positivism); perception may need to be transcended to access underlying reality (critical realism)	*Value realist*: accepts that findings and methodology may be influenced by the researcher's values, and seeks to remedy bias	*Post-positivism:* Popper (1959) Gettier (1963) *Critical realism:* Bhaskar (1975, 1979, 1987)	*Bounded empiricism:* Mixed methods Observation Interpretation (content analysis) Axiological reflection Researcher bias control techniques
Social constructionism	*Constructionist*: multiple realities are co-constructed by those who participate within them	*Subjectivist*: as meanings of realities are socially created; perception filters through these created meanings	*Value dependent*: as both reality and meaning are socially constructed, they carry the values of those who constructed them; (researcher's) values are inescapable so should be assumed	Berger and Luckman (1966) Weick (1995) Latour (2005)	Ethnography Interpretation (thematic analysis) Axiological reflection Deconstruction Actor network analysis
Critical inquiry and critical theory	Ranging from realist to constructionist (e.g. about power structures)	*Inter-subjectivist*: reality is perceived according to meanings co-created by groups and communities in which perceiving subjects participate	*Critical*: rejects the idea of research and knowledge as being value neutral; researcher explicitly adopts values and goals of social resistance, emancipation and change	Adorno (1966) Horkheimer (1974) Habermas (1971, 1984, 1985)	Critical analysis Critical discourse analysis Critical reflexivity Participative methods Action research
Pragmatism	*Contextualist*: reality reflects the desirability of action, and this will depend on contextual detail	*Purposive (teleological)*: neither objectivist nor subjectivist a priori; embraces that epistemology which may best support purposeful action aiming at practically beneficial outcomes	*Utilitarian*: embraces values, goals and purposes that are useful to the community	James (1907) Dewey (1916, 1929) Peirce (1934) Rorty (1992)	Pragmatic inquiry Practice research methodology Case study methodology
Postmodernism	*Relativist*: there are no 'great laws' of reality – all is contingent	*Subjectivist*: our perception of reality is heavily influenced by our experiences and social contexts	*Radical*: questions all systems of value (including the researcher's) and the context of their creation	Derrida (1967, 1992) Levinas (1985) Foucault (1979, 1984) Bauman (1993)	Concept analysis and synthesis Radical reflection Radical deconstruction Re-imagination techniques

this space – though, as observed earlier, some fields (e.g. critical inquiry and theory, and pragmatism) are better represented than others (e.g. critical realism and postmodernism). But, to reiterate previous evaluations, we feel that the unfulfilled potential in these fields illuminates an opportunity for further exploration and application in RMLE research and practice.

Secondly, a more recent but growing phenomenon in RMLE research methodology is the specific fusion of the traditions of critical inquiry and pragmatic thought. Studies such as Grey (2002), Louw (2014) and Millar and Price (2018), which are representative of this fusion, conclude with calls for a greater focus on critical theory and reflexivity, and even for moving away from the ideological constraints of the PRME to more fully embrace CME.

Thirdly, summarizing the first two insights, we note that two methodological streams continue to dispute priority in RMLE research – one seeking measurable improvements in responsible management education and corporate impacts at individual, organizational, national and global levels; the other opposing the methods underpinning measurable improvements and seeking more radical methodological change for more substantive impact.

PREFIGURING (OR SHAPING?) THE FUTURE

As our evaluation suggests, RMLE research has progressed substantially from both its SRE roots and its initial reactions to the PRME. However, despite complementary contributions from a variety of paradigms, there is room for improvement in many directions – such as, addressing contextual interpretations of the core values that should underpin RMLE; relativizing the ideological underpinnings of the PRME; expanding the range of social constructionist perspectives and interpretive tools available to RMLE

researchers; challenging the fundamental assumptions informing their research philosophies; and striking a productive middle ground when using pragmatic utilitarianism to overcome the inhibitions caused by critical and postmodern challenges.

The ongoing tensions between positivistic and the critical-reflective approaches in RMLE research point to certain limitations in using paradigmatic thinking – or at least single paradigm applications – for methodology design in this field. While much research here is grounded in a single paradigm, some of the authors discussed above (e.g. Mingers, 2009; Newton, 2002; Raelin, 2007) have actually applied multiple paradigms. This has enabled them to comparatively analyse, and draw from, paradigms across disciplines.

Here, it is worth observing the tension between the very idea of a paradigm and some of the emphases of the SRE disciplines from which the PRME literature draws inspiration. Firstly, echoing this tension, Perriton and Reynolds (2004) find that paradigms enforce – or at least recommend – a structure in disciplines that are traditionally oriented towards contesting structure. Secondly, the use of paradigms tends to homogenize discourse, whereas many of the disciplines discussed oppose abstract, generalizable concepts and favour contextualized subjectivity that emphasizes differences over similarities. Thirdly, as a consequence of these homogenizing tendencies, paradigms risk de-individuating and de-personalizing discourse in disciplines that contest rule-following and privilege experiential and intuitive accounts of both the ontological and the epistemological. This is particularly the case with RMLE research, where, by way of example, Fenwick (2005) suggests that the top-down application of paradigms may be inferior to interacting more personally with the object of study: '[t]hough an understanding of theoretical constructions is important to any serious vocational endeavor, it is more efficacious to think in terms of engaging thoughtfully with theory and, then, putting ourselves into practice rather than putting theory into practice' (Fenwick, 2005: 47). This position critiques the adequacy of any single paradigm in capturing the complexities of lived experience and human action.

So, how can we address the above challenges? One option is to de-construct the existing paradigms and re-construct new ones. As discussed, each paradigm is based on certain philosophical assumptions, but we do not need to maintain these assumptions in a 'pre-packaged' combination. For example, ontological realism may blend with epistemological inter-subjectivism, axiological normativism and praxeological teleology – to support a research programme that acknowledges the existence of a reality that is independent of our conscience but admits of social knowledge in so far as it is inter-subjectively constructed, asserts its values based on a fully assumed normative stance (without denying others the possibility of divergent stances), and confers significant purpose to human action. We are yet to find an adequate label for this paradigmatic possibility. More importantly, this sort of paradigm re-thinking has to be oriented to the needs of RMLE research. A pragmatist's emphasis on purposeful action, for instance, accords with the goal-directed nature of RMLE (including as shaped by the PRME and post-PRME), yet those goals still require examination and contextualization. Critical and postmodern inquiry can aid this examination and contextualization but not at the expense of beneficial action. Striking an appropriate balance is the key.

We therefore suggest that making one's paradigmatic positioning explicit is not sufficient to allow for methodological reflection and improvement. Using references to pre-packaged research paradigm theory should not be regarded as an acceptable substitute for first-order philosophical reflection. We encourage RMLE researchers to consider and confidently promote first-order reflections involving new types of philosophical premises, as well as new combinations of already utilized premises, across paradigms. For example, the nature of responsible management may require new emphases on axiology by refining distinct assumptions about normative and applied ethics, aesthetics, and theory of value. Furthermore, the nature of management learning and education may require new praxeological assumptions about management, learning and teaching as different forms of purposeful human action in interaction with each other. In agreement with Laasch and Gherardi (2019), we particularly encourage doctoral candidates and junior faculty to actively engage in first-order philosophical reflection on their own profile and role as researchers, and to approach methodological traditions in this field with a personalized evaluation agenda. The methodological horizon is still widely open for creative approaches as RMLE research comes of age.

REFERENCES

Adorno, T. W. (1966). *Lectures on negative dialectics* (trans. R. Livingstone). Cambridge: Polity Press.

Ählström, J., Macquet, M., & Richter, U. (2009). The lack of a critical perspective in environmental management research: distortion in the scientific discourse. *Business Strategy and the Environment*, *18*(5), 334–346.

Archer, M. (2012). *The reflexive imperative in late modernity*. Cambridge: Cambridge University Press.

Asirvatham, S., & Humphries-Kil, M. (2017). Feminist reflections on life in (im)balance, career praxis, and the PRME. *International Journal of Management Education*, *15*(2), 126–137.

Aylesworth, G. (2015). Postmodernism. *The Stanford Encyclopedia of Philosophy*. Available at: https://plato.stanford.edu/entries/postmodernism/.

Banerjee, S. B. (2003). The practice of stakeholder colonialism: national interest and colonial discourses in the management of indigenous stakeholders. In Prasad A. (Ed.), *Postcolonial theory and organizational analysis* (pp. 255–279). New York: Palgrave Macmillan.

Basu, K., & Palazzo, G. (2008). Corporate social responsibility: a process model of sensemaking. *Academy of Management Review*, *33*(1), 122–136.

Bauman, Z. (1993). *Postmodernist ethics*. Oxford: Blackwell.

Bauman, Z. (1997). *Postmodernity and its discontents*. Cambridge: Polity Press.

Benn, S., Edwards, M., & Angus-Leppan, T. (2013). Organizational learning and the sustainability community of practice: the role of boundary objects. *Organization & Environment*, *26*(2), 184–202.

Berger, P. L., & Luckmann, T. (1966). *The social construction of reality: a treatise in the sociology of knowledge*. Garden City, NY: Anchor Books.

Berman, S. L., Wicks, A. C, Kotha, S., & Jones, T. M. (1999). Does stakeholder orientation matter? The relationship between stakeholder management models and firm financial performance. *Academy of Management Journal*, *42*, 488–506.

Bhaskar, R. (1975). *A realist theory of science*. London: Verso.

Bhaskar, R. (1979). *The possibility of naturalism*. London: Routledge.

Bhaskar, R. (1987). *Scientific realism and human emancipation*. London: Verso.

Blasco, M. (2012). Aligning the hidden curriculum of management education with PRME: an inquiry-based framework. *Journal of Management Education*, *36*(3), 364–388.

Borges, J. C., Ferreira, T. C., Borges de Oliveira, M. S., Macini, N., & Caldana, A. C. F. (2017). Hidden curriculum in student organizations: learning, practice, socialization, and responsible management in a business school. *International Journal of Management Education*, *15*(2B), 153–161.

Bowie, N. E. (1999). *Business ethics: a Kantian perspective*. Oxford: Blackwell.

Brand, V. (2009). Empirical business ethics research and paradigm analysis. *Journal of Business Ethics*, *86*(4), 429–449.

Buchholz, R. A., & Rosenthal, S. B. (2008). The unholy alliance of business and science. *Journal of Business Ethics*, *78*(1–2), 199–206.

Buckley, M. (2013). A constructivist approach to business ethics. *Journal of Business Ethics*, *117*(4), 695–706.

Burchell, J., Murray, A., & Kennedy, S. (2014). Responsible management education in UK business schools: critically examining the role of the United Nations Principles for Responsible Management Education as a driver for change. *Management Learning*, *46*(4), 479–497.

Burrell, G., & Morgan, G. (1979/2017). *Sociological paradigms and organisational analysis: elements of the sociology of corporate life*. London: Routledge.

Carolan, M. S. (2005). Society, biology, and nature: bringing nature back into sociology's disciplinary narrative through critical realism. *Organization and Environment*, *18*(4), 393–421.

Carroll, A. B. (1979). A three-dimensional conceptual model of corporate social performance. *Academy of Management Review*, *4*, 497–505.

Clegg, S., Kornberger, M., & Rhodes, C. (2007). Business ethics as practice. *British Journal of Management*, *18*, 107–122.

Clegg, S., & Ross-Smith, A. (2003). Revising the boundaries: management education and learning in a postpositivist world. *Academy of Management Learning and Education*, *2*(1), 85–98.

Comte, A. (1844/2019). *A general view of positivism*. New Delhi: General Press.

Cramer, J., Van Der Hiejden, A., & Jonker, J. (2006). Corporate social responsibility: making sense through thinking and acting. *Business Ethics*, *15*(4), 380–389.

Crane, A. (1999). Are you ethical? Please tick yes or no: on researching ethics in business organizations. *Journal of Business Ethics*, *20*, 237–248.

Cunliffe, A. (2002). Reflexive dialogical practice in management learning. *Management Learning*, *33*(1), 35–61.

Dehler, G. (2007). Prospects and possibilities of critical management education: critical beings and a pedagogy of critical action. *Management Learning*, *40*(1), 31–49.

Derrida, J. (1967) *De la grammatologie*. Paris: Minuit.

Derrida, J. (1992). Force of law: the mystical foundation of authority. In Cornell, D., Rosenfeld, M., & Carlson, D. G. (Eds.), *Deconstruction and the possibility of justice* (pp. 3–68). London: Routledge.

Derrida, J. (2002). *Negotiations: interventions and interviews, 1971–2001* (trans. E. Rottenberg). Stanford, CA: Stanford University Press.

Dewey, J. (1916). The pragmatism of Peirce. *Journal of Philosophy, Psychology and Scientific Methods, 13*(26), 709–715.

Dewey, J. (1929). The quest for certainty. In Boydston, J. A. (Ed.), *The later works, 1929–1953*. Carbondale, IL: Illinois University Press.

Dey, P., & Steyaert, C. (2007). The troubadours of knowledge: passion and invention in management education. *Organization, 14*, 437–461.

Donaldson, T., & Dunfee, T. W. (1999). *Ties that bind*. Boston, MA: Harvard Business School Press.

Durkheim, É. (1895/2013). *The rules of sociological method* (Ed. S. Lukes). New York: Free Press.

Eiríksdóttir, L., & Engelmark, K. (2016). Sensemaking of sustainability in business education: the case of PRME in Swedish business schools and universities. Available at: www.diva-portal.org/smash/record.jsf?pid=diva2%3A953749&dswid=2666.

Elias, N. (1994). *The civilizing process* (vols. 1 and 2). Oxford: Blackwell.

Ellsworth, E. (1989). Why doesn't this feel empowering? Working through the repressive myths of critical pedagogy. *Harvard Educational Review, 59*, 297–324.

Fairclough, N. (2010). *Critical discourse analysis: the critical study of language* (2nd ed.). Harlow: Longmans.

Fenwick, T. (2005). Ethical dilemmas of critical management education: within classrooms and beyond. *Management Learning, 36*(4), 31–48.

Flyvbjerg, B. (2006). Making organization research matter: power, values and phronesis. In Clegg, S. R., Hardy, C., Lawrence, T. B., & Nord, W. R. (Eds.), *The Sage handbook of organization studies* (2nd ed.) (pp. 370–387). London: Sage.

Forray, J. M., & Leigh, J. S. (2012). A primer on the principles of responsible management education intellectual roots and waves of change. *Journal of Management Education, 36*(6), 295–309.

Foucault, M. (1979). *Discipline and punish: the birth of the prison* (trans. A. Sheridon). New York: Vintage Books.

Foucault, M. (1984). *The history of sexuality: an introduction* (trans. R. Hurley). London: Penguin Books.

Fougère, M., Solitander, N., & Young, S. (2014). Exploring and exposing values in management education: problematizing final vocabularies in order to enhance moral imagination. *Journal of Business Ethics, 120*, 175–187.

Frederick, W. C. (2000). Pragmatism, nature, and norms. *Business and Society Review, 105*, 467–479.

Freeman, R. E. (2002). A stakeholder theory of the modern corporation. In Hartman, L. P. (Ed.), *Perspectives in business ethics* (pp. 171–181). Boston, MA: McGraw-Hill.

Freire, P., & Freire, A. M. A. (1994). *Pedagogy of hope: reliving pedagogy of the oppressed*. New York: Continuum.

Gettier, E. L. (1963). Is justified true belief knowledge? *Analysis, 23*(6), 121–123.

Godemann, J., Bebbington, J., Herzig, C., & Moon, J. (2014). Higher education and sustainable development: exploring possibilities for organisational change. *Accounting, Auditing & Accountability Journal, 27*(2), 218–233.

Grey, C. (2002). What are business schools for? On silence and voice in management education. *Journal of Management Education, 26*(5), 496–511.

Grey, C. (2004). Reinventing business schools: the contribution of critical management education. *Academy of Management Learning & Education, 3*(2), 178–186.

Guba, E. G., & Lincoln, Y. S. (1994). Competing paradigms in qualitative research. In Guba, E. G., Lincoln, Y. S., & Denzin, N. K. (Eds.), *Handbook of qualitative research* (pp. 105–117). Thousand Oaks, CA: Sage.

Guba, E. G., & Lincoln, Y. S. (2005). Paradigmatic controversies, contradictions, and emerging influences. In Denzin, N. K., & Lincoln, Y. S. (Eds.), *The Sage handbook of qualitative research* (3rd ed.). London: Sage.

Habermas, J. (1971/2015). *Knowledge and human interests*. New York: John Wiley and Sons.

Habermas, J. (1984). *The theory of communication* (vol. 1). Boston, MA: Beacon Press.

Habermas, J. (1985). *The theory of communication* (vol. 2). Boston, MA: Beacon Press.

Haski-Leventhal, D., Pournader, M., & McKinnon, A. (2017). The role of gender and age in business students' values, CSR attitudes, and responsible management education: learnings from the PRME international survey. *Journal of Business Ethics, 146*(1), 219–239.

Hay, A., & Hodgkinson, M. (2008). More success than meets the eye – a challenge to critiques of the MBA: possibilities for critical management education? *Management Learning, 39*(1), 21–40.

Heisenberg, W. (1930/2015). *The physical principles of quantum theory.* Mansfield Centre, CT: Martino Publishing.

Heller, A., & Feher, F. (1989). *The postmodern political condition.* Cambridge: Polity Press.

Hervieux, C., McKee, M., & Driscoll, C. (2017). Room for improvement: using GRI principles to explore potential for advancing PRME SIP reporting. *International Journal of Management Education, 15*(2), 219–237.

Horkheimer, M. (1974). *Eclipse of reason.* New York: Continuum.

Jacobs, D. C. (2004). A pragmatist approach to integrity in business ethics. *Journal of Management Inquiry, 13*(3), 215–223.

James, W. (1907). *Pragmatism: a new name for some old ways of thinking.* New York: Longmans.

Jensen, T. (2007). Moral responsibility and the business and sustainable development assemblage: a Jonasian ethics for the technological age. *International Journal of Innovation and Sustainable Development, 2*(1), 116–129.

Jones, C. (2003). 'As if business ethics were possible, "within such limits" ….'. *Organization, 10*(2), 223–248.

Jones, C. (2007). Friedman with Derrida. *Business and Society Review, 112*(4), 511–532.

Jones, M. T., & Fleming, P. (2003). Unpacking complexity through critical stakeholder analysis the case of globalization. *Business and Society, 42*(4), 430–454.

Jones, T. M. (1995). Instrumental stakeholder theory: a synthesis of ethics and economics. *Academy of Management Review, 20,* 404–437.

Kelley, S., & Nahser, R. (2017). Integrating the six Principles of PRME in practice through pragmatic inquiry: a sustainable management case study. In Sunley, R., & Leigh, J. (Eds.), *Educating for responsible management:* *putting theory into practice* (e-book). London: Routledge.

Kuhn, T. S. (1962). *The structure of scientific revolutions.* Chicago, IL: University of Chicago Press.

Laasch, O. (2018). Delineating and reconnecting responsible management, learning, and education (RMLE): Towards a social practices perspective on the field, 4(5), 1–28. *CRME Working Papers.*

Laasch, O., & Gherardi, S. (2019). Delineating and reconnecting responsible management, learning, and education (RMLE): a research agenda through a social practices lens. In *Academy of Management Annual Meeting,* Boston, 9–13 August 2019.

Laasch, O., & Moosmayer, D. (2015). Responsible management learning: reflecting on the role and use of paradigms in sustainability, responsibility, ethics research. *CRME Working Papers, 2.* Available at: http://responsible-management.net/wp-content/uploads/2015/08/LaaschMoosmayer2015Responsible MgmtLearningWorkingPaper.pdf.

Latour, B. (2005). *Reassembling the social: an introduction to actor network theory.* Oxford: Oxford University Press.

Levinas, E. (1985). *Ethics and infinity* (trans. R. Cohen). Pittsburgh, PA: Duquesne University Press.

Louw, J. (2014). Paradigm change or no change at all? A critical reading of the UN Principles for Responsible Management Education. *Journal of Management Education, 39*(2), 184–208.

Lozano, J. F. (2012). Educating responsible managers. the role of university ethos. *Journal of Academic Ethics, 10*(3), 213–226.

Lyotard, J. F. (1984). *The postmodern condition: a report on knowledge* (vol. 10). Minneapolis, MN: University of Minnesota Press.

Meppem, T., & Gill, R. (1998). Planning for sustainability as a learning concept. *Ecological Economics, 26*(2), 121–137.

Millar, J., & Price, M. (2018). Imagining management education: a critique of the contribution of the United Nations PRME to critical reflexivity and rethinking management education. *Management Learning, 49*(3), 346–362.

Mingers, J. (2009). Discourse ethics and critical realist ethics: an evaluation in the context of business. *Journal of Critical Realism, 8*(2), 172–202.

Moosmayer, D. C., Waddock, S., Wang, L., Hühn, M. P., Dierksmeier, C., & Gohl, C. (2018). Leaving the road to Abilene: a pragmatic approach to addressing the normative paradox of responsible management education. *Journal of Business Ethics*, 1–20.

Morrow, R. A., & Torres, C.A. (2002). *Reading Freire and Habermas: critical pedagogy and transformative social change*. New York: Teachers College Press.

Morsing, M., & Schultz, M. (2006). Corporate social responsibility communication: stakeholder information, response and involvement strategies. *Business Ethics: A European Review*, *15*(4), 323–338.

Murdoch, J. (2001). Ecologising sociology: actor-network theory, co-construction and the problem of human exemptionalism. *Sociology*, *35*(1), 111–133.

Neesham, C. (2018). Philosophical foundations of qualitative research. In Mir, R., & Jain, S. (Eds.), *The Routledge companion to qualitative research in organization studies* (pp. 21–39). London: Routledge.

Newton, T. J. (2002). Creating the new ecological order: Elias and actor-network theory. *Academy of Management Review*, *27*(4), 523–540.

Nijhof, A., & Jeurissen, R. (2006). Editorial: a sensemaking perspective on corporate social responsibility: introduction to the special issue. *Business Ethics: A European Review*, *15*(3), 316–322.

Nonet, G., Kassel, K., & Meijs, L. (2016). Understanding responsible management: emerging themes and variations from European business school programs. *Journal of Business Ethics*, *139*(4), 717–736.

Painter-Morland, M. (2015). Philosophical assumptions undermining responsible management education. *Journal of Management Development*, *34*(1), 61–75.

Palazzo, G., & Scherer, A. G. (2006). Corporate legitimacy as deliberation: a communicative framework. *Journal of Business Ethics*, 66, 71–88.

Pater, A., & van Lierop, L. (2006). Sense and sensitivity: the roles of organisation and stakeholders in managing corporate social responsibility. *Business Ethics: A European Review*, *15*(4), 339–351.

Peirce, C.S. (1934). Pragmatism and pragmaticism. In Hartshorne, C., & Weiss, P. (Eds.), *Collected papers* (vol. 5). Cambridge, MA: Harvard University Press.

Perriton, L., & Reynolds, M. (2004). Critical management education: from pedagogy of possibility to pedagogy of refusal? *Management Learning*, *35*(1), 61–77.

Perry, M., & Win, S. (2013). An assessment of PRME's contribution to responsibility in higher education. *Journal of Corporate Citizenship*, *49*(March), 48–70.

Popper, K. (1959/2005). *The logic of scientific discovery*. London: Routledge.

Prandini, M., Vervoort Isler, P., & Barthelmess, P. (2012). Responsible management education for 21st century leadership. *Central European Business Review*, *1*(2), 16–22.

Raelin, J. A. (2007). Toward an epistemology of practice. *Academy of Management Learning & Education Journal*, *6*(4), 495–519.

Reed, D. (1999). Stakeholder management theory: a critical theory perspective. *Business Ethics Quarterly*, *9*(3), 453–483.

Rorty, R. (1992). Metaphilosophical difficulties of linguistic philosophy. In Rorty, R. (Ed.), *The linguistic turn: essays in the philosophical method* (pp. 1–39). Chicago, IL: University of Chicago Press.

Rosenthal, S. B., & Buchholz, R. A. (2000). The empirical-normative split in business ethics: a pragmatic alternative. *Business Ethics Quarterly*, *10*(2), 399–408.

Ruhe, J., & Nahser, F. B. (2001). Putting American pragmatism to work in the classroom. *Journal of Business Ethics*, *34*(3–4), 317–330.

Scherer, A. G., & Palazzo, G. (2007). Toward a political conception of corporate responsibility: business and society seen from a Habermasian perspective. *Academy of Management Review*, *32*(4), 1096–1120.

Scholz, R. W., Lang, D. J., Wiek, A., Walter, A. I., & Stauffacher, M. (2006). Transdisciplinary case studies as a means of sustainability learning: historical framework and theory. *International Journal of Sustainable Higher Education*, *7*, 226–251.

Schouten, E. M. J., & Remme, J. (2006). Making sense of corporate social responsibility in international business: experiences from Shell. *Business Ethics: A European Review*, *15*(4), 365–379.

Smith, J. D. (2004). A précis of a communicative theory of the firm. *Business Ethics: A European Review*, *13*(4), 317–331.

Solomon, R. C. (1993). *Ethics and excellence*. Oxford: Oxford University Press.

Stachowicz-Stanusch, A. (2011). The implementation of Principles for Responsible Management Education in practice: research results. *Journal of Intercultural Management*, *3*(2), 241–257.

Sunley, R., & Leigh, J. (Eds.), (2016) *Educating for responsible management: putting theory into practice*. Sheffield: Greenleaf Publishing.

Wartick, S. L., & Cochran, P. _. (1985). The evolution of the corporate social performance model. *Academy of Management Review*, *4*, 758–769.

Weick, K. E. (1995). *Sensemaking in organizations*. Thousand Oaks, CA: Sage.

Welford, R. J. (1998). Corporate environmental management, technology, and sustainable development: postmodern perspectives and the need for a critical research agenda. *Business Strategy and the Environment*, *7*(1), 1–12.

Wersun, A. (2017). Context and the institutionalisation of PRME: the case of the University for the Common Good. *International Journal of Management Education*, *15*(2), 249–262.

Wicks, A. C., & Freeman, R. E. (1998). Organization studies and the new pragmatism: positivism, anti-positivism, and the search for ethics. *Organization Science*, *9*, 123–140.

Willmott, H. (1998). Towards a new ethics? The contributions of poststructuralism and post-humanism. In Parker, M. (Ed.), *Ethics and organizations* (pp. 76–121). London: Sage.

Wood, D. J. (1991). Corporate social performance revisited. *Academy of Management Review*, *16*, 691–718.

Wry, T. E. (2009). Does business and society scholarship matter to society: pursuing a normative agenda with critical realism and neoinstitutional theory. *Journal of Business Ethics*, *89*(2), 151–171.

Young, S., & Nagpal, S. (2013). Meeting the growing demand for sustainability-focused management education: a case study of a PRME academic institution. *Higher Education Research & Development*, *32*(3), 493–506.

31

Methods in Responsible Management Learning and Education – A Review

Tine Köhler and Jennifer Gao

This chapter provides a review of the research methods and methodologies employed in current responsible management learning and education (RMLE) research. In general, reviewing the research methods (including data collection and analysis) of any given field is useful to determine how it has arrived at its current knowledge base. Research methods are the tools with which we explore our phenomena of interest and the contexts in which they exist. The research methods we use allow us to discover, explore, develop, examine, reflect on, assess, test, challenge, and refute knowledge. Over time, the use of research methods helps researchers create a knowledge base on a given phenomenon and the context in which it operates.

Yet, all research methods also have limitations. As McGrath (1995) discusses, all research methods are inherently flawed. Research methods are rooted in research philosophies about what exists (ontology) and how we can know what exists (epistemology). This means that employing a particular research method inherently imposes a specific lens through which a phenomenon and its context can be explored and understood. Furthermore, all research methods have strengths and weaknesses such that no one research method can fully capture a phenomenon and its context. Rather, a particular research method allows the researcher to explore certain characteristics of a phenomenon but not others or certain aspects related to how the phenomenon operates in its context but not in others. As such, the existing knowledge base on a phenomenon of interest and its context is strongly influenced by the research methods a field employs.

The purpose of this chapter is to examine which research methods have been employed to study RMLE phenomena and their contexts. This review allows us to determine if certain tools to generate knowledge are favored over others, which may indicate that the knowledge base created on RMLE may be stronger in some ways than in others. We also examine how research methods

METHODS IN RESPONSIBLE MANAGEMENT LEARNING AND EDUCATION – A REVIEW

have been applied and provide examples of excellent applications of research methods in RMLE research.

First, we describe the method we employed to systematically review the use of research methods in RMLE research. We then report findings from our review that highlight which methods are most commonly employed. We also evaluate the current applications of these methods in RMLE research and provide specific examples for excellent applications of the method. We then discuss more generally some of the specific methodological challenges researchers face in RMLE research and offer suggestions for addressing and managing these challenges. Finally, we highlight alternative research approaches that show great promise for the future study of RMLE.

REVIEW OF RMLE METHODS

In this section we describe the method we employed for our review of the research methods currently used in RMLE research. We also discuss the strengths and limitations of our chosen approach.

Search for Empirical Papers

For our review, we evaluated papers published over the five years 2013–2018 in the journals *Academy of Management Learning and Education (AMLE)*, *Journal of Management Education (JME)*, *Management Learning (ML)*, *Management Teaching Review (MTR)*, and *International Journal of Management Education (IJME)*. We limited our review to this five-year period to ensure that our observations reflect the most current practices.

We chose the five journals above for several reasons. First, these journals all cover general management learning and education research, rather than more specific sub-topics, such as learning and education specifically related to leadership (e.g., *Journal of*

Leadership Education), marketing (e.g., *Journal of Marketing Education*), or international business (e.g. *Journal of Teaching in International Business*). In this way, we ensure that we do not overrepresent particular research topics and associated research methods by reviewing published articles in journals that limit themselves to specific topics.

Second, the five chosen journals each have different research foci and serve slightly different communities of learning and education researchers. A review of their mission statements shows that *AMLE* focuses on the process and results of management teaching as well as the institutional environment of business schools (Academy of Management Learning & Education, 2018). *JME* publishes articles that 'reflect changes and developments in the conceptualization, organization, and practice of management education' (Journal of Management Education, 2018). *MTR* publishes short teaching and learning resources (Management Teaching Review, 2018). *IJME* seeks to publish 'reflective papers which bring together pedagogy and theories of management learning' (International Journal of Management Education, 2018). *ML* 'provide[s] a unique forum for critical inquiry, innovative ideas and dialogue' (Management Learning, 2018).

Furthermore, our assertion that these journals publish different types of papers is also based on the personal experiences of the first author of this chapter. While being an Associate Editor for *AMLE*, Köhler has held several workshops with Editors and Associate Editors of *JME*, *MTR* and *ML* that have focused on how the journals differ in the content they publish, in the ontological and epistemological traditions in which most of their publications are rooted, and in the associated research methods that are frequently employed in the published papers. As such, in reviewing articles published in these five journals we can ensure a plurality of ontological and epistemological foundations as well as a plurality of specific approaches to research methods such as experimental research, simulations, survey research, different qualitative research methods and many more.

Third, the five journals chosen for this review include arguably the most influential journals in MLE research. The journals are ranked consistently highly in popular publication ranking systems. Furthermore, the submission rates to these journals have increased over recent years (based on journal statistics from editorial board meetings and on personal conversations with the journals' editors), indicating that they are a popular and respected outlet for MLE research. Consequently, our review of research methods related to RMLE research in these five journals should allow us to review the most relevant methods for RMLE researchers.

In order to search for articles published on RMLE topics in these five journals, we used the following search terms: sustainab* (which finds all matches related to this word stem, such as sustainability, sustainable, sustainably, and other words with the same word stem), ethic* (i.e., ethics, ethical, ethically, business ethics, ethic, etc.), and responsib* (i.e., responsibility, corporate social responsibility, responsible, responsibly, etc.). Table 31.1 lists the initial search hits produced by the use of these search terms.

Inclusion Criteria

To be included in our review, an article had to meet several inclusion criteria. First, the article had to be a research piece on RMLE topics. For example, several articles might have included the word 'responsible', but the use of the word was not related to responsible management learning and education. It might have been used in the sense of a manager being responsible for her or his employees or an antecedent being responsible for a certain effect. Similarly, an article may have included the word 'sustainable' but only to say that certain teaching practices were not sustainable over the course of a semester. To be included in our review, an article's main research topic had to be either a topic related to communicating learning content on sustainability, responsibility, or ethics or a topic related to teaching and educating in a responsible, sustainable, or ethical way.

Second, the article had to include an empirical component, i.e., a data collection and analysis. Conceptual, anecdotal, editorial, or opinion pieces were not included in our review. Consequently, our review included 11 papers from *AMLE*, 17 papers from *JME*, 0 papers from *MTR* (no empirical data was found in any of the RMLE studies we assessed in *MTR*), 19 papers from *ML*, and 18 papers from *IJME*.

Coding Approach

From each of the included articles we coded the following information about the employed research methods:

- Journal
- Publication year.

Table 31.1 Overview of search results using the selected keywords

Journal	Number of articles on			Row total	Included in review
	Responsib*	Ethic*	Sustainab*		
AMLE	22	33	16	71	11
JME	12	28	7	47	17
ML	14	20	9	43	19
MTR	5	8	1	14	0
IJME	7	3	8	18	18
Total	60	92	41	193	65

For journal abbreviations, see text.

- Did the paper follow a qualitative, quantitative, mixed method or other approach?
- Was the topic of the paper re ated to communicating RMLE content or relat=d to RMLE as a characteristic of the educational experience?
- General approach employed ¡qualitative: e.g., grounded theory, case study analysis, ethnography, action research; quantitative: e.g., survey methodology, experiment, archival, vignette study).
- Data collection approach (qualitative: e.g., interviews, observations, artifacts, field notes; quantitative: e.g., panel survey, longitudinal measurement, repeated measures, archival data).
- Data analysis approach (qualitative: e.g. thematic analysis, discursive analysis, content analysis, grounded theory coding; quantitative: e.g. descriptive statistics, t-test, ANOVA, regression, SEM, HLM, social networks analysis).

For papers using a different approach than we would usually classify in the management discipline as quantitative, qualitative, or mixed method we collected all available information about the employed method. Table 31.2 presents the articles we coded and our coding decisions.

FINDINGS

Over the last five years, we found 65 empirical articles in 5 journals, out of which we classified 10 as quantitative, 39 as qualitative, 15 employed some form of mixed methods, and 1 paper used another type of approach not commonly captured under these prior approaches.

Quantitative

Amongst the 10 papers using quantitative approaches, 9 papers used a survey approach. Out of these 9 survey papers, 6 used one-time measurement, 1 used measures at different points in time, and 3 used repeated measurement (note: some papers featured multiple data collections). In addition to using a

survey approach, the paper by Rasche, Gilbert, and Schedel, (2013) also featured a longitudinal design, the paper by Klapper and Farber (2016) a quasi-experimental design, and the paper by Koris, Örtenblad, and Ojala (2017) used vignettes as stimulus material. The one quantitative paper that d:d not use a survey (Décamps, Barbat, Carteron, Hands, & Parkes, 2017) introduced the Sustainability Literacy Test platform (to demonstrate how higher education institutions can evaluate their sustainability teaching and learning) and reported statistics on sustainability literacy worldwide at present time. For data analysis, 3 papers used SEM or path modeling, 3 papers used t-tests, 2 papers used regression techniques, 2 papers used only descriptive statistics, 1 paper used factor analysis, and 1 paper used ANOVA techniques (note: some papers used several techniques).

Qualitative

Amongst the 39 papers using a qualitative approach, 18 papers employed a case study analysis approach, 3 papers a grounded theory approach, 4 papers a narrative approach, 4 papers discourse analysis, 8 papers a content analysis approach, 4 papers an action research approach and 3 papers an ethnographic approach (again, several papers combined multiple approaches). Data collection means included interviews (15 papers), focus groups (2 papers), observations (14 papers), surveys (9 papers), other documents or archival textual data (18 papers), non-textual data (e.g. photos; 4 papers), co-created materials (4 papers), personal reflections (2 papers), field notes (3 papers), journaling (3 papers) and vignettes (1 paper). Data in the qualitative papers were analyzed using thematic analysis (15 papers), analysis of discursive practices (5 papers), narrat:ve analysis (4 papers), visual semiotic analysis (1 paper), grounded theory analysis (5 papers), inductive coding (2 papers), critical

Table 31.2   Coded studies over the period 2013–2018 in *AMLE, JME, ML* and *IJME*

Journal	Study	RMLE as content to teach (Content) vs. RMLE as a characteristic of the educational experience (Ed. experience)	General research method used	Data collection approach	Data analysis approach
AMLE	Aragon-Correa, Marcus, Rivera & Kenworthy (2017)	Content	Quantitative survey	Survey	Descriptive statistics
AMLE	Arieli, Sagiv & Cohen-Shalem (2016)	Content	Mixed methods case study; longitudinal study	Survey; documents and other archival data	Content analysis; MANOVA; t-test
AMLE	Baden (2014)	Content	Qualitative	Survey	Thematic analysis
AMLE	Butler, Delaney & Spoelstra (2017)	Content	Qualitative	Interviews	Thematic analysis
AMLE	Cummings & Bridgman (2016)	Content	Different approach	Publication analysis; textbook review; comparative analysis to other disciplines	Maps; textbook analysis; descriptive statistic; content coding
AMLE	Hanson & Moore (2014)	Content	Qualitative case study	Interviews, observations, survey	Thematic analysis
AMLE	Hanson et al. (2017)	Content	Qualitative case study	Interviews, observations, survey, documents, field notes	Grounded theory
AMLE	Montiel, Antolin-Lopez & Gallo (2018)	Content	Qualitative	Documents	Grounded theory
AMLE	Rasche, Gilbert & Schedel (2013)	Content	Quantitative survey	Survey – repeated measurement; longitudinal measurement; textual data	Descriptive statistics; content coding
AMLE	Snelson-Powell, Grosvold & Millington (2016)	Ed. experience	Mixed methods – case study; survey; longitudinal study	Survey interviews; documents and other archival data	Content analysis; fs/QCA; descriptive statistics
AMLE	Sutherland, Gosling & Jelinek (2015)	Content AND Ed. experience	Qualitative case study	Interviews, observations	Grounded theory
IJME	Annan-Diab & Molinari (2017)	Content	Qualitative case study (limited information on data collection and analysis)		
IJME	Awaysheh & Bonfiglio (2017)	Content	Qualitative case study (limited information on data collection and analysis)		
IJME	Beddewela, Warin, Hesselden & Coslet (2017)	Content AND Ed. experience	Mixed methods (case study)	Survey; documents and other archival data	Thematic analysis; descriptive statistics

Journal	Authors	Focus	Method	Data collection	Data analysis
IJME	Borges et al. (2017)	Ed. experience	Mixed methods (content coding; survey)	Survey	Content analysis; descriptive statistics (count of comments)
IJME	Borges, Ferreira, de Oliveira, Macini & Caldana (2017)	Content AND Ed. experience	Qualitative content coding	Questionnaire	Thematic analysis
IJME	Burga, Leblanc & Rezania (2017)	Content	Quantitative survey	Survey (repeated measurement)	t-test; regression
IJME	Carreira, Aguiar, Onça & Monzoni (2017)	Content	Qualitative content coding (limited)	Observation	Thematic analysis
IJME	Cicmil, Gough & Hills (2017)	Ed. experience	Qualitative case study	Observation	Thematic analysis
IJME	Décamps, Barbat, Carteron, Hands & Parkes (2017)	Content	Introduces Sulitest as a method to assess sustainability learning		
IJME	Greenberg et al. (2017)	Content AND Ed. experience	Mixed methods (case study)	Interviews; survey	Narrative analysis; descriptive statistics (no actual description of data analysis process)
IJME	Jagger & Volkman (2014)	Content	Qualitative content coding	Interviews	Thematic analysis
IJME	Klapper & Farber (2016)	Content	Quantitative survey	Survey – repeated measurement; quasi-experiment	Saturated model specification test
IJME	Kolb, Fröhlich & Schmidpeter (2017)	Content AND Ed. experience	Qualitative case study (claims to be mixed methods, but no info on quantitative)	Documents and other archival data	More of description than analysis
IJME	Ortiz & Huber-Heim (2017)	Content	Qualitative case study (more of a description rather than analysis)		
IJME	Rive, Bonnet, Parmentier, Pelazzo-Plat & Pignet-Fall (2017)	Ed. experience	Qualitative case study	Documents and other archival data	Description rather than analysis
IJME	Ross, Valenzuela, Intindola & Flinchbaugh (2017)	Content	Mixed methods (content analysis and survey)	Survey; documents and other archival data	Thematic analysis; descriptive statistics; MANOVA
IJME	Tyran (2017)	Content	Qualitative narrative analysis	Observations; documents and other archival data	Narrative analysis (limited)
IJME	Warwick, Wyness & Conway (2017)	Content	Qualitative action research	Interviews; focus groups; observations	Thematic analysis
ML	Burchell, Kennedy & Murray (2015)	Content	Mixed methods (case study; survey)	Survey; interviews	Thematic analysis; descriptive statistics

(Continued)

Table 31.2   Coded studies over the period 2013–2018 in *AMLE, JME, ML* and *IJME* (Continued)

Journal	Study	RMLE as content to teach (Content) vs. RMLE as a characteristic of the educational experience (Ed. experience)	General research method used	Data collection approach	Data analysis approach
ML	Crevani & Hallin (2017)		Qualitative case study	Interviews; observations; documents and other archival data; non-textual data; co-creating or interaction; journaling	Inductive coding
ML	Dwyer & Hardy (2016)	Content	Qualitative interpretive case study	Documents and other archival data	Interpretive analysis
ML	García-Rosell (2013)	Content	Qualitative case study; action research	Observations; questionnaire; co-creating or interaction; personal reflections; field notes; journaling	Discourse analysis
ML	Gearty, Bradbury-Huang & Reason (2015)	Content	Qualitative action research	Interviews; co-creating or interaction	Co-creating learning histories
ML	Gherardi & Murgia (2015)	Content	Qualitative case study	Documents and other archival data	Discourse analysis
ML	Gherardi & Rodeschini (2016)	Content	Qualitative ethnography	Interviews; observations; documents and other archival data	Grounded theory; critical incident analysis
ML	Hawkins, Pye & Correia (2017)	Content	Qualitative case study	Observations; vignettes; action learning	Thematic analysis
ML	Heizmann & Liu (2018)	Content	Qualitative discourse analysis	Documents and other archival data; non-textual data	Discourse analysis
ML	Kassinis & Panayiotou (2017)	Content	Qualitative case study	Documents and other archival data; non-textual data	Narrative analysis; visual semiotic analysis
ML	Koris, Örtenblad & Ojala (2017)	Content	Quantitative vignette study	Survey	ANOVA/ANCOVA
ML	Mangan, Kelemen & Moffat (2016)	Content	Qualitative case study (Auto-ethnography)	Focus groups; personal reflections; field notes; journaling	Reflective conversations
ML	Millar & Price (2018)	Ed. experience	Qualitative case study	Interviews	Discourse analysis; thematic analysis
ML	Page, Grisoni & Turner (2014)	Content	Qualitative action research	Observations; non-textual data; co-creating or interaction	

ML	Porschitz, Smircich & Calás (2016)	Ed. experience	Qualitative ethnography	Interviews; observations; documents and other archival data; field notes	Inductive coding
ML	Smolović Jones, Smolović Jones, Winchester & Grint (2016)	Content	Qualitative case study	Interviews; observations	
ML	Toubiana (2014)	Content	Qualitative grounded theory	Interviews; questionnaire	Grounded theory
ML	Warhurst & Black (2017)	Content	Qualitative narrative analysis	Interviews; non-textual data	Discourse analysis; narrative analysis
ML	Zwack, Kraiczy, von Schlippe & Hack (2016)	Content	Mixed methods (case study; survey; vignette study)	Survey; interviews	Thematic analysis; narrative analysis; ANOVA/MANOVA; other non-linear simple comparison tests
JME	Bergman, Westerman, Bergman, Westerman & Daly (2014)	Content AND Ed. experience	Quantitative survey	Survey	SEM/Path modeling
JME	Bruni-Bossio & Willness (2016)	Content	Mixed methods (content analysis; survey)	Survey; documents and other archival data	Thematic analysis; Descriptive statistics
JME	Deer & Zarestky (2017)	Content	Qualitative narrative analysis	Documents and other archival data	Content coding (thematic analysis; narrative analysis)
JME	Huster, Petrillo, O'Malley, Glassman, Rush & Wasserheit (2017)	Content	Mixed methods (content analysis; survey)	Survey	Thematic analysis; descriptive statistics
JME	Kuechler & Stedham (2018)	Content	Mixed methods (content analysis; survey)	Survey (repeated measure); documents and other archival data	Thematic analysis; t-test
JME	Ledley & Holt (2014)	Content	Quantitative survey	Survey	t-test; correlation
JME	Louw (2015)	Content	Qualitative discourse analysis	Documents and other archival data	Discourse analysis
JME	McDonald (2013)	Content	Mixed methods (Content analysis; survey)	Survey; documents and other archival data	Thematic analysis; descriptive statistics (limited information on data analysis)
JME	O'Brien, Wittmer & Ebrahimi (2017)	Content	Mixed methods content analysis	Student assessments; documents and other archival data	Thematic analysis; descriptive statistics (limited information on data analysis)
JME	Parris & McInnis-Bowers (2017)	Content	Qualitative content coding	Questionnaire; documents and other archival data	Thematic analysis

(Continued)

Table 31.2   Coded studies over the period 2013–2018 in *AMLE*, *JME*, *ML* and *IJME* (Continued)

Journal	Study	RMLE as content to teach (Content) vs. RMLE as a characteristic of the educational experience (Ed. experience)	General research method used	Data collection approach	Data analysis approach
JME	Rennie, Byrum, Tidwell & Chitkara (2018)	Content	Qualitative content coding	Interviews; documents and other archival data	Thematic analysis
JME	Roberts et al. (2018)	Content AND Ed. experience	Quantitative survey	Survey (different measures at different times, but not a pre-post design)	SEM/ path modelling; EFA/CFA/ PCA; t-test (post-hoc)
JME	Sroufe, Sivasubramaniam, Ramos & Saiia (2015)	Content	Qualitative content coding	Documents and other archival data	Thematic analysis
JME	Tomlin, Metzger, Bradley-Geist & Gonzalez-Padron (2017)	Content	Qualitative content coding	Questionnaire	Thematic analysis
JME	Vidal, Smith & Spetic (2015)	Content	Mixed methods (content analysis; survey)	Survey; documents and other archival data	Thematic analysis; Descriptive statistics; cluster analysis
JME	Volkema & Kapoutsis (2016)	Content	Mixed methods (content analysis; survey)	Survey (student feedback)	Thematic analysis; narrative analysis; t-test
JME	Walker (2018)	Content	Quantitative survey	Survey	Regression

For journal abbreviations, see text.

incident analysis (1 paper), interpretive analysis (1 paper) and reflective conversations (1 paper).

Mixed and Other

Amongst the mixed methods papers, 5 papers used a case study approach, 11 papers a content analysis approach, 13 papers a survey approach (with 1 longitudinal design among them), 1 paper a vignette study and 1 paper student assessments. The data collection of these papers included surveys (13 papers with one-time measurement, 1 with repeated measures), interviews (3 papers) and the analysis of other documents or archival textual data (9 papers). Data analysis techniques included thematic analysis (11 papers), narrative analysis (3 papers), content analysis (3 papers), fuzzy set qualitative comparative analysis (1 paper), descriptive statistics as the dominant technique (11 papers), ANOVA/MANOVA (3 papers), t-tests (3 papers), other non-linear comparison tests (1 paper) and cluster analysis (1 paper).

We only found one paper that used a different approach than we would usually classify in the management discipline as quantitative, qualitative, or mixed method. The paper by Cummings and Bridgman (2016) created geographical maps using an algorithm into which textual data was fed. They also used a narrative textbook review as well as publication analyses.

As such, the most commonly employed techniques that we see in RMLE research are survey methodology, case study analysis and content analysis of textual data. Quantitative data analysis techniques focus predominantly on descriptive statistics and some of the simpler mean comparison techniques. Qualitative data analysis techniques predominantly favor thematic analysis. In the following, we will highlight four example papers that have used different methods to examine their research questions. We chose these articles because of the demonstrated fit between the research

question posed and the research method applied, which allowed each author team to address interesting research questions and uncover new knowledge.

Examples of Different Research Method Applications

Employing a qualitative multiple-case study analysis approach, Hanson et al. (2017) examine students' moral development across three different cultural contexts (United States, Morocco and Brazil). The researchers adopted a constructionist epistemology in which they explored moral beliefs as being 'created, altered, and affirmed in their daily experiences within the communities in which they are embedded' (Hanson et al., 2017: 396). Of specific interest to the researchers was how students' interactions with their institutions shaped their moral development process. Using triangulation in data collection (surveys, observations, artifacts, and interviews) and data analysis (coding notes, field notes, prolonged researcher engagement, member checks, the use of multiple coders, within- and across-case analysis), the authors were able to draw strong inferences about the model of moral development they were re-examining. Their study allowed them to confirm several dimensions of their theoretical model, modify two of the original dimensions, and add another influence factor to the model. In this paper, the case study approach was used very effectively for model elaboration and extension.

Gherardi and Rodeschini (2016) employed an ethnographic approach to study caring. Using a post-humanist approach to explore the practice of caring as an organizational competence, the authors conducted ethnographic field work in a nursing home for the elderly. The authors analyzed data from interviews, observations, prolonged field exposure, and official documents via a grounded theory approach focusing on critical incidents (i.e. 'an emotional event in the life of a person or an organization in that it is a period of intense feelings'; Gherardi & Rodeschini, 2016: 272). Core insights from this research uncovered caring to be a common orientation of actors that is collectively performed, encoded in practices and adapted through situated decision-making. The paper is a great example of the opportunities that ethnographic studies can provide for studying ethical decision-making and the enactment of responsible practices.

Adopting a quantitative survey approach, Roberts et al. (2018) developed an integrated moral conviction theory of student academic dishonesty. Drawing on models and concepts of moral philosophies, moral identity and moral conviction, the authors propose multiple paths through which moral conviction may affect unethical decision-making among students. The authors collected survey data from undergraduate business students on the measures of moral conviction, moral identity, moral philosophy, moral disengagement and unethical decision-making. Based on the results of a confirmatory factor analysis and structural equation modeling, the research confirms moral conviction as a key factor that reduces student moral disengagement and unethical decision-making. This paper illustrates how quantitative modeling can be applied to examine factors that predict (un) ethical decision-making.

In their mixed methods study, Beddewela, Warin, Hesselden, and Coslet (2017) examined staff and students' views on responsible management education (RME) and deficiencies in the existing curriculum. The authors used a three-phase data collection approach, which combined qualitative data from two business faculty workshops aimed at targeting a list of terms faculty associate with RME, qualitative data from a document analysis of the existing curriculum (e.g. syllabi, course descriptions, etc.), and quantitative data from a student survey. Results from thematic analysis and descriptive statistics revealed that while some faculty and student perceptions aligned, for example, with regard to the need of a more widespread and systematic incorporation of RME into the program's curriculum, some perceptions differed widely, for example, with regard to the importance of RME to students. Faculty members thought that students were less enthusiastic about RME, while students reported that RME weighs strongly in their consideration of program quality and choice. From their findings, the authors conclude that effective responsible management education requires business school-wide support.

In the next section, we discuss specific challenges that arise from the study of the three reviewed research topics in RMLE, i.e. ethics, sustainability and responsibility. We review how current papers have addressed these challenges when selecting and applying specific research methods. In addition, we make some alternative suggestions for future RMLE work.

UNIQUE CHALLENGES OF THE RMLE CONTEXT

Studying research topics grounded in ethics, sustainability and responsibility poses some specific challenges on the research methods being employed. Furthermore, there are specific challenges arising out of the two main research purposes, i.e. RMLE as content to be taught versus RMLE as a characteristic of the educational experience.

Teaching RMLE Content

Authors are often interested in an evaluation of the effectiveness of their approach for teaching RMLE content. Much of the published research we reviewed for this chapter highlights, though, that the teaching of RMLE content goes beyond teaching declarative, tangible knowledge. Rather, teaching RMLE content often involves, among other things, instilling moral values, changing existing beliefs and behavioral patterns, becoming aware of taken-for-granted thought patterns and challenging one's own identity. On the one hand, these are complex topics to teach that require innovative learning approaches. Furthermore, when it comes to research methods, authors also need to take into account specific characteristics inherent in assessing these learning contexts.

In the papers we reviewed, it was noticeable that the number of qualitative studies far outweighed the number of quantitative studies (by about 4 to 1). It seems that authors consider qualitative work to be much more suitable to the research topic and context in RMLE. A closer look at the unique challenges presented in RMLE research may explain why. As mentioned in the previous paragraph, the teaching content chosen is complex. For example, changing values or morals to foster responsible and sustainable leadership or developing an ethical identity are topics that are hard to capture in a survey for two reasons.

First, the concepts themselves are hard to assess with static survey questions. Morals and values are malleable, and students may not assign the same meaning to them. As such, asking pre-worded questions about them negates the importance of the sense-making process that students may engage in when being taught about morals and values. Second, if the process of changing morals, values or identities is of interest to the researcher, then the research method needs to be able to account for the fact that learning trajectories may differ between individuals. It also needs to accommodate that learning rarely unfolds in a linear process (Wright & Gilmore, 2012). As such, a research method needs to be able to capture dynamic change over time. Qualitative methods are uniquely qualified to cater to these requirements, especially methods that explore and uncover patterns alongside the research participants.

Along these lines, it is noteworthy that several of the qualitative papers that focus on teaching RMLE content have used action

research approaches (García-Rosell, 2013; Gearty, Bradbury-Huang & Reason, 2015; Page, Grisoni & Turner, 2014; Warwick, Wyness & Conway, 2017), ethnography (Gherardi & Rodeschini, 2016; Mangan, Kelemen & Moffat, 2016), grounded theory (Montiel, Antolin-Lopez & Gallo, 2018; Sutherland, Gosling & Jelinek, 2015; Toubiana, 2014), narrative analysis (Deer & Zaretsky, 2017; Kassinis & Panayiotou, 2017; Tyran, 2017; Warhurst & Black, 2017), or discourse analysis (García-Rosell, 2013; Heizmann & Liu, 2018; Louw, 2015). All of these approaches focus in one way or another on the lived experiences of the participants, their sensemaking processes, development over time and the importance of context (physical context or relevant relationships and interactions) for said development. Furthermore, many of these approaches are rooted in epistemologies that assume the subjectivity of participants' experiences and focus on how experiences, sensemaking, meaning-making, and identities are created. These include social constructionism, social constructivism, critical realism, interpretivism and phenomenology.

If researchers are interested in RMLE research questions and do not expect change in the underlying construct specification of the main construct over time, then researchers may want to consider using quantitative techniques that can assess different learning trajectories, such as hierarchical linear modeling or time series analysis. For example, if the research question was to determine the most effective method to deliver knowledge surrounding sustainability or to increase engagement in sustainable practices, then researchers could administer different instructional techniques in different classes (i.e. a nested design) and compare the learning curve slopes over time. Hierarchical linear modeling should be of interest to MLE researchers as they could use it to compare the effectiveness of different instructional designs administered to different groups of students. Time series analysis could be of interest to assess how learning unfolds, i.e. how the students' standing on the construct of interest changes over time. This type of data collection requires multiple measurement points at equally spaced time intervals and strives to learn about the nature of a phenomenon by understanding how it changes over time.

Generally, these types of quantitative research are still rare in RMLE research (and more generally in learning and teaching research) but could be very valuable in assessing the value of different teaching techniques. The construct complexity in RMLE research, though, often makes the use of quantitative techniques difficult. Before quantitative techniques can be used more widely, we need to arrive at more appropriate and stable construct specifications, which may be very difficult if we know that constructs are malleable, subjective and fickle.

Beyond the complexity of the chosen topic, RMLE research topics are challenging because they deal with potentially sensitive issues, such as discovering that one is not being as ethical, sustainable or responsible as one thought. Sensitive topics can bring with them a whole range of psychological adjustments, distortions, and coping mechanisms to ameliorate the negative conclusions we may draw about ourselves. For example, we may engage in some form of positivity bias or self-deception (Goleman, 1996) to maintain an image that we are not as bad as we may have to conclude from a particular learning experience. Or we respond to questions on a survey in a way that is influenced by social desirability, i.e. we may acknowledge we are not the ethical or sustainable posterchild, but we do not want others to know that or judge us for it. In these cases, qualitative research that follows the participant over time can again be quite useful. On the one hand, researchers can specifically explore self-deception or social desirability biases. Beyond procedures in survey research that may statistically correct for such biases to create data that is assumed to be largely free

from its influence, qualitative work allows the researcher to explore why participants engage in these behaviors. Insights from such explorations may be particularly helpful to understand obstacles to learning and identity development.

Finally, many of the papers we reviewed have highlighted the importance of introducing reflexivity and reflection activities in their research on teaching RMLE content, including reflexivity of the researcher, i.e. reflexivity as a characteristic of the research approach. Through reflections, students observe, analyze and reconsider different interpretations of their evaluations of a given situation. In order to change something as deeply rooted as values, morals, beliefs, or identities, deep reflection is often necessary (Hibbert & Cunliffe, 2015; Mirvis, 2008). Assessing this reflection process can provide important insights to researchers about appropriate teaching content, stimuli for initiating reflection, or offering assistance for reflection (Sutherland et al., 2015; Tomkins & Ulus, 2015, 2016).

RMLE as Characteristic of the Educational Experience

Many of the studies on RMLE as a characteristic of the educational experience focus on business schools' implementation of the United Nations' Principles for Responsible Management Education (PRME) to increase business schools' positive societal impact. Others focus on issues with student cheating or the influence of student organizations on students' moral development. The predominant research methods used for studies on educational experiences were case study analyses followed by surveys and content analysis. Many of the studies included analyses of business curricula, business school websites, or textual data from reports. The survey studies gathered data directly from different stakeholders such as students, business school faculty, or career services staff.

When using secondary data, researchers face the challenge that they often do not have access to the thought processes involved in creating the secondary data. For example, when analyzing business school curricula across different business schools, researchers are often not privy to the decision-making processes underlying what was included in the curriculum and what was not. When studying PRME reports, researchers do not know if information was strategically left out of the report or if some aspects were worded a bit more optimistically than maybe warranted. In short, when studying secondary data, researchers must rely on the edited nature of the content they are analyzing. We can argue that this is likely going to be true for all business schools and thus, would ensure that we are still comparing like with like. However, this also means that we would never get the full picture of how business schools incorporate RMLE-related characteristics into their organizational and educational context.

When collecting primary data, for example, through surveys or interviews, researchers essentially face many of the same issues related to social desirability, self-deception, or the discussion of sensitive issues as outlined above. Furthermore, in order to rigorously carry out a survey research project, statistical power for running analyses needs to be strong. In the published studies, many of the surveys had a couple of hundred participants. However, practically none of the papers examined issues with the base rate of the behavior they were trying to assess. For example, if cheating practices are the topic of research, we have to take into account first how prevalent cheating is. If cheating is not prevalent in the data, then power for finding relationships between cheating and other variables of interest may be low.

Alternative Research Methods

To address unique challenges of RMLE research, we suggest a few specific research contexts and their associated methods. These may better allow for an assessment of how to teach RMLE content and how to create educational experiences anchored in RMLE.

The first research context relates to the use of games or simulations to teach RMLE content. Games and simulations are not just the teaching approach, but also an approach to research. Games and simulations have the advantage that students get experiential learning while being in a controlled environment (Köhler, Fischlmayr, Lainema, & Saarinen, 2013). Many business simulations include ethical decision-making or decision-making under difficult conditions. This means that students can experience RMLE content in a research context that is akin to a quasi-experimental setting, in which instructors can manipulate aspects of the simulation or the context to foster specific learning. At the same time, by creating certain contexts and situations, researchers can study RMLE-related issues in a more targeted fashion.

An interesting example is the ViBu simulation (Köhler et al., 2013), where teams of students work together as either part of a company that produces medical equipment or as part of a sub-producer company that produces parts for the medical equipment. In a simulated market place, students in the sub-producer teams have to ensure the continuation of their production process and offer their products to the medical company. They are in competition with other sub-producer teams that are also negotiating deals with the medical company. Research using the simulation has shown that student teams often engage in unethical practices as they are competing with other teams (e.g. Fischlmayr, Lähteenmäki, & Saarinen, 2007). In some simulations, teams hacked the simulation of other teams to run the other team's company into financial loss, so their own company could prosper. In other simulations, sub-producer teams colluded to create an alliance against the medical company to control price in the market.

Experiences such as these lend themselves to investigation of learning from and in difficult decisions. Rather than relying on students' previous experiences or the general context of their classes, simulations and games can be used to replicate contexts that foster questionable behaviors. In that way, researchers can more specifically study how students learn RMLE content and develop ethical, responsible, and sustainable mindsets and decision-making. In this context, qualitative research methods can be used to observe and track the students' learning process, especially when simulations are used in conjunction with student reflections on their learning experiences. Quantitative research methods could be employed, for example, using a quasi-experimental design, in which different student groups might be set up to isolate demographic or context factors and explore how they affect students' engagement in questionable practices. Students could then learn about these factors and how they impact on their decision-making.

As a note of caution though, we would like to remind researchers about the importance of researcher and instructor reflexivity about the learning process in these type of learning contexts. As Forray and Lund Dean (Wright, Forray & Lund Dean, 2019) have argued, many learning experiences like the one suggested here may be potentially challenging for students to process as they make students aware of their own susceptibility for practicing unethical behaviors. In addition, there may be unintended challenges to the students' identity and self-perception that instructors need to be prepared to manage and ameliorate. Thorough debriefing is necessary under such conditions to ensure the ethical treatment of research participants.

The second alternative research context we would like to highlight is real-life engagement projects, in which students engage directly with organizations, such as service learning projects or student consultancies. Prior research has shown that engagement projects can be highly effective in teaching students about RMLE content in a relevant context.

Furthermore, by anchoring students' learning in real-life settings that are often designed to have a positive impact on the engaged stakeholders, instructors also achieve RMLE as a characteristic of the educational experience. In many of these learning contexts, students create 'good' with their engaged partners and experience first-hand the challenges of responsible, ethical and sustainable management. Furthermore, they are encouraged to find real solutions.

Different types of research questions could be explored in these contexts. In-depth qualitative research methods, for instance, allow researchers to examine the students' sense-making and learning. Prior service learning projects have used qualitative approaches such as content analysis of learning narratives (e.g., Pless, Maak & Stahl, 2011) or case study analysis of specific projects, their unique settings and the learning generated by them (e.g. Brower, 2011; Smith & Woodworth, 2012). Quantitative research methods, such as regression or ANOVA techniques (especially those employing longitudinal designs), might be used to assess the benefits of institutionalizing service learning in a given curriculum. Researchers could, for example, assess whether a curriculum that incorporates service learning projects increases beneficial collaborations with industry partners, increases student employability, helps improve community issues, develops core student learning outcomes, or increases the attractiveness of their programs to new student cohorts (e.g., Beddewela et al., 2017; Simons & Cleary, 2006; Yorio & Ye, 2012).

CONCLUSION

This chapter has reviewed the research methods currently employed by researchers studying RMLE topics related to ethics, sustainability and responsibility. The most common research methods employed were case study analysis, content analysis of textual data and survey methodology. Quantitative data analysis techniques focus predominantly on descriptive statistics and some of the simpler mean comparison techniques. Qualitative data analysis techniques predominantly favor thematic analysis. Our review indicated that qualitative studies outnumbered quantitative studies by 4 to 1. This indicates a strong preference for qualitative work that accounts for the complexity of the topics studied, captures dynamic change and differences in sensemaking and meaning-making, and explores the important role of context. Furthermore, we discussed alternative research approaches of games, simulations, service learning and student consultancies that may offer interesting and valuable opportunities for studying RMLE topics in future research.

REFERENCES

Academy of Management Learning & Education (2018). *Mission Statement*. Retrieved on September 10, 2018 from http://aom.org/Publications/AMLE/Academy-of-Management-Learning—Education.aspx.

Beddewela, E., Warin, C., Hesselden, F., & Coslet, A. (2017). Embedding responsible management education – staff, student and institutional perspectives. *International Journal of Management Education*, *15*(2), 263–279.

Brower, H. H. (2011). Sustainable development through service learning: a pedagogical framework and case example in a third world context. *Academy of Management Learning & Education*, *10*(1), 58–76.

Cummings, S., & Bridgman, T. (2016). The limits and possibilities of history: how a wider, deeper, and more engaged understanding of business history can foster innovative thinking. *Academy of Management Learning & Education*, *15*(2), 250–267. doi:10.5465/amle.2014.0373.

Deer, S., & Zarestky, J. (2017). Balancing profit and people: corporate social responsibility in business education. *Journal of Management Education*, *41*(5), 727–749.

Fischlmayr, I., Lähteenmäki, S., & Saarinen, E. (2007). Cultural differences in the role of

trust in virtual multicultural teams. In *3rd colloquium of the European Group of Organizational Studies in Vienna, Austria*.

García-Rosell, J.-C. (2013). Struggles over corporate social responsibility meanings in teaching practices: the case of hybrid problem-based learning. *Management Learning*, *44*(5), 537–555. doi:10.1177/1350507612451228.

Gearty, M. R., Bradbury-Huang, H., & Reason, P. (2015). Learning history in an open system: creating histories for sustainable futures. *Management Learning*, *46*(1), 44–66. doi:10.1177/1350507613501735.

Gherardi, S., & Rodeschini, G. (2016). Caring as a collective knowledgeable doing: about concern and being concerned. *Management Learning*, *47*(3), 266–284. doi:10.1177/1350507615610030.

Goleman, D. (1996). *Vital lies, simple truths: the psychology of self deception*. New York: Simon and Schuster.

Hanson, W. R., Moore, J. R., Bachleda, C., Canterbury, A., Franco Jr, C., Marion, A., & Schreiber, C. (2017). Theory of moral development of business students: case studies in Brazil, North America, and Morocco. *Academy of Management Learning & Education*, *16*(3), 393–414. doi.5465/amle.2014.312.

Heizmann, H., & Liu, H. (2018). Becoming green, becoming leaders: identity narratives in sustainability leadership development. *Management Learning*, *49*(1), 40–58. doi:10.1177/1350507617725189.

Hibbert, P., & Cunliffe, A. (2015). Responsible management: engaging moral reflexive practice through threshold concepts. *Journal of Business Ethics*, *127*(1), 177–188.

International Journal of Management Education (2018). *The International Journal of Management Education*. Retrieved on September 10, 2018 from www.journals.elsevier.com/the-international-journal-of-management-education.

Journal of Management Education (2018). *Description*. Retrieved on September 10, 2018 from https://au.sagepub.com/en-gb/oce/journal/journal-management-education#description.

Kassinis, G., & Panayiotou, A. (2017). Website stories in times of distress. *Management Learning*, *48*(4), 397–415. doi:10.1177/1350507617690684.

Klapper, R. G., & Farber, V. A. (2016). In Alain Gibb's footsteps: evaluating alternative approaches to sustainable enterprise education (SEE). *International Journal of Management Education*, *14*(3), 422–439.

Köhler, T., Fischlmayr, I., Lainema, T., & Saarinen, E. (2013). Bringing the world into our classrooms: the benefits of engaging students in an international business simulation. In Charles. W. and Patrick B. (Eds.), *Increasing student engagement and retention using classroom technologies: classroom response systems and mediated discourse technologies* (Cutting-Edge Technologies in Higher Education, Vol. 6 Part E, pp. 163–198). Sheffield: Emerald.

Koris, R., Örtenblad, A., & Ojala, T. (2017). From maintaining the status quo to promoting free thinking and inquiry: business students' perspective on the purpose of business school teaching. *Management Learning*, *48*(2), 174–186. doi:10.1177/1350507616668480.

Louw, J. (2015). 'Paradigm change' or no real change at all? A critical reading of the UN Principles for responsible management education. *Journal of Management Education*, *39*(2), 184–208.

Management Learning (2018). *About this journal*. Retrieved on September 10, 2018 from http://journals.sagepub.com/home/mlq.

Management Teaching Review (2018). *About this journal*. Retrieved on September 10, 2018 from http://journals.sagepub.com/home/mtr.

Mangan, A., Kelemen, M., & Moffat, S. (2016). Animating the classroom: pedagogical responses to internationalisation. *Management Learning*, *47*(3), 285–304. doi:10.1177/1350507615598908.

McGrath, J. E. (1995). Methodology matters: doing research in the behavioral and social sciences. In Baecker, R. M., Grudin, J., Buxton, W. A. S., & Greenberg, S. (Eds.), *Readings in human–computer interaction: toward the year 2000* (2nd ed.) (pp. 152–169). San Francisco, CA: Morgan Kaufman.

Mirvis, P. (2008). Executive development through consciousness-raising experiences. *Academy of Management Learning & Education*, *7*(2), 173–188.

Montiel, I., Antolin-Lopez, R., & Gallo, P. J. (2018). Emotions and sustainability: a literary genre-based framework for environmental sustainability management education. *Academy of Management Learning & Education*, *17*(2), 155–183. doi:10.5465/amle.2016.0042.

Page, M., Grisoni, L., & Turner, A. (2014). Dreaming fairness and re-imagining equality and diversity through participative aesthetic inquiry. *Management Learning*, *45*(5), 577–592. doi:10.1177/1350507613486425.

Pless, N. M., Maak, T., & Stahl, G. K. (2011). Developing responsible global leaders through international service-learning programs: the Ulysses experience. *Academy of Management Learning & Education*, *10*(2), 237–260.

Roberts, F., Thomas, C. H., Novicevic, M. M., Ammeter, A., Garner, B., Johnson, P., & Popoola, I. (2018). Integrated moral conviction theory of student cheating: an empirical test. *Journal of Management Education*, *42*(1), 104–134.

Simons, L., & Cleary, B. (2006). The influence of service learning on students' personal and social development. *College Teaching*, *54*(4), 307–319.

Smith, I. H., & Woodworth, W. P. (2012). Developing social entrepreneurs and social innovators: a social identity and self-efficacy approach. *Academy of Management Learning & Education*, *11*(3), 390–407.

Sutherland, I. A. N., Gosling, J. R., & Jelinek, J. (2015). Aesthetics of power: why teaching about power is easier than learning for power, and what business schools could do about it. *Academy of Management Learning & Education*, *14*(4), 607–624. doi:10.5465/amle.2014.0179.

Tomkins, L., & Ulus, E. (2015). Is narcissism undermining critical reflection in our business schools? *Academy of Management Learning & Education*, *14*(4), 595–606.

Tomkins, L., & Ulus, E. (2016). 'Oh, was that "experiential learning"?!' Spaces, synergies and surprises with Kolb's learning cycle. *Management Learning*, *47*(2), 158–178.

Toubiana, M. (2014). Business pedagogy for social justice? An exploratory investigation of business faculty perspectives of social justice in business education. *Management Learning*, *45*(1), 81–102. doi:10.1177/1350507612454097.

Tyran, K. L. (2017). Transforming students into global citizens: international service learning and PRME. *International Journal of Management Education*, *15*(2), 162–171.

Warhurst, R., & Black, K. (2017). What do managers know? Wisdom and manager identity in later career. *Management Learning*, *48*(4), 416–430. doi:10.1177/1350 507616679346.

Warwick, P., Wyness, L., & Corway, H. (2017). 'Think of the future': Managing educational change from students' perspectives of an undergraduate sustainable business programme. *International Journal of Management Education*, *15*(2), 192–204.

Wright, A. L., & Gilmore, A. (2012). Threshold concepts and conceptions: student learning in introductory management courses. *Journal of Management Education*, *36*(5), 614–635.

Wright, S., Forray, J. M., & Lund Dean, K. (2019). From advocacy to accountability in experiential learning practices. *Management Learning*, *50*(3), 261–281.

Yorio, P. L., & Ye, F. (2012). A meta-analysis on the effects of service-learning on the social, personal, and cognitive outcomes of learning. *Academy of Management Learning & Education*, *11*(1), 9–27.

REFERENCES FOR RESEARCH METHODS CODING

AMLE

Aragon-Correa, J. A., Marcus, A. A., Rivera, J. E., & Kenworthy, A. L. (2017). Sustainability management teaching resources and the challenge of balancing planet, people, and profits. *Academy of Management Learning & Education*, *16*(3), 469–483. doi:10.5465/ amle.2017.0180.

Arieli, S., Sagiv, L., & Cohen-Shalem, E. (2016). Values in business schools: the role of self-selection and socialization. *Academy of Management Learning & Education*, *15*(3), 493–507. doi:10.5465/amle.2014.0064.

Baden, D. (2014). Look on the bright side: a comparison of positive and negative role models in business ethics education. *Academy of Management Learning & Education*, *13*(2), 154–170. doi:10.5465/amle.2012.0251.

Butler, N., Delaney, H., & Spoelstra, S. (2017). The gray zone: questionable research practices in the business school. *Academy of Management Learning & Education*, *16*(1), 94–109. doi:10.5465/amle.2015.0201.

Cummings, S., & Bridgman, T. (2016). The limits and possibilities of history: how a wider, deeper, and more engaged understanding of business history can foster innovative thinking. *Academy of Management Learning & Education*, *15*(2), 250–267. doi:10.5465/amle.2014.0373.

Hanson, W. R., & Moore, J. R. (2014). Business student moral influencers: unseen opportunities for development? *Academy of Management Learning & Education*, *13*(4), 525–546. doi:10.5465/amle.2012. 0325.

Hanson, W. R., Moore, J. R., Bachleda, C., Canterbury, A., Franco Jr, C., Marion, A., & Schreiber, C. (2017). Theory of moral development of business students: case studies in Brazil, North America, and Morocco. *Academy of Management Learning & Education*, *16*(3), 393–414. doi:10.5465/ amle.2014.0312.

Montiel, I., Antolin-Lopez, R., & Gallo, P. J. (2018). Emotions and sustainability: a literary genre-based framework for environmental sustainability management education. *Academy of Management Learning & Education*, *17*(2), 155–183. doi:10.5465/ amle.2016.0042.

Rasche, A., Gilbert, D. U., & Schedel, I. (2013). Cross-disciplinary ethics education in MBA programs: rhetoric or reality? *Academy of Management Learning & Education*, *12*, 71–85.

Snelson-Powell, A., Grosvold, J., & Millington, A. (2016). Business school legitimacy and the challenge of sustainability: a fuzzy set analysis of institutional decoupling. *Academy of Management Learning & Education*, *15*(4), 703–723. doi:10.5465/amle. 2015.0307.

Sutherland, I. A. N., Gosling, J. R., & Jelinek, J. (2015). Aesthetics of power: why teaching about power is easier than learning for power, and what business schools could do about it. *Academy of Management Learning & Education*, *14*(4), 607–624. doi:10.5465/ amle.2014.0179.

ML

Burchell, J., Kennedy, S., & Murray, A. (2015). Responsible management education in UK business schools: critically examining the role of the United Nations Principles for Responsible Management Education as a driver for change. *Management Learning, 46*(4), 479–497. doi:10.1177/1350507614549117.

Crevani, L., & Hallin, A. (2017). Performative narcissism: when organizations are made successful, admirable, and unique through narcissistic work. *Management Learning, 48*(4), 431–452. doi:10.1177/1350507617692295.

Dwyer, G., & Hardy, C. (2016). We have not lived long enough: sensemaking and learning from bushfire in Australia. *Management Learning, 47*(1), 45–64. doi:10.1177/1350507615577047.

García-Rosell, J.-C. (2013). Struggles over corporate social responsibility meanings in teaching practices: the case of hybrid problem-based learning. *Management Learning, 44*(5), 537–555. doi:10.1177/1350507612451228.

Gearty, M. R., Bradbury-Huang, H., & Reason, P. (2015). Learning history in an open system: creating histories for sustainable futures. *Management Learning, 46*(1), 44–66. doi:10.1177/1350507613501735.

Gherardi, S., & Murgia, A. (2015). Imagine being asked to evaluate your CEO …: using the constructive controversy approach to teach gender and management in times of economic crisis. *Management Learning, 46*(1), 6–23. doi:10.1177/1350507614549119.

Gherardi, S., & Rodeschini, G. (2016). Caring as a collective knowledgeable doing: about concern and being concerned. *Management Learning, 47*(3), 266–284. doi:10.1177/1350507615610030.

Hawkins, B., Pye, A., & Correia, F. (2017). Boundary objects, power, and learning: the matter of developing sustainable practice in organizations. *Management Learning, 48*(3), 292–310. doi:10.1177/1350507616677199.

Heizmann, H., & Liu, H. (2018). Becoming green, becoming leaders: identity narratives in sustainability leadership development. *Management Learning, 49*(1), 40–58. doi:10.1177/1350507617725189.

Kassinis, G., & Panayiotou, A. (2017). Website stories in times of distress. *Management Learning, 48*(4), 397–415. doi:10.1177/1350507617690684.

Koris, R., Örtenblad, A., & Ojala, T. (2017). From maintaining the status quo to promoting free thinking and inquiry: business students' perspective on the purpose of business school teaching. *Management Learning, 48*(2), 174–186. doi:10.1177/1350507616668480.

Mangan, A., Kelemen, M., & Moffat, S. (2016). Animating the classroom: pedagogical responses to internationalisation. *Management Learning, 47*(3), 285–304. doi:10.1177/1350507615598908.

Millar, J., & Price, M. (2018). Imagining management education: a critique of the contribution of the United Nations PRME to critical reflexivity and rethinking management education. *Management Learning, 49*(3), 346–362. doi:10.1177/1350507618759828.

Page, M., Grisoni, L., & Turner, A. (2014). Dreaming fairness and re-imagining equality and diversity through participative aesthetic inquiry. *Management Learning, 45*(5), 577–592. doi:10.1177/1350507613486425.

Porschitz, E. T., Smircich, L., & Calás, M. B. (2016). Drafting 'foot soldiers': the social organization of the war for talent. *Management Learning, 47*(3), 343–360. doi:10.1177/1350507615598906.

Smolović Jones, S., Smolović Jones, O., Winchester, N., & Grint, K. (2016). Putting the discourse to work: on outlining a praxis of democratic leadership development. *Management Learning, 47*(4), 424–442. doi:10.1177/1350507616631926.

Toubiana, M. (2014). Business pedagogy for social justice? An exploratory investigation of business faculty perspectives of social justice in business education. *Management Learning, 45*(1), 81–102. doi:10.1177/1350507612454097.

Warhurst, R., & Black, K. (2017). What do managers know? Wisdom and manager identity in later career. *Management Learning, 48*(4), 416–430. doi:10.1177/1350507616679346.

Zwack, M., Kraiczy, N. D., von Schlippe, A., & Hack, A. (2016). Storytelling and cultural family value transmission: value perception of stories in family firms. *Management Learning, 47*(5), 590–614. doi:10.1177/1350507616659833.

JME

Bergman, J. Z., Westerman, J. W., Bergman, S. M., Westerman, J., & Daly, J. P. (2014). Narcissism, materialism, and environmental ethics in business students. *Journal of Management Education*, *38*(4), 489–510.

Bruni-Bossio, V., & Willness, C. (2016). The 'Kobayashi Maru' meeting: high-fidelity experiential learning. *Journal of Management Education*, *40*(5), 619–647.

Deer, S., & Zarestky, J. (2017). Balancing profit and people: corporate social responsibility in business education. *Journal of Management Education*, *41*(5), 727–749.

Huster, K., Petrillo, C., O'Malley, G., Glassman, D., Rush, J., & Wasserheit, J. (2017). Global social entrepreneurship competitions: incubators for innovations in global health? *Journal of Management Education*, *41*(2), 249–271.

Kuechler, W., & Stedham, Y. (2018). Management education and transformational learning: the integration of mindfulness in an MBA course. *Journal of Management Education*, *42*(1), 8–33.

Ledley, F. D., & Holt, S. S. (2014). Learning objectives and content of science curricula for undergraduate management education. *Journal of Management Education*, *38*(1), 86–113.

Louw, J. (2015). 'Paradigm change' or no real change at all? A critical reading of the UN Principles for responsible management education. *Journal of Management Education*, *39*(2), 184–208.

McDonald, L. M. (2013). Using student-constructed cases to investigate crises. *Journal of Management Education*, *37*(1), 115–134.

O'Brien, K., Wittmer, D., & Ebrahimi, B. P. (2017). Behavioral ethics in practice: integrating service learning into a graduate business ethics course. *Journal of Management Education*, *41*(4), 599–616.

Parris, D. L., & McInnis-Bowers, C. (2017). Business not as usual: developing socially conscious entrepreneurs and intrapreneurs. *Journal of Management Education*, *41*(5), 687–726.

Rennie, K. D., Byrum, K., Tidwell, M., & Chitkara, A. K. (2018). Strategic communication in MBA curricula: a qualitative study of student outcomes. *Journal of Management Education*, *42*(5), 594–617. doi: 1052 562918774593.

Roberts, F., Thomas, C. H., Novicevic, M. M., Ammeter, A., Garner, B., Johnson, P., & Popoola, I. (2018). Integrated moral conviction theory of student cheating: an empirical test. *Journal of Management Education*, *42*(1), 104–134.

Sroufe, R., Sivasubramaniam, N., Ramos, D., & Saiia, D. (2015). Aligning the PRME: how study abroad nurtures responsible leadership. *Journal of Management Education*, *39*(2), 244–275.

Tomlin, K. A., Metzger, M. L., Bradley-Geist, J., & Gonzalez-Padron, T. (2017). Are students blind to their ethical blind spots? An exploration of why ethics education should focus on self-perception biases. *Journal of Management Education*, *41*(4), 539–574.

Vidal, N., Smith, R., & Spetic, W. (2015). Designing and teaching business & society courses from a threshold concept approach. *Journal of Management Education*, *39*(4), 497–530.

Volkema, R. J., & Kapoutsis, I. (2016). From restaurants to board rooms: how initiating negotiations teaches management principles and theory. *Journal of Management Education*, *40*(1), 76–101.

Walker, J. L. (2018). Do methods matter in global leadership development? Testing the global leadership development ecosystem conceptual model. *Journal of Management Education*, *42*(2), 239–264.

IJME

Annan-Diab, F., & Molinari, C. (2017). Interdisciplinarity: practical approach to advancing education for sustainability and for the sustainable development goals. *International Journal of Management Education*, *15*(2), 73–83.

Awaysheh, A., & Bonfiglio, D. (2017). Leveraging experiential learning to incorporate social entrepreneurship in MBA programs: a case study. *International Journal of Management Education*, *15*(2), 332–349.

Beddewela, E., Warin, C., Hesselden, F., & Coslet, A. (2017). Embedding responsible management education – staff, student and institutional perspectives. *International Journal of Management Education*, *15*(2), 263–279.

Borges, J. C., Cezarino, L. O., Ferreira, T. C., Sala, O. T. M., Unglaub, D. L., & Caldana, A. C. F. (2017). Student organizations and communities of practice: actions for the 2030 Agenda for Sustainable Development. *International Journal of Management Education*, *15*(2), 172–182.

Borges, J. C., Ferreira, T. C., de Oliveira, M. S. B., Macini, N., & Caldana, A. C. F. (2017). Hidden curriculum in student organizations: learning, practice, socialization and responsible management in a business school. *International Journal of Management Education*, *15*(2), 153–161.

Burga, R., Leblanc, J., & Rezania, D. (2017). Analysing the effects of teaching approach on engagement, satisfaction and future time perspective among students in a course on CSR. *International Journal of Management Education*, *15*(2), 306–317.

Carreira, F., Aguiar, A. C., Onça, F., & Monzoni, M. (2017). The Celsius Game: an experiential activity on management education simulating the complex challenges for the two-degree climate change target. *International Journal of Management Education*, *15*(2), 350–361.

Cicmil, S., Gough, G., & Hills, S. (2017). Insights into responsible education for sustainable development: the case of UWE, Bristol. *The International Journal of Management Education*, *15*(2), 293–305.

Décamps, A., Barbat, G., Carteron, J. C., Hands, V., & Parkes, C. (2017). Sulitest: a collaborative initiative to support and assess sustainability literacy in higher education. *International Journal of Management Education*, *15*(2), 138–152.

Greenberg, D. N., Deets, S., Erzurumlu, S., Hunt, J., Manwaring, M., Rodgers, V., & Swanson, E. (2017). Signing to living PRME: learning from a journey towards responsible management education. *International Journal of Management Education*, *15*(2), 205–218.

Jagger, S., & Volkman, R. (2014). Helping students to see for themselves that ethics matters. *International Journal of Management Education*, *12*(2), 177–185.

Klapper, R. G., & Farber, V. A. (2016). In Alain Gibb's footsteps: evaluating alternative approaches to sustainable enterprise education (SEE). *International Journal of Management Education*, *14*(3), 422–439.

Kolb, M., Fröhlich, L., & Schmidpeter, R. (2017). Implementing sustainability as the new normal: responsible management education – from a private business school's perspective. *International Journal of Management Education*, *15*(2), 280–292.

Ortiz, D., & Huber-Heim, K. (2017). From information to empowerment: teaching sustainable business development by enabling an experiential and participatory problem-solving process in the classroom. *International Journal of Management Education*, *15*(2), 318–331.

Rive, J., Bonnet, M., Parmentier, C., Pelazzo-Plat, V., & Pignet-Fall, L. (2017). A contribution to the laying of foundations for dialogue between socially responsible management schools. *International Journal of Management Education*, *15*(2), 238–248.

Ross, J., Valenzuela, M., Intindola, M., & Flinchbaugh, C. (2017). Preparing potential leaders: facilitating a learning experience on LMX and fairness in the workplace. *International Journal of Management Education*, *15*(1), 84–97.

Tyran, K. L. (2017). Transforming students into global citizens: international service learning and PRME. *International Journal of Management Education*, *15*(2), 162–171.

Warwick, P., Wyness, L., & Conway, H. (2017). 'Think of the future': Managing educational change from students' perspectives of an undergraduate sustainable business programme. *International Journal of Management Education*, *15*(2), 192–204.

32

A Pragmatist Approach to Responsible Management Learning and Education

Christopher Gohl

LITERATURE REVIEW: PRAGMATISM FOR RESPONSIBLE MANAGEMENT LEARNING AND EDUCATION?

Responsible management and responsible management education are taken to be inclusive conceptions of managerial and educational practice shaped by ethics, responsibility and sustainability (Laasch & Conaway, 2015; Laasch & Moosmayer, 2015; Rasche & Gilbert, 2015). From a pragmatist perspective on responsible management that is recounted here, ethics, responsibility and sustainability are not separate domains but rather integral and related aspects of a certain conception of human life and conduct employed by pragmatists. Fundamentally, pragmatism is a method of inquiry. Its foundation is an epistemology of relational holism that rejects the duality between theory and practice, body and mind, intellect and senses, and other such distinctions. Pragmatism's unique epistemology has direct consequences for its understanding of ethics, responsibility and sustainability. Epistemologically understood, and roughly speaking at the outset of this inquiry, life is a process of learning, at once personal and communal; and learning is the inherently ethical intelligent exercise of responsibility in response to (social) expectations and (environmental) challenges, with the aim and reward of sustaining the continuity of a harmonious life experience. In consequence, learning means becoming ethically responsible for the sustainable development of life amongst its stakeholders.

As the literature review that comprises the first section of this chapter reveals, this full and comprehensive perspective of pragmatism on responsible management has not yet impressed itself upon the debate. As any growth of understanding builds on existing knowledge, though, it is conducive to such growth to zoom in on pragmatist conceptions in the field of business ethics; on pragmatist inspirations to the theories of learning at use in the discourse on responsible management learning; and on existing building blocks of a pragmatist argument on sustainability. The second section of the chapter will reconstruct the epistemological foundation and conceptions of pragmatism that illuminate and smooth out the first rough sketch given above on the interrelation of epistemology, ethics, learning, sustainability and that fundamental and consequential conception of responsibility that pervades all aspects. The outlook of the final section will, amongst other issues, feature the central function of responsibility for sustainable development.

First, the chapter recounts a fruitful pragmatist debate in business ethics. In the field of responsible management learning, the presence of pragmatism is strong at first sight, as various theories of learning claim roots in pragmatism. However, a closer look reveals, that, as in business ethics, pragmatism has often been more an inspiration than a fully developed program. The same is true of potential pragmatist contributions to the sustainability discourse.

Pragmatist Ethics: More than Overcoming the Separation Fallacy

In the past two decades, business ethics has taken a stronger interest in pragmatism, mainly in John Dewey, Charles Sanders Peirce and William James (Nahser, 1997; Wicks & Freeman, 1998; Margolis, 1998; Rosenthal & Buchholz, 2000; Fontrodona, 2002). This interest in pragmatist business ethics is closely related to the rise of stakeholder theory, especially because its leading pioneers, R. Edward Freeman and his colleagues, inquired and found roots of their thinking in pragmatism (Freeman, Harrison, Wicks, Parmar & De Colle, 2010). As Freeman et al. have extensively shown, pragmatism not only supports the general criticism of neoclassical models (2010: 63–79), it also offers a way out of a central problem of business ethics and responsible management – the 'separation

fallacy', according to which theories of business treat business and ethics as different realms (Freeman et al., 2010: 6).

From a pragmatist perspective, the early stakeholder theorists' reading of pragmatism from Wicks and Freeman (1998) to Freeman et al. (2010) may not have done full justice to classical pragmatism (Taylor & Bell 2013), a shortcoming that has since been addressed and is being mitigated (Jensen & Sandström, 2013; Parmar, Phillips & Freeman, 2017). The pragmatist understanding of participative inquiry and problem resolution not only sheds light on ethical aspects of managerial processes of value creation and trade among stakeholders, but the meliorative intention of pragmatism conceives of economic actors as change agents for a better world. It thus insists on reflection not only on the ethical aspects and means, but on the very purpose of meaningful conduct in business as part of leading better lives, and on the interdependence and continuity of ends and means (Jacobs, 2004; Parmar et al., 2017; Taylor & Bell, 2013: 165). As organizational (business) purposes can only be achieved cooperatively with, or possibly in conflict with stakeholders, responsibility – framed not as 'corporate social responsibility' but as 'company stakeholder responsibility' – becomes a central principle in stakeholder theory, marking its fundamental disagreement with shareholder capitalism as espoused by Milton Friedman (Freeman et al., 2010).

Just how one is to inquire into moral problems is subject of the pragmatist approach to ethical business decision-making (McVea, 2007). Pragmatist inquiry into moral problems can be taught in the classroom (Nahser & Ruhe, 2001), arguably to a point of developing 'wisdom as a habit' (Statler, 2014). For Dewey, only a curriculum and pedagogy that nurture moral character deserved to be described as education (Prakash, 1995). Insofar as Dewey can be said to be concerned with the 'naturalization of the idealist ethics of self-realization' (Westbrook, 1991: 152), he aims at the cultivation of one's self, providing seeds of a mature model of virtue ethics (Carden, 2006; Teehan, 1995).

In conclusion, pragmatism proves, far from misrepresentations as an ethically indifferent, merely instrumental and utility-oriented approach, to possess emancipatory potential in much the same vein as critical theory (Visser, 2019). It may be strengthened by looking further into the work of Jane Addams, 'the first practicing pragmatist', and perhaps the most intriguing, but also the most neglected pioneer among the classical pragmatists (Shields, Whetsell & Hanks, 2013). The pragmatist approach to building ethical capacity in the classroom (Lynch, 2017) also shines through in various approaches to management learning that primarily build on the pragmatist philosophy of education, rather than on pragmatist ethics.

Pragmatist Inspirations in the Discourse on Responsible Management Learning

A philosophy of education is a central effort of classical pragmatism, and the aim of education is to enable individuals to keep learning, 'the object and reward' of which is 'continued capacity for growth' (Dewey, MW9: 107[1]). Pragmatist founding fathers William James (1842–1910), Charles Sanders Peirce (1839–1914), John Dewey (1859–1952) and, to a lesser known but important degree, George Herbert Mead (1863–1931) had built an empiricist conception of learning deep into and around their understanding of experience. 'Learning by doing' is 'learning through intelligent action', where knowledge becomes not the resource of a subject before an object but a relation within the continuity of experience (Fourcade & Go, 2012: 199–200). Vince and Reynolds portray '[t]he philosopher John Dewey [as] arguably the founding father of our modern conceptualization of reflection in management learning', drawing a line from Dewey to Lindeman to Kolb's Learning Cycle and to Donald Schön's work

on the manager as reflective practitioner (Vince & Reynolds, 2009: 89; Schön, 2005).

This basic approach of pragmatism has contributed to various discourses within the field of learning in management education. Pragmatist conceptions of learning have inspired various fields of management research and managerial practice: organizational learning, the especially influential theory of experiential learning of David Kolb, service learning, and learning for sustainability.

Journals within the field of management learning have professed the inspiration they have drawn from pragmatism. As editors of the *Journal of Management Education* (*JME*), Lund Dean and Forray have declared the journal's allegiance to a Deweyan approach to teaching and learning that ultimately enacts 'Dewey's emphasis on experience in learning' (Lund Dean & Forray, 2018: 699). Assessing the far-reaching impact of Chris Argyris on the journal *Academy of Management Learning and Education* (*AMLE*) in an editorial obituary marking his passing in 2013, editor Jean M. Bartunek reminded readers that Argyris and his long-time research partner Donald Schön had always thought of as practitioners, in their own words, 'not as passive recipients of expertise, but as Deweyan inquirers' (Bartunek, 2014: 1).

Organizational learning

John Dewey's views on learning from experience and through social interactions have earned him recognition as a classical source in the field of organizational learning (Easterby-Smith & Lyles, 2011: 9), with certain strands of the discussion such as individual learning theory (Argyris & Schön, 1996) or social learning theory (Elkjaer, 2004) turning Dewey's insights into pragmatist contributions to the field. Brandi and Elkjaer have traced the impact of John Dewey's pragmatism on founding figures of organizational learning such as Herbert

Simon, Chris Argyris and Donald Schön (Brandi & Elkjaer, 2013). Likewise, Dewey is the main inspiration for Elkjaer's understanding of organizational learning, which she has called the 'Third Way', 'defined as the development of experience and knowledge by inquiry (or reflective thinking) in social worlds held together by commitment' (Elkjaer, 2004: 419).

Experiential learning

It is also often taken as an article of faith that the legacy of the pragmatist founding fathers lives on in David Kolb's influential experiential learning theory (Yamazaki & Kayes, 2004: 363). Kolb himself has based his theory on his analysis of John Dewey, Kurt Lewin and Jean Piaget (Kolb, 1984), later elevating William James to the status of a foundational scholar (Kolb, 2014: 23–24). From a pragmatist point of view, though, Kolb's concept of phases of immediate, concrete experience misses elements of continuous reflection and interaction that are crucial for Dewey's conception of learning, which makes his approach 'phonetically close', though 'theoretically and epistemologically quite far apart', indeed a testimony to 'psychological reductionism that Dewey considered a misinterpretation of his antidualist conception of experience' (Miettinen, 2000: 70). Kolb's ultimately unconvincing attempt to reply to Miettinen's critique draws on James (Kolb, 2014: 56–59). This is not the place to argue these points further.

Service learning

It is sometimes argued that service learning is a community-based variant of the experiential learning approach inspired by Kolb (Pless, Maak & Stahl, 2011). However, John Dewey's educational philosophy ought to be counted as the main influence of the modern pedagogical practice and movement of service learning (Giles & Eyler, 1994; Ord & Leather, 2011; Pacho, 2015; Speck & Hoppe, 2004; Tai-Seale, 2000). Literature reviews on the effects of service learning (Pless et al., 2011: 243; Yorio & Ye, 2012; Fougère, Solitander & Maheshwari, 2019) and of experiential learning (Walker, Dyck, Zhang & Starke, 2019: 203) demonstrate that these pedagogies contribute greatly to different aspects of an engaged, ethical, or responsible conduct of management students.

Pragmatism on Sustainability: Learning for Sustainable Business Practices

Sustainability is a diverse field of research and practice. In contrast to business ethics and theories of learning, a comprehensive pragmatistic discourse has yet to emerge on sustainability. A literature review reveals clusters of arguments that could become building blocks of a more consequential pragmatist theory on sustainable development. A starting point may be the argument that managing or leading for sustainability requires the craftsmanship of reflective practitioners who are capable of integrating different forms of knowledge as they fit specific situations and goals (De Graaf, 2019). Preparing graduates to be such reflective promoters and enactors of responsible and sustainable business practices, however, raises a few new challenges.

For one, the challenge to inform and create sustainable attitudes, commitments and lifestyles in management students really extends to the fluid, yet habitual, plurality of patterns, preferences, morals, identities and relationships that shape (un)sustainable consumption and their radical or gradual change (Hiller & Woodall, 2019; Painter, Hibbert & Cooper, 2018). That involves, secondly, an understanding of societal change and the role of business as (entrepreneurial) change agent. Pragmatists place no trust in adopting a *final or fixed telos* for effecting changes towards sustainability as a future state. Rather, the pragmatist argument opts for a re-dedication of *intentions* towards 'a desirable, prized future that offers a response to the problems and challenges we face in the present' (Painter et al., 2018: 888), a procedural inclination that turns 'sustainability' into 'sustainable development'. For businesses, that requires an entrepreneurial and experimental reflection of purposes and means of businesses models in the light of sustainable value creation (Davies and Doherty, 2019; Osorio-Vega, 2018, Surie & Ashley, 2008). York (2009) offers solace: 'Under a pragmatic approach to ethics, the choice for sustainability becomes self-evident for business performance and moral reasons.'

However – third challenge – the freedom to reflect upon the purposes of business may not be a practice encouraged by dominant economic and business theories. Moosmayer, Waddock, Wang, Hühn, Dierksmeier and Gohl (2018) argue that, in contrast to a pragmatist approach, ubiquitous neoclassical theories and the mechanistic models and motifs of the past century of economic thinking may be epistemologically and methodologically unfit or downright harmful to responsible and sustainable business conduct (Dierksmeier, 2016; Painter-Morland 2014). Where and how, then – fourth challenge – do students learn to engage in the relational transactions, collaborative partnerships and hybrid alliances so instrumental to sustainable change (Gillett, Loader, Doherty & Scott, 2019; Lorino, 2018)?

At last, learning for sustainability, not surprisingly, already is a stronghold of pragmatist argument. Building on pioneer work by Nahser (1997, 2009; Nahser & Ruhe, 2001), Kelley and Nahser (2014) lay out a pragmatist agenda for implementing the PRME in the service of developing sustainable strategies: '(1) it must confront the cognitional myth that knowing is like looking, (2) it must move beyond mere analysis to systems thinking, and (3) it must transition from a values-neutral stance to a values-driven stance'. Similarly, Prakash (1995) builds on Dewey's holistic approach to attack divisive specialization and argue for ecological literacy and '[moral] education for postmodern sustainability'. Van Poeck, Östman and Block (2018) likewise draw on Dewey to develop 'an analytical tool that allows to open-up the black box of learning in sustainability transitions'. In the context of education for sustainability (EfS), Earl, VanWynsberghe, Walter and Straka (2018) build on Dewey's theory of behavior change as 'applied to educative experiences based on habit disruption and real-world learning, leading to creativity in the formation of new habits', effectively coming full circle to educate reflective practitioners.

PRESENT: RESPONSIBLE MANAGEMENT EDUCATION FROM A PRAGMATIST PERSPECTIVE

This section considers, first, how the pragmatist perspective on responsible management education is fundamentally shaped by the *pragmatist epistemology of experience*. Secondly, it distinguishes between *learning* which requires reflection of experience from *education* which ensures that individuals can learn to partake in the social reflection of experience, thus becoming members of their communities and sustaining their continuity. Thirdly, it shows how learning, as a process of growth, relies on the *freedom of intelligence*, while enhancing *freedom as the power of self-directed conduct and purposive action*. Lastly, it shows how intelligent self-directed activity inherently entails the responsive habit to consider the consequences of one's conduct on others, the world, and one's self, thus profiling the exercise of *responsibility* as an inherent, central, and consequential feature of learning so conceived. All of these conceptions have consequences for the pragmatist perspective on responsible management education.

Pragmatist Epistemology: From Experience to Experimental Inquiry

Rejection of dualism

As a matter of epistemology, pragmatism rejects the separations of dualistic conception that have marked Western thinking from Plato and the stoics to Descartes, Locke and Kant, such as between mind and body, spirit and flesh, faith and reason, reason and emotion, intellect and senses, subjective and objective, rational and empirical, fact and value, or duty and desire (Kaplan, 1980: x). The comprehensive understanding of pragmatist pedagogy (and ethics) relies on psychology (Anacker, 2018) as well as sociology (Nungesser & Pettenkofer, 2018), together illuminating the constitutive continuity of the inner and the outer dimensions of a learner's natural dispositions here and the functions, subject and context of learning there. Thus, two other approaches to education are rejected – the formation from without as well as the targeted development of a supposed inner nature of the learner (MW9: 75–78). Embracing the continuity, rather than the duality, of goal and process, pragmatism rejects the idea that education is a process of growth of certain qualities towards pre-determined fixed goals of perfection, such as they may be divined by prophets, argued for by philosophers, set by the example of elders, or determined by teachers of management classes. Rather, the process of learning (and of education) relies on that interaction of inner disposition and outer circumstances that pragmatists call 'experience'.

Experience as interaction

Experience is a central as well as a contested concept within pragmatism (Volbers, 2018: 78). It is conceived of as at once embodied, situated and socialized; and it encompasses material, mental and aesthetic factors such as vagueness and determination, conflict and reorganization (Joas, 1996; Volbers,

2018). Dewey defined experience as 'a matter of the interaction of organism with its environment'. This environment 'is human as well as physical' and 'includes the materials of tradition and institutions as well as local surroundings'. The organism, for its part, 'brings with it through its own structure, native and acquired, forces that play a part in the interaction'. The interaction, as an effort of coordination by the acting organism, has an active and a passive side: 'The self acts as well as undergoes, and its undergoings are not impressions stamped upon an inert wax but depend upon the way the organism reacts and responds' (LW10: 251). Conceived as a reciprocal interaction that involves feedback between organism and environment, 'experience is primarily an active–passive affair; it is not primarily cognitive' (MW9: 147).

Experience as raw material of learning

Such experience becomes the raw material of learning, and ultimately, of education. Dewey's argument is concisely captured in a motto often attributed to, but likely never authored by him: 'we do not learn from experience; we learn from reflecting on experience' (Lagueux, 2014). Deliberate reflection means to organize experience by engaging with 'all the objects, ideas, and principles which enter as resources or obstacles into the continuous intentional pursuit of a course of action' which we undertake (MW9: 145).

> To 'learn from experience' is to make a backward and forward connection between what we do to things and what we enjoy or suffer from things in consequence. Under such conditions, doing becomes a trying; an experiment with the world to find out what it is like; the undergoing becomes instruction – discovery of the connection of things. (MW9: 147)

Intelligent experimental inquiry

As learners face their environment, this either constitutes an unproblematic situation, resulting in a harmonious experience; or a problematic situation marked by ambiguities, unresolved tensions, or open conflict that triggers a quest for the certainty of a satisfying, harmonious experience. The contingency of the situation gives rise to creative (intelligent, deliberate, innovating) action (Festl, 2018), consummating in an experimental process of inquiry, transformation and reflective learning (Miettinen, 2000: 66–67). Experiments are active, intelligent and rationally controlled forms of experience. Its fruit is better knowledge of the factors of a given situation, driving individual growth and social learning up to the point of experimentalism as a central mode of democracy (Serrano Zamora, 2018).

Experimental inquiry is driven not so much by reason but by intelligence. According to Dewey, philosophy had long seen reason as an independent source of moral authority, 'a faculty of insight into universals, laws, and principles' (Edel & Flower, 1985: xxiii–xxv). In the naturalist account of ethics offered by Dewey and Tufts (LW7), the centrality of reason was substituted by the centrality of a related, but different concept – intelligence. 'Reason thus becomes Intelligence – the power of using past experience to shape and transform future experience. It is constructive and creative', Dewey wrote (MW11: 346). While both reason and intelligence 'imply considering a proposed or performed act as a whole, in its relations, and with a view especially to consequences, intelligence involves not only empirical observation on past experience, already formulated concepts, and deduction, but "that rarer quality which in the presence of a situation discerns a meaning not obvious, suggests an idea, 'injustice,' to interpret the situation"' (Edel & Flower, 1985: xxiv, citing Tufts, 1917: 364).

The notion of intelligent experimentation infuses Dewey's Logic of Inquiry (LW12). Here, Dewey defines inquiry as 'the controlled or directed transformation of an indeterminate situation into one that is so determinate in constituent distinctions and relations as to convert the elements of

the original situation into a unified whole' (MW12: 108). The two main components of the inquiry are ideas and facts: 'Ideas are operational in that they instigate and direct further operations of observation; they are proposals and plans for acting upon existing conditions to bring new facts to light and to organize all the selected facts into a coherent whole.' Facts, on the other hand, 'are selected and described [...] for a purpose, namely the statement of the problem involved in such a way that its material both indicates a meaning relevant to resolution of the difficulty and serves to test its worth and validity' (MW12: 116). From a pragmatist perspective, values are a subset of such operational ideas. They prescribe a certain unified effect of conduct that is not just (through impulse) desired, but, all experience considered (through reflection), judged as desirable (Joas, 2000).

Ideas for action, taken as directions of consequential action, are tested by manipulating the facts of a given problem, resulting not only in the change of the problematic situation, but also in the knowledge of the consequence of an idea that was put to action (Serrano Zamora, 2018: 81–82). In Dewey's model, experimental and reflective problem resolution includes all steps from analysis to implementation: the qualification of a situation as problematic, the experimental and rational test of a hypothesis, the reflexive establishment of a relationship between conception and reality, and the construction of judgment (Krüger, 2000: 212–227). In such a dialectical process, a problematic situation is purposefully transformed until it is deemed satisfactory.

The inquiry may either be conducted individually, or it is a social inquiry of a community of inquirers who understand themselves to be affected by a shared problem that none of them can solve by herself. It is a prototypical participatory process where participants go through a whole cycle of problem resolution together. They do so in a cooperative, experimental manner. Such social inquiry aims to reach agreement in regard to consequences, and thus to jointly confirm or correct results or outcomes of action (Krüger, 2000; Visser, 2019: 47). As these processes inquire into shared problems, they often address problems of a social, political, ethical and moral nature. Moral reflection is the *'activity called forth and directed by ideas of value or worth, where the values concerned are so mutually incompatible as to require consideration and selection before an overt action is entered upon'* (Dewey & Tufts, MW5: 194, emphasis in original; Westbrook, 1991: 153). This raises the question of the genesis of shared insights, conventions and habits, to which we now turn.

The rise of habits to character, customary morality, ethical inquiry and institutions

Inquiry is a creative learning process that involves adaptation of the self as well as transformation of the environment. Through repetition in similar and typical situations, successful patterns of action that restore and avouch equilibrium between the self and the environment become habits, relieving us of the need for constant conscious reflection (Joas, 1996). In their first edition of Ethics in 1908, Dewey and Tufts had conceived of shared social habits and their normative import as inherently conservative, cohesive customs that signaled the authoritative approval of individual conduct by a group (MW5: 7, 54–73). As such, the habits of customary morality were to be overcome by reflective morality. In the second edition of Ethics in 1932, Dewey and Tufts reconstruct these shared social habits differently (LW7). Habit now 'gives social shape to impulse', while intelligence is exercised to make sense of conflicting habits and 'disrupt unsatisfying habits (…) Habits constitute the self, character is the interpenetration of habits', and even the notions of reason and its updated iterations of reflection and intelligence may themselves be understood as constituted by certain habits and customs of perception (Edel & Flower, 1985: xxii).

As an inheritance of purposive conduct that has proven valuable in certain prior situations, customs are shared traditional habits that regulate our behavior and define our conceptions of the world. Not necessarily as a drag and determination of the past, though – just until inquiry into new circumstances may prove these habits no longer serve a continuous purpose and should be discontinued. To Dewey 'ethical inquiry is the use of reflective intelligence to revise our judgments in light of the consequences of acting on them', with value judgments as 'tools for satisfactorily redirecting conduct when habits fail' (Anderson, 2019). Individuals into which education has instilled habits of independent inquiry and experimentation, may through such inquiry change old habits and develop new habits which predispose them to certain choices in certain situations, and which may be cultivated as virtues (Teehan, 1995). Virtues, in that sense, are values that have become so habitualized and embodied that their prescriptions for desirable conduct permeate and organize one's actions in their entirety. Likewise, pragmatists reconstruct (political, but also economic) institutions as social habits that (1) have emerged in past problematic situations through intentional inquiry (not: rational design), and (2) now regulate social interactions, either as general law or in the form of social conventions (Bromley, 2006; Beckert, 2009).

The Aim of Education: Growth Through the Reconstruction of Experience Adds Powers of Control

We learn not from experience, but from reflection on it. Education is the social process of ensuring that individuals can partake not only in the continuous social reflection of experience as members of their communities, but that they participate 'in the social consciousness of the race' (EW5: 84), that is, partake in its accumulated knowledge and customs as well as in its challenges. The basic idea of education advanced by Dewey 'is formally summed up in the idea of continuous reconstruction of experience' (MW9: 86). Its aim is that learners can continually grow: 'We have laid it down that the educative process is a continuous process of growth, having as its aim at every stage an added capacity of growth' (p. 59). The functional aim of education is 'to enable individuals to continue their education – or that the object and reward of learning is continued capacity for growth' (p. 107). As 'life is a self-renewing process through action upon the environment', so education becomes a process of learning in, through and for such interactions. In a very basic sense, education sustains the continuity of individual life and the continued existence of society by expanding the individual's capacity for growth (pp. 4–7).

As reconstruction of experience, education adds powers of subsequent direction and control. First, by adding to the meaning of present experience (MW9: 82–84). Learning raises the perception of connections and continuities of a given activity. The learner acquires the kind of knowledge of the context and factors of an experience that allows for a better understanding of what one is about to do or bring about. Secondly, the reflective learner adds knowledge of a successful procedure – as prototype of a future habit – that widens the meaning-horizon and aids her in directing her own future actions towards even more satisfying experiences (MW9: 84–85). With such awareness, the learner can realize her intention of certain (desirable) consequences rather than being reduced to suffer (undesirable) consequences of acting without proper knowledge: 'Knowing marks the conversion of undirected changes into changes directed toward an intended conclusion' (LW4: 163); and the present problem may be resolved more easily through the reconstruction and (possibly habitualized) reorganization of experience, transforming the quality of experience by enriching its perceptible meaning (MW9: 82). Continuous reconstruction of experience

entails that the outcome of a course of action informs and reconstructs our understanding of the earlier elements of action, so that we gain an understanding of the whole of the process only after experiencing its result.

The Nexus of Responsibility and Freedom in Ethics and Learning

The understanding of freedom as an idea and value is central not only to modern economics but also to business ethics and its conceptions of (managerial and corporate, social and ecological) responsibility (Dierksmeier & Pirson, 2010; Dierksmeier, 2011; 2016; 2019). By reconstructing freedom and its nexus to responsibility as central features and aims of the learning processes sustained by education, Deweyan pragmatism offers its own conception of *responsible freedom* that is, as shall be shown in the conclusion of this argument, at the heart of perspectives on Humanistic Management and sustainable development.

In their account of the civilizational process, Dewey and Tufts (LW7) describe how an increase of freedom and individuality over the centuries since antiquity led to the emergence of the conception of responsibility. The once dominant forces of external approval of traditional authorities gave way to the rising importance of inner determination and individual ethical reflection. With greater individuality came greater responsibility – including in economics (LW7: 121–148). The following argument aims to show how education adds powers of control and strengthens the freedom of the individual as well as of the group to engage in even more intelligent inquiry sustaining further growth.

Freedom as the capacity to learn self-direction in purposive and effective conduct

'[F]reedom in its practical and moral sense is connected with possibility of growth, learning and modification of character ... Freedom in the practical sense develops when one is aware of this possibility and takes an interest in converting it into a reality' (Dewey & Tufts, LW7: 306). If freedom is realized as the power of self-direction and the recreation of ourselves, '['t]he only freedom that is of enduring importance is the freedom of intelligence, that is to say, freedom of observation and of judgment, exercised in behalf of purposes that are intrinsically worth while' (LW13: 39). Dewey calls it a 'sound instinct which identifies freedom with power to frame purposes and to execute or carry into effect purposes so framed. Such freedom is in turn identical with self-control; for the formation of purposes and the organization of means to execute them are the work of intelligence' (LW13: 43). Such freedom of intelligence – the freedom of creative and constructive 'power of using past experience to shape and transform future experience' (MW11: 346) – is itself a product of other freedoms, such as the modes of freedom guaranteed by the Bill of Rights. Edel and Flower conclude that for Dewey 'freedom is essentially the capacity to learn and to make creative and innovative use of learning in guiding conduct' (Edel & Flower, 1985: xxv).

Responsibility as habitual consideration of consequences of one's self-directed conduct

With an increase in individuality, responsibility becomes important: 'The ethical problems connected with the fact of self-hood culminate in the ideas of responsibility and freedom' (Dewey & Tufts, LW7: 303). In Dewey's and Tufts' Ethics of 1908 (MW5), responsibility is rooted in responsiveness to (social or environmental) experiences and exercised in creative anticipation of future consequences. In their revised edition of Ethics in 1932 (LW7), Dewey and Tufts also emphasize how responsibility so conceived reforms the self, and thus the world shaped through the acts therein.

For Dewey and Tufts, responsibility denotes not just obligations, either enforced

by law or settled by custom, to which we react (MW5: 391–392). In their nuanced account of different forms of responsibility, they constrict obligations to the sphere of legal rights, and define liability as the external, negative aspect of responsibility. Responsibility in a positive, creative and constructive sense is defined as the '[habitual formation of] purposes after consideration of the social consequences of their execution' (MW5: 392). As a responsive habit, responsibility may be jump-started by fear of disapproval. But as individuals understand that living together requires a mutual balance of interests, they begin to be susceptible and apprehensive to the rights and interests of others and actively factor them into their course of conduct, 'which is the essence of responsibility, which in turn is the sole ultimate guarantee of social order' (Dewey & Tufts, MW5: 391–392).

This responsibility extends to our holding others accountable 'in such a manner that this responsiveness develops', and indeed to ideally become comprehensively responsible in all of our actions (Dewey & Tufts, LW7: 305). As individuals become responsive to and react with social demands, approval or condemnation towards the conduct of others, holding them accountable or liable, they do so with the expectation of effecting a prospective change in future courses of action, or even a modification of character: 'The fact that each act tends to form, through habit, a self which will perform a certain kind of acts, is the foundation, theoretically and practically, of responsibility' (p. 304). In that view, the self is capable of forming, moving, learning and changing, as the future import of one's course of action on others is considered: 'The possibility of a desirable *modification* of character and the selection of the course of action which will make that possibility a reality is the central fact in responsibility' (p. 303, emphasis in original). Understood as a mode of responsive and reconstructive self-transformation, the exercise of responsibility is inherent to the process of growth through learning – of reconstructing, enriching and habitualizing the forms of that continuous satisfactory interaction of the self and the world which constitutes experience.

CONCLUSION: RESPONSIBLE MANAGEMENT EDUCATION FROM A PRAGMATIST PERSPECTIVE

As we have seen, the pragmatist perspective on responsible management education is rooted in an epistemology that models learning as the reflection of experience, and education as the effort to enable every individual to participate in, contribute to and benefit from the growth of the consciousness and knowledge of all. Freedom and responsibility as powers of satisfactory self-directed, purposive, and effective conduct and of controlled growth in a responsive world have been reconstructed as integral aims and desirable features of educative efforts aiming to ensure successful learning processes. Learning is understood to be a transformational process where learners are practicing the responsible exercise of their freedom of intelligence to ensure the continuity of satisfactory experiences through the transactional adaptations of their selves and the practices and circumstances undermining or sustaining the world they share and shape as stakeholders together.

Pragmatism: an epistemological strategy to overcome an epistemological barrier to responsible management education

One of the main arguments why business schools too often fail to educate responsible managers is the argument that theory and practice are separated. Managers in the field often find management research, conducted with academic standards of excellence and rigor in mind (Bennis & O'Toole, 2005: 96), simply irrelevant in practice (Markides, 2011; Mintzberg, 2010). Two

approaches can be distinguished to overcome this divide between theory and practice, first an institutional approach that supports new communities of inquiry (Anderson, Mason, Hibbert, and Rivers, 2018: 427; Beech, MacIntosh & MacLean, 2010); and secondly, a theoretical approach concerned with epistemological and methodological assumptions that inhibit a meaningful conception of responsibility in management (Dierksmeier, 2016; Moosmayer et al., 2018; Painter-Morland, 2014). Pragmatism, in its epistemology and methodology, is deeply committed to overcome this 'separation fallacy' (Freeman et al., 2010) by embracing 'relational holism' (MacMullan, 2013). As has been shown, social life is always already conceived as a 'community of inquiry'; and inquiry aims at a practical understanding that makes a difference for the harmonious continuation of life.

Responsible management as intelligent, self-directed and responsible inquiry

It has been shown that from a pragmatist view, ethics, responsibility and sustainability are not separate domains but rather integral and related aspects of how intelligent inquiry into problems and their resolutions are organized – namely, in the mode and to the effect of responsible freedom:

1 Pragmatist (business) ethics is not conceived as a distant exercise of reasoning about the good and right best learned about in an extra class, but is always part of reflective activity and intelligent inquiry that best permeates all classes and subjects. Moreover, ethical reflection is inherently a social inquiry into concrete circumstances that shape a given community of inquiry. As central conceptions that shape the precondition and practice of any inquiry into one's world, freedom and responsibility are at once functional and ethical conceptions.

2 Responsibility arises as a responsive habit of forming, and redirecting, one's own purposes in deliberate consideration of the possible effects of one's intended course of action on others, the environment, and ultimately one's own self and

identity. It is not simply a burden to be accepted in relation to stakeholders, but a function of intelligent self-conduct among others, ultimately leading to learners adopting values and embodying virtues as proven ideas prescribing desirable and habitual conduct.

3   Sustainability is a function of sustaining the harmonious continuity of one's community of inquiry. In that sense, it is a learning program. Sustainability strategies arise through intelligent inquiry into concrete practices and circumstances, the harmful effects of factors at play, and the critical search for corrective, ameliorative action, carrying into effect modes of the responsible exercise of freedom and resulting in better practices and habits.

These general ideas on the main components of responsible management education have many further consequences, some of which will be pointed to in the final section of this chapter.

Changing aim, content, and process of responsible management education

Introducing pragmatism as a foundation has implications for (1) the aim, (2) the content and (3) the process of responsible management education:

1   Pragmatist responsible management education aims to empower executives to lead (often transformative) change processes in an increasingly diverse, complex and dynamic business world, treating other management theories, including even those built on self-interest that may actually impair students to conceive of themselves as change agents to lead that kind of change, as resources for intelligent inquiry.

2   A pragmatist approach gives legitimacy to, and places importance on, a stakeholder orientation in the process of problem resolution and value creation, including the self as a stakeholder. Its conception of economic responsibility offers guidance on virtue and virtuosity in management by rendering clear the connection and continuity between individual actions, social habits and economic institutions, thus empowering students to build better habits, business practices, and cultural codes.

3   A pragmatist pedagogy aims to build methods of critical reflection and inquiry by integrating real-life challenges into a consideration of one's own role in problem resolution and value-creation processes. It empowers executives to distinguish between different forms of formal, methodological and explicit knowledge and intuitive, strategic and tacit competence.

Taken together, these aspects are not just a learning program for students but for teachers as well. If Edel and Flower are correct in asserting that 'freedom is essentially the capacity to learn and to make creative and innovative use of learning in guiding conduct', teachers must ensure the Deweyan 'freedom of intelligence' of students above all. As freedom of comprehensive reconstruction of one's experience, this is a relational and dialogic kind of freedom that can only grow and prosper when exercised with responsibility, or more bluntly: when exercised as reciprocal responsibility. Rather than pressing information upon their students or raising bars for them to jump over, teachers are to conceive of themselves as guiding students as self-directed, responsible learners, a role that implies teachers are becoming learners themselves.

OUTLOOK: FUTURE DEVELOPMENTS

In the account given here, pragmatism has been offered as a philosophical foundation for responsible management education that also supports the institutional strategy to search for new knowledge in new and open communities of inquiry, overcoming theoretical rigor in favor of practical relevance, and building the capacity for responsible change processes. Its true potential, though, lies not within the classroom or the university, but in building, sustaining and protecting the habits of societies that conceive of themselves as civil communities of free and equal citizens. These societies have come under pressure, not the least by disruptive megatrends, such as digitization and climate change. In this final section two perspectives will be further clarified. First we consider pragmatistic management as humanistic management, as an economic practice of human beings creating value with human beings for human beings (Dierksmeier, 2016).

Pragmatistic Management as Humanistic Management

Drawing on liberal thought from Immanuel Kant to Amartya Sen's capability approach, philosopher Claus Dierksmeier has made a case for *humanistic management* by arguing that any agenda to replace 'the atomistic models of the *homo economicus* with an economics based on the relational nature of the *conditio humana*' (...) should promote the theoretical as well as practical realization of responsible freedom on part of management', conceiving of economic actors as human beings within specific socio-cultural contexts (Dierksmeier, 2011: 280, emphasis in original). Deweyan pragmatism can reconstruct and support the perspectives of humanistic management and related conceptions of the capability approach and of sustainable development because its conception of learning inherently entails an understanding of responsible freedom as a method of learning to sustain conditions conducive to continuous self-determined and responsible conduct.

The Humanistic Management Project entails efforts to advance a theoretical, practical and political agenda of forms of management in business which are focused on protecting and promoting human dignity in freedom (Amann, Pirson, Dierksmeier, von Kimakowitz & Spitzeck, 2001; Dierksmeier, 2016; Pirson, 2017). In the tradition of William James and John Dewey, pragmatism has always been described as humanism (Dooley, 1974; James, 1979 [1907]). At the center of pragmatism is the human being who inquires into the world in association with others in order to ameliorate the world.

Like other humanist approaches, it rejects neoclassical accounts of freedom and contract theories, while raising awareness for the powerful effects, as well as the limitations, of individual and collective action. Pragmatist epistemology holds that truth as meaning is found in the practical effects it predicts for an object or action in a given situation. Thus, it 'is impossible to strip the human element out from even our most abstract theorizing' (James, 1979 [1907]), and the explicit task of pragmatist theory is to transcend traditional dualisms such as nature and man, mind and body, and practical and theoretical inquiry: 'What Humanism means to me is an expansion, not a contraction, of human life, an expansion in which nature and the science of nature are made the willing servants of human good.'

By bringing a fully developed epistemology to the project of humanistic management, pragmatism deepens the base of human-centered approaches to responsible management education, and establishes a perspective that is decidedly non-idealistic, thus adding legitimacy and appeal to the discourse of humanistic management. The reflexive and responsible consideration of the impact of one's own actions on the self and the world is an integral feature of pragmatism, not just a deduction. Pragmatism conceives of humanity as a learning society of learning communities of individuals in the constant process of learning. It views habits as reservoirs of previous experiences, which shape our conception of the world, but do not determine it. Pragmatism encourages individuals to think of themselves and their roles as creative change agents and cooperative participants in a process of social melioration, aiming to build practical knowledge.

A Pragmatist Conception of Sustainable Development

Going beyond the building blocks that have been sketched out, comprehensive pragmatist understanding of sustainability might with good reasons be conceived with a focus on sustainable development as a process of integrative and transformational learning. In a pragmatist perspective, the basic problem of sustainability is that various forms of interdependencies are playing out in processes with negative consequences. Interdependencies are temporal in their intergenerational extension, spatial in the correlation of local practices and global effects, and sectional in the confluence of social, environmental and economic, if not also cultural and political, concerns and aspects. The concurrence of interdependent effects is unfolding with undesirable and often unforeseen consequences.

Pragmatist education is conceptually prepared for such circumstances, at least in principle. Pragmatism not only entails a mode of continuous intelligent and deliberate adaptation to changing and ambiguous environments but also a preparation of the mind and its modes of thinking for future requirements of action in more complex challenges. 'To live signifies that a connected continuity of acts is effected in which preceding ones prepare the conditions under which later ones occur', and in the 'particular cumulative continuity' of human life, the results of interactions with its environs are a matter of life (satisfactorily lived) and death, Dewey writes (LW4: 179). He continues: 'As organisms become more complex in structure and thus related to a more complex environment, the importance of a particular act in establishing conditions favorable to subsequent acts that sustain the continuity of the life process, becomes at once more difficult and more imperative.'

Challenges to mankind such as climate change urgently demonstrate a central insight of pragmatism, namely that any action has dynamic effects on the condition of others. As we meet this global challenge of unprecedented scope, we must succeed in the continuous critique and correction of past habits, practices, codes and modes of production and consumption. This requires a global learning program for which pragmatism provides a fitting source

code. Relational holism as the quintessential pragmatist premise (MacMullan, 2013: 229) results in a pragmatist action theory that is best understood as a continuous and transformational process of searching, learning, innovating and reshaping our course of action, and thus: in sustainable development (Schneidewind, 2018). Pragmatism makes no distinction between learning *about* sustainability (knowledge) and learning *for* sustainability (competences). Rather, pragmatist learning is ultimately itself a form of sustainable development that strengthens collaborative power as 'power in the making' and may bring together communities of inquiry as coalitions for change (Hafting & Lindhult, 2013). Our global problems have often been stated already. They seem worth exploring, at least and at last, with a mindset of freedom exercised in responsibility, through resolute and comprehensive pragmatist inquiry and transformation.

Note

1   Throughout this article, the works of John Dewey are cited according to *The Collected Works of John Dewey, 1882–1953*, edited by Jo Ann Boydston (Carbondale and Edwardsville: Southern Illinois University Press, 1969–199) which are divided into *The Early Works* (EW), *The Middle Works* (MW) and *The Later Works* (LW). Citations employ the standard formula: (volume number: page number), hence MW9: 107 refers to Middle Works, volume 9, page 107.

REFERENCES

Amann, W., Pirson, M., Dierksmeier, C., von Kimakowitz, E., & Spitzeck, H. (Eds.). (2011). *Business schools under fire: humanistic management education as the way forward.* Basingstoke: Palgrave Macmillan.

Anacker, M. (2018). *Psychologie.* In Festl, M. (Ed.), *Handbuch Pragmatismus* (pp. 207–214). Stuttgart: J. B. Metzler.

Anderson, E. (2019). Dewey's moral philosophy. In Zalta, E. N. (Ed.), *The Stanford encyclopedia of philosophy*, Winter 2019 edition. Retrieved from: https://plato.stanford.edu/archives/win2019/entries/dewey-moral.

Anderson, L., Mason, K., Hibbert, P., & Rivers, C. (2018). Management education in turbulent times. *Journal of Management Education*, *42*(4), 423–440.

Argyris, C., & Schön, D. (1996). *Organizational learning II*. Reading, MA: Addison-Wesley.

Bartunek, J. M. (2014). From the Editors: Honoring the legacy of Chris Argyris by devoting attention to how managers learn. *Academy of Learning and Education*, *13*(1), 1–4.

Beckert, J. (2009). *Pragmatismus und wirtschaftliches Handeln. MPIfG Working Paper 09/4*. Cologne: Max-Planck-Institut für Gesellschaftsforschung.

Beech, N., MacIntosh, R., & MacLean, D. (2010). Dialogues between academics and practitioners: The role of generative dialogic encounters. *Organization Studies*, *31*, 1341–1367.

Bennis, W. G., & O'Toole, J. (2005). *How business schools lost their way. Harvard Business Review*, *83*(5), 96–104.

Brandi, U., & Elkjaer, B. (2013). Organizational learning: knowing in organizing. In Kelemen, M., & Rumens, N. (Eds.), *American pragmatism and organization* (pp. 147–161). Aldershot, UK: Gower.

Bromley, D. W. (2006). *Sufficient reason: volitional pragmatism and the meaning of economic institutions*. Princeton, NJ: Princeton University Press.

Carden, S. D. (2006). *Virtue ethics: Dewey and MacIntyre*. London: Continuum International.

Davies, I., & Doherty, B. (2019). Balancing a hybrid business model: the search for equilibrium at Cafédirect. *Journal of Business Ethics*, *157*(4), 1043–1066.

De Graaf, F. J. (2019). Ethics and behavioural theory: how do professionals assess their mental models? *Journal of Business Ethics*, *157*(4), 933–947.

Dierksmeier, C., & Pirson, M. (2010). The modern corporation and the idea of freedom. *Philosophy of Management*, *9*(3), 5–25.

Dewey, J., (1897 / 1972). My pedagogic creed. In Boydston, J. A. (Ed.), *The Early Works of John Dewey, v. 5 1895–1898* (pp. 84–95). Carbondale: Southern Illinois University Press.

Dewey, J. (1916 / 1980). Democracy and education. In Boydston, J. A. (Ed.), *The Middle Works of John Dewey, v. 9 1916*. Carbondale: Southern Illinois University Press.

Dewey, J. (1919 / 1982). Syllabus of eight lectures on 'Problems of Philosophic Reconstruction'. In Boydston, J. A. (Ed.), *The Middle Works of John Dewey, v. 11 1918–1919* (pp. 341–349). Carbondale: Southern Illinois University Press.

Dewey, J. (1920 / 1982). Reconstruction in philosophy. In Boydston, J. A. (Ed.), *The Middle Works of John Dewey, v. 12 1920* (pp. 77–201). Carbondale: Southern Illinois University Press.

Dewey, J. (1929 / 1984). The quest for certainty. In Boydston, J. A. (Ed.), *The Later Works of John Dewey, v. 4 1929*. Carbondale: Southern Illinois University Press.

Dewey, J., (1930 / 1984). What Humanism Means to Me, In Boydston, J. A. (Ed.), *The Later Works of John Dewey, v. 5 1929–1930* (pp. 263–266). Carbondale: Southern Illinois University Press.

Dewey, J. (1934 / 1987). Art as experience. In Boydston, J. A. (Ed.), *The Later Works of John Dewey, v. 10 1934*. Carbondale: Southern Illinois University Press.

Dewey, J. (1938 / 1986). Logic: The Theory of Inquiry. In Boydston, J. A. (Ed.), *The Later Works of John Dewey, v. 12 1938*. Carbondale: Southern Illinois University Press.

Dewey, J. (1938 / 1988). Experience and education. In Boydston, J. A. (Ed.), *The Later Works of John Dewey, v. 13 1938–1939* (pp. 1–62). Carbondale: Southern Illinois University Press.

Dewey, J., & Tufts, J. H. (1908 / 1978). Ethics. In Boydston, J. A. (Ed.), *The Middle Works of John Dewey, v. 5 1908*. Carbondale: Southern Illinois University Press.

Dewey, J., & Tufts, J. H. (1932 / 1985). Ethics. In Boydston, J. A. (Ed.), *The Later Works of John Dewey, v. 7 1932*. Carbondale: Southern Illinois University Press.

Dierksmeier, C. (2011). The freedom–responsibility nexus in management philosophy and business ethics. *Journal of Business Ethics*, *101*, 263–283.

Dierksmeier, C. (2016). *Reframing economic ethics. The philosophical foundations of humanistic management*. Basingstoke: Palgrave Macmillan.

Dierksmeier, C. (2019). *Qualitative freedom – autonomy in cosmopolitan responsibility*. Cham, Switzerland: Springer.

Dierksmeier, C., & Pirson, M. (2010). The modern corporation and the idea of freedom. *Philosophy of Management, 9*(3), 5–25.

Dooley, P. K. (1974). *Pragmatism as humanism: the philosophy of William James*. Chicago: Nelson-Hall.

Earl, A., VanWynsberghe, R., Walter, P., & Straka, T. (2018). Adaptive education applied to higher education for sustainability. *International Journal of Sustainability in Higher Education, 19*(6), 1111–1130.

Easterby-Smith, M., & Lyles, M. (2011). *Handbook of organizational learning and knowledge management*. Hoboken, NJ: John Wiley & Sons.

Edel, A., & Flower, E. (1985). Introduction. In Boydston, J. A. (Ed.), *John Dewey: The Later Works, 1925–1953*, Vol. 7 (pp. vii–xxxv). Carbondale: Southern Illinois University Press.

Elkjaer, B. (2004). Organizational learning: The 'Third way'. *Management Learning, 35*(4), 419–434.

Festl, M. (2018). *Kontingenz und Kreativität*. In Festl, M. (Ed.), *Handbuch Pragmatismus* (pp. 65–73). Stuttgart: J. B. Metzler.

Fontrodona, J. (2002). *Pragmatism and management inquiry: insights from the thought of Charles S. Peirce*. London: Quorum Books.

Fougère, M., Solitander, N., & Maheshwari, S. (2019). Achieving responsible management learning through enriched reciprocal learning: service-learning projects and the role of boundary spanners. *Journal of Business Ethics*, 1–18. doi:10.1007/s10551-019-04365-8.

Fourcade, F., & Go, N. (2012). Towards a new paradigm in experiential learning: lessons learned from kindergarten. *Journal of Management, 31*(3), 198–208.

Freeman, R. E., Harrison, J. S., Wicks, A. C., Parmar, B. L., & De Colle, S. (2010). *Stakeholder theory: the state of the art*. Cambridge: Cambridge University Press.

Giles, D. E., Jr., & Eyler, J. (1994). The theoretical roots of service-learning in John Dewey: toward a theory of service-learning. *Service Learning, General*. 150. https://digitalcommons.unomaha.edu/slceslgen/150.

Gillett, A., Loader, K., Doherty, B., & Scott, J. M. (2019). An examination of tensions in a hybrid collaboration: a longitudinal study of an empty homes project. *Journal of Business Ethics, 157*(4), 949–967.

Hafting, T., & Lindhult E. (2013). Developing collaborative power in working life: linking american pragmatism and action research. In Kelemen, M., & Rumens, N. (Eds.), *American pragmatism and organization: issues and controversies* (pp. 205–221). Aldershot: Gower.

Hiller, A. J., & Woodall, T. (2019). Everything flows: a pragmatist perspective of trade-offs and value in ethical consumption. *Journal of Business Ethics, 157*(4), 893–912.

Jacobs, D. C. (2004). A pragmatist approach to integrity in business ethics. *Journal of Management Inquiry, 13*(3), 215–223.

James, W. (1979 [1907]). *Pragmatism: a new name for some old ways of thinking*. Cambridge, MA: Harvard University Press.

Jensen, T., & Sandström, J. (2013). In defence of stakeholder pragmatism. *Journal of Business Ethics, 114*, 225–237.

Joas, H. (1996). *The creativity of action*. Chicago: University of Chicago Press.

Joas, H. (2000). *The genesis of values*. Chicago: University of Chicago Press.

Kaplan, A. (1980). Introduction. In Boydston, J. (Ed.) *The Later Works of John Dewey, 1925–1953*, Vol. 10. Carbondale: Southern Illinois University Press.

Kelley, S., & Nahser, R. (2014). Developing sustainable strategies: foundations, method, and pedagogy. *Journal of Business Ethics, 123*(4), 631–644.

Kolb, D. A. (1984). *Experiential learning. Experience as the source of learning and development*. Upper Saddle River, NJ: Prentice Hall.

Kolb, D. A. (2014). *Experiential learning. Experience as the source of learning and development*. Second Edition. Upper Saddle River, NJ: Prentice Hall.

Krüger, H. (2000). Prozesse der öffentlichen Untersuchung. Zum Potential einer zweiten Modernisierung in John Dewey's 'Logic: The Theory of Inquiry'. In Joas, H. (Ed.), *Philosophie der Demokratie. Beiträge zum Werk von John Dewey* (pp. 194–234). Frankfurt-am-Main: Suhrkamp.

Laasch, O., & Conaway, R. N. (2015). *Principles of responsible management: glocal sustainability, responsibility, ethics*. Mason: Cengage.

Laasch, O., & Moosmayer, D. C. (2015). Responsible management learning: reflecting on the role and use of paradigms n sustainability, responsibility, ethics research *CRME Working Papers*, Vol. 2.

Lagueux, R. C. (2014). *A spurious John Dewey quotation on reflection*. Retrieved from https://www.academia.edu/17358587/A_Spurious_John_Dewey_Quotation_on_ Reflection.

Lorino, P. (2018). *Pragmatism and organization studies*. Oxford: Oxford University Press.

Lund Dean, K., & Forray, J. (2018). On positioning, domains, and readerships: some thoughts on management education journals. *Journal of Management Education*, *42*(6), 695–703.

Lynch, S. (2017). Building ethica capacity: inclusiveness and the reflective dimensions of service-learning. In *Service-learning: international perspectives on inclusive education*, Vol. 12 (pp. 53–71). Bingley: Emerald Publishing.

MacMullan, T. (2013). The fly wheel of society: habit and social meliorism in the pragmatist tradition. In Sparrow, T., & Hutchinson, A. (Eds.), *A history of habit from Aristotle to Bourdieu* (pp. 229–253). Lanham, MD: Lexington Books.

Margolis, J. D. (1998). Psychological pragmatism and the imperative of aims: a new approach for business ethics. *Business Ethics Quarterly*, *8*(3), 409–430.

Markides, C. (2011). Crossing the chasm: How to convert relevant research into managerially useful research. *Journal of Applied Behavioral Science*, *47*, 121–134.

McVea, J. F. (2007). Constructing good decisions in ethically charged situations: the role of dramatic rehearsal. *Journal of Business Ethics*, *70*, 375–390.

Miettinen, R. (2000). The conceot of experiential learning and John Dewey's theory of reflective thought and action. *International Journal of Lifelong Education*, *19*(1), 54–72.

Mintzberg, H. (2010), *Managers not MBAs. A hard look at the soft practice of managing and management development*. San Francisco, CA: Berrett-Koehler.

Moosmayer, D. C., Waddock, S., Wang, L., Hühn, M. P., Dierksmeier, C., & Gohl, C. (2018). Leaving the road to Abilene: a pragmatic approach to addressing the normative paradox of responsible management education. *Journal of Business Ethics*, *157*(4), 913–932.

Nahser, F. B. (1997). *Learning to read the signs: reclaiming pragmatism in business*. Oxford: Butterworth-Heinemann.

Nahser, F. B. (2009). *Journeys to Oxford: nine pragmatic inquiries into the practice of values in business and education*. New York: Global Scholarly Publications.

Nahser, F. B., & Ruhe, J. (2001). Putting American pragmatism to work in the classroom. *Journal of Business Ethics*, *34*(3–4), 317–330.

Nungesser, F., & Pettenkofer, A. (2018) Soziologie. In Festl, M. (Ed.), *Handbuch Pragmatismus* (pp. 193–199). Stuttgart: J. B. Metzler.

Ord, J., & Leather, M. (2011). The substance beneath the labels of experiential learning: the importance of John Dewey for outdoor educators. *Journal of Outdoor and Environmental Education*, *15*, 13–25.

Osorio-Vega, P. (2018). The ethics of entrepreneurial shared value. *Journal of Business Ethics*, *157*(4), 981–995.

Pacho, T. O. (2015). Unpacking John Dewey's connection to service-learning. *Journal of Education*, *2*(3), 9.

Painter, M., Hibbert, S., & Cooper, T. (2018). The development of responsible and sustainable business practice: value, mind-sets, business-models. *Journal of Business Ethics*, *157*, 885–891.

Painter-Morland, M. (2014). Philosophical assumptions undermining responsible management education. *Journal of Management Development*, *34*(1), 61–75.

Parmar, B. L., Phillips, R., & Freeman, R. E. (2017). Pragmatism and organization studies. In Mir, R., Willmott, H., & Greenwood, M. (Eds.), *The Routledge companion to philosophy in organization studies*. New York: Routledge.

Pirson, M. (2017). *Humanistic management. Protecting dignity and promoting well-being*. Cambridge: Cambridge University Press.

Pless, N. M., Maak, T., & Stahl, G. K. (2011). Developing responsible global leaders through international service-learning programs: the Ulysses experience. *Academy of Management Learning and Education*, *10*(2), 237–260.

Prakash, M. S. (1995). Ecological literacy for moral virtue: Orr on [moral] education for postmodern sustainability. *Journal of Moral Education*, *24*(1), 3–18.

Rasche, A., & Gilbert, D. U. (2015). Decoupling responsible management education: why business schools may not walk their talk. *Journal of Management Inquiry*, *24*(3), 1–14.

Rosenthal, S. B., & Buchholz, R. A. (2000). *Rethinking business ethics*. New York: Oxford University Press.

Schneidewind, U. (2018). *Die große Transformation: Eine Einführung in die Kunst gesellschaftlichen Wandels*. Frankfurt: Fischer Verlag.

Schön, D. (2005). *The reflective practitioner*. New York: Basic Books.

Serrano Zamora, J. (2018). Experiment. In Festl, M. (Ed.), *Handbuch Pragmatismus* (pp. 81–85). Stuttgart: J.B. Metzler.

Shields, P., Whetsell, T., & Hanks, E. (2013). Pragmatism and public administration: looking back, looking forward. In Rumens, N., & Kelemen, M. (Eds.), *American pragmatism and organization studies: researching management practices* (pp. 175–199). Aldershot, UK: Gower.

Speck, B. W., & Hoppe, S. L. (2004). *Service-learning: history, theory, and issues*. Westport, CT: Greenwood Publishing.

Statler, M. (2014). Developing wisdom in a business school? Critical reflections on pedagogical practice. *Management Learning*, *45*(4), 397–417.

Surie, G., & Ashley, G. (2008). Integrating pragmatism and ethics in entrepreneurial leadership for sustainable value creation. *Journal of Business Ethics*, *81*(1), 235–246.

Tai-Seale, T. (2000). Service-learning: historical roots, present forms, and educational potential for training health educators. *Journal of Health Education*, *31*(5), 256–263.

Taylor, S., & Bell, E. (2013) Believing in a pragmatist business ethics. In Kelemen, M., & Rumens, N. (Eds.), *American pragmatism and organization: issues and controversies* (pp. 163–174). Aldershot, UK: Gower.

Teehan, J. (1995). Character, integrity and Dewey's virtue ethics. *Transactions of the Charles S. Peirce Society*, *31*(4), 841–863.

Tufts, J. H. (1917). The moral life and the construction of values and standards. In Dewey, J. et al. (Eds.), *Creative intelligence: essays in the pragmatic attitude* (pp. 354–408). New York, NY: Henry Holt and Company.

Van Poeck, K., Östman, L., & Block, T. (2018). Opening up the black box of learning-by-doing in sustainability transitions. *Environmental Innovation and Societal Transitions*, https://doi.org/10.1016/j.eist.2018.12.006.

Vince, R., & Reynolds, M, (2009). Reflection, reflective practice and organizing reflection. In Armstrong, S., & Fukami, C. (Eds.), *The SAGE handbook of management learning, education and development* (pp. 89–103). London, U.K.: Sage Publications.

Visser, M. (2019). Pragmatism, critical theory and business ethics: converging lines. *Journal of Business Ethics*, *156*(1), 45–57.

Volbers, J. (2018). Reclaiming the power of thought. *European Journal of Pragmatism and American Philosophy*, *10*(2), 2–19.

Walker, K., Dyck, B., Zhang, Z., & Starke, F. (2019). The use of Praxis in the classroom to facilitate student transformation. *Journal of Business Ethics*, *157*(1), 199–216.

Westbrook, R. B. (1991). *John Dewey and American democracy*. Ithaca, NY: Cornell University Press.

Wicks A., & Freeman, E. (1998). Organization studies and the new pragmatism: positivism, anti-positivism and the search for ethics. *Organization Science*, *9*(2), 123–140.

Yamazaki, Y., & Kayes, D. C. (2004). An experiential approach to cross-cultural learning: a review and integration of competencies for successful expatriate adaptation. *Academy of Management Learning and Education*, *3*(4), 362–379.

Yorio, P. L., & Ye, F. (2012). A meta-analysis on the effects of service-learning on the social, personal, and cognitive outcomes of learning. *Academy of Management Learning and Education*, *11*(1), 9–27.

York, J. G. (2009). Pragmatic sustainability: translating environmental ethics into competitive advantage. *Journal of Business Ethics*, *85*, 97–109.

Responsible Management Learning and Education in Need of Inter- and Transdisciplinarity

Markus Beckmann and Stefan Schaltegger

To be effective, responsible management learning and education requires adequate forms of interaction that uncover what responsibility could mean and how it could be realized in practice. To introduce and enhance responsibility in learning thus goes hand in hand with implications for management research and practice (Laasch & Moosmayer, 2015), one being the need for inter- and transdisciplinarity. This chapter discusses why inter- and transdisciplinarity play an important role for responsible management learning beyond acquiring facts. In a nutshell, interdisciplinarity combines different academic research perspectives to jointly analyze an object or issue (Jantsch, 1970; Scholz, Lang, Wiek & Walter, 2006). Transdisciplinarity goes one step further by combining not only different academic disciplines but, in addition, also diverse practitioner perspectives to jointly address complex real world problems (Max-Neef, 2005; Thompson Klein, Grossenbacher-Mansuy, Häberli, Bill, Scholz & Welti, 2001).

Inter- and transdisciplinary research approaches are relevant with regard to the specific purpose of responsible management learning and education. A key purpose of responsible management education is to endow future managers with the capabilities to create contributions to sustainable development (UN PRME, 2018) by creating value for stakeholders, society and the natural environment. Sustainability challenges in business, however, are typically complex and multidimensional, bringing together economic with ethical, social and ecological considerations (Pohl, 2005; Schaltegger, Beckmann & Hansen, 2013). No single academic discipline can fully capture all of these various dimensions. This is why the complexity to realize responsible management calls for *interdisciplinarity* – as the collaboration between various academic disciplines in order to capture a range of different perspectives.

At the same time, responsible management issues are in practice characterized by the interplay of various stakeholders.

Sustainability problems are furthermore not just intellectual challenges but real-world problems, which can only be understood by engaging with the empirical phenomena and involved practitioners. Practitioners have expertise and knowledge which is different and goes beyond abstract academic constructs but that is necessary to complement disciplinary and interdisciplinary analyses to fully understand real-world challenges. This is one of the reasons why *transdisciplinarity* is particularly promising to create a richer, more realistic analysis of the existing challenges and to support transformative change towards responsible management and creating contributions to sustainable development (Nicolescu, 2014).

In the following, we discuss the general idea of inter- and transdisciplinarity and its specific role for responsible management learning and education in more detail. The book chapter is organized in six steps.

The first step places the role of research within the context of responsible management learning and education. Using the UN Principles of Responsible Management Education (PRME) as a starting point, we show that a transition towards a more responsible and sustainable business and society requires adequate forms of knowledge creation, knowledge dissemination and knowledge application. Given the complexity and urgency of sustainability challenges and responsible management issues, however, the question arises as to what kind of research approaches are available and effective in this regard.

Addressing this question, the second step analyzes the context of responsible management and links it to a comparative discussion of different research approaches. The key claim here is that responsible management and current sustainability challenges are characterized by significant and often increasing degrees of complexity (Schaltegger et al., 2013) that create the need for specialization. Discussing options for aligning specialization with re-integration, we define and compare the different approaches of disciplinary, multidisciplinary, interdisciplinary and transdisciplinary research.

Building upon this distinction, we zoom in a third step into the concept of transdisciplinarity. As key principles of transdisciplinarity, we discuss (a) taking a real-life challenge as starting point, (b) organizing fruitful collaboration to address complexity, (c) joint clarification with diverse partners of what the actual problem is, (d) iterative process of joint problem-solving and re-definition, as well as (e) crossing the divide between knowledge creation, knowledge transfer and knowledge application (Lang et al., 2012; Schaltegger et al., 2013).

Having clarified the general concept of transdisciplinarity, our fourth step then shifts the focus towards perspectives of implementing and managing transdisciplinary research processes.

In the fifth section, we discuss the educational context and how transdisciplinary approaches invite transcending a strict separation between knowledge creation (research) and knowledge application (management) on the one hand and knowledge dissemination (education and learning) on the other. Transdisciplinarity then inspires learning formats in which research, education and the management application of knowledge are intertwined (Scholz et al., 2006).

While inter- and transdisciplinary research and learning perspectives can contribute significantly to sharpening the ideal of responsible management education, their implementation is not always easy (Jahn et al., 2012). For this reason, the sixth step of this chapter looks at barriers and limitations that come along with this approach.

Our chapter concludes with a short summary and brief discussion of future research questions.

THE ROLE OF MANAGEMENT, RESEARCH AND EDUCATION FOR RESPONSIBLE VALUE CREATION

Any discussion about responsible management learning and education is incomplete if it does not take into account the role of research and its links to management practice as well. In fact, academic institutions best realize their potential as places for learning when the teaching, dissemination, learning and application of knowledge is strongly intertwined with its creation. It is therefore not surprising that one of the six UN Principles of Responsibility Management *Education* (see Chapter 2 by Librizzi & Parkes in this Handbook) explicitly addresses the role of *research*. Principle 4 of the UN PRME (2018) maintains:

> We will engage in conceptual and empirical research that advances our understanding about the role, dynamics, and impact of corporations in the creation of sustainable social, environmental and economic value.

This principle highlights that research plays a pivotal role in making responsible learning and education for sustainable value creation possible. In fact, research, education and management have complementary contributions for responsibility. As expressed in PRME Principle 1, the key purpose of responsible management education is to enable future managers to create 'sustainable value for business and society at large and to work for an inclusive and sustainable global economy' (UN PRME, 2018). The role of education, then, is to endow students with the

knowledge, skills and capabilities needed for sustainable value creation. To this end, however, further adequate research is needed that advances our understanding of sustainable value creation and that creates the knowledge base on which effective management education can build. Yet, what does *adequate* research mean in this regard?

In the past, this interplay of research, education and management was often understood in a rather linear way that distinguishes knowledge creation, knowledge dissemination and knowledge application as separable and sequential steps (Figure 33.1). Given the complexity and urgency of today's sustainability challenges, however, such a linear model runs against its limits for at least four reasons.

First, if researchers want to create relevant knowledge that eventually helps practitioners solve actual problems, they benefit from integrating these practitioner perspectives (including experiences, practical issues of implementation, etc.) into the research process. Second, given the multi-dimensional complex nature of many sustainability challenges, interdisciplinary research is needed where different disciplines generate different pieces of the knowledge puzzle (Pohl, 2005). Yet, integrating these pieces into a coherent picture does not happen automatically. It rather requires a context of learning and

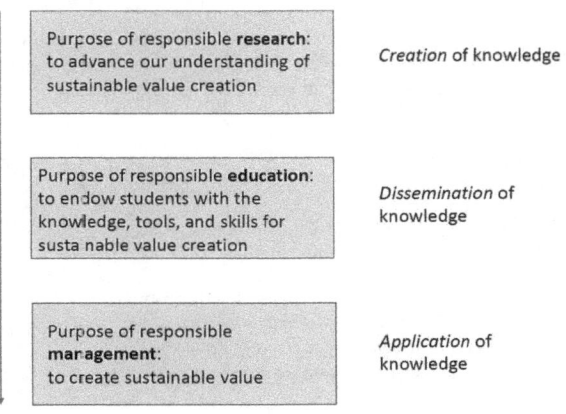

Figure 33.1   A linear model of knowledge creation, dissemination and application

application that is informative for the research process itself. Third, if knowledge creation is separated from those who later apply it, concepts for change may lack the acceptance and 'social robustness' (Nowotny, Scott, Gibbons & Scott, 2001) by practitioners. Finally, in the face of a rapidly changing world with urgent challenges, the linear model is often too slow and not responsive enough. If students prepare for the challenges of the future by learning today what researchers have learned about problems of the past, then knowledge always has a substantial time lag and is referenced to the past. To be sure, there are deep insights and basic competences that are timeless. Yet, given pressing current real-life challenges, there are benefits in speeding up societal adaptation by preventing a separation of research, education and application in management practice.

Against this background, Figure 33.2 illustrates an alternative perspective on the interplay of responsible research, education and management. Instead of assuming a strict separation and a linear logic,

Figure 33.2 highlights the interdependencies of knowledge creation, dissemination and application. Here, research, education and management have interlinkages that work in both directions. In fact, real-life challenges such as the implementation of the UN Sustainable Development Goals are characterized by high levels of complexity, by multiple dimensions (ecological, social, economic and ethical), and by multiple stakeholders. Such complexity calls for forms of exchange where the boundaries of knowledge creation, dissemination and application overlap to allow the simultaneous co-creation of solutions for an inclusive and sustainable global economy.

In short, both the complexity and urgency of sustainability challenges and responsible management issues call for research approaches that can handle complexity, multi-dimensionality and multi-stakeholder challenges. The next section therefore reviews different science paradigms and discusses how they relate to the challenges just introduced.

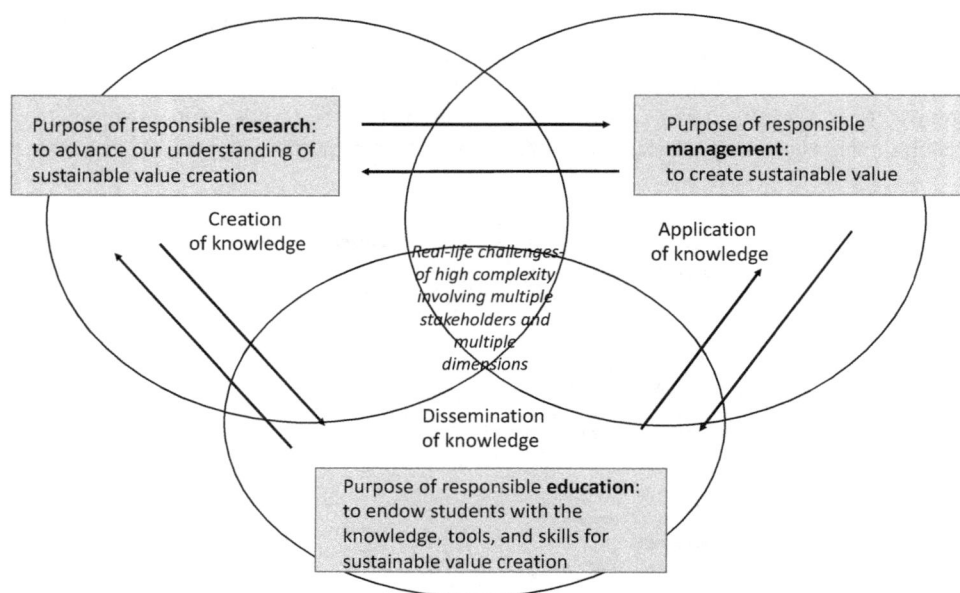

Figure 33.2 Knowledge creation, diffusion and application as overlapping spheres

ADDRESSING COMPLEXITY THROUGH SPECIALIZATION AND REINTEGRATION: FROM DISCIPLINARITY TO INTER- AND TRANSDISCIPLINARITY

A key challenge for responsible management are the ever-higher levels of complexity that come along with dynamic challenges such as climate change, poverty, the UN SDGs, or managing within the planetary boundaries that define a safe operating space for humanity (Rockström et al., 2009; Schaltegger, Beckmann & Hockerts, 2018a and 2018b).

Both in management practice and in scholarly research one important reaction to complexity is specialization: to divide complex phenomena into sub-questions (see, e.g., Hirsch Hadorn, Bradley, Pohl & Rist, 2006). In management practice, specialization leads to the emergence of specialized corporate functions, specialized professions, and specialized management tools. Similarly, the scientific process is characterized by an ever-increasing differentiation that leads to specialized disciplines with specialized theories and methodologies (Nicolescu, 2002).

Disciplinarity, understood as the emergence of highly specialized scientific perspectives with advanced theories and methodologies, is thus an important and primary step within the academic system to advance its ability to address complex phenomena. Only based on the specialization and division of labor of diverse disciplines can the scientific process dig deeper into understanding complex challenges (Schaltegger et al., 2013). Take the example of climate change. To understand how the climate changed in the past, paleo-climatologists have developed elaborate methodologies such as drilling out and analyzing ice-cores from ancient glaciers. This form of specialization thus generates knowledge at a depth that would otherwise not be possible.

Specialization is thus necessary and highly productive. However, highly specialized knowledge comes at the price of illuminating only a partial aspect of the larger phenomenon (Thompson Klein et al., 2001). Take again the challenge of climate change. No single researcher and no single methodology could ever grasp individually the complexity of atmospheric chemistry, the role of cloud formation, sun radiation, glacier melting, or ocean currents, as well as the impacts of rain forest fires, NO_x-pollution, change in land patterns, CO_2 emissions, cattle farming and plane trails in the sky. What is therefore needed is to extend disciplinarity.

Multidisciplinarity, both in science and corporate practice, refers to an approach in which different disciplines address different aspects of the same phenomenon or issue, yet without a systematic exchange between these efforts or the attempt to integrate the different pieces into a larger perspective. In a way, multidisciplinarity is therefore merely the multiplication of disciplinarity as the different disciplinary perspectives remain 'untouched' in parallel and continue to produce their research output individually (Schaltegger et al., 2013). Multidisciplinarity thus contributes to addressing complexity by understanding more pieces of the puzzle, yet it stops short of integrating these pieces into a bigger picture. In sum, both disciplinarity and multidisciplinarity thus address the challenge of complexity through specialization and division of labor yet fail to answer the question as to how the results of division of labor and specialization can be re-integrated.

In contrast, *interdisciplinarity* aims at the purposeful and problem-driven integration and cooperation of specialized disciplinary knowledge (see, e.g., Pohl, 2005; Scholz et al., 2006; Thompson Klein et al., 2001). Note that any integration of knowledge pieces into a bigger picture starts with a common perspective (which can be inspired by a theoretical or a real-world problem). Take again climate change. The work of the IPCC (the Intergovernmental Panel on Climate Change) is highly interdisciplinary. When estimating, for example, the economic costs of global warming, climatologists, economists and others combine their different disciplinary sets of knowledge and methodologies. As a result, interdisciplinarity allows addressing scientific questions of higher complexity that no single discipline can answer alone. It seeks to reap the benefits of both scientific specialization and knowledge re-integration. At the same time, however, interdisciplinarity refers to the inner-academic exchange between scientific disciplines (and often between disciplines that are close to each other, Scholz & Steiner, 2015a).

Transcending the boundaries of purely inner-scientific learning is at the core of *transdisciplinarity*. For Nicolescu (2002), transdisciplinarity is what is between, across and beyond disciplines. In doing so, transdisciplinarity seeks to transcend boundaries in two ways, namely by transcending boundaries between scientific disciplines and by transcending the boundaries between the scientific process and the real world of the stakeholders that matter in and for a given problem context. By giving voice to different stakeholder perspectives, transdisciplinarity departs from an objectivist viewpoint that aims at 'scientific' neutrality and technocentrism but rather engages in *reflexivity* to question 'what we, and others might be taking for granted' (Cunliffe, 2016: 741). Cunliffe, Aguiar, Góes and Carreira (2020) spell out how radical reflexivity can help

contextualize with regard to real-life problems how 'we are embedded within our social and material world and therefore need to interrogate our place, activities and responsibilities from within our experience'. Against this background, reflexivity and '[m]utual learning among scientists and practitioners about a complex, societally relevant problem may be seen as the kernel of transdisciplinary processes' (Scholz & Steiner; 2015a: 528). Transdisciplinarity is thus always problem-driven with real life challenges in mind. Table 33.1 summarizes the distinctions between disciplinarity, multi-, inter- and transdisciplinarity. The subsequent section zooms in and discusses transdisciplinarity and its relevance for responsible management education in more detail.

TRANSDISCIPLINARITY: KEY PRINCIPLES AND IMPLICATIONS FOR RESPONSIBLE MANAGEMENT

By spanning the boundaries both between disciplines and between research and practice, transdisciplinarity provides a potentially powerful contribution to the field of responsible management. Before discussing these potential benefits, however, it is worth elaborating the following key principles that

Table 33.1 Disciplinarity, multi-, inter-, and transdisciplinarity in comparison (adapted from Schaltegger et al., 2013: 222)

	Disciplinary	*Multidisciplinary*	*Interdisciplinary*	*Transdisciplinary*
Research object	Individual	Same object	Jointly defined object	Complex real world problem jointly defined
Focus	As specific as possible (breaking down complexity)	As specific as possible (breaking down complexity)	Combining different disciplinary sets of knowledge	Combining different disciplinary and practitioner sets of knowledge
Real-world problem as starting point	Possible	Possible	Possible	Necessary
Collaboration with other disciplines	Not given	Not given	Given	Given
Collaboration with practitioners	Possible but not necessary	Possible but not necessary	Possible but not necessary	Defining characteristic

characterize the transdisciplinarity approach (Lang et al., 2012; Schaltegger, Beckmann & Hansen, 2011):

- *Taking a real-world problem as a starting point.* Just like interdisciplinarity, transdisciplinarity aims at the synthesis of new knowledge through the integration of fragmented knowledge pieces. Yet, while interdisciplinary projects might do this by addressing inner-academic theory problems, transdisciplinarity always starts with a real-life problem that affects societal actors outside the academia. Instead of being model- or theory-driven, transdisciplinary research endeavors are phenomenon-driven without drawing on prior assumptions (Scholz & Steiner, 2015a).
- *Multiple partners jointly define the relevant problem.* Any purposeful research investigation and knowledge integration needs a guiding problem perspective. In interdisciplinary research, this problem formulation emerges from within the scientific system. Given complex, ambiguous and sometimes 'messy problems', however, the relevant problem definition can be unclear and difficult to formulate. In this situation, transdisciplinarity requests that researchers and societal stakeholders engage in the joint clarification of the actual problem. As Thompson Klein (2004: 518, emphasis in original) maintains, '[t]ransdisciplinarity raises the question of not only problem *solution* but problem *choice*'. In doing so collaboratively, transdisciplinarity does not only empower stakeholders by strengthening their voice but also adjusts the research process towards relevance.
- *Need to organize collaboration to address complexity.* As high levels of complexity and ambiguity result in the fact that no single actor can understand, leave alone solve complex challenges, collaboration is needed. However, such collaboration may not necessarily be an easy addition of partial pieces of knowledge puzzles but requires additional knowledge taking a broader picture of interplay, dependencies, trade-offs and synergies into account (Scholz & Tietje, 2002). Transdisciplinarity thus needs organizing (Binder, Absenger-Helmli & Schilling, 2015), which the next section discusses in more detail.
- *Joint problem-definition, -solving and -re-definition as an iterative process.* Conventional research problems often follow a linear logic according to which a problem is posed and then solved step

by step. In light of complexity and ambiguity, however, transdisciplinarity research has a 'rolling character' where steps of problem-solving iteratively feed back into re-formulating the problem. Here, transdisciplinarity transcends the boundaries between academics and practitioners not only with regard to the initial problem definition. By engaging societal stakeholders not just as interview partners but as providers of expertise and co-owners of the research process (Scholz & Steiner, 2015a), transdisciplinarity aims at a co-evolutionary process in which academics and practitioners jointly work towards workable solutions.

- *Bridging the divide between knowledge-creation, knowledge transfer, and knowledge application.* Since the created solutions and knowledge address specific real-world problems, they often do not fit into conventional knowledge schemes. At the same time, the iterative problem-solving process creates feedback from the empirical context that can test, validate, disconfirm and elaborate research insights. Consequently, as potential solutions are developed with practitioners and often tested in their real-life context, the creation of knowledge and the diffusion of knowledge overlap and happen in parallel as in Figure 33.2 instead of after each other as in the linear model illustrated in Figure 33.1.

This brief review of key transdisciplinarity principles may suffice as a basis to show why transdisciplinary approaches have a lot to offer for responsible management (RM), responsible management research (RMR) and notably also for responsible management education (RME). Responsibility in RM, RMR and RME derive their relevance because of the positive and negative impacts that management and managers unfold for society – that is their contributions to foster 'sustainable value for business and society at large and to work for an inclusive and sustainable global economy' (UN PRME, 2018, Principle 1). In other words, responsibility in this perspective is always about the '*response-ability*', that is, the ability to respond to societal needs and expectations (see Beckmann, Schaltegger & Landrum, 2020).

So how does transdisciplinarity influence the 'response-ability' of RM, RMR and

RME? One way to address this question is to borrow the distinction between *rigor* and *relevance* from the more general discussion about criteria for valuable research (Gulati, 2007; for a thoughtful discussion of this debate regarding the mission of business schools see also McKiernan and Tsui, 2020). To start with the latter, *relevance* can be interpreted as the degree to which research addresses real-world problems that are meaningful and whose solution affects societal actors in their well-being. Against this background, working towards 'an inclusive and sustainable global economy' focuses in its core on relevance. Relevance, in other words, thus refers to the 'response' part of response-ability. Yet, merely somehow addressing an important issue is not enough. Rather, the specific contribution of science and the academic research process lies in finding solutions that cannot be generated by common sense alone, that build upon a deeper level of understanding, and that qualify as true. By this logic, *rigor* reflects the methodological soundness, empirical grounding and theoretical consistency of the research process. Rigor, in other words, could thus be interpreted as referring to the 'ability' part in response-ability. Seen from this perspective, transdisciplinarity provides an interesting research approach for RM, RMR and RME because it offers the potential to address both rigor and relevance in the following ways.

- *Selecting empirical problems of relevance.* Most obviously, starting with a real-world problem and formulating it jointly with societal stakeholders can serve to systematically direct the research endeavor towards problems of relevance. After all, stakeholders will only be willing to invest their time and dedication if they perceive the research problem to be meaningful and salient. Transdisciplinary projects are therefore less prone to get stuck in the (rigorous) ivory tower.
- *Richer empirical foundation.* Co-creating solutions with diverse societal stakeholders can provide qualitatively different sources of knowledge as personally involved stakeholders contribute their unique first-hand, often intangible knowledge and personal in-depth field experience (see the following section). If used appropriately, such a richer empirical foundation can result in more rigorously grounded results.
- *Empowering stakeholders by giving them voice.* One indirect way to respond to societal needs and to make research relevant is to give stakeholders a voice in the first place. This is where transdisciplinarity goes further than other research approaches.
- *Increased epistemological robustness through iterative feedback*: By testing and refining knowledge and potential solutions in an iterative process, the increased epistemological robustness is translated into more rigorous results.
- *Increased speed of knowledge diffusion.* By transcending the separation of knowledge creation, knowledge dissemination and knowledge application, transdisciplinary projects may require more time at the beginning but can speed up impact, thus also fostering relevance for real-world challenges.

Finally, one important benefit of transdisciplinarity that goes beyond the rigor–relevance debate is the importance of social robustness. In light of complex challenges, it is not enough that a group of researchers finds a rigorous solution for a relevant problem. Rather, if multiple actors are involved and need to be brought on board for a solution (Freeman, 1984), they will only support a suggested solution if they perceive it as legitimate. Involving stakeholders into the problem-solving process is therefore relevant not only because of their implicit knowledge but also for generating legitimizing policy options (Scholz & Steiner, 2015a). Solutions that derive from participatory processes are considered more just and can ultimately lead to more 'socially robust knowledge' (Gibbons, 2000: 161).

In short, transdisciplinary projects hold the potential to address highly complex real-world problems by transcending the boundaries between disciplines as well as between the spheres of knowledge creation, knowledge diffusion and knowledge application. Transdisciplinarity thus offers an interesting perspective to illuminate the area of overlap as illustrated in the center of Figure 33.2. The next section looks at perspectives on how to organize such a process.

TRANSDISCIPLINARITY AND RESPONSIBLE MANAGEMENT RESEARCH: PERSPECTIVES ON METHODOLOGY AND RESEARCH DESIGN

Transdisciplinarity can be understood as aiming at the purposeful transgression of boundaries among and between fields and disciplines. Two things are worth noting here. First, the 'transgression' part of this definition acknowledges that no predefined viewpoint or no existing methodological blueprint can fully address the complexity of most sustainability and responsibility issues. Second, however, transdisciplinarity does not transgress boundaries for the sake of transgression but with a purpose. Transdisciplinarity is about mutual learning (Scholz & Tietje, 2002).

It seeks to advance our knowledge and ability to change society towards the better. Against this background, transdisciplinary methodologies serve to organize the orchestrated transgression of boundaries and to purposefully direct the process towards more effective problem-solving. For brevity, we highlight three helpful and interrelated perspectives on transdisciplinary (TD) research methodology, namely regarding (1) different *phases*, (2) different *levels of knowledge* and (3) the interplay of different *types of knowledge production* in the TD process. Figure 33.3 visualizes all three perspectives and how they relate.

First, regarding the time dimension, the TD research process can be distinguished into three *phases* (Lang et al., 2012), namely phase A of problem framing and team building, phase B of co-creation of solution-oriented transferable knowledge and phase C of (re-)integration and application of created knowledge (see upper part of Figure 33.3). More specifically, phase A is about the collaborative framing of the problem. This requires to build the collaborative research

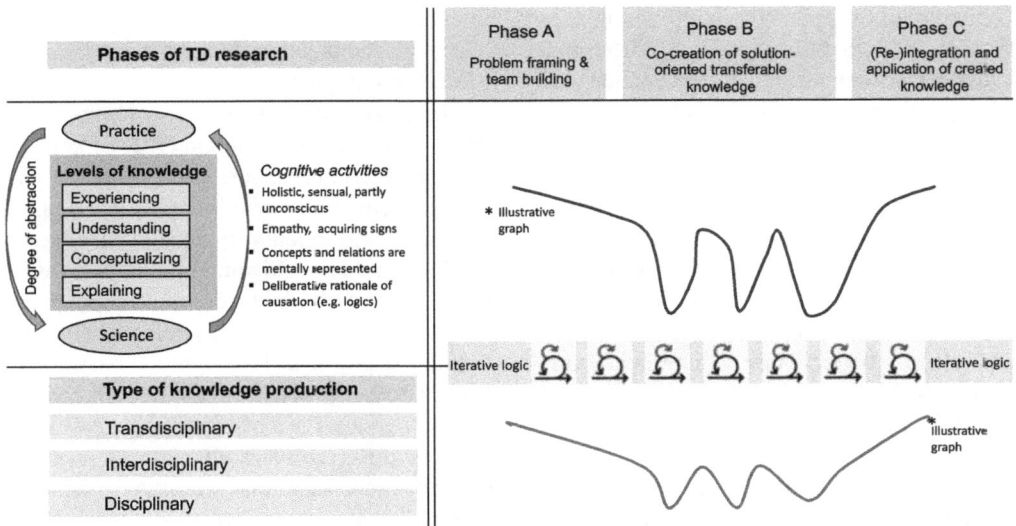

Figure 33.3   The transdisciplinary research process (based on Scholz, 2000; Scholz & Steiner, 2015a; Lang et al., 2012; Binder, 2014)

team and to decide which stakeholders and disciplines are brought on board. Here, it is also important to translate the real-world-problem into a boundary object that can actually be researched (Lang et al., 2012). Phase B refers to the actual doing of the research. Here, the jointly defined problem is linked to the diverse perspectives of the different stakeholders. As Lang et al. (2012: 28) put it, '[f]or each step of the research process, it needs to be defined who contributes what, supported by which means and to what end'. Finally, phase C serves to re-integrate the knowledge. Here, the application of newly created knowledge serves both to validate and refine the research findings but also to change social practices and to feed back into the scientific process. This three-phase model highlights that TD research systematically works towards achieving a purpose. Yet, given the iterative character of TD (as illustrated by the iteration arrows in Figure 33.3), it is important to note that these three phases do not follow a strictly linear logic (Scholz et al., 2006). Rather, the research process can also iterate back where necessary.

Second, regarding the knowledge dimension, TD research acknowledges and seeks to integrate different *levels of knowledge* (Scholz, 2000; Scholz & Steiner, 2015a) that differ (a) in their degree of abstraction and (b) in their relevance for practice and science, respectively (Figure 33.3, middle left). According to this 'architecture of knowledge' (Scholz, 2000), the first form of knowledge is *experiencing*. Experiencing builds upon personal sensations and perceptions. Operating also subconsciously, it creates a particularly holistic form of knowledge that is highly relevant in practice. Here, practitioners may hold valuable experiential system knowledge that distinguishes them from scientists. Building upon experience, *understanding* relates to the material or social world (e.g. through empathy) and uses cues and signs to provide meaning to experience and phenomena. The next form of knowledge is *conceptualizing*. Conceptualizing is about relating

concepts, e.g. through the representation by mental maps. Using language and grammar to express relationships, the conceptual level is relevant for the discourse amongst stakeholders and for communicating and understanding their different rationales. Finally, *explaining* refers to the highest level of abstraction. It serves to explain causal (if–then) relationships, e.g. through logical or inductive–empirical methods (Scholz & Steiner, 2015a).

The 'architecture of knowledge' model is helpful in pointing out that knowledge comes in different forms where each form can make a valuable contribution for mutual learning. While deeper levels of abstraction may isolate relevant causal relationships, more holistic notions acknowledge the richness of context, systemic interdependencies, and the closer link to social practices. Against this background, the idea of TD research is to acknowledge and combine all knowledge types. As Figure 33.3 shows, experiencing and understanding are particularly relevant in phase A for jointly formulating the guiding research problem. Similarly, both knowledge forms are also highly relevant and informative when created knowledge is applied in integrated social practices. On the other hand, conceptualizing and explaining play a central role in phase B.

Third, and closely related, the TD research process builds upon different types of knowledge production (Binder, 2014; Binder et al., 2015). Here, transdisciplinary, interdisciplinary and disciplinary types of knowledge production do not substitute but complement each other with their respective strengths. Transdisciplinary perspectives serve to jointly define the problem, to tap into experiencing knowledge, to formulate shared objectives and to deduce the corresponding questions that the different research partners want to address. Interdisciplinary research management and integration serves to define how the different sub-questions relate, how the different sub-tasks contribute to or necessitate each other (Lang et al., 2012). Disciplinary research then carries out the individual sub-projects. Here, specialized methodologies, data sources and modes of causal reasoning then contribute to advancing explanatory knowledge. As findings from one disciplinary project feed into and potentially refine other projects, the TD process in phase B often goes back and forth between disciplinary and interdisciplinary knowledge work.

The important message from the third element in Figure 33.3 is that TD research does not dispense disciplinary research, including its methodological and theoretical specialization. On the contrary, the power of transdisciplinarity hinges on strong and differentiated disciplinary foundations that it can build upon: effective transdisciplinarity is 'disciplined transdisciplinarity'. The next section will discuss how these principles of TD research can inspire transdisciplinarity in responsible management education and learning.

LINKING TRANSDISCIPLINARY RESEARCH AND FORMATS FOR LEARNING/EDUCATION

Building upon the principles of TD discussed above, we can now distinguish three basic options for bringing TD to responsible management education and learning: first, learning about TD in the classroom; second, learning by emulating TD in the classroom; and, third, learning in TD projects that reach out beyond the classroom (for a similar discussion, see also Cunliffe et al., 2020). This distinction will serve us in the next section to discuss not only the potential but also the inherent challenges and barriers for TD in responsible management, RM research and RM education and learning.

(1) Learning *about* TD in the classroom is the most conventional form of learning and education. For responsible management, this form of teaching can use established formats such as lectures and seminars in which

students learn about the theory and need for inter- and transdisciplinarity. Students can learn about society's grand challenges such as the UN SDGs and managing within the planetary boundaries and why such complex challenges require collaborative, multi-stakeholder solutions (Schaltegger et al., 2018a, 2018b). In terms of theory foundations, students can engage with transdisciplinary theory including complexity theory, sustainability science (Komiyama & Takeuchi, 2006) and systems thinking (Meadows, 2008).

Such learning about TD can contribute relevant background knowledge and may provide students with useful theoretical concepts. It falls short, however, of engaging more deeply with TD.

(2) Allowing students to learn *by emulating* TD in the classroom relates to several formats that are at the core of many responsible management education programs. Key principles addressed here are the idea to focus on real-life problems, to highlight their complexity and uncertainty, to bring together different stakeholder voices, and to engage the students in the changing of perspectives, reflective thinking and critical dialogue. Teaching approaches to address these aims include the use of case studies, co-teaching, role-plays, classroom discussions, presentations by practitioners and engaged discussion with them, and ethical reflections. To illustrate, in their article on 'transdisciplinary learning and reflexivity in responsible management education', Parkes and Blewitt (2011) discuss how MBA students from around the world address grand sustainability challenges in a format that was taught by staff from disciplines, used ethical dilemma discussions and built on case studies, including live case studies with invited business practitioners.

For responsible management education, a key difference of this second option compared to merely learning about TD is that emulating TD departs from a conventional teaching context in which mere facts and the 'right way to think about an issue' are passed on from the lecturer to the student. By engaging in role-plays students can access their own emotions and experiential knowledge. Similarly, co-teaching, invited speeches and classroom discussions (particularly with a diverse student body) can highlight the relevance and value of poly-perspectivity. Furthermore, discussing complex cases and ethical dilemmas creates awareness that in the real-world there is typically no clear-cut, right answer. While this is an important prerequisite for open and mutual learning, students also experience, however, that the departure from certainty can feel challenging (Parkes & Blewitt, 2011). At the same time, emulating TD research may contribute to creating habits of mind for transdisciplinarity (McGregor, 2017), yet falls short of actually applying knowledge, changing social practices and directly solving problems of unsustainability. This is where the third option to be discussed next goes further.

(3) Learning *in and through TD projects* not only inside but above all outside the classroom is the most ambitious and sophisticated, yet also most challenging form of wedding TD with responsible management education

and learning. Jantsch (1972: 114), one of the conceptual founding fathers of TD thinking, already highlighted that 'the essential characteristic of a transdisciplinary approach is the coordination of activities at all levels of the education/innovation system towards a common purpose'. TD transcends the boundaries of knowledge creation, knowledge diffusion and knowledge application. Following this idea, truly transdisciplinary forms of learning are embedded in the full TD research process described above where real problems are addressed, new knowledge is created and social practices are changed through the application of newly created solutions.

A useful methodology to organize such TD research and learning is the embedded case study approach (Scholz & Tietje, 2002). Figure 33.4 helps to explain the approach's underlying components and rationale. Explicitly designed as a TD methodology, in an embedded case study, 'the starting and end points are the comprehension of the case as a whole in its real-world context' (Scholz & Tietje, 2002: 2). After formulating a shared problem and objectives, subprojects are identified that can be addressed with

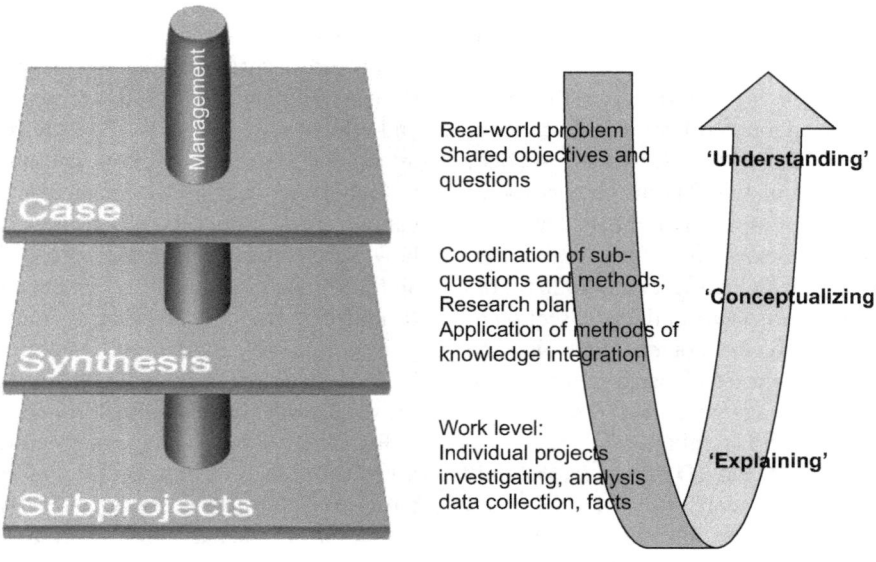

Figure 33.4   The embedded case study approach (based on Scholz & Tietje, 2002)

(disciplinary) specialization. At the core of the methodology, however, stands the level of knowledge integration where the case serves as the unit of analysis for knowledge *synthesis*. Knowledge synthesis can be achieved through various methods such as formative scenario analysis, integrated risk management or life-cycle assessment, with the choice of an appropriate method depending on the problem formulation and other factors.

While the embedded case study approach provides a general methodology for TD research, it can be and is also used as a framework for TD in higher education for responsible management (Hesselbarth & Schaltegger, 2014). Steiner and Posch (2006) discuss an example of such a transdisciplinary case study in which the students were actively involved throughout the TD process. The real-world case was the abandoned iron ore mining region of Eisenerz in central Austria. The shared problem was to develop solutions for an ecologically, economically and socially sustainable development of this area. Students were organized in four subgroups that looked at the sub-questions of analyzing the potential for tourism (1), infrastructure and traffic (2), further business opportunities (3) and social sustainability (4). Acting as both researchers and experiential learners, each student group had a corresponding stakeholder expert group. Furthermore, regional advisory boards and case study offices provided further stakeholder input and spaces for mutual change. Finally, the case study management as well as the knowledge synthesis was coordinated by researchers from the University of Graz assisted by an additional scientific and regional advisory board.

What such implementations of TD in higher education show is that truly embedding and doing TD has a highly promising potential for responsible management education (Hesselbarth & Schaltegger, 2014). Through embedded case study work, 'students' problem-solving abilities are improved by their gaining an understanding of open and complex systems' (Steiner & Posch, 2006: 889).

Moreover, such projects give voice to stakeholders and can contribute to positive change in the community. At the same time, the above example also illustrates that truly TD experiential and research-based learning is complex, time-consuming and challenging. Against this background, the next section takes a more critical look at TD in RMR/RME and discusses some of the relevant barriers to and limitations of inter- and transdisciplinarity.

LIMITATIONS OF AND BARRIERS FOR TRANSDISCIPLINARITY: A CRITICAL PERSPECTIVE

No doubt, TD has enormous potential for responsible management (education). Yet, given the constraints of the broader research, education and management reality, the same principles that generate the potential of TD also go along with significant barriers and limitations, of which the following seven challenges may be particularly relevant:

1   *Career trade-offs for (young) researchers.* While TD holds the promise to increase the impact and relevance of scientific research, the standards for academic rigor are usually defined in disciplinary terms. In journal rankings, most A+ or 4-star journals reflect the disciplinary core of a field whereas most interdisciplinary journals typically rank much lower. Moreover, TD projects are time-consuming, complex and depend on many critical factors which the individual research can hardly control (engagement of practitioners, unpredictable outcome of project, etc.). For young researchers competing in the academic job market or facing strict tenure criteria, there are therefore strong incentives *not* to engage in TD projects.

2   *Assessing the quality of TD work.* Although there are valuable and sophisticated criteria for high quality TD projects (Scholz & Steiner, 2015b), journal reviewers, grant agencies and career committees still struggle to assess the quality of inter- and transdisciplinary projects. Most senior reviewers have a disciplinary background and refer to the disciplinary criteria which they learnt

and which have shaped their own careers. One typical challenge is the lack of interdisciplinary qualified reviewers who can assess both the disciplinary excellence of a research project and its inter- and transdisciplinary quality.

3 *Qualification of academics.* In TD learning projects, 'teachers and researchers have to abandon the role paradigm of the teacher as provider of information and the students as "consumers" of the provided information' (Steiner & Posch, 2006: 877). While this paradigm shift is highly promising for inquiry-based learning, it raises questions of role understanding, self-esteem and as to where teachers gain the competences for such a role change. As shown above, academics need to take on the role of instructors, tutors, project managers, synthesizers and (disciplinary) researchers. Being an expert in all areas can overtax academics. Furthermore, as Easton (2017) found, finding and maintaining faculty leadership across disciplines can be challenging.

4 *Organizational and institutional constraints in the classroom.* TD projects require a lot of time. Against this background, a teaching term of one tri- or semester is simply not long enough to conduct the full cycle of the three phases reviewed above. Moreover, given the non-linear logic of the TD process, the time schedule is less predictable and creates uncertainty, particularly with regard to the student examination. Furthermore, the student examination raises further questions. As no pre-defined 'right' answers exist, it is more challenging to assess student performance. Besides, student performance typically depends on stakeholder collaboration which is out of their control. Finally, TD favors group work which sometimes may not be used for the individual grading of students. In light of increasingly regulated teaching contexts, TD requires levels of teaching flexibility that are not always given.

5 *Linking local and global challenges.* As the example from the Austrian embedded case study illustrates, a critical step in any TD project is the definition of meaningful boundaries. Otherwise, if the research question is too broad, the stakeholder and issue scope would no longer be manageable. In other words, TD projects cannot escape the necessity to be selective in addressing certain fragments of reality. One way to achieve this and to have a clearer definition of relevant stakeholders is to focus on local/regional problems, e.g. with regard to climate change adaptation. This raises the question as to how these fragmented TD projects can be integrated on the global level without passing the boundaries of what can actually be managed and synthesized.

6 *Selecting an adequate number and choice of partners.* As the quality of TD processes and projects is strongly influenced by the engagement and input of involved actors, the choice of partners from different disciplines and practice may strongly influence the quality of the research and education processes as well as the outcome. While choosing representatives from similar or adjoining disciplines increases the likelihood for easier communication, a larger variety of more diverse disciplines may increase the innovation potential very different perspectives can provide.

7 *Transdisciplinary excellence requires effective communication and reliable disciplinary foundations.* One challenge of TD projects is that different actors find it hard to communicate effectively. For example, Kieser and Leiner (2012) criticize that the idea of collaborative research underestimates the communicative difficulties between practitioners and researchers. Differences exist with regard to language, goals, incentives, organizational embedding, etc. Similarly, already on the level of interdisciplinarity, different academic disciplines speak different languages whose translation is challenging. Here, a risk is that the TD dialogue choses the lowest common conceptual denominator. Furthermore, as Figure 33.3 illustrated, TD builds on inter- and disciplinary foundations. For learning projects, this means that undergraduate students first and foremost need to develop disciplinary foundations before engaging in TD projects.

In short, just like any project, TD projects need to weigh costs and benefits and to deal with trade-offs between different project objectives. While a larger and more diverse stakeholder- and researcher-team, for example, can address more aspects of a real-life problem, larger and more diverse research teams also provoke more communication issues, time requirements, transaction costs and are less easy to plan and control (Scholz & Steiner, 2015c). At the same time, the success of TD projects critically hinges upon the appropriate configuration of project partners as well as institutional support. TD projects are an interesting perspective for RMR and RME, yet neither easy nor a panacea. Finally, as McKiernan and Tsui, 2020 spell out a change towards responsible research and education in business management needs to start with transforming doctoral education in a way that focuses research (again) onto real-life problems of relevance and that prepares future researchers to be change-makers in their fields.

CONCLUSION

This chapter has served to review and discuss the contribution of inter- and transdisciplinarity for responsible management education and learning. We started with a short review of the UN Principles for Responsible Management Education. As expressed in Principle 4, adequate (disciplinary) research is needed as a prerequisite for responsible management education. Given the complexity, multi-dimensionality and ambiguity of real-life problems such as the goal of sustainable development, disciplinary research is however not enough to heed this call. Interdisciplinarity calls for the actual and effective collaboration of multiple academic disciplines. Yet, partnership for responsible management does not stop here. In fact, Principle 5 of the UN PRME (2018) can be interpreted as going one step further and as calling for a transdisciplinary approach:

> We will interact with managers of business corporations to extend our knowledge of their challenges in meeting social and environmental responsibilities and to explore jointly effective approaches to meeting these challenges.

Transdisciplinarity aims at mutual learning between practitioners and academics from diverse disciplines. For responsible management, TD offers interesting approaches to align and integrate knowledge creation, diffusion and application in a way that can foster sustainable development. We reviewed

principles of TD and their application to education and learning. In the current academic system, however, TD projects still encounter relevant barriers and limitations. This unveils that any future discussion of transdisciplinarity in responsible management (education) cannot be separated from the broader context of how we organize education, learning and university governance systems.

REFERENCES

Beckmann, M., Schaltegger, S., & Landrum, N. E. (2020). Sustainability management from a responsible management perspective. In Laasch, O., Suddaby, R., Freeman, E., & Jamali, D. (Eds.), *The research handbook of responsible management* (pp. 122–137). Cheltenham: Edward Elgar.

Binder, C. R. (2014) Transdisciplinarity: co-creation of knowledge for the future. In Emmet, R., & Zelko, F. (Eds.), *Minding the gap working across disciplines in environmental studies. RCC Perspectives*, 2014, no. 2. doi.org/10.5282/rcc/6313.

Binder, C. R., Absenger-Helmli, I., & Schilling, T. (2015). The reality of transdisciplinarity: a framework-based self-reflection from science and practice leaders. *Sustainability Science*, 10(4), 545–562.

Cunliffe, A. L. (2016). 'Becoming a critically reflexive practitioner' redux: what does it mean to be reflexive? *Journal of Management Education*, 40, 740–746.

Cunliffe, A. L., Aguiar, A. C., Góes, V., & Carreira, F. (2020). Radical-Reflexivity and Transdisciplinarity as Paths to Developing Responsible Management Education, In: Dirk, C. M., Oliver, L., Carole, P., & Kenneth, G. B. (Eds.), *Responsible Management Learning and Education*, Sage, 298–314.

Easton, P. (2017). Lessons learned in transdisciplinary graduate education: Claremont Graduate University's decade-long experiment. In Gibbs, P. (Ed.), *Transdisciplinary higher education* (pp. 109–119). Cham: Springer.

Freeman, R. E. (1984). *Strategic management: a stakeholder approach*. Boston, MA: Pitman.

Gibbons, M. (2000). Mode 2 society and the emergence of context-sensitive science. *Science and Public Policy*, *27*(3), 159–163.

Gulati, R. (2007). Tent poles, tribalism, and boundary spanning: the rigor–relevance debate in management research. *Academy of Management Journal*, 50(4), 775–782.

Hesselbarth, C., & Schaltegger, S. (2014). Educating change agents for sustainability. Learnings from the first sustainability management master of business administration, *Journal of Cleaner Production*, *62*, 24–36.

Hirsch Hadorn, G., Bradley, D., Pohl, C., & Rist, S. (2006). Implications of transdisciplinarity for sustainability research. *Ecological Economics*, *60*, 119–128.

Jahn, T., Bergmann, M., & Keil, F. (2012) Transdisciplinarity: between mainstreaming and marginalization. *Ecological Economics*, *79*, 1–10.

Jantsch, E. (1970). Interdisciplinary and transdisciplinary university – systems approach to education and innovation. *Policy Sciences*, *1*(4), 403–428.

Jantsch, E. (1972). Towards interdisciplinarity and transdisciplinarity in education and innovation. In Apostel, L., Berger, G., Briggs, A., Michaud, G. (Eds.), *Interdisciplinarity: problems of teaching and research in universities* (pp. 97–121). University of Nice, Nice.

Kieser, A., & Leiner, L. (2012). Collaborate with practitioners: but beware of collaborative research. *Journal of Management Inquiry*, *21*(1), 14–28.

Komiyama, H., & Takeuchi, K. (2006). Sustainability science: building a new discipline. *Sustainability Science*, *1*, 1–6.

Laasch, O., & Moosmayer, D. (2015). Responsible management learning: reflecting on the role and use of paradigms for research in sustainability, responsibility, and ethics. *CRME Working Papers*, *1*(1).

Lang, D. J., Wiek, A., Bergmann, M., Stauffacher, M., Martens, P., & Moll, P. (2012). Transdisciplinary research in sustainability science: practice, principles, and challenges. *Sustainability Science*, *7*(S1), 25–43.

Max-Neef, M. A. (2005). Foundations of transdisciplinarity. *Ecological Economics*, *5*, 5–16.

McGregor, S. L. (2017). Transdisciplinary pedagogy in higher education: transdisciplinary learning, learning cycles and habits of minds. In Gibbs, P. (Ed.), *Transdisciplinary higher education* (pp. 3–16). Cham: Springer.

McKiernan, P., & Tsui, A.S. (2020). Responsible Research in Business and Management: Transforming Doctoral Education, In: Dirk, C. M., Oliver, L., Carole, P., & Kenneth, G. B. (Eds.), *Responsible Management Learning and Education*, Sage, 485–501.

Meadows, D. H. (2008). *Thinking in systems: a primer*. Chelsea: Green Publishing.

Nicolescu, B. (2002). *Manifesto of transdisciplinarity*. Albany, NY: SUNY Press.

Nicolescu, B. (2014). Methodology of transdisciplinarity. *World Futures*, *70*(3–4), 186–199.

Nowotny, H., Scott, P., Gibbons, M., & Scott, P. B. (2001). *Re-thinking science: knowledge and the public in an age of uncertainty* (p. 12). Cambridge: Polity Press.

Parkes, C., & Blewitt, J. (2011). 'Ignorance was bliss, now I'm not ignorant and that is far more difficult'. Transdisciplinary learning and reflexivity in responsible management education. *Journal of Global Responsibility*, *2*(2), 206–221.

Pohl, C. (2005). Transdisciplinary collaboration in environmental research. *Futures*, *37*(10), 1159–1178.

Rockström, J., Steffen, W., Noone, K., Persson, A., Chapin, F. S., Lambin, E. F., Lenton, T. M., Scheffer, M., Folke, C., Schellnhuber, H. J., Nykvist, B., de Wit, C. A., Hughes, T., van der Leeuw, S., Rodhe, H., Sorlin, S., Snyder, P. K., Costanza, R., Svedin, U., Falkenmark, M., Karlberg, L., Corell, R. W., Fabry, V. J., Hansen, J., Walker, B., Liverman, D., Richardson, K., Crutzen, P., & Foley, J. A. (2009). A safe operating space for humanity. *Nature*, *461*(7263), 472–475.

Schaltegger, S., Beckmann, M., & Hansen, E. G. (2011). Transdisciplinarity in corporate sustainability. *Business Strategy and the Environment*, *20*, 348–350.

Schaltegger, S., Beckmann, M., & Hansen, E. G. (2013). Transdisciplinarity in corporate sustainability: mapping the field. *Business Strategy and the Environment*, *22*(4), 219–229.

Schaltegger, S., Beckmann, M., & Hockerts, K. (2018a). Collaborative entrepreneurship for sustainability: creating solutions in light of the UN sustainable development goals. *Inter-*

national *Journal of Entrepreneurial Venturing*, *10*(2), 131–152.

Schaltegger, S., Beckmann, M., & Hockerts, K. (2018b). Sustainable entrepreneurship: creating environmental solutions in light of planetary boundaries. *International Journal of Entrepreneurial Venturing*, *10*(1), 1–16.

Scholz, R. W. (2000). Mutual learning as a basic principle of transdisciplinarity In Scholz, R. W., Häberli, R., Bill, A., & Welti, W. (Eds.), *Transdisciplinarity: joint problem-solving among science, technology and society. Workbook II: mutual learning sessions* (pp. 13–17). Zürich: Haffmans Sachbuch.

Scholz, R. W., Lang, D., Wiek, A., & Walter, A. (2006). Transdisciplinarity case studies as means of sustainability learning. Historical framework and theory. *International Journal of Sustainability in Higher Education*, *7*(3), 226–251.

Scholz, R. W., & Steiner, G. (2015a). The real type and ideal type of transdisciplinary processes: part I – theoretical foundations. *Sustainability Science*, *10*(4), 527–544.

Scholz, R. W., & Steiner, G. (2015b). The real type and ideal type of transdisciplinary processes: part II – what constraints and obstacles do we meet in practice? *Sustainability Science*, *10*(4), 653–671.

Scholz, R. W., & Steiner, G. (2015c). Transdisciplinarity at the crossroads. *Sustainability Science*, *10*(4), 521–526.

Scholz, R. W., & Tietje, O. (2002). *Embedded case study methods: integrating quantitative and qualitative knowledge*. London: Sage.

Steiner, G., & Posch, A. (2006). Higher education for sustainability by means of transdisciplinary case studies: an innovative approach for solving complex, real-world problems. *Journal of Cleaner Production*, *14*(9–11), 877–890.

Thompson Klein, J. (2004). Prospects for transdisciplinarity. *Futures*, *36*(4), 515–526.

Thompson Klein, J., Grossenbacher-Mansuy, W., Häberli, R., Bill, A., Scholz, R.W., & Welti, M. (Eds.). (2001). *Transdisciplinarity: Joint problem solving among science, technology, and society. An effective way for managing complexity*. Basel: Birkhäuser.

UN PRME (2018). The Principles for Responsible Management Education (PRME). United Nations, New York. Available at: www.unprme.org/resource-docs/PRMEBrochure2018.pdf.

Index

Page numbers in *italic* denote figures and in **bold** indicate tables, end of chapter notes are denoted by a letter n between page number and note number.